Why Do You Need This N S0-CFK-291

If you're wondering why you should buy this eleventh edition of *Writing and Reading Across the Curriculum,* here are 7 good reasons!

1 Over 40 brand new readings span the disciplines and help stimulate your writing by offering new, engaging perspectives on all themes found in Part II: An Anthology of Readings.

2 A new Chapter 7, "The Changing Landscape of Work in the Twenty-first Century" challenges you to rethink the dynamic role of work in contemporary society and examines how the workplace of today is distinctly different from that of our parents' and grandparents' generations. Drawing on such disciplines as economics, management consulting, sociology, labor statistics, history, and education, the chapter provides a wide variety of perspectives to stimulate your thinking and writing.

3 "Green Power" moves to the forefront in an all-new Chapter 8. Cutting-edge coverage offers numerous opportunities to think and write about the hot topics of climate crisis and renewable energy. Scientific research, reportage, and individual analyses presented by scientists, environmentalists, businesspeople, members of government, and journalists at the heart of the debate will help you develop your own position on global warming and energy independence.

4 An updated Chapter 11, "New and Improved: Six Decades of Advertising," features a new section on TV commercials, in addition to 28 full-page print ads from popular American magazines of the mid-1940s through today. This wealth of carefully selected advertisements and commercials will prompt you to analyze and comment upon our changing cultural and consumerist values.

5 An enhanced Chapter 13, "Obedience to Authority," revisits Stanley Milgram's groundbreaking obedience experiment with a contemporary replication of this famous study. These experiments, along with Solomon Asch's and Philip Zimbardo's work on groupthink provide an in-depth look at the social forces that influence individual behavior. New readings—each providing a distinctive scientific or literary perspective—illustrate both the danger and the powerful appeal of blind obedience to authority.

6 Chapter 1, "Summary," presents a new article by economist Alan Blinder—Will Your Job Be Exported?—as the basis for a fresh example summary. A revised section on Summarizing Figures and Tables features new material on energy production and consumption. Strategies for careful reading prepare you to highlight key information and make notes towards summarizing college-level materials.

7 Chapter 5, "Argument Synthesis," features a new model synthesis focusing on the debate over student privacy rights and campus safety in the wake of the 2007 Virginia Tech shooting. Employing articles, editorials, investigative reports, and the law as sources, the argument synthesis demonstrates how to fully support a well-developed position on a complex topic.

PEARSON

Writing and Reading Across the Curriculum

ELEVENTH EDITION

Laurence Behrens
University of California Santa Barbara

Leonard J. Rosen
Bentley University

Longman

Boston   Columbus   Indianapolis   New York   San Francisco   Upper Saddle River
Amsterdam   Cape Town   Dubai   London   Madrid   Milan   Munich   Paris   Montreal
Toronto   Delhi   Mexico City   Sao Paulo   Sydney   Hong Kong   Seoul   Singapore   Taipei   Tokyo

Executive Editor: Suzanne Phelps Chambers
Editorial Assistant: Erica Schweitzer
Senior Marketing Manager: Sandra McGuire
Senior Media Producer: Stefanie Liebman
Senior Supplements Editor: Donna Campion
Production Manager: Savoula Amanatidis
Project Coordination and Text Design: Elm Street Publishing Services
Electronic Page Makeup: Integra Software Services Pvt. Ltd.
Cover Design Manager: Wendy Ann Fredericks
Cover Designer: Kay Petronio
Photo Researcher: Julie Tesser
Senior Manufacturing Buyer: Dennis J. Para
Printer and Binder: Edwards Brothers, Inc.
Cover Printer: Lehigh-Phoenix Color Corporation

For permission to use copyrighted material, grateful acknowledgment is made to the copyright holders on pp. 757–762, which are hereby made part of this copyright page.

Library of Congress Cataloging-in-Publication Data
Behrens, Laurence.
    Writing and reading across the curriculum / Laurence Behrens, Leonard J. Rosen. — 11th ed.
        p. cm.
    Includes bibliographical references and index.
    ISBN 0-205-72765-4
        1. College readers.   2. Interdisciplinary approach in education—Problems, exercises, etc.
3. English language—Rhetoric—Problems, exercises, etc.   4. Academic writing—Problems,
exercises, etc.   I. Rosen, Leonard J.   II. Title.
    PE1417.B396 2010
    808'.0427—dc22

2009022629

1 2 3 4 5 6 7 8 9 10—EDW—13 12 11 10

Longman
is an imprint of

www.pearsonhighered.com

ISBN-13: 978-0-205-72765-0
ISBN-10:   0-205-72765-4

To: Keiko and Charlotte

Detailed Contents

Chapter   4   Explanatory Synthesis   91

Chapter 5   Argument Synthesis   132

Part
An Anthology of Readings   203

ENVIRONMENT/PUBLIC POLICY
Chapter 8   Green Power   279

BUSINESS

Chapter 11   New and Improved: Six Decades of Advertising   536

FOLKLORE

Chapter 12   Fairy Tales: A Closer Look at Cinderella   614

PSYCHOLOGY

Chapter 13   Obedience to Authority   680

Preface

When *Writing and Reading Across the Curriculum* was first published in 1982, it was—viewed from one angle—an experiment. We hoped to prove our hypothesis that both students and teachers would respond favorably to a composition reader organized by the kinds of specific topics that were typically studied in general education courses.

The response was both immediate and enthusiastic. Instructors found the topics in that first edition of *WRAC* both interesting and teachable, and students appreciated the links that such topics suggested to the courses they were taking concurrently in the humanities, the social sciences, and the sciences. Readers also told us how practical they found our "summary, synthesis, and critique" approach to writing college-level papers. Instructors, and students as well, welcomed the addition of "analysis" to our coverage in Part I of the ninth edition.

In developing each edition of *WRAC*, we have been guided by the same principle: to retain the essential multidisciplinary character of the text while providing ample new topics and individual readings to keep it fresh and timely. Some topics have proven particularly enduring—our "Cinderella" and "Obedience" chapters have been fixtures of *WRAC* since the first edition. But we take care to make sure that at least a third of the book is completely new every time, both by extensively revising existing chapters and by creating new ones. While we have retained an emphasis on summary, critique, and synthesis—and now, analysis—we continue to develop content on such issues as the process of writing and argumentation that addresses the issues and interests of today's classrooms.

STRUCTURE

Like its predecessors, the eleventh edition of *Writing and Reading Across the Curriculum* is divided into two parts. The first part introduces the strategies of summary, critique, synthesis, and analysis. We take students step-by-step through the process of writing papers based on source material, explaining and demonstrating how summaries, critiques, syntheses, and analyses can be generated from the kinds of readings students will encounter later in the book—and throughout their academic careers. The second part of the text consists of a series of seven subject chapters drawn from both academic and professional disciplines. Each subject is not only interesting in its own right but is also representative of the kinds of topics typically studied during the course of an undergraduate education. We also believe that students and teachers will discover connections among the thematic chapters of this edition that further enhance opportunities for writing, discussion, and inquiry.

CONTINUED FOCUS ON ARGUMENTATION

Part I of *Writing and Reading Across the Curriculum* is designed to prepare students for college-level assignments across the disciplines. The eleventh edition continues the previous edition's strengthened emphasis on the writing process and on argument, in particular. In treating argument, we emphasize the following:

- **The Elements of Argument: Claim, Support, Assumption.** This section adapts the Toulmin approach to argument to the kinds of readings that students will encounter in Part II of the text.
- **The Three Appeals of Argument:** *Logos, Ethos, Pathos.* This discussion may be used to analyze and develop arguments in the readings that students will encounter in Part II of the book.
- **Developing and Organizing the Support for Your Arguments.** This section helps students to mine source materials for facts, expert opinions, and examples that will support their arguments.
- **Annotated Student Argument Paper.** A sample student paper highlights and discusses argumentative strategies that a student writer uses in drafting and developing a paper.

PART I: NEW APPARATUS, TOPICS, READINGS, AND STUDENT PAPERS

Chapter 1: Summary, Paraphrase, and Quotation

Students are taken through the process of writing a summary of economist Alan S. Blinder's "Will Your Job Be Exported?" (a selection new to this edition). We demonstrate how to annotate a source and divide it into sections, how to develop a thesis, and how to write and smoothly join section summaries. The entirely rewritten section "Summarizing Figures and Tables" focuses now on the world's dwindling supply of oil. And, as in previous editions, students learn how to

- summarize figures and tables;
- paraphrase sources;
- quote sources.

Chapter 4: Explanatory Synthesis

Chapter 4 features an updated model synthesis: Several brief selections on the topic of alternative energy vehicles precede discussion of the planning and writing of a student paper, "The Car of the Future?" The first draft is accompanied by detailed instructor comments and guides to revision.

Chapter 5: Argument Synthesis

Chapter 5 provides a new argument synthesis focusing on the debate over student privacy rights and campus safety that was generated by the Virginia Tech shootings in April 2007. The synthesis builds on several articles and editorials on the subject, the report of the panel that investigated the shootings, and the applicable federal laws on student privacy.

Chapter 6: Analysis

The chapter now includes a new section, "When *Your* Perspective Guides the Analysis," highlighting an alternative, more personal approach to analysis than the type that is based on the use of formal principles and definitions and that continues to underlie the greater part of this chapter.

PART II: NEW THEMATIC CHAPTERS

As in earlier editions, Part II of *Writing and Reading Across the Curriculum* provides students with opportunities to practice the skills of summary, synthesis, critique—and now analysis—that they have learned in Part I. We have prepared two new chapters for the eleventh edition of *WRAC*.

Chapter 7: The Changing Landscape of Work in the Twenty–first Century

"The Changing Landscape of Work in the Twenty–first Century," new to this edition, offers students a wealth of information and informed opinion on how the workplace they are about to enter already differs markedly from the workplaces their parents and grandparents have known. Emphasizing the promise and perils of the new economy, the chapter draws from a number of disciplines: economics, management consulting, sociology, labor studies, history, and education. Among the numerous questions posed by the readings: How has the nature of work changed? What role has technology played in its change? Which jobs of the future look to be secure and insecure? Are careers (as the term was once understood) still possible in an economy in which workers can expect to change jobs, and skill sets, multiple times?

We open with definitions of *work* and related terms. Subsequent readings divide into two broad sections: The first distinguishes work of the present and future from work of the past; the second explores expected changes in specific professions. To supplement the coverage of particular professions in this chapter, we point students to an extraordinarily rich Web site maintained by the Bureau of Labor Statistics, a site that provides information on virtually every job category. Ultimately, the chapter invites students to explore through writing the ways in which their choices now can position them strategically for the workplace they will soon enter.

Chapter 8: Green Power

A growing body of evidence points to a global climate crisis caused by massive levels of carbon dioxide and other greenhouse gases continuously spewed into the atmosphere by the burning of coal and oil. Reducing our dependence on these fossil fuels involves developing renewable sources of clean energy that can power our cars, our homes, our businesses, and our public buildings. In this new chapter, students will consider the views of scientists, environmentalists, businesspeople, members of a government task force, and reporters about the nature of the problem and about ways of addressing it.

In the first section of the chapter, students will discover how scientists measure climate change; they will review the enormous challenge of significantly reducing our carbon footprint; and they will consider how government and business can work together to reduce the nation's dependence on oil. The intensity of the debate is unmistakable: While former Vice President Al Gore urges the country to commit itself to producing all of its electricity from renewable sources within ten years, an energy expert warns of "the dangerous delusions of energy independence." In the second part of the chapter, the focus shifts to some of the most promising—though often controversial—sources of renewable energy: nuclear, solar, and wind. Two articles consider whether electric cars are likely to replace gasoline-powered vehicles in the near future. All told, the selections in this chapter will provide students with an occasion to write and an opportunity to contribute to the public debate about climate change and renewable energy. Students will increase their understanding of the energy-related problems we face and also expand their awareness of available options for moving into an era of green power.

PART II: REVISED THEMATIC CHAPTERS

Five anthology chapters are carried over from the tenth edition; many of the reading selections for each, however, are new to this edition.

Chapter 9: Marriage and Family in America

Definitions of marriage and family, husband and wife, mother and father are changing before our eyes. A once-stable (or so we thought) institution seems under attack—an unusually fertile context in which to offer a chapter on "Marriage and Family in America." The chapter pivots on the work of marriage scholars like historian Stephanie Coontz, sociologist David Popenoe, and sociologist Andrew J. Cherlin. Other selections, such as those by Terry Martin Hekker, Hope Edelman, and Eric Bartels, offer personal, often charged accounts of marriage from the inside. Students will follow the debate over gay marriage; they will also examine two ongoing controversies concerning working mothers versus stay-at-home mothers (often referred to as "the Mommy Wars") and the so-called "stalled revolution"—the feminist complaint that, in an age of working women, men have not shouldered their share of household work. A powerful short story, Lore Segal's "The Arbus Factor," rounds out the chapter with a fresh perspective. We've selected readings that will challenge student assumptions and produce writing informed not only by the provocative and sometimes emotionally raw views of chapter authors but also by their own personal experiences. For each of our students has direct experience with marriage and family—some positive, some not; and each, we believe, can bring the authority of that experience to bear in mature, college-level writing.

Chapter 10: To Sleep

Sleep is the most common and, until recently, one of the least understood of human behaviors. Annually, tens of millions of dollars fund basic research on sleep; but experts do not yet know precisely *why* we sleep. This chapter gathers the work of biologists, neurologists, psychologists, and journalists who specialize in science writing to investigate what one author in this chapter terms a "state so familiar yet so strange." Students will read an overview of sleep and an introduction to the physiology of sleep before moving on to the principal focus of the chapter: the sleep of adolescents—particularly of college-age adolescents. Various researchers report on the state of adolescent sleep (generally insufficient) and the causes and consequences of, and potential solutions to, adolescent sleep debt. The chapter concludes with three poems on sleep by Keats, Coleridge, and Byron. Quite aside from providing an insight into the science of sleep, this chapter serves a practical function: to educate college students on the mechanics and dangers of sleep debt. Even for those not intending a career in the sciences, learning what happens cognitively and physically when we deprive ourselves of sleep should make for fascinating reading—and create ample opportunities to practice college-level writing.

Chapter 11: New and Improved: Six Decades of Advertising

The centerpiece of this chapter is a set of two portfolios of memorable advertising: 28 full-page print ads and 18 TV commercials. The print ads, which have appeared in popular American magazines since the mid-1940s, promote cigarettes, liquor and beer, automobiles, food, and beauty and cleaning products. This edition also features a new section on TV commercials, referring students to historical and current gems of the genre viewable on YouTube. Like genetic markers, print advertisements and TV commercials are key indicators of our consumerism, our changing cultural values, and our less variable human psychology. Students will find this material both entertaining and well-suited for practicing and honing their analysis skills.

Chapter 12: Fairy Tales: A Closer Look at Cinderella

This popular chapter includes variants of "Cinderella" along with the perspectives of a folklorist (Stith Thompson), a psychologist (Bruno Bettelheim), a historian (Bonnie Cullen), a novelist (Judith Rossner), and literary and cultural critic (Elisabeth Panttaja). New to this edition are three selections. The first, by historian

Arthur Schlesinger, Jr., is a first-person recollection of reading and being read to as a child and, more generally, a meditation on the importance of classic children's literature. The second, by media critic James Poniewozik, observes the ways in which contemporary movie versions of "Cinderella" try to incorporate feminist themes so that the heroine can "wear [her] tiara while spurning it too." The third, by Peggy Orenstein, investigates the merchandising of Cinderella and other Disney princesses. This chapter develops in students two basic skills: the ability to analyze by applying elements of a theoretical reading to one or more variants of "Cinderella" and the ability to think and write comparatively by reading multiple versions of the story and developing criteria by which to clarify similarities and differences.

Chapter 13: Obedience to Authority

The Obedience chapter, which continues to build on the profoundly disturbing Milgram obedience experiments, features important additions: first, a sharpened focus on the power of situations to influence personal behavior, the context for which is set by sociologists Lee Ross and Richard E. Nisbett; second, a report on the first sanctioned American replication of Milgram's work, some forty-five years after the initial obedience experiments (Jerry M. Burger's findings, reported in 2009, were essentially identical to Milgram's); third, an essay by novelist Doris Lessing on "Group Minds" and the general perfectibility of our species; and finally, an excerpt from novelist Ian McEwan's novel *Atonement*, in which British soldiers at Dunkirk form a mob, demonstrating the power of groups to affect individual conscience. The chapter continues to offer selections by Erich Fromm, Solomon Asch, Philip Zimbardo, and Ian Parker.

RESOURCES FOR TEACHERS AND STUDENTS

- The *Instructor's Manual* for the eleventh edition of *Writing and Reading Across the Curriculum* provides sample syllabi and course calendars, chapter summaries, classroom ideas for writing assignments, introductions to each set of readings, and answers to review questions. Materials for each subject chapter in the anthology include a listing of Videolinks—materials students can access online (usually through YouTube) that complement the chapter readings. Included as well are tips on how to incorporate MyCompLab into the course material. ISBN: 0-205-73467-7.

- PEARSON mycomplab   The Web site *MyCompLab* integrates the market-leading instruction, multimedia tutorials, and exercises for writing, grammar, and research that users have come to identify with the program, along with a new online composing space and new assessment tools. The result is a revolutionary application that offers a seamless and flexible teaching and learning environment built specifically for writers. Created by faculty and students across the country, the new MyCompLab provides help for writers in the context of their writing, with instructor and peer commenting functionality, proven tutorials and exercises for writing, grammar and research, an e-portfolio, an assignment-builder, a bibliography tool, tutoring services, and a gradebook and course management organization created specifically for writing classes. Visit www.mycomplab.com, <http://www.mycomplab.com/> for information.

- An e-book version of *Writing and Reading Across the Curriculum,* Part One, "How to Write Summaries, Critiques, Syntheses, and Analyses" is also available in MyCompLab. This online version of Part One integrates the many resources of MyCompLab, such as extra help with composing, researching, and documenting sources, thereby creating an enriched, interactive learning experience for writing students. This version additionally provides access to the videolinks correlated to each thematic chapter as described in the *Instructor's Manual.*

ACKNOWLEDGMENTS

We have benefited over the years from the suggestions and insights of many teachers—and students—across the country. We would especially like to thank these reviewers of the eleventh edition: Angela Adams, Loyola University Chicago; Fabián Álvarez, Western Kentucky University; Laurel Bollinger, University of Alabama in Huntsville; David Elias, Eastern Kentucky University; Wanda Fries, Somerset Community College; Kerrie Kawasaki-Hull, Ohlone College; Kathy Mendt, Front Range Community College, Larimer Campus; RoseAnn Morgan, Middlesex County College; Alison Reynolds, University of Florida; Deborah L. Ruth, Owensboro Community & Technical College; and Mary R. Seel, Broome Community College.

We would also like to thank the following reviewers for their help in the preparation of past editions: James Allen, College of DuPage; Chris Anson, North Carolina State University; Phillip Arrington, Eastern Michigan University; Anne Bailey, Southeastern Louisiana University; Carolyn Baker, San Antonio College; Bob Brannan, Johnson County Community College; Joy Bashore, Central Virginia Community College; Nancy Blattner, Southeast Missouri State University; Mary Bly, University of California, Davis; Paul Buczkowski, Eastern Michigan University; Jennifer Bullis, Whatcom Community College; Paige Byam, Northern Kentucky University; Susan Callendar, Sinclair Community College; Anne Carr, Southeast Community College; Jeff Carroll, University of Hawaii; Joseph Rocky Colavito, Northwestern State University; Michael Colonneses, Methodist College; James A. Cornette, Christopher Newport University; Timothy Corrigan, Temple University; Kathryn J. Dawson, Ball State University; Cathy Powers Dice, University of Memphis; Kathleen Dooley, Tidewater Community College; Judith Eastman, Orange Coast College; David Elias, Eastern Kentucky University; Susan Boyd English, Kirkwood Community College; Kathy Evertz, University of Wyoming; Kathy Ford, Lake Land College; University of Wyoming; Bill Gholson, Southern Oregon University; Karen Gordon, Elgin Community College; Deborah Gutschera, College of DuPage; Lila M. Harper, Central Washington University; M. Todd

Harper, University of Louisville; Kip Harvigsen, Ricks College; Michael Hogan, Southeast Missouri State University; Sandra M. Jensen, Lane Community College; Anita Johnson, Whatcom Community College; Mark Jones, University of Florida; Daven M. Kari, Vanguard University; Jane Kaufman, University of Akron; Rodney Keller, Ricks College; Walt Klarner, Johnson County Community College; Jeffery Klausman, Whatcom Community College; Alison Kuehner, Ohlone College; William B. Lalicker, West Chester University; Dawn Leonard, Charleston Southern University; Lindsay Lewan, Arapahoe Community College; Clifford L. Lewis, U Mass Lowell; Signee Lynch, Whatcom Community College; Jolie Martin; San Francisco State University; Krista L. May, Texas A&M University; Stella Nesanovich, McNeese State University; Kathy Mendt, Front Range Community College–Larimer Campus; RoseAnn Morgan, Middlesex County College; David Moton, Bakersfield College; Roark Mulligan, Christopher Newport University; Joan Mullin, University of Toledo; Susie Paul, Auburn University at Montgomery; Thomas Pfau, Bellevue Community College; Aaron Race, Southern Illinois University–Carbondale; Nancy Redmond, Long Beach City College; Deborah Reese, University of Texas at Arlington; Priscilla Riggle, Bowling Green State University; Jeanette Riley, University of New Mexico; Robert Rongner, Whatcom Community College; Sarah C. Ross, Southeastern Louisiana University; Amy Rybak, Bowling Green State University; Raul Sanchez, University of Utah; Rebecca Shapiro, Westminster College; Mary Sheldon, Washburn University; Horacio Sierra, University of Florida; Philip Sipiora, University of Southern Florida; Joyce Smoot, Virginia Tech; Bonnie A. Spears, Chaffey College; Bonnie Startt, Tidewater Community College; R. E. Stratton, University of Alaska–Fairbanks; Katherine M. Thomas, Southeast Community College; Victor Villanueva, Washington State University; Deron Walker, California Baptist University; Jackie Wheeler, Arizona State University; Pat Stephens Williams, Southern Illinois University at Carbondale; and Kristin Woolever, Northeastern University.

We gratefully acknowledge the work of Michael Behrens, who made significant contributions to the Argument Synthesis and the "Marriage and Family in America" chapters.

A special thanks to Suzanne Phelps Chambers, Erica Schweitzer, Beth Keister, and Martha Beyerlein for helping shepherd the manuscript through the editorial and production process. And our continued gratitude to Joe Opiela, longtime friend, supporter, and publisher.

LAURENCE BEHRENS
LEONARD J. ROSEN

Your sociology professor asks you to write a paper on attitudes toward the homeless population of an urban area near your campus. You are expected to consult books, articles, Web sites, and other online sources on the subject, and you are also encouraged to conduct surveys and interviews.

Your professor is making a number of assumptions about your capabilities. Among them:

- that you can research and assess the value of relevant sources;
- that you can comprehend college-level material, both print and electronic;
- that you can use theories and principles learned from one set of sources as tools to investigate other sources (or events, people, places, or things);
- that you can synthesize separate but related sources;
- that you can intelligently respond to such material.

In fact, these same assumptions underlie practically all college writing assignments. Your professors will expect you to demonstrate that you can read and understand not only textbooks but also critical articles and books, primary sources, Internet sources, online academic databases, CD-ROMs, and other material related to a particular subject of study. For example: For a paper on the progress of the Human Genome Project, you would probably look to articles and Internet sources for the most recent information. Using an online database, you would find articles on the subject in such print journals as *Nature, Journal of the American Medical Association,* and *Bioscience,* as well as leading newspapers and magazines. A Web search engine might lead you to a useful site called "A New Gene Map of the Human Genome" (http://www.ncbi.nlm.nih.gov/genemap99/) and the site of the "Human Genome Sequencing Department" at the Lawrence Berkeley National Laboratory (http://www-hgc.lbl.gov/). You would be expected to assess the relevance of such sources to your topic and to draw from them the information and ideas you need. It's even possible that the final product of your research and reading may not be a conventional paper at all, but rather a Web site you create that explains the science behind the Human Genome Project, explores a particular controversy about the project, or describes the future benefits geneticists hope to derive from the project.

You might, for a different class, be assigned a research paper on the films of director Martin Scorsese. To get started, you might consult your film studies textbook, biographical sources on Scorsese, and anthologies of criticism. Instructor and peer feedback on a first draft might lead you to articles in both popular magazines (such as *Time*) and scholarly journals (such as *Literature/Film Quarterly*), a CD-ROM data-base (such as *Film Index International*), and relevant Web sites (such as the "Internet Movie Database," http://us.imdb.com).

These two example assignments are very different, of course, but the skills you need to work with them are the same. You must be able to research relevant sources. You must be able to read and comprehend these sources. You must be able to perceive the relationships among several pieces of source material. And you must be able to apply your own critical judgments to these various materials.

Writing and Reading Across the Curriculum provides you with the opportunity to practice the essential college-level skills we have just outlined and the forms of writing associated with them, namely:

- the *summary*
- the *critique*
- the *synthesis*
- the *analysis*

Each chapter of Part II of this text represents a subject from a particular area of the academic curriculum: Sociology, Psychology, Economics, Biology, Folklore, Public Policy, Business, and Advertising. These chapters, dealing with such topics as "Marriage and Family in America," "Obedience to Authority," and "Green Power," illustrate the types of material you will study in your other courses.

Questions following the readings will allow you to practice typical college writing assignments. Review Questions help you recall key points of content. Discussion and Writing Suggestions ask you for personal, sometimes imaginative, responses to the readings. Synthesis Activities allow you to practice assignments of the type that are covered in detail in Part I of this book. For instance, you may be asked to *summarize* the Milgram experiment and the reactions to it, or to *compare and contrast* a controlled experiment with a real-life (or fictional) situation. Finally, Research Activities ask you to go beyond the readings in this text in order to conduct your own independent research on these subjects.

In this book, you'll find articles and essays written by physicians, literary critics, sociologists, psychologists, lawyers, folklorists, political scientists, journalists, and specialists from other fields. Our aim is that you become familiar with the various subjects and styles of academic writing and that you come to appreciate the interrelatedness of knowledge. Fairy tales can be studied by literary critics, folklorists, psychologists, and feminists. Human activity and human behavior are classified into separate subjects only for convenience. The novel you read in your literature course may be able to shed some light upon an assigned article for your economics course—and vice versa.

We hope, therefore, that your writing course will serve as a kind of bridge to your other courses and that as a result of this work you will become more skillful at perceiving relationships among diverse topics. Because it involves such critical and widely applicable skills, your writing course may well turn out to be one of the most valuable—and one of the most interesting—of your academic career.

LAURENCE BEHRENS
LEONARD J. ROSEN

How to Write Summaries, Critiques, Syntheses, and Analyses

Summary, Paraphrase, and Quotation

WHAT IS A SUMMARY?

The best way to demonstrate that you understand the information and the ideas in any piece of writing is to compose an accurate and clearly written summary of that piece. By a *summary* we mean a *brief restatement, in your own words, of the content of a passage* (a group of paragraphs, a chapter, an article, a book). This restatement should focus on the *central idea* of the passage. The briefest of summaries (one or two sentences) will do no more than this. A longer, more complete summary will indicate, in condensed form, the main points in the passage that support or explain the central idea. It will reflect the order in which these points are presented and the emphasis given to them. It may even include some important examples from the passage. But it will not include minor details. It will not repeat points simply for the purpose of emphasis. And it will not contain any of your own opinions or conclusions. A good summary, therefore, has three central qualities: *brevity, completeness*, and *objectivity*.

CAN A SUMMARY BE OBJECTIVE?

Objectivity could be difficult to achieve in a summary. By definition, writing a summary requires you to select some aspects of the original and leave out others. Since deciding what to select and what to leave out calls for your personal judgment, your summary really is a work of interpretation. And, certainly, your interpretation of a passage may differ from another person's.

One factor affecting the nature and quality of your interpretation is your *prior knowledge* of the subject. For example, if you're attempting to summarize an anthropological article and you're a novice in that field, then your summary of the article will likely differ from that of your professor, who has spent twenty years studying this particular area and whose judgment about what is more or less significant is undoubtedly more reliable than your own. By the same token, your personal or professional *frame of reference* may also affect your interpretation. A union representative and a management representative attempting to summarize the latest management offer would probably come up with two very different accounts. Still, we believe that in most cases it's possible to produce a reasonably objective summary of a passage if you make a conscious, good-faith effort to be unbiased and to prevent your own feelings on the subject from coloring your account of the author's text.

USING THE SUMMARY

In some quarters, the summary has a bad reputation—and with reason. Summaries are often provided by writers as substitutes for analyses. As students, many of us have summarized books that we were supposed to *review critically*. All the same, the summary does have a place in respectable college work. First, writing a summary is an excellent way to understand what you read. This in itself is an important goal of academic study. If you don't understand your source material, chances are you won't be able to refer to it usefully in a paper. Summaries help you understand what you read because they force you to put the text into your own words. Practice with writing summaries also develops your general

WHERE DO WE FIND WRITTEN SUMMARIES?

Here are just a few of the types of writing that involve summary:

Academic Writing
- **Critique papers** summarize material in order to critique it.
- **Synthesis papers** summarize to show relationships between sources.
- **Analysis papers** summarize theoretical perspectives before applying them.
- **Research papers:** note-taking and reporting research require summary.
- **Literature reviews:** overviews of work are presented in brief summaries.
- **Argument papers** summarize evidence and opposing arguments.
- **Essay exams** demonstrate understanding of course materials through summary.

Workplace Writing
- **Policy briefs** condense complex public policy.
- **Business plans** summarize costs, relevant environmental impacts, and other important matters.
- **Memos, letters, and reports** summarize procedures, meetings, product assessments, expenditures, and more.
- **Medical charts** record patient data in summarized form.
- **Legal briefs** summarize relevant facts and arguments of cases.

writing habits, because a good summary, like any other piece of good writing, is clear, coherent, and accurate.

Second, summaries are useful to your readers. Let's say you're writing a paper about the McCarthy era in the United States, and in part of that paper you want to discuss Arthur Miller's *The Crucible* as a dramatic treatment of the subject. A summary of the plot would be helpful to a reader who hasn't seen or read—or who doesn't remember—the play. Or perhaps you're writing a paper about the politics of recent American military interventions. If your reader isn't likely to be familiar with American actions in Kosovo and Afghanistan, it would be a good idea to summarize these events at some early point in the paper. In many cases (an exam, for instance), you can use a summary to demonstrate your knowledge of what your professor already knows; when writing a paper, you can use a summary to inform your professor about some relatively unfamiliar source.

Third, summaries are required frequently in college-level writing. For example, on a psychology midterm, you may be asked to explain Carl Jung's theory of the collective unconscious and to show how it differs from Sigmund Freud's theory of the personal unconscious. You may have read about Jung's theory in your textbook or in a supplementary article, or your instructor may have outlined it in her lecture. You can best demonstrate your understanding of it by summarizing it. Then you'll proceed to contrast it with Freud's theory—which, of course, you must also summarize.

THE READING PROCESS

It may seem to you that being able to tell (or retell) in summary form exactly what a passage says is a skill that ought to be taken for granted in anyone who can read at high school level. Unfortunately, this is not so: For all kinds of reasons, people don't always read carefully. In fact, it's probably safe to say that usually they don't. Either they read so inattentively that they skip over words, phrases, or even whole sentences, or, if they do see the words in front of them, they see them without registering their significance.

When a reader fails to pick up the meaning and implications of a sentence or two, usually there's no real harm done. (An exception: You could lose credit on an exam or paper because you failed to read or to realize the significance of a crucial direction by your instructor.) But over longer stretches—the paragraph, the section, the article, or the chapter—inattentive or haphazard reading interferes with your goals as a reader: to perceive the shape of the argument, to grasp the central idea, to determine the main points that compose it, to relate the parts of the whole, and to note key examples. This kind of reading takes a lot more energy and determination than casual reading. But in the long run it's an energy-saving method because it enables you to retain the content of the material and to draw upon that content in your own responses. In other words, it allows you to develop an accurate and coherent written discussion that goes beyond summary.

CRITICAL READING FOR SUMMARY

- *Examine the context.* Note the credentials, occupation, and publications of the author. Identify the source in which the piece originally appeared. This information helps illuminate the author's perspective on the topic he or she is addressing.
- *Note the title and subtitle.* Some titles are straightforward; the meanings of others become clearer as you read. In either case, titles typically identify the topic being addressed and often reveal the author's attitude toward that topic.
- *Identify the main point.* Whether a piece of writing contains a thesis statement in the first few paragraphs or builds its main point without stating it up front, look at the entire piece to arrive at an understanding of the overall point being made.
- *Identify the subordinate points.* Notice the smaller subpoints that make up the main point, and make sure you understand how they relate to the main point. If a particular subpoint doesn't clearly relate to the main point you've identified, you may need to modify your understanding of the main point.
- *Break the reading into sections.* Notice which paragraphs make up a piece's introduction, body, and conclusion. Break up the body paragraphs into sections that address the writer's various subpoints.
- *Distinguish between points, examples, and counterarguments.* Critical reading requires careful attention to what a writer is *doing* as well as what he or she is *saying*. When a writer quotes someone else, or relays an example of something, ask yourself why this is being done. What point is the example supporting? Is another source being quoted as support for a point or as a counterargument that the writer sets out to address?
- *Watch for transitions within and between paragraphs.* In order to follow the logic of a piece of writing, as well as to distinguish between points, examples, and counterarguments, pay attention to the transitional words and phrases writers use. Transitions function like road signs, preparing the reader for what's next.
- *Read actively and recursively.* Don't treat reading as a passive, linear progression through a text. Instead, read as though you are engaged in a dialogue with the writer: Ask questions of the text as you read, make notes in the margin, underline key ideas in pencil, put question or exclamation marks next to passages that confuse or excite you. Go back to earlier points once you finish a reading, stop during your reading to recap what's come so far, and move back and forth through a text.

HOW TO WRITE SUMMARIES

Every article you read will present its own challenge as you work to summarize it. As you'll discover, saying in a few words what has taken someone else a great many can be difficult. But like any other skill, the ability to summarize improves with practice. Here are a few pointers to get you started. They represent possible stages, or steps, in the process of writing a summary. These pointers are not meant to be ironclad rules; rather, they are designed to encourage habits of thinking that will allow you to vary your technique as the situation demands.

GUIDELINES FOR WRITING SUMMARIES

- *Read the passage carefully.* Determine its structure. Identify the author's purpose in writing. (This will help you distinguish between more important and less important information.) Make a note in the margin when you get confused or when you think something is important; highlight or underline points sparingly, if at all.
- *Reread.* This time divide the passage into sections or stages of thought. The author's use of paragraphing will often be a useful guide. *Label*, on the passage itself, each section or stage of thought. *Underline* key ideas and terms. Write notes in the margin.
- *Write one-sentence summaries,* on a separate sheet of paper, of each stage of thought.
- *Write a thesis—a one- or two-sentence summary of the entire passage.* The thesis should express the central idea of the passage, as you have determined it from the preceding steps. You may find it useful to follow the approach of most newspaper stories—naming the *what, who, why, where, when,* and *how* of the matter. For persuasive passages, summarize in a sentence the author's conclusion. For descriptive passages, indicate the subject of the description and its key feature(s). Note: In some cases, *a suitable thesis statement may already be in the original passage.* If so, you may want to quote it directly in your summary.
- *Write the first draft of your summary* by (1) combining the thesis with your list of one-sentence summaries or (2) combining the thesis with one-sentence summaries *plus* significant details from the passage. In either case, eliminate repetition and less important information. Disregard minor details or generalize them (e.g., Bill Clinton and George W. Bush might be generalized as "recent presidents"). Use as few words as possible to convey the main ideas.
- *Check your summary against the original passage* and make whatever adjustments are necessary for accuracy and completeness.
- *Revise your summary,* inserting transitional words and phrases where necessary to ensure coherence. Check for style. *Avoid a series of short, choppy sentences.* Combine sentences for a smooth, logical flow of ideas. Check for grammatical correctness, punctuation, and spelling.

DEMONSTRATION: SUMMARY

To demonstrate these points at work, let's go through the process of summarizing a passage of expository material—that is, writing that is meant to inform and/or persuade. Read the following selection carefully. Try to identify its parts and understand how they work together to create an overall statement.

WILL YOUR JOB BE EXPORTED?

Alan S. Blinder

Alan S. Blinder is the Gordon S. Rentschler Memorial Professor of Economics at Princeton University. He has served as vice chairman of the Federal Reserve Board and was a member of President Clinton's original Council of Economic Advisers.

The great conservative political philosopher Edmund Burke, who probably would not have been a reader of *The American Prospect,* once observed, "You can never plan the future by the past."* But when it comes to preparing the American workforce for the jobs of the future, we may be doing just that.

For about a quarter-century, demand for labor appears to have shifted toward the college-educated and away from high school graduates and dropouts. This shift, most economists believe, is the primary (though not the sole) reason for rising income inequality, and there is no end in sight. Economists refer to this phenomenon by an antiseptic name: skill-biased technical progress. In plain English, it means that the labor market has turned ferociously against the low skilled and the uneducated.

In a progressive society, such a worrisome social phenomenon might elicit some strong policy responses, such as more compensatory education, stepped-up efforts at retraining, reinforcement (rather than shredding) of the social safety net, and so on. You don't fight the market's valuation of skills; you try to mitigate its more deleterious effects. We did a bit of this in the United States in the 1990s, by raising the minimum wage and expanding the Earned Income Tax Credit.† Combined with tight labor markets, these measures improved things for the average worker. But in this decade, little or no mitigation has been attempted. Social Darwinism has come roaring back.‡

---

*Edmund Burke (1729–1797) was a conservative British statesman, philosopher, and author. *The American Prospect*, in which "Will Your Job Be Exported?" first appeared in the November 2006 issue, describes itself as "an authoritative magazine of liberal ideas."

†The Earned Income Tax Credit, an anti-poverty measure enacted by Congress in 1975 and revised in the 1980s and 1990s, provides a credit against federal income taxes for any filer who claims a dependent child.

‡Social Darwinism, a largely discredited philosophy dating from the Victorian era and espoused by Herbert Spenser, asserts that Charles Darwin's observations on natural selection apply to human societies. Social Darwinists argue that the poor are less fit to survive than the wealthy and should, through a natural process of adaptation, be allowed to die out.

With one big exception: We have expended considerable efforts to keep more young people in school longer (e.g., reducing high-school dropouts and sending more kids to college) and to improve the quality of schooling (e.g., via charter schools and No Child Left Behind*). Success in these domains may have been modest, but not for lack of trying. You don't have to remind Americans that education is important; the need for educational reform is etched into the public consciousness. Indeed, many people view education as the silver bullet. On hearing the question "How do we best prepare the American workforce of the future?" many Americans react reflexively with: "Get more kids to study science and math, and send more of them to college."

5   Which brings me to the future. As I argued in a recent article in *Foreign Affairs* magazine, the greatest problem for the next generation of American workers may not be lack of education, but rather "offshoring"—the movement of jobs overseas, especially to countries with much lower wages, such as India and China. Manufacturing jobs have been migrating overseas for decades. But the new wave of offshoring, of *service* jobs, is something different.

Traditionally, we think of service jobs as being largely immune to foreign competition. After all, you can't get your hair cut by a barber or your broken arm set by a doctor in a distant land. But stunning advances in communication technology, plus the emergence of a vast new labor pool in Asia and Eastern Europe, are changing that picture radically, subjecting millions of presumed-safe domestic service jobs to foreign competition. And it is not necessary actually to move jobs to low-wage countries in order to restrain wage increases; the mere threat of offshoring can put a damper on wages.

Service-sector offshoring is a minor phenomenon so far, Lou Dobbs notwithstanding; probably well under 1 percent of U.S. service jobs have been outsourced.[†] But I believe that service-sector offshoring will eventually exceed manufacturing-sector offshoring by a hefty margin—for three main reasons. The first is simple arithmetic: There are vastly more service jobs than manufacturing jobs in the United States (and in other rich countries). Second, the technological advances that have made service-sector offshoring possible will continue and accelerate, so the range of services that can be moved offshore will increase ineluctably. Third, the number of (e.g., Indian and Chinese) workers capable of performing service jobs offshore seems certain to grow, perhaps exponentially.

I do not mean to paint a bleak picture here. Ever since Adam Smith and David Ricardo, economists have explained and extolled the gains in living standards that derive from international trade.[‡] Those arguments are just as valid for

---

*Charter schools are public schools with specialized missions to operate outside of regulations that some feel restrict creativity and performance in traditional school settings. The No Child Left Behind Act of 2001 (NCLB) mandates standards-based education for all schools receiving federal funding. Both the charter schools movement and NCLB can be understood as efforts to improve public education.

[†]Lou Dobbs, a conservative columnist and political commentator for CNN, is well known for his anti-immigration views.

[‡]Adam Smith (1723–1790), Scottish author of *An Inquiry into the Nature and Causes of the Wealth of Nations* (1776), established the foundations of modern economics. David Ricardo (1772–1823) was a British businessman, statesman, and economist who founded the classical school of economics and is best known for his studies of monetary policy.

trade in services as for trade in goods. There really *are* net gains to the United States from expanding service-sector trade with India, China, and the rest. The offshoring problem is not about the adverse nature of what economists call the economy's eventual equilibrium. Rather, it is about the so-called transition—the ride from here to there. That ride, which could take a generation or more, may be bumpy. And during the long adjustment period, many U.S. wages could face downward pressure.

Thus far, only American manufacturing workers and a few low-end service workers (e.g., call-center operators) have been competing, at least potentially, with millions of people in faraway lands eager to work for what seems a pittance by U.S. standards. But offshoring is no longer limited to low-end service jobs. Computer code can be written overseas and e-mailed back to the United States. So can your tax return and lots of legal work, provided you do not insist on face-to-face contact with the accountant or lawyer. In writing and editing this article, I communicated with the editors and staff of *The American Prospect* only by telephone and e-mail. Why couldn't they (or I, for that matter) have been in India? The possibilities are, if not endless, at least vast.

10   What distinguishes the jobs that cannot be offshored from the ones that can? The crucial distinction is not—and this is the central point of this essay—the required levels of skill and education. These attributes have been critical to labor-market success in the past, but may be less so in the future. Instead, the new critical distinction may be that some services either require personal delivery (e.g., driving a taxi and brain surgery) or are seriously degraded when delivered electronically (e.g., college teaching—at least, I hope!), while other jobs (e.g., call centers and keyboard data entry) are not. Call the first category personal services and the second category impersonal services. With this terminology, I have three main points to make about preparing our workforce for the brave, new world of the future.

First, we need to think about, plan, and redesign our educational system with the crucial distinction between personal service jobs and impersonal service jobs in mind. Many of the impersonal service jobs will migrate offshore, but the personal service jobs will stay here.

Second, the line that divides personal services from impersonal services will move in only one direction over time, as technological progress makes it possible to deliver an ever-increasing array of services electronically.

Third, the novel distinction between personal and impersonal jobs is quite different from, and appears essentially unrelated to, the traditional distinction between jobs that do and do not require high levels of education.

For example, it is easy to offshore working in a call center, typing transcripts, writing computer code, and reading X-rays. The first two require little education; the last two require quite a lot. On the other hand, it is either impossible or very difficult to offshore janitorial services, fast-food restaurant service, college teaching, and open-heart surgery. Again, the first two occupations require little or no education, while the last two require a great deal. There seems to be little or no correlation between educational requirements (the old concern) and how "offshorable" jobs are (the new one).

15   If so, the implications could be startling. A generation from now, civil engineers (who must be physically present) may be in greater demand in the United States than computer engineers (who don't). Similarly, there might be more divorce lawyers (not offshorable) than tax lawyers (partly offshorable). More imaginatively, electricians might earn more than computer programmers. I am not predicting any of this; lots of things influence relative demands and supplies for different types of labor. But it all seems within the realm of the possible as technology continues to enhance the offshorability of even highly skilled occupations. What does seem highly likely is that the relative demand for labor in the United States will shift away from impersonal services and toward personal services, and this shift will look quite different from the familiar story of skill-biased technical progress. So Burke's warning is worth heeding.

I am *not* suggesting that education will become a handicap in the job market of the future. On the contrary, to the extent that education raises productivity and that better-educated workers are more adaptable and/or more creative, a wage premium for higher education should remain. Thus, it still makes sense to send more of America's youth to college. But, over the next generation, the kind of education our young people receive may prove to be more important than how much education they receive. In that sense, a college degree may lose its exalted "silver bullet" status.

Looking back over the past 25 years, "stay in school longer" was excellent advice for success in the labor market. But looking forward over the next 25 years, more subtle occupational advice may be needed. "Prepare yourself for a high-end personal service occupation that is not offshorable" is a more nuanced message than "stay in school." But it may prove to be more useful. And many non-offshorable jobs—such as carpenters, electricians, and plumbers—do not require college education.

The hard question is how to make this more subtle advice concrete and actionable. The children entering America's educational system today, at age 5, will emerge into a very different labor market when they leave it. Given gestation periods of 13 to 17 years and more, educators and policy-makers need to be thinking now about the kinds of training and skills that will best prepare these children for their future working lives. Specifically, it is essential to educate America's youth for the jobs that will actually be available in America 20 to 30 years from now, not for the jobs that will have moved offshore.

Some of the personal service jobs that will remain in the United States will be very high-end (doctors), others will be less glamorous though well paid (plumbers), and some will be "dead end" (janitor). We need to think long and hard about the types of skills that best prepare people to deliver high-end personal services, and how to teach those skills in our elementary and high schools. I am not an education specialist, but it strikes me that, for example, the central thrust of No Child Left Behind is pushing the nation in exactly the wrong direction. I am all for accountability. But the nation's school system will not build the creative, flexible, people-oriented workforce we will need in the future by drilling kids incessantly with rote preparation for standardized tests in the vain hope that they will perform as well as memory chips.

20   Starting in the elementary schools, we need to develop our youngsters' imaginations and people skills as well as their "reading, writing, and 'rithmetic." Remember that kindergarten grade for "works and plays well with others"? It may become increasingly important in a world of personally delivered services. Such training probably needs to be continued and made more sophisticated in the secondary schools, where, for example, good communications skills need to be developed.

More vocational education is probably also in order. After all, nurses, carpenters, and plumbers are already scarce, and we'll likely need more of them in the future. Much vocational training now takes place in community colleges; and they, too, need to adapt their curricula to the job market of the future.

While it is probably still true that we should send more kids to college and increase the number who study science, math, and engineering, we need to focus on training more college students for the high-end jobs that are unlikely to move offshore, and on developing a creative workforce that will keep America incubating and developing new processes, new products, and entirely new industries. Offshoring is, after all, mostly about following and copying. America needs to lead and innovate instead, just as we have in the past.

Educational reform is not the whole story, of course. I suggested at the outset, for example, that we needed to repair our tattered social safety net and turn it into a retraining trampoline that bounces displaced workers back into productive employment. But many low-end personal service jobs cannot be turned into more attractive jobs simply by more training—think about janitors, fast-food workers, and nurse's aides, for example. Running a tight labor market would help such workers, as would a higher minimum wage, an expanded Earned Income Tax Credit, universal health insurance, and the like.

Moving up the skill ladder, employment is concentrated in the public or quasi-public sector in a number of service occupations. Teachers and health-care workers are two prominent examples. In such cases, government policy can influence wages and working conditions directly by upgrading the structure and pay of such jobs—developing more professional early-childhood teachers and fewer casual daycare workers for example—as long as the taxpayer is willing to foot the bill. Similarly, some service jobs such as registered nurses are in short supply mainly because we are not training enough qualified personnel. Here, too, public policy can help by widening the pipeline to allow more workers through. So there are a variety of policy levers that might do some good—if we are willing to pull them.

25   But all that said, education is still the right place to start. Indeed, it is much more than that because the educational system affects the entire population and because no other institution is nearly as important when it comes to preparing our youth for the world of work. As the first industrial revolution took hold, America radically transformed (and democratized) its educational system to meet the new demands of an industrial society. We may need to do something like that again. There is a great deal at stake here. If we get this one wrong, the next generation will pay dearly. But if we get it (close to) right, the gains from trade promise coming generations a prosperous future.

The somewhat inchoate challenge posed here—preparing more young Americans for personal service jobs—brings to mind one of my favorite Churchill quotations: "You can always count on Americans to do the right thing—after they've tried everything else." It is time to start trying.

Read, Reread, Highlight

Let's consider our recommended pointers for writing a summary.

As you reread the passage, note in the margins of the essay important points, shifts in thought, and questions you may have. Consider the essay's significance as a whole and its stages of thought. What does it say? How is it organized? How does each part of the passage fit into the whole? What do all these points add up to?

Here is how several paragraphs from the middle of Blinder's article might look after you have marked the main ideas by highlighting and by marginal notations.

Offshored service jobs will eclipse lost manufacturing jobs—3 reasons

Service-sector offshoring is a minor phenomenon so far, Lou Dobbs notwithstanding; probably well under 1 percent of U.S. service jobs have been outsourced. But I believe that service-sector offshoring will eventually exceed manufacturing-sector offshoring by a hefty margin—for three main reasons. The first is simple arithmetic: There are vastly more service jobs than manufacturing jobs in the United States (and in other rich countries). Second, the technological advances that have made service-sector offshoring possible will continue and accelerate, so the range of services that can be moved offshore will increase ineluctably. Third, the number of (e.g., Indian and Chinese) workers capable of performing service jobs offshore seems certain to grow, perhaps exponentially.

Long-term economy will be ok. Short-to-middle term will be "bumpy"

I do not mean to paint a bleak picture here. Ever since Adam Smith and David Ricardo, economists have explained and extolled the gains in living standards that derive from international trade. Those arguments are just as valid for trade in services as for trade in goods. There really *are* net gains to the United States from expanding service-sector trade with India, China, and the rest. The offshoring problem is not about the adverse nature of what economists call the economy's eventual equilibrium. Rather, it is about the so-called transition—the ride from here to there. That ride, which could take a generation or more, may be bumpy. And during the long adjustment period, many U.S. wages could face downward pressure.

High-end jobs to be lost

Thus far, only American manufacturing workers and a few low-end service workers (e.g., call-center operators) have been competing, at least potentially, with millions of people in faraway lands eager to work for what seems a pittance by U.S. standards. But offshoring is no longer limited to low-end service jobs. Computer code can be written overseas and e-mailed back to the United States. So can your tax return and lots of legal work, provided you do not insist on face-to-face contact with the accountant or lawyer. In writing and editing this article, I communicated with the editors and staff of *The American Prospect* only by telephone and e-mail. Why couldn't they (or I, for that matter) have been in India? The possibilities are, if not endless, at least vast.

What distinguishes the jobs that cannot be offshored from the ones that can? The crucial distinction is not—and this is the central point of this essay—the required levels of skill and education. These attributes have been critical to labor-market success in the past, but may be less so in the future. Instead, the new critical distinction may be that some services either require personal delivery (e.g., driving a taxi and brain surgery) or are seriously degraded when delivered electronically (e.g., college teaching—at least, I hope!), while other jobs (e.g., call centers and keyboard data entry) are not. Call the first category personal services and the second category impersonal services. With this terminology, I have three main points to make about preparing our workforce for the brave, new world of the future.

First, we need to think about, plan, and redesign our educational system with the crucial distinction between personal service jobs and impersonal service jobs in mind. Many of the impersonal service jobs will migrate offshore, but the personal service jobs will stay here.

Second, the line that divides personal services from impersonal services will move in only one direction over time, as technological progress makes it possible to deliver an ever-increasing array of services electronically.

Third, the novel distinction between personal and impersonal jobs is quite different from, and appears essentially unrelated to, the traditional distinction between jobs that do and do not require high levels of education.

Margin notes:

B's main point: key distinction: Personal service jobs stay; impersonal jobs go

3 points re: prep of future workforce

Movement: impersonal → personal

Level of ed. not related to future job security

Divide into Stages of Thought

When a selection doesn't contain sections with topic headings, as is the case with "Will Your Job Be Exported?" how do you determine where one stage of thought ends and the next one begins? Assuming that what you have read is coherent and unified, this should not be difficult. (When a selection is unified, all of its parts pertain to the main subject; when a selection is coherent, the parts follow one another in logical order.) Look particularly for transitional sentences at the beginning of paragraphs. Such sentences generally work in one or both of two ways: (1) they summarize what has come before; (2) they set the stage for what is to follow.

Look at the sentences that open paragraphs 5 and 10: "Which brings me to the future" and "What distinguishes the jobs that cannot be offshored from the ones that can?" In both cases Blinder makes a clear announcement. Grammatically speaking, "Which brings me to the future" is a fragment, not a sentence. Experienced writers will use fragments on occasion to good effect, as in this case. The fragment clearly has the sense of a complete thought: the pronoun "which" refers readers to the content of the preceding paragraphs, asking readers to summarize that content and then, with the predicate "brings me to the future," to move forward into the next part of the article. Similarly, the question "What distinguishes the jobs that cannot be offshored from the ones that can?" implicitly asks readers to recall an important distinction just made (the definitions of offshorable and non-offshorable jobs) and then clearly moves readers forward to new, related content. As you can see, the openings of paragraphs 5 and 10 announce new sections in the article.

Each section of an article generally takes several paragraphs to develop. Between paragraphs, and almost certainly between sections of an article, you will usually find transitions that help you understand what you have just read and what you are about to read. For articles that have no subheadings, try writing your own section headings in the margins as you take notes. Blinder's article can be divided into five sections.

> **Section 1:** *Recent past: education of workers important*—For twenty-five years, the labor market has rewarded workers with higher levels of education (paragraphs 1–4).

> **Section 2:** *Future: ed level won't always matter—workers in service sector will lose jobs offshore*—Once thought immune to outsourcing, even highly trained service workers will lose jobs to overseas competition (paragraphs 5–9).

> **Section 3:** *Which service jobs at highest risk?*—Personal service workers are safe; impersonal service workers, both highly educated and not, will see jobs offshored (paragraphs 10–15).

> **Section 4:** *Educating the future workforce*—Emphasizing the kind, not amount, of education will help to prepare workers for jobs of the future (paragraphs 16–22).

> **Section 5:** *Needed policy reforms*—Government can improve conditions for low-end service workers and expand opportunities for higher-end service workers; start with education (paragraphs 23–26).

Write a Brief Summary of Each Stage of Thought

The purpose of this step is to wean you from the language of the original passage, so that you are not tied to it when writing the summary. Here are brief summaries, one for each stage of thought in "Will Your Job Be Exported?"

> *Section 1:* Recent past: education of workers important (paragraphs 1–4).

> > For the past twenty-five years, the greater a worker's skill or level of education, the better and more stable the job.

> *Section 2:* Future: ed level won't always matter—workers in service sector will lose jobs offshore (paragraphs 5–9).

> > Advances in technology have brought to the service sector the same pressures that forced so many manufacturing jobs offshore to China and India. The rate of offshoring in the service sector will accelerate and "eventually exceed" job losses in manufacturing, says Blinder, and jobs

requiring both relatively little education (like call-center staffing) and extensive education (like software development) will be lost to workers overseas.

Section 3: Which service jobs at highest risk? (paragraphs 10–15).

While "personal services" workers (like barbers and surgeons) will be relatively safe from offshoring because their work requires close physical proximity to customers, "impersonal services" workers (like call-center operators and radiologists), regardless of their skill or education, will be at risk because their work can be completed remotely without loss of quality and then delivered via phone or computer. Blinder believes that "the relative demand for labor in the United States will [probably] shift away from impersonal services and toward personal services."

Section 4: Educating the future workforce (paragraphs 16–22).

Blinder advises young people to plan for "a high-end personal service occupation that is not offshorable." He also urges educators to prepare the future workforce by anticipating the needs of a personal services economy and redesigning classroom instruction and vocational training accordingly.

Section 5: Needed policy reforms (paragraphs 23–26).

Blinder urges the government to develop policies that will improve wages and conditions for low-wage personal service workers (like janitors); to encourage more low-wage workers (like daycare providers) to retrain and take on better jobs; and to increase opportunities for professional and vocational training in high-demand areas (like nursing and carpentry).

Write a Thesis: A Brief Summary of the Entire Passage

The thesis is the most general statement of a summary (or any other type of academic writing). It is the statement that announces the paper's subject and the claim that you or—in the case of a summary—another author will be making about that subject. Every paragraph of a paper illuminates the thesis by providing supporting detail or explanation. The relationship of these paragraphs to the thesis is analogous to the relationship of the sentences within a paragraph to the topic sentence. Both the thesis and the topic sentences are general statements (the thesis being the more general) that are followed by systematically arranged details.

To ensure clarity for the reader, *the first sentence of your summary should begin with the author's thesis, regardless of where it appears in the article itself.* An author may locate her thesis at the beginning of her work, in which case the thesis operates as a general principle from which details of the presentation follow. This is called a *deductive* organization: thesis first, supporting details second. Alternatively, an author may locate his thesis at the end of the work, in which case the author begins with specific details and builds toward a more general conclusion, or thesis. This is called an *inductive* organization. And, as you might expect, an author might locate the thesis anywhere between beginning and end, at whatever point it seems best positioned.*

A thesis consists of a subject and an assertion about that subject. How can we go about fashioning an adequate thesis for a summary of Blinder's article? Probably no two versions of Blinder's thesis statement would be worded identically, but it is fair to say that any reasonable thesis will indicate that Blinder's subject is the future loss to offshoring of American jobs in the service sector—that part of the economy that delivers services to consumers, from low end (e.g., janitorial services) to high end (e.g., neurosurgery). How does Blinder view the situation? How secure will service jobs be if Blinder's distinction between personal and impersonal services is valid? Looking back over our section summaries, we find that Blinder insists on three points: (1) that education and skill matter less than they once did in determining job quality and security; (2) that the distinction between personal and impersonal services will increasingly determine which jobs remain and which are offshored; and (3) that the distinction between personal and impersonal has implications for both the future of education and public policy.

Does Blinder make a statement anywhere in this passage that pulls all this together? Examine paragraph 10 and you will find his thesis—two sentences that answer his question about which jobs will and will not be sent offshore: "The crucial distinction is not—and this is the central point of this essay—the required levels of skill and education.... Instead, the new critical distinction may be that some services either require personal delivery (e.g., driving a taxi and brain surgery) or are seriously degraded when delivered electronically (e.g., college teaching—at least, I hope!), while other jobs (e.g., call centers and keyboard data entry) are not."

You may have learned that a thesis statement must be expressed in a single sentence. We would offer a slight rewording of this generally sound advice and say that a thesis statement must be *expressible* in a single sentence. For reasons of emphasis or style, a writer might choose to distribute a thesis across two or more sentences. Certainly, the sense of Blinder's thesis can take the form of a single statement: "The critical distinction is X, not Y." For reasons largely of emphasis, he divides his thesis into two sentences—in fact, separating these sentences with another sentence that explains the first part of the thesis: "These attributes [that is, skill and education] have been critical to labor-market success in the past, but may be less so in the future."

---

*Blinder positions his thesis midway through his five-section article. He opens the selection by discussing the role of education in the labor market during the past twenty-five years (Section 1, pars. 1–4). He continues by summarizing an earlier article on the ways in which service jobs are following manufacturing jobs offshore (Section 2, pars. 5–9). He then presents a two-sentence thesis in answer to the question that opens paragraph 10: "What distinguishes the jobs that cannot be offshored from the ones that can?" The remainder of the article either develops this thesis (Section 3, pars. 10–15) or follows its implications for education (Section 4, pars. 16–22) and public policy (Section 5, pars. 23–26).

Here is a one-sentence version of Blinder's two-sentence thesis:

> The quality and security of future jobs in America's service sector will be determined by how "offshorable" those jobs are.

Notice that the statement anticipates a summary of the *entire* article: both the discussion leading up to Blinder's thesis and his discussion after. To clarify for our readers the fact that this idea is Blinder's and not ours, we might qualify the thesis as follows:

> In "Will Your Job Be Exported?" economist Alan S. Blinder argues that the quality and security of future jobs in America's service sector will be determined by how "offshorable" those jobs are.

The first sentence of a summary is crucially important, for it orients readers by letting them know what to expect in the coming paragraphs. In the example above, the first sentence refers directly to an article, its author, and the thesis for the upcoming summary. The author and title reference could also be indicated in the summary's title (if this were a free-standing summary), in which case their mention could be dropped from the thesis statement. And lest you become frustrated too quickly with how much effort it takes to come up with this crucial sentence, keep in mind that writing an acceptable thesis for a summary takes time. In this case, it took three drafts, roughly ten minutes, to compose a thesis and another few minutes of fine-tuning after a draft of the entire summary was completed. The thesis needed revision because the first draft was vague; the second draft was improved but too specific on a secondary point; the third draft was more complete but too general on a key point:

> **Draft 1:** We must begin now to train young people for high-quality personal service jobs.
> (Vague. The question of why we should begin training isn't clear, nor is the phrase "high-quality personal service jobs." Define this term or make it more general.)
>
> **Draft 2:** Alan S. Blinder argues that unlike in the past, the quality and security of future American jobs will not be determined by skill level or education but rather by how "offshorable" those jobs are.
> (Better, but the reference to "skill level or education" is secondary to Blinder's main point about offshorable jobs.)
>
> **Draft 3:** In "Will Your Job Be Exported?" economist Alan S. Blinder argues that the quality and security of future jobs will be determined by how "offshorable" those jobs are.
> (Close—but not "all" jobs. Blinder specifies which types of jobs are "offshorable.")

Final Draft: In "Will Your Job Be Exported?" economist Alan S. Blinder argues that the quality and security of future jobs in America's service sector will be determined by how "offshorable" those jobs are.

Write the First Draft of the Summary

Let's consider two possible summaries of Blinder's article: (1) a short summary, combining a thesis with brief section summaries, and (2) a longer summary, combining thesis, brief section summaries, and some carefully chosen details. Again, keep in mind that you are reading final versions; each of the following summaries is the result of at least two full drafts. Highlighting indicates transitions added to smooth the flow of the summary.

Summary 1: Combine Thesis Sentence with Brief Section Summaries

In "Will Your Job Be Exported?" economist Alan S. Blinder argues that the quality and security of future jobs in America's service sector will be determined by how "offshorable" those jobs are. For the past twenty-five years, the greater a worker's skill or level of education, the better and more stable the job. No longer. Advances in technology have brought to the service sector the same pressures that forced so many manufacturing jobs offshore to China and India. The rate of offshoring in the service sector will accelerate, and jobs requiring both relatively little education (like call-center staffing) and extensive education (like software development) will increasingly be lost to workers overseas.

These losses will "eventually exceed" losses in manufacturing, but not all services jobs are equally at risk. While "personal services" workers (like barbers and surgeons) will be relatively safe from offshoring because their work requires close physical proximity to customers, "impersonal services" workers (like call-center operators and radiologists), regardless of their skill or education, will be at risk because their work can be completed remotely without loss of quality and then delivered via phone or computer. "[T]he relative demand for labor in the United States will [probably] shift away from impersonal services and toward personal services."

Blinder recommends three courses of action: He advises young people to plan for "a high-end personal service occupation that is not offshorable." He urges educators to prepare the future workforce by anticipating the needs of a personal services economy and redesigning classroom instruction and vocational training accordingly. Finally, he urges the government to adopt policies that will improve existing personal services jobs by increasing wages for low-wage workers; retraining workers to take on better jobs; and increasing opportunities in high-demand, well-paid areas like nursing and carpentry. Ultimately, Blinder wants America to prepare a new generation to "lead and innovate" in an economy that will continue exporting jobs that require "following and copying."

The Strategy of the Shorter Summary

This short summary consists essentially of a restatement of Blinder's thesis plus the section summaries, modified or expanded a little for stylistic purposes. You'll recall that Blinder locates his thesis midway through the article, in paragraph 10. But note that this model summary *begins* with a restatement of his thesis. Notice also the relative weight given to the section summaries within the model. Blinder's main point, his "critical distinction" between personal and impersonal services jobs, is summarized in paragraph 2 of the model. The other paragraphs combine summaries of relatively less important (that is, supporting or explanatory) material. Paragraph 1 combines summaries of the article's Sections 1 and 2; paragraph 3 combines summaries of Sections 4 and 5.

Between the thesis and the section summaries, notice the insertion of three (highlighted) transitions. The first—a fragment (*No longer*)—bridges the first paragraph's summaries of Sections 1 and 2 of Blinder's article. The second transition links a point Blinder makes in his Section 2 (*Losses in the service sector will "eventually exceed" losses in manufacturing*) with an introduction to the key point he will make in Section 3 (*Not all service jobs are equally at risk*). The third transition (*Blinder recommends three courses of action*) bridges the summary of Blinder's Section 3 to summaries of Sections 4 and 5. Each transition, then, links sections of the whole: each casts the reader back to recall points just made; each casts the reader forward by announcing related points about to be made. Our model ends with a summary of Blinder's motivation for writing, the sense of which is implied by the section summaries but nowhere made explicit.

Summary 2: Combine Thesis Sentence, Section Summaries, and Carefully Chosen Details

The thesis and brief section summaries could also be used as the outline for a more detailed summary. However, most of the details in the passage won't be necessary in a summary. It isn't necessary even in a longer summary of this passage to discuss all of Blinder's examples of jobs that are more or less likely to be sent offshore. It would be appropriate, though, to mention one example of such a job; to review his reasons for thinking "that service-sector offshoring will eventually exceed manufacturing-sector offshoring by a hefty margin"; and to expand on his point that a college education in itself will no longer ensure job security.

None of these details appeared in the first summary; but in a longer summary, a few carefully selected details might be desirable for clarity. How do you decide which details to include? First, working with Blinder's point that one's job type (personal services vs. impersonal services) will matter more for future job quality and security than did the once highly regarded "silver bullet" of education, you may want to cite some of the most persuasive evidence supporting this idea. For example, you could explore why some highly paid physicians, like radiologists, might find themselves competing for jobs with lower-paid physicians overseas. Further, your expanded summary might reflect the relative weight Blinder gives to education (seven paragraphs, the longest of the article's five sections).

You won't always know which details to include and which to exclude. Developing good judgment in comprehending and summarizing texts is largely a matter of reading skill and prior knowledge (see page 3). Consider the analogy of the seasoned mechanic who can pinpoint an engine problem by simply listening to a characteristic sound that to a less-experienced person is just noise. Or consider the chess player who can plot three separate winning strategies from a board position that to a novice looks like a hopeless jumble. In the same way, the more practiced a reader you are, the more knowledgeable you become about the subject and the better able you will be to make critical distinctions between elements of greater and lesser importance. In the meantime, read as carefully as you can and use your own best judgment as to how to present your material.

Here's one version of a completed summary with carefully chosen details. Note that we have highlighted phrases and sentences added to the original, briefer summary.

> In "Will Your Job Be Exported?" economist Alan S. Blinder argues that the quality and security of future jobs in America's service sector will be determined by how "offshorable" those jobs are. For the past twenty-five years, the greater a worker's skill or level of education, the better and more stable the job. Americans have long regarded education as the "silver bullet" that could propel motivated people to better jobs and a better life. No longer. Advances in technology have brought to the service sector the same pressures that forced so many manufacturing jobs offshore to China and India. The rate of offshoring in the service sector will accelerate, says Blinder, and jobs requiring both relatively little education (like call-center staffing) and extensive education (like software development) will increasingly be lost to workers overseas.
>
> Blinder expects that job losses in the service sector will "eventually exceed" losses in manufacturing, for three reasons. Developed countries have more service jobs than manufacturing jobs; as technology speeds communications, more service jobs will be offshorable; and the numbers of qualified offshore workers is increasing. Service jobs lost to foreign competition may cause a "bumpy" period as the global economy sorts out what work gets done where, by whom. In time, as the global economy finds its "eventual equilibrium," offshoring will benefit the United States; but the consequences in the meantime may be painful for many.
>
> That pain will not be shared equally by all service workers, however. While "personal service" workers (like barbers and surgeons) will be relatively safe from offshoring because their work requires close physical proximity to customers, "impersonal service" workers (like audio transcribers and radiologists), regardless of their skill or education, will be at risk because their work can be completed remotely without loss of quality and then delivered via phone or computer. In the coming decades, says Blinder, "the relative demand for labor in the United States will [probably] shift away from impersonal services and toward personal services." This shift will be influenced by the desire to keep good jobs in the United States while exporting jobs that require "following and copying." Highly trained computer coders will face the same pressures of outsourcing as relatively untrained call-center attendants. A tax

attorney whose work requires no face-to-face interaction with clients may see her work migrate overseas while a divorce attorney, who must interact with clients on a case-by-case basis, may face no such competition. Same educations, different outcomes: what determines their fates in a global economy is the nature of their work (that is, personal vs. impersonal), not their level of education.

Based on this analysis, Blinder recommends three courses of action: First, he advises young people to plan for "a high-end personal service occupation that is not offshorable." Many good jobs, like carpentry and plumbing, will not require a college degree. Next, Blinder urges educators to prepare the future workforce by anticipating the needs of a personal services economy and redesigning classroom instruction and vocational training accordingly. These efforts should begin in elementary school and develop imagination and interpersonal skills rather than capacities for rote memorization. Finally, Blinder urges the government to develop policies that will improve wages and conditions for low-wage personal services workers (like janitors); to encourage more low-wage workers (like daycare providers) to retrain and take on better service jobs; and to increase opportunities for professional and vocational training for workers in high-demand services areas (like nurses and electricians). Ultimately, Blinder wants America to prepare a new generation of workers who will "lead and innovate . . . just as we have in the past."

The Strategy of the Longer Summary

Compared to the first, briefer summary, this effort (seventy percent longer than the first) includes Blinder's reasons for suggesting that job losses in the services sector will exceed losses in manufacturing. It emphasizes Blinder's point that job type (personal vs. impersonal services), not a worker's education level, will ensure job security. It includes Blinder's point that offshoring in the service sector is part of a larger global economy seeking "equilibrium." And it offers more on Blinder's thoughts concerning the education of future workers.

The final two of our suggested steps for writing summaries are (1) to check your summary against the original passage, making sure that you have included all the important ideas, and (2) to revise so that the summary reads smoothly and coherently. The structure of this summary generally reflects the structure of the original article—with one significant departure, as noted earlier. Blinder uses a modified inductive approach, stating his thesis midway through the article. The summary, however, states the thesis immediately, then proceeds deductively to develop that thesis.

HOW LONG SHOULD A SUMMARY BE?

The length of a summary depends both on the length of the original passage and on the use to which the summary will be put. If you are summarizing an entire article, a good rule of thumb is that your summary should be no longer than one-fourth the length of the original passage. Of course, if you were summarizing an entire chapter or even an entire book, it would have to be much shorter than that. The longer summary above is one-quarter the length of Alan Blinder's original. Although it shouldn't be very much longer, you have seen (p. 19) that it could be quite a bit shorter.

The length as well as the content of the summary also depends on the *purpose* to which it will be put. Let's suppose you decided to use Blinder's piece in a paper that dealt with the loss of manufacturing jobs in the United States and the rise of the service economy. In this case, in an effort to explain the complexities of the service economy to your readers, you might summarize *only* Blinder's core distinction between jobs in personal services and impersonal services, likely mentioning that jobs in the latter category are at risk of offshoring. If, instead, you were writing a paper in which you argued that the forces of globalization will eventually collapse the world's economies into a single, global economy, you would likely give less attention to Blinder's distinction between personal and impersonal services. More to the point might be his observation that highly skilled, highly educated workers in the United States are now finding themselves competing with qualified, lower-wage workers in China and India. Thus, depending on your purpose, you would summarize either selected portions of a source or an entire source. We will see this process more fully demonstrated in the upcoming chapters on syntheses.

Exercise 1.1

Individual and Collaborative Summary Practice

Turn to Chapter 13 and read Solomon A. Asch's article "Opinions and Social Pressures" (pp. 723–727). Follow the steps for writing summaries outlined above—read, underline, and divide into stages of thought. Write a one- or two-sentence summary of each stage of thought in Asch's article. Then gather in groups of three or four classmates and compare your summary sentences. Discuss the differences in your sentences, and come to some consensus about the divisions in Asch's stages of thought—and the ways in which to best sum them up.

As a group, write a one- or two-sentence thesis statement summing up the entire passage. You could go even further, and, using your individual summary sentences—or the versions of them your group revised—put together a brief summary of Asch's essay. Model your work on the brief summary of Blinder's article, on pp. 19–20.

SUMMARIZING FIGURES AND TABLES

In your reading in the sciences and social sciences, you will often find data and concepts presented in nontext forms—as figures and tables. Such visual devices offer a snapshot, a pictorial overview of material that is more quickly and clearly communicated in graphic form than as a series of (often complicated) sentences. Note that in essence, figures and tables are themselves summaries. The writer uses a graph, which in an article or book is labeled as a numbered "figure," and presents the quantitative results of research as points on a line or a bar or as sections ("slices") of a pie. Pie charts show relative proportions, or percentages. Graphs, especially effective in showing patterns, relate one variable to another: for instance, income to years of education, or sales figures of a product over a period of three years.

Writers regularly draw on graphs, charts, and tables to provide information or to offer evidence for points they are arguing. Consider the following passage from an op-ed article by Michael Klare arguing that the United States and China should cooperate, rather than compete, in order to supply their future energy needs:

> In 2007, according to Energy Department figures, the United States consumed about 21 million barrels of oil a day, nearly three times as much as China. Even more significant, we imported 13 million barrels every day, a vastly greater amount than China's import tally. So, although it is indeed true that Chinese and American consumers are competing for access to overseas supplies, thereby edging up prices, American consumption still sets the pace in international oil markets.
>
> The reality is that as far as the current run-up in gasoline prices is concerned, other factors are more to blame: shrinking oil output from such key producers as Mexico, Russia and Venezuela; internal violence in Iraq and Nigeria; refinery inadequacies in the U.S. and elsewhere; speculative stockpiling by global oil brokers, and so on. These conditions are likely to persist for the foreseeable future, so prices will remain high.
>
> Peer into the future, however, and the China factor starts looming much larger.
>
> With its roaring economy and millions of newly affluent consumers—many of whom are now buying their first automobiles—China is rapidly catching up with the United States in its net oil intake. According to the most recent projections, Chinese petroleum consumption is expected to jump from 8 million barrels a day in 2008 to an estimated 12 million in 2020 and to 16 million in 2030. American consumption will also climb, but not as much, reaching an estimated 27 million barrels a day in 2030. In terms of oil imports, moreover, the gap will grow even smaller. Chinese imports are projected to hit 10.8 million barrels a day in 2030, compared with 16.4 million for the United States. Clearly, the Sino-American competition for foreign oil supplies will grow ever more intense with every passing year.*

A good deal of the data Klare provides in this passage likely came from graphs, charts, and tables.

In the following pages, we present four figures and a table from various sources, all related to the world's rising oil consumption and its dwindling supply. (Some promising alternative sources of energy for automobiles and other vehicles are discussed in our model explanatory synthesis, "The Car of the Future?" in Chapter 4, pp. 123–130.)

---

*Michael T. Klare, "The U.S. and China are over a Barrel," *Los Angeles Times* 28 Apr. 2008: 17. Klare is professor of peace and world security studies at Hampshire College and the author of *Rising Powers, Shrinking Planet: The New Geopolitics of Energy.*

Bar Graphs

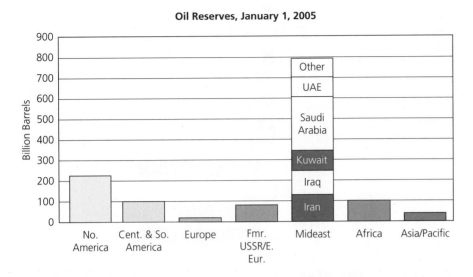

Oil Reserves, January 1, 2005

Figure 1.1   World Oil Reserves by Region, January 1, 2005*

Figure 1.1 is a bar graph indicating the world's known oil reserves as of January 2005. The vertical axis of this graph indicates the number of barrels, in billions, estimated to be available. The horizontal axis indicates various regions of the world. The vertical bar above each region indicates the number of billions of barrels. Note that the bar indicating the largest available supplies, the Mideast, is subdivided into the nations of that region in control of the largest oil reserves.

Here is a summary of the information presented in Figure 1.1:

> As of January 1, 2005, the Middle East had by far the largest quantities of oil re-serves in the world, almost 800 billion barrels. North America, the region with the next highest oil reserves, has slightly more than a quarter of this quantity, just over 200 billion barrels. Central and South America and Africa come next, each with about 100 billion barrels. Russia and Eastern Europe have slightly less than this quantity. Compared to these oil-rich regions, Asia and the Pacific region and Europe have relatively minimal amounts. Within the Middle East region, Saudi Arabia has the largest oil reserves, about 250 billion barrels. This one country therefore has more oil than any other entire region in the world. Iran, Iraq, and Kuwait each have at least 100 million barrels of oil. Each of these countries, therefore, has at least as much in oil reserves as all of the African countries or all of the Central and South American countries combined.

Oil and Gas Journal 1 Jan. 2005. <http://www.eia.doe.gov/pub/oil_gas/petroleum/analysis_ publications/oil_market_basics/sup_image_reserves.htm>.

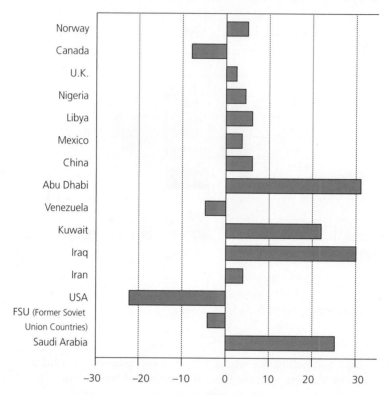

Time to Depletion Midpoint of Oil Reserves, 2003 (Years)

Figure 1.2   This graph illustrates the number of years to the midpoint of the depletion of oil reserves for various major oil-producing nations in 2003. A negative value means that the midpoint was in the past. The only countries a significant distance from their midpoints are the major Middle East producers.*

Figure 1.2, another bar graph, indicates the number of years (from 2003—the "zero" point on the horizontal axis) until the midpoint of depletion of national oil reserves for fifteen countries. Note that this graph features bars stretching in opposite directions: The bars to the left indicate negative values; the bars to the right indicate positive values. Thus, Norway will have used up half of its total oil reserves by 2008, five years after the date the chart was prepared. Canada, by contrast, reached the midpoint of its depletion about eight years *before* 2003.

*The Hubbert Peak for World Oil. Chart updated 2003. <http://www.oilcrisis.com/summary.htm>.

Pie Charts

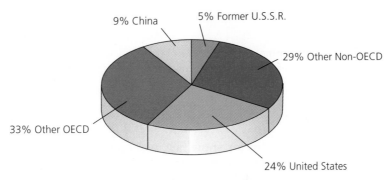

Figure 1.3   The Oil Consumption Pie

Exercise 1.2

Summarizing Graphs

Write a brief summary of the data in Figure 1.2. Use our summary of Figure 1.1 as a model.

Bar graphs are useful for visually comparing numerical quantities. Pie charts, on the other hand, are useful for visually comparing percentages of a whole. The pie represents the whole; the individual slices represent the relative sizes of the parts. Figure 1.3 is a pie chart indicating the relative oil consumption of various regions of the world in 2007. Each slice represents a percentage of the world's total oil consumption.

In this chart, OECD stands for the Organization for Economic Cooperation and Development.* Note that only two of the five pie slices represent individual countries: the United States (an OECD country) and China. Two additional slices represent "other OECD countries" and "other Non–OECD countries" (i.e., countries other than China and the former USSR, which are separately represented in the chart). Finally, note that the "former USSR" slice indicates Russia and Eastern

---

*The OECD is a Paris-based international group, founded in 1961, that collects and analyzes economic data. According to its Web site <http://www.oecd.org>, "[I]ts mission [is] to help...member countries to achieve sustainable economic growth and employment and to raise the standard of living in member countries while maintaining financial stability...[and contributing] to the development of the world economy." OECD countries, democracies with market economies, include Australia, Austria, Belgium, Canada, the Czech Republic, Denmark, Finland, France, Germany, Greece, Hungary, Iceland, Ireland, Italy, Japan, Korea, Luxembourg, Mexico, Netherlands, New Zealand, Norway, Poland, the Slovak Republic, Spain, Switzerland, Sweden, Turkey, the United Kingdom, and the United States.

European countries—such as Bulgaria, Romania, and Estonia—that are not presently members of the OECD (as are Hungary and Poland).

Exercise 1.3

Summarizing Pie Charts

Write a brief summary of the data in Figure 1.3. Use our summary of Figure 1.1 (or your summary of Figure 1.2) as a model.

Line Graphs

Line graphs are useful for showing trends over a period of time. Usually, the horizontal axis indicates years, months, or shorter periods, and the vertical axis indicates a quantity: dollars, barrels, personnel, sales, anything that can be counted. The line running from left to right indicates the changing values, over a given period, of the object of measurement. Frequently, a line graph will feature multiple lines (perhaps in different colors, perhaps some solid, others dotted, etc.), each indicating a separate variable to be measured. Thus, a line graph could show the changing approval ratings of several presidential candidates over the

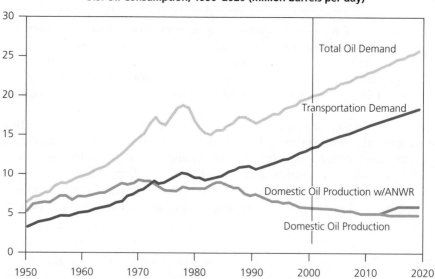

Figure 1.4   U.S. Oil Consumption, 1950–2020*

---

*Energy Information Administration (EIA), Annual Energy Outlook, 2001: "Potential Oil Production from the Coastal Plain of ANWR [Arctic National Wildlife Refuge [ANWR]," EIR Reserves and Production Division. <http://energy.senate.gov/legislation/energybill/charts/chart8.pdf>.

course of a campaign season. Or it could indicate the number of iPhones vs. Blackberries sold in a given year.

The line graph shown in Figure 1.4 indicates the changes in several U.S. oil consumption variables, over time: (1) total oil demand (in millions of barrels per day), (2) oil consumption demand for transportation alone, and (3) domestic oil production. Note that because the graph was produced in 2001, the fifty-year period before that indicates historical data; the twenty-year period following is a projection based on estimates. Note also that somewhere around 2015, the domestic oil production line splits in two: The upper range indicates the level of oil production if Alaskan oil reserves were included; the lower range indicates domestic production without this particular resource.

Exercise 1.4

Summarizing Line Graphs

Write a brief summary of the key data in Figure 1.4. Use our summary of Figure 1.1 (or your summary of Figure 1.2) as a model.

Tables

A table presents numerical data in rows and columns for quick reference. If the writer chooses, tabular information can be converted to graphic information. Charts and graphs are preferable when the writer wants to emphasize a pattern or relationship; tables are preferable when the writer wants to emphasize numbers. While the previous charts and graphs represented a relatively small number of factors (regions or countries, quantities of oil produced or consumed in a given year or over a period of time), Table 1.1 breaks down oil production into numerous countries, organized by region.* Note that since production is represented in thousands of barrels daily, each number should be multiplied by 1000. The number at the upper left corner of page 30, 8295, therefore represents the 8,295,000 barrels a day produced by the USA in 1996. "Total World" production that year (p. 32, lower left) was 69,931,000 barrels per day.

A table may contain so much data that you would not want to summarize *all* of it for a particular paper. In this case, you would summarize the *part* of a table that you find useful. Here is a summary drawn from the information from Table 1.1 focusing just on the North American and Middle Eastern sections. Notice that the summary requires the writer to read closely and discern which information is significant. The table reports raw data and does not speak for itself. At the end of

---

*"British Petroleum Statistical Review of World Energy 2006: Oil Production." British Petroleum, 2007. <http://www.bp.com/liveassets/bp_internet/globalbp/globalbp_uk_english/reports_and_ publications/statistical_energy_review_2007/STAGING/local_assets/downloads/pdf/table_of_world_ oil_production_2007.pdf>.

Table 1.1 Oil Production by Country, 1997–2007*

Producer	Thousands of barrels daily											Change: 2007 over 2006	2007 share of total
	1997	1998	1999	2000	2001	2002	2003	2004	2005	2006	2007		
USA	8269	8011	7731	7733	7669	7626	7400	7228	6895	6841	**6879**	0.4%	8.0%
Canada	2588	2672	2604	2721	2677	2858	3004	3085	3041	3208	**3309**	3.6%	4.1%
Mexico	3410	3499	3343	3450	3560	3585	3789	3824	3760	3683	**3477**	−5.5%	4.4%
Total North America	**14,267**	**14,182**	**13,678**	**13,904**	**13,906**	**14,069**	**14,193**	**14,137**	**13,695**	**13,732**	**13,665**	**−0.5%**	**16.5%**
Argentina	877	890	847	819	830	818	806	754	725	716	**698**	−2.5%	0.9%
Brazil	868	1003	1133	1268	1337	1499	1555	1542	1716	1809	**1833**	1.4%	2.3%
Colombia	667	775	838	711	627	601	564	551	554	559	**561**	0.4%	0.7%
Ecuador	397	385	383	409	416	401	427	535	541	545	**520**	−4.5%	0.7%
Peru	120	116	107	100	98	98	92	94	111	116	**114**	−1.3%	0.1%
Trinidad & Tobago	135	134	141	138	135	155	164	152	171	174	**154**	−12.5%	0.2%
Venezuela	3321	3480	3126	3239	3142	2895	2554	2907	2937	2808	**2613**	−7.2%	3.4%
Other S. & Cent. America	108	125	124	130	137	152	153	144	143	141	**141**	**	0.2%
Total S. & Cent. America	**6493**	**6908**	**6699**	**6813**	**6722**	**6619**	**6314**	**6680**	**6899**	**6866**	**6633**	**−3.6%**	**8.5%**
Azerbaijan	182	231	279	282	301	311	313	315	452	654	**868**	31.7%	1.1%
Denmark	230	238	299	363	348	371	368	390	377	342	**312**	−8.8%	0.4%
Italy	124	117	104	95	86	115	116	113	127	120	**122**	1.6%	0.2%
Kazakhstan	536	537	631	744	836	1018	1111	1297	1356	1426	**1490**	3.9%	1.8%
Norway	3280	3138	3139	3346	3418	3333	3264	3188	2969	2779	**2556**	−7.7%	3.0%
Romania	141	137	133	131	130	127	123	119	114	105	**105**	1.0%	0.1%
Russian Federation	6227	6169	6178	6536	7056	7698	8544	9287	9552	9769	**9978**	2.2%	12.6%
Turkmenistan	108	129	143	144	162	182	202	193	192	186	**198**	6.5%	0.3%
United Kingdom	2702	2807	2909	2667	2476	2463	2257	2028	1809	1636	**1636**	0.2%	2.0%
Uzbekistan	182	191	191	177	171	171	166	152	126	125	**114**	−8.9%	0.1%
Other Europe & Eurasia	524	506	474	465	465	501	509	496	469	459	**456**	−0.2%	0.6%
Total Europe & Eurasia	**14,235**	**14,199**	**14,480**	**14,950**	**15,450**	**16,289**	**16,973**	**17,579**	**17,542**	**17,600**	**17,835**	**1.5%**	**22.0%**
Iran	3776	3855	3603	3818	3794	3543	4183	4308	4359	4388	**4401**	0.4%	5.4%
Iraq	1166	2121	2610	2614	2523	2116	1344	2030	1833	1999	**2145**	7.3%	2.7%
Kuwait	2137	2232	2085	2206	2148	1995	2329	2475	2618	2682	**2626**	−2.1%	3.3%
Oman	909	905	911	959	961	900	824	756	787	752	**718**	−4.6%	0.9%

Table 1.1 (continued)

Producer	1997	1998	1999	2000	2001	2002	2003	2004	2005	2006	2007	Change: 2007 over 2006	2007 share of total
						Thousands of barrels daily							
Qatar	692	701	723	757	754	764	879	992	1028	1110	**1197**	5.3%	1.4%
Saudi Arabia	9482	9502	8853	9491	9209	8928	10,164	10,638	11,114	10,853	**10,413**	-4.1%	12.6%
Syria	577	576	579	548	581	548	527	495	450	421	**394**	-6.5%	0.5%
United Arab Emirates	2567	2643	2511	2626	2534	2324	2611	2656	2753	2971	**2915**	-2.3%	3.5%
Yemen	375	380	405	450	455	457	448	420	416	380	**336**	-11.6%	0.4%
Other Middle East	50	49	48	48	47	48	48	48	34	32	**32**	—	**
Total Middle East	**21,731**	**22,964**	**22,328**	**23,516**	**23,006**	**21,623**	**23,357**	**24,818**	**25,393**	**25,589**	**25,176**	**-1.8%**	**30.8%**
Algeria	1421	1461	1515	1578	1562	1680	1852	1946	2014	2003	**2000**	-0.1%	2.2%
Angola	741	731	745	746	742	905	862	976	1246	1421	**1723**	20.7%	2.2%
Cameroon	124	105	95	88	81	72	67	89	82	87	**82**	-5.7%	0.1%
Chad	—	—	—	—	—	—	24	168	173	153	**144**	-6.3%	0.2%
Rep. of Congo (Brazzaville)	225	264	266	254	234	231	215	216	246	262	**222**	-15.3%	0.3%
Egypt	873	857	827	781	758	751	749	721	696	697	**710**	1.4%	0.9%
Equatorial Guinea	60	83	100	91	177	204	242	345	373	358	**363**	1.6%	0.5%
Gabon	364	337	340	327	301	295	240	235	234	235	**230**	-2.1%	0.3%
Libya	1491	1480	1425	1475	1427	1375	1485	1624	1751	1834	**1848**	0.5%	2.2%
Nigeria	2316	2167	2066	2155	2274	2103	2263	2502	2580	2474	**2356**	-4.8%	2.9%
Sudan	9	12	63	174	217	241	265	301	305	331	**457**	38.1%	0.6%
Tunisia	81	85	84	78	71	74	68	71	73	70	**98**	40.2%	0.1%
Other Africa	64	63	56	56	53	63	71	75	72	69	**85**	24.7%	0.1%
Total Africa	**7768**	**7644**	**7583**	**7804**	**7897**	**7994**	**8402**	**9268**	**9846**	**9995**	**10,318**	**3.2%**	**12.5%**
Australia	669	644	625	809	733	730	624	582	580	554	**561**	1.8%	0.6%
Brunei	163	157	182	193	203	210	214	210	206	221	**194**	-12.1%	0.2%
China	3211	3212	3213	3252	3306	3346	3401	3481	3627	3684	**3743**	1.6%	4.8%
India	800	787	788	780	780	801	798	812	776	795	**801**	0.9%	1.0%

(continued)

Table 1.1 (continued)

Producer	Thousands of barrels daily											Change: 2007 over 2006	2007 share of total
	1997	1998	1999	2000	2001	2002	2003	2004	2005	2006	2007		
Indonesia	1557	1520	1408	1456	1389	1289	1183	1129	1087	1017	969	-4.9%	1.2%
Malaysia	777	779	737	735	719	757	776	793	744	748	755	1.0%	0.9%
Thailand	126	130	140	176	191	204	236	223	265	286	309	7.4%	0.3%
Vietnam	205	245	296	328	350	354	364	427	398	367	340	-7.6%	0.4%
Other Asia Pacific	229	217	218	200	195	193	195	186	198	206	234	13.1%	0.3%
Total Asia Pacific	**7737**	**7692**	**7608**	**7928**	**7866**	**7884**	**7791**	**7843**	**7880**	**7877**	**7907**	**0.3%**	**9.7%**
TOTAL WORLD	72,231	73,588	72,377	74,918	74,847	74,478	77,031	80,326	81,255	81,659	81,533	−0.2%	100.0%
of which													
European Union	3454	3553	3684	3493	3285	3339	3128	2902	2659	2422	2394	-0.9%	2.9%
OECD	21669	21,500	21,103	21,521	21,303	21,430	21,165	20,766	19,861	19,458	**19,170**	-1.4%	23.0%
OPEC	30666	31,892	30,671	32,160	31,498	29,917	31,709	34,183	35,321	35,560	**35,204**	-1.2%	43.0%
Non-OPEC‡	34191	34,305	34,153	34,742	34,689	35,028	34,823	34,735	34,095	33,780	**33,524**	-0.7%	41.0%
Former Soviet Union	7374	7391	7552	8014	8660	9533	10,499	11,407	11,839	12,318	**12,804**	3.9%	16.0%

*Includes crude oil, shale oil, oil sands and NGLs (the liquid content of natural gas where this is recovered separately). Excludes liquid fules from other sources such as biomass and coal derivatives.
‡Excludes Former Soviet Union.
**Less than 0.05%

Note: Annual changes and shares of total are calculated using million tons per annum figures.

the summary the writer, using information not only from this table but also from Figure 1.4, "U.S. Oil Consumption, 1950–2020," draws her own conclusions:

> In 1996, the United States produced 8.3 million barrels of oil daily, or 89% of Saudia Arabia's production of 9.3 million barrels. By 2006, the United States was producing less than 7 million barrels, or 62% of Saudi Arabia's 11 million barrels. If we compare by region, the figures are only marginally more favorable to Americans. In 1996, the countries of North America produced 68% of the oil produced by the countries of the Middle East. Ten years later, that 68% had declined to 54%. Though the years between 1996 and 2006 have seen ups and downs in oil production by both regions, the overall trend is clear: North American production is falling and Middle East production is rising. Further, North American production is falling primarily because of declines in U.S. production; generally, Canadian and Mexican production have seen small but steady rises. Canada, for example, was producing about 2.5 million barrels of oil in 1996 and just over 3 million barrels in 2006. But this half-million-barrel rise was dwarfed by the 1.5-million-barrel rise in production by Saudi Arabia during that same period. The implications are clear: far from being self-sufficient in oil production, the United States is becoming less self-sufficient every year and is becoming ever more dependent for its petroleum supplies on a region whose political stability and reliability as a petroleum source are in serious question.

Exercise 1.5

Summarizing Tables

Focus on other data in Table 1.1 and write a brief summary of your own. Or locate another table on the general topic of oil production or consumption and summarize part or all of its data. Suggestion: "Oil Production and Consumption Country Comparison Table" from the World Factbook <http://education.yahoo.com/reference/factbook/countrycompare/oil/1a.html>.

PARAPHRASE

In certain cases, you may want to *paraphrase* rather than summarize material. Writing a paraphrase is similar to writing a summary: It involves recasting a passage into your own words, so it requires your complete understanding of the material. The difference is that while a summary is a shortened version of the original, the paraphrase is approximately the same length as the original.

Why write a paraphrase when you can quote the original? You may decide to offer a paraphrase of material written in language that is dense, abstract, archaic, or possibly confusing.

Let's consider some examples. If you were investigating the ethical concerns relating to the practice of in vitro fertilization, you might conclude that you should read some medical literature. You might reasonably want to hear from the doctors who are themselves developing, performing, and questioning the procedures that you are researching. In professional journals and bulletins, physicians write to one another, not to the general public. They use specialized language. If you wanted to refer to the following technically complex selection, you might need to write a paraphrase.

> [I]t is not only an improvement in the success-rate that participating research scientists hope for but, rather, developments in new fields of research in in-vitro gene diagnosis and in certain circumstances gene therapy. In view of this, the French expert J. F. Mattei has asked the following question: "Are we forced to accept that in vitro fertilization will become one of the most compelling methods of genetic diagnosis?" Evidently, by the introduction of a new law in France and Sweden (1994), this acceptance (albeit with certain restrictions) has already occurred prior to the application of in vitro fertilization reaching a technically mature and clinically applicable phase. This may seem astonishing in view of the question placed by the above-quoted French expert: the idea of embryo production so as to withhold one or two embryos before implantation presupposes a definite "attitude towards eugenics." And to destroy an embryo merely because of its genetic characteristics could signify the reduction of a human life to the sum of its genes. Mattei asks: "In face of a molecular judgment on our lives, is there no possibility for appeal? Will the diagnosis of inherited monogenetic illnesses soon be extended to genetic predisposition for multi-factorial illnesses?"*

Like most literature intended for physicians, the language of this selection is somewhat forbidding to nonspecialists, who will have trouble with phrases such as "predisposition for multi-factorial illnesses." As a courtesy to your readers and in an effort to maintain a consistent tone and level in your essay, you could paraphrase this paragraph from a medical newsletter. First, of course, you must understand the meaning of the passage, perhaps no small task. But, having read the material carefully (and consulted a dictionary), you might prepare a paraphrase like this one:

> Writing in *Biomedical Ethics*, Dietmar Mieth reports that fertility specialists today want not only to improve the success rates of their procedures but also to diagnose and repair genetic problems before they implant fertilized eggs. Because the result of the in vitro process is often more fertilized eggs than can be used in a procedure, doctors may examine test-tube embryos for genetic defects and "withhold one or two" before implanting them. The practice of selectively implanting embryos raises concerns about eugenics and the rights of rejected embryos. On what genetic grounds will specialists distinguish flawed from healthy embryos and make a decision whether or not to implant? The appearance of single genes linked directly to specific, or "monogenetic," illnesses could be grounds for destroying an embryo. More complicated would be genes that predispose people to an illness but in no way guarantee the onset of that illness. Would these genes, which are only one

*Dietmar Mieth, "In Vitro Fertilization: From Medical Reproduction to Genetic Diagnosis," *Biomedical Ethics: Newsletter of the European Network for Biomedical Ethics* 1.1 (1996): 45.

factor in "multi-factorial illnesses" also be labeled undesirable and lead to embryo destruction? Advances in fertility science raise difficult questions. Already, even before techniques of genetic diagnosis are fully developed, legislatures are writing laws governing the practices of fertility clinics.

We begin our paraphrase with the same "not only/but also" logic of the original's first sentence, introducing the concepts of genetic diagnosis and therapy. The next four sentences in the original introduce concerns of a "French expert." Rather than quote Mieth quoting the expert, and immediately mentioning new laws in France and Sweden, we decided (first) to explain that in vitro fertilization procedures can give rise to more embryos than needed. We reasoned that non-medical readers would appreciate our making explicit the background knowledge that the author assumes other physicians possess. Then we quote Mieth briefly ("withhold one or two" embryos) to provide some flavor of the original. We maintain focus on the ethical questions and wait until the end of the paraphrase before mentioning the laws to which Mieth refers. Our paraphrase is roughly the same length as the original, and it conveys the author's concerns about eugenics. As you can see, the paraphrase requires a writer to make decisions about the presentation of material. In many, if not most, cases, you will need to do more than simply "translate" from the original, sentence by sentence, to write your paraphrase.

When you come across a passage that you don't understand, the temptation is to skip over it. Resist this temptation! Use a paraphrase as a tool for explaining to yourself the main ideas of a difficult passage. By translating another writer's language into your own, you clarify what you understand and pinpoint what you don't. The paraphrase therefore becomes a tool for learning the subject.

The following pointers will help you write paraphrases.

HOW TO WRITE PARAPHRASES

- Make sure that you understand the source passage.
- Substitute your own words for those of the source passage; look for synonyms that carry the same meaning as the original words.
- Rearrange your own sentences so that they read smoothly. Sentence structure, even sentence order, in the paraphrase need not be based on that of the original. A good paraphrase, like a good summary, should stand by itself.

Paraphrases are generally about the same length as (and sometimes shorter than) the passages on which they are based. But sometimes clarity requires that a paraphrase be longer than a tightly compacted source passage. For example, suppose you wanted to paraphrase this statement by Sigmund Freud:

> We have found out that the distortion in dreams which hinders our understanding of them is due to the activities of a censorship, directed against the unacceptable, unconscious wish-impulses.

If you were to paraphrase this statement (the first sentence in the Tenth Lecture of his *General Introduction to Psychoanalysis*), you might come up with something like this:

> It is difficult to understand dreams because they contain distortions. Freud believed that these distortions arise from our internal censor, which attempts to suppress unconscious and forbidden desires.

Essentially, this paraphrase does little more than break up one sentence into two and somewhat rearrange the sentence structure for clarity.

Like summaries, then, paraphrases are useful devices, both in helping you to understand source material and in enabling you to convey the essence of this source material to your readers. When would you choose to write a summary instead of a paraphrase (or vice versa)? The answer depends on your purpose in presenting the source material. As we've said, summaries are generally based on articles (or sections of articles) or books. Paraphrases are generally based on particularly difficult (or important) paragraphs or sentences. You would seldom paraphrase a long passage, or summarize a short one, unless there were particularly good reasons for doing so. (A lawyer might want to paraphrase several pages of legal language so that his or her client, who is not a lawyer, could understand it.) The purpose of a summary is generally to save your reader time by presenting him or her with a brief version of a lengthy source. The purpose of a paraphrase is generally to clarify a short passage that might otherwise be unclear. Whether you summarize or paraphrase may also depend on the importance of your source. A particularly important source—if it is not too long—may rate a paraphrase. If it is less important, or peripheral to your central argument, you may write a summary instead. And, of course, you may choose to summarize only part of your source—the part that is most relevant to the point you are making.

Exercise 1.6

Paraphrasing

Locate and photocopy three relatively complex, but brief, passages from readings currently assigned in your other courses. Paraphrase these passages, making the language more readable and understandable. Attach the photocopies to the paraphrases.

QUOTATIONS

A *quotation* records the exact language used by someone in speech or writing. A *summary*, in contrast, is a brief restatement in your own words of what someone else has said or written. And a *paraphrase* is also a restatement, although one that is often as long as the original source. Any paper in which you draw upon sources will rely heavily on quotation, summary, and paraphrase. How do you choose among the three?

Remember that the papers you write should be your own—for the most part: your own language and certainly your own thesis, your own inferences, and your own conclusion. It follows that references to your source materials should be written primarily as summaries and paraphrases, both of which are built on restatement, not quotation. You will use summaries when you need a *brief* restatement, and paraphrases, which provide more explicit detail than summaries, when you need to follow the development of a source closely. When you quote too much, you risk losing ownership of your work: More easily than you might think, your voice can be drowned out by the voices of those you've quoted. So *use quotation sparingly*, as you would a pungent spice.

Nevertheless, quoting just the right source at the right time can significantly improve your papers. The trick is to know when and how to use quotations.

Quotations can be direct or indirect. A *direct* quotation is one in which you record precisely the language of another. An *indirect* quotation is one in which you report what someone has said without repeating the words exactly as spoken (or written):

Direct quotation: Franklin D. Roosevelt said, "The only thing we have to fear is fear itself."
Indirect quotation: Franklin D. Roosevelt said that we have nothing to fear but fear itself.

The language in a direct quotation, which is indicated by a pair of quotation marks (" "), must be faithful to the language of the original passage. When using an indirect quotation, you have the liberty of changing words (although not changing meaning). For both direct and indirect quotations, *you must credit your sources*, naming them either in (or close to) the sentence that includes the quotation or in a parenthetical citation.

Choosing Quotations

You'll find that using quotations can be particularly helpful in several situations:

Quoting Memorable Language

You should quote when the source material is worded so eloquently or powerfully that to summarize or paraphrase it would be to sacrifice much of the impact and significance of the meaning. Here, for example, is the historian John Keegan describing how France, Germany, Austria, and Russia slid inexorably in 1914 into the cataclysm of World War I:

> In the event, the states of Europe proceeded, as if in a dead march and a dialogue of the deaf, to the destruction of their continent and its civilization.

No paraphrase could do justice to the power of Keegan's words, as they appear in his book *The First World War* (1998). You would certainly want to quote them in any paper dealing with the origins of this conflict.

WHEN TO QUOTE

- Use quotations when another writer's language is particularly memorable and will add interest and liveliness to your paper.
- Use quotations when another writer's language is so clear and economical that to make the same point in your own words would, by comparison, be ineffective.
- Use quotations when you want the solid reputation of a source to lend authority and credibility to your own writing.

Quoting Clear and Concise Language

You should quote a source when its language is particularly clear and economical— when your language, by contrast, would be wordy. Read this passage from a biology text by Patricia Curtis:

> The honeybee colony, which usually has a population of 30,000 to 40,000 workers, differs from that of the bumblebee and many other social bees or wasps in that it survives the winter. This means that the bees must stay warm despite the cold. Like other bees, the isolated honeybee cannot fly if the temperature falls below 10°C (50°F) and cannot walk if the temperature is below 7°C (45°F). Within the wintering hive, bees maintain their temperature by clustering together in a dense ball; the lower the temperature, the denser the cluster. The clustered bees produce heat by constant muscular movements of their wings, legs, and abdomens. In very cold weather, the bees on the outside of the cluster keep moving toward the center, while those in the core of the cluster move to the colder outside periphery. The entire cluster moves slowly about on the combs, eating the stored honey from the combs as it moves.*

A summary of this paragraph might read:

> Honeybees, unlike many other varieties of bee, are able to live through the winter by "clustering together in a dense ball" for body warmth.

A paraphrase of the same passage would be considerably more detailed:

> Honeybees, unlike many other varieties of bee (such as bumblebees), are able to live through the winter. The 30,000 to 40,000 bees within a honeybee hive could not, individually, move about in cold winter temperatures. But when "clustering together in a dense ball," the bees generate heat by constantly moving their body parts. The cluster also moves slowly about the hive, those on the periphery of the cluster moving into the center, those in the center moving to the periphery, and all eating honey stored in the combs. This nutrition, in addition to the heat generated by the cluster, enables the honeybee to survive the cold winter months.

---

*Patricia Curtis, "Winter Organization," *Biology*, 2nd ed. (New York: Worth, 1976) 822–23.

In both the summary and the paraphrase we've quoted Curtis's "clustering together in a dense ball," a phrase that lies at the heart of her description of wintering honeybees. For us to describe this clustering in any language other than Curtis's would be pointless when her description is admirably brief and precise.

Quoting Authoritative Language

You should use quotations that lend authority to your work. When quoting an expert or a prominent political, artistic, or historical figure, you elevate your own work by placing it in esteemed company. Quote respected figures to establish background information in a paper, and your readers will tend to perceive that information as reliable. Quote the opinions of respected figures to endorse a statement that you've made, and your statement becomes more credible to your readers. Here, in a discussion of space flight, the writer David Chandler refers to a physicist and a physicist-astronaut:

> A few scientists—notably James Van Allen, discoverer of the Earth's radiation belts—have decried the expense of the manned space program and called for an almost exclusive concentration on unmanned scientific exploration instead, saying this would be far more cost-effective.
>
> Other space scientists dispute that idea. Joseph Allen, physicist and former shuttle astronaut, says, "It seems to be argued that one takes away from the other. But before there was a manned space program, the funding on space science was zero. Now it's about $500 million a year."

In the first paragraph Chandler has either summarized or used an indirect quotation to incorporate remarks made by James Van Allen into the discussion on space flight. In the second paragraph, Chandler directly quotes Joseph Allen. Both quotations, indirect and direct, lend authority and legitimacy to the article, for both James Van Allen and Joseph Allen are experts on the subject of space flight. Note that Chandler provides brief but effective biographies of his sources, identifying each one, so that their qualifications to speak on the subject are known to all:

James Van Allen, *discoverer of the Earth's radiation belts* . . .

Joseph Allen, *physicist and former shuttle astronaut* . . .

The phrases in italics are *appositives*. Their function is to rename the nouns they follow by providing explicit, identifying detail. Any information about a person that can be expressed in the following sentence pattern can be made into an appositive phrase:

James Van Allen is the *discoverer of the Earth's radiation belts*.

He has decried the expense of the manned space program.

Sentence with an appositive:

James Van Allen, *discoverer of the Earth's radiation belts*, has decried the expense of the manned space program.

Appositives (in the example above, "discoverer of the Earth's radiation belts") efficiently incorporate identifying information about the authors you quote, while adding variety to the structure of your sentences.

Incorporating Quotations into Your Sentences

Quoting Only the Part of a Sentence or Paragraph That You Need

We've said that a writer selects passages for quotation that are especially vivid, memorable, concise, or authoritative. Now put these principles into practice. Suppose that while conducting research on college sports, you've come across the following, written by Robert Hutchins, former president of the University of Chicago:

> If athleticism is bad for students, players, alumni, and the public, it is even worse for the colleges and universities themselves. They want to be educational institutions, but they can't. The story of the famous halfback whose only regret, when he bade his coach farewell, was that he hadn't learned to read and write is probably exaggerated. But we must admit that pressure from trustees, graduates, "friends," presidents, and even professors has tended to relax academic standards. These gentry often overlook the fact that a college should not be interested in a fullback who is a half-wit. Recruiting, subsidizing and the double educational standard cannot exist without the knowledge and the tacit approval, at least, of the colleges and universities themselves. Certain institutions encourage susceptible professors to be nice to athletes now admitted by paying them for serving as "faculty representatives" on the college athletic board.*

Suppose that in this paragraph you find a gem, a sentence with striking language that will enliven your discussion:

> These gentry often overlook the fact that a college should not be interested in a fullback who is a half-wit.

Incorporating the Quotation into the Flow of Your Own Sentence

Once you've selected the passage you want to quote, you need to work the material into your paper in as natural and fluid a manner as possible. Here's how we would quote Hutchins:

> Robert Hutchins, former president of the University of Chicago, asserts that "a college should not be interested in a fullback who is a half-wit."

Note that we've used an appositive to identify Hutchins. And we've used only the part of the paragraph—a single clause—that we thought memorable enough to quote directly.

---

*Robert Hutchins, "Gate Receipts and Glory," *Saturday Evening Post* 3 Dec. 1983: 38.

Avoiding Freestanding Quotations

A quoted sentence should never stand by itself, as in the following example:

> Various people associated with the university admit that the pressures of athleticism have caused a relaxation of standards. "These gentry often overlook the fact that a college should not be interested in a fullback who is a half-wit." But this kind of thinking is bad for the university and even worse for the athletes.

Even if it were followed by a parenthetical citation, a freestanding quotation would be jarring to the reader. You need to introduce the quotation with a *signal phrase* that attributes the source, not in a parenthetical citation but in some other part of the sentence—beginning, middle, or end. Thus, you could write:

> As Robert Hutchins notes, "These gentry often overlook the fact that a college should not be interested in a fullback who is a half-wit."

Here's a variation with the signal phrase in the middle:

> "These gentry," asserts Robert Hutchins, "often overlook the fact that a college should not be interested in a fullback who is a half-wit."

Another alternative is to introduce a sentence-long quotation with a colon:

> But Robert Hutchins disagrees: "These gentry often overlook the fact that a college should not be interested in a fullback who is a half-wit."

Use colons also to introduce indented quotations (as when we introduce long quotations in this chapter).

When attributing sources in signal phrases, try to vary the standard *states, writes, says,* and so on. Stronger verbs you might consider are: *asserts, argues, maintains, insists, asks,* and even *wonders.*

Exercise 1.7

Incorporating Quotations

Return to the article (pp. 8–13) by Alan S. Blinder, "Will Your Job Be Exported?" Find sentences that you think make interesting points. Imagine you want to use these points in a paper you're writing on job prospects in the twenty-first century. Write five different sentences that use a variety of the techniques discussed thus far to incorporate whole sentences as well as phrases from Blinder's article.

Using Ellipses

Using quotations becomes somewhat complicated when you want to quote the beginning and end of a passage but not its middle. Here's part of a paragraph from Thoreau's *Walden*:

> To read well, that is to read true books in a true spirit, is a noble exercise, and one that will task the reader more than any exercise which the customs of the day esteem. It requires a training such as the athletes underwent, the

steady intention almost of the whole life to this object. Books must be read as deliberately and reservedly as they were written.*

And here is how we can use this material in a quotation:

> Reading well is hard work, writes Henry David Thoreau in *Walden*, "that will task the reader more than any exercise which the customs of the day esteem . . . . Books must be read as deliberately and reservedly as they were written."

Whenever you quote a sentence but delete words from it, as we have done, indicate this deletion to the reader with three spaced periods—called an "ellipsis"—in the sentence at the point of deletion. The rationale for using an ellipsis mark is that a direct quotation must be reproduced *exactly* as it was written or spoken. When writers delete or change any part of the quoted material, readers must be alerted so they don't think the changes were part of the original. When deleting an entire sentence or sentences from a quoted paragraph, as in the example above, end the sentence you have quoted with a period, place the ellipsis, and continue the quotation.

If you are deleting the middle of a single sentence, use an ellipsis in place of the deleted words:

> "To read well . . . is a noble exercise, and one that will task the reader more than any exercise which the customs of the day esteem."

If you are deleting material from the end of one sentence through to the beginning of another sentence, add a sentence period before the ellipsis:

> "It requires a training such as the athletes underwent. . . . Books must be read as deliberately and reservedly as they were written."

If you begin your quotation of an author in the middle of his or her sentence, you need not indicate deleted words with an ellipsis. Be sure, however, that the syntax of the quotation fits smoothly with the syntax of your sentence:

> Reading "is a noble exercise," writes Henry David Thoreau.

Using Brackets to Add or Substitute Words

Use brackets whenever you need to add or substitute words in a quoted sentence. The brackets indicate to the reader a word or phrase that does not appear in the original passage but that you have inserted to avoid confusion. For example, when a pronoun's antecedent would be unclear to readers, delete the pronoun from the sentence and substitute an identifying word or phrase in brackets. When you make such a substitution, no ellipsis mark is needed. Assume that you wish to quote either of the underlined sentences in the following passage by Jane Yolen:

> Golden Press's *Walt Disney's Cinderella* set the new pattern for America's Cinderella. This book's text is coy and condescending. (Sample: "And her best friends of all were—guess who—the mice!") The illustrations are

---

*Henry David Thoreau, *Walden* (New York: Signet Classic, 1960) 72.

poor cartoons. And Cinderella herself is a disaster. She cowers as her sisters rip her homemade ball gown to shreds. (Not even homemade by Cinderella, but by the mice and birds.) She answers her stepmother with whines and pleadings. She is a sorry excuse for a heroine, pitiable and useless. She cannot perform even a simple action to save herself, though she is warned by her friends, the mice. She does not hear them because she is "off in a world of dreams." Cinderella begs, she whimpers, and at last has to be rescued by—guess who—the mice!*

In quoting one of these sentences, you would need to identify to whom the pronoun *she* refers. You can do this inside the quotation by using brackets:

> Jane Yolen believes that "[Cinderella] is a sorry excuse for a heroine, pitiable and useless."

When the pronoun begins the sentence to be quoted, you can identify the pronoun outside the quotation and begin quoting your source one word later:

> Jane Yolen believes that in the Golden Press version, Cinderella "is a sorry excuse for a heroine, pitiable and useless."

Here's another example of a case where the pronoun needing identification occurs in the middle of the sentence to be quoted. Newspaper reporters must use brackets when quoting a source, who in an interview might say this:

> After the fire they did not return to the station house for three hours.

WHEN TO SUMMARIZE, PARAPHRASE, AND QUOTE

Summarize:

- To present main points of a lengthy passage (article or book)
- To condense peripheral points necessary to discussion

Paraphrase:

- To clarify a short passage
- To emphasize main points

Quote:

- To capture another writer's particularly memorable language
- To capture another writer's clearly and economically stated language
- To lend authority and credibility to your own writing

---

*Jane Yolen, "America's 'Cinderella,'" *Children's Literature in Education* 8 (1977): 22.

If the reporter wants to use this sentence in an article, he or she needs to identify the pronoun:

> An official from City Hall, speaking on the condition that he not be identified, said, "After the fire [the officers] did not return to the station house for three hours."

You will also need to add bracketed information to a quoted sentence when a reference essential to the sentence's meaning is implied but not stated directly. Read the following paragraph from Walter Isaacson's recent biography of Albert Einstein, *Einstein: His Life and Universe:*

> Newton had bequeathed to Einstein a universe in which time had an absolute existence that tick-tocked along independent of objects and observers, and in which space likewise had an absolute existence. Gravity was thought to be a force that masses exerted on one another rather mysteriously across empty space. <u>Within this framework, objects obeyed mechanical laws that had proved remarkably accurate—almost perfect—in explaining everything from the orbits of the planets, to the diffusion of gases, to the jiggling of molecules, to the propagation of sound (though not light) waves.</u>

If you wanted to quote only the underlined sentence above, you would need to provide readers with a bracketed explanation; otherwise, the phrase "this framework" would be unclear. Here is how you would manage the quotation:

> According to Walter Isaacson, Newton's universe was extremely regular and predictable:
>
>> Within this framework [that time and space exist independently of their observation and that gravity results from masses exerting a remote attraction on one another], objects obeyed mechanical laws that had proved remarkably accurate—almost perfect—in explaining everything from the orbits of the planets, to the diffusion of gases, to the jiggling of molecules, to the propagation of sound (though not light) waves. (223)

INCORPORATING QUOTATIONS INTO YOUR SENTENCES

- *Quote only the part of a sentence or paragraph that you need*. Use no more of the writer's language than necessary to make or reinforce your point.
- *Incorporate the quotation into the flow of your own sentence*. The quotation must fit, both syntactically and stylistically, into your surrounding language.
- *Avoid freestanding quotations*. A quoted sentence should never stand by itself. Use a *signal phrase*—at the beginning, the middle, or the end of the sentence—to attribute the source of the quotation.

- *Use ellipsis marks*. Indicate deleted language in the middle of a quoted sentence with ellipsis marks. Deleted language at the beginning or end of a sentence generally does not require ellipsis marks.
- *Use brackets to add or substitute words*. Use brackets to add or substitute words in a quoted sentence when the meaning of the quotation would otherwise be unclear—for example, when the antecedent of a quoted pronoun is ambiguous.

Exercise 1.8

Using Brackets

Write your own sentences incorporating the following quotations. Use brackets to clarify information that isn't clear outside its original context—and refer to the original sources to remind yourself of this context.

From the David Chandler paragraph on James Van Allen (p. 39):

a.   Other space scientists *dispute that idea*.

b.   Now *it's about $500 million a year*.

From the Jane Yolen excerpt on Cinderella (pp. 42–43):

a.   *This book's* text is coy and condescending.

b.   *She* cannot perform even a simple action to save herself, though she is warned by her friends, the mice.

c.   She does not hear *them* because she is "off in a world of dreams."

Remember that when you quote the work of another, you are obligated to credit—or cite—the author's work properly; otherwise, you may be guilty of plagiarism.

AVOIDING PLAGIARISM

Plagiarism is generally defined as the attempt to pass off the work of another as one's own. Whether born out of calculation or desperation, plagiarism is the least tolerated offense in the academic world. The fact that most plagiarism is unintentional—arising from an ignorance of the conventions rather than deceitfulness—makes no difference to many professors.

The ease of cutting and pasting whole blocks of text from Web sources into one's own paper makes it tempting for some to take the easy way out and avoid doing their own research and writing. But, apart from the serious ethical issues involved, the same technology that makes such acts possible also makes it possible for instructors to detect them. Software marketed to instructors allows them to conduct Web searches, using suspicious phrases as keywords. The results often provide irrefutable evidence of plagiarism.

Of course, plagiarism is not confined to students. Recent years have seen a number of high-profile cases—some of them reaching the front pages of newspapers—of well-known scholars who were shown to have copied passages from sources into their own book manuscripts, without proper attribution. In some cases, the scholars maintained that these appropriations were simply a matter of carelessness, that in the press and volume of work they had lost track of which words were theirs and which were the words of their sources. But such excuses sounded hollow: These careless acts inevitably embarrassed the scholars professionally, tarnished their otherwise fine work and reputations, and disappointed their many admirers.

You can avoid plagiarism and charges of plagiarism by following the basic rules provided on page 47.

Following is a passage from an article by Richard Rovere on Senator Joseph P. McCarthy, along with several student versions of the ideas represented.

> McCarthy never seemed to believe in himself or in anything he had said. He knew that Communists were not in charge of American foreign policy. He knew that they weren't running the United States Army. He knew that he had spent five years looking for Communists in the government and that—although some must certainly have been there, since Communists had turned up in practically every other major government in the world— he hadn't come up with even one.*

One student version of this passage reads:

> McCarthy never believed in himself or in anything he had said. He knew that Communists were not in charge of American foreign policy and weren't running the United States Army. He knew that he had spent five years looking for Communists in the government, and although there must certainly have been some there, since Communists were in practically every other major government in the world, he hadn't come up with even one.

Clearly, this is intentional plagiarism. The student has copied the original passage almost word for word.

Here is another version of the same passage:

> McCarthy knew that Communists were not running foreign policy or the Army. He also knew that although there must have been some Communists in the government, he hadn't found a single one, even though he had spent five years looking.

This student has attempted to put the ideas into her own words, but both the wording and the sentence structure are so heavily dependent on the original passage that even if it *were* cited, most professors would consider it plagiarism.

---

*Richard Rovere, "The Most Gifted and Successful Demagogue This Country Has Ever Known," *New York Times Magazine*, 30 Apr. 1967.

In the following version, the student has sufficiently changed the wording and sentence structure, and she uses a *signal phrase* (a phrase used to introduce a quotation or paraphrase, signaling to the reader that the words to follow come from someone else) to properly credit the information to Rovere, so that there is no question of plagiarism:

> According to Richard Rovere, McCarthy was fully aware that Communists were running neither the government nor the Army. He also knew that he hadn't found a single Communist in government, even after a lengthy search (192).

And although this is not a matter of plagiarism, as noted above, it's essential to quote accurately. You are not permitted to change any part of a quotation or to omit any part of it without using brackets or ellipses.

RULES FOR AVOIDING PLAGIARISM

- Cite *all* quoted material and *all* summarized and paraphrased material, unless the information is common knowledge (e.g.: the Civil War was fought from 1861 to 1865).
- Make sure that both the *wording* and the *sentence structure* of your summaries and paraphrases are substantially your own.

Chapter 2

Critical Reading and Critique

CRITICAL READING

When writing papers in college, you are often called on to respond critically to source materials. Critical reading requires the abilities to both summarize and evaluate a presentation. As you have seen in Chapter 1, a *summary* is a brief restatement in your own words of the content of a passage. An *evaluation*, however, is a more ambitious undertaking. In your college work, you read to gain and *use* new information; but because sources are not equally valid or equally useful, you must learn to distinguish critically among them by evaluating them.

There is no ready-made formula for determining validity. Critical reading and its written equivalent—the *critique*—require discernment, sensitivity, imagination, knowledge of the subject, and above all, willingness to become involved in what you read. These skills are developed only through repeated practice. You must begin somewhere, though, and we recommend that you start by posing two broad questions about passages, articles, and books that you read: (1) To what extent does the author succeed in his or her purpose? (2) To what extent do you agree with the author?

Question 1: To What Extent Does the Author Succeed in His or Her Purpose?

All critical reading *begins with an accurate summary.* Thus, before attempting an evaluation, you must be able to locate an author's thesis and identify the selection's content and structure. You must understand the author's *purpose.* Authors write to inform, to persuade, and to entertain. A given piece may be primarily *informative* (a summary of the research on cloning), primarily *persuasive* (an argument on why the government must do something to alleviate homelessness), or primarily *entertaining* (a play about the frustrations of young lovers). Or it may be all three (as in John Steinbeck's novel *The Grapes of Wrath,* about migrant workers during the Great Depression). Sometimes authors are not fully conscious of their purpose. Sometimes their purpose changes as they write. Also, multiple purposes can overlap: An essay may need to inform the reader about an issue in order to make a persuasive point. But if the finished piece is coherent, it will have a primary reason for having been written, and it should be apparent that the author is attempting primarily to inform, persuade, or entertain a particular audience. To identify this primary reason—this purpose—is your first job as a critical reader. Your next job is to determine how successful the author has been.

As a critical reader, you bring various criteria, or standards of judgment, to bear when you read pieces intended to inform, persuade, or entertain.

Writing to Inform

A piece intended to inform will provide definitions, describe or report on a process, recount a story, give historical background, and/or provide facts and figures. An informational piece responds to questions such as:

What (or who) is _____?

How does _____ work?

What is the controversy or problem about?

What happened?

How and why did it happen?

What were the results?

What are the arguments for and against _____?

WHERE DO WE FIND WRITTEN CRITIQUES?

Here are just a few of the types of writing that involve critique:

Academic Writing

- **Research papers** critique sources in order to establish their usefulness.
- **Position papers** stake out a position by critiquing other positions.
- **Book reviews** combine summary with critique.
- **Essay exams** demonstrate understanding of course material by critiquing it.

Workplace Writing

- **Legal briefs and legal arguments** critique previous arguments made by opposing counsel.
- **Business plans and proposals** critique other less cost-effective, efficient, or reasonable approaches.
- **Policy briefs** communicate failings of policies and legislation through critique.

To the extent that an author answers these and related questions and the answers are a matter of verifiable record (you could check for accuracy if you had the time and inclination), the selection is intended to inform. Having determined this, you can organize your response by considering three other criteria: accuracy, significance, and fair interpretation of information.

Evaluating Informative Writing

Accuracy of Information   If you are going to use any of the information presented, you must be satisfied that it is trustworthy. One of your responsibilities as a critical reader, then, is to find out if it is accurate. This means you should check facts against other sources. Government publications are often good resources for verifying facts about political legislation, population data, crime statistics, and the like. You can also search key terms in library databases and on the Web. Since material on the Web is essentially self-published, however, you must be especially vigilant in assessing its legitimacy. A wealth of useful information is now available on the Internet—but there is also a tremendous amount of misinformation, distorted "facts," and unsupported opinion.

Significance of Information   One useful question that you can put to a reading is "So what?" In the case of selections that attempt to inform, you may reasonably wonder whether the information makes a difference. What can the reader gain from this information? How is knowledge advanced by the publication of this material? Is the information of importance to you or to others in a particular audience? Why or why not?

Fair Interpretation of Information   At times you will read reports, the sole purpose of which is to relate raw data or information. In these cases, you will build your response on Question 1, introduced on page 48: To what extent does the author succeed in his or her purpose? More frequently, once an author has presented information, he or she will attempt to evaluate or interpret it—which is only reasonable, since information that has not been evaluated or interpreted is of little use. One of your tasks as a critical reader is to make a distinction between the author's presentation of facts and figures and his or her attempts to evaluate them. Watch for shifts from straightforward descriptions of factual information ("20 percent of the population") to assertions about what this information means ("a *mere* 20 percent of the population"), what its implications are, and so on. Pay attention to whether the logic with which the author connects interpretation with facts is sound. You may find that the information is valuable but the interpretation is not. Perhaps the author's conclusions are not justified. Could you offer a contrary explanation for the same facts? Does more information need to be gathered before firm conclusions can be drawn? Why?

Writing to Persuade

Writing is frequently intended to persuade—that is, to influence the reader's thinking. To make a persuasive case, the writer must begin with an assertion that is arguable, some statement about which reasonable people could disagree. Such an assertion, when it serves as the essential organizing principle of the article or book, is called a *thesis*. Here are two examples:

> Because they do not speak English, many children in this affluent land are being denied their fundamental right to equal educational opportunity.

> Bilingual education, which has been stridently promoted by a small group of activists with their own agenda, is detrimental to the very students it is supposed to serve.

Thesis statements such as these—and the subsequent assertions used to help support them—represent conclusions that authors have drawn as a result of researching and thinking about an issue. You go through the same process yourself when you write persuasive papers or critiques. And just as you are entitled to evaluate critically the assertions of authors you read, so your professors—and other students—are entitled to evaluate *your* assertions, whether they be written arguments or comments made in class discussion.

Keep in mind that writers organize arguments by arranging evidence to support one conclusion and oppose (or dismiss) another. You can assess the validity of an argument and its conclusion by determining whether the author has (1) clearly defined key terms, (2) used information fairly, and (3) argued logically and not fallaciously (see pp. 55–59).

Exercise 2.1

Informative and Persuasive Thesis Statements

With a partner from your class, identify at least one informative and one persuasive thesis statement from two passages of your own choosing. Photocopy these passages and highlight the statements you have selected.

As an alternative, and also working with a partner, write one informative and one persuasive thesis statement for *three* of the topics listed in the last paragraph of this exercise. For example, for the topic of prayer in schools, your informative thesis statement could read:

> Both advocates and opponents of school prayer frame their position as a matter of freedom.

Your persuasive thesis statement might be worded:

> As long as schools don't dictate what kinds of prayers students should say, then school prayer should be allowed and even encouraged.

> Don't worry about taking a position that you agree with or feel you could support; this exercise doesn't require that you write an essay. The topics:

school prayer

gun control

stem cell research

grammar instruction in English class

violent lyrics in music

teaching computer skills in primary schools

curfews in college dormitories

course registration procedures

Evaluating Persuasive Writing

Read the argument that follows on the nation's troubled "star" system for producing elite athletes and dancers. We will illustrate our discussion on defining terms, using information fairly, and arguing logically by referring to Joan Ryan's argument. The model critique that follows these illustrations will be based on this same argument.

WE ARE NOT CREATED EQUAL IN EVERY WAY

Joan Ryan

In an opinion piece for the San Francisco Chronicle *(December 12, 2000), columnist and reporter Joan Ryan takes a stand on whether the San Francisco Ballet School did or did not discriminate against 8-year-old Fredrika Keefer when it declined to admit her on the grounds that she had the wrong body type to be a successful ballerina. Keefer's mother subsequently sued the ballet school for discrimination, claiming that the rejection had caused her daughter confusion and humiliation. Ryan examines the question of setting admissions standards and also the problems some parents create by pushing their young children to meet these standards.*

Fredrika Keefer is an 8-year-old girl who likes to dance, just like her mother and grandmother before her. She relishes playing the lead role of Clara in the Pacific Dance Theater's "Petite Nutcracker." So perhaps she is not as shy as many fourth-graders. But I wonder how she feels about her body being a topic of public discussion.

Fredrika and her mother filed suit because, as her mother puts it, she "did not have the right body type to be accepted" by the San Francisco Ballet School. "My daughter is very sophisticated, so she understands why we're doing this," Krissy Keefer said. "And the other kids think she's a celebrity."

There is no question Keefer raises a powerful point in her complaint. The values placed on an unnaturally thin body for female performers drives some dancers to potentially fatal eating disorders. But that isn't exactly the issue here. This is: Does the San Francisco Ballet School have the right to give preference to leaner body types in selecting 300 students from this year's 1,400 applicants?

Yes, for the same reason UC Berkeley can reject students based on mental prowess and a fashion modeling school can reject students based on comeliness. Every institution has standards that weed out those who are less likely to succeed. I know this flies in the face of American ideals. But the reality is that all men and women are not created equal.

5   Like it or not, the ethereal, elongated body that can float on air is part of the look and feel of classical ballet. You and I might think ballet would be just as pleasing with larger bodies. But most of those who practice the art disagree, which is their right. This doesn't mean that women with different body types cannot become professional dancers. They just have to find a different type of dance—jazz, tap, modern—just as athletes have to find sports that fit certain body types. A tall, blocky man, for example, could not be a jockey but he could play baseball.

Having written extensively about the damaging pressures on young female gymnasts and figure skaters, I understand Keefer's concerns about body type. But for me, the more disturbing issue in this story isn't about weight but age.

The San Francisco Ballet School is very clear and open about the fact it is strictly a training ground for professional dancers. "We are not a recreation department," said a ballet spokeswoman.

In other words, children at age 8 are already training for adult careers. By age 12 or 13, the children are training so much that they either begin home-schooling or attend a school that accommodates the training schedule. The child has thrown all her eggs into this one little basket at an age when most kids can barely decide what to wear to school in the morning. And the child knows the parents are paying lots of money for this great opportunity.

The ballet school usually has a psychologist to counsel the students, but at the moment there is not one on staff. And the parents are given no training by the school on the pitfalls their daughters might encounter as they climb the ballet ladder: weight issues, physical ailments, social isolation, psychological pressure.

10   Just as in elite gymnastics and figure skating, these children are in the netherland of the law. They are neither hobbyists nor professionals. There is no safety net for them, no arm of government that makes sure that the adults in their lives watch out for their best interests.

Keefer said she would drop her lawsuit if the school accepted her daughter. The San Francisco Ballet School offers the best training in the Bay Area, she said. Fredrika, however, has said she is quite happy dancing where she is. Still, the mother gets to decide what's best for her daughter's dancing career. The child is clearly too young to make such a decision. Yet, in the skewed logic of elite athletics and dancing, she is not too young to pay the price for it.

Exercise 2.2

Critical Reading Practice

Look back at the Critical Reading for Summary box on p. 6 of Chapter 1. Use each of the guidelines listed there to examine the essay by Joan Ryan. Note in the margins of the selection, or on a separate sheet of paper, the essay's main point, subpoints, and use of examples.

Persuasive Strategies

Clearly Defined Terms   The validity of an argument depends to some degree on how carefully an author has defined key terms. Take the assertion, for example, that American society must be grounded in "family values." Just what do people who use this phrase mean by it? The validity of their argument depends on whether they and their readers agree on a definition of "family values"—as well as what it means to be "grounded in" family values. If an author writes that in the recent past "America's elites accepted as a matter of course that a free society can sustain itself only through virtue and temperance in the people" (Charles Murray, "The Coming White Underclass," *Wall Street Journal,* October 20, 1993), readers need to know what exactly the author means by "elites" and by "virtue and temperance" before they can assess the validity of the argument. In such cases, the success of the argument—its ability to persuade—hinges on the definition of a term. So, in responding to an argument, be sure you (and the author) are clear on what exactly is being argued. Unless you are, no informed response is possible.

Ryan uses several terms important for understanding her argument. The primary one is the "body type" that the San Francisco Ballet School uses as an application standard. Ryan defines this type (paragraph 5) as the "elongated body that can float on air." Leaving other terms undefined, she writes that the ballet school's use of body type as a standard "flies in the face of American ideals" (paragraph 4). Exactly *which* ideals she leaves for the reader to define: They might include fair play, equality of access, or the belief that decisions ought to be based on talent, not appearance. The reader cannot be sure. When she reports that a spokeswoman for the school stated that "We are not a recreation department," Ryan assumes the reader will understand the reference. The mission of a recreation department is to give *all* participants equal access. In a youth recreation league, children of all abilities would get to play in a baseball game. In a league for elite athletes, in which winning was a priority, coaches would permit only the most talented children to play.

When writing a paper, you will need to decide, like Ryan, which terms to define and which you can assume the reader will define in the same way you do. As the writer of a critique, you should identify and discuss any undefined or ambiguous term that might give rise to confusion.

Fair Use of Information   Information is used as evidence in support of arguments. When you encounter such evidence, ask yourself two questions: (1) "Is the information accurate and up to date?" At least a portion of an argument becomes invalid when the information used to support it is inaccurate or out of date. (2) "Has the author cited *representative* information?" The evidence used in an argument must be presented in a spirit of fair play. An author is less than ethical when he presents only evidence favoring his own views even though he is well aware that contrary evidence exists. For instance, it would be dishonest to argue that an economic recession is imminent and to cite only indicators of economic downturn while ignoring and failing to cite contrary (positive) evidence.

As you have seen, "We Are Not Created Equal in Every Way" is not an information-heavy essay. The success of the piece turns on the author's use of logic, not facts and figures. In this case, the reader has every reason to trust that Ryan has presented the facts accurately: An 8-year-old girl has been denied admission to a prestigious ballet school. The mother of the girl has sued the school.

Logical Argumentation: Avoiding Logical Fallacies

At some point, you will need to respond to the logic of the argument itself. To be convincing, an argument should be governed by principles of *logic*—clear and orderly thinking. This does *not* mean that an argument should not be biased. A biased argument—that is, an argument weighted toward one point of view and against others, which is in fact the nature of argument—may be valid as long as it is logically sound.

Let's examine several types of faulty thinking and logical fallacies you will need to watch for.

Emotionally Loaded Terms Writers sometimes attempt to sway readers by using emotionally charged words. Words with positive connotations (e.g., "family values") are intended to sway readers to the author's point of view; words with negative connotations (e.g., "paying the price") try to sway readers away from an opposing point of view. The fact that an author uses emotionally loaded terms does not necessarily invalidate an argument. Emotional appeals are perfectly legitimate and time-honored modes of persuasion. But in academic writing, which is grounded in logical argumentation, they should not be the *only* means of persuasion. You should be sensitive to *how* emotionally loaded terms are being used. In particular, are they being used deceptively or to hide the essential facts?

Ryan appeals to our desire to protect children in "We Are Not Created Equal in Every Way." She writes of "disturbing issue[s]," lack of a "safety net" for young people on the star track to elite performance, and an absence of adults "watch[ing] out for [the children's] best interests." Ryan understands that no reader wants to see a child abused; and while she does not use the word *abuse* in her essay, she implies that parents who push young children too hard to succeed commit abuse. That implication is enough to engage the sympathies of the reader. As someone evaluating the essay, you should be alert to this appeal to your emotions and then judge whether or not the appeal is fair and convincing. Above all, you should not let an emotional appeal blind you to shortcomings of logic, ambiguously defined terms, or a misuse of facts.

***Ad Hominem* Argument** In an *ad hominem* argument, the writer rejects opposing views by attacking the person who holds them. By calling opponents names, an author avoids the issue. Consider this excerpt from a political speech:

> I could more easily accept my opponent's plan to increase revenues by collecting on delinquent tax bills if he had paid more than a hundred dollars in state taxes in each of the past three years. But the fact is, he's a millionaire with a millionaire's tax shelters. This man hasn't paid a wooden nickel for the state services he and his family depend on. So I ask you: Is *he* the one to be talking about taxes to *us*?

It could well be that the opponent has paid virtually no state taxes for three years; but this fact has nothing to do with, and is used as a ploy to divert attention from, the merits of a specific proposal for increasing revenues. The proposal is lost in the attack against the man himself, an attack that violates principles of logic. Writers (and speakers) should make their points by citing evidence in support of their views and by challenging contrary evidence.

Does Ryan attack Fredrika Keefer's mother in this essay? You be the judge. Here are lines referring directly or indirectly to Krissy Keefer. Is Ryan criticizing the mother, directly or indirectly? Cite specific words and phrases to support your conclusion.

> Fredrika and her mother filed suit because, as her mother puts it, she "did not have the right body type to be accepted" by the San Francisco Ballet School. "My daughter is very sophisticated, so she understands why we're doing this," Krissy Keefer said. "And the other kids think she's a celebrity."

> There is no question Keefer raises a powerful point in her complaint.

> Keefer said she would drop her lawsuit if the school accepted her daughter. The San Francisco Ballet School offers the best training in the Bay Area, she said. Fredrika, however, has said she is quite happy dancing where she is. Still, the mother gets to decide what's best for her daughter's dancing career. The child is clearly too young to make such a decision. Yet, in the skewed logic of elite athletics and dancing, she is not too young to pay the price for it.

Faulty Cause and Effect   The fact that one event precedes another in time does not mean that the first event has caused the second. An example: Fish begin dying by the thousands in a lake near your hometown. An environmental group immediately cites chemical dumping by several manufacturing plants as the cause. But other causes are possible: A disease might have affected the fish; the growth of algae might have contributed to the deaths; or acid rain might be a factor. The origins of an event are usually complex and are not always traceable to a single cause. So you must carefully examine cause-and-effect reasoning when you find a writer using it. In Latin, this fallacy is known as *post hoc, ergo propter hoc* ("after this, therefore because of this").

TONE

Tone refers to the overall emotional effect produced by a writer's choice of language. Writers might use especially emphatic words to create a tone: A film reviewer might refer to a "magnificent performance," or a columnist might criticize "sleazeball politics."

These are extreme examples of tone; but tone can be more subtle, particularly if the writer makes a special effort *not* to inject emotion into the writing. As we indicated in the section on emotionally loaded terms, the fact that a writer's tone is highly emotional does not necessarily mean that the writer's argument is invalid. Conversely, a neutral tone does not ensure an argument's validity.

Many instructors discourage student writing that projects a highly emotional tone, considering it inappropriate for academic or preprofessional work. (One sure sign of emotion: the exclamation mark, which should be used sparingly.)

The debate over the San Francisco Ballet School's refusal to admit Fredrika Keefer involves a question of cause and effect. Fredrika Keefer's rejection by the ballet school was caused by the school's insistence that its students have an "ethereal, elongated body." If the school changes that standard, the outcome could change: Fredrika Keefer might be admitted.

Ryan also uses cause-and-effect logic in her essay to suggest that Fredrika Keefer's mother, and by extension all parent managers, can cause their children harm by pushing them too hard in their training. At the end of the essay, Ryan writes that Fredrika is too young "to decide what's best for her...dancing career" but that "she is not too young to pay the price for" the decisions her mother makes to promote that career. The "price" Fredrika pays will be "caused" by her mother's (poor) decisions.

Either/Or Reasoning   Either/or reasoning also results from an unwillingness to recognize complexity. If in analyzing a problem an author artificially restricts the range of possible solutions by offering only two courses of action, and then rejects the one that he opposes, he cannot logically argue that the remaining course of action, which he favors, is therefore the only one that makes sense. Usually, several other options (at least) are possible. For whatever reason, the author has chosen to overlook them. As an example, suppose you are reading a selection on genetic engineering in which the author builds an argument on the basis of the following:

> Research in gene splicing is at a crossroads: Either scientists will be carefully monitored by civil authorities and their efforts limited to acceptable applications, such as disease control; or, lacking regulatory guidelines, scientists will set their own ethical standards and begin programs in embryonic manipulation that, however well intended, exceed the proper limits of human knowledge.

Certainly other possibilities for genetic engineering exist beyond the two mentioned here. But the author limits debate by establishing an either/or choice. Such a limitation is artificial and does not allow for complexity. As a critical reader, you need to be on the alert for either/or reasoning.

Hasty Generalization   Writers are guilty of hasty generalization when they draw their conclusions from too little evidence or from unrepresentative evidence. To argue that scientists should not proceed with the human genome project because a recent editorial urged that the project be abandoned is to make a hasty generalization. That lone editorial may be unrepresentative of the views of most individuals—both scientists and laypeople—who have studied and written about the matter. To argue that one should never obey authority because Stanley Milgram's Yale University experiments in the 1960s showed the dangers of obedience is to ignore the fact that Milgram's experiments were concerned primarily with obedience to *immoral* authority. Thus the experimental situation was unrepresentative of most routine demands for obedience—for example, to obey a parental rule or to comply with a summons for jury duty—and a conclusion about the malevolence of all authority would be a hasty generalization.

False Analogy   Comparing one person, event, or issue to another may be illuminating, but it can also be confusing or misleading. Differences between the two may be more significant than their similarities, and conclusions drawn from one may not necessarily apply to the other. A writer who argues that it is reasonable to quarantine people with AIDS because quarantine has been effective in preventing the spread of smallpox is assuming an analogy between AIDS and smallpox that is not valid (because of the differences in transmission between the two diseases).

Ryan compares the San Francisco Ballet School's setting an admissions standard to both a university's and a modeling school's setting standards. Are the analogies apt? Certainly one can draw a parallel between the standards used by the ballet school and those of a modeling school: Both emphasize a candidate's appearance, among other qualities. Are the admissions standards of a university based on appearance? In principle, no. At least that's not a criterion any college admissions office would post on its Web site. A critical reader might therefore want to object that one of Ryan's analogies is faulty.

Ryan attempts to advance her argument by making another comparison:

> [The rejection of a candidate because she does not have a body suited to classical ballet] doesn't mean that women with different body types cannot become professional dancers. They just have to find a different type of dance—jazz, tap, modern—just as athletes have to find sports that fit certain body types. A tall, blocky man, for example, could not be a jockey but he could play baseball.

The words "just as" signal an attempt to advance the argument by making an analogy. What do you think? Is the analogy sufficiently similar to Fredrika Keefer's situation to persuade you?

Begging the Question   To beg the question is to assume as proven fact the very thesis being argued. To assert, for example, that America is not in decline because it is as strong and prosperous as ever does not prove anything: It merely repeats the claim in different words. This fallacy is also known as *circular reasoning*.

When Ryan writes that "There is no safety net for [children placed into elite training programs], no arm of government that makes sure that the adults in their lives watch out for their best interests," she assumes that there should be such a safety net. But, as you will read in the model critique, this is a point that must be argued, not assumed. Is such intervention wise? Under what circumstances would authorities intervene in a family? Would authorities have the legal standing to get involved if there were no clear evidence of physical abuse? Ryan is not necessarily wrong in desiring "safety nets" for young, elite athletes and dancers, but she assumes a point that she should be arguing.

Non Sequitur   *Non sequitur* is Latin for "it does not follow"; the term is used to describe a conclusion that does not logically follow from a premise. "Since minorities have made such great strides in the past few decades," a writer may argue, "we no longer need affirmative action programs." Aside from the fact that the premise itself is arguable (*have* minorities made such great strides?), it does not follow that because minorities *may* have made great strides, there is no further need for affirmative action programs.

Oversimplification   Be alert for writers who offer easy solutions to complicated problems. "America's economy will be strong again if we all 'buy American,'" a politician may argue. But the problems of America's economy are complex and cannot be solved by a slogan or a simple change in buying habits. Likewise, a writer who argues that we should ban genetic engineering assumes that simple solutions ("just say no") will be sufficient to deal with the complex moral dilemmas raised by this new technology.

Exercise 2.3

Understanding Logical Fallacies

Make a list of the nine logical fallacies discussed in the preceding section. Briefly define each one in your own words. Then, in a group of three or four classmates, review your definitions and the examples we've provided for each logical fallacy. Collaborate with your group to find or invent examples for each of the fallacies. Compare your examples with those generated by the other groups in your class.

Writing to Entertain

Authors write not only to inform and persuade but also to entertain. One response to entertainment is a hearty laugh, but it is possible to entertain without encouraging laughter: A good book or play or poem may prompt you to reflect, grow wistful, become elated, get angry. Laughter is only one of many possible reactions. Like a response to an informative piece or an argument, your response to an essay, poem, story, play, novel, or film should be precisely stated and carefully developed. Ask yourself some of the following questions (you won't have space to explore all of them, but try to consider the most important): Did I care for the portrayal of a certain character? Did that character (or a group of characters united by occupation, age, ethnicity, etc.) seem overly sentimental, for example, or heroic? Did his adversaries seem too villainous or stupid? Were the situations believable? Was the action interesting or merely formulaic? Was the theme developed subtly or powerfully, or did the work come across as preachy or shrill? Did the action at the end of the work follow plausibly from what had come before? Was the language fresh and incisive or stale and predictable? Explain as specifically as possible what elements of the work seemed effective or ineffective and why. Offer an overall assessment, elaborating on your views.

Question 2: To What Extent Do You Agree with the Author?

When formulating a critical response to a source, try to distinguish your evaluation of the author's purpose and success at achieving that purpose from your own agreement or disagreement with the author's views. The distinction allows you to respond to a piece of writing on its merits. As an unbiased, evenhanded critic, you evaluate an author's clarity of presentation, use of evidence, and adherence to principles of logic. To what extent has the author succeeded in achieving his or her purpose? Still withholding judgment, offer your assessment and give the author (in effect) a grade. Significantly, your assessment of the presentation may not coincide with your views of the author's conclusions: You may agree with an author entirely but feel that the presentation is superficial; you may find the author's logic and use of evidence to be rock solid but at the same time you may resist certain conclusions. A critical evaluation works well when it is conducted in two parts. After evaluating the author's purpose and design for achieving that purpose, respond to the author's main assertions. In doing so, you'll want to identify points of agreement and disagreement and also evaluate assumptions.

Identify Points of Agreement and Disagreement

Be precise in identifying where you agree and disagree with an author. You should state as clearly as possible what *you* believe, and an effective way of doing this is to define your position in relation to that presented in the piece. Whether you agree enthusiastically, agree with reservations, or disagree, you can organize your reactions in two parts: (1) summarize the author's position; and (2) state your own position and elaborate on your reasons for holding it. The elaboration, in effect, becomes an argument itself, and this is true regardless of the position you take. An opinion is effective when you support it by supplying evidence from your reading (which should be properly cited), your observation, or your personal experience. Without such evidence, opinions cannot be authoritative. "I thought the article on inflation was lousy." Or: "It was terrific." Why? "I just thought so, that's all." This opinion is worthless because the criticism is imprecise: The critic has taken neither the time to read the article carefully nor the time to explore his or her own reactions carefully.

Exercise 2.4

Exploring Your Viewpoints—in Three Paragraphs

Go to a Web site that presents short persuasive essays on current social issues, such as reason.com, opinion-pages.org, drudgereport.com, or Speakout.com. Or go to an Internet search engine and type in a social issue together with the word "articles," "editorials," or "opinion," and see what you find. Locate a selection on a topic of interest that takes a clear, argumentative position. Print out the selection on which you choose to focus. Write one paragraph summarizing the author's key argument. Write two paragraphs articulating your agreement or disagreement with the author. (Devote each paragraph to a *single* point of agreement or disagreement.) Be sure to explain why you think or feel the way you do and, wherever possible, cite relevant evidence—from your reading, experience, or observation.

Explore the Reasons for Agreement and Disagreement:
Evaluate Assumptions

One way of elaborating your reactions to a reading is to explore the underlying *reasons* for agreement and disagreement. Your reactions are based largely on assumptions that you hold and how those assumptions compare with the author's. An *assumption* is a fundamental statement about the world and its operations that you take to be true. A writer's assumptions may be explicitly stated; but just as often, assumptions are implicit and you can only infer them.

Assumptions provide the foundation on which entire presentations are built. When you find an author's assumptions invalid—that is, not supported by factual evidence—or if you disagree with value-based assumptions underlying an author's position, you may well disagree with the conclusions that follow from these assumptions. Alternatively, if you find that your own assumptions are contradicted by actual experience, you may be forced to conclude that your premises were mistaken.

An interesting example of an assumption fatally colliding with reality was revealed during a recent congressional investigation into the financial meltdown of late 2008 precipitated by the collapse of the home mortgage market—itself precipitated, many believed, by an insufficiently regulated banking and financial system run amuck. During his testimony before the House Oversight Committee in October of that year, former Federal Reserve chairman Alan Greenspan was grilled by committee chairman Henry Waxman (D-CA) about his "ideology"—essentially an assumption or set of assumptions raised to the level of a governing principle.

Greenspan responded, "I do have an ideology. My judgment is that free, competitive markets are by far the unrivaled way to organize economies. We have tried regulation; none meaningfully worked." Greenspan defined an ideology as "a conceptual framework [for] the way people deal with reality. Everyone has one. You have to. To exist, you need an ideology." And he pointed out that the assumptions on which he and the Federal Reserve operated were supported by "the best banking lawyers in the business…and an outside counsel of expert professionals to advise on regulatory matters."

Greenspan then admitted that in light of the economic disaster engulfing the nation, he had found a "flaw" in his ideology. The testimony continues:

> Chairman Waxman: You found a flaw?
>
> Mr. Greenspan: I found a flaw in the model that I perceived is the critical functioning structure that defines how the world works, so to speak.
>
> Chairman Waxman: In other words, you found that your view of the world, your ideology, was not right, it was not working.
>
> Mr. Greenspan: Precisely. That's precisely the reason I was shocked, because I had been going for 40 years or more with very considerable evidence that it was working exceptionally well.*

---

*United States. Cong. House Committee on Oversight and Government Reform. *The Financial Crisis and the Role of Federal Regulators.* 110th Cong. 2nd sess. Washington: GPO, 2008.

The lesson? All the research, expertise, and logical argumentation in the world will fail if the premise (assumption, ideology) on which it is based turns out to be "flawed."

How do you determine the validity of assumptions once you have identified them? In the absence of more scientific criteria, you may determine validity by how well the author's assumptions stack up against your own experience, observations, reading, and values. A caution, however: The overall value of an article or book may depend only to a small degree on the validity of the author's assumptions. For instance, a sociologist may do a fine job of gathering statistical data on the incidence of crime in urban areas along the eastern seaboard. The sociologist might also be a Marxist, and you may disagree with the subsequent analysis of the data. Yet you may still find the data extremely valuable for your own work.

Readers will want to examine two assumptions at the heart of Ryan's essay on Fredrika Keefer and the San Francisco Ballet School's refusal to admit her. First, Ryan assumes that setting a standard for admission based on a candidate's appearance is equivalent to setting a standard based on a candidate's "mental prowess," the admissions standard (presumably) used by universities. An appearance-based standard, Ryan writes, will "weed out those who are less likely to succeed" in professional ballet. The writer of the critique that follows agrees with Ryan's assumption. But you may not. You may assume, by contrast, that standards based on appearance are arbitrary while those based on intellectual ability rest on documented talent (SAT scores or high school transcripts, for instance). Ryan makes a second assumption: that there are appropriate and inappropriate ways to raise children. She does not state the ways explicitly, but that does not keep her from using them to judge Krissy Keefer harshly. You may disagree with her and find a reason to cheer Krissy Keefer's defense of her daughter's rights. That's your decision. What you must do as a critical reader is recognize assumptions whether they are stated or not. You should spell them out and then accept or reject them. Ultimately, your agreement or disagreement with an author will rest on your agreement or disagreement with the author's assumptions.

CRITIQUE

In Chapter 1 we focused on summary—the condensed presentation of ideas from another source. Summary is key to much of academic writing because it relies so heavily on the works of others for the support of claims. It's not going too far to say that summarizing is the critical thinking skill from which a majority of academic writing builds. However, most academic thinking and writing do not stop at summary; usually we use summary to restate our understanding of things we see or read. Then we put that summary to use. In academic writing, one typical use of summary is as a prelude to critique.

A *critique* is a *formalized, critical reading of a passage*. It is also a personal response, but writing a critique is considerably more rigorous than saying that a movie is "great," or a book is "fascinating," or "I didn't like it." These are all responses, and, as such, they're a valid, even essential, part of your understanding of what you see and read. But such responses don't illuminate the subject—even for you—if you haven't explained how you arrived at your conclusions.

GUIDELINES FOR WRITING CRITIQUES

- *Introduce.* Introduce both the passage under analysis and the author. State the author's main argument and the point(s) you intend to make about it.

  Provide background material to help your readers understand the relevance or appeal of the passage. This background material might include one or more of the following: an explanation of why the subject is of current interest; a reference to a possible controversy surrounding the subject of the passage or the passage itself; biographical information about the author; an account of the circumstances under which the passage was written; a reference to the intended audience of the passage.
- *Summarize.* Summarize the author's main points, making sure to state the author's purpose for writing.
- *Assess the presentation.* Evaluate the validity of the author's presentation, as distinct from your points of agreement or disagreement. Comment on the author's success in achieving his or her purpose by reviewing three or four specific points. You might base your review on one or more of the following criteria:

  Is the information accurate?

  Is the information significant?

  Has the author defined terms clearly?

  Has the author used and interpreted information fairly?

  Has the author argued logically?

- *Respond to the presentation.* Now it is your turn to respond to the author's views. With which views do you agree? With which do you disagree? Discuss your reasons for agreement and disagreement, when possible tying these reasons to assumptions—both the author's and your own. Where necessary, draw on outside sources to support your ideas.
- *Conclude.* State your conclusions about the overall validity of the piece—your assessment of the author's success at achieving his or her aims and your reactions to the author's views. Remind the reader of the weaknesses and strengths of the passage.

Your task in writing a critique is to turn your critical reading of a passage into a systematic evaluation in order to deepen your reader's (and your own) understanding of that passage. Among other things, you're interested in determining what an author says, how well the points are made, what assumptions underlie the argument, what issues are overlooked, and what implications can be drawn from such an analysis. Critiques, positive or negative, should include a fair and accurate summary of the passage; they may draw on and cite information and ideas from other sources (your reading or your personal experience and observations); and they should also include a statement of your own assumptions. It is important to remember that you bring to bear an entire set of assumptions about the world. Stated or not, these assumptions underlie every evaluative comment you make; you therefore have an obligation, both to the reader and to yourself, to clarify your standards by making your assumptions explicit. Not only do your readers stand to gain by your forthrightness, but so do you. In the process of writing a critical assessment, you are forced to examine your own knowledge, beliefs, and assumptions. Ultimately, the critique is a way of learning about yourself— yet another example of the ways in which writing is useful as a tool for critical thinking.

How to Write Critiques

You may find it useful to organize a critique into five sections: introduction, summary, assessment of the presentation (on its own terms), your response to the presentation, and conclusion.

The box on p. 63 offers guidelines for writing critiques. They do not constitute a rigid formula. Thousands of authors write critiques that do not follow the structure outlined here. Until you are more confident and practiced in writing critiques, however, we suggest you follow these guidelines. They are meant not to restrict you, but rather to provide a workable sequence for writing critiques.

DEMONSTRATION: CRITIQUE

The critique that follows is based on Joan Ryan's op-ed piece "We Are Not Created Equal in Every Way" (pp. 52–53), which we have already begun to examine. In this formal critique, you will see that it is possible to agree with an author's main point, at least provisionally, yet disagree with other elements of the argument. Critiquing a different selection, you could just as easily accept the author's facts and figures but reject the conclusion he draws from them. As long as you carefully articulate the author's assumptions and your own, explaining in some detail your agreement and disagreement, the critique is yours to take in whatever direction you see fit.

Let's summarize the preceding sections by returning to the core questions that guide critical reading. You will see how, when applied to Joan Ryan's argument, they help to set up a critique.

To What Extent Does the Author Succeed in His or Her Purpose?

To answer this question, you will need to know the author's purpose. Joan Ryan's "We Are Not Created Equal in Every Way" is an argument—actually, *two* related arguments. She wants readers to accept her view that (1) a school of performing arts has the right to set admissions standards according to criteria it believes will ensure the professional success of its graduates; and (2) parents may damage their children by pushing them too hard to meet the standards set by these schools.

By supporting a ballet school's right to set admission standards based on appearance, Ryan supports the star system that produces our elite athletes and performers. At the same time, she disapproves of parents who risk their children's safety and welfare by pushing them through this system. Ryan both defends the system and attacks it. Her ambivalence on the issue keeps the argument from succeeding fully.

To What Extent Do You Agree with the Author? Evaluate Assumptions

Ryan's views on the debate surrounding Fredrika Keefer's rejection by the San Francisco School of Ballet rest on the assumption that the school has the right to set its own admissions standards—even if we find those standards harsh. All private institutions, she claims, have that right. The writer of the critique that follows agrees with Ryan, although we have seen how it is possible to disagree.

Ryan's second argument concerns the wisdom of subjecting an 8-year-old to the rigors of professional training. Ryan disapproves. The writer of the critique, while sympathetic to Ryan's concerns, states that as a practical and even as a legal matter it would be nearly impossible to prevent parents such as Krissy Keefer from doing exactly as they please in the name of helping their children. In our culture, parents have the right (short of outright abuse) to raise children however they see fit.

Finally, the writer of the critique notes a certain ambivalence in Ryan's essay: her support of the ballet school's admission standards on the one hand and her distaste for parent managers like Krissy Keefer on the other. The writer does not find evidence of a weak argument in Ryan's mixed message but rather a sign of confusion in the broader culture: We love our young stars, but we condemn parents for pushing children to the breaking point in the name of stardom.

The selections you are likely to critique will be those, like Ryan's, that argue a specific position. Indeed, every argument you read is an invitation to agree or disagree. It remains only for you to speak up and justify your position.

MODEL CRITIQUE

Eric Ralston

Professor Reilly

Writing 2

11 January 2008

A Critique of "We Are Not Created Equal

in Every Way" by Joan Ryan

(1)   Most freshmen know how it feels to apply to a school and be rejected. Each year, college admissions offices mail thousands of thin letters that begin: "Thank you for your application. The competition this year was unusually strong...." We know that we will not get into every college on our list or pass every test or win the starring role after every audition, but we believe that we deserve the chance to try. And we can tolerate rejection if we know that we compete on a level playing field. But when that field seems to arbitrarily favor some candidates over others, we take offense. At least that's when an ambitious mother took offense, bringing to court a suit that claimed her eight-year-old daughter, Fredrika Keefer, was denied admission to the prestigious San Francisco Ballet School because she had the wrong "body type" (A29).

(2)   In an opinion piece for the *San Francisco Chronicle* (12 December 2000), Joan Ryan asks: "Does [a ballet school] have the right to give preference to leaner body types?" Her answer is a firm yes. Ryan argues that institutions have the right to set whatever standards they want to ensure that those they admit meet the physical or intellectual requirements for professional success. But she also believes that some parents push their children too hard to meet those standards. Ryan offers a questionable approach to protecting children from the possible abuses of such parents. Overall, however, she raises timely issues in discussing the star system that produces our world-class athletes and performers. The sometimes conflicting concerns she expresses reflect contradictions and tensions in our larger culture.

(3)   The issue Ryan discusses is a particularly sensitive one because the child's mother charged the ballet school with discrimination. As a society we have made great strides over the past few decades in combating some of the more blatant forms of discrimination—racial, ethnic, and sexual. But is it possible, is it desirable, to eliminate *all* efforts to distinguish one person from another? When is a standard that permits some (but not all) people entry to an institution discriminatory and when is it a necessary part of doing business? Ryan believes that schools discriminate all the time, and rightly so

Ralston 2

when candidates for admission fail to meet the stated criteria for academic or professional success. That UC Berkeley does not accept every applicant is *discriminating,* not discriminatory. Ryan recognizes the difference.

She maintains, correctly, that the San Francisco Ballet School, like any other private institution, has the right to set standards by which it will accept or reject applicants. Rejection is a part of life, she writes, expressing the view that gives her essay its title: "We Are Not Created Equal in Every Way." And because we are not created equal, not everyone will be admitted to his or her number one school or get a turn on stage. That's the inevitable consequence of setting standards: Some people will meet them and gain admission, others won't. Ryan quotes the spokesperson who explained that the San Francisco Ballet School is "'not a recreation department'" (A29). In other words, a professional ballet school, like a university, is within its rights to reject applicants with body types unsuited to its view of success in professional ballet. The standard may be cruel and to some even arbitrary, but it is understandable. To put the matter bluntly, candidates with unsuitable body types, however talented or otherwise attractive, are less likely to succeed in professional ballet than those with "classical" proportions. Female dancers, for example, must regularly be lifted and carried, as if effortlessly, by their male counterparts—a feat that is difficult enough even with "leaner body types." Ryan points out that candidates without the ideal body type for ballet are not barred from professional dance: "[t]hey just have to find a different type of dance...just as athletes have to find sports that fit certain body types" (A29).

The San Francisco Ballet School is *not* saying that people of a certain skin color or religious belief are not welcome. That *would* be discriminatory and wrong. But the standard concerning body type cuts across *all* people, rich or poor, black or white, Protestant or Jew, male or female. Such a broad standard could be termed an equal opportunity standard: If it can be used to distinguish among all people equally, it is discriminating, not discriminatory.

Ryan's parallel concern in this essay is the damage done to children by parents who push them at an early age to meet the high standards set by professional training programs. Children placed onto such star tracks attend special schools (or receive home schooling) in order to accommodate intense training schedules that sometimes lead to physical or psychological injuries. In healthy families, we might expect parents to protect children from such dangers. But parents who manage what they view as their children's "careers" may be too single-minded to realize that their actions may place Johnny and Susie at risk.

(7)   Ryan disapproves of a star track system that puts children into professional training at a young age. In pursuing a career in dance, for instance, a young "child has thrown all her eggs into this one little basket at an age when most kids can barely decide what to wear to school in the morning" (A29). The law makes no provision for protecting such elite performers in training, writes Ryan: "There is no safety net for them, no arm of government that makes sure that the adults in their lives watch out for their best interests" (A29).

(8)   Like the rest of us, Ryan assumes there are appropriate and less appropriate ways to raise children. While she does not explicitly share her preferred approach, she uses language effectively (both her own and her subjects') to suggest what does not work: pushing an otherwise "quite happy" eight-year-old who "relishes" dancing into professional ballet school. Ryan is subtle enough not to attack Krissy Keefer directly, instead letting the mother undermine herself with a comment few could take seriously: "My daughter is very sophisticated, so she understands why we're [bringing a lawsuit]." No eight-year-old could fully understand the motivations behind a lawsuit, and the statement suggests a mother pursuing her own—not her daughter's—agenda. Ryan suggests that Krissy Keefer has succumbed to "the skewed logic of elite athletics and dancing" that has damaged too many young people. When Ryan points out that "no arm of government" looks out for children like Frederika, she implies the need for a Department of Youth Services to supervise parent managers. This is not a good idea.

(9)   There is no sure way to tell when a parent's managing of a child's dance or athletic schedule is abusive or constructive. Intense dedication is necessary for would-be elite athletes and performers to succeed, and such dedication often begins in childhood. Since young children are not equipped to organize their lives in pursuit of a single goal, parents step in to help. That's what the parents of Tiger Woods did on recognizing his talents:

> [H]is father...[started] him very early....[Tiger] was on the Mike Douglas show hitting golf balls when he was three years old. I mean, this is a prodigy type thing. This is like Mozart writing his first symphony when he was six, that sort of thing, and he did show unique ability right from the beginning. And his life has been channeled into being a pro. His father has devoted his life to bringing him to this point. His father hasn't worked full-time since 1988. That's what it's been all about. (Feinstein)

(10)   Ryan would point out, correctly, that for every Tiger Woods or Michelle Kwan there are many child-athletes and performing artists who fall short of their goals. They may later regret the single-minded focus that robbed them of their childhood, but there is no way to

Ralston 4

know before committing a child to years of dedicated practice whether he or she will become the next Tiger or an embittered also-ran. We simply do not have the wisdom to intervene in a parent manager's training program for her child. And Joan Ryan is not going to find an "arm of government" to intervene in the child rearing of Fredrika Keefer, however much she may "pay the price for" (A29) her mother's enthusiasm.

The tension in Ryan's essay over high standards and the intense preparation to meet them mirrors a tension in the larger culture. On the one hand, Ryan argues persuasively that elite institutions like the San Francisco Ballet School have the right to set standards for admission. At such institutions, high standards give us high levels of achievement—dancers, for instance, who "can float on air" (A29). We cheer brilliant performers like Tiger Woods and Michelle Kwan who started on their roads to success while still children. The star system produces stars. On the other hand, Ryan condemns parents who buy into the star system by pushing their children into professional training programs that demand a single-minded focus. We are horrified to learn that Macaulay Culkin of the *Home Alone* movies never really had a childhood (Peterson). Of course Culkin and others like him didn't have childhoods: They were too busy practicing their lines or their jumps and spins. If Ryan defends high standards in one breath and criticizes parents in the next for pushing children to achieve these standards, she is only reflecting a confusion in the larger culture: We love our stars, but we cannot have our stars without a star system that demands total (and often damaging) dedication from our youngest and most vulnerable citizens. That parents can be the agent of this damage is especially troubling.

⑪

Joan Ryan is right to focus on the parents of would-be stars, and she is right to remind us that young children pressured to perform at the highest levels can suffer physically and psychologically. Perhaps it was better for Fredrika Keefer the child (as opposed to Fredrika Keefer the future professional dancer) that she was not admitted to the San Francisco School of Ballet. For Keefer's sake and that of other child performers, we should pay attention to the dangers of the star system and support these children when we can. But without clear evidence of legally actionable neglect or abuse, we cannot interfere with parent managers, however much we may disagree with their decisions. We may be legitimately concerned, as is Ryan, that such a parent is driving her child to become not the next Tiger Woods but the next admission to a psychiatric ward. In a free society, for better or for worse, parents have the right to guide (or misguide) the lives of their children. All the rest of us can do is watch—and hope for the best.

⑫

Ralston 5

Works Cited

Feinstein, John. "Year of the Tiger." Interview by Jim Lehrer. *Online News Hour.*

    PBS, 14 Apr. 1997. Web. 8 Jan. 2008.

Peterson, Paul. Interview by Gary James. *ClassicBands.com.* Classic Bands, 12 Feb. 2000.

    Web. 8 Jan. 2008. <http://www.classicbands.com/PaulPetersonInterview.html>.

Ryan, Joan. "We Are Not Created Equal in Every Way." *San Francisco Chronicle*

    12 Dec. 2000: A29. Print.

Exercise 2.5

Informal Critique of the Model Critique

Before reading our analysis of this model critique, write your own informal response to the critique. What are its strengths and weaknesses? To what extent does the critique follow the general Guidelines for Writing Critiques that we outlined on p. 63? To the extent it varies from the guidelines, speculate on why. Jot down ideas for a critique that takes a different approach to Ryan's essay.

CRITICAL READING FOR CRITIQUE

- *Use the tips from Critical Reading for Summary on p. 6.* Remember to examine the context; note the title and subtitle; identify the main point; identify the subpoints; break the reading into sections; distinguish between points, examples, and counterarguments; watch for transitions within and between paragraphs; and read actively.
- *Establish the writer's primary purpose in writing.* Is the piece meant primarily to inform, persuade, or entertain?
- *Evaluate informative writing. Use these criteria (among others):*
  Accuracy of information
  Significance of information
  Fair interpretation of information
- *Evaluate persuasive writing. Use these criteria (among others):*
  Clear definition of terms
  Fair use and interpretation of information
  Logical reasoning

> • *Evaluate writing that entertains. Use these criteria (among others):*
>   Interesting characters
>   Believable action, plot, and situations
>   Communication of theme
>   Use of language
> • *Decide whether you agree or disagree with the writer's ideas, position, or message.* Once you have determined the extent to which an author has achieved his or her purpose, clarify your position in relation to the writer's.

The Strategy of the Critique

- Paragraph 1 of the model critique introduces the issue to be reviewed. It provides brief background information and sets a general context that explains why the topic of fair (and unfair) competition is important.

- Paragraph 2 introduces the author and the essay and summarizes the author's main claims. The paragraph ends (see the final three sentences) with the writer's overall assessment of the essay.

- Paragraph 3 sets a specific context for evaluating Ryan's first claim concerning admissions standards. The writer summarizes Ryan's position by making a distinction between the terms *discriminating* and *discriminatory.*

- Paragraph 4 evaluates Ryan's first claim, that the ballet school has the right to set admission standards. The writer supports Ryan's position.

- Paragraph 5 continues the evaluation of Ryan's first claim. Again, the writer of the critique supports Ryan, returning to the distinction between *discriminating* and *discriminatory.*

- Paragraphs 6–7 summarize Ryan's second claim, that parents can damage their children by pushing them too hard through professional training programs at too early an age.

- Paragraphs 8–10 evaluate Ryan's second claim. In paragraph 8 the writer states that Ryan makes a mistake in implying that a government agency should safeguard the interests of children like Fredrika Keefer. Paragraphs 9–10 present the logic for disagreeing with Ryan on this point.

- Paragraph 11 evaluates the essay as a whole. Ryan defends the right of schools in the star system to set high standards but objects when parents push young children into this system. This "tension" in the essay reflects a confusion in the larger culture.

- Paragraph 12 concludes the critique. The writer offers qualified support of Ryan's position, agreeing that children caught in the star system can suffer. The writer also states that there is not much we can do about the problem except watch and hope for the best.

Introductions, Theses, and Conclusions

WRITING INTRODUCTIONS

All writers must face the task of writing their paper's introduction and conclusion. How to start? What's the best way to approach your topic? With a serious tone, a light touch, an anecdote? How to end? How best to make the connection from your work back to the reader's world?

Many writers avoid such decisions by putting them off—and productively so. Bypassing careful planning for the introduction and conclusion, they begin writing the body of the piece; only after they've finished the body do they go back to write the opening and closing paragraphs. There's a lot to be said for this approach: Because you have presumably spent more time thinking and writing about the topic itself than about how you're going to introduce or conclude it, you are in a better position to set out your ideas. And often it's not until you've actually seen the piece on paper and read it over once or twice that a natural way of introducing or concluding it becomes apparent. You are generally in better psychological shape to write both the introduction and the conclusion after the major task of writing is behind you and you know exactly what your major points are.

The purpose of an introduction is to prepare the reader to enter the world of your paper. The introduction makes the connection between the more familiar world inhabited by the reader and the less familiar world of the writer's topic; it places a discussion in a context that the reader can understand. If you find yourself getting stuck on an introduction at the beginning of a first draft, skip over it for the moment. State your working thesis directly and move on to the body of the paper.

There are many strategies for opening a paper; we'll consider the most common ones.

Quotation

Here are the two introductory paragraphs to an article titled "The Radical Idea of Marrying for Love," from Stephanie Coontz's *Marriage: A History.*

> George Bernard Shaw described marriage as an institution that brings together two people "under the influence of the most violent, most insane, most delusive, and most transient of passions. They are required to swear that they will remain in that excited, abnormal, and exhausting condition continuously until death do them part."
>
> Shaw's comment was amusing when he wrote it at the beginning of the twentieth century, and it still makes us smile today, because it pokes fun at the unrealistic expectations that spring from a dearly held cultural ideal— that marriage should be based on intense, profound love and a couple should maintain their ardor until death do them part. But for thousands of years the joke would have fallen flat.*

The provocative quotation by Shaw is intended by Coontz to puncture our romantic assumptions about the role of love and passion in marriage. She follows the quotation with an explanation of why Shaw's statement "makes us smile" before setting out on her main undertaking in this article—as indicated in the final sentence of the second paragraph—a historical survey demonstrating that for most of the last few thousand years, love and marriage have had little to do with one another. Quoting the words of others offers you many points of departure for your paper: You can agree with the quotation. You can agree and expand. You can sharply disagree. You can use the quotation to set a context or tone.

Historical Review

In many cases, the reader will be unprepared to follow the issue you discuss unless you provide some historical background. Consider this introduction to a paper on the film-rating system:

> Sex and violence on the screen are not new issues. In the Roaring Twenties there was increasing pressure from civic and religious groups to ban depictions of "immorality" from the screen. Faced with the threat of federal censorship, the film producers decided to clean their own house. In 1930, the Motion Picture Producers and Distributors of America established the Production Code. At first, adherence to the Code was voluntary; but in 1934 Joseph Breen, newly appointed head of the MPPDA, gave the Code teeth. Henceforth all newly produced films had to be submitted for approval to the Production Code Administration, which had the power to award or withhold

---

*"The Radical Idea of Marrying for Love," from *Marriage: A History,* by Stephanie Coontz, copyright 2005 by the S.J. Coontz Company. Viking Penguin, a division of Penguin Group (USA), Inc.

the Code seal. Without a Code seal, it was virtually impossible for a film to be shown anywhere in the United States, since exhibitors would not accept it. At about the same time, the Catholic Legion of Decency was formed to advise the faithful which films were and were not objectionable. For several decades the Production Code Administration exercised powerful control over what was portrayed in American theatrical films. By the 1960s, however, changing standards of morality had considerably weakened the Code's grip. In 1968, the Production Code was replaced with a rating system designed to keep younger audiences away from films with high levels of sex or violence. Despite its imperfections, this rating system has proved more beneficial to American films than did the old censorship system.

The paper examines the relative benefits of the rating system. By beginning with some historical background on the rating system, the writer helps readers understand his arguments. (Notice the chronological development of details.)

Review of a Controversy

A particular type of historical review provides the background on a controversy or debate. Consider this introduction:

> The *American Heritage Dictionary*'s definition of civil disobedience is rather simple: "the refusal to obey civil laws that are regarded as unjust, usually by employing methods of passive resistance." However, despite such famous (and beloved) examples of civil disobedience as the movements of Mahatma Gandhi in India and the Reverend Martin Luther King, Jr., in the United States, the question of whether or not civil disobedience should be considered an asset to society is hardly clear cut. For instance, Hannah Arendt, in her article "Civil Disobedience," holds that "to think of disobedient minorities as rebels and truants is against the letter and spirit of a constitution whose framers were especially sensitive to the dangers of unbridled majority rule." On the other hand, a noted lawyer, Lewis Van Dusen, Jr., in his article "Civil Disobedience: Destroyer of Democracy," states that "civil disobedience, whatever the ethical rationalization, is still an assault on our democratic society, an affront to our legal order and an attack on our constitutional government." These two views are clearly incompatible. I believe, though, that Van Dusen's is the more convincing. On balance, civil disobedience is dangerous to society.*

The negative aspects of civil disobedience, rather than Van Dusen's essay, are the topic of this paper. But to introduce this topic, the writer has provided quotations that represent opposing sides of the controversy over civil disobedience, as well as brief references to two controversial practitioners. By focusing at the outset on the particular rather than on the abstract qualities of the topic, the writer hopes to secure the attention of her readers and involve them in the controversy that forms the subject of her paper.

---

*Michele Jacques, "Civil Disobedience: Van Dusen vs. Arendt," unpublished paper, 1993, 1. Used by permission.

From the General to the Specific

Another way of providing a transition from the reader's world to the less familiar world of the paper is to work from a general subject to a specific one. The following introduction begins a paper on improving our air quality by urging people to trade the use of their cars for public transportation.

> While generalizations are risky, it seems pretty safe to say that most human beings are selfish. Self-interest may be part of our nature, and probably aids the survival of our species, since self-interested pursuits increase the likelihood of individual survival and genetic reproduction. Ironically, however, our selfishness has caused us to abuse the natural environment upon which we depend. We have polluted, deforested, depleted, deformed, and endangered our earth, water, and air to such an extent that now our species' survival is gravely threatened. In America, air pollution is one of our most pressing environmental problems, and it is our selfish use of the automobile that poses the greatest threat to clean air, as well as the greatest challenge to efforts to stop air pollution. Very few of us seem willing to give up our cars, let alone use them less. We are spoiled by the individual freedom afforded us when we can hop into our gas-guzzling vehicles and go where we want, when we want. Somehow, we as a nation will have to wean ourselves from this addiction to the automobile, and we can do this by designing alternative forms of transportation that serve our selfish interests.*

Anecdote and Illustration: From the Specific to the General

The following two paragraphs offer an anecdote in order to move from the specific to a general subject:

> The night of March 24, 1989, was cold and calm, the air crystalline, as the giant *Exxon Valdez* oil tanker pulled out of Valdez, Alaska, into the tranquil waters of Prince William Sound. In these clearest of possible conditions the ship made a planned turn out of the shipping channel and didn't turn back in time. The huge tanker ran aground, spilling millions of gallons of crude oil into the sound. The cost of the cleanup effort was over $2 billion. The ultimate cost of continuing environmental damage is incalculable. Furthermore, when the civil trial was finally over in the summer of 1995, the Exxon Corporation was assessed an additional $5 billion in punitive damages. Everyone I query in my travels vividly recalls the accident, and most have the impression that it had something to do with the master's alcohol consumption. No one is aware of the true cause of the tragedy. In its final report, the National Transportation Safety Board (NTSB) found that sleep deprivation and sleep debt were direct causes of the accident. This stunning result got a brief mention in the back pages of the newspapers.

---

*Travis Knight, "Reducing Air Pollution with Alternative Transportation," unpublished paper, 1998, 1. Used by permission.

> Out of the vast ocean of knowledge about sleep, there are a few facts that are so important that I will try to burn them into your brain forever. None is more important than the topic of sleep debt. If we can learn to understand sleep indebtedness and manage it, we can improve everyday life as well as avoid many injuries, *horribly diminished lives, and premature deaths.**

The previous introduction went from the general (the statement that human beings are selfish) to the specific (how to decrease air pollution). This one goes from the specific (a calamitous oil spill by a giant oil tanker in Alaskan waters) to the general (the enormous financial and human costs of "sleep debt," or not getting enough sleep). The anecdote is one of the most effective means at your disposal for capturing and holding your reader's attention. It is also one of the most commonly used types of introduction in popular articles. For decades, speakers have begun their remarks with a funny, touching, or otherwise appropriate story. (In fact, plenty of books are nothing but collections of such stories, arranged by subject.)

Question

Frequently you can provoke the reader's attention by posing a question or a series of questions:

> **Which of the following people** would you say is the most admirable: Mother Teresa, Bill Gates, or Norman Borlaug? And which do you think is the least admirable? For most people, it's an easy question. Mother Teresa, famous for ministering to the poor in Calcutta, has been beatified by the Vatican, awarded the Nobel Peace Prize and ranked in an American poll as the most admired person of the 20th century. Bill Gates, infamous for giving us the Microsoft dancing paper clip and the blue screen of death, has been decapitated in effigy in "I Hate Gates" Web sites and hit with a pie in the face. As for Norman Borlaug...who the heck is Norman Borlaug?
>
> Yet a deeper look might lead you to rethink your answers. Borlaug, father of the "Green Revolution" that used agricultural science to reduce world hunger, has been credited with saving a billion lives, more than anyone else in history. Gates, in deciding what to do with his fortune, crunched the numbers and determined that he could alleviate the most misery by fighting everyday scourges in the developing world like malaria, diarrhea and parasites. Mother Teresa, for her part, extolled the virtue of suffering and ran her well-financed missions accordingly: their sick patrons were offered plenty of prayer but harsh conditions, few analgesics and dangerously primitive medical care.
>
> It's not hard to see why the moral reputations of this trio should be so out of line with the good they have done....[†]

---

*From "The Promise of Sleep," copyright 1999 by William C. Dement. Used by permission of Dell Publishing, a division of Random House, Inc.

[†]Steven J. Pinker, "The Moral Instinct," *New York Times Magazine* 12 Jan. 2008.

In this introduction to "The Moral Instinct," Steven Pinker asks a question that appears to be easy; but the answer turns out to be more complex than the average reader would have suspected. Pinker uses the rest of the first paragraph to explain why the question appears to be so easy. (After all, no one was more widely admired than Mother Teresa; and for many people—especially Apple partisans!—former Microsoft CEO Bill Gates was an emblem of capitalist greed.) In the second paragraph, Pinker overturns these assumptions as he begins his exploration of the moral sense. Opening your paper with a question can be provocative because it places the reader in an active role. Put on the spot by the author, he or she must consider answers—in this case, Who *is* the most admirable? What kind of qualities or activities *should* we admire? An opening question, chosen well, will engage readers and launch them into your paper.

Statement of Thesis

Perhaps the most direct method of introduction is to begin immediately with the thesis:

> The contemporary American shopping mall is the formal garden of late twentieth-century culture, a commodified version of the great garden styles of Western history with which it shares fundamental characteristics. Set apart from the rest of the world as a place of earthly delight like the medieval walled garden; filled with fountains, statuary, and ingeniously devised machinery like the Italian Renaissance garden; designed on grandiose and symmetrical principles like the seventeenth-century French garden; made up of the fragments of cultural and architectural history like the eighteenth-century irregular English garden; and set aside for the public like the nineteenth-century American park, the mall is the next phase of this garden history, a synthesis of all these styles that have come before. But it is now joined with the shopping street, or at least a sanitized and standardized version of one, something that never before has been allowed within the garden.*

This selection begins with a general assertion—that the American shopping mall is analogous to the great formal gardens of Western history. This idea is Richard Keller Simon's thesis, for an article titled "The Formal Garden in the Age of Consumer Culture," which he begins to develop in his second sentence with comparisons between the modern shopping mall and various types of gardens throughout history. In the paragraphs following this introduction, Simon draws correspondences between contemporary shopping malls in Houston, Philadelphia, and Palo Alto and such classic formal gardens as Henry VIII's Hampton

---

*Excerpted from "The Formal Garden in the Age of Consumer Culture: A Reading of the Twentieth-Century Shopping Mall," copyright 1992 by Richard Keller Simon. Reprinted from *Mapping the American Culture*, ed. Wayne Franklin and Michael Steiner, by permission of the University of Iowa Press.

Court. The "promenades, walls, vistas, mounts, labyrinths, statues, archways" of classic gardens, he writes, all have their analogs in the modern mall. Beginning with a thesis statement (as opposed to a quotation, question, or anecdote) works well when you want to develop an unexpected, or controversial, argument. The mall as a formal garden? Who would think so? We read on.

Or perhaps you open with the provocative assertion that "Reading is dead" in a paper examining the problem of declining literacy in the digital age. The reader sits up and takes notice, perhaps even protesting ("No, it's not—I read all the time!"). This strategy "hooks" a reader, who is likely to want to find out how you will support such an emphatic thesis.

One final note about our model introductions: They may be longer than introductions you have been accustomed to writing. Many writers (and readers) prefer a shorter, snappier introduction. The length of an introduction can depend on the length of the paper it introduces, and it is also largely a matter of personal or corporate style. There is no rule concerning the correct length of an introduction. If you feel that a short introduction is appropriate, use one. Or you may wish to break up what seems like a long introduction into two paragraphs.

Exercise 3.1

Drafting Introductions

Imagine that you are writing a paper using the topic, ideas, and thesis you developed in the exercises in this chapter. Conduct some preliminary research on the topic, using an Internet search engine such as *Google* or an article database available at your college. Choose one of the seven types of introductions we've discussed—preferably one you have never used before—and draft an introduction that would work to open a paper on your topic. Use our examples as models to help you draft your introduction.

WRITING A THESIS

A thesis, as we have seen, is a one- or two-sentence summary of a paper's content. Whether it is explanatory, mildly argumentative, or strongly argumentative, the thesis is an assertion about that content—for instance, about what the content is, how it works, what it means, if it is valuable, if action should be taken, and so on. A thesis is similar, actually, to a paper's conclusion, but it lacks the conclusion's concern for broad implications and significance. The thesis is the product of your thinking; it therefore represents *your* conclusion about the topic on which you're writing, and therefore you have to have spent some time thinking (that is, in the invention stage) in order to arrive at the thesis that governs your paper.

For a writer in the drafting stages, the thesis establishes a focus, a basis on which to include or exclude information. For the reader of a finished product, the thesis anticipates the author's discussion. *A thesis, therefore, is an essential tool for both writers and readers of academic papers.*

The Components of a Thesis

Like any other sentence, a thesis includes a subject and a predicate that makes an assertion about the subject. In the sentence "Lee and Grant were different kinds of generals," "Lee and Grant" is the subject and "were different kinds of generals" is the predicate. What distinguishes a thesis from any other sentence with a subject and a predicate is that *the thesis presents the controlling idea of the paper.* The subject of a thesis, and the assertion about it, must present the right balance between the general and the specific to allow for a thorough discussion within the allotted length of the paper. The discussion might include definitions, details, comparisons, contrasts—whatever is needed to illuminate a subject and support the assertion. (If the sentence about Lee and Grant were a thesis, the reader would assume that the rest of the paper contained comparisons and contrasts between the two generals.)

Bear in mind when writing theses that the more general your subject and the more complex your assertion, the longer your paper will be. The broadest theses require book-length treatments, as in this case:

> Meaningful energy conservation requires a shrewd application of political, financial, and scientific will.

One could not write an effective ten-page paper based on this thesis. The topic alone would require pages merely to define carefully what is meant by "energy conservation" and then by "meaningful." Energy can be conserved in homes, vehicles, industries, appliances, and power plants, and each of these areas would need consideration. Having accomplished this task, the writer would then turn his or her attention to the claim, which entails a discussion of how politics, finance, and science individually and collectively influence energy conservation. Moreover, the thesis requires the writer to argue that "shrewd application" of politics, finance, and science is required. The thesis may very well be accurate and compelling. Yet it promises entirely too much for a ten-page paper.

To write an effective thesis and thus a controlled, effective paper, you need to limit your subject and your claims about it, in that way arriving at a manageable topic. You will convert that topic to a thesis when you make an assertion about it—a *claim* that you will explain and support in the paper.

Making an Assertion

Thesis statements constitute an assertion or claim that you wish to make *about* your paper's topic. If you have spent enough time reading and gathering information, and brainstorming ideas about the assignment, you will be knowledgeable enough to have something to say based on a combination of your own thinking and the thinking of your sources.

If you have trouble making an assertion, devote more time to invention strategies: Try writing your subject at the top of a page and then listing everything you now know and feel about it. Often from such a list you will discover an assertion that you can then use to fashion a working thesis. A good way to gauge the reasonableness of your claim is to see what other authors have asserted about the same topic. Your keeping good notes on the views of others will provide you with a useful counterpoint to your own views as you write and think about your claim, and you may want to use those notes in your paper. Next, make several assertions about your topic, in order of increasing complexity, as in the following:

1. Fuel-cell technology has emerged as a promising approach to developing energy-efficient vehicles.

2. To reduce our dependence on nonrenewable fossil fuel, the federal government should encourage the development of fuel-cell vehicles.

3. The federal government should subsidize the development of fuel-cell vehicles as well as the hydrogen infrastructure needed to support them; otherwise, the United States will be increasingly vulnerable to recession and other economic dislocations resulting from our dependence on the continued flow of foreign oil.

Keep in mind that these are *working theses*. Because you haven't begun a paper based on any of them, they remain *hypotheses* to be tested. You might choose one and use it to focus your initial draft. After completing a first draft, you would revise it by comparing the contents of the paper to the thesis and making adjustments as necessary for unity. The working thesis is an excellent tool for planning broad sections of the paper, but—again—don't let it prevent you from pursuing related discussions as they occur to you.

Starting with a Working Thesis

As a student, you are not yet an expert on the subject of your paper and, therefore, won't generally have the luxury of beginning your writing tasks with a definite thesis in mind. But let's assume that you *do* have an area of expertise, that you are in your own right a professional (albeit not in academic matters). We'll assume that you understand some nonacademic subject—say, backpacking—and have been given a clear purpose for writing: to discuss the relative merits of backpack designs. Your job is to write a recommendation for the owner of a sporting-goods chain, suggesting which line of backpacks the chain should carry. Because you already know a good deal about backpacks, you may have some well-developed ideas on the subject before you start doing additional research.

Yet even as an expert in your field, you will find that crafting a thesis is challenging. After all, a thesis is a summary, and it is difficult to summarize a presentation yet to be written—especially if you plan to discover what you want to say during the process of writing. Even if you know your material well, the best you can do at first is to formulate a working thesis—a hypothesis of sorts, a well-informed hunch about your topic and the claim to be made about it. After you have completed a draft, you can evaluate the degree to which your working thesis accurately summarizes the content of your paper. If the match is a good one, the working thesis becomes the thesis. If, however, sections of the paper drift from the focus of the working thesis, you'll need to revise the thesis and the paper itself to ensure that the presentation is unified. (You'll know that the match between content and thesis is a good one when every paragraph directly refers to and develops some element of the thesis.)

This model works whether you are writing about a subject in your area of expertise—backpacking, for example—or one that is more in your professor's territory, such as government or medieval poetry. The difference is that when approaching subjects that are less familiar to you, you will have to spend more time gathering data and brainstorming in order to make assertions about your subject.

Using the Thesis to Plan a Structure

A working thesis will help you sketch the structure of your paper, for the structure flows directly from the thesis. Consider, for example, the third thesis (see p. 80) on fuel-cell technology:

> The federal government should subsidize the development of fuel-cell vehicles as well as the hydrogen infrastructure needed to support them; otherwise, the United States will be increasingly vulnerable to recession and other economic dislocations resulting from our dependence on the continued flow of foreign oil.

This thesis is *strongly argumentative,* or *persuasive.* The economic catastrophes mentioned by the writer indicate a strong degree of urgency in the need for the solution recommended: the federal subsidy of a national hydrogen infrastructure to support fuel-cell vehicles. If a paper based on this thesis is to be well developed, the writer must commit him- or herself to explaining (1) why fuel-cell vehicles are a preferred alternative to gasoline-powered vehicles; (2) why fuel-cell vehicles require a hydrogen infrastructure (i.e., the writer must explain that fuel cells produce power by mixing hydrogen and oxygen, generating both electricity and water in the process); (3) why the government needs to subsidize industry in developing fuel-cell vehicles; and (4) how continued reliance on fossil fuel technology could make the country vulnerable to economic dislocations. This thesis therefore helps the writer plan the paper, which should include a section on each of the four topics. Assuming that the paper follows the organizational plan we've proposed, the working thesis would become the final thesis, on the basis of which a reader could anticipate sections of the paper to come. In a finished product, the thesis becomes an essential tool for guiding readers.

Note, however, that this thesis is still provisional. It may turn out, as you do research or begin drafting, that the paper to which this thesis commits you will be too long and complex. You may therefore decide to drop the second clause of the thesis dealing with the country's vulnerability to economic dislocations and focus

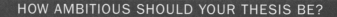

HOW AMBITIOUS SHOULD YOUR THESIS BE?

Writing tasks vary according to the nature of the thesis.

- The *explanatory thesis* is often developed in response to short-answer exam questions that call for information, not analysis (e.g., "How does James Barber categorize the main types of presidential personality?").
- The *mildly argumentative thesis* is appropriate for organizing reports (even lengthy ones), as well as essay questions that call for some analysis (e.g., "Discuss the qualities of a good speech").
- The *strongly argumentative thesis* is used to organize papers and exam questions that call for information, analysis, *and* the writer's forcefully stated point of view (e.g., "Evaluate the proposed reforms of health maintenance organizations").

The strongly argumentative thesis, of course, is the riskiest of the three because you must state your position unequivocally and make it appear reasonable—which requires that you offer evidence and defend against logical objections. But such intellectual risks pay dividends, and if you become involved enough in your work to make challenging assertions, you will provoke challenging responses that enliven classroom discussions and your own learning.

on the need for the government to subsidize the development of fuel-cell vehicles and a hydrogen infrastructure, relegating the economic concerns to your conclusion (if at all). If you make this change, your final thesis could read: "The federal government should subsidize the development of fuel-cell vehicles as well as the hydrogen infrastructure needed to support them."

This revised thesis makes an assertive commitment to the subject even though the assertion is not as complex as the original. Still, it is more assertive than the second proposed thesis:

> To reduce our dependence on nonrenewable fossil fuel energy sources, the federal government should encourage the development of fuel-cell vehicles.

Here we have a *mildly argumentative* thesis that enables the writer to express an opinion. We infer from the use of the words "should encourage" that the writer endorses the idea of the government's promoting fuel-cell development. But a government that "encourages" development is making a lesser commitment than one that "subsidizes," which means that it allocates funds for a specific policy. So the writer who argues for mere encouragement takes a milder position than the one who argues for subsidies. Note also the contrast between the second thesis and the first one, in which the writer is committed to no involvement in the debate and suggests no government involvement whatsoever.

> Fuel-cell technology has emerged as a promising approach to developing energy-efficient vehicles.

This, the first of the three thesis statements, is *explanatory,* or *informative.* In developing a paper based on this thesis, the writer is committed only to explaining how fuel-cell technology works and why it is a promising approach to energy-efficient vehicles. Given this thesis, a reader would *not* expect to find the author strongly recommending, for instance, that fuel-cell engines replace internal combustion engines in the near future. Neither does the thesis require the writer to defend a personal opinion; he or she need only justify the use of the relatively mild term "promising."

As you can see, for any topic you might explore in a paper, you can make any number of assertions—some relatively simple, some complex. It is on the basis of these assertions that you set yourself an agenda for your writing—and readers set for themselves expectations for reading. The more ambitious the thesis, the more complex will be the paper and the greater will be the readers' expectations.

To review: A thesis (a one-sentence summary of your paper) helps you organize your discussion, and it helps your reader anticipate it. Theses are distinguished by their carefully worded subjects and predicates, which should be just broad enough and complex enough to be developed within the length limitations of the assignment. Both novices and experts typically begin the initial draft of a paper with a working thesis—a statement that provides writers with structure enough to get started but with latitude enough to discover what they want to say as they write. Once you have completed a first draft, however, you test the "fit" of your thesis with what you have written. When you have a good fit, every element of the thesis is developed in the paper that follows. Discussions that drift from your thesis should be deleted, or the thesis revised to accommodate the new discussions.

Exercise 3.2 ◯

Drafting Thesis Statements

Work individually or in small groups to narrow a subject and to draft three theses on this narrowed subject. Draft one explanatory thesis, one mildly argumentative thesis, and one strongly argumentative thesis.

CONCLUSIONS

One way to view the conclusion of your paper is to see it as an introduction in reverse, a bridge from the world of your paper back to the world of your reader. A conclusion is the part of your paper in which you restate and (if necessary) expand on your thesis. Essential to many conclusions is the summary, which is not merely a repetition of the thesis but a restatement that takes advantage of the material you've presented. *The simplest conclusion is a summary of the paper, but you should want more than this.* Depending on your needs, you might offer a summary and then build onto it a discussion of the paper's significance or its implications for future study, for choices that individuals might make, for policy, and so on.

You might also want to urge readers to change an attitude or modify behavior. Certainly, you are under no obligation to discuss the broader significance of your work (and a summary, alone, will satisfy the formal requirement that your paper have an ending); but the conclusions of better papers often reveal that authors are "thinking large" and want to connect their concerns with the broader concerns of society.

Two words of advice: First, no matter how clever or beautifully executed, a conclusion cannot salvage a poorly written paper. Second, by virtue of its placement, the conclusion carries rhetorical weight; it is the last statement a reader will encounter before turning from your work. Realizing this, writers who expand on the basic summary conclusion often wish to give their final words a dramatic flourish, a heightened level of diction. Soaring rhetoric and drama in a conclusion are fine as long as they do not unbalance the paper and call attention to themselves. Having labored long hours over your paper, you may be inclined at this point to wax eloquent. But keep a sense of proportion and timing; make your points quickly and end crisply.

Statement of the Subject's Significance

One of the more effective ways to conclude a paper is to discuss the larger significance of what you have written, providing readers with one more reason to regard your work as a serious effort. When using this strategy, you move from the specific concern of your paper to the broader concerns of the reader's world. Often, you will need to choose among a range of significances: A paper on the Wright brothers might end with a discussion of air travel as it affects economies, politics, or families; a paper on contraception might end with a discussion of its effect on sexual mores, population, or the church. But don't overwhelm your reader with the importance of your remarks. Keep your discussion well focused.

The following paragraph by June J. Pilcher and Amy S. Walters concludes a paper on how "sleep debt" hurts college students.

> In sum, our findings suggest that college students are not aware of the extent to which sleep deprivation impairs their ability to complete cognitive tasks successfully because they consistently overrate their concentration and effort, as well as their estimated performance. In addition, the current data suggest that 24 hours of sleep deprivation significantly affects only fatigue and confusion and does not have a more general effect on positive or negative mood states. The practical implication of these findings is that many college students are unknowingly sabotaging their own performance by choosing to deprive themselves of sleep [while] they complete complex cognitive tasks.*

---

*"How Sleep Deprivation Affects Psychological Variables Related to College Students' Cognitive Performance" by June J. Pilcher and Amy S. Walters, from *Journal of American College Health*, Vol. 46, issue 3, November 1997, pp. 121–126. Reprinted with permission of the Helen Dwight Reid Educational Foundation. Published by Heldref Publications, 1319 Eighteenth St., N.W., Washington, DC 20036-1802. Copyright 1997.

The first sentence (as the initial phrase indicates) summarizes the chief finding of the study on which the authors have written. They expand on this conclusion before ending with a statement of the subject's significance ("The practical implication of these findings is that..."). Ending the paper in this fashion is another way of saying, "The conclusions of this paper matter." If you have taken the trouble to write a good paper, the conclusions *do* matter. Don't be bashful: State the larger significance of the point(s) you have made. Just don't claim too great a significance for your work, lest by overreaching you pop the balloon and your reader thinks, "No, the paper's not *that* important."

Call for Further Research

In the scientific and social scientific communities, papers often end with a review of what has been presented (as, for instance, in an experiment) and the ways in which the subject under consideration needs to be further explored. *A word of caution:* If you raise questions that you call on others to answer, make sure you know that the research you are calling for hasn't already been conducted.

The following conclusion comes from a sociological report on the placement of elderly men and women in nursing homes.

> Thus, our study shows a correlation between the placement of elderly citizens in nursing facilities and the significant decline of their motor and intellectual skills over the ten months following placement. What the research has not made clear is the extent to which this marked decline is due to physical as opposed to emotional causes. The elderly are referred to homes at that point in their lives when they grow less able to care for themselves—which suggests that the drop-off in skills may be due to physical causes. But the emotional stress of being placed in a home, away from family and in an environment that confirms the patient's view of himself as decrepit, may exacerbate—if not itself be a primary cause of— the patient's rapid loss of abilities. Further research is needed to clarify the relationship between depression and particular physical ailments as these affect the skills of the elderly in nursing facilities. There is little doubt that information yielded by such studies can enable health care professionals to deliver more effective services.*

Notice how this call for further study locates the author in a larger community of researchers on whom he depends for assistance in answering the questions that have come out of his own work. The author summarizes his findings (in the first sentence of the paragraph), states what his work has not shown, and then extends his invitation.

---

*Adam Price, "The Crisis in Nursing Home Care," unpublished paper, 2001. Used by permission.

Solution/Recommendation

The purpose of your paper might be to review a problem or controversy and to discuss contributing factors. In such a case, it would be appropriate, after summarizing your discussion, to offer a solution based on the knowledge you've gained while conducting research, as the writer of the following conclusion does. If your solution is to be taken seriously, however, your knowledge must be amply demonstrated in the body of the paper.

> The major problem in college sports today is not commercialism—it is the exploitation of athletes and the proliferation of illicit practices which dilute educational standards.
>
> Many universities are currently deriving substantial benefits from sports programs that depend on the labor of athletes drawn from the poorest sections of America's population. It is the responsibility of educators, civil rights leaders, and concerned citizens to see that these young people get a fair return for their labor both in terms of direct remuneration and in terms of career preparation for a life outside sports.
>
> Minimally, scholarships in revenue-producing sports should be designed to extend until graduation, rather than covering only four years of athletic eligibility, and should include guarantees of tutoring, counseling, and proper medical care. At institutions where the profits are particularly large (such as Texas A & M, which can afford to pay its football coach $280,000 a year), scholarships should also provide salaries that extend beyond room, board, and tuition. The important thing is that the athlete be remunerated fairly and have the opportunity to gain skills from a university environment without undue competition from a physically and psychologically demanding full-time job. This may well require that scholarships be extended over five or six years, including summers.
>
> Such a proposal, I suspect, will not be easy to implement. The current amateur system, despite its moral and educational flaws, enables universities to hire their athletic labor at minimal cost. But solving the fiscal crisis of the universities on the backs of America's poor and minorities is not, in the long run, a tenable solution. With the support of concerned educators, parents, and civil rights leaders, and with the help from organized labor, the college athlete, truly a sleeping giant, will someday speak out and demand what is rightly his—and hers—a fair share of the revenue created by their hard work.*

In this conclusion, the author summarizes his article in one sentence: "The major problem in college sports today is not commercialism—it is the exploitation of athletes and the proliferation of illicit practices which dilute educational standards." In paragraph 2, he continues with an analysis of the problem just stated and follows with a general recommendation that "educators, civil rights leaders, and concerned citizens" be responsible for the welfare of college athletes. In paragraph 3, he makes a specific proposal, and in the final paragraph, he anticipates resistance to the proposal. He concludes by discounting this resistance and returning to the general point, that college athletes should receive a fair deal.

---

*Mark Naison, "Scenario for Scandal," *Commonweal* 109.16 (1982).

Anecdote

As you learned in the context of introductions, an anecdote is a briefly told story or joke, the point of which is to shed light on your subject. The anecdote is more direct than an allusion. With an allusion, you merely refer to a story ("Too many people today live in Plato's cave..."); with the anecdote, you retell the story. The anecdote allows readers to discover for themselves the significance of a reference to another source—an effort most readers enjoy because they get to exercise their creativity.

The following anecdote concludes a political-philosophical essay. First, the author sums up her argument in a paragraph, then she follows that with a brief story.

> Ironically, our economy is fueled by the very thing that degrades our value system. But when politicians call for a return to "traditional family values," they seldom criticize the business interests that promote and benefit from our coarsened values. Consumer capitalism values things over people; it thrives on discontent and unhappiness since discontented people make excellent consumers, buying vast numbers of things that may somehow "fix" their inadequacies. We buy more than we need, the economy chugs along, but such materialism is the real culprit behind our warped value systems. Anthony de Mello tells the following story:
>
>> Socrates believed that the wise person would instinctively lead a frugal life, and he even went so far as to refuse to wear shoes. Yet he constantly fell under the spell of the marketplace and would go there often to look at the great variety and magnificence of the wares on display.
>>
>> A friend once asked him why he was so intrigued with the allures of the market. "I love to go there," Socrates replied, "to discover how many things I am perfectly happy without."*

The writer chose to conclude her article with this anecdote. She could have developed an interpretation, but this would have spoiled the dramatic value for the reader. The purpose of using an anecdote is to make your point with subtlety, to resist the temptation to interpret. When selecting an anecdote, keep in mind four guidelines: The anecdote should fit your content, it should be prepared for (readers should have all the information they need to understand it), it should provoke the readers' interest, and it should not be so obscure as to be unintelligible.

Quotation

A favorite concluding device is the quotation—the words of a famous person or an authority in the field on which you are writing. The purpose of quoting another is to link your work to theirs, thereby gaining for your work authority and credibility. The first criterion for selecting a quotation is its suitability to

---

*Frances Wageneck, "Family Values in the Marketplace," unpublished paper, 2000. Used by permission.

your thesis. But consider carefully what your choice of sources says about you. Suppose you are writing a paper on the American work ethic. If you could use a line by the comedian Jon Stewart or one by the current secretary of labor to make the final point of your conclusion, which would you choose and why? One source may not be inherently more effective than the other, but the choice certainly sets a tone for the paper. The following paragraph concludes an article on single-sex education:

> But schools, inevitably, present many curriculums, some overt and some subtle; and critics argue that with Sax's* model comes a lesson that our gender differences are primary, and this message is at odds with one of the most foundational principles of America's public schools. Given the myriad ways in which our schools are failing, it may be hard to remember that public schools were intended not only to instruct children in reading and math but also to teach them commonality, tolerance and what it means to be American. "When you segregate, by any means, you lose some of that," says Richard Kahlenberg, a senior fellow at the Century Foundation. "Even if one could prove that sending a kid off to his or her own school based on religion or race or ethnicity or gender did a little bit better job of raising the academic skills for workers in the economy, there's also the issue of trying to create tolerant citizens in a democracy."[†]

In the article leading up to this conclusion, Elizabeth Weil takes a somewhat skeptical view of the virtues of "teaching boys and girls separately." She concludes with an apt quotation by Richard Kahlenberg who, while conceding some value for single-sex education, supports Weil's own skepticism by suggesting that single-sex education may not create citizens as tolerant as those who have been through classes that include both genders.

Using quotations poses one potential problem: If you end with the words of another, you may leave the impression that someone else can make your case more eloquently than you. The language of the quotation will put your own prose into relief. If your prose suffers by comparison—if the quotations are the best part of your paper—you need to spend time revising. Avoid this kind of problem by making your own presentation a strong one.

Question

Questions are useful for opening papers, and they are just as useful for closing them. Opening and closing questions function in different ways, however. The introductory question promises to be addressed in the article that follows. But the concluding question leaves issues unresolved, calling on the readers to assume an

---

[*]Leonard Sax is a psychologist and physician who gave up medicine to devote himself to promoting single-sex public education.
[†]Elizabeth Weil, "Teaching Boys and Girls Separately," *New York Times Magazine* 2 Mar.2008.

active role by offering their own answers. Consider the following two paragraphs, written to conclude an article on genetically modified (GM) food:

> Are GM foods any more of a risk than other agricultural innovations that have taken place over the years, like selective breeding? Do the existing and potential future benefits of GM foods outweigh any risks that do exist? And what standard should governments use when assessing the safety of transgenic crops? The "frankenfood" frenzy has given life to a policy-making standard known as the "precautionary principle," which has been long advocated by environmental groups. That principle essentially calls for governments to prohibit any activity that raises concerns about human health or the environment, even if some cause-and-effect relationships are not fully established scientifically. As Liberal Democrat MP [Member of Parliament] Norman Baker told the BBC: "We must always apply the precautionary principle. That says that unless you're sure of adequate control, unless you're sure the risk is minimal, unless you're sure nothing horrible can go wrong, you don't do it."
>
> But can any innovation ever meet such a standard of certainty—especially given the proliferation of "experts" that are motivated as much by politics as they are by science? And what about those millions of malnourished people whose lives could be saved by transgenic foods?*

Rather than end with a question, you may choose to *raise* a question in your conclusion and then answer it, based on the material you've provided in the paper. The answered question challenges a reader to agree or disagree with you and thus places the reader in an active role. The following brief conclusion ends a student paper titled "Is Feminism Dead?"

> So the answer to the question "Is the feminist movement dead?" is no, it's not. Even if most young women today don't consciously identify themselves as "feminists"—due to the ways in which the term has become loaded with negative associations—the principles of gender equality that lie at feminism's core are enthusiastically embraced by the vast number of young women, and even a large percentage of young men.

Speculation

When you speculate, you ask about and explore what has happened or what might happen. Speculation involves a spinning out of possibilities. It stimulates readers by immersing them in your discussion of the unknown, implicitly challenging them to agree or disagree. The following paragraph concludes a brief article, "The Incandescent Charisma of the Lonely Light Bulb" by Dan Neil. The author laments the passing of the familiar electric light bulb (in favor of lower wattage compact fluorescent lights) as one more indication of the end of the

---

*"Frankenfoods Frenzy," *Reason* 13 Jan. 2000

analog age and the triumph of the digital: "The demise of the light bulb marks the final transition from electrics to electronics":

> The passing of any technology provokes nostalgia. I'm sure someone bemoaned the rise of the push-button phone and eulogized the rotary dialer. (*What a beautiful sound, the "shickity-shick" of a well-spun number....*) But the Edisonian light bulb is a more fundamental thing—so much the proverbial better idea that it came to symbolize the eureka moment, the flash of insight, when it appeared over a cartoon character's head. The fact is, how we light the world inevitably affects how we see the world. I predict we're going to miss the soft, forgiving light of the incandescent bulb with its celestial geometry. *I predict a more harshly lighted future.**

The author's concluding speculation may not be entirely serious (though a few people do lament the passing of the manual typewriter and the phonograph record), but it does highlight what is often lost, and subsequently missed, in the relentless journey of technological progress. If you have provided the necessary information prior to a concluding speculation, you will send readers back into their lives (and away from your paper) with an implicit challenge: Do they regard the future as you do? Whether they do or do not, you have set an agenda. You have got them thinking.

Exercise 3.3

Drafting Conclusions

Imagine that you have written a paper using the topic, ideas, and thesis you developed in the earlier exercises in this chapter. Conduct some preliminary research on the topic, using an Internet search engine such as *Google* or an article database available at your college. Choose one of the seven types of conclusions we've discussed—preferably one you have never used before—and draft a conclusion that would work to end your paper. Use our examples as models to help you draft your conclusion.

---

*Dan Neil, "The Incandescent Charisma of the Lonely Light Bulb," *Los Angeles Times Magazine* 3 Feb. 2008: 70.

4

Explanatory Synthesis

WHAT IS A SYNTHESIS?

A *synthesis* is a written discussion that draws on two or more sources. It follows that your ability to write syntheses depends on your ability to infer relationships among sources—essays, articles, fiction, and also nonwritten sources such as lectures, interviews, visual media, and observations. This process is nothing new for you because you infer relationships all the time—say, between something you've read in the newspaper and something you've seen for yourself, or between the teaching styles of your favorite and least favorite instructors. In fact, if you've written research papers, you've already written syntheses. In a *synthesis,* you make explicit the relationships that you have inferred among separate sources.

The skills you've already learned and practiced in the previous two chapters will be vital in writing syntheses. Before you're in a position to draw relationships between two or more sources, you must understand what those sources say; you must be able to *summarize* those sources. Readers will frequently benefit from at least partial summaries of sources in your synthesis essays. At the same time, you must go beyond summary to make judgments—judgments based on your *critical reading* of your sources: what conclusions you've drawn about the quality and validity of these sources, whether you agree or disagree with the points made in your sources, and why you agree or disagree.

In a synthesis, you go beyond the critique of individual sources to determine the relationships among them. Is the information in source B, for example, an extended illustration of the generalizations in source A? Would it be useful to compare and contrast source C with source B? Having read and considered sources A, B, and C, can you infer something else— in other words, D (not a source, but your own idea)?

Because a synthesis is based on two or more sources, you will need to be selective when choosing information from each. It would be neither possible nor desirable, for instance, to discuss in a ten-page paper on the American Civil War every point that the authors of two books make about their subject. What you as a writer must do is select from each source the ideas and information that best allow you to achieve your purpose.

PURPOSE

Your purpose in reading source materials and then drawing on them to write your own material is often reflected in the wording of an assignment. For instance, consider the following assignments on the Civil War:

American History: Evaluate the author's treatment of the origins of the Civil War.

Economics: Argue the following proposition, in light of your readings: "The Civil War was fought not for reasons of moral principle but for reasons of economic necessity."

Government: Prepare a report on the effects of the Civil War on Southern politics at the state level between 1870 and 1917.

Mass Communications: Discuss how the use of photography during the Civil War may have affected the perceptions of the war by Northerners living in industrial cities.

Literature: Select two Southern writers of the twentieth century whose work you believe was influenced by the divisive effects of the Civil War. Discuss the ways this influence is apparent in a novel or a group of short stories written by each author. The works should not be *about* the Civil War.

Applied Technology: Compare and contrast the technology of warfare available in the 1860s with the technology available a century earlier.

WHERE DO WE FIND WRITTEN SYNTHESES?

Here are just a few of the types of writing that involve synthesis:

Academic Writing

- **Analysis papers** synthesize and apply several related theoretical approaches.
- **Research papers** synthesize multiple sources.
- **Argument papers** synthesize different points into a coherent claim or position.
- **Essay exams** demonstrate understanding of course material through comparing and contrasting theories, viewpoints, or approaches in a particular field.

Workplace Writing

- **Newspaper and magazine articles** synthesize primary and secondary sources.
- **Position papers and policy briefs** compare and contrast solutions for solving problems.
- **Business plans** synthesize ideas and proposals into one coherent plan.
- **Memos and letters** synthesize multiple ideas, events, and proposals into concise form.
- **Web sites** synthesize information from various sources to present in Web pages and related links.

Each of these assignments creates a particular purpose for writing. Having located sources relevant to your topic, you would select for possible use in a paper only the parts of those sources that helped you in fulfilling this purpose. And how you used those parts—how you related them to other material from other sources—would also depend on your purpose. For instance, if you were working on the government assignment, you might draw on the same source as a student working on the literature assignment by referring to Robert Penn Warren's novel *All the King's Men,* about Louisiana politics in the early part of the twentieth century. But because the purposes of the two assignments are different, you and the other student would make different uses of this source. The parts or aspects of the novel that you find worthy of detailed analysis might be mentioned only in passing—or not at all—by the other student.

USING YOUR SOURCES

Your purpose determines not only what parts of your sources you will use but also how you will relate them to one another. Since the very essence of synthesis is the combining of information and ideas, you must have some basis on which to combine them. *Some relationships among the material in your sources must make them worth synthesizing.* It follows that the better able you are to discover such relationships, the better able you will be to use your sources in writing syntheses. Notice that the mass communications assignment requires you to draw a *cause-and-effect* relationship between photographs of the war and Northerners' perceptions of the war. The applied technology assignment requires you to *compare and contrast* state-of-the-art weapons technology in the eighteenth and nineteenth centuries. The economics assignment requires you to *argue* a proposition. In each case, *your purpose will determine how you relate your source materials to one another.*

Consider some other examples. You may be asked on an exam question or in the instructions for a paper to *describe* two or three approaches to prison reform during the past decade. You may be asked to *compare and contrast* one country's approach to imprisonment with another's. You may be asked to *develop an argument* of your own on this subject, based on your reading. Sometimes (when you are not given a specific assignment) you determine your own purpose: You are interested in exploring a particular subject; you are interested in making a case for one approach or another. In any event, your purpose shapes your essay. Your purpose determines which sources you research, which ones you use, which parts of them you use, at which points in your paper you use them, and in what manner you relate them to one another.

TYPES OF SYNTHESES: EXPLANATORY AND ARGUMENT

In this and the next chapter we categorize syntheses into two main types: *explanatory* and *argument.* The easiest way to recognize the difference between the two types may be to consider the difference between a news article and an editorial on the same subject. For the most part, we'd say that the main purpose of the news article is to convey *information,* and the main purpose of the editorial is to convey *opinion* or *interpretation.* Of course, this distinction is much too simplified: News articles often convey opinion or bias, sometimes subtly, sometimes openly; and editorials often convey unbiased information along with opinion. But as a practical matter we can generally agree on the distinction between a news article that primarily conveys information and an editorial that primarily conveys opinion. You should be able to observe this distinction in the selections shown here as Explanation and Argument.

Explanation: News Article from the New York Times

PRIVATE GETS 3 YEARS FOR IRAQ PRISON ABUSE

By David S. Cloud
September 28, 2005

Pfc. Lynndie R. England, a 22-year-old clerk in the Army who was photographed with naked Iraqi detainees at Abu Ghraib prison, was sentenced on Tuesday to three years in prison and a dishonorable discharge for her role in the scandal.

After the sentence was announced, Private England hung her head and cried briefly before hugging her mother, one of the few signs of emotion she showed in the six-day trial.

She had been found guilty on Monday of one count of conspiracy to maltreat prisoners, four counts of maltreatment and one count of committing an indecent act.

She made no comment on Tuesday as she was led out of the courthouse in handcuffs and leg shackles.

5   Earlier in the day, though, she took the stand and apologized for abusing the prisoners, saying her conduct was influenced by Specialist Charles A. Graner Jr., her boyfriend at the time.

She said she was "embarrassed" when photographs showing her posing next to naked detainees became public in 2004.

"I was used by Private Graner," she said. "I didn't realize it at the time."

Specialist Graner was reduced in rank after he was convicted in January as ringleader of the abuse.

Often groping for words and staring downward, Private England directed her apology to the detainees and to any American troops and their families who might have been injured or killed as a result of the insurgency in Iraq gaining strength.

10   Prosecutors argued on Tuesday that the anti-American feeling generated in Arab and Muslim countries by the Abu Ghraib scandal justified sentencing Private England to four to six years in prison and dishonorably discharging her from the Army. The charges the jury found her guilty of on Monday carried a maximum penalty of nine years....

Argument: Editorial from the Boston Globe

MILITARY ABUSE

September 28, 2005

The court-martial conviction Monday of reservist Lynndie England for her role in the abuse of Iraqi prisoners at Abu Ghraib should fool no one that the Pentagon is taking seriously the mistreatment of Iraqis, especially after the release last Friday of a report on torture by members of the 82d Airborne Division stationed near Fallujah....

If the [new] allegations are found credible, they further demolish the contention by officials that the abuse first reported at Abu Ghraib in 2004 was an isolated case of a few bad apples. Pentagon brass also tried to explain away the activities of England's unit as the actions of relatively untrained reservists. It is less easy to dismiss as a fluke such abuse when it occurs at the hands of the 82d Airborne, a thoroughly trained and highly decorated division.

The new charges, along with other accusations of abuse that have emerged since Abu Ghraib, including 28 suspicious detainee deaths, provide strong evidence that both reservist and active duty troops throughout Iraq were confused about their responsibility to treat detainees as prisoners of war under the terms of the Geneva Conventions....Congress should have long since created a special commission, as proposed in a bill by Senator Carl Levin of Michigan, to investigate the issue of prisoner abuse....

A truly independent inquiry, along the lines of the one done by the 9/11 commission, could trace accountability for prisoner abuse through statements and policies by ranking civilian and military officials in the Bush administration. Accountability for the shame of prisoner torture and abuse should not stop with Lynndie England and her cohort.

We'll say, for the sake of convenience, that the news article provides an *explanation* of England's sentence and that the editorial provides an *argument* for investigating responsibility *beyond* England.

As a further example of the distinction between explanation and argument, read the following paragraph:

> Researchers now use recombinant DNA technology to analyze genetic changes. With this technology, they cut and splice DNA from different species, then insert the modified molecules into bacteria or other types of cells that engage in rapid replication and cell division. The cells copy the foreign DNA right along with their own. In short order, huge populations produce useful quantities of recombinant DNA molecules. The new

technology also is the basis of genetic engineering, by which genes are isolated, modified, and inserted back into the same organism or into a different one.*

Now read this paragraph:

> Many in the life sciences field would have us believe that the new gene splicing technologies are irrepressible and irreversible and that any attempt to oppose their introduction is both futile and retrogressive. They never stop to even consider the possibility that the new genetic science might be used in a wholly different manner than is currently being proposed. The fact is, the corporate agenda is only one of two potential paths into the Biotech Century. It is possible that the growing number of anti-eugenic activists around the world might be able to ignite a global debate around alternative uses of the new science—approaches that are less invasive, more sustainable and humane and that conserve and protect the genetic rights of future generations.†

Both of these passages deal with the topic of biotechnology, but the two take quite different approaches. The first passage comes from a biology textbook, while the second appears in a magazine article. As we might expect from a textbook on the broad subject of biology, the first passage is explanatory and informative; it defines and explains some of the key concepts of biotechnology without taking a position or providing commentary about the implications of the technology. Magazine articles often present information in the same ways; however, many magazine articles take specific positions, as we see in the second passage. This passage is argumentative or persuasive: its primary purpose is to convey a point of view regarding the topic of biotechnology.

While each of these excerpts presents a clear instance of writing that is either explanatory or argumentative, it is important to note that both the textbook chapter and the magazine article contain elements of both explanation and argument. The textbook writers, while they refrain from taking a particular position, do note the controversies surrounding biotechnology and genetic engineering. They might even subtly reveal a certain bias in favor of one side of the issue, through their word choice and tone, and perhaps through devoting more space and attention to one point of view. Explanatory and argumentative writing are not mutually exclusive. The overlap of explanation and argument is also found in the magazine article: In order to make his case against genetic engineering, the writer has to explain certain elements of the issue. Yet even while these categories overlap to a certain extent, the second passage clearly has argument as its primary purpose, and the first passage is primarily explanatory.

In Chapter 2 we noted that the primary purpose in a piece of writing may be informative, persuasive, or entertaining (or some combination of the three). Some scholars of writing argue that all writing is essentially persuasive, and even without

---

*Cecie Starr and Ralph Taggart, "Recombinant DNA and Genetic Engineering," *Biology: The Unity and Diversity of Life* (New York: Wadsworth, 1998).

†Jeremy Rifkin, "The Ultimate Therapy: Commercial Eugenics on the Eve of the Biotech Century," *Tikkun* May-June 1998: 35.

entering into that complex argument, we've just seen how the varying purposes in writing do overlap. In order to persuade others of a particular position, we typically must inform them about it; conversely, a primarily informative piece of writing must also work to persuade the reader that its claims are truthful. Both informative and persuasive writing often include entertaining elements, and writing intended primarily to entertain also typically contains information and persuasion. For practical purposes, however, it is possible—and useful—to identify the *primary* purpose in a piece of writing as informative/explanatory, persuasive/argumentative, or entertaining. Entertainment as a primary purpose is the one least often practiced in purely academic writing—perhaps to your disappointment!—but information and persuasion are ubiquitous. So, while recognizing the overlap that will occur between these categories, we distinguish in this chapter between two types of synthesis writing: explanatory (or informative) and argument (or persuasive). Just as distinguishing the primary purpose in a piece of writing helps you to critically read and evaluate it, distinguishing the primary purpose in your own writing will help you to make the appropriate choices regarding your approach.

HOW TO WRITE SYNTHESES

Although writing syntheses can't be reduced to a lockstep method, it should help you to follow the guidelines listed in the box below.

GUIDELINES FOR WRITING SYNTHESES

- *Consider your purpose in writing.* What are you trying to accomplish in your paper? How will this purpose shape the way you approach your sources?
- *Select and carefully read your sources,* according to your purpose. Then reread the passages, mentally summarizing each. Identify those aspects or parts of your sources that will help you fulfill your purpose. When rereading, *label* or *underline* the sources for main ideas, key terms, and any details you want to use in the synthesis.
- *Take notes on your reading.* In addition to labeling or underlining key points in the readings, you might write brief one- or two-sentence summaries of each source. This will help you in formulating your thesis statement and in choosing and organizing your sources later.
- *Formulate a thesis.* Your thesis is the main idea that you want to present in your synthesis. It should be expressed as a complete sentence. You might do some predrafting about the ideas discussed in the readings in order to help you work out a thesis. If you've written one-sentence summaries of the readings, looking them over will help you to brainstorm connections between readings and to devise a thesis.

(continued)

When you write your synthesis drafts, you will need to consider where your thesis fits in your paper. Sometimes the thesis is the first sentence, but more often it is *the final sentence of the first paragraph.* If you are writing an *inductively arranged* synthesis (see p. 156), the thesis sentence may not appear until the final paragraphs.

- *Decide how you will use your source material.* How will the information and the ideas in the passages help you fulfill your purpose?
- *Develop an organizational plan,* according to your thesis. How will you arrange your material? It is not necessary to prepare a formal outline. But you should have some plan that will indicate the order in which you will present your material and that will indicate the relationships among your sources.
- *Draft the topic sentences for the main sections.* This is an optional step, but you may find it a helpful transition from organizational plan to first draft.
- *Write the first draft* of your synthesis, following your organizational plan. Be flexible with your plan, however. Frequently, you will use an outline to get started. As you write, you may discover new ideas and make room for them by adjusting the outline. When this happens, reread your work frequently, making sure that your thesis still accounts for what follows and that what follows still logically supports your thesis.
- *Document your sources.* You must do this by crediting sources within the body of the synthesis—citing the author's last name and the page number from which the point was taken—and then providing full citation information in a list of "Works Cited" at the end. Don't open yourself to charges of plagiarism! (See pp. 45–47.)
- *Revise your synthesis*, inserting transitional words and phrases where necessary. Make sure that the synthesis reads smoothly, logically, and clearly from beginning to end. Check for grammatical correctness, punctuation, and spelling.

Note: The writing of syntheses is a recursive process, and you should accept a certain amount of backtracking and reformulating as inevitable. For instance, in developing an organizational plan (Step 6 of the procedure), you may discover a gap in your presentation that will send you scrambling for another source—back to Step 2. You may find that formulating a thesis and making inferences among sources occur simultaneously; indeed, inferences are often made before a thesis is formulated. Our recommendations for writing syntheses will give you a structure that will get you started. But be flexible in your approach; expect discontinuity and, if possible, be assured that through backtracking and reformulating you will produce a coherent, well-crafted paper.

In this chapter we'll focus on explanatory syntheses. In the next chapter, we'll discuss the argument synthesis.

THE EXPLANATORY SYNTHESIS

Many of the papers you write in college will be more or less explanatory in nature. An explanation helps readers understand a topic. Writers explain when they divide a subject into its component parts and present them to the reader in a clear and orderly fashion. Explanations may entail descriptions that recreate in words some object, place, emotion, event, sequence of events, or state of affairs. As a student reporter, you may need to explain an event—to relate when, where, and how it took place. In a science lab, you would observe the conditions and results of an experiment and record them for review by others. In a political science course, you might review research on a particular subject—say, the complexities underlying the debate over gay marriage—and then present the results of your research to your professor and the members of your class.

Your job in writing an explanatory paper—or in writing the explanatory portion of an argumentative paper—is not to argue a particular point, but rather *to present the facts in a reasonably objective manner*. Of course, explanatory papers, like other academic papers, should be based on a thesis (see pp. 108–109). But the purpose of a thesis in an explanatory paper is less to advance a particular opinion than to focus the various facts contained in the paper.

DEMONSTRATION: EXPLANATORY SYNTHESIS—THE CAR OF THE FUTURE?

To illustrate how the process of synthesis works, we'll begin with a number of short extracts from several articles on the same subject.

Suppose you were writing a paper on a matter that auto manufacturers, along with many drivers upset by escalating gasoline prices, are discussing: efficient, environmentally sound alternatives to the internal combustion engine. Some writers and thinkers are excited about the possibility that one alternative energy source in particular, hydrogen fuel cells, could both free Americans of reliance on foreign oil and slow the degradation of the earth's atmosphere. Others, recognizing the need for new ways to power automobiles, cite difficulties with the current state-of-the-art fuel cell technology and favor other approaches, including the hybrid (gasoline and electric) engine.

Exercise 4.1

Exploring the Topic

Before reading what others have written on the subject of alternative energy vehicles, write a page or so exploring what you know and what you think about this topic. You might focus your first paragraph on your own experience with alternative energy sources—for instance, water power, steam, solar, wind, or hybrid. If you have no direct experience with the topic, recall what you have read, seen, or heard about levels of petroleum consumption in the United States, the controversies surrounding the search for oil in this country, or the advertising buzz surrounding hybrid cars. What do you imagine are some concerns people have about alternative energy vehicles? What do you think would be of most interest to journalists, politicians, and businesspeople?

Because the topic of hydrogen fuel cells is a technical one and you may not have the expertise to write knowledgeably on it just yet, and also because you are aware that the hydrogen fuel cell is but one of several technologies being discussed as replacements to the internal combustion engine, you decide to investigate what has been written on the subject, in both print and electronic texts. In the following pages we present several excerpts from the kinds of articles your research might locate.

Note: To save space and for the purpose of demonstration, we offer excerpts from four sources only; a full list of sources appears in the "Works Cited" of the model synthesis on pp. 129–130. In preparing your paper, of course, you would draw on the entire articles from which these extracts were made. (The discussion of how these passages can form the basis of an explanatory synthesis resumes on p. 107.)

THE FUEL SUBSIDY WE NEED

Ricardo Bayon

A fellow at the New America Foundation, Ricardo Bayon writes on the intersection of finance, public policy, and environmental studies. The following is excerpted from an article in the Atlantic Monthly, *January/February 2003.*

The American economy is, after Canada's, the most energy-dependent in the advanced industrialized world, requiring the equivalent of a quarter ton of oil to produce $1,000 of gross domestic product. We require twice as much energy as Germany—and three times as much as Japan—to produce the same amount of GDP. Overall the United States consumes 25 percent of the oil produced in the world each year. This binds us to the Middle East, which still holds more than 65 percent of the world's proven oil reserves. Even if we were to buy all our oil from Venezuela, Canada, and Russia, or to find more oil here in the United States (which currently holds only 2.9 percent of proven reserves), Persian Gulf producers with excess capacity, such as Saudi Arabia and the United Arab Emirates, would still largely dictate the price we paid for it.

America's economic vulnerability to oil-price fluctuations has led Washington to strike a tacit bargain with Saudi Arabia and other Persian Gulf oil producers. In return for U.S. military protection and silence about the more unsavory aspects of their societies, these countries increase production when prices get too high and cut it when they get too low. In addition, they price their oil in dollars and recycle their petro-profits through U.S. financial institutions. But this has made the United States vulnerable not only to a sustained spike in oil prices but also to the possible fall of the dollar. In part because the dollar has been strong, we have been able to consume more than we produce and then to make up the difference by borrowing from abroad. As a result, our current net international debt has risen to $2.3 trillion, or 22.6 percent of GDP. What would happen if a war in Iraq went badly or if Islamic extremists gained ground in key oil-producing states? Oil prices could rise and the dollar could fall, inflicting a double blow to the U.S. economy from which it could not easily recover.

The way to escape this abiding insecurity is to wean the U.S. economy—and the world economy, too—off oil. And the way to do that is to encourage the commercial development of a technology called the hydrogen fuel cell. Solar power and windmills will surely be important parts of our energy future, but only the fuel cell can address our oil dependency by challenging the primacy of the internal-combustion engine.

Fuel cells are actually a relatively old technology (they were invented in 1839, Jules Verne wrote about them in the 1870s, and they were used by U.S. astronauts in the 1960s), and the concept underlying them is simple: by mixing hydrogen and oxygen, fuel cells generate both water and electricity. Not only do fuel cells turn two of nature's most abundant elements into enough energy to power a car, but they create no toxic emissions (drinkable water is their only by-product). And fuel cells are completely quiet, meaning that it is now realistic to imagine living in a world of silent cars and trucks.

5   The technology is not science fiction: fuel cells are on their way toward commercial viability. Fuel-cell-powered buses are running in Vancouver, Chicago, London, and parts of Germany. BMW has a prototype car powered solely by fuel cells. Honda, Toyota, and DaimlerChrysler announced recently that they would begin shipping fuel-cell cars to retail customers around the world; General Motors and Ford are not far behind. Honda's car was shipped to its first major customer—the city of Los Angeles—at the beginning of December.

Geoffrey Ballard, the founder of the Canadian manufacturer Ballard Power Systems, has said, "The internal-combustion engine will go the way of the horse. It will be a curiosity to my grandchildren." Even large oil companies believe that they must embrace hydrogen power.

PUTTING THE HINDENBURG TO REST

Jim Motavalli

Jim Motavalli is editor of the environmentally focused E Magazine *and writes extensively on environmental matters for newspapers and magazines nationally. This article appeared in the* New York Times *on June 5, 2005.*

Some transportation experts are betting that hydrogen will eventually power most cars, while others see substantial, perhaps insurmountable, hurdles. Here is a primer on the benefits and disadvantages:

Q. *What is hydrogen, and where does it come from?*

A. *It is the lightest gas and the simplest, most abundant element in the universe. Because it is present in so many compounds, including water, supplies cannot be exhausted. But hydrogen is not actually a fuel, and can be used in a vehicle only after it is separated from other elements. This process itself consumes energy.*

Q. How is hydrogen used to power a car? And what's a fuel cell?

A. A fuel cell uses a chemical process, similar to that in a battery, to produce electricity—in this case, from hydrogen that flows into the cell from a storage tank. This electricity drives the fuel-cell car's electric motor; the only byproducts are heat and water.

Q. What are the potential advantages?

A. Because hydrogen is found everywhere, supplies are not only infinite, they pose no geographic challenges. It can be produced, albeit expensively, from emission-free sources like solar panels, wind turbines or even nuclear plants. Fuel cells can be easily scaled up or down in size, so they could replace small computer batteries or large power plants. A hydrogen car emits no pollution or global warming gases, aside from what might have resulted from producing the hydrogen itself.

Q. If it's so great, why aren't we driving hydrogen cars right now?

A. Widespread use of fuel-cell cars will have to wait until the cells become cheaper and more efficient, and until storage methods have evolved to give vehicles a travel range of perhaps 300 miles. Hydrogen production will have to be scaled up and standardized, and pumping stations equipped for hydrogen refueling at an affordable price.

Q. I've heard about the Hindenburg—is hydrogen safe?

A. Hydrogen is very flammable, and poses special challenges: it burns without a visible flame, for instance. But it is arguably no more dangerous than gasoline, and fuel-cell cars are built with leak detectors and very strong crash-resistant tanks. As for the Hindenburg tragedy of 1937, a retired NASA engineer, Addison Bain, theorizes that the dirigible burned not because it contained hydrogen, but because its cloth skin was coated with highly flammable paint. Others disagree with his assessment.

Q. How will a car carry hydrogen?

A. Hydrogen can be stored as a gas, as a liquid or in metal hydrides, which are chemical sponges, but each form has advantages and disadvantages. Still, much of automakers' current research focuses on pressurized hydrogen gas.

Q. When will I have a hydrogen car in my driveway?

A. Joseph Romm, a former Department of Energy official and author of "The Hype About Hydrogen" (Island Press, 2004), says, "I doubt that in the next 20 years an affordable, durable and efficient vehicle will be delivered that will be attractive to the public." But a renewable energy advocate, Amory Lovins of the Rocky Mountain Institute, says the nation's car fleet could be converted to hydrogen in less than a decade, and a network of small hydrogen reformers (devices that produce hydrogen from natural gas or other sources) could be quickly installed in 10 to 20 percent of the nation's 180,000 gas stations for $2 billion to $4 billion.

Q. Is this just a lot of hype?

A. Some overblown claims have already been disproved. But there is also groundbreaking research backed by serious testing programs. Lawrence D. Burns, General Motors' vice president for research and planning, says G.M. aims to have a production-ready fuel-cell vehicle (built on an innovative "skateboard" platform that could support a variety of bodies) by 2010. DaimlerChrysler is running 30 fuel-cell buses in Europe and helping to seed a hydrogen infrastructure in Iceland.

Fuel-cell Toyota Highlanders are being tested at two California universities; both the City of Los Angeles and the State of New York are using Honda FCX's. Nissan will reportedly lease a few X-Trail fuel-cell S.U.V.'s to American businesses in 2007.

Q. *Will fuel-cell cars be cheap to operate? Where will I fill up?*

A. *Hydrogen's current price is three to four times that of gasoline. The Department of Energy has issued optimistic cost estimates, but they assume widespread commercial acceptance of hydrogen fuel—which is at least a decade away. There are only a few hydrogen stations scattered around the country, though California envisions a 170-station "hydrogen highway" by 2010; Florida has announced a similar plan.*

Q. *How long will fuel cells last?*

A. *The journal of the American Institute of Chemical Engineers says the life of fuel cells may be only a fifth as long as that of a typical gasoline engine—about 30,000 miles versus 150,000. Ben Knight, vice president for automotive engineering at Honda, agrees that the durability of fuel-cell stacks is "a work in progress," but promises "a significantly longer life" from newer designs.*

Q. *Can you run a regular engine with hydrogen, without fuel cells?*

A. *Yes. A hydrogen Cadillac was featured at President Jimmy Carter's inauguration in 1977. A Mini with a hydrogen-powered internal combustion engine was displayed at the Frankfurt auto show in 2001, and Ford has shown prototypes. BMW plans to offer a "dual fuel" 7 Series sedan, which could run on either gasoline or hydrogen, by 2008. That V-12 car would have a range of 125 miles on hydrogen and 185 on gasoline.*

USING FOSSIL FUELS IN ENERGY PROCESS GETS US NOWHERE

Jeremy Rifkin

Jeremy Rifkin, a prolific writer well known for his cautionary views on technology (especially genetic technologies), is the author of The Hydrogen Economy: The Creation of the World Wide Energy Web and the Redistribution of Power on Earth *(2002). This selection is excerpted from an article in the* Los Angeles Times, *November 9, 2003.*

Hydrogen—the lightest and most abundant element of the universe—is the next great energy revolution. Scientists call it the "forever fuel" because it never runs out. And when hydrogen is used to produce power, the only byproducts are pure water and heat.

The shift to fuel cells and hydrogen energy—when it happens—will be as significant and far-reaching in its effect on the American and global economy as the steam engine and coal in the 19th century and the internal combustion engine and oil in the 20th century.

Hydrogen has the potential to end the world's reliance on oil from the Persian Gulf. It will dramatically cut down on carbon dioxide emissions and mitigate the effects of global warming. And because hydrogen is so plentiful, people who have never before had access to electricity will be able to generate it.

The environmental community is up in arms over the Bush hydrogen agenda. Why? Hydrogen has a Janus face. Though it is found everywhere on Earth, it rarely exists free-floating in nature. Hydrogen has to be extracted from fossil fuels or water or biomass.

5   In other words, there is "black" hydrogen and "green" hydrogen. And it is this critical difference that separates Bush's vision of a hydrogen future from the vision many of us hold in the environmental movement.

Bush and Secretary of Energy Spencer Abraham say hydrogen can free us from dependence on foreign oil. What they leave unsaid is that their plan calls for extracting hydrogen from all of the old energy sources—oil, natural gas and coal—and by harnessing nuclear power. Bush would like to take us into a hydrogen future without ever leaving the fossil fuels and nuclear past.

Today, most commercial hydrogen is extracted from natural gas via a steam reforming process. Although natural gas emits less carbon dioxide than other fossil fuels in producing hydrogen, it is a finite resource and in relatively short supply.

Hydrogen can also be extracted from coal, and enthusiasts point out that the U.S. enjoys ample coal reserves. The problem is that coal produces twice as much carbon dioxide as natural gas, which means a dramatic increase in global warming.

The coal industry counters that it might be possible to safely store the carbon dioxide emissions underground or in the ocean depths for thousands of years and has convinced the White House to subsidize further research into this. For many environmentalists, the issue of storing carbon dioxide seems eerily reminiscent of the arguments used by the nuclear industry about nuclear waste.

10   The nuclear industry would like to produce hydrogen, but there are still unresolved issues surrounding the safe storage of nuclear waste, the skyrocketing costs of building new reactors and the vulnerability of nuclear power plants to terrorist attacks.

There is another way to produce hydrogen—the green way—that uses no fossil fuels or nuclear power. Renewable sources of energy—wind, hydro- and geothermal power and photovoltaic cells—are increasingly being used to produce electricity. That electricity, in turn, can be used, in a process called electrolysis, to split water into hydrogen and oxygen.

Hydrogen could also be extracted from sustainable energy crops and agricultural waste in a process called gasification. There would be no increase in carbon dioxide emissions because the carbon taken from the atmosphere by the plants is released back during hydrogen production.

The White House proposal calls for large subsidies to the coal and nuclear industries to extract hydrogen. The Secretary of Energy claims that the administration is equally committed to research and development of renewable sources of energy to extract hydrogen.

However, the White House and the Republican Party have systematically blocked efforts in Congress to establish target dates for the phasing in of renewable sources of energy in the generation of electricity and for transport.

15   If the U.S. is successful in steering the International Partnership for the Hydrogen Economy toward a black hydrogen future, it could lock the global economy into the old energy regime for much of the 21st century, with dire environmental and economic consequences.

The real benefits of a hydrogen future can be realized only if renewable sources of energy are phased in and eventually become the primary source for extracting hydrogen. In the interim, the U.S. government should be supporting much tougher automobile fuel standards, hybrid cars, the overhaul of the nation's power grid with emphasis on smart technology, the Kyoto Protocol on global warming and benchmarks for renewable energy adoption.

All of these other initiatives should be carried on concurrently with an ambitious national effort to subsidize and underwrite the research and development of renewable energy technology, hydrogen and fuel cells.

The goal should be a fully integrated green hydrogen economy by the end of the first half of the 21st century.

LOTS OF HOT AIR ABOUT HYDROGEN

Joseph J. Romm

Joseph Romm is a former Acting Assistant Secretary of Energy and author of the book The Hype About Hydrogen: Fact and Fiction in the Race to Save the Climate. *The selection originally appeared in the* Los Angeles Times, *Opinion section, March 29, 2004.*

WASHINGTON—Earlier this month, the South Coast Air Quality Management District approved a $4-million program to put a mustache on the Mona Lisa—at least that's how it seems to me. What the agency actually did was approve spending millions to take 35 or so of the greenest, most energy-efficient sedans ever made—the hybrid gasoline-electric Toyota Prius—and turn them all into dirty energy guzzlers.

It is going to achieve this giant leap backward by converting the hybrids to run on hydrogen, the most overhyped alternative fuel since methyl tertiary-butyl ether, or MTBE.

Hybrids are already extremely efficient. The Prius, for example, generates only about 210 grams of carbon dioxide—the principal heat-trapping gas that causes global warming—per mile. The car is also a partial zero-emission vehicle, which means that when it uses California's low-sulfur gasoline, it produces very little of the smog-forming pollutants, like nitrogen oxides.

Hydrogen is not a primary fuel, like oil, that we can drill for. It is bound up tightly in molecules of water, or hydrocarbons like natural gas. A great deal of energy must be used to unbind it—something the AQMD plans to do by electrolyzing water into its constituents: hydrogen and oxygen. And because the resulting hydrogen is a gas, additional energy must be used to compress it to very high pressures to put it in the tank of your car.

5   With all the energy needed to create and compress that hydrogen—even with the relatively clean electric grid of California—a Prius running on hydrogen would result in twice as much greenhouse gas emissions per mile as an unmodified car. It would result in more than four times as much nitrogen oxides per mile.

I own a Prius, so that's the hybrid I am most familiar with. But Honda also makes a hybrid vehicle, and thanks to California's leadership in vehicle emissions regulations, many other car companies plan to introduce them soon. These cars will get even greener over time as technology improves.

Sadly, two of the features I love most about my car would be wiped out by the AQMD's expensive "upgrade." First, the hybrid has cut my annual fuel bill by half. Hydrogen is so expensive to make that even with California's high gasoline prices, the hydrogen hybrid will have more than four times the annual fuel bill of a gasoline hybrid. Second, my car can go twice as far on a tank of gas as my old Saturn, so I have to make those unpleasant trips to the gas station only half as often. The hydrogen hybrid would have less than half the range of my car. With hydrogen fueling stations so scarce, hydrogen hybrid drivers will constantly be scampering back to the fueling stations before the tanks get too low.

Why is the AQMD spending millions of dollars to increase pollution and destroy all the desirable features of one of the greenest, most efficient cars ever made? It has bought into the hype about hydrogen, the myth that this miracle fuel will somehow solve all of our energy and environmental problems.

When I was helping to oversee clean-energy programs at the U.S. Department of Energy in the mid-1990s, I too was intrigued by hydrogen, mainly because of recent advances in fuel cells. Fuel cells are electrochemical devices that take in hydrogen and oxygen and generate electricity and heat with high efficiency. The only "emission" is water. They have been an elusive technological goal since the first fuel cell was invented in 1839. During the 1990s, we increased funding for hydrogen tenfold and for transportation fuel cells threefold.

10   I began to change my mind about hydrogen while researching a book over the last 12 months. After speaking to dozens of experts and reviewing the extensive literature, I came to realize that hydrogen cars still needed several major breakthroughs and a clean-energy revolution to be both practical and desirable.

A recent Energy Department report noted that transportation fuel cells were 100 times more expensive than internal combustion engines. Historically, even the most aggressively promoted energy technologies, such as wind and solar power, have taken 20 years just to see a tenfold decline in prices.

The most mature onboard hydrogen storage systems—using ultrahigh pressure—contain 10 times less energy per unit volume than gasoline, in addition to requiring a significant amount of compression energy. A National Academy of Sciences panel concluded in February that such storage had "little promise of long-term practicality for light-duty vehicles" and urged the Department of Energy to halt research in this area. Yet this kind of storage is precisely what the AQMD plans to put in its hydrogen hybrids.

Another problem with hydrogen is in how it is made. Although people seem to view hydrogen as a pollution-free elixir, hydrogen is just an energy carrier, like electricity. And, like electricity, it is no cleaner than the fuels used to make it. For the next several decades, the National Academy panel concluded, "it is highly likely that fossil fuels will be the principal sources of hydrogen." Making hydrogen from fossil fuels won't solve our major environmental problems.

It's possible, of course, to make hydrogen with renewable electricity, such as solar and wind power, but that is a lousy use for renewables, since they can directly displace more than four times as much carbon dioxide from coal power compared with using that renewable power to make hydrogen for vehicles. And these savings can all be achieved without spending hundreds of billions of dollars on a new hydrogen infrastructure and hydrogen vehicles.

15   As one 2002 British study concluded, "Until there is a surplus of renewable electricity, it is not beneficial in terms of carbon reduction to use renewable electricity to produce hydrogen—for use in vehicles, or elsewhere." That surplus is, sadly, a long way off, given that Congress hasn't been willing to pass legislation requiring that even 10% of U.S. electricity in 2020 be from renewables like wind and solar.

Finally, delivering renewable hydrogen to a car in usable form is prohibitively expensive today—equal to gasoline at $7 to $10 a gallon—and likely to remain so for decades in the absence of major technology advances.

For at least several decades, hydrogen cars are exceedingly unlikely to be a cost-effective solution for global warming. Until we achieve major breakthroughs in vehicle technology, hydrogen storage, hydrogen infrastructure and renewable hydrogen production, hydrogen cars will remain inferior to the best hybrids in cost, range, annual fueling bill, convenience, roominess, safety and greenhouse gas emissions.

While we wait, California should continue to lead the way in building renewable-power generation and in advancing the most environmentally responsible cars in the world—hybrid partial zero-emission vehicles.

Consider Your Purpose

We asked a student, Janice Hunte, to read these four selections and to use them (and others) as sources in an explanatory paper on fuel cell technology. (We also asked her to write additional comments describing the process of developing her ideas into a draft.) Her paper (the final version begins on p. 123) drew on more than twenty selections on hydrogen fuel cell technology. How did she—how do you—go about synthesizing the sources?

First, remember that before considering the *how*, you must consider the *why*. In other words, what is your *purpose* in synthesizing these sources? You might use them for a paper dealing with a broader issue: "green," or environmentally friendly, technologies, for instance. If this were your purpose, these sources would be used in your sections on the problems associated with petroleum-based technologies and on the eco-neutral potential of fuel cells. Because such a broader paper would consider power sources other than fuel cells (for instance, wind, solar, and geothermal), it would also need to draw on additional sources. For a marketing course, you might consider strategies for encouraging public acceptance of fuel cells, the challenge being that at first they may be more expensive or less convenient than gasoline engines. The sources would clarify for you how fuel cells work, their potential, and the technical challenges that must be overcome in order for them to become a reasonable energy source. For a paper on the challenges of promoting acceptance of fuel cells, you would (again) need to consult more sources than we've gathered here in order to write an effective synthesis. Moving out of the academic world and into the commercial one, you might be an engineer preparing a brochure for your company's new fuel cell design. In this brochure, you might want to address the challenges of conventional designs and the advantages that your company's product offers.

But for now let's keep it simple: You want to write a paper, or a section of a paper, that simply explains the potential of fuel cell technology to alleviate our dependence on foreign oil and to provide a power source for cars that does not degrade the environment. Your job, then, is to write an *explanatory* synthesis—one that presents information but does not advance your own opinion on the subject.

Exercise 4.2

Critical Reading for Synthesis

Look over the four readings on hydrogen fuel cell technology and make a list of the ways they address the problems associated with petroleum-based technology and the potential of alternative technologies, especially fuel cells. Make your list as specific and detailed as you can. Assign a source to each item on the list.

Formulate a Thesis

The difference between a purpose and a thesis is primarily a difference of focus. Your purpose provides direction to your research and gives a focus to your paper. Your thesis sharpens this focus by narrowing it and formulating it in the words of a single declarative statement. (Chapter 3 has more on formulating thesis statements.)

Since Hunte's purpose in this case was to synthesize source material with little or no comment, her thesis would be the most obvious statement she could make about the relationship among the source readings. By "obvious" we mean a statement that is broad enough to encompass the main points of all the readings. Taken as a whole, what do they *mean*? Here Hunte describes the process she followed in coming up with a preliminary thesis for her explanatory synthesis:

> I began my writing process by looking over all the readings and noting the main point of each reading in a sentence on a piece of paper.
>
> Then I reviewed all of these points and identified the patterns in the readings. These I listed underneath my list of main points:—All the readings focus on the energy needed to power cars and, more generally, the American economy. The readings

explain America's dependence on foreign oil, the wisdom of that dependence, technologies that could free us of this dependence, and the plusses and minuses of two technologies in particular, hydrogen fuel cell and gasoline/electric hybrids.

Looking over these points, I drafted a preliminary thesis. This thesis summed up the different issues in the sources and stated how they were interrelated.

> America's dependence on dwindling foreign oil reserves has spurred research into alternative technologies for powering cars.

This was a true statement, but it sounded too vague and too obvious. I didn't feel it adequately represented the readings' points, especially since several experts hotly debate the advantages of fuel cells vs. hybrids. I wanted my thesis to more fully reflect the complexity of people's concerns regarding how these technologies are evolving as auto manufacturers search for ever more efficient designs. My next version followed:

> Many people believe hybrids will solve our energy needs, but since hybrids still depend on gasoline, others insist that another technology will take its place: fuel cells.

This thesis reflected the disagreement among experts concerning the two technologies, but I didn't feel I said enough about what makes fuel cells so attractive—namely, that they are powered by hydrogen, which is a clean-burning fuel with a virtually inexhaustible supply (unlike petroleum). In my next attempt, I tried to be more specific and a little more emphatic:

> Although many see hybrids as merely transitional vehicles, since they require gasoline, others believe that fuel-cell vehicles powered by hydrogen, a clean-burning and abundant energy source, will become the norm for roadway and highway travel.

Although this sentence was too long and sounded awkward to me, I thought it could be a good working thesis because it would help to define important parts of my paper: for instance, what are hybrids, why would they be transitional, what are fuel cells, what are their advantages over hybrids? Now I proceeded to the next step in writing—organizing my material.

Decide How You Will Use Your Source Material

The easiest way to deal with sources is to summarize them. But because you are synthesizing *ideas* rather than sources, you will have to be more selective than if you were writing a simple summary. You don't have to treat *all* the ideas in your sources, only the ones related to your thesis. Some sources might be summarized in their entirety; others, only in part. Look over your earlier notes or sentences discussing the topics covered in the readings, and refer back to the readings themselves. Focusing on the more subtle elements of the issues addressed by the authors, expand your earlier summary sentences. Write brief phrases in the margin of the sources, underline key phrases or sentences, or take notes on a separate sheet of paper or in a word processing file or electronic data filing program. Decide how your sources can help you achieve your purpose and support your thesis. For example, how might you use a diagram explaining the basics of fuel cell technology? How would you present disagreements over the perceived problems with and the potential of fuel cell technology? How much would you discuss gasoline/electric hybrids?

Develop an Organizational Plan

An organizational plan is your map for presenting material to the reader. What material will you present? To find out, examine your thesis. Do the content and structure of the thesis (that is, the number and order of assertions) suggest an organizational plan for the paper? Expect to devote at least one paragraph of your paper to developing each section of this plan. Having identified likely sections, think through the possibilities of arrangement. Ask yourself: What information does the reader need to understand first? How do I build on this first section—what block of information will follow? Think of each section in relation to others until you have placed them all and have worked your way through to a plan for the whole paper.

Study your thesis, and let it help suggest an organization. Bear in mind that any one paper can be written—successfully—according to a variety of plans. Your job before beginning your first draft is to explore possibilities. Sketch a series of rough outlines: Arrange and rearrange your paper's likely sections until you develop a plan that both facilitates the reader's understanding and achieves your objectives as a writer. Think carefully about the logical order of your points: Does one idea or point lead to the next? If not, can you find a more logical place for the point, or are you just not clearly articulating the connections between the ideas?

Your final paper may well deviate from your final sketch; in the act of writing you may discover the need to explore new material, to omit planned material, to refocus or to reorder your entire presentation. Just the same, a well-conceived organizational plan will encourage you to begin writing a draft.

Summary Statements

In her notes describing the process of organizing her material, Hunte refers to all the sources she used, including the four excerpted in this chapter.

> In reviewing my sources and writing summary statements, I noted the most important aspects of problems associated with reliance on petroleum and the promise and problems of fuel cells and other alternative technologies:
>
> - Saudi Arabia is running out of oil, and when it does the "Petroleum Age" will end with catastrophic results, unless economies prepare by changing their patterns of energy consumption (Sherman).
> - America is dangerously dependent on foreign oil. We can "wean" our economy off oil by developing hydrogen fuel cell technology (Bayon).
> - Hydrogen fuel cells work by combining hydrogen and oxygen. Because "free hydrogen" does not exist in nature, hydrogen must be separated

from the substance to which it has bonded. This process requires energy ("Hydrogen Fuel Cell").

- There are eco-friendly (green) ways to isolate hydrogen and unfriendly (black) ways. Unless we focus on the green approaches, the environmental costs of producing hydrogen for fuel cells will be unacceptably high (Rifkin).
- The energy required to isolate hydrogen is "prohibitively expensive" and the much dreamed of "hydrogen economy" creates more problems than it solves (Anthrop).
- High gasoline prices have sparked interest in gasoline/electric hybrid cars such as Toyota's Prius. Though hybrids may not be the technology that ultimately replaces the gasoline engine, hybrids are selling "briskly" today (Mackinnon and Scott).
- Because of the energy needed to isolate hydrogen, the technical problems of storing hydrogen once it is isolated, and the cost of hydrogen to the consumer, hydrogen fuel cell technology should not replace hybrid technology (Romm).

I tried to group some of these topics into categories that would have a logical order. The first thing that I wanted to communicate was the growing awareness that our dependence on petroleum is an increasing problem, both because of the dwindling reserves of the world's oil and because of the greenhouse emissions that result from burning oil.

Next, I thought I should explain what technologies are being developed to replace the gasoline engine: chiefly hybrids and fuel cells.

I also wanted to explain the problems people find with each of these technologies. Because the emphasis of my paper is on hydrogen fuel cells, this is the technology that should receive most of my attention. Still, because hybrid cars are gaining in popularity, I thought I should devote some attention to them—both to their potential and to their limitations.

Finally, I intended to present the serious doubts people have about hydrogen as the fuel of the future. With all the optimism, there are still reasons to be cautious.

I returned to my thesis, converting it to two sentences to make it less awkward and adding a phrase or two:

> Many see hybrids, which use gasoline, as merely transitional vehicles. In the future, they believe, fuel-cell vehicles powered by hydrogen, a clean-burning and abundant energy source, will become the norm for roadway and highway transportation.

Based on her thesis, Hunte developed an outline for a thirteen-paragraph paper, including introduction and conclusion:

A. Set a context. Introduce the problem of global warming.
B. Review the history of alternatives to gasoline-powered internal combustion engines, including compressed natural gas, hybrids, and flexible-fuel hybrids.

    C. Present hydrogen as an alternative fuel, including its history. Explain how a hydrogen fuel cell works.

    D. Explain the problems that limit widespread use of hydrogen fuel at present. Provide examples of current (limited) use.

    E. Report on U.S. government backing for hydrogen fuel cell technology.

    F. Conclude.

Write the Topic Sentences

Writing draft versions of topic sentences (an optional step) will get you started on each main idea of your synthesis and will help give you the sense of direction you need to proceed. Here are Hunte's draft topic sentences for sections, based on the thesis and organizational plan she developed. Note that when read in sequence following the thesis, these sentences give an idea of the logical progression of the essay as a whole.

- In recent years, the major automakers have been exploring alternatives to the gasoline-powered internal combustion engine.
- Over the years, many alternative fuel technologies have been proposed, but all have shown limited practicality or appeal.
- The most popular alternative energy vehicle in this country is the hybrid, which combines an electric motor with a standard gasoline engine.
- Hybrids may not be a long-term solution.
- A variation on the standard hybrid is the plug-in, flexible fuel-tank hybrid.
- There are two advantages that make hydrogen stand out from other alternative energy sources.
- The fuel cell was first proposed by a British physicist.
- At present, widespread use of hydrogen technology is not practical.
- Some major automakers recognize the inevitable end of the petroleum era. They have committed themselves to developing and producing fuel-cell vehicles.
- The federal government is supporting the new technology.
- Successful development of hydrogen fuel-cell vehicles faces significant roadblocks.
- There is also the problem of hydrogen leakage from large numbers of fuel-cell vehicles.
- Hydrogen fuel cells use platinum, which is a precious and expensive metal in limited supply.
- Taking these concerns into account, many experts believe that evolving technology will eventually solve the major problems and obstacles.

ORGANIZE A SYNTHESIS BY IDEA, NOT BY SOURCE

A synthesis is a blending of sources organized by *ideas*. The following rough sketches suggest how to organize and how *not* to organize a synthesis. The sketches assume you have read seven sources on a topic, Sources A–G.

Incorrect: Organizing by Source + Summary

Thesis

Summary of source A in support of the thesis.

Summary of source B in support of the thesis.

Summary of source C in support of the thesis.

(Etc.)

Conclusion

This is *not* a synthesis because it does not blend sources. Each source stands alone as an independent summary. No dialogue among sources is possible.

Correct: Organizing by Idea

Thesis

First idea: Refer to and discuss *parts* of sources (perhaps A, C, F) in support of the thesis.

Second idea: Refer to and discuss *parts* of sources (perhaps B, D) in support of the thesis.

Third idea: Refer to and discuss *parts* of sources (perhaps A, E, G) in support of the thesis.

(Etc.)

Conclusion

This *is* a synthesis because the writer blends and creates a dialogue among sources in support of an idea. Each organizing idea, which can be a paragraph or group of related paragraphs, in turn supports the thesis.

Write Your Synthesis

Here is the first draft of Hunte's explanatory synthesis. Thesis and topic sentences are highlighted. Modern Language Association (MLA) documentation style is followed throughout.

Alongside this first draft we have included comments and suggestions for revision from Hunte's instructor. For purposes of demonstration, these comments are likely to be more comprehensive than the selective comments provided by most instructors.

MODEL EXPLANATORY SYNTHESIS (FIRST DRAFT)

Janice Hunte

Professor Case

English 101

22 January 2009

The Hydrogen Fuel-Cell Car

① One of the most serious problems facing the world today is global warming. According to Michael D. Mastrandrea and Stephen H. Schneider in their article *Global Warming,* "Global warming is an increase in the average temperature of the Earth's surface. Since the Industrial Revolution, that temperature has gone up by 0.7 to 1.4 °F." The authors point out that Americans are responsible for almost 25% of the greenhouse gas pollution that causes global warming, even though they make up only 5% of the world's population. The authors also note that global warming is caused primarily by the burning of fossil fuels, such as coal, natural gas, and oil, and that much of this burning occurs in the gasoline engines that power automobiles, as well as "in factories, and in electric power plants that provide energy for houses and office buildings (47)." It is clear, then, that gasoline-powered cars are a major cause of the greenhouse gas pollution that is responsible for global warming. In the future, some believe, this problem may be solved by vehicles powered by hydrogen, a clean-burning and abundant energy source, which will become the norm for roadway and highway transportation.

② In recent years, the major automakers have been exploring alternatives to the gasoline-powered internal combustion engine. A few years ago, the electric car was widely seen as one viable alternative. Between 1996 and 2003, the Big Three U.S. automakers produced prototype electric vehicles, among them G.M.'s EVI, that were leased to a limited number of consumers. But these battery-powered, zero-emission cars proved problematic. Most had to be recharged every 100 miles or so, considerably limiting their range; and drivers found relatively few recharging stations. Manufacturers could never figure out how to reduce the batteries to manageable size or how to produce

Title and Paragraph ①

Your title could be more interesting and imaginative. The first paragraph gets off on the wrong foot because it provides a misleading impression of what the synthesis is going to be about. A reader might reasonably conclude from this paragraph that the paper was going to deal with global warming, rather than with alternative energy vehicles, and particularly with the hydrogen fuel-cell car. By the end of the first paragraph you do get to a thesis that more accurately reflects the subject of the paper, but this thesis seems awkwardly tacked on to the end of a paragraph about something else.

Suggestions for Revision

Make the title more interesting. Rewrite the first paragraph so that it provides a clear indication of the subject of the synthesis as a whole. You could begin with an anecdote that illustrates the subject, a provocative quotation, a set of questions, or a historical review of attempts to develop alternatives to the internal combustion engine. Fix mechanics errors: The article title "Global Warming" should be within quotation marks, not set in italics. Later in the paragraph, the close quotation mark should *precede,* rather than follow, the parenthetical page reference.

Paragraph ②

This paragraph does make the transition to the true subject of the synthesis: alternative energy vehicles, particularly the hydrogen fuel-cell car. But it could be more fully developed: Consider discussing other reasons (besides the need to

Hunte 2

them at reasonable cost. In the end, the automakers reclaimed all but a few of the leased electric vehicles and destroyed them (Ortiz D1).

Over the years, many alternative fuel technologies have been proposed, but all have shown limited practicality or appeal. Compressed natural gas (CNG), which powers the Honda Civic GX, is a reliable, clean-burning, renewable (though fossil) fuel, in plentiful supply. But because of their limited range (about 200 miles) and the absence of a significant CNG infrastructure, natural gas vehicles are employed primarily in fleets that have relatively short routes and access to their own filling stations (Neil). A third alternative-fuel vehicle, powered by compressed air, is being developed by a French company, Moteur Developpement International. A prototype car can achieve a speed of 70 miles an hour and has a range of 120 miles. It takes about four hours to recharge the onboard air tanks, using a compressor that can be plugged into a wall outlet. So far, the company's U.S. representative has not sold any manufacturing franchises in this country and has had trouble attracting investment capital (Weikel B2). Another alternative energy source, biodiesel fuel, was promoted in mid-2005 by President Bush. Biodiesel fuel can be made from soybeans (which can be produced domestically). "Biodiesel burns more completely and produces less air pollution than gasoline or regular diesel," declared the president. "And every time we use homegrown diesel, we support American farmers, not foreign oil producers." Critics point out, however, that biodiesel fuel can be as much as 20 cents a gallon more expensive than gasoline (Chen 15). And diesel-powered cars have never caught on in the United States, as they have in Europe.

The most popular alternative energy vehicle in this country is the hybrid, which combines an electric motor with a standard gasoline engine. The battery is used to accelerate the car from a standing position to 30 to 35 miles an hour; then the gasoline engine takes over. Unlike all-electric vehicles, hybrid cars are self-charging; they don't need to be regularly plugged in (Mackinnon and Scott D1). Priuses have been so much in demand that there is an average waiting period of 6 months for new purchasers

③

reduce greenhouse gas pollution) for the inevitable end of the internal combustion engine era. For example, we are rapidly exhausting our supplies of petroleum, a fact that may be more significant to automobile manufacturers—as well as to consumers—than the dangers of global warming.

Suggestions for Revision
Devise a clearer thesis and place it at the end of the first or second paragraph (depending on how you introduce the synthesis). Expand your discussion of why gasoline will soon become impractical as the primary means of powering automobiles.

Paragraph ③
Since this paper is largely about the hydrogen fuel-cell car, you devote too much space to discussing vehicles powered by other energy sources. While you could mention natural gas, compressed air, and biodiesel vehicles in passing, your extensive discussion of them here tends to blur what should be a sharp focus on hydrogen fuel cell vehicles.

Suggestions for Revision
Reduce the information in this paragraph to just two or three sentences. Consider appending these sentences to the paragraph discussing electric cars. This paragraph, then, would concern the least practical, appealing, or marketable alternative fuel technologies.

④

Paragraphs ④, ⑤ and ⑥

These paragraphs cover the subject of hybrids well, but this section is still too long, given that the real subject of the paper is the hydrogen fuel cell car.

Suggestions for Revision

Consider combining these three paragraphs into one shorter paragraph, cutting the discussion by at least one third. Perhaps reduce the block quotation from *Consumer Reports* to a summary sentence.

(McDonald 1). In 2004 Toyota announced that it would step up production of the vehicles and double the number for sale in the U.S. (Ohnsman E3). In 2006 the automaker plans to introduce a hybrid version of its popular Camry. Other automakers have also been getting into the act: Honda is currently producing Civic, Insight, and Accord hybrids; Ford has introduced the hybrid Mercury Mariner and the Ford Escape (Mackinnon and Scott D1). Hybrids win praise from both consumers and critics. One satisfied customer, Wendy Brown of Akron, Ohio, said that she went "from Akron to Virginia Beach on one tank of gas. It was awesome" (qtd. in Mackinnon and Scott D1). In its April 2005 Auto Issue, *Consumer Reports* had this to say about the Prius:

> Toyota's second-generation Prius is unbeatable for its economy, acceleration and interior room. It couples a 1.5 liter gasoline engine with an electric motor, and it automatically switches between them or runs on both as needed. The car shuts the engine off at idle. We got an excellent 44 mpg overall in our tests. . . . Reliability has been outstanding. (77)

⑤ But hybrids may not be a long-term solution. Most Americans remain wary of the new technology, perhaps some thinking that with their gasoline engines, they may remain transitional vehicles. From 1999 to mid-2005, 340,000 hybrids have been sold worldwide. But in 2004 alone, Americans bought 900,000 gas-hungry SUVs (McDonald 1). Hybrids may use less gasoline than standard cars, but they still use gasoline, and therefore rely on a rapidly depleting resource. And hybrids aren't cheap: consumers pay a premium of about $3,000 over similarly sized cars: "The higher initial purchase price, coupled with higher insurance premiums and related expenses, offset the gasoline savings, the recent Edmunds study concluded. Edmunds said a typical hybrid might actually cost its owner $5,283 more over five years than its nonhybrid counterpart" (Mackinnon and Scott D1).

⑥ A variation of the standard hybrid is the plug-in, flexible-fuel tank hybrid. According to *Newsweek* columnist Fareed Zakaria, a standard hybrid that gets 50 miles to the gallon could get 75 if the electric motor could be

Hunte 4

recharged by plugging in to a 120-volt outlet. And "[r]eplace the conventional fuel tank with a flexible-fuel tank that can run on a combination of 15 percent petroleum and 85 percent ethanol or methanol, and you get between 400 and 500 miles per gallon of gasoline" (Zakaria 27). According to Max Boot, "[t]hat's not science fiction; that's achievable right now." Other advantages of plug-in, flexible-fuel hybrids: such technology would reduce U.S. dependence on foreign (i.e., Middle East) oil, reduce toxic emissions, and give a boost to U.S. carmakers, who could manufacture such vehicles, and sell them not only domestically, but also in Europe and Asia (Boot B5).

There are two advantages that make hydrogen stand out from other alternative energy sources. First, it is clean burning (the only by-products from the combining of hydrogen and oxygen are water and electricity), and secondly, it is an inexhaustible and widely available element. The principle behind the fuel-cell vehicle is simple. Essentially, an electric current is used to separate hydrogen from other elements with which it is bonded, such as oxygen. When the hydrogen is recombined with oxygen in a fuel cell, the reverse process occurs and electricity is generated. As reporter Elizabeth Kolbert notes, "[t]he elegance of hydrogen technology is hard to resist" (40). She describes a visit to the office of Bragi Aronson. Aronson is a chemistry professor whose office is in Reykjavik, Iceland, a country that relies heavily on clean energy sources:

> On the counter was a device with a photovoltaic cell on one end and a little fan on the other. In between was a cylinder of water, some clear plastic tubes, and a fuel cell, which looked like two sheets of cellophane stretched over some wire mesh. When Aronson turned on a desk lamp, the photovoltaic cell began to produce electricity, which electrolyzed the water. Hydrogen and oxygen ran through the tubes to the fuel cell, where they recombined to produce more water, in the process turning the fan. It was an impressive display. (Kolbert 40)

(7)

Paragraph ⑦

This paragraph provides a clear description of hydrogen fuel-cell technology, with good use of block quotation. But the transition from other alternative energy vehicles to hydrogen fuel-cell cars, by means of the topic (first) sentence, is overly abrupt. The writing is occasionally wordy and overly passive.

Suggestions for Revision

Develop an introductory sentence that more smoothly and effectively makes the transition between what has come before (a discussion of various alternative energy-source vehicles) and what is to follow (a discussion of hydrogen fuel-cell vehicles). For emphasis, consider making this paragraph a short one and leaving the discussion of the mechanics of the fuel cell to the next paragraph. Rewrite the *weak* "There are" sentence opening ("There are two advantages…"), making the sentence more *active* ("Two advantages combine…"). Fix surface problems, like the inconsistency of "First" followed by "secondly." Toward the end of the paragraph, the repetition of "Aronson" is awkward. Rewrite, perhaps converting the sentence beginning "Aronson is a chemistry professor" into an appositive phrase ("a chemistry professor") and combining this phrase with the previous sentence. You could also create a stronger transition, after the block quotation, to the historical development of the hydrogen fuel cell.

The fuel cell was first proposed in 1839 by a British physicist (and justice of the high court) William Grove. Jules Verne wrote about hydrogen fuel cells in his 1875 novel *The Mysterious Island*. And fuel cells have been used by American astronauts since the 1960s (Bayon 117). It is only in recent years that hydrogen fuel cells have been proposed and tested for use in automobiles and other vehicles. The fuel-cell vehicle operates on the same principle as the fan in Aronson's office. Pressurized or supercooled liquid hydrogen from a storage canister in the vehicle flows into a stack of fuel cells, where it is combined with oxygen. This chemical process generates electricity (and water), which impels the electric motor, which turns the vehicle's wheels (Kolbert 38; Motavalli 12.1). The process is clean, cool, and virtually silent (Kolbert 39–40).

⑧   At present, widespread use of hydrogen technology (corresponding to widespread use of hybrid cars) is not practical. For one thing, fuel cells are expensive. It costs more to generate a kilowatt of electricity from a fuel cell than it does to generate a corresponding quantity of power from an internal combustion engine. Second, the nation has no hydrogen infrastructure through which hydrogen can be extracted from water or natural gas and then delivered to customers through a network of hydrogen stations (Bayon 118). But this situation is likely to change, if not over the next few years, then over the next few decades. Hydrogen fuel cells are more promising than that of other alternative fuel technologies, such as electric cars or natural gas or compressed air vehicles. This is because some of the major automakers recognize the inevitable end of the petroleum era. Accordingly, they have to a significant degree committed themselves to developing and producing fuel-cell vehicles. Some of these vehicles are now in operation. In 2003 General Motors developed an early fuel-cell prototype vehicle, the Hy-Wire, which it proudly showed off to reporters and National Highway Traffic Safety Administration officials (Kolbert 38). GM's vice president

Paragraph ⑧

This paragraph does a nice job of presenting some of the advantages of hydrogen fuel-cell vehicles, but it gets off on the wrong foot by focusing initially on the problems with the technology. Since you deal at some length with these problems later in the synthesis, it would be better to move the opening sentences of the paragraph to a later point. And while the examples of hydrogen prototype vehicles are fine, they may be more than you need to establish the fact that auto manufacturers are interested in developing the new technology.

Suggestions for Revision

Move the first few sentences of this paragraph to a later paragraph where you begin focusing on the problems with and drawbacks of hydrogen fuel technology. Cut some of the repetitive examples of prototype hydrogen fuel-cell vehicles in operation around the world. Fix occasionally awkward phrases ("are more promising than that of other alternative fuel technologies"), choppy sentence structure ("This is because…"), and illogical series.

Hunte 6

for research and planning, Lawrence D. Burns, says that the company "aims to have a production-ready fuel-cell vehicle...by 2010" (Motavalli 12.1). In January 2005, GM introduced its hydrogen fuel-cell prototype, the Sequel. This is the first hydrogen fuel-cell vehicle with a range of 300 miles, the minimum necessary to render it marketable. The Ford Motor Company will provide hydrogen-powered buses for passengers at Dallas–Fort Worth International Airport (Schneider A.01). BMW, Honda, Toyota, and DaimlerChrysler are all developing vehicles using the new technology. As Bayon reports, "[f]uel cell-powered buses are running in Vancouver, Chicago, London, and parts of Germany" (Bayon 117). Hydrogen fuel-cell buses are also undergoing trials in other cities, including Perth, Stockholm, Barcelona, Amsterdam, and Madrid ("Buses" 12). Nissan plans to lease fuel-cell SUVs to selected American businesses in 2007 (Motavalli 12.1). And in November 2004, "a Shell station in Washington, D.C. became the first in the nation to provide a hydrogen-fuel dispenser alongside its gasoline pumps" to service the six HydroGen3 minivans that GM uses to demonstrate hydrogen technology to members of Congress (Solheim).

    The federal government has also supported the new technology. In ⑨ 2003 President Bush, who has long been identified with the oil industry, proposed, in his State of the Union address, a $1.2 billion research program for the development of hydrogen cars (Kolbert 36). The following year he recommended spending $227 million for fuel cell research and development in 2005. The ultimate goal is to make hydrogen fuel-cell vehicles "road ready by 2020" (Durbin).

    In spite of these promising steps, successful development of ⑩ hydrogen fuel-cell vehicles faces significant roadblocks. As indicated above, hydrogen fuel cells are expensive to produce and the nation has no hydrogen infrastructure. But there may be more fundamental problems. According to Peter Eisenberger, chairman of the American Physical Society, "major scientific breakthroughs are needed for the hydrogen economy to

Paragraph ⑨
This paragraph is fine as a means of illustrating federal government support of hydrogen fuel-cell technology.

Suggestions for Revision
Only minor tinkering needed here: perhaps combine the first two and the last two sentences.

Paragraph ⑩
Since, in this generally well-developed paragraph, you begin discussing the drawbacks of hydrogen fuel-cell technology, you can move some of the material in the opening sentences of paragraph 8 here (as discussed in the comments above) and combine it with the opening sentences of the present paragraph. Otherwise, fix wordy sentences and awkward constructions.

Suggestions for Revision
Combine opening sentences of paragraph 8 and paragraph 10 here. Fix wordiness later in the paragraph by replacing "who is" constructions with appositive phrases. Make "a proven vehicle technology" into another appositive.

Hunte 7

succeed" (qtd. in Durbin). Though hydrogen is the most abundant element in the universe (Motavalli 12.1), it rarely occurs in free form in nature: it is typically bound up with other elements, such as oxygen or carbon. Significant quantities of energy must be employed to unbind it. Donald F. Anthrop, who is a professor of environmental science at San Jose State University, points out that the energy required to operate fuel cells will exceed the energy that they produce. He further argues that "[t]he cost of this energy will be prohibitively expensive" (Anthrop 10). Joseph Romm, who is a former acting assistant Secretary of Energy, believes that hybrids are a proven vehicle technology, and that they are preferable to hydrogen fuel-cell vehicles. He argues that it is likely that fossil fuels such as coal and natural gas are likely to be our major sources of hydrogen, and that the process of extracting hydrogen from these sources and then compressing the gas for storage in tanks will not only consume large quantities of energy, it will also generate significant quantities of carbon dioxide. Thus, "[m]aking hydrogen...won't solve our major environmental problems" (Romm M3).

(11) There is also the problem of hydrogen leakage from large numbers of fuel-cell vehicles. Over time this process could increase the level of greenhouse gases and affect the world's climate. "Hydrogen is not necessarily more benign," maintains Werner Zittel, a German energy consultant. "It depends on how you produce it" (qtd. in Ananthaswamy 6). Jeremy Rifkin, who is a supporter of hydrogen fuel-cell development, cautions that we should focus on the development of "green hydrogen" rather than "black hydrogen." The latter, extracted from such fossil fuels as oil, coal, and natural gas, or derived from nuclear power, generates large quantities of carbon dioxide and other toxic emissions. "Green hydrogen," on the other hand, derives from renewable energy sources such as wind, water, geothermal power, energy crops, and agricultural waste (Rifkin M5).

(12) Plus, hydrogen fuel cells use platinum, which is a precious and expensive metal in limited supply. There is not enough platinum in the

Paragraph (11)

This paragraph works well to establish the potential environmental drawbacks of hydrogen fuel cell technology. It begins awkwardly, however, with a "There is" topic sentence.

Suggestions for Revision

Make the first sentence more active and perhaps combine it with the second sentence. Eliminate the "who is" construction after "Jeremy Rifkin"; create an appositive phrase here.

Paragraph (12)

This paragraph needs a better topic sentence to introduce a paragraph that deals both with shortage and safety issues.

Suggestions for Revision

Write a topic sentence that covers both the platinum supply and safety concerns. Eliminate the awkward repetition of "people" ("Some people...These people") later in the paragraph. Provide a transitional word or term before the final sentence of the paragraph.

Hunte 8

world to replace all the existing internal combustion engines with fuel cells—at least not with fuel cells built on existing technology (Mackintosh and Morrison 22). Some people are concerned about the safety of hydrogen. These people remember the Hindenburg disaster in 1937 in which the hydrogen-filled transatlantic German airship burst into flames shortly before landing in Lakehurst, New Jersey, killing 36 persons (Motavalli 12.1). But others downplay both concerns. Alternatives to platinum may be found and future hydrogen fuel cells will use considerably less of the metal (Mackintosh and Morrison 22). Safety measures can prevent another Hindenburg-type disaster (Motavalli 12.1).

Taking these concerns into account, many experts believe that evolving technology will eventually solve the major problems and obstacles. But whether the car of the future is powered by hydrogen fuel cells or by some other form of energy, it is clear that gasoline-powered cars are going the way of the dinosaurs. We must take steps, as soon as possible, to reduce our dependence upon the internal combustion engine. Hopefully, human ingenuity will prevail in solving this critical problem.

(13)

Paragraph ⑬

The conclusion is overgeneralized. While the first sentence provides the beginning of an effective transition to the closing, what follows merely summarizes what has come before ("We must take steps…to reduce our dependence on the internal combustion engine"). The final sentence is vague and anticlimactic.

Suggestions for Revision

Develop a conclusion more rooted in specific facts and quotations by those who believe the problems described in the preceding paragraphs will be overcome. Appeal to reader interest in the subject as a way of closing strongly.

Revise Your Synthesis: Global, Local, and Surface Revisions

Many writers find it helpful to plan for three types of revision: global, local, and surface.

Global revisions affect the entire paper: the thesis, the type and pattern of evidence employed, the overall organization, the tone. A global revision may also emerge from a change in purpose. For example, the writer of this paper might decide to rewrite, focusing not on a broad introduction to and explanation of fuel-cell technology but on plans to create a national hydrogen infrastructure, similar to the existing network of gas stations, that would enable drivers to re-fuel their hydrogen-powered vehicles at their convenience.

Local revisions affect paragraphs: topic and transitional sentences; the type of evidence presented within a paragraph; evidence added, modified, or dropped within a paragraph; logical connections from one sentence or set of sentences within a paragraph to another.

Surface revisions deal with sentence style and construction, word choice, and errors of grammar, mechanics, spelling, and citation form.

Revising the First Draft: Highlights

Global

- Refocus the paper so that it emphasizes hydrogen fuel-cell vehicles and de-emphasizes (while still briefly covering) such other alternative energy vehicles as hybrids and electrics.
- Sharpen the *thesis* so that it focuses on hydrogen fuel-cell vehicles.
- In the body of the paper (e.g., paragraphs 3–6), cut back on references to alternative energy vehicles other than hydrogen fuel-cell cars.

Local

- More fully develop paragraph 2, providing additional reasons for the inevitable end of the internal combustion engine era.
- Combine information in paragraphs 4, 5, and 6 into one shorter paragraph, cutting the discussion by at least one third.
- Improve topic and transitional sentences in paragraphs 7, 8, and 12.
- Move the opening sentences of paragraph 8 to a corresponding position in paragraph 10 to improve coherence and logic.
- In paragraph 8, cut some of the repetitive examples of prototype hydrogen fuel-cell vehicles around the world.
- Improve the conclusion, making it more specific and appealing more strongly to reader interest.

Surface

- Avoid passive phrases such as "is used."
- Avoid phrases such as "there is" and "there are."
- Fix errors in mechanics: place titles of articles (like "Global Warming") within quotation marks, rather than italicizing them.
- Follow principles of parallelism for items in a series: "First" should be followed by "Second," not "Secondly."
- Reduce wordiness throughout.
- Fix awkward phrases (e.g., "are more promising than that of other alternative fuel technologies").

Exercise 4.3

Revising the Explanatory Synthesis

Try your hand at creating a final draft of the paper on pp. 114–121 by following the revision suggestions above and using your own best judgment about how to improve the first draft. Make global, local, and surface changes. After writing your own version of the paper, compare it to the revised version of our student paper below.

MODEL EXPLANATORY SYNTHESIS (FINAL DRAFT)

Hunte 1

Janice Hunte

Professor Case

English 101

31 January 2009

The Car of the Future?

In July 2005 a California family, the Spallinos, took proud possession of a new silver
and blue Honda FCX. Never heard of the FCX? That's because this particular model is not a
part of Honda's standard product line. It's a prototype powered by hydrogen fuel cells.
Although companies like Honda, Toyota, GM, and Chrysler have been experimenting with
hydrogen-powered vehicles for some years, the Spallinos' car is the first to be placed in
private hands for road testing. The family was selected by Honda because they already own a
Civic powered by natural gas and so are used to the inconveniences of driving a vehicle that
needs the kind of fuel available only in a limited number of commercial outlets. Mr. Spallino
is excited at the prospect of test driving the FCX: "Maybe this is the technology of the
future. Maybe it isn't," says Spallino, who commutes 77 miles a day. "But if I can be part of
the evolution of this technology, that would be a lot of fun" (Molloy).

Are hydrogen fuel-cell cars the wave of the future? In recent years, the major
automakers, with some financial incentives from the federal government, have been
exploring alternatives to the gasoline-powered internal combustion engine. We've seen
vehicles powered by electricity, natural gas, even compressed air. Diesel engines have been
popular in Europe for decades, though they have a much smaller customer base in the United
States. Currently, the most popular alternative energy vehicles are the hybrids, such as the
Toyota Prius, vehicles that run on both gasoline engines and electric motors. But many see
hybrids, which use gasoline, as merely transitional vehicles. In the future, they believe, fuel-
cell vehicles powered by hydrogen, a clean-burning and abundant energy source, will become
the norm for roadway and highway transportation.

But why not continue to rely indefinitely on gasoline? The answer is that the days of
the gasoline-powered internal combustion engine are numbered. First, gasoline is an
environmentally dirty fuel that, when burned, creates the toxic greenhouse gas pollution
that contributes to global warming. Second, oil is a rapidly depleting resource. As energy
expert Paul Roberts points out, "the more you produce, the less remains in the ground, and

the harder it is to bring up that remainder." Today, we import most of our oil from Saudi Arabia, a country previously thought to have virtually inexhaustible supplies of oil. But many experts believe that the Saudi fields are in decline, or have at least "matured," with most of their easily extractable petroleum already gone (Klare A19). Such "peak oil" theorists predict that in the near future, the Saudis may no longer be able to meet world demand (Sherman 7). Roberts notes that the demand for oil today stands at 29 billion barrels of oil a year. Currently, the supply matches the demand; but by 2020, with increasing demands for oil by emerging industrial countries like India and China, the demand will far outstrip the supply. Prices, typically around $60 a barrel, may soar. (For a few months in 2008, prices rose to $140 a barrel.) If the U.S. does not reduce its demand for oil, a future shortage could mean that "the global economy is likely to slip into a recession so severe that the Great Depression will look like a dress rehearsal" (Roberts).

4   Over the years, many alternative fuel technologies have been proposed, but all have shown limited practicality or appeal. Fifteen to twenty years ago, electric cars looked attractive. But those battery-powered, zero-emission cars proved problematic: most had to be recharged every 100 miles or so, considerably limiting their range. Manufacturers could never figure out how to reduce the batteries to manageable size or how to produce them at reasonable cost. Currently, not a single full-sized electric car capable of reaching highway speeds is in mass production (Ulrich A8). Other alternative fuel sources include compressed natural gas (CNG), compressed air, and biodiesel fuel. While prototype vehicles using these various technologies have been built, none appears likely to succeed in the American mass market. In fact, a recent congressional initiative to convert food stocks to biofuel may have backfired--with critics accusing such biofuel of damaging the environment and contributing to a global food shortage blamed for food riots in countries like Haiti (Brown A19).

5   Currently, the most popular alternative energy vehicle in this country is the hybrid, which combines an electric motor with a standard gasoline engine. The battery is used to accelerate the car from a standing position to 30 to 35 miles an hour; then the gasoline engine takes over. Unlike all-electric vehicles, hybrid cars are self-charging; they don't need to be regularly plugged in (Mackinnon and Scott D1). The most popular hybrid, the Toyota Prius, is in so much demand that new purchasers must typically wait six months to get one. Other manufacturers, including Honda, Ford, and General Motors, also sell or soon plan to

offer hybrid vehicles. *Consumer Reports* called the Prius "unbeatable for its economy, acceleration and interior room" and in 2005 declared the Honda Accord hybrid its highest scoring family sedan ("Best" 76–77). Despite their advantages, however, hybrids may still be transitional vehicles. They may use less gasoline than standard cars, but they still use gasoline and therefore rely on a rapidly depleting resource. And hybrids aren't cheap: consumers pay a premium of about $3,000 over similarly sized cars, an amount that could easily offset for years any savings in gasoline expenses. A variation of the standard hybrid, the plug-in, flexible-fuel tank hybrid, offers greatly improved fuel economy. In these vehicles, gasoline could be mixed with cheaper fuels like ethanol or methanol. Of course, consumers may find plugging in their cars inconvenient or (if they are on the road) impractical; and flexible-fuel hybrids would be reliant on a national ethanol/methanol infrastructure, which doesn't yet exist.

6

With these alternatives to the standard gasoline-powered internal combustion engine, what is the special appeal of the hydrogen fuel-cell vehicle? Two advantages combine to make hydrogen stand out from the rest: it is clean burning (the only by-products from the combining of hydrogen and oxygen are water and electricity), and it is an inexhaustible and widely available element.

7

The principle behind the fuel-cell vehicle is simplicity itself. Essentially, an electric current is used to separate hydrogen from other elements with which it is bonded, such as oxygen. When the hydrogen is recombined with oxygen in a fuel cell, the reverse process occurs and electricity is generated. As reporter Elizabeth Kolbert notes, "[t]he elegance of hydrogen technology is hard to resist" (40). She describes a visit to the office of Bragi Aronson, a chemistry professor, in his office in Reykjavik, Iceland, a country that relies heavily on clean energy sources:

> On the counter was a device with a photovoltaic cell on one end and a little
> fan on the other. In between was a cylinder of water, some clear plastic
> tubes, and a fuel cell, which looked like two sheets of cellophane stretched
> over some wire mesh. When Aronson turned on a desk lamp, the photo-
> voltaic cell began to produce electricity, which electrolyzed the water.
> Hydrogen and oxygen ran through the tubes to the fuel cell, where they
> recombined to produce more water, in the process turning the fan. It was
> an impressive display. (40)

(8)   The fuel cell is not exactly cutting-edge technology: the concept itself was first proposed in 1839 by British physicist (and justice of the high court) William Grove. Jules Verne wrote about hydrogen fuel cells in his 1875 novel *The Mysterious Island*. And fuel cells have been used by American astronauts since the 1960s (Bayon 117). It is only in recent years, however, that hydrogen fuel cells have been proposed and tested for use in automobiles and other vehicles. The fuel-cell vehicle operates on the same principle as the fan in Aronson's office. Pressurized or supercooled liquid hydrogen from a storage canister in the vehicle flows into a stack of fuel cells, where it is combined with oxygen. This chemical process generates electricity (and water), which impels the electric motor, which turns the vehicle's wheels (Kolbert 38; Motavalli, "Putting"). (See Figure 1.) The process is clean, cool, and virtually silent (Kolbert 39–40).

(9)   What makes the successful development of hydrogen fuel cells more promising than that of other alternative fuel technologies, such as electric cars or natural gas or compressed air vehicles, is that a number of major automakers, recognizing the inevitable end of the petroleum era, have to a significant degree committed themselves to developing and producing fuel-cell vehicles. In 2003 General Motors developed an early fuel-cell prototype vehicle, the Hy-Wire (Kolbert 38). In January 2005, GM introduced the Sequel, a hydrogen vehicle with a range of 300 miles--the minimum necessary to render it marketable (Schneider

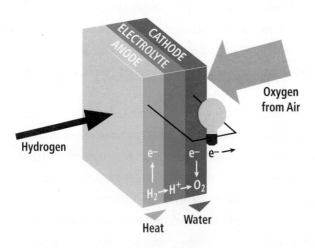

Fig. 1.   How a hydrogen fuel cell works

A.01). The company "aims to have a production-ready fuel-cell vehicle...by 2010" (Motavalli, "Putting"). The Ford Motor Company produces the E-450 Shuttle, a hydrogen-powered bus now in operation around airport parking lots and hotels. Teamed with the British oil company BP, Ford has built a fleet of 30 E-450 Shuttle buses (Sherman 7). BMW, Honda, Toyota, and Chrysler are all developing vehicles using the new technology; Honda said it would begin leasing its FCX fuel cell-powered vehicles in limited quantities in 2008 (Motavalli, "Universe" 5). As Bayon reports, "[f]uel cellpowered buses are running in Vancouver, Chicago, London, and parts of Germany" (118), and they are undergoing trials elsewhere. Nissan planned to lease fuel-cell SUVs to selected American businesses in 2007 (Motavalli, "Putting").

The federal government has also supported the new technology: in 2003 President Bush, long identified with the oil industry, proposed in his State of the Union address a $1.2 billion research program for the development of hydrogen cars (Kolbert 36). The following year he recommended spending $227 million for fuel-cell research and development in 2005, with the ultimate goal of making hydrogen fuel-cell vehicles "road ready by 2020" (Durbin). ⑩

At present, widespread use of hydrogen technology (corresponding to widespread use of hybrid cars) is not practical (Committee 116–17). For one thing, fuel cells are expensive. It costs more to generate a kilowatt of electricity from a fuel cell than it does to generate a corresponding quantity of power from an internal combustion engine. For another, the nation has no hydrogen infrastructure through which hydrogen can be extracted from water or natural gas and then delivered to customers through a network of hydrogen stations (Bayon 118). This situation is likely to change, however, if not over the next few years, then over the next few decades. But there may be more fundamental problems with hydrogen fuel cell technology. According to Peter Eisenberger, chairman of the American Physical Society, "major scientific breakthroughs are needed for the hydrogen economy to succeed" (qtd. in Durbin). Though hydrogen is the most abundant element in the universe (Motavalli, "Putting"), it rarely occurs in free form in nature: it is typically bound up with other elements, such as oxygen or carbon. Significant quantities of energy must be employed to unbind it. Donald F. Anthrop, a professor of environmental science at San Jose State University, points out that the energy required to operate fuel cells will exceed the energy that they produce. He further argues that "[t]he cost of this energy will be prohibitively expensive" (10). Joseph Romm, a former Acting Assistant Secretary of Energy, believes that ⑪ hybrids, a proven vehicle technology, are preferable to hydrogen fuel-cell vehicles. He argues fossil fuels such as coal and natural gas are likely to be our major sources of hydrogen and that the process of extracting hydrogen from these sources and then compressing the gas for storage in tanks will not only consume large quantities of energy but will also generate significant quantities of carbon dioxide. Thus, "[m]aking hydrogen...won't solve our major environmental problems" (Romm).

(12)   Others worry about hydrogen leakage from large numbers of fuel-cell vehicles, which could, over time, increase the level of greenhouse gases and affect the world's climate. "Hydrogen is not necessarily more benign," maintains Werner Zittel, a German energy consultant. Its ecological impact "depends on how you produce it" (qtd. in Ananthaswamy 6). Jeremy Rifkin, a supporter of hydrogen fuel cell development, cautions that we should focus on the development of "green hydrogen" rather than "black hydrogen." The latter, extracted from such fossil fuels as oil, coal, and natural gas, or derived from nuclear power, generates large quantities of carbon dioxide and other toxic emissions. "Green hydrogen," on the other hand, derives from renewable energy sources such as wind, water, geothermal power, energy crops, and agricultural waste (Rifkin).

(13)   Other problems confront hydrogen advocates. Hydrogen fuel cells use platinum, a precious and expensive metal in limited supply. There is not enough platinum in the world to replace all the existing internal combustion engines with fuel cells--at least not with fuel cells built on existing technology (Mackintosh and Morrison). Some are concerned about the safety of hydrogen--mindful of the Hindenburg disaster in 1937, when the hydrogen-filled transatlantic German airship burst into flames shortly before landing in Lakehurst, New Jersey, killing 36 persons (Motavalli, "Putting"). As an extremely light gas, hydrogen is something of an "escape artist," easily able to leak out of pipelines and holding tanks. This makes it unforgiving and expensive to transport (Motavalli, "Universe" 5). But others downplay both concerns: alternatives to platinum may be found and future hydrogen fuel cells will use considerably less of the metal (Mackintosh and Morrison). And safety measures--which in time will become more efficient--can prevent another Hindenburg-type disaster (Motavalli, "Putting").

(14)   Taking these concerns into account, many experts believe that evolving technology will eventually solve the major problems and obstacles. To critics like Max Boot, widespread use of hydrogen fuel-cell cars is "science fiction." But it's worth remembering that in 1870 the

telephone was science fiction, as was the airplane in 1900, home television in 1920, the desktop computer in 1970, and the World Wide Web in 1990. In none of those years was the know-how and technology yet available for the corresponding scientific development. Such developments were made possible--and, in later years, both affordable and indispensable to modern life--because of the commitment and hard work of one or more individuals. One reader of Joseph Romm's article "Lots of Hot Air About Hydrogen" responded, "Had bureaucrats like Romm discouraged James Watt in the eighteenth century regarding the harnessing of steam energy, our economic engines would still be powered by horses" (Hoffman). It may indeed turn out that the problems of developing affordable and practical hydrogen vehicles on a large scale prove insurmountable. But many believe that the promise of hydrogen fuel cells as a provider of clean and virtually inexhaustible energy makes further research and development vital for the transportation needs of the twenty-first century. As for the internal combustion engine-- according to Geoffrey Ballard, founder of Ballard Power Systems, it "will go the way of the horse. It will be a curiosity to my grandchildren" (qtd. in Bayon 118).

Works Cited

Ananthaswamy, Anil. "Reality Bites for the Dream of a Hydrogen Economy." *New Scientist* 15 Nov. 2003: 6+. Print.

Anthrop, Donald F. Letter. "Renewable Energy and Fuel Cells." *Oil and Gas Journal* 10 Oct. 2004: 10. Print.

Bayon, Ricardo. "The Fuel Subsidy We Need." *Atlantic Monthly* Jan./Feb. 2003: 117-18. Print.

"Best 2005 Cars." *Consumer Reports* Apr. 2005: 76 (Toyota Prius); 77 (Honda Accord). Print.

Board on Energy and Environmental Systems. Committee on Alternatives and Strategies for Future Hydrogen Production and Use. *The Hydrogen Economy: Opportunities, Costs, Barriers, and RD Needs*. Washington: National Academies P, 2004. Print.

Boot, Max. "The 500-Mile-Per-Gallon Solution." *Los Angeles Times* 24 Mar. 2005: B5. *LexisNexis*. Web. 20 Jan. 2009.

Brown, Lester, and Jonathan Lewis. "Ethanol's Failed Promise." *Washington Post* 22 Apr. 2008: A19. *Academic Search Complete*. Web. 19 Jan. 2009.

Hunte 9

Durbin, Dee-Ann. "Official Defends Fuel Cell Study Funds." *Los Angeles Times* 8 Mar.
    2004: B1. *ProQuest*. Web. 18 Jan. 2009.

Hoffman, Robert D. Letter. *Los Angeles Times* 3 Apr. 2004: B4. *LexisNexis*. Web. 20 Jan. 2009.

"How a Hydrogen Fuel Cell Works." *Creating a Sustainable Energy System for New Zealand*.
    Ministry of Economic Development, New Zealand, Oct. 2004. Web. 18 Jan. 2009.

Klare, Michael T. "The Vanishing Mirage of Saudi Oil: Dwindling Reserves May End the Pe-
    troleum Age." *Los Angeles Times* 2 June 2005: B9. *LexisNexis*. Web. 20 Jan. 2009.

Kolbert, Elizabeth. "The Car of Tomorrow." *New Yorker* 11 Aug. 2003: 36–40. Print.

Mackinnon, Jim, and Dave Scott. "Prices Fueling Hybrid Interest." *Akron Beacon Journal*
    24 July 2005: D1+. *Academic Search Complete*. Web. 18 Jan. 2009.

Mackintosh, James, and Kevin Morrison. "Car Makers Gear Up for the Next Shortage--
    Platinum." *Financial Times* [London] 6 July 2005: 22. *Academic Search Complete*.
    Web. 19 Jan. 2009.

Molloy, Tim. "Tomorrow's Car: It's a Gas to Drive." *Courier Mail* [Queensland, Australia]
    2 July 2005: 18. *ProQuest*. Web. 17 Jan. 2009.

Motavalli, Jim. "Putting the Hindenburg to Rest." *New York Times* 5 June 2005: 12.1.
    InfoTrac. Web. 18 Jan. 2009.

---. "A Universe of Promise (and a Tankful of Caveats)." *New York Times* 29 Apr. 2007: 1+.
    InfoTrac. Web. 18 Jan. 2009.

Rifkin, Jeremy. "Using Fossil Fuels in Energy Process Gets Us Nowhere." *Los Angeles Times*
    9 Nov. 2003: M5. *LexisNexis*. Web. 19 Jan. 2009.

Roberts, Paul. "Running Out of Oil—and Time." *Los Angeles Times* 7 Mar. 2004: M1.
    Academic Search Complete. Web. 21 Jan. 2009.

Romm, Joseph J. "Lots of Hot Air about Hydrogen." *Los Angeles Times* 28 Mar. 2004: M3.
    Academic Search Complete. Web. 21 Jan. 2009.

Schneider, Greg. "Automakers Put Hydrogen Power on the Fast Track." *Washington Post*
    9 Jan. 2005: A.01. *LexisNexis*. Web. 21 Jan. 2009.

Sherman, Don. "On the Road, Hope for a Zero-Pollution Car." *New York Times* 29 Apr. 2007:
    A1+. *InfoTrac*. Web. 19 Jan. 2009.

Ulrich, Lawrence. "They're Electric, but Can They Be Fantastic?" *New York Times* 23 Sept.
    2007: A1+. *InfoTrac*. Web. 19 Jan. 2009.

CRITICAL READING FOR SYNTHESIS

- *Use the tips from Critical Reading for Summary on p. 6.* Remember to examine the context; note the title and subtitle; identify the main point; identify the subpoints; break the reading into sections; distinguish between points, examples, and counterarguments; watch for transitions within and between paragraphs; and read actively and recursively.
- *Establish the writer's primary purpose.* Use some of the guidelines discussed in Chapter 2. Is the piece primarily informative, persuasive, or entertaining? Assess whether the piece achieves its purpose.
- *Read to identify a key idea.* If you begin reading your source materials with a key idea or topic already in mind, read to identify what your sources have to say about the idea.
- *Read to discover a key idea.* If you begin the reading process without a key idea in mind, read to discover a key idea that your sources address.
- *Read for relationships.* Regardless of whether you already have a key idea or you are attempting to discover one, your emphasis in reading should be on noting the ways in which the readings relate to each other, to a key idea, and to your purpose in writing the synthesis.

5

Argument Synthesis

WHAT IS AN ARGUMENT SYNTHESIS?

An argument is an attempt to persuade a reader or listener that a particular and debatable claim is true. Writers argue in order to establish facts, to make statements of value, and to recommend policies. For instance, answering the question *Why do soldiers sometimes commit atrocities in wartime?* would involve making an argument. To develop this argument, researchers might conduct experiments, collect historical evidence, and examine and interpret data. The researchers might then present their findings at professional conferences and in journals and books. The extent to which readers (or listeners) accept these findings will depend on the quality of the supporting evidence and the care with which the researchers have argued their case. What we are calling an argument *synthesis* draws upon evidence from a variety of sources in an attempt to persuade others of the truth or validity of a debatable claim.

By contrast, the explanatory synthesis, as we have seen, is fairly modest in purpose. It emphasizes the sources themselves, not the writer's use of sources to persuade others. The writer of an explanatory synthesis aims to inform, not persuade. Here, for example, is a thesis devised for an explanatory synthesis on the ubiquity of cell phones in contemporary life:

> Cell phones make it possible for us to be always within reach, though many people would prefer *not* to be always within reach.

This thesis summarizes two viewpoints about the impact of cell phones on contemporary life, arguing neither for nor against either viewpoint.

An argumentative thesis, however, is *persuasive* in purpose. A writer working with the same source material might conceive and support an opposing thesis:

> Cell phones have ruined our ability to be isolated, to be willfully *out of touch* with the rest of the world.

So the thesis for an argument synthesis is a claim about which reasonable people could disagree. It is a claim with which—given the right arguments—your audience might be persuaded to agree. The strategy of your argument synthesis is therefore to find and use convincing *support* for your *claim.*

The Elements of Argument: Claim, Support, and Assumption

One way of looking at an argument is to see it as an interplay of three essential elements: claim, support, and assumption. A *claim* is a proposition or conclusion that you are trying to prove. You prove this claim by using *support* in the form of fact or expert opinion. Linking your supporting evidence to your claim is your *assumption* about the subject. This assumption, also called a *warrant,* is—as we've discussed in Chapter 2—an underlying belief or principle about some aspect of the world and how it operates. By nature, assumptions (which are often unstated) tend to be more general than either claims or supporting evidence.

Here are the essential elements of an argument advocating parental restriction of television viewing for high school children:

Claim

High school students should be restricted to no more than two hours of TV viewing per day.

Support

An important new study and the testimony of educational specialists reveal that students who watch more than two hours of TV a night have, on average, lower grades than those who watch less TV.

Assumption

Excessive TV viewing adversely affects academic performance.

For another example, here's an argumentative claim on the topic of what some call computer-mediated communication (CMC):

CMC threatens to undermine human intimacy, connection, and ultimately community.

Here are the other elements of this argument:

Support

- While the Internet presents us with increased opportunities to meet people, these meetings are limited by geographical distance.
- People are spending increasing amounts of time in cyberspace: In 1998, the average Internet user spent over four hours per week online, a figure that has nearly doubled recently.
- College health officials report that excessive Internet use threatens many college students' academic and psychological well-being.
- New kinds of relationships fostered on the Internet often pose challenges to pre-existing relationships.

Assumptions

- The communication skills used and the connections formed during Internet contact fundamentally differ from those used and formed during face-to-face contact.
- "Real" connection and a sense of community are sustained by face-to-face contact, not by Internet interactions.

For the most part, arguments should be constructed logically so that assumptions link evidence (supporting facts and expert opinions) to claims. As we'll see, however, logic is only one component of effective arguments.

Exercise 5.1

Practicing Claim, Support, and Assumption

Devise two sets of claims, support, and assumptions. First, in response to the example above on computer-mediated communication and relationships, write a one-sentence claim addressing the positive impact (or potentially positive impact) of CMC on relationships—whether you personally agree with the claim or not. Then list the supporting statements on which such a claim might rest, and the assumption that underlies them. Second, write a claim that states your own position on any debatable topic you choose. Again, devise statements of support and relevant assumptions.

The Three Appeals of Argument: Logos, Ethos, Pathos

Speakers and writers have never relied on logic alone in advancing and supporting their claims. More than 2000 years ago, the Athenian philosopher and rhetorician Aristotle explained how speakers attempting to persuade others to their point of view could achieve their purpose by relying on one or more *appeals*, which he called *logos*, *ethos*, and *pathos*.

Since we frequently find these three appeals employed in political argument, we'll use political examples in the following discussion. But keep in mind that these appeals are also used extensively in advertising, legal cases, business documents, and many other types of argument.

Logos

Logos is the rational appeal, the appeal to reason. If speakers expect to persuade their audiences, they must argue logically and must supply appropriate evidence to support their case. Logical arguments are commonly of two types (often combined): deductive and inductive. The *deductive* argument begins with a generalization, then cites a specific case related to that generalization, from which follows a conclusion.

An example of a deductive argument may be seen in President John F. Kennedy's address to the nation in June 1963 on the need for sweeping civil rights legislation. Kennedy begins with the generalizations that it "ought to be possible...for American students of any color to attend any public institution they select without having to be backed up by troops" and that "it ought to be possible for American citizens of any color to register and vote in a free election without interference or fear of reprisal." Kennedy then provides several specific examples (primarily recent events in Birmingham, Alabama) and statistics to show that this was not the case. He concludes:

> We face, therefore, a moral crisis as a country and a people. It cannot be met by repressive police action. It cannot be left to increased demonstrations in the streets. It cannot be quieted by token moves or talk. It is time to act in the Congress, in your state and local legislative body, and, above all, in all of our daily lives.

Underlying Kennedy's argument is this reasoning:

All Americans should enjoy certain rights. (*assumption*)

Some Americans do not enjoy these rights. (*support*)

We must take action to ensure that all Americans enjoy these rights. (*claim*)

Another form of logical argumentation is *inductive* reasoning. A speaker or writer who argues inductively begins not with a generalization, but with several pieces of specific evidence. The speaker then draws a conclusion from this evidence. For example, in a 1990 debate on gun control, Senator Robert C. Byrd cited specific examples of rampant crime involving guns: "I read of young men being viciously murdered for a pair of sneakers, a leather jacket, or $20." He also offered statistical evidence of the increasing crime rate: "in 1951, there were 3.2 policemen for every felony committed in the United States; this year nearly 3.2 felonies will be committed per every police officer." He concluded, "Something has to change. We have to stop the crimes that are distorting and disrupting the way of life for so many innocent, law-respecting Americans. The bill that we are debating today attempts to do just that."

Senator Edward M. Kennedy also used statistical evidence in arguing for passage of the Racial Justice Act of 1990, which was designed to ensure that minorities were not disproportionately singled out for the death penalty. Kennedy pointed out that between 1973 and 1980, 17 defendants in Fulton County, Georgia, were charged with killing police officers, but the only defendant who received the death sentence was a black man. Kennedy also cited statistics to show that "those who killed whites were 4.3 times more likely to receive the death penalty than were killers of blacks," and that "in Georgia, blacks who killed whites received the death penalty 16.7 percent of the time, while whites who killed received the death penalty only 4.2 percent of the time."

Of course, the mere piling up of evidence does not in itself make the speaker's case. As Donna Cross explains in "Politics: The Art of Bamboozling,"* politicians are very adept at "card-stacking." And statistics can be selected and manipulated to prove anything, as demonstrated in Darrell Huff's landmark book *How to Lie with Statistics* (1954). Moreover, what appears to be a logical argument may in fact be fundamentally flawed. (See Chapter 2 for a discussion of logical fallacies and

---

*Donna Cross, *Word Abuse: How the Words We Use Use Us* (New York: Coward, 1979).

faulty reasoning strategies.) On the other hand, the fact that evidence can be distorted, statistics misused, and logic fractured does not mean that these tools of reason can be dispensed with or should be dismissed. It means only that audiences have to listen and read critically—perceptively, knowledgeably, and skeptically (though not necessarily cynically).

Sometimes in political disagreements, people can turn their opponents' faulty logic against them. For example, in the wake of the meltdown in 2008 of the mortgage loan industry, with more than 1.2 million homes in foreclosure, some argued that it would be bad policy to help homeowners who had lost their homes as a consequence of no longer being able to make mortgage payments. Their argument worked like this:

> Financially irresponsible behavior should not be rewarded with government bailouts. (*assumption*)
>
> Taking on a mortgage that one cannot afford is financially irresponsible behavior. (*support*)
>
> Taking on a mortgage that one cannot afford should not be rewarded with government bailouts. (*claim*)

But this argument was made to work for the opposite position by those who favored government assistance. Their strategy was simply to change the middle term—the *support*. In light of the almost immediate massive financial support provided by the Federal Reserve to assist the large investment banking house Bear Stearns when it was threatened with bankruptcy, the middle term was switched to:

> Large-scale investing in subprime mortgages is financially irresponsible behavior.

Thus, the inescapable conclusion—the *claim*—of this argument inevitably became:

> Banks threatened with bankruptcy as a result of having made poor investments in subprime mortgages should not be rewarded with government bailouts.

The inconsistency of helping out investment banks while not helping out homeowners was illogical enough that Congress rushed to consider legislation that would also help out homeowners. But beyond being illogical, the initial decision not to help out individual homeowners created a powerful appeal to *pathos*: Legislators did not want to be seen as unsympathetic to families who, because of large-scale economic factors beyond their control, would lose their homes and, in effect, be thrown out on the streets.

Exercise 5.2

Using Deductive and Inductive Logic

Choose an issue currently being debated at your school, or a college-related issue about which you are concerned. Write a claim about this issue. Then write two paragraphs addressing your claim—one in which you organize your points deductively, and one in which you organize them inductively. Possible issues might include college admissions policies, classroom crowding, or grade inflation. Alternatively, you could base your paragraphs on a claim generated in Exercise 5.1.

Ethos

Ethos, or the ethical appeal, is based not on the ethical rationale for the subject under discussion, but rather on the ethical status of the person making the appeal. A person making an argument must have a certain degree of credibility: That person must be of good character, have sound sense, and be qualified to hold the office or recommend policy.

For example, Elizabeth Cervantes Barrón, running for senator as the Peace and Freedom candidate, begins her statement with "I was born and raised in central Los Angeles. I grew up in a multiethnic, multicultural environment where I learned to respect those who were different from me....I am a teacher and am aware of how cutbacks in education have affected our children and our communities."

On the other end of the political spectrum, the American Independent gubernatorial candidate Jerry McCready also begins with an ethical appeal: "As a self-employed businessman, I have learned firsthand what it is like to try to make ends meet in an unstable economy being manipulated by out-of-touch politicians." Both candidates are making an appeal to *ethos*, an appeal based on the strength of their personal qualities for the office they seek.

L. A. Kauffman is not running for office but writing an article arguing against socialism as a viable ideology for the future ("Socialism: No," *Progressive*, April 1, 1993). To defuse objections that he is simply a tool of capitalism, Kauffman begins with an appeal to *ethos:* "Until recently, I was executive editor of the journal *Socialist Review*. Before that I worked for the Marxist magazine, *Monthly Review*. My bookshelves are filled with books of Marxist theory, and I even have a picture of Karl Marx up on my wall." Thus, Kauffman establishes his credentials to argue knowledgeably about Marxist ideology.

The conservative commentator Rush Limbaugh frequently makes use of the ethical appeal by linking himself with the kind of Americans he assumes his audiences to be (the writer Donna Cross calls this "glory by association"):

> In their attacks [on me], my critics misjudge and insult the American people. If I were really what liberals claim—racist, hatemonger, blowhard—I would years ago have deservedly gone into oblivion. The truth is, I provide information and analysis the media refuses to disseminate, information and analysis the public craves. People listen to me for one reason: I am effective. And my credibility is judged in the marketplace every day....I represent America's rejection of liberal elites....I validate the convictions of ordinary people.*

Exercise 5.3

Using Ethos

Return to the claim you used for Exercise 5.2 and write a paragraph in which you use an appeal to *ethos* to make a case for that claim.

---

*Rush Limbaugh, "Why I Am a Threat to the Left," *Los Angeles Times* 9 Oct. 1994.

Pathos

Finally, speakers and writers appeal to their audiences by using *pathos*, the appeal to the emotions. Nothing is inherently wrong with using an emotional appeal. Indeed, because emotions often move people far more powerfully than reason alone, speakers and writers would be foolish not to use emotion. And it would be a drab, humorless world if human beings were not subject to the sway of feeling as well as reason. The emotional appeal becomes problematic only when it is the *sole* or *primary* basis of the argument. This imbalance of emotion over logic is the kind of situation that led, for example, to the internment of Japanese Americans during World War II or that leads to periodic political spasms that call for enacting anti-flag-burning legislation.

President Ronald Reagan was a master of emotional appeal. He closed his first Inaugural Address with a reference to the view from the Capitol to the Arlington National Cemetery, where lie thousands of markers of "heroes":

> Under one such marker lies a young man, Martin Treptow, who left his job in a small-town barbershop in 1917 to go to France with the famed Rainbow Division. There, on the western front, he was killed trying to carry a message between battalions under heavy artillery fire. We're told that on his body was found a diary. On the flyleaf under the heading, "My Pledge," he had written these words: "America must win this war. Therefore, I will work, I will save, I will sacrifice, I will endure, I will fight cheerfully and do my utmost, as if the issue of the whole struggle depended on me alone." The crisis we are facing today does not require of us the kind of sacrifice that Martin Treptow and so many thousands of others were called upon to make. It does require, however, our best effort and our willingness to believe in ourselves and to believe in our capacity to perform great deeds, to believe that together with God's help we can and will resolve the problems which now confront us.

Surely, Reagan implies, if Martin Treptow can act so courageously and so selflessly, we can do the same. His logic is somewhat unclear because the connection between Martin Treptow and ordinary Americans of 1981 was rather tenuous (as Reagan concedes); but the emotional power of Martin Treptow, whom reporters were sent scurrying to research, carried the argument.

President Bill Clinton also used *pathos*. Addressing an audience of the nation's governors about his welfare plan, Clinton closed his remarks by referring to a conversation he had had with a welfare mother who had gone through the kind of training program Clinton was advocating. Asked by Clinton whether she thought that such training programs should be mandatory, the mother said, "I sure do." Clinton in his remarks explained what she said when he asked her why:

> "Well, because if it wasn't, there would be a lot of people like me home watching the soaps because we don't believe we can make anything of ourselves anymore. So you've got to make it mandatory." And I said, "What's the best thing about having a job?" She said, "When my boy goes to school, and they say, 'What does your mama do for a living?' he can give an answer."

Clinton uses the emotional power he counts on in that anecdote to set up his conclusion: "We must end poverty for Americans who want to work. And we must do it on terms that dignify all of the rest of us, as well as help our country to work better. I need your help, and I think we can do it."

Exercise 5.4

Using Pathos

Return to the claim you used for Exercises 5.2 and 5.3, and write a paragraph in which you use an appeal to *pathos* to argue for that claim.

The Limits of Argument

Our discussion of *ethos* and *pathos* indicates a potentially troubling but undeniable reality: Arguments are not won on the basis of logic and evidence alone. In the real world, arguments don't operate like academic debates. If the purpose of argument is to get people to change their minds or to agree that the writer's or speaker's position on a particular topic is the best available, then the person making the argument must be aware that factors other than evidence and good reasoning come into play when readers or listeners are considering the matter.

These factors involve deep-seated cultural, religious, ethnic, racial, and gender identities, moral predilections, and the effects of personal experiences (either pleasant or unpleasant) that are generally impervious to the weight of reasoning, however well-framed. Try—using the best available arguments—to convince someone who is pro-life to agree with the pro-choice position (or vice versa). Try to persuade someone who opposes capital punishment to believe that state-endorsed executions are necessary for deterrence (or for any other reason). Marshall your evidence and logic to persuade someone whose family members have had run-ins with the law that police efforts are directed at protecting the law-abiding. On such emotionally loaded topics, it is extremely difficult, if not impossible, to get people to change their minds because they are so personally invested in their beliefs. (See the discussion of *assumptions* in Chapter 2, pp. 61–62.) It is not just a matter of their forming or choosing an opinion on a particular topic; it is a matter of an opinion's emerging naturally from an often long-established component of the person's psyche. Someone who believes that all life is sacred is not likely to be swayed by an argument that abortion or stem-cell research that involves the destruction of a fetus is acceptable. As Susan Jacoby, author of *The Age of American Unreason*, notes, "Whether watching television news, consulting political blogs, or (more rarely) reading books, Americans today have become a people in search of validation for opinions that they already hold."*

---

*Susan Jacoby, "Talking to Ourselves: Americans Are Increasingly Close-Minded and Unwilling to Listen to Opposing Views," *Los Angeles Times* 20 Apr. 2008: M10.

The tenacity with which people hold on to longtime beliefs does not mean, however, that they cannot change their minds or that subjects like abortion, capital punishment, gun control, and gay marriage should be off-limits to reasoned debate. It means only that you should be aware of the limits of argument. The world is not populated by Mr. and Ms. Spocks of *Star Trek* fame, whose brains function by reason alone. Even those who claim to be open-minded on a given topic are often captive to deeply held beliefs and, so, deceive themselves concerning their willingness to respond rationally to arguments. As one letter writer to the *New York Times Book Review* observed, "[P]eople often fail to identify their own biases because of a compelling human desire to believe they are fair-minded and decent."*

The most fruitful topics for argument in a freshman composition setting, therefore, tend to be those on which most people are persuadable, either because they know relatively little about the topic or because deep-rooted cultural, religious, or moral beliefs are not involved. At least initially in your career as a writer of academic papers, it's probably best to avoid "hot button" topics that are the focus of broader cultural debates, and to focus instead on topics in which *pathos* plays less of a part. Most people are not heavily invested in plug-in hybrid or hydrogen-powered vehicles, so an argument on behalf of the more promising technology for the coming decades will not be complicated by deep-seated beliefs. Similarly, most people don't know enough about the mechanics of sleep to have strong opinions on how to deal with sleep deprivation. Your arguments on such topics, therefore, will provide opportunities both to inform your readers or listeners and to persuade them that your arguments, if well reasoned and supported by sound evidence, are at least plausible if not entirely convincing.

DEMONSTRATION: DEVELOPING AN ARGUMENT SYNTHESIS—BALANCING PRIVACY AND SAFETY IN THE WAKE OF VIRGINIA TECH

To demonstrate how to plan and draft an argument synthesis, let's suppose you are taking a course on Law and Society or Political Science or (from the Philosophy Department) Theories of Justice, and you find yourself considering the competing claims of privacy and public safety. The tension between these two highly prized values burst anew into public consciousness in 2007 after a mentally disturbed student at the Virginia Polytechnic Institute shot to death 32 fellow students and faculty members and injured 17 more. Unfortunately, this incident was only the latest in a long history of mass killings at American schools.† It was later revealed that the shooter had a documented history of mental instability, but

---

*Susan Abendroth, letter in *New York Times Book Review* 30 Mar. 2008: 12.
†In 1966 a student at the University of Texas at Austin, shooting from the campus clock tower, killed 14 people and wounded 31. In 2006 a man shot and killed five girls at an Amish school in Lancaster, Pennsylvania.

because of privacy rules this information was not made available to university officials. Many people demanded to know why this information was not shared with campus police or other officials so that Virginia Tech could take measures to protect members of the university community. Didn't the safety of those who were injured and killed outweigh the privacy of the shooter? At what point, if any, *does* the right to privacy outweigh the right to safety? What *should* the university have done before the killing started? Should federal and state laws on privacy be changed or even abandoned in the wake of this and other similar incidents?

Suppose, in preparing to write a paper on balancing privacy and safety, you located (among others) the following sources:

- *Mass Shootings at Virginia Tech, April 16, 2007: Report of the Review Panel Presented to Governor Kaine, Commonwealth of Virginia*, August 2007 (a report)
- "Laws Limit Schools Even After Alarms" (a newspaper article)
- "Perilous Privacy at Virginia Tech" (an editorial)
- "Colleges Are Watching Troubled Students" (a newspaper article)
- "Virginia Tech Massacre Has Altered Campus Mental Health Systems" (a newspaper article)
- *The Family Educational Rights and Privacy Act (FERPA)*, sec.1232g (a federal statute)

Read these sources (which follow) carefully, noting the kinds of information and ideas you could draw on to develop an *argument synthesis*. Some of these passages are excerpts only; in preparing your paper, you would draw on the entire articles, reports, and book chapters from which these passages were taken. And you would draw on more sources than these in your search for supporting materials (as the writer of the model synthesis has done; see pp. 159–165). But these six sources provide a good introduction to the subject. Our discussion of how these passages can form the basis of an argument synthesis resumes on p. 155.

Mass Shootings at Virginia Tech, April 16, 2007

*Report of the Review Panel
Presented to Governor Kaine, Commonwealth of Virginia,
August 2007*

The following passage leads off the official report of the Virginia Tech shootings by the panel appointed by Virginia Governor Tim Kaine to investigate the incident. The mission of the panel was "to provide an independent, thorough, and objective incident review of this tragic event, including a review of educational laws, policies and institutions, the public safety and health care procedures and responses, and the mental health delivery system." Panel members included the chair, Colonel Gerald Massenghill, former Virginia State Police Superintendent; Tom Ridge, former Director of Homeland Security and former governor of Pennsylvania; Gordon Davies; Dr Roger L. Depue; Dr. Aradhana A. "Bela" Sood; Judge Diane Strickland; and Carol L. Ellis. The panel Web site may be found at <http://www.vtreviewpanel.org/panel_info/>.

Summary of Key Findings

On April 16, 2007, Seung Hui Cho, an angry and disturbed student, shot to death 32 students and faculty of Virginia Tech, wounded 17 more, and then killed himself.

The incident horrified not only Virginians, but people across the United States and throughout the world.

Tim Kaine, Governor of the Commonwealth of Virginia, immediately appointed a panel to review the events leading up to this tragedy; the handling of the incidents by public safety officials, emergency services providers, and the university; and the services subsequently provided to families, survivors, caregivers, and the community.

The Virginia Tech Review Panel reviewed several separate but related issues in assessing events leading to the mass shootings and their aftermath:

- The life and mental health history of Seung Hui Cho, from early childhood until the weeks before April 16.
- Federal and state laws concerning the privacy of health and education records.
- Cho's purchase of guns and related gun control issues.
- The double homicide at West Ambler Johnston (WAJ) residence hall and the mass shootings at Norris Hall, including the responses of Virginia Tech leadership and the actions of law enforcement officers and emergency responders.
- Emergency medical care immediately following the shootings, both onsite at Virginia Tech and in cooperating hospitals.
- The work of the Office of the Chief Medical Examiner of Virginia.
- The services provided for surviving victims of the shootings and others injured, the families and loved ones of those killed and injured, members of the university community, and caregivers.

5   The panel conducted over 200 interviews and reviewed thousands of pages of records, and reports the following major findings:

1. Cho exhibited signs of mental health problems during his childhood. His middle and high schools responded well to these signs and, with his parents' involvement, provided services to address his issues. He also received private psychiatric treatment and counseling for selective mutism and depression.

    In 1999, after the Columbine shootings, Cho's middle school teachers observed suicidal and homicidal ideations in his writings and recommended psychiatric counseling, which he received. It was at this point that he received medication for a short time. Although Cho's parents were aware that he was troubled at this time, they state they did not specifically know that he thought about homicide shortly after the 1999 Columbine school shootings.

2. During Cho's junior year at Virginia Tech, numerous incidents occurred that were clear warnings of mental instability. Although various individuals and departments within the university knew about each of these incidents, the university did not intervene effectively. No one knew all the information and no one connected all the dots.

3. University officials in the office of Judicial Affairs, Cook Counseling Center, campus police, the Dean of Students, and others explained their failures to communicate with one another or with Cho's parents by noting their belief that such communications are prohibited by the federal laws governing the privacy of health and education records. In reality, federal laws and their state counterparts afford ample leeway to share information in potentially dangerous situations.

4. The Cook Counseling Center and the university's Care Team failed to provide needed support and services to Cho during a period in late 2005 and early 2006. The system failed for lack of resources, incorrect interpretation of privacy laws, and passivity. Records of Cho's minimal treatment at Virginia Tech's Cook Counseling Center are missing.

5. Virginia's mental health laws are flawed and services for mental health users are inadequate. Lack of sufficient resources results in gaps in the mental health system including short term crisis stabilization and comprehensive outpatient services. The involuntary commitment process is challenged by unrealistic time constraints, lack of critical psychiatric data and collateral information, and barriers (perceived or real) to open communications among key professionals.

6. There is widespread confusion about what federal and state privacy laws allow. Also, the federal laws governing records of health care provided in educational settings are not entirely compatible with those governing other health records.

7. Cho purchased two guns in violation of federal law. The fact that in 2005 Cho had been judged to be a danger to himself and ordered to outpatient treatment made him ineligible to purchase a gun under federal law.

8. Virginia is one of only 22 states that report any information about mental health to a federal database used to conduct background checks on would-be gun purchasers. But Virginia law did not clearly require that persons such as Cho—who had been ordered into out-patient treatment but not committed to an institution—be reported to the database. Governor Kaine's executive order to report all persons involuntarily committed for outpatient treatment has temporarily addressed this ambiguity in state law. But a change is needed in the Code of Virginia as well.

9. Some Virginia colleges and universities are uncertain about what they are permitted to do regarding the possession of firearms on campus.

10. On April 16, 2007, the Virginia Tech and Blacksburg police departments responded quickly to the report of shootings at West Ambler Johnston

residence hall, as did the Virginia Tech and Blacksburg rescue squads. Their responses were well coordinated.

11. The Virginia Tech police may have erred in prematurely concluding that their initial lead in the double homicide was a good one, or at least in conveying that impression to university officials while continuing their investigation. They did not take sufficient action to deal with what might happen if the initial lead proved erroneous. The police reported to the university emergency Policy Group that the "person of interest" probably was no longer on campus.

12. The VTPD erred in not requesting that the Policy Group issue a campus-wide notification that two persons had been killed and that all students and staff should be cautious and alert.

13. Senior university administrators, acting as the emergency Policy Group, failed to issue an all-campus notification about the WAJ killings until almost 2 hours had elapsed. University practice may have conflicted with written policies.

14. The presence of large numbers of police at WAJ led to a rapid response to the first 9-1-1 call that shooting had begun at Norris Hall.

15. Cho's motives for the WAJ or Norris Hall shootings are unknown to the police or the panel. Cho's writings and videotaped pronouncements do not explain why he struck when and where he did.

16. The police response at Norris Hall was prompt and effective, as was triage and evacuation of the wounded. Evacuation of others in the building could have been implemented with more care.

17. Emergency medical care immediately following the shootings was provided very effectively and timely both onsite and at the hospitals, although providers from different agencies had some difficulty communicating with one another. Communication of accurate information to hospitals standing by to receive the wounded and injured was somewhat deficient early on. An emergency operations center at Virginia Tech could have improved communications.

18. The Office of the Chief Medical Examiner properly discharged the technical aspects of its responsibility (primarily autopsies and identification of the deceased). Communication with families was poorly handled.

19. State systems for rapidly deploying trained professional staff to help families get information, crisis intervention, and referrals to a wide range of resources did not work.

20. The university established a family assistance center at The Inn at Virginia Tech, but it fell short in helping families and others for two reasons: lack of leadership and lack of coordination among service providers. University volunteers stepped in but were not trained or able to answer many questions and guide families to the resources they needed.

21. In order to advance public safety and meet public needs, Virginia's colleges and universities need to work together as a coordinated system of state-supported institutions.

As reflected in the body of the report, the panel has made more than 70 recommendations directed to colleges, universities, mental health providers, law enforcement officials, emergency service providers, lawmakers, and other public officials in Virginia and elsewhere.

*Laws Limit Schools Even After Alarms**

Jeff Gammage and Stacey Burling

This article first appeared in the *Philadelphia Inquirer* on April 19, 2007, just three days after the Virginia Tech shootings. *Inquirer* staff writer Paul Nussbaum contributed to the article.

If Cho Seung-Hui had been a warning light, he would have been blinking bright red.

Two female students complained to campus police that he was stalking them. His poetry was so twisted that his writing professor said she would quit if he weren't removed from her room. Some students found him so menacing that they refused to attend class with him.

Yet Virginia Tech, like other colleges trying to help emotionally troubled students, had little power to force Cho off campus and into treatment.

"We can't even pick up the phone and call their family. They're adults. You have to respect their privacy," said Brenda Ingram-Wallace, director of counseling and chair of the psychology department at Albright College in Reading.

5   In the aftermath of the deadliest shooting in U.S. history, counselors, police authorities, and mental-health professionals say privacy laws prevent colleges from taking strong action regarding students who might be dangerous.

Many at Tech saw Cho as a threat—and shared those fears with authorities. In 2005, after the second stalking complaint, the school obtained a temporary detention order that resulted in Cho undergoing a psychiatric evaluation. But the 23-year-old remained enrolled at the university until the moment he shot himself to death.

Federal laws such as the 1974 Family Educational Rights and Privacy Act (FERPA) and the 1996 Health Insurance Portability and Accountability Act (HIPAA) protect students' right to privacy by banning disclosure of any mental-health problems—even to family members—without a signed waiver.

Patient-therapist confidentiality is crucial, privacy advocates say. Students may shy from treatment for fear of exposure.

FERPA does allow colleges to release information without permission in cases of "health and safety emergencies." But the criteria are so vague, and the

*Philadelphia Inquirer 19 Apr. 2007: A01.

potential liability so severe, that administrators say they hesitate to act in any but the most dire circumstances.

10   "The law tends to be protective of individual autonomy rather than getting in there and forcing people to get treatment," said Anthony Rostain, associate professor of psychiatry at the University of Pennsylvania School of Medicine.

Lots of students write violent stories, he noted. How do you distinguish between a future Cho Seung-Hui and a future Quentin Tarantino?*

"This kind of problem happens all the time across college campuses," Rostain said.

The law puts colleges in a tough position, said Dana Fleming, a lawyer with the college and university practice group at Nelson, Kinder, Mousseau & Saturley in Manchester, N.H. Schools may face legal trouble if they try to keep ill students out, if they try to send them home, or if they let them stay.

"No matter which decision they make," she said, "they can find liability on the other end."

15   Colleges can't screen students for mental illnesses during the admissions process because that violates the Americans With Disabilities Act. As a result, schools know which students will need tutoring or want to play soccer, but have no idea who is likely to need mental-health care, Fleming said.

Virginia Tech and most other universities cannot summarily suspend a student. Formal disciplinary charges must be filed and hearings held. Students who initiate a complaint often end up dropping the matter.

Nor can schools expect courts to hospitalize a student involuntarily without solid evidence that he poses a danger to himself or others.

That has left many colleges trying to find creative ways to identify and help troubled students.

At Albright College, administrators recently updated a program where anyone concerned about a student's behavior—a work supervisor, a professor or another student—can fill out a "student alert form."

20   Perhaps friends notice a student has become withdrawn or has stopped showing up for class. If multiple forms arrive concerning the same person, counseling director Ingram-Wallace said, the counseling center investigates by contacting housing officials or by reaching the student via phone or e-mail.

But the choice to speak with a psychological counselor stays with the student. The center can't send a therapist to knock on the student's door, she said.

"On the surface, it sounds like a caring thing to do," she said, but "if they haven't been dangerous to themselves or others, there's no reason to mandate them into any kind of services."

Among students who have been referred to the counseling center, "the responses are mixed," she said. "Some people felt imposed upon."

At St. Lawrence University in Canton, N.Y., every student who visits the health center—even for a head cold—is screened for depression and signs of

---

*Director, screenwriter, and producer of frequently violent films such as *Reservoir Dogs* (1992), *Pulp Fiction* (1994), and *Kill Bill* (vol. 1, 2003; vol. 2, 2004).

other mental illness. The effort follows a national study that showed depression rising among college students.

25   If a screening shows someone needs help from the health center, "we literally walk them over there," said Patricia Ellis, director of counseling services.

More than a year before Monday's massacre of 32 students and staff members, Cho was twice accused of stalking female students and taken to a mental-health facility amid fears he was suicidal, police said yesterday.

After the first incident, in November 2005, police referred him to the university disciplinary system. Ed Spencer, Tech's assistant vice president of student affairs, said he could not comment on any proceedings against the gunman because federal law protects students' medical privacy even after death.

The university obtained the detention order after the second stalking complaint, in December 2005. "His insight and judgment are normal," an examiner at the psychiatric hospital concluded.

Yet poet Nikki Giovanni, one of his professors, told CNN that students were so unnerved by Cho's behavior, which included taking cell-phone photos of them in class, that most stopped attending the course. She insisted that he be removed.

30   Lucinda Roy, a codirector of the creative writing program, tutored Cho after that, and tried to get him into counseling. He always refused. Roy sent samples of Cho's writing, with its images of people attacking each other with chain saws, to the campus police, student-affairs office, and other agencies.

PERILOUS PRIVACY AT VIRGINIA TECH

This editorial appeared in the *Christian Science Monitor* on September 4, 2007.

Colleges didn't need last week's report on the Virginia Tech shootings to address a key finding: a faster alert during the crisis may have saved lives. Many colleges have already set blast-notice plans. But here's what needs careful study: the report's conclusions about privacy.

Privacy is a huge issue on campuses. Colleges and universities are dealing with young people who have just become legal adults, but who may still require supervision and even intervention.

That was the case with Seung-Hui Cho, the student who killed 32 people and then himself on April 16. According to the report, which was commissioned by Virginia Gov. Timothy Kaine, this troubled student's behavior raised serious questions about his mental stability while he was at VT, yet no one contacted his parents, and communication about his case broke down among school, law-enforcement, and mental-health officials.

A big reason? A "widespread perception" that privacy laws make it difficult to respond to troubled students, according to the report. But this is "only partly correct."

5   Lack of understanding about federal and state laws is a major obstacle to helping such students, according to the report. The legal complexity, as well as concerns about liability, can easily push teachers, administrators, police, and mental-health workers into a "default" position of withholding information, the report found.

There's no evidence that VT officials consciously decided not to inform Mr. Cho's parents. But the university's lawyer told the panel investigating Cho's case that privacy laws prevent sharing information such as that relating to Cho.

That's simply not true. The report listed several steps that could quite legally have been taken:

The Virginia Tech police, for instance, could have shared with Cho's parents that he was temporarily detained, pending a hearing to commit him involuntarily to a mental-health institution, because that information was public.

And teachers and administrators could have called Cho's parents to notify them of his difficulties, because only student records—not personal observations or conversations—are shielded by the federal privacy law that covers most secondary schools.

10   Notifying Cho's parents was intuitively the right course. Indeed, his middle school contacted his parents to get him help, and they cooperated. His high school also made special arrangements. He improved.

The report points out that the main federal privacy laws that apply to a college student's health and campus records recognize exceptions for information sharing in emergencies that affect public health and safety.

Privacy is a bedrock of American law and values. In a mental-health case, it gives a patient the security to express innermost thoughts, and protects that person from discrimination. But the federal law, at least, does recognize a balance between privacy and public safety, even when colleges can't, or won't.

The report is to be commended for pointing out this disconnect, and for calling for greater clarification of privacy laws and school policies.

Perhaps now, common sense can match up with legal obligations so both privacy and public safety can be served.

COLLEGES ARE WATCHING TROUBLED STUDENTS

Jeffrey McMurray

During the year following the Virginia Tech shootings, many colleges and universities took a hard look at their policies on student privacy and their procedures for monitoring and sharing information about troubled students. This article, by the Associated Press, was first published on March 28, 2008. AP writer Sue Lindsay contributed to this report.

On the agenda: A student who got into a shouting match with a faculty member. Another who harassed a female classmate. Someone found sleeping in a car. And a student who posted a threat against a professor on Facebook.

In a practice adopted at one college after another since the massacre at Virginia Tech, a University of Kentucky committee of deans, administrators, campus police and mental health officials has begun meeting regularly to discuss a watch list of troubled students and decide whether they need professional help or should be sent packing.

These "threat assessment groups" are aimed at heading off the kind of bloodshed seen at Virginia Tech a year ago and at Northern Illinois University last month.

"You've got to be way ahead of the game, so to speak, expect what may be coming. If you're able to identify behaviors early on and get these people assistance, it avoids disruptions in the classrooms and potential violence," said Maj. Joe Monroe, interim police chief at Kentucky.

5   The Kentucky panel, called Students of Concern, held its first meeting last week and will convene at least twice a month to talk about students whose strange or disturbing behavior has come to their attention.

Such committees represent a change in thinking among U.S. college officials, who for a long time were reluctant to share information about students' mental health for fear of violating privacy laws.

"If a student is a danger to himself or others, all the privacy concerns go out the window," said Patricia Terrell, vice president of student affairs, who created the panel.

Terrell shared details of the four discussed cases with The Associated Press on the condition that all names and other identifying information be left out.

Among other things, the panel can order a student into counseling or bar him or her from entering a particular building or talking to a certain person. It can also order a judicial hearing that can lead to suspension or expulsion if the student's offense was a violation of the law or school policy.

10   Although the four cases discussed last week were the ones administrators deemed as needing the most urgent attention, a database listing 26 other student cases has been created, providing fodder for future meetings.

Students are encouraged during their freshman orientation to report suspicious behavior to the dean of students, and university employees all the way down to janitors and cafeteria workers are instructed to tell their supervisors if they see anything.

Virtually every corner of campus is represented in the group's closed-door meetings, including dorm life, academics, counseling, mental health and police.

"If you look back at the Virginia Tech situation, the aftermath, there were several people who knew that student had problems, but because of privacy and different issues, they didn't talk to others about it," said Lee Todd, UK president.

High schools have been doing this sort of thing for years because of shootings, but only since Virginia Tech, when a disturbed student gunman killed 32 people and committed suicide, have colleges begun to follow suit, said Mike Dorn, executive director of Safe Havens International, a leading campus safety firm.

15   "They didn't think it was a real threat to them," Dorn said.

Virginia Tech has added a threat assessment team since the massacre there. Boston University, the University of Utah, the University of Illinois–Chicago and numerous others also have such groups, said Gwendolyn Dungy, executive director of the National Association of Student Personnel Administrators.

Bryan Cloyd, a Virginia Tech accounting professor whose daughter Austin was killed in the rampage, welcomed the stepped-up efforts to monitor troubled students but stressed he doesn't want to turn every college campus into a "police state."

"We can't afford to overreact," Cloyd said, but "we also can't afford to underreact."

Seung-Hui Cho, the Virginia Tech gunman, was ruled a danger to himself in a court hearing in 2005 that resulted from a roommate's call to police after Cho mentioned suicide in an e-mail. He was held overnight at a mental health center off campus and was ordered into outpatient treatment, but he received no follow-up services, despite his sullen, withdrawn behavior and his twisted, violence-filled writings.

20   Mary Bolin-Reece, director of counseling and testing at Kentucky, attends the threat assessment group's meetings but cannot share what she knows or, in most cases, even whether a student has been undergoing counseling. But participants can share information on other possible red flags.

"We always look at, 'Is there a change in the baseline?'" Bolin-Reece said. "The student had previously gotten very good grades, and then there was a drop-off. Something has happened. Is there some shift in their ability to function? If a student is coming to the attention of various parties around the university, we begin to be able to connect the dots."

The University of Kentucky has not had a murder on campus since 1984. Still, the threat-assessment effort has the strong backing of Carol Graham of Fort Carson, Colo., whose son Kevin was a Kentucky student when he committed suicide before leaving for an ROTC summer camp in 2003.

"UK is such a huge university," Graham said. "It's important to know there's a safety net—that people are looking out for each other. With Kevin, his professors thought he was perfect. He'd be an A student. But the people around him were noticing differences."

As for the four cases taken up by the committee: The student who got into an argument with a faculty member—and had also seen a major dip in grades and exhibited poor hygiene—was ordered to meet with the dean of students.

25   The one accused of harassment was referred to a judicial hearing, during which he was expelled from university housing. The student who made the Facebook threat was given a warning. In the case of the student sleeping in a car, a committee member was dispatched to check on the person. No further details were released.

VIRGINIA TECH MASSACRE HAS ALTERED CAMPUS MENTAL HEALTH SYSTEMS

This article, prepared by the Associated Press, is representative of numerous reports of how college administrators across the nation responded to the Virginia Tech killings. Many schools reviewed their existing policies on student privacy and communication and instituted new procedures. The article appeared in the *Los Angeles Times* on April 14, 2008.

The rampage carried out nearly a year ago by a Virginia Tech student who slipped through the mental health system has changed how American colleges reach out to troubled students.

Administrators are pushing students harder to get help, looking more aggressively for signs of trouble and urging faculty to speak up when they have concerns. Counselors say the changes are sending even more students their way, which is both welcome and a challenge, given that many still lack the resources to handle their growing workloads.

Behind those changes, colleges have edged away in the last year from decades-old practices that made student privacy paramount. Now, they are more likely to err on the side of sharing information—with the police, for instance, and parents—if there is any possible threat to community safety. But even some who say the changes are appropriate worry it could discourage students from seeking treatment.

Concerns also linger that the response to shooters like Seung-hui Cho at Virginia Tech and Steven Kazmierczak, who killed five others at Northern Illinois University, has focused excessively on boosting the capacity of campus police to respond to rare events. Such reforms may be worthwhile, but they don't address how to prevent such a tragedy in the first place.

5   It was last April 16, just after 7 a.m., that Cho killed two students in a Virginia Tech dormitory, the start of a shooting spree that continued in a classroom building and eventually claimed 33 lives, including his own.

Cho's behavior and writing had alarmed professors and administrators, as well as the campus police, and he had been put through a commitment hearing where he was found to be potentially dangerous. But when an off-campus psychiatrist sent him back to the school for outpatient treatment, there was no follow-up to ensure that he got it.

People who work every day in the campus mental health field—counselors, lawyers, advocates and students at colleges around the country—say they have seen three major types of change since the Cho shootings:

Faculty are speaking up more about students who worry them. That's accelerating a trend of more demand for mental health services that was already under way before the Virginia Tech shootings.

Professors "have a really heightened level of fear and concern from the behavior that goes on around them," said Ben Locke, assistant director of the counseling center at Penn State University.

10   David Wallace, director of counseling at the University of Central Florida, said teachers are paying closer attention to violent material in writing assignments—warning bells that had worried Cho's professors.

"Now people are wondering, 'Is this something that could be more ominous?'" he said. "Are we talking about the Stephen Kings of the future or about somebody who's seriously thinking about doing something harmful?"

The downside is officials may be hypersensitive to any eccentricity. Says Susan Davis, an attorney who works in student affairs at the University of Virginia: "There's no question there's some hysteria and there's some things we don't need to see."

Changes are being made to privacy policies. In Virginia, a measure signed into law Wednesday by Gov. Tim Kaine requires colleges to bring parents into the loop when dependent students may be a danger to themselves or others.

Even before Virginia Tech, Cornell University had begun treating students as dependents of their parents unless told otherwise—an aggressive legal strategy that gives the school more leeway to contact parents with concerns without students' permission.

15   In Washington, meanwhile, federal officials are trying to clarify privacy guidelines so faculty won't hesitate to report potential threats.

"Nobody's throwing privacy out the window, but we are coming out of an era when individual rights were paramount on college campuses," said Brett Sokolow, who advises colleges on risk management. "What colleges are struggling with now is a better balance of those individual rights and community protections."

The big change since the Virginia Tech shootings, legal experts say, is colleges have shed some of their fear of violating the federal Family Educational Rights and Privacy Act.

Many faculty hadn't realized that the law applies only to educational records, not observations of classroom behavior, or that it contains numerous exceptions.

The stigma of mental illness, in some cases, has grown. "In general, the attention to campus mental health was desperately needed," said Alison Malmon, founder of the national Active Minds group. But some of the debate, she added, "has turned in a direction that does not necessarily support students."

20   All the talk of "threat assessments" and better-trained campus SWAT teams, she said, has distracted the public from the fact that the mentally ill rarely commit violence—especially against others.

"I know that, for many students, it made them feel more stigmatized," Malmon said. "It made them more likely to keep their mental health history silent."

Sokolow, the risk consultant for colleges, estimated in the aftermath of the Virginia Tech and NIU shootings, the schools he works with spent $25 on police and communications for every $1 on mental health. Only recently has he seen a shift.

"Campuses come to me, they want me to help them start behavioral intervention systems," Sokolow said. "Then they go to the president to get the money and, oh, well, the money went into the door locks."

Phone messaging systems and security are nice, he said, but "there is nothing about text-messaging that is going to prevent violence."

THE FAMILY EDUCATIONAL RIGHTS AND PRIVACY ACT

United States Code
Title 20. Education
CHAPTER 31. General Provisions Concerning Education
§ 1232g. Family Educational and Privacy Rights

Following are excerpts from the *Family Educational Rights and Privacy Act (FERPA)*, the federal law enacted in 1974 that governs restrictions on the release of student educational records. FERPA provides for the withholding of federal funds to educational institutions that violate its provisions, and it is the federal guarantor of the privacy rights of post-secondary students.

(1)(A) No funds shall be made available under any applicable program to any educational agency or institution which has a policy of denying, or which effectively prevents, the parents of students who are or have been in attendance at a school of such agency or at such institution, as the case may be, the right to inspect and review the education records of their children. If any material or document in the education record of a student includes information on more than one student, the parents of one of such students shall have the right to inspect and review only such part of such material or document as relates to such student or to be informed of the specific information contained in such part of such material. Each educational agency or institution shall establish appropriate procedures for the granting of a request by parents for access to the education records of their children within a reasonable period of time, but in no case more than forty-five days after the request has been made....

(C) The first sentence of subparagraph (A) shall not operate to make available to students in institutions of postsecondary education the following materials:

  (i) financial records of the parents of the student or any information contained therein;

  (ii) confidential letters and statements of recommendation, which were placed in the education records prior to January 1, 1975, if such letters or statements are not used for purposes other than those for which they were specifically intended;

  (iii) if the student has signed a waiver of the student's right of access under this subsection in accordance with subparagraph (D), confidential recommendations—

    (I) respecting admission to any educational agency or institution,
    (II) respecting an application for employment, and
    (III) respecting the receipt of an honor or honorary recognition.

....

(B) The term "education records" does not include—

  (i) records of instructional, supervisory, and administrative personnel and educational personnel ancillary thereto which are in the sole possession of the maker thereof and which are not accessible or revealed to any other person except a substitute;

(ii) records maintained by a law enforcement unit of the educational agency or institution that were created by that law enforcement unit for the purpose of law enforcement;

(iii) in the case of persons who are employed by an educational agency or institution but who are not in attendance at such agency or institution, records made and maintained in the normal course of business which relate exclusively to such person in that person's capacity as an employee and are not available for use for any other purpose; or

(iv) records on a student who is eighteen years of age or older, or is attending an institution of postsecondary education, which are made or maintained by a physician, psychiatrist, psychologist, or other recognized professional or paraprofessional acting in his professional or paraprofessional capacity, or assisting in that capacity, and which are made, maintained, or used only in connection with the provision of treatment to the student, and are not available to anyone other than persons providing such treatment, except that such records can be personally reviewed by a physician or other appropriate professional of the student's choice....

(h) Certain disciplinary action information allowable. Nothing in this section shall prohibit an educational agency or institution from—

(1) including appropriate information in the education record of any student concerning disciplinary action taken against such student for conduct that posed a significant risk to the safety or well-being of that student, other students, or other members of the school community; or

(2) disclosing such information to teachers and school officials, including teachers and school officials in other schools, who have legitimate educational interests in the behavior of the student.

Exercise 5.5

Critical Reading for Synthesis

Having read the selections relating to privacy and safety, pp. 141–154, write a one-sentence summary of each. On the same page, list two or three topics that you think are common to several of the selections. Beneath each topic, list the authors who have something to say and briefly note what they have to say. Finally, for each topic, jot down what *you* have to say. Now regard your effort: With each topic you have created a discussion point suitable for inclusion in a paper. (Of course, until you determine the claim of such a paper, you won't know to what end you would put the discussion.) Write a paragraph or two in which you introduce the topic and then conduct a brief conversation among the interested parties (including yourself).

Consider Your Purpose

Your specific purpose in writing an argument synthesis is crucial. What exactly you want to do will affect your claim and how you organize the evidence. Your purpose may be clear to you before you begin research, or it may not emerge until after you have completed your research. Of course, the sooner your purpose is clear to you, the fewer wasted motions you will make. On the other hand, the more you approach research as an exploratory process, the likelier that your conclusions will emerge from the sources themselves rather than from preconceived ideas. Each new writing project will have its rhythm in this regard. Be flexible in your approach: through some combination of preconceived structures and invigorating discoveries, you will find your way to the source materials that will yield a promising paper.

Let's say that while reading these six (and additional) sources on the debate about campus safety and student privacy you shared the outrage of many who blamed the university (and the federal privacy laws on which it relied) for not using the available information in a way that might have spared the lives of those who died. Perhaps you also blamed the legislators who wrote the privacy laws for being more concerned about the confidentiality of the mental health records of the individual person than with the safety of the larger college population. Perhaps, you concluded, society has gone too far in valuing privacy more than it appears to value safety.

On the other hand, in your own role as a student, perhaps you share the high value placed on the privacy of sensitive information about yourself. After all, one of the functions of higher education is to foster students' independence as they make the transition from adolescence to adulthood. You can understand that many students like yourself might not want parents or others to know details about academic records or disciplinary measures, much less information about therapy sought and undertaken at school. Historically, in the decades since the university officially stood *in loco parentis*—in place of parents—students have struggled hard to win the same civil liberties and rights (including the right to privacy) of their elders.

Further, you may wonder whether federal privacy laws do in fact forbid the sharing of information about potentially dangerous students when the health and safety of others are at stake. A little research may begin to confirm your doubts about whether Virginia Tech officials were as helpless as they claim they were.

Your purpose in writing, then, emerges from these kinds of responses to the source materials you find.

Making a Claim: Formulate a Thesis

As we indicated in the introduction to this chapter, one useful way of approaching an argument is to see it as making a *claim*. A claim is a proposition, a conclusion that you have made, that you are trying to prove or demonstrate. If your purpose is to argue that we should work to ensure campus safety without enacting restrictive laws that overturn the hard-won privacy rights of students, then that claim (generally expressed in one-sentence form as a *thesis*) is at the heart of your argument. You will draw support from your sources as you argue logically for your claim.

Not every piece of information in a source is useful for supporting a claim. You must read with care and select the opinions, facts, and statistics that best advance your position. You may even find yourself drawing support from sources that make claims entirely different from your own. For example, in researching the subject of student privacy and campus safety, you may come across editorials arguing that in the wake of the Virginia Tech shootings student privacy rights should be greatly restricted. Perhaps you will find information in these sources to help support your own contrary arguments.

You might use one source as part of a *counterargument*—an argument opposing your own—so you can demonstrate its weaknesses and, in the process, strengthen your own claim. On the other hand, the author of one of your sources may be so convincing in supporting a claim that you will adopt it yourself, either partially or entirely. The point is that *the argument is in your hands.* You must devise it yourself and use your sources in ways that will support the claim you present in your thesis.

You may not want to divulge your thesis until the end of the paper, thereby drawing the reader along toward your conclusion, allowing that thesis to flow naturally out of the argument and the evidence on which it is based. If you do this, you are working *inductively.* Or you may wish to be more direct and (after an introduction) *begin* with your thesis, following the thesis statement with evidence and reasoning to support it. If you do this, you are working *deductively.* In academic papers, deductive arguments are far more common than inductive ones.

Based on your reactions to reading sources—and perhaps also on your own inclinations as a student—you may find yourself essentially in sympathy with the approach to privacy taken by one of the schools covered in your sources, M.I.T. At the same time, you may feel that M.I.T.'s position does not demonstrate sufficient concern for campus safety and that Cornell's position, on the other hand, restricts student privacy too much. Perhaps most important, you conclude that we don't need to change the law because, if correctly interpreted, the law already incorporates a good balance between privacy and safety. After a few tries, you develop this thesis:

> In responding to the Virginia Tech killings, we should resist rolling back federal rules protecting student privacy; for as long as college officials effectively respond to signs of trouble, these rules already provide a workable balance between privacy and public safety.

Decide How You Will Use Your Source Material

Your claim commits you to (1) arguing that student privacy should remain protected, and (2) demonstrating that federal law already strikes a balance between privacy and public safety. The sources (some provided here, some located elsewhere) offer information and ideas—evidence—that will allow you to support your claim. The excerpt from the official report on the Virginia Tech shootings reveals a finding that school officials failed to correctly interpret federal privacy rules and failed to "intervene effectively." The article "Virginia Tech Massacre Has Altered Campus Mental Health Systems" outlines some of the ways that campuses around the country have instituted policy changes regarding troubled students and privacy in the wake of Virginia Tech. And the excerpt from the Family Educational Rights and Privacy Act (FERPA), the federal law, reveals that restrictions on revealing students' confidential information have a crucial exception for "the safety or well-being of...students, or other members of the school community." (These and several other sources not included in this chapter will be cited in the model argument paper.)

Develop an Organizational Plan

Having established your overall purpose and your claim, having developed a thesis (which may change as you write and revise the paper), and having decided how to draw upon your source materials, how do you logically organize your paper? In many cases, a well-written thesis will suggest an organization. Thus, the first part of your paper will deal with the debate over rolling back student privacy. The second part will argue that as long as educational institutions behave proactively—that is, as long as they actively seek to help troubled students and foster campus safety—existing federal rules already preserve a balance between privacy and safety. Sorting through your material and categorizing it by topic and subtopic, you might compose the following outline:

I. Introduction. Recap Va. Tech shooting. College officials, citing privacy rules, did not act on available info about shooter with history of mental problems.

II. Federal rules on privacy. Subsequent debate over balance between privacy and campus safety. Pendulum now moving back toward safety. *Thesis.*

III. Developments in student privacy in recent decades.
   A. Doctrine of *in loco parentis* defines college-student relationship.
   B. Movement away from *in loco parentis* begins in 1960s, in context not only of student rights but also broader civil rights struggles of the period.
   C. FERPA, enacted 1974, establishes new federal rules protecting student privacy.

IV. Arguments *against* student privacy.
   A. In wake of Virginia Tech, many blame FERPA protections and college officials, believing privacy rights have been taken too far, putting campus community at risk.
   B. Cornell rolls back some FERPA privacy rights.

V. Arguments *for* student privacy.
   A. M.I.T. strongly defends right to privacy.
   B. Problem is not federal law but incorrect interpretation of federal law. FERPA provides health and safety exceptions. Virginia Tech officials erred in citing FERPA for not sharing info about shooter earlier.

    C. Univ. of Kentucky offers good balance between competing claims of privacy and safety.
      1. watch lists of troubled students
      2. threat assessment groups
      3. open communication among university officials

VI. Conclusion.
    A. Virginia Tech incident was tragic but should not cause us to overturn hard-won privacy rights.
    B. We should support a more pro-active approach to student mental health problems and improve communication between departments.

Formulate an Argument Strategy

The argument that emerges through this outline will build not only on evidence drawn from sources but also on the writer's assumptions. Consider the bare-bones logic of the argument:

Laws protecting student privacy serve a good purpose. (*assumption*)

If properly interpreted and implemented, federal law as currently written is sufficient both to protect student privacy and to ensure campus safety. (*support*)

We should not change federal law to overturn or restrict student privacy rights. (*claim*)

The crucial point about which reasonable people will disagree is the *assumption* that laws protecting student privacy serve a good purpose. Those who wish to restrict the information made available to parents are likely to agree with this assumption. Those who favor a policy that allows college officials to inform parents of problems without their children's permission are likely to disagree.

Writers can accept or partially accept an opposing assumption by making a *concession*, in the process establishing themselves as reasonable and willing to compromise (see p. 172). David Harrison does exactly this in the model synthesis that follows when he summarizes the policies of the University of Kentucky. By raising objections to his own position and conceding some validity to them, he blunts the effectiveness of *counterarguments*. Thus, Harrison concedes the absolute requirement for campus safety, but he argues that this requirement can be satisfied as long as campus officials correctly interpret existing federal law and implement proactive procedures aimed at dealing more effectively with troubled students.

The *claim* of the argument about privacy vs. safety is primarily a claim about *policy*, about actions that should (or should not) be taken. An argument can also concern a claim about *facts* (Does X exist? How can we define X? Does X lead to Y?), a claim about *value* (What is X worth?), or a claim about *cause and effect* (Why did X happen?). The present argument rests to some degree on a dispute about cause and effect. No one disputes that the primary cause of this tragedy was that a disturbed student was not stopped before he killed people. But many have disputed the secondary cause: Did the massacre happen, in part, because federal law prevented officials from sharing crucial information about the disturbed student? Or did it happen, in part, because university officials failed to interpret correctly what they could and could not do under the law? As you read the following paper, observe how these opposing views are woven into the argument.

Draft and Revise Your Synthesis

The final draft of an argument synthesis, based on the outline above, follows. Thesis, transitions, and topic sentences are highlighted; Modern Language Association (MLA) documentation style is used throughout (except in the citing of federal law).

A cautionary note: When writing syntheses, it is all too easy to become careless in properly crediting your sources. Before drafting your paper, always review the section on Avoiding Plagiarism (pp. 45–47).

MODEL ARGUMENT SYNTHESIS

Harrison 1

David Harrison

Professor Shanker

Law and Society I

14 February 2009

Balancing Privacy and Safety in the Wake of Virginia Tech

On April 16, 2007, Seung Hui Cho, a mentally ill student at Virginia Polytechnic Institute, shot to death 32 fellow students and faculty members, and injured 17 others, before killing himself. It was the worst mass shooting in U.S. history, and the fact that it took place on a college campus lent a special horror to the event. In the days after the tragedy, several facts about Seung Hui Cho came to light. According to the official Virginia State Panel report on the killings, Cho had exhibited signs of mental disturbance, including "suicidal and homicidal ideations" dating back to high school. And during Cho's junior year at Virginia Tech, numerous incidents occurred that provided clear warnings of Cho's mental instability and violent impulses (Virginia Tech Review 1). University administrators, faculty, and officials were aware of these incidents but failed to intervene to prevent the impending tragedy.

In the search for answers, attention quickly focused on federal rules governing student privacy that Virginia Tech officials said prevented them from communicating effectively with each other or with Cho's parents regarding his troubles. These rules, the officials argued, prohibit the sharing of information concerning students' mental health with parents or other students. The publicity about such restrictions revived an ongoing debate over university policies that balance student privacy against campus safety. In the wake of the Virginia Tech tragedy, the pendulum seems to have swung in favor of safety. In April 2008, Virginia Governor Tim Kaine signed into law a measure requiring colleges to alert parents when dependent students may be a danger to themselves or to others ("Virginia Tech Massacre" 1). Peter Lake, an educator at Stetson University College of Law, predicted that in the wake of Virginia Tech, "people will go in a direction of safety over privacy" (qtd. in Bernstein, "Mother").

③   The shootings at Virginia Tech demonstrate, in the most horrifying way, the need for secure college campuses. Nevertheless, privacy remains a crucial right to most Americans-- including college students, many of whom for the first time are exercising their prerogatives as adults. Many students who pose no threat to anyone will, and should, object strenuously to university administrators peering into and making judgments about their private lives. Some might be unwilling to seek professional therapy if they know that the records of their counseling sessions might be released to their parents or to other students. In responding to the Virginia Tech killings, we should resist rolling back federal rules protecting student privacy; for as long as college officials effectively respond to signs of trouble, these rules already provide a workable balance between privacy and public safety.

④   In these days of *Facebook* and reality TV, the notion of privacy rights, particularly for young people, may seem quaint. In fact, recently a top lawyer for the search engine *Google* claimed that in the Internet age, young people just don't care about privacy the way they once did (Cohen A17). Whatever the changing views of privacy in a wired world, the issue of student privacy rights is a serious legal matter that must be seen in the context of the student-college relationship, which has its historical roots in the doctrine of *in loco parentis*, Latin for "in the place of the parents." Generally, this doctrine is understood to mean that the college stands in place as the student's parent or guardian. The college therefore has "a duty to protect the safety, morals, and welfare of their students, just as parents are expected to protect their children" (Pollet).

⑤   Writing of life at the University of Michigan before the 1960s, one historian observes that "*in loco parentis* comprised an elaborate structure of written rules and quiet understandings enforced in the trenches by housemothers [who] governed much of the what,

Harrison 3

where, when, and whom of students' lives, especially women: what to wear to dinner, what time to be home, where, when, and for how long they might receive visitors" (Tobin).

During the 1960s court decisions began to chip away at the doctrine of *in loco parentis*. These rulings illustrate that the students' rights movement during that era was an integral part of a broader contemporary social movement for civil rights and liberties. In *Dixon v. Alabama State Board of Education*, Alabama State College invoked *in loco parentis* to defend its decision to expel six African-American students without due process for participating in a lunchroom counter sit-in. Eventually, a federal appeals court rejected the school's claim to unrestrained power, ruling that students' constitutional rights did not end once they stepped onto campus (Weigel).   ⑥

Students were not just fighting for the right to hold hands in dorm rooms; they were also asserting their rights as the vanguard of a social revolution. As Stetson law professor Robert Bickel notes: "The fall of *in loco parentis* in the 1960s correlated exactly with the rise of student economic power and the rise of student civil rights" (qtd. in Weigel).   ⑦

The students' rights movement received a further boost with the Family Educational Rights and Privacy Act (FERPA), signed into law by President Ford in 1974. FERPA barred schools from releasing educational records--including mental health records--without the student's permission. The Act provides some important exceptions: educational records *can* be released in the case of health and safety emergencies or if the student is declared a dependent on his or her parents' tax returns (*Federal*).   ⑧

In the wake of Virginia Tech, however, many observers pointed the finger of blame at federal restrictions on sharing available mental health information. Also held responsible were the school's officials, who admitted knowing of Cho's mental instability but claimed that FERPA prevented them from doing anything about it. The State of Virginia official report on the killings notes as follows: ⑨

> University officials...explained their failures to communicate with one an-
> other or with Cho's parents by noting their belief that such communications
> are prohibited by the federal laws governing the privacy of health and edu-
> cation records. (Virginia Tech Review 2)

Observers were quick to declare the system broken. "Laws Limit Schools Even after Alarms," trumpeted a headline in the *Philadelphia Inquirer* (Gammage and Burling). Commentators attacked federal privacy law, charging that the pendulum had swung too far   ⑩ away from campus safety. Judging from this letter to the editor of the *Wall Street Journal*, many agreed wholeheartedly: "Parents have a right to know if their child has a serious problem, and they need to know the progress of their child's schoolwork, especially if they are paying the cost of the education. Anything less than this is criminal" (Guerriero).

(11)   As part of this public clamor, some schools have enacted policies that effectively curtail student privacy in favor of campus safety. For example: after Virginia Tech, Cornell University began assuming that students were dependents of their parents. Exploiting what the *Wall Street Journal* termed a "rarely used legal exception" in FERPA allows Cornell to provide parents with confidential information without students' permission (Bernstein, "Bucking" A9).

(12)   Conversely, the Massachusetts Institute of Technology lies at the opposite end of the spectrum from Cornell in its staunch defense of student privacy. M.I.T. has stuck to its position even in the wake of Virginia Tech, recently demanding that the mother of a missing M.I.T. student obtain a subpoena in order to access his dorm room and e-mail records. That student was later found dead, an apparent suicide (Bernstein, "Mother"). Even in the face of lawsuits, M.I.T. remains committed to its stance. Its Chancellor explained the school's position this way:

> Privacy is important. . . . Different students will do different things they ab-
> solutely don't want their parents to know about. . . . Students expect this kind
> of safe place where they can address their difficulties, try out lifestyles, and
> be independent of their parents. (qtd. in Bernstein, "Mother")

(13)   One can easily understand how parents would be outraged by the M.I.T. position. No parent would willingly let his or her child enter an environment where that child's safety cannot be assured. Just as the first priority for any government is to protect its citizens, the first priority of an educational institution must be to keep its students safe. But does this responsibility justify rolling back student privacy rights or returning to a more traditional interpretation of *in loco parentis* in the relationship between a university and its students? No, for the simple reason that the choice is a false one.

(14)   As long as federal privacy laws are properly interpreted and implemented, they do nothing to endanger campus safety. The problem at Virginia Tech was not the federal government's policy; it was the university's own practices based on a faulty interpretation of that policy. The breakdown began with the failure of Virginia Tech officials to understand

federal privacy laws. Interpreted correctly, these laws would *not* have prohibited officials from notifying appropriate authorities of Cho's problems. The Virginia Tech Review Panel report was very clear on this point: "[F]ederal laws and their state counterparts afford ample leeway to share information in potentially dangerous situations" (2). FERPA does, in fact, provide for a "health and safety emergencies" exception; educational records *can* be released without the student's consent "in connection with an emergency, [to] appropriate persons if the knowledge of such information is necessary to protect the health or safety of the student or other person..." (232g (b) (1) (g-h)). But Virginia Tech administrators did not invoke this important exception to FERPA's privacy rules.

An editorial in the *Christian Science Monitor* suggested several other steps that the university could legally have taken, including informing Cho's parents that he had been briefly committed to a mental health facility, a fact that was public information. The editorial concluded, scornfully, that "federal law, at least, does recognize a balance between privacy and public safety, even when colleges can't, or won't" ("Perilous"). ⑮

To be fair, such confusion about FERPA's contingencies appears widespread among college officials. For this reason, the U.S. Department of Education's revised privacy regulations, announced in March 2008 and intended to "clarify" when schools may release student records, are welcome and necessary. But simply reassuring anxious university officials that they won't lose federal funds for revealing confidential student records won't be enough to ensure campus safety. We need far more effective intervention for troubled students than the kind provided by Virginia Tech, which the Virginia Tech Review Panel blasted for its "lack of resources" and "passivity" (2). ⑯

Schools like the University of Kentucky offer a positive example of such intervention, demonstrating that colleges can adopt a robust approach to student mental health without infringing on privacy rights. At Kentucky, "threat assessment groups" meet regularly to discuss a "watch list" of troubled students and decide what to do about them (McMurray). These committees emphasize proactiveness and communication--elements that were sorely missing at Virginia Tech. The approach represents a prudent middle ground between the extreme positions of M.I.T. and Cornell. ⑰

Schools such as Kentucky carry out their policies with a firm eye toward student privacy rights. For example, the University of Kentucky's director of counseling attends the threat assessment group's meetings but draws a clear line at what information she can share--for ⑱ instance, whether or not a student has been undergoing counseling. Instead, the group looks for other potential red flags, such as a sharp drop-off in grades or difficulty functioning in the campus environment (McMurray). This open communication between university officials will presumably also help with delicate judgments--whether, for example, a student's violent story written for a creative writing class is an indication of mental instability or simply an early work by the next Stephen King ("Virginia Tech Massacre" 1).

(19)   What happened at Virginia Tech was a tragedy. Few of us can appreciate the grief of the parents of the shooting victims at Virginia Tech, parents who trusted that their children would be safe and who were devastated when that faith was betrayed. To these parents, the words of the MIT chancellor quoted earlier--platitudes about students "try[ing] out lifestyles" or "address[ing] their difficulties"--must sound hollow. But we must guard against allowing a few isolated incidents, however tragic, to restrict the rights of millions of students, the vast majority of whom graduate college safely and without incident. Schools must not use Virginia Tech as a pretext to bring back the bad old days of resident assistants snooping on the private lives of students and infringing on their privacy. That step is the first down a slippery slope of dictating morality. Both the federal courts and Congress have rejected that approach and for good reason have established the importance of privacy rights on campus. These rights must be preserved.

(20)   The Virginia Tech shooting does not demonstrate a failure of current policy, but rather a breakdown in the enforcement of policy. In its wake, universities have undertaken important modifications to their procedures. We should support changes that involve a more proactive approach to student mental health and improvements in communication between departments, such as those at the University of Kentucky. Such measures will not only bring confidential help to the troubled students who need it, they will also improve the safety of the larger college community. At the same time, these measures will preserve hard-won privacy rights on campus.

Works Cited

Bernstein, Elizabeth. "Bucking Privacy Concerns, Cornell Acts as Watchdog." *Wall Street Journal* 27 Dec. 2007: A1+. *LexisNexis*. Web. 10 Feb. 2009.

---. "A Mother Takes On MIT." *Wall Street Journal* 20 Sept. 2007: A1. *LexisNexis*. Web. 10 Feb. 2009.

Harrison 8

Cohen, Adam. "One Friend Facebook Hasn't Made Yet: Privacy Rights." *New York Times*
18 Feb. 2008: A1+. *Academic Search Complete*. Web. 9 Feb. 2009.

Federal Educational Rights and Privacy Act (FERPA). 20 U.S.C. §1232g (b) (1) (g–h)
(2006). Print.

Gammage, Jeff, and Stacy Burling. "Laws Limit Schools Even after Alarms." *Philadelphia
Inquirer* 19 Apr. 2007: A1. *Academic Search Complete*. Web. 10 Feb. 2009.

Guerriero, Dom. Letter. *Wall Street Journal* 7 Jan. 2008. *LexisNexis*. Web. 11 Feb. 2009.

McMurray, Jeffrey. "Colleges Are Watching Troubled Students." *AP Online*. Associated Press,
28 Mar. 2008. Web. 11 Feb. 2009.

"Perilous Privacy at Virginia Tech." Editorial. *Christian Science Monitor* 4 Sept. 2007:
8. *Academic Search Complete*. Web. 10 Feb. 2009.

Pollet, Susan J. "Is 'In Loco Parentis' at the College Level a Dead Doctrine?" *New York Law
Journal* 288 (2002): 4. Print.

Tobin, James. "The Day 'In Loco Parentis' Died." *Michigan Today*. U of Michigan,
Nov. 2007. Web. 10 Feb. 2009.

"Virginia Tech Massacre Has Altered Campus Mental Health Systems." *Los Angeles Times*
14 Apr. 2008: A1+. *LexisNexis*. Web. 8 Feb. 2009.

Virginia Tech Review Panel. *Mass Shootings at Virginia Tech, April 16, 2007: Report of the
Virginia Tech Review Panel Presented to Timothy M. Kaine, Governor, Commonwealth of
Virginia*. Arlington, VA: n.p., 2007. Print.

Weigel, David. "Welcome to the Fun-Free University: The Return of *In Loco Parentis* Is Killing
Student Freedom." *Reasononline*. Reason Magazine, Oct. 2004. Web. 7 Feb. 2009.

The Strategy of the Argument Synthesis

In his argument synthesis, Harrison attempts to support a *claim*—one that favors laws protecting student privacy while at the same time helping to ensure campus safety—by offering *support* in the form of facts (what campuses such as the University of Kentucky are doing, what Virginia Tech officials did and failed to do) and opinions (testimony of persons on both sides of the issue). However, because Harrison's claim rests on an *assumption* about the value of student privacy laws, its effectiveness depends partially on the extent to which we, as readers, agree with this assumption. (See our discussion of assumptions in Chapter 2, pp. 61–62.) An assumption (sometimes called a warrant) is a generalization or principle about how the world works or should work—a fundamental statement of belief about facts or values. In this case, the underlying assumption is that college students, as emerging adults, and as citizens with civil rights, are entitled to keep their educational records private. Harrison makes this assumption explicit. Though you are under no obligation to do so, stating assumptions explicitly will clarify your arguments to readers.

Assumptions are often deeply rooted in people's psyches, sometimes derived from lifelong experiences and observations and not easily changed, even by the most logical of arguments. People who lost loved ones in incidents such as Virginia Tech, or people who believe that the right to safety of the larger campus community outweighs the right of individual student privacy, are not likely to accept the assumption underlying this paper, nor are they likely to accept the support provided by Harrison. But readers with no firm opinion might well be persuaded and could come to agree with him that existing federal law protecting student privacy is sufficient to protect campus safety, provided that campus officials act responsibly.

A discussion of the model argument's paragraphs, along with the argument strategy for each, follows. Note that the paper devotes one paragraph to developing each section of the outline on pp. 157–158. Note also that Harrison avoids plagiarism by the careful attribution and quotation of sources.

- **Paragraph 1:** Harrison summarizes the key events of the Virginia Tech killings and establishes that Cho's mental instability was previously known to university officials.

  Argument strategy: Opening with the bare facts of the massacre, Harrison proceeds to lay the basis for the reaction against privacy rules that will be described in the paragraphs to follow. To some extent, Harrison encourages the reader to share the outrage by many in the general public that university officials failed to act to prevent the killings before they started.

- **Paragraph 2:** Harrison now explains the federal rules governing student privacy and discusses the public backlash against such rules and the new law signed by the governor of Virginia restricting privacy at colleges within the state.

  Argument strategy: This paragraph highlights the debate over student privacy—and in particular the sometimes conflicting demands of student privacy and campus safety that will be central to the rest of the paper. Harrison cites both fact (the new Virginia law) and opinion (the quotation by Peter Lake) to develop this paragraph.

- **Paragraph 3:** Harrison further clarifies the two sides of the apparent conflict between privacy and safety, maintaining that both represent important social values but concluding with a thesis that argues for not restricting privacy.

  Argument strategy: For the first time, Harrison reveals his own position on the issue. He starts the paragraph by conceding the need for secure campuses but begins to make the case for privacy (for example, without privacy rules students might be reluctant to enter therapy). In his thesis he emphasizes that the demands of both privacy and safety can be satisfied because existing federal rules incorporate the necessary balance.

- **Paragraphs 4–7:** These paragraphs constitute the next section of the paper (see outline, pp. 157–158), covering the developments in student privacy over the past few decades. Paragraphs 4 and 5 treat the doctrine of *in loco parentis*; paragraph 6 discusses how court decisions like *Dixon v. Alabama State Board of Education* began to erode this doctrine.

   Argument strategy: This section of the paper establishes the situation that existed on college campuses before the 1960s—and presumably would exist again were privacy laws to be rolled back. By linking the erosion of the *in loco parentis* doctrine to the civil rights struggle, Harrison attempts to bestow upon pre-1960s college students (especially women), who were "parented" by college administrators, something of the ethos of African–Americans fighting for full citizenship during the civil rights era. Essentially, Harrison is making an analogy between the two groups—one that readers may or may not accept.

- **Paragraph 8:** This paragraph on FERPA constitutes the final part of the section of the paper dealing with the evolution of student privacy since before the 1960s. Harrison explains what FERPA is and introduces an exception to its privacy rules that will be more fully developed later in the paper.

   Argument strategy: FERPA is the federal law central to the debate over the balance between privacy and safety, so Harrison introduces it here as the culmination of a series of developments that weakened *in loco parentis* and guaranteed a certain level of student privacy. But since Harrison in his thesis argues that federal law on student privacy already establishes a balance between privacy and safety, he ends the paragraph by referring to the "health and safety" exception, an exception that will become important later in his argument.

- **Paragraphs 9–11:** These paragraphs constitute the section of the paper that covers the arguments **against** student privacy. Paragraph 9 treats public reaction against both FERPA and Virginia Tech officials who were accused of being more concerned with privacy than with safety. Paragraph 10 cites anti-privacy sentiments expressed in newspapers. Paragraph 11 explains how, in the wake of Virginia Tech, schools like Cornell have enacted new policies restricting student privacy.

   Argument strategy: Harrison sufficiently respects the sentiments of those whose position he opposes to deal at some length with the counterarguments to his thesis. He quotes the official report on the mass shootings to establish that Virginia Tech officials believed that they were acting according to the law. He quotes the writer of an angry letter about parents' right to know without attempting to rebut its arguments. In outlining the newly restrictive Cornell policies on privacy, Harrison also establishes what he considers an extreme reaction to the massacres: essentially gutting student privacy rules. He is therefore setting up one position on the debate which will later be contrasted with other positions—those of M.I.T. and the University of Kentucky.

- **Paragraphs 12–18:** These paragraphs constitute the section of the paper devoted to arguments **for** student privacy. Paragraphs 12 and 13 discuss the M.I.T. position on privacy, as expressed by its chancellor. Paragraph 14 refocuses on FERPA and quotes language to demonstrate that existing federal law provides a health and safety exception to the enforcement of privacy rules. Paragraph 15 quotes an editorial supporting this interpretation of FERPA. Paragraph 16 concedes the existence of confusion about federal rules and makes the transition to an argument about the need for more effective action by campus officials to prevent tragedies like this one.

  Argument strategy: Because these paragraphs express Harrison's position, as embedded in his thesis, this is the longest segment of the discussion. Paragraphs 12 and 13 discuss the M.I.T. position on student privacy, which (given that school's failure to accommodate even prudent demands for safety) Harrison believes is too extreme. Notice the transition at the end of paragraph 13: conceding that colleges have a responsibility to keep students safe, Harrison poses a question: Does the goal of keeping students safe justify the rolling back of privacy rights? In a pivotal sentence, he responds, "No, for the simple reason that the choice is a false one." Paragraph 14 develops this response and presents the heart of Harrison's argument. Recalling the health and safety exception introduced in paragraph 8, Harrison now explains *why* the choice is false: he quotes the exact language of FERPA to establish that the problem at Virginia Tech was not due to federal law that prevented campus officials from protecting students, but rather to campus officials who *misunderstood* the law. Paragraph 15 amplifies Harrison's argument with a reference to an editorial in the *Christian Science Monitor*. Paragraph 16 marks a transition, within this section, to a position (developed in paragraphs 17 and 18) that Harrison believes represents a sensible stance in the debate over campus safety and student privacy. Harrison bolsters his case by citing here, as elsewhere in the paper, the official report on the Virginia Tech killings. The report, prepared by an expert panel that devoted months to investigating the incident, carries considerable weight as evidence in this argument.

- **Paragraphs 17–18:** These paragraphs continue the arguments in favor of Harrison's position. They focus on new policies in practice at the University of Kentucky that offer a "prudent middle ground" in the debate.

  Argument strategy: Having discussed schools such as Cornell and M.I.T. where the reaction to the Virginia Tech killings was inadequate or unsatisfactory, Harrison now outlines a set of policies and procedures in place at the University of Kentucky since April 2007. Following the transition at the end of paragraph 16 on the need for more effective intervention on the part of campus officials, Harrison explains how Kentucky established a promising form of such intervention: watch lists of troubled students, threat assessment groups, and more open communication among university officials. Thus Harrison positions what is happening at the University of Kentucky—as opposed to rollbacks of federal rules—as the most effective way of preventing future killings like those at Virginia Tech. Kentucky therefore becomes a crucial example for Harrison of how to strike a good balance between the demands of student privacy and campus safety.

- **Paragraphs 19–20:** In his conclusion, Harrison reiterates points made in the body of the paper. In paragraph 19 he agrees that what happened at Virginia Tech was a tragedy but maintains that an isolated incident should not become an excuse for rolling back student privacy rights and bringing back "the bad old days" when campus officials took an active, and intrusive, interest in students' private lives. In paragraph 20, Harrison reiterates the position stated in his thesis: that the problem at Virginia Tech was not a restrictive federal policy that handcuffed administrators but a breakdown in enforcement. He concludes on a hopeful note that new policies established since Virginia Tech will both protect student privacy and improve campus safety.

  Argument strategy: The last two paragraphs provide Harrison with a final opportunity for driving home his points. These two paragraphs to some degree parallel the structure of the thesis itself. In paragraph 19, Harrison makes a final appeal against rolling back student privacy rights. This appeal parallels the first clause of the thesis ("In responding to the Virginia Tech killings, we should resist rolling back federal rules protecting student privacy"). In paragraph 20, Harrison focuses not on federal law itself but rather on the kind of measures adopted by schools like the University of Kentucky that go beyond mere compliance with federal law—and thereby demonstrate the validity of part two of Harrison's thesis ("As long as college officials effectively respond to signs of trouble, these rules already provide a workable balance between privacy and public safety"). Harrison thus ends a paper on a grim subject with a note that provides some measure of optimism and that attempts to reconcile proponents on both sides of this emotional debate.

Another approach to an argument synthesis based on the same and additional sources could argue (along with some of the sources quoted in the model paper) that safety as a social value should never be outweighed by the right to privacy. Such a position could draw support from other practices in contemporary society—searches at airports, for example—illustrating that most people are willing to give up a certain measure of privacy, as well as convenience, in the interest of the safety of the community. Even if such an argument were not to call for a rollback of federal privacy rules, it could recommend modifying the language of the law to make doubly clear that safety trumps privacy. Some have even argued that safety would be improved if students and teachers were permitted to bring guns to campus and were thereby able to defend themselves and others in the event of being confronted by a deranged gunman. In the wake of Virginia Tech and other recent mass killings (such as the shooting deaths of five Amish children at their schoolhouse in 2006), it is difficult to conceive of support for an extreme claim that the rights of the individual are paramount and that privacy should always trump safety. A more reasonable argument might be made, working in counterpoint to the pro–privacy position of the M.I.T. chancellor, specifying more precisely the criteria that would constitute (in the language of FERPA) "significant risk to the safety or well-being" of the campus community. Having met the clearly defined threshold of a grave risk, university officials could then breach student privacy in the interest of the greater good.

Whatever your approach to a subject, in first *critically examining* the various sources and then *synthesizing* them to support a position about which you feel strongly, you are engaging in the kind of critical thinking that is essential to success in a good deal of academic and professional work.

DEVELOPING AND ORGANIZING THE SUPPORT FOR YOUR ARGUMENTS

Experienced writers seem to have an intuitive sense of how to develop and present supporting evidence for their claims; this sense is developed through much hard work and practice. Less experienced writers wonder what to say first, and having decided on that, wonder what to say next. There is no single method of presentation. But the techniques of even the most experienced writers often boil down to a few tried and tested arrangements.

As we've seen in the model synthesis in this chapter, the key to devising effective arguments is to find and use those kinds of support that most persuasively strengthen your claim. Some writers categorize support into two broad types: *evidence* and *motivational appeals*. Evidence, in the form of facts, statistics, and expert testimony, helps make the appeal to reason. Motivational appeals—appeals grounded in emotion and upon the authority of the speaker—are employed to get people to change their minds, to agree with the writer or speaker, or to decide upon a plan of activity.

Following are the most common strategies for using and organizing support for your claims.

Summarize, Paraphrase, and Quote Supporting Evidence

In most of the papers and reports you will write in college and in the professional world, evidence and motivational appeals derive from your summarizing, paraphrasing, and quoting of material in sources that either have been provided to you or that you have independently researched. For example, in paragraph 9 of the model argument synthesis, Harrison uses a long quotation from the Virginia Tech Review Panel report to make the point that college officials believed they were prohibited by federal privacy law from communicating with one another about disturbed students like Cho. You will find another long quotation later in the synthesis and a number of brief quotations woven into sentences throughout. In addition, you will find summaries and paraphrases. In each case, Harrison is careful to cite a source.

Provide Various Types of Evidence and Motivational Appeals

Keep in mind that you can use appeals to both reason and emotion. The appeal to reason is based on evidence that consists of a combination of *facts* and *expert testimony*. The sources by Tobin and Weigel, for example, offer facts about the evolution over the past few decades of the *in loco parentis* doctrine. Bernstein and McMurray interview college adminstrators at Cornell, M.I.T., and the University of Kentucky who explain the changing policies at those institutions. The model synthesis makes an appeal to emotion by engaging the reader's self-interest: If campuses are to be made more secure from the acts of mentally disturbed persons, then college officials should take a proactive approach to monitoring and intervention.

Use Climactic Order

Climactic order is the arrangement of examples or evidence in order of anticipated impact on the reader, least to greatest. Organize by climactic order when you plan to offer a number of categories or elements of support for your claim. Recognize that some elements will be more important—and likely more persuasive—than others. The basic principle here is that you should *save the most important evidence for the end* because whatever you say last is what readers are likely to remember best. A secondary principle is that whatever you say first is what they are *next* most likely to remember. Therefore, when you have several reasons to offer in support of your claim, an effective argument strategy is to present the second most important, then one or more additional reasons, and finally the most important reason. Paragraphs 7–11 of the model synthesis do exactly this.

Use Logical or Conventional Order

Using logical or conventional order involves using as a template a pre-established pattern or plan for arguing your case.

- One common pattern is describing or arguing a *problem/solution*. Using this pattern, you begin with an introduction in which you typically define the problem, perhaps explain its origins, then offer one or more solutions, then conclude.
- Another common pattern presents *two sides of a controversy*. Using this pattern, you introduce the controversy and (in an argument synthesis) your own point of view or claim, then you explain the other side's arguments, providing reasons why your point of view should prevail.
- A third common pattern is *comparison-and-contrast*. This pattern is so important that we will discuss it separately in the next section.

The order in which you present elements of an argument is sometimes dictated by the conventions of the discipline in which you are writing. For example, lab reports and experiments in the sciences and social sciences often follow this pattern: *Opening* or *Introduction, Methods and Materials* (of the experiment or study), *Results, Discussion.* Legal arguments often follow the so-called IRAC format: *Issue, Rule, Application, Conclusion.*

Present and Respond to Counterarguments

When developing arguments on a controversial topic, you can effectively use *counterargument* to help support your claims. When you use counterargument, you present an argument *against* your claim and then show that this argument is weak or flawed. The advantage of this technique is that you demonstrate that you are aware of the other side of the argument and that you are prepared to answer it.

Here is how a counterargument is typically developed:

   I. Introduction and claim
  II. Main opposing argument
 III. Refutation of opposing argument
  IV. Main positive argument

Use Concession

Concession is a variation of counterargument. As in counterargument, you present an opposing viewpoint, but instead of dismissing that position you *concede* that it has some validity and even some appeal, although your own position is the more reasonable one. This concession bolsters your standing as a fair-minded person who is not blind to the virtues of the other side. In the model synthesis, Harrison acknowledges the grief and sense of betrayal of the parents of the students who were killed. He concedes that parents have a right to expect that "the first priority of an educational institution must be to keep students safe." But he insists that this goal of achieving campus safety can be accomplished without rolling back hard-won privacy rights.

Here is an outline for a typical concession argument:

   I. Introduction and claim
  II. Important opposing argument
 III. Concession that this argument has some validity
  IV. Positive argument(s)

Sometimes, when you are developing a counterargument or concession argument, you may become convinced of the validity of the opposing point of view and change your own views. Don't be afraid of this happening. Writing is a tool for learning. To change your mind because of new evidence is a sign of flexibility and maturity, and your writing can only be the better for it.

DEVELOPING AND ORGANIZING SUPPORT FOR YOUR ARGUMENTS

- *Summarize, paraphrase, and quote supporting evidence.* Draw on the facts, ideas, and language in your sources.
- *Provide various types of evidence and motivational appeal.*
- *Use climactic order.* Save the most important evidence in support of your argument for the *end*, where it will have the most impact. Use the next most important evidence *first*.
- *Use logical or conventional order.* Use a form of organization appropriate to the topic, such as problem/solution; sides of a controversy; comparison/contrast; or a form of organization appropriate to the academic or professional discipline, such as a report of an experiment or a business plan.
- *Present and respond to counterarguments.* Anticipate and evaluate arguments against your position.
- *Use concession.* Concede that one or more arguments against your position have some validity; re-assert, nonetheless, that your argument is the stronger one.

Avoid Common Fallacies in Developing and Using Support

In Chapter 2, in the section on critical reading, we considered criteria that, as a reader, you may use for evaluating informative and persuasive writing (see pp. 50–52, 59). We discussed how you can assess the accuracy, the significance, and the author's interpretation of the information presented. We also considered the importance in good argument of clearly defined key terms and the pitfalls of emotionally loaded language. Finally, we saw how to recognize such logical fallacies as either/or reasoning, faulty cause-and-effect reasoning, hasty generalization, and false analogy. As a writer, no less than as a critical reader, you need to be aware of these common problems and to avoid them.

Be aware, also, of your responsibility to cite source materials appropriately. When you quote a source, double- and triple-check that you have done so accurately. When you summarize or paraphrase, take care to use your own language and sentence structures (though you can, of course, also quote within these forms). When you refer to someone else's idea—even if you are not quoting, summarizing, or paraphrasing—give the source credit. By being ethical about the use of sources, you uphold the highest standards of the academic community.

THE COMPARISON-AND-CONTRAST SYNTHESIS

A particularly important type of argument synthesis is built on patterns of comparison and contrast. Techniques of comparison and contrast enable you to examine two subjects (or sources) in terms of one another. When you compare, you consider *similarities*. When you contrast, you consider *differences*. By comparing and contrasting, you perform a multifaceted analysis that often suggests subtleties that otherwise might not have come to your (or your reader's) attention.

To organize a comparison-and-contrast argument, you must carefully read sources in order to discover *significant criteria for analysis*. A *criterion* is a specific point to which both of your authors refer and about which they may agree or disagree. (For example, in a comparative report on compact cars, criteria for *comparison and contrast* might be road handling, fuel economy, and comfort of ride.) The best criteria are those that allow you not only to account for obvious similarities and differences—those concerning the main aspects of your sources or subjects—but also to plumb deeper, exploring subtle yet significant comparisons and contrasts among details or subcomponents, which you can then relate to your overall thesis.

Note that comparison-and-contrast is frequently not an end in itself but serves some larger purpose. Thus, a comparison-and-contrast synthesis may be a component of a paper that is essentially a critique, an explanatory synthesis, an argument synthesis, or an analysis.

Organizing Comparison-and-Contrast Syntheses

Two basic approaches to organizing a comparison-and-contrast synthesis are organization by *source* and organization by *criteria*.

Organizing by Source or Subject

You can organize a comparative synthesis by first summarizing each of your sources or subjects and then discussing the significant similarities and differences between them. Having read the summaries and become familiar with the distinguishing features of each source, your readers will most likely be able to appreciate the more obvious similarities and differences. In the discussion, your task is to consider both the obvious and the subtle comparisons and contrasts, focusing on the most significant—that is, on those that most clearly support your thesis.

Organization by source or subject works best with passages that can be briefly summarized. If the summary of your source or subject becomes too long, your readers might have forgotten the points you made in the first summary when they are reading the second. A comparison-and-contrast synthesis organized by source or subject might proceed like this:

  I. Introduce the paper; lead to thesis.

 II. Summarize source/subject A by discussing its significant features.

III. Summarize source/subject B by discussing its significant features.

IV. Discuss in a paragraph (or two) the significant points of comparison and contrast between sources or subjects A and B. Alternatively, begin the comparison-contrast in Section III as you introduce source/subject B.

 V. Conclude with a paragraph in which you summarize your points and, perhaps, raise and respond to pertinent questions.

Organizing by Criteria

Instead of summarizing entire sources one at a time with the intention of comparing them later, you could discuss two sources simultaneously, examining the views of each author point by point (criterion by criterion), comparing and contrasting these views in the process. The criterion approach is best used when you have a number of points to discuss or when passages or subjects are long and/or complex. A comparison-and-contrast synthesis organized by criteria might look like this:

I. Introduce the paper; lead to thesis.

II. Criterion 1

    A. Discuss what author #1 says about this point. Or present situation #1 in light of this point.

    B. Discuss what author #2 says about this point, comparing and contrasting #2's treatment of the point with #1's. Or present situation #2 in light of this point and explain its differences from situation #1.

III. Criterion 2

    A. Discuss what author #1 says about this point. Or present situation #1 in light of this point.

    B. Discuss what author #2 says about this point, comparing and contrasting #2's treatment of the point with #1's. Or present situation #2 in light of this point and explain its differences from situation #1.

And so on, proceeding criterion by criterion until you have completed your discussion. Be sure to arrange criteria with a clear method; knowing how the discussion of one criterion leads to the next will ensure smooth transitions throughout your paper. End by summarizing your key points and perhaps raising and responding to pertinent questions.

However you organize your comparison-and-contrast synthesis, keep in mind that comparing and contrasting are not ends in themselves. Your discussion should point to a conclusion, an answer to the question "So what—why bother to compare and contrast in the first place?" If your discussion is part of a larger synthesis, point to and support the larger claim. If you write a stand-alone comparison-and-contrast synthesis, though, you must by the final paragraph answer the "Why bother?" question. The model comparison-and-contrast synthesis that follows does exactly this.

Exercise 5.5

Comparing and Contrasting

Review the model argument synthesis (pp. 159–165) for elements of comparison-and-contrast—specifically those paragraphs concerning how Cornell University, M.I.T. and the University of Kentucky balance student privacy with the parental right to know about the health and welfare of their children.

1. From these paragraphs in the model paper, extract raw information concerning the positions of the three schools on the issue of student privacy and then craft your own brief comparison-and-contrast synthesis. Identify criteria for comparison and contrast, and discuss the positions of each school in relation to these criteria. *Note:* For this exercise, do not concern yourself with parenthetical citation (that is, with identifying your source materials).

2. Write a paragraph or two that traces the development of comparison-and-contrast throughout the model paper. Having discussed the *how* and *where* of this development, discuss the *why*. Answer this question: Why has the writer used comparison-and-contrast? (Hint: it is not an end in itself.) To what use is it put?

A Case for Comparison-and-Contrast: World War I and World War II

Let's see how the principles of comparison-and-contrast can be applied to a response to a final examination question in a course on modern history. Imagine that having attended classes involving lecture and discussion, and having read excerpts from John Keegan's *The First World War* and Tony Judt's *Postwar: A History of Europe Since 1945,* you were presented with this examination question:

> Based on your reading to date, compare and contrast the two world wars in light of any four or five criteria you think significant. Once you have called careful attention to both similarities and differences, conclude with an observation. What have you learned? What can your comparative analysis teach us?

Comparison-and-Contrast Organized by Criteria

Here is a plan for a response, essentially a comparison-and-contrast synthesis, organized by *criteria* and beginning with the thesis—and the *claim*.

> *Thesis*: In terms of the impact on cities and civilian populations, the military aspects of the two wars in Europe, and their aftermaths, the differences between World War I and World War II considerably outweigh the similarities.

> I. Introduction. World Wars I and II were the most devastating conflicts in history. *Thesis*

> II. Summary of main similarities: causes, countries involved, battlegrounds, global scope.

> III. First major difference: Physical impact of war.
>   A. WWI was fought mainly in rural battlegrounds.
>   B. In WWII cities were destroyed.

> IV. Second major difference: Effect on civilians.
>   A. WWI fighting primarily involved soldiers.
>   B. WWII involved not only military but also massive noncombatant casualties: civilian populations were displaced, forced into slave labor, and exterminated.

   V. Third major difference: Combat operations.
      A. World War I, in its long middle phase, was characterized by trench warfare.
      B. During the middle phase of World War II there was no major military action in Nazi-occupied Western Europe.

   VI. Fourth major difference: Aftermath.
      A. Harsh war terms imposed on defeated Germany contributed significantly to the rise of Hitler and World War II.
      B. Victorious allies helped rebuild West Germany after World War II but allowed Soviets to take over Eastern Europe.

   VII. Conclusion. Since the end of World War II, wars have been far smaller in scope and destructiveness, and warfare has expanded to involve stateless combatants committed to acts of terror.

The following model exam response, a comparison-and-contrast synthesis organized by criteria, is written according to the preceding plan. (Thesis and topic sentences are highlighted.)

MODEL EXAM RESPONSE

World War I (1914–18) and World War II (1939–45) were the most catastrophic and destructive conflicts in human history. For those who believed in the steady but inevitable progress of civilization, it was impossible to imagine that two wars in the first half of the twentieth century could reach levels of barbarity and horror that would outstrip those of any previous era. Historians estimate that more than 22 million people, soldiers and civilians, died in World War I; they estimate that between 40 and 50 million died in World War II. In many ways, these two conflicts were similar: they were fought on many of the same European and Russian battlegrounds, with more or less the same countries on opposing sides. Even many of the same people were involved: Winston Churchill and Adolf Hitler figured in both wars. And the main outcome in each case was the same: total defeat for Germany. However, in terms of the impact on cities and civilian populations, the military aspects of the two wars in Europe, and their aftermaths, the differences between World Wars I and II considerably outweigh the similarities.

The similarities are clear enough. In fact, many historians regard World War II as a continuation--after an intermission of about twenty years--of World War I. One of the main causes of each war was Germany's dissatisfaction and frustration with what it perceived as its diminished place in the world. Hitler launched World War II partly out of revenge for

(1)

(2)

Germany's humiliating defeat in World War I. In each conflict Germany and its allies (the Central Powers in WWI, the Axis in WWII) went to war against France, Great Britain, Russia (the Soviet Union in WWII), and eventually, the United States. Though neither conflict included literally the entire world, the participation of countries not only in Europe but also in the Middle East, the Far East, and the Western hemisphere made both conflicts global in scope. And as indicated earlier, the number of casualties in each war was unprecedented in history, partly because modern technology had enabled the creation of deadlier weapons-- including tanks, heavy artillery, and aircraft--than had ever been used in warfare.

(3)   Despite these similarities, the differences between the two world wars are considerably more significant. One of the most noticeable differences was the physical impact of each war in Europe and in Russia--the western and eastern fronts. The physical destruction of World War I was confined largely to the battlefield. The combat took place almost entirely in the rural areas of Europe and Russia. No major cities were destroyed in the first war; cathedrals, museums, government buildings, urban houses and apartments were left untouched. During the second war, in contrast, almost no city or town of any size emerged unscathed. Rotterdam, Warsaw, London, Minsk, and--when the Allies began their counterattack--almost every major city in Germany and Japan, including Berlin and Tokyo, were flattened. Of course, the physical devastation of the cities created millions of refugees, a phenomenon never experienced in World War I.

(4)   The fact that World War II was fought in the cities as well as on the battlefields meant that the second war had a much greater impact on civilians than did the first war. With few exceptions, the civilians in Europe during WWI were not driven from their homes, forced into slave labor, starved, tortured, or systematically exterminated. But all of these crimes happened routinely during WWII. The Nazi occupation of Europe meant that the civilian populations of France, Belgium, Norway, the Netherlands, and other conquered lands, along with the industries, railroads, and farms of these countries, were put into the service of the Third Reich. Millions of people from conquered Europe--those who were not sent directly to the death camps--were forcibly transported to Germany and put to work in support of the war effort.

(5)   During both wars, the Germans were fighting on two fronts--the western front in Europe and the eastern front in Russia. But while both wars were characterized by intense military activity during their initial and final phases, the middle and longest phases--at least in Europe--differed considerably. The middle phase of the First World War was

characterized by trench warfare, a relatively static form of military activity in which fronts seldom moved, or moved only a few hundred yards at a time, even after major battles. By contrast, in the years between the German conquest of most of Europe by early 1941 and the Allied invasion of Normandy in mid-1944, there was no major fighting in Nazi-occupied Western Europe. (The land battles then shifted to North Africa and the Soviet Union.)

And of course, the two world wars differed in their aftermaths. The most significant   ⑥
consequence of World War I was that the humiliating and costly war reparations imposed on the defeated Germany by the terms of the 1919 Treaty of Versailles made possible the rise of Hitler and thus led directly to World War II. In contrast, after the end of the Second World War in 1945, the Allies helped rebuild West Germany (the portion of a divided Germany which it controlled), transformed the new country into a democracy, and helped make it one of the most thriving economies of the world. But perhaps the most significant difference in the aftermath of each war involved Russia. That country, in a considerably weakened state, pulled out of World War I a year before hostilities ended so that it could consolidate its 1917 Revolution. Russia then withdrew into itself and took no significant part in European affairs until the Nazi invasion of the Soviet Union in 1941. In contrast, it was the Red Army in World War II that was most responsible for the crushing defeat of Germany. In recognition of its efforts and of its enormous sacrifices, the Allies allowed the Soviet Union to take control of the countries of Eastern Europe after the war, leading to fifty years of totalitarian rule--and the Cold War.

While the two world wars that devastated much of Europe were similar in that, at least   ⑦
according to some historians, they were the same war interrupted by two decades, and similar in that combatants killed more efficiently than armies throughout history ever had, the differences between the wars were significant. In terms of the physical impact of the fighting, the impact on civilians, the action on the battlefield at mid-war, and the aftermaths, World Wars I and II differed in ways that matter to us decades later. Recently, the wars in Iraq, Afghanistan, and Bosnia have involved an alliance of nations pitted against single nations; but we have not seen, since the two world wars, grand alliances moving vast armies across continents. The destruction implied by such action is almost unthinkable today. Warfare is changing, and "stateless" combatants like Hamas and Al Qaeda wreak destruction of their own. But we may never see, one hopes, the devastation that follows when multiple nations on opposing sides of a conflict throw millions of soldiers--and civilians--into harm's way.

The Strategy of the Exam Response

The general strategy of this argument is an organization by *criteria*. The writer argues that although the two world wars exhibited some similarities, the differences between the two conflicts were more significant. Note that the writer's thesis doesn't merely establish these significant differences; it enumerates them in a way that anticipates both the content and the structure of the response to follow.

In argument terms, the *claim* the writer makes is the conclusion that the two global conflicts were significantly different, if superficially similar. The *assumption* is that careful attention to the impact of the wars upon cities and civilian populations and to the consequences of the Allied victories is the key to understanding the differences between them. The *support* comes in the form of historical facts regarding the levels of casualties, the scope of destruction, the theaters of conflict, the events following the conclusions of the wars, and so on.

- **Paragraph 1:** The writer begins by commenting on the unprecedented level of destruction of World Wars I and II and concludes with the thesis summarizing the key similarities and differences.

- **Paragraph 2:** The writer summarizes the key similarities in the two wars: the wars' causes, their combatants, their global scope, the level of destructiveness made possible by modern weaponry.

- **Paragraph 3:** The writer discusses the first of the key differences: the fact that the battlegrounds of World War I were largely rural, but in World War II cities were targeted and destroyed.

- **Paragraph 4:** The writer discusses the second of the key differences: the impact on civilians. In World War I, civilians were generally spared from the direct effects of combat; in World War II, civilians were targeted by the Nazis for systematic displacement and destruction.

- **Paragraph 5:** The writer discusses the third key difference: Combat operations during the middle phase of World War I were characterized by static trench warfare. During World War II, in contrast, there were no major combat operations in Nazi-occupied Western Europe during the middle phase of the conflict.

- **Paragraph 6:** The writer focuses on the fourth key difference: the aftermath of the two wars. After World War I, the victors imposed harsh conditions on a defeated Germany, leading to the rise of Hitler and the Second World War. After World War II, the Allies helped Germany rebuild and thrive. However, the Soviet victory in 1945 led to its postwar domination of Eastern Europe.

- **Paragraph 7:** In the conclusion, the writer sums up the key similarities and differences just covered and makes additional comments about the course of more recent wars since World War II. In this way, the writer responds to the questions posed at the end of the assignment: "What have you learned? What can your comparative analysis teach us?"

SUMMARY OF SYNTHESIS CHAPTERS

In this chapter and in Chapter 4 we've considered three main types of synthesis: the *explanatory synthesis*, the *argument synthesis*, and the *comparison-and-contrast synthesis*. Although for ease of comprehension we've placed them in separate categories, these types are not mutually exclusive. Both explanatory syntheses and argument syntheses often involve elements of one another, and comparison-and-contrast syntheses can fall into either of the other two categories. Which approach you choose will depend on your *purpose* and the method that you decide is best suited to achieve this purpose.

If your main purpose is to help your audience understand a particular subject, and in particular to help them understand the essential elements or significance of this subject, then you will be composing an explanatory synthesis. If your main purpose, on the other hand, is to persuade your audience to agree with your viewpoint on a subject, or to change their minds, or to decide on a particular course of action, then you will be composing an argument synthesis. If one effective technique of making your case is to establish similarities or differences between your subject and another one, then you will compose a comparison-and-contrast synthesis—which may well be just *part* of a larger synthesis.

In planning and drafting these syntheses, you can draw on a variety of strategies: supporting your claims by summarizing, paraphrasing, and quoting from your sources; using appeals to *logos*, *pathos*, and *ethos*; and choosing from among strategies such as climactic or conventional order, counterargument, and concession the approach that will best help you to achieve your purpose.

We turn, now, to analysis, which is another important strategy for academic thinking and writing. Chapter 6, Analysis, will introduce you to a strategy that, like synthesis, draws upon all the strategies you've been practicing as you move through *Writing and Reading Across the Curriculum*.

Chapter

Analysis

WHAT IS AN ANALYSIS?

An *analysis* is an argument in which you study the parts of something to understand how it works, what it means, or why it might be significant. The writer of an analysis uses an analytical tool: a *principle* or *definition* on the basis of which an object, an event, or a behavior can be divided into parts and examined. Here are excerpts from two analyses of the movie version of L. Frank Baum's *The Wizard of Oz:*

> At the dawn of adolescence, the very time she should start to distance herself from Aunt Em and Uncle Henry, the surrogate parents who raised her on their Kansas farm, Dorothy Gale experiences a hurtful reawakening of her fear that these loved ones will be rudely ripped from her, especially her Aunt (Em—M for Mother!).*

> [*The Wizard of Oz*] was originally written as a political allegory about grassroots protest. It may seem harder to believe than Emerald City, but the Tin Woodsman is the industrial worker, the Scarecrow [is] the struggling farmer, and the Wizard is the president, who is powerful only as long as he succeeds in deceiving the people.†

As these paragraphs suggest, what you discover through an analysis depends entirely on the principle or definition you use to make your insights. Is *The Wizard of Oz* the story of a girl's psychological development, or is it a story about politics? The answer is *both*. In the first example, the psychiatrist Harvey Greenberg applies the principles of his profession and, not surprisingly, sees *The Wizard of Oz* in psychological terms. In the second example, a newspaper reporter applies the political theories of Karl Marx and, again not surprisingly, discovers a story about politics.

Different as they are, these analyses share an important quality: Each is the result of a specific principle or definition used as a tool to divide an object into parts in order to see what it means and how it works. The writer's choice of analytical tool

---

*Harvey Greenberg, *The Movies on Your Mind* (New York: Dutton, 1975).
†Peter Dreier, "The Politics of Oz," *San Francisco Chronicle*, 24 Sept. 1989.

simultaneously creates and limits the possibilities for analysis. Thus, working with the principles of Freud, Harvey Greenberg sees *The Wizard of Oz* in psychological, not political, terms; working with the theories of Karl Marx, Peter Dreier understands the movie in terms of the economic relationships among characters. It's as if the writer of an analysis who adopts one analytical tool puts on a pair of glasses and sees an object in a specific way. Another writer, using a different tool (and a different pair of glasses), sees the object differently.

You might protest: Are there as many analyses of *The Wizard of Oz* as there are people to read the book or to see the movie? Yes, or at least as many analyses as there are analytical tools. This does not mean that all analyses are equally valid or useful. Each writer must convince the reader. In creating an essay of analysis, the writer must organize a series of related insights, using the analytical tool to

WHERE DO WE FIND WRITTEN ANALYSES?

Here are just a few of the types of writing that involve analysis:

Academic Writing

- **Experimental and lab reports** analyze the meaning or implications of the study results in the Discussion section.
- **Research papers** analyze information in sources or apply theories to material being reported.
- **Process analyses** break down the steps or stages involved in completing a process.
- **Literary analyses** examine characterization, plot, imagery, or other elements in works of literature.
- **Essay exams** demonstrate understanding of course material by analyzing data using course concepts.

Workplace Writing

- **Grant proposals** analyze the issues you seek funding for in order to address them.
- **Reviews of the arts** employ dramatic or literary analysis to assess artistic works.
- **Business plans** break down and analyze capital outlays, expenditures, profits, materials, and the like.
- **Medical charts** record analytical thinking and writing in relation to patient symptoms and possible options.
- **Legal briefs** break down and analyze facts of cases and elements of legal precedents and apply legal rulings and precedents to new situations.
- **Case studies** describe and analyze the particulars of a specific medical, social service, advertising, or business case.

examine first one part and then another of the object being studied. To read Harvey Greenberg's essay on *The Wizard of Oz* is to find paragraph after paragraph of related insights—first about Aunt Em, then the Wicked Witch, then Toto, and then the Wizard. All these insights point to Greenberg's single conclusion: that "Dorothy's 'trip' is a marvelous metaphor for the psychological journey every adolescent must make." Without Greenberg's analysis, we would probably not have thought about the movie as a psychological journey. This is precisely the power of an analysis: its ability to reveal objects or events in ways we would not otherwise have considered.

The writer's challenge is to convince readers that (1) the analytical tool being applied is legitimate and well matched to the object being studied; and (2) the analytical tool is being used systematically to divide the object into parts and to make a coherent, meaningful statement about these parts and the object as a whole.

When *Your* Perspective Guides the Analysis

In some cases a writer's analysis of a phenomenon or a work of art may not result from anything as structured as a principle or a definition. It may follow from the writer's cultural or personal outlook, perspective, or interests. Imagine reading a story or observing the lines of a new building and being asked to analyze it—not based on someone else's definition or principle, but on your own. Analyses in this case continue to probe the parts of things to understand how they work and what they mean. And they continue to be carefully structured, examining one part of a phenomenon at a time. The essential purpose of the analysis, to *reveal*, remains unchanged. This goal distinguishes the analysis from the critique, whose main purpose is to *evaluate* and *assess validity*.

Consider this passage from an op-ed article by Terri Martin Hekker, "The Satisfactions of Housewifery and Motherhood in an Age of 'Do Your Own Thing,'" which appeared in the *New York Times* in 1977:

> I come from a long line of women...who never knew they were unfulfilled. I can't testify that they were happy, but they *were* cheerful. And if they lacked "meaningful relationships," they cherished relations who meant something. They took pride in a clean, comfortable home and satisfaction in serving a good meal because no one had explained to them that the only work worth doing is that for which you get paid.
>
> They enjoyed rearing their children because no one ever told them that little children belonged in church basements and their mothers belonged somewhere else. They lived, very frugally, on their husbands' paychecks because they didn't realize that it's more important to have a bigger house and a second car than it is to rear your own children. And they were so incredibly ignorant that they died never suspecting they'd been failures.
>
> That won't hold true for me. I don't yet perceive myself as a failure, but it's not for want of being told I am.

The other day, years of condescension prompted me to fib in order to test a theory. At a party where most of the guests were business associates of my husband, a Ms. Putdown asked me who I was. I told her I was Jack Hekker's wife. That had a galvanizing effect on her. She took my hand and asked if that was all I thought of myself—just someone's wife? I wasn't going to let her in on the five children but when she persisted I mentioned them but told her that they weren't mine, that they belonged to my dead sister. And then I basked in the glow of her warm approval.

It's an absolute truth that whereas you are considered ignorant to stay home to rear *your* children, it is quite heroic to do so for someone else's children. Being a housekeeper is acceptable (even to the Social Security office) as long as it's not *your* house you're keeping. And treating a husband with attentive devotion is altogether correct as long as he's not *your* husband.

Sometimes I feel like Alice in Wonderland. But lately, mostly, I feel like an endangered species.

Hekker's view of the importance of what she calls "housewifery"—the role of the traditional American wife and mother—derives from her own personal standards and ideals, which themselves derive from a cultural perspective that she admits is no longer in fashion in the late 1970s. This cultural and personal perspective places great value on such aspects of marriage and motherhood as having "a clean, comfortable home," the satisfaction of "serving a good meal," and the enjoyment of rearing "your own children," and it places less value on "having a big house and a second car." She refuses to consider herself a failure (as she believes others do) because she takes pride in identifying herself as her husband's wife. Hekker's analysis of her own situation, in contrast to the situation of the more "liberated" working wife, throws a revealing light on the cultural conflicts of that period regarding marriage.

Almost thirty years after she wrote this op-ed article, Hekker's perspective had dramatically shifted. Her shattering experiences in the wake of her unexpected divorce had changed her view—and as a result, her analysis—of the status, value, and prospects of the traditional wife:

> Like most loyal wives of our generation, we'd contemplated eventual widowhood but never thought we'd end up divorced. And "divorced" doesn't begin to describe the pain of this process. "Canceled" is more like it.... If I had it to do over again, I'd still marry the man I married and have my children: they are my treasure and a powerful support system for me and for one another. But I would have used the years after my youngest started school to further my education. I could have amassed two doctorates using the time and energy I gave myself to charitable and community causes and been better able to support myself.

Hekker's new analysis of the role of the traditional wife (published in the *New York Times* in 2006) derives from her changed perspective, based on her own experience and the similar experiences of a number of her divorced friends. Notice, again, that the analysis is meant to *reveal*. (The complete versions of these two op-eds by Terri Martin Hekker appear in Chapter 9, "Marriage and Family in America," pp. 412–417.)

If you find yourself writing an analysis guided by your own insights, not by someone else's, then you owe your reader a clear explanation of your guiding principles and the definitions by which you will probe the subject under study. Continue using the Guidelines for Writing Analyses (see p. 196), modifying this advice as you think fit to accommodate your own personal outlook, perspective, or interests. Above all, remember to structure your analysis with care. Proceed systematically and emerge with a clear statement about what the subject means, how it works, or why it might be significant.

DEMONSTRATION: ANALYSIS

Two examples of analyses follow. The first was written by a professional writer; the second was written by a student in response to an assignment in his sociology class. Each analysis illustrates the two defining features of analysis just discussed: a statement of an analytical principle or definition, and the use of that principle or definition in closely examining an object, behavior, or event. As you read, try to identify these features. An exercise with questions for discussion follows each example.

THE PLUG-IN DRUG

Marie Winn

This analysis of television viewing as an addictive behavior appeared originally in Marie Winn's book *The Plug-In Drug: Television, Computers, and Family Life (2002).* A writer and media critic, Winn has been interested in the effects of television on both individuals and the larger culture. In this passage, she carefully defines the term addiction and then applies it systematically to the behavior under study.

The word "addiction" is often used loosely and wryly in conversation. People will refer to themselves as "mystery-book addicts" or "cookie addicts." E. B. White wrote of his annual surge of interest in gardening: "We are hooked and are making an attempt to kick the habit." Yet nobody really believes that reading mysteries or ordering seeds by catalogue is serious enough to be compared with addictions to heroin or alcohol. In these cases the word "addiction" is used jokingly to denote a tendency to overindulge in some pleasurable activity.

People often refer to being "hooked on TV." Does this, too, fall into the light-hearted category of cookie eating and other pleasures that people pursue with unusual intensity? Or is there a kind of television viewing that falls into the more serious category of destructive addiction?

Not unlike drugs or alcohol, the television experience allows the participant to blot out the real world and enter into a pleasurable and passive mental state. To be sure, other experiences, notably reading, also provide a temporary respite from reality. But it's much easier to stop reading and return to reality than to stop watching television. The entry into another world offered by reading includes an easily accessible return ticket. The entry via television does not. In this way television viewing, for those vulnerable to addiction, is more like drinking or taking drugs—once you start it's hard to stop.

Just as alcoholics are only vaguely aware of their addiction, feeling that they control their drinking more than they really do ("I can cut it out any time I want—I just like to have three or four drinks before dinner"), many people overestimate their control over television watching. Even as they put off other activities to spend hour after hour watching television, they feel they could easily resume living in a different, less passive style. But somehow or other while the television set is present in their homes, it just stays on. With television's easy gratifications available, those other activities seem to take too much effort.

5   A heavy viewer (a college English instructor) observes:

> I find television almost irresistible. When the set is on, I cannot ignore it. I can't turn it off. I feel sapped, will-less, enervated. As I reach out to turn off the set, the strength goes out of my arms. So I sit there for hours and hours.

Self-confessed television addicts often feel they "ought" to do other things—but the fact that they don't read and don't plant their garden or sew or crochet or play games or have conversations means that those activities are no longer as desirable as television viewing. In a way, the lives of heavy viewers are as unbalanced by their television "habit" as drug addicts' or alcoholics' lives. They are living in a holding pattern, as it were, passing up the activities that lead to growth or development or a sense of accomplishment. This is one reason people talk about their television viewing so ruefully, so apologetically. They are aware that it is an unproductive experience, that by any human measure almost any other endeavor is more worthwhile.

It is the adverse effect of television viewing on the lives of so many people that makes it feel like a serious addiction. The television habit distorts the sense of time. It renders other experiences vague and curiously unreal while taking on a greater reality for itself. It weakens relationships by reducing and sometimes eliminating normal opportunities for talking, for communicating.

And yet television does not satisfy, else why would the viewer continue to watch hour after hour, day after day? "The measure of health," wrote the psychiatrist Lawrence Kubie, "is flexibility...and especially the freedom to cease when sated." But heavy television viewers can never be sated with their television experiences. These do not provide the true nourishment that satiation requires, and thus they find that they cannot stop watching.

Exercise 6.1

Reading Critically: Winn

In an analysis, an author first presents the analytical principle in full and then systematically applies parts of the principle to the object or phenomenon under study. In her brief analysis of television viewing, Marie Winn pursues an alternative, though equally effective, strategy by *distributing* parts of her analytical principle across the essay. Locate where Winn defines key elements of addiction. Locate where she uses each element as an analytical lens to examine television viewing as a form of addiction.

What function does paragraph 4 play in the analysis?

In the first two paragraphs, how does Winn create a funnel-like effect that draws readers into the heart of her analysis?

Recall a few television programs that genuinely moved you, educated you, humored you, or stirred you to worthwhile reflection or action. To what extent does Winn's analysis describe your positive experiences as a television viewer? (Consider how Winn might argue that from within an addicted state, a person may feel "humored, moved or educated" but is in fact—from a sober outsider's point of view—deluded.) If Winn's analysis of television viewing as an addiction does *not* account for your experience, does it follow that her analysis is flawed? Explain.

Edward Peselman wrote the following paper as a first-semester sophomore, in response to this assignment from his English professor:

> Read Chapter 3, "The Paradoxes of Power," in Randall Collins's *Sociological Insight: An Introduction to Non-Obvious Sociology* (2nd ed., 1992). Use any of Collins's observations to examine the sociology of power in a group with which you are familiar. Write for readers much like yourself: freshmen or sophomores who have taken one course in sociology. Your object in this paper is to use Collins as a way of learning something "nonobvious" about a group to which you belong or have belonged.

> Note: This paper is formatted in MLA style.

MODEL ANALYSIS

Peselman 1

Edward Peselman

Professor Sladko

Everyday Life Reconsidered

Murray State University

23 March 2010

The Coming Apart of a Dorm Society

(1)   During my first year of college, I lived in a dormitory, like most freshmen on campus. We inhabitants of the dorm came from different cultural and economic backgrounds. Not surprisingly, we brought with us many of the traits found in people outside of college. Like many on the outside, we in the dorm sought personal power at the expense of others. The gaining and maintaining of power can be an ugly business, and I saw people hurt and in

Peselman 2

turn hurt others all for the sake of securing a place in the dorm's prized social order. Not until one of us challenged that order did I realize how fragile it was.

Randall Collins, a sociologist at the University of California, Riverside, defines the exercise of power as the attempt "to make something happen in society" (61). A society can be understood as something as large and complex as "American society"; something more sharply defined, such as a corporate or organizational society; or something smaller still—a dorm society like my own, consisting of six 18-year-old men who lived at one end of a dormitory floor in an all-male dorm.

In my freshman year, my society was a tiny but distinctive social group in which people exercised power. I lived with two roommates, Dozer and Reggie. Dozer was an emotionally unstable, excitable individual who vented his energy through anger. His insecurity and moodiness contributed to his difficulty in making friends. Reggie was a friendly, happy-go-lucky sort who seldom displayed emotions other than contentedness. He was shy when encountering new people, but when placed in a socially comfortable situation he would talk for hours.

Eric and Marc lived across the hall from us and therefore spent a considerable amount of time in our room. Eric could be cynical and was often blunt: He seldom hesitated when sharing his frank and sometimes unflattering opinions. He commanded a grudging respect in the dorm. Marc could be very moody and, sometimes, was violent. His temper and stubborn streak made him particularly susceptible to conflict. The final member of our miniature society was Benjamin, cheerful yet insecure. Benjamin had certain characteristics which many considered effeminate, and he was often teased about his sexuality—which in turn made him insecure. He was naturally friendly but, because of the abuse he took, he largely kept to himself. He would join us occasionally for a pizza or late-night television.

Together, we formed an independent social structure. Going out to parties together, playing cards, watching television, playing ball: These were the activities through which we got to know each other and through which we established the basic pecking order of our community. Much like a colony of baboons, we established a hierarchy based on power relationships. According to Collins, what a powerful person wishes to happen must be achieved by controlling others. Collins's observation can help to define who had how much power in our social group. In the dorm, Marc and Eric clearly had the most power. Everyone feared them and agreed to do pretty much what they wanted. Through violent words or threats of violence, they got their way. I was next in line: I wouldn't dare to manipulate Marc or Eric, but the others I could manage through occasional quips. Reggie, then Dozer, and finally Benjamin.

(6)   Up and down the pecking order, we exercised control through macho taunts and challenges. Collins writes that "individuals who manage to be powerful and get their own way must do so by going along with the laws of social organization, not by contradicting them" (61). Until mid-year, our dorm motto could have read: "You win through rudeness and intimidation." Eric gained power with his frequent and brutal assessments of everyone's behavior. Marc gained power with his temper—which, when lost, made everyone run for cover. Those who were not rude and intimidating drifted to the bottom of our social world. Reggie was quiet and unemotional, which allowed us to take advantage of him because we knew he would back down if pressed in an argument. Yet Reggie understood that on a "power scale" he stood above Dozer and often shared in the group's tactics to get Dozer's food (his parents were forever sending him care packages). Dozer, in turn, seldom missed opportunities to take swipes at Benjamin, with references to his sexuality. From the very first week of school, Benjamin could never—and never wanted to—compete against Eric's bluntness or Marc's temper. Still, Benjamin hung out with us. He lived in our corner of the dorm, and he wanted to be friendly. But everyone, including Benjamin, understood that he occupied the lowest spot in the order.

(7)   That is, until he left mid-year. According to Collins, "any social arrangement works because people avoid questioning it most of the time" (74). The inverse of this principle is as follows: When a social arrangement is questioned, that arrangement can fall apart. The more fragile the arrangement (the flimsier the values on which it is based), the more quickly it will crumble. For the entire first semester, no one questioned our rude, macho rules, and because of them we pigeon-holed Benjamin as a wimp. In our dorm society, gentle men had no power. To say the least, ours was not a compassionate community. From a distance of one year, I am shocked to have been a member of it. Nonetheless, we had created a mini-society that somehow served our needs.

(8)   At the beginning of the second semester, we found Benjamin packing up his room. Marc, who was walking down the hall, stopped by and said something like: "Hey buddy, the kitchen get too hot for you?" I was there, and I saw Benjamin turn around and say: "Do you practice at being such a _____, or does it come naturally? I've never met anybody who felt so good about making other people feel lousy. You'd better get yourself a job in the army or in the prison system, because no one else is going to put up with your _____." Marc said something in a raised voice. I stepped between them, and Benjamin said: "Get out." I was cheering.

Benjamin moved into an off-campus apartment with his girlfriend. This astonished us,   ⑨
first because of his effeminate manner (we didn't know he had a girlfriend) and second
because none of the rest of us had been seeing girls much (though we talked about it
constantly). Here was Benjamin, the gentlest among us, and he blew a hole in our macho
society. Our social order never really recovered, which suggests its flimsy values. People in
the dorm mostly went their own ways during the second semester. I'm not surprised,
and I was more than a little grateful. Like most people in the dorm, save for Eric and
Marc, I both got my lumps and I gave them, and I never felt good about either. Like
Benjamin, I wanted to fit in with my new social surroundings. Unlike him, I didn't have the
courage to challenge the unfairness of what I saw.

By chance, six of us were thrown together into a dorm and were expected, on the basis   ⑩
of proximity alone, to develop a friendship. What we did was sink to the lowest possible
denominator. Lacking any real basis for friendship, we allowed the forceful, macho
personalities of Marc and Eric to set the rules, which for one semester we all subscribed
to—even those who suffered.

The macho rudeness couldn't last, and I'm glad it was Benjamin who brought us down. By   ⑪
leaving, he showed a different and a superior kind of power. I doubt he was reading Randall
Collins at the time, but he somehow had come to Collins's same insight: As long as he played
by the rules of our group, he suffered because those rules placed him far down in the dorm's
pecking order. Even by participating in pleasant activities, like going out for pizza, Benjamin
supported a social system that ridiculed him. Some systems are so oppressive and small-minded
that they can't be changed from the inside. They've got to be torn down. Benjamin had to
move, and in moving he made me (at least) question the basis of my dorm friendships.

Works Cited

Collins, Randall. *Sociological Insight: An Introduction to Non-obvious Sociology.* 2nd ed.
    New York: Oxford UP, 1992. Print.

Reading Critically: Peselman

What is the function of paragraph 1? Though Peselman does not use the word *sociology*, what signals does he give that this will be a paper that examines the social interactions of a group? Peselman introduces Collins in paragraph 2. Why? What does Peselman accomplish in paragraphs 3–4? How does his use of Collins in paragraph 5 logically follow the presentation in paragraphs 3–4? The actual analysis in this paper takes place in paragraphs 5–11. Point to where Peselman draws on the work of Randall Collins, and explain how he uses Collins to gain insight into dorm life.

HOW TO WRITE ANALYSES

Consider Your Purpose

Whether you are assigned a topic to write on or are left to your own devices, you inevitably face this question: What is my idea? Like every paper, an analysis has at its heart an idea you want to convey. For Edward Peselman, it was the idea that a social order based on flimsy values is not strong enough to sustain a direct challenge to its power and thus will fall apart eventually. From beginning to end, Peselman advances this one idea: first, by introducing readers to the dorm society he will analyze; next, by introducing principles of analysis (from Randall Collins); and finally, by examining his dorm relationships in light of those principles. The entire set of analytical insights coheres as a paper because the insights are *related* and point to Peselman's single idea.

Peselman's paper offers a good example of the personal uses to which analysis can be put. Notice that he gravitates toward events in his life that confuse him and about which he wants some clarity. Such topics can be especially fruitful for analysis because you know the particulars well and can provide readers with details; you view the topic with some puzzlement; and, through the application of your analytical tool, you may come to understand it. When you select topics to analyze from your own experience, you provide yourself with a motivation to write and learn. When you are motivated in this way, you spark the interest of readers.

Using Randall Collins as a guide, Edward Peselman returns again and again to the events of his freshman year in the dormitory. We sense that Peselman himself wants to understand what happened in that dorm. He writes, "I saw people hurt and in turn hurt others all for the sake of securing a place in the dorm's prized social order." Peselman does not approve of what happened, and the analysis he launches is meant to help him understand.

Locate an Analytical Principle

When you are given an assignment that asks for analysis, use two specific reading strategies to identify principles and definitions in source materials.

- **Look for a sentence that makes a general statement about the way something works.** The statement may strike you as a rule or a law. The line that Edward Peselman quotes from Randall Collins has this quality: "[A]ny social arrangement works because people avoid questioning it most of the time." Such statements are generalizations—conclusions to sometimes complicated and extensive arguments. You can use these conclusions to guide your own analyses as long as you are aware that for some audiences you will need to re-create and defend the arguments that resulted in these conclusions.

- **Look for statements that take this form: X can be defined as (or X consists of) A, B, and C.** The specific elements of the definition—A, B, and C—are what you use to identify and analyze parts of the object being studied. You've seen an example of this approach in Marie Winn's multipart definition of addiction, which she uses to analyze television viewing. As a reader looking for definitions suitable for conducting an analysis, you might come across Winn's definition of addiction and then use it for your own purposes, perhaps to analyze the playing of video games as an addiction.

Essential to any analysis is the validity of the principle or definition being applied, the analytical tool. Make yourself aware, as both writer and reader, of a tool's strengths and limitations. Pose these questions of the analytical principles and definitions you use: Are they accurate? Are they well accepted? Do *you* accept them? What are the arguments against them? What are their limitations? Since every principle or definition used in an analysis is the end product of an argument, you are entitled—even obligated—to challenge it. If the analytical tool is flawed, the analysis that follows from it will be flawed.

A page from Randall Collins's *Sociological Insight* follows; Edward Peselman uses a key sentence from this extract as an analytical tool in his essay on power relations in his dorm (see p. 190). Notice that Peselman underlines the sentence he will use in his analysis.

1.   Try this experiment some time. When you are talking to someone, make them explain everything they say that isn't completely clear. The result, you will discover, is a series of uninterrupted interruptions:

   A: Hi, how are you doing?
   B: What do you mean when you say "how"?
   A: You know. What's happening with you?
   B: What do you mean, "happening"?
   A: Happening, you know, what's going on.
   B: I'm sorry. Could you explain what you mean by "what"?
   A: What do you mean, what do I mean? Do you want to talk to me or not?

2.   It is obvious that this sort of questioning could go on endlessly, at any rate if the listener doesn't get very angry and punch you in the mouth. But it illustrates two important points. First, virtually everything can be called into question. We are able to get along with other people not because everything is clearly spelled out, but because we are willing to take most

things people say without explanation. Harold Garfinkel, who actually performed this sort of experiment, points out that there is an infinite regress of assumptions that go into any act of social communication. Moreover, some expressions are simply not explainable in words at all. A word like "you," or "here," or "now" is what Garfinkel calls "indexical." You have to know what it means already; it can't be explained.

3.   "What do you mean by 'you'?"

4.   "I mean *you, you!*" About all that can be done here is point your finger.

5.   The second point is that people get mad when they are pressed to explain things that they ordinarily take for granted. This is because they very quickly see that explanations could go on forever and the questions will never be answered. If you really demanded a full explanation of everything you hear, you could stop the conversation from ever getting past its first sentence. The real significance of this for a sociological understanding of the way the world is put together is not the anger, however. It is the fact that people try to avoid these sorts of situations. They tacitly recognize that we have to avoid these endless lines of questioning. Sometimes small children will start asking an endless series of "whys," but adults discourage this.

6.   In sum, <u>any social arrangement works because people avoid questioning it most of the time.</u> That does not mean that people do not get into arguments or disputes about just what ought to be done from time to time. But to have a dispute already implies there is a considerable area of agreement. An office manager may dispute with a clerk over just how to take care of some business letter, but they at any rate know more or less what they are disputing about. They do not get off into a...series of questions over just what is meant by everything that is said. You could very quickly dissolve the organization into nothingness if you followed that route: there would be no communication at all, even about what the disagreement is over.

7.   Social organization is possible because people maintain a certain level of focus. If they focus on one thing, even if only to disagree about it, they are taking many other things for granted, thereby reinforcing their social reality.*

The statement that Peselman has underlined—"any social arrangement works because people avoid questioning it most of the time"—is the end result of an argument that takes Collins several paragraphs to develop. Peselman agrees with the conclusion and uses it in paragraph 7 of his analysis. Observe that for his own purposes Peselman does *not* reconstruct Collins's argument. He selects *only* Collins's conclusion and then imports that into his analysis, which concerns an entirely different subject. Once he identifies in Collins a principle he can use in his analysis, he converts the principle into questions

---

*Randall Collins, *Sociological Insight: An Introduction to Non–obvious Sociology,* 2nd ed. (New York: Oxford UP, 1992) 73–74.

that he then directs to his topic, life in his freshman dorm. Two questions follow directly from Collins's insight:

1. What was the social arrangement in the dorm?
2. How was this social arrangement questioned?

Peselman clearly defines his dormitory's social arrangement in paragraphs 3–6 (with the help of another principle borrowed from Collins). Beginning with paragraph 7, he explores how one member of his dorm questioned that arrangement:

> That is, until he left mid-year. According to Collins, "any social arrangement works because people avoid questioning it most of the time" (p. 74). The inverse of this principle is as follows: When a social arrangement is questioned, that arrangement can fall apart. The more fragile the arrangement (the flimsier the values on which it is based), the more quickly it will crumble. For the entire first semester, no one questioned our rude, macho rules, and because of them we pigeon-holed Benjamin as a wimp. In our dorm society, gentle men had no power. To say the least, ours was not a compassionate community. From a distance of one year, I am shocked to have been a member of it. Nonetheless, we had created a mini-society that somehow served our needs.

Formulate a Thesis

An analysis is a two-part argument. The first part states and establishes the writer's agreement with a certain principle or definition.

Part One of the Argument

This first part of the argument essentially takes this form:

> **Claim #1:** Principle X (or definition X) is valuable.

Principle X can be a theory as encompassing and abstract as the statement that *myths are the enemy of truth*. Principle X can be as modest as the definition of a term such as *addiction* or *comfort*. As you move from one subject area to another, the principles and definitions you use for analysis will change, as these assignments illustrate:

Sociology: *Write a paper in which you place yourself in American society by locating both your absolute position and relative rank on each single criterion of social stratification used by Lenski & Lenski. For each criterion, state whether you have attained your social position by yourself or if you have "inherited" that status from your parents.*

Literature: *Apply principles of Jungian psychology to Hawthorne's "Young Goodman Brown." In your reading of the story, apply Jung's principles of the* shadow, persona, *and* anima.

Physics: *Use Newton's second law (F = ma) to analyze the acceleration of a fixed pulley, from which two weights hang:* m_1 *(.45 kg) and* m_2 *(.90 kg). Explain in a paragraph the principle of Newton's law and your method of applying it to solve the* *problem. Assume your reader is not comfortable with mathematical explanations: do not use equations in your paragraph.*

Finance: *Using Guidford C. Babcock's "Concept of Sustainable Growth"* [Financial Analysis 26 (May–June 1970): 108–14], *analyze the stock price appreciation of the XYZ Corporation, figures for which are attached.*

The analytical tools to be applied in these assignments must be appropriate to the discipline. Writing in response to the sociology assignment, you would use sociological principles developed by Lenski and Lenski. In your literature class, you would use principles of Jungian psychology; in physics, Newton's second law; and in finance, a particular writer's concept of "sustainable growth." But whatever discipline you are working in, the first part of your analysis will clearly state which (and whose) principles and definitions you are applying. For audiences unfamiliar with these principles, you will need to explain them; if you anticipate objections, you will need to argue that they are legitimate principles capable of helping you conduct the analysis.

GUIDELINES FOR WRITING ANALYSES

Unless you are asked to follow a specialized format, especially in the sciences or the social sciences, you can present your analysis as a paper by following the guidelines below. As you move from one class to another, from discipline to discipline, the principles and definitions you use as the basis for your analyses will change, but the following basic components of analysis will remain the same.

- *Create a context for your analysis.* Introduce and summarize for readers the object, event, or behavior to be analyzed. Present a strong case about why an analysis is needed: Give yourself a motivation to write, and give readers a motivation to read. Consider setting out a problem, puzzle, or question to be investigated.
- *Introduce and summarize the key definition or principle that will form the basis of your analysis.* Plan to devote an early part of your analysis to arguing for the validity of this principle or definition if your audience is not likely to understand it or if they are likely to think that the principle or definition is not valuable.
- *Analyze your topic.* Systematically apply elements of this definition or principle to parts of the activity or object under study. You can do this by posing specific questions, based on your analytic principle or definition, about the object. Discuss what you find part by part (organized perhaps by question), in clearly defined sections of the essay.
- *Conclude by stating clearly what is significant about your analysis.* When considering your analytical paper as a whole, what new or interesting insights have you made concerning the object under study? To what extent has your application of the definition or principle helped you to explain how the object works, what it might mean, or why it is significant?

Part Two of the Argument

In the second part of an analysis, you *apply* specific parts of your principle or definition to the topic at hand. Regardless of how it is worded, this second argument in an analysis can be rephrased to take this form:

> **Claim #2:** By applying principle (or definition) X, we can understand *(topic)* as *(conclusion based on analysis)*.

This is your thesis, the main idea of your analytical paper. Fill in the first blank with the specific object, event, or behavior you are examining. Fill in the second blank with your conclusion about the meaning or significance of this object, based on the insights you made during your analysis. Mary Winn completes the second claim of her analysis this way:

> By applying my multipart definition, we can understand *television viewing* as *an addiction.*

Develop an Organizational Plan

You will benefit enormously in the writing of a first draft if you plan out the logic of your analysis. Turn key elements of your analytical principle or definition into questions and then develop the paragraph-by-paragraph logic of the paper.

Turning Key Elements of a Principle or a Definition into Questions

Prepare for an analysis by phrasing questions based on the definition or principle you are going to apply, and then directing those questions to the activity or object to be studied. The method is straightforward: State as clearly as possible the principle or definition to be applied. Divide the principle or definition into its parts and, using each part, form a question. For example, Marie Winn develops a multipart definition of addiction, each part of which is readily turned into a question that she directs at a specific behavior: television viewing. Her analysis of television viewing can be understood as *responses* to each of her analytical questions. Note that in her brief analysis, Winn does not first define addiction and then analyze television viewing. Rather, *as* she defines aspects of addiction, she analyzes television viewing.

Developing the Paragraph-by-Paragraph Logic of Your Paper

The following paragraph from Edward Peselman's essay illustrates the typical logic of a paragraph in an analytical essay:

> Up and down the pecking order, we exercised control through macho taunts and challenges. Collins writes that "individuals who manage to be powerful and get their own way must do so by going along with the laws of social organization, not by contradicting them" (p. 61). Until mid-year, our dorm motto could have read: "You win through rudeness and intimidation." Eric gained power with his frequent and brutal assessments of everyone's behavior. Marc gained power with his temper—which, when

lost, made everyone run for cover. Those who were not rude and intimidating drifted to the bottom of our social world. Reggie was quiet and unemotional, which allowed us to take advantage of him because we knew he would back down if pressed in an argument. Yet Reggie understood that on a "power scale" he stood above Dozer and often shared in the group's tactics to get Dozer's food (his parents were forever sending him care packages). Dozer, in turn, seldom missed opportunities to take swipes at Benjamin, with references to his sexuality. From the very first week of school, Benjamin could never—and never wanted to—compete against Eric's bluntness or Marc's temper. Still, Benjamin hung out with us. He lived in our corner of the dorm, and he wanted to be friendly. But everyone, including Benjamin, understood that he occupied the lowest spot in the order.

We see in this paragraph the typical logic of analysis:

- *The writer introduces a specific analytical tool.* Peselman quotes a line from Randall Collins:

  "[I]ndividuals who manage to be powerful and get their own way must do so by going along with the laws of social organization, not by contradicting them."

- *The writer applies this analytical tool to the object being examined.* Peselman states his dorm's law of social organization:

  Until mid-year, our dorm motto could have read: "You win through rudeness and intimidation."

- *The writer uses the tool to identify and then examine the meaning of parts of the object.* Peselman shows how each member (the "parts") of his dorm society conforms to the laws of "social organization":

  Eric gained power with his frequent and brutal assessments of everyone's behavior. Marc gained power with his temper—which, when lost, made everyone run for cover. Those who were not rude and intimidating drifted to the bottom of our social world.

An analytical paper takes shape when a writer creates a series of such paragraphs and then links them with an overall logic. Here is the logical organization of Edward Peselman's paper:

- Paragraph 1: Introduction states a problem—provides a motivation to write and to read.
- Paragraph 2: Randall Collins is introduced—the author whose work will provide principles for analysis.
- Paragraphs 3–4: Background information is provided—the cast of characters in the dorm.
- Paragraphs 5–9: The analysis proceeds—specific parts of dorm life are identified and found significant, using principles from Collins.
- Paragraphs 10–11: Summary and conclusion are provided—the freshman dorm society disintegrates for reasons set out in the analysis. A larger point is made: Some oppressive systems must be torn down.

Draft and Revise Your Analysis

You will usually need at least two drafts to produce a paper that presents your idea clearly. The biggest changes in your paper will typically come between your first and second drafts. No paper that you write, including an analysis, will be complete until you revise and refine your single compelling idea: your analytical conclusion about what the object, event, or behavior being examined means or how it is significant. You revise and refine by evaluating your first draft, bringing to it many of the same questions you pose when evaluating any piece of writing:

- Are the facts accurate?
- Are my opinions supported by evidence?
- Are the opinions of others authoritative?
- Are my assumptions clearly stated?
- Are key terms clearly defined?
- Is the presentation logical?
- Are all parts of the presentation well developed?
- Are significant opposing points of view presented?

Address these same questions to the first draft of your analysis, and you will have solid information to guide your revision.

Write an Analysis, Not a Summary

The most common error made in writing analyses—an error that is *fatal* to the form—is to present readers with a summary only. For analyses to succeed, you must *apply* a principle or definition and reach a conclusion about the object, event, or behavior you are examining. By definition, a summary (see Chapter 1) includes none of your own conclusions. Summary is naturally a part of analysis; you will need to summarize the object or activity being examined and, depending on the audience's needs, summarize the principle or definition being applied. But in an analysis you must take the next step and share insights that suggest the meaning or significance of some object, event, or behavior.

Make Your Analysis Systematic

Analyses should give the reader the sense of a systematic, purposeful examination. Marie Winn's analysis illustrates the point: She sets out specific elements of addictive behavior in separate paragraphs and then uses each, within its paragraph, to analyze television viewing. Winn is systematic in her method, and we are never in doubt about her purpose.

Imagine another analysis in which a writer lays out four elements of a definition and then applies only two, without explaining the logic for omitting the others. Or imagine an analysis in which the writer offers a principle for analysis but directs it to only a half or a third of the object being discussed, without providing a rationale for doing so. In both cases the writer would be failing to deliver on a promise basic to analyses: Once a principle or definition is presented, it should be thoroughly and systematically applied.

Answer the "So What?" Question

An analysis should make readers *want* to read. It should give readers a sense of getting to the heart of the matter, that what is important in the object or activity under analysis is being laid bare and discussed in revealing ways. If when rereading the first draft of your analysis, you cannot imagine readers saying, "I never thought of _____ this way," then something may be seriously wrong. Reread closely to determine why the paper might leave readers flat and exhausted, as opposed to feeling that they have gained new and important insights. Closely reexamine your own motivations for writing. Have *you* learned anything significant through the analysis? If not, neither will readers, and they will turn away. If you have gained important insights through your analysis, communicate them clearly. At some point, pull together your related insights and say, in effect, "Here's how it all adds up."

Attribute Sources Appropriately

In an analysis you work with one or two sources and apply insights from them to some object or phenomenon you want to understand more thoroughly. Because you are not synthesizing a great many sources, and because the strength of an analysis derives mostly from *your* application of a principle or definition, the opportunities for not appropriately citing sources are diminished. Take special care to cite and quote, as necessary, the one or two sources you use throughout the analysis.

CRITICAL READING FOR ANALYSIS

- ***Read to get a sense of the whole in relation to its parts.*** Whether you are clarifying for yourself a principle or a definition to be used in an analysis, or you are reading a text that you will analyze, understand how parts function to create the whole. If a definition or principle consists of parts, use them to organize sections of your analysis. If your goal is to analyze a text, be aware of its structure: Note the title and subtitle; identify the main point and subordinate points and where they are located; break the material into sections.
- ***Read to discover relationships within the object being analyzed.*** Watch for patterns. When you find them, be alert—for they create an occasion to analyze, to use a principle or definition as a guide in discussing what the patterns may mean.

  In fiction, a pattern might involve responses of characters to events or to each other, the recurrence of certain words or phrasings, images, themes, or turns of plot (to name a few).

  In poetry, a pattern might involve rhyme schemes, rhythm, imagery, figurative or literal language, and more.

The challenge to you as a reader is first to see a pattern (perhaps using a guiding principle or definition to do so) and then to locate other instances of that pattern. Reading carefully in this way prepares you to conduct an analysis.

ANALYSIS: A TOOL FOR UNDERSTANDING

As this chapter has demonstrated, analysis involves applying principles as a way to probe and understand. With incisive principles guiding your analysis, you will be able to pose questions, observe patterns and relationships, and derive meaning. Do not forget that this meaning will be one of several possible meanings. Someone else, or even you, using different analytical tools, could observe the same phenomena and arrive at very different conclusions regarding meaning or significance. We end the chapter, then, as we began it: with the two brief analyses of *The Wizard of Oz*. The conclusions expressed in one look nothing like the conclusions expressed in the other, save for the fact that both seek to interpret the same movie. And yet we can say that both are useful, that both reveal meaning.

> At the dawn of adolescence, the very time she should start to distance herself from Aunt Em and Uncle Henry, the surrogate parents who raised her on their Kansas farm, Dorothy Gale experiences a hurtful reawakening of her fear that these loved ones will be rudely ripped from her, especially her Aunt (Em—M for Mother!).*

> [*The Wizard of Oz*] was originally written as a political allegory about grass-roots protest. It may seem harder to believe than Emerald City, but the Tin Woodsman is the industrial worker, the Scarecrow [is] the struggling farmer, and the Wizard is the president, who is powerful only as long as he succeeds in deceiving the people.†

You have seen in this chapter how it is possible for two writers, analyzing the same object or phenomenon but applying different analytical principles, to reach vastly different conclusions about what the object or phenomenon may mean or why it is significant. *The Wizard of Oz* is both an inquiry into the psychology of adolescence and a political allegory. What else the classic film may be awaits revealing with the systematic application of other analytical tools. The insights you gain as a writer of analyses depend entirely on your choice of tools and the subtlety with which you apply them.

---

*Greenberg, Movies.
†Dreier, "Politics."

Part II

An Anthology of Readings

Chapter 7

The Changing Landscape of Work in the Twenty-first Century

Along with the well-wishes of friends and family, you bring to college many expectations. Some involve your emergence as an independent thinker; others, your emergence as an adult, social being. But perhaps no expectations weigh so heavily as thoughts of future employment and the hope of financial independence—especially in an uncertain economy. On the far end of this journey you have begun in higher education, you will seek meaningful employment. If you already devote long hours to supporting your family or paying your way through school, then you know *exactly* why so many pursue a degree: the conviction that a diploma will ensure a better, more secure job. Learn, apply yourself, and succeed: This has always been the formula for achieving the American dream.

The times, however (to paraphrase Bob Dylan), are changing. In the second half of the twentieth century, the labor market rewarded the educated, conferring on those who attended college an "education premium." Even as the forces of globalization reshaped the American economy and workers began losing manufacturing jobs to competitors offshore in China and India, college-educated workers were generally spared severe disruptions. Today, education no longer promises such protection. The relentless search for cheap labor and plentiful raw materials, together with advances in technology, have opened the information-based service economy to foreign competition. According to economists and other analysts, the American, college-educated workforce will increasingly face the same pressures that decades ago so unsettled the automotive and manufacturing sectors. Employers are already offshoring computer coding, certain types of accounting, and medical consultation (the reading of X-rays, MRIs, CT scans, and such)—services that require extensive training.

Experts predict that more American jobs will be lost to foreign competition and fewer will entail a lifelong commitment between employer and employee (pensions, for instance, are quickly disappearing). What implications will these developments hold for you and your intended career? Will they affect the courses you take, the major (and minors) you choose, the summer jobs and internships you pursue? Could you undertake an analysis *now* that will help you anticipate and avoid major disruptions to your working life tomorrow?

This chapter gives you an opportunity to learn what economists, policy analysts, sociologists, historians, management consultants, statisticians, and educators are forecasting about the world of work in the twenty-first century. Readings in the first section of the chapter set a broad context for your investigations; readings in the second section focus on particular kinds of work. We open with varying definitions of *work* and the related terms *career, profession,* and *vocation.* As you will learn, *work* is not one thing and is not easily defined: Its meaning has shifted over time and across cultures. Next, an expert in international labor studies, Ursula Huws, examines the impact of twin "upheavals" that characterize the new economy: the migration of jobs to workers (think outsourcing on a global scale) and the migration of workers who sometimes travel great distances to find jobs. Sociologist Richard Sennett follows with a startling portrait of a man whose adaptability allowed him to succeed in a corporate culture of downsizing but at the same time "corroded" his character.

Many find reasons for optimism in the new economy. Management consultant Tom Peters sees "gargantuan opportunity" in the emerging business environment and offers six survival skills for success. Writing for a policy think tank, Richard Judy and Carol D'Amico offer a map to the twenty-first century workplace and project winners and losers. In an excerpt from *The World is Flat,* Thomas Friedman advises that if you expect your work life to flourish, you had better make yourself "untouchable." Next, former presidential advisor Alan Blinder traces the migration of service jobs (even those requiring a college degree) away from American shores. He, too, offers a strategy for succeeding in the global economy. Rounding out this first section of the chapter, writers for the *Economist* argue that those worried about the loss of jobs to downsizing and globalization should relax: Through a process of "creative destruction," the economy inevitably adds more jobs than it destroys.

The chapter concludes with five selections that examine either the prospects for work in the coming decades or changes that are already well underway. Any study of work in twenty-first century America should include a close look at the Bureau of Labor Statistics' "Occupational Outlook Handbook" and report on "Tomorrow's Jobs." Next, Jill Casner-Lotto and Linda Barrington present the results of a questionnaire asking 400 employers to assess the readiness of new entrants to the American workforce. Following, the president of Olin College, a new and innovative school of engineering, offers undergraduates advice that extends well beyond the technical disciplines. Two selections on developments in the legal and medical professions follow. Tom McGrath examines what happens when law firms seek ever-higher profits, and Matt Richtel reports on a new development in medicine: Rookie doctors expect a career *and* a life. Read these job-specific selections—even those of little or no present interest to you. Your current plans may change; and even if they do not, the writers raise issues almost certain to touch on your working life, whatever your interests.

As you search for employment now and in the future, the selections in this chapter will inform your efforts at a doubly uncertain time—when the economy is struggling and when the very foundations of work itself are shifting.

Definitions: Work, Career, Profession, Vocation

The history of work is as old as the human race, and the meaning of the word has changed over time. Tracing the evolution of that meaning is a study unto itself. To ground the present discussion in a common vocabulary, we provide from that literature several definitions of work and related terms.

Work

1. Work has an end beyond itself, being designed to produce or achieve something; it involves a degree of obligation or necessity, being a task that others set us or that we set ourselves; and it is arduous, involving effort and persistence beyond the point at which the task ceases to be wholly pleasurable.

   Keith Thomas, The Oxford Book of Work, 1999 [qtd. in "Changing Boundaries and Definitions of Work Over Time and Space," Jurgen Kocka]

2. No, I don't like work. I had rather laze about and think of all the fine things that can be done. I don't like work—no man does—but I like what is in the work—the chance to find yourself. Your own reality—for yourself, not for others—what no other man can ever know. They can only see the mere show, and never can tell what it really means.

   Joseph Conrad, Heart of Darkness

3. The word *work* is not only a kind of activity but a set of ideas and values related to that activity. Consider why we say the following are performing work: a construction worker digging a ditch, an executive at a meeting, a professional basketball player practicing his shots, a critic watching a movie she has to review, a student reading a novel for class, a volunteer bathing a patient in a hospital, an artist painting a picture, a secretary typing a letter for the boss, a monk meditating, and a man washing his kitchen floor. What do these activities have in common? Essentially nothing, except for the fact that, as we say, all of these people are working. We usually don't term shooting baskets, watching movies, and reading short stories *work*. Some might say that getting paid for these activities makes them work. If I pay a group of noisy children to get out of the house and go to a movie, are they working? Students don't get paid to read stories, nor do hospital volunteers or people who wash their own floors get paid to do their tasks. And what about the monk? He doesn't seem to be doing anything.

   A common thread of necessity runs through all of these examples. There is a sense in which all the people *have* to do what they are doing or feel that they *must* do what they are doing. This is clear for the wage earners, including people who play games for a living. They have a particular agreement with their employers to be at a certain place at a certain time, and to perform a particular task. It's also true of the student who must read the book to pass the course, but the student has fewer restrictions on when and where she'll do her work. The floor washer also has few external restrictions. He can choose to let the floor remain dirty. However, if he finds the filth distasteful and doesn't want to live with it, he must wash the floor.

The painter seems to have the most amount of choice, particularly if he actually earns his living as a cabdriver. While external necessities such as bosses, agreements on time and uses of energy, and dirty floors are strong defining features of work, they do not account for the artist who paints from the internal necessity of his or her desire. It is tempting to say that he or she is not working, but as Karl Marx wrote, "Really free work, e.g., composing, is at the same time the most damned serious, the most intense exertion." Most artists would agree. The drive and motivation to work that come from inside a person can be far more powerful than outside forces. This is certainly true for the monk, who is driven by his spirituality.

Joanne B. Ciulla
The Working Life: The Promise and Betrayal of Modern Work

4. The story of work is a story of humanity's trials and triumphs—from the ordeal of hard work, sometimes under conditions of slavery with obedience mandated by the whip, to the development of tools and machines, which take the burdens off human backs and even human minds. These advances in technology, which are still taking place, extend the reach of the hand, expand muscle power, enlarge the senses, and multiply the capacities of the mind. This story of work is still unfolding, with great changes taking place throughout the world and in a more accelerated fashion than ever before.

But work involves more than the use of tools and techniques. The form and nature of the work process help determine the character of a civilization, but, in turn, a society's economic, political, and cultural characteristics shape the form and nature of the work process as well as the role and status of the worker within the society.

Work is essential in providing the basic physical needs of food, clothing, and shelter, and different explanations have been given at different times for its existence and purpose in human survival. Thus, in Chinese civilization, work became part of the Taoist flow of nature to which a person must adapt as part of the natural world. However, in the Judeo-Christian religious tradition (and in pagan religions as well), it was regarded as a punishment sent by God (or by the gods or spirits) to punish human beings for some deviation from the wishes or rules of the divine.

The human spirit, however, is too resilient and optimistic to face an eternal and damning process of hard physical labour, as most was during most of human history for most people, so more benign explanations of the meaning and purpose of work came into use. For example, in western Christendom the Benedictine monks enunciated the rule that "to work is to pray," to fulfill one's duty to God and thus achieve salvation. This notion of work bringing spiritual rewards, in addition to physical survival, was carried further during the 17th century by the Puritans, whose work ethic led them to regard the accumulation of material wealth through labour as a sign of God's favour as well as of the individual's religious fervour. This attitude still appears in the American expression, "You are what you do," implying that people define themselves by the nature of their work.

With the onset of the industrial Revolution and the development of powered machinery during the 18th and 19th centuries, much onerous physical effort was gradually removed from work in factories and fields. Work was still regarded, however, as something separate from pleasure, and the dichotomy between work and play persists even in today's highly industrialized society.

Melvin Kranzberg
"History of the Organization of Work"

Career

NINETEENTH CENTURY   The word career derives from forms meaning "carry." The original definitions of career all referred to rapid and continuous action, movement, and procedure. For instance, an 1819 American edition of Samuel Johnson's eighteenth century Dictionary of the English Language listed the following items: "1. The ground on which a race is run; the length of a course. 2. A course, a race. 3. Height of speed; swift motion. 4. Course of action; uninterrupted procedure." The most common usage of the word related to horse racing and falconry. As the nineteenth century progressed, however, the meaning of career took on a new dimension, cultural rather than physical, abstract rather than visual. The Oxford English Dictionary dated as 1803 the first example of the following usage: "A person's course for progress through life (or a distinct portion of life) so of a nation, party, etc. A profession affording opportunities of advancement." But it was not until midcentury that Oxford found an example of a person actively being told to "go and make a career for himself." The usage of the word was maturing. In American English by the late nineteenth century, to make the career meant to make a success, to become famous. The 1893 edition of the Funk and Wagnalls dictionary in America added the following definitions of career to the familiar ones: "1. A complete course or progress extending through the life or a portion of it, especially when abounding in remarkable actions or incidents, or when publicly conspicuous: said of persons, political parties, nations, etc. 2. A course of business activity, or enterprise; especially, a course of professional life or employment, that offers advancement or honor."

When speaking of occupational activities in the new usage of *career*, an individual no longer confined himself to the description of a random series of jobs, projects, or businesses which provided a livelihood. The individual could now speak of a larger and more absorbing experience—a career: a pre-established total pattern of organized professional activity, with upward movement through recognized preparatory stages, and advancement based on merit and bearing honor. By the late nineteenth century, *The Century Dictionary* and *Funk and Wagnalls* were acknowledging a new social concept.

Burton J. Bledstein
The Culture of Professionalism: The Middle Class
and the Development of Higher Education in America

TWENTY-FIRST CENTURY   Work has changed out of all recognition in less than a generation.

- Unprecedented change and uncertainty has led employers to seek flexible and adaptable employees.
- Globalization, competition and financial constraints have led to massive restructuring, more short-term contracts, and an emphasis on skills development. All sectors have been affected, including higher education.
- Employment in small organizations is more common.
- Continuous learning is vital to keep up with change.

How Careers Have Changed   If the future feels uncertain and you sometimes wonder if you have a career, remember that the conventional idea of a "job for life," steadily rising up a hierarchy, is now less relevant. Careers now

- are less likely to be set within a single organization or even a single occupation over a lifetime;
- can include paid or unpaid work, part-time or full-time, within an employing organization or self-employment; and
- develop in a global job market.

The balance of responsibility for career management has shifted from employer to individual. As job opportunities in one specialty or geographic region fade, others blossom. To maintain employability, you need to be able to adapt to these changes by continuously developing and transferring your skills.

WHAT SHAPE IS YOUR CAREER?   A range of career forms now coexist.

- **Linear career**—the conventional notion of upward progression through an organization. Now, with flatter organizations, promotions may be less available so you may have to move out to move up.
- **Professional career** (Dalton et al.)—career development is seen as series of stages (dependent apprentice, expert colleague, mentor/manager, figurehead). Again, movement between organizations may be necessary to gain experience for growth into the next professional stage.
- **Entrepreneurial career** (Rosabeth Moss Kanter)—career growth through creation of new income and capacity. Not only a feature of the private sector; this is as relevant to public sector organizations (including research) competing for funding.
- **Portfolio** (attributed to Charles Handy)—here the career is viewed as a project portfolio, each activity overlapping or running in parallel and using a slightly different mix of skills. Consultants typically grow their careers in this way.
- **Crazy paving or patchwork** (attributed to Robin Linnecar)—a career made up of a variety of different roles or even different occupations for which a pattern may only be apparent with hindsight. In periods of rapid change, this pattern is about adaptability and survival. It can create a rich career history.

- **Steady-state**—a career where work is enjoyed, development is related to keeping up to date to sustain employability and making an ongoing contribution, but desire for promotion is not significant.

A career can encompass several of these patterns. For example, higher education careers are based in bureaucratic organizations with linear career structures and progression is through stages identifiable with the professional career model. Growing a research group involves bidding competitively for funding providing entrepreneurial career growth, and experienced academics often carry out consultancy for a number of clients or develop spin-out activities giving portfolio career growth.... Contemporary careers can be viewed as a *journey through life, work and learning*. To ensure you are in control of this journey, learn how to manage your own career. How much you invest in your career and how fulfilling you find it is up to you.

*Vitae: The Career and Development Organization**
http://www.vitae.ac.uk/1332/What-is-a-career.html

Profession

Professions are one of the main forms of institutionalizing expertise in western societies. The term "profession" is a curious one. It immediately conjures up images drawn from television shows featuring lawyers or medical doctors. Such representations point to the hold that certain professions have on our imagination. In *Bleak House*, Charles Dickens's celebrated novel, Richard Carstone considers which profession he wants to take up. The realm of possibilities—according to the definitional criteria of the age—is the military, the clergy, the law, and medicine. Professions such as law and medicine have successfully maintained both their power and status across several centuries and are seen as quintessential examplars of what constitutes a profession. In the late nineteenth century and throughout the twentieth, a raft of new professions emerged. Some, like accountancy, have accured considerable power.

While the dazzling array of different professions renders a definition of a profession difficult,... research suggests that features of a profession include: a body of abstract and specialized knowledge; a professional's autonomy over the labor process; self-regulation by the profession; legal rights restricting those who can practice; control of the supply and licensing of practitioners by the professional body; altruism; and the enjoyment of high status within society. Such characteristics form an "ideal type" of professional labor—one which is rarely observed in professions themselves.

The professional associations of many so-called "new" professions, such as marketers and human resource specialists, have expended considerable effort in

---

*Vitae is a U.K. based organization that champions the personal, professional and career development of doctoral researchers and research staff in higher education institutions and research institutes. To find out more about vitae visit the organzation's Web site at www.vitae.ac.uk. © 2009 Careers Research and Advisory Centre (CRAC).

trying to emulate the traits of the more established professions. Professions are complex and variegated and there are crucial distinction in their relative status, the length of their history, and power.

Chris Carter
The Blackwell Encyclopedia of Sociology

Vocation

1. Vocation, or calling, is an answer to the question "for what purpose was I born?" The word vocation comes from the Latin *vocare*, to call. While many people are fortunate to find career tracks that make pursuit of their vocation easier, there are others who have careers in medicine and education, for example, who are not called to heal or to teach. In other words you *may* find a well-trod career path in which to live out your vocation and you may have to find a career or a job (job = anything you do for a paycheck) to support living out your vocation, at least in the early years. (Think of all the people waiting tables and doing auditions.)

   Don't narrow the field too quickly when thinking of vocation. Try to separate vocation from job slots, to use the verb form rather than the noun: "I'm called to heal others," not, "I'm called to be a doctor." "Doctor" limits too quickly what you can imagine. Maybe a side interest in herbology will pull you into Chinese medicine, or your contemplative nature into spiritual direction.

   Parker Palmer says your vocation is what you can't *not* do. I have a friend who understands her calling to be that of bringing love into the world. I can imagine very few jobs from the least to the greatest where this calling could not be lived out. "Liz" enjoys math and is a natural teacher, so teaching high school math was an easy first step. At some point it seemed right to take courses at the local seminary, as she was able; the school invited her to declare a degree when she nearly had enough courses to graduate. Taking clinical pastoral education, she felt pulled into training to be a pastoral counselor and during that time also worked with inner city girls at high-risk of becoming pregnant. A deeply spiritual person, Liz always worked hard to listen for the appropriate place to offer her gifts, whether or not she understood why. Discovering a gift for being present to the dying, she worked with hospice for a while and then as hospital chaplain. Still called to bring love into the world, Liz is now in higher education administration and in her spare time partners with a nurse to work with the ill and dying and their families. She cannot help but live her vocation in the places she finds herself.

   Frederick Buechner defines vocation as "the place where your deep gladness and the world's deep hunger meet." Vocation is the thing that will make your heart sing while at the same time meeting a need for someone else.

Guilford College Web Site
http://www.guilford.edu/academics/vocation.html

2. Through work man must earn his daily bread[1] and contribute to the continual advance of science and technology and, above all, to elevating unceasingly the

---

[1]Cf. Ps. 127 (128): 2; cf. also Gn. 3:17–19; Prv. 10:22; Ex. 1:8–14; Jer. 22:13.

cultural and moral level of the society within which he lives in community with those who belong to the same family. And work means any activity by man, whether manual or intellectual, whatever its nature or circumstances; it means any human activity that can and must be recognized as work, in the midst of all the many activities of which man is capable and to which he is predisposed by his very natures, by virtue of humanity itself. Man is made to be in the visible universe and image and likeness of God himself,[2] and he is placed in it in order to subdue the earth.[3] From the beginning therefore he is *called to work*. *Work is one of the characteristics that distinguish* man from the rest of creatures, whose activity for sustaining their lives cannot be called work. Only man is capable of work, and only man works, at the same time by work occupying his existence on earth. Thus work bears a particular mark of man and of humanity, the mark of a person operating within a community of persons. And this mark decides its interior characteristics; in a sense it constitutes its very nature.

Pope John Paul II
Laborem exercens (On Human Work)

Review Questions

1. Both Ciulla and Thomas use the word *necessity* in defining work. What do they mean by this word?

2. According to Kranzberg, what major transformation regarding attitudes toward work occurred in the Western Christian tradition?

3. What are major differences in the definition of *career* as the word was understood in the late nineteeth and much of the twentieth centuries and the word as it is understood today?

4. What are the defining characteristics of a profession?

5. What is a vocation?

Discussion and Writing Suggestions

1. Locate the definition of work in the *Oxford English Dictionary*. Read the entire entry. Report on what you find in a paragraph or two.

2. Write your own definition of work. Compare your effort to that of others in this selection. In the context of that comparison, consider Joanne Ciulla's observation that "[t]here may be no one particular feature present in everything we call work,

---

[2]Cf. Gn. 1:26.
[3]Cf. Gn. 1:28.

but rather many characteristics that overlap and intersect" (*The Working Life*, 23). To what extent does your comparison confirm Ciulla's statement?

3. Research the definition of a work-related word not defined in this selection. Possibilities include *toil, labor, job, drudgery, indentured servitude, slavery, livelihood, trade, craft, hobby,* and *occupation.* Report on the history of the word.

4. Consider an activity you know well in which it is possible to both play and work (e.g., tennis, basketball, or chess), and discuss the point at which play *becomes* work. Use Thomas's definition of work as involving "persistence beyond the point at which the task ceases to be wholly pleasurable" to clarify the distinction between play and work.

5. What work do you do that would qualify as a vocation, as opposed to a job? To what extent would you want your job to be your vocation? Do you see this combination as practical? desirable? Discuss.

6. According to the authors in this section, modern careers differ considerably from their historical counterparts. You may know of people who have pursued or are pursuing careers in the old sense of the word and the new. Discuss the advantages and disadvantages you find in each.

7. Describe differences between work that you do for yourself and work that you do for others. Build your description around two specific examples of work. Conrad writes that it is possible to "find yourself" in work. Consider working this idea into your response.

FIXED AND FOOTLOOSE: WORK AND IDENTITY IN THE TWENTY-FIRST CENTURY

Ursula Huws

Sociologist Ursula Huws, professor of international labor studies at the Working Lives Research Institute at London Metropolitan University, is the author of *Making of a Cybertariat: Virtual Work in a Real World* (2003). In this article, she reviews changes in the modern workplace that have left us "with a . . . shifting and largely uncharted landscape in which jobs are created (and disappear) with great rapidity, often without even a concrete designation—just a mix-and-match combination of 'skills,' 'aptitudes,' and 'competences.'" As you read, notice the structure of Huws's article: after a general introduction, she devotes paragraphs 6–11 to "fixed" jobs; paragraphs 12–15 to "footloose" jobs; and paragraphs 16–18 to "fractured" jobs. This article first appeared in *Monthly Review* (March 2006).

The combination of technological change and globalization is bringing about fundamental changes in who does what work where, when, and how. This has implications which are profoundly contradictory for the nature of jobs [and] for the people who carry them out. . . .

On one hand, work which has previously been geographically tied to a particular place has become footloose to a historically unprecedented extent; on the other, there have been vast migrations of people crossing the planet in search of both jobs and personal safety. There has thus been a double uprooting—a movement of jobs to people and a movement of people to jobs. Between them, these upheavals are transforming the character of cities in both developed and developing countries.

In the process, they are also transforming social identities and structures. Most classic accounts of social stratification place a central importance on occupational identity. The basic building block of class identity has traditionally been the occupation, normally a stable identity acquired slowly either by inheritance or through a training process intended to equip the student or apprentice with skills for life. Once entered into this occupation and practicing those skills, the holder has a recognized position in the social division of labor which gives him or her a "place" in that society for life, barring some calamity such as illness, unemployment, or bankruptcy—risks against which the welfare states of most European countries provide some form of social insurance....

The unprecedented movements of people and jobs around the world have coincided with a breakdown of many traditional occupational identities. Specific skills linked to the use of particular tools or machinery have increasingly given way to more generic and fast-changing skills linked to the use of information and communications technologies (for work involving the processing of information) or to new labor-saving technologies for manual work, for instance in construction, manufacturing, packing, or cleaning. In many countries, this disintegration of occupational identities has also coincided with a collapse in the institutional forms of representation of workers, such as trade unions, which have in the past served to give some coherent shape and social visibility to these identities. We are left with a rapidly shifting and largely uncharted landscape in which jobs are created (and disappear) with great rapidity, often without even a concrete designation— just a mix-and-match combination of "skills," "aptitudes," and "competences."...

5   One of the ironies of the present situation is that many of the most fixed jobs are often carried out by the most footloose people, while some of the most footloose jobs may be carried out by people with deep ancestral roots in the location where they work.

Let us start with some of the fixed jobs. One of the most obvious characteristics of fixedness is the need for physical proximity to a particular spot, because the job directly involves the making, mending, cleaning, or moving of physical goods or the delivery of real personal services to people in real time and real space.

Starting with my own real space, I look around at the fixed jobs that sustain it. I live on a street of nineteenth-century three-story houses in London, where around a third of the houses are occupied by single middle-class households, the remainder having been converted into apartments or occupied by larger, poorer extended families. Most of the middle-class households employ a cleaner for three or four hours a week. Of the cleaners I know on this street, one is Bolivian, one Mauritian, one Ugandan, and one Colombian. Not a single one is white; not a single one was born in Europe, let alone London. At the end of the road there are two restaurants, a café, a fish-and-chip shop, and a fried chicken takeout outlet. One of the restaurants serves European-style dishes of various origins, mainly French. Its owner is a Montenegrin married to an Irish woman. The waitresses are Brazilian, Polish, and Russian. The other restaurant advertises an Italian menu but is owned and staffed (with the exception of one Albanian waitress) by Turkish men, as is the café. The fish-and-chip shop is staffed by Chinese men. The fried chicken outlet, which is open most of the night and caters to a rather rough clientele, is, despite its American name, staffed by a transient crew of exhausted-looking workers of African or Asian origins.

Periodically the houses on the street that are publicly owned (around 20 percent of the total) are renovated together. This happened last year, and for several weeks the neighborhood was filled with construction workers. This time, as far as we could tell, all the skilled workers were Polish; some of the less-skilled laborers were from various Balkan states. Apart from one surveyor (a black Londoner) I saw no women in the crew.

Not having a car, I make frequent use of a local minicab (cheap taxi) service. The drivers are constantly changing but include men from a large number of South Asian and African countries. To my knowledge there is only one woman driver, a feisty Nigerian who refuses to get out of her car but leans heavily on the horn to announce her arrival. I cannot remember the last time I was assigned a white driver.

10   This diversity of ethnic origin is not unique to manual work. The small company that maintains my computer network is run by a Greek Cypriot man. His deputy is Syrian and when he is too busy he sends a Turkish engineer to attend to my problem. All are highly skilled and educated. The reception desk in our local health center is staffed by two very efficient women—one Nigerian and one Somali.

Such examples could be multiplied many times, not just in London but in many cities across the globe where the maintenance of fixed infrastructure and customer-facing service activities are increasingly in the hands of people who were born in other countries or continents. Their presence as newcomers or temporary migrants has multiple effects on the shape and character of the host cities now dependent on their labor, both in the areas where they live and the areas where they work. As service workers and service users they are often at the interface of consumption and production in both public and private services and in the process both are transformed: markets are created for new kinds of food and personal services; health and educational institutions revise the hours and the languages in which services are available; and new codes of dress or behavior, tacit or explicit, are introduced making multiple demands on both new and established residents whose social survival depends on learning how to decode them....

So much for the fixed jobs; what of the footloose ones? The development of a global division of labor is not new. Regions have traded their goods with each other for as long as recorded history, and raiding other parts of the world for raw materials or slave labor is at least as old as colonialism. At the end of the nineteenth century the British Empire exhibited a remarkably developed pattern of regional industrial specialization knitted together into a global trade network. The twentieth century saw multinational corporations operating with increasing independence of the interests of the nation states in which they were based, ushering in a period after the Second World War that was characterized by Baran and Sweezy as "monopoly capitalism."[1] By the 1970s, it was clear that a "new global division of labor" was coming into being in manufacturing industry with companies breaking down their production processes into separate subprocesses and redistributing these activities around the globe to wherever conditions were most favorable.[2] These trends continued in the 1980s with industries as diverse as clothing, electronics, and auto manufacture dispersing their production facilities away from developed economies with high labor costs and strong environmental controls to developing countries, often in "free trade zones" where various tax incentives were offered and labor and environmental-protection regulations were suspended in an effort to attract as much foreign direct investment as possible. Workers in these zones were disproportionately young and female, and they received wages below subsistence level. Nevertheless, they were by no means passive and many actively organized to improve their lot.[3] This is one of the reasons why some of the regions once regarded as low wage, for instance Southeast Asia and Central America, are now seen as relatively high wage, and the companies have left them to exploit even cheaper workforces in places such as China, sub-Saharan Africa, and other parts of Latin America....

Less well studied—at least until very recently—has been the new global division of labor in white-collar work. Nevertheless, this too has been progressing since the 1970s when low-skilled work such as data entry or typesetting began to be exported in bulk from North America and Europe to low-cost economies in the Caribbean, as well as South and Southeast Asia, while higher-skilled services, such as computer programming, started to be exported to the developed world from developing economies such as India, the Philippines, and Brazil.[4]...

Even more striking than the overall extent of "eWork" is the form it takes. Most literature on remote work, telecommuting, teleworking, or any of the other pseudonyms for "eWork" presupposes that the dominant form is home-based work. Yet these results show that the stereotypical "eWorker" employee based solely at home is in fact one of the least popular forms. Moreover, in-house "eWorking" is heavily outweighed by "eOutsourcing" as a mechanism for organizing work remotely, with some 43 percent of European employers and 26 percent of Australians making use of this practice. Much "eOutsourcing" is carried out within the region where the employer is based (34.5 percent), but substantial numbers (18.3 percent) outsource to other regions within the same country, and 5.3 percent outsource outside their national borders. These inter-regional and international (sometimes inter-continental) relocations of work provide clues to the geography of the emerging international division of labor in "eServices."

• • •

15   What has happened since 2000?...What was still a risky experiment at the turn of the millennium had become normal, not to say routine, business practice three years later. Value chains were getting longer and more complex, with more and more intermediaries involved. The world was witnessing the emergence of huge new companies involved in the supply of business services, often many times bigger than their clients, with an internal global division of labor. When a large organization in the private or public sector decides to outsource a major contract to supply business services, it is increasingly not so much a case of choosing between India or Russia, Canada or China, but more a question of deciding on a particular company (for instance Accenture, EDS, or Siemens Business Services). Once that company has the contract, it may decide to divide up the work between teams in many parts of the world, depending on the particular balance of skills, languages, cost, and quality

criteria involved. This type of work could be regarded in many ways as a paradigmatic case of footlooseness, sliding without friction between teams across the globe
who are linked by telecommunications networks and a common corporate culture
but may nevertheless be physically located in strongly contrasting environments.

●   ●   ●

So far I have drawn a strongly dichotomous picture of a world in which the
fixed is counterposed to the footloose in relation both to jobs and to people. For most
of us, of course, the reality is much more complex than that, exhibiting both fixed
and footloose features in complex configurations. I have termed this condition
fractured. In a fractured existence, the characteristics of fixedness and footlooseness
are in constant, tense interaction with each other. Rooted real-time activities (like
putting the children to bed or eating a meal) are constantly interrupted by "virtual"
ones (like the ringing of the telephone), while "virtual" activities (like checking one's
e-mail) are disturbed by the physical realities of the situation in which one is placed
(the pain of a stiff neck, for instance, or the impact of a power outage). The traditional
diurnal rhythms of life are disrupted by requirements to respond to global demands.
The interpenetration of time zones in one sphere of life leads inexorably to the development of a twenty-four-hour economy as people forced to work non-traditional
hours then need to satisfy their needs as consumers during abnormal times, which
in turn obliges another group to be on duty to provide these services, ratcheting up a
process where-by opening hours are slowly extended right across the economy, and
with them the expectation that it is normal for everything always to be open.

●   ●   ●

This fractured experience...is mirrored in the fracturing of occupational identities. Although many job descriptions retain a mix of fixed and footloose features,
these are increasingly volatile. There has been an erosion of the clear boundaries
of the workplace and the working day, with a spillover of many activities into the
home or other locations, including an expectation that you should continue to be
productive while traveling, whether you are a truck driver taking orders over a
mobile phone during your lunch break or an executive working on a spreadsheet
in an airport departure lounge. In a world in which the responsibilities for home
and children are unevenly distributed between the sexes, these impacts are far
from gender neutral and have contributed to an invisible redrawing of the boundaries between the jobs that can easily and safely be done by women and those that
announce themselves subliminally as masculine.

Accompanying these dissolutions...there has also been a redesign of many
work processes involving some subtle and other not-so-subtle shifts in responsibility for particular tasks within most workplaces. Some of these changes have the
cumulative effect of tipping the balance between fixedness and footlooseness. For
example, a job that previously combined meeting and greeting customers with
more backroom activities might become wholly computerbased, making it easy to
relocate it either wholly or in part to another location. If that other location is the

existing worker's own home, then this might be experienced as quite liberating, but if the skills are not unique to the worker, the chances are the other location could be somebody else's desk on the other side of the world; far from being liberating this would then constitute a new source of precariousness....

It is easy to caricature as rigid and hierarchical the old world [of work] in which everyone knew "this task is what I do; that task is what you do; that task is reserved for new young trainees; that one is only done by very experienced older workers who know what can go wrong." Apart from anything else, it could easily lead to a set of unspoken rules which assigned certain tasks to women or to members of particular ethnic groups or people with a particular educational background. This would pose unacceptable barriers to social mobility and equality of opportunity. But [today] without [the old, hierarchical rules], what do we have? A world in which you are always only as good as last week's performance; where to keep your job you must always be prepared to learn new skills and change the old ways you were trained in (and in which you may have taken pride in the past); where you cannot know reliably in advance when you will be free and when you will have to work; where you can never say "no, that is not my responsibility" without fear of reprisal. A world without occupational boundaries could very easily become a world in which social solidarity is well-nigh impossible because you no longer have any clear way of defining who are your co-workers or your neighbors, and one where so many of your interactions are with strangers that it is hard to tell friend or ally from threat or enemy.

Notes

1. Paul Baran and Paul Sweezy, *Monopoly Capital: An Essay on the American Economic and Social Order* (New York: Monthly Review Press, 1966).

2. F. Froebel, J. Heinrichs, & O. Krey, *The New International Division of Labor* (Cambridge: Cambridge University Press, 1979).

3. See for instance *Women Working Worldwide, Common Interests: Women Organising in Global Electronics* (London: Women Working Worldwide, 1991).

4. Ursula Huws, *The Making of a Cybertariat: Virtual Work in a Real World* (New York: Monthly Review Press & London: Merlin Books, 2003).

● Review Questions

1. Reread paragraphs 3 and 4 of Huws's article and the equally important final paragraph. These three paragraphs rest on the same set of facts, but the final paragraph is notably different. How so?

2. According to Huws, a worker's occupation has traditionally defined his or her personal identity and social identity. How so? How have changes in technology and globalization affected these identities?

3. What does Huws mean by "fixed" work? What changes have new technologies and globalization brought to fixed work?

4. What does Huws mean by "footloose" work, and what were its origins? How has footloose work changed in modern times? Specifically, what is the new "paradigmatic case of footlooseness"?

5. What does Huws mean by "fractured" work, and what are its implications?

● Discussion and Writing Suggestions

1. What evidence do you find that we live in a world in which "jobs are created (and disappear) with great rapidity, often without even a concrete designation— just a mix-and-match combination of 'skills,' 'aptitudes,' and 'competences'"?

2. Would you expect the "rapidly shifting . . . landscape of work" that Huws describes to have the same effect on a worker of your generation as it might on a worker of your parents' generation? Explain.

3. What are some of the ways in which people are defined by their occupation— both individually and as members of a group? In developing your answer, describe someone you know well and the work he or she does.

4. One of the assumptions on which Huws builds her article is the "classic" view of occupation as having "central importance" in the individual's identity and position in the larger social order (see paragraph 3). Assume for a moment that identity is based less on "what you do" than on "what kind of person you are" and on "how other people see you." (On this point, see the story of Enrico that follows below.) In what ways would this new, competing assumption change Huws's argument?

5. Huws claims (in paragraph 4) that "[t]he unprecedented movements of people and jobs around the world have coincided with a breakdown of many traditional occupational identities." By the end of her paper, Huws comes to regard this breakdown with alarm—evidence of which we find in her final paragraph. What is your response to the breakdown? Do you expect, for instance, that the world of work you will enter post-college will be incoherent and anxiety provoking? (Note that other writers in this chapter find reasons for optimism in this same "rapidly shifting . . . landscape.")

No Long Term: New Work and the Corrosion of Character

Richard Sennett

Richard Sennett, a sociologist best known for his writing about cities, labor, and culture, is Centennial Professor of Sociology at the London School of Economics and Professor of the Humanities at New York University. During the 1980s he served as president of the American Council on Work. He is the author of three novels and numerous scholarly studies, including the much-cited *The Corrosion of Character: The Personal Consequences of Work in the New Capitalism* (1998), in which the following passage initially appeared. *Corrosion* is the first in a series of four books that explores "modern capitalism [and]...its personal consequences for workers."

Recently I met someone in an airport whom I hadn't seen for fifteen years. I had interviewed the father of Rico (as I shall call him) a quarter century ago when I wrote a book about blue-collar workers in America, *The Hidden Injuries of Class*. Enrico, his father, then worked as a janitor, and had high hopes for this boy, who was just entering adolescence, a bright kid good at sports. When I lost touch with his father a decade later, Rico had just finished college. In the airline lounge, Rico looked as if he had fulfilled his father's dreams. He carried a computer in a smart leather case, dressed in a suit I couldn't afford, and sported a signet ring with a crest.

Enrico had spent twenty years by the time we first met cleaning toilets and mopping floors in a downtown office building. He did so without complaining, but also without any hype about living out the American Dream. His work had one single and durable purpose, the service of his family. It had taken him fifteen years to save the money for a house, which he purchased in a suburb near Boston, cutting ties with his old Italian neighborhood because a house in the suburbs was better for the kids. Then his wife, Flavia, had gone to work, as a presser in a dry-cleaning plant; by the time I met Enrico in 1970, both parents were saving for the college education of their two sons.

What had most struck me about Enrico and his generation was how linear time was in their lives: year after year of working in jobs which seldom varied from day to day. And along that line of time, achievement was cumulative: Enrico and Flavia checked the increase in their savings every week, measured their domesticity by the various improvements and additions they had made to their ranch house. Finally, the time they lived was predictable. The upheavals of the Great Depression and World War II had faded, unions protected their jobs; though he was only forty when I first met him, Enrico knew precisely when he would retire and how much money he would have.

Time is the only resource freely available to those at the bottom of society. To make time accumulate, Enrico needed what the sociologist Max Weber called an "iron cage," a bureaucratic structure which rationalized the use of time; in Enrico's case, the seniority rules of his union about pay and the regulations organizing his government pension provided this scaffolding. When he added to these resources his own self-discipline, the result was more than economic.

5   He carved out a clear story for himself in which his experience accumulated materially and psychically; his life thus made sense to him as a linear narrative. Though a snob might dismiss Enrico as boring, he experienced the years as a dramatic story moving forward repair by repair, interest payment by interest payment. The janitor felt he became the author of his life, and though he was a man low on the social scale, this narrative provided him a sense of self-respect.

Though clear, Enrico's life story was not simple. I was particularly struck by how Enrico straddled the worlds of his old immigrant community and his new suburban-neutral life. Among his suburban neighbors he lived as a quiet, self-effacing citizen; when he returned to the old neighborhood, however, he received much more attention as a man who had made good on the outside, a worthy elder who returned each Sunday for Mass followed by lunch followed by gossipy coffees. He got recognition as a distinctive human being from those who knew him long enough to understand his story; he got a more anonymous kind of respect from his new neighbors by doing what everyone else did, keeping his home and garden neat, living without incident. The thick texture of Enrico's particular experience lay in the fact that he was acknowledged in both ways, depending in which community he moved: two identities from the same disciplined use of his time.

If the world were a happy and just place, those who enjoy respect would give back in equal measure the regard which has been accorded them. This was Fichte's idea in "The Foundations of National Law"; he spoke of the "reciprocal effect" of recognition. But real life does not proceed so generously.

Enrico disliked blacks, although he had labored peaceably for many years with other janitors who were black; he disliked non-Italian foreigners like the Irish, although his own father could barely speak English. He could not acknowledge kindred struggles; he had no class allies. Most of all, however, Enrico disliked middle-class people. We treated him as though he were invisible, "as a zero," he said; the janitor's resentment was complicated by his fear that because of his lack of education and his menial status, we had a sneaking right to do so. To his powers of endurance in time he contrasted the whining self-pity of blacks, the unfair intrusion of foreigners, and the unearned privileges of the bourgeoisie.

Though Enrico felt he had achieved a measure of social honor, he hardly wanted his son Rico to repeat his own life. The American dream of upward mobility for the children powerfully drove my friend. "I don't understand a word he says," Enrico boasted to me several times when Rico had come home from school and was at work on math. I heard many other parents of sons and daughters like Rico say something like "I don't understand him" in harder tones, as though the kids had abandoned them. We all violate in some way the place assigned us in the family myth, but upward mobility gives that passage a peculiar twist. Rico and other youngsters headed up the social ladder sometimes betrayed shame about their parents' working-class accents and rough manners, but more often felt suffocated by the endless strategizing over pennies and the reckoning of time in tiny steps. These favored children wanted to embark on a less constrained journey.

10   Now, many years later, thanks to the encounter at the airport, I had the chance to see how it had turned out for Enrico's son. In the airport lounge, I must confess, I didn't much like what I saw. Rico's expensive suit could have been just business plumage, but the crested signet ring—a mark of elite family background—seemed both a lie and a betrayal of the father. However, circumstances threw Rico and me together on a long flight. He and I did not have one of those American journeys in which a stranger spills out his or her emotional guts to you, gathers more tangible baggage when the plane lands, and disappears forever. I took the seat next to Rico without being asked, and for the first hour of a long flight from New York to Vienna had to pry information out of him.

Rico, I learned, has fulfilled his father's desire for upward mobility, but has indeed rejected the way of his father. Rico scorns "time-servers" and others wrapped in the armor of bureaucracy; instead he believes in being open to change and in taking risks. And he has prospered; whereas Enrico had an income in the bottom quarter of the wage scale, Rico's has shot up to the top 5 percent. Yet this is not an entirely happy story for Rico.

After graduating from a local university in electrical engineering, Rico went to a business school in New York. There he married a fellow student, a young Protestant woman from a better family. School prepared the young couple to move and change jobs frequently, and they've done so. Since graduation, in fourteen years at work Rico has moved four times.

Rico began as a technology adviser to a venture capital firm on the West Coast, in the early, heady days of the developing computer industry in Silicon Valley; he then moved to Chicago, where he also did well. But the next move was for the sake of his wife's career. If Rico were an ambition-driven character out of the pages of Balzac, he would never have done it, for he gained no larger salary, and he left hotbeds of high-tech activity for a more retired, if leafy, office park in Missouri. Enrico felt somewhat ashamed when Flavia went to work; Rico sees Jeannette, his wife, as an equal working partner, and has adapted to her. It was at this point, when Jeannette's career took off, that their children began arriving.

In the Missouri office park, the uncertainties of the new economy caught up with the young man. While Jeannette was promoted, Rico was downsized—his firm was absorbed by another, larger firm that had its own analysts. So the couple made a fourth move, back East to a suburb outside New York. Jeannette now manages a big team of accountants, and he has started a small consulting firm.

15   Prosperous as they are, the very acme of an adaptable, mutually supportive couple, both husband and wife often fear they are on the edge of losing control over their lives. This fear is built into their work histories.

In Rico's case, the fear of lacking control is straightforward: it concerns managing time. When Rico told his peers he was going to start his own consulting firm, most approved; consulting seems the road to independence. But in getting started he found himself plunged into many menial tasks, like doing his own photocopying, which before he'd taken for granted. He found himself plunged into the sheer flux of networking; every call had to be answered, the slightest acquaintance pursued. To find work, he has fallen subservient to the schedules of people who are in no way obliged to respond to him. Like other consultants, he wants to work in accordance with contracts setting out just what the consultant will do. But these contracts, he says, are largely fictions. A consultant usually has to tack one way and another in response to the changing whims or thoughts of those who pay; Rico has no fixed role that allows him to say to others, "This is what I do, this is what I am responsible for."

Jeannette's lack of control is more subtle. The small group of accountants she now manages is divided among people who work at home, people usually in the office, and a phalanx of low-level back-office clerks a thousand miles away connected to her by computer cable. In her present corporation, strict rules and surveillance of phones and e-mail disciplines the conduct of the accountants who work from home; to organize the work of the back-office clerks a thousand miles away, she can't make hands-on, face-to-face judgments, but instead must work by formal written guidelines. She hasn't experienced less bureaucracy in this seemingly flexible work arrangement; indeed, her own decisions count for less than in the days when she supervised workers who were grouped together, all the time, in the same office.

As I say, at first I was not prepared to shed many tears for this American Dream couple. Yet as dinner was served to Rico and me on our flight, and he began to talk more personally, my sympathies increased. His fear of losing control, it developed, went much deeper than worry about losing power in his job. He feared that the actions he needs to take and the way he has to live in order to survive in the modern economy have set his emotional, inner life adrift.

Rico told me that he and Jeannette have made friends mostly with the people they see at work, and have lost many of these friendships during the moves of the last twelve years, "though we stay 'netted.'" Rico looks to electronic communications for the sense of community which Enrico most enjoyed when he attended meetings of the janitors' union, but the son finds communications on-line short and hurried. "It's like with your kids—when you're not there, all you get is news later."

20   In each of his four moves, Rico's new neighbors have treated his advent as an arrival which closes past chapters of his life; they ask him about Silicon Valley or the Missouri office park, but, Rico says, "they don't *see* other places"; their imaginations are not engaged. This is a very American fear. The classic American suburb was a bedroom community; in the last generation a different kind of suburb has arisen, more economically independent of the urban core, but not really town or village either; a place springs into life with the wave of a developer's wand, flourishes, and begins to decay all within a generation. Such communities are not empty of sociability or neighborliness, but no one in them becomes a long-term witness to another person's life.

The fugitive quality of friendship and local community form the background to the most important of Rico's inner worries, his family. Like Enrico, Rico views work as his service to the family; unlike Enrico, Rico finds that the demands of the job interfere with achieving the end. At first I thought he was talking about the all too familiar conflict between work time and time for family. "We get home at seven, do dinner, try to find an hour for the kids' homework, and then deal with our own paperwork." When things get tough for months at a time in his consulting firm, "it's like I don't know who my kids are." He worries about the frequent anarchy into which his family plunges, and about neglecting his children, whose needs can't be programmed to fit into the demands of his job.

Hearing this, I tried to reassure him; my wife, stepson, and I had endured and survived well a similarly high-pressure life. "You aren't being fair to yourself," I said. "The fact you care so much means you are doing the best for your family you can." Though he warmed to this, I had misunderstood.

As a boy, I already knew, Rico had chafed under Enrico's authority; he had told me then he felt smothered by the small-minded rules which governed the janitor's life. Now that he is a father himself, the fear of a lack of ethical discipline haunts him, particularly the fear that his children will become "mall rats," hanging out aimlessly in the parking lots of shopping centers in the afternoons while the parents remain out of touch at their offices.

He therefore wants to set for his son and daughters an example of resolution and purpose, "but you can't just tell kids to be like that"; he has to set an example.

The objective example he could set, his upward mobility, is something they take for granted, a history that belongs to a past not their own, a story which is over. But his deepest worry is that he cannot offer the substance of his work life as an example to his children of how they should conduct themselves ethically. The qualities of good work are not the qualities of good character.

25   As I came later to understand, the gravity of this fear comes from a gap separating Enrico and Rico's generations. Business leaders and journalists emphasize the global marketplace and the use of new technologies as the hallmarks of the capitalism of our time. This is true enough, but misses another dimension of change: new ways of organizing time, particularly working time.

The most tangible sign of that change might be the motto "No long term." In work, the traditional career progressing step by step through the corridors of one or two institutions is withering; so is the deployment of a single set of skills through the course of a working life. Today, a young American with at least two years of college can expect to change jobs at least eleven times in the course of working, and change his or her skill base at least three times during those forty years of labor.

An executive for ATT points out that the motto "No long term" is altering the very meaning of work:

> In ATT we have to promote the whole concept of the work force being contingent, though most of the contingent workers are inside our walls. "Jobs" are being replaced by "projects" and "fields of work."[1]

Corporations have also farmed out many of the tasks they once did permanently in-house to small firms and to individuals employed on short-term contracts. The fastest-growing sector of the American labor force, for instance, is people who work for temporary job agencies.[2]

"People are hungry for [change]," the management guru James Champy argues, because "the market may be 'consumer-driven' as never before in history."[3] The market, in this view, is too dynamic to permit doing things the same way year after year, or doing the same thing. The economist Bennett Harrison believes the source of this hunger for change is "impatient capital," the desire for rapid return; for instance, the average length of time stocks have been held on British and American exchanges has dropped 60 percent in the last fifteen years. The market believes rapid market return is best generated by rapid institutional change.

The "long-term" order at which the new regime takes aim, it should be said, was itself short-lived—the decades spanning the mid-twentieth century. Nineteenth-century capitalism lurched from disaster to disaster in the stock markets and in irrational corporate investment; the wild swings of the business cycle provided people little security. In Enrico's generation after World War II, this disorder was brought somewhat under control in most advanced economies; strong unions, guarantees of the welfare state, and large-scale corporations combined to produce an era of relative stability. This span of thirty or so years defines the "stable past" now challenged by a new regime.

30   A change in modern institutional structure has accompanied short-term, contract, or episodic labor. Corporations have sought to remove layers of bureaucracy, to become flatter and more flexible organizations. In place of organizations

as pyramids, management wants now to think of organizations as networks. "Networklike arrangements are lighter on their feet" than pyramidal hierarchies, the sociologist Walter Powell declares; "they are more readily decomposable or redefinable than the fixed assets of hierarchies."[4] This means that promotions and dismissals tend not to be based on clear, fixed rules, nor are work tasks crisply defined; the network is constantly redefining its structure.

An IBM executive once told Powell that the flexible corporation "must become an archipelago of related activities."[5] The archipelago is an apt image for communications in a network, communication occurring like travel between islands—but at the speed of light, thanks to modern technologies. The computer has been the key to replacing the slow and clogged communications which occur in traditional chains of command. The fastest-growing sector of the labor force deals in computer and data-processing services, the area in which Jeanette and Rico work; the computer is now used in virtually all jobs, in many ways, by people of all ranks....

For all these reasons, Enrico's experience of long-term, narrative time in fixed channels has become dysfunctional. What Rico sought to explain to me—and perhaps to himself—is that the material changes embodied in the motto "No long term" have become dysfunctional for him too, but as guides to personal character, particularly in relation to his family life.

Take the matter of commitment and loyalty. "No long term" is a principle which corrodes trust, loyalty, and mutual commitment. Trust can, of course, be a purely formal matter, as when people agree to a business deal or rely on another to observe the rules in a game. But usually deeper experiences of trust are more informal, as when people learn on whom they can rely when given a difficult or impossible task. Such social bonds take time to develop, slowly rooting into the cracks and crevices of institutions.

The short time frame of modern institutions limits the ripening of informal trust. A particularly egregious violation of mutual commitment often occurs when new enterprises are first sold. In firms starting up, long hours and intense effort are demanded of everyone; when the firms go public—that is, initially offer publicly traded shares—the founders are apt to sell out and cash in, leaving lower-level employees behind. If an organization whether new or old operates as a flexible, loose network structure rather than by rigid command from the top, the network can also weaken social bonds. The sociologist Mark Granovetter says that modern institutional networks are marked by "the strength of weak ties," by which he partly means that fleeting forms of association are more useful to people than long-term connections, and partly that strong social ties like loyalty have ceased to be compelling.[6] These weak ties are embodied in teamwork, in which the team moves from task to task and the personnel of the team changes in the process.

35 Strong ties depend, by contrast, on long association. And more personally they depend on a willingness to make commitments to others. Given the typically short, weak ties in institutions today, John Kotter, a Harvard Business School professor, counsels the young to work "on the outside rather than on the inside" of organizations. He advocates consulting rather than becoming "entangled" in long-term employment; institutional loyalty is a trap in an economy where "business concepts, product designs, competitor intelligence, capital equipment, and all kinds of knowledge have shorter credible life spans."[7]

A consultant who managed a recent IBM job shrinkage declares that once employees "understand [they can't depend on the corporation] they're marketable."[8] Detachment and superficial cooperativeness are better armor for dealing with current realities than behavior based on values of loyalty and service.

It is the time dimension of the new capitalism, rather than high-tech data transmission, global stock markets, or free trade, which most directly affects people's emotional lives outside the workplace. Transposed to the family realm, "No long term" means keep moving, don't commit yourself, and don't sacrifice. Rico suddenly erupted on the plane, "You can't imagine how stupid I feel when I talk to my kids about commitment. It's an abstract virtue to them; they don't see it anywhere." Over dinner I simply didn't understand the outburst, which seemed apropos of nothing. But his meaning is now clearer to me as a reflection upon himself. He means the children don't see commitment practiced in the lives of their parents or their parents' generation.

Similarly, Rico hates the emphasis on teamwork and open discussion which marks an enlightened, flexible workplace once those values are transposed to the intimate realm. Practiced at home, teamwork is destructive, marking an absence of authority and of firm guidance in raising children. He and Jeannette, he says, have seen too many parents who have talked every family issue to death for fear of saying "No!," parents who listen too well, who understand beautifully rather than lay down the law; they have seen as a result too many disoriented kids.

"Things have to hold together," Rico declared to me. Again, I didn't at first quite get this, and he explained what he meant in terms of watching television. Perhaps unusually, Rico and Jeannette make it a practice to discuss with their two sons the relation between movies or sitcoms the boys watch on the tube and events in the newspapers. "Otherwise it's just a jumble of images." But mostly the connections concern the violence and sexuality the children see on television. Enrico constantly spoke in little parables to drive home questions of character; these parables he derived from his work as a janitor—such as "You can ignore dirt but it won't go away." When I first knew Rico as an adolescent, he reacted with a certain shame to these homely snippets of wisdom. So now I asked Rico if he too made parables or even just drew ethical rules from his experience at work. He first ducked answering directly—"There's not much on TV about that sort of thing"—then replied, "And well, no, I don't talk that way."

Behavior which earns success or even just survival at work thus gives Rico little to offer in the way of a parental role model. In fact, for this modern couple, the problem is just the reverse: how can they protect family relations from succumbing to the short-term behavior, the meeting mind-set, and above all the weakness of loyalty and commitment which mark the modern workplace? In place of the chameleon values of the new economy, the family—as Rico sees it—should emphasize instead formal obligation, trustworthiness, commitment, and purpose. These are all long-term virtues.

40   This conflict between family and work poses some questions about adult experience itself. How can long-term purposes be pursued in a short-term society? How can durable social relations be sustained? How can a human being develop a narrative of identity and life history in a society composed of episodes and fragments? The conditions of the new economy feed instead on experience

which drifts in time, from place to place, from job to job. If I could state Rico's dilemma more largely, short-term capitalism threatens to corrode his character, particularly those qualities of character which bind human beings to one another and furnishes each with a sense of sustainable self.

$$\bullet \quad \bullet \quad \bullet$$

Rico's experiences with time, place, and work are not unique; neither is his emotional response. The conditions of time in the new capitalism have created a conflict between character and experience, the experience of disjointed time threatening the ability of people to form their characters into sustained narratives.

At the end of the fifteenth century, the poet Thomas Hoccleve declared in *The Regiment of Princes*, "Allas, wher ys this worldes stabylnesse?"—a lament that appears equally in Homer or in Jeremiah in the Old Testament.[9] Through most of human history, people have accepted the fact that their lives will shift suddenly due to wars, famines, or other disasters, and that they will have to improvise in order to survive. Our parents and grandparents were filled with anxiety in 1940, having endured the wreckage of the Great Depression and facing the looming prospect of a world war.

What's peculiar about uncertainty today is that it exists without any looming historical disaster; instead it is woven into the everyday practices of a vigorous capitalism. Instability is meant to be normal, Schumpeter's entrepreneur served up as an ideal Everyman. Perhaps the corroding of character is an inevitable consequence. "No long term" disorients action over the long term, loosens bonds of trust and commitment, and divorces will from behavior.

I think Rico knows he is both a successful and a confused man. The flexible behavior which has brought him success is weakening his own character in ways for which there exists no practical remedy. If he is an Everyman for our times, his universality may lie in that dilemma.

Notes

1. Quoted in *New York Times,* Feb. 13, 1996, pp. D1, D6.

2. Corporations like Manpower grew 240 percent from 1985 to 1995. As I write, the Manpower firm, with 600,000 people on its payroll, compared with the 400,000 at General Motors and 350,000 at IBM, is now the country's largest employer.

3. James Champy, *Re-engineering Management* (New York: HarperBusiness, 1995) p. 119, pp. 39–40.

4. Walter Powell and Laurel Smith-Doerr, "Networks and Economic Life," in Neil Smelser and Richard Swedberg, eds., *The Handbook of Economic Sociology* (Princeton: Princeton University Press, 1994), p. 381.

5. Ibid.

6. Mark Granovetter, "The Strength of Weak Ties, " *American Journal of Sociology* 78 (1973), 1360–80.

7. John Kotter, *The New Rules* (New York: Dutton, 1995) pp. 81, 159.

8. Anthony Sampson, *Company Man* (New York: Random House, 1995), pp. 226–27.

9. Quoted in Ray Pahl, *After Success: Fin de Siècle Anxiety and Identity* (Cambridge, U.K.: Polity Press, 1995), pp. 163–64.

● Review Questions

1. What does "No long term" mean—as compared to "Long term"? How does Sennett use "No long term" as a "motto" to describe changes in the new economy?

2. Sennett describes Rico and his father, Enrico, as having different life narratives. What are these narratives? How do they differ? How do they lead to Rico's distress?

3. In the new economy, what changes have occurred in the structure of businesses and the ways in which workers are assigned and do work?

4. Why does Rico feel that he needs to protect his family from behavior patterns and values now commonplace in the new economy?

5. Reread paragraphs 39 and 43, in which Sennett summarizes Rico's "dilemma." What is that dilemma?

● Discussion and Writing Suggestions

1. Rico's "deepest worry," according to Sennett, "is that he cannot offer the substance of his work life as an example to his children of how they should conduct themselves ethically. The qualities of good work are not the qualities of good character" (paragraph 24). As a reader, you are obliged to accept Sennett's description of Rico's "deepest worry." At the same time, Rico's turmoil need not be yours. In your experience, how closely tied are the qualities of "good character" to your activities at a job? Can doing a job well elicit from a worker good character? How so?

2. To what extent have you seen evidence that the behaviors demanded of both employees and employers in the new economy jeopardize the link between good work and good character?

3. According to Sennett, "a young American with at least two years of college can expect to change jobs at least eleven times in the course of working, and change his or her skill base at least three times during those forty years of labor" (paragraph 26). What is your "gut-level" response to these projections concerning changes in jobs and skill bases?

4. As an undergraduate, how do you *prepare* for a working life characterized by the changes Sennett projects?

5. In describing the life of Rico, Sennett shows us how identity is tied to work—an important correlation among sociologists. (See, for instance, paragraph 3

in the selection by Ursula Huws, who makes the same assumption about the relationship of identity, social status, and occupation.) Reflect on your experiences of work and the working lives of people you know well. Is the assumption concerning the relationship between work and identity true? Is it possible to have a self-respecting identity if you do not respect what you do (or how you must do what you do) on the job?

6. Sennett contrasts "No long term" and "Long term" employment and also the lives of Enrico and his son, Rico. For Sennett, "Long-term" equals stable employment, stable values, and a stable identity; "No long-term" equals the instability of all three. Enrico's life in long-term employment was stable; Rico's life in short-term employment is not. Is Sennett proposing some sort of "law" here? That is, *if* identity is tied to occupation (as many sociologists believe) *and* the "qualities of good work are not the qualities of good character" (paragraph 24), then must one's identity be in crisis, as Rico's is? Given the demands on workers in the new economy, must the identities of all or most workers be thrown into crisis? If you don't think so, then where does Sennett's argument break down?

I FEEL SO DAMN LUCKY!

Tom Peters

Tom Peters, a well-known management consultant, prolific writer, and much sought-after speaker, coauthored the influential *In Search of Excellence* (1982). The selection that follows, originally titled "The New Wired World of Work: A More Transparent Workplace Will Mean More White-collar Accountability and Less Tolerance for Hangers-on," first appeared in *Business Week* (August 28, 2008). The new title is taken from the last line of the selection itself.

You're hiking along near the Grand Canyon in August, 2000, but fretting about the progress your virtual partner in Kuala Lumpur has made in the past 24 hours? No problem! Your local Kampgrounds of America campsite now has Internet access.

Call it the new wired world of work. Depending on how you view it, it's intrusive, pervasive, or merely ubiquitous. But it's definitely not your dad's office. And this perpetually plugged-in existence is just the beginning of the changes we'll see in the 21st century white-collar workplace.

Work in the '50s and '60s meant trudging to the same office for decades. Same colleagues. Same processes, mostly rote. Former MCI Communications Chief Bill McGowan called yesterday's middle managers "human message switches." And the information was laughably dated. Closing the account books at month's end could drag on for weeks. Customer data were nonexistent, or hopelessly unreliable.

But in the next few years, whether at a tiny company or behemoth, we will be working with an eclectic mix of contract teammates from around the globe, many of whom we'll never meet face-to-face. Every project will call for a new team, composed of specially tailored skills. Info that's more than hours old will be viewed with concern.

5   Every player on this team will be evaluated—pass by pass, at-bat by at-bat—for the quality and uniqueness and timeliness and passion of her or his contribution. And therein lies the peril, and the remarkable opportunity, of this weird, wired, wild new age of work. White-collar accountability has until now been mostly an oxymoron. Show up, suck up, process your paper flow with a modicum of efficiency, and you could count on a pretty decent end-of-year evaluation, a cost-of-living-plus raise, and a sure-as-death-and-taxes 40-year tenure at Desk No. 263.

Now you are like a New York Yankees or Los Angeles Dodgers closer. A couple of blown saves following a night on the town and your pressured and performance-driven teammates, more than your manager, are ready to show you the exit. This will hold for the freshly minted University of Wisconsin grad as well as the 56-year-old who had envisioned himself on a pain-free coast toward retirement. There may be a tight labor market for stellar performers, but the flip side is much less tolerance for hangers-on.

As enterprise resource-planning software and other such systems wreak havoc on the vast majority of staff jobs in the next decade, what will it take for you and me to navigate and win? Here's a list of minimal survival skills for the 21st century office worker:

- Mastery: To thrive in tomorrow's transparent team environment, the typical white-collar worker will have to be noticeably good at something the world values. "HR guy" doesn't cut it. Nor does "CPA." What subset of, say, techie recruiting skills or international accountancy excellence makes you a clearly valued contributor? I firmly believe that if you can't describe your distinction in the space of a one-sixteenth-page Yellow Pages ad, you will be doomed.

- Who Do You Know?: The new Rolodex will deemphasize bosses and traditional power figures, focusing more on peers (future project mates!) who appreciate your clear-cut contributions. I consider my own electronic Rolodex to be my Extended Global University, colleagues I can call upon (and who can call upon me) to further my current and future projects.

- Entrepreneurial Instinct: You do not have to start your own business. But as I see it, all these projects are entrepreneurial. So you must act as if you were running your own business. Think of yourself as Maggie Inc., who happens to be at General Electric Capital Services Inc. at the moment. And speaking of which, I fully expect women to dominate managerial roles. I think they tend to handle ambiguity better than we guys do. The new world is a floating crap game, with new projects, new teammates, and a constant need to adjust. Those who can operate in the absence of laid-out bounds will be the leaders.

- Love of Technology: Technology is changing everything. Believe the hype—if anything, it's understated. You need not be a technologist per se, but you must embrace technology. "Coping" with it is not enough.

- Marketing: You do not have to become a shameless self-promoter, a la Martha Stewart. But you must get your story out on the airwaves. Do it via your personal Web site. Do it by telling your project's story at a trade show.

- Passion for Renewal: You've got to constantly improve and, on occasion, reinvent yourself. My bread and butter—at age 57—are my lectures. But I imagine that the Internet will devour many conventional meetings in a few years. Hence I am madly working with several groups that will deliver my message via the new technologies.

I love to read Dilbert and usually choke with laughter. But I have a problem with the subtext: My company stinks, my boss stinks, my job stinks. If that's your take—at this moment of monumental change and gargantuan opportunity—then I can only feel sad for you. We get to reinvent the world. I feel so damn lucky!

● Review Questions

1. What are some of the main differences between "your dad's office" and the workplace of the twenty-first century?

2. In the view of Tom Peters, what are the minimal survival skills for office workers in the twenty-first century?

3. Peters uses a sports analogy in this selection. To what end?

● Discussion and Writing Suggestions

1. "The new world is a floating crap game, with new projects, new teammates, and a constant need to adjust. Those who can operate in the absence of laid-out bounds will be the leaders." How significant a departure is the world described here from the world of work just a generation ago? (See, for instance, the example of Enrico in Richard Sennett's article.) How comfortable are you operating "in the absence of laid-out bounds"?

2. Age 57 when writing this piece, Tom Peters is an unabashed optimist comfortable with the changing landscape of work he describes. Fifty-seven is close to the traditional age of retirement. Do you know other fifty-somethings in the workforce? Contact them and ask how they're adapting to recent changes on the job. What accounts for the anxiety of some in the face of these changes and the optimism of others?

3. Peters regards workers of the twenty-first century as occupying a "moment of monumental change and gargantuan opportunity" in which he and his readers get to "reinvent the world." Peters is thrilled at the prospect. Do you feel up to the challenge? Do you have an appetite to continually renew and promote yourself in the ways he is suggesting? Explain.

4. Peters suggests that in the new world of work you will be evaluated on a what-have-you-done-for-me-lately basis, much as an athlete is. In your view, what is lost and what is gained in such an intensely performance-driven view of the workplace?

WORK AND WORKERS IN THE TWENTY-FIRST CENTURY

Richard W. Judy and Carol D'Amico

The selection that follows forms the opening section of the Hudson Institute's *Workforce 2020* (published in 1997), which appeared ten years after its predecessor, *Workforce 2000* (published in 1987). That book challenged policymakers and employers to consider and respond to trends that were revolutionizing the landscape of work at the end of the twentieth century. In this update, Hudson analysts Richard Judy and Carol D'Amico similarly ask us to project current trends into the near future so that we can respond meaningfully. The Hudson Institute describes itself as "a non-partisan policy research organization dedicated to innovative research and analysis that promotes global security, prosperity, and freedom."

You have before you a map, one that describes the journey America's labor force is now beginning. It lays out the general contours of the employment landscape, not the fine details or the specific landmarks, depicting the many roads to what we call "Workforce 2020." Some will be superhighways and some will be dead ends for American workers. Although immense forces shape the employment landscape, we believe that we know the difference between the superhighways and the dead ends.

Skilled cartographers in the guise of economists, education experts, and policy researchers at Hudson Institute helped prepare this map. It offers our best ideas about what lies ahead and what Americans—collectively and individually, in large and small firms, in federal agencies and in small-town development commissions—should do to prepare for the journey to Workforce 2020.

Our map is needed because American workers at the threshold of the twenty-first century are embarking on mysterious voyages. They seek glittering destinations but travel along roads with numerous pitfalls and unexpected diversions. Many workers—more than at any time in America's history—will reach the glittering destinations. They will enjoy incomes unimaginable to their parents, along with working and living conditions more comfortable than anyone could have dreamed of in centuries past. But many other workers will be stymied by the pitfalls along the road or baffled by the diversions. Their standard of living may stagnate or even decline. Much is already known today about what will divide the hopeful from the anxious along these roads, and we will share that knowledge here.

What makes America's voyage to the workforce of 2020 unique is not merely the heights to which some will climb or the difficulties others will endure. Two qualities give a truly unprecedented character to the roads ahead. First, the gates have lifted before almost every American who wishes to embark on the journey of work. Age, gender, and race barriers to employment opportunity have broken down. What little conscious discrimination remains will be swept away soon—not by government regulation but by the enlightened self-interest of employers. Second, more and more individuals now undertake their own journeys through the labor force, rather than "hitching rides" on the traditional mass transportation provided by unions, large corporations, and government bureaucracies. For most workers, this "free agency" will be immensely liberating. But for others, it will provoke anxiety and anger. For all workers, the premium on education, flexibility, and foresight has never been greater than it will be in the years ahead.

5   What explains the immense satisfactions and dangers ahead? What makes possible the unprecedented expansion of opportunities in the labor force? What forces conspire, for better or worse, to demand that we compete as individuals and contend with ever-changing knowledge and skill requirements? We highlight four forces in particular.

First, the pace of technological change in today's economy has never been greater. It will accelerate still further, in an exponential manner. Innovations in biotechnology, computing, telecommunications, and their confluences will bring new products and services that are at once marvelous and potentially frightening. And the "creative destruction"* wrought by this technology on national economies, firms, and individual workers will be even more powerful in the twenty-first century than when economist Joseph Schumpeter coined the phrase fifty years ago. We cannot know what innovations will transform the global economy by 2020, any more than analysts in the mid-1970s could have foreseen the rise of the personal computer or the proliferation of satellite, fiber-optic, and wireless communications. However, the computer and telecommunications revolutions enable us to speculate in an informed manner on the implications of today's Innovation Age for the American workforce:

- Automation will continue to displace low-skilled or unskilled workers in America's manufacturing firms and offices. Indeed, machines will substitute for increasingly more sophisticated forms of human labor. Even firms that develop advanced technology will be able to replace some of their employees with technology (witness the "CASE tools" that now assist in writing routine computer code) or with lower-paid workers in other countries (witness the rise of India's computer programmers and data processors).

- However, experience suggests that the development, marketing, and servicing of ever more sophisticated products—and the use of those products in an ever richer ensemble of personal and professional services—almost certainly will create more jobs than the underlying technology will destroy. On the whole, the new jobs will also be safer, more stimulating, and better paid than the ones they replace.

- The best jobs created in the Innovation Age will be filled by Americans (and workers in other advanced countries) to the extent that workers possess the skills required to compete for them and carry them out. If jobs go unfilled in the U.S., they will quickly migrate elsewhere in our truly global economy.

---

*In *Capitalism, Socialism and Democracy* (1942), Joseph Schumpeter coined the term "creative destruction" to describe the process by which capitalism, operating through "new consumers, goods, the new methods of production or transportation, the new markets, [and] the new forms of industrial organization,…incessantly revolutionizes the economic structure *from within*, incessantly destroying the old one, incessantly creating a new one" (New York, Harper: 1975, pp. 82–85; http://transcriptions.english.ucsb.edu/archive/courses/liu/english25/materials/schumpeter.html).

- Because the best new jobs will demand brains rather than brawn, and because physical presence in a particular location at a particular time will become increasingly irrelevant, structural barriers to the employment of women and older Americans will continue to fall away. Americans of all backgrounds will be increasingly able to determine their own working environments and hours.

Second, the rest of the world matters to a degree that it never did in the past. We can no longer say anything sensible about the prospects for American workers if we consider only the U.S. economy or the characteristics of the U.S. labor force. Fast-growing Asian and Latin American economies present us with both opportunities and challenges. Meanwhile, communications and transportation costs have plummeted (declining to almost zero in the case of information exchanged on the Internet), resulting in what some have called "the death of distance." Whereas the costs of shipping an automobile or a heavy machine tool remain consequential, the products of the world's most dynamic industries—such as biological formulas, computers, financial services, microchips, and software—can cross the globe for a pittance. Investment capital is also more abundant and more mobile than ever before, traversing borders with abandon in search of the best ideas, the savviest entrepreneurs, and the most productive economies. The implications of this globalization for U.S. workers are no less complex than the implications of new technology:

- Manufacturing will continue to dominate U.S. exports. Almost 20 percent of U.S. manufacturing workers now have jobs that depend on exports; that figure will continue to escalate. America's growing export dependence in the early twenty-first century will benefit most of America's highly productive workers, because many foreign economies will continue to expand more rapidly than our own, thereby generating massive demand for U.S. goods. Skilled workers whose jobs depend on exports are better paid than other U.S. manufacturing workers as a rule, because the U.S. enjoys a comparative advantage in the specialized manufacturing and service sectors that create their jobs. These workers also tend to earn more than similar workers in other countries.

- But globalization will affect low-skilled or unskilled American workers very differently. They will compete for jobs and wages not just with their counterparts across town or in other parts of the U.S., but also with low-skilled workers around the globe. As labor costs become more important to manufacturers than shipping costs, the U.S. will retain almost no comparative advantage in low-skilled manufacturing. Jobs in that sector will disappear or be available only at depressed wages. Second or third jobs and full-time employment for both spouses—already the norm in households headed by low-skilled workers—will become even more necessary.

- Manufacturing's share of total U.S. employment will continue to decline, due to the combined effects of automation and globalization. But the millions of high-productivity manufacturing jobs that remain will be more highly skilled and therefore better paid than at any other time in U.S. history. Employment growth, meanwhile, will remain concentrated in services, which also will benefit increasingly from export markets and will offer high salaries for skilled workers.

- Globalization and technological change will make most segments of the U.S. economy extremely volatile, as comparative advantages in particular market segments rise and then fall away. Small- and medium-sized firms will be well situated to react to this volatility, and their numbers will grow. Labor unions will cope badly with this rapidly evolving economy of small producers, and their membership and influence will shrink. Individual workers will change jobs frequently over time. For those who maintain and improve their skills, the changes should bring increasing rewards. But the changes may be traumatic for those who fall behind the skills curve and resist retraining.

Third, America is getting older. At some level, all of us are aware of this. Our parents and grandparents are living longer, and we are having fewer children. But U.S. public policy as well as many employers have yet to come to grips with the full implications of America's aging. The oldest among America's so-called baby boomers—the massive cohort born between 1945 and 1965—will begin to reach age 65 in 2010. By 2020, almost 20 percent of the U.S. population will be 65 or older. There will be as many Americans of "retirement age" as there are 20–35-year-olds. America's aging baby boomers will decisively affect the U.S. workforce, through their departure from and continued presence in it, and as recipients of public entitlements and purchasers of services:

- America's taxpayer-funded entitlements for its aging population—Medicare and Social Security—are likely to undergo profound changes in the next two decades. The tax rates necessary to sustain the current "pay-as-you-go" approach to funding these programs as the baby boomers retire will rise, perhaps precipitously, unless the expectations of retirees regarding their benefits become more modest, the economy grows more strongly than expected, or the programs receive fundamental overhauls.

- Depending on how the funding of entitlement programs is resolved and how well individual baby boomers have prepared for retirement, some who reach age 65 will continue to require outside income and will be unable to retire. Many others will not want to retire and will seek flexible work options. As average life expectancies extend past 80 years of age, even many of the well-heeled will conclude that twenty years on golf courses and cruise ships do not present enough of a challenge.

- Whether they continue working or simply enjoy the fruits of past labors, America's aging baby boomers will constitute a large and powerful segment of the consumer market. Their resulting demand for entertainment, travel, and other leisure-time pursuits; specialized health care; long-term care facilities; and accounting, home-repair, and other professional services will fuel strong local labor markets throughout the U.S., but particularly in cities and regions that attract many retirees. The jobs created by this boom in the service sector in local economies may replace many of the low-skilled or unskilled manufacturing jobs the U.S. stands to lose, though not always at comparable wages.

Fourth, the U.S. labor force continues its ethnic diversification, though at a fairly slow pace. Most white non-Hispanics entering America's early twenty-first century workforce simply will replace exiting white workers; minorities will constitute slightly more than half of net new entrants to the U.S. workforce. Minorities will account for only about a third of total new entrants over the next decade. Whites constitute 76 percent of the total labor force today and will account for 68 percent in 2020. The share of African-Americans in the labor force probably will remain constant, at 11 percent, over the next twenty years. The Asian and Hispanic shares will grow to 6 and 14 percent, respectively. Most of this change will be due to the growth of Asian and Hispanic workforce representation in the South and West. The changes will not be dramatic on a national scale. The aging of the U.S. work-force will be far more dramatic than its ethnic shifts.

10   In summary, Hudson Institute's *Workforce 2020* offers a vision of a bifurcated U.S. labor force in the early twenty-first century. As we envision the next twenty-plus years, the skills premium appears even more powerful to us than it did to our predecessors who wrote *Workforce 2000*. Millions of Americans with proficiency in math, science, and the English language will join a global elite whose services will be in intense demand. These workers will command generous and growing compensation. Burgeoning local markets for services in some parts of the U.S. will continue to sustain some decent-paying, low-skill jobs. But other Americans with inadequate education and no technological expertise—how many depends in large part on what we do to improve their training—will face declining real wages or unemployment, particularly in manufacturing.

● Review Questions

1. What two qualities give an "unprecedented character" to the prospects for work in America in the coming years?

2. What major factors do researchers at the Hudson Institute think will shape the employment landscape in the coming years?

3. The writers claim that "the best new jobs will demand brains rather than brawn." Explain what they mean.

4. What are the implications of globalization for U.S. workers?

5. What are the implications of an aging American population for U.S. workers?

6. What is the "skills premium"?

● Discussion and Writing Suggestions

1. How appropriate and how effective do you find the "map" metaphor in the opening of the selection? Trace its use throughout the piece, and comment.

2. Given the Hudson Institute's forecast for work in the coming decades, how well do think your education to date, and your intended field of study, prepare you to take your place in the global economy? To what extent are you poised to join what the authors anticipate will be "a global elite"?

3. Those who endorse the principle of "creative destruction" (see paragraph 6) expect that the loss of industries and jobs to mechanization, computerization, or outsourcing will in time create new industries and jobs. Cite one example of a job category or industry lost. Do you see evidence of new jobs or industries forming?

4. Judy and D'Amico write that "more and more individuals [will] undertake their own journeys through the labor force, rather than 'hitching rides' on the traditional mass transportation provided by unions, large corporations, and government bureaucracies. For most workers, this 'free agency' will be immensely liberating. But for others, it will provoke anxiety and anger." What do you imagine your response will be to the likely "free agency" of working life? Do you expect to (or do you already) feel liberated? Angry or anxious? Explain.

5. Locate the Hudson Institute's *Workforce 2000*, written in 1987. Assess its accuracy in predicting contours of our present-day workforce.

The Untouchables

Thomas L. Friedman

Thomas Friedman, an investigative reporter and a columnist for the *New York Times,* won the National Book Award for *From Beirut to Jerusalem* (1989) and three Pulitzer Prizes for international reporting and commentary. Most recently he has written *Hot, Flat, and Crowded* (2008). The selection that follows appears in his best seller *The World Is Flat: A Brief History of the Twenty-First Century* (2005), in which Friedman explores the opportunities and dangers associated with globalization. Friedman uses the word "flat" to describe "the stunning rise of middle classes all over the world." In this newly flat world, "we are now connecting all the knowledge centers on the planet together into a single global network, which—if politics and terrorism do not get in the way—could usher in an amazing era of prosperity, innovation, and collaboration, by companies, communities, and individuals."

If the flattening of the world is largely (but not entirely) unstoppable, and if it holds out the potential to be as beneficial to American society in general as past market evolutions have been, how does an individual get the best out of it? What do we tell our kids?

My simple answer is this: There will be plenty of good jobs out there in the flat world for people with the right knowledge, skills, ideas, and self-motivation to seize them. But there is no sugar-coating the new challenge: Every young American today would be wise to think of himself or herself as competing against every young Chinese, Indian, and Brazilian. In Globalization 1.0, countries had to think globally to thrive, or at least survive. In Globalization 2.0, companies had to think globally to thrive, or at least survive. In Globalization 3.0, individuals have to think globally to thrive, or at least survive. This requires not only a new level of technical skills but also a certain mental flexibility, self-motivation, and psychological mobility. I am certain that we Americans can indeed thrive in this world. But I am also certain that it will not be as easy as it was in the last fifty years. Each of us, as an individual, will have to work a little harder and run a little faster to keep our standard of living rising.

"Globalization went from globalizing industries to globalizing individuals," said Vivek Paul, the Wipro president.* "I think today that people working in most jobs can sense how what they are doing integrates globally: 'I am working with someone in India. I am buying from someone in China. I am selling to someone in England.' As a result of the ability to move work around, we have created an amazing awareness on the part of every individual that says: 'Not only does my work have to fit into somebody's global supply chain, but I myself have to understand how I need to compete and have the skill sets required to work at a pace that fits the supply chain. And I had better be able to do that as well or better than anyone else in the world.' " That sense of responsibility for one's own advancement runs deeper than ever today. In many global industries now, you have got to justify your job every day with the value you create and the unique skills you contribute. And if you don't, that job can fly away farther and faster than ever.

In sum, it was never good to be mediocre in your job, but in a world of walls, mediocrity could still earn you a decent wage. You could get by and then some. In a flatter world, you *really* do not want to be mediocre or lack any passion for what you do. You don't want to find yourself in the shoes of Willy Loman in *Death of a Salesman*, when his son Biff dispels his idea that the Loman family is special by declaring, "Pop! I'm a dime a dozen, and so are you!" An angry Willy retorts, "I am not a dime a dozen! I am Willy Loman, and you are Biff Loman!"

5   I don't care to have that conversation with my girls, so my advice to them in this flat world is very brief and very blunt: "Girls, when I was growing up, my parents used to say to me, 'Tom, finish your dinner—people in China and India are starving.' My advice to you is: Girls, finish your homework—people in China and India are starving for your jobs." And in a flat world, they can have them, because in a flat world there is no such thing as an American job. There is just a job, and in more cases than ever before it will go to the best, smartest, most productive, or cheapest worker—wherever he or she resides.

---

*Wipro is a global technology company that provides "integrated business, technology, and process solutions" in North and South America, Europe, the Middle East, Asia, and Australia.

The New Middle

It is going to take more than just doing your homework to thrive in a flat world, though. You are going to have to do the *right kind* of homework as well. Because the companies that are adjusting best to the flat world are not just making minor changes, they are changing the whole model of the work they do and how they do it—in order to take advantage of the flat-world platform and to compete with others who are doing the same. What this means is that students also have to fundamentally reorient what they are learning and educators how they are teaching it. They can't just keep the same old model that worked for the past fifty years, when the world was round. This set of issues is what I will explore in this and the next chapter: What kind of good middle-class jobs are successful companies and entrepreneurs creating today? How do workers need to prepare themselves for those jobs, and how can educators help them do just that?

Let's start at the beginning. The key to thriving, as an individual, in a flat world is figuring out how to make yourself an "untouchable." That's right. When the world goes flat, the caste system gets turned upside down. In India, untouchables are the lowest social class, but in a flat world everyone should want to be an untouchable. "Untouchables," in my lexicon, are people whose jobs cannot be outsourced, digitized, or automated. And remember, as analyst David Rothkopf notes, most jobs are not lost to outsourcing to India or China— most lost jobs are "outsourced to the past." That is, they get digitized and automated. *The New York Times*'s Washington bureau used to have a telephone operator–receptionist. Now it has a recorded greeting and voice mail. That reception job didn't go to India; it went to the past or it went to a microchip. The flatter the world gets, the more anything that can be digitized, automated, or outsourced will be digitized, automated, or outsourced. As Infosys CEO Nandan Nilekani likes to say, in a flat world there is "fungible and nonfungible work." Work that can be easily digitized, automated, or transferred abroad is fungible. One of the most distinguishing features of the flat world is how many jobs—not just blue-collar manufacturing jobs but now also *white-collar service jobs*—are becoming fungible. Since more of us work in those service jobs than ever before, more of us will be affected.

• • •

[W]ho will the untouchables be? What jobs are not likely to become fungible, easy to automate, digitize, or outsource? I would argue that the untouchables in a flat world will fall into three broad categories. First are people who are really "special or specialized." This label would apply to Michael Jordan, Madonna, Elton John, J. K. Rowling, your brain surgeon, and the top cancer researcher at the National Institutes of Health. These people perform functions in ways that are so special or specialized that they can never be outsourced, automated, or made tradable by electronic transfer. They are untouchables. They have a global market for their goods and services and can command global wages.

Second are people who are really "localized" and "anchored." This category includes many, many people. They are untouchables because their jobs must be done in a specific location, either because they involve some specific local knowledge or because they require face-to-face, personalized contact or interaction with a customer, client, patient, colleague, or audience. All these people are untouchables because they are anchored: my barber, the waitress at lunch, the chefs in the kitchen, the plumber, nurses, my dentist, lounge singers, masseurs, retail sales clerks, repairmen, electricians, nannies, gardeners, cleaning ladies, and divorce lawyers. Note that these people can be working in high-end jobs (divorce lawyer, dentist), vocational jobs (plumber, carpenter), or low-end jobs (garbage collector, maid). Regardless of that worker's level of sophistication, their wages will be set by the local market forces of supply and demand.

10   That then brings me to the third broad category. This category includes people in many formerly middle-class jobs—from assembly line work to data entry to securities analysis to certain forms of accounting and radiology—that were once deemed nonfungible or nontradable and are now being made quite fungible and tradable thanks to the ten flatteners.* Let's call these the "old middle" jobs. Many of them are now under pressure from the flattening of the world. As Nandan Nilekani puts it: "The problem [for America] is in the middle. Because the days when you could count on being an accounts-payable clerk are gone. And a lot of the middle class are where that [old] middle is.... This middle has not yet grasped the competitive intensity of the future. Unless they [do], they will not make the investments in reskilling themselves and you will end up with a lot of people stranded on an island."

That is not something we want. The American economy used to look like a bell curve, with a big bulge in the middle. That bulge of middle-class jobs has been the foundation not only of our economic stability but of our political stability as well. Democracy cannot be stable without a broad and deep middle class. We cannot afford to move from a bell curve economy to a barbell economy—with a big high end and a bigger low end and nothing in the middle. It would be economically unfair and politically unstable. As former Clinton national economic adviser Gene Sperling rightly argues, "We either grow together or we will grow apart."

So if the next new thing is the automation and outsourcing of more and more old middle-class jobs, then the big question for America—and every other developed country—is this: What will be the jobs of the new middle, and what skills will they be based on? In the United States, new middle jobs are coming into being all the time; that is why we don't have large-scale unemployment, despite the flattening of the world. But to get and keep these new middle jobs you need certain skills that are suited to the flat world—skills that can make you, at least temporarily, special, specialized, or anchored, and therefore, at least temporarily, an untouchable. In the new middle, we are all temps now.

---

*In *The World Is Flat*, Friedman argues that ten forces have "flattened" the world. These forces include the fall of the Berlin Wall (November 1989), the emergence of Internet connectivity, and the outsourcing of work.

● Review Questions

1. Why in a "flat" world do you not want to be mediocre in your work?

2. Why does one want to be "untouchable" in a flat world, according to Friedman?

3. What kinds of workers are likely to remain untouchable in the global economy?

4. What are the differences between a bell-curve and a barbell economy? What implications do these differences hold for the future?

● Discussion and Writing Suggestions

1. Read Alan S. Blinder's "Will Your Job Be Exported?" (summary, page 243; article, pages 8–13). Compare and contrast his analysis of the future job market with Friedman's.

2. Tell the story of someone you know well—a grandparent, perhaps— who has never quite felt comfortable in the digital age. Maybe remote controls, cell phones, or computers are a challenge to this individual. Speculate on the ways in which retraining for the new economy might also be a challenge.

3. Consider your work history and the work you intend to do in the future. Use Friedman's distinction of fungible/nonfungible as a lens to analyze your past and intended work. What observations can you make?

4. Having read this piece, to what extent are you inclined at all to rethink your course selections in the coming semesters? Has Friedman's argument prompted you to reconsider your major? Explain.

5. Friedman writes: "In Globalization 3.0, individuals have to think globally to thrive, or at least survive. This requires not only a new level of technical skills but also a certain mental flexibility, self-motivation, and psychological mobility." What technical skills do you plan to develop in college? How mentally flexible do you see yourself? Self-motivated? Psychologically mobile? Aside from the technical, how does one *learn* these attributes?

6. Do you find challenges in "thinking globally" about your intended work? As you prepare yourself to take on rewarding work in the twenty-first century, to what degree do you anticipate competition from workers in India or China?

WILL YOUR JOB BE EXPORTED? [SUMMARY]

Alan S. Blinder

Alan S. Blinder is the Gordon S. Rentschler Memorial Professor of Economics at Princeton University. He has served as vice chairman of the Federal Reserve Board and was a member of President Clinton's original Council of Economic Advisers. This article first appeared in *The American Prospect* in November 2006. The following summary of "Will Your Job Be Exported?" appears in Chapter 1, in the context of a discussion on how to write summaries. See pp. 8–13 for the complete text of this important article.

In "Will Your Job Be Exported?" economist Alan S. Blinder argues that the quality and security of future jobs in America's services sector will be determined by how "offshorable" those jobs are. For the past 25 years, the greater a worker's skill or level of education, the better and more stable the job. No longer. Advances in technology have brought to the service sector the same pressures that forced so many manufacturing jobs offshore to China and India. The rate of offshoring in the service sector will accelerate, and jobs requiring both relatively little education (like call-center staffing) and extensive education (like software development) will increasingly be lost to workers overseas.

These losses will "eventually exceed" losses in manufacturing, but not all service jobs are equally at risk. While "personal services" workers (like barbers and surgeons) will be relatively safe from offshoring because their work requires close physical proximity to customers, "impersonal services" workers (like call-center operators and radiologists), regardless of their skill or education, will be at risk because their work can be completed remotely without loss of quality and then delivered via phone or computer. "[T]he relative demand for labor in the United States will [probably] shift away from impersonal services and toward personal services."

Blinder recommends three courses of action. He advises young people to plan for "a high-end personal services occupation that is not offshorable." He urges educators to prepare the future workforce by anticipating the needs of a personal services economy and redesigning classroom instruction and vocational training accordingly. Finally, he urges the government to adopt policies that will improve existing personal services jobs by increasing wages for low-wage workers; retraining workers to take on better jobs; and increasing opportunities in high-demand, well-paid areas like nursing and carpentry. Ultimately, Blinder wants America to prepare a new generation to "lead and innovate" in an economy that will continue exporting jobs that require "following and copying."

● Review Questions

1. What is "offshoring"? Why have service jobs been thought "immune to foreign competition"?

2. Explain Blinder's distinction between "personal services" and "impersonal services." Why is this distinction important?

3. In the past 25 years, what role has education played in preparing people for work? How does Blinder see that role changing in the coming decades?

4. What advice does Blinder offer to young people preparing for future work in the coming decades?

5. Why will the United States eventually lose more service-sector than manufacturing-sector jobs?

● **Discussion and Writing Suggestions**

1. Identify a worker (real or imagined) in a job that may be at risk for offshoring, according to Blinder. Write a letter to that person, apprising him or her of the potential danger and offering advice you think appropriate.

2. What is your reaction to Blinder's claim that educational achievement, in and of itself, will be less of a predictor of job quality and security than it once was?

3. Describe a well-paying job that would not require a college education but that should, according to Blinder, be immune to offshoring. Compare your responses to those of your classmates.

4. What work can you imagine doing in ten years? Describe that work in a concise paragraph. Now analyze your description as Blinder might. How secure is your future job likely to be?

5. Approach friends who have not read the Blinder article with his advice on preparing for future work (see Review Question 4). Report on their reactions.

6. What were your *emotional* reactions to Blinder's article? Did the piece leave you feeling hopeful, anxious, apprehensive, excited? Explain.

INTO THE UNKNOWN

The Economist

The following piece first appeared in *The Economist* (November 13, 2004).

Where will the jobs of the future come from?

"Has the machine in its last furious manifestation begun to eliminate workers faster than new tasks can be found for them?" wonders Stuart Chase, an American writer. "Mechanical devices are already ousting skilled clerical workers and replacing them with operators....Opportunity in the white-collar services is being steadily undermined." The anxiety sounds thoroughly contemporary. But Mr. Chase's publisher, MacMillan, "set up and electrotyped" his book, *Men and Machines*, in 1929.

The worry about "exporting" jobs that currently grips America, Germany and Japan is essentially the same as Mr. Chase's worry about mechanization 75 years ago. When companies move manufacturing plants from Japan to China, or call-center workers from America to India, they are changing the way they produce things. This change in production technology has the same effect as automation: some workers in America, Germany and Japan lose their jobs as machines or foreign workers take over. This fans fears of rising unemployment.

What the worriers always forget is that the same changes in production technology that destroy jobs also create new ones. Because machines and foreign workers can perform the same work more cheaply, the cost of production falls. That means higher profits and lower prices, lifting demand for new goods and services. Entrepreneurs set up new businesses to meet demand for these new necessities of life, creating new jobs.

5   As Alan Greenspan, chairman of America's Federal Reserve Bank, has pointed out, there is always likely to be anxiety about the jobs of the future, because in the long run most of them will involve producing goods and services that have not yet been invented.* William Nordhaus, an economist at Yale University, has calculated that under 30% of the goods and services consumed at the end of the 20th century were variants of the goods and services produced 100 years earlier. "We travel in vehicles that were not yet invented that are powered by fuels not yet produced, communicate through devices not yet manufactured, enjoy cool air on the hottest days, are entertained by electronic wizardry that was not dreamed of and receive medical treatments that were unheard of," writes Mr. Nordhaus. What hardy late 19th-century American pioneer would have guessed that, barely more than a century later, his country would find employment for (by the government's latest count) 139,000 psychologists, 104,000 floral designers and 51,000 manicurists and pedicurists?

Even relatively short-term labor-market predictions can be hazardous. In 1988, government experts at the Bureau of Labor Statistics confidently predicted strong demand in America over the next 12 years for, among others, travel agents and [gas]-station attendants. But by 2000, the number of travel agents had fallen by 6% because more travellers booked online, and the number of pump attendants was down to little more than half because drivers were filling up their cars themselves. Of the 20 occupations that the government predicted would suffer the most job losses between 1988 and 2000, half actually gained jobs. Travel agents have now joined the government's list of endangered occupations for 2012. Maybe they are due for a modest revival. You never know.

The bureau's statisticians are now forecasting a large rise in the number of nurses, teachers, salespeople, "combined food preparation and serving workers, including fast food" (a fancy way of saying burger flippers), waiters, truck

---

*Alan Greenspan served as chairman of the Federal Reserve Bank from 1987 to 2006.

drivers and security guards over the next eight years. If that list fails to strike a chord with recent Stanford graduates, the bureau also expects America to create an extra 179,000 software-engineering jobs and 185,000 more places for computer-systems analysts over the same period.

Has the bureau forgotten about Bangalore? Probably not. Catherine Mann of the Institute for International Economics points out that the widely quoted number of half a million for [Information Technology] jobs "lost" to India in the past couple of years takes as its starting point the year 2001, the top of the industry's cycle. Most of the subsequent job losses were due to the recession in the industry rather than to an exodus to India. Measured from 1999 to 2003, the number of IT-related white-collar jobs in America has risen. . . .

Ms. Mann thinks that demand will continue to grow as falling prices help to spread IT more widely through the economy, and as American companies demand more tailored software and services. Azim Premji, the boss of Wipro,* is currently trying to expand his business in America. "IT professionals are in short supply in America," says Mr. Premji. "Within the next few months, we will have a labor shortage."

10   If that seems surprising, it illustrates a larger confusion about jobs and work. Those who worry about the migration of white-collar work abroad like to talk about "lost jobs" or "jobs at risk." Ashok Bardhan, an economist at the University of California at Berkeley, thinks that 14 [million] Americans, a whopping 11% of the workforce, are in jobs "at risk to outsourcing." The list includes computer operators, computer professionals, paralegals and legal assistants. But what Mr. Bardhan is really saying is that some of this work can now also be done elsewhere.

What effect this has on jobs and pay will depend on supply and demand in the labor market and on the opportunity, willingness and ability of workers to retrain. American computer professionals, for instance, have been finding recently that certain skills, such as maintaining standard business-software packages, are no longer in such demand in America, because there are plenty of Indian programmers willing to do this work more cheaply. On the other hand, IT firms in America face a shortage of skills in areas such as tailored business software and services. There is a limited supply of fresh IT graduates to recruit and train in America, so companies such as IBM and Accenture are having to retrain their employees in these sought-after skills.

Moreover, Mr. Bardhan's list of 14 [million] jobs at risk features many that face automation anyway, regardless of whether the work is first shipped abroad. Medical transcriptionists, data-entry clerks and a large category of 8.6 [million] miscellaneous "office support" workers may face the chop as companies find new ways of mechanizing paperwork and capturing information.

Indeed, the definition of the sort of work that Indian outsourcing firms are good at doing remotely—repetitive and bound tightly by rules—sounds just like

---

*See footnote on p. 239.

the sort of work that could also be delegated to machines. If offshoring is to be blamed for this "lost" work, then mechanical diggers should be blamed for usurping the work of men with shovels. In reality, shedding such lower-value tasks enables economies to redeploy the workers concerned to jobs that create more value.

Stuart Chase understood the virtuous economics of technological change, but he still could not stop himself from fretting. "An uneasy suspicion has gathered that the saturation point has at last been reached" he reflected darkly. Could it be that, with the invention of the automobile, central heating, the phonograph and the electric refrigerator, entrepreneurs had at long last emptied the reservoir of human desires? He need not have worried. Today's list of human desires includes instant messaging, online role-playing games and internet dating services, all unknown in the 1920s. And there will be many more tomorrow.

Review Questions

1. What is the main mechanism by which the economy creates jobs even as it eliminates jobs through automation, computerization, and outsourcing?

2. The *Economist* believes that while our anxiety at being unable to identify future jobs that will replace current jobs lost to outsourcing is understandable, our apprehensions are not warranted. Why not?

3. What types of jobs are most easily outsourced, and how does such outsourcing create opportunities for American companies and their employees?

4. What is the role of human desire in fueling the economy?

Discussion and Writing Suggestions

1. The writers open this article by playing a trick of sorts on readers: quoting Stuart Chase on the topic of job loss to advancing technology. Discuss this strategy. Did you find it effective?

2. The *Economist* trusts the economy to create new jobs. Do you? In developing your response, reread paragraphs 3 and 4.

3. How would you describe the mood of this piece—relatively optimistic or pessimistic? Explain.

4. How does the economic news of the day color your reading of the piece? In your view, does the validity of the *Economist's* basic argument change at all in tough economic times?

5. Briefly research the term "market fundamentalism." What does it mean, and to what extent does it apply to the *Economist's* position in this essay?

OCCUPATIONAL OUTLOOK HANDBOOK, 2008–09 EDITION

Bureau of Labor Statistics

The Bureau of Labor Statistics, a division of the U.S. Department of Labor, regularly publishes its *Occupational Outlook Handbook,* which for hundreds of occupations provides current, thorough information on the following: "the training and education needed, earnings, expected job prospects, what workers do on the job, and working conditions." Use these categories to learn more about the occupations that interest you. And draw on the *OOH* Web site as a dependable resource while writing papers associated with this chapter.

Access the OOH Web site at *http://www.bls.gov/oco/.* To prepare for more detailed use later, devote 15 or 20 minutes to exploring the site and its offerings.

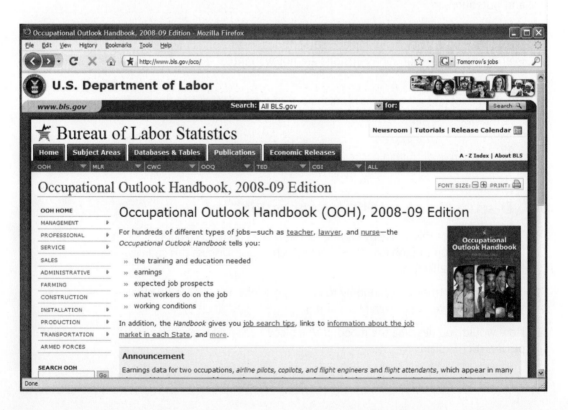

TOMORROW'S JOBS: 2006–2016

Bureau of Labor Statistics

An important document that can be accessed from the Occupational Outlook Handbook Web site is the BLS study "Tomorrow's Jobs." The U.S. Department of Labor releases these ten-year employment projections every two years as part of a "60-year tradition of providing information to individuals who are making education and training choices, entering the job market, or changing careers." This is not likely a report you will read in its entirety. The more appropriate strategy would be to download the pdf file (or browse the Web site online) and skim its contents, returning to sections as needed when writing your papers. You will find statistically backed projections on changes in the age and ethnic makeup of the labor pool and expanding and shrinking employment opportunities by industry sector.

Access "Tomorrow's Jobs" at *http://www.bls.gov/oco/oco2003.htm*.

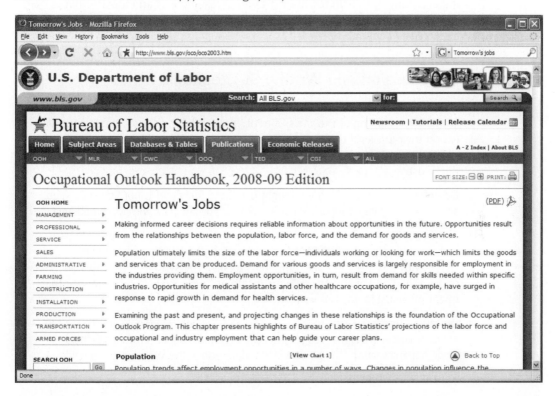

Review Questions

Go the Web site http://www.bls.gov/oco and answer these questions:

1. How is the *Occupational Outlook Handbook (OOH)* organized?

2. What nine specific types of information can a researcher find for every job listed in the *OOH* database?

3. From the *OOH* page for a particular occupation, follow a link to an associated OES (Occupational Employment Statistics) page. What information do you find there?

Under "Related Links" on the above Web site, go to "Tomorrow's Jobs"—or find that Bureau of Labor Statistics (BLS) Web site directly at http://www.bls.gov/oco/oco2003.htm. Answer these questions:

4. What is the purpose of the BLS report "Tomorrow's Jobs"?

5. How is "Tomorrow's Jobs" organized?

6. Under the heading of "Labor Force" in "Tomorrow's Jobs," find the BLS projection for the youth labor force's share of the overall labor force by 2016.

7. Under the "Industry" heading, what do you learn about the goods-producing economy of the United States? Offer an example of an industry that is expected to grow between now and 2016. Offer an example of an industry expected to decline.

● Discussion and Writing Suggestions

1. Your evaluation of every Web site can begin (but should not necessarily end) with a close reading of the site's "About" page, which most reputable sites will list on their top-level (or home) pages. Locate the "About BLS" Web page and report on what you find. How, for instance, does BLS gather the statistics you might use in a paper?

2. Describe the ways in which you might use these Bureau of Labor Statistics Web sites to investigate either broad career areas or specific jobs within a broad area.

3. The *Occupational Outlook Handbook* is a vast resource that can provide you with credible statistical information as you complete writing assignments associated with this chapter. Take a moment to skim the synthesis activities on pages 276–278. For any *one* activity, locate on these Web pages a statistic that might prove useful in your writing.

4. Peruse the Teacher's Guide to the *Occupational Outlook Handbook*, which you can access from the OOH main page or directly at http://www.bls.gov/oco/teachers_guide.htm#navigating. The guide will introduce you to the Web site and provide additional resources for research related to this chapter.

ARE THEY REALLY READY TO WORK?

Jill Casner-Lotto and Linda Barrington

The following selection, "Are They Really Ready to Work? Employers' Perspectives on the Basic Knowledge and Applied Skills of New Entrants to the 21st Century U.S. Workforce," is part of a collaborative report produced by four organizations devoted to promoting a robust business environment in the 21st century.[1] During the spring of 2006, these organizations commissioned a survey of more than 400 employers for the purpose of ascertaining their views on the readiness of new entrants to the workforce to assume responsibilities in the modern economy. You can read the full report at http://www.conferenceboard.org/Publications/describe.cfm?id=1218.

Jill Casner-Lotto and Linda Barrington prepared this report. Casner-Lotto, a former senior vice president for policy studies at Work in America Institute, conducts research on human resources and labor-management issues. Barrington is a labor economist and Research Director at The Conference Board.

Presidents' Letter

What skills are necessary for success in the workplace of the 21st century? And do new entrants to the workforce, graduates of high school, two-year and four-year colleges have those skills? These and other questions were posed in a survey of human resource professionals mounted in the spring of 2006 by The Conference Board, Corporate Voices for Working Families, the Partnership for 21st Century Skills and the Society for Human Resource Management. It is our hope that through our combined resources, reputations, and strong member bases ... the business community, educators, policy makers, students and their families will listen to what employers collectively think of the new workforce in America. The results indicate that the U.S. is not doing enough, fast enough, to prepare for a vibrant economic future for our children and our nation.

Young people need a range of skills, both basic academic skills as well as the ability to apply these skills and knowledge in the workplace. The survey results indicate that far too many young people are inadequately prepared to be successful in the workplace. At the high school level, well over one-half of new entrants are deficiently prepared in the most important skills—*Oral* and *Written Communications, Professionalism/Work Ethic*, and *Critical Thinking/Problem Solving*. College graduates are better prepared, with lower levels of deficiency on the most important skills, but too few are excelling. Only about one-quarter of four-year college graduates are perceived to be excellent in many of the most important skills, and more than one-quarter of four-year college graduates are perceived to be deficiently prepared in *Written Communications.*

How can the United States continue to compete in a global economy if the entering workforce is made up of high school graduates who lack the skills they need, and of college graduates who are mostly "adequate" rather than "excellent"? The quandary is particularly problematic because it comes just as the workforce is entering a period of realignment. As the baby-boomers retire—taking their skills and knowledge with them—America faces a shortage of available workers. This report indicates that the pool of talented workers available is even smaller.

So, what are the solutions? All of us must do our part to ensure that our students are well-prepared for the workforce demands of the 21st century. The

---

[1]The four organizations are The Conference Board, Corporate Voices for Working Families, The Partnership for 21st Century Skills, and The Society for Human Resource Management.

education and business communities must agree that applied skills integrated with core academic subjects are the "design specs" for creating an educational system that will prepare our high school and college graduates to succeed in the modern workplace and community life. These skills are in demand for all students, regardless of their future plans, and will have an enormous impact on our students' ability to compete.

5   Business leaders must take an active role in outlining the kinds of skills we need from our employees for our companies and economy to thrive. This report is a first step in articulating these necessary skills. But we can do much more than that. As business leaders, we must also play a role in creating opportunities for young people to obtain the skills they need. Businesses can partner with schools and other organizations that work with young people to provide internships, job shadowing programs and summer jobs. Businesses can encourage their employees to serve as mentors and tutors. Businesses can invest in programs at the local and national level that have demonstrated their ability to improve outcomes for young people. Finally, business leaders can use their expertise in innovation and management to help identify new and creative solutions.

This report underscores the importance of increased workforce readiness. This requirement is now more important than ever because of our increasingly complex knowledge- and technology-based global economy. The business community must speak with one voice: new entrants to the U.S. workforce must be equipped with the basic knowledge and applied skills necessary to be competitive in the global economy of the 21st century. We hope the messages found in the results of this study will inspire action.

Richard E. Cavanagh
President and CEO
The Conference Board

Ken Kay
President
Partnership for 21st Century Skills

Donna Klein
President and CEO
Corporate Voices for Working
    Families

Susan R. Meisinger
President and CEO
Society for Human Resource
    Management

Executive Summary

The future U.S. workforce is here—and it is woefully ill-prepared for the demands of today's (and tomorrow's) workplace. So say employers in a unique study by The Conference Board, Corporate Voices for Working Families, Partnership for 21st Century Skills, and the Society for Human Resource Management, which looks at the readiness of new entrants to the workforce. Knowing how employers view these new entrants is an important first step in enabling both these new entrants and U.S. business to succeed on the global economic playing field.

The four participating organizations jointly surveyed over 400 employers across the United States. These employers articulate the skill sets that new entrants—recently hired graduates from high school, two-year colleges or technical schools, and four-year colleges—need to succeed in the workplace. Among the most important skills cited by employers:

- Professionalism/Work Ethic
- Oral and Written Communications
- Teamwork/Collaboration and
- Critical Thinking/Problem Solving.

In fact, the findings indicate that applied skills[1] on all educational levels trump basic knowledge and skills, such as *Reading Comprehension* and *Mathematics*. In other words, while the "three Rs" are still fundamental to any new workforce entrant's ability to do the job, employers emphasize that applied skills like *Teamwork/ Collaboration* and *Critical Thinking* are "very important" to success at work.

Basic Knowledge/Skills	*Applied Skills**
English Language (spoken)	Critical Thinking/Problem Solving
Reading Comprehension (In English)	Oral Communications
	Written Communications
Writing in English (grammar, spelling, etc.)	Teamwork/Collaboration Diversity
Mathematics	Information Technology Application
Science	
Government/Economics Humanities/Arts	Leadership
	Creativity/Innovation
Foreign Languages	Lifelong Learning/Self Direction
History/Geography	Professionalism/Work Ethic
	Ethics/Social Responsibility

10   *A Poor Report Card*   When asked to assess new workforce entrants, employers report that many of the new entrants lack skills essential to job success. A Workforce Readiness Report Card[2] presents each of the three educational

---

[1]Applied skills refer to those skills that enable new entrants to use the basic knowledge acquired in school to perform in the workplace.

[2]Skills rated "very important" by a majority of employer respondents appear on either the Excellence List or on the Deficiency List of the Report Card if at least 1 in 5 employer respondents rate new entrants' skill readiness as "excellent" or "deficient," respectively.

*See definitions of these applied skills on p. 259.

levels considered in the study. Employers expect young people to arrive in the workplace with a set of basic and applied skills, and the Workforce Readiness Report Card makes clear that the reality is not matching expectations.

- The Workforce Readiness Report Card for new entrants with a high school diploma does not have a single item in the Excellence List. All 10 skills that a majority of employer respondents rate as "very important" to workforce success are on the Deficiency List.

- For two-year college-educated entrants, one "very important" applied skill— *Information Technology Application*—appears on the Excellence List while seven skills appear on the Deficiency List.

- Only for the four-year college-educated entrants to the workforce is the Excellence List longer than the Deficiency List on the Report Card.

Encouraging news, however, is the appearance of *Creativity/Innovation* on the Excellence List for four-year college-educated entrants. Creativity and innovation are important drivers for the economic progress of individual businesses and for the economy-at-large. It should be noted, however, that *Creativity/Innovation* barely clears the threshold for placement on the Excellence List.

The report's findings reflect employers' growing frustrations over the lack of skills they see in new workforce entrants. Which skills do employers view as "very important" now and which are increasing in importance?

A combination of basic knowledge and applied skills are perceived to be critical for new entrants' success in the 21st century U.S. workforce, but when basic knowledge and applied skills rankings are combined for each educational level, the top five "most important" are almost always applied skills.

- *Professionalism/Work Ethic, Teamwork/Collaboration* and *Oral Communications* are rated as the three "most important" applied skills needed by entrants into today's workforce.

- *Knowledge of Foreign Languages* will "Increase in importance" in the next five years, more than any other basic skill, according to over 60 percent (63.3 percent) of the employer respondents.

- *Making Appropriate Choices Concerning Health and Wellness* is the No.1 emerging content area for future graduates entering the U.S. workforce as reported by three-quarters of the employer respondents (76.1 percent).[3]

- *Creativity/Innovation* is projected to "Increase in importance" for future workforce entrants, according to more than 70 percent (73.6 percent) of employer respondents. Currently, however, more than half of employer respondents (54.2 percent) report new workforce entrants with a high school diploma to be "deficient" in this skill set, and relatively few consider two-year and four-year college-educated entrants to be "excellent" (4.1 percent and 21.5 percent, respectively).

---

[3]Emerging content areas refer to topics not typically emphasized in schools today, such as personal financial responsibility.

In the next five years, college graduates will continue to increase in number among new hires. More than one-quarter of employer respondents (27.7 percent) project that over the next five years their companies will reduce hiring of new entrants with only a high school diploma. Almost 60 percent (58.8 percent) project that their companies will increase hiring of four-year college graduates and about half (49.5 percent) project increased hiring of two-year college/technical school graduates.

15 *Improvements Needed*   The results of this study leave little doubt that improvements are needed in the readiness of new workforce entrants, if "excellence" is the standard for global competitiveness. While the employer respondents report that some new workforce entrants have "excellent" basic knowledge and applied skills, significant "deficiencies" exist among entrants at every educational level, especially those coming directly from high school.

High School Graduates are:

- "Deficient" in the basic knowledge and skills of *Writing in English, Mathematics*, and *Reading Comprehension*.
- "Deficient" in *Written Communications* and *Critical Thinking/Problem Solving*, both of which may be dependent on basic knowledge and skills,
- "Deficient" in *Professionalism/Work Ethic*, and
- "Adequate" in three "very important" applied skills: *Information Technology Application, Diversity*, and *Teamwork/Collaboration*.

Two-Year and Four-College Graduates are:

- Better prepared than high school graduates for the entry-level jobs they fill,
- "Deficient" in *Writing in English* and *Written Communications*, and
- "Deficient" in *Leadership*.

DEMOGRAPHIC ISSUES WARRANT ACTION

With significant numbers of workers retiring over the next 10 years, the United States is facing a serious challenge in preparing students to meet workplace demands in an increasingly complex, knowledge-and technology-based, global economy. The results of this study reinforce the need for action. The demographic and economic changes facing the United States today have major implications for the worker, the workplace, and for U.S. competitiveness.

- Over half (57 percent) of U.S. CEOs report education and workforce preparedness is a "very important" or "most important" policy issue. Nearly three-quarters (73 percent) of those CEOs who report having difficulty

(continued)

finding qualified workers in the U.S. rate global competitiveness as "very important" or "most important."[4]

- Between 2000 and 2010, the number of workers ages 35–44 will decrease by 10 percent and those aged 16–24 will increase by 15 percent.[5]
- Between 2000 and 2015, about 85 percent of newly created U.S. jobs will require education beyond high school.[6]

[4]*The Business Council Survey of Chief Executives: CEO Survey Results, February 2006.* The Business Council and The Conference Board, Chart 4 and p. 7.
[5]U.S. Bureau of Labor Statistics, *Occupational Outlook Quarterly*, Winter 2001–02.
[6]Gunderson, Steve; Jones, Roberts; and Scanland, Kathryn, *The Jobs Revolution: Changing How America Works*, 2005. Copywriters Incorporated, a division of The Greystone Group, Inc.

The study's findings are valuable to new (and future) workforce entrants, as well as to business people, educators, policy makers, and members of community organizations—anyone who has an interest in ensuring the success of new entrants into the U.S. workforce. The preparedness and skill levels of its workforce are critical factors in the ability of the United States to stay competitive in the 21st century.

Across the U.S. alarm bells are sounding in the business community about educating tomorrow's workforce. This study's results are consistent with important initiatives launched by a number of other business organizations in response to a growing talent gap and to the impact that gap has on the United States' ability to maintain its competitive lead in the world economy.[7] The business community, as represented in part by this research consortium, is speaking with one voice, calling for higher standards of workforce excellence consistent with the demands of the 21st century.

Summary of Results by Educational Level

HIGH SCHOOL GRADUATE ENTRANTS

Falling Short in *Overall Preparation* for Entry-Level Jobs   Over 40 percent (42.4 percent) of employer respondents rate new entrants with a high school diploma as "deficient" in their *Overall Preparation* for the entry-level jobs they typically fill. Almost the same percentage (45.6 percent) rate the *Overall Preparation* of high school graduate entrants as "adequate," but almost no one (less than 1/2 of 1 percent—0.2 percent) rates their *Overall Preparation* as "excellent."

[7]*Tapping America's Potential,* July 2005. The Business Roundtable; *Innovate America: Thriving in a World of Challenge and Change.* July 2004. National Innovation Initiative. Council on Competitiveness; Pawloski, Brett, *Notes from the 2005 Business Education Network Summit,* October 2005. U.S. Chamber of Commerce, DeHavill and Associates; *2005 Skills Gap Report—A Survey of the American Manufacturing Workforce,* November 2005. National Association of Manufacturers, Manufacturers Institute, and Deloitte Consulting LLP.

Many Report "Deficiencies" in Three "Very Important" Basic Skills

Writing in English—72.0 percent of employer respondents rate new entrants with a high school diploma as "deficient." Almost half (49.4 percent) of them say basic *Writing in English*, including grammar and spelling, are "very important" for high school graduates' successful job performance.

20   *Mathematics*—53.5 percent of employer respondents report high school graduate entrants as "deficient." Almost one-third of respondents (30.4 percent) say knowledge of *Mathematics* is "very important" for this group of entrants.

     Reading Comprehension—38.4 percent of employer respondents report high school graduate entrants as "deficient." Nearly two-thirds of respondents (62.5 percent) say *Reading Comprehension* is "very important" for high school graduate entrants' success in the workforce.

Most Report "Deficiencies" in Applied Skills

Written Communications—80.9 percent of employer respondents report high school graduate entrants as "deficient." More than half (52.7 percent) say *Written Communications*, which includes writing memos, letters, complex reports clearly and effectively, is "very important" for high school graduates' successful job performance.

     Professionalism/Work Ethic—70.3 percent of employer respondents report high school graduate entrants as "deficient." *Professionalism/Work Ethic*, defined as "demonstrating personal accountability, effective work habits, e.g., punctuality, working productively with others, time and workload management" is rated "very important" for high school graduates' successful job performance by 80.3 percent of employer respondents.

25   *Critical Thinking/Problem Solving*—69.6 percent of employer respondents report high school graduate entrants as "deficient." More than half of the employer respondents (57.5 percent) indicate that *Critical Thinking/Problem Solving* abilities are "very important" to successful performance on the job for this group of new entrants.

"Adequate" in Three "Very Important" Applied Skills

While "excellence" is infrequently reported, over 60 percent of employer respondents rate the preparation of high school graduate entrants as "adequate" in three applied skills considered "very important" for successful job performance by a majority of employers—*Information Technology* (IT) *Application, Diversity,* and *Teamwork/Collaboration*.

     IT Application—62.8 percent report high school graduate entrants' preparation is "adequate."

     IT Application is rated "very important" by 53.0 percent of employer respondents.

     Diversity—61.8 percent report high school graduate entrants' preparation is "adequate."

     Diversity is rated "very important" by 52.1 percent of employer respondents.

     Teamwork/Collaboration—60.9 percent of employer respondents rate high school graduate entrants' preparation as "adequate." *Teamwork/Collaboration* is considered "very important" by nearly three-quarters (74.7 percent) of employer respondents.

TWO-YEAR AND FOUR-YEAR COLLEGE GRADUATES

"Adequate" in General Preparation for the Entry-Level Jobs They Typically Fill
Employer respondents were asked, in general, how they rated the preparation of recent graduates hired for entry-level jobs in their U.S. workplaces (*Overall Preparation*). The majority of employer respondents rate *Overall Preparation* of both two-year and four-year college graduates as "adequate" (70.1 percent and 64.5 percent, respectively) for the entry-level jobs they fill. A small percentage reports that two-year and four-year college-educated entrants are "excellent" in terms of their *Overall Preparation* (10.3 percent and 23.9 percent, respectively). On a more positive note, only a small percentage of employer respondents (10.8 percent and 8.7 percent, respectively) rates two-year and four-year college graduates as "deficient" in their *Overall Preparation* for work.

30   **"Deficiencies" in Basic Knowledge of *Writing in English* and in *Written Communications*, Even with a College Diploma**
Writing in English—46.4 percent of employer respondents report new workforce entrants with a two-year college diploma as "deficient," and over a quarter (26.2 percent) report that new workforce entrants with a four-year college diploma are "deficient." Almost two-thirds of employer respondents (64.9) say *Writing in English* is "very important" for two-year college graduates; almost 90 percent (89.7 percent) say these skills are "very important" for four-year college graduates.

   Written Communications—47.3 percent and 27.8 percent of employer respondents, respectively, report new entrants with two-year and four-year college diplomas as "deficient." Almost three-quarters of the employer respondents (71.5 percent) say *Written Communications* is "very important" for two-year college graduates. For four-year college graduates, 93.1 percent say *Written Communications* is "very important."

"Deficiencies" in a "Very Important" Applied Skill: *Leadership*
Leadership—42.6 percent of employer respondents report two-year college-educated entrants as "deficient," and almost a quarter (23.8 percent) report four-year college-educated entrants "deficient." This "deficiency" is the second most frequently rated "deficient" skill for both two-and four-year college graduates. *Leadership* is rated as a "very important" applied skill for new entrants with a two-year college diploma by 45.4 percent of employer respondents. An overwhelming majority (81.8 percent) rate *Leadership* as "very important" for new entrants with a four-year college diploma.

Skills: Basic and Applied

LIST OF SKILLS

Basic Knowledge/Skills*

English Language (spoken)	Government/Economics
Reading Comprehension (in English)	Humanities/Arts

---

*For the most part, this list of basic knowledge and skill areas includes the core academic subjects as identified by the No Child Left Behind Act of 2001.

Writing in English (grammar, spelling, etc.)	Foreign Languages
Mathematics	History/Geography
Science	

Applied Skills*

Critical Thinking/Problem Solving—Exercise sound reasoning and analytical thinking; use knowledge, facts, and data to solve workplace problems; apply math and science concepts to problem solving.

Oral Communications—Articulate thoughts, ideas clearly and effectively; have public speaking skills.

Written Communications—Write memos, letters and complex technical reports clearly and effectively.

Teamwork/Collaboration—Build collaborative relationships with colleagues and customers; be able to work with diverse teams, negotiate and manage conflicts.

Diversity—Learn from and work collaboratively with individuals representing diverse cultures, races, ages, gender, religious, lifestyles, and viewpoints.

Information Technology Application—Select and use appropriate technology to accomplish a given task, apply computing skills to problem-solving.

Leadership—Leverage the strengths of others to achieve common goals; use interpersonal skills to coach and develop others.

Creativity/Innovation—Demonstrate originality and inventiveness in work; communicate new ideas to others; integrate knowledge across different disciplines.

Lifelong Learning/Self Direction—Be able to continuously acquire new knowledge and skills; monitor one's own learning needs; be able to learn from one's mistakes.

Professionalism/Work Ethic—Demonstrate personal accountability, effective work habits, e.g., punctuality, working productively with others, and time and workload management.

Ethics/Social Responsibility—Demonstrate integrity and ethical behavior; act responsibly with the interests of the larger community in mind.

APPLIED SKILLS AND BASIC KNOWLEDGE: COMBINING AND RANKING   Before examining the specific applied skills, it is valuable to consider the relative rankings of a combined list of basic knowledge areas and applied skills. One difficulty

---

*The list of applied skills was derived primarily from the Partnership for 21st Century Skills. In addition, several members of The Conference Board's Business and Education Council were consulted.

in defining the ideal skill set needed for new entrants' workforce readiness is determining the relative importance of basic knowledge, such as *Reading Comprehension, Writing in English, Mathematics* and *English Language* skills, and the applied skills, which are often considered to be more social or behavioral. While several of the applied skills are social or behavioral in nature, others, such as *Critical Thinking/ Problem Solving* and *Creativity/Innovation*, are also based on cognitive abilities. To determine how employers view the relative importance of basic knowledge versus applied skills, both skill sets are combined and the overall rankings are considered for each of the three educational levels in Tables 3, 4, and 5.[8]

Table 3

For new entrants with a high school diploma, applied skills are four of the top five "very important" skills in combined ranking with basic knowledge and skills.

Rank	Skill	
1	Professionalism/Work Ethic*	80.3%
2	Teamwork/Collaboration*	74.7
3	Oral Communications*	70.3
4	Ethics/Social Responsibility*	63.4
5	Reading Comprehension	62.5
6	English Language	61.8
7	Critical Thinking/ Problem Solving*	57.5
8	Information Technology Application*	53.0
9	Written Communications*	52.7
10	Diversity*	52.1
11	Writing in English	49.4
12	Lifelong Learning/ Self Direction*	42.5
13	Creativity/Innovation*	36.3
14	Mathematics	30.4
15	Leadership*	29.2
16	Foreign Languages	11.0
17	Science	9.0
18	Government/Economics	3.5
19	History/Geography	2.1
20	Humanities/Arts	1.8

Basic and applied skills rank ordered by percent rating as "very important."
Number of respondents varied for each question, ranging from 336 to 361.
* Indicates an applied skill

Table 4

For new entrants with a two-year college/technical school diploma, applied skills are four of the top five "very important" skills in combined ranking with basic knowledge and skills.

Rank	Skill	
1	Professionalism/Work Ethic*	83.4%
2	Teamwork/Collaboration*	82.7
3	Oral Communications*	82.0
4	Critical Thinking/ Problem Solving*	72.7
5	Reading Comprehension	71.6
6	Written Communications*	71.5
7	English Language	70.6
8	Ethics/Social Responsibility*	70.6
9	Information Technology Application*	68.6
10	Writing in English	64.9
11	Lifelong Learning/ Self Direction*	58.3
12	Diversity*	56.9
13	Creativity/Innovation*	54.2
14	Leadership*	45.4
15	Mathematics	44.0
16	Science	21.2
17	Foreign Languages	14.1
18	Government/Economics	6.7
19	Humanities/Arts	4.4
20	History/Geography	3.6

Basic and applied skills rank ordered by percent rating as "very important."
Number of respondents varied for each question, ranging from 334 to 360.
* Indicates an applied skill

Table 5

For new entrants with a four-year college diploma, applied skills are four of the top five "very important" skills in combined ranking with basic knowledge and skills.

Rank	Skill	
1	Oral Communications*	95.4%
2	Teamwork/Collaboration*	94.4
3	Professionalism/Work Ethic*	93.8
4	Written Communications*	93.1
5	Critical Thinking/ Problem Solving*	92.1
6	Writing in English	89.7
7	English Language	88.0
8	Reading Comprehension	87.0
9	Ethics/Social Responsibility*	85.6
10	Leadership*	81.8
11	Information Technology Application*	81.0
12	Creativity/Innovation*	81.0
13	Lifelong Learning/ Self Direction*	78.3
14	Diversity*	71.8
15	Mathematics	64.2
16	Science	33.4
17	Foreign Languages	21.0
18	Government/Economics	19.8
19	History/Geography	14.1
20	Humanities/Arts	13.2

Basic and applied skills rank ordered by percent rating as "very important."
Number of respondents varied for each question, ranging from 382 to 409.
* Indicates an applied skill

[8]It should be noted that employers may assess as more important those skills they can observe directly. Applied skills rather than basic skills are more likely to be observed in day-to-day job performance.

● Review Questions

1. What are the goals of this report? On what information is the report based?

2. What are the differences between academic skills (or "basic knowledge") and applied skills? How do employers rank the relative importance of basic knowledge versus applied skills for new entrants (high school, two-year college, and four-year college) to the workforce?

3. Which four applied skills did survey respondents view as "critical" or "important"?

4. What percentage of four-year college graduates are perceived to be deficiently prepared in written communications? What percentage of businesses ranked *Written Communications* as "very important" for four-year college graduates?

5. What one bit of "encouraging news" do the authors report for four-year college entrants to the workforce? Why is this news encouraging?

6. Why is the timing of this report significant, according to the authors?

● Discussion and Writing Suggestions

1. Study the list of "Applied Skills" and their definitions (p. 259). Rate yourself on each. In terms of your applied skills, how prepared are you to enter the new economy? Specifically note areas where you could improve. What are some ways in which you might approach your coursework this semester so that you could, in fact, improve?

2. As you read the "Report Card" section of "Are They Really Ready," what do you find to be the standout facts? Why?

3. "Across the U.S. alarm bells are sounding in the business community about educating tomorrow's workforce. This study's results are consistent with important initiatives launched by a number of other business organizations in response to a growing talent gap and to the impact this gap has on the United States' ability to maintain its competitive lead in the world economy. The business community . . . is speaking with one voice, calling for higher standards of workforce excellence consistent with the demands of the 21st century." The business community is worried. Are you? Explain.

4. Study Table 5, in which the business community ranks the importance of basic knowledge and applied skills for new four-year college entrants to the workforce. What is the role, do you suppose, of items 15–20 on the list (ranked relatively unimportant) in helping one to develop the five most important applied skills at the top of the list? That is, what role do you think content courses in mathematics or the arts play in helping one learn to think critically or write well?

5. If you used this report as "the tail" to wag "the dog" of your college education—that is, to design your undergraduate degree—what courses would you take? At the end of four years, would you be satisfied calling this academic record a college education? Would your college? Is the ranking of "History/Geography" and "Humanities/Arts" last in Tables 3 through 5 sufficient reason for you *not* to take courses in these areas?

6. What are the difficulties in teaching the "applied skills" of professionalism and work ethic? Are these not elements of what we call "character"? Can character be taught? If so, how?

Engineering

Richard K. Miller

Think "engineering school," and you're likely to imagine an institution that focuses almost entirely on imparting technical knowledge. But this is by no means true of the Olin College of Engineering in Needham, Massachusetts. This innovative college was founded in 1997 by the Franklin W. Olin Foundation to implement a vision for engineering education in the twenty-first century. Directors of the National Science Foundation and other organizations believed that traditional engineering programs could not easily implement changes that called for teaching young engineers "business and entrepreneurship skills, creativity and an understanding of the social, political and economic contexts of engineering." Rather than work incrementally with existing colleges and universities, the Olin Foundation launched an altogether new college of engineering, with Richard Miller serving as its first president. The following passage is part of an address Miller delivered at the college on October 16, 2001.

All of us need to set aside some time periodically to make plans—to assess where we are, what opportunities and challenges we face, and think deliberately about our future in preparation for making decisions. In particular, we plan to talk about where the field of engineering is headed, what a career in engineering might be like, and what some of the possibilities are for our graduates....

Historical Perspective

It might be appropriate to begin by considering some of the changes in the engineering profession in the last two decades that led to the call for reform in engineering education. The call for reform, in turn, led to the creation of Olin College by the F.W. Olin Foundation.

Since the end of the Cold War, the practice of engineering has changed significantly. To deliberately over-simplify for the purpose of clarity, before the end of the war, the defense department was a major consumer of engineering talent. Many high tech companies had one primary client—the federal government. So, marketing efforts were not focused on the consumers in the way that they are today. In addition, the technical challenges that attracted many engineering students were focused solely on high technology. They were exciting and grand, but limited in scope. These challenges included such tasks as putting a man on the moon by the end of the decade—no matter what the cost. "Just do it if it's possible" was the request. And do it quickly—we needed to beat the Russians. Since we were not planning to manufacture large quantities of such spacecraft or sell them widely, manufacturing and marketing—or business considerations generally—were not very important by today's standards. Furthermore, since the technology was highly confidential, it was a disadvantage for a company to have business relationships with foreigners. Security was the principal objective, and this meant keeping important ideas protected from foreigners by avoiding unnecessary business interactions with them. Finally, technical companies were often organized internally with "silos" in which engineers worked only with other engineers—usually with exactly the same technical degrees. This situation minimized the need of engineers to understand the perspective of others not exactly like them, and also minimized the importance of a global perspective or understanding of other cultures.

When the Cold War ended, many things changed. A simple story that illustrates this well is that of the development of the Boeing 777 aircraft. Again to oversimplify a little for clarity in the time we have available, Boeing predicted a shift away from defense and toward commercial aircraft in their business. In order to beat the competition in designing and building the next generation of jetliner, Boeing took a bold step. It invested heavily in new computer simulation technology so accurate that it is capable not only of designing but also simulating the behavior of a complete jetliner. This cost them nearly everything they had, and it was a huge risk. But the potential benefits were also huge. The software eliminated the need to cut metal to test prototypes before finalizing the design. Such hardware tests are very costly and cause a lot of delays in the design process. Then, they partnered with foreign firms in Asia and Europe, so they could download their daily progress over the Internet to a partner on another continent at the end of the day. The partner was just beginning the workday at their location, so they were able to work essentially continuously—24 hours a day—without shutting down at night. The result was amazing. They finished the design of the 777 in a small fraction of the time—and at far less cost—than their competitors. As a result, Boeing now owns McDonnell Douglas. In fact, today, if you do not have international partners or advanced simulation technology, you are not even in the game in the commercial aircraft business.

5   In the process of pioneering this new way of doing business, Boeing learned many lessons. In particular, they learned that their engineering workforce was not well prepared to work in this new way. Many other companies have also learned this lesson, and have been calling for changes in the education of engineers.

Boeing has been a leading voice in this call for reform. Their list of proposed changes mirrors those called for by the National Science Foundation and many other businesses. They include better teamwork and communication skills, and familiarity with basic business principles. They found that to be successful in this new way of doing business, engineers needed to be able to work well on teams with real diversity—including diversity of functional responsibility (since engineers no longer work in silos with only engineers on projects), and also foreign cultures. They also reported that for their purposes, all engineering graduates they hired were essentially over-qualified in technical subjects for the type of work they were asked to do, but badly uneducated in other important areas, like the nature of business, and also in the ability to communicate effectively with others. Also, they found that in many cases, young engineers were not familiar with the design process or with manufacturing....

ABET Criteria for All Accredited Engineering Programs

The changes proposed by Boeing and others have found their way into the accreditation criteria recently adopted by the Accreditation Board for Engineering and Technology (ABET) in their "Criteria 2000." The following list of basic ABET requirements for all engineering programs provides a definition of the expected competencies of all engineers in the US at this time:

- An ability to apply knowledge of mathematics, science, and engineering
- An ability to design and conduct experiments, as well as to analyze and interpret data
- An ability to design a system, component, or process to meet desired needs
- An ability to function on multi-disciplinary teams
- An ability to identify, formulate, and solve engineering problems
- An understanding of professional and ethical responsibility
- An ability to communicate effectively
- The broad education necessary to understand the impact of engineering solutions in a global and societal context
- A recognition of the need for, and an ability to engage in life-long learning
- A knowledge of contemporary issues
- An ability to use the techniques, skills, and modern engineering tools necessary for engineering practice

Of the 11 criteria listed by ABET, it is significant that 6 of them—over half—relate to the non-technical abilities of engineers. I believe there is an important message here. What does it take to succeed in an engineering career today?

Recently I asked a couple of industry leaders to tell me what the path is today for career advancement among engineering employees in their companies. The detailed description I received from one of them—which was quickly endorsed by the other—is as follows, and I will quote for a while:

> [H]ere is the process that usually leads to our identifying potential successful leaders.... First and foremost, it starts early in the career path of the [engineer] with technical competence. We sometimes make the mistake of believing that an engineer who is very good technically makes a good leader. This is not always the case. Yet the first promotions are based more on technical ability than other factors. The first level of promotion

is to go from a discipline lead on a project to a project manager. Usually, the discipline lead who has always performed on schedule and met his/her budget gets the nod. To be successful as a project manager, this individual needs to have good organizational ability, team building skills, client management skills and definitely good business acumen. Success at this level is based on successfully completing the projects assigned on schedule, within budget and to the satisfaction of our clients. As a private business, there is a strong correlation between financial success and project manager performance. Although not the primary evaluation factor, a project manager performs well only if we do not lose money on the aggregate of the engagements managed (not just one project) and that we have satisfied clients. This will not happen if people skills and business skills are lacking.

From the group of successful project managers, we look for line managers who start out as Department Heads, and progressively move up as Group Heads, Regional Managers and President of the firm. Not all successful project managers make good line managers. Supervisory leadership requires more team building, motivating the staff and taking a strong position with subordinates when needed and leading by example. Many of our engineers are poor supervisors who do not communicate well and are not willing to make appropriate decisions when they need to do so. The higher in the line organization the position is, the more there needs to be a good balance between internal and external relationship building. Bottom line, growing the business becomes the standard yardstick of measure.

[I]t is clear from this very detailed picture of career advancement in a contemporary engineering firm that communication and people skills as well as an understanding of basic business principles are essential to career advancement. Essentially every corporate CEO or chief technology officer I have met for the last 10 years has urged that we do all we can to provide better preparation for these aspects of engineering practice.

I think there are several points here. One is that without a solid technical background, an engineer will never get that first job in industry. Our first job—and our students' first priority—is to obtain an excellent understanding of the technical fundamentals that form the foundation of engineering. That is implicit, and should need no special emphasis from me....

10   But, technical competence alone will not provide for the career advancement that most [engineering] graduates will seek. Communication, people skills, and a basic understanding of business will also be required. Although we do not have a lot of time specifically dedicated to these topics in our curriculum, we are attempting to weave this into technical courses [and] projects...wherever we can.

Since communication skills has topped the list of needed improvements in engineering education for nearly 50 years, it may not be well understood, and therefore is probably worth a few additional comments. As I talk with industry leaders, I get the strong impression that they mean much more by this than being able to write an effective business letter or lab report. It certainly includes writing of all types, as well as oral communication, visual communication, and also listening. But more importantly, the type of communication I hear about involves looking people in the eyes and answering questions openly, communicating and gaining trust, persuading without pressure, and establishing lasting relationships. This has a clear dimension of attitude and personality, as well as values and good judgment. It includes knowing that preserving relationships may be more important than being right in every instance. Knowing how to be honest in your criticism without coming across as disrespectful is an extremely important communication skill—especially for building and preserving teamwork. Some important suggestions I hear frequently include: always postpone any judgment until after you have listened to both sides; use praise and criticism in equal measure; and especially, never attribute to malice that which could possibly be attributed instead to carelessness, oversight, or even incompetence or ignorance. People are nearly always deeply distressed and they rarely forget when they have been accused of being dishonest or deceitful. When I have been thoughtful enough to use [these principles of effective communication], I have always found them highly useful in building teamwork.

● ● ●

What Will Be the Most Important New Technologies in the Next 20 Years?

A natural question in planning a future career is which one of [the many] emerging topics will become important in the future? How important is it to identify the right one? How can you be sure the one you have chosen has a bright future?

While I think it is important to obtain a broad foundation in the fundamentals of emerging research themes, it is not possible to know for sure which if any of these new areas will become and remain important in industry. It is probably more important to learn how to engage in research in a new and emerging field that is unfamiliar to you. That skill is undoubtedly going to be useful for your entire career, no matter what emerging research area turns out to be most important.

A brief illustration from my own career might be helpful here. When I was an undergraduate, it was widely assumed that nuclear energy would soon replace petroleum as the primary source of energy on the planet, and everyone believed that space would quickly become an important commercial frontier. Nuclear power plants were being constructed across the country, and we had recently put a man on the moon. Arthur C. Clark's movie, *2001: A Space Odyssey*, was so convincing—with images of a PanAm cruiser taking tourists into space, and American astronauts in route to Mars. As a result, all undergraduate engineers were required to take at least one course in modern physics so they could at least read the literature in nuclear technology. In addition, aerospace engineering was regarded as the safest major on campus for anyone wanting to assure his or her future in a high technology company.

15   Of course, both of these impressions turned out to be wrong. Nuclear energy is still an illusive dream—and nuclear engineering departments have largely been eliminated from schools of engineering since careers in this area are quite limited. In addition, shortly after the movie, aerospace engineers were driving

taxicabs in Los Angeles as the aerospace industry collapsed. Many schools merged aerospace engineering departments with more robust and general programs in mechanical engineering.

The moral is that even the brightest minds are not capable of predicting which technologies will become the most important. In fact, history has shown that many of the most important technical innovations have come from small businesses or independent inventors, without support from the major research labs and universities. Hence, it may be wisest not to make career decisions based on estimates of the future technologies. Instead, for students as talented and capable as you, I would recommend pursuing those topics that truly fascinate you. Topics that have the power to hold your interest, in spite of a lack of obvious career potential, may well provide a lifetime of inspiration for you. You are likely to do your best work on topics that are of deep personal interest to you. And if you do your best work—given your talent and drive—I have to believe there is almost certainly going to be successful career waiting for you. Those who are excellent at what they do—almost independent of what that is—are almost always in demand. Concentrate on selecting topics that you are both deeply interested in and also very good at, and you are most likely to succeed.

● Review Questions

1. Summarize Miller's account of the significant changes in the engineering profession over the last two decades.

2. What major reforms have businesses and the National Science Foundation called for in engineering education?

3. Businesses have reported that engineers entering the workforce are both overqualified and underqualified. In what sense?

4. Miller writes: "technical competence alone will not provide for the career advancement that most . . . graduates will seek." Why not?

5. Why should one not make career decisions based on the promise of new technologies, according to Miller? Instead, how should one plan for future employment?

● Discussion and Writing Suggestions

1. Miller offers advice to engineers in training: he sets out criteria for advancement (see paragraphs 7–15); and he offers suggestions on the best preparation for finding a job on graduation (see paragraph 20). Assuming you are *not* an engineer in training, to what extent do you think Miller's advice generalizes to those not seeking an engineering (or technical) career?

2. Reread paragraph 7, in which Miller reviews the accreditation standards for engineering and technical schools, as revised in 2000. Why would a "knowledge of contemporary issues" be important for an engineer or for any person in a technical field to have? For example, if you were designing a brake pad for an airplane, how aware of contemporary issues would you need to be?

3. In paragraph 15, drawing on his conversations with business leaders, Miller expands upon the traditional definition of "communication skills." Recall experiences in which you have worked with people (perhaps managers) who either possess or lack these expanded skills. What difference do these skills make in your relations with these people? Insofar as they are *skills* that can be learned, do you intend to learn them? How?

Law

Tom McGrath

The selection that follows, originally titled "The Last Days of the Philadelphia Lawyer," first appeared in *Philadelphia* magazine (April 2008). While nominally the writer investigates changes in the legal profession in Philadelphia, the changes he observes are occurring nationwide, throughout the profession.

Lawyers, it probably goes without saying, like to argue, but the one thing they all agree on is that over the past two decades, their once high-minded profession has been transformed into a high-stakes business. "A revolution has occurred," says Michael Coleman, one of the city's preeminent legal recruiters. That revolution may only be a prologue to an even bigger transformation now taking place: the high-stakes business slamming head-on into the fast-moving, and generally unforgiving, 21st-century global economy.

"The world is flat," Alderman tells his Penn Law students one day, as they're seated around a seminar table. Alderman's course is called "The Law of Law Firms," and in contrast to the legal-reasoning courses that make up the bulk of a law student's education, this class attempts to give the next generation of lawyers a realistic view of the business they're getting themselves into.

... [T]he technological and economic changes affecting all of us are certainly making an impact on lawyers—particularly on the dozen or so largest, most prestigious firms in Philadelphia. For starters, the pressure is on firms to be bigger and broader—to open offices in all the places around the world where their clients are doing business. ...

Even more important, though, is that the market for legal services has been, if not globalized, at least nationalized—which means that Philly firms are now competing for clients with firms in New York and Chicago and Charlotte and anywhere else easily reachable with a BlackBerry and some frequent-flier miles.

5   The heightened competition—combined with the bottom-line mentality that began taking hold at least 15 years ago—has spun off its own consequences. While lawyers at big firms make more money than ever, there's a certain sense

of ennui among many in the profession. Previous generations of attorneys had the sense that in practicing law, they were serving the public good. A fair number of lawyers today fret that what they do has no more value than selling used cars. "It can suck the soul out of you," one lawyer complains of the constant focus on billable hours and client development and all the other things lawyers now do that aren't actually practicing law. Says another, of the pressure to make more and more profits, "How much is enough?"

The answer to…the broader question of why the legal profession in America currently operates the way it does—can be traced back to changes that started in the 1980s….

The impact of the *American Lawyer* rankings over the past two decades is tough to overestimate. For starters, they've transformed the mind-sets of many lawyers—or at least those who run large law firms. Twenty years ago, a partner at a Philadelphia firm might have been very happy making $150,000 per year— until he saw that lawyers at a firm in, say, Boston were making $ 250,000 per year. Telling competitive people like lawyers how much their peers were making was like giving someone with an addictive personality his first hit on a crack pipe.

Just as important, though, is that over the years, large firms have come to realize that the Am Law rankings are their best marketing tool when it comes to attracting the best law-school graduates and, now, the best partners from other firms—partners who bring with them books of clients that contribute handsomely to the bottom line. After all, why stay at a firm with profits per partner of only $400,000 per year when folks at the firm down the road are making 20 percent more?

…[T]he Am Law rankings—both literally, in the sense that firms care enormously about where they fall on them, and figuratively, in the sense that they represent a legal world all about the Benjamins—have become the dominant measuring stick in the legal industry.

10   If there's an irony in law having become a business, it's that law, it turns out, isn't a very *good* business—or at least doesn't have a very efficient business model. While manufacturers typically make money through economies of scale, and other service professionals, like investment bankers or architects, make money by taking a percentage of a deal or the cost of a project, lawyers for the most part still work for an hourly wage. In short, they're in the business of selling their time.

The problem, of course, is that time is finite, so even if you're selling those hours for an exorbitantly high rate—a handful of lawyers in Philadelphia can charge up to $1,000 an hour—it can be tough to build a successful, globally competitive business.

To compensate for that labor-intensive business model, firms have adopted various strategies. Strategy number one: Make young lawyers—associates—bill as many hours as humanly possible. In the 1960s and '70s, associates at big firms were expected to bill between 1,600 and 1,800 per year; today, the expectation is generally around 2,200 hours per year. And since not every hour you spend at the office can be billed to a client, associates typically end up putting in 80-to-90-hour weeks. With starting associate salaries approaching $150,000 at Philly's biggest firms, this might not be so bad—if the work was consistently challenging intellectually, and if the path to becoming a partner was as fast as it used to be. But some associates complain that they spend their days locked in the office, pushing through paper. As for partnership, it's a reward that takes longer and longer to realize these days.

But associates aren't the only ones for whom the rules of the game have changed. While once it was enough for a partner at a firm simply to be a smart practitioner who understood the law and served his clients well, today the focus is less on what you do in the courtroom or boardroom than on what kind of business you bring in the door. In the past, becoming a partner at a big firm was pretty much like becoming a tenured college professor—you were there for as long as you wanted to be. Today, it's not unheard-of for a partner to be de-equitized—essentially, pushed back to being a salaried employee—or driven out completely. "I know some lawyers in their 50s who have been asked to leave their firms because they don't have a book of business," says Steve Cozen, of Cozen O'Connor. "The problem is, they were never told they *had* to have a book of business. It used to be enough for them just to be good lawyers."

In some firms, it's no longer enough even to have clients—they must be clients who can pay hourly rates hefty enough to support an insatiable appetite for profits. Over the past few years, Dechert [Philadelphia's most profitable law firm] has rid itself of several practice areas that simply didn't command high enough rates from clients, including media law, which was led by respected First Amendment attorney Amy Ginensky, who last year moved to Pepper Hamilton after 28 years at Dechert. Ginensky says she could have stayed, but she didn't like the constraints the firm's economic strategy placed on her. "I didn't want to decide what cases to take based solely on how much money they would make," she says. Dechert's strategy is one any businessman would understand instantly—if a product line isn't profitable enough, you discontinue it and move on to something else. But for the lawyers involved, who were asked to practice a different type of law or simply to leave, it's a tough adjustment to make. "We're dealing with human capital, not widgets," says legal recruiter Michael Coleman. "I don't know if when you're 45, you want to be retooled."

● Review Questions

1. What are some of the changes occurring in the legal profession? What has caused these changes?

2. McGrath reports on the "ennui" that a "fair number of lawyers today" feel. What is this ennui? How is it new to the profession of law?

3. As compared to other professions, why is law not a "very *good* business"? How have law firms attempted to compensate for their business model?

● Discussion and Writing Suggestions

1. "A fair number of lawyers today fret that what they do has no more value than selling used cars." Your comment?

2. If you are considering a career in law, how does McGrath's article affect you?

3. Much of the legal world, according to McGrath, seems to be "all about the Benjamins"—that is, all about money. If one works to earn money, then what's the problem with working to earn "Benjamins"? Why do some attorneys seem to resist this objective? Pursue the matter further: What is the conflict here between work as livelihood and work as vocation? (For a definition of vocation, see pp. 212–213).

4. Interview an attorney—someone who could speak with you for 15 or 20 minutes on a nonbillable basis! Prepare several questions about "work" and "vocation" that cannot be answered with a simple *yes* or *no*. Discuss your findings in a brief paper that answers this question: What important ideas emerged from the interview?

MEDICINE

Matt Richtel

The selection that follows, originally titled "Young Doctors and Wish Lists: No Weekend Calls, No Beepers," first appeared in the *New York Times* (January 7, 2004).

Jennifer C. Boldrick lights up when the topic turns to blisters, eczema and skin cancer. She is also a big fan of getting a full night of sleep. And the combination of these interests has led Dr. Boldrick to become part of a marked shift in the medical profession.

Dr. Boldrick, 31, a graduate of Stanford University Medical School, is training to become a dermatologist. Dermatology has become one of the most competitive fields for new doctors, with a 40 percent increase in students pursuing the profession over the last five years, compared with a 40 percent drop in those interested in family practice.

The field may have acquired its newfound chic from television shows like "Nip/Tuck" and the vogue for cosmetic treatments like Botox, but for young doctors it satisfies another longing. Today's medical residents, half of them women, are choosing specialties with what experts call a "controllable lifestyle." Dermatologists typically do not work nights or weekends, have decent control over their time and are often paid out of pocket, rather than dealing with the inconveniences of insurance.

"The surgery lifestyle is so much worse," said Dr. Boldrick, who rejected a career in plastic surgery. "I want to have a family. And when you work 80 or 90 hours a week, you can't even take care of yourself."

5   Other specialties also enjoying a surge in popularity are radiology, anesthesiology and even emergency-room medicine, which despite their differences all allow doctors to put work behind them when their shifts end, and make medicine less all-encompassing, more like a 9-to-5 job.

What young doctors say they want is that "when they finish their shift, they don't carry a beeper; they're done," said Dr. Gregory W. Rutecki, chairman of medical education at Evanston Northwestern Healthcare, a community hospital affiliated with the Feinberg School of Medicine at Northwestern University.

Lifestyle considerations accounted for 55 percent of a doctor's choice of specialty in 2002, according to a paper in the *Journal of the American Medical Association* in September by Dr. Rutecki and two co-authors. That factor far outweighs income, which accounted for only 9 percent of the weight prospective residents gave in selecting a specialty.

Many of the brightest students vie for several hundred dermatology residency spots. The National Residency Matching Program, which matches medical school graduates to residency openings, reported that in 2002, 338 medical school seniors were interested in dermatology, up from 244 in 1997—though the 2002 figure still represented only 2.3 percent of the potential doctor pool.

In 2002, 944 seniors wanted to pursue anesthesiology, compared with 243 five years earlier—while the interest in radiology almost doubled, to 903 from 463, according to the matching program's figures.

10   Numerous medical educators noted that the growth of interest in these fields coincided with a drop in students drawn to more traditional—and all-consuming—fields. In 2002, the number of students interested in general surgery dropped to 1,123 from 1,437, for example.

And that has many doctors and educators concerned. "There's a brain drain to dermatology, radiology and anesthesia," Dr. Rutecki said. He said that students who are not selected for residencies in these lifestyle-friendly specialties are choosing internal medicine by default.

"Not only are we getting interest from people lower in the class, but we're getting a number of them because they have nowhere else to go," Dr. Rutecki said.

This notion of a "brain drain" to subspecialties from the bread and butter fields of medicine is not new. But in recent years it has come to be associated with a flight to more lucrative fields. What is new, say medical educators, is an emphasis on way of life. In some cases, it even means doctors are willing to take lower-paying jobs—say, in emergency room medicine—or work part time. In other fields, like dermatology and radiology, doctors can enjoy both more control over their time and a relatively hefty paycheck.

According to the American Medical Association, a dermatologist averages $221,000 annually for 45.5 hours of work per week. That's more lucrative—and less time-consuming—than internal medicine or pediatrics, where doctors earn around $135,000 and spend more than 50 hours a week at work. A general surgeon averages $238,000 for a 60-hour week, while an orthopedist makes $323,000 for a 58-hour week. The number of dermatology residencies has been steadily growing. The American Academy of Dermatology says there are 343 dermatology residents in their third year, 377 in their second year, and 392 in their first.

15   The trend comes as the medical profession is already struggling to balance the demands of patient care with the strain put on doctors from overwork. Since last year, new rules have limited a resident's hours to 80 hours a week.

Some medical careers, like radiology, entail working long hours but not responding to patient emergencies on nights and weekends.

Educators point to a number of factors to explain the newfound emphasis on lifestyle. Dr. Elliott Wolfe, director of professional development for medical students at Stanford, cites the growing proportion of medical students who are women; in the 2002–3 year they made up 49.1 percent of entering students, according to the American Medical Association. Dermatology offers more control and income than, say, pediatrics and family medicine, which have traditionally drawn women.

Lee Ann Michelson, director of premedical and health care advising at Harvard University, said undergraduates considering a future in medicine are extremely concerned about whether they can have a life outside of medicine. She said she talks to numerous children of physicians who are concerned they will be as absent in the lives of their children, as their parents were.

The symbol for "controllable lifestyle" is dermatology. And when residents graduate they can count on plenty of faces and bodies to heal and reconstruct, thanks to an aging, and affluent, population. One-stop dermatology spas seem to open weekly in Manhattan, offering lunchtime visitors quick-fix lip fillers, laser procedures and face peels. It's not fast food, it's fast facial.

20   "You make your own hours. You can see 15 patients a day, or 10 patients a day. There are very few emergencies. It's not an acute situation, ever," said Dr. Dennis Gross, a Manhattan dermatologist. Plus, he said the procedures dermatologists perform can be lucrative; a 12-minute Botox treatment can cost a patient $400, with the doctor keeping half, for instance.

And the procedures often are elective, meaning that patients pay out of their own pockets. "It's cash, check or credit card," said Dr. Wolfe of Stanford.

The difference in lives is well illustrated by the experience of Z. Paul Lorenc and Marek M. Lorenc, 48-year-old twin brothers who chose careers on different ends of the spectrum.

Marek is a dermatologist in Santa Rosa, Calif., north of San Francisco. He gets into work at 8 a.m., leaves at 6 p.m., and is rarely called to the hospital at night, giving him ample time to spend with his wife and two children. "When I'm done," he said, "I'm a husband and a father. I go to soccer games. I coach soccer games."

His brother is a plastic surgeon in Manhattan. He arrives at work before 7, kissing his two sleeping children before he leaves the house. He performs face lifts, breast augmentations, brow lifts and liposuction, intensive surgical procedures that demand round-the-clock availability at the hospital. He often does not get home until after 9 p.m., and he goes into the office on Saturday. He doesn't see his children nearly as much as he would like, but he said that is what the pursuit of excellence in his specialty requires.

25   He is bothered by what he sees as a lack of devotion by today's medical students. A faculty member at New York University's medical school, he said the interest in way of life is across the board.

"When residents come looking for jobs, they ask, 'How often do I have to take night calls,' " he said. "There's less intensity, less determination and less devotion."

But Dr. Boldrick said she is not trying to avoid hard work. While she intends to have two children, she still plans to work full time.

What she wants to avoid is chaos and uncertainty and the lack of control that comes with other specialties. "I see people around me who like to do those things, and I think, 'Thank God,' " said Dr. Boldrick, who added that she feels she can make a contribution without taking on the meat and potatoes of say, internal medicine. "If I force myself to do something that didn't make me happy in order to pay a debt to society, that wouldn't do anyone any good," she said.

The reasoning resonates with Dr. Clara Choi, 32, a resident in radiation oncology at Stanford. Dr. Choi finds her field fascinating but pointed out that it also demands few unexpected calls to the hospital.

30   Married, she plans to have a family. "I'd have to get someone to take care of the baby if I spent every third or fourth night in the hospital," Dr. Choi said.

Dr. Rutecki says he completely understands, having missed out on a lot in the lives of his own two children.

"I missed a lot because I was on call three to five days a week," he said. "Rather than take this data as an opportunity to criticize, I think we recognize that this is the way medicine is moving."

● Review Questions

1. What trend do observers of residency programs note about the interests of young doctors in choosing a specialty?

2. What is the appeal of the most sought-after specialties in medicine?

3. In selecting a specialty, what relative value do young doctors place on considerations of "lifestyle" versus "income"? As a result, how are the choices of these doctors creating a "brain drain"?

4. How has the increasing number of women physicians affected the trends that Richtel reports on in this selection?

● Discussion and Writing Suggestions

1. One physician quoted by Richtel "is bothered by what he sees as a lack of devotion by today's medical students." To what extent do you expect your doctor to be interested in or concerned for you in a different way than a postal worker, say, is concerned about delivering a letter to the correct address? Why would we expect "devotion" more from a doctor than from the others?

2. How understandable to you are the desires of medical students who are selecting a specialty? Are you sympathetic to their concerns? If you were a medical student selecting a specialty, would your concerns be any different?

3. If the present trends in selecting specialties continue, what difficulties do you see emerging in medicine? What solutions can you envision?

SYNTHESIS ACTIVITIES

1. Write an explanatory synthesis that reviews the developments responsible for the accelerating changes in the American workplace and the jobs that are most—and least—at risk from these changes. What are these changes? How did they come about? How do they affect workers?

2. In "Are They Really Ready to Work?" Casner-Lotto and Barrington draw a distinction between basic knowledge and applied skills. In his speech to engineering students at Olin College, Richard Miller quotes "industry leaders" who stress the importance of communication skills as opposed to "technical knowledge." In an explanatory synthesis, draw on these sources and others to establish how—and why—the workplace of the future will especially value applied skills.

3. According to the authors in this chapter, what are the attributes of workers likeliest to succeed in the new economy? Consult Peters, Judy and D'Amico, Blinder, and Friedman. Given this information, how likely is it that you will succeed? No one has a crystal ball, of course, but take stock of your character: Use your answer to the first question as a lens to analyze your attributes as a worker, and make a projection from there. How prepared would Peters or Friedman, for instance, find you to take on a job that would not likely be lost to outsourcing or rendered obsolete by technology?

4. Use any of the definitions from the first selection of this chapter, or one of the definitions from the articles by Blinder or Friedman, to analyze a job that interests you. First, carefully research that job (or a similar one) at the Bureau of Labor Statistics Web site. Recall that in your analysis you can use a definition or principle to generate questions, which you can then use as a lens to study key features of the object under analysis—in this case, a particular job. What insights does your analysis yield?

5. Sennett concludes that the skills needed to succeed in the new economy may "corrode" one's character. Use his insight as a principle to analyze the working life of someone you know well, much as Sennett has analyzed the life of Rico.

6. Both Sennett and Huws suggest that developments in the new economy can assault a worker's identity. If identity is tied to occupation (a common assumption among sociologists—see Huws, paragraph 3) and the "qualities of good work [in the new economy] are not the qualities of good character" (see Sennett, paragraph 24), then are you as a worker in the new economy destined to become as conflicted as Rico? Where does the Sennett/Huws argument break down? In a synthesis that draws on selections in this chapter for support, critique the Sennett/Huws argument.

7. In the articles by Sennett and Huws, you may have detected a tone of lament—a sense that something of value from the old world of work has

been lost in the new economy. Other writers, like Peters, Judy and D'Amico, Blinder, Friedman, and the Economist, sound more hopeful notes. Compare and contrast the degrees of optimism and pessimism among authors in this chapter, considering their reasons (stated or not) for taking the positions they do. This paper could be an explanatory or an argument synthesis. If an argument, agree or disagree that an author's optimism or pessimism is warranted; conclude with a statement of your own regarding optimism or pessimism. Remember to organize your synthesis by idea, not by source.

8. Sennett writes that "a young American with at least two years of college can expect to change jobs at least eleven times in the course of working, and change his or her skill base at least three times during those forty years of labor" (paragraph 26). Assuming this claim to be true, how will you prepare for a working life in which change is the one constant? Recall from "Are They Really Ready to Work?" the distinction between basic knowledge and applied skills. What mix of knowledge and skills will you pursue? Develop your response into an argument synthesis that draws on Sennett, Judy and D'Amico, Blinder, Friedman, Casner-Lotto and Barrington, and any other selections you think pertinent. You may enjoy framing your argument around either of the following statements:

    a. College years are not only a preparation for the world of work; they are also a safe harbor from it—a time to think broadly, impractically even, and look beyond the narrow needs of the workplace. Because no one can predict the future with certainty, a college student is best served by training broadly, developing core skills (such as critical thinking, writing, and speaking), and later meeting the challenges of the future workplace as they arise.

    b. A favorite uncle or aunt tells you: "You'd better be realistic about your studies. Changes are coming, and you need to be prepared....A college education is expensive. It's unconscionable to spend all that money and not get the training you need for a good job immediately after graduation."

9. Define work and its essential features. Recall the multiple definitions that open this chapter (and there are many that were not included in the opening selection); recall also the definitions either assumed or stated explicitly by various writers in the chapter. Your definition will necessarily be an argument: one claim among many, the purpose of which will be to convince readers that the way you define work is reasonable, even compelling.

10. Reread, in the first selection of this chapter, the definitions of work and vocation. Consider the differences between approaching work as a livelihood and approaching it as a vocation. How might a confusion concerning these words complicate your working life? In your paper allude to the tensions that McGrath and Richtel discuss in the lives of lawyers and doctors.

RESEARCH ACTIVITIES

1. Interview several workers you know who are in their forties or, preferably, in their fifties. Ask them to describe changes they've seen in the workplace and ask how they're adapting to these changes. Frame the results of your interview in the context of several of the readings in this chapter. That is, use the readings to help make sense of the information you record in the interviews. Your research paper could take the form of an argument or an analysis.

2. Take a thorough accounting of the "Occupational Outlook Handbook" at the Bureau of Labor Statistics Web site, as previewed in this chapter. Prepare a report that presents (1) the range of information available at the OOH site—and closely linked sites; (2) a strategy for mining useful information. Essentially, you will be preparing a "User's Guide" to the OOH.

3. Find a copy of Studs Terkel's Working; select one of the interviewees reporting on his or her experiences at a particular job; and research the current status of this job or career field at the Bureau of Research Statistics Web site. Compare and contrast the experiences of the Terkel subject (mid-1970s) with those of a present-day worker.

4. Visit the career counseling office at your school; interview one or more of the staff people there and survey the publications available at the office to determine facts about the interests and employment prospects of the student body at your school. Write a report on the success your fellow students have had in securing internships at local businesses or job placements with local employers.

5. Writing for the Hudson Institute, Judy and D'Amico claim that the emergence of new jobs and services will "almost certainly…create more jobs than the underlying [emerging] technology will destroy." This view on the "creative destruction" in the economy is shared by the Economist and also Blinder, who cautions that we must do our best to anticipate coming changes and train the U.S. workforce accordingly. Research the work of Joseph Schumpeter, originator of the concept of creative destruction, and report on the acceptance of this concept by present-day economists.

6. Trace the changing attitudes toward work in Western culture. Authors of interest will likely include Hebert Applebaum, Melvin Kranzberg and Joseph Gies, Richard Donkin, and Joanne Ciulla.

7. Research the origins of the Puritan work ethic and its persistence in American culture. Puritans, writes Melvin Kranzberg, "regard[ed] the accumulation of material wealth through labor as a sign of God's favor as well as of the individual's religious fervor." Be sure, in your research, to look at The Protestant Ethic and the Spirit of Capitalism by economist and sociologist Max Weber.

8. Read the entire report, "Are They Really Ready to Work? Employers' Perspectives on the Basic Knowledge and Applied Skills of New Entrants to the 21st Century U.S. Workforce." Then investigate the mission and publications of any one of the organizations that sponsored this report: The Conference Board, Corporate Voices for Working Families, the Partnership for 21st Century Skills, or the Society for Human Resource Management. As part of your research, investigate the organization's membership. Write an explanatory paper that introduces this organization to your classmates.

8

Green Power

Our wealth, our society, our being is driven by oil and carbon. And when we say that we have to make a shift, that is extremely difficult. It is intellectually dishonest to say that we can get some lightbulbs, or we can get a Prius, and we're all done. No—this is going to take massive technological innovation. It's going to take changes in the way we live and work. It's going to take cooperation of unprecedented degrees among businesses and government and among countries. That's where we are. There's no other word except "daunting."

—Jerry Brown, Attorney General of California

In 2006 climber and filmmaker David Braeshears made his way up to a Himalayan outcrop on a steep ridge 19,000 feet high. From that familiar vantage point he had a clear view of the Rongbuk Glacier in Tibet, a frozen river of ice that flows from the north slope of Mount Everest. Comparing what he was seeing to a photograph taken in 1921 from the same vantage point by British explorer George Mallory, he was appalled by how much the ice had melted. "The glacier's just gone," he remarked to *Frontline* producer Martin Smith. It had, in fact, lost some 40 percent of its mass in the past 85 years.

The shrunken Himalayan glacier is but one more indication—along with collapsing ice shelves in Antarctica and polar bears stranded on ice floes—of the extent of climate change since the middle of the twentieth century. Climate experts warn of nothing short of an apocalypse unless current global warming trends are reversed. The earth's population faces the prospect of more frequent and severe hurricanes, fires, declining agricultural yields, the extinction of species, and rising ocean levels that threaten to flood coastal cities. Author and *New York Times* columnist Thomas Friedman quotes environmental consultant Rob Watson on the nature of the challenge we confront: "People don't seem to realize . . . that it is not like we're on the *Titanic* and we have to avoid the iceberg. *We've already hit the iceberg.* The water is rushing in below. But some people just don't want to leave the dance floor; others don't want to give up on the buffet."

What's causing climate change? Experts point to inceasing levels of greenhouse gases—chiefly carbon dioxide or CO_2. (Other greenhouse gases include methane, ozone, and water vapor.) These gases trap the sun's heat in the atmosphere by preventing infrared rays from escaping into space—and therefore, they keep living things from freezing to death. (Like cholesterol, a certain quantity of greenhouse gases is essential to survival.) For most of human history, greenhouse gases have remained at a life-supporting equilibrium. But accelerating levels of industrialization during the nineteenth and twentieth centuries have changed this equilibrium by measurably increasing atmospheric levels of CO_2, a byproduct of burning fossil fuels such as coal and oil, energy sources that are integral to the existence of modern civilization. More than half of the nation's electricity is generated by burning coal. It takes $9 \frac{1}{2}$ tons of coal to produce the quantity of electricity used by the average American each year. And, of course, the overwhelming majority of the world's vehicles are fueled by gasoline, or refined petroleum.

The internal-combustion, CO_2-spewing engine that has powered vehicles of every type since the dawn of the automobile era in the early twentieth century has long been viewed as one of the greatest culprits in creating air pollution—and, more recently, in contributing to climate change. And bad as the situation is now, it is expected to get far worse. The number of cars in the world, about 625 million, is anticipated to double by 2020. China and India—whose populations account for a third of humanity—will soon replace the United States as the world's biggest importers of oil, a development that will generate significantly increased levels of CO_2 in the atmosphere.

In recent years, interest in and development of alternative energy sources that do not release CO_2 (or, at least, as *much* CO_2) into the atmosphere—and thus that serve to slow, if not reverse, the pace of global climate change—have intensified. Automakers are taking the first serious steps away from gasoline-powered vehicles. The popularity of the Toyota Prius hybrid, the development of the all-electric Chevrolet Volt, ongoing research into hydrogen fuel-cell vehicles, and the increased use of biofuels and natural gas to power cars and buses are all evidence of the slow greening of the transportation industry. And wind and solar power are gaining ground as sources of electricity for home and industry. In 2008 Texas oilman T. Boone Pickens launched a highly visible public relations campaign explaining his plan to build the world's largest wind farm in the Texas Panhandle, which would generate and transmit enough electricity to power one million homes. Pickens also proposed conversion of all of the nation's automobiles to run on natural gas, instead of gasoline. As the recession that began later that year deepened, however, the scarcity of credit and the fall-off in natural gas prices (making wind power less economically attractive) forced Pickens to scale back his ambitious project in favor of a series of smaller wind farms in the Midwest.

More controversial than wind power is nuclear power, owing chiefly to questions of safety and cost. Building a nuclear power plant costs between $5 and $10 billion, and no application for a new nuclear power plant has been approved since 1979 (the year of the Three Mile Island reactor accident). Other renewable sources of electrical power include hydroelectric (generated by the force of flowing water); geothermal (generated by heat from the earth's core, transmitted to the surface); and biomass (generated by the burning of organic matter such as wood, leaves, manure, and crops). As of 2007, however, according to the U.S. Department of Energy's EIA (Energy Information Administration), only about

7 percent of the nation's energy consumption was being generated from renewable sources—as opposed to 40 percent from fossil fuels like petroleum and 22 percent from coal. (Natural gas provides 23 percent of the total consumption; nuclear power provides 8 percent.)

The development of green power, of renewable energy sources, is not only a global imperative; it is also a matter of public policy. That is, it involves questions of what government does or does not do to encourage or discourage particular activities by businesses, nonprofit organizations, educational institutions, and individuals. Governments issue regulations, pass laws, tax and spend, subsidize, make grants, reward those who comply with their rules, and penalize those who do not. In the 1970s, the U.S. government attempted to impose CAFE (Corporate Average Fuel Efficiency Standards) regulations mandating minimum fuel efficiency standards for vehicles. But automakers have long resisted such standards and have pressured the government to ease or abandon them. Other government efforts to curb greenhouse gas emissions have not survived industry opposition. In 2007 Senators Joseph Lieberman (ID-CT) and John Warner (R-VA) proposed the Climate Security Act, which would have imposed caps on CO_2 emissions; penalized companies for exceeding their allowable emissions limits; and mandated a 60 percent reduction in greenhouse gases by 2050. That measure, too, was resisted by business interests, and the matter never came to a vote.

The election of the environmentally conscious Barack Obama as president in 2008 (who, in his inaugural address, called for the country to "harness the sun and the winds and the soil to fuel our cars and run our factories") raised new hopes that public policy would now favor dramatic steps to reverse climate change, to encourage the development of renewable energy sources, and to reduce the nation's reliance on fossil fuels. In his campaign Obama supported cap-and-trade programs, which impose gradually reduced limits on the quantities of carbon dioxide that large industries may emit. Environmentalists were also encouraged by Obama's announced intent to raise federal fuel economy standards, to provide government subsidies for the development of more fuel-efficient vehicles, and to make significant federal investments in green technologies—including the construction of a national "smart grid" to transmit electrical power from wind and solar generators to energy-hungry cities.

The selections in this chapter offer multiple perspectives on how we can reduce (if not entirely eliminate) our dependence on fossil fuels and support the development of alternative, renewable energy sources. As you might expect, experts disagree not only about the nature of the problem and its causes but also about needed solutions. In the chapter that follows, we present some of these disagreements, which will give you ample opportunity to evaluate, respond, and form your own informed opinions.

The chapter is organized into two sections. The first lays out the more general challenges we face in addressing a carbon emission-related climate crisis and in working to reduce our dependence on fossil fuels. The second section considers particular alternative, renewable energy sources such as nuclear, wind, and solar power.

We begin with Michael Lemonick's "Global Warming: Beyond the Tipping Point." Writing for *Scientific American*, Lemonick explains the science behind global warming, focusing on the work of James Hansen, an environmental scientist who heads NASA's Goddard Institute for Space Studies and whose models of the pace of climate change, owing to increased atmospheric levels of CO_2, are likely to alarm most readers. This piece is followed by Thomas Friedman's "205 Easy Ways to Save the Earth," a chapter in his book *Hot, Flat, and Crowded: Why We Need a Green Revolution—And How it Can Save America* (2008). Friedman argues that contrary to his ironic title, there are no easy ways to save the earth: The task ahead is both gigantic and daunting. "If we can pull this off," he declares, "it will be the biggest single peacetime project humankind will ever have undertaken." Friedman's piece is followed by an op-ed by Al Gore, former vice president, Nobel laureate, and Oscar-winning creator of the documentary *An Inconvenient Truth* (2007). In this 2008 editorial, "The Climate for Change," anticipating the environment-friendly policies of the incoming Obama administration, Gore returns to the theme of an influential speech he made earlier in the year in which he challenged the nation to commit to producing all of our electricity from carbon sources within the next decade. "It is a plan," he argues, "to simultaneously move us forward toward solutions to the climate crisis and the economic crisis—and create millions of new jobs that cannot be outsourced."

In "The Dangerous Delusions of Energy Independence," Robert Bryce throws cold water on those who believe that we can free ourselves of reliance upon oil produced in other countries. "Energy independence is hogwash," he declares. "Worse yet, the inane obsession with the idea of energy independence is preventing the U.S. from having an honest and effective discussion about the energy challenges it now faces." We follow Bryce's piece with two selections that focus on the public policy challenges of dealing with climate change. In "National Security Consequences of U.S. Oil Dependency," an independent task force sponsored by the Council on Foreign Relations lays out policy alternatives by which government could provide incentives to reduce the nation's dependence on petroleum, a dependence it views as a national security issue. In "Balance Sheets and the Climate Crisis: How American Businesses Can Help," Mindy S. Lubber, who leads a network of investor groups working on global sustainability issues, recommends steps that companies can take—and have taken—to reduce their carbon footprint and simultaneously improve their bottom line. The first part of the chapter concludes with "Stop the Energy Insanity," an editorial by *U.S. News & World Report* publisher (and real estate billionaire) Mortimer Zuckerman, who deplores the bipartisan wrangling that has stalled effective public policy on energy and who attempts to reconcile the conflicting demands of those who want to continue using fossil fuels and those who want to rapidly convert to alternative energy technologies.

The second half of the chapter begins with Don Sherman's "G.M. at 100: Is Its Future Electric?" which considers the potential benefits and drawbacks of the Chevrolet Volt, a prototype plug-in electric car scheduled to be available to the general public in 2010. But in "Why the Gasoline Engine Isn't Going Away Any Time Soon," *Wall Street Journal* reporter Joseph P. White cautions that the challenges facing alternative energy vehicles like the Volt are sufficiently daunting that there is no prospect in the near term of their supplanting vehicles powered by internal-combustion. Next, in "The Case for and Against Nuclear Power," Michael Totty argues both sides of the issue while striving for objectivity. See if you can decide which case he finds stronger. Two pairs of pro-con pieces follow. In "The Island in the Wind" *New Yorker* writer Elizabeth Kolbert reports on the fascinating case of the Danish island of Samso, whose citizens decided to convert to electrical power generated entirely by wind turbines. Their experience raises intriguing questions about what might be done in this country, given the will. However, in "Wind Power Puffery," another doubter, H. Sterling Burnett, dismisses the prospect of wind power as a significant response to our energy problems. Next, in "State Solar Power Plans Are as Big as All Outdoors," *Los Angeles Times* reporter Marla Dickerson discusses what the state of California, facing new mandates on renewable power, has done to convert a significant part of its power generation from coal to solar. In the final selection, "Environmentalists Against Solar Power," the *New York Times'* Peter Maloney reports on a split in the environmentalist ranks between big solar and small solar. Big solar is represented by power companies that build large, ground-based solar projects capable of producing thousands of megawatts, and small solar is represented by individual homeowners who install rooftop solar panels. The small solar advocates object to the toll taken by the industrial solar projects on the environment and on wildlife.

And so the debate continues, not only between business people and environmentalists, but also among environmentalists themselves. To return to Thomas Friedman, "there is no 'Easy' button we can press to make the world green."

GLOBAL WARMING: BEYOND THE TIPPING POINT

Michael D. Lemonick

We begin with an article that presents some of the scientific underpinnings of climate change. While it is misleading, if not untrue, to claim that environmental scientists dispute the reality of global warming, it *is* the case that scientists disagree on the mechanisms of climate change: the relationship between global mean temperatures and concentrations of carbon dioxide, the pace at which climate change is occurring, and the precision with which it can be measured. In this piece Michael Lemonick focuses on the findings of James Hansen and his coauthors, who explain in a recent issue of *Open Atmospheric Science Journal* that mean temperatures are rising much faster than expected. Some scientists remain skeptical about Hansen's methods and conclusions.

Michael Lemonick is a senior science writer for *Time* magazine and has also worked for *Discover* magazine and *Science Digest*. This article first appeared in a special edition of *Scientific American*, October 6, 2008.

The basic proposition behind the science of climate change is so firmly rooted in the laws of physics that no reasonable person can dispute it. All other things being equal, adding carbon dioxide (CO_2) to the atmosphere—by, for example, burning millions of tons of oil, coal and natural gas—will make it warm up. That, as the Nobel Prize–winning chemist Svante Arrhenius first explained in 1896, is because CO_2 is relatively transparent to visible light from the sun, which heats the planet during the day. But it is relatively opaque to infrared, which the earth tries to reradiate back into space at night. If the planet were a featureless, monochromatic billiard ball without mountains, oceans, vegetation and polar ice caps, a steadily rising concentration of CO_2 would mean a steadily warming earth. Period.

But the earth is not a billiard ball. It is an extraordinarily complex, messy geophysical system with dozens of variables, most of which change in response to one another. Oceans absorb vast amounts of heat, slowing the warm-up of the atmosphere, yet they also absorb excess CO_2. Vegetation soaks up CO_2 as well but eventually rereleases the gas as plants rot or burn—or, in a much longer-term scenario—drift to the bottom of the ocean to form sedimentary rock such as limestone. Warmer temperatures drive more evaporation from the oceans; the water vapor itself is a heat-trapping gas, whereas the clouds it forms block some of the sun's warming rays. Volcanoes belch CO_2, but they also spew particulates that diffuse the sun's rays. And that's just a partial list.

Because including all these factors in calculations about the effects of CO_2 increase is hugely difficult, it is no surprise that climate scientists are still struggling to understand how it all will likely turn out. It is also no surprise, given his track record as something of a climate change agitator, that James Hansen, director of the NASA Goddard Institute for Space Studies, has been circulating a preprint of a journal paper saying that the outcome is likely to turn out worse than most people think. The most recent major report from the Intergovernmental Panel on Climate Change in 2007 projects a temperature rise of three degrees Celsius, plus or minus 1.5 degrees—enough to trigger serious impacts on human life from rising sea level, widespread drought, changes in weather patterns, and the like.

But according to Hansen and his nine co-authors, who have submitted their paper to *Open Atmospheric Science Journal,* the correct figure is closer to six degrees C. "That's the equilibrium level," he says. "We won't get there for a while. But that's where we're aiming." And although the full impact of this temperature increase will not be felt until the end of this century or even later, Hansen says, the point at which major climate disruption is inevitable is already upon us. "If humanity wishes to preserve a planet similar to that on which civilization developed and to which life on Earth is adapted," the paper states, "CO_2 will need to be reduced from its current 385 ppm [parts per million] to at most 350 ppm." The situation, he says, "is much more sensitive than we had implicitly been assuming."

5   As with many of Hansen's assertions, this one pushes the science further than some of his colleagues would be willing to go. Back in 1998, for example, Hansen was arguing that the human impact on climate was unquestionable, even as other leading climate scientists continued to question it. He was subsequently proved right, not only about the human influence but about the approximate pace of future temperature rise. But just as in 1998, the underlying motivation for his claims, if not all of his conclusions, is shared pretty much universally.

The problem is that conventional projections for how warm things will get come out of a calculation everyone knows is wrong. Called the Charney sensitivity, it estimates how much the global mean temperature will rise if atmospheric CO_2 is doubled from its preindustrial levels, before people began burning coal and oil on a grand scale. In the mid-1800s carbon dioxide concentrations stood at about 280 ppm. Double that to 560 ppm, and the Charney sensitivity calculation tells you that temperatures should rise about three degrees C.

But the Charney sensitivity, though not quite as stripped down as the billiard ball model, is still an oversimplification. The calculation does take into account some feedback mechanisms that can modify the effects of increasing temperatures on short timescales—changes in water vapor, clouds and sea ice, for example. But for the sake of simplicity, it assumes no change in other, longer-term factors, including changes in glaciation and vegetation; in particulates, such as dust; and in the ability of the ocean to absorb carbon dioxide, which diminishes as sea temperature rises.

Climate Models Struggle with Reality

"Many people, ourselves included, have tended to take [the Charney sensitivity] and apply it to the real world," says Gavin Schmidt, who is also a climatologist at Goddard (though not a co-author on the new paper). "But the real world isn't a model where a few things can change while others stay fixed." At some point, Schmidt says, "we have to talk about the real climate."

That's what Hansen has attempted to do. He isn't the first: other scientists, including Stephen H. Schneider of Stanford University, have talked for years about bringing additional real-world factors to standard climate models. The difficulty is that to add those factors, you have to come up with a reasonable way to weight them.

10   Like other climate scientists, Hansen and his co-authors use evidence from the deep past to sort out these feedback mechanisms. Over the past 800,000 years, for example, we know that the climate has oscillated between long ice ages and much shorter periods of interglacial warmth—much like the conditions we are in now. The relation between air temperature and CO_2 is pretty well understood for that period, thanks largely to air bubbles trapped in ancient ice cores that have been drilled in Greenland and Antarctica (the CO_2 concentration inside them can be measured directly; the global mean temperature can be calculated from the relative abundances of two different oxygen isotopes, which vary with how warm it gets).

But Hansen points out that the record contains other clues. "We also know how sea level changed over that period," he says, from studies tracing the height of ancient shorelines. Because sea level rises and falls as continental ice sheets retreat and advance, you have a measure of what fraction of the earth was covered with a bright white, heat-reflecting coating. As ice retreats in a warming world, more dark surface is exposed to absorb solar radiation, which makes the world even warmer, melting even more of the ice. Conversely, a cooling world gets cold faster as ice sheets advance. This is one of the key feedback mechanisms left out of the Charney sensitivity calculation, partly because it is thought to happen only over hundreds of years, and, Hansen says, partly because "it just hadn't sunk in that the paleoclimate record is a remarkable source of info on climate sensitivity."

Using that record, for example, Hansen concludes that even if the human race could maintain today's level of atmospheric CO_2, which stands at 385 ppm—not even halfway to the atmospheric doubling we are headed for—sea level would rise several meters thanks to the disintegration of continental ice sheets. Moreover, he thinks disintegration may happen much faster than one might naively expect. "We didn't have convincing data on this until we had the gravity satellites," he says, referring to GRACE, a pair of orbiters that can detect tiny local changes in the earth's gravitational field. "Greenland has gone from stable mass in 1990 to increasing ice loss. Another big surprise is West Antarctica, where despite little actual warming, the ice shelves are melting." As those partially floating ice shelves melt, land-based glaciers are free to slide more rapidly to the sea. In Greenland, meltwater from the top of the glaciers is evidently pouring down through cracks to lubricate the underside of the ice sheets, easing their flow out to the ocean.

Warming temperatures, Hansen says, not only increase the amount of meltwater on the surface of the ice but also increase rainfall. "Ice-sheet growth," he says, "is a dry process. Disintegration is a wet process, so it goes a lot faster."

If today's CO_2 levels would lead to several meters of sea-level rise—putting many coastal areas, housing hundreds of millions of people, completely underwater—then letting CO_2 rise to 560 ppm could lead to a disaster of unimaginable proportions. Even a rise to 450 ppm could be catastrophic, according to Hansen's team's analysis. Before about 35 million years ago, the planet was completely ice free, so warm-water alligators and lush redwood forests thrived above the Arctic Circle. The transition to large-scale glaciation in Antarctica began, the researchers estimate, when CO_2 dropped to 425 ppm, plus or minus 75 ppm. Most of the ice should therefore disappear again if we reach that point—and if all of Antarctica's and Greenland's glaciers were to melt, sea level would rise many tens of meters. The only way to keep CO_2 concentrations as low as that, Schneider says, is to have the entire world adopt California's strictest-in-the-nation proposals for limiting carbon emissions—something that is hard to imagine even the other U.S. states agreeing to, let alone developing nations such as India and China.

15   That's only taking the feedback from melting glaciers into account. "Changes in vegetation, in atmospheric and ocean chemistry, and in aerosols and dust in the atmosphere all appear to be positive feedbacks on temperature changes," Schmidt says. "If global average temperatures change for any reason, those other elements will amplify the change." Other positive feedbacks include the release of CO_2 dissolved in the oceans, which will happen as they warm up, and the accelerated release of other greenhouse gases—methane, for example, from biomass that will begin rotting as permafrost melts in the Arctic.

Given Hansen's eminence as a climate scientist, one might expect that his analysis would have triggered a general panic. And it has—but not among scientists. "This month may have been the most important yet in the two-decade history of the fight against global warming," wrote journalist and author Bill McKibben in the *Washington Post* this past December, shortly after Hansen spoke about his new calculations at a conference: "[350 ppm is] the number that may define our future." McKibben has even created an organization he calls 350.org to spread the word. Other activists and bloggers have reacted with similar alarm.

Most climate experts turn out to be much less exercised, even though they take the danger of global warming very seriously. The reason: Hansen and his colleagues base their new estimate of climate sensitivity and of the various tipping points represented by different feedback mechanisms on a record of ancient conditions that are not really well understood. "The problem," Schmidt says, "is that the further back you go, the less you really know. The error bars get very large." The planet's ice-free periods are, he admits, "very interesting—they're like the periods we think we're heading for, and in principle they can tell us a lot about the climate sensitivity to CO_2 changes."

And although you can infer atmospheric CO_2 levels indirectly, from changes in the acidity of ocean sediments, for instance, Schmidt notes that this involves assumptions that might be wrong. "People generally think CO_2 was higher then, but you can't get a precise number or a precise time series. Jim would say that the true climate sensitivity is twice the Charney sensitivity, but it could be three times, it could be one." Similar uncertainties surround the ebb and flow of continental ice sheets. "It's quite possible," Schmidt says, "that the ice sheets across North America might have been more sensitive than those in Greenland, which would explain why Greenland's have persisted."

That appears to be a widespread consensus. "Jim's analysis is very shrewd," says Michael Oppenheimer, a professor of geosciences and international affairs at Princeton University. "It's something we all should be thinking about, but the uncertainties are so large that it's a weak point." Schneider, too, offers praise overall but caution about specifics. "Jim's doing great work," he says, "but I wish he'd get off absolute numbers. It's not as though the world is okay with 1.8 degrees of warming but turns into a pumpkin at 2.2 or something."

Seeking a Workable Solution

20   Indeed, although few climate scientists are ready to buy Hansen's argument in detail, they agree that the changes already observed are ominous. "Where I've come down on this," says Fred Krupp, president of the Environmental Defense Fund, "not sparked by Jim Hansen but by watching coral reefs die and Antarctic ice sheets break off sooner than we ever expected, is that we need to stabilize CO_2 at current levels or below."

Lurking behind this general tone of caution is the sense that reducing the growth of CO_2 emissions is a daunting enough prospect by itself, given that the world's population continues to grow and that countries such as India and China are determined to catch up to the developed world economically. Halting that growth entirely would be even more difficult, and actually drawing down the amount of CO_2 in the atmosphere seems largely inconceivable. Nevertheless, Hansen and his co-authors lay out a possible strategy. "The only way I can see of doing it," Hansen says, "is, first of all, to cut off emissions from coal entirely by 2030." Coal, he points out, is the single biggest fossil-fuel reservoir of carbon, and because it is only burned in power plants, not as transportation fuel, "it can be captured at just a few sources rather than millions of tailpipes."

To push coal-based carbon emissions down to zero, he and his colleagues suggest, the world has to agree that, starting right away, no new plants will be built unless they have the capability to capture waste CO_2 before it leaves the smokestack. At the same time, existing plants will either have to be retrofitted with capture technology or phased out by 2030.

A second major effort, the authors say, would involve massive reforestation of areas that been denuded of trees. "Deforestation contributed a net emission of 60 ± 30 ppm over the past few hundred years," they write, "of which ~20 ppm CO_2 remains in the air today." Regrowing forests, they argue, could absorb all of that excess and more. And finally, they favor the use of "biochar," or charcoal made from agricultural waste and other biomass. If burned or left to decay, this biomass releases CO_2. When converted to charcoal and tilled into the soil, it does two things. First, it is exceptionally stable, so it keeps carbon sequestered for centuries, at least. Second, it increases soil fertility, because it adsorbs nutrients and keeps them available for new crops. "Replacing slash-and-burn agriculture with slash-and-char," they write, "could provide a CO_2 drawdown of ~8 ppm in half a century." More speculative technologies might also eventually be able to draw CO_2 out of the atmosphere and lock it up in minerals, although their potential scale and expense are still guesswork.

But possibility and plausibility are two different things. Hansen and his colleagues have produced a road map; getting all the biggest carbon emitters to go along will be tough. The scheme would take decades to implement even if every nation agreed to it today. The task, the scientists admit, "is Herculean yet feasible when compared with the efforts that went into World War II." Schneider, though just as concerned as Hansen about the dangers posed by increasing atmospheric carbon, has a less optimistic view. "It has no chance in hell," he says. "None. Zero. The best thing we can do is to overshoot, reach 450 or 550 parts per million, then come back as quickly as possible on the back end." And even that, given the political barriers to quick and effective action, will be difficult.

● Review Questions

1. Summarize the conclusions of James Hansen and his colleagues about climate change and safe levels of CO_2.

2. How does the burning of fossil fuels like coal and oil change the earth's climate?

3. What is the Charney sensitivity? What are the limits of this calculation?

4. How are the climate changes in Greenland and Western Antarctica harbingers of larger climate shifts?

5. Why are some climate experts skeptical about Hansen's findings?

● Discussion and Writing Suggestions

1. Hansen and his colleagues have offered a grim prognostication of the effects of increased levels of CO_2 on global climate. Why do you think that such scientific findings have not generated a greater sense of urgency and crisis among other climate experts, the general population, and their elected representatives? In the last paragraph Lemonick refers to the "political barriers to quick and effective action." What are some of these political barriers? How might they be overcome?

2. To what extent do you feel the urgency of the climate crisis, as presented by Lemonick? List some of the steps that you believe should be taken to address the problem (and specifically to reduce carbon emissions) by individuals, by business, and by the government.

3. To what extent did you find this piece, which originally appeared in *Scientific American*, difficult to follow? Cite examples of technical vocabulary that may have presented a problem. Did you find that you needed to reread sections of the article to fully comprehend it?

4. Lemonick reports that to combat climate change Hansen and his colleagues recommend (1) assuring that present and future industrial plants are able to capture CO_2 emissions; (2) massive reforestation of areas where trees (which use CO_2) have been cleared. Would you favor such steps if they resulted in (1) your having to pay significantly more for products affected by these plans (e.g., electricity, automobiles); (2) your having to pay increased taxes to pay for government incentives for reforestation?

205 EASY WAYS TO SAVE THE EARTH

Thomas L. Friedman

Thomas Friedman, foreign affairs columnist for the *New York Times*, has won three Pulitzer Prizes for his books, which include *From Beirut to Jerusalem* (1989), *The Lexus and the Olive Tree* (1999), and *The World is Flat* (2005). (We offer an excerpt from *The World is Flat* in Chapter 9, The Changing Landscape of Work in the twenty-first Century.) The following passage is from his most recent book *Hot, Flat, and Crowded: Why We Need a Green Revolution—And How it Can Renew America* (2008). Friedman expresses his opinions forcefully and is not afraid of initially offending readers with his tongue-in-cheek dismissal of quick-fix solutions to the climate crisis. But he also has the ability—and the facts—to make people reconsider their basic assumptions about important issues, whether or not they end up agreeing with him.

> *"Oh God, here they come—act green."*
> –A husband and wife speaking as another couple approaches them at a cocktail party. Cartoon in *The New Yorker*, August 20, 2007

A recent study found the average American golfer walks about 900 miles a year. Another study found American golfers drink, on average, 22 gallons of alcohol a year. That means, on average, American golfers get about 41 miles to the gallon.
Kind of makes you proud.

—From the Internet

What do you mean? We're not having a green revolution? But I just picked up *Working Mother* magazine at the doctor's office and read the cover story: "205 Easy Ways to Save the Earth" (November 2007). It so whetted my appetite for easy ways to save the planet that I Googled for more books and magazine articles on this topic—and boy, did I find more: "20 Easy Ways You Can Help the Earth," "Easy Ways to Protect Our Planet," "Simple Ways to Save the Earth," "10 Ways to Save the Earth," "20 Quick and Easy Ways to Save the Planet," "Five Ways to Save the Earth," "The 10 Easiest Ways to Green Your Home," "365 Ways to Save the Earth," "100 Ways You Can Save the Earth," "1001 Ways to Save the Earth," "101 Ways to Heal the Earth," "10 Painless Ways to Save the Planet," "21 Ways to Save the Earth and Make More Money," "14 Easy Ways to Be an Everyday Environmentalist," "Easy Ways to Go Green," "40 Easy Ways to Save the Planet," "10 Simple Ways to Save the Earth," "Help Save the Planet: Easy Ways to Make a Difference," "50 Ways to Save the Earth," "50 Simple Ways to Save the Earth and Get Rich Trying," "Top Ten Ways to Green Up Your Sex Life" (vegan condoms, solar vibrators—I'm not making this up), "Innovative Ways to Save Planet Earth," "101 Thing Designers Can Do to Save the Earth," "Five Weird and Wacky Ways to Save the Earth," "Five Ways to Save the World," and for those with a messianic streak but who are short of both cash and time: "10 Ways to Save the Earth (& Money) in Under a Minute."

Who knew that saving the earth could be so easy—and in under a minute!

There is some good news in this trend. Thinking about how to live and work in a greener fashion—with cleaner electrons, greater energy and resource productivity, and an ethic of conservation—is being popularized and democratized. It is no longer an elite issue for those living on the West and East coasts or in the backwoods of Colorado or Vermont.

If you are in the technology business today and you have not been invited to a green-tech conference somewhere, you must not be breathing, or everybody has lost your e-mail address. To say that green is the color du jour is an understatement. "Green" was actually the single most trademarked term in 2007, according to the U.S. Patent and Trademark office. Environmental reporters in newsrooms, who used to sit in the corner farthest from the editor's desk, are suddenly cool. Universities are adding classes on environmentalism and looking to shrink their carbon footprints, as are more and more companies. No candidate can get elected today without uttering the trilogy: I will support cleaner fuels. I will liberate America from its oil dependence. I will combat climate change.

5 The politics of this issue have shifted so much that even al-Qaeda supporters, who always have their fingers on the global pulse, are getting in on the green

branding thing. *Newsweek* (September 10, 2007) reported that in July 2007 "an umbrella group of Islamists that advocates a Sharia state in Indonesia—and whose leaders have publicly supported Osama bin Laden—hoisted placards bearing the name Friends of the Earth-Indonesia at a rally protesting a U.S. mining company and the Bush Administration…[The real] Friends of the Earth denounced the unauthorized use of their logo and denied any links. But don't be surprised if radical Islamists make more attempts to cloak their work in the garb of social activism."

Not to be outdone by the Muslims, the Jews are also getting in on the act. UPI reported (December 5, 2007): "A group of Israeli environmentalists has launched an Internet campaign encouraging Jews around the world to light at least one fewer candle this Hanukkah…The founders of the Green Hanukkia campaign say each candle burning all the way down produces 15 grams of carbon dioxide," and that many candles multiplied around Jewish households all over the world starts to add up to a kosher carbon footprint. "'The campaign calls for Jews around the world to save the last candle and save the planet, so we won't need another miracle,' Liad Ortar, a founder of the campaign, told *The Jerusalem Post*." (One blog I saw said in response: Why not ask everyone in the world to stop smoking cigarettes?)

You'll pardon me, though, if I've become a bit cynical about all of this. I have read or heard so many people saying, "We're having a green revolution." Of course, there is certainly a lot of green buzz out there. But whenever I hear that "we're having a green revolution" line I can't resist firing back: "Really? Really? A green revolution? Have you ever seen a revolution where no one got hurt? That's the green revolution we're having." In the green revolution we're having, everyone's a winner, nobody has to give up anything, and the adjective that most often modifies "green revolution" is "easy." That's not a revolution. That's a party. We're actually having a green party. And, I have to say, it's a lot of fun. I get invited to all the parties. But in America, at least, it is mostly a costume party. It's all about *looking* green—and everyone's a winner. There are no losers. The American farmers are winners. They're green. They get to grow ethanol and garner huge government subsidies for doing so, even though it makes no real sense as a CO_2-reduction strategy. Exxon Mobil says it's getting green and General Motors does too. GM put yellow gas caps on its cars that are flex-fuel, meaning they can run on a mix of gasoline and ethanol. For years, GM never bothered to highlight that its cars were flex-fuel, or use it as a selling point with customers, because the only reason GM made a certain number of cars flex-fuel was that, if it did so, the government would allow it to build even more gas-guzzling Hummers and pickup trucks and still remain under the CAFE fuel economy standard mandated by Congress—but why quibble?

Coal companies are going green by renaming themselves "energy" companies and stressing how sequestration of CO_2, something none of them has ever done, will give us "clean coal." I am sure Dick Cheney is green. He has a home in Wyoming, where he goes hunting, and he favors liquefied coal. We're all green. "Yes, step right up, ladies and gentlemen, in the green revolution we're having in America today, everybody gets to play, everybody's a winner, nobody gets hurt, and nobody has to do anything hard."

As I said, that's not the definition of a revolution. That's the definition of a party.

10   Thankfully, more than a few people are onto this green party. A blogger at Greenasathistle.com, which tracks environmental issues, wryly observed:

> Raising awareness about global warming, enviro-friendly products and people doing green deeds is obviously a good thing—but does every single magazine on the rack have to come out with a green issue? I'm starting to believe that there actually can be too much publicity when it comes to climate change, especially when it reaches the fashion world. Seriously, if I read the word "eco-chic" one more time, I'll jab my eyes out with my biodegradable pen...I just fear that as soon as all the magazines get these green issues out of the way, they'll feel like it's out of their system, over and done with, like any other passing trend. By next month they'll probably declare...gas guzzling "in" and earnest recycling "out," with headlines like "Littering is the new black!"

The amount of time, energy, and verbiage being spent on making people "aware" of the energy-climate problem, and asking people to make symbolic gestures to call attention to it, is out of all proportion to the time, energy, and effort going into designing a systemic solution. We've had too many Live Earth concerts and Barneys "Have a Green Holiday" Christmas catalogs and too few focused lobbying efforts to enact transformational green legislation. If the money and mobilization effort spent on Live Earth had gone into lobbying the U.S. Congress for more generous and longer-term production and investment tax credits for renewable energy, and for other green legislation, the impact would have been vastly more meaningful. Moving from the symbolic to the substantive is not easy. I live in Montgomery County, Maryland, which is chock-full of people who identify themselves as green and recycle and do all the other good things. But when I wanted to install two solar arrays in my side yard, I was told that it was against the law. Too unsightly. Zoning laws said they could go only in the backyard. Our backyard doesn't get enough sun. Our solar firm had to hire a lawyer and appeal to get the law changed, which we managed to do after almost a year.

Pentagon planners like to say: "A vision without resources is a hallucination." Right now we are having a green hallucination, not a green revolution. Because we are offering ourselves and our kids a green vision without the resources—without a systemic response shaped by an intelligent design and buttressed by market forces, higher efficiency standards, tougher regulations, and an ethic of conservation that might have a chance of turning that vision into reality. We have willed the ends, but not the means.

Sure, if you look at how far we have come in just the last five years, it can feel like we're having a green revolution. But if you look at where we have to go in the next ten years, we're having a party. No one has said it better than Michael Maniates, a professor of political science and environmental science at Allegheny College, who wrote in *The Washington Post* (November 22, 2007): "Never has so little been asked of so many at such a critical moment."

Several best-selling books "offer advice about what we must ask of ourselves and one another," Maniates noted.

Their titles suggest that we needn't break much of a sweat: "It's Easy Being Green," "The Lazy Environmentalist," or even "The Green Book: The Everyday Guide to Saving the Planet One Simple Step at a Time."

Although each offers familiar advice ("reuse scrap paper before recycling" or "take shorter showers"), it's what's left unsaid by these books that's intriguing. Three assertions permeate the pages: (1) We should look for easy, cost-effective things to do in our private lives as consumers, since that's where we have the most power and control; these are the best things to do because (2) if we all do them the cumulative effect of these individual choices will be a safe planet; which is fortunate indeed because (3) we, by nature, aren't terribly interested in doing anything that isn't private, individualistic, cost-effective and, above all, easy. This glorification of easy isn't limited to the newest environmental self-help books. The Web sites of the big U.S. environmental groups, the Environmental Protection Agency and even the American Association for the Advancement of Science offer markedly similar lists of actions that tell us we can change the world through our consumer choices, choices that are economic, simple, even stylish.

15   Of course, we are not going to consume our way out of this problem. And there is no "Easy" button we can press to make the world green. Maniates went on:

> The hard facts are these: If we sum up the easy, cost-effective, eco-efficiency measures we should all embrace, the best we get is a slowing of the growth of environmental damage...Obsessing over recycling and installing a few special light bulbs won't cut it. We need to be looking at fundamental change in our energy, transportation and agricultural systems rather than technological tweaking on the margins, and this means changes and costs that our current and would-be leaders seem afraid to discuss. Which is a pity, since Americans are at their best when they're struggling together, and sometimes with one another, toward difficult goals...Surely we must do the easy things: They slow the damage and themselves become enabling symbols of empathy for future generations. But we cannot permit our leaders to sell us short. To stop at "easy" is to say that the best we can do is accept an uninspired politics of guilt around a parade of uncoordinated individual action.

The problem is, the minute we leave the comforting realm of "the easy ways to go green," whatever facile consensus for action exists around this issue breaks down. The truth is, for all that we talk about going green, "we have not agreed as a society on what being 'green' actually means," remarked Peter Gleick, the climate expert from the Pacific Institute. That opens a door to everyone claiming to be green, without any benchmarks.

What I hope to do in the remainder of this book is lay out what a systemic green strategy would look like. But before we go there, we need to stop for just one moment at the weight scale.

You know how after you put on a few pounds, you stop weighing yourself—or at least I do—because you just don't want to know how many pounds you are going to have to shed? Well, the same has been true of the green issue. People tend to talk about it in the total abstract, without any connection to the actual scale of the challenge we have to meet in order to significantly reduce CO_2

emissions and become more energy and resource efficient. So before we take another step, we need to put this challenge on the scale, look down at the digital readout, and behold, without blinking, just how big a project this really is.

For starters, let's remember what we're trying to do: *We're trying to change the climate system—to avoid the unmanageable and manage the unavoidable!* We are trying to affect how much the rain falls, how strong the winds blow, how fast the ice melts. In addition to all that, *we're trying to preserve and restore the world's rapidly depleting ecosystems*—our forests, rivers, savannahs, oceans, and the cornucopia of plant and animal species they contain. Finally, we are trying to break a collective addiction to gasoline that is having not only profound climate effects, but also geopolitical ones. It doesn't get any bigger than this. This is not something you do as a hobby, and the adjective "easy" should never—ever, ever—accompany this task.

20   The truth is: Not only are there not 205 easy ways to *really go green,* there isn't *one easy way to really go green*! If we can pull this off, it will be the biggest single peacetime project humankind will have ever undertaken. Rare is the political leader anywhere in the world who will talk straight about the true size of this challenge.

As a result, the task often falls to oil, gas, and coal company executives. They are happy to tell us about the scale of the problem—but usually with secret delight, because they want us to believe that a real green revolution is impossible to pull off, so we have no choice but to remain addicted to oil, gas, and coal. They want to break our will to resist. Their hidden message is: "Surrender now, give in to your inner gas guzzler; the scale of what we need to do to really make a difference is too great. Surrender now, surrender now, surrender now . . ."

I am instinctively wary of their analysis—but I do make exceptions, for companies that have actually made substantial bets in renewable energy and are actually looking to build real businesses there—if there is a market. Chevron, for instance, is the world's biggest private producer of electricity from clean geothermal sources (steam, heat, and hot water produced underground by volcanic material from the earth's core, which provides the force to spin turbine generators and produce electricity.) Here's how Chevron's CEO, David O'Reilly, sees the scope and scale of our clean energy challenge:

"There is a problem with energy literacy," O'Reilly argues. "If you look at energy consumption in the world each day and convert it all into oil equivalent, we are consuming ten million barrels an hour—that is 420 million gallons per hour. Think about that. That means if we take all the hydro, coal, oil, and renewables—everything—and put them together, that is how much we are using. To really make a difference, there are three issues: There is the scale of the demand, the scale of the investment needed to produce alternatives at scale, and the scale of time it takes to produce alternatives. Many alternatives are just at the embryonic phase.

"Now let's look at the rising demand. I've heard people talk about 'the golden billion'—the billion people on the planet who [already] have the quality of life and standard of living we [Americans] are used to. But there are another two billion on the way up and three billion still in poverty. The two billion who are moving up want to get to where we are, and then the three billion want to move up—and from a global prosperity point of view, we want them to move up. Then there's another three billion coming along who have not even been born yet [but will be here by 2050]. This energy supply we have today is focused on meeting the demands of the one billion and the two billion—not the three billion who are still in poverty, let alone the three billion who have not been born yet. So this ten million barrels per hour [that we are consuming] is not static," said O'Reilly. "It is going to rise, because there is an inexorable connection between energy use and well-being."

Now, said O'Reilly, let's look at the challenge of creating new ways to produce and use energy. "People are overestimating the ability of the alternatives that are out there to get to scale," he explained. "Let's talk about efficiency: If you shut down the whole transportation system—I am talking about every car, truck, train, ship, and plane, anything that flies or is on wheels—and another vehicle never moved on planet earth, you would reduce carbon emission by 14 percent, globally. If you shut down all industrial activity, all commercial activity, all residential activity—shut everything off to every home—you would reduce carbon emissions by 68 percent...So efficiency can help, but let's not make false promises. We still need oil and natural gas. We need to make coal work, and we need to make energy efficiency work more."

25   As if that scenario doesn't already boggle the mind, O'Reilly argues that, absent some unexpected breakthrough, it will take decades for alternatives to be brought to scale. "I want my grandchildren to live in a world that has energy, environment, and economy in balance. But you cannot get there overnight," he insisted. "The system we have today is the product of over a hundred years of investments, and the next one will require a hundred years of investments. [So,] these quick promises that we hear in Washington and other places—be careful. My prediction [is that] global greenhouse gases will be higher ten years from now than they are today, but when my grandchildren are in my stage of life—their sixties—they could be substantially lower. We need leaders who will stand up and say this is hard, this is big, and it [requires] massive amounts of investment."

What about the $5 billion or so that I keep reading about that went into green venture capital investing in 2007? I asked O'Reilly. That would not even buy a sophisticated new oil refinery, he snapped. "If you want to really change the path we are on, you need a number that starts with a *T* in front of it"—*T* for *trillion*. "Otherwise we will stay on the path we are on."

But let's say you are an optimist. You believe that the renewable energy technologies available today, and opportunities for energy efficiency, are advanced enough to make a fundamental impact on both climate change and energy prices. What exactly would we have to do by way of deploying these existing clean power technologies and energy-efficiency programs—starting today—to make that fundamental impact?

The answer to that question—and another way to look at the scale of the problem—is offered by Robert Socolow, an engineering professor at Princeton, and Stephen Pacala, an ecology professor there, who together lead the Carbon Mitigation Initiative, a consortium that has set out to design scalable solutions for the climate problem. Socolow and Pacala first argued in a now famous paper published by the journal *Science* (August 2004) that human beings can emit only so much carbon dioxide into the atmosphere before the buildup of CO_2 reaches a level unknown in recent geologic history, and the earth's climate system starts to go haywire. Like the Intergovernmental Panel on Climate Change, they argued that the risk of really weird global weirding grows rapidly as CO_2 levels approach a doubling of the concentration of CO_2 that was in the atmosphere before the Industrial Revolution, which was 280 parts per million (ppm).

"Think of the climate-change issue as a closet, and behind the door are lurking all kinds of monsters—and there's a long list of them," Pacala said. All of our scientific work says the most damaging monsters start to come out from behind that door when you hit the doubling of CO_2 levels."

30 So, as a simple goal everyone can understand, the doubling of CO_2 is what we want to avoid. Here's the problem: If we basically do nothing, and global CO_2 emissions continue to grow at the current trajectory, we will easily pass the doubling level—an atmospheric concentration of carbon dioxide of 560 ppm—around mid-century, and we'll likely hit a tripling sometime around 2075, said Pacala. You don't want to live in a 560 ppm world, let alone an 800 ppm world. To avoid that—and still leave room for developed countries to grow, while using less carbon, and for developing countries like India and China to grow, emitting double or triple their current carbon levels, until they climb out of poverty and are able to become more energy efficient—will require a huge global industrial energy project.

To convey the scale involved, Socolow and Pacala created a pie chart with fifteen different wedges. Some wedges represent carbon-free or carbon-diminishing power-generating technologies; other wedges represent efficiency programs that could conserve large amounts of energy and prevent CO_2 emissions. Socolow and Pacala argue that beginning today—right now—the world needs to deploy any eight of these fifteen wedges on a grand scale, or sufficient amounts of all fifteen, in order to generate enough clean power, conservation, and energy efficiency to grow the world economy and still avoid the doubling of CO_2 in the atmosphere by mid-century.

Each of these wedges, when phased in over fifty years, would avoid the release of twenty-five billion tons of carbon, for a total of 200 billion tons of carbon avoided between now and mid-century, which is the amount that Pacala and Socolow believe would keep us below the doubling. To qualify as one of the fifteen wedges, though, the technology must exist today and must be capable of large-scale deployment, and the emissions reductions it offers have to be measurable.

So now we have a target: We want to avoid the doubling of CO_2 by mid-century, and to do it we need to avoid the emission of 200 billion tons of carbon as we grow between now and then. So let's get to the wedges. Choose your favorite "easy" eight:

- Double fuel efficiency of two billion cars from 30 miles per gallon to 60 mpg.
- Drive two billion cars only 5,000 miles per year rather than 10,000, at 30 miles per gallon.
- Raise efficiency at 1,600 large coal-fired plants from 40 to 60 percent.

- Replace 1,400 large coal-fired electric plants with natural-gas-powered facilities.
- Install carbon capture and sequestration capacity at eight hundred large coal-fired plants, so that the CO_2 can be separated and stored underground.
- Install carbon capture and sequestration at new coal plants that would produce hydrogen for 1.5 billion hydrogen-powered vehicles.
- Install carbon capture and sequestration at 180 coal gasification plants.
- Add twice today's current global nuclear capacity to replace coal-based electricity.
- Increase wind power fortyfold to displace all coal-fired power.
- Increase solar power seven-hundred-fold to displace all coal-fired power.
- Increase wind power eightyfold to make hydrogen for clean cars.
- Drive two billion cars on ethanol, using one-sixth of the world's cropland to grow the needed corn.
- Halt all cutting and burning of forests.
- Adopt conservation tillage, which emits much less CO_2 from the land, in all agricultural soils worldwide.
- Cut electricity use in homes, offices, and stores by 25 percent, and cut carbon emissions by the same amount.

If the world managed to take just one of those steps, it would be a miracle. Eight would be the miracle of miracles, but this is the scale of what will be required. "There has never been a deliberate industrial project in history as big as this," Pacala said. Through a combination of clean power technology and conservation, "we have to get rid of 200 billion tons of carbon over the next fifty years—and still keep growing. It is possible to accomplish this if we start today. But every year that we delay, the job becomes more difficult. Because every year you delay, you have to do that much more the next year—and if we delay a decade or two, avoiding the doubling or more will become impossible."

Nate Lewis, the California Institute of Technology chemist and energy expert, uses a somewhat different set of calculations than Socolow and Pacala, but his approach is also useful in conveying the challenge. Lewis puts it this way: In the year 2000, the world's total average rate of energy usage was roughly 13 trillion watts (13 terawatts). That means that at any given moment, on average, the world was using about 13 trillion watts. That is what the world's electric meter would read. Even with aggressive conservation, that figure is expected to double by 2050 to around 26 trillion watts. But if we want to avoid the doubling of CO_2 in the atmosphere, and accommodate our own growth and that of India and China and other developing countries, we would actually have to cut global CO_2 emissions by 2050 by close to 80 percent, relative to current levels—starting today.

35   That means by 2050 we could use only about 2.6 trillion watts from carbon-emitting energy sources. But we know total demand is going to double by then, to about 26 terawatts. "That means, roughly speaking," said Lewis, "between now and 2050 we have to conserve almost as much energy as we are currently using, by

becoming more energy efficient, and we also have to make almost as much clean energy as we currently use, by developing non-carbon-emitting energy sources."

An average nuclear power plant today produces about a billion watts—one gigawatt—of electricity at any given time. So if we tried to get all the new clean power we would need between now and 2050 (almost 13 trillion watts) just from nuclear power, we would have to build 13,000 new nuclear reactors, or roughly one new reactor every day for the next thirty-six years—starting today.

"It will take all of our investment capital and intellectual capital to meet this challenge," said Lewis. "Some people say it will ruin our economy and is a project which we can't afford to do. I'd say it is a project at which we simply can't afford to fail."

And make no mistake: We are failing right now. For all the talk of a green revolution, said Lewis, "things are not getting better. In fact, they are actually getting worse. From 1990 to 1999, global CO_2 emissions increased at a rate of 1.1 percent per year. Then everyone started talking about Kyoto [see Footnote 4, p. 317], so we buckled up our belts, got serious, and we showed 'em what we could do: In the years 2000 to 2006, we *tripled* the rate of global CO_2 emission increases, to an average [increase] for that period of over 3 percent a year! That'll show 'em that we mean business! Hey, look what we can do when we're serious—we can emit even more carbon even faster."

This is where politics meets climate meets energy meets technology. Do we have the political energy—does anyone have the political energy—to undertake and deploy an industrial project of this scale?

40   Of course, being green at the rhetorical level we're at right now is not inconsistent with the broadly professed principles of either the Democratic or the Republican party. But implementing a green revolution at speed and scale is going to mean confronting some of the economic, regional, and corporate vested interests that live at the heart of both parties—from farmers in Iowa to coal lobbies in West Virginia. Therefore, without a real clash within the Republican and Democratic parties on this issue, there will be no real green revolution in America.

"When everyone—Democrats and Republicans, corporations and consumers—claims to embrace your cause, you should suspect that you have not really defined the problem, or framed it as a real political question," said the Harvard philosopher Michael J. Sandel. "Serious social, economic, and political change is controversial. It is bound to provoke argument and opposition. Unless you think there is a purely technological fix, meeting the energy challenge will require shared sacrifice, and political will. There is no real politics without disagreement and competing interests. Politics is about hard choices, not feel-good posturing. Only when a real debate breaks out—between or within the political parties—will we be on our way to a politically serious green agenda."

You can't call something a revolution when the maximum changes that are politically feasible still fall well short of the minimum needed to start making even a dent in the problem. The challenges posed by the Energy-Climate Era "can't be solved at the level of current political thinking," said Hal Harvey, an energy expert at the William and Flora Hewlett Foundation. "You cannot solve a problem from the same level of thinking that created it."

Rob Watson, the environmental consultant, said to me one day that meeting this challenge—for real—reminded him of an experience he had in the Boy Scouts. "I was overweight, and there were things I thought I could do in my head that I couldn't always do in real life," he explained. "Once my Boy Scout troop had a fifty-mile hike. And to prepare we had to do a series of training hikes. So I took hikes on my own. I thought I was going nine to twelve miles each time to prepare, but actually I was just going three or four. When I finally got out in the wilderness with my troop, I collapsed with heatstroke, because I was not really in shape. I endangered myself and everyone in my group, because I was not being real. I know the need to want to feel that you are doing well and doing right—but if we are not real about where we are, we are not going to do what we need to do to survive in this wilderness."

People don't seem to realize, he added, that it is not like we're on the *Titanic* and we have to avoid the iceberg. *We've already hit the iceberg.* The water is rushing in down below. But some people just don't want to leave the dance floor; others don't want to give up on the buffet. But if we don't make the hard choices, nature will make them for us. Right now, that acute awareness of the true scale and speed of this problem remains confined largely to the expert scientific community, but soon enough it will be blindingly obvious to everyone.

45   Don't get me wrong: I take succor from the number of young people being engaged by this issue. And as the Greenasathistle.com blogger rightly observed, "it's better to be hypocritical than apathetic when it comes to the environment"— as long as you know that's what you're doing, as long as you keep moving in the right direction, and as long as you don't prematurely declare victory. It's planting our flag prematurely that will get us in the most trouble. And that's what we've started doing lately—a green brand, some green buzz, a green concert, and we're on our way to solving the problem. Not a chance.

"It is as if we were climbing Mount Everest and we reached base camp six, the lowest rung on the mountain climb, and decided to look around, put down our gear, pat our Sherpas on the back, and open a celebratory brandy," said Jack Hidary, the energy entrepreneur. "But meanwhile, Mount Everest, all 29,000 feet of it, still looms before us."

● Review Questions

1. Why is Friedman "cynical" about all of the "green buzz"?

2. What does Friedman propose in place of a "green hallucination"?

3. What is the scale problem, discussed by Chevron CEO David O'Reilly?

4. Explain the purpose of Socolow and Pacala's fifteen-wedge pie chart.

5. Why are China and India mentioned so often by Friedman and others in discussions of the global climate problem?

● Discussion and Writing Suggestions

1. Friedman appears to make fun of the "205 Easy Ways to Save the Earth" approach to climate change. Why? To what extent do you agree with him? To what extent have you bought into the kind of "eco-chic" for which Friedman has such scorn? Do you think he is not sufficiently appreciative of well-intentioned (if ineffectual) efforts on the part of individuals?

2. Throughout this piece, Friedman writes in a breezy, punchy style. (See, for example, the opening of paragraph 4). Was this style effective for you,? Cite examples of sentences that worked for you (in advancing Friedman's argument) or that didn't.

3. Write a critique of this selection. Use as guidelines the principles discussed in Chapter 2. Consider first the main questions: (1) To what extent does Friedman succeed in his purpose? (2) To what extent do you agree with him? Then move to the specifics: Do you find Friedman's strategies (for example, dismissing the effectiveness of what he calls "easy ways to save the earth") effective? Has he argued logically? What are his assumptions, and how do you assess their validity?

4. Friedman lays partial blame on the government—and particularly, the Bush administration—for not effectively responding to the threat of climate change. Based on what you have seen and read so far about the Obama administration's approach to global warming, to what extent do you believe that the current administration is responding effectively to this crisis? Explain.

5. Locate a specific principle or definition that Friedman uses in this selection. For example, in paragraph 6 in which he discusses the "green revolution," Friedman asks, "Have you ever seen a revolution where no one got hurt?" The underlying principle here is that in real revolutions people *do* get hurt—not necessarily physically, but perhaps economically, or in such a way as to significantly change their preferred lifestyle. Write an analysis in which you apply this or another of Friedman's principles or definitions to a particular situation of which you have personal knowledge or about which you have read. See the guidelines and model analyses in Chapter 6 for ideas on how to proceed.

6. Toward the end of this selection (paragraph 41), Friedman quotes philosopher Michael J. Sandal as follows: "Serious social, economic, and political change is controversial. It is bound to provoke argument and opposition. . . . There is no real politics without disagreement and competing interests." (You may wish to reread the rest of this paragraph.) Assuming that you agree, why do you think that this is the case?

7. At the end of this selection, Friedman makes use of vivid imagery: boy scouts on a fifty-mile hike, the Titanic hitting the iceberg, mountain climbers on Everest. What does he achieve with such imagery? To what extent do you find it effective?

THE CLIMATE FOR CHANGE

Al Gore

Albert Arnold Gore, Jr., forty-fifth vice president of the United States (1993–2001) and environmental activist, won the Nobel Peace Prize in 2007 (shared with Rajendra Pachauri, head of the Intergovernmental Panel on Climate Change) in recognition of his work "to build up and disseminate greater knowledge about man-made climate change, and to lay the foundations for the measures that are needed to counteract such change." That year Gore also won the Oscar for his documentary on the environment *An Inconvenient Truth.* In 2004 he founded Generation Investment Management, a fund management firm that handles environment-friendly portfolios; and two years later he founded The Alliance for Climate Protection. He has written several books, including *The Assault on Reason* (2007) and *The Path to Survival* (2009).

In July 2008 Gore gave a major speech in DAR Constitution Hall in Washington, D.C., in which he challenged the United States to end its reliance on petroleum-based fuels and to generate 100 percent of its electricity from renewable sources within ten years. The speech provoked considerable discussion and no little controversy as to whether its goals were achievable. The following selection, which follows up on the subject of Gore's Constitution Hall speech, appeared as an op-ed in the *New York Times* on November 9, 2008.

The inspiring and transformative choice by the American people to elect Barack Obama as our 44th president lays the foundation for another fateful choice that he—and we—must make this January to begin an emergency rescue of human civilization from the imminent and rapidly growing threat posed by the climate crisis.

The electrifying redemption of America's revolutionary declaration that all human beings are born equal sets the stage for the renewal of United States leadership in a world that desperately needs to protect its primary endowment: the integrity and livability of the planet.

The world authority on the climate crisis, the Intergovernmental Panel on Climate Change, after 20 years of detailed study and four unanimous reports, now says that the evidence is "unequivocal." To those who are still tempted to dismiss the increasingly urgent alarms from scientists around the world, ignore the melting of the north polar ice cap and all of the other apocalyptic warnings from the planet itself, and who roll their eyes at the very mention of this existential threat to the future of the human species, please wake up. Our children and grandchildren need you to hear and recognize the truth of our situation, before it is too late.

Here is the good news: the bold steps that are needed to solve the climate crisis are exactly the same steps that ought to be taken in order to solve the economic crisis and the energy security crisis.

5   Economists across the spectrum—including Martin Feldstein and Lawrence Summers—agree that large and rapid investments in a jobs-intensive infrastructure initiative is the best way to revive our economy in a quick and sustainable way. Many also agree that our economy will fall behind if we continue spending hundreds of billions of dollars on foreign oil every year. Moreover, national security experts in both parties agree that we face a dangerous strategic vulnerability if the world suddenly loses access to Middle Eastern oil.

As Abraham Lincoln said during America's darkest hour, "The occasion is piled high with difficult, and we must rise with the occasion. As our case is new, so we must think anew, and act anew." In our present case, thinking anew requires discarding an outdated and fatally flawed definition of the problem we face.

Thirty-five years ago this past week, President Richard Nixon created Project Independence, which set a national goal that, within seven years, the United States would develop "the potential to meet our own energy needs without depending on any foreign energy sources." His statement came three weeks after the Arab oil embargo had sent prices skyrocketing and woke America to the dangers of dependence on foreign oil. And—not coincidentally—it came only three years after United States domestic oil production had peaked.

At the time, the United States imported less than a third of its oil from foreign countries. Yet today, after all six of the presidents succeeding Nixon repeated some version of his goal, our dependence has doubled from one-third to nearly two-thirds—and many feel that global oil production is at or near its peak.

Some still see this as a problem of domestic production. If we could only increase oil and coal production at home, they argue, then we wouldn't have to rely on imports from the Middle East. Some have come up with even dirtier and more expensive new ways to extract the same old fuels, like coal liquids, oil shale, tar sands and "clean coal" technology.

10   But in every case, the resources in question are much too expensive or polluting, or, in the case of "clean coal," too imaginary to make a difference in protecting either our national security or the global climate. Indeed, those who spend hundreds of millions promoting "clean coal" technology consistently omit the fact that there is little investment and not a single large-scale demonstration project in the United States for capturing and safely burying all of this pollution. If the coal industry can make good on this promise, then I'm all for it. But until that day comes, we simply cannot any longer base the strategy for human survival on a cynical and self-interested illusion.

Here's what we can do—now: we can make an immediate and large strategic investment to put people to work replacing 19th-century energy technologies that depend on dangerous and expensive carbon-based fuels with 21st-century technologies that use fuel that is free forever: the sun, the wind and the natural heat of the earth.

What follows is a five-part plan to repower America with a commitment to producing 100 percent of our electricity from carbon-free sources within 10 years. It is a plan that would simultaneously move us toward solutions to the climate crisis and the economic crisis—and create millions of new jobs that cannot be outsourced.

First, the new president and the new Congress should offer large-scale investment in incentives for the construction of concentrated solar thermal plants in the Southwestern deserts, wind farms in the corridor stretching from Texas to the Dakotas and advanced plants in geothermal hot spots that could produce large amounts of electricity.

Second, we should begin the planning and construction of a unified national smart grid for the transport of renewable electricity from the rural places where it is mostly generated to the cities where it is mostly used. New high-voltage, low-loss underground lines can be designed with "smart" features that provide consumers with sophisticated information and easy-to-use tools for conserving electricity, eliminating inefficiency and reducing their energy bills. The cost of this modern grid—$400 billion over 10 years—pales in comparison with the annual loss to American business of $120 billion due to the cascading failures that are endemic to our current balkanized and antiquated electricity lines.

15   Third, we should help America's automobile industry (not only the Big Three but the innovative new startup companies as well) to convert quickly to plug-in hybrids that can run on the renewable electricity that will be available as the rest of this plan matures. In combination with the unified grid, a nationwide fleet of plug-in hybrids would also help to solve the problem of electricity storage. Think about it: with this sort of grid, cars could be charged during off-peak energy-use hours; during peak hours, when fewer cars are on the road, they could contribute their electricity back into the national grid.

Fourth, we should embark on a nationwide effort to retrofit buildings with better insulation and energy-efficient windows and lighting. Approximately 40 percent of carbon dioxide emissions in the United States come from buildings— and stopping that pollution saves money for homeowners and businesses. This initiative should be coupled with the proposal in Congress to help Americans who are burdened by mortgages that exceed the value of their homes.

Fifth, the United States should lead the way by putting a price on carbon here at home, and by leading the world's efforts to replace the Kyoto treaty [see Footnote 4, p. 317] next year in Copenhagen with a more effective treaty that caps global carbon dioxide emissions and encourages nations to invest together in efficient ways to reduce global warming pollution quickly, including by sharply reducing deforestation.

Of course, the best way—indeed the only way—to secure a global agreement to safeguard our future is by re-establishing the United States as the country with the moral and political authority to lead the world toward a solution.

Looking ahead, I have great hope that we will have the courage to embrace the changes necessary to save our economy, our planet and ultimately ourselves.

20   In an earlier transformative era in American history, President John F. Kennedy challenged our nation to land a man on the moon within 10 years. Eight years and two months later, Neil Armstrong set foot on the lunar surface. The average age of the systems engineers cheering on Apollo 11 from the Houston control room that day was 26, which means that their average age when President Kennedy announced the challenge was 18.

This year similarly saw the rise of young Americans, whose enthusiasm electrified Barack Obama's campaign. There is little doubt that this same group of energized youth will play an essential role in this project to secure our national future, once again turning seemingly impossible goals into inspiring success.

● **Review Questions**

1. How does Gore tie the environmental crisis to the nation's economic and national security challenges?

2. In terms of energy independence, what policy should the United States adopt as its ultimate goal in the immediate future?

3. Summarize Gore's five-part plan.

● Discussion and Writing Suggestions

1. Why do you think Gore begins and ends his op-ed with references to president-elect Barack Obama?

2. To what extent do you support the use of public funds to help pay for the costs of realizing Al Gore's five-part plan? To what degree do you believe that such projects should be financed by private industry? Explain.

3. Gore's plan to make America independent of fossil fuels within such a short period of time was attacked by many critics. How does Gore attempt to respond to such criticism and to address particular objections and concerns?

4. Based on your own understanding of the matter (and perhaps, also, what you have read of Thomas Friedman and other authors in this chapter, such as Bryce), to what extent do you think that Gore's plan is achievable? What are the primary stumbling blocks, in your view? Explain.

5. Write a critique of Gore's argument. Use as guidelines the principles discussed in Chapter 2. Consider first the main questions: (1) To what extent does Gore succeed in his purpose? (2) To what extent do you agree with him? Then move to the specifics: Do you find Gore's recommendations (for example, his five-part plan) practical? Has he argued logically? Before writing your critique, you may want to read other selections in that chapter that deal with similar concerns: Robert Bryce's "The Dangerous Delusions of Energy Independence," Mortimer B. Zuckerman's "Stop the Energy Insanity," and Joseph P. White's "Why the Gasoline Engine Isn't Going Away Anytime Soon." To what extent do you find one or more of these authors challenging Gore's assumptions?

THE DANGEROUS DELUSIONS OF ENERGY INDEPENDENCE

Robert Bryce

In the following selection Robert Bryce argues that it is neither possible nor desirable for the United States to become independent of foreign energy supplies. Those who advocate such independence, he claims, are "woefully ignorant about the fundamentals of energy and the energy business." Bryce's provocative conclusion flies in the face of often unexamined assumptions held by many politicians, as well as environmentalists.

Robert Bryce, a fellow at the Institute for Energy Research, and a managing editor of *the Energy Tribune,* has written about energy for more than two decades. His articles have appeared in such publications as the *Atlantic Monthly,* the *Guardian,* and *the Nation.* His books include *Cronies: Oil, the Bushes, and the Rise of Texas, America's Superstate* (2004) and *Pipe Dreams: Greed, Ego, and the Death of Enron* (2002). This selection is excerpted from the Introduction ("The Persistent Delusion") to his book *Gusher of Lies: The Dangerous Delusions of "Energy Independence"* (2008).

Americans love independence.

Whether it's financial independence, political independence, the Declaration of Independence, or grilling hotdogs on Independence Day, America's self-image is inextricably bound to the concepts of freedom and autonomy. The promises laid out by the Declaration—life, liberty, and the pursuit of happiness—are the shared faith and birthright of all Americans.

Alas, the Founding Fathers didn't write much about gasoline.

Nevertheless, over the past 30 years or so—and particularly over the past 3 or 4 years—American politicians have been talking as though Thomas Jefferson himself warned about the dangers of imported crude oil. Every U.S. president since Richard Nixon has extolled the need for energy independence. In 1974, Nixon promised it could be achieved within 6 years.[1] In 1975, Gerald Ford promised it in 10.[2] In 1977, Jimmy Carter warned Americans that the world's supply of oil would begin running out within a decade or so and that the energy crisis that was then facing America was "the moral equivalent of war."[3]

The phrase "energy independence" has become a prized bit of meaningful-sounding rhetoric that can be tossed out by candidates and political operatives eager to appeal to the broadest cross section of voters. When the U.S. achieves energy independence, goes the reasoning, America will be a self-sufficient Valhalla, with lots of good-paying manufacturing jobs that will come from producing new energy technologies. Farmers will grow fat, rich, and happy by growing acre upon acre of corn and other plants that can be turned into billions of gallons of oil-replacing ethanol. When America arrives at the promised land of milk, honey, and supercheap motor fuel, then U.S. soldiers will never again need visit the Persian Gulf, except, perhaps, on vacation. With energy independence, America can finally dictate terms to those rascally Arab sheikhs from troublesome countries. Energy independence will mean a thriving economy, a positive balance of trade, and a stronger, better America.

5   The appeal of this vision of energy autarky has grown dramatically since the terrorist attacks of September 11. That can be seen through an analysis of news stories that contain the phrase "energy independence." In 2000, the Factiva news database had just 449 stories containing that phrase. In 2001, there were 1,118 stories. By 2006, that number had soared to 8,069.

The surging interest in energy independence can be explained, at least in part, by the fact that in the post–September 11 world, many Americans have been hypnotized by the conflation of two issues: oil and terrorism. America was attacked, goes this line of reasoning, because it has too high a profile in the parts of the world where oil and Islamic extremism are abundant. And buying oil from the countries of the Persian Gulf stuffs petrodollars straight into the pockets of terrorists like Mohammad Atta and the 18 other hijackers who committed mass murder on September 11.

Americans have, it appears, swallowed the notion that all foreign oil—and thus, presumably, all foreign energy—is bad. Foreign energy is a danger to the economy, a danger to America's national security, a major source of funding for terrorism, and, well, just not very patriotic. Given these many assumptions, the common wisdom is to seek the balm of energy independence. And that balm is being peddled by the Right, the Left, the Greens, Big Agriculture, Big Labor, Republicans, Democrats, senators, members of the House, [former president] George W. Bush, the opinion page of the *New York Times*, and the neoconservatives. About the only faction that dismisses the concept is Big Oil. But then few people are listening to Big Oil these days.

Environmental groups like Greenpeace and Worldwatch Institute continually tout energy independence.[4] The idea has long been a main talking point of Amory Lovins, the high priest of the energy-efficiency movement and the CEO of the Rocky Mountain Institute.[5] One group, the Apollo Alliance, which represents labor unions, environmentalists, and other left-leaning groups, says that one of its primary goals is "to achieve sustainable American energy independence within a decade."[6]

Al Gore's 2006 documentary about global warming, *An Inconvenient Truth*, implies that America's dependence on foreign oil is a factor in global warming.[7] The film, which won two Academy Awards (for best documentary feature and best original song), contends that foreign oil should be replaced with domestically produced ethanol and that this replacement will reduce greenhouse gases.[8] (In October 2007, Gore was awarded the Nobel Peace Prize.)

10   The leading Democratic candidates for the White House in 2008 have made energy independence a prominent element of their stump speeches. [Former] Illinois senator Barack Obama has declared that "now is the time for serious leadership to get us started down the path of energy independence."[9] In January 2007, in the video that she posted on her Website that kicked off her presidential campaign, New York senator Hillary Clinton said she wants to make America "energy independent and free of foreign oil."[10]

The Republicans are on board, too. In January 2007, shortly before Bush's State of the Union speech, one White House adviser declared that the president would soon deliver "headlines above the fold that will knock your socks off in terms of our commitment to energy independence."[11] In February 2007, Arizona senator and presidential candidate John McCain told voters in Iowa, "We need energy independence. We need it for a whole variety of reasons."[12] In March 2007, former New York mayor Rudolph Giuliani insisted that the federal government "must treat energy independence as a matter of national security." He went on, saying that "we've been talking about energy independence for over 30 years and it's been, well, really, too much talk and virtually no action.... I'm impatient and I'm single-minded about my goals, and we will achieve energy independence."[13]

•   •   •

Polls show that an overwhelming majority of Americans are worried about foreign oil. A March 2007 survey by Yale University's Center for Environmental Law and Policy found that 93 percent of respondents said imported oil is a serious problem and 70 percent said it was "very" serious.[14] That finding was confirmed by an April 2007 poll by Zogby International, which found that 74 percent of Americans believe that cutting oil imports should be a high priority for the federal government. And a majority of those surveyed said that they support expanding the domestic production of alternative fuels.[15]

The energy independence rhetoric has become so extreme that some politicians are even claiming that lightbulbs will help achieve the goal. In early 2007, U.S. Representative Jane Harman, a California Democrat, introduced a bill that would essentially outlaw incandescent bulbs by requiring all bulbs in the U.S. to be as efficient as compact fluorescent bulbs. Writing about her proposal in the *Huffington Post*, Harman declared that such bulbs could "help transform America into an energy efficient and energy independent nation."[16]

While Harman may not be the brightest bulb in the chandelier, there's no question that the concept of energy independence resonates with American voters and explains why a large percentage of the American populace believes that energy independence is not only doable but desirable.

15　　But here's the problem: It's not and it isn't.

Energy independence is hogwash. From nearly any standpoint—economic, military, political, or environmental—energy independence makes no sense. Worse yet, the inane obsession with the idea of energy independence is preventing the U.S. from having an honest and effective discussion about the energy challenges it now faces.

[Let's] acknowledge, and deal with, the difference between rhetoric and reality. The reality is that the world—and the energy business in particular—is becoming ever more interdependent. And this interdependence will likely only accelerate in the years to come as new supplies of fossil fuel become more difficult to find and more expensive to produce. While alternative and renewable forms of energy will make minor contributions to America's overall energy mix, they cannot provide enough new supplies to supplant the new global energy paradigm, one in which every type of fossil fuel—crude oil, natural gas, diesel fuel, gasoline, coal, and uranium—gets traded and shipped in an ever more sophisticated global market.

Regardless of the ongoing fears about oil shortages, global warming, conflict in the Persian Gulf, and terrorism, the plain, unavoidable truth is that the U.S., along with nearly every other country on the planet, is married to fossil fuels. And that fact will not change in the foreseeable future, meaning the next 30 to 50 years. That means that the U.S. and the other countries of the world will continue to need oil and gas from the Persian Gulf and other regions. Given those facts, the U.S. needs to accept the reality of *energy interdependence*.

The integration and interdependence of the $5-trillion-per-year global energy business can be seen by looking at Saudi Arabia, the biggest oil producer on the planet.[17] In 2005, the Saudis *imported* 83,000 barrels of gasoline and other refined oil products per day.[18] It can also be seen by looking at Iran, which imports 40 percent of its gasoline needs. Iran also imports large quantities of natural gas from Turkmenistan.[19] If the Saudis, with their 260 billion barrels of oil reserves, and the Iranians, with their 132 billion barrels of oil and 970 trillion cubic feet of natural gas reserves, can't be energy independent, why should the U.S. even try?[20]

20　　An October 2006 report by the Council on Foreign Relations put it succinctly: "The voices that espouse 'energy independence' are doing the nation a disservice by focusing on a goal that is unachievable over the foreseeable future and that encourages the adoption of inefficient and counterproductive policies."[21]

America's future when it comes to energy—as well as its future in politics, trade, and the environment—lies in accepting the reality of an increasingly interdependent world. Obtaining the energy that the U.S. will need in future decades requires American politicians, diplomats, and business people to be actively engaged with the energy-producing countries of the world, particularly the Arab and Islamic producers. Obtaining the country's future energy supplies means that the U.S. must embrace the global market while acknowledging the practical limits on the ability of wind power and solar power to displace large amounts of the electricity that's now generated by fossil fuels and nuclear reactors.

The rhetoric about the need for energy independence continues largely because the American public is woefully ignorant about the fundamentals of energy and the energy business.[22] It appears that voters respond to the phrase, in part, because it has become a type of code that stands for foreign policy isolationism—the idea being that if only the U.S. didn't buy oil from the Arab and Islamic countries, then all would be better. The rhetoric of energy independence provides political cover for protectionist trade policies, which have inevitably led to ever larger subsidies for politically connected domestic energy producers, the corn ethanol industry being the most obvious example.

But going it alone with regard to energy will not provide energy security or any other type of security. Energy independence, at its root, means protectionism and isolationism, both of which are in direct opposition to America's long-term interests in the Persian Gulf and globally.

Once you move past the hype and the overblown rhetoric, there's little or no justification for the push to make America energy independent. And that's the purpose of this book: to debunk the concept of energy independence and show that none of the alternative or renewable energy sources now being hyped—corn ethanol, cellulosic ethanol, wind power, solar power, coal-to-liquids, and so on—will free America from imported fuels. America's appetite is simply too large and the global market is too sophisticated and too integrated for the U.S. to secede.

25   Indeed, America is getting much of the energy it needs because it can rely on the strength of an ever-more-resilient global energy market. In 2005, the U.S. bought crude oil from 41 different countries, jet fuel from 26 countries, and gasoline from 46.[23] In 2006, it imported coal from 11 different countries and natural gas from 6 others.[24] American consumers in some border states rely on electricity imported from Mexico and Canada.[25] Tens of millions of Americans get electricity from nuclear power reactors that are fueled by foreign uranium. In 2006, the U.S. imported the radioactive element from 8 different countries.[26]

Yes, America does import a lot of energy. But here's an undeniable truth: It's going to continue doing so for decades to come. Iowa farmers can turn all of their corn into ethanol, Texas and the Dakotas can cover themselves in windmills, and Montana can try to convert all of its coal into motor fuel, but none of those efforts will be enough. America needs energy, and lots of it. And the only way to get that energy is by relying on the vibrant global trade in energy commodities so that each player in that market can provide the goods and services that it is best capable of producing.

Notes

1. Richard Nixon, State of the Union address, January 30, 1974. Available: http://www. thisnation.com/library/sotu/1974rn.html.

2. Gerald Ford, State of the Union address, January 15, 1975. Available: http://www.ford.utexas.edu/LIBRARY/SPEECHES/750028.htm.

3. Jimmy Carter, televised speech on energy policy, April 18, 1977. Available: http://www.pbs.org/wgbh/amex/carter/filmmore/ps_energy.html.

4. Greenpeace is perhaps the most insistent of the environmental groups regarding energy independence. This 2004 statement is fairly representative: http://www.greenpeace.org/ international/campaigns/no-war/war-on-iraq/it-s-about-oil. For Worldwatch, see its press release after George W. Bush's 2007 State of the Union speech, which talks about "increased energy independence." Available: http://www.worldwatch.org/node/4873.

5. See any number of presentations by Lovins on energy independence. One sample: his presentation before the U.S. Senate Committee on Energy and Natural Resources on March 7, 2006. Available: http://energy.senate.gov/public/index.cfm? FuseAction=Hearings.Testimony&Hearing_ID=1534&Witness_ID=4345. Or see *Winning the Energy Endgame*, by Lovins et al., 228, discussing the final push toward "total energy independence" and the move to the hydrogen economy.

6. National Apollo Alliance Steering Committee statement. Available: http://www. apolloalliance.org/about_the_alliance/who_we_are/steeringcommittee.cfm.

7. At approximately 1:32 into the movie, in a section that discusses what individuals can do to counter global warming, a text message comes onto the screen: "Reduce our dependence on foreign oil, help farmers grow alcohol fuels."

8. AMPAS data. Available: http://www.oscars.org/79academyawards/nomswins.html.

9. Barack Obama, "Energy Security Is National Security," Remarks of Senator Barack Obama to the Governor's Ethanol Coalition, February 28, 2006. Available: http://obama.senate.gov/speech/060228-energy_security_is_national_security/ index.html.

10. Original video at www.votehillary.org. See also, http://www.washingtonpost.com/ wp-dyn/content/article/2007/01/20/AR2007012000426.html.

11. *New York Times*, "Energy Time: It's Not about Something for Everyone," January 16, 2007.

12. Shailagh Murray, "Ethanol Undergoes Evolution as Political Issue," *Washington Post*, March 13, 2007, A06. Available: http://www.washingtonpost.com/ wp-dyn/content/article/2007/03/12/AR2007031201722_pf.html.

13. Richard Perez-Pena, "Giuliani Focuses on Energy," *The Caucus: Political Blogging from the New York Times*, March 14, 2007. Available: http://thecaucus.blogs. nytimes.com/2007/03/14/giuliani-focuses-on-energy.

14. Yale Center for Environmental Law and Policy, 2007 Environment survey. Available: http://www.yale.edu/envirocenter/YaleEnvironmentalPoll2007Keyfindings.pdf.

15. UPI, "Americans Want Energy Action, Poll Says," April 17, 2007. Available: http://www.upi.com/Energy/Briefing/2007/04/17/americans_want_energy_action _poll_says.

16. Jane Harman, "A Bright Idea for America's Energy Future," *Huffington Post*, March 15, 2007. Available: http://www.huffingtonpost.com/rep-jane-harman/a-bright-idea-for-america_b_43519.html.

17. http://www.infoplease.com/ipa/A0922041.html.

18. Organization of Arab Petroleum Exporting Countries (OPEC), *Annual Statistical Report 2006*, 75. Available: http://www.oapecorg.org/images/A%20S%20R%202006.pdf.

19. Nazila Fathi and Jad Mouawad, "Unrest Grows amid Gas Rationing in Iran," *New York Times*, June 29, 2007. According to this story, Iran imports gasoline from 16 countries. Iran has been importing natural gas from Turkmenistan since the late 1990s. In 2008, those imports will likely be about 1.3 billion cubic feet of natural gas per day. The fuel will be used to meet demand in northern Iran. For more, see, David Wood, Saeid Mokhatab, and Michael J. Economides, "Iran Stuck in Neutral," *Energy Tribune*, December 2006, 19.

20. EIA oil reserve data for Saudi Arabia available:http://www.eia.doe.gov/emeu/cabs/saudi.html. EIA oil reserve data for Iran available: http://www.eia.doe.gov/emeu/cabs/Iran/Oil.html. EIA natural gas data for Iran available: http://www.eia.goe.gov/emeu/cabs/Iran/NaturalGas.html.

21. Council on Foreign Relations, "National Security Consequences of U.S. Oil Dependency," October 2006, 4. Available: http://www.cfr.org/content/publications/attachments/EnergyTFR.pdf.

22. A June 2007 survey done by Harris Interactive for the American Petroleum Institute found that only 9 percent of the respondents named Canada as America's biggest supplier of oil for the year 2006. For more on this, see Robert Rapier, "America's Energy IQ," R-Squared Energy Blog, June 29, 2007. Available: http://i-r-squared.blogspot.com/2007/06/americas-energy-iq.html#links. For the results of the entire survey, see: http://www.energytomorrow.org/energy_issues/energy_iq/energy_iq_survey.html.

23. EIA crude import data available: http://tonto.eia.doe.gov/dnav/pet/pet_move_impcus_a2_nus_epc0_im0_mbbl_a.htm. EIA data for jet fuel available: http://tonto.eia.doe.gov/dnav/pet/pet_move_impcus_a2_nus_EPJK_im0_mbbl_a.htm. EIA data for finished motor gasoline available: http://tonto.eia.doe.gov/dnav/pet/pet_move_impcus_a2_nus_epm0f_im0_mbbl_a.htm.

24. EIA coal data available: http://www.eia.doe.gov/cneaf/coal/quarterly/html/t18p01p1.html. For gas imports, EIA data available: http://tonto.eia.doe.gov/dnav/ng/ng_move_impc_sl_a.htm.

25. EIA data available: http://www.eia.doe.gov/cneaf/electricity/epa/epat6p3.html.

26. Information from 2006, EIA data available: http://www.eia.doe.gov/cneaf/nuclear/umar/table3.html.

Review Questions

1. Why are Americans so obsessed with independence, according to Bryce?

2. Why does Bryce believe that renewable energy sources such as wind power and solar power cannot supplant fossil fuels in the foreseeable future?

3. How does Bryce explain the American public's (and their leaders') rhetoric about independence?

● Discussion and Writing Suggestions

1. What is Bryce's chief objection to the premise that the United States should strive to become energy independent? To what extent do you agree with his objection?

2. To what extent do you believe that Bryce is overly pessimistic about the prospects for renewable energy sources supplanting fossil fuels in the near term? Explain.

3. Bryce employs sarcasm plentifully throughout this piece. Cite examples. Do you think that he uses this rhetorical device effectively? Explain.

4. Bryce argues that "the U.S. needs to accept the reality of *energy interdependence*." What implications does such an acceptance have for (1) domestic suppliers of fossil fuels (coal, oil, natural gas); (2) domestic consumption of energy from both fossil and renewable sources; (3) our relations with oil-supplying nations of the Middle East?

5. Critique Bryce's argument. Use as guidelines the principles discussed in Chapter 2. Consider first the main questions: (1) To what extent does Bryce succeed in his purpose? (2) To what extent do you agree with him? Then move to the specifics: Do you find Bryce's arguments compelling? Has he argued logically? What are his assumptions, and how do you assess their validity? You may want to draw upon other authors in this chapter—for example, Friedman or Gore—to provide support in your critique of Bryce. Keep in mind that this selection by Bryce is part of the Introduction to a book-length treatment of the subject during which he goes into much greater detail and a more extended argument than you will find in this relatively brief excerpt. Nevertheless, the heart of Bryce's argument is contained in this passage.

6. Locate a specific principle or definition that Bryce uses in this selection. For example, in paragraph 1 he asserts that "Americans love independence" and in paragraph 17 he contends that "the world—and the energy business in particular—is becoming ever more interdependent. And this interdependence will likely only accelerate in the years to come..." Write an analysis in which you apply this or another principle or definition by Bryce to a particular situation of which you have personal knowledge or about which you have read. See the guidelines and model analyses in Chapter 6 for ideas on how to proceed.

NATIONAL SECURITY CONSEQUENCES OF U.S. OIL DEPENDENCE

Report of an Independent Task Force

The following selection is excerpted from the "Overview and Introduction" of a Task Force report issued in October 2006 by the Council on Foreign Relations. The Task Force chairs were John Deutch, who served as Deputy Secretary of Defense from 1994 to 1995, and as Director of Central Intelligence from 1995 to 1996; and James Schlesinger, Secretary of Defense from 1973 to 1975 and America's first Secretary of Energy under President Carter. The blue ribbon group included twenty-four other members.

The lack of sustained attention to energy issues is undercutting U.S. foreign policy and U.S. national security. Major energy suppliers—from Russia to Iran to Venezuela—have been increasingly able and willing to use their energy resources to pursue their strategic and political objectives. Major energy consumers—notably the United States, but other countries as well—are finding that their growing dependence on imported energy increases their strategic vulnerability and constrains their ability to pursue a broad range of foreign policy and national security objectives. Dependence also puts the United States into increasing competition with other importing countries, notably with today's rapidly growing emerging economies of China and India. At best, these trends will challenge U.S. foreign policy; at worst, they will seriously strain relations between the United States and these countries.

This report focuses on the foreign policy issues that arise from dependence on energy traded in world markets and outlines a strategy for response. And because U.S. reliance on the global market for oil, much of which comes from politically unstable parts of the world, is greater than for any other primary energy source, this report is mainly about oil. To a lesser degree it also addresses natural gas.

Put simply, the reliable and affordable supply of energy—"energy security"—is an increasingly prominent feature of the international political landscape and bears on the effectiveness of U.S. foreign policy. At the same time, however, the United States has largely continued to treat "energy policy" as something that is separate and distinct—substantively and organizationally—from "foreign policy." This must change. The United States needs not merely to coordinate but to integrate energy issues with its foreign policy.

The challenge over the next several decades is to manage the consequences of unavoidable dependence on oil and gas that is traded in world markets and to begin the transition to an economy that relies less on petroleum. The longer the delay, the greater will be the subsequent trauma. For the United States, with 4.6 percent of the world's population using 25 percent of the world's oil, the transition could be especially disruptive.

5   During the next twenty years (and quite probably beyond), it is infeasible to eliminate the nation's dependence on foreign energy sources. The voices that espouse "energy independence" are doing the nation a disservice by focusing on a goal that is unachievable over the foreseeable future and that encourages the adoption of inefficient and counterproductive policies. Indeed, during the next two decades, it is unlikely that the United States will be able to make a sharp reduction in its dependence on imports, which currently stand at 60 percent of consumption. The central task for the next two decades must be to manage the consequences of dependence on oil, not to pretend the United States can eliminate it.

A popular response to the steep rise in energy prices in recent years is the false expectation that policies to lower imports will automatically lead to a decline in prices. The public's continuing expectation of the availability of cheap energy alternatives will almost surely be disappointed. While oil prices may retreat from their current high levels, one should not expect the price of oil to return, on a sustained basis, to the low levels seen in the late 1990s. In fact, if more costly domestic supply is used to substitute for imported oil, then prices will not moderate. Yet the public's elected representatives have allowed this myth to survive, as they advocate policies that futilely attempt to reduce import dependence quickly while simultaneously lowering prices. Leaders of both political parties, especially when seeking public office, seem unable to resist announcing unrealistic goals that are transparent efforts to gain popularity rather than inform the public of the challenges the United States must overcome. Moreover, the political system of the United States has so far proved unable to sustain the policies that would be needed to manage dependence on imported fuels. As history since 1973 shows, the call for policy action recedes as prices abate.

These problems rooted in the dependence on oil are neither new nor unique to the United States. Other major world economies that rely on imported oil—from Western Europe to Japan, and now China and India—face similar concerns. All are having difficulties in meeting the challenges of managing demand for oil. But these countries do not share the foreign policy responsibilities of the United States. And the United States, insufficiently aware of its vulnerability, has not been as attentive as the other large industrialized countries in implementing policies to slow the rising demand for oil. Yet even if the United States were self-sufficient in oil (a condition the Task Force considers wholly infeasible in the foreseeable future), U.S. foreign policy would remain constrained as long as U.S. allies and partners remained dependent on imports because of their mutual interdependence. Thus, while reducing U.S. oil imports is desirable, the underlying problem is the high and growing demand for oil worldwide.

The growing worldwide demand for oil in the coming decades will magnify the problems that are already evident in the functioning of the world oil market. During that period, the availability of low-cost oil resources is expected to decline; production and transportation costs are likely to rise. As more hydrocarbon resources in more remote areas are tapped, the world economy will become even more dependent on elaborate and vulnerable infrastructures to bring oil and gas to the markets where they are used.

For the last three decades, the United States has correctly followed a policy strategy that, in large measure, has stressed the importance of markets. Energy markets, however, do not operate in an economically perfect and transparent manner. For example, the Organization of Petroleum Exporting Countries (OPEC), quite notably, seeks to act as a cartel. Most oil and gas resources are controlled by state-run companies, some of which enter into supply contracts with consumer countries that are accompanied by political arrangements that distort the proper functioning of the market. These agreements, such as those spearheaded by the Chinese government in oil-rich countries across Africa and elsewhere, reflect many intentions, including the desire to "lock up" particular supplies for the Chinese market. Some of the state companies that control these resources are inefficient, which imposes further costs on the world market. And some governments use the revenues from hydrocarbon sales for political purposes that harm U.S. interests. Because of these realities, an active public policy is needed to correct these market failures that harm U.S. economic and national security. The market will not automatically deliver the best outcome.

· · ·

10   [W]hile the United States has limited leverage to achieve its energy security objectives through foreign policy actions, it has considerable ability to manage

its energy future through the adoption of domestic policies that complement both a short- and long-term international strategy.

The Task Force is unanimous in recommending the adoption of incentives to slow and eventually reverse the growth in consumption of petroleum products, especially transportation fuels such as motor gasoline. However, the Task Force did not agree about the particular options that would best achieve this objective. The Task Force considered three measures:

- A tax on gasoline (with the tax revenue recycled into the economy with a fraction possibly earmarked for specific purposes such as financing of energy technology research and development [R&D]);
- Stricter and broader mandated Corporate Average Fuel Economy standards, known as CAFE standards; and
- The use of tradable gasoline permits that would cap the total level of gasoline consumed in the economy.

Used singly or in combination, these measures would not only encourage higher-efficiency vehicles (although these will take time to find their way into the fleet), but also encourage the introduction of alternative fuels, as well as promote changes in behavior such as the greater use of public transportation. While there are other domestic policies that could be adopted to limit demand for fuels, no strategy will be effective without higher prices for transportation fuels or regulatory incentives to use more efficient vehicles....

At the same time that the United States promotes measures to reduce oil demand, it should also be prepared to open some new areas for exploration and production of oil and gas, for example, in Alaska, along the East and West coasts, and in the Gulf of Mexico. In addition to modestly increasing supply, encouraging domestic production is a valuable, if not essential, element for increasing the credibility of U.S. efforts to persuade other nations to expand their exploration and production activities.

Ultimately, technology will be vital to reducing the dependence on oil and gas, and to making a transition away from petroleum fuels. These benefits of improved technology will come in the future only if investments are made today in research, development, and demonstration (RD&D).

15   The Task Force notes that higher energy prices are unleashing remarkable forces for innovation in this country. Entrepreneurs are seeking new ideas for products and services, such as batteries, fuel cells, and biofuels. Private equity capital is seeking opportunities to invest in new energy technologies. Large corporations are investing in RD&D in all aspects of energy production and use. These activities will undoubtedly result in a steady improvement in the ability of the U.S. economy to meet energy needs.

The U.S. government has an important role in supporting this innovation in the private sector, especially for technologies that require significant development efforts to demonstrate commercial potential. The Task Force recommends that the federal government offer greatly expanded incentives and investments aimed at both short- and long-term results to address a wide range of technologies that includes higher-efficiency vehicles, substitutes for oil in transportation (such as biomass and electricity), techniques to enhance production from existing oil wells, and technologies that increase the energy efficiency of industrial processes that use oil and gas. Government spending is appropriate in this context because the market alone does not make as much effort as is warranted by national security and environmental considerations....

● Discussion and Writing Suggestions

1. In what ways does the Task Force report support Robert Bryce's conclusions about the prospects for U.S. energy independence?

2. The authors of the report assert that "[t]he central task for the next two decades must be to manage the consequences of dependence on oil, not to pretend the United States can eliminate it." To what extent do you agree with this conclusion, especially given Al Gore's challenge to the country? Are the authors of the report being too pessimistic, even defeatist, about the prospects for nationwide conversion to renewable energy?

3. The authors of this report fault politicians of both parties for misleading the public about the prospects of reducing the nation's dependence on foreign oil in the near term (paragraph 5). Conduct a short Google or Bing (or other database) search—using, among other search terms, "energy independence"—and report on whether or not you agree with the Task Force authors on this matter.

4. The Task Force considered three measures that would help reduce American dependence on foreign oil and spur the development of higher-efficiency vehicles and alternative fuels: (1) increased taxes on gasoline, (2) raised fuel economy (CAFE) standards, (3) and a cap-and-trade system for gasoline. Which of these measures do you find the most (and least) desirable? The most (and least) practical? Explain.

5. The Task Force recommends increasing domestic production of oil and gas by opening "new areas [within the United States and in the Gulf of Mexico] for the exploration of oil and gas"—that is, by drilling. During the 2008 presidential campaign, "Drill, baby, drill!" became a campaign slogan. To what extent do you favor increased drilling? Explain.

BALANCE SHEETS AND THE CLIMATE CRISIS: HOW AMERICAN BUSINESSES CAN HELP

Mindy S. Lubber

Mindy Lubber (pronounced *Loober*) is president of Ceres, a national coalition of investors, environmental organizations, and public interest groups that has defined global climate change as a financial issue. Working with coalition members, Ceres reports on corporations that expose themselves to financial risk by not reducing their carbon foot-prints and simultaneously steers investment dollars (some seven trillion dollars aggre-gated across coalition members) toward companies that carefully manage these risks. A former Regional Administrator of the U.S. Environmental Protection Agency, Lubber has won international awards for her work on combating climate change and is a frequent speaker at national and international forums on the subject. The following is adapted from a speech delivered in October 2008 at a Deutsche Bank conference, "Women on Wall Street," during the financial downturn that followed the subprime lending crisis.

A Global Crisis

For the first time in history, we are about to leave to our children a future in which the natural resources we take for granted, such as clean air and abundant, clean water, are imperiled. That means that my son, Abe, and my daughter, Jessie, and your children will be living in a world that is not sustainable. And I am standing here on behalf of my children, and your children and nieces and nephews, who are going to be inheriting this planet and for whose sake we must now act.

We have reached a critical moment, for we can now name a problem that is world changing and life changing, a problem that must be addressed yester-day—not in two years, a problem so vast that we have finally reached a tipping point that portends a collapse in the natural systems we depend on for our col-lective health and security. That problem, of course, is global climate change. We talk about action, but we are not yet acting in a manner that is anywhere near what is required to save the planet.

Many of us in this room think of ourselves as the "good guys" who want to do the right thing for our children and for the environment. That's well and good. But I stand before you as an analyst who sees in climate change a signifi-cant, material risk to our financial markets.[1] Hurricane Katrina was not just a devastating event on a human scale but also a monumental financial disaster. When we look at the tens of billions of dollars in losses that insurance compa-nies paid out for Katrina, and the even greater sums in uninsured losses, we rec-ognize that climate change may be the biggest financial risk that companies have ever faced—bigger, say, than spiking oil prices, bigger than labor unrest, bigger than unstable currencies. The threats that climate change poses to corporate profitability are enormous; and even if we weren't the "good guys" who want to save the planet for the planet's sake or our children's, we had better pay atten-tion as business leaders whose enterprises are at risk. We know that ignoring the sub-prime lending disaster led to a stunning financial collapse on Wall Street and Main Street. If we make that same mistake with respect to the climate, we jeopardize not only our capital markets but our very survival.

So it's time we pay attention and stop thinking of climate change as an off-balance sheet risk.[2] It's a risk that needs to appear on our balance sheets and be

---

[1] A "material" risk is any risk sizeable enough to affect the value of a company. [Eds.]

[2] To assess financial health, a business will record assets and liabilities on a "balance sheet." Risks known to affect profitability are "on-balance sheet" risks. Known risks that are kept "off-balance sheet"—that is, not reported to shareholders—can open a company to charges of dishonest accounting. [Eds.]

woven into the fabric of everyday decision-making on Wall Street, from the copy room to the boardroom.

5   When I mentioned this speaking opportunity to a friend, she suggested that this is a stunningly poor time to give a talk on Wall Street. "Isn't everyone depressed? Isn't it a moment when we are suffering from the results of a broken economic model—a time of cutbacks, limited new ideas, turmoil and complete uncertainty?"

    Perhaps. But what better time to address capital market[3] leaders who are actively rethinking the fundamentals of our economy? The new 21st-century reality must be one in which we acknowledge the substantial risks of short-term thinking in capital markets and commit to rethinking and rebuilding our economy so that it can endure the test of time. Because unchecked carbon emissions will cause untold damage to this world, we must commit now to building long-term shareholder value and creating new high-paying jobs that do not revolve around oil and coal. The near collapse of our economy has got your attention; so while you are paying attention, let's talk about your exposure to climate risk—and also the opportunities that await those who lead on this crucial issue.

    Let's talk about the actions needed to confront the climate crisis so that we can build a global economy that sustains not only the hopes of the 6.7 billion people on the planet today, but also the 9 billion people expected to be here in 2050. Specifically, I want to discuss the varied, mutually reinforcing roles of government, regulatory agencies, corporations, and investors in meeting the challenges ahead.

The Need for Public Policy on Climate Change

What needs to happen to reverse rising temperatures on our planet? How can we be audacious enough to build a future economy that allows us to reduce our carbon emissions while building a robust economy for our present and future?

    First, we need government action.

10   The scientific community is clear: to limit the worst impacts of climate change, we must reduce global warming pollution by at least 25 percent below 1990 levels by 2020 and 80 percent by 2050. The only way to achieve these reductions is through strong government policies that set mandatory limits on carbon dioxide emissions—which means putting a price on carbon emissions.

    Many-governments around the world are already making this shift. The Kyoto Protocol[4] is now in full force and many industrialized countries are participating. In Europe, there is a price on carbon. In the United States, there is not. The European Union has been limiting carbon emissions for three years

---

[3]"Capital markets": the market place in which shares of a company are bought and sold. [Eds.]
[4]The Kyoto Protocol (a component of the United Nations Convention on Climate Change), adopted in Kyoto, Japan, in 1997, and taking effect in 2005, was aimed at reducing global greenhouse gases. The protocol has been adopted by 183 countries—but *not* the United States. [Eds.]

and carbon emission allowances are now trading at $30 to $40 a ton. A similar cap-and-trade carbon-reducing program was launched last month for power plants operating in the Northeast, including New York and New Jersey. Forcing the operators of these power plants, especially high CO_2-emitting coal plants, to pay for every ton of CO_2 they emit will impact their bottom line, creating a meaningful incentive to pursue technologies that will reduce CO_2 output.

The government can also help by investing in our future. Three hundred fifty billion dollars invested over the next three years could create 5 million high quality jobs—jobs that are needed now. Developing our nation's vast *clean* energy resources can move us toward energy security, climate stability, and economic prosperity. Such a shift will transform America into becoming the global leader of the new green economy.

A new and massive economic stimulus package could pay for itself in energy savings and in tax dollars generated by new jobs and businesses. We just found 700 billion.[5] Let's find another 350 billion. That is half the price tag of the Wall Street rescue package, which has no guarantee of success. But with the 350 billion dollar investment, we absolutely and positively could retrofit and repower America using clean, green energy—and create millions of jobs in the process. A green bailout could give America a start to rebuilding our economy.

It makes sense for government to act because mandatory change is often the only way to assure results. And the reach of government should be precise and deal with the problems appropriately. It is essential that we not regulate for regulation's sake, but instead be smart and clear. We need a cap on carbon pollution and a cost on carbon pollution. We also need investment.

15   The government has an enormous role to play, but non-governmental organizations (NGOs) must also be part of the plan. Outside advocates have historically been important and effective engines for passing legislation that protects our natural resources—such as the Clean Air and Clean Water Acts. Every day, administrations get pressured by business lobbyists who advocate for policies that favor business. Advocates for the health of our natural resources must be equally as effective—and insistent.

From Crisis to Economic Opportunity

It is important to keep in mind that the challenges we face create enormous economic opportunities. Transitioning to low-carbon energy sources and energy-efficient technologies will be in John Doerr's[6] words, "the biggest economic opportunity of the 21st century," an opportunity worth—literally—trillions of dollars.

---

[5]In late 2008, the Congress approved a $700 billion package to rescue the nation's financial system by purchasing "toxic" real estate securities and other assets from banks and large insurance companies threatened with collapse because of the rippling effects of the sub-prime mortgage crisis. [Eds.]
[6]John Doerr: venture capitalist to many Silicon Valley high technology firms, such as Google, Sun Microsystems, Symantec, Compaq, and Netscape. [Eds.]

Some companies and some investors are waking up to the opportunity—they are beginning to integrate environmental threats into their day-to-day decision-making and are actually putting a price on carbon, on water, on social impacts, and on workforce issues. Most importantly, they're seeing the financial benefit of doing so.

Our partners at Sun Microsystems, for example, now have 40% of their workforce working from home, in order to cut down on transportation costs. Google has invested in a bus system so that fewer employees are getting in their cars and driving to work everyday. When I was out in California visiting with Pacific Gas and Electric, CEO Peter Darbee told me that the response he got from his workforce when he announced his company's new initiative on climate change was the most positive he has ever received for any initiative. He said his e-mail box was flooded with e-mails supporting new approaches to promoting energy efficiency, investing in renewables, and, with the Governor of California, calling for comprehensive climate policy in the state. PG&E employees recognized their company was making wise choices both for the planet and for their business, and their support was overwhelming. This is the kind of leadership we need.

You know the times *are* changing when the *Wall Street Journal, Forbes, Fortune,* the *Economist* and the New York Stock Exchange all invite Ceres to speak to them about sustainability and its impacts on corporate finances. When Dell and Nike integrate climate goals into their strategic planning, we know that we are making progress. When leading Wall Street firms are now producing dozens of analyst reports on climate-related business impacts, we sense a change coming. Major corporations are recognizing the need for action.

The New Metrics: A Way Forward

20 But these efforts of forward-looking businesses are still not enough—in fact, not nearly enough. Most leading companies, including most of the financial firms represented in this room, are undervaluing climate risks and are continuing to invest in carbon-intensive projects that will make it all but impossible to reduce global warming pollution to the levels we need.

This is hard-core economics and our capital markets must begin to factor in the costs and opportunities of climate change, water shortages, depleted forests, and other sustainability issues. To not do so is to have these same issues savage our bottom lines in the future—at an hour late enough in the day that corrective action will either be prohibitively inexpensive or altogether ineffective.

Capital markets cannot operate effectively until *all* costs are recognized and factored into business decisions. We need to build an economy that recognizes the real risks of resource pollution and depletion and opportunities, and builds them into the fabric of business planning. That is to say, we need new metrics that will create a level playing field for all companies—a new standard of reporting by which corporations and investors alike can measure progress toward a greener way of doing business. Here are some specific ways to move forward.

Stock exchanges must examine their role with respect to the global climate. Exchanges the world over require comprehensive information to be disclosed from public companies that wish to trade on a given exchange. Stock exchanges could demand that companies fully disclose natural resource costs. The Securities and Exchange Commission could do the same, as could the Federal Accounting Standards Board, which sets universal accounting practices for corporate reporting. When all companies are required to report on the same array of climate- and resource-related risks, investors large and small can assess these risks and the markets will sort out winners or losers.

Investors, both individual and institutional, must also change. They need to broaden their short-term horizons to account for the very real, substantial risks of climate change. These risks can't be measured in hours or even months. But that does not make them any less real. Reducing our carbon footprint by 80% by 2050 and building a clean energy economy starting today is as clear a material risk as is currency risk, inflation risk, and sub-prime risk. We knew the sub-prime crisis was looming and chose to ignore it. We do not have the luxury of making a similar mistake on climate change.

25   Certified Financial Analysts need to teach those whose job it is to report on companies how to analyze exposure to climate risk. Real numbers need to go in those quarterly analyst reports on which the public's perception of a company's financial health rises and falls. The issues need to be raised on earnings calls, and they need to be addressed because there are metrics available to measure the very real costs of climate change, water shortages, and so on.

Corporate Responsibility

Finally, corporate leaders need to act—to see sustainability, diversity, and social issues as key aspects of their corporate strategy, where they are material as major factors.

We need to tie CEO compensation to accomplishing specific goals related to climate change, in the same way that CEO compensation is currently tied to other metrics like profitability, and we need to hold people accountable.

We need a complete integration of climate risk into strategic planning, and we need a Chief Sustainability executive with direct reporting to the CEO or COO [Chief Operating Officer]. Such an officer would be charged, for instance, with examining a company's supply chain. Wal-Mart, for example, has made impressive progress in analyzing its supply chain in its entirety, making sure that at every step in moving from raw material to finished goods to packaging and display it is taking action to reduce greenhouse gas emissions.

Corporations must come to see sustainability reporting as a fundamental responsibility. All companies should disclose and measure the same risks, because what gets measured gets managed.

30   My point is this: Global warming, water shortages, and other mega risks here in the US and across the globe can no longer be dismissed as environmental issues—off-balance sheet risks—externalities—or problems that deserve focus *only* during the good years. These sustainability issues must be woven into the fabric of our capital markets if we are to rebuild our economy into a healthy, robust, and enduring system.

Our long-held models, driven by a short-term view, have made it difficult to build the mega risks of global warming into our capital markets. Yet the fiscal crises on Wall Street has been a painful lesson in how entire industries can delude themselves into ignoring fundamental issues—in this current economic crisis, the hidden risks from subprime mortgages. That fiasco revealed the pitfalls of an economic system that focuses on short-term gains and growth at all costs while ignoring long-term shareholder value. As we confront mega issues like global climate change—perhaps the biggest challenge mankind has ever faced—business, investors, regulatory agencies, and government leaders have an opportunity to learn from the present crises and get it right.

There is work to do. Given the risks, we have no choice but to roll up our sleeves. We owe our children and our children's children our very best. Let it not be said of us that we faced a grave challenge, a surmountable challenge, but chose instead short-term profits, imperiling the world in the process. Together, today, we *can* take a long-term view. Together, we *can* build a sustainable economy.

Discussion and Writing Suggestions

1. Lubber begins and ends with allusions to children. How does this strategy help advance her case?

2. How is the focus of Lubber's piece different from—if related to—Al Gore's?

3. Lubber argues that we need "a cap on carbon pollution and a cost on carbon pollution." One way to do this is to levy significantly increased gas taxes, as do governments in Europe. In July 2008, when gasoline prices in the United States topped out at more than $4 a gallon, gasoline prices in Europe—due to high gas taxes—reached more than $9 (and in some cases, $10) a gallon. To what extent would you—and the American public—be prepared to pay increased taxes that would raise the price of gasoline to such levels in an attempt to put a cost and a cap on carbon pollution?

4. Locate a specific principle or definition that Lubber uses in this selection. For example, consider her assertion in paragraph 2 that "We talk about action, but we are not yet acting in a manner that is anywhere near what is required to save the planet." Write an analysis in which you apply this or another principle or definition by Lubber to a particular situation of which you have personal knowledge or about which you have read. See the guidelines and model analyses in Chapter 6 for ideas on how to proceed.

5. Lubber notes that some companies and investors "are beginning to integrate environmental threats into their day-to-day decision-making. . . ." To what extent do you see evidence of this new environmental concern among American businesses? How does this tendency relate to some of Thomas Friedman's findings in "205 Easy Ways to Save the Earth"?

6. Lubber advocates significantly increased reporting requirements for companies concerning the impact of their carbon footprints on climate. What other steps do you believe that companies with large carbon footprints should be required to take to reduce the risks of climate change? Note that in the past, large companies such as automobile manufacturers generally argued that much as they cared for the environment, it was not economically feasible to operate in a greener fashion. To what extent can reducing carbon footprints be both good for business as well as good for the environment?

7. In the report "American's Energy 'Independence'" published on the Web (http://www.abc.net.au/unleashed/stories/s2274315.htm), Dennis Phillips, a professor of foreign policy at the University of Sydney in Australia, notes that the environmental agenda often clashes with the economic and employment agenda, particularly in third world countries. He argues:

> All the world's poor are entitled to a much higher standard of living, but in order to progress, the world's poorest three billion will need to access and consume vastly increased quantities of energy. "Renewables" like wind and solar power are not going to do the job in the short term.
>
> Do we tell the world's poor to be patient and wait? In the "ethanol fiasco" we have done worse than that. We have processed staple crops like corn and soybeans to pour into our fuel tanks, forcing up food prices that ignited riots around the world.

How is it possible to reconcile such sometimes conflicting agendas: ensuring economic development—and indeed, survival itself—in third world countries while at the same time ensuring, as Mindy Lubber and others advocate, that we secure the future for our children and grandchildren by capping carbon pollution?

STOP THE ENERGY INSANITY

Mortimer B. Zuckerman

In the following selection, Mort Zuckerman decries the "special-interest-driven politics" that have long paralyzed intelligent policymaking on energy and calls for "imperatives" that involve both fossil-based and renewable fuels. Zuckerman, a Canadian-born naturalized American citizen, is editor-in-chief of *U.S. News & World Report* and publisher/owner of the *New York Daily News*. He is also a real estate billionaire who in 2007 was ranked as the 188th wealthiest American by *Forbes* magazine. This editorial appeared in *U.S. News & World Report* on July 21, 2008.

We are in a hole—and still digging. We have oil at a catastrophic $140 a barrel yet no sign of a bipartisan energy policy assured of passage—let alone the forceful execution needed to expand domestic supplies and restrict domestic consumption. Instead, we have the blame game about greedy speculators, careless consumers, and cowardly politicians, inevitable maybe in an election year but a betrayal of the promise of America.

In the meantime, as gasoline soars over $4 a gallon, the availability of credit for enterprise shrinks, home values collapse, and food and fuel prices skyrocket, afflicting the American consumer with a triple whammy so devastating that the economic stimulus of the $120 billion tax rebate has been wiped out. And where is the wealth going? To enemies of America, to some of the world's worst leaders, such as the oil autocrats of Iran, Venezuela, and Russia.

It's pathetic that we have had to beg a begrudging Saudi Arabia to pump a few more barrels. Ever since the oil crisis of the 1970s, report after report has warned us about the U.S addiction to oil. The United States may constitute 4 percent of the world's population, but we account for around one quarter of worldwide oil consumption—twice the combined rate of the Chinese and the Indians. The core of the problem is parked in U.S driveways. Nearly 70 percent of the 21 million barrels of oil we burn every day goes to transportation, most of which is used by individual drivers.

The American people are not foolish. Every day we have a lesson in the surging cost of oil; we know that the dream of energy independence is really just a delusion for a country that produces only a third of the oil it uses. Whatever the rhetoric, no combination of solar, wind, ethanol, biodiesel, or anything else will allow us independence in the foreseeable future.

5   The public also sees the role of our special-interest-driven politics. The farm and ethanol lobbies have succeeded in getting Congress to pay huge subsidies to farmers to grow corn to be converted into ethanol—at the same time, we set high tariffs to keep out cheaper, imported ethanol. Americans see that acreage once devoted to growing food now grows corn for fuel, thus contributing to higher food prices; they see the oil, gas, and nuclear power lobbies winning for their industries the lion's share of government support, compared with the relatively modest support for U.S. alternative energy approaches; they see that the strength of the oil lobby has only increased the subsidies and tax breaks under the Bush administration—and they are disgusted.

What is to be done?

Consumption

The first fuel economy standard law, known as Corporate Average Fuel Economy, or CAFE, was passed in 1975—a mandate that doubled the fuel efficiency of the typical car sold in the United States between 1974 and 1985 from 13.8 mpg to 27.5 mpg (even though these measurements took place in favorable controlled conditions rather than on actual highways). It has flattened out since then, in contrast to Europe, which now demands 44 mpg. An effort here in 1990 to lift the fuel standard to 40 mpg for cars aroused furious opposition led by Democrats from automaking states, like Michigan's Sen. Carl Levin and Rep. John Dingell. Had that bill been passed, we would be using 3 million fewer barrels a day.

Only in 2007, with gasoline nearing $3 a gallon, did Congress approve the first major increase in fuel efficiency in 32 years, requiring the fleet average to reach 35 mpg by 2020—a measure that would save only 1 million barrels a day by then. Attempts to raise taxes on gasoline to reduce consumption have essentially failed, except for a small tax increase of 4.3 cents per gallon in 1993.

Supply

10 As costs of oil imports have soared, the benefits of increasing our own supplies have multiplied—while the environmental costs have been reduced by technologies and practices developed over the past two decades. In other words, the benefits exceed the costs.

We can get past the lame repetition of the decades-old argument over the virtues of offshore drilling. Simply put: To refuse to exploit our vast oil reserves is insane. The United States is one of the few countries in the world that choose to lock up their natural resources by dramatically restricting production and exploration. At least, until now. That $4 pump price is changing public attitudes. In a recent Gallup Poll, 57 percent favored drilling in U.S coastal and wilderness areas that were once off limits. How shocking is that? In the Arctic National Wildlife Refuge, we're talking about a tiny corner of 2,200 acres (an area the size of a small airport) out of 19 million acres. The proposed drilling promises to yield an estimated 10.4 billion barrels, representing well over 20 years of imports from Saudi Arabia. Drilling in ANWR would take place on the coastal plain, a mosquito-plagued tundra and bog in the summer, not in the snowcapped mountains of ANWR that television pictures would have you believe are at stake. In the winter, the area would also be traversed on ice roads that melt in the spring. This would do no permanent damage to an environment in one of the bleakest, most remote places on this continent—except to inconvenience some caribou that might have to find a different place to mate. We cannot lose over $40 billion a year to serve the caribou.

Similarly, the outer continental shelf is estimated to contain some 86 billion barrels of oil, plus 420 trillion cubic feet of natural gas that is overwhelmingly off limits and underdeveloped—even though those reserves could be tapped now with minimal environmental disturbance. This is supported by the fact that there were virtually no oil spills when Hurricanes Katrina and Rita flattened terminals around the Gulf of Mexico. Offshore drilling rigs would be far beyond beach sightlines. The stellar environmental records of eco-sensitive regions such as Scandinavia, the Netherlands, and Great Britain have shown that the greatest oil spills would be avoided because they typically come from tankers importing oil, not from drilling or other offshore locations. The same can be said of the eastern Gulf of Mexico, where there is an estimated 3.7 billion barrels in relatively shallow waters.

If this sounds like a remedy that's a long way off from fixing $4-a-gallon gas, it must be remembered that prices for crude and gasoline are set by future expectations. Any policy that pushes the future supply to increase or leads future demand to drop can cause today's prices to fall or to rise less than they otherwise would. That is why to open up new areas would cause the oil futures markets to respond relatively quickly.

Oil out of the ground is only a start. For new crude to yield lower gasoline prices, we need to reduce the barriers to building or expanding our refineries. Refineries face multiple regulatory barriers in a world of NIMBY ("not in my backyard") and the inevitable litigation from the environmental lobbies.

15   Here are five more energy imperatives we need to move on quickly:

1. Reallocate resources to concentrate funds on providing the necessary R&D [research and development] support for energy efficiency. We must do this with the real menace of global warming in mind. James Hansen, the director of NASA's Goddard Institute for Space Studies, frames the issue this way: Our biggest worry is not what we put in our cars but what we put in our power plants. He believes that we should stop the use of coal by 2030, except with those power plants that can capture the carbon dioxide.

2. Fix our mass transit system for both freight and passengers. When you consider rail in terms of energy, steel wheels on steel rails are some 10 times as efficient as rubber on roads. A real rail program could probably have the single greatest impact on our oil consumption and on the release of carbon dioxide. A single locomotive run by two men can haul the same amount of freight as 70 modern semitrailer truck rigs with 70 drivers. One passenger train can take 1,000 cars off the road.

3. Raise fuel economy standards for new cars and trucks immediately.

4. Substantially increase the gas tax, offsetting it with other tax cuts to induce people to buy fuel-efficient vehicles.

5. Pursue alternative energy technologies within the limits of the market.

Such measures as these would send a signal to the world that the United states is no longer putting its fate fully in the hands of foreign nations and that we are determined to reduce the financial drain costing us at least $300 billion a year. None of this will happen without a sensible compromise among liberals, conservatives, and environmentalists. We simply cannot afford a political system that is incapable of addressing such a critical national issue. In other words, we need real leadership in Washington.

● Review Questions

1. Summarize Zuckerman's recommendations to "stop the energy insanity."

2. What evidence does Zuckerman provide to show that it is safe to drill for oil in the Arctic National Wildlife Reserve (ANWR) as well as offshore and on the outer continental shelf of the United States?

3. Why is mass rail transit more energy-efficient than "rubber on roads," according to Zuckerman?

● Discussion and Writing Suggestions

1. Zuckerman asserts that "[t]o refuse to exploit our vast oil reserves is insane." He adds, "We cannot lose over $40 billion a year to serve the caribou." To what extent do you find his argument persuasive? Note that Zuckerman does not rule out—indeed he strongly advocates—the development of alternative energy sources.

2. Which of Zuckerman's five "energy imperatives" do you find most appealing? Most practical? Least appealing and least practical? Explain.

3. To what extent do you find that Zuckerman is sensitive to environmental concerns? Explain, pointing to particular sections in his editorial.

4. With which of the other authors in this chapter (so far) do you find Zuckerman in most agreement, in terms of their attitudes toward the energy/environmental crisis? Which authors would most disagree with his analysis and recommendations? For example, Zuckerman, like other authors in this chapter, lays a good deal of the blame on politicians and "special-interest-driven politics." Who else shares this view?

5. Zuckerman concludes by asserting that "we need real leadership in Washington." Based on what you have learned from newspapers, magazines, or TV or Internet news about the Obama administration's energy policies, do you believe that we now have such leadership on this particular issue? Explain, providing specific examples.

6. Critique Zuckerman's argument. Use as guidelines the principles discussed in Chapter 2. Consider first the main questions: (1) To what extent does Zuckerman succeed in his purpose? (2) To what extent do you agree with him? Then move to the specifics: Do you find use of the term "insanity" reasonable? Has he argued logically? Before writing your critique, you may want to read other selections in that chapter that deal with similar concerns: Friedman's "205 Easy Ways to Save the Earth," Gore's "The Climate for Change," Lubber's "Balance Sheets and the Climate Crisis." To what extent do you find one or more of these authors challenging Zuckerman's assumptions?

G.M. AT 100: IS ITS FUTURE ELECTRIC?

Don Sherman

The Chevrolet Volt—which G.M. categorizes as an "extended range electric vehicle" or E-REV—is one of the most eagerly anticipated cars on the horizon. (The Tesla Roadster, an electric sports car, is available now; but since it costs upward of $100,000, its appeal is limited.) Many see the success of electric cars like the Volt as key to the very survival of General Motors, which emerged from bankruptcy in July 2009 as a considerably smaller corporation than before. Ford Motor Company is also working on an electric car, as are Chrysler, Toyota, Nissan, and Mitsubishi, parent company of Subaru.

Still under development, and not expected in dealer showrooms until at least late 2010, the Volt has many wondering if this is truly a reinvention of the automobile, a victory in the battle for oil independence—or if it will prove to be (like its predecessor in the electric car division, the late lamented EV1) an expensive money loser for General Motors that will fail to gain widespread consumer acceptance.

In his 2008 *Atlantic* article, "Electro-Shock Therapy," detailing the early development of the Volt, Jonathan Rauch sums up the difference between the Volt and conventional hybrids:

> Because it will have both an electric and a gasoline motor on board, the Volt will be a hybrid. But it will be like no other hybrid on the road today. Existing hybrids are gasoline-powered cars, with an electric assist to improve the gas mileage. The Volt will be an electric-powered car, with a gasoline assist to increase the battery's range.

Electric vehicles have been around since the dawn of the automobile era (you may have ridden on golf carts); but they have never been equipped with batteries that could take them more than short distances without recharging. With its lithium ion battery (and that assist from the small gasoline engine), the makers of the Volt hope to neutralize that limitation.

"G.M. at 100: Is Its Future Electric?" updates the Volt's status as of September 14, 2008, when the article appeared in the *New York Times*. Don Sherman, who has a degree in mechanical engineering, has also written for magazines such as *Car and Driver* (which he edited from 1985 to 1987), *Popular Science*, and *Sports Car International*.

The Chevrolet Volt is expected to be the icing on General Motors' 100th birthday cake this week. The much-promoted sedan, which will operate as an electric car in typical local driving, is intended to provide a jump-start for the company's second century.

The timing of the Tuesday event is fortuitous, for much more is riding on the Volt than whether a new model using experimental technologies will be a hit. For if the Volt succeeds, it could put the troubled company on a whole new path after 10 decades tethered to the internal-combustion engine. If it fails, it could drag G.M., and perhaps the entire struggling American auto industry, even further behind Asian competitors.

It was on Sept. 16, 1908, that William Crapo Durant filed the incorporation papers that formed G.M., with a revitalized Buick as its foundation. The centennial should be a time of joy at the company. But, with losses since 2005 approaching $70 billion, and Toyota having accelerated past G.M. into the No. 1 spot in global auto sales, the company's staff won't be dancing in party hats.

Instead of toasting the glory days when G.M. owned half of the United States car and truck market—its share peaked at 51 percent in 1962 amid suggestions that it should be broken up under antitrust laws—G.M. executives are looking expectantly ahead to November 2010. That's when the Volt, expected to break cover this week in close to final form, is due to reach customers.

5   By mobilizing its formidable marketing resources, G.M. has piqued interest in the Volt. Anticipation is high; when unauthorized photos and surreptitious video footage emerged recently, they spread across the Internet with viral intensity. (The photos and video can be seen at autobloggreen.com.) [See also YouTube (Eds.)]

The interest goes beyond the usual curiosity about the styling and features of a wholly new model. The public, like industry veterans and seasoned experts, seems to grasp the potential: the Volt could revive Detroit's fortunes while loosening OPEC's stranglehold.

Burt Rutan, the aerospace visionary whose accomplishments include the Voyager round-the-world aircraft and who is also an electric-car enthusiast, is among the believers. "I expect the Chevy Volt to be both a success and a transportation game-changer," he said.

Though electric cars were common in the early 20th century, gasoline models had won out by the 1920s. Since then, the concept has surfaced again and again, but never in a car with mass-market appeal. Still, throughout the 20th century G.M. was developing breakthroughs in electrical systems—coil ignitions, electric starters, computerized powertrains and digital infotainment systems—that mainly ended up advancing its fossil-fueled vehicles.

But at the same time, G.M. researchers were quietly investigating alternatives to internal combustion. In the 1960s, the research and development staff experimented with fuel cells, hybrids and plug-in electric cars.

10   By the mid-1990s, G.M. took a gamble that electric propulsion was ready for public consumption. It leased 1,100 two-seat EV1 commuter cars, based on the Impact electric concept car.

The EV1 was stymied by its short range—sometimes only 50 miles on a charge. And unlike the Volt it had no backup power if the batteries ran down. Yet the EV1 had a devoted following, and lessees protested when G.M. took back the cars to crush them. G.M. called the EV1 a $1 billion learning experience.

Those lessons, and recent knowledge gained developing vastly superior lithium-ion batteries, are the Volt's great enablers. But despite widespread enthusiasm for G.M.'s brilliant 2007 Volt concept car, there are growing doubts about the Volt's chances of success.

Some of that uncertainty can be traced to G.M.'s reluctance to put its cards on the table, potentially ceding a competitive advantage more than two years before the car goes on sale.

But there is also considerable doubt about whether lithium-ion batteries can meet the public's high expectations for range and durability. It is clear that both Toyota and Honda, which have done lithium-ion research, are taking a wait-and-see approach toward lithium-ion—and may actually be moving to other technologies. (All current hybrid cars use nickel-metal-hydride batteries, an older but hardly ideal technology.)

15   Finally, there are questions about the cost. G.M. executives concede that they are revising the price upward. While the company initially hinted at a $30,000 starting price, executives have recently suggested that the Volt might end up in the mid-to high-$40,000 range.

What is not in doubt is that the Volt will be a four-passenger, front-drive compact sedan. But the high-style design of the Volt concept, which captivated crowds at the 2007 Detroit auto show, has given way to a more conventional look that fits without flamboyance into the Chevrolet family. Recent spy photos reveal that the roof has been raised and the window sills altered, presumably to provide a more usable passenger cabin.

G.M. still stands behind its pledge that the Volt will be able to travel at least 40 miles with no exhaust emissions on a fully charged battery. The sole propulsion source is a 160-horsepower alternating-current motor. The 1.4-liter gas engine runs only when necessary to power a generator, which in turn supplies electrical current to both the battery pack and the drive motor.

The concept had a turbocharged 3-cylinder; the production car will have a naturally aspirated 4-cylinder.

Electric motors, generators and engines are old hat at G.M., in contrast to the Volt's lithium-ion battery pack, a leap into uncharted territory. The 400-pound T-shaped pack provides 16 kilowatt-hours of electricity (equivalent to 21 horsepower for one hour), and is nestled between and behind the seats.

20   After studying lithium-ion batteries for decades, G.M. began working last year with two organizations to move them from the lab onto the road. The development partners are Compact Power, a subsidiary of the Korean battery maker LG Chem, and Continental Automotive Systems of Germany, using battery cells designed by A123Systems of Watertown, Mass. G.M. recently decided which of two competing lithium-ion chemistries it will use and which company will make the batteries, but it has made no public announcement.

The Volt is such a departure from the fossil-fuel age that there are different views on how to categorize it. Mr. Rutan calls it a "proper hybrid" because owners have the option of driving on electricity or on a combination of electricity and gasoline. Most engineers prefer "series hybrid," which means an electrically driven car that employs a second form of power conversion to supplement the battery's energy reserve.

G.M. hopes to distinguish the Volt from ordinary hybrids by labeling it an electric car. Plugging into a standard household socket for six or so hours to charge the batteries, and topping off the 12-gallon gas tank, will provide 400 miles of driving range, G.M. says.

An electric car that spews no emissions and consumes only a few pennies' worth of energy commuting to work, while also capable of several hundred miles of range, is the better mousetrap that appeals to green advocates and auto industry pundits alike. The actor Ed Begley Jr., a former EV1 leaseholder who owns a Toyota Prius, said: "I think the Volt's going to be good for everybody. None of us needs a sledgehammer to install a carpet tack. By that, I mean most trips are short—to and from work, to a restaurant or store."

Mr. Begley said he and his wife used their Prius for long trips, and an electric car (a 2003 Toyota RAV4 EV) in town.

25   "The arrival of the Volt and other electric cars will reduce not only America's dependence on foreign oil, but also the smog I experience every day in L.A.," he said.

Chris Paine, who wrote and directed the documentary "Who Killed the Electric Car?" concurs. "G.M. seems motivated and ahead of the competition," he said. "It's a cultural shift of huge proportions for a vast auto company to embrace the concept of a car that's more than an internal-combustion engine.

"Of course, there are huge technical and financial challenges," he added. Still, "The price of oil and consumer interest in change should make the Volt a success."

Industry watchers are more cautious in their optimism. Csaba Csere, editor in chief of *Car and Driver* magazine, said, "The Volt could put G.M. in the most positive light it's enjoyed in 30 years, but its success depends on solving two issues: battery durability and cost."

Mr. Csere (pronounced *CHED-uh*) noted that lithium-ion batteries had proved successful in laptop computers. "But to serve the car world, they'll have to last 10 years, versus the typical two-or three-year laptop lifespan."

30   Manahem Anderman, president of Advanced Automotive Batteries and an electric-car consultant, is also unconvinced. "Without three or four years to test battery life in both the laboratory and in the field, prudent engineering steps have to be bypassed," he said. "Lacking long-term data, G.M. might have to include the cost of a battery replacement in the Volt's price."

Mr. Anderman added: "Rushing to deliver 60,000 electric vehicles per year poses a phenomenal risk. The business case for a vehicle with a $10,000 battery is problematic. I predict G.M. will end up building only a few thousand of them." He said he did not expect the Volt "to be either a commercial success or a long-term benefit" to G.M.'s image.

An auto industry analyst, Jim Hall of 2953 Analytics in Birmingham, Michigan, takes a more sanguine view. "You've got to consider the Volt an investment in new technology," he said. "As was the case with the Prius, G.M. won't earn a profit during the life cycle of the first-generation Volt, but they will gain a foot in the door with this new technology."

G.M. has said that its next-generation Saturn Vue hybrid, due in fall 2010, will also receive lithium-ion batteries and be capable of plug-in recharging.

Robert C. Stempel, the former chairman of both General Motors and Energy Conversion Devices, the Michigan company that developed the nickel-metal-hydride battery, relishes what lies ahead. "The Volt has the possibility of being one of the most successful vehicles in G.M. history," he said.

35   While the Volt is on track to be the first quasi-electric car capable of replacing the conventional sedan, there is no guarantee that it will trump the Prius to become the new green-car king.

Mr. Hall said: "If G.M. were alone in this initiative, the Volt probably would be enough to boost it back to the top of the technological heap. But in Toyota City, there's a seven-story tower called the Electric Powertrain Building. And Chrysler has a hybrid project called ENVI that's progressing more quickly than expected. So the best that can be hoped is that the Volt will move G.M. to the front row of companies with contemporary propulsion technology."

Maintaining front-row status is the key to a G.M. that thrives in its second century. David Cole, the chairman of the Center for Automotive Research in Ann Arbor, Michigan, put a fine point on what lies ahead. "The plug-in hybrid is the most notable technological advancement of the past 50 years," he said. "G.M.'s challenge is making them profitable and continuing to invent a broad range of advanced vehicles."

● Review Questions

1. What was the fate of G.M.'s first all-electric vehicle, the EV1? What was the EV1's chief problem?

2. In what ways is the Chevy Volt seen as an improvement over the EV1? What are the Volt's chief drawbacks? What is the main challenge faced by G.M.'s engineers in bringing the Volt successfully to production?

3. The Volt uses both electricity and gasoline. Why is this vehicle not considered a conventional hybrid, like the Toyota Prius?

● Discussion and Writing Suggestions

1. Assuming that you were gainfully employed or otherwise financially self-sufficient (and assuming a personal situation of your choosing), would you consider buying a Chevy Volt? Why or why not?

2. Since peaking in mid-2008, the price of gasoline has dropped from more than $4 a gallon to—as of early 2009—under $2 a gallon. To what extent do you think that the drop in gasoline prices (assuming they remain more or less steady) bodes ill for electric vehicles like the Volt?

3. Sherman quotes some observers who predict that the Volt will be a breakthrough vehicle, both for G.M. and for the driving public. He quotes others who take a more cautious view and yet others who predict that the Volt will fail both to become profitable and to significantly change vehicle purchasing and driving habits. Where do you stand on this issue, based upon what you have read of the Volt and upon your own sense of consumer preferences? Explain.

4. To a considerable degree, and for better or for worse, G.M. has come to represent the American automobile industry. Of course, foreign auto companies like Toyota and Honda also build cars in the United States and sell them—by the millions—to Americans. In the long term, to what extent do you think it makes a difference if American auto companies like G.M., Chrysler, and Ford lose market share to foreign car companies—or even go out of business, as long as many of their employees and suppliers can find employment and new customer contracts with the foreign auto companies?

WHY THE GASOLINE ENGINE ISN'T GOING AWAY ANY TIME SOON

Joseph B. White

In the following article, Joseph B. White, who covers automobile and energy-related stories for the *Wall Street Journal,* explains why, despite its numerous critics and its massive carbon footprint, the internal-combustion engine still has miles to go before it sleeps. This article first appeared in the *Journal* on September 15, 2008.

An automotive revolution is coming—but it's traveling in the slow lane.

High oil prices have accomplished what years of pleas from environmentalists and energy-security hawks could not: forcing the world's major auto makers to refocus their engineers and their capital on devising mass-market alternatives to century-old petroleum-fueled engine technology.

With all the glitzy ads, media chatter and Internet buzz about plug-in hybrids that draw power from the electric grid or cars fueled with hydrogen, it's easy to get lulled into thinking that gasoline stations soon will be as rare as drive-in theaters. The idea that auto makers can quickly execute a revolutionary transition from oil to electricity is now a touchstone for both major presidential candidates.

That's the dream. Now the reality: This revolution will take years to pull off—and that's assuming it isn't derailed by a return to cheap oil. Anyone who goes to sleep today and wakes up in five years will find that most cars for sale in the U.S. will still run on regular gas—with a few more than today taking diesel fuel. That will likely be the case even if the latter-day Rip Van Winkle sleeps until 2020.

Free to Drive

5 Cars aren't iPods or washing machines. They are both highly complex machines and the enablers of a way of life that for many is synonymous with freedom and opportunity—not just in the U.S., but increasingly in rising nations such as China, India and Russia.

Engineering and tooling to produce a new vehicle takes three to five years—and that's without adding the challenge of major new technology. Most car buyers won't accept "beta" technology in the vehicles they and their families depend on every day. Many senior industry executives—including those at Japanese companies—have vivid memories of the backlash against the quality problems that resulted when Detroit rushed smaller cars and new engines into the market after the gas-price shocks of the 1970s. The lesson learned: Technological change is best done incrementally.

Integral to Modern Life

Technological inertia isn't the only issue. Cars powerful enough and large enough to serve multiple functions are integral to modern life, particularly in suburban and rural areas not well served by mass transit.

Ditching the internal-combustion engine could mean ditching the way of life that goes with it, and returning to an era in which more travel revolves around train and bus schedules, and more people live in smaller homes in dense urban neighborhoods.

Economic and cultural forces—high gas prices and empty-nest baby boomers bored with the suburbs—are encouraging some Americans to return to city life, but by no means all. In rising economies such as China, meanwhile, consumers are ravenous for the mobility and freedom that owning a car provides.

Desire Isn't Enough

10 That doesn't mean auto makers and their technology suppliers aren't serious about rethinking the status quo. But displacing internal-combustion engines fueled by petroleum won't be easy and it won't be cheap.

It also may not make sense. Over the past two decades, car makers have at times declared the dawn of the age of ethanol power, hydrogen power and electric power—only to wind up back where they started: confronting the internal-combustion engine's remarkable combination of low cost, durability and power. One effect of higher oil prices is that car makers now have strong incentives to significantly improve the technology they already know.

"There are a lot of improvements coming to the internal-combustion engine," says John German, manager for environmental and energy analysis at Honda Motor Co.'s U.S. unit.

Refinements to current gasoline motors, driven by advances in electronic controls, could result in motors that are a third to half the size and weight of current engines, allowing for lighter, more-efficient vehicles with comparable power. That, Mr. German says, "will make it harder for alternative technologies to succeed."

By 2020, many mainstream cars could be labeled "hybrids." But most of these hybrids will run virtually all the time on conventional fuels. The "hybrid" technology will be a relatively low-cost "micro hybrid" system that shuts the car off automatically at a stop light, and then restarts it and gives it a mild boost to accelerate.

Cheaper Than Water

15 Gasoline and diesel are the world's dominant motor-vehicle fuels for good reasons. They are easily transported and easily stored. They deliver more power per gallon than ethanol or other biofuels. And until recently petroleum fuels were a bargain, particularly for consumers in the U.S. Even now, gasoline in the U.S. is cheaper by the gallon than many brands of bottled water.

Car makers have made significant advances in technology to use hydrogen as a fuel, either for a fuel cell that generates electricity or as a replacement for gasoline in an internal-combustion engine. But storing and delivering hydrogen remains a costly obstacle to mass marketing of such vehicles.

Natural gas has enjoyed a resurgence of interest in the wake of big new gas finds in the U.S., and Honda markets a natural-gas version of its Civic compact car.

But there are only about 1,100 natural-gas fueling stations around the country, of which just half are open to the public, according to the Web site for Natural Gas Vehicles for America, a group that represents various natural-gas utilities and technology providers.

Among auto-industry executives, the bet now is that the leading alternative to gasoline will be electricity. Electric cars are a concept as old as the industry itself. The big question is whether battery technology can evolve to the point where a manufacturer can build a vehicle that does what consumers want at a cost they can afford.

20   "The No. 1 obstacle is cost," says Alex Molinaroli, head of battery maker Johnson Controls Inc.'s Power Solutions unit. Johnson Controls is a leading maker of lead-acid batteries—standard in most cars today—and is working to develop advanced lithium-ion automotive batteries in a joint venture with French battery maker Saft Groupe SA.

The Costs Add Up

Cost is a problem not just with the advanced batteries required to power a car for a day's driving. There's also the cost of redesigning cars to be lighter and more aerodynamic so batteries to power them don't have to be huge.

There's the cost of scrapping old factories and the workers that go with them—a particular challenge for Detroit's Big Three auto makers, which have union agreements that make dismissing workers difficult and costly.

A world full of electricity-driven cars would require different refueling infrastructure but the good news is that it's already largely in place, reflecting a century of investment in the electric grid.

The refueling station is any electric outlet. The key will be to control recharging so it primarily happens when the grid isn't already stressed, but controllers should be able to steer recharging to off-peak hours, likely backed by discount rates for electricity.

25   Big utilities in the two most populous states, California and Texas, are adding millions of smart meters capable of verifying that recharging happens primarily in periods when other electricity use is slack. Studies show the U.S. could easily accommodate tens of millions of plug-in cars with no additional power plants. Three big utilities in California are planning to install smart meters capable of managing off-peak recharging. The estimated cost: $5 billion over the next five years.

Remembering the Past

Americans often reach for two analogies when confronted with a technological challenge: The Manhattan Project, which produced the first atomic bomb during World War II, and the race to put a man on the moon during the 1960s. The success of these two efforts has convinced three generations of Americans that all-out, spare-no-expense efforts will yield a solution to any challenge.

This idea lives today in General Motors Corp.'s crash program to bring out the Chevrolet Volt plug-in hybrid by 2010—even though the company acknowledges the battery technology required to power the car isn't ready.

Even if GM succeeds in meeting its deadline for launching the Volt, the Volt won't be a big seller for years, especially if estimates that the car will be priced at $40,000 or more prove true.

Moon-shot efforts like the Volt get attention, but the most effective ways to use less energy may have less to do with changing technology than with changing habits.

30   A 20-mile commute in an electric car may not burn gasoline, but it could well burn coal—the fuel used to fire electric power plants in much of the U.S. The greener alternative would be to not make the drive at all, and fire up a laptop and a broadband connection instead.

[The following table accompanied White's article.]

The Road Ahead

Gasoline has powered the vast majority of the world's automobiles for the past century. But now amid rising oil prices and increasing concern about tailpipe emissions and global warming, new types of propulsion technologies are starting to emerge. Here's an overview of what's here now, and what's ahead.

—*Kelly McDaniel-Timon*

	Pros	Cons	Vehicles	Availability/ Starting Prices
Hybrids Have a battery and electric motor to power the car at low speeds and a gas engine for accelerating and highway driving.	Increases fuel-economy significantly, especially in heavy stop-and-go driving.	Price premium over standard models can be $2,500 or more for a Toyota Prius, $8,000 and up for large hybrid SUVs. Mileage improvements modest in some larger vehicles.	Toyota Prius, Ford Escape Hybrid, GMC Yukon Hybrid, Lexus LS600h, Lexus RX400h, Chrysler Aspen Hybrid, Dodge Durango Hybrid.	On the market now. Prius $23,375, Yukon $50,920, Lexus RX400h $43,480.
Mild Hybrids Electric motor only assists the gasoline engine; it can't drive wheels on its own.	Cost. Generally less expensive than full hybrids.	Only modest improvement in fuel economy.	Honda Civic Hybrid, Chevrolet Malibu Hybrid, Saturn Aura Hybrid.	On the market now. Honda Civic $22,600, Chevy Malibu $24,695, Saturn Aura $24,930.
Plug-In Hybrids A full hybrid with a large battery that drivers can recharge by plugging the car into an AC outlet.	Dramatic boost in fuel economy- can go up to perhaps 120 miles on the battery alone.	The advanced batteries required are not yet available. They are also expensive and can overheat.	None on the market today. Some "hackers" can convert Priuses to plug-ins.	Many auto makers working to offer them in 2-4 years.

	Pros	Cons	Vehicles	Availability/ Starting Prices
Flex Fuel Vehicles Have standard internal combustion engines that can run on gasoline or a mix of gasoline and ethanol.	No price premium, can be used in vehicles of all sizes. Reduces greenhouse gas emissions.	Ethanol not widely available. A gallon of ethanol has less energy than a gallon of gas, so mile per gallon is lower.	Almost all GM, Ford and Chrysler models.	On the market now.
Fuel Cell Vehicles Use hydrogen gas and a chemical process to generate electricity that powers an electric motor.	Uses no fossil fuel, hydrogen is widely available and the only tailpipe emission is water vapor.	Still in experimental stage, hydrogen not widely available as fuel, technology still far too expensive for commercial use.	Models now in tests include Honda FCX Clarity and Chevrolet Equinox among others.	Small number of Clarity and Equinox available for lease through test programs.
Electric Car Powered by a long-lasting battery and electric motor. Can have a small gas engine on board to charge the battery.	Practically no emission or engine noise. Can be recharged from AC outlet.	Technology still unproven. Batteries not available.	GM working on Chevy Volt. Also start-up electric car makers Tesla, Fisker and others.	Volt due by 2011. Tesla, Fisker and others possibly sooner.
Clean Diesel New, advanced diesel engines that burn fuel more cleanly and use low-sulfur fuel.	20% to 40% more miles per gallon and more torque than gas engines, reduced greenhouse gas emissions.	More expensive than models with gas engines. Diesel fuel more expensive than gasoline. Unclear if Americans will embrace diesel.	Jeep Grand Cherokee and Volkswagen Jetta are two examples. BMW and Mercedes-Benz also offering clean diesel models.	VW Jetta diesel $21,999, Grand Cherokee $31,390.

Source: WSJ Reporting

● Review Questions

1. Summarize White's answer to the implied question in the title of his article.

2. What are the main stumbling blocks, according to White, to broad consumer acceptance of alternative energy vehicles?

3. What are the chief drawbacks of hydrogen and natural gas as automobile fuels? To what extent do electric-powered vehicles share such drawbacks?

● Discussion and Writing Suggestions

1. White argues, "Most car buyers won't accept 'beta' [developmental] technology in the vehicles that they and their families depend on every day." To what extent do you agree with this assertion as it applies to alternative energy vehicles? Would you be hesitant to buy a first-generation Chevy Volt or any other plug-in hybrid vehicle if there were no guarantee of its reliability?

2. White cites "mobility and freedom" as one reason that the internal-combustion engine will persist for the foreseeable future. To what extent are such values sufficiently important that you would hesitate to purchase or refuse to consider purchasing an all-electric vehicle?

3. Locate a specific principle or definition that White uses in this selection. For example, he asserts in paragraph 5 that cars "are both highly complex machines and the enablers of a way of life that for many is synonymous with freedom and opportunity." Write an analysis in which you apply this or another principle or definition by White to a particular situation of which you have personal knowledge or about which you have read. See the guidelines and model analyses in Chapter 6 for ideas on how to proceed.

4. If the next generation of gasoline-powered vehicles were built with motors "a third to half the size and weight of [motors in] current vehicles" (and therefore, with an equivalent decrease in their carbon footprint), would there be any reason to convert the nation's vehicle fleet to electric, fuel-cell, or other forms of power?

5. Toward the end of this article, White suggests that "the most effective ways to use less energy may have less to do with changing technology than with changing habits." To what extent do you agree with this conclusion? Is the goal of using less energy better achieved by changing our habits than by changing our technology? In what particular ways might changing our habits affect the way we live and work?

THE CASE FOR AND AGAINST NUCLEAR POWER

Michael Totty

In the following article *Wall Street Journal* staff reporter Michael Totty attempts the tricky task of arguing on both sides of the same issue: whether or not we should build more nuclear reactors to help satisfy our energy needs. Can you determine which argument Totty himself finds more persuasive? This article appeared in a special energy section of the *Journal* on June 30, 2008.

Is nuclear power the answer for a warming planet? Or is it too expensive and dangerous to satisfy future energy needs?

Interest in nuclear power is heating up, as the hunt intensifies for "green" alternatives to fossil fuels like coal and natural gas. Even some environmentalists have come on board, citing the severity of the global-warming threat to explain their embrace of the once-maligned power source.

But the issue is far from settled. Proponents insist that nuclear is a necessary alternative in an energy-constrained world. They say that the economics make sense—and that the public has a warped image of the safety risks, thanks to Three Mile Island, Chernobyl and *The China Syndrome*. [See paragraph 25.] Opponents, meanwhile, are convinced that the costs are way too high to justify the safety hazards, as well as the increased risks of proliferation.

Has nuclear's time come? The debate rages on.

Nuclear's the Answer

5   The argument for nuclear power can be stated pretty simply: We have no choice.

If the world intends to address the threat of global warming and still satisfy its growing appetite for electricity, it needs an ambitious expansion of nuclear power.

Scientists agree that greenhouse gases, mainly carbon dioxide, are building up in the atmosphere and contributing to a gradual increase in global average temperatures. At the same time, making electricity accounts for about a third of U.S. greenhouse emissions, mostly from burning fossil fuels to produce power.

Nuclear power plants, on the other hand, emit virtually no carbon dioxide—and no sulfur or mercury either. Even when taking into account "full life-cycle emissions"—including mining of uranium, shipping fuel, constructing plants and managing waste—nuclear's carbon-dioxide discharges are comparable to the full life-cycle emissions of wind and hydropower and less than solar power.

Nuclear power, of course, isn't the only answer. We need to get more energy from other nonpolluting sources such as solar and wind. Conservation is crucial. So is using technology to make more efficient use of fossil-fuel power.

10   But we have to be realistic about the limits of these alternatives. As it is, the 104 nuclear power plants in the U.S. generate about a fifth of the nation's energy. Wind accounts for about 1%, and solar even less than that. Any increase in the number of nuclear power plants can help—even if they won't solve the whole problem.

HOW A NUCLEAR REACTOR WORKS

All power plants convert a source of energy or fuel into electricity. Most large plants do that by heating water to create steam, which turns a turbine that drives an electric generator. Inside the generator, a large electromagnet spins within a coil of wire, producing electricity.

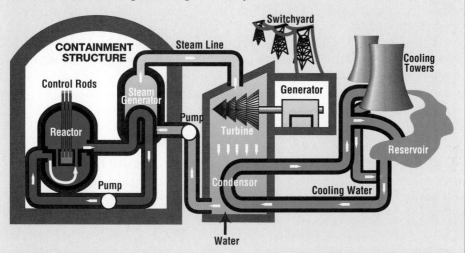

A fossil plant burns coal or oil to make the heat that creates the steam. Nuclear power plants...make the steam from heat that is created when atoms split apart—called fission.

The fuel for nuclear power plants is uranium, which is made into pellets and sealed inside long metal tubes, called fuel rods. The rods are located in the reactor vessel.

The fission process takes place when the nucleus of a uranium atom is split when struck by a neutron. The "fissioning" of the nucleus releases two or three new neutrons and energy in the form of heat. The released neutrons then repeat the process, releasing more neutrons and producing more nuclear energy. The repeating of the process is called a chain reaction and creates the heat needed to turn water into steam.

In a pressurized water reactor...water is pumped through the reactor core and heated by the fission process. The water is kept under high pressure inside the reactor so it does not boil.

The heated water from the reactor passes through tubes inside four steam generators, where the heat is transferred to water flowing around the tubes. The water boils and turns to steam.

The steam is piped to the turbines. The force of the expanding steam drives the turbines, which spin a magnet in coil of wire—the generator—to produce electricity.

(continued)

After passing through the turbines, the steam is converted back to water by circulating it around tubes carrying cooling water in the condenser. The condensed steam—now water—is returned to the steam generators to repeat the cycle.

The cooling water from the condenser is sprayed into the air inside the cooling tower and falls about 60 feet, which cools it before it is continuously recycled to condense more steam. Water in the vapor rising from the cooling tower is replenished to the condenser cooling system using [pumped-in water, generally from a nearby river].

The three water systems at [a nuclear power plant] are separate from each other, and the radioactive water is not permitted to mix with other non-radioactive water systems.

Adapted from "How Sequoyah Works," Tennessee Valley Authority, http://www.tva.gov/power/nuclear/sequoyah_howworks.htm.

More important from the standpoint of displacing fossil fuel, nuclear can meet power demand 24 hours a day. Solar and wind can't do that. Nuclear is the only current technology that fits the bill.

The Real Economics   So, what's the case against nuclear power? It boils down to two things: economics and safety.

Neither holds up to scrutiny.

First, economics. Critics argue that the high cost of building and financing a new plant makes nuclear power uneconomical when compared with other sources of power.

15   But that's misleading on a number of levels. One reason it's so expensive at this point is that no new plant has been started in the U.S. since the last one to begin construction in 1977. Lenders—uncertain how long any new plant would take because of political and regulatory delays—are wary of financing the first new ones. So financing costs are unusually high. As we build more, the timing will be more predictable, and financing costs will no doubt come down as lenders become more comfortable.

Loan guarantees and other federal incentives are needed to get us over this hump. They are not permanent subsidies for uneconomical ventures. Instead, they're limited to the first half dozen of plants as a way to reassure investors that regulatory delays won't needlessly hold up construction. It's important to remember that although nuclear energy has been around a while, it's hardly a "mature" industry, as some critics say. Because of the lack of new plants in so many years, nuclear in many ways is more like an emerging technology, and so subsidies make sense to get it going.

It's also true that a shortage of parts and skills is raising the cost of new plants. But if we start building more plants, the number of companies supplying parts will increase to meet the demand, lowering the price.

Most important, nuclear power appears economically uncompetitive primarily because the price of "cheaper" fossil fuels, mainly coal, don't reflect the high cost that carbon emissions pose for the environment. Add those costs, and suddenly, nuclear power will look like a bargain.

That's likely to happen soon. Governments are expected to assign a cost to greenhouse gases, through either a direct tax (based on the carbon content of a fuel) or a so-called cap-and-trade system, which would set a limit on emissions while allowing companies whose discharges are lower than the cap to sell or trade credits to companies whose pollution exceeds the cap.

20 　　Suddenly, big carbon polluters like coal-produced electricity are going to look a lot more expensive compared with low-carbon sources—in particular, nuclear, wind and hydropower.

It's estimated that a carbon "price" of between $25 and $50 a ton makes nuclear power economically competitive with coal. That should be enough to ease investor concerns about utilities that build new nuclear plants.

Even without a carbon tax, rising natural-gas prices are beginning to make nuclear power more competitive. That's true even in some deregulated markets, such as Texas.

NRG Energy Inc., based in Princeton, New Jersey has filed an application to build a reactor adjacent to an existing plant in Texas. Though it's too early to know how much the plant will eventually cost—or even if it ultimately will get built—high natural-gas prices alone are enough to justify construction, according to NRG.

One other point on cost: Solar and wind advocates say these sources are cheaper than nuclear—and getting cheaper. But again, even if true, the intermittent nature of these sources make them flawed replacements for carbon-emitting sources. Nuclear is the only clean-energy way to address that gap.

25 *No 'China Syndrome'*　　Let's turn to the critics' other argument: safety. We're still living in a world whose viewpoints have been warped by the 1979 accident at the Three Mile Island plant in Pennsylvania and the 1986 explosion at the Chernobyl plant in the Ukraine, as well as by the anti-nuclear movie *The China Syndrome*.

The truth is that there's little doubt that in the U.S., at least, plants are much safer now than they were in the past. Those accidents led regulators and the industry to bolster safety at U.S. nuclear plants. There are more safety features at the plants, plant personnel are better trained and reactors have been redesigned so that accidents are far less likely to occur. For instance, every U.S. plant has an on-site control-room simulator where employees can hone their skills and handle simulated emergencies, and plant workers spend one week out of every six in the simulator or in the classroom.

The next generation of plants is designed to be even safer, using fewer pumps and piping and relying more on gravity to move water for cooling the hot nuclear core. This means fewer possible places where equipment failure could cause a serious accident.

And even if a serious accident does occur, U.S. plants are designed to make sure that no radiation is released into the environment. Reactors are contained inside a huge structure of reinforced concrete with walls that are as much as four feet thick; the Chernobyl reactor lacked such a structure.

What's more, you can't look at safety in a vacuum. Consider the hazards of the world's reliance on coal-fired plants: Coal mining world-wide results in several thousand deaths every year, most of them in China, and burning coal is a leading source of mercury in the atmosphere.

30   Furthermore, look at safety more broadly—from an environmental perspective. The death and destruction stemming from global warming far exceed what is likely to happen if there is a nuclear accident. And yet, when we talk about safety, we seem to focus only on the risks of nuclear power.

Politics of Disposal   The long-term disposal of nuclear waste is also a problem—but it's mainly a policy issue, not a technical one.

Most experts agree that the best way to dispose of waste is deep underground, where radioactive materials can be prevented from entering the environment and where it can be guarded against theft or terrorist attack. In the U.S., the Energy Department picked Yucca Mountain in southwestern Nevada for a repository, but political wrangling has so far blocked proceeding with the site, and final approval is considered a long shot. Even if approved, it won't be able to begin accepting waste for a decade or more.

In the meantime, interim storage in deep pools next to nuclear plants is considered sufficiently safe to meet the industry's needs until well into the future. The amount of waste produced is relatively small; all the waste produced so far in the U.S. would only cover a football field about five yards deep. Older, cooler fuel can also be stored for decades in dry casks.

Longer term, advanced fuel recycling and reprocessing can reduce the amount of waste that needs to be stored. While reprocessing wouldn't eliminate the need for a long-term repository, it can reduce the amount, heat and radioactivity of the remaining waste.

35   *Stopping the Spread*   Finally, critics say that an expansion of nuclear power will increase the danger that potentially hostile nations will use nuclear material from a power program to develop atomic weapons, or that rogue states or terrorists will steal nuclear material to make bombs.

While nonproliferation is an important consideration, the proliferation problem won't be solved by turning away from nuclear power.

To curtail these risks, governments need to strengthen current international anti-proliferation efforts to, among other things, give the International Atomic Energy Agency more information about a country's nuclear-related activities and IAEA inspectors greater access to suspect locations. Further, current fuel-reprocessing techniques are limited and new processing technologies are being developed to limit the amount and accessibility of weapons-grade materials (by, for instance, producing a form of plutonium that needs further reprocessing before it could be used in bombs).

One final point about security: One of the biggest dangers to our security is from oil nations providing support to anti-U.S. terrorist groups. The faster we can move away from carbon-based energy, the faster we take away that funding source. Nuclear energy offers the fastest and most direct path to that safer future.

No to Nuclear

Nuclear power isn't a solution to global warming. Rather, global warming is just a convenient rationale for an obsolete energy source that makes no sense when compared to the alternatives.

40   Sure, nuclear power generates lots of electricity while producing virtually no carbon dioxide. But it still faces the same problems that have stymied the development of new nuclear plants for the past 20 years—exorbitant costs, the risks of an accident or terrorist attack, the threat of proliferation and the challenge of disposing of nuclear waste.

The cost issue alone will mean that few if any new nuclear power stations will get built in the next few years, at least in the U.S., and any that do will require expensive taxpayer subsidies. Instead of subsidizing the development of new plants that have all these other problems, the U.S. would be better off investing in other ways to meet growing energy demands and reduce carbon-dioxide emissions.

In fact, the sheer number of nuclear plants needed to make a major dent in greenhouse emissions means the industry hasn't a prayer of turning nuclear power into the solution to global warming. One study from last year determined that to make a significant contribution toward stabilizing atmospheric carbon dioxide, about 21 new 1,000-megawatt plants would have to be built each year for the next 50 years, including those needed to replace existing reactors, all of which are expected to be retired by 2050. That's considerably more than the most ambitions industry growth projections.

Too Expensive   But let's start with the biggest problem with nuclear power: the cost.

While no one knows what a new reactor will cost until one gets built, estimates for new construction continue to rise. Building a new plant could cost as much as $6,000 a kilowatt of generating capacity, up from estimates of about $4,000 a kilowatt just a year ago. FPL Group, of Juno Beach, Florida, estimates that two new reactors planned for southeast Florida would cost between $6 billion and $9 billion each.

45   Part of the reason for the rising cost estimates is the small number of vendors able to supply critical reactor components, as well as shortage of engineering and construction skills in the nuclear industry. Perhaps the biggest bottleneck is in the huge reactor vessels that contain a plant's radioactive core. Only one plant in the world is capable of forging the huge vessels in a single piece, and it can produce only a handful of the forgings a year. Though the plant intends to expand capacity in the next couple of years, and China has said it plans to begin making the forgings, this key component is expected to limit development for many years.

The only way to make nuclear power economically competitive would be the imposition of steep "prices" on carbon-emitting power sources. Nobody knows precisely how high those prices would have to go—there are too many variables to consider. But estimates range as high as $60 a ton of carbon dioxide. This imposes an unacceptably high price on consumers.

More important, though, there are less-costly ways of weaning ourselves off these carbon-emitting energy sources. Even if a high price of carbon makes nuclear economical, the costs of renewable energy such as wind and solar power are cheaper, and getting cheaper all the time. By contrast, nuclear is more expensive, and getting more expensive all the time.

Solving a Problem   And yes, it's true that wind and solar suffer from the problem of not being available 24 hours a day. But new technology is already beginning to solve that problem. And we'd be better off—from both an economic and safety standpoint—if we used natural gas to fill in the gaps, rather than nuclear.

Subsidies to the industry distort the financial picture further. In the U.S., Washington assumes liability for any catastrophic damages above $10.5 billion for an accident, and has taken on responsibility for the disposal of nuclear waste. The 2005 federal Energy Policy Act also provides loan guarantees for as much as 80% of the cost of new reactors and additional financial guarantees of up to $2 billion for costs arising from regulatory delays.

50   The 2005 act saw subsidies as a way to prime the pump of a nuclear-energy revival in the U.S.; increased demand and a stable regulatory environment would ultimately reduce the cost of building new plants. However, the industry for 50 years has shown only a trend toward higher costs, and there's no evidence that subsidies will spur any reduction in those costs.

And besides, if nuclear power is such a great deal, it should be able to stand on its own, and not require such subsidies from the taxpayer. Government subsidies should sponsor research and development into new or emerging energy technologies where prices are already falling and the subsidies can jump-start demand to help further bring down costs. They're inappropriate for mature industries, like nuclear power, where market forces should be allowed to do their work.

The Safety Issue   Cost isn't the only reason an expansion of nuclear power is a bad idea.

The safety of nuclear plants has certainly improved, thanks to changes adopted in the wake of the Three Mile Island accident. But safety problems persist, because the U.S. Nuclear Regulatory Commission isn't adequately enforcing existing safety standards. What's more, countries where nuclear power is likely to expand don't have a strong system for regulating nuclear safety.

The important thing to remember about safety is this: The entire nuclear power industry is vulnerable to the safety standards of its worst performers, because an accident anywhere in the world would stoke another antinuclear backlash among the public and investors.

55   There's also the question of waste disposal. Proponents of nuclear power say disposal of the industry's waste products is a political problem. That's true.

But it doesn't make the problem any less real. California, for instance, won't allow construction of more plants until the waste issue is resolved.

Opposition to a long-term waste repository at Yucca Mountain shows how difficult it will be to come up with a politically acceptable solution. Yucca Mountain has been plagued by questions about the selection process and its suitability as a repository, and even if it is ultimately approved, it won't be available for at least another decade—and it will be filled to capacity almost immediately. If it isn't approved, any replacement site will face the same opposition from neighbors and local political leaders.

Proliferation Threat   By far the greatest risk is the possibility that an expansion of nuclear power will contribute to the proliferation of nuclear weapons. Plants that enrich uranium for power plants can also be used to enrich for bombs; this is the path Iran is suspected of taking in developing a weapons program. An ambitious expansion of nuclear power would require a lot more facilities for enriching uranium, broadening this risk. Facilities for reprocessing spent nuclear fuel for reuse pose the danger that the material can be diverted for weapons.

Expansion of nuclear power in the U.S. doesn't pose a great proliferation risk, but a nuclear renaissance will put a strain on the current anti-proliferation system. Most of the growth world-wide is expected to be in countries—such as those in the Middle East and Africa—where a nuclear-energy program could give cover to surreptitious weapons development and create the local expertise in handling and processing nuclear materials.

The dangers of nuclear proliferation would be heightened if a nuclear revival turned to reprocessing of spent fuel to reduce the amount of high-level waste that builds up and to maintain adequate fuel supplies. Reprocessing is a problem because it can produce separated plutonium—which is easier to steal or divert for weapons production, as North Korea has done, than plutonium contained in highly radioactive fuel. And commercial reprocessing plants produce so much plutonium that keeping track of it all is difficult, making it easier to divert enough for weapons without the loss being detected.

60   If nuclear power really were able to make a big dent in greenhouse emissions, then it would be worth the time and resources necessary to address all these problems. Instead, though, the magnitude of these difficulties will keep any nuclear renaissance too small to make a difference, and will require expensive government support just to achieve modest gains. Those resources are better spent elsewhere.

● Review Questions

1. Why is nuclear power seen as a viable way of dealing with the global warming problem?

2. Summarize the chief arguments against nuclear power.

3. Why are current nuclear power plant designs safer than older designs?

4. In outline form, summarize the pro-con arguments regarding (1) costs of nuclear power plants; (2) safety of nuclear power plants; and (3) nuclear proliferation.

● Discussion and Writing Suggestions

1. Totty argues (rather than summarizes) both the pros and cons of nuclear power. To what extent, if any, can you detect his own position on the subject as he attempts to present the arguments made by each side?

2. Which arguments for or against nuclear power presented by Totty are the most persuasive to you? The least persuasive? Since the same author presents both sides of the case, how is one to determine whether the pro or the con arguments are the stronger ones?

3. Which of the concerns about nuclear power do you most share? To what extent do Totty's arguments rebutting these concerns in the first section of his article allay your concerns? Explain.

4. Many solutions to social or technological problems, while appealing in theory, fall victim to the NIMBY (not in my back yard) syndrome. People who vigorously support building more prisons often don't want a prison built in or near their own home town, citing safety concerns. The same appears to apply to nuclear power plants. If you were convinced that building more nuclear power plants would significantly decrease carbon emissions caused by power generation, would you be willing to see one constructed several miles away from where you live? Explain, offering alternatives if your answer is in the negative.

5. In "205 Easy Ways to Save the Earth," Thomas Friedman notes that if we were to try to derive all the renewable energy we need between now and the year 2050 from nuclear power, "we would have to build 13,000 new nuclear reactors or roughly one new reactor every day for the next thirty-six years—starting today." Given the obstacles noted by Totty to building even one nuclear power plant, is it unrealistic to expect that nuclear power can play a significant role in reducing carbon emissions over the next few decades? Assuming that what Friedman says is true, do such considerations doom nuclear power as a viable power source?

THE ISLAND IN THE WIND

Elizabeth Kolbert

In the following selection, excerpted from a longer article in the *New Yorker,* Elizabeth Kolbert describes in vivid imagery "an unlikely social movement": how the people of the Danish island of Samsø got all their homes and farms to run on electricity generated entirely by wind power. Their experience is a testament to determination and "people power"—though whether that experience can be duplicated in other areas is an open question.

Kolbert is a journalist who specializes in environmental issues. She wrote for the *New York Times* from 1984 to 1999 and has been a staff reporter for the *New Yorker* since 1999. She is the author of *Field Notes from a Catastrophe: Man and Nature and Climate Change* (2006).

Jørgen Tranberg is a farmer who lives on the Danish island of Samsø. He is a beefy man with a mop of brown hair and an unpredictable sense of humor. When I arrived at his house, one gray morning this spring, he was sitting in his kitchen, smoking a cigarette and watching grainy images on a black-and-white TV. The images turned out to be closed-circuit shots from his barn. One of his cows, he told me, was about to give birth, and he was keeping an eye on her. We talked for a few minutes, and then, laughing, he asked me if I wanted to climb his wind turbine. I was pretty sure I didn't, but I said yes anyway.

We got into Tranberg's car and bounced along a rutted dirt road. The turbine loomed up in front of us. When we reached it, Tranberg stubbed out his cigarette and opened a small door in the base of the tower. Inside were eight ladders, each about twenty feet tall, attached one above the other. We started up, and were soon huffing. Above the last ladder, there was a trapdoor, which led to a sort of engine room. We scrambled into it, at which point we were standing on top of the generator. Tranberg pressed a button, and the roof slid open to reveal the gray sky and a patchwork of green and brown fields stretching toward the sea. He pressed another button. The rotors, which he had switched off during our climb, started to turn, at first sluggishly and then much more rapidly. It felt as if we were about to take off. I'd like to say the feeling was exhilarating; in fact, I found it sickening. Tranberg looked at me and started to laugh.

Samsø, which is roughly the size of Nantucket, sits in what's known as the Kattegat, an arm of the North Sea. The island is bulgy in the south and narrows to a bladelike point in the north, so that on a map it looks a bit like a woman's torso and a bit like a meat cleaver. It has twenty-two villages that hug the narrow streets; out back are fields where farmers grow potatoes and wheat and strawberries. Thanks to Denmark's peculiar geography, Samsø is smack in the center of the country and, at the same time, in the middle of nowhere.

For the past decade or so, Samsø has been the site of an unlikely social movement. When it began, in the late nineteen-nineties, the island's forty-three hundred inhabitants had what might be described as a conventional attitude toward energy: as long as it continued to arrive, they weren't much interested in it. Most Samsingers heated their houses with oil, which was brought in on tankers. They used electricity imported from the mainland via cable, much of which was generated by burning coal. As a result, each Samsinger put into the atmosphere, on average, nearly eleven tons of carbon dioxide annually.

Catching the wind

Alternative energy sources are getting a new look as demand for fossil fuels increases worldwide, and as technical innovations help reduce the costs of alternatives. California produces more wind-generated electricity than any state except Texas and Iowa. A look at wind farms:

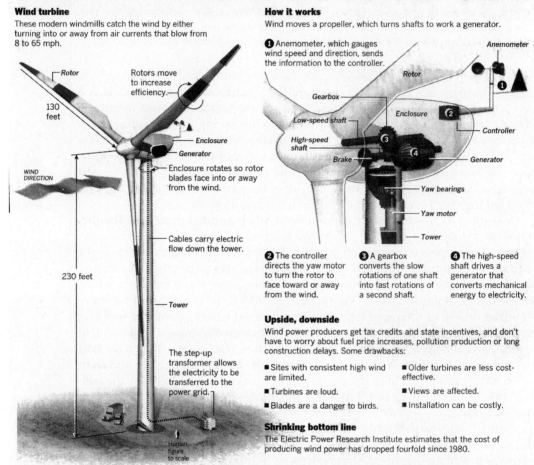

Wind turbine

These modern windmills catch the wind by either turning into or away from air currents that blow from 8 to 65 mph.

Rotor

Rotors move to increase efficiency.

130 feet

WIND DIRECTION

Enclosure

Generator

Enclosure rotates so rotor blades face into or away from the wind.

Cables carry electric flow down the tower.

230 feet

Tower

The step-up transformer allows the electricity to be transferred to the power grid.

Human figure to scale

How it works

Wind moves a propeller, which turns shafts to work a generator.

❶ Anemometer, which gauges wind speed and direction, sends the information to the controller.

Anemometer

Rotor

Gearbox

Low-speed shaft

Enclosure

High-speed shaft

Brake

Controller

Generator

Yaw bearings

Yaw motor

Tower

❷ The controller directs the yaw motor to turn the rotor to face toward or away from the wind.

❸ A gearbox converts the slow rotations of one shaft into fast rotations of a second shaft.

❹ The high-speed shaft drives a generator that converts mechanical energy to electricity.

Upside, downside

Wind power producers get tax credits and state incentives, and don't have to worry about fuel price increases, pollution production or long construction delays. Some drawbacks:

- Sites with consistent high wind are limited.
- Turbines are loud.
- Blades are a danger to birds.
- Older turbines are less cost-effective.
- Views are affected.
- Installation can be costly.

Shrinking bottom line

The Electric Power Research Institute estimates that the cost of producing wind power has dropped fourfold since 1980.

Sources: California Energy Commission, National Wind Technology Center, U.S. Department of Energy's Energy Information Administration, National Renewable Energy Laboratory

DOUG STEVENS Los Angeles Times

5   Then, quite deliberately, the residents of the island set about changing this. They formed energy coöperatives and organized seminars on wind power. They removed their furnaces and replaced them with heat pumps. By 2001, fossil-fuel use on Samsø had been cut in half. By 2003, instead of importing electricity, the island was exporting it, and by 2005 it was producing from renewable sources more energy than it was using.

     The residents of Samsø that I spoke to were clearly proud of their accomplishment. All the same, they insisted on their ordinariness. They were, they noted, not wealthy, nor were they especially well educated or idealistic. They weren't even terribly adventuresome. "We are a conservative farming community" is how one

Samsinger put it. "We are only normal people," Tranberg told me. "We are not some special people."

This year, the world is expected to burn through some thirty-one billion barrels of oil, six billion tons of coal, and a hundred trillion cubic feet of natural gas. The combustion of these fossil fuels will produce, in aggregate, some four hundred quadrillion B.T.U.s of energy. It will also yield around thirty billion tons of carbon dioxide. Next year, global consumption of fossil fuels is expected to grow by about two per cent, meaning that emissions will rise by more than half a billion tons, and the following year consumption is expected to grow by yet another two per cent.

When carbon dioxide is released into the air, about a third ends up, in relatively short order, in the oceans. (CO_2 dissolves in water to form a weak acid; this is the cause of the phenomenon known as "ocean acidification.") A quarter is absorbed by terrestrial ecosystems—no one is quite sure exactly how or where—and the rest remains in the atmosphere. If current trends in emissions continue, then sometime within the next four of five decades the chemistry of the oceans will have been altered to such a degree that many marine organisms—including reef-building corals—will be pushed toward extinction. Meanwhile, atmospheric CO_2 levels are projected to reach five hundred and fifty parts per million—twice pre-industrial levels—virtually guaranteeing an eventual global temperature increase of three or more degrees. The consequences of this warming are difficult to predict in detail, but even broad, conservative estimates are terrifying: at least fifteen and possibly as many as thirty per cent of the planet's plant and animal species will be threatened; sea levels will rise by several feet; yields of crops like wheat and corn will decline significantly in a number of areas where they are now grown as staples; regions that depend on glacial runoff or seasonal snowmelt—currently home to more than a billion people—will face severe water shortages; and what now counts as a hundred-year drought will occur in some parts of the world as frequently as once a decade.

Today, with CO_2 levels at three hundred and eighty-five parts per million, the disruptive impacts of climate change are already apparent. The Arctic ice cap, which has shrunk by half since the nineteen-fifties, is melting at an annual rate of twenty-four thousand square miles, meaning that an expanse of ice the size of West Virginia is disappearing each year. Over the past ten years, forests covering a hundred and fifty million acres in the United States and Canada have died from warming-related beetle infestations. It is believed that rising temperatures are contributing to the growing number of international refugees—"Climate change is today one of the main drivers of forced displacement," the United Nations' high commissioner for refugees, António Guterres, said recently—and to armed conflict: some experts see a link between the fighting in Darfur, which has claimed as many as three hundred thousand lives, and changes in rainfall patterns in equatorial Africa.

10   "If we keep going down this path, the Darfur crisis will be only one crisis among dozens of other," President Nicolas Sarkozy, of France, told a meeting of world leaders in April. The Secretary-General of the United Nations, Ban Ki-moon, has called climate change "the defining challenge of our age."

In the context of this challenge, Samsø's accomplishments could be seen as trivial. Certainly, in numerical terms they don't amount to much: all the island's avoided emissions of the past ten years are overwhelmed by the CO_2 that a single coal-fired *power* plant will emit in the next three weeks, and China is building new coal-fired plants at the rate of roughly four a month. But it is also in this context that the island's efforts are most significant. Samsø transformed its energy systems in a single decade. Its experience suggests how the carbon problem, as huge as it is, could be dealt with, if we were willing to try.

Samsø set out to reinvent itself thanks to a series of decisions that it had relatively little to do with. The first was made by the Danish Ministry of Environment and Energy in 1997. The ministry, looking for ways to promote innovation, decided to sponsor a renewable-energy contest. In order to enter, a community had to submit a plan showing how it could wean itself off fossil fuels. An engineer who didn't actually live on Samsø thought the island would make a good candidate. In consultation with Samsø's mayor, he drew up a plan and submitted it. When it was announced that Samsø had won, the general reaction among residents was puzzlement. "I had to listen twice before I believed it," one farmer told me.

The brief surge of interest that followed the announcement soon dissipated. Besides its designation as Denmark's "renewable-energy island," Samsø received basically nothing—no prize money or special tax breaks, or even government assistance. One of the few people on the island to think the project was worth pursuing was Søren Hermansen.

Hermansen, who is now forty-nine, is a trim man with close-cropped hair, ruddy cheeks, and dark-blue eyes. He was born on Samsø and, save for a few stints away, to travel and go to university, has lived there his entire life. His father was a farmer who grew, among other things, beets and parsley. Hermansen, too, tried his hand at farming—he took over the family's hundred acres when his father retired—but he discovered he wasn't suited to it. "I like to talk, and vegetables don't respond," he told me. He leased his fields to a neighbor and got a job teaching environmental studies at a local boarding school. Hermansen found the renewable-energy-island concept intriguing. When some federal money was found to fund a single staff position, he became the project's first employee.

15   For months, which stretched into years, not much happened. "There was this conservative hesitating, waiting for the neighbor to do the move," Hermansen recalled. "I know the community and I know this is what usually happens." Rather than working against the islanders' tendency to look to one another, Hermansen tried to work with it.

"One reason to live here can be social relations," he said. "This renewable-energy project could be a new kind of social relation, and we used that." Whenever there was a meeting to discuss a local issue—any local issue—Hermansen attended and made his pitch. He asked Samsingers to think about what it would be like to work together on something they could all be proud of. Occasionally, he brought free beer along to the discussions. Meanwhile, he began trying to enlist the support of the island's opinion leaders. "This is where the hard work starts, convincing the first movers to be active," he said. Eventually, much as Hermansen had hoped, the social dynamic that had stalled the project began to work in its favor. As more people got involved, that prompted others to do so. After a while, enough Samsingers were participating that participation became the norm.

"People on Samsø started thinking about energy," Ingvar Jørgensen, a farmer who heats his house with solar hot water and a straw-burning furnace, told me. "It became a kind of sport."

"It's exciting to be a part of this," Brian Kjær, an electrician who installed a small-scale turbine in his back yard, said. Kjær's turbine, which is seventy-two feet tall generates more current than his family of three can use, and also more than the power lines leading away from his house can handle, so he uses the excess to heat water, which he stores in a tank that he rigged up in his garage. He told me that one day he would like to use the leftover electricity to produce hydrogen, which could potentially run a fuel-cell car.

"Søren, he has talked again and again, and slowly it's spread to a lot of people," he said.

20   Since becoming the "renewable energy island," Samsø has increasingly found itself an object of study. Researchers often travel great distances to get there, a fact that is not without its own irony. The day after I arrived, from New York via Copenhagen, a group of professors from the University of Toyama, in Japan, came to look around. They had arranged a tour with Hermansen, and he invited me to tag along. We headed off to meet the group in his electric Citroën, which is painted blue with white puffy clouds on the doors. It was a drizzly day, and when we got to the dock the water was choppy. Hermansen commiserated with the Japanese, who had just disembarked from the swaying ferry; then we all boarded a bus.

Our first stop was a hillside with a panoramic view of the island. Several wind turbines exactly like the one I had climbed with Tranberg were whooshing nearby. In the wet and the gray, they were the only things stirring. Off in the distance, the silent fields gave way to the Kattegat, where another group of turbines could be seen, arranged in a soldierly line in the water.

All told, Samsø has eleven large land-based turbines. (It has about a dozen additional micro-turbines.) This is a lot of turbines for a relatively small number of people, and the ratio is critical to Samsø's success, as is the fact that the wind off the Kattegat blows pretty much continuously; flags on Samsø, I noticed, do not wave—they stick straight out, as in children's drawings. Hermansen told us that the land-based turbines are a hundred and fifty feet tall, with rotors that are eighty feet long. Together, they produce some twenty-six million kilowatt-hours a year, which is just about enough to meet all the island's demands for electricity. (This is true in an arithmetic sense; as a practical matter, Samsø's production of electricity and its needs fluctuate, so that sometimes it is feeding power into the grid and sometimes it is drawing power from it.) The offshore turbines, meanwhile, are even taller—a hundred and ninety-five feet high, with rotors that extend a hundred and twenty feet. A single offshore turbine generates roughly eight million kilowatt-hours of electricity a year, which, at Danish rates of energy use, is enough to satisfy the needs of some two thousand homes. The offshore turbines—there are ten of them—were erected to compensate for Samsø's continuing use of fossil fuels in its cars, trucks, and ferries. Their combined output, of around eighty million kilowatt-hours a year, provides the energy equivalent of all the gasoline and diesel oil consumed on the island, and then some; in aggregate, Samsø generates about ten per cent more power than it consumes.

"When we started, in 1997, nobody expected this to happen," Hermansen told the group. "When we talked to local people, they said, Yes, come on, maybe in your dreams." Each land-based turbine cost the equivalent of eight hundred and fifty thousand dollars. Each offshore turbine cost around three million dollars. Some of Samsø's turbines were erected by a single investor, like Tranberg; others were purchased collectively. At least four hundred and fifty island residents own shares in the onshore turbines, and a roughly equal number own shares in those offshore. Shareholders, who also include many nonresidents, receive annual dividend checks based on the prevailing price of electricity and how much their turbine has generated.

"If I'm reduced to being a customer, then if I like something I buy it, and if I don't like it I don't buy it," Hermansen said. "But I don't care about the production. We care about the production, because we own the wind turbines. Every time they turn around, it means money in the bank. And, being part of it, we also feel responsible." Thanks to a policy put in place by Denmark's government in the late nineteen-nineties, utilities are required to offer ten-year fixed-rate contracts for wind power that they can sell to customers elsewhere. Under the terms of these contracts, a turbine should—barring mishap—repay a shareholder's initial investment in about eight years.

25   From the hillside, we headed to the town of Ballen. There we stopped at a red shed-shaped building made out of corrugated metal. Inside, enormous bales of straw were stacked against the walls. Hermansen explained that the building was a district heating plant that had been designed to run on biomass. The bales, each representing the equivalent of fifty gallons of oil, would be fed into a furnace, where water would be heated to a hundred and fifty-eight degrees. This hot water would then be piped underground to two hundred and sixty houses in Ballen and in the neighboring town of Brundby. In this way, the energy of the straw burned at the plant would be transferred to the homes, where it could be used to provide heat and hot water.

Samsø has two other district heating plants that burn straw—one in Tranebjerg, the other in Onsbjerg—and also a district plant, in Nordby, that burns wood chips. When we visited the Nordby plant, later that afternoon, it was filled with what looked like mulch. (The place smelled like a potting shed.) Out back was a field covered in rows of solar panels, which provide additional hot water when the sun is shining. Between the rows, sheep with long black faces were munching on the grass. The Japanese researchers pulled out their cameras as the sheep snuffled toward them, expectantly.

Of course, burning straw or wood, like burning fossil fuels, produces CO_2. The key distinction is that while fossil fuels release carbon that otherwise would have remained sequestered, biomass releases carbon that would have entered the atmosphere anyway, through decomposition. As long as biomass regrows, the CO_2 released in its combustion should be reabsorbed, meaning that the cycle is—or at least can be—carbon neutral. The wood chips used in the Nordby plant come from fallen trees that previously would have been left to rot. The straw for the Ballen-Brundby plant comes mainly from wheat stalks that would previously have been burned in the fields. Together, the biomass heating plants prevent the release of some twenty-seven hundred tons of carbon dioxide a year.

In addition to biomass, Samsø is experimenting on a modest scale with biofuels: a handful of farmers have converted their cars and tractors to run on canola oil. We stopped to visit one such farmer, who grows his own seeds, presses his own oil, and feeds the leftover mash to his cows. The farmer couldn't be located, so Hermansen started up the press himself. He stuck a finger under the spout, then popped it into his mouth. "The oil is very good," he announced. "You can use it in your car, and you can use it on your salad."

After the tour, I went back with Hermansen to his office, in a building known as the Energiakademi. The academy, which looks like a Bauhaus interpretation of a barn, is covered with photovoltaic cells and insulated with shredded newspapers. It is supposed to serve as a sort of interpretive center, though when I visited, the place was so new that the rooms were mostly empty. Some high-school students were kneeling on the floor, trying to put together a miniature turbine.

30   I asked Hermansen whether there were any projects that hadn't worked out. He listed several, including a plan to use natural gas produced from cow manure and an experiment with electric cars that failed when one of the demonstration vehicles spent most of the year in the shop. The biggest disappointment, though, had to do with consumption.

"We made several programs for energy savings," he told me. "But people are acting—what do you call it?—irresponsibly. They behave like monkeys." For example, families that insulated their homes better also tended to heat more rooms, "so we ended up with zero." Essentially, he said, energy use on the island has remained constant for the past decade.

I asked why he thought the renewable-energy-island effort had got as far as it did. He said he wasn't sure, because different people had had different motives for participating. "From the very egoistic to the more over-all perspective, I think we had all kinds of reasons."

Finally, I asked what he thought other communities might take from Samsø's experience.

"We always hear that we should think globally and act locally," he said. "I understand what that means—I think we as a nation should be part of the global consciousness. But each individual cannot be part of that. So 'Think locally, act locally' is the key message for us."

35   "There's this wish for showcases," he added. "When we are selected to be the showcase for Denmark, I feel ashamed that Denmark doesn't produce anything bigger than that. But I feel proud because we are the showcase. So I did my job, and my colleagues did their job, and so did the people of Samsø."

● Review Questions

1. Locate the one or two sentences in Kolbert's article that make the connection between Samsø's experience with wind power and the reduction of global CO_2 emissions.

2. How did Samsø's geographical circumstances play a role in the success of its conversion to renewable energy?

3. Why is the process of burning biomass substances, such as bales of straw or wood chips, more carbon-neutral than burning coal, according to Kolbert?

● Discussion and Writing Suggestions

1. Why do you think Kolbert begins this article as she does, with a verbal picture of Jørgen Tranberg, rather than with, say, the data on CO_2 emissions in paragraph 7 or the consequences of heightened levels of CO_2 in the atmosphere in paragraphs 8 and 9?

2. Kolbert describes a "social dynamic" through which one committed citizen convinced a number of his fellow citizens to participate in a community project; and they in turn convinced others, some with particular skills, until the committed few became a community-wide movement dedicated to productive change. Have you witnessed or been a part of such a movement in your own or another community? Describe what happened and the conclusions you draw from this experience. What obstacles did you face? How were they overcome? Which factors or events were most helpful? Most surprising? Most frustrating? Most rewarding? What advice do you have for others considering such community projects?

3. To what extent do you think the experience of Samsø concerning renewable energy sources such as wind is repeatable elsewhere, particularly in the United States? In what ways might the different geographical, cultural, and political circumstances in the United States make it difficult to repeat Samsø's experience here? In what respects might the circumstances be similar?

4. What conclusions, if any, can you draw from the Samsø experience with wind power about the role of government in encouraging the use of renewable energy? About the role of entrepreneurship? The role of individual initiative? The role of civic duty?

WIND POWER PUFFERY

H. Sterling Burnett

In this op-ed H. Sterling Burnett discusses the limitations and drawbacks of wind power. Burnett is a senior fellow with the National Center for Policy Analysis. In 2000 he served as a member of the Environment and Natural Resources Task Force in the Texas Comptroller's e-Texas commission. His articles and opinion pieces have been published in *Environmental*

Ethics, International Studies in Philosophy, and daily newspapers nationwide. This piece appeared in the *Washington Times* on February 4, 2004.

Whenever there is a discussion of energy policy, many environmentalists and their political allies tout wind power as an alternative to burning fossil fuels. Even if electricity from wind power is more expensive than conventional fuel sources, and it is, wind advocates argue its environmental benefits are worth it. In particular, proponents claim increased reliance on wind power would reduce air pollution and greenhouse gas emissions.

But is this assertion correct? No, the truth is wind power's environmental benefits are usually overstated, while its significant environmental harms are often ignored.

Close inspection of wind power finds the promised air pollution improvements do not materialize. There are several reasons, the principal one being that wind farms generate power only when the wind blows within a certain range of speed. When there is too little wind, wind towers don't generate power. Conversely, when the wind is too strong, they must be shut off for fear of being blown down.

Due to this fundamental limitation, wind farms need conventional power plants to supplement the power they supply and to replace a wind farm's expected supply to the grid when the towers are not turning. After all, the power grid requires a regulated constant flow of energy to function properly.

5 Yet bringing a conventional power plant on line to supply power is not as simple as turning on a switch. Most "redundant" fossil fuel power stations must run, even if at reduced levels, continuously. When these factors are combined with the emissions of pollutants and CO_2 caused by the manufacture and maintenance of wind towers and their associated infrastructure, very little of the air quality improvements actually result from expansion of wind power.

There are other problems. A recent report from Great Britain—where wind power is growing even faster than in the U.S.—says that as wind farms grow, wind power is increasingly unpopular. Why? Wind farms are noisy, land-intensive and unsightly. The industry has tricked its way into unspoiled countryside in "green" disguise by portraying wind farms as "parks." In reality, wind farms are more similar to highways, industrial buildings, railways and industrial farms. This wouldn't be a major consideration if it weren't that, because of the prevailing wind currents, the most favorable locations for wind farms usually are areas with particularly spectacular views in relatively wild places.

Worse, wind farms produce only a fraction of the energy of a conventional power plant but require hundreds of times the acreage. For instance, two of the biggest wind "farms" in Europe have 159 turbines and cover thousands of acres between them. But together they take a year to produce less than four days' output from a single 2,000-megawatt conventional power station—which takes up 100 times fewer acres. And in the U.S., a proposed wind farm off the coast of Massachusetts would produce only 450 megawatts of power but require 130 towers and more than 24 square miles of ocean.

Perhaps the most well-publicized harmful environmental impact of wind power relates to its effect on birds and bats. For efficiency, wind farms must be located where the wind blows fairly constantly. Unfortunately, such locations are prime travel routes for migratory birds, including protected species like Bald and Golden Eagles. This motivated the Sierra Club to label wind towers "the Cuisinarts of the air."

Indeed, scientists estimate as many as 44,000 birds have been killed over the past 20 years by wind turbines in the Altamont Pass, east of San Francisco. The victims include kestrels, red-tailed hawks and golden eagles—an average of 50 golden eagles are killed each year.

10   These problems are exacerbated explains one study as "Wind farms have been documented to act as both bait and executioner—rodents taking shelter at the base of turbines multiply with the protection from raptors, while in turn their greater numbers attract more raptors to the farm."

Deaths are not limited to the United States or to birds. For example, at Tarif, Spain, thousands of birds from more than 13 species protected under European Union law have been killed by the site's 269 wind turbines. During last fall's migration, at least 400 bats, including red bats, eastern pipistrelles, hoary bats and possible endangered Indiana bats, were killed at a 44-turbine wind farm in West Virginia.

As a result of these problems and others, lawsuits are either pending or being considered to prevent expansion of wind farms in West Virginia and California and to prevent the construction of offshore wind farms in a number of New England states.

Indeed, the Audubon society has called for a moratorium on new wind development in bird-sensitive areas—which, because of the climatic conditions needed for wind farms, includes the vast majority of the suitable sites for proposed construction.

Wind power is expensive, doesn't deliver the environmental benefits it promises and has substantial environmental costs. In short, wind power is no bargain. Accordingly, it doesn't merit continued government promotion or funding.

● Discussion and Writing Suggestions

1. To what extent do you view the problems with wind power cited by Burnett as serious enough to rule out this energy source as viable? To what extent do you think we should proceed with large-scale construction of wind farms, considering the realities of (1) intermittent power that must be periodically supplemented by conventional power plants; (2) the poor ratio of power generated to acreage of land consumed by wind turbines; (3) the danger to birds?

2. Conduct a brief Google (or other database) search, and then respond to some of Burnett's concerns about wind power with the information you find. To what extent are Burnett's objections well-founded? To what extent might it be possible to deal effectively with the problems he discusses?

3. The danger to birds posed by spinning wind turbines is analogous to the danger to whales posed by sonar tests conducted by Navy submarines. In one case, the benefit is renewable energy; in the other case, the benefit is (according to the military and civilian Dept. of Defense officials) enhanced national security. How should we weigh such conflicting interests and decide between them?

4. Critique Burnett's argument. Use as guidelines the principles discussed in Chapter 2. Consider first the main questions: (1) To what extent does Burnett succeed in his purpose? (2) To what extent do you agree with him? Then move to the specifics: for example, to what extent do you agree with his contention that wind turbines pose too great a risk to birds? Before writing your critique, you may want to reread what Elizabeth Kolbert and other authors in this chapter have written about wind power.

STATE SOLAR PLANS ARE AS BIG AS ALL OUTDOORS

Marla Dickerson

In the following selection, Marla Dickerson reports on the expansion of solar power construction in California in compliance with that state's mandate to generate 20 percent of its electricity from renewable power sources by 2010. In a more recent article ("Solar Farm Cuts Gap with Fossil Fuel"), Dickerson reported that Sempra Energy, a San Diego-based power company that recently installed a 10-megawatt solar farm in Nevada, has employed a new form of panel technology that has enabled it to achieve the critical goal of "grid parity"—that is, to produce renewable energy at a cost equal to or lower than the cost of a comparable amount of power generated from carbon-based fuels such as coal or natural gas. The key to this "Wal-Mart of solar panels" is an array of solar cells made from a cadmium telluride semiconductor that is less expensive to make than its silicon-based equivalent.

Dickerson is an economics and business writer for the *Los Angeles* Times, where this article appeared on December 3, 2008. Previously, Dickerson wrote for the *Detroit News* and the *Rochester Times-Union*.

Just up the road, past pump jacks bobbing in California's storied oil patch, look sharp and you'll catch a glimpse of the state's energy future.

Rows of gigantic mirrors covering an area bigger than two football fields have sprouted alongside almond groves near California 99. This is a power plant that uses the sun's heat to produce electricity for thousands of homes.

Owned by Palo Alto-based Ausra Inc., it's the first so-called solar thermal facility to open in California in nearly two decades. It's part of a drive to build clean electricity generation using the sun, wind and other renewable sources with an urgency not seen since the days of environmentalist Gov. Jerry Brown. Add President-elect Barack Obama's stated intention to push for more renewable power, and you've got the equivalent of a green land rush.

At least 80 large solar projects are on the drawing board in California, more than in any other place in the country. The scale of some is unrivaled on the planet. One facility planned for the Mojave Desert is projected to take up a land mass the size of Inglewood.*

5   "The expectation is that renewables will transform California's electricity system," said Terry O'Brien, who helps vet sites for new facilities for the California Energy Commission.

It's a daunting challenge for the world's eighth-largest economy. Despite the nation's toughest mandates for boosting green energy and reducing greenhouse gases, California remains addicted to burning fossil fuels to keep the lights on.

Excluding large hydroelectric operations, less than 12% of the state's electricity came from renewable sources in 2007, according to the commission. Solar ranked last, supplying just 0.2% of California's needs. Rooftop photovoltaic panels are unaffordable or impractical for most Californians even with generous state incentives.

Enter Big Solar.

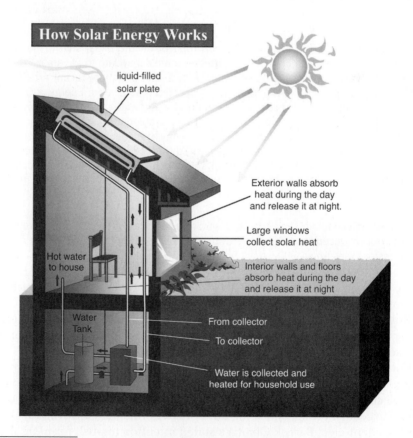

How Solar Energy Works

liquid-filled solar plate

Exterior walls absorb heat during the day and release it at night.

Large windows collect solar heat

Hot water to house

Interior walls and floors absorb heat during the day and release it at night

Water Tank

From collector

To collector

Water is collected and heated for household use

*Inglewood: a city in southwestern Los Angeles County; area: 9.1 square miles.

Proponents say utility-scale solar is a way to get lots of clean megawatts on-line quickly, efficiently and at lower costs. Solar thermal plants such as Ausra's are essentially giant boilers made of glass and steel. They use the sun's heat to create steam to power turbines that generate electricity.

10   Costing about 18 cents a kilowatt-hour at present, solar thermal power is roughly 40% cheaper than that generated by the silicon-based panels that sit on the roofs of homes and businesses, according to a June report by Clean Edge Inc. and the Co-op American Foundation. Analysts say improved technology and economies of scale should help lower the cost of solar thermal to about 5 cents a kilowatt-hour by 2025. That would put it on par with coal, the cheap but carbon-spewing fuel that generates about half the nation's electricity.

Size matters, said Sun Microsystems Inc. co-founder-turned-venture-capitalist Vinod Khosla, whose Khosla Ventures has invested more than $30 million in Ausra. A square patch of desert about 92 miles long on each side blanketed with Ausra's technology could generate enough electricity to meet the entire nation's demand, company executives say. "Utility-scale solar is probably the only way to achieve real scale...and reduce our carbon emissions" significantly, Khosla said.

Critics fear that massive solar farms would create as many environmental problems as they purport to solve. This new-age electricity still requires old-fashioned power towers and high-voltage lines to get it to people's homes. A proposed 150-mile transmission line known as the Sunrise Powerlink that would carry renewable power from Imperial County to San Diego has run into stiff resistance from grass-roots groups and environmentalists.

Solar plants require staggering amounts of land, which could threaten fragile ecosystems and mar the stark beauty of America's deserts. And in contrast to rooftop panels, which enable homeowners to pursue energy independence, these centralized facilities keep consumers tethered to utility companies.

"They are trying to perpetuate the old Big Energy paradigm into the renewable-energy era," said Sheila Bowers, a Santa Monica attorney and environmental activist. "They have a monopoly agenda."

15   California already has the largest operating collection of solar thermal facilities in the world: nine plants totaling just over 350 megawatts in San Bernardino County. Built in the 1980s, they were part of a drive toward energy self-sufficiency stemming from the '70s oil shocks. The boom ended when California dropped requirements forcing utilities to buy renewable power.

The push is back. The 2000–01 energy crisis exposed California's continued dependence on outsiders—more than 30% of its electricity still comes from out of state. Renewable forms of energy are once again central to efforts to shore up supply and fight global warming.

State lawmakers have told investor-owned utilities that they must procure 20% of their electricity from renewable sources by 2010; Gov. Arnold Schwarzenegger is pushing for a minimum of 33% by 2020. A landmark 2006 state law forcing California to reduce its greenhouse gas emissions to 1990 levels within 12 years also is boosting green generation. Most of the proposed utility-scale solar plants are slated for San Bernardino and Riverside counties, whose vast deserts offer abundant sunshine and plenty of open space for the behemoths. The U.S. Bureau of Land Management is juggling so many requests from companies looking to build on federal land—79 at last count, covering more than 690,000 acres—that it had to stop accepting applications for a few weeks last summer. Many of these facilities may never get built. Environmentalists are mobilizing. U.S. credit markets are in a deep freeze. Oil and natural gas prices are falling, reducing some of the urgency to go green.

Still, the obstacles haven't clouded the ambitions of solar start-ups such as Ausra.

"Our investors perceive there is a huge opportunity here," said Bob Fishman, Ausra's president and chief executive. A group of dignitaries that included Schwarzenegger gathered near here in October to get a close-up look at the 5-megawatt operation Ausra opened.

20   The company uses a technology known as a compact linear Fresnel reflector. Acres of mirrors are anchored to metal frames and held roughly 6 feet off the ground in parallel rows. Controlled by computers, these panels make hundreds of barely perceptible movements throughout the day, tracking the sun's path across the sky.

The mirrors catch the sun's rays and reflect them onto a cluster of water pipes overhead. The intense heat—it can reach 750 degrees—generates pressurized steam inside the pipes. That steam is then fed into a turbine whose spinning generates electricity.

"It's like when you were a kid and you used a magnifying glass to fry a bug" on a sunny day, said Dave DeGraaf, vice president of product development. "We're focusing all that energy."

Despite its mammoth size, this pilot plant generates a modest amount of electricity, enough to power just 3,500 homes when the sun is shining. Ausra is thinking much bigger.

It has set up a manufacturing facility in Nevada that will supply a 177-megawatt solar plant planned for a site near Carrizo Plain National Monument in eastern San Luis Obispo County.

The facility's mirrors will occupy a full square mile of terrain. The project is still in the permitting process. Ausra has never tried something on this scale. But Pacific Gas & Electric is confident enough that is has agreed to buy the power from Carrizo to help it meet its green energy needs.

25   Other companies looking to shine in California with utility-scale plants include Solel Inc., whose proposed 553-megawatt project in the Mojave Desert would span nine square miles; BrightSource Energy Inc. of Oakland; SunPower Corp. of San Jose; OptiSolar Inc. of Hayward, Calif.; Stirling Energy Systems Inc. of Phoenix; and FPL Energy of Juno Beach, Fla.

"Climate change is the greatest challenge that mankind has ever faced," said Peter Darbee, president and chief executive of Pacific Gas & Electric and head of its parent, San Francisco-based PG&E Corp. "It's imperative to seek out the most cost-effective solutions."

● **Review Questions**

1. "Size matters," says Sun Microsystems co-founder Vinod Khosla, referring to solar power systems. What does he mean?

2. What are the disadvantages of the solar thermal power systems of the kind described by Dickerson?

3. What forces are helping to spur the development of solar power, especially in California?

● **Discussion and Writing Suggestions**

1. How do you think Thomas Friedman would feel about the kind of solar projects described in this article? Might such projects fall into the category of "205 Easy Ways to Save the Earth"? Why or why not?

2. Dickerson contrasts the key features of "massive solar farms" with rooftop solar panels. Considering the pros and cons of each system, which type of solar power generation do you believe the government should most encourage, through subsidies, tax credits, etc.? Explain your reasoning.

3. The NIMBY (not in my backyard) issue raised in Discussion and Writing Suggestion no. 4 for Michael Totty's article on nuclear power (p. 346) applies equally to large-scale solar power projects, as the following article by Peter Maloney also makes clear. Would you be prepared to live in an area near one of the large-scale solar facilities described in this article, knowing that the generation of solar power in large quantities could significantly reduce the volume of carbon dioxide released into the atmosphere from the burning of coal? Explain.

ENVIRONMENTALISTS AGAINST SOLAR POWER

Peter Maloney

One might think that environmentalists would be all for solar power generation; but as Peter Maloney indicates, this is not necessarily so. There is solar power and there is solar power. Writing for the *New York Times* in a story published on September 24, 2008, Maloney explains the difference.

What's not to like about solar power? Sunlight is clean, quiet and abundant. If enough of it were harnessed and turned into electricity, it could be the solution to the energy crisis. But surprisingly, solar power projects are running into mounting opposition—and not from hard-nosed, coal-fired naysayers, but from environmentalists.

The opposition is particularly strong in Southern California. Aside from abundant sunshine and virtually cloudless skies, the California desert has altitude, so there is less atmospheric interference for the sun's rays, as well as broad swaths of level land for installing equipment, and proximity to large, electricity-hungry cities.

But it is also home to the Mojave ground squirrel, the desert tortoise and the burrowing owl, and to human residents who describe themselves as desert survivors and who are unhappy about the proliferation of solar projects planned for their home turf.

"We're tired of everyone looking at the desert like a wasteland," said Donna Charpied, who lives with her husband, Larry, in Desert Center, California, where they have been farming jojoba, a native shrub cultivated for its oil, for 27 years. She is also the policy advocate for the Desert Communities Protection Campaign of the Center for Community Action and Environmental Justice.

5   The United States Bureau of Land Management said it had applications for solar power projects that would cover 78,490 acres in the area around the Charpieds' farm, which abuts Joshua Tree National Park. For the entire United States, the total number of applications is far greater, growing from zero less than two years ago to more than 125 projects with a combined electrical potential of 70,000 megawatts, the equivalent of the electrical capacity of about 70 large coal-fired power plants.

Investors, developers and speculators filed so many applications with the bureau that in May it declared a moratorium on new ones. On July 2, overwhelmed by protests, it reversed itself and ended the moratorium.

The land rush is being driven in large part by a California law that calls for 20 percent of the state's electricity to come from renewable resources by 2010.

The California Public Utilities Commission said the state was falling behind in meeting that goal. It estimated that California's electric utilities would have to build or buy 3,000 megawatts of renewable resources over the next two years to meet the 20 percent target. So the utilities are scrambling to find renewable resources, and developers are working furiously to build projects.

Last month, Pacific Gas and Electric, based in San Francisco, signed contracts to buy the electricity produced by projects under development in San Luis Obispo County by two companies, OptiSolar and the SunPower Corporation, which are expected to come on line between 2010 and 2013.

10   This sudden flood of solar power projects not only caught the staff of the Bureau of Land Management off guard, it also surprised some environmentalists. "Many community groups are up in arms" about the projects planned in the Mojave Desert and Coachella Valley regions, said D'Anne Albers, the California desert associate for Defenders of Wildlife, citing plans by OptiSolar, BrightSource Energy and FPL Energy.

Jim Harvey, a founder of the Alliance for Responsible Energy Policy, an environmental group in Joshua Tree, said: "Our position is that none of this is needed. We support renewable energy, and we support California's renewable energy targets, but we think it can be done through rooftop solar."

Mr. Harvey said that if Germany, which is as far north as the Canadian city of Calgary, could have a successful solar power program that relies heavily on rooftops, so could the United States. Germany's solar program works, he said, because the government offers so-called feed-in tariffs—fixed-rate payments for electricity generated from solar panels.

The tariff is the equivalent of about 50 cents a kilowatt hour. The average residential retail rate in the United States is about 11 cents a kilowatt hour, according to the Department of Energy.

Mr. Harvey said the tariff would not have to be that high in the United States. Matching wholesale rates would be sufficient to spur a rush to small solar power. "It's all about policy," he said. "Our lawmakers have sold out to the big solar lobby."

15   In addition to obstructing views and disrupting habitats, large solar power projects take a toll on the desert's scarce water supply, environmentalists like Mr. Harvey said. Mirrors and solar panels have to be washed, and some solar projects incorporate steam turbines, which require even more water.

In addition, some solar projects call for grading the land and spraying it with chemicals to inhibit dust or plant growth that can reduce the efficiency of solar panels. Others require backup generators powered by fossil fuels.

These environmentalists favor "distributed generation," like solar panels on rooftops, and they argue that the leadership of national environmental organizations such as the Sierra Club and the Natural Resources Defense Council has gone in the wrong direction.

Terry Frewin, the chairman of the Sierra Club's California/Nevada desert committee, wrote to the club's executive director, Carl Pope, in July, criticizing him for backing large-scale solar projects.

"Remote solar arrays destroy all native resources on site, and have indirect and irreversible impacts on surrounding wildernesses," Mr. Frewin wrote. He urged the Sierra Club to embrace distributed generation as an alternative to the "industrial renewable" option.

20   Carl Zichella, Western renewable projects director for the Sierra Club, said in response to the letter, "We don't take a back seat to anyone in caring for the desert." But he said the group's position was unchanged.

At the current rate of adding 200 megawatts of rooftop solar power a year, it would take 100 years to meet the 20 percent renewable target that California must meet by 2010, Mr. Zichella said. "What they are proposing is not a solution at all."

One of the first tests of public land use for large, privately owned solar projects is likely to be over BrightSource Energy's planned 400-megawatt solar project, which would occupy 3,400 acres on the California border near Primm, Nev.

The project would use an array of mirrors to concentrate the sun's rays on a boiler. Steam produced in the boiler would turn a turbine that would generate enough electricity to power 250,000 homes.

John Woolard, the chief executive of BrightSource, cited several ways in which the company was trying to have as little impact as possible on the desert. He said the project would use "dry cooling" technology to condense the steam in the turbines for reuse, keeping water usage to a minimum, and that Bright-Source had purposely sought out already disrupted land (it had been used for cattle grazing) for its project.

25   But in the end, the scale of BrightSource's project is driven by the efficiencies of the technology. "You get half as much bang for your buck from rooftop solar" as with concentrating solar technology, Mr. Woolard said, adding, "Rooftop solar will never put a dent in California's renewable targets."

Currently available commercial photovoltaic technology converts sunlight to electricity at an efficiency rate of 12 percent to 14 percent. (The most efficient power plants can achieve efficiencies of nearly 60 percent.)

Absent an economic incentive, solar power just does not make sense, said Al Forte, principal and director of the clean energy solutions practice at Nexant, an energy industry consulting firm. Lucrative incentives like Germany's feed-in tariff "tend to warp the reality of the market," he said.

One of the first battles over a large solar power project was fought on the outskirts of Victorville, California, on the western edge of the Mojave. Inland Energy is building a "hybrid" project on 250 acres there for the city of Victorville that will combine solar panels with conventional technology.

In compliance with state law, Inland hired a firm to look for endangered species, including the Mojave ground squirrel and the desert tortoise. No squirrels were found, but three or four tortoises were found. Because no squirrels were found, Inland proposed to the California Department of Fish and Game that it buy one acre of land to offset every acre of lost habitat, said Tom Barnett, executive vice president at Inland. But the department insisted on the three-to-one ratio its rules call for, he said.

30   "Time is more important than anything else" in project development, Mr. Barnett said, explaining why Inland agreed to the three-to-one ratio. But he noted that it would cost $6.5 million to $10 million to buy and maintain the offsetting acreage for the tortoises.

A family—of human beings—was also living on the site. Inland reached a deal to relocate them at a total cost of $250,000.

"One of the biggest concerns we have," Mr. Barnett said, "is that ours is just a 50-megawatt project."

The much larger projects being proposed will be that much more complicated, but Mr. Barnett, who has a master's degree in environmental science, is not giving up easily. He has begun work on an identical project in Palmdale, California, where the wildlife survey, once again, found no squirrels. He said he was prepared to fight the habitat battle again.

Meanwhile, on the other side off the desert, south of Joshua Tree National Park, Donna Charpied said desert residents of California and Nevada were planning some unspecified action within two months. "The desert will not go quietly into that dark night," she said.

● Review Questions

1. Summarize the chief objections of some environmentalists to large-scale solar power farms.

2. What is the "feed-in" tariff used in Germany and recommended for use here by some environmentalists as a way of offering incentives to homeowners to install rooftop solar panels?

3. Contrast the key benefits of ground-based solar power plants to rooftop panels.

● Discussion and Writing Suggestions

1. Maloney's article develops more fully some of the environmental concerns about solar power raised in Dickerson's article immediately preceding. To what extent do you take such objections seriously? How should we weigh the competing interests—both ultimately involving the environment—of (1) the need for large-scale renewable energy and (2) the need to protect the environment?

2. Currently, California law mandates that 20 percent of the state's electricity must be generated from renewable resources by 2010. To what extent do you favor a policy that imposes government mandates on power generation?

3. Maloney quotes environmentalist Tim Harvey: "We support renewable energy, and we support California's renewable energy targets, but we think it can be done through rooftop solar." To what extent do you agree? In developing your response, draw upon Dickerson's article, preceding, as well as Maloney's.

SYNTHESIS ACTIVITIES

1. Write an explanatory synthesis, as if it were a cover story for a weekly newsmagazine, in which you (1) lay out the essential features of the environmental crisis posed by the burning of fossil fuels and (2) discuss the range of alternative, renewable energy sources available now or in the near future. Your synthesis will therefore roughly follow the organization of the "Green Power" chapter itself.

   Begin by drawing on authors like Lemonick, Friedman, and Gore to indicate the nature and scope of the problem posed by increasing levels of carbon dioxide and other greenhouse gases. Describe some of the proposals for dealing with the problem discussed by authors like Friedman, Bryce, the members of the Council of Foreign Relations

Task Force, Lubber, and Zuckerman. In the second half of your synthesis, summarize some of the particular forms of renewable energy—nuclear, wind, and solar power, as well as the prospect of plug-in hybrid vehicles, drawing upon the authors represented in the second half of this chapter.

Conclude by indicating which of these forms of green energy, and which policies, appear to the authors of your sources as the most promising or practical.

2. Write an argument synthesis in which you advocate a policy or a set of policies that you believe should govern the nation's use of energy over the next fifty years. Mindy Lubber and the authors of the Task Force offer some policies for consideration, as do Thomas Friedman, Al Gore, and Morton Zuckerman. Some of the articles in the latter half of the chapter cover policies already in place (such as California's mandate to derive 20 percent of the state's energy sources from renewable energy by 2010, as reported by Marla Dickerson).

Based upon your reading in this chapter and elsewhere, as well as on your your own sense of what must be done, make the case for your policies. Remember that it is not sufficient to simply advocate broad goals (we must steadily convert to renewable energy sources): You must also indicate what government, industry, smaller business, and individuals must *do* to achieve significant reductions in greenhouse gas emissions.

3. How, in the years ahead, are green technologies likely to change our daily lives? Write an article for a magazine dated December 2025 (or 2050) on the subject of how the national quest to address the climate crisis and to develop alternative energy sources has, since 2000, changed the way Americans live and work. Draw upon as many sources in this chapter as are helpful; but use your imagination (and a reasonable degree of probability) to analyze how the world of the near future developed from policy decisions and technological innovations being made now and over the next few years.

4. Thomas Friedman, Al Gore, and Mindy Lubber offer analyses of the environmental perils we face at the beginning of the twenty-first century and propose some solutions. Compare and contrast these analyses and these solutions. Review the guidelines for comparison-and-contrast syntheses on pp.174–175.

5. Given what you have read about the need for renewable energy, what do you believe are an *individual's* responsibilities, if any, in reducing energy use? Thomas Friedman appears to believe that the climate crisis cannot effectively be addressed by individuals, arguing that unless solutions are "scaled" to a massive degree, they are token and inconsequential in resolving the larger problem. What, amid all this incoming

data, is your position? Is it necessary or useful for an individual to have an energy policy? What would your policy be? How effective would this policy be in reducing carbon emissions? If it is symbolic only (or mostly), is that still important and necessary? Draw upon Friedman, Gore, Lubber, and any other authors in this chapter that seem relevant to you.

6. Imagine that you work for an advertising agency that is competing for a contract with a large company that generates either nuclear, wind, or solar power for a particular state or a particular region. Your job is to try to win the contract by preparing a brief plan that lays out to the power company execs a potential advertising campaign. Draw upon some of the authors in this chapter to prepare your written prospectus. (Include a Works Cited list on a separate page at the end of the document.) Indicate the key idea of your proposed campaign that will sell nuclear/wind/solar power. Explain why the type of energy the company is offering is superior to other types of energy. Do not misrepresent or distort the information presented by the authors in this chapter, but use their information and their arguments to best advantage. Organize your plan so that it has an introductory section, a body section containing specifics and a persuasive argument, and a conclusion.

7. Explain how some of the selections in this chapter may have changed your perception of the way you and those around you use energy, and how your life may be affected by the necessity of developing alternative sources of energy. Which authors' analyses have done the most to impress upon you the seriousness of the challenge? Which have most concerned you? For example, when Friedman asks, "Have you ever seen a revolution where no one got hurt?" he implies that saving the earth will require considerable sacrifice. To what extent are you prepared to make sacrifices: to pay increased taxes to help ensure a cleaner, safer environment and a more stable climate; to give up a degree of ease of movement; to take different jobs; to buy different cars, homes, and appliances; to live in places located near power generation stations, whether wind, solar, or nuclear? Draw upon whichever authors in the chapter seem best suited to help you grapple with such questions.

8. In the latter part of his article, Thomas Friedman discusses the scope of the environmental problems facing us by describing the fifteen-wedge pie chart created by engineering professor Robert Socolow and ecology professor Stephen Pacala. Discuss the prospects of achieving the goals in some of these wedges by drawing upon information in the latter half of this chapter about nuclear, wind, and solar power by authors like Sherman, White, Totty, Kolbert, and Maloney.

9. Robert Bryce forcefully argues that we should not succumb to the "delusions of energy independence." Much as we (and Al Gore) would prefer, he asserts, there is no prospect of achieving independence from Middle Eastern oil during the next few decades. Which other authors in this chapter might support that position? Write an argument supporting or refuting Bryce's conclusion, based upon arguments made and information presented by other authors in the second part of this chapter.

10. Thomas Friedman and others have argued that the most effective way to spur the development of energy-efficient vehicles and alternative fuels for transportation is to make gasoline so expensive that it becomes financially painful to drive vehicles powered by internal-- combustion engines. "As long as gas is cheap," he writes, "people will go out and buy used SUVs and Hummers." Imposing a steep gas tax will force people to change their habits and their preferred modes of transportation. In an editorial, argue for or against the federal government's imposing a gas tax sufficient to make gasoline in the United States as expensive as it is in Europe—between $5 and $7 a gallon. Draw upon some of the authors in this chapter to help you make the case for or against such a tax.

11. Don Sherman reports on the Chevrolet Volt, G.M.'s potentially break-through electric vehicle that, along with other forthcoming plug-in hybrids, may go a long way toward helping the nation break its dependence upon Middle Eastern oil—or not. Chapter 4, on explanatory synthesis, includes a model paper and a set of short readings on the hydrogen fuel cell vehicle, consumer models of which are still only a distant prospect. Drawing upon Sherman, Joseph P. White ("Why the Gasoline Engine Isn't Going Away Anytime Soon"), and some of the readings in Chapter 4, compare and contrast the features, advantages, and disadvantages of electric, fuel cell, and internal-combustion (gasoline-powered) vehicles.

12. You have read about the conflicts between those who would pursue renewable energy projects (such as solar power in California) and locals who scream NIMBY (not in my backyard). Many people live in remote areas, away from cities and suburbs, because they like the view, and they don't want to see wind turbines or solar power arrays cluttering the landscape. The construction of a national electric power grid, necessary to send electricity from a wind farm in Texas to office buildings in Los Angeles, may be delayed, according to a recent *Los Angeles Times* article, because "municipalities and landowners have protested plans to string transmission networks through their backyards."

    What can we do to get beyond the NIMBY syndrome? Draw particularly upon the readings in the latter part of this chapter, as well as any others than seem relevant.

RESEARCH ACTIVITIES

1. After the presidential election of 2008, many people were hopeful that the policies of the incoming Obama administration would be far more responsive to environmental concerns than the policies of the previous administration. The new president campaigned partially on the promise to take climate change seriously, to transform the automobile industry to make more energy-efficient vehicles, and to build a high-tech energy infrastructure to transmit electricity from wind and solar power plants in rural areas to the cities. The president also promised to push for higher federal fuel-economy standards and to support a cap-and-trade program with the goal of reducing carbon emissions by 80 percent by mid-century.

   Investigate what the Obama administration has done so far to achieve these goals. What policies and programs have been proposed, what regulations have been issued, what laws have been passed? What kind of hurdles has the federal government encountered as it attempts to achieve its green energy goals?

2. Robert Bryce is one of many who dismiss as impractical the goal of energy independence. To what degree are we more independent of Middle Eastern oil than we were five or ten years ago? To what degree are plug-in hybrids more of a reality than they were at the turn of the present century? To what extent has the amount of power generated by wind and solar power significantly supplanted coal-fired electricity during the last few years? Write a report summarizing your findings.

3. In the report "American's Energy 'Independence'" published on the Web (http://www.abc.net.au/unleashed/stories/s2274315.htm), Dennis Phillips, a professor of foreign policy at the University of Sydney in Australia, notes that the environmental agenda often clashes with the economic and employment agenda, particularly in third world countries. He argues:

   > All the world's poor are entitled to a much higher standard of living, but in order to progress, the world's poorest three billion will need to access and consume vastly increased quantities of energy. "Renewables" like wind and solar power are not going to do the job in the short term.

   > Do we tell the world's poor to be patient and wait? In the "ethanol fiasco" we have done worse than that. We have processed staple crops like corn and soybeans to pour into our fuel tanks, forcing up food prices that ignited riots around the world.

   Research the energy situation in one or two non-European countries to determine (1) energy requirements for sustainability and economic development; (2) chief energy sources; (3) carbon footprints; and

(4) prospects for developing and using clean, renewable energy. How, if at all, have governments and businesses in these countries attempted to reconcile the environmental costs of increased energy use, on the one hand, and the need for increased energy to spur economic development, on the other?

4. To what extent are other countries, particularly in Europe, further along in developing and using clean energy than the United States? Select one European country and research its government's energy policy, its patterns of energy use, and its development of renewable energy plants and infrastructure. Determine the extent to which the experiences of this country, particularly its successes, may be transferable to the United States.

5. In 2008 Texas oilman T. Boone Pickens, declaring that "the United States is the Saudi Arabia of wind power," attempted to counteract our dependence upon foreign oil by launching an ambitious plan to build the world's largest wind farm in Texas. Investing millions of dollars of his own money, Pickens founded Mesa Power to oversee the project, which involved over 2,500 wind turbines, sufficient, he anticipated, to eventually produce electricity to power 1.3 million homes. Launching a nationwide publicity campaign on television, in newspapers, and in magazines to promote his plan, Pickens also proposed that natural gas—which is abundant in this country and which does not produce CO_2—should replace gasoline as the fuel for all automobiles. Pickens's plan ran into a snag with the credit crunch of late 2008 (it was difficult for him to get the necessary financing), but he remained hopeful that the setback would be temporary.

   Research the Pickens plan and its current status and prospects. How many wind turbines have been built? How much power is being supplied? What kind of progress has been made converting automobiles to use natural gas? To what extent do energy experts and environmentalists view the Pickens plan as offering a viable solution to the environmental crisis?

6. Opponents of nuclear power argue that previous nuclear accidents such as occurred at the Three Mile Island reactor in Pennsylvania (1979) and at the Chernobyl reactor in the former Soviet Union (1986) risk a cataclysm that makes nuclear power generation too dangerous. Others point to the perfect safety record of nuclear reactors in France, where, after a twenty-five-year conversion process, 80 percent of the country's energy comes from nuclear reactors. Investigate the safety factor of nuclear reactors used for power generation. What steps have been taken since Three Mile Island and Chernobyl to decrease the risks of radioactive particles being released into the atmosphere following a nuclear accident? Have experts arrived at a consensus about the safety issues, or is there still significant controversy over this issue?

7. Investigate the attempts to discourage use of fossil fuels and to encourage renewable power generation by one of the following methods: (1) cap and trade; (2) carbon taxes; (3) increased gasoline

taxes. Consider not only proposed U.S. government programs, but also state programs, such as California's mandate to generate at least 20 percent of its power from renewable sources by 2010. Consider also policies proposed at international environmental conferences such as occurred at the United Nations Conference on Environment and Development (the "Earth Summit," Rio de Janeiro, 1992), in Kyoto (the Kyoto Protocol, 1997), and at the United Nations Climate Change Conference (Bali, 2007). Which proposals and programs to discourage carbon greenhouse gas pollution and to encourage green energy generation have met with most success? Which have been the most controversial? To what extent can successful programs in one state (or one country) be transferred, in the opinion of experts, to other states (or other countries)?

8. Research the latest developments in either (1) plug-in hybrid technology or (2) hydrogen fuel cell technology. If you choose to study plug-in hybrid technology, pay particular attention to the quest to develop relatively low cost, long-range batteries. If you choose hydrogen fuel cell technology, pay particular attention to the quest to separate pure hydrogen from its other bound elements, as well as to store and distribute hydrogen through a national infrastructure. You may wish to begin by considering the readings and model synthesis on fuel cell cars in Chapter 4.

9. Investigate the latest developments in either wind or solar power. For the energy source you select, investigate the actual growth of this technology over the past decade or so and the projected growth over the next ten years. How much of the nation's power requirements are currently being supplied by this particular technology? How much is projected to be supplied ten, twenty, or fifty years down the road? What government incentives are available for the construction and operation of wind power or solar power? If you research solar power, to what extent are large-scale ground arrays overtaking rooftop solar panels in popularity? To what extent are environmental concerns, political wrangling, and bureaucratic roadblocks hindering the development of wind or solar power?

10. For many years there was great excitement about ethanol, an alcohol-based fuel which is blended with gasoline. The most popular formulation, known as E85, consists of 85 percent corn ethanol and 15 percent gasoline. Presidential candidates campaigning in Iowa felt compelled to express their undying support for ethanol because Iowan and other Midwestern farmers grew and sold the corn necessary for its manufacture. More recently, ethanol's stock has fallen. Research the history of ethanol as an alternative fuel, focusing on the economic and political aspects of its role in the search for alternatives to straight gasoline.

11. Research another form of alternative energy not significantly covered in this chapter: biomass, diesel, biodiesel, geothermal, natural gas, algae. To what extent does this form of energy promise to help us achieve a greater degree of energy independence? To what degree is it likely to supplant fossil fuels, such as oil and coal? What are its advantages and disadvantages? What are the implications for the environment of large-scale use of this form of energy? What major players currently control or are likely to control the supply of this energy? Which parties stand most to gain by such large-scale use? Which stand most to lose?

9

Marriage and Family
in America

etween 40 and 50 percent of all American marriages will fail. An even
higher percentage of second marriages will end in divorce. Failed marriages
of young couples have become cynically known as "Starter Marriages."
Cohabitation is on the rise, and more people than ever before are choosing to stay
single. A survey released by the U.S. Census Bureau in October 2006 found that
domiciles led by married couples were now in the minority—just 49.7 percent of
all households. Yet marriage continues to fascinate and inspire us—as it has every
known culture throughout human history. The wedding industry generates over
$60 billion a year in expenses ranging from embossed invitations to rented tuxe-
dos to $10,000 video shoots. Newsstands are choked with bridal magazines.
Tabloids splash celebrity weddings across their covers; and most Hollywood
comedies still end with the prospect of a wedding. Everybody, it seems, plans on
getting married. According to one set of statistics, 85 percent of Americans will
marry at some point in their lives, and 99 percent say they plan to do so.

Why? What is it about the marital state that is so universally appealing? Why
do we continue to wed, despite the fact that most of us, statistically, have experienced or witnessed divorce? For some young people, marriage is simply another fact of life—perhaps part of a dimly glimpsed future, along with 401(k)
plans, 9-to-5 jobs, and other pillars of adulthood. Others may see the institution
in more specific terms—for instance, a teenage girl obsessing over the color of
her future bridesmaids' dresses and the merits of white versus pink roses for the
centerpieces.

Whether marriage fuels our childhood fantasies or fulfills (or frustrates) our expectations as adults, very few of us can describe what it means to be married—if
it ever occurred to us to do so. Doesn't this seem odd? After all, most people have
no trouble describing "friendship" as a form of human relationship or "employment" or "citizenship." Yet marriage, an institution to which nearly all of us
aspire, and a condition in which most of us will spend many years of our lives,
resists easy interpretation. If pressed, most of us would probably characterize the
marriage relationship as primarily romantic. The most idealistic and starry-eyed
of us, who see marriage as a way for soul mates to pledge unending devotion to

one another, dwell at one end of this spectrum. Others, aware that love can be fickle and ephemeral, sense that marriage must be about other things: maturity and commitment, an indication that one has "settled down," perhaps even a rite of passage to adulthood. (Yes, you are marrying someone you love, but you loved at twenty and didn't marry. What changed? *You* did.)

Sociologists Maria Kefalas and Kathryn Edin have demonstrated how, among poorer Americans, marriage has become a luxury item, to be purchased only when a couple has "arrived" financially, last on a "to-do" list, behind a home mortgage and new furniture. And at least some of us suspect that marriage involves pragmatic considerations of a social, political, or even avaricious nature. As they say, it's just as easy to fall in love with and marry a rich girl (or guy) as a poor one.

As the selections in this chapter will show, these conflicting and tangled motives for marrying are no accident. The very meaning of marriage has been changing over the centuries, an evolution that can be traced to broad cultural, intellectual, and economic trends. If anything, these changes seem to be accelerating. (To borrow from Hemingway—the changes seem to be happening slowly, and all at once.) But what significance can we draw from this evolution? Conservative cultural commentators point to the muddled state of contemporary marriage as proof that our society has taken a wrong turn. Yet a wrong turn from what—some historical, universally acclaimed ideal of marriage? As marriage historian Stephanie Coontz notes:

> Everyone agrees that marriage isn't what it used to be, and everyone is quite right. But most of what "everyone knows" about what matrimony used to be and just how it has changed is wrong.

With Coontz's observation as our starting point, this chapter examines the state of marriage and family in contemporary America. Historians, sociologists, anthropologists, political scientists, legal scholars, political activists, and journalists have studied marriage from their various perspectives; and they have offered observations about its impact on our culture, our lives, and indeed our very sense of who we are. Some call marriage a vital public institution that must be safeguarded for the civic good (we allude, here, to the debate over gay marriage). Others view marriage as a private concern between two consenting adults. Some venerate marriage as the ultimate partnership between the sexes. Others charge that marriage forces men and women into rigid—and unequal—gender roles.

The selections in this chapter reveal an institution in flux, the mutable nature of which forces Americans to create their own definitions—not just of marriage and family, but also of what it means to be a wife, a husband, a mother, and a father. The viewpoint in these selections ranges from the scholarly to the personal. A common theme, as you will notice, revolves around the female half of the marriage equation. Debates over the role of women, both in families and in society as a whole, underlie the most contentious debates regarding modern marriages and families. We will examine two of these disputes—working versus stay-at-home mothers, and the continued gender divide between women and men over the subject of child care and housework. As you read the selections, think about your own experiences with marriage and family. You may not be married yourself, or have even thought much about marriage; but certainly you have witnessed the marriages of family members and of friends. Ask yourself whether the viewpoint being expressed in the selections squares with your own observations and your own beliefs on the subject.

The chapter opens with a "pop quiz" by historian Stephanie Coontz that may challenge some of your assumptions about marriage. Next, Coontz describes the horror with which many societies treated the "The Radical Idea of Marrying for Love"—an idea most of us now take for granted. Following, in "The State of Our Unions," marriage researchers David Popenoe and Barbara Whitehead use national marriage statistics to argue that the institution of marriage now faces its gravest crisis.

The next two selections take on the contentious topic of gay marriage as debated by two prominent cultural commentators. First, Andrew Sullivan argues why conservatives ought to support gay marriage. Then, conservative commentator William Bennett charges that opening marriage to homosexuals would destroy the institution itself.

The chapter next turns to an extended examination of two ongoing debates regarding marriage: working mothers versus stay-at-home mothers (often referred to as the "Mommy Wars" or the "opt-out debate") and the "stalled revolution"—the feminist complaint that, in an age of working women, men still refuse to shoulder their share of the housework or childcare. First, we offer two opposing perspectives, written twenty-nine years apart, by one woman, Terri Martin Hekker, on the subject of stay-at-home mothers. Taken together, these essays paint a stark portrait of marital disillusionment and personal despair that you are unlikely to forget anytime soon. Next, the author of *The Feminine Mistake*, Leslie Bennetts, argues that despite the common assumption that we are living in an age of gender equality, many husbands still expect that their wives (rather than they) will quit their jobs and abandon their careers after the arrival of the first child. Following, linguist Deborah Tannen challenges her mother's traditional assumptions about whether or not wives should work—or want to work—at professional careers; but she then attempts to see things from her mother's point of view.

We step back from the personal perspective, as sociologist Andrew Cherlin examines the two major transformations of American marriage since the 1950s. Following are two selections detailing another skirmish on the marital front: housework. According to recent research, the amount of time men spend on housework has not changed in forty years. While an increasing number of women have joined the workforce, often earning more than their husbands, women still do the bulk of the cooking, laundry, and child-rearing. Naturally, this state of affairs has occasioned anger and bitterness among wives. Is this a private issue among spouses or a more systemic, feminist one? The next two selections, by Hope Edelman and Eric Bartels, offer personal perspectives on married life that range across several of the issues raised by previous selections in the chapter. Their writings provide a raw, honest, look at the daily reality of married life.

Next, Aviva Patz reports on a study that responds to the key question confronting many hopeful engaged couples: "Can Success in Marriage be Predicted?" The answer may surprise you. The chapter concludes with a haunting short story by Lore Segal, "The Arbus Factor," about aging, love, and marriage.

These selections on marriage are intended to be provocative—to challenge assumptions about what marriage and family mean to you. After all, if you are like 90 percent of Americans, one day you too will be married.

A POP QUIZ ON MARRIAGE; THE RADICAL IDEA OF MARRYING FOR LOVE

Stephanie Coontz

Our chapter selections begin with a "pop quiz" designed to ferret out your assumptions about marriage. There's no penalty for getting the answers wrong; but you may be interested to discover that you know less about the subject than you thought. After taking the quiz (and checking the correct answers), you'll proceed to an in-depth historical survey of love, as it relates to marriage.

One of the bedrock assumptions of modern marriage is the once-radical idea that newlyweds be in love. Marriage and love have existed through the ages, of course. But according to historian Stephanie Coontz, only in the relatively recent past, beginning in the eighteenth century, did the political and economic institution of marriage take on romantic associations. Reminding us through historical and cultural examples that many people were (and still are) horrified by the idea of marrying for love, and loving the one you marry, Coontz traces the intellectual development of this subversive notion back to the Enlightenment. She then hints at the long-term consequences it held for the institution of marriage.

Stephanie Coontz teaches history and family studies at The Evergreen State College in Olympia, Washington, and has written numerous books on marriage and family in America, including *The Way We Never Were: American Families and the Nostalgia Trap* (1992) and *The Way We Really Are: Coming to Terms with America's Changing Families* (1998). The following selection first appeared in *Marriage: A History: From Obedience to Intimacy, or How Love Conquered Marriage* (2005).

1. Women are more eager to marry than men. *True or False?*

2. Men are threatened by women who are their intellectual and occupational equals, preferring to be with much younger, less accomplished women. *True or False?*

3. There are more long-term marriages today than in the past. *True or False?*

4. Americans have become much more tolerant of all sexual activity. *True or False?*

5. The growth in the number of couples living together and even having children without formal marriage ceremonies or licenses reflects a sharp break with centuries old tradition. *True or False?*

6. Educated married women are increasingly "opting out" of work to stay home with their children. *True or False?*

7. Men and women who hold nontraditional views about gender roles are less likely to marry and more likely to divorce than those with traditional values. *True or False?*

8. Divorce rates in the 1950's were lower than at any other time in the 20th century. *True or False?*

9. Throughout history, philosophers and theologians have always believed that strong marital commitments form the foundation of a virtuous society. *True or False?*

10. American women have more positive attitudes toward marriage than Japanese women do. *True or False?*

11. Divorce has always been a disaster for women and children. *True or False?*

12. The preferred form of marriage through the ages has been between one man and one woman. *True or False?*

13. Born-again Christians are just as likely to divorce as more secular Americans. *True or False?**

● Discussion and Writing Suggestions

1. Assess your score on this quiz. How many of the answers surprised you? Why? How did one or more of the answers (or a fact contained in one of the answers) run counter to your own preconceptions about or attitudes toward marriage?

2. How do you account for the correct answer to Question 1? To what extent does this answer corroborate (or contradict) your own observations of the marriages and divorces you have observed?

3. Coontz notes in her answer to Question 7 that "women's views on gender [i.e., on traditional gender roles] are changing more rapidly than men's." Do you believe that this is the case? If so, what might be the reasons? Provide examples from your own experience or observation.

4. Coontz's Question 8 focuses on divorce rates. Access the National Center for Health Statistics (NCHS) "Fast Stats A–Z" page <www.cdc.gov/nchs/fastats/divorce.htm>, click on one of the links about marriage and divorce, and write a short paragraph based on the statistics you find. As an alternative, write a paragraph based on statistics you find at the DivorceMagazine.com site: <http://www.divorcemag.com/statistics/statsUS.shtml>.

5. Question 10 concerns attitudes toward marriage by Japanese women. If you are an immigrant to the United States or an immigrant one generation removed, discuss how attitudes toward marriage in your culture of origin may significantly differ from attitudes you have encountered in this country.

---

*For Answer key, please turn to p. 457.

THE RADICAL IDEA OF MARRYING FOR LOVE

George Bernard Shaw described marriage as an institution that brings together two people "under the influence of the most violent, most insane, most delusive, and most transient of passions. They are required to swear that they will remain in that excited, abnormal, and exhausting condition continuously until death do them part."

Shaw's comment was amusing when he wrote it at the beginning of the twentieth century, and it still makes us smile today, because it pokes fun at the unrealistic expectations that spring from a dearly held cultural ideal—that marriage should be based on intense, profound love and a couple should maintain their ardor until death do them part. But for thousands of years the joke would have fallen flat.

For most of history it was inconceivable that people would choose their mates on the basis of something as fragile and irrational as love and then focus all their sexual, intimate, and altruistic desires on the resulting marriage. In fact, many historians, sociologists, and anthropologists used to think romantic love was a recent Western invention. This is not true. People have always fallen in love, and throughout the ages many couples have loved each other deeply.

But only rarely in history has love been seen as the main reason for getting married. When someone did advocate such a strange belief, it was no laughing matter. Instead, it was considered a serious threat to social order.

5   In some cultures and times, true love was actually thought to be incompatible with marriage. Plato believed love was a wonderful emotion that led men to behave honorably. But the Greek philosopher was referring not to the love of women, "such as the meaner men feel," but to the love of one man for another.

Other societies considered it good if love developed after marriage or thought love should be factored in along with the more serious considerations involved in choosing a mate. But even when past societies did welcome or encourage married love, they kept it on a short leash. Couples were not to put their feelings for each other above more important commitments, such as their ties to parents, siblings, cousins, neighbors, or God.

In ancient India, falling in love before marriage was seen as a disruptive, almost antisocial act. The Greeks thought lovesickness was a type of insanity, a view that was adopted by medieval commentators in Europe. In the Middle Ages the French defined love as a "derangement of the mind" that could be cured by sexual intercourse, either with the loved one or with a different partner. This cure assumed, as Oscar Wilde once put it, that the quickest way to conquer yearning and temptation was to yield immediately and move on to more important matters.

In China, excessive love between husband and wife was seen as a threat to the solidarity of the extended family. Parents could force a son to divorce his wife if her behavior or work habits didn't please them, whether or not he loved her. They could also require him to take a concubine if his wife did not produce a son. If a son's romantic attachment to his wife rivaled his parents' claims on the couple's time and labor, the parents might even send her back to her parents. In the Chinese language the term *love* did not traditionally apply to feelings between husband and wife. It was used to describe an illicit, socially disapproved relationship. In the 1920s a group of intellectuals invented a new word for love between spouses because they thought such a radical new idea required its own special label.

In Europe, during the twelfth and thirteenth centuries, adultery became idealized as the highest form of love among the aristocracy. According to the Countess of Champagne, it was impossible for true love to "exert its powers between two people who are married to each other."

10   In twelfth-century France, Andreas Capellanus, chaplain to Countess Marie of Troyes, wrote a treatise on the principles of courtly love. The first rule was that "marriage is no real excuse for not loving." But he meant loving someone outside the marriage. As late as the eighteenth century the French essayist Montaigne wrote that any man who was in love with his wife was a man so dull that no one else could love him.

Courtly love probably loomed larger in literature than in real life. But for centuries, noblemen and kings fell in love with courtesans rather than the wives they married for political reasons. Queens and noblewomen had to be more discreet than their husbands, but they too looked beyond marriage for love and intimacy.

This sharp distinction between love and marriage was common among the lower and middle classes as well. Many of the songs and stories popular among peasants in medieval Europe mocked married love.

The most famous love affair of the Middle Ages was that of Peter Abelard, a well-known theologian in France, and Héloïse, the brilliant niece of a fellow churchman at Notre Dame. The two eloped without marrying, and she bore him a child. In an attempt to save his career but still placate Héloïse's furious uncle, Abelard proposed they marry in secret. This would mean that Héloïse would not be living in sin, while Abelard could still pursue his church ambitions. But Héloïse resisted the idea, arguing that marriage would not only harm his career but also undermine their love.

"Nothing Is More Impure Than to Love One's Wife as if She Were a Mistress"

Even in societies that esteemed married love, couples were expected to keep it under strict control. In many cultures, public displays of love between husband and wife were considered unseemly. A Roman was expelled from the Senate because he had kissed his wife in front of his daughter. Plutarch conceded that the punishment was somewhat extreme but pointed out that everyone knew that it was "disgraceful" to kiss one's wife in front of others.

15   Some Greek and Roman philosophers even said that a man who loved his wife with "excessive" ardor was "an adulterer." Many centuries later Catholic and Protestant theologians argued that husbands and wives who loved each other too much were committing the sin of idolatry. Theologians chided wives who used endearing nicknames for their husbands, because such familiarity on

a wife's part undermined the husband's authority and the awe that his wife should feel for him. Although medieval Muslim thinkers were more approving of sexual passion between husband and wife than were Christian theologians, they also insisted that too much intimacy between husband and wife weakened a believer's devotion to God. And, like their European counterparts, secular writers in the Islamic world believed that love thrived best outside marriage.

Many cultures still frown on placing love at the center of marriage. In Africa, the Fulbe people of northern Cameroon do not see love as a legitimate emotion, especially within marriage. One observer reports that in conversations with their neighbors, Fulbe women "vehemently deny emotional attachment to a husband." In many peasant and working-class communities, too much love between husband and wife is seen as disruptive because it encourages the couple to withdraw from the wider web of dependence that makes the society work.

As a result, men and women often relate to each other in public, even after marriage, through the conventions of a war between the sexes, disguising the fondness they may really feel. They describe their marital behavior, no matter how exemplary it may actually be, in terms of convenience, compulsion, or self-interest rather than love or sentiment. In Cockney rhyming slang, the term for *wife* is *trouble and strife*.

Whether it is valued or not, love is rarely seen as the main ingredient for marital success. Among the Taita of Kenya, recognition and approval of married love are widespread. An eighty-year-old man recalled that his fourth wife "was the wife of my heart. . . . I could look at her and no words would pass, just a smile." In this society, where men often take several wives, women speak wistfully about how wonderful it is to be a "love wife." But only a small percentage of Taita women experience this luxury, because a Taita man normally marries a love wife only after he has accumulated a few more practical wives.

In many cultures, love has been seen as a desirable outcome of marriage but not as a good reason for getting married in the first place. The Hindu tradition celebrates love and sexuality in marriage, but love and sexual attraction are not considered valid reasons for marriage. "First we marry, then we'll fall in love" is the formula. As recently as 1975, a survey of college students in the Indian state of Karnataka found that only 18 percent "strongly" approved of marriages made on the basis of love, while 32 percent completely disapproved.

20   Similarly, in early modern Europe most people believed that love developed after marriage. Moralists of the sixteenth and seventeenth centuries argued that if a husband and wife each had a good character, they would probably come to love each other. But they insisted that youths be guided by their families in choosing spouses who were worth learning to love. It was up to parents and other relatives to make sure that the woman had a dowry or the man had a good yearly income. Such capital, it was thought, would certainly help love flower.

"[I]t Made Me Really Sick, Just as I Have Formerly Been When in Love with My Wife"

I don't believe that people of the past had more control over their hearts than we do today or that they were incapable of the deep love so many individuals now hope to achieve in marriage. But love in marriage was seen as a bonus, not as a necessity. The great Roman statesman Cicero exchanged many loving letters with his wife, Terentia, during their thirty-year marriage. But that didn't stop him from divorcing her when she was no longer able to support him in the style to which he had become accustomed.

Sometimes people didn't have to make such hard choices. In seventeenth-century America, Anne Bradstreet was the favorite child of an indulgent father who gave her the kind of education usually reserved for elite boys. He later arranged her marriage to a cherished childhood friend who eventually became the governor of Massachusetts. Combining love, duty, material security, and marriage was not the strain for her that it was for many men and women of that era. Anne wrote love poems to her husband that completely ignored the injunction of Puritan ministers not to place one's spouse too high in one's affections. "If ever two were one," she wrote him, "then surely we; if ever man were loved by wife, then thee....I prize thy love more than whole mines of gold, or all the riches that the East doth hold; my love is such that rivers cannot quench, nor ought but love from thee, give recompense."

The famous seventeenth-century English diarist Samuel Pepys chose to marry for love rather than profit. But he was not as lucky as Anne. After hearing a particularly stirring piece of music, Pepys recorded that it "did wrap up my soul so that it made me really sick, just as I have formerly been when in love with my wife." Pepys would later disinherit a nephew for marrying under the influence of so strong yet transient an emotion.

There were always youngsters who resisted the pressures of parents, kin, and neighbors to marry for practical reasons rather than love, but most accepted or even welcomed the interference of parents and others in arranging their marriages. A common saying in early modern Europe was "He who marries for love has good nights and bad days." Nowadays a bitter wife or husband might ask, "Whatever possessed me to think I loved you enough to marry you?" Through most of the past, he or she was more likely to have asked, "Whatever possessed me to marry you just because I loved you?"

"Happily Ever After"

25 Through most of the past, individuals hoped to find love, or at least "tranquil affection," in marriage. But nowhere did they have the same recipe for marital happiness that prevails in most contemporary Western countries. Today there is general agreement on what it takes for a couple to live "happily ever after." First, they must love each other deeply and choose each other unswayed by outside pressure. From then on, each must make the partner the top priority in life, putting that relationship above any and all competing ties. A husband and wife, we believe, owe their highest obligations and deepest loyalties to each other and the children they raise. Parents and in-laws should not be allowed to interfere in the marriage. Married couples should be best friends, sharing their most intimate feelings and secrets. They should express affection openly but also talk candidly about problems. And of course they should be sexually faithful to each other.

This package of expectations about love, marriage, and sex, however, is extremely rare. When we look at the historical record around the world, the customs of modern America and Western Europe appear exotic and exceptional.

Leo Tolstoy once remarked that all happy families are alike, while every unhappy family is unhappy in its own way. But the more I study the history of marriage, the more I think the opposite is true. Most unhappy marriages in history share common patterns, leaving their tear-stained—and sometimes bloodstained—records across the ages. But each happy, successful marriage seems to be happy in its own way. And for most of human history, successful marriages have not been happy in *our* way.

A woman in ancient China might bring one or more of her sisters to her husband's home as backup wives. Eskimo couples often had cospousal arrangements, in which each partner had sexual relations with the other's spouse. In Tibet and parts of India, Kashmir, and Nepal, a woman may be married to two or more brothers, all of whom share sexual access to her.

In modern America, such practices are the stuff of trash TV: "I caught my sister in bed with my husband"; "My parents brought their lovers into our home"; "My wife slept with my brother"; "It broke my heart to share my husband with another woman." In other cultures, individuals often find such practices normal and comforting. The children of Eskimo cospouses felt that they shared a special bond, and society viewed them as siblings. Among Tibetan brothers who share the same wife, sexual jealousy is rare.

30   In some cultures, cowives see one another as allies rather than rivals. In Botswana, women add an interesting wrinkle to the old European saying "Woman's work is never done." There they say: "Without cowives, a woman's work is never done." A researcher who worked with the Cheyenne Indians of the United States in the 1930s and 1940s told of a chief who tried to get rid of two of his three wives. All three women defied him, saying that if he sent two of them away, he would have to give away the third as well.

Even when societies celebrated the love between husband and wife as a pleasant by-product of marriage, people rarely had a high regard for marital intimacy. Chinese commentators on marriage discouraged a wife from confiding in her husband or telling him about her day. A good wife did not bother her husband with news of her own activities and feelings but treated him "like a guest," no matter how long they had been married. A husband who demonstrated open affection for his wife, even at home, was seen as having a weak character.

In the early eighteenth century, American lovers often said they looked for "candor" in each other. But they were not talking about the soul-baring intimacy idealized by modern Americans, and they certainly did not believe that couples should talk frankly about their grievances. Instead candor meant fairness, kindliness, and good temper. People wanted a spouse who did *not* pry too deeply. The ideal mate, wrote U.S. President John Adams in his diary, was willing "to palliate faults and Mistakes, to put the best Construction upon Words and Action, and to forgive Injuries."

Modern marital advice books invariably tell husbands and wives to put each other first. But in many societies, marriage ranks very low in the hierarchy of meaningful relationships. People's strongest loyalties and emotional connections may be reserved for members of their birth families. On the North American plains in the 1930s, a Kiowa Indian woman commented to a researcher that "a woman can always get another husband, but she has only one brother." In China it was said that "you have only one family, but you can always get another wife." In Christian texts prior to the seventeenth century, the word *love* usually referred to feelings toward God or neighbors rather than toward a spouse.

In Confucian philosophy, the two strongest relationships in family life are between father and son and between elder brother and younger brother, not between husband and wife. In thirteenth-century China the bond between father and son was so much stronger than the bond between husband and wife that legal commentators insisted a couple do nothing if the patriarch of the household raped his son's wife. In one case, although the judge was sure that a woman's rape accusation against her father-in-law was true, he ordered the young man to give up his sentimental desire "to grow old together" with his wife. Loyalty to parents was paramount, and therefore the son should send his wife back to her own father, who could then marry her to someone else. Sons were sometimes ordered beaten for siding with their wives against their father. No wonder that for 1,700 years women in one Chinese province guarded a secret language that they used to commiserate with each other about the griefs of marriage.

35   In many societies of the past, sexual loyalty was not a high priority. The expectation of mutual fidelity is a rather recent invention. Numerous cultures have allowed husbands to seek sexual gratification outside marriage. Less frequently, but often enough to challenge common preconceptions, wives have also been allowed to do this without threatening the marriage. In a study of 109 societies, anthropologists found that only 48 forbade extramarital sex to both husbands and wives.

When a woman has sex with someone other than her husband and he doesn't object, anthropologists have traditionally called it wife loaning. When a man does it, they call it male privilege. But in some societies the choice to switch partners rests with the woman. Among the Dogon of West Africa, young married women publicly pursued extramarital relationships with the encouragement of their mothers. Among the Rukuba of Nigeria, a wife can take a lover at the time of her first marriage. This relationship is so embedded in accepted custom that the lover has the right, later in life, to ask his former mistress to marry her daughter to his son.

Among the Eskimo of northern Alaska, as I noted earlier, husbands and wives, with mutual consent, established comarriages with other couples. Some anthropologists believe cospouse relationships were a more socially acceptable outlet for sexual attraction than was marriage itself. Expressing open jealousy about the sexual relationships involved was considered boorish.

Such different notions of marital rights and obligations made divorce and remarriage less emotionally volatile for the Eskimo than it is for most modern Americans. In fact, the Eskimo believed that a remarried person's partner had an obligation to allow the former spouse, as well as any children of that union, the right to fish, hunt, and gather in the new spouse's territory.

Several small-scale societies in South America have sexual and marital norms that are especially startling for Europeans and North Americans. In these groups, people believe that any man who has sex with a woman during her pregnancy contributes part of his biological substance to the child. The husband is recognized as the primary father, but the woman's lover or lovers also have paternal responsibilities, including the obligation to share food with the woman and her child in the future. During the 1990s researchers taking life histories of elderly Bari women in Venezuela found that most had taken lovers during at least one of their pregnancies. Their husbands were usually aware and did not object. When a woman gave birth, she would name all the men she had slept with since learning she was pregnant, and a woman attending the birth would tell each of these men: "You have a child."

40   In Europe and the United States today such an arrangement would be a surefire recipe for jealousy, bitter breakups, and very mixed-up kids. But among the Bari people this practice was in the best interests of the child. The secondary fathers were expected to provide the child with fish and game, with the result that a child with a secondary father was twice as likely to live to the age of fifteen as a brother or sister without such a father.

Few other societies have incorporated extramarital relationships so successfully into marriage and child rearing. But all these examples of differing marital and sexual norms make it difficult to claim there is some universal model for the success or happiness of a marriage.

About two centuries ago Western Europe and North America developed a whole set of new values about the way to organize marriage and sexuality, and many of these values are now spreading across the globe. In this Western model, people expect marriage to satisfy more of their psychological and social needs than ever before. Marriage is supposed to be free of the coercion, violence, and gender inequalities that were tolerated in the past. Individuals want marriage to meet most of their needs for intimacy and affection and all their needs for sex.

Never before in history had societies thought that such a set of high expectations about marriage was either realistic or desirable. Although many Europeans and Americans found tremendous joy in building their relationships around these values, the adoption of these unprecedented goals for marriage had unanticipated and revolutionary consequences that have since come to threaten the stability of the entire institution.

• • •

[B]y the beginning of the seventeenth century a distinctive marriage system had taken root in Western Europe, with a combination of features that together not only made it different from marriage anywhere else in the world but also made it capable of very rapid transformation. Strict divorce laws made it difficult to end a marriage, but this was coupled with more individual freedom to choose or refuse a partner. Concubinage had no legal status. Couples tended to marry later and to be closer to each other in age. And upon marriage a couple typically established an independent household.

45   During the eighteenth century the spread of the market economy and the advent of the Enlightenment wrought profound changes in record time. By the

end of the 1700s personal choice of partners had replaced arranged marriage as a social ideal, and individuals were encouraged to marry for love. For the first time in five thousand years, marriage came to be seen as a private relationship between two individuals rather than one link in a larger system of political and economic alliances. The measure of a successful marriage was no longer how big a financial settlement was involved, how many useful in-laws were acquired, or how many children were produced, but how well a family met the emotional needs of its individual members. Where once marriage had been seen as the fundamental unit of work and politics, it was now viewed as a place of refuge from work, politics, and community obligations.

The image of husbands and wives was also transformed during the eighteenth century. The husband, once the supervisor of the family labor force, came to be seen as the person who, by himself, provided for the family. The wife's role was redefined to focus on her emotional and moral contributions to family life rather than her economic inputs. The husband was the family's economic motor, and the wife its sentimental core.

Two seismic social changes spurred these changes in marriage norms. First, the spread of wage labor made young people less dependent on their parents for a start in life. A man didn't have to delay marriage until he inherited land or took over a business from his father. A woman could more readily earn her own dowry. As day labor replaced apprenticeships and provided alternatives to domestic service, young workers were no longer obliged to live in a master's home for several years. They could marry as soon as they were able to earn sufficient wages.

Second, the freedoms afforded by the market economy had their parallel in new political and philosophical ideas. Starting in the mid-seventeenth century, some political theorists began to challenge the ideas of absolutism. Such ideas gained more adherents during the eighteenth-century Enlightenment, when influential thinkers across Europe championed individual rights and insisted that social relationships, including those between men and women, be organized on the basis of reason and justice rather than force. Believing the pursuit of happiness to be a legitimate goal, they advocated marrying for love rather than wealth or status. Historian Jeffrey Watts writes that although the sixteenth-century Reformation had already "enhanced the dignity of married life by denying the superiority of celibacy," the eighteenth-century Enlightenment "exalted marriage even further by making love the most important criterion in choosing a spouse."

The Enlightenment also fostered a more secular view of social institutions than had prevailed in the sixteenth and seventeenth centuries. Marriage came to be seen as a private contract that ought not be too closely regulated by church or state. After the late eighteenth century, according to one U.S. legal historian, marriage was increasingly defined as a private agreement with public consequences, rather than as a public institution whose roles and duties were rigidly determined by the family's place in the social hierarchy.

50   The new norms of the love-based, intimate marriage did not fall into place all at once but were adopted at different rates in various regions and social groups. In England, the celebration of the love match reached a fever pitch as

early as the 1760s and 1770s, while the French were still commenting on the novelty of "marriage by fascination" in the mid-1800s. Many working-class families did not adopt the new norms of marital intimacy until the twentieth century.

But there was a clear tipping point during the eighteenth century. In England, a new sentimentalization of wives and mothers pushed older anti-female diatribes to the margins of polite society. Idealization of marriage reached such heights that the meaning of the word *spinster* began to change. Originally an honorable term reserved for a woman who spun yarn, by the 1600s it had come to mean any woman who was not married. In the 1700s the word took on a negative connotation for the first time, the flip side of the new reverence accorded to wives.

In France, the propertied classes might still view marriage as "a kind of joint-stock affair," in the words of one disapproving Englishwoman, but the common people more and more frequently talked about marriage as the route to "happiness" and "peace." One study found that before the 1760s fewer than 10 percent of French couples seeking annulments argued that a marriage should be based on emotional attachment to be fully valid, but by the 1770s more than 40 percent thought so.

Romantic ideals spread in America too. In the two decades after the American Revolution, New Englanders began to change their description of an ideal mate, adding companionship and cooperation to their traditional expectations of thrift and industriousness.

These innovations spread even to Russia, where Tsar Peter the Great undertook westernizing the country's army, navy, bureaucracy, and marriage customs all at once. In 1724 he outlawed forced marriages, requiring bride and groom to swear that each had consented freely to the match. Russian authors extolled "the bewitchment and sweet tyranny of love."

55   The court records of Neuchâtel, in what is now Switzerland, reveal the sea change that occurred in the legal norms of marriage. In the sixteenth and seventeenth centuries, judges had followed medieval custom in forcing individuals to honor betrothals and marriage contracts that had been properly made, even if one or both parties no longer wanted the match. In the eighteenth century, by contrast, judges routinely released people from unwanted marriage contracts and engagements, so long as the couple had no children. It was no longer possible for a man to force a woman to keep a marriage promise.

In contrast to the stories of knightly chivalry that had dominated secular literature in the Middle Ages, late eighteenth-century and early nineteenth-century novels depicted ordinary lives. Authors and audiences alike were fascinated by domestic scenes and family relations that had held no interest for medieval writers. Many popular works about love and marriage were syrupy love stories or melodramatic tales of betrayals. But in the hands of more sophisticated writers, such as Jane Austen, clever satires of arranged marriages and the financial aspects of courtship were transformed into great literature.

One result of these changes was a growing rejection of the legitimacy of domestic violence. By the nineteenth century, male wife-beaters rather than female "scolds" had become the main target of village shaming rituals in much of Europe. Meanwhile, middle- and upper-class writers condemned wife beating as a "lower-class" vice in which no "respectable" man would indulge.

Especially momentous for relations between husband and wife was the weakening of the political model upon which marriage had long been based. Until the late seventeenth century the family was thought of as a miniature monarchy, with the husband king over his dependents. As long as political absolutism remained unchallenged in society as a whole, so did the hierarchy of traditional marriage. But the new political ideals fostered by the Glorious Revolution in England in 1688 and the even more far-reaching revolutions in America and France in the last quarter of the eighteenth century dealt a series of cataclysmic blows to the traditional justification of patriarchal authority.

In the late seventeenth century John Locke argued that governmental authority was simply a contract between ruler and ruled and that if a ruler exceeded the authority his subjects granted him, he could be replaced. In 1698 he suggested that marriage too could be seen as a contract between equals. Locke still believed that men would normally rule their families because of their greater strength and ability, but another English writer, Mary Astell, pushed Locke's theories to what she thought was their logical conclusion, "If Absolute Sovereignty be not necessary in a State," Astell asked, "how comes it to be so in a Family?" She answered that not only was absolutism unnecessary within marriage, but it was actually "more mischievous in Families than in kingdomes," by exactly the same amount as "100,000 tyrants are worse than one."

60 During the eighteenth century people began to focus more on the mutual obligations required in marriage. Rejecting analogies between the absolute rights of a husband and the absolute rights of a king, they argued that marital order should be based on love and reason, not on a husband's arbitrary will. The French writer the Marquis de Condorcet and the British author Mary Wollstonecraft went so far as to call for complete equality within marriage.

Only a small minority of thinkers, even in "enlightened" circles, endorsed equality between the sexes. Jean Jacques Rousseau, one of the most enthusiastic proponents of romantic love and harmonious marriage, also wrote that a woman should be trained to "docility ... for she will always be in subjection to a man, or to man's judgment, and she will never be free to set her own opinion above his." The German philosopher J. G. Fichte argued in 1795 that a woman could be "free and independent only as long as she had no husband." Perhaps, he opined, a woman might be eligible to run for office if she promised not to marry. "But no rational woman can give such a promise, nor can the state rationally accept it. For woman is destined to love, and ... when she loves, it is her duty to marry."

In the heady atmosphere of the American and French revolutions of 1776 and 1789, however, many individuals dared draw conclusions that anticipated feminist demands for marital reform and women's rights of the early twentieth century. And even before that, skeptics warned that making love and companionship the core of marriage would open a Pandora's box.

The Revolutionary Implications of the Love Match

The people who pioneered the new ideas about love and marriage were not, by and large, trying to create anything like the egalitarian partnerships that modern Westerners associate with companionship, intimacy, and "true love." Their aim was to make marriage more secure by getting rid of the cynicism that accompanied mercenary marriage and encouraging couples to place each other first in their affections and loyalties.

But basing marriage on love and companionship represented a break with thousands of years of tradition. Many contemporaries immediately recognized the dangers this entailed. They worried that the unprecedented idea of basing marriage on love would produce rampant individualism.

65   Critics of the love match argued—prematurely, as it turns out, but correctly—that the values of free choice and egalitarianism could easily spin out of control. If the choice of a marriage partner was a personal decision, conservatives asked, what would prevent young people, especially women, from choosing unwisely? If people were encouraged to expect marriage to be the best and happiest experience of their lives, what would hold a marriage together if things went "for worse" rather than "for better"?

If wives and husbands were intimates, wouldn't women demand to share decisions equally? If women possessed the same faculties of reason as men, why would they confine themselves to domesticity? Would men still financially support women and children if they lost control over their wives' and children's labor and could not even discipline them properly? If parents, church, and state no longer dictated people's private lives, how could society make sure the right people married and had children or stop the wrong ones from doing so?

Conservatives warned that "the pursuit of happiness," claimed as a right in the American Declaration of Independence, would undermine the social and moral order. Preachers declared that parishioners who placed their husbands or wives before God in their hierarchy of loyalty and emotion were running the risk of becoming "idolaters." In 1774 a writer in England's *Lady Magazine* commented tartly that "the idea of matrimony" was not "for men and women to be always taken up with each other" or to seek personal self-fulfillment in their love. The purpose of marriage was to get people "to discharge the duties of civil society, to govern their families with prudence and to educate their children with discretion."

There was a widespread fear that the pursuit of personal happiness could undermine self-discipline. One scholar argues that this fear explains the extraordinary panic about masturbation that swept the United States and Europe at the end of the eighteenth century and produced thousands of tracts against "the solitary vice" in the nineteenth. The threat of female masturbation particularly repelled and fascinated eighteenth-century social critics. To some it seemed a short step from two people neglecting their social duties because they were "taken up with each other" to one person pleasuring herself without fulfilling a duty to anyone else at all.

As it turned out, it took another hundred years for the contradictions that gave rise to these fears to pose a serious threat to the stability of the new system of marriage.

● Review Questions

1. What are the two main reasons, according to Coontz, that the norms about the relationship between love and marriage began to change in the eighteenth century?

2. According to Coontz, what was the aim of people who championed the "love match" model of marriage in the eighteenth century?

3. What did a conservative writer in a 1774 issue of England's *Lady Magazine* claim was the purpose of marriage?

4. Describe the two values that critics of the "love match" feared could lead to widespread individualism. Cite at least one feared consequence of each value.

● Discussion and Writing Suggestions

1. Coontz begins the selection with a cynical observation of marriage by George Bernard Shaw: that marriage brings together two people "under the influence of the most violent, most insane, most delusive, and most transient of passions. They are required to swear that they will remain in that excited, abnormal, and exhausting condition until death do them part." To what extent—before your reading of this selection—would you (or others you know) have subscribed to the assumptions about marriage that are the object of Shaw's scorn? To what extent do you think that Shaw is overstating the case? Explain.

2. Coontz notes that only a "small minority" of the Enlightenment thinkers who called for greater equality within marriage actually endorsed equality between the sexes. Is there a difference between equality within marriage and equality between the sexes? Is it contradictory to believe in one but not the other? Explain your answer.

3. Coontz writes that with the advent of the love-based marriage, "The measure of a successful marriage was no longer how big a financial settlement was involved, how many useful in-laws were acquired, or how many children were produced, but how well a family met the emotional needs of its individual members." To what degree would you agree that this statement describes the reality of modern marriages? Do you feel that issues such as money, number of offspring, and in-laws can or should be separated from the "emotional needs" of husband and wife? If possible, when stating your opinion, cite specific examples of marriages you have known about or witnessed.

4. Critics of the love match argued that allowing people to choose their mates would also allow them to choose badly. But presumably some arranged marriages also resulted in bad matches. Do you feel that one sort of bad match is worse than the other? And what does a "bad match" mean, exactly?

5. In her historical and cultural survey of attitudes toward love in marriage, Coontz notes that many cultures have believed that married people should "love" one another. But these cultures have also differentiated married love from romantic love, which they felt was transitory and fleeting. Do you see any distinction(s) between married love and romantic love?

THE STATE OF OUR UNIONS

David Popenoe and Barbara Dafoe Whitehead

At the end of the previous selection, Stephanie Coontz hinted at the consequences that the rise of the "love match" would have for the institution of marriage. So how is marriage faring? In the following selection, the codirectors of the National Marriage Project at Rutgers State University warn that the institutions of marriage and family are in a state of crisis. David Popenoe is a professor of sociology at Rutgers University in New Brunswick, New Jersey. An expert in the study of marriage and family life, he has written or edited ten books, most recently *War Over the Family* (2005). Barbara Dafoe Whitehead lectures and writes on the well-being of families and children for scholarly and popular audiences. She is the author of *The Divorce Culture: Rethinking Our Commitment to Marriage and Family* (1997). The following selection combines sections of Popenoe and Whitehead's 2002 and 2005 reports on marriage, presented here in three parts: Marriage, Divorce, and Unmarried Cohabitation. The earlier report appeared in *USA Today Magazine* in July 2002. The later report appears on the National Marriage Project Web site at http://marriage.rutgers.edu/Publications/SOOO/TEXTSOOU2005.htm. Data in figures have been updated to reflect those contained in the authors' 2007 report.

Each year, the National Marriage Project at Rutgers University publishes an assessment of the health of marriage and marital relationships in America entitled "The State of Our Unions." It is based on a thorough review and evaluation of the latest statistics and research findings about marriage, family, and courtship trends, plus our own special surveys.

Americans haven't given up on marriage as a cherished ideal. Indeed, most continue to prize and value it as an important life goal, and the vast majority (an estimated 85%) will marry at least once in a lifetime. Almost all couples enter marriage with a strong desire and determination for a life-long, loving partnership, and this desire may even be increasing among the young. Since the 1980s, the percentage of high school seniors who say that having a good marriage is extremely important to them as a life goal has gone up, though only slightly.

• • •

Marriage

Key Finding: Marriage trends in recent decades indicate that Americans have become less likely to marry, and the most recent data show that the marriage rate in the United States continues to decline. Of those who do marry, there has been a moderate drop since the 1970s in the percentage of couples who consider their marriages to be "very happy," but in the past decade this trend has swung in a positive direction.

Americans have become less likely to marry. This is reflected in a decline of nearly 50 percent, from 1970 to 2004, in the annual number of marriages per 1,000 unmarried adult women (Figure 1). Some of this decline—it is not clear just how much—results from the delaying of first marriages until older ages: the median age at first marriage went from 20 for females and 23 for males in 1960 to about 26 and 27, respectively, in 2004. Other factors accounting for the decline are the growth of unmarried cohabitation and a small decrease in the tendency of divorced persons to remarry.

5   The decline also reflects some increase in lifelong singlehood, though the actual amount cannot be known until current young and middle-aged adults pass through the life course.

The percentage of adults in the population who are currently married has also diminished. Since 1960, the decline of those married among all persons age 15 and older has been 14 percentage points—and over 29 points among black females (Figure 2). It should be noted that these data include both people who have never married and those who have married and then divorced. (For some economic implications of the decline of marriage, see the accompanying box: "The Surprising Economic Benefits of Marriage.")

In order partially to control for a decline in married adults simply due to delayed first marriages, we have looked at changes in the percentage of

Figure 1　Number of Marriages per 1,000 Unmarried Women Age 15 and Older, by Year, United States[a]

Year	Number[b]
1960	73.5
1970	76.5
1975	66.9
1980	61.4
1985	56.2
1990	54.5
1995	50.8
2000	46.5
2005	40.7

a. We have used the number of marriages per 1,000 unmarried women age 15 and older, rather than the Crude Marriage Rate of marriages per 1,000 population to help avoid the problem of compositional changes in the population, that is, changes which stem merely from there being more or less people in the marriageable ages. Even this more refined measure is somewhat susceptible to compositional changes.
b. Per 1,000 unmarried women age 14 and older.

Source: U.S. Department of the Census, Statistical Abstract of the United States, 2001, Page 87, Table 117; and Statistical Abstract of the United States, 1986, Page 79, Table 124. Figure for 2004 was obtained using data from the Current Population Surveys, March 2004 Supplement, as well as Births, Marriages, Divorces, and Deaths: Provisional Data for 2004, National Vital Statistics Report 53:21, June 26, 2005, Table 3. (http://www.cdc.gov/nchs/data/nvsr/nvsr53/nvsr53_21.pdf) The CPS, March Supplement, is based on a sample of the U.S. population, rather than an actual count such as those available from the decennial census. See sampling and weighting notes at http://www.bis.census.gov:80/cps/ads/2002/ssampwgt.htm

Figure 2   Percentage of All Persons Age 15 and Older Who Were Married, by Sex and Race, 1960–2006, United States[a]

Year	Total Males	Black Males	White Males	Total Females	Black Females	White Females
1960	69.3	60.9	70.2	65.9	59.8	66.6
1970	66.7	56.9	68	61.9	54.1	62.8
1980	63.2	48.8	65	58.9	44.6	60.7
1990	60.7	45.1	62.8	56.9	40.2	59.1
2000	57.9	42.8	60	54.7	36.2	57.4
2006[b]	56.3	40.9	58.5	53.4	34.3	56.3

a. Includes races other than Black and White.
b. In 2003, the U.S. Census Bureau expanded its racial categories to permit respondents to identify themselves as belonging to more than one race. This means that racial data computations beginning in 2004 may not be strictly comparable to those in prior years.

Source: U.S. Bureau of the Census, Current Population Reports, Series P20-506; America's Families and Living Arrangements: March 2000 and earlier reports; and data calculated from the Current Population Surveys, March 2004 Supplement.

persons age 35 through 44 who were married (Figure 3). Since 1960, there has been a drop of 22 percentage points for married men and 20 points for married women.

Marriage trends in the age range of 35 to 44 are suggestive of lifelong single-hood. In times past and still today, virtually all persons who were going to marry during their lifetimes had married by age 45. More than 90 percent of women have married eventually in every generation for which records exist, going back to the mid-1800s. By 1960, 94 percent of women then alive had been

Figure 3   Percentage of Persons Age 35 through 44 Who Were Married, by Sex, 1960–2006, United States

Year	Males	Females
1960	88.0	87.4
1970	89.3	86.9
1980	84.2	81.4
1990	74.1	73.0
2000	69.0	71.6
2006	67.9	69.5

Source: U.S. Bureau of the Census, Statistical Abstract of the United States, 1961, Page 34, Table 27; Statistical Abstract of the United States, 1971, Page 32, Table 38; Statistical Abstract of the United States, 1981, Page 38, Table 49; and U.S. Bureau of the Census, General Population Characteristics, 1990, Page 45, Table 34; and Statistical Abstract of the United States, 2001, Page 48, Table 51; internet tables (http://www.census.gov/population/socdemo/hh-fam/cps2003/tabA1-all.pdf) and data calculated from the Current Population Surveys, March 2004 Supplement. Figure for 2004 was obtained using data from the Current Population Surveys rather than data from the census. The CPS, March Supplement, is based on a sample of the U.S. population, rather than an actual count such as those available from the decennial census. See sampling and weighting notes at http://www.bls.census.gov:80/cps/ads/2002/ssampwgt.htm

married at least once by age 45—probably an historical high point.[1] For the generation of 1995, assuming a continuation of then current marriage rates, several demographers projected that 88 percent of women and 82 percent of men would ever marry.[2] If and when these figures are recalculated for the early years of the 21st century, the percentage of women and men ever marrying will almost certainly be lower.

It is important to note that the decline in marriage does not mean that people are giving up on living together with a sexual partner. On the contrary, with the incidence of unmarried cohabitation increasing rapidly, marriage is giving ground to unwed unions. Most people now live together before they marry for the first time. An even higher percentage of those divorced who subsequently remarry live together first. And a growing number of persons, both young and old, are living together with no plans for eventual marriage.

10   There is a common belief that, although a smaller percentage of Americans are now marrying than was the case a few decades ago, those who marry have marriages of higher quality. It seems reasonable that if divorce removes poor marriages from the pool of married couples and cohabitation "trial marriages" deter some bad marriages from forming, the remaining marriages on average should be happier. The best available evidence on the topic, however, does not support these assumptions. Since 1973, the General Social Survey periodically has asked representative samples of married Americans to rate their marriages as either "very happy," "pretty happy," or "not too happy."[3]

Figure 4   Percentage of Married Persons Age 18 and Older Who Said Their Marriages Were "Very Happy," by Period, United States

Period	Men	Women
1973–1976	69.6	68.6
1977–1981	68.3	64.2
1982–1986	62.9	61.7
1987–1991	66.4	59.6
1993–1996	63.2	59.7
1998–2004	64.4	60.4

Source: The General Social Survey, conducted by the National Opinion Research Center of the University of Chicago. The trend for both men and women is statistically significant (p < .01 on a two-tailed test).

---

[1]Andrew J. Cherlin, *Marriage, Divorce, and Remarriage* (Cambridge, MA: Harvard University Press, 1992): 10; Michael R. Haines, "Long-Term Marriage Patterns in the United States from Colonial Times to the Present," *The History of the Family* 1-1 (1996): 15–39.

[2]Robert Schoen and Nicola Standish, "The Retrenchment of Marriage: Results from Marital Status Life Tables for the United States, 1995." *Population and Development Review* 27-3 (2001): 553–563.

[3]Conducted by the National Opinion Research Center of the University of Chicago, this is a nationally representative study of the English-speaking, non-institutionalized population of the United States age 18 and over.

As Figure 4 indicates, the percentage of both men and women saying "very happy" has declined moderately over the past 25 years.[4] This trend, however, is now heading in a positive direction.

THE SURPRISING ECONOMIC BENEFITS OF MARRIAGE

When thinking of the many benefits of marriage, the economic aspects are often overlooked. Yet the economic benefits of marriage are substantial, both for individuals and for society as a whole. Marriage is a wealth generating institution. Married couples create more economic assets on average than do otherwise similar singles or cohabiting couples. A 1992 study of retirement data concluded that "individuals who are not continuously married have significantly lower wealth than those who remain married throughout their lives." Compared to those continuously married, those who never married have a reduction in wealth of 75% and those who divorced and didn't remarry have a reduction of 73%.[a]

One might think that the explanation for why marriage generates economic assets is because those people who are more likely to be wealth creators are also more likely to marry and stay married. And this is certainly true, but only in part. The institution of marriage itself provides a wealth-generation bonus. It does this through providing economies of scale (two can live more cheaply than one), and as implicitly a long-term personal contract it encourages economic specialization. Working as a couple, individuals can develop those skills in which they excel, leaving others to their partner.

Also, married couples save and invest more for the future, and they can act as a small insurance pool against life uncertainties such as illness and job loss.[b] Probably because of marital social norms that encourage healthy, productive behavior, men tend to become more economically productive after marriage; they earn between 10 and 40% more than do single men with similar education and job histories.[c] All of these benefits are independent of the fact that married couples receive more work-related and government-provided support, and also more help and support from their extended families (two sets of in-laws) and friends.[d]

Beyond the economic advantages of marriage for the married couples themselves, marriage has a tremendous economic impact on society. It is a major contributor to family income levels and inequality. After more than doubling between 1947 and 1977, the growth of median family income has slowed over the past 20 years, increasing by just 9.6%. A big reason is that married couples, who fare better economically than their single counterparts,

---

[4]Using a different data set that compared marriages in 1980 with marriages in 1992, equated in terms of marital duration, Stacy J. Rogers and Paul Amato found similarly that the 1992 marriages had less marital interaction, more marital conflict, and more marital problems. "Is Marital Quality Declining? The Evidence from Two Generations," *Social Forces* 75 (1997): 1089.

have been a rapidly decreasing proportion of total families. In this same 20 year period, and largely because of changes in family structure, family income inequality has increased significantly.[e]

Research has shown consistently that both divorce and unmarried child-bearing increase child poverty. In recent years the majority of children who grow up outside of married families have experienced at least one year of dire poverty.[f] According to one study, if family structure had not changed between 1960 and 1998, the black child poverty rate in 1998 would have been 28.4% rather than 45.6%, and the white child poverty rate would have been 11.4% rather than 15.4%.[g] The rise in child poverty, of course, generates significant public costs in health and welfare programs.

Marriages that end in divorce also are very costly to the public. One researcher determined that a single divorce costs state and federal governments about $30,000, based on such things as the higher use of food stamps and public housing as well as increased bankruptcies and juvenile delinquency. The nation's 1.4 million divorces in 2002 are estimated to have cost the taxpayers more than $30 billion.[h]

Notes

a. Janet Wilmoth and Gregor Koso, "Does Marital History Matter? Marital Status and Wealth Outcomes Among Preretirement Adults," *Journal of Marriage and the Family* 64:254–68, 2002.

b. Thomas A. Hirschl, Joyce Altobelli, and Mark R. Rank, "Does Marriage Increase the Odds of Affluence? Exploring the Life Course Probabilities," *Journal of Marriage and the Family* 65-4 (2003): 927–938; Joseph Lupton and James P. Smith, "Marriage, Assets and Savings," in Shoshana A. Grossbard-Schectman (ed.) *Marriage and the Economy* (Cambridge: Cambridge University Press, 2003): 129–152.

c. Jeffrey S. Gray and Michael J. Vanderhart, "The Determination of Wages: Does Marriage Matter?," in Linda Waite, et al. (eds.) *The Ties that Bind: Perspectives on Marriage and Cohabitation* (New York: Aldine de Gruyter, 2000): 356–367; S. Korenman and D. Neumark, "Does Marriage Really Make Men More Productive?" *Journal of Human Resources* 26-2 (1991): 282–307; K. Daniel, "The Marriage Premium," in M. Tomassi and K. Ierulli (eds.) *The New Economics of Human Behavior* (Cambridge: Cambridge University Press, 1995) 113–125.

d. Lingxin Hao, "Family Structure, Private Transfers, and the Economic Well-Being of Families with Children," *Social Forces* 75 (1996): 269–292.

e. U.S. Bureau of the Census, Current Population Reports, P60-203, *Measuring 50 Years of Economic Change Using the March Current Population Survey,* U.S. Government Printing Office, Washington, DC, 1998; John Iceland, "Why Poverty Remains High: The Role of Income Growth, Economic Inequality, and Changes in Family Structure, 1949–1999," *Demography* 40-3:499–519, 2003.

f. Mark R. Rank and Thomas A. Hirschl, "The Economic Risk of Childhood in America: Estimating the Probability of Poverty Across the Formative Years," *Journal of Marriage and the Family* 61:1058–1067, 1999.

g. Adam Thomas and Isabel Sawhill, "For Richer or For Poorer: Marriage as an Antipoverty Strategy," *Journal of Policy Analysis and Management* 21:4, 2002.

h. David Schramm, "The Costly Consequences of Divorce in Utah: The Impact on Couples, Community, and Government," Logan, UT: Utah State University, 2003. Unpublished preliminary report.

Divorce

Key Finding: The American divorce rate today is nearly twice that of 1960, but has declined slightly since hitting the highest point in our history in the early 1980s. For the average couple marrying in recent years, the lifetime probability of divorce or separation remains between 40 and 50 percent.

The increase in divorce, shown by the trend reported in Figure 5, probably has elicited more concern and discussion than any other family-related trend in the United States. Although the long-term trend in divorce has been upward since colonial times, the divorce rate was level for about two decades after World War II during the period of high fertility known as the baby boom. By the middle of the 1960s, however, the incidence of divorce started to increase and it more than doubled over the next fifteen years to reach an historical high point in the early 1980s. Since then the divorce rate has modestly declined, a trend described by many experts as "leveling off at a high level." The decline apparently represents a slight increase in marital stability.[5] Two probable reasons for this are an increase in the age at which people marry for the first time, and a higher educational level of those marrying, both of which are associated with greater marital stability.[6]

Figure 5   Number of Divorces per 1,000 Married Women Age 15 and Older, by Year, United States[a]

Year	Divorces
1960	9.2
1965	10.6
1970	14.9
1975	20.3
1980	22.6
1985	21.7
1990	20.9
1995	19.8
2000	18.8
2005	16.4

a. We have used the number of divorces per 1,000 married women age 15 and older, rather than the Crude Divorce Rate of divorces per 1,000 population to help avoid the problem of compositional changes in the population. Even this more refined measure is somewhat susceptible to compositional changes.

Source: Statistical Abstract of the United States, 2001, Page 87, Table 117; National Vital Statistics Reports, August 22, 2001; California Current Population Survey Report: 2000, Table 3, March 2001; Births, Marriages, Divorces, and Deaths: Provisional Data for 2004, National Vital Statistics Report 53:21, June 26, 2005, Table 3, (http://www.cdc.gov/nchs/data/nvsr/nvsr53/nvsr53_21.pdf) and calculations by the National Marriage Project for the U.S. [not including] California, Georgia, Hawaii, Indiana, Louisiana and Oklahoma using the Current Population Surveys, 2004.

---

[5]Joshua R. Goldstein, "The Leveling of Divorce in the United States," *Demography* 36 (1999): 409–414.
[6]Tim B. Heaton, "Factors Contributing to Increased Marital Stability in the United States," *Journal of Family Issues* 23 (2002): 392–409.

Figure 6 Percentage of All Persons Age 15 and Older Who Were Divorced, by Sex and Race, 1960–2006, United States

Year	Males			Females		
	Total	Blacks	Whites	Total	Blacks	Whites
1960	1.8	2	1.8	2.6	4.3	2.5
1970	2.2	3.1	2.1	3.5	4.4	3.4
1980	4.8	6.3	4.7	6.6	8.7	6.4
1990	6.8	8.1	6.8	8.9	11.2	8.6
2000	8.3	9.5	8.4	10.2	11.8	10.2
2006[a]	8.6	9.4	8.7	10.9	12.9	10.9

a. In 2003, the U.S. Census Bureau expanded its racial categories to permit respondents to identify themselves as belonging to more than one race. This means that racial data computations beginning in 2004 may not be strictly comparable to those of prior years.

Source: U.S. Bureau of the Census, Current Population Reports, Series P20-537; America's Families and Living Arrangements: March 2000 and earlier reports; and Current Population Surveys, March 2004 supplement, raw data.

Although a majority of divorced persons eventually remarry, the growth of divorce has led to a steep increase in the percentage of all adults who are currently divorced (Figure 6). This percentage, which was only 1.8 percent for males and 2.6 percent for females in 1960, quadrupled by the year 2000. The percentage of divorce is higher for females than for males primarily because divorced men are more likely to remarry than divorced women. Also, among those who do remarry, men generally do so sooner than women.

Overall, the chances remain very high—estimated between 40 and 50 percent—that a marriage started in recent years will end in either divorce or separation before one partner dies.[7] (But see the accompanying box: "Your Chances of Divorce May Be Much Lower Than You Think.") The likelihood of divorce has varied considerably among different segments of the American population, being higher for Blacks than for Whites, for instance, and higher in the West than in other parts of the country. But these variations have been diminishing. The trend toward a greater similarity of divorce rates between Whites and Blacks is largely attributable to the fact that fewer blacks are marrying.[8] Divorce rates in the South and Midwest have come to resemble those in the West, for reasons that are not well understood, leaving only the Eastern Seaboard and the Central Plains with significantly lower divorce.

15 At the same time, there has been little change in such traditionally large divorce rate differences as between those who marry when they are teenagers compared to those who marry after age 21, high-school drop outs versus college graduates, and the non-religious compared to the religiously committed. Teenagers, high-school drop outs, and the non-religious who marry have considerably higher divorce rates.[9]

---

[7]Robert Schoen and Nicola Standish, "The Retrenchment of Marriage: Results from Marital Status Life Tables for the United States, 1995," *Population and Development Review* 27-3 (2001): 553–563; R. Kelly Raley and Larry Bumpass, "The Topography of the Divorce Plateau: Levels and Trends in Union Stability in the United States after 1980," *Demographic Research* 8-8 (2003): 245–259.
[8]Jay D. Teachman, "Stability across Cohorts in Divorce Risk Factors," *Demography* 39-2 (2002): 331–351.
[9]Raley and Bumpass, 2003.

Unmarried Cohabitation

Key Finding: The number of unmarried couples has increased dramatically over the past four decades, and the increase is continuing. Most younger Americans now spend some time living together outside of marriage, and unmarried cohabitation commonly precedes marriage.

YOUR CHANCES OF DIVORCE MAY BE MUCH LOWER THAN YOU THINK

By now almost everyone has heard that the national divorce rate is close to 50% of all marriages. This is true, but the rate must be interpreted with caution and several important caveats. For many people, the actual chances of divorce are far below 50/50.

The background characteristics of people entering a marriage have major implications for their risk of divorce. Here are some percentage point decreases in the risk of divorce or separation *during the first ten years of marriage,* according to various personal and social factors:[a]

Factors	Percent Decrease in Risk of Divorce
Annual income over $50,000 (vs. under $25,000)	−30
Having a baby seven months or more after marriage (vs. before marriage)	−24
Marrying over 25 years of age (vs. under 18)	−24
Own family of origin intact (vs. divorced parents)	−14
Religious affiliation (vs. none)	−14
Some college (vs. high-school dropout)	−13

So if you are a reasonably well-educated person with a decent income, come from an intact family and are religious, and marry after age twenty-five without having a baby first, your chances of divorce are very low indeed.

Also, it should be realized that the "close to 50%" divorce rate refers to the percentage of marriages entered into during a particular year that are projected to end in divorce or separation before one spouse dies. Such projections assume that the divorce and death rates occurring that year will continue indefinitely into the future—an assumption that is useful more as an indicator of the instability of marriages in the recent past than as a predictor of future events. In fact, the divorce rate has been dropping, slowly, since reaching a peak around 1980, and the rate could be lower (or higher) in the future than it is today.[b]

Notes

a. Matthew D. Bramlett and William D. Mosher, *Cohabitation, Marriage, Divorce and Remarriage in the United States,* National Center for Health Statistics, Vital and Health Statistics, 23 (22), 2002. The risks are calculated for women only.

b. Rose M. Kreider and Jason M. Fields, "Number, Timing and Duration of Marriages and Divorces, 1996," *Current Population Reports,* P70–80, Washington, DC: U.S. Census Bureau, 2002.

Between 1960 and 2004, as indicated in Figure 7, the number of unmarried couples in America increased by nearly 1200 percent. Unmarried cohabitation—the status of couples who are sexual partners, not married to each other, and sharing a household—is particularly common among the young. It is estimated that about a quarter of unmarried women age 25 to 39 are currently living with a partner and an additional quarter have lived with a partner at some time in the past. Over half of all first marriages are now preceded by living together, compared to virtually none 50 years ago.[10]

For many, cohabitation is a prelude to marriage, for others, simply an alternative to living alone, and for a small but growing number, it is considered an alternative to marriage. Cohabitation is more common among those of lower educational and income levels. Recent data show that among women in the 19 to 44 age range, 60 percent of high-school dropouts have cohabited compared to 37 percent of college graduates.[11] Cohabitation is also more common among

Figure 7   Number, in Thousands, of Cohabiting, Unmarried, Adult Couples of the Opposite Sex, by Year, United States

Year	Number
1960	439
1970	523
1980	1,589
1990	2,856
2000	4,736
2006	5,368

Source: U.S. Bureau of the Census, Current Population Reports, Series P20–537; America's Families and Living Arrangements: March 2000; and U.S. Bureau of the Census, Population Division, Current Population Survey, 2004 Annual Social and Economic Supplement (http://www.census.gov/population/socdemo/hh-fam/cps2004).

---

[10]Larry Bumpass and Hsien-Hen Lu, "Trends in Cohabitation and Implications for Children's Family Contexts in the U. S.," *Population Studies* 54 (2000) 29–41.

[11]Bumpass and Lu, 2000.

those who are less religious than their peers, those who have been divorced, and those who have experienced parental divorce, fatherlessness, or high levels of marital discord during childhood. A growing percentage of cohabiting couple households, now over 40 percent, contain children.

The belief that living together before marriage is a useful way "to find out whether you really get along," and thus avoid a bad marriage and an eventual divorce, is now widespread among young people. But the available data on the effects of cohabitation fail to confirm this belief. In fact, a substantial body of evidence indicates that those who live together before marriage are more likely to break up after marriage. This evidence is controversial, however, because it is difficult to distinguish the "selection effect" from the "experience of cohabitation effect." The selection effect refers to the fact that people who cohabit before marriage have different characteristics from those who do not, and it may be these characteristics, and not the experience of cohabitation, that leads to marital instability. There is some empirical support for both positions. Also, a recent study based on a nationally representative sample of women concluded that premarital cohabitation (and premarital sex), when limited to a woman's future husband, is not associated with an elevated risk of marital disruption.[12] What can be said for certain is that no evidence has yet been found that those who cohabit before marriage have stronger marriages than those who do not.[13]

Conclusions

20   As a **stage in the life course of adults,** marriage is shrinking. Americans are living longer, marrying later, exiting marriages more quickly, and choosing to live together before marriage, after marriage, in between marriages, and as an alternative to marriage. A small but growing percentage, an estimated 15% [as of 2002], will never marry, compared to about five percent during the 1950s. As a consequence, marriage gradually is giving way to partnered and unpartnered singlehood, with or without children. Since 1960, the percentage of persons age 35 through 44 who were married has dropped from 88% to 68% for men and 87% to 70% for women.

As an **institution,** marriage has lost much of its legal, social, economic, and religious meaning and authority. The marital relationship once consisted of an economic bond of mutual dependency, a social bond supported by the extended family and larger community, and a spiritual bond upheld by religious doctrine, observance, and faith. Today, there are many marriages that have none of these elements. The older ideal of marriage as a permanent

---

[12]Jay Teachman, "Premarital Sex, Premarital Cohabitation, and the Risk of Subsequent Marital Disruption among Women," *Journal of Marriage and the Family* 65 (2003): 444–455.

[13]For a full review of the research on cohabitation see: Pamela J. Smock, "Cohabitation in the United States," *Annual Review of Sociology* 26 (2000); and David Popenoe and Barbara Dafoe Whitehead, *Should We Live Together? What Young Adults Need to Know About Cohabitation Before Marriage—A Comprehensive Review of Recent Research,* 2nd Edition (New Brunswick, NJ: The National Marriage Project, Rutgers University, 2002).

contractual union, strongly supported by society and designed for procreation and childrearing, is giving way to a new reality of it as a purely individual contract between two adults. Moreover, marriage is also quietly losing its place in the language and in popular culture. Unmarried people now tend to speak inclusively about "relationships" and "intimate partners." In the entertainment industry—including films, television, and music—marriage is often neglected or discredited.

If these have been the main changes, what, then, has marriage become in 21st-century America? First, let us not forget that many of the marriage-related trends of recent decades have been positive. The legal, sexual, and financial emancipation of women has become a reality as never before in history. With few restrictions on divorce, a married woman who is seriously abused by her husband can get out of the relationship, which she previously might have been stuck in for life. Due to great tolerance of family diversity, adults and children who through no fault of their own end up in nontraditional families are not marked for life by social stigma. Moreover, based on a companionship of equals, many marriages today may be more emotionally satisfying than ever before.

We have described the new marriage system as "emotionally deep, but socially shallow." For most Americans, marriage is a "couples relationship" designed primarily to meet the sexual and emotional needs of the spouses. Increasingly, happiness in marriage is measured by each partner's sense of psychological well-being, rather than the more-traditional measures of getting ahead economically, boosting children up to a higher rung on the educational ladder than the parents, or following religious teachings on marriage. People tend to be puzzled or put off by the idea that marriage has purposes or benefits that extend beyond fulfilling individual adult needs for intimacy and satisfaction. Eight out of 10 of the young adults in our survey agreed that "marriage is nobody's business, but that of the two people involved."

It is a sign of the times that the overwhelming majority (94%) of never-married singles in our survey agreed that "when you marry, you want your spouse to be your soul mate, first and foremost." This perspective, surely encouraged not only by the changing nature of marriage, but by the concern about divorce and therefore the seeming necessity of finding the one right person, is something that most people in the older generation would probably consider surprising. In times past, people married to start a new family, and therefore they looked for a competent and reliable mate to share life's tasks. To the degree that a soul mate was even considered, it was more likely to have been thought of as the end result of a lifetime of effort put into making a marriage work, not something you start out with.

25   Of course, having a soul mate as a marriage partner would be wonderful. In many ways, it is reassuring that today's young people are looking for a marriage that is both meaningful and lasting. Yet, there is a danger that the soul mate expectation sets a standard so high it will be hard to live up to. Also, if people believe that there is just one soul mate waiting somewhere out there for them, as most of today's youths in fact do according to our survey, doesn't it

seem more likely that a marriage partner will be dropped when the going gets rough? Isn't it easier to say, "I must have picked the wrong person"? In other words, perhaps we have developed a standard for marriage that tends to destabilize the institution.

There are some hopeful signs in the recent statistics that may bode well for the future of marriage. The divorce rate has slowly been dropping since the early 1980s. Since the early 1990s, the teen birthrate has decreased by about 20%, with some indications that teenagers have become sexually more conservative. Overall, the percentage of unwed births has remained at its current level for the past five years. Indeed, due to fewer divorces and stabilized unwed births, the percentage of children living in single-parent families dropped slightly in the past few years, after having increased rapidly and continuously since 1960.

Moreover, one can see glimmers of hope here and there on the cultural scene. There are stirrings of a grassroots "marriage movement." Churches in several hundred communities have joined together to establish a common set of premarital counseling standards and practices for engaged couples. Marriage education has emerged as a prominent theme among some family therapists, family life educators, schoolteachers, and clergy. In several states, legislatures have passed bills promoting marriage education in the schools and even seeking ways to cut the divorce rate, mainly through educational means. More books are being published with the theme of how to have a good marriage, and seemingly fewer with the theme of divorcing to achieve personal liberation. Questions are being raised more forcefully by members of Congress, on both sides of the aisle, about the "family values" of the entertainment industry. These positive trends bear watching and are encouraging, but it is too soon to tell whether they will persist or result in the revitalization of this critical social institution.

● Review Questions

1. What factors significantly reduce the incidence of divorce, according to Popenoe and Whitehead?

2. According to Popenoe and Whitehead, which two factors are most likely responsible for the slight increase in marital stability (i.e., a decline in the divorce rate) since the early 1980s?

3. The data show that the percentage of divorced females is higher than that of males. Why?

4. Popenoe and Whitehead suggest that it might it be erroneous to claim that, based on recent data, people who live together before marriage are more likely to experience marital instability. Explain.

● Discussion and Writing Suggestions

1. Popenoe and Whitehead's key finding is that "Marriage trends in recent decades indicate that Americans have become less likely to marry, and . . . that the marriage rate in the United States continues to decline." To what extent does this finding square with your own observations and impressions of contemporary marriage? How do you account for the declining marriage rate?

2. Popenoe and Whitehead assert that, despite the conventional wisdom among many young people that living together before marriage is a useful way to discover whether a couple is really compatible, and therefore to avoid a bad marriage and eventual divorce, "No evidence has yet been found that those who cohabit before marriage have stronger marriages than those who do not." In light of this assertion, have your opinions about whether or not people should live together before marriage changed? Explain your answer.

3. Noting that 94% of never-married singles agreed with the statement that "when you marry, you want your spouse to be your soul mate, first and foremost," Popenoe and Whitehead worry that this "soul mate expectation" sets up an unrealistically high standard for marriage. How do you define "soul mate"? Do you agree that expecting a spouse to be a soul mate can destabilize the institution of marriage?

4. Popenoe and Whitehead claim that, as an institution, marriage has lost much of its "legal, social, economic, and religious meaning and authority," and that marriage is becoming devalued in popular culture. Contrast these statements with the multitudes of bridal magazines on sale at every newsstand and the breathless attention with which tabloids follow celebrity marriages. To what extent does such evidence of our culture's fascination with marriage contradict Popenoe and Whitehead's thesis? Explain your answer.

A DEBATE ON GAY MARRIAGE

There are few more hot-button topics in American politics today than gay marriage. In the Defense of Marriage Act of 1996, the federal government defined marriage as the legal union of a man as husband and a woman as wife. Similar legislation has been passed in 38 states. In November 2003, however, the Massachusetts Supreme Court ruled that denying marriage licenses to gay couples violated the state's Equal Protection Clause. The following year, the city of San Francisco began issuing marriage licenses to gay couples. Hundreds of same-sex couples were legally married in the aftermath of these rulings. Responding in outrage, many conservative state legislatures rushed to pass or reaffirm laws banning gay marriage. In July 2006, court rulings in New York, Nebraska, and Washington limited marriage to unions between a man and a woman. In November 2008, Proposition 8, an initiative to ban gay marriage in California, was passed by 52% of voters; the initiative was subsequently upheld by California's Supreme Court.

FOR GAY MARRIAGE

Andrew Sullivan

The debate over gay marriage highlights a vast cultural divide that typically hinges on core beliefs regarding the nature of marriage itself. In the following selection from Andrew Sullivan's book *Virtually Normal: An Argument about Homosexuality* (1995), Sullivan articulates a vision of marriage as a public contract that should be available to any two citizens. Andrew Sullivan is a former editor of the *New Republic* magazine who writes on a wide range of political and social topics, including gay and lesbian issues. He lives in Washington, D.C.

Marriage is not simply a private contract; it is a social and public recognition of a private commitment. As such, it is the highest public recognition of personal integrity. Denying it to homosexuals is the most public affront possible to their public equality.

This point may be the hardest for many heterosexuals to accept. Even those tolerant of homosexuals may find this institution so wedded to the notion of heterosexual commitment that to extend it would be to undo its very essence. And there may be religious reasons for resisting this that, within certain traditions, are unanswerable. But I am not here discussing what churches do in their private affairs. I am discussing what the allegedly neutral liberal state should do in public matters. For liberals, the case for homosexual marriage is overwhelming. As a classic public institution, it should be available to any two citizens.

Some might argue that marriage is by definition between a man and a woman; and it is difficult to argue with a definition. But if marriage is articulated beyond this circular fiat, then the argument for its exclusivity to one man and one woman disappears. The center of the public contract is an emotional, financial, and psychological bond between two people; in this respect, heterosexuals and homosexuals are identical. The heterosexuality of marriage is intrinsic only if it is understood to be intrinsically procreative; but that definition has long been abandoned in Western society. No civil marriage license is granted on the condition that the couple bear children; and the marriage is no less legal and no less defensible if it remains childless. In the contemporary West, marriage has become a way in which the state recognizes an emotional commitment by two people to each other for life. And within that definition, there is no public way, if one believes in equal rights under the law, in which it should legally be denied homosexuals.

Of course, no public sanctioning of a contract should be given to people who cannot actually fulfill it. The state rightly, for example, withholds marriage from minors, or from one adult and a minor, since at least one party is unable to understand or live up to the contract. And the state has also rightly barred close family relatives from marriage because familial emotional ties are too strong and powerful to enable a marriage contract to be entered into freely by two autonomous, independent individuals, and because incest poses a uniquely dangerous threat to the trust and responsibility that the family needs to survive. But do homosexuals fall into a similar category? History and experience strongly suggest they don't. Of course, marriage is characterized by a kind of commitment that is rare—and perhaps declining—even among heterosexuals. But it isn't necessary to prove that homosexuals or lesbians are less—or more—able to form long-term relationships than straights for it to be clear that at least *some* are. Moreover, giving these people an equal right to affirm their commitment doesn't reduce the incentive for heterosexuals to do the same.

5   In some ways, the marriage issue is exactly parallel to the issue of the military. Few people deny that many homosexuals are capable of the sacrifice, the commitment, and the responsibilities of marriage. And indeed, for many homosexuals and lesbians, these responsibilities are already enjoined—as they have been enjoined for centuries. The issue is whether these identical relationships should be denied equal legal standing, not by virtue of anything to do with the relationships themselves but by virtue of the internal, involuntary nature of the homosexuals involved. Clearly, for liberals, the answer to this is clear. Such a denial is a classic case of unequal protection of the laws.

But perhaps surprisingly, . . . one of the strongest arguments for gay marriage is a conservative one. It's perhaps best illustrated by a comparison with the alternative often offered by liberals and liberationists to legal gay marriage, the concept of "domestic partnership." Several cities in the United States have domestic partnership laws, which allow relationships that do not fit into the category of heterosexual marriage to be registered with the city and qualify for benefits that had previously been reserved for heterosexual married couples. In these cities, a variety of interpersonal arrangements qualify for health insurance, bereavement leave, insurance, annuity and pension rights, housing rights (such as rent-control apartments), adoption, and inheritance rights. Eventually, the aim is to include federal income tax and veterans' benefits as well. Homosexuals are not the only beneficiaries; heterosexual "live-togethers" also qualify.

The conservative's worries start with the ease of the relationship. To be sure, potential domestic partners have to prove financial interdependence, shared living arrangements, and a commitment to mutual caring. But they don't need to have a sexual relationship or even closely mirror old-style marriage. In principle, an elderly woman and her live-in nurse could qualify, or a pair of frat buddies. Left as it is, the concept of domestic partnership could open a Pandora's box of litigation and subjective judicial decision making about who qualifies. You either are or you're not married; it's not a complex question. Whether you are in a domestic partnership is not so clear.

More important for conservatives, the concept of domestic partnership chips away at the prestige of traditional relationships and undermines the priority we give them. Society, after all, has good reasons to extend legal advantages to heterosexuals who choose the formal sanction of marriage over simply living together. They make a deeper commitment to one another and to society; in exchange, society extends certain benefits to them. Marriage provides an anchor, if an arbitrary and often weak one, in the maelstrom of sex and relationships to which we are all prone. It provides a mechanism for emotional stability and economic security. We rig the law in its favor not because we disparage all forms of relationship other than the nuclear family, but because we recognize that not to promote marriage would be to ask too much of human virtue.

For conservatives, these are vital concerns. There are virtually no conservative arguments either for preferring no social incentives for gay relationships or for preferring a second-class relationship, such as domestic partnership, which really does provide an incentive for the decline of traditional marriage. Nor, if conservatives are concerned by the collapse of stable family life, should they be dismayed by the possibility of gay parents. There is no evidence that shows any deleterious impact on a child brought up by two homosexual parents, and considerable evidence that such a parental structure is clearly preferable to single parents (gay or straight) or no effective parents at all, which, alas, is the choice many children now face. Conservatives should not balk at the apparent radicalism of the change involved, either. The introduction of gay marriage would not be some sort of leap in the dark, a massive societal risk. Homosexual marriages have always existed, in a variety of forms; they have just been euphemized. Increasingly they exist in every sense but the legal one. As it has become more acceptable for homosexuals to acknowledge their loves and commitments publicly, more and more have committed themselves to one another for life in full view of their families and friends. A law institutionalizing gay marriage would merely reinforce a healthy trend. Burkean conservatives should warm to the idea.

10   It would also be an unqualified social good for homosexuals. It provides role models for young gay people, who, after the exhilaration of coming out can easily lapse into short-term relationships and insecurity with no tangible goal in sight. My own guess is that most homosexuals would embrace such a goal with as much (if not more) commitment as heterosexuals. Even in our society as it is, many lesbian and gay male relationships are virtual textbooks of monogamous commitment; and for many, "in sickness and in health" has become a vocation rather than a vow. Legal gay marriage could also help bridge the gulf often found between homosexuals and their parents. It could bring the essence of gay life—a gay couple—into the heart of the traditional family in a way the family can most understand and the gay offspring can most easily acknowledge. It could do more to heal the gay-straight rift than any amount of gay rights legislation.

More important, perhaps, as gay marriage sank into the subtle background consciousness of a culture, its influence would be felt quietly but deeply among gay children. For them, at last, there would be some kind of future; some older faces to apply to their unfolding lives, some language in which their identity could be properly discussed, some rubric by which it could be explained—not in terms of sex, or sexual practices, or bars, or subterranean activity, but in terms of their future life stories, their potential loves, their eventual chance at some kind of constructive happiness. They would be able to feel by the intimation of myriad examples that in this respect their emotional orientation was not merely about pleasure, or sin, or shame, or otherness (although it might always be involved in many of those things), but about the ability to love and be loved as complete, imperfect human beings. Until gay marriage is legalized, this fundamental element of personal dignity will be denied a whole segment of humanity. No other change can achieve it.

Any heterosexual man who takes a few moments to consider what his life would be like if he were never allowed a formal institution to cement his relationships will see the truth of what I am saying. Imagine life without a recognized family; imagine dating without even the possibility of marriage. Any heterosexual woman who can imagine being told at a young age that her attraction to men was wrong, that her loves and crushes were illicit, that her destiny was singlehood and shame, will also appreciate the point. Gay marriage is not a radical step; it is a profoundly humanizing, traditionalizing step. It is the first step in any resolution of the homosexual question—more important than any other institution, since it is the most central institution to the nature of the problem, which is to say, the emotional and sexual bond between one human being and another. If nothing else were done at all, and gay marriage were legalized, 90 percent of the political work necessary to achieve gay and lesbian equality would have been achieved. It is ultimately the only reform that truly matters.

So long as conservatives recognize, as they do, that homosexuals exist and that they have equivalent emotional needs and temptations as heterosexuals, then there is no conservative reason to oppose homosexual marriage and many conservative reasons to support it. So long as liberals recognize, as they do, that citizens deserve equal treatment under the law, then there is no liberal reason to oppose it and many liberal reasons to be in favor of it. So long as intelligent people understand that homosexuals are emotionally and sexually attracted to the same sex as heterosexuals are to the other sex, then there is no human reason on earth why it should be granted to one group and not the other.

● Review Questions

1. According to Sullivan, what definition of marriage prohibits any public way for marriage to be legally denied to homosexuals "if one believes in equal rights under the law"?

2. Which two classes of people, according to Sullivan, does the state believe cannot fulfill the contract of marriage?

3. Summarize Sullivan's "conservative" arguments preferring gay marriage to "domestic partnership."

4. How does Sullivan believe that gay marriage will "bridge the gulf" that is often found between homosexuals and their parents?

● Discussion and Writing Suggestions

1. Write a critique of Sullivan's argument in favor of gay marriage. To what extent do you agree, for example, that "the marriage issue [for gays] is exactly parallel to the issue of the military"? Or that "[l]egal gay marriage could...help bridge the gulf often found between homosexuals and their parents"? Follow the principles discussed in Chapter 2.

2. Sullivan makes the surprising case that conservatives should support, rather than oppose, gay marriage because marriage is a fundamentally conservative institution (more conservative, for instance, than domestic partnership). To what extent do you agree with his reasoning?

3. Imagine for a moment, as Sullivan suggests, that you belong to a class of people that has been denied the right to marry or have a recognized family. To what extent do you feel that this restriction would affect your approach to life? For example, do you feel that you would be drawn more to short-term relationships—as Sullivan suggests is true of some young gays? To what extent do you feel that the lack of these rights would adversely affect your life?

4. Sullivan writes: "[G]iving [homosexuals] an equal right to affirm their commitment doesn't reduce the incentive for heterosexuals to do the same." However, many antigay marriage activists make precisely that argument—that gay marriage "devalues" heterosexual marriage, by implication making it less attractive to men and women. To what degree does the value you place on marriage depend on its being an institution reserved for a heterosexual man and woman?

5. Sullivan writes that marriage provides a bulwark against the "maelstrom of sex and relationships to which we are all prone." Do you agree that people who have undertaken the public commitment of marriage are less likely to yield to temptation than, say, people who have made a private commitment that has not been publicly recognized? If so, describe what it is about the public nature of the commitment that would tend to encourage fidelity.

6. Noting that "it is difficult to argue with a definition," Sullivan bypasses the argument that marriage is by definition between a man and a woman. Instead, he insists on articulating for the sake of his argument a broader and more complex definition of the nature of marriage: as a public contract that has, at its center, an "emotional, financial, and psychological bond between two people." However, since other relationships—such as that between a father and son—are often characterized by emotional, financial, and psychological bonds, clearly more is needed before this definition could be called comprehensive. In a sentence beginning "Marriage is...," craft your own comprehensive definition of marriage, one that reflects your own beliefs.

AGAINST GAY MARRIAGE

William J. Bennett

In the following selection, William J. Bennett, a prominent cultural conservative, explains why he thinks that allowing gays to marry would damage the institution of marriage. Note that Bennett attempts to rebut Andrew Sullivan's pro-gay marriage arguments. Bennett served as chairman of the National Endowment for the Humanities (1981–85) and secretary of education (1985–88) under President Ronald Reagan, and as President George H. W. Bush's "drug czar" (1989–90). His writings on cultural issues in America include *The Book of Virtues* (1997) and *The Broken Hearth: Reversing the Moral Collapse of the American Family* (2001). He has served as senior editor of the conservative journal *National Review* and is codirector of Empower America, a conservative advocacy organization. This piece first appeared as an op-ed column in the *Washington Post* on May 21, 1996.

We are engaged in a debate which, in a less confused time, would be considered pointless and even oxymoronic: the question of same-sex marriage.

But we are where we are. The Hawaii Supreme Court has discovered a new state constitutional "right"—the legal union of same-sex couples. Unless a "compelling state interest" can be shown against them, Hawaii will become the first state to sanction such unions. And if Hawaii legalizes same-sex marriages, other states might well have to recognize them because of the Constitution's Full Faith and Credit Clause. Some in Congress recently introduced legislation to prevent this from happening.*

Now, anyone who has known someone who has struggled with his homosexuality can appreciate the poignancy, human pain and sense of exclusion that are often involved. One can therefore understand the effort to achieve for homosexual unions both legal recognition and social acceptance. Advocates of homosexual marriages even make what appears to be a sound conservative argument: Allow marriage in order to promote faithfulness and monogamy. This is an intelligent and politically shrewd argument. One can even concede that it might benefit some people. But I believe that overall, allowing same-sex marriages would do significant, long-term social damage.

Recognizing the legal union of gay and lesbian couples would represent a profound change in the meaning and definition of marriage. Indeed, it would be the most radical step ever taken in the deconstruction of society's most important institution. It is not a step we ought to take.

5   The function of marriage is not elastic; the institution is already fragile enough. Broadening its definition to include same-sex marriages would stretch it almost beyond recognition—and new attempts to broaden the definition still further would surely follow. On what principled grounds could the advocates of same-sex marriage oppose the marriage of two consenting brothers? How could they explain

---

*As of September 2009, six states (Massachusetts, Connecticut, Vermont, New Hampshire, Maine and Iowa) and the District of Columbia have recognized the right of same-sex couples to marry. Nine states (including Oregon, Washington, and New Jersey) recognize some form of civil union for same-sex couples. Legislatures in several other states are actively debating the issue.

why we ought to deny a marriage license to a bisexual who wants to marry two people? After all, doing so would be a denial of that person's sexuality. In our time, there are more (not fewer) reasons than ever to preserve the essence of marriage.

Marriage is not an arbitrary construct; it is an "honorable estate" based on the different, complementary nature of men and women—and how they refine, support, encourage and complete one another. To insist that we maintain this traditional understanding of marriage is not an attempt to put others down. It is simply an acknowledgment and celebration of our most precious and important social act.

Nor is this view arbitrary or idiosyncratic. It mirrors the accumulated wisdom of millennia and the teaching of every major religion. Among worldwide cultures, where there are so few common threads, it is not a coincidence that marriage is almost universally recognized as an act meant to unite a man and a woman.

To say that same-sex unions are not comparable to heterosexual marriages is not an argument for intolerance, bigotry or lack of compassion (although I am fully aware that it will be considered so by some). But it is an argument for making distinctions in law about relationships that are themselves distinct. Even Andrew Sullivan, among the most intelligent advocates of same-sex marriage, has admitted that a homosexual marriage contract will entail a greater understanding of the need for "extramarital outlets." He argues that gay male relationships are served by the "openness of the contract," and he has written that homosexuals should resist allowing their "varied and complicated lives" to be flattened into a "single, moralistic model."

But this "single, moralistic model" is precisely the point. The marriage commitment between a man and a woman does not—it cannot—countenance extramarital outlets. By definition it is not an open contract; its essential idea is fidelity. Obviously that is not always honored in practice. But it is normative, the ideal to which we aspire precisely because we believe some things are right (faithfulness in marriage) and others are wrong (adultery). In insisting that marriage accommodate the less restrained sexual practices of homosexuals, Sullivan and his allies destroy the very thing that supposedly has drawn them to marriage in the first place.

10   There are other arguments to consider against same-sex marriage—for example, the signals it would send, and the impact of such signals on the shaping of human sexuality, particularly among the young. Former Harvard professor E. L. Pattullo has written that "a very substantial number of people are born with the potential to live either straight or gay lives." Societal indifference about heterosexuality and homosexuality would cause a lot of confusion. A remarkable 1993 article in *The Post* supports this point. Fifty teenagers and dozens of school counselors and parents from the local area were interviewed. According to the article, teenagers said it has become "cool" for students to proclaim they are gay or bisexual—even for some who are not. Not surprisingly, the caseload of teenagers in "sexual identity crisis" doubled in one year. "Everything is front page, gay and homosexual," according to one psychologist who works with the schools. "Kids are jumping on it... [counselors] are saying, 'What are we going to do with all these kids proclaiming they are bisexual or homosexual when we know they are not?' "

If the law recognizes homosexual marriages as the legal equivalent of heterosexual marriages, it will have enormous repercussions in many areas. Consider just two: sex education in the schools and adoption. The sex education curriculum of public schools would have to teach that heterosexual and homosexual marriage are equivalent. "Heather Has Two Mommies" would no longer be regarded as an anomaly; it would more likely become a staple of a sex education curriculum. Parents who want their children to be taught (for both moral and utilitarian reasons) the privileged status of heterosexual marriage will be portrayed as intolerant bigots; they will necessarily be at odds with the new law of matrimony and its derivative curriculum.

Homosexual couples will also have equal claim with heterosexual couples in adopting children, forcing us (in law at least) to deny what we know to be true: that it is far better for a child to be raised by a mother and a father than by, say, two male homosexuals.

The institution of marriage is already reeling because of the effects of the sexual revolution, no-fault divorce and out-of-wedlock births. We have reaped the consequences of its devaluation. It is exceedingly imprudent to conduct a radical, untested and inherently flawed social experiment on an institution that is the keystone in the arch of civilization. That we have to debate this issue at all tells us that the arch has slipped. Getting it firmly back in place is, as the lawyers say, a "compelling state interest."

Review Questions

1. What is the "intelligent and politically shrewd" conservative argument for marriage, according to Bennett?

2. What "enormous repercussion" does Bennett predict in the area of sex education, if the law recognizes homosexual marriage?

3. Summarize two of Bennett's arguments against broadening "the meaning and definition" of marriage to include same-sex marriages.

4. According to Bennett, what distinguishes the sexual behavior of heterosexuals from that of homosexuals?

Discussion and Writing Suggestions

1. Write a critique of Bennett's arguments against gay marriage. Follow the principles discussed in Chapter 2. For example, to what extent do you agree with Bennett's assertion that one argument against same-sex marriage is that it sends "the wrong signals"? Or his assertion that "it is far better for a child to be raised by a mother and a father than by, say, two male homosexuals"? You may wish to include some of Andrew Sullivan's points in your discussion.

2. Contending that homosexual relationships involve "less restrained sexual practices" than heterosexual ones, Bennett quotes Andrew Sullivan, who admits that a homosexual marriage contract will need to feature an acknowledgment of the need for "extramarital outlets." Propose a definition of marriage that allows for such outlets.

3. Imagine that you are one of the advocates of same-sex marriage to whom Bennett refers in the fifth paragraph of his op-ed column. In a brief paragraph, argue why same-sex marriages should be allowed, but not the marriage of two consenting brothers.

THE SATISFACTIONS OF HOUSEWIFERY AND MOTHERHOOD/PARADISE LOST (DOMESTIC DIVISION)

Terry Martin Hekker

We begin with a matched set of op-ed columns written nearly 30 years apart for the *New York Times* by the same author. At the time her December 20, 1977, column "The Satisfactions of Housewifery and Motherhood" was published, Terry Martin Hekker was a housewife living in South Nyack, New York, who had been married 22 years to her husband, John Hekker, a lawyer and South Nyack village judge. The column deals with Hekker's experiences as a "stay-at-home" mom at a time—the late 1970s—when many women were opting to enter the workforce rather than stay home to raise their children. As a result of the extraordinary response to Hekker's column—some of which she describes in her follow-up 2006 piece, "Paradise Lost"—she expanded the essay into a book, *Ever Since Adam and Eve,* published by William Morrow in 1979. "Paradise Lost" was published on January 1, 2006. Like her first column, it aroused much comment in op-ed pieces and blogs around the nation.

(1977)

My son lied about it on his college application. My husband mutters it under his breath when asked. And I had grown reluctant to mention it myself.

The problem is my occupation. But the statistics on women that have come out since the Houston conference have given me a new outlook. I have ceased thinking of myself as obsolete and begun to see myself as I really am—an endangered species. Like the whooping crane and the snow leopard, I deserve attentive nurturing and perhaps a distinctive metal tag on my foot. Because I'm one of the last of the dying breed of human females designated, "Occupation: Housewife."

I know it's nothing to crow about. I realize that when people discuss their professions at parties I am more of a pariah than a hooker or a loan shark is. I have been castigated, humiliated and scorned. In an age of do-your-own-thing, it's clear no one meant me. I've been told (patiently and a little louder than necessary, as one does with a small child) that I am an anachronism (except that they avoid such a big word). I have been made to feel so outmoded that I wouldn't be surprised to discover that, like a carton of yogurt, I have an expiration date stamped on my bottom.

I once treasured a small hope that history might vindicate me. After all, nursing was once just such a shameful occupation, suitable for only the lowest women. But I abandoned any thought that my occupation would ever become fashionable again, just as I had to stop counting on full-figured women coming back into style. I'm a hundred years too late on both counts.

5   Now, however, thanks to all these new statistics, I see a brighter future for myself. Today, fewer than 16 percent of American families have a full-time housewife-mother. Comparing that with previous figures, at the rate it's going I calculate I am less than eight years away from being the last housewife in the country. And then I intend to be impossible.

I shall demand enormous fees to go on talk shows, and will charge for my autograph. Anthropologists will study my feeding and nesting habits through field glasses and keep notebooks detailing my every move. That is, if no one gets the bright idea that I'm so unique that I must be put behind sealed glass like the Book of Kells. In any event, I can expect to be a celebrity and to be pampered. I cannot, though, expect to get even.

There's no getting even for years of being regarded as stupid or lazy, or both. For years of being considered unproductive (unless you count five children, which no one does). For years of being viewed as a parasite, living off a man (except by my husband whose opinion doesn't seem to matter). For years of fetching other women's children after they'd thrown up in the lunchroom, because I have nothing better to do, or probably there is nothing I do better, while their mothers have "careers." (Is clerking in a drug store a bona fide career?) For years of caring for five children and a big house and constantly being asked when I'm going to work.

I come from a long line of women, most of them more Edith Bunker* than Betty Friedan,[†] who never knew they were unfulfilled. I can't testify that they were happy, but they *were* cheerful. And if they lacked "meaningful relationships," they cherished relations who meant something. They took pride in a clean, comfortable home and satisfaction in serving a good meal because no one had explained to them that the only work worth doing is that for which you get paid.

They enjoyed rearing their children because no one ever told them that little children belonged in church basements and their mothers belonged somewhere else. They lived, very frugally, on their husbands' paychecks because they didn't realize that it's more important to have a bigger house and a second car than it is to rear your own children. And they were so incredibly ignorant that they died never suspecting they'd been failures.

10   That won't hold true for me. I don't yet perceive myself as a failure, but it's not for want of being told I am.

---

*Edith Bunker (wife of Archie Bunker) was a character in the 1970s sitcom *All in the Family;* in the first few years of the series, she was a traditional stay-at-home housewife.
[†]Betty Friedan (1921–2006) was an author and activist; her 1963 book *The Feminine Mystique,* documenting the stifling and vaguely dissatisfied lot of the mid-20th century traditional housewife, launched the "second wave" feminist revolution.

The other day, years of condescension prompted me to fib in order to test a theory. At a party where most of the guests were business associates of my husband, a Ms. Putdown asked me who I was. I told her I was Jack Hekker's wife. That had a galvanizing effect on her. She took my hand and asked if that was all I thought of myself—just someone's wife? I wasn't going to let her in on the five children but when she persisted I mentioned them but told her that they weren't mine, that they belonged to my dead sister. And then I basked in the glow of her warm approval.

It's an absolute truth that whereas you are considered ignorant to stay home to rear *your* children, it is quite heroic to do so for someone else's children. Being a housekeeper is acceptable (even to the Social Security office) as long as it's not *your* house you're keeping. And treating a husband with attentive devotion is altogether correct as long as he's not *your* husband.

Sometimes I feel like Alice in Wonderland. But lately, mostly, I feel like an endangered species.

PARADISE LOST (DOMESTIC DIVISION)

(2006)

A while back, at a baby shower for a niece, I overheard the expectant mother being asked if she intended to return to work after the baby was born. The answer, which rocked me, was, "Yes, because I don't want to end up like Aunt Terry."

That would be me.

In the continuing case of Full-Time Homemaker vs. Working Mother, I offer myself as Exhibit A. Because more than a quarter-century ago I wrote an Op-Ed article for *The New York Times* on the satisfaction of being a full-time housewife in the new age of the liberated woman. I wrote it from my heart, thoroughly convinced that homemaking and raising my children was the most challenging and rewarding job I could ever want.

"I come from a long line of women," I wrote, "most of them more Edith Bunker than Betty Friedan, who never knew they were unfulfilled. I can't testify that they were happy, but they were cheerful. They took pride in a clean, comfortable home and satisfaction in serving a good meal because no one had explained that the only work worth doing is that for which you get paid."

5   I wasn't advocating that mothers forgo careers to stay home with their children; I was simply defending my choice as a valid one. The mantra of the age may have been "Do your own thing," but as a full-time homemaker, that didn't seem to mean me.

The column morphed into a book titled *Ever Since Adam and Eve*, followed by a national tour on which I, however briefly, became the authority on homemaking as a viable choice for women. I ultimately told my story on *Today* and to Dinah Shore, Charlie Rose and even to Oprah, when she was the host of a local TV show in Baltimore.

In subsequent years I lectured on the rewards of homemaking and house-wifery. While others tried to make the case that women like me were parasites and little more than legalized prostitutes, I spoke to rapt audiences about the importance of being there for your children as they grew up, of the satisfactions of "making a home," preparing family meals and supporting your hard-working husband.

So I was predictably stunned and devastated when, on our 40th wedding anniversary, my husband presented me with a divorce. I knew our first anniversary would be paper, but never expected the 40th would be papers, 16 of them meticulously detailing my faults and flaws, the reason our marriage, according to him, was over.

We had been married by a bishop with a blessing from the pope in a country church filled with honeysuckle and hope. Five children and six grandchildren later we were divorced by a third-rate judge in a suburban courthouse reeking of dust and despair.

10   Our long marriage had its full share of love, complications, illnesses, joy and stress. Near the end we were in a dismal period, with my husband in treatment for alcoholism. And although I had made more than my share of mistakes, I never expected to be served with divorce papers. I was stunned to find myself, at this stage of life, marooned. And it was small comfort that I wasn't alone. There were many other confused women of my age and circumstance who'd been married just as long, sharing my situation.

I was in my teens when I first read Dickens's *Great Expectations,* with the tale of Miss Haversham, who, stood up by her groom-to-be, spent decades in her yellowing wedding gown, sitting at her cobweb-covered bridal banquet table, consumed with plotting revenge. I felt then that to be left waiting at the altar with a church full of people must be the most crushing thing that could happen to a woman.

I was wrong. No jilted bride could feel as embarrassed and humiliated as a woman in her 60's discarded by her husband. I was confused and scared, and the pain of being tossed aside by the love of my life made bitterness unavoidable. In those first few bewildering months, as I staggered and wailed through my life, I made Miss Haversham look like a good sport.

Sitting around my kitchen with two friends who had also been dumped by their husbands, I figured out that among the three of us we'd been married 110 years. We'd been faithful wives, good mothers, cooks and housekeepers who'd married in the 50's, when "dress for success" meant a wedding gown and "wife" was a tenured position.

Turns out we had a lot in common with our outdated kitchen appliances. Like them we were serviceable, low maintenance, front loading, self-cleaning and (relatively) frost free. Also like them we had warranties that had run out. Our husbands sought sleeker models with features we lacked who could execute tasks we'd either never learned or couldn't perform without laughing.

15   Like most loyal wives of our generation, we'd contemplated eventual widowhood but never thought we'd end up divorced. And "divorced" doesn't begin to describe the pain of this process. "Canceled" is more like it. It began

with my credit cards, then my health insurance and checkbook, until, finally, like a used postage stamp, I felt canceled too.

I faced frightening losses and was overwhelmed by the injustice of it all. He got to take his girlfriend to Cancun, while I got to sell my engagement ring to pay the roofer. When I filed my first nonjoint tax return, it triggered the shocking notification that I had become eligible for food stamps.

The judge had awarded me alimony that was less than I was used to getting for household expenses, and now I had to use that money to pay bills I'd never seen before: mortgage, taxes, insurance and car payments. And that princely sum was awarded for only four years, the judge suggesting that I go for job training when I turned 67. Not only was I unprepared for divorce itself, I was utterly lacking in skills to deal with the brutal aftermath.

I read about the young mothers of today—educated, employed, self-sufficient—who drop out of the work force when they have children, and I worry and wonder. Perhaps it is the right choice for them. Maybe they'll be fine. But the fragility of modern marriage suggests that at least half of them may not be.

Regrettably, women whose husbands are devoted to their families and are good providers must nevertheless face the specter of future abandonment. Surely the seeds of this wariness must have been planted, even if they can't believe it could ever happen to them. Many have witnessed their own mothers jettisoned by their own fathers and seen divorced friends trying to rear children with marginal financial and emotional support.

20   These young mothers are often torn between wanting to be home with their children and the statistical possibility of future calamity, aware that one of the most poverty-stricken groups in today's society are divorced older women. The feminine and sexual revolutions of the last few decades have had their shining victories, but have they, in the end, made things any easier for mothers?

I cringe when I think of that line from my Op-Ed article about the long line of women I'd come from and belonged to who were able to find fulfillment as homemakers "because no one had explained" to us "that the only work worth doing is that for which you get paid." For a divorced mother, the harsh reality is that the work for which you do get paid is the only work that will keep you afloat.

These days couples face complex negotiations over work, family, child care and housekeeping. I see my children dealing with these issues in their marriages, and I understand the stresses and frustrations. It becomes evident that where traditional marriage through the centuries had been a partnership based on mutual dependency, modern marriage demands greater self-sufficiency.

While today's young women know from the start they'll face thorny decisions regarding careers, marriage and children, those of us who married in the 50's anticipated lives similar to our mothers' and grandmothers'. Then we watched with bewilderment as all the rules changed, and the goal posts were moved.

If I had it to do over again, I'd still marry the man I married and have my children: they are my treasure and a powerful support system for me and for one another. But I would have used the years after my youngest started school to further my education. I could have amassed two doctorates using the time and energy I gave to charitable and community causes and been better able to support myself.

25   But in a lucky twist, my community involvement had resulted in my being appointed to fill a vacancy on our Village Board. I had been serving as titular deputy mayor of my hometown (Nyack, N.Y.) when my husband left me. Several weeks later the mayor chose not to run again because of failing health, and I was elected to succeed him, becoming the first female mayor.

I held office for six years, a challenging, full-time job that paid a whopping annual salary of $8,000. But it consumed me and gave me someplace to go every day and most nights, and as such it saved my sanity. Now, mostly retired except for some part-time work, I am kept on my toes by 12 amazing grandchildren.

My anachronistic book was written while I was in a successful marriage that I expected would go on forever. Sadly, it now has little relevance for modern women, except perhaps as a cautionary tale: never its intended purpose. So I couldn't imagine writing a sequel. But my friend Elaine did come up with a perfect title: "Disregard First Book."

● Discussion and Writing Suggestions

1. Hekker discovered that events have a way of reversing our most cherished beliefs. To what extent, based on your own life and on your observations of others, does Hekker's sadder-but-wiser experience appear to be universal? Can one—should one—prepare for such reversals in life? What is gained, and what is lost, by such preparation?

2. In her 1977 column, Hekker writes that traditional mothers "lived, very frugally, on their husbands' paychecks because they didn't realize that it's more important to have a bigger house and a second car than it is to rear your own children." Based on your own observations of working mothers, to what extent do you feel that Hekker's suggestion that most mothers choose to work in order to maintain an affluent lifestyle is fair and/or accurate?

3. In her 2006 column, Hekker writes, "It becomes evident that where traditional marriage through the centuries had been a partnership based on mutual dependency, modern marriage demands greater self-sufficiency." Assuming the truth of this statement, which type of marriage would you prefer—traditional or modern? Why?

4. In 2006, notwithstanding her divorce and the bitter lessons learned, Hekker maintained that she would still have stayed at home with her children until the youngest was school-age. Presumably that choice in 2006, as in the 1970s, would have involved some sacrifice of money and/or career goals. Assume that you faced this same choice. That is, assume that you are married, have a career you care about, yet also want to raise a family. Based on your values regarding childrearing, would you stay at home until the youngest is school-age? What

financial and career sacrifices would you be willing to make in order to maintain this arrangement? Describe your ideal child-care arrangement.

5. In her 2006 column, Hekker writes, "Women whose husbands are devoted to their families and are good providers must nevertheless face the specter of future abandonment." To what extent do you agree with this statement? Assuming it is true, would you want to live in this way—either being a suspicious woman or an implicitly distrusted man?

6. To what extent do you feel that the self-confident Hekker of the 1977 column got her comeuppance? To what extent do you feel that she deserves your sympathy and support? On a blog site in response to the 2006 column, one poster criticized Hekker as self-pitying and bitter. Do you agree with this assessment? Describe your own reaction upon reading the paragraphs beginning, "So I was predictably stunned and devastated when, on our 40th wedding anniversary, my husband presented me with a divorce."

A MOTHER'S DAY KISS-OFF

Leslie Bennetts

Hekker's bitter experience in the wake of her divorce, particularly her sense of abandonment and lack of preparedness to enter the world of work and earn her own living, is all too typical of many women in her situation. In the following selection, Leslie Bennetts, a contributing editor at *Vanity Fair* since 1988, and the author of *The Feminine Mistake* (2008) further explores these issues. Echoing Hekker, Bennetts has written of the "millions of women [who] continue to be misled by the fairy-tale version of life, in which Prince Charming comes along and takes care of you forever."

This passage first appeared as an op-ed in the *Los Angeles Times* on Mother's Day 2007 (May 13), alongside the Deborah Tannen piece that immediately follows.

This morning, millions of proud mothers will be presented with special, homemade breakfasts by their beaming children. There will be Mother's Day presents and cards, including precious handmade creations from the kids and joking or romantic ones from Dad.

But then the world, having made its annual perfunctory nod to the contributions of American mothers, will move on, leaving us once again to cope with our inordinate responsibilities, largely on our own.

Those responsibilities—and the personal sacrifices they typically entail—generate a permanent state of simmering anger in all too many women. Some deny it even to themselves. But the evidence is everywhere.

Last month, a *Washington Post* review of my new book asked why it is that so many mothers are so angry. After noting that lack of sleep doesn't fully explain this pervasive phenomenon, the writer suggested that motherhood represents the first time most women run headfirst into fundamental inequities—not just the biological differences between men and women but also the disproportionate burdens imposed by a culture that still regards the raising of children as the mother's responsibility.

5   The result is often a painful collision between family needs and workplace realities. Even all these years after the women's movement emerged, working mothers must still confront the intransigence of a corporate culture whose extreme hours, inflexible structures and hostility toward caretaking needs can make the juggling act very difficult. Most husbands still view child care and household chores as women's work, even when those women are working full time.

Stressed and resentful, the majority of women nonetheless continue to work, many out of financial necessity. Others quit their jobs to stay home, although the price may include conflicted feelings about having had to make such a "choice."

Both working mothers and stay-at-home moms have good reason for resentment, but it's the latter group that is most at risk. Although our culture tends to romanticize full-time motherhood, forgoing an independent income can make mothers and their children profoundly vulnerable to economic hardship, among other problems.

If a breadwinner dies, divorces his wife or becomes unemployed, homemakers often cannot find decent jobs to support their families. Years later, they often remain shocked and furious as well as grief-stricken, feeling deeply betrayed.

But even among women who enjoy stable marriages with employed spouses, many wives who give up their careers to stay home are also angry. While researching a book about the dangers of economic dependency and the rewards of work, I interviewed a woman who had wanted to be a lawyer since she was in second grade. As a successful commercial litigator, she regarded stay-at-home wives with disdain—until she had children and found that her employer's unforgiving demands made it impossible for her to continue to excel at her own job, and that her husband's heavy travel schedule and brutal work hours made it equally impossible for him to share the child-care duties with her.

10   "It was horrible," she said. "My husband understood my stress level, but his answer was, 'Then *you* leave work.' It was my problem."

So she became a stay-at-home mother, even as she continued to seethe about the sacrifice she had been forced to make. Months after our interview, when she received a pre-publication copy of my book, she was so upset by the explosiveness of her own words on the page that she asked me to change her name, which I did.

But her decision made me sad. Having given up a career she loved to accept domestic responsibilities she often found to be thankless, she then gave up even her right to sound off about it without hiding behind a pseudonym. Her retreat seemed like a powerful metaphor for the ways in which women sacrifice parts of themselves that they shouldn't have to give up. Frightened by the toxic feelings that result, they then sacrifice their own voices, feeling that they must even refrain from admitting how angry they really are.

But their resentment often festers just below the surface of their lives, erupting into full-blown rage at the slightest provocation. Sometimes it's directed against their husbands for not sharing the domestic burdens in a remotely equitable manner. Often, however, this anger is directed against other women, as in the vicious back-and-forth of the so-called Mommy Wars.

Since publishing my book, I have been pilloried in print and in cyberspace by hundreds of enraged stay-at-home mothers who have attacked everything from my appearance to my marriage and children. Their rage is genuinely frightening, as is their choice of targets. Ridiculing my weight or writing that my kids must be "scarred and dysfunctional" because I'm a working mother doesn't exactly advance the public debate over important work-family issues.

15   And yet the real problems are systemic, not personal. Women are indeed giving up too much, which may be why so many are so angry.

We accept unacceptable inequities in the workplace, quitting and retiring to our homes instead of organizing to demand reforms. Why do any of us accept the fact that childless women earn 10% less than their male counterparts, or that women with children earn 27% less, or that single mothers earn up to 44% less?

We accommodate our husbands' careers at the expense of our own interests, thereby leaving ourselves and our children vulnerable to future hardship. Can any of us defend the fact that women's standard of living drops by 36% after divorce, whereas that of men rises by 28%?

We put up with elected officials who pay lip service to family values but do little or nothing to address the real needs of American families, from flexible work schedules to affordable, quality child care.

Compared with other Western nations, the family-related policies of the United States are a disgrace. The United States and Australia are the only industrialized countries that don't provide paid maternity leave by law.

20   But nothing will change here until we insist on it. And men won't truly commit themselves to the effort until they too must be responsive to family needs. It's only when fathers as well as mothers get the call from the school nurse at 11:30 a.m. that their 6-year-old is vomiting and has to be picked up immediately that men will understand the need for workplace flexibility—and the imperative to make it happen.

It's long past time for women to stop venting their anger on each other and redirect it to changing the institutions, policies and practices that oppress us all. We need solutions, not scapegoats.

Mother's Day would be an even happier occasion if it didn't leave so many women feeling that their most important concerns had been kissed off by a greeting card holiday.

● Discussion and Writing Suggestions

1. Bennetts argues that "[m]ost husbands still view child care and household chores as women's work, even when those women are working full time." Canvass some of your friends to see whether or not they agree with this statement. Then conduct separate votes, by gender, on the same question. Discuss the results of your survey.

2. Bennetts points out that even professional women in stable marriages are often forced to give up their professions to become stay-at-home moms. Does her story of the commercial litigator who decided to become a stay-at-home mother resonate with you? Do you believe that this woman was justifiably angry? What kind of cultural or legal changes might be required to allow such women to continue working if they so choose?

3. Bennetts notes that after the publication of her book *The Feminine Mistake*, she was "pilloried in print and in cyberspace by hundreds of enraged stay-at-home mothers." A sampling of this type of backlash:

   • In a review published in the online version of *Commentary* (April 17, 2007), reviewer David Blum wrote, "[Bennetts] wants all women to live by her playbook, and scolds those who do otherwise. But Ms. Bennetts has spent far too much time hanging around presidents and movie stars in her charmed life to understand the difficult choices the rest of us make and the easy ones, too, such as wanting to spend as much time with our children as humanly possible."

   • In an otherwise favorable review, Joan Walsh, writing for the online magazine *Salon* (April 3, 2007) wrote "Any piece about women grappling with the choice to abandon careers for children has to make clear how rare it is to have that option."

   • Another advocate for professional working mothers, Linda Hirschman, was met with similar arguments. Responding to her April 25, 2007 *New York Times* article, "Off to Work She Should Go," one stay-at-home mother wrote, "Could anyone who has ever waited on tables, sold clothes, or worked for a soul-numbing large corporation find that more valuable than teaching a child to read or care about others? I doubt it."

   • Another declared, "Perhaps mothers are opting out of the work force because they believe that they can do the job of raising their children better than anyone else."

   • Yet another: "Linda Hirschman neglects to mention the fulfillment and pleasure mothers receive from caring for their children."

   To what extent do you believe that Bennetts and other advocates of American working mothers are justified in arguing that "[w]omen are . . . giving up too much" and that women "accommodate our husbands' careers at the expense of our own interests"? To what extent are they dismissing—and possibly insulting—those working mothers who choose to opt out of work to take care of their children?

4. Bennetts recommends that women redirect their anger from one another (and from men) to "changing the institutions, policies and practices that oppress us all." What kind of changes does she recommend? How desirable, how practical do you find her recommendations? What steps can individuals take to help promote and foster such changes?

UNDERSTANDING MOM

Deborah Tannen

Professional women often confront a generational gap when discussing their life choices with their mothers, who grew up assuming that the highest calling of a woman was to marry, raise children, and run a household. In the following piece, Deborah Tannen stands her ground as she justifies her choice to divorce her husband and return to school; at the same time, she makes a generous and touching effort to understand the worlds of gender and marriage from her mother's perspective.

Deborah Tannen is a linguist who teaches at George Washington University in Washington, D.C. She has published numerous articles and books on interpersonal communication, social interaction, and public discourse. Her book *You Just Don't Understand: Women and Men in Conversation* (1990) remained on the *New York Times* Best Sellers list for four years. She has written nine other books, including *That's Not What I Meant! How Conversational Style Makes or Breaks Relationships* (1986) and *You're Wearing That?: Mothers and Daughters in Conversation* (2006).

This article first appeared as an op-ed in the *Los Angeles Times* on Mother's Day 2007 (May 13), opposite Leslie Bennetts's, which precedes it in this chapter.

"My mother never saw me," several women have told me.

I think they meant that their mothers didn't perceive—or didn't value—the qualities these women most valued in themselves. But I wonder how many of us really saw our mothers.

My mother wanted for me the gifts of an ordinary life—a husband, children, a comfortable home. What I wanted was anything but. As a teenager, I identified with the heroine of "The Fantasticks," who whispered, "Please God, don't let me be ordinary."

Growing up in the 1960s, I disdained makeup even as my mother insisted, "Put on a little lipstick when you go out with me." My passion for books was so consuming that I frequently read while walking home from school—so engrossed that I didn't see my mother standing on the porch, worrying that I'd trip and fall on the sidewalk. And when I divorced at 29, my mother was not pleased that I decided to enroll in graduate school and work toward a doctorate instead of working toward finding a replacement husband.

5   All that time, I was convinced that it was unfair of my mother to scorn my values. It didn't occur to me that it was unfair of me to scorn hers.

Soon after I received my doctorate and joined the faculty at Georgetown University, my mother visited me. I was eager to prove to her that my life was good even though I hadn't remarried. I showed her my office with my name on the door and my publications on the shelf, hoping that she'd be proud of my success. And she was. But then she asked, "Do you think you would have accomplished all this if you'd stayed married?"

"I'm sure I wouldn't have," I replied. "If I'd stayed married, I wouldn't have gone back to school to get a PhD."

My mother thought for a moment, then said, "Well, if you'd stayed married, you wouldn't have had to."

I have told this story often, knowing my listeners would groan or gasp at how my mother hurtfully denigrated my professional success, caring only about my marital state. More recently, however, I tell this story for a different purpose: to understand her point of view.

10 My mother was born in Russia in 1911 and came to the United States before she turned 12. She left high school without graduating because she had to go to work to help support her family. What on Earth was she to make of a woman getting a doctorate and becoming a university professor—and of this unimaginable fate befalling her own daughter?

Surely every mother is proud of a daughter who soars. But from the perspective of the earthbound onlooker, a soaring daughter is receding in the sky, heading toward a universe her mother cannot know. Along with pride must come the pain of separation and of loss—plus the jolt of seeing the child she reared behaving as if she were an entirely different species.

Faced with the trappings of my professional life, my mother was probably trying to figure out how it all had happened. In her world, marriage ensured a woman's financial stability. An unmarried woman had to achieve that goal by going to work. "If you had stayed married, you wouldn't have had to" reflects this view.

Thinking of my mother's perspective reminds me of a remark a woman once made to me. "The shock of my life," she said, "was that my daughter didn't turn out exactly like me."

Though my mother would not have put that insight into words, I'll bet it describes what she was grappling with: trying to make sense of a life so different from any she could have imagined for herself.

15 We want our mothers to see us and love us for who we are, but we are often disappointed in them for falling short of who we think they should be. Mother's Day is a good time to try to see our mothers and love them for who they are: creations of their lives and their worlds, which doubtless are different from our own.

● Discussion and Writing Suggestions

1. Tannen's mother represents a generation of wives who believed that the goal of a young woman should be "a husband, children, a comfortable home." To what extent do you believe that hers is one of the last generations in this country to hold such a belief? In the future, will all—or most—women believe that their daughters should aspire to professional careers or to lives of work? Do you envision a significant percentage of women continuing to hold that a mother's primary job is to stay at home and take care of the children?

2. Consider the decisions women that you know have made regarding work and family. Approximately what proportion of these women has the economic means to opt out of the workforce to stay at home and raise children? Of

those who can afford to choose whether to continue to work or to stay at home, how many chose full-time motherhood? Why? What support do these women receive personally and culturally for choosing as they did?

3. Tannen writes poignantly about the different perspectives of her mother and herself. In a paragraph or two recount an anecdote between you and your mother (or father) that similarly demonstrates a difference in perspectives. To what extent can you, like Tannen, empathize with your parent's point of view, one based on a different set of cultural or generational values—a different "world"?

AMERICAN MARRIAGE IN TRANSITION

Andrew J. Cherlin

How has the institution of marriage changed in the United States during the past sixty years? In the following selection—originally titled "The Deinstitutionalization of American Marriage," Andrew J. Cherlin, a sociologist at Johns Hopkins University, attempts to answer this question. Cherlin defines "deinstitutionalization" as "the weakening of the social norms that define people's behavior in a social institution such as marriage." These norms include such tacit or explicit understandings regarding which partner assumes the role of chief breadwinner, which assumes the role of chief homemaker; which is the chief source of authority, which is the "loyal and supportive spouse."

Andrew Cherlin specializes in the sociology of families and public policy. He has published numerous books and articles on marriage and divorce, children's well-being, intergenerational relations, family policy, and welfare policy. The following is an excerpted version of an article that first appeared in the *Journal of Marriage and Family* in November 2004.

By 1978, the changing division of labor in the home and the increase in childbearing outside marriage were undermining the *institutionalized* basis of marriage. The distinct roles of homemaker and breadwinner were fading as more married women entered the paid labor force. Looking into the future, I thought that perhaps an equitable division of household labor might become institutionalized. But what happened instead was the "stalled revolution," in Hochschild's (1989) well-known phrase. Men do somewhat more home work than they used to do, but there is wide variation, and each couple must work out their own arrangement without clear guidelines. In addition, in 1978 1 out of 6 births in the United States occurred outside marriage, already a much higher ratio than at midcentury (U.S. National Center for Health Statistics, 1982). Today, the comparable figure is 1 out of 3 (U.S. National Center for Health Statistics, 2003). The percentage is similar in Canada (Statistics Canada, 2003) and in the United Kingdom and Ireland (Kiernan, 2002). In the Nordic countries of Denmark, Iceland, Norway, and Sweden, the figure ranges from about 45% to about 65% (Kiernan). Marriage is no longer the nearly universal setting for childbearing that it was a half century ago.

• • •

Two Transitions in the Meaning of Marriage

In a larger sense, the changing division of labor, childbearing outside of marriage, cohabitation, and gay marriage are the result of long-term cultural and material trends that altered the meaning of marriage during the 20th century. The cultural trends included, first, an emphasis on emotional satisfaction and romantic love that intensified early in the century. Then, during the last few decades of the century, an ethic of expressive individualism—which Bellah, Marsden, Sullivan, Swidler, & Tipton (1985) describe as the belief that "each person has a unique core of feeling and intuition that should unfold or be expressed if individuality is to be realized" (p. 334)—became more important. On the material side, the trends include the decline of agricultural labor and the corresponding increase in wage labor; the decline in child and adult mortality; rising standards of living; and, in the last half of the 20th century, the movement of married women into the paid workforce.

These developments, along with historical events such as the Depression and World War II, produced two great changes in the meaning of marriage during the 20th century. Ernest Burgess famously labeled the first one as a transition "from an institution to a companionship" (Burgess & Locke, 1945). In describing the rise of the *companionate marriage,* Burgess was referring to the single-earner, breadwinner-homemaker marriage that flourished in the 1950s. Although husbands and wives in the companionate marriage usually adhered to a sharp division of labor, they were supposed to be each other's companions—friends, lovers—to an extent not imagined by the spouses in the institutional marriages of the previous era. The increasing focus on bonds of sentiment within nuclear families constituted an important but limited step in the individualization of family life, Much more so than in the 19th century, the emotional satisfaction of the spouses became an important criterion for marital success. However, through the 1950s, wives and husbands tended to derive satisfaction from their participation in a marriage-based nuclear family (Roussel, 1989). That is to say, they based their gratification on playing marital roles well: being good providers, good homemakers, and responsible parents.

During this first change in meaning, marriage remained the only socially acceptable way to have a sexual relationship and to raise children in the United States, Canada, and Europe, with the possible exception of the Nordic countries. In his history of British marriages, Gillis (1985) labeled the period from 1850 to 1960 the "era of mandatory marriage." In the United States, marriage and only marriage was one's ticket of admission to a full family life. Prior to marrying, almost no one cohabited with a partner except among the poor and the avant garde. As recently as the 1950s, premarital cohabitation in the United States was restricted to a small minority (perhaps 5%) of the less educated (Bumpass, Sweet, & Cherlin, 1991). In the early 1950s, only about 4% of children were born outside marriage (U.S. National Center for Health Statistics, 1982). In fact, during the late 1940s and the 1950s, major changes that increased the importance of marriage occurred in the life course of young adults. More people married—about 95% of young adults in the United States in the 1950s, compared with about 90% early in the century (Cherlin, 1992)—and they married at younger ages. Between 1900 and 1960, the estimated median age at first marriage in the United States fell from 26 to 23 for men, and from 22 to 20 for women (U.S. Census Bureau, 2003a). The birth rate, which had been falling for a century or more, increased sharply, creating the "baby boom." The post-World War II increase in marriage and childbearing also occurred in many European countries (Roussel, 1989).

5   But beginning in the 1960s, marriage's dominance began to diminish, and the second great change in the meaning of marriage occurred. In the United States, the median age at marriage returned to and then exceeded the levels of the early 1900s. In 2000, the median age was 27 for men and 25 for women (U.S. Census Bureau, 2003a). Many young adults stayed single into their mid to late 20s, some completing college educations and starting careers. Cohabitation prior to (and after) marriage became much more acceptable. Childbearing outside marriage became less stigmatized and more accepted. Birth rates resumed their long-term declines and sunk to all-time lows in most countries. Divorce rates rose to unprecedented levels. Same-sex unions found greater acceptance as well.

During this transition, the companionate marriage lost ground not only as the demographic standard but also as a cultural ideal. It was gradually overtaken by forms of marriage (and non-marital, families) that Burgess had not foreseen, particularly marriages in which both the husband and the wife worked outside the home. Although women continued to do most of the housework and child care, the roles of wives and husbands became more flexible and open to negotiation. And an even more individualistic perspective on the rewards of marriage took root. When people evaluated how satisfied they were with their marriages, they began to think more in terms of the development of their own sense of self and the expression of their feelings, as opposed to the satisfaction they gained through building a family and playing the roles of spouse and parent. The result was a transition from the companionate marriage to what we might call the *individualized marriage*.

The transition to the individualized marriage began in the 1960s and accelerated in the 1970s, as shown by an American study of the changing themes in popular magazine articles offering marital advice in every decade between 1900 and 1979 (Cancian, 1987). The author identified three themes that characterized beliefs about the post-1960-style marriage. The first was self-development: Each person should develop a fulfilling, independent self instead of merely sacrificing oneself to one's partner. The second was that roles within marriage should be flexible and negotiable. The third was that communication and openness in confronting problems are essential. She then tallied the percentage of articles in each decade that contained one or more of these three themes. About one third of the articles in the first decade of the century, and again at mid-century, displayed these themes, whereas about two thirds displayed these themes in the 1970s. The author characterized this transition as a shift in emphasis "from role to self" (Cancian).

During this second change in the meaning of marriage, the role of the law changed significantly as well. This transformation was most apparent in divorce law. In the United States and most other developed countries, legal restrictions on divorce were replaced by statutes that recognized consensual and even unilateral divorce. The transition to "private ordering" (Mnookin & Kornhauser, 1979) allowed couples to negotiate the details of their divorce agreements within broad limits. Most European nations experienced similar legal developments (Glendon, 1989; Théry, 1993). Indeed, French social demographer Louis Roussel (1989) wrote of a "double deinstitutionalization" in behavior and in law: a greater hesitation of young adults to enter into marriage, combined with a loosening of the legal regulation of marriage.

Sociological theorists of late modernity (or postmodernity) such as Anthony Giddens (1991, 1992) in Britain and Ulrich Beck and Elisabeth Beck-Gemsheim in Germany (1995, 2002) also have written about the growing individualization of personal life. Consistent with the idea of deinstitutionalization, they note the declining power of social norms and laws as regulating mechanisms for family life, and they stress the expanding role of personal choice. They argue that as traditional sources of identity such as class, religion, and community lose influence, one's intimate relationships become central to self-identity. Giddens (1991, 1992) writes of the emergence of the "pure relationship": an intimate partnership entered into for its own sake, which lasts only as long as both partners are satisfied with the rewards (mostly intimacy and love) that they get from it. It is in some ways the logical extension of the increasing individualism and the deinstitutionalization of marriage that occurred in the 20th century. The pure relationship is not tied to an institution such as marriage or to the desire to raise children. Rather, it is "free-floating," independent of social institutions or economic life. Unlike marriage, it is not regulated by law, and its members do not enjoy special legal rights. It exists primarily in the realms of emotion and self-identity.

10   Although the theorists of late modernity believe that the quest for intimacy is becoming the central focus of personal life, they do not predict that *marriage* will remain distinctive and important. Marriage, they claim, has become a choice rather than a necessity for adults who want intimacy, companionship, and children. According to Beck and Beck-Gernsheim (1995), we will see "a huge variety of ways of living together or apart which will continue to exist side by side" (pp. 141–142). Giddens (1992) even argues that marriage has already become "just one life-style among others" (p. 154), although people may not yet realize it because of institutional lag.

The Current Context of Marriage

Overall, research and writing on the changing meaning of marriage suggest that it is now situated in a very different context than in the past. This is true in at least two senses. First, individuals now experience a vast latitude for choice in their personal lives. More forms of marriage and more alternatives to marriage are socially acceptable. Moreover, one may fit marriage into one's life in many ways: One may first live with a partner, or sequentially with several partners, without an explicit consideration of whether a marriage will occur. One may have children with one's eventual spouse or with someone else before marrying. One may, in some jurisdictions, marry someone of the same gender and build a shared marital world with few guidelines to rely on. Within marriage, roles are more flexible and negotiable, although women still do more than their share of the household work and childrearing.

The second difference is in the nature of the rewards that people seek through marriage and other close relationships. Individuals aim for personal growth and deeper intimacy through more open communication and mutually shared disclosures about feelings with their partners. They may feel justified in insisting on changes in a relationship that no longer provides them with individualized rewards. In contrast, they are less likely than in the past to focus on the rewards to be found in fulfilling socially valued roles such as the good parent or the loyal and supportive spouse. The result of these changing contexts has been a deinstitutionalization of marriage, in which social norms about family and personal life count for less than they did during the heyday of the companionate marriage, and far less than during the period of the institutional marriage. Instead, personal choice and self-development loom large in people's construction of their marital careers.

• • •

The Symbolic Significance of Marriage

What has happened is that although the practical importance of being married has declined, its symbolic importance has remained high, and may even have increased. Marriage is at once less dominant and more distinctive than it was. It has evolved from a marker of conformity to a marker of prestige. Marriage is a status one builds up to, often by living with a partner beforehand, by attaining steady employment or starting a career, by putting away some savings, and even by having children. Marriage's place in the life course used to come before those investments were made, but now it often comes afterward. It used to be the foundation of adult personal life; now it is sometimes the capstone. It is something to be achieved through one's own efforts rather than something to which one routinely accedes.

● Review Questions

1. Which factors were chiefly responsible for what Cherlin calls the "deinstitutionalization of marriage"?

2. Summarize the major features of the three types of marriage Cherlin describes.

3. In what two ways does Cherlin believe that marriages today are significantly different from marriage before the 1960s?

● Discussion and Writing Suggestions

1. Consider some of the marriages you have seen first hand. To what extent do you recognize the features described by Cherlin in surveying the three types of marriages he describes: institutional, companionate, and individualistic? To what extent do the marriages you discuss appear to blend features of two or three of these types of marriages?

2. To what extent can you draw correlations between the types of marriages you see and their degree of success? To what extent can you draw correlations between the types of marriages and the ages (either similar or different) of the partners?

3. Cherlin reports that since the 1950s young people have tended to delay getting married (the first time). Do you think it is best to wait until one's later twenties or even ones thirties before getting married? Explain.

4. Cherlin discusses the relationship between the rise of the individualistic marriage and the "growing individualization of personal life" apart from marriage. What do you see as the advantages and disadvantages of this growing individualism of personal life? Cite examples from your own observation or knowledge.

5. Cherlin observes that some believe that marriage "has become a choice rather than a necessity for adults who want intimacy, companionship, and children." Argue either for or against this claim. Do you imagine (or do you know from experience) that intimacy, companionship, and/or having children can be as satisfying for all concerned *outside* a marriage as *inside?*

6. Cherlin concludes this passage by noting that marriage "has evolved from a marker of conformity to a marker of prestige." Reread this final paragraph and restate Cherlin's point in your own words. Then agree or disagree. In explaining your response, consider your own goals for marriage, the marital goals of those you know, and some of the marriages that you have observed.

THE MYTH OF CO-PARENTING: HOW IT WAS SUPPOSED TO BE. HOW IT WAS.

Hope Edelman

The previous selections in the chapter (Hekker excepted) have dealt with issues of modern marriage from a journalistic, scholarly, or activist viewpoint. In the following two essays, two professional writers—a woman and a man—offer personal perspectives on their own marriages. You are already familiar with some of the issues they will discuss. What is distinctive about these selections is their tone: The writing is by turns raw, wounded, angry, and defensive and offers an unflinchingly honest, if brutal, assessment of each writer's marriage. These essays strikingly reveal the miscommunication and resentment that can afflict even mature, thoughtful, dedicated couples. In the first, Hope Edelman describes the disillusionment and anger she felt when, after the birth of their child, her husband immersed himself in his career, leaving her to run their household alone.

Hope Edelman has written three nonfiction books, including *Motherless Daughters* (1995). Her essays and articles have appeared in the *New York Times,* the *Chicago Tribune,* the *San Francisco Chronicle,* and *Seventeen* magazine. She lives with her husband and two children in Los Angeles. This essay was written for the anthology *The Bitch in the House (2002).*

Throughout much of 1999 and 2000, my husband spent quite a lot of time at work. By "quite a lot" I mean the kind of time Fermilab scientists spent trying to split the atom, which is to say, every waking moment. The unofficial count one week came in at ninety-two hours, which didn't include cell phone calls answered on grocery checkout lines or middle-of-the-night brainstorms that had to be e-mailed before dawn. Often I would wake at 3:00 A.M. and find him editing a business plan down in the living room, drinking herbal tea in front of his laptop's ethereal glow. If he had been a lawyer tallying billable hours, he would have made some firm stinking rich.

He was launching an Internet company back then, and these were the kind of hours most people in his industry were putting in. Phrases like "window of opportunity" and "ensuring our long-term security" were bandied about our house a lot, usually during the kind of exasperating late-night conversations that began with "The red-eye to New York? *Again?*" and included "I mean, it's not like you're trying to find a cure for cancer," somewhere within. I was working nearly full-time myself, though it soon became clear this would have to end. Our daughter was a year and a half old, and the phrase "functionally orphaned" was also getting thrown around our house a lot, usually by me.

So as my husband's work hours exponentially increased, I started cutting back on mine. First a drop from thirty-five per week to twenty-five, and then a dwindle down to about eighteen. At first I didn't really mind. With the exception of six weeks postpartum, this was the first time since high school that I had a good excuse not to work like a maniac, and I was grateful for the break. Still, there was something more than vaguely unsettling about feeling that my choice hadn't been much of an actual choice. When one parent works ninety-two hours a week, the other one, by necessity, has to start picking up the slack. Otherwise, some fairly important things—like keeping the refrigerator stocked, or filing income taxes, or finding a reliable baby-sitter, not to mention giving a child some semblance of security and consistency around this place, for God's sake—won't get done. A lot of slack was starting to pile up around our house. And because I was the only parent spending any real time there, the primary de-slacker was me.

How did I feel about this? I don't mind saying. I was extremely pissed off.

5   Like virtually every woman friend I have, I entered marriage with the belief that co-parenting was an attainable goal. In truth, it was more of a vague assumption, a kind of imagined parity I had superimposed on the idea of marriage without ever really thinking it through. *If I'm going to contribute half of the income, then he'll contribute half of the housework and child care.* Like that. If you'd asked me to elaborate, I would have said something impassioned and emphatic, using terms like "shared responsibility" and "equal division of labor." The watered-down version of feminism I identified with espoused those catchphrases, and in lieu of a more sophisticated blueprint for domestic life, I co-opted the talk as my own. But really, I didn't know what I was talking about beyond the fact that I didn't want to be the dominant parent in the house.

When I was growing up in suburban New York, my mother seemed to do everything. *Everything.* Carpooling, haircuts, vet appointments, ice cream cakes, dinners in the Crock-Pot, book-report dioramas—the whole roll call for a house-wife of the 1960s and 1970s. My father, from my child's point of view, did three things. He came home from work in time for dinner. He sat at the kitchen table once a month and paid the bills. And, on weekend trips, he drove the car. Certainly he did much more than that, including earn all of our family's income, but my mother's omnipresence in our household meant that anyone else felt, well, incidental in comparison. The morning after she died, of breast cancer at forty-two, my younger siblings and I sat at the kitchen table with our father as dawn filtered through the yellow window shades. I looked at him sitting there, in a polo shirt and baseball cap, suddenly so small beneath his collapsed shoulders. I was barely seventeen. He was fifty-one. *Huh,* I thought. *Who are* you?

There were no chore charts taped to the refrigerator, no family powwows, no enthusiastic TV nannies suddenly materializing outside our front door. My father taught himself to use a microwave and I started driving my siblings for their haircuts and that, as they say, was that.

My cousin Lorraine, a devout Baha'i, once told me it doesn't matter how many orgasms a potential husband gives you; what really matters is the kind of father he'll be. At first I thought she said this because Baha'is disavow premarital sex, but the more men I dated, the more I realized Lorraine was right. Loyalty and devotion are undoubtedly better traits to have in a spouse than those fleeting moments of passion, though I can't deny the importance of the latter. When I met John, it was like winning the boyfriend jackpot. He was beautiful and sexy, and devoted and smart, *so* smart, and he had the kindest green eyes. The first time I saw those eyes, when I was negotiating an office sublease from him in New York, he smiled right at me and it happened, just the way you dream about when you're twelve: I knew this was someone I would love. *And* he wanted children, which immediately separated him from a cool three-quarters of the men I'd dated before. I was thirty-two when we started dating, and just becoming acutely aware that I didn't have unlimited time to wait.

What happened next happened fast. Within two years, John and I were parents and homeowners in a canyon outside Los Angeles. By then he was deep into the process of starting his own company, which left us with barely an hour to spend together at the end of each day. And even though I so badly wanted him to succeed, to get the acclaim a smart, hardworking, honest person deserves—and even though I was grateful that his hard, honest work earned enough to support us both—well, let me put it bluntly. Back there when I was single and imagining the perfect partnership? This wasn't what I had in mind.

10   When John became so scarce around our house, I had to compensate by being utterly present in every way: as a kisser of boo-boos; a dispenser of discipline; an employer of baby-sitters; an assembler of child furniture; a scary-monster slayer, mortgage refinancer, reseeder of dying backyards. And that's before I even opened my office door for the day. Balancing act? I was the whole damn circus, all three rings.

It began to make me spitting mad, the way the daily duties of parenting and home ownership started to rest entirely on me. It wasn't even the additional work I minded as much as the total responsibility for every decision made. The frustration I felt after researching and visiting six preschools during my so-called work hours, trying to do a thorough job for both of us, and then having

John offhandedly say, "Just pick the one you like best." Or the irritation I felt when, after three weeks of weighing the options, I finally made the choice, and then he raised his eyebrows at the cost. *I didn't sign up for this!* I began shouting at my sister over the phone.

How does it happen, I wondered both then and now, that even today, in this post–second wave, post-superwoman, dual-income society we're supposed to live in, the mother nearly always becomes the primary parent, even when she, too, works full-time—the one who meets most or all of the children's and the household's minute-by-minute needs? We start out with such grand intentions for sharing the job, yet ultimately how many fathers handle the dental appointments, shop for school clothes, or shuttle pets to and from the vet? Nine times out of ten, it's still the mother who plans and emcees the birthday parties, the mother who cuts the meeting short when the school nurse calls. Women have known about this Second Shift for years, the way the workday so often starts up again for women when they walk through the door at the end of the *other* workday—a time mandated perhaps by the baby-sitter's deadline, but also by their own guilt, sense of responsibility, tendency to prioritize their husband's job first, or a combination of all three. Still, I—like many other enlightened, equality-oriented women having babies in this era—had naïvely thought that a pro-feminist partner, plus my own sheer will power, would prevent this from happening to me. I hadn't bargained for how deeply the gender roles of "nurturer" and "provider" are ingrained in us all, or—no matter how much I love being a mother to my daughter—how much I would grow to resent them.

When it became clear that my husband and I were not achieving the kind of co-parenting I'd so badly wanted us to achieve, I felt duped and infuriated and frustrated and, beneath it all, terribly, impossibly sad. Sad for myself, and sad for my daughter, who—just like me as a child—had so little one-on-one time with her father. No matter how sincerely John and I tried to buck convention, no matter how often I was the one who sat down at the kitchen table to pay the bills, there we were: he absorbed in his own world of work, me consumed by mine at home. My parents all over again.

The intensity of John's workplace was, originally, supposed to last for six months, then for another six months, then for only about three months more. But there was always some obstacle on the horizon: first-round funding, second-round funding, hirings, firings, had to train a sales force, had to meet a new goal. And meetings, all those meetings. Seven in the morning, nine at night. How were all those other dot-com wives managing?

15   There was no time together for anything other than the most pragmatic exchanges. When he walked through the door at 10:00 P.M., I'd lunge at him with paint chips to approve, or insurance forms to sign, or leaks to examine before I called the plumber first thing in the morning. Fourteen hours of conversation compressed into twenty highly utilitarian minutes before we fell, exhausted, into bed. A healthy domestic situation, it was not.

I was angry with the kind of anger that had nothing to do with rationality. A lot of the time, I was mad at Gloria Steinem for having raised women's expectations when I was just a toddler—but at least she lived by her principles, marrying late and never trying to raise kids; so then I got mad at Betty Friedan for having started it all with *The Feminine Mystique,* and when that wasn't satisfying enough, I got mad at all the women in my feminist criticism class in graduate school, the ones who'd sat there and so smugly claimed it was impossible for a strong-willed woman to ever have an equal partnership with a man. Because it was starting to look as if they'd been right.

But mostly I was mad at John, because he'd never actually sat down with me to say, "This is what starting a dot-com company will involve," or even, "I'd like to do this—what do you think?"—the way I imagine I would have with him before taking on such a demanding project (which, of course, we'd then have realized together was not feasible unless he quit his job or cut back dramatically, which—of course—was out of the question). Legitimate or not, I felt that at least partly because he was "the husband" and his earning power currently eclipsed mine, his career took precedence, and I had to pick up the household slack, to the detriment of my own waning career—or in addition to it. Before our marriage, I had never expected that. I don't remember the conversation where I asked him to support me financially in exchange for me doing everything else. In fact, I'd never wanted that and still decidedly didn't. I was not only happy to put in my portion of the income (though it would inevitably be less than usual during any year I birthed and breast-fed an infant), I expected to and *wanted* to contribute as much as I could: Part of who I was—what defined me and constituted a main source of my happiness and vitality—was my longtime writing and teaching career. I didn't want to give it up, but I also didn't want hired professionals running my household and raising my child. It felt like an impossible catch-22.

Face-to-face, John and I didn't give ultimatums. At first, we didn't even argue much out loud. Instead we engaged in a kind of low-level quibbling where the stakes were comfortably low. Little digs that didn't mean much in isolation but eventually started to add up. Like bickering about whose fault it was we never took vacations. (He said mine, I said his.) And whether we should buy our daughter a swing set. (I said yes, he said not now.) And about who forgot to roll the trash cans to the bottom of the driveway, again. (Usually him.)

I'd been through therapy. I knew the spiel. How you were supposed to say, "When you're gone all the time, it makes me feel angry and resentful and lonely," instead of, "How much longer do you realistically think I'm going to put up with this crap?" I tried that first approach, and there was something to it, I admit. John listened respectfully. He asked what he could do to improve. Then it was his turn. He told me how he'd begun to feel like a punching bag in our home. How my moods ruled our household, how sometimes he felt like wilting when he heard that sharp edge in my voice. Then he said he was sorry and I said I was sorry, and he said he'd try to be home more and I said I'd try to lighten up. And this would work, for a while. Until the night John would say he'd be home at eight to put Maya to bed but would forget to call about the last-minute staff meeting that started at six, and when he'd walk through the door at ten I'd be too pissed off to even say hello. Instead, I'd snap, "How much longer do you realistically think I'm going to put up with this crap?" And the night would devolve from there.

20   Neither of us was "wrong." Neither was completely right. The culpability was shared. Both of us were stuck together on that crazy carousel, where the more time John spent away from home, the more pissed off I got, and the more pissed off I got, the less he wanted to be around.

One day I said fuck it, and I took John's credit card and bought a swing set. Not one of those fancy redwood kinds that look like a piece of the Alamo, but a sturdy wood one nonetheless with a tree house at the top of the slide, and I paid for delivery and assembly, too. On the way home I stopped at one of those places that sell the fancy redwood kind and ordered a playground-quality bucket swing for another seventy bucks.

Fuck it.

There were other purchases I'd made like this, without John's involvement—the silk bedroom curtains, the Kate Spade wallet I didn't really need—each one thrilling me with a momentary, devilish glee. But the swing set: the swing set was my gutsiest act of rebellion thus far. Still, when it was fully installed on our side lawn, the cloth roof of the tree house gently flapping in the breeze, I felt oddly unfulfilled. Because, after all, what had I really achieved? My daughter had a swing set, but I was still standing on the grass by myself, furiously poking at gopher holes with my foot, thinking about whether I'd have time on Thursday to reseed the lawn alone. When what I really wanted was for my husband to say, "Honey, let me help you with that reseeding, and then we'll all three go out for dinner together." I just wanted him to come home, to share with me—and Maya—all the joys and frustrations and responsibilities of domestic life.

On bad days, when the baby-sitter canceled or another short-notice business trip had just been announced, he would plead with me to hire a full-time nanny—we'd cut corners elsewhere, we'd go into savings, whatever it took, he said. I didn't want to hear it. "I don't need a nanny, I need a husband!" I shouted. Didn't he understand? My plan hadn't been to hire someone to raise our child. My plan had been to do it together: two responsible parents with two fulfilling jobs, in an egalitarian marriage with a well-adjusted kid who was equally bonded to us both.

25   In writing class I tell my students there are just two basic human motivators: desire and fear. Every decision we make, every action we take, springs from this divided well. Some characters are ruled by desire. Others are ruled by fear. So what was my story during the year and a half that John spent so much time at work? He claimed that I was fear-driven, that I was threatened by the loss of control, which may in fact have been true. When I try to dissect my behavior then, reaching beneath all the months of anger and complaints, I do find fear: the fear that I'd never find a way to balance work and family life without constantly compromising one, the other, or both. But mostly what I find is desire. For my daughter to have a close relationship with her father, for my husband to have more time to spend with me, for me to find a way to have some control over my time, even with a husband and a child factored into the mix. And then there was the big one: for my husband to fulfill the promise I felt he made to me on our

wedding day, which was to be my partner at home and in life. Somewhere along the way, we'd stopped feeling like a team, and I wanted that fellowship back.

I wish, if only to inject a flashy turning point into this story right about now, that I could say some climactic event occurred from which we emerged dazed yet transformed, or that one of us delivered an ultimatum the other couldn't ignore and our commitment to each other was then renewed. But in reality, the way we resolved all this was gradual, and—in retrospect—surprisingly simple. John got the company stabilized and, as he'd promised, finally started working fewer hours. And I, knowing he would be home that much more, slowly started adding hours to my workday. With the additional income, we hired a live-in nanny, who took over much of the housework as well. And then, a few months after Francis arrived, Maya started preschool two mornings a week. Those became blessed writing hours for me, time when I was fully released of the guilt of paying others to watch my child. Between 9:00 A.M. and 12:30 P.M. Maya was exactly where she was supposed to be and, within that time frame, so was I.

With Francis came an additional benefit: a baby-sitter on Friday nights. For the first time since Maya's birth, John and I had a set night each week to devote to each other, and as we split combination sushi plates and did side-by-side chatarangas in a 6:00 P.M. yoga class, we began to slowly build upon the foundation we'd laid with our marriage—and, thankfully, even in the darkest months, we'd always trusted hadn't disappeared. Yes, there were still some Friday nights when I watched TV alone because John was flying back from New York, and other Fridays when I had to sit late in front of the computer to meet a deadline. And there were some weekend days when John still had to take meetings, though they became fewer and fewer over time.

It has taken real effort for me to release the dream of completely equal co-parenting, or at least to accept that we may not be the family to make it real. We're still quite a distance from that goal, and even further when you factor in the amount of household support we now have. Does John do 50 percent of the remaining child care? No. But neither do I contribute 50 percent of the income, as I once did. Ours is still an imbalanced relationship in some ways, but imbalance I've learned to live with—especially after the extreme inequity we once had.

What really matters now—more than everything being absolutely equal, more than either my husband or me "striking it rich"—is that John is home before Maya's bedtime almost every night now to join the pileup on her bed, and that we took our first real family vacation last December. This is the essence of what I longed for during those bleak, angry months of my daughter's first two years. It was a desire almost embarrassing in its simplicity, yet one so strong that, in one of the greatest paradoxes of my marriage, it might have torn my husband and me apart: the desire to love and be loved, with reciprocity and conviction, with fairness and respect; the desire to capture that elusive animal we all grow up believing marriage is, and never stop wanting it to be.

● Discussion and Writing Questions

1. Reread paragraph 5, which begins, "Like virtually every woman friend I have." To what extent does this paragraph describe your own expectations regarding co-parenting with your (eventual) spouse? To what extent has reading about an experience such as Edelman's caused you to adjust these expectations? Explain.

2. In a brief paragraph, describe the parenting roles played by your own parents when you were growing up. How much of the parenting did your mother perform? Your father? What were your feelings about this parenting arrangement then, and what are your feelings now? How likely is it that your parents' example will affect your own expectations of your husband or wife, when you are married and attempting to divide household responsibilities between yourself and your spouse?

3. Edelman writes that even though she wanted her husband to succeed and was glad for the money he was making, she couldn't escape the feeling that the life she was living "wasn't what [she] had in mind" when she had been single and "imagining the perfect partnership." In a brief paragraph, describe your own "perfect partnership" with a spouse. Be sure to take into account the "reality check" that essays such as Edelman's (and Shulman's) provide—that is, it's probably unrealistic to imagine a high-earning spouse who is also able to perform at least half of the housework and child-raising duties.

4. Edelman writes, "I hadn't bargained for how deeply the gender roles of 'nurturer' and 'provider' are ingrained in us all." To what extent do you agree that the kinds of division-of-household-labor problems Edelman describes stem from ingrained gender roles? In responding, draw upon your own experiences and observations.

5. Edelman writes: "Neither of us was 'wrong.' Neither was completely right." Do you agree? Explain your response.

6. Edelman explains that her problem was eventually solved when, among other things, she and her husband hired a nanny. However, elsewhere in the essay Edelman describes her resistance to the idea of hiring professional help. Describe your reaction to her (presumed) compromise. To what extent do you feel it was a betrayal of her ideals? To what extent do you feel it was the right thing to do in her situation?

7. *For men only:* Write a response to Edelman's essay, as if you were her husband.

MY PROBLEM WITH HER ANGER

Eric Bartels

In the previous selection, Hope Edelman describes how her husband's absence made her feel "angry and resentful and lonely." In the following essay, Eric Bartels writes about what it is like to be on the receiving end of such spousal anger. Eric Bartels is a feature writer for the *Portland Tribune* in Portland, Oregon, where he lives with his wife and two children.

This is a revised version of the essay by this title that appeared in The Bastard on the Couch: 27 Men Try Really Hard to Explain Their Feelings About Love, Loss, Fatherhood, and Freedom *(2004), an anthology edited by Daniel Jones.*

My wife and kids were sleeping when I finished the dishes the other night, shook the water off my hands and smudged them dry with one of the grimy towels hanging on the door to the oven. I gave the kitchen floor a quick sweep, clearing it of all but the gossamer tufts of cat hair that always jet away from the broom as if under power.

I turned to shut the lights, but then I noticed the two metal grills I had left to soak in the basin. They're the detachable, (cast iron type) (stove-top kind) that we occasionally use to affect a kind of indoor, open-flame cooking experience. Submerging them in water for awhile makes it easier to remove the carbonized juices and bits of flesh that get welded on during use. It's a good, sensible way to save labor.

The problem was that they'd been in the sink for several days now. And then it occurred to me: What I was staring at was the dark heart of the divide between men and women.

It's unlikely I was any less harried or less tired the previous few nights as I went about my kitchen duties, a responsibility that has fallen to me more or less exclusively of late. No, my energy level is fairly constant—that is to say depleted—at that particular point of just about any day. I could, and probably should have finished the grill-cleaning project sooner. Just as I should make the bed every morning instead of occasionally. Just as I should always throw my underwear into the hamper before showering, rather than leaving them on top of it, or on the floor next to it.

5   These are the things men do that quietly annoy the living shit out of a woman. Until she becomes a mother. Then they inspire a level of fury unlike anything she has ever experienced. And that fury won't be kept secret. On the receiving end, the husband will be left to wonder why the punishment is so wildly out of line with the crime. This is the kind of vitriol that should be reserved for lying politicians, corporate greed and hitters who don't take a pitch when their team trails in the late innings—not a dedicated marriage partner with garden-variety human foibles.

Yet here we are, my wife and me. We're both good people. We have lots of friends. We make a decent living at relatively satisfying professional jobs: She, half-time at a small advertising firm; I, as a newspaper writer. And we're dedicated, attentive parents to a six-year old daughter and a two-year old son.

We don't use profanity in front of the children, unless we're arguing angrily. We don't talk to each other disrespectfully, except when arguing angrily. And we don't say bad things about each other to the kids, unless, of course, we just finished arguing angrily.

I know my wife's life is hard. She spends more time with the kids than I do and is almost completely responsible for running them around to day care and school. I contribute regularly and earnestly to the shopping, cooking and cleaning, but a fair amount of it still falls to her. And her job, although part-time for the last six years, presents her with Hell's own revolving door of guilt over neglecting her work for kids and vice versa.

I work hard to take pressure off her and have given up some freedoms myself since our first child was born: time with friends, regular pickup basketball games, beer. And I honestly don't mind living without these things. What gets me, though, is how little credit I get for the effort. My wife gets tired. She gets frustrated. She gets angry. And she seems to want to take it out on me.

10   Then logic starts moving backward in an ugly zigzag pattern. If, in her mind, my shortcomings provide the justification for her anger, then the perception of my behavior must be groomed like the playing field of a game I can't seem to win. The things I do that don't conform to my new loser image—and to think this woman once thought I was cooler than sliced bread—don't even show up on the scoreboard. Until, finally, nothing I do is right.

My efforts to organize the contents of the armoire one day—a project she had suggested—led to a screaming fight. The clutter I was planning to move to the basement would just create more junk down there, she said. But we hardly use the basement, I thought, and besides, why couldn't we just make another, separate project of sorting out the basement later? Doesn't it solve the more pressing armoire problem in the meantime? Isn't that logical?

Evidently not.

One night she stomped into the kitchen as I was cleaning up after a dinner that I may well have cooked and served and announced in angry tones that she needed more help getting the kids ready for bed than I had been providing, as if she had just found me drinking beer and playing video games. Isn't that something we could discuss rationally, I asked her, when we're not both right in the middle of our respective (unpleasant) (demanding) nightly routines?

It didn't occur to her, I guess.

15   And a few nights later, after bathing the kids in succession, putting them in their pajamas and feeding them their vitamins, I was rocking our son to sleep when I heard my wife approach. I think she had been downstairs doing laundry. She walks into the bathroom and scornfully asks no one in particular "Why is there still water in the bathtub?"

I missed it.

I make a nice dinner after a long day at work, broiled pork chops with steamed zuccini, perhaps, and she asks why I made rice instead of pasta. At the grocery store, I try to buy food that's somewhere between not entirely toxic and prohibitively expensive, but I often disappoint her. I wash clothes the wrong way, not separating them properly by color. I spend too much time rinsing off dishes before loading them into the dishwasher.

If this is my castle, it is under siege. From within.

At times, the negativity threatens to grind my spirit into dust. I make it through an arduous week, gleeful to have it behind me, only to come home to the sound of her loudly and impatiently scolding our son for standing on a chair or turning on the TV or dumping his cheese puffs on the floor, exactly the stuff two-year old boys are supposed to do. Okay, children need to learn "no," and my wife does a lot of the teaching, but I'm certain there's a gentler way to pronounce the word.

20   I try to make this point calmly, and when that doesn't work, I make it more forcefully. Then we fight, until the (shame and) futility of that leaves me feeling deflated and distant, in a place where passion of any kind has slipped into a coma. And then it's time to start all over.

At times I watch my wife's mercury rise steadily, predictably to that point where she lashes out, almost as if she wanted to get there. I tell her, in the quietest, most reasonable tone I can manage, to please relax. Choose: "(You, Your Daughter, Your Son) did/did not do (this, that, the other)," she replies, her ire mounting. But, I think to myself, I didn't ask her what she's angry about, I asked her to stay calm. Aren't those different things?

I think it's fairly well established by now that marriage is a challenge, a creaky, old institution that may not have fully adapted itself to modern life, one that now fails in this country more often than not. Put children in the picture and you have an exponentially higher degree of difficulty.

Motherhood asks the modern woman, who has grown up seeing professional success as hers for the taking, to add the loss of a linear career path to an already considerable burden: child rearing, body issues, a shifting self-image and a husband who fell off his white horse long, long ago. I suppose this would make anyone angry.

Perhaps for women of recent generations, anger has replaced the quiet desperation of the past. That seems like a healthy development to me. But that doesn't mean there aren't several good reasons why, having seen the frustrated, angry, resentful place that the demands of modern motherhood will almost certainly take them, women shouldn't take the next logical, evolutionary step.

25   It seems to me that a woman should now focus only secondarily on what the world, and more specifically, her partner can do for her during the challenging early years of child rearing. She must now truly empower herself by turning to the more important issue: Controlling the monstrous effects that motherhood can have on her own emotional landscape.

In other words, buck up.

For better or worse, men don't experience life the way women do. Absent the degree of intuition and empathy that seem an integral (natural) part of a woman's nurturing instinct, men grow up in a simpler milieu in which challenges are to be quickly surmounted, without a great deal of fanfare. Something breaks, you fix it and move on. (But don't throw it out, it could come in handy at some point.)

It's not a mindset that lends itself to a great deal of introspection and deep thought. That's not to say that women can't fix things or that men are shallow-minded. These (just seem like) are philosophical tendencies propelled by disparate biological imperatives. The result in men is an inclination not to worry about things before they happen. This imbues them with a confidence that, however vexing a problem might seem, it can and will be resolved.

I don't think most women share this confidence. A friend of mine says that everything in a woman's world starts with fear. Everything becomes tied in some way to fears of disapproval and abandonment and loss of control and God knows what else. To make matters worse, a man's more measured response to (in) certain situations is likely to suggest to his wife that he is not sufficiently engaged. Indifferent. Oblivious.

30   Am I the only guy who feels like he forever stands accused of not understanding the pressures my wife is under? That I can't possibly fathom her frustrations? After all, what would a man know about controlling his impulses?

What would he know? I like that one. Remember, we're talking about men here, the people with the built-in testosterone factory. The ones whose favorite childhood entertainments run to breaking windows, starting fires and dismembering small animals. The ones who instantly want to know if their first car will do 100 mph. The ones who attend beery high school parties with the goal of getting laid, but who'll settle for a good fistfight. Women should be eager to learn what most men know about managing anger.

For many years, I made a living as a bartender. I was good at it and loved the challenge of having to nimbly beat back the surging, immediate gallery of tasks that a big crowd and a busy night present. But it's a job where things go wrong pretty much constantly and I would occasionally lose my cool, kicking a cooler door closed or angrily sending an empty bottle smashing into a bin with an ear-splitting explosion. I imagined I was just blowing off a little steam.

I didn't know what I was really doing until I was a patron at someone else's bar one night. I watched a bartender momentarily capture everyone's attention with a loud fit of pique and realized quickly that witnesses saw the whole thing as landing somewhere between laughable and pathetic. We didn't care what was bothering him. We were having drinks and a good time. Too bad he wasn't enjoying the evening himself.

Was the guy under a lot of pressure? Yes. Was he being vexed by all manner of impediments to his ability to do his job? Almost certainly. Did anybody care? No.

35   I did a lot less kicking doors and throwing things after that.

Of course I care about my wife's happiness. Whether we're bothered by the same things or react to challenges the same way is irrelevant. She is my partner and I love her. We have important things to do together. The life we've built depends heavily on her ability to find contentment.

But she's not the only one in the family who has tough days. I have my own stuff to deal with and so do our kids, young as they are. When my wife decides it's okay to look darkly at her self or the day she's having, she's giving herself permission to ignore what's going on in other's lives. However little she regards the obligations and pressures of my existence, the fact is that I have some less than radiant days myself.

Women could try to accept that it is theoretically possible for a man to be tired, feel stress and even need a bit of emotional support himself. The children can certainly provide a lift, but they are also notoriously inconsistent about refraining from imperfect, untimely behaviors: talking in loud, excited voices, soiling themselves and moving at high speed in close proximity to valued objects and unforgiving hardwood furniture.

An overworked wife is certainly within her rights, as ever, to express her concerns and wishes at these moments. But that is not the same as a bilious, ill-timed attack that suggests her husband, through arrogance and selfishness, knows absolutely nothing of the realities of her world. In fact, he probably has a pretty good idea. He's probably even willing to meet any reasonable request to help. He'd just like it if someone would ask him nicely.

40   I'm amazed at how willing my wife is to push my buttons sometimes. And it's not like she's unfamiliar with the instrument panel. She evidently hasn't noticed that I occasionally ignite like dry kindling.

I should probably admit about now that I'm not always a model of decorum. I'm a personable, intelligent guy, but I'm not one of those wise, super-evolved aliens with the massive cranium from science fiction. I've said unkind things to people. I've thrown elbows on the basketball court. Gripped by paroxysmic anger, I've sent any number of small appliances to the promised land. And I do like to win. But this is about not fighting.

Anyone who's ever watched a young child's face crumple in fear and bewilderment as parents unleash their anger, in any direction, knows instantly what the stakes are. Parents do not need the toxic stew of anger coursing through them while in charge of small, impressionable children. And partners who are struggling to remember what particular disease of the brain led to their union won't be helped back to the right path by the rotating wheel of frustration, resentment and blame.

I fear that when anger is allowed to manifest itself regularly, it becomes less and less necessary to question its origins. No need to examine it, no need to work backward in the hope of identifying and defusing the triggers to the fast-replicating chain of events. And what is the hope of altering a behavior if you don't know where it came from and never see it coming?

It baffles me that someone of my wife's intelligence would shout at our son to stop yelling or demand in a voice twisted with exasperation that our daughter stop whining. Can't she see what she's doing? It's like hitting someone to curb his or her violent tendencies. Of course I understand her frustration. But to let the expression of that frustration take any form, however inappropriate or unproductive, is indefensible.

45   Anger can spread quickly and I don't want us to poison the house where our kids are growing up. I don't know for a fact that whiney, self-centered children are always the product of undisciplined, self-indulgent parents, but what reasonable person would want to take that chance? Isn't a bit of restraint a rather small price to pay?

Anger is not power. Managing anger is power. A good friend of many years, with whom I've had many passionate debates on all manner of issues, used to tell me how his father would sit impassively during their own lively exchanges. His father, a university department head, would never lose his temper, never so much as raise his voice. I think I dismissed it as humanly impossible. My friend said it drove him crazy. But he is now an eloquent, engaging orator who runs a weekly literary discussion group out of his home. Then again, he also has two young sons and is divorced.

The level of discipline my friend learned from his father doesn't generally reside where my wife grew up. Individually, my in-laws are charming, intelligent, accomplished people. But together, they struggle mightily to break old habits. You can get one or another of them to acknowledge the familiar cycle of intolerance, blame and recrimination that often cripples their dealings with each other, but no one seems to have the will to fix it. As if the patience it would require would be seen as weakness.

My wife is the black sheep of that family. She has a quick mind, both analytical and imaginative. She has no love for convention and looks easily through hypocrisy of all kinds. She also has big-time Type A tendencies, character traits that make her the choice for many of the organizational and administrative duties in our shared life like paying bills and scheduling the kids' activities.

But these proclivities also work against her. The chaotic, unpredictable reality of having two small children threatens and at times overwhelms her compulsion for order. She breaks down. Traveling, with the on-the-fly time-management it requires, makes her crazy. I watched her walk face-first into a glass door at the airport. Another time, near the baggage carousel, she distractedly pushed our son's stroller into another child. The child was seated at the time. A pointless quarrel over a trip to the Home Depot led to her backing out of the driveway and into a parked mail truck one morning.

50   My wife and I need to fix this anger thing. We knew, or should have known, what we were getting into. We signed the contract. Shook on it. Kissed, actually. But I think we missed some of the small print. We wanted kids and had a vague idea that it would involve some work. Well, I have a news flash: It can be really, really hard.

And that goes for guys, too. I don't recall being told about spending more money each year than I actually earn, with no exotic vacations, nice cars or fancy anything else to show for it. I wasn't informed that I would give up golf altogether, just as I was pushing my handicap down toward single digits. And I'm certain I was not warned that sex would become a rarer commodity than at any time in the thirty years since I learned to participate in it.

But I've gotten used to all that. I do what most men do. I take a deep breath and push ahead, fairly confident that if I can just soldier on, the things I've sacrificed and more will be my reward down the road.

I suppose the anger issues in our household loom as large as they do, in part, because of my fervor to confront (defeat) them. It's been a battlefield at times. My wife and I have been mean and fought dirty and we've hurt each other. We need to recognize that and make up our minds to change, no matter how much work it requires.

But hey, we're still here. Our children, who we love so dearly, are growing up and every day we can count on the reassuring rhythms of life: the sun rises in the morning, a weather system slips over the Oregon Cascades and blots it out, cats barf up hairballs on the carpet. I'm optimistic. I don't think we've done any permanent damage. I don't think it's anything we can't fix.

55   But that's just me.

● Discussion and Writing Questions

1. Reflecting on his wife and other working mothers, Bartels concludes: "To truly empower herself, she will need to find a way to get beyond—on her own, with help, or however—the destructive impulses that the frustrations of modern motherhood can bring out in her." Your response?

2. Bartels suggests that women "of his generation" seem more comfortable expressing anger than women of previous generations did, and he attributes this, in part, to the fact that they have been in the workforce. To what extent do you find this explanation plausible? Explain your answer.

3. Bartels describes his failure to promptly clean the indoor grill, as well as a propensity for leaving dirty underwear on the floor, as typical "domestic lapses" common to men. To what extent does this square with your own observations of male behavior? To what extent do you feel, as Bartels implies, that such behavior cannot be modified?

4. Write a critique of Bartels's argument that, for the sake of their marriage and family, his wife needs to move past her "destructive impulses." Pay particular attention to the persuasive strategies he employs to support his thesis. Now respond to his argument. With which of his points do you agree, and with which do you disagree? State your overall conclusion as to the validity of the piece. Follow the principles in Chapter 2.

5. With the goal of suggesting a possible solution to the challenges Bartels and his wife face, evaluate his marriage according to one or more of the principles you have read about in previous selections. If Bartels's grievances are to be assuaged, to what extent do he and his wife need to fundamentally reexamine their assumptions regarding, say, the household division of labor? How much of that change should be Bartels's? How much his wife's?

6. *For women only:* Write a response to Bartels, as if you were his wife.

WILL YOUR MARRIAGE LAST?

Aviva Patz

Every newly wedded couple expects—or at least hopes—that their marriage will endure the test of time. But in most parts of the world the statistics are not encouraging. As of 2002, the highest divorce rate was found in Sweden, where 55 percent of new marriages ended in divorce; Guatemala had the lowest rate: 0.13 percent. The divorce rate in the United States is on the high end of the scale: 46 percent.

Is it possible to predict, in the early stages of a marriage, whether it will likely succeed or fail? In the following selection, Aviva Patz, executive editor of *Psychology Today,* reports on a study designed to answer that intriguing question. Ted Huston, a professor of human ecology and psychology at the University of Texas at Austin, designed and conducted the PAIR Project (Processes of Adaptation in Intimate Relationships), which followed the experiences of 168 couples from their wedding day through the next thirteen years. The results should surprise you and may overturn some of your assumptions about what makes for a successful marriage.

This article first appeared in the *Los Angeles Times* on March 15, 2000, and, in slightly different form, in *Psychology Today* on April 23 of that year. The present selection is drawn from both versions of the article.

What if I told you that there is a man in America who can predict, from the outset, whether your marriage will last? He doesn't need to hear you arguing; he doesn't need to know what you argue about. He doesn't even care whether you argue at all.

I was dubious, too, but I was curious enough to attend a lecture on the subject at the most recent American Psychological Association convention in Boston. Ted Huston, a professor of human ecology and psychology at the University of Texas at Austin, was showcasing the results of a long-term study of married couples that pierces the heart of social-psychological science: the ability to forecast whether a husband and wife, two years after taking their vows, will stay together and whether they will be happy.

My press pass notwithstanding, I went to the seminar for reasons of my own. Fresh out of college I had gotten married—and burned. Some part of me was still reeling from three years of waking up angry every morning, not wanting to go home after work, feeling lonely even as my then-husband sat beside me. I went because I have recently remarried and just celebrated my one-year anniversary. Needless to say, I'd like to make this one work. So I scribbled furiously in my notebook, drinking in the graphs and charts—for psychology, for husbands and wives everywhere, but mostly for myself.

Huston, a pioneer in the psychology of relationships, launched the Processes of Adaptation in Intimate Relationships (the "PAIR Project") in 1981, in which he followed 168 couples—drawn from marriage license records in four counties in a rural and working-class area of Pennsylvania—from their wedding day through thirteen years of marriage.

Examining a Marriage's Early Stages

5 Through multiple interviews, Huston looked at the way partners related to one another during courtship, as newlyweds and through the early years of marriage. Were they "gaga"? Comfortable? Unsure? He measured their positive and negative feelings for each other and observed how those feelings changed over time. Are newlyweds who hug and kiss more likely than other couples to have a happy marriage, he wondered, or are they particularly susceptible to divorce if their romance dissipates? Are newlyweds who bicker destined to part ways?

Since one in two marriages ends in divorce in this country, there ought to be tons of research explaining why. But the existing literature provides only pieces of the larger puzzle.

Past research has led social scientists to believe that newlyweds begin their life together in romantic bliss and can then be brought down by their inability to navigate the issues that inevitably crop up during the marriage. When Benjamin Karny and Thomas Bradbury did a comprehensive review of the literature in 1995, they confirmed studies such as those of John Gottman and Neil Jacobson, maintaining that the best predictors of divorce are interactive difficulties, such as frequent expressions of antagonism, lack of respect for each other's ideas and similar interpersonal issues.

But most of this research was done on couples who had been married a number of years, with many of them already well on their way to divorce. It came as no surprise, then, that researchers thought their hostility toward one another predicted the further demise of the relationship.

Huston's study was unique in that it looked at couples much earlier, when they were courting and during the initial years of marriage, thus providing the first complete picture of the earliest stages of distress. Its four main findings were quite surprising.

10　First, contrary to popular belief, Huston found that many newlyweds are far from blissfully in love. Second, couples whose marriages begin in romantic bliss are particularly divorce-prone because such intensity is too hard to maintain. Believe it or not, marriages that start out with less "Hollywood romance" usually have more promising futures.

Accordingly, and this is the third major finding, spouses in lasting but lackluster marriages are not prone to divorce, as one might suspect; their marriages are less fulfilling to begin with, so there is no erosion of a Western-style romantic ideal. Lastly, and perhaps most important, it is the loss of love and affection, not the emergence of interpersonal issues, that sends couples journeying toward divorce.

By the end of Huston's study in 1994, the couples looked a lot like the rest of America, falling into four groups. They were either married and happy; married and unhappy; divorced early, within seven years; or divorced later, after seven years—and each category showed a distinct pattern.

Satisfied Spouses Were Happy Newlyweds

Those who remained happily married were very "in love" and affectionate as newlyweds. They showed less ambivalence, expressed negative feelings less often and viewed their mate more positively than other couples. Most important, these feelings remained stable over time. By contrast, although many couples who divorced later were very affectionate as newlyweds, they gradually became less loving, more negative and more critical of their spouse.

Indeed, Huston found that how well spouses got along as newlyweds affected their future, but the major distinguishing factor between those who divorced and those who remained married was the amount of change in the relationship over its first two years.

15　"The first two years are key—that's when the risk of divorce is particularly high," he says. "And the changes that take place during this time tell us a lot about where the marriage is headed."

What surprised Huston most was the nature of the changes that led to divorce: The experiences of the 56 participating couples who divorced showed that loss of initial levels of love and affection, rather than conflict, was the most salient predictor of distress and divorce. This loss sends that relationship into a downward spiral, leading to increased bickering and fighting, and to the collapse of the union.

"This ought to change the way we think about the early roots of what goes wrong in marriage," Huston said. "The dominant approach has been to work with couples to resolve conflict, but it should focus on preserving the positive feelings. That's a very important take-home lesson."

Feelings May Determine a Union's Fate

"Huston's research fills an important gap in the literature by suggesting that there is more to a successful relationship than simply managing conflict,' said Harry Reis, of the University of Rochester, a leading social psychologist.

"My own research speaks to 'loss of intimacy,' in the sense that when people first become close they feel a tremendous sense of validation from each other, like their partner is the only other person on earth who sees things as they do. That feeling sometimes fades, and when it does, it can take a heavy toll on the marriage."

20   Social science has a name for that fading dynamic—"disillusionment": Lovers initially put their best foot forward, ignoring each other's—and the relationship's—shortcomings. But after they tie the knot, hidden aspects of their personalities emerge, and idealized images give way to more realistic ones. This can lead to disappointment, loss of love and, ultimately, distress and divorce.

When Marriage Fails

The story of Peter and Suzie, participants in the PAIR Project, shows classic disillusionment. When they met, Suzie was 24, a new waitress at the golf course where Peter, then 26, played. He was "awed" by her beauty. After a month, the two considered themselves an exclusive couple. Peter said Suzie "wasn't an airhead; she seemed kind of smart, and she's pretty." Suzie said Peter "cared a lot about me as a person, and was willing to overlook things."

By the time they strolled down the aisle on Valentine's Day in 1981, Peter and Suzie had dated only nine months, experiencing many ups and downs along the way.

Huston says couples are most vulnerable to disillusionment when their courtship is brief. In a whirlwind romance, it's easy to paint an unrealistically rosy picture of the relationship, one that cannot be sustained.

Sure enough, reality soon set in for Peter and Suzie. Within two years, Suzie was less satisfied with almost every aspect of their marriage. She expressed less affection for Peter and felt her love decline continuously. She considered him to have "contrary" traits, such as jealousy and possessiveness, and resented his propensity to find fault with her.

25   Peter, for his part, was disappointed that his wife did not become the flaw-less parent and homemaker he had envisioned.

Another danger sign for relationships is a courtship filled with drama and driven by external circumstances. For this pair, events related to Peter's jealousy propelled the relationship forward. He was the force behind their destroying let-ters and pictures from former lovers. It was a phone call between Suzie and an old flame that prompted him to bring up the idea of marriage in the first place. And it was a fit of jealousy—over Suzie's claiming to go shopping and then com-ing home suspiciously late—that convinced Peter he was ready to marry.

Theirs was a recipe for disaster: A short courtship, driven largely by Peter's jealousy, enabled the pair to ignore flaws in the relationship and in each other, setting them up for disappointment. That disappointment eroded their love and affection, which soured their perception of each other's personalities, creating feelings of ambivalence.

Ten years after saying "I do," the disaffected lovers were in the midst of di-vorce. When Suzie filed the papers, she cited as the primary reason a gradual loss of love.

The parallels between Peter and Suzie's failed marriage and my own are striking: My courtship with my first husband was short, also about nine months. Like Peter, I had shallow criteria: This guy was cool; he had long hair, wore a leather jacket, played guitar and adored the same obscure band that I did.

30   When it came time to build a life together, however, we were clearly mis-matched. I wanted a traditional family with children; he would have been happy living on a hippie commune. In college, when we wanted to move in together, we thought our parents would be more approving if we got engaged first. So we did, even though we weren't completely sold on the idea of marriage.

The road to divorce was paved early, by the end of the first year: I had said I wanted us to spend more time together; he accused me of trying to keep him from his hobbies, and told me, in so many words, to "get a life." Well I did, and two years later, he wasn't in it.

When Marriage Succeeds

While the disillusionment model best describes those who divorce, Huston found that another model suits those who stay married, whether or not they are happy: The "enduring dynamics model," in which partners establish pat-terns of behavior early and maintain them over time, highlights stability in the relationship—the feature that distinguishes those who remain together from those who eventually split up.

The major difference between the unhappily married couples and their happy counterparts is simply a lower level of satisfaction across the board. Yet, oddly enough, this relative unhappiness by itself does not doom the marriage. "We have a whole group of people who are stable in unhappy marriages and not necessarily dissatisfied," Huston said. "It's just a different model of marriage. It's not that they're happy about their marriage; it's just that the discontent does-n't spill over and soil the rest of their lives."

And while all married couples eventually lose a bit of that honeymoon euphoria, Huston notes, those who remain married don't consider this a crushing blow, but rather a natural transition from "romantic relationship" to "working partnership." And when conflict does arise, they diffuse it with various constructive coping mechanisms.

35   Nancy and John, participants in Huston's study, are a shining example of happy, healthy balance. They met in February 1978 and were immediately attracted to each other. John said Nancy was "fun to be with" and he "could take her anywhere." Nancy said John always complimented her and liked to do things she enjoyed, things "other guys wouldn't do."

During their courtship, they spent a lot of time together, going to dances at their high school and hanging out with friends. They became comfortable with each other and began to openly disclose their opinions and feelings, realizing they had a lot in common and enjoyed each other's company.

John paid many surprise visits to Nancy and bought her a number of gifts. Toward the end of the summer, John gave Nancy a charm necklace with a "genuine diamond." She recalls his saying: "This isn't your ring, honey, but you're going to get one." And she did. The two married on Jan. 17, 1981, nearly three years after they began dating.

The prognosis for this relationship is good. Nancy and John have a solid foundation of love and affection, built on honesty and intimacy. A three-year courtship enabled them to paint realistic portraits of one another.

In 1994, when they were last interviewed, Nancy and John were highly satisfied with their marriage. They were very compatible, disagreeing only about politics. Both felt they strongly benefited from the marriage and said they had no desire to leave.

40   When the seminar ends, I can't get to a pay phone fast enough. After two rings, the phone is answered. He's there, of course. Dependable. Predictable. That's one of the things that first set my husband apart. At the close of one date, he'd lock in the next. "Can I see you tomorrow for lunch?"

"Will you have dinner with me next week?"

Unlike the fantasy-quality of my first marriage, I felt a deep sense of comfort and companionship with him, and did not harbor outrageous expectations. We exchanged vows 3 1/2 years later, in August, 1998.

There at the convention center, I try to tell my husband about Huston's study, about the critical first few years, about "enduring dynamics," it all comes out in a jumble.

"You're saying we have a good marriage, that we're not going to get divorced?" he asks.

45   "Yes," I say breathlessly, relieved of the burden of explanation.

"Well I'm glad to hear that," he says, "but I wasn't really worried."

Sometimes I wonder: Knowing what I know now, could I have saved my first marriage? Probably not. Huston's research suggests that the harbingers of disaster were present even before my wedding day.

And he blames our culture. Unlike many other world cultures, he says Western society makes marriage the key adult relationship, which puts pressure on people to marry. "People feel they have to find a way to get there and one way is to force it, even if it only works for the time being," he says.

Our culture is also to blame, Huston says, for perpetuating the myth of storybook romance, which is more likely to doom a marriage than strengthen it. He has few kind words for Hollywood, which brings us unrealistic passion.

50   So if your new romance starts to resemble a movie script, try to remember: The audience never sees what happens after the credits roll.

Are you headed for bliss or a bust-up?

Review Questions

1. What was the purpose of the PAIR project? Who were its subjects and what procedures did investigators use? What were the chief conclusions?

2. What is the critical period in a marriage that tends to determine whether the marriage will endure or will end in divorce?

3. How do the findings of Huston's study suggest a need to shift focus in marital counseling?

4. What is the "enduring dynamics" model of marriage?

Discussion and Writing Suggestions

1. Do the results of Ted Huston's study surprise you? To what extent did his findings contradict your expectations of what causes marriages to succeed or fail? In what ways do some of the marriages with which you are familiar support or rebut the conclusions of the study?

2. Huston's study was based on a study of 168 couples from "a rural and working-class area of Pennsylvania." Based on your own observations and knowledge, do you have any reason to believe that the results of the study would have been significantly different had the study been conducted with a different demographic—say, using professional couples from Chicago or from the suburbs of New York City? Explain.

3. Does the story of Suzie and Peter seem a familiar one? Describe one or two couples you know (changing the names and disguising their relationship to you) who fit the pattern indicated by Suzie and Peter. To what extent do Huston's findings allow you to better understand the factors at work in the marriage(s) you describe?

4. For generations, novelists and filmmakers have entertained and enthralled us with stories that end with the wedding, or the prospect of a wedding, between a happy couple. But as Patz observes, "[t]he audience never sees what happens after the credits roll." Drawing upon the results of Huston's study, imagine the

life of a well-known fictional couple that follows their wedding day. Categorize the state of their marriage using Huston's template: "married and happy; married and unhappy; divorced early, within seven years; or divorced later, after seven years." Trace the developments of this marital state to factors that may have been apparent in the *premarital* relationship. An example: Do you detect anything in the personal qualities or background of Romeo or Juliet that might have spelled trouble for the marriage, had these characters actually lived to marry? See, also, Anne Sexton's ironic treatment of the "Cinderella" story on pp. 643–645, especially the final two stanzas dealing with Cinderella's life after the wedding.

5. According to Patz, Huston blames our culture for creating conditions that work against marital success. Apart from Hollywood, which aspects of contemporary culture do you believe tend to pressure people to marry before they may be ready or foster unrealistic expectations about life after the wedding? Provide specific examples from your own knowledge or observation.

THE ARBUS FACTOR

Lore Segal

We conclude our chapter on marriage and family with a poignant short story—a miniature gem. To tease out its meaning, relate your discussions about it to some of the other discussions provoked by earlier selections in this chapter.

Born in Vienna, Lore Segal subsequently lived in England (where she received her B.A. in English from the University of London in 1948), the Dominican Republic, and (starting in 1951), New York. She has taught writing at Columbia University's School of the Arts, Princeton, Bennington College, the University of Illinois at Chicago, and Ohio State University. A prolific writer, her novels include *Other People's Houses* (1964), *Lucinella* (1978), and *Her First American* (1985). Her children's books include *Tell Me a Mitzi* (1970), *Morris the Artist* (2003), and *Why Mole Shouted and Other Stories* (2004). Thirteen interrelated stories, seven of which appeared in *the New Yorker*, were collected into *Shakespeare's Kitchen* (2007). "The Arbus Factor" appeared in the Winter Fiction issue of *the New Yorker* on December 24 and 31, 2007.

On one of the first days of the New Year, Jack called Hope. "Let's have lunch," he said. "I've got an agenda." No need to specify the Café Provence on upper Broadway, or the time—fifteen minutes before noon, when they were sure of getting their table by the window.

They did the menu, heard the specials. Hope said, "I'm always going to order something different," but ordered the onion soup. Jack ordered the cassoulet, saying, "I *should* have the fish."

"And a bottle of your Merlot," he told the unsmiling proprietress, "which we will have right away."

"We'll share a salad," Hope said. She saw Jack watch the proprietress walk off in the direction of the bar, in a remarkably short skirt for a woman of fifty. Hope saw the long, brown, athletic legs, bare even in January, with Jack's eyes. Jack, a large man, with a heavy, dark face, turned to Hope. "So?"

5   "O.K., I guess. You?"

Jack said, "My agenda: if we were still making resolutions, what would yours be?"

Hope's interest pricked right up. "I'm thinking. You go first."

Jack said, "I'm going to watch what I eat. It's not the weight; it's the constantly thinking of eating. I don't eat real meals unless Jeremy comes over." Jeremy was Jack's son.

Hope said, "I'm going to watch what I watch and then I'm going to turn the TV off. It's ugly waking mornings with the thing flickering. It feels debauched."

10   Jack said, "I'm not going to order books from Amazon till I've read the ones on my shelves."

Hope said, "I'm going to hang up my clothes even when nobody is coming over. Nora is very severe with me." Nora was Hope's daughter.

The wine arrived. Jack did the label-checking, cork-sniffing, tasting, and nodding. The salad came. Hope served their two plates. Jack indicated Hope's hair, which she had done in an upsweep. "Very fetching," he commented.

"Thank you. Here's an old new resolution: Going to learn French. What was the name of my teacher when we got back from Paris? I once counted eleven years of school French, but it was you who always had to do the talking."

Jack said, "I want to learn how to pray."

15   Hope looked across the table to see if he was being cute. Jack was concentrating on folding a whole lettuce leaf into his mouth.

Hope said, "I'll never understand the principle of not cutting it into bite size."

The onion soup came, the cassoulet came. Jack asked Hope if she would like to go back.

"Go back? Back to Paris!" Jack and Hope had lived together before marrying two other people. Jack subsequently divorced his wife, who had subsequently died. Hope was widowed.

"To Paris. To Aix," Jack said.

20   "Something I've been meaning to ask you," Hope said. "Were you and I ever together in an old, old garden? Did we walk under century-old trees? Did we lie down in the grass and look into tree crowns in France, or was that in England? Was it an old English garden or is this a garden in a book?"

"What's to keep us?" Jack said.

There were a lot of reasons, of course, to keep them from going back. Two of the littlest were at this moment flattening their noses against the outside of the restaurant window. Ten-year-old Benjamin stuck his thumbs in his ears and wiggled his fingers at his grandfather. Hope made as if to catch her granddaughter's hand through the glass. This made little Miranda laugh. And there was Hope's daughter, Nora, with baby Julie in a stroller, and Jack's son, Jeremy, standing out on the sidewalk.

"I'm just going to the bathroom," Hope mouthed to her daughter.

"What?" Nora mouthed back, her face sharpened with irritation. The baby was crying.

25   "She knows I can't hear her through the glass," Nora said to Jeremy.

Jeremy said, "You stay with the kids. I'll go in and get him. I'll see what your mother wants." Jeremy walked into the restaurant, passing Jack and Hope on his way to the corner where, an hour ago, he had folded up his father's wheelchair. Hope stood and came around the table to kiss Jack and be kissed goodbye.

"On the double, Dad," Jeremy said. "I need to get back to the office."

"I'll call you," Jack said to Hope. "We'll have lunch."

Hope was mouthing through the window again and Nora said, "Julie, shut up, please! Mom, *what*?" The baby had started screeching.

30   Hope pointed in the direction of the ladies' room. Nora signalled, You need me to go with you? Hope shook her head no. One of the reasons for the Café Provence was that its bathrooms were on the street floor, not in the basement, down a long stair.

Gathering her coat and bag, Hope opened the door to the ladies' room and saw, in the mirror above the basins, that her hair was coming out of its pins. She removed all the pins and stood gazing at the crone with the gray, shoulder-length hair girlishly loosened. Hope saw what Diane Arbus might have seen and was appalled, and being appalled pricked her interest right up. "I've got an agenda: the Arbus factor of old age," Hope looked forward to saying to Jack the next time it would be convenient for Jeremy and Nora to arrange lunch for them at the Café Provence.

● Discussion and Writing Suggestions

1. As you began reading this story, what were your initial impressions of Jack and Hope when they meet at the restaurant? How did you picture these characters? What did you infer about their relationship? What kind of details provided by Segal caused your initial impressions to change?

2. When did you realize that Jack and Hope are older, possibly elderly? Were you surprised? Why do you think Segal withheld this information at the outset of the story?

3. At what point do we learn of Jack and Hope's prior relationship? What kind of relationship do you believe it was? Do you think that during this prior relationship they contemplated marriage to one another? If so, what might have prevented such a marriage from happening?

4. Aging and the consequences of aging are a recurring motif in this story. What evidence does Segal provide of these consequences? How does this evidence relate to what you take to be the theme of "The Arbus Factor"?

5. How would you characterize Jeremy and Nora's attitudes toward each other, their parents, and their own children? Have we caught Jeremy and Nora on a

bad day, at a bad moment? If not, what does Segal's characterization of them suggest to you about marriage?

6. To what extent do Jeremy and Nora's attitudes toward one another and their parents make you reassess Hope and Jack's prospects for a successful marriage at the time they were living together in Paris? Might their intimacy, as it is revealed over lunch at the restaurant, have *suffered* had they decided to marry?

7. Why do you think this story is called "The Arbus Factor"? Look up Diane Arbus, using Google or Bing, and study some of her photographs. (The *New Yorker*, where this story originally appeared, accompanied the text with an Arbus photograph of an old woman's wrinkled face.) Do you think Jack sees what Diane Arbus might have seen when looking at Hope—or what Hope herself sees when looking in the mirror?

8. In what ways might this story suggest that young people and old people share closer views (or experiences) relating to idealized romantic love than do married people (such as Jeremy and Nora) with stay-at-home children?

9. Segal opens the story by giving Jack an "agenda." The story closes with Hope's having an "agenda." What is Hope's agenda, and how does it compare with Jack's? Discuss the effect—on the story and on you—of this symmetry.

10. View the film *Away from Her* (2006), about a Canadian woman (played by Julie Christie) with worsening Alzheimer's disease, who is placed by her loving husband into an assisted living facility. There, as she gradually forgets who her husband is, she falls in love with another man—a relationship eventually accepted and even encouraged by her husband. How are the themes of this Sarah Polley film (and the Alice Munro story, "The Bear Came Over the Mountain," on which it is based) reminiscent of those in "The Arbus Factor"? What is the role of age and memory in strengthening—and weakening—love and/or marriage?

SYNTHESIS ACTIVITIES

1. Write an explanatory synthesis focused on the development of the "love match" model of marriage. Why did it emerge? When? How does it differ from previous models? Explain the effect of the rise of the "love match" model on the institution of marriage as a whole. Focus particularly on the effect this model has had on people's expectations of marriage and on who should get married. For your sources, draw upon Coontz, Popenoe and Whitehead, Sullivan, Cherlin, Edelman, Bartels, and Patz. *An option:* As part of an extended conclusion that might be as long as a third of the final paper, explore the role you expect (hope?) love to play in your own marriage. So that your conclusion remains a part of

the overall synthesis, let your exploration emerge from your awareness of the historical determinants of the love match. You now know that there have been other models for marriage—the "economic" match, for instance, the "institutional" match, or the "compatibility" match. As you contemplate your own (prospective) marriage, to what extent will you insist on a love match?

2. Explain the working mother versus stay-at-home mother debate. Focus in particular on the struggles women face as they try to balance the concerns of work versus family. You may also wish to touch upon the issue of house-work, as the two issues sometimes overlap. Because this is an *explanatory* synthesis, make sure that your explanation of the varying viewpoints re-mains objective. Draw primarily upon the selections by Hekker, Bennetts, Tannen, and Edelman (as well as Bartels, if you find it relevant).

3. Argue that one parent should—or should not—stop working (at least for a time) when children are born. In formulating your argument, be sure to acknowledge the various arguments on all sides of the issue. Then assert which course of action, overall, would best benefit Ameri-can families. Draw upon as many of the articles in this chapter as will support your case.

4. Devise a blueprint for contemporary wives and husbands to avoid (or at least effectively address) common marital conflicts. First explain elements of your blueprint and then argue for its viability. For example, first ex-plain how best to take care of the children when both parents must work or prefer to work. Then argue that your plan is reasonable. You could do the same for devising a fair division of household labor. In developing this combination explanatory/argument synthesis, consult such sources as Coontz, Popenoe and Whitehead, Bennetts, Edelman, and Bartels.

5. To what extent is it a good idea for young people to delay getting mar-ried until their late twenties or beyond? In supporting your argument for earlier or later marriage, draw upon such sources as Popenoe and White-head, Cherlin, Edelman, and Bartels.

6. Compare and contrast Terry Martin Hekker's first essay, on the satisfac-tions of being a stay-at-home mother, with the selection by Edelman. How does each of these women feel about her married and family lives? As points of comparison and contrast, consider their attitudes toward housework, their children, their husbands, and their desire for self-fulfill-ment. In writing your conclusion, consider what factors might have been responsible for these women's differing views on these matters.

7. Analyze a marital relationship—real or fictional—using one or more of the principles in articles from the chapter. (If you have read any Jane Austen novels or Leo Tolstoy's *Anna Karenina* or Gustave Flaubert's *Madame Bovary*, you may wish to use the marriages of characters in those books.) Focus on how the principle you have chosen allows one to better

understand the relationship in question. Follow the general format for writing analyses discussed in Chapter 6.

8. Compare and contrast Andrew Sullivan's and William J. Bennett's arguments on gay marriage. In particular, focus on the assumptions regarding the nature of marriage that each brings to his argument. (You may want to consider how Sullivan's argument follows from a principle found in the selection by Coontz.)

9. Discuss whether or not, as Eric Bartels writes, "marriage is a creaky, old institution that may not have fully adapted itself to modern life." In supporting your argument, draw upon Coontz, Popenoe and Whitehead, Hekker, Cherlin, Edelman, Bartels, and any of the other selections you think relevant. Follow the "Guidelines for Writing Syntheses," pp. 97–98 in Chapter 4.

10. Conduct an analysis of a bridal or newlywed magazine, movie, or television show, guided by a principle you select from one or more selections in this chapter. Use this analytical principle to understand more clearly how popular culture, as expressed in the magazine, movie, or television show you have selected, helps to form, reinforce, or (perhaps) undermine our expectations of marriage. Follow the "Guidelines for Writing Analyses," p. 196.

11. Offer—and explain—the one piece of advice that you would give to someone who is about to get married. In supporting your argument that this is the single most important advice that anybody who is getting married should follow, draw from among the following selections: Coontz, Popenoe and Whitehead, Hekker, Edelman, Bartels, and Patz.

RESEARCH ACTIVITIES

1. Do an Internet search, using Google, Bing, or another search engine, for reaction to the Terry Martin Hekker 2006 essay "Paradise Lost (Domestic Division)." Locate mentions of the piece on blogs (try sites dealing with the "Mommy Wars," working mothers, or stay-at-home mothers), in letters to the editor of the *New York Times*, and in op-ed pieces; then synthesize some of the responses that Hekker's essay inspired.

2. Find and report on additional articles dealing with the "Mommy Wars"—the dispute over whether mothers should stay at home to take care of the children or whether they should pursue careers, leaving their children with other caregivers. To what extent has the controversy evolved over the past few years? To what extent does a critical consensus appear to be forming—perhaps by feminists, perhaps by traditionalists—over what young mothers should do? Write a synthesis explaining your findings, and, perhaps, arguing your own position.

3. What is the state of gay marriage in the United States today? How many states, for example, allow gay marriage? Prohibit gay marriage? How many recognize civil unions? What has been the position of the federal government over the past fifteen years? What kinds of state and federal legislation have been passed (or debated) in recent years, and what kinds of decisions have been made by state and federal courts in response? What do recent polls about the subject reveal? Based on your findings, do you believe that the social and political climate for gay marriage is improving or deteriorating?

4. Research arranged marriages—either in an ethnic subculture in the United States or in a foreign country. On the whole, how happy do people report being in these marriages? Provide statistical and/or anecdotal evidence concerning this rate of satisfaction. Compare this rate to that of people in nonarranged marriages, preferably in that same culture—or, if that information is not available, compare it to the rate of marital satisfaction in our country, as reported by sources such as the National Marriage Project (http://marriage.rutgers.edu/). If you know people who have been in an arranged marriage, ask for their views on the subject.

5. The prenuptial agreement has become a common feature of marriages where at least one partner has significant assets. Research and write an overview of prenuptial contracts (including, if possible, some of the more notorious lawsuits they have engendered). Search, in particular, for pieces that express an opinion regarding their use (op-ed pieces, magazine articles, letters to the editor). You may also wish to conduct an informal poll among your friends as to whether or not they approve of their use, whether or not they might insist, before their own marriage, on a prenuptial contract, etc. Report on your findings.

6. Investigate the effect that no-fault divorce laws have had on marriage in this country. Write a synthesis summarizing the circumstances under which the states passed such laws, the effect of these laws on the national divorce rate, and a brief overview of the controversy over the laws and their effect on the institution of marriage.

7. President John Adams and First Lady Abigail Adams had one of the more famous marriages in the history of the presidency. Abigail Adams's letters to her husband, in which she counseled him on matters public and private and in which she was an early advocate for women's issues, are still widely read, and in part form the lyrics for the Broadway musical *1776*. Research John and Abigail Adams's marriage. In which ways was it typical of its time and place? In which ways was it atypical—i.e., in which ways did it seem more like a modern marriage?

8. The 1950s are often considered the "Golden Age" of marriage. When conservative commentators evoke the "good old days" of marriage, it is almost always the 1950s model they have in mind—a father with a good job, a mother who stays home and raises the children, a house in the

suburbs, and an extended family that is usually located in another town or even state. Such marriages were the basis of popular contemporary 1950s sitcoms like *Father Knows Best* and *Ozzie and Harriet,* and they were also satirized in the 1998 film *Pleasantville.*

Research the realities of marriage in the 1950s. (Stephanie Coontz has written extensively on this subject.) To what extent is the stereotype accurate? Was there a "dark side" to marriage in the 1950s? Consider the political, economic, and cultural climate of the 1950s. What effect did these factors have on marriages of the day?

9. Research the issue of day care in this country. Locate studies that have shown positive or negative consequences to putting kids in day care. Draw also upon op-ed pieces, articles, sections in books, or personal opinions you have discovered (for example, on blogs concerning motherhood, working mothers, or stay-at-home mothers), and write a synthesis reporting on your findings.

10. Andrew Cherlin has noted how weddings, once events controlled by kinship groups or parents, are now increasingly controlled by the couples themselves. One result is that the wedding has become a status symbol—"an important symbol of the partners' personal achievements and a stage in their self-development." Research the wedding industry in this country, which generates over $60 billion annually. On what is all this money being spent? What kinds of services are most popular among clients—and why? Where are people getting married? Examine a bridal magazine. What do you think the industry is *really* selling? Try to find quotations from wedding industry professionals on this topic.

11. Leslie Bennetts writes: "Compared with other Western nations, the family-related policies of the United States are a disgrace." Research some of the policies relating to families—ranging "from flexible work schedules to affordable quality child care"—in one or more other Western countries, such as Canada, the United Kingdom, France, or Sweden.

Answer Key to "A Pop Quiz on Marriage"

1. **FALSE.** From 1970 to the late 1990's, men's attitudes toward marriage became more favorable, while women's became less so. By the end of the century, more men than women said that marriage was their ideal lifestyle. And on average, men become more content with their marriages over time, while women grow less so. A majority of divorced men and women report that the wife was the one who wanted out of the marriage. A recent study of divorces that occurred after age 40 found that wives initiated two-thirds of them.

2. **FALSE.** The difference in the ages of men and women at first marriage has been narrowing for the past 80 years and is now at a historic low. By the end of the 1990, 39 percent of women age 35 to 44 lived with younger men. Men still rate youth and good looks higher than women do when looking for a

mate, but those criteria no longer outweigh all others. Men are much more likely now to seek a mate who has the same level of education and similar earnings potential. College educated women are more likely to marry and less likely to divorce than women with less education.

3. **TRUE.** Although divorce rates have risen, death rates have fallen even more steeply, so that more couples will celebrate their 40th wedding anniversaries now than at any time in the past. Furthermore, the divorce rate reached its height more than 25 years ago. It has fallen by more than 25 percent since 1981.

4. **FALSE.** Americans are now more tolerant of consenting sexual relations between unmarried adults than in the past. But surveys show that disapproval of adultery, sexual coercion, rape and sex with minors has increased over the past 30 years and is now at a historic high. In 1889, a girl could legally consent to sex at 10, 11 or 12 in half the states, and in Delaware the age of consent was 7. There were many more prostitutes per capita in late 19th century America than there are today—resulting in a high incidence of venereal disease among respectably married women infected by their husbands.

5. **FALSE.** For the first thousand years of its existence, the church held that a marriage was valid if a couple claimed they had exchanged words of consent—even if there were no witnesses and no priest to officiate. Not until 1754 did England require issuance of a license for a marriage to be valid. Informal marriage and cohabitation were so common in early 19th-century America that one judge estimated that one third of all children were born to couples who were not legally married.

6. **FALSE.** The likelihood that college-educated women will drop out of the labor force because of having children declined by half from 1984 to 2004. And among all mothers with children under 6, the most highly educated are the least likely to leave their jobs, with that likelihood declining with each level of educational attainment.

7. **TRICK QUESTION.** Women with nontraditional values are indeed more likely to divorce than women with traditional views, but they are also more likely to get married in the first place. As for men, those with traditional values about gender are more likely to marry than nontraditional men, but they are also more likely to divorce. We don't precisely know why this discrepancy exists, but it probably has something to do with the fact that women's views on gender are changing more rapidly than men's.

8. **FALSE.** Aside from a huge spike in divorce immediately after World War II, divorce rates in the 1950's were higher than in any previous decade aside from the Depression, and almost one in three marriages formed in the 1950's eventually ended in divorce. Divorce rates rose steadily from the 1890's through the 1960's (with a dip in the Depression and a spike after World War II), soared in the 1970's, and have fallen since 1981. Marriage rates, however, have also fallen significantly in the past 25 years.

9. **FALSE.** Ancient Roman philosophers and medieval theologians thought that loving your spouse too much was a form of "adultery," a betrayal of one's obligations to country or God. The ancient Greeks held that the purest form of love was between two men. In China, Confucian philosophers ranked the relationship between husband and wife as second from the bottom on their list of the most important family ties, with the father-eldest son relationship topping the list. Early Christians thought marriage was inescapably tainted by the presence of sex. According to the medieval church, virgins ranked highest in godliness, widows were second and wives a distant third.

10. **TRUE.** In 2001 schoolgirls around the world were asked whether they agreed with the statement that everyone needed to marry. Three-quarters of American schoolgirls agreed. But in Japan, 88 percent of schoolgirls disagreed.

11. **FALSE.** Divorce in modern America often does cause a sharp drop in the economic standard of living for women and children. But states that legalize no-fault divorce experienced an average 10 percent decline in suicide rates among married women over the following five years. And a recent study suggests that while divorce worsens the emotional well being of 55 percent to 60 percent of children, it improves the well-being of 40 percent to 45 percent.

12. **FALSE.** The form of marriage that has been approved by more societies than any other through the ages has been polygamy—one man and many women. That family form is the one mentioned most often in the first five books of the Bible. In some societies, one woman could marry several men. In others, two families could forge an alliance by marrying off a son or daughter to the "ghost" of the other family's dead child. For most of history; the main impetus for marriage was getting in-laws and managing property, not love or sex.

13. **TRUE.** Thirty-five percent of born-again Christians in this country have divorced, almost the same as the 37 percent of atheists and agnostics who have divorced—and 23 percent of born-again Christians have divorced twice. Among Pentecostals, the divorce rate is more than 40 percent. The region with the highest divorce rate is the Bible Belt.

Chapter 10

To Sleep

Every night nearly every person on the planet undergoes an astounding metamorphosis. As the sun sets, a delicate timing device at the base of our brain sends a chemical signal throughout our body, and the gradual slide toward sleep begins. Our body becomes inert, and our lidded eyes roll slowly from side to side. Later, the eyes begin the rapid eye movements that accompany dreams, and our mind enters a highly active state where vivid dreams trace our deepest emotions. Throughout the night we traverse a broad landscape of dreaming and nondreaming realms, wholly unaware of the world outside. Hours later, as the sun rises, we are transported back to our bodies and to waking consciousness.

And we remember almost nothing.

So begins *The Promise of Sleep* by researcher and sleep pioneer William Dement, who for fifty years has investigated what happens each night after we close our eyes. Later in this chapter you will hear more from Dement; but for the moment, let his sense of wonder about what another author in this chapter calls that "state so familiar yet so strange" spark your own interest in sleep, a behavior that will occupy one-third of your life.

Not until 1929 did Johannes Berger use a new device called the electroencephalogram (EEG) to confirm that far from shutting down while asleep, our brains remain highly active. With the insight that sleep is not merely the absence of wakefulness, and the subsequent discovery that each night's sleep unfolds in five classifiable stages, sleep research accelerated in the twentieth century. Yet for thousands of years sleep (and its frustrating absence) has sparked the inquiries of physicians, scientists, and philosophers. As early as 1300 BCE, the Egyptians used opium as a medication to treat insomnia. Nearly a thousand years later, Aristotle framed his inquiry into sleep with questions that occupy us still:

> With regard to sleep and waking, we must consider what they are: whether they are peculiar to soul or to body, or common to both; and if common, to what part of soul or body they appertain: further, from what cause it arises that they are attributes of animals, and whether all animals share in them both....
>
> *"On Sleep and Sleeplessness"*

Allowing for the fact that modern sleep researchers do not investigate the "soul," per se, they nevertheless retain a high level of interest in the nature of consciousness and what happens to it when we sleep. The ancients thought of sleep as a daily, metaphorical death. If sleep is not a death, then what precisely *is* it? Does sleep repair the body? Does it consolidate the day's learning? Is it a strategy for keeping the sleeper safe? Does it aid in development and maintenance of the central nervous system? Researchers have investigated each of these questions but have found no definitive answers. Theoretical explanations of sleep aside, at the clinical level specialists cannot yet remedy all eighty-four known sleep disorders, which rob sufferers of needed rest and keep them, according to the famous insomniac poet and critic Samuel Taylor Coleridge, in "anguish and in agony." The investigations, therefore, continue.

Up to forty million Americans suffer from sleep disruptions that for some trigger serious health risks, including cardiovascular disease, obesity, and depression. Sleep loss leads to measurable cognitive and physical deficits comparable to those observed in people impaired by alcohol. The sleep that *we don't* get each day adds up to a cumulative debt that we must "repay" in order to function at full capacity, say sleep specialists. Failure to sleep enough (eight hours is the norm, though individual requirements vary) leads to quantifiable costs:

- Americans spend $15 billion per year in direct health care costs related to problems with sleeping.
- The U.S. economy loses $50 billion per year in diminished productivity due to problems with sleeping.
- The National Highway Traffic and Safety Administration estimates that sleep-deprived drivers cause 100,000 accidents each year, resulting in 1,500 fatalities and 71,000 injuries.

The literature of sleep research is vast. Investigators study the sleep of insects, fish, amphibians, birds, and mammals (including humans) with the tools of biology, neurology, chemistry, psychology, and a host of other disciplines. This chapter brings the study of sleep to a focus very close to home for readers of this book: the sleep of adolescents, one of the many subspecialties of sleep medicine. You may know that the sleep of infants and toddlers merits special attention from specialists since, when children don't sleep well, few others in the home do, either. And you may be aware that the sleep of older people, which can grow troubled due to both physiological and psychological changes, has been the subject of intense study. An equally active area among researchers is the sleep of ten- to nineteen-year-olds, who require one hour more of sleep each night (due to rapidly maturing bodies) than do adults or children who no longer nap—and this at a time in life when the scheduling demands of school and work tend to decrease the amount of sleep available to adolescents.

If you find yourself at the threshold of late adolescence and early adulthood, or are otherwise connected to an adolescent who is a sibling or friend, you will discover much of interest in this chapter on the "strange state" of sleep. We begin with an overview of the subject, "A Third of Life" by Paul Martin, in which you will learn (among other things) that certain dolphins put one-half of their brains to sleep at a time so that the other half can keep them swimming—and surfacing for air. "Improving Sleep" edited by Lawrence Epstein, MD, reviews the fundamentals of sleep medicine, including REM (rapid eye movement) and non-REM sleep. We move next to a news release on the troubled state of adolescent sleep, based on a poll conducted by the National Sleep Foundation. Researcher Mary A. Carskadon then explains how the biological, behavioral, and social worlds converge to make sleeping so difficult for many adolescents. William C. Dement and Christopher Vaughan follow with "Sleep Debt and the Mortgaged Mind," an inquiry into what happens to a body deprived of sleep.

So that you can assess the current state of your own sleep, we offer the Pittsburgh Sleep Quality Index, a self-scoring assessment used in many sleep studies. Use the PSQI to rate your sleep along seven dimensions and determine your overall sleep score. In "How Sleep Debt Hurts College Students," June J. Pilcher and Amy S. Walters deprive students of a night's sleep and test their cognitive functioning the next day. (The news is not good for those who pull "all-nighters.") A second sleep study examines the correlations between the sleepiness of students and their incidence of auto crashes when school start times are delayed by one hour. We conclude the chapter with several nonscientific reflections on sleep by the English Romantic poets John Keats ("To Sleep"), Samuel Taylor Coleridge ("The Pains of Sleep"), and Lord Byron ("The Dream").

The National Institutes of Health distributes $200 million a year for sleep research, with some of that money reserved for new curricula that alert science students to the importance of good sleep hygiene. In effect, this chapter offers such a curriculum. In reading the selections that follow, not only will you gain an opportunity to practice the skills of summary, synthesis, critique, and analysis; you will also gain information that can help you feel and function better in your daily life.

A THIRD OF LIFE

Paul Martin

In our chapter opening, Paul Martin, who holds a PhD in behavioral biology from Cambridge University, provides an overview of sleep and its place in both human and animal evolution. Martin introduces the concept of sleep debt and its consequences—a principal focus of this chapter—and then reviews the behavioral characteristics of sleep. The present selection forms the first chapter of Martin's *Counting Sheep: The Science and Pleasures of Sleep and Dreams* (2002).

> Man…consumes more than one third of his life in this his irrational situation.
>
> Erasmus Darwin, *Zoonomia (1801)*

Sleep: a state so familiar yet so strange. It is the single most common form of human behaviour and you will spend a third of your life doing it—25 years or more, all being well. When you die, a bigger slice of your existence will have passed in that state than in making love, raising children, eating, playing games, listening to music, or any of those other activities that humanity values so highly.

Sleep *is* a form of behaviour, just as eating or socialising or fighting or copulating are forms of behaviour, even if it is not the most gripping to observe. Most of the action goes on inside the brain. It is also a uniquely private experience, even when sharing a bed. When we are awake we all inhabit a common world, but when we sleep each of us occupies a world of our own. Most of us, however, have precious little awareness of what we experience in that state. Our memories of sleeping and dreaming mostly evaporate when we awake, erasing the record every morning.

Many of us do not get enough sleep and we suffer the consequences, often without realising what we are doing to ourselves. The demands of the 24-hour society are marginalising sleep, yet it is not an optional activity. Nature imposes it upon us. We can survive for longer without food. When our sleep falls short in quantity or quality we pay a heavy price in depressed mood, impaired performance, damaged social relationships and poorer health. But we usually blame something else.

Sleep is an active state, generated within the brain, not a mere absence of consciousness. You are physiologically capable of sleeping with your eyelids held open by sticking plaster, bright lights flashing in your eyes and loud music playing in your ears. We shall later see how science has revealed the ferment of electrical and chemical activity that goes on inside the brain during sleep, and how the sleeping brain operates in a quite different mode from waking consciousness. We shall see too how lack of sleep erodes our quality of life and performance while simultaneously making us more vulnerable to injuries and illness. Science amply supports William Shakespeare's view that sleep is the 'chief nourisher in life's feast'.

5   What is sleep and what is it for? Why do so many people have such problems with it? Why do we dream? Although sleep forms a central strand of human and animal life it is still poorly understood and widely neglected. It is an inglorious example of familiarity breeding contempt. Sleep is so much a part of our everyday existence that we take it for granted. We are ignorant even of our ignorance. In 1758, Doctor Samuel Johnson summed it up like this:

> Among the innumerable mortifications that waylay human arrogance on every side may well be reckoned our ignorance of the most common objects and effects…Vulgar and inactive minds confound familiarity with knowledge, and conceive themselves informed of the whole nature of things when they are shown their form or told their use…Sleep is a state in which a great part of every life is passed. No animal has been yet discovered whose existence is not varied with intervals of insensibility. Yet of this change so frequent, so great, so general, and so necessary, no searcher has yet found either the efficient or final cause; or can tell by what power the mind and body are thus chained down in irresistible stupefaction; or what benefits the animal receives from this alternate suspension of its active powers.

The scientists who do know something about sleep often bemoan society's ignorance of it. They point to the vast gap between current scientific understanding of sleep, patchy though it is, and the practical benefits it could bring if that knowledge were absorbed and acted upon by society. Our collective indifference towards sleep has enormous and largely avoidable costs.

A sleep-sick society?

> The mere presence of an alarm clock implies sleep deprivation, and what bedroom lacks an alarm clock?
>
> James Gleick, *Faster (1999)*

All is not well with the state of sleep. Many of us depend on an alarm clock to prise us out of bed each morning, and children's bedrooms increasingly resemble places of entertainment rather than places of sleep. When given the opportunity, we sleep in at the weekends and feel only half awake when we do get up. On that long-awaited holiday we find the change of scenery (or is it the air?) makes us even sleepier. We are told that lying around and sleeping too much will only make us sleepier. But in truth we feel sleepy at weekends and on holidays not because we are sleeping too much, but because we have slept too little the rest of the time.

A century ago the majority toiled long hours while the affluent few idled away their time. Today, however, the more conventionally successful you are, the less free time you will probably have. Having nothing to do is seen as a sign of worthlessness, while ceaseless activity signifies status and success. Supposedly unproductive activities are deprioritised or delegated. And according to prevailing cultural attitudes, sleeping is one of the least productive of all human activities.... In their ceaseless pursuit of work and pleasure the cash-rich buy time from others, hiring them to clean their houses, look after their children and cook their food. But one of the activities you simply cannot delegate to anyone else is sleeping.

Evolution equipped humans, in common with all other animals, with biological mechanisms to make us sleep at roughly the same time every day. However, those mechanisms evolved to cope with a pre-industrial world that was vastly different from the one we now inhabit.

Our daily cycles of sleep and activity are no longer driven by dawn and dusk, but by clocks, electric lighting and work schedules. Sleep has become increasingly devalued in the 24-hour society. Many regard sleep as wasted time and would prefer to sacrifice less of their busy lives to it. We live in a world where there are too many tired, sleep-deprived people. Think of those pinched, yawning faces you can see every day on the trains and in buses and in cars crawling through jams. They look as if they have been brainwashed, but they are just tired.

10   We pay a steep price for neglecting sleep, in our ignorance and indifference. The scientific evidence tells us that far too many people in industrialised societies are chronically sleep-deprived, with damaging consequences for their mental and physical health, performance at work, quality of life and personal relationships. William Dement, a pioneering scientist in the field, believes that we now live in a 'sleep-sick society'. Scientists have not yet reached a consensus

about the precise extent of sleep deprivation in society, but they do all agree that sleepiness is a major cause of accidents and injuries. In fact, sleepiness is responsible for far more deaths on the roads than alcohol or drugs.

Everyone has heard about the need for a balanced diet and physical exercise, even if many of us fail to follow the advice. But sleep is lost in a deep well of ignorance and apathy. Even the medical profession pays it scant regard. Sleep and its disorders barely feature in the teaching of medicine, and few physicians are fully equipped to deal with the sleep problems they regularly encounter. When researchers from Oxford University investigated British medical education in the late 1990s, they discovered that the average amount of time devoted to sleep and sleep disorders in undergraduate teaching was five minutes, rising to a princely peak of 15 minutes in preclinical training. Your doctor is therefore unlikely to be an expert on the subject.

The general public and the medical profession are not the only ones to display a remarkable indifference to sleep. So too do most contemporary writers. Considering that sleep accounts for a third of human existence, it features remarkably rarely in novels, biographies, social histories or learned texts on neurobiology, psychology and medicine. And the few accounts that have made it into print are mostly concerned with what happens when it goes wrong. Insomnia and nightmares loom large in the tiny literature of sleep.

Few biographies mention the sleep behaviour or dreams of their subjects. That part of their story is almost invariably missing, as if somehow we all cease to exist at night. And most of those scholarly books that set out to explain how the human mind works say little or nothing about what goes on during the several hours of every day when the mind is sleeping and dreaming. They are really just books about how the brain works when it is awake. Our neglect of sleep is underlined by its absence from our literature.

Vladimir Nabokov once said that all the great writers have good eyes. What has happened to the eyes of writers as far as sleep and dreams are concerned? It was not always so. Older literature is distinctly richer in references to sleeping and dreaming, perhaps because darkness and sleep and dreams were much more prominent aspects of everyday life before the invention of the electric light bulb and the advent of the 24-hour society. Shakespeare's works are thick with allusions to sleep and dreams, as are Dickens's. We shall encounter some of them later. Meanwhile, to set the right tone, here is Sancho Panza's eulogy to sleep from *Don Quixote:*

> God bless the inventor of sleep, the cloak that covers all man's thoughts, the food that cures all hunger, the water that quenches all thirst, the fire that warms the cold, the cold that cools the heat; the common coin, in short, that can purchase all things, the balancing weight that levels the shepherd with the king and the simple with the wise.

The universal imperative

> Almost all other animals are observed to partake of sleep, aquatic, winged, and terrestrial creatures alike. For every kind of fish and the soft-shelled species have been seen sleeping, as has every other creature that has eyes.
>
> Aristotle *(384–322 B.C.), On Sleep and Waking*

15 Sleep is a universal human characteristic, like eating and drinking. Absolutely everybody does it. Sleep occupies about one third of each human life, and up to two thirds of a baby's time. (According to Groucho Marx, the proportion rises to three thirds if you live in Peoria.) It is a common bond that ties us all together. We have no choice: the longer we go without sleep, the stronger our desire for it grows. Tiredness, like hunger and thirst, will eventually force us to do the right thing whether we want to or not.

The dreams that accompany sleep are equally ubiquitous features of human life, even if many of us retain little memory of them after we awake. Dreaming is a classless activity that unites monarchs and paupers, a thought that Charles Dickens mused upon in one of his essays:

> Here, for example, is her Majesty Queen Victoria in her palace, this present blessed night, and here is Winking Charley, a sturdy vagrant, in one of her Majesty's jails...It is probable that we have all three committed murders and hidden bodies. It is pretty certain that we have all desperately wanted to cry out, and have had no voice; that we have all gone to the play and not been able to get in; that we have all dreamed much more of our youth than of our later lives.

Sleep is not a specifically human trait, of course. On the contrary, it is a universal characteristic of complex living organisms, as Aristotle deduced more than 23 centuries ago. Sleep is observed in animals of every sort, including insects, molluscs, fish, amphibians, birds and mammals. Within the animal world, sleep does vary enormously in quantity, quality and timing, accounting for anything up to 80 per cent of some animals' lifespans. But they all do it, one way or another. Some species, especially predators, spend more of their lives asleep than they do awake, a fact that TV documentaries and natural-history books seldom mention.

How do we know that an animal is sleeping? It is hard enough sometimes to be sure that a human is asleep, let alone a fish or a fly. The ultimate indicator of whether an animal or person is asleep is the distinctive pattern of electrical activity in its brain. During deep sleep the billions of individual nerve cells in the brain synchronise their electrical activity to some extent, generating characteristic waves of tiny voltage changes that can be detected by electrodes placed on the scalp. We shall be exploring the nature and internal structure of sleep later. The easiest way to recognise sleep, however, is from overt behaviour.

Sleep has several rather obvious distinguishing characteristics. A sleeping person or animal will generally remain in the same place for a prolonged period, perhaps several hours. There will be a certain amount of twitching, shifting of posture and fidgeting. Young animals will suckle while they sleep and ruminants will carry on chewing the cud. But sleepers normally do not get up and change their location. (When they do, we recognise it as a curious phenomenon and call it sleepwalking.)

Sleeping organisms also adopt a characteristic posture. Sloths and bats, for example, sleep hanging upside down from a branch. The Mediterranean flour moth sleeps with its antennae swivelled backwards and the tips tucked under its wings. If you are careful, you can gently lift the sleeping moth's wing without disturbing it—a trick that will definitely not work when it is awake. A lizard will settle on a branch during the hours before sunset, curl up its tail, close its eyelids, retract its eyeballs and remain in that distinctly sleep-like posture all night unless it is disturbed. A partridge, like many birds, will rest its weight on one leg while it sleeps. It is said that some gourmets can tell *which* leg, from its taste.

20   Monkeys and apes, including humans, usually sleep lying down. Indeed, we are built in such a way that we find it difficult to sleep properly unless we are lying down. People can and sometimes do sleep after a fashion while sitting, notably in aeroplanes, business meetings and school classrooms. If you are really exhausted, you might even manage to snatch some sleep standing up. But sleep taken while standing or sitting upright is generally fitful, shallow and unrefreshing. The non-horizontal sleeper may repeatedly nod off, but as soon as they descend beyond the shallowest stages of sleep their muscles relax, they begin to sway and their brain wakes them up again. That is why we 'nod off'. If you travel frequently on trains or buses, you might have had the dubious pleasure of sitting next to a weary commuter who has nodded off all over your shoulder. Recordings of brain-wave patterns show that people sleeping in an upright sitting position achieve only the initial stages of light sleep, not the sustained, deep sleep we require to wake up feeling truly refreshed. The reason is simple. Our muscles relax when we are fully asleep and we would fall over if we were not already lying down. Our brains therefore do not permit us to enter sustained, deep sleep unless we are in a physically stable, horizontal (or near-horizontal) posture.

Despite the virtual impossibility of sleeping deeply while sitting upright, we are sometimes forced to try. In *Down and Out in Paris and London,* George Orwell describes a particularly unwelcoming form of overnight accommodation that was known to the homeless of prewar London as the Twopenny Hangover. At the Twopenny Hangover the night's residents would sit in a row along a bench. In front of them was a rope, and the would-be sleepers would lean on this rope as though leaning over a fence. In that posture they were supposed to sleep. At five o'clock the next morning an official, wittily known as the valet, would cut the rope so that the residents could begin another day of wandering the streets.

Nowadays, tourist-class airline passengers travelling long distances can enjoy an experience similar to the Twopenny Hangover, albeit at vastly greater expense. George Orwell's autobiographical account of grinding poverty in the late 1920s is also a sharp reminder that lack of money is often accompanied by lack of decent sleep. Rough sleepers rarely get a good night's sleep.

Sleep has several other distinctive characteristics besides immobility and posture. In many species, including humans, individuals return to the same place each night (or each day, if they are nocturnal) in order to sleep. More generally, all members of a given species will tend to choose the same sorts of sleeping places. The distinctive feature of those places is often their security. Birds usually sleep on inaccessible branches or ledges. Many small mammals sleep in underground burrows where they are safer from predators. Fishes lie on the bottom, or wedge themselves into a crevice or against the underside of a rock. We humans prefer to sleep in relatively private and secure places. Given the choice, we rarely opt to sleep on busy streets or in crowded restaurants.

One obvious feature of sleep is a marked reduction in responsiveness to sights, sounds and other sensory stimuli. To provoke a response from a sleeping organism, stimuli have to be more intense or more relevant to the individual. For example, the reef fish known as the slippery dick sleeps during the hours of darkness, partly buried in the sand. While it is in this state, the sleeping slippery dick can be gently lifted to the surface by hand without it waking up and swimming off.

25   A sort of perceptual wall is erected during sleep, insulating the mind from the outside world. You would still be able to sleep if you had no eyelids, because your sleeping brain would not register what your eyes could see. This sensory isolation is highly selective, however. You can sleep through relatively loud noises from traffic or a radio, but a quiet mention of your name can rouse you immediately. Your brain is not simply blocked off during sleep. Moreover, this reduced responsiveness is rapidly reversible—a characteristic that distinguishes sleep from states such as unconsciousness, coma, anaesthesia and hibernation. A suitable stimulus, particularly one signifying immediate danger, can snap a sleeping person into staring-eyed alertness in an instant.

Another diagnostic feature of sleep is its regular cycle of waxing and waning. Living organisms sleep and wake according to a regular 24-hour cycle, or circadian rhythm. All members of a given species tend to sleep during the same part of the 24-hour cycle, when their environment is least favourable for other activities such as looking for food. For most species this means sleeping during the hours of darkness, but some species do the reverse. Many small mammals, which would be more vulnerable to predators during daylight, sleep by day and forage at night. Aside from a few nocturnal specialists such as owls, birds cannot easily fly in the dark, and most reptiles find it hard to maintain a sufficiently high body temperature to be active during the cool of night. Most birds and reptiles therefore sleep at night. Predators tend to sleep when their prey are asleep and hunt when their prey are up and about.

Sleep, then, is characterised by a special sleeping place and posture, prolonged immobility, a selective and rapidly reversible reduction in responsiveness to stimuli, and a 24-hour cycle. According to these and other criteria, all mammals, birds, fish, amphibians, reptiles and insects that have been inspected have been found to sleep.

• • •

Half asleep

> And the small fowl are making melody
> That sleep away the night with open eye
>
> Geoffrey Chaucer, *A Prologue to The Canterbury Tales (c. 1387)*

Sleep is such an overriding biological imperative that evolution has found ingenious ways of enabling animals to do it in the face of formidable obstacles. Nature, it seems, will do almost anything to ensure that animals sleep.

Consider dolphins, for example. They are air-breathing mammals like us, so they must swim to the surface each time they want to take a breath. They would drown if they fell into deep sleep while deep underwater. One possible solution to this biological design conundrum would be to wake up each time a breath of air was required. However, evolution has produced a more elegant solution: only one half of the dolphin's brain goes to sleep at a time.

30   Dolphins are capable of what is known as unihemispheric sleep, in which one hemisphere of the brain submerges into deep sleep while the other hemisphere remains awake. The two halves of the brain take it in turns to sleep, swapping at intervals of between one and three hours. This cerebral juggling trick enables dolphins to sleep underwater without drowning, which is just as well considering that they spend a good third of their lives asleep. Unihemispheric sleep has been recorded in several species of dolphins, porpoises and whales, including bottlenosed and Amazonian dolphins, Black Sea porpoises and white whales.

Despite the apparent convenience of being able to sleep and stay awake simultaneously, very few mammals are capable of unihemispheric sleep. The biological benefits of sleeping with only half of the brain at a time presumably outweigh the disadvantages only under unusual conditions, such as those encountered by air-breathing mammals living in the deep oceans.

Unihemispheric sleep is widespread in birds, however. They do it for a different biological reason. Sleeping with half the brain awake and one eye open allows them to sleep while simultaneously remaining vigilant for predators. In birds, each eye exclusively feeds the visual processing areas in the opposite half of the brain: thus, all the nerve fibres coming from the right eye connect to the left hemisphere of the brain and vice versa. When a bird is in unihemispheric sleep its open eye is the one corresponding to the waking half of the brain, while the closed eye is connected to the sleeping half. If a bird feels relatively safe, it closes both eyes, and both sides of its brain go to sleep.

An experiment with mallard ducks demonstrated how unihemispheric sleep helps birds to stay safe from predators. Four ducks were placed in a row along a perch, the idea being that the ducks at either end of the row would feel more vulnerable to predators than the two in the middle. In the natural world it is generally a bad idea to be on the edge of a group if you might end up as some other animal's dinner. As predicted, video recordings showed that the outer two birds were much more likely to sleep with one eye open than the two on the inside; their unihemispheric sleep increased by 150 per cent. The amount of unihemispheric sleep rose further when the ducks were shown frightening video images of an approaching predator.

The relationship between unihemispheric sleep and vigilance was finely controlled. The exposed birds on the ends of the row preferentially opened their outward-facing eye—the one directed towards potential danger. From time to time, a bird would turn round and switch eyes, so that the open eye was still the one facing out. Simultaneous recordings of brain activity confirmed that the brain hemisphere corresponding to the open eye was always awake, while the hemisphere corresponding to the closed eye was the one in deep sleep.

35 The one-eyed tactic was effective: when an attacking predator was simulated on a video screen, the birds sleeping with one eye open were able to react in a fraction of a second—far faster than if they had been in deep sleep with both eyes shut.

Humans are not capable of unihemispheric sleep, although at least one writer has played with the fantasy. Damon Runyon wrote of how he once played cards with a fading champion card player who now lacked the stamina to stay awake during marathon games of gin rummy lasting eight or ten hours. When the man lost a game after making a bad play, the punters betting on him to win clamoured to remove their bets from the next game, on the grounds that he was asleep. Then someone pointed out that the allegedly sleeping player's eyes were open, so he must be awake. 'The one on your side is', retorted one of the backers, 'but the one on the other side is closed. He is sleeping one-eye.'

● Review Questions

1. What are some of the qualities of sleep that make it "so strange," in Martin's view?

2. Cite some signs of sleep deprivation, and indicate some aspects of modern life that lead to lack of sleep.

3. What are the distinguishing characteristics of sleep, and which species have been observed to sleep?

4. What is unihemispheric sleep, and why is it a characteristic of some marine mammals and birds?

● Discussion and Writing Suggestions

1. Before reading Martin's article, to what extent did you consider sleep a "behavior"? How did you think of it, if not as a behavior? Explain.

2. What accounts for the relatively scant attention sleep has received in popular culture? In developing your answer, read what Samuel Johnson said on the matter in 1758 (see paragraph 5). To what extent does his response answer this question today?

3. What single observation about sleep stands out for you from this article? Explain your fascination.

4. Martin writes that "[e]volution equipped humans...to...sleep at roughly the same time every day...to cope with a pre-industrial world that was vastly different from the one we now inhabit" (paragraph 8). Imagine the world before the invention of electric or gas lighting. (If you go camping, you have direct experience

with this world.) In what ways do you think that modern life is working at odds
with bodily rhythms that evolved over tens of thousands of years?

5. Do you consider yourself sleep deprived? Several other authors in this chapter
   will address the issue; but based on the signs of sleep deprivation that Martin
   reviews, how serious is your sleep debt? Write about one incident that
   prompted you to consider getting more sleep.

IMPROVING SLEEP*

Lawrence Epstein, MD, Editor

Of the hundreds of introductions to the physiology of sleep, this selection appearing in a
Harvard Special Health Report edited by Lawrence Epstein, MD is among the clearest for
audiences without a formal background in medicine. We excerpt the opening sections of
the larger report: overviews of sleep mechanics, sleep throughout life, and consequences
of sleep deprivation.

Some nights, sleep comes easily, and you sail through the night in a satisfying
slumber. Waking up after a night of good sleep feels wonderful—you're
refreshed, energized, and ready to take on the world. Other nights, sleep comes
slowly or not until the wee hours. Or you may fall asleep, only to awaken
throughout the night.

If you have trouble sleeping, you're not alone. Almost everyone occasionally
suffers from short-term insomnia. According to the National Institutes of Health,
about 60 million Americans a year have insomnia frequently or for extended periods of time. About half of all people over 65 have frequent sleeping problems,
and an estimated 40 million Americans have a chronic sleep disorder such as
sleep apnea, restless legs syndrome, or narcolepsy. We pay a high price for all
the sleep deprivation caused by sleep problems. For example:

- Insufficient sleep is directly linked to poor health, with new research suggesting it increases the risk of diabetes, heart disease, obesity, and even
  premature death. Even a few nights of bad sleep can be detrimental.

- The combination of sleep deprivation and driving can have deadly consequences. A 2006 review by the Institute of Medicine of the National Academy
  of Sciences found that almost 20% of all serious car accidents and 57% of fatal
  accidents are associated with driver sleepiness.

- Sleep deprivation played a role in catastrophes such as the Exxon Valdez
  oil spill off the coast of Alaska, the space shuttle Challenger explosion, and
  the nuclear accident at Three Mile Island.

---

*Excerpted from the Harvard Health Publications Special Report, "Improving Sleep," © 2008, Presi-
dent and Fellows of Harvard College. For more information visit: www.health.harvard.edu. Harvard
Health Publications does not endorse any products or medical procedures. Reprinted by permission.

Sleep problems affect virtually every aspect of day-to-day living, including mood, mental alertness, work performance, and energy level. Yet few Americans seek treatment for their sleep problems. If you aren't getting your share of sleep, you needn't fumble about in a fog of fatigue. This report describes the complex nature of sleep, the latest in sleep research, the factors that can disturb sleep, and, most importantly, what you can do to get the sleep you need for optimal health, safety, and well-being.

Sleep Mechanics

For centuries, scientists scrutinized minute aspects of human activity, but showed little interest in the time that people spent in sleep. Sleep seemed inaccessible to medical probing and was perceived as an unvarying period of inactivity—a subject best suited to poets and dream interpreters who could conjure meaning out of the void. All that changed in the 1930s, when scientists learned

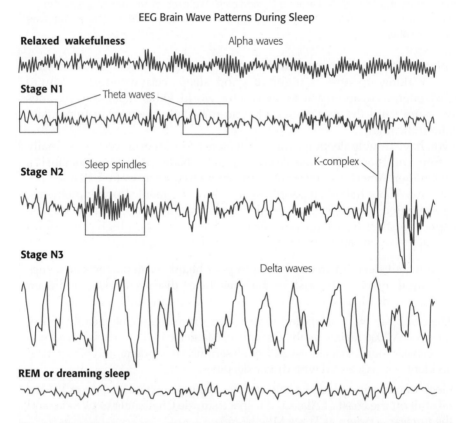

Fig. 1. These brain waves, taken by electroencephalogram, are used by sleep experts to identify the stages of sleep. Close your eyes and your brain waves will look like the first band, "relaxed wakefulness." Theta waves indicate Stage N1 sleep. (The "N" designates non-REM sleep.) Stage N2 sleep shows brief bursts of activity as sleep spindles and K-complex waves. Deep sleep is represented by large, slow delta waves (Stage N3).

to place sensitive electrodes on the scalp and record the signals produced by electrical activity in the brain. These brain waves can be seen on an electroencephalogram, or EEG (see Figure 1), which today is captured on a computer screen. Since then, researchers gradually came to appreciate that sleep is a highly complex activity. Using electrodes to monitor sleepers' eye movements, muscle tone, and brain wave patterns, they identified several discrete stages of sleep. And today, researchers continue to learn how certain stages of sleep help to maintain health, growth, and functioning.

5   Scientists divide sleep into two major types: rapid eye movement (REM) sleep or dreaming sleep, and non-REM or quiet sleep. Surprisingly, they are as different from one another as sleeping is from waking.

Quiet Sleep   Sleep specialists have called non-REM or quiet sleep "an idling brain in a movable body." During this phase, thinking and most physiological activities slow down, but movement can still occur, and a person often shifts position while sinking into progressively deeper stages of sleep.

To an extent, the convention of describing people "dropping" into sleep actually parallels changes in brain wave patterns at the onset of non-REM sleep. When you are awake, billions of brain cells receive and analyze sensory information, coordinate behavior, and maintain bodily functions by sending electrical impulses to one another. If you're fully awake, the EEG will record a messy, irregular scribble of activity. Once your eyes are closed and your nerve cells no longer receive visual input, brain waves settle into a steady and rhythmic pattern of about 10 cycles per second. This is the alpha-wave pattern, characteristic of calm, relaxed wakefulness.

The transition to quiet sleep is a quick one that might be likened to flipping a switch—that is, you are either awake (switch on) or asleep (switch off), according to recent research. Some brain centers and pathways stimulate the entire brain to wakefulness; others promote falling asleep. One chemical, hypocretin, seems to play an important role in regulating when the flip between states occurs and keeping you in the new state. Interestingly, people with narcolepsy often lack hypocretin, and they consequently flip back and forth between sleep and wakefulness frequently.

Three Stages of Quiet Sleep   Unless something disturbs the process, you will soon proceed smoothly through the three stages of quiet sleep.

10 STAGE N1.   In making the transition from wakefulness into light sleep, you spend about five minutes in Stage N1 sleep. On the EEG, the predominant brain waves slow to four to seven cycles per second, a pattern called theta waves. Body temperature begins to drop, muscles relax, and eyes often move slowly from side to side. People in Stage N1 sleep lose awareness of their surroundings, but they are easily jarred awake. However, not everyone experiences Stage N1 sleep in the same way: If awakened, one person might recall being drowsy, while another might describe having been asleep.

STAGE N2.   This first stage of true sleep lasts 10 to 25 minutes. Your eyes are still, and your heart rate and breathing are slower than when awake. Your brain's electrical activity is irregular. Large, slow waves intermingle with brief bursts of activity called sleep spindles, when brain waves speed up for roughly half a second or longer. About every two minutes, EEG tracings show a pattern called a K-complex, which scientists think represents a sort of built-in vigilance system that keeps you poised to awaken if necessary. K-complexes can also be provoked by certain sounds or other external or internal stimuli. Whisper someone's name during Stage N2 sleep, and a K-complex will appear on the EEG. You spend about half the night in Stage N2 sleep, which leaves you moderately refreshed.

STAGE N3.   Eventually, large slow brain waves called delta waves become a major feature on the EEG. This is Stage N3, known as deep sleep or slow-wave sleep. During this stage, breathing becomes more regular. Blood pressure falls, and pulse rate slows to about 20% to 30% below the waking rate. The brain becomes less responsive to external stimuli, making it difficult to wake the sleeper.

Slow-wave sleep seems to be a time for your body to renew and repair itself. Blood flow is directed less toward your brain, which cools measurably. At the beginning of this stage, the pituitary gland releases a pulse of growth hormone that stimulates tissue growth and muscle repair. Researchers have also detected increased blood levels of substances that activate your immune system, raising the possibility that slow-wave sleep helps the body defend itself against infection.

Normally, young people spend about 20% of their sleep time in stretches of slow-wave sleep lasting up to half an hour, but slow-wave sleep is nearly absent in most people over age 65. Someone whose slow-wave sleep is restricted will wake up feeling unrefreshed, no matter how long he or she has been in bed. When a sleep-deprived person gets some sleep, he or she will pass quickly through the lighter sleep stages into the deeper stages and spend a greater proportion of sleep time there, suggesting that slow-wave sleep fills an essential need.

15   *Dreaming (REM) Sleep*   Dreaming occurs during REM sleep, which has been described as an "active brain in a paralyzed body." Your brain races, thinking and dreaming, as your eyes dart back and forth rapidly behind closed lids. Your body temperature rises. Your blood pressure increases, and your heart rate and breathing speed up to daytime levels. The sympathetic nervous system, which creates the fight-or-flight response, is twice as active as when you're awake. Despite all this activity, your body hardly moves, except for intermittent twitches; muscles not needed for breathing or eye movement are quiet.

Just as slow-wave sleep restores your body, scientists believe that REM or dreaming sleep restores your mind, perhaps in part by helping clear out irrelevant information. Recent studies of students' ability to solve a complex puzzle involving abstract shapes suggest the brain processes information overnight; students who got a good night's sleep after seeing the puzzle fared much better than those asked to solve the puzzle immediately. Earlier studies found that REM sleep facilitates learning and memory. People tested to measure how well they had learned a new task improved their scores after a night's sleep. If they were roused from REM sleep, the improvements were lost. On the other hand, if they were awakened an equal number of times from slow-wave sleep, the improvements in the scores were unaffected. These findings may help explain why students who stay up all night cramming for an examination generally retain less information than classmates who get some sleep.

About three to five times a night, or about every 90 minutes, a sleeper enters REM sleep. The first such episode usually lasts only for a few minutes, but REM time increases progressively over the course of the night. The final period of REM sleep may last a half-hour. Altogether, REM sleep makes up about 25% of total sleep in young adults. If someone who has been deprived of REM sleep is left undisturbed for a night, he or she enters this stage earlier and spends a higher proportion of sleep time in it—a phenomenon called REM rebound.

Sleep Architecture   During the night, a normal sleeper moves between different sleep stages in a fairly predictable pattern, alternating between REM and non-REM sleep. When these stages are charted on a diagram, called a hypnogram (see Figure 2), the different levels resemble a drawing of a city skyline. Sleep experts call this pattern sleep architecture.

In a young adult, normal sleep architecture usually consists of four or five alternating non-REM and REM periods. Most deep sleep occurs in the first half of the night. As the night progresses, periods of REM sleep get longer and alternate with Stage N2 sleep. Later in life, the sleep skyline will change, with less Stage N3 sleep, more Stage N1 sleep, and more awakenings.

20 *Your Internal Clock*   Scientists have discovered that certain brain structures and chemicals produce the states of sleeping and waking.

A pacemaker-like mechanism in the brain regulates the circadian rhythm of sleeping and waking. ("Circadian" means "about a day.") This internal clock, which gradually becomes established during the first months of life, controls the daily ups and downs of biological patterns, including body temperature, blood pressure, and the release of hormones.

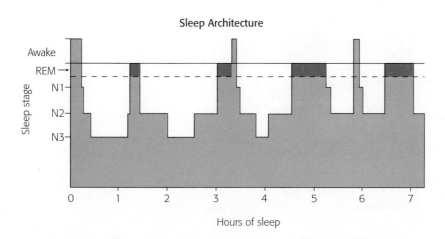

Fig. 2.   When experts chart sleep stages on a hypnogram, the different levels resemble a drawing of a city skyline. This pattern is known as sleep architecture. The hypnogram above shows a typical night's sleep of a healthy young adult.

The circadian rhythm makes people's desire for sleep strongest between midnight and dawn, and to a lesser extent in midafternoon. In one study, researchers instructed a group of people to try to stay awake for 24 hours. Not surprisingly, many slipped into naps despite their best efforts not to. When the investigators plotted the times when the unplanned naps occurred, they found peaks between 2 a.m. and 4 a.m. and between 2 p.m. and 3 p.m.

Most Americans sleep during the night as dictated by their circadian rhythms, although many nap in the afternoon on the weekends. In societies where taking a siesta is the norm, people can respond to their bodies' daily dips in alertness with a one- to two-hour afternoon nap during the workday and a correspondingly shorter sleep at night.

Mechanisms of Your "Sleep Clock"   In the 1970s, studies in rats identified the suprachiasmatic nucleus as the location of the internal clock. This cluster of cells is part of the hypothalamus, the brain center that regulates appetite and other biological states (see Figure 3). When this tiny area was damaged, the sleep/wake rhythm disappeared and the rats no longer slept on a normal schedule. Although the clock is largely self-regulating, its location allows it to respond to several types of external cues to keep it set at 24 hours. Scientists call these cues "zeitgebers," a German word meaning "time givers."

25   LIGHT.   Light striking your eyes is the most influential zeitgeber. When researchers invited volunteers into the laboratory and exposed them to light at intervals that were at odds with the outside world, the participants unconsciously reset their biological clocks to match the new light input. The circadian rhythm disturbances and sleep problems that affect up to 90% of blind people demonstrate the importance of light to sleep/wake patterns.

The Sleep Wake Control Center

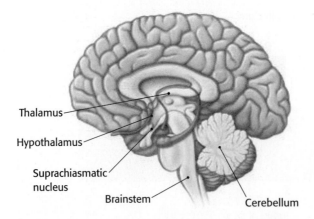

Thalamus

Hypothalamus

Suprachiasmatic nucleus

Brainstem

Cerebellum

Fig. 3.   The pacemaker-like mechanism in your brain that regulates the circadian rhythm of sleeping and waking is thought to be located in the suprachiasmatic nucleus. This cluster of cells is part of the hypothalamus, the brain center that regulates appetite, body temperature, and other biological states.

TIME. As a person reads clocks, follows work and train schedules, and demands that the body remain alert for certain tasks and social events, there is cognitive pressure to stay on schedule.

MELATONIN. Cells in the suprachiasmatic nucleus contain receptors for melatonin, a hormone produced in a predictable daily rhythm by the pineal gland, which is located deep in the brain between the two hemispheres. Levels of melatonin begin climbing after dark and ebb after dawn. The hormone induces drowsiness in some people, and scientists believe its daily light-sensitive cycles help keep the sleep/wake cycle on track.

Your Clock's Hour Hand As the circadian rhythm counts off the days, another part of the brain acts like the hour hand on a watch. This timekeeper resides in a nugget of nerve cells within the brain stem, the area that controls breathing, blood pressure, and heartbeat. Fluctuating activity in the nerve cells and the chemical messengers they produce seem to coordinate the timing of wakefulness, arousal, and the 90-minute changeover between REM and non-REM sleep.

Several neurotransmitters (brain chemicals that neurons release to communicate with adjacent cells) play a role in arousal. Their actions help explain why medications that mimic or counteract their effects can influence sleep. Adenosine and gamma-aminobutyric acid (GABA) are believed to promote sleep. Acetylcholine regulates REM sleep. Norepinephrine, epinephrine, dopamine, and the recently discovered hypocretin stimulate wakefulness. Individuals vary greatly in their natural levels of neurotransmitters and in their sensitivity to these chemicals.

Sleep Throughout Life

30 To a certain extent, heredity determines how people sleep throughout their lives. Identical twins, for example, have much more similar sleep patterns than nonidentical twins or other siblings. Differences in sleeping and waking seem to be inborn. There are night owls and early-morning larks, sound sleepers and light ones, people who are perky after five hours of sleep and others who are groggy if they log less than nine hours. Nevertheless, many factors can affect how a person sleeps. Aging is the most important influence on basic sleep rhythms—from age 20 on, it takes longer to fall asleep [a period of time called *sleep latency*], you sleep less at night, Stages N1 and N2 sleep increase, Stage N3 sleep and REM sleep decrease, and nighttime awakenings increase (see Table 1).

Childhood For an adult to sleep like a baby is not only unrealistic but also undesirable. A newborn may sleep eight times a day, accumulating 18 hours of sleep and spending about half of it in REM sleep. The REM to non-REM cycle is shorter, usually lasting less than an hour.

At about the age of 4 weeks, a newborn's sleep periods get longer. By 6 months, infants spend longer and more regular periods in non-REM sleep; most begin sleeping through the night and taking naps in the morning and afternoon. During the preschool years, daytime naps gradually shorten, until by age 6 most children are awake all day and sleep for about 10 hours a night.

Table 1	Sleep Changes During Adulthood				

As people age, it takes longer to fall asleep (increased sleep latency). And sleep efficiency—or the percentage of time spent asleep while in bed—decreases as people grow older.

	Age 20	Age 40	Age 60	Age 70	Age 80
Sleep latency	16 minutes	17 minutes	18 minutes	18.5 minutes	19 minutes
Total sleep time	7.5 hours	7 hours	6.2 hours	6 hours	5.8 hours
% of time in Stage N2 sleep	47%	51%	53%	55%	57%
% of time in Stage N3 sleep	20%	15%	10%	9%	7.5%
% of time in REM sleep	22%	21%	20%	19%	17%
Sleep efficiency	95%	88%	84%	82%	79%

Source: Ohayon MM, et al. "Meta-analysis of quantitative sleep parameters from childhood to old age in healthy individuals; Developing normative sleep values across the human lifespan," *Sleep* (2004), Vol. 27, No. 7, pp. 1255–73.

Between age 7 and puberty, nocturnal melatonin production is at its lifetime peak, and sleep at this age is deep and restorative. At this age, if a child is sleepy during the day, parents should be concerned.

Adolescence In contrast, adolescents are noted for their daytime drowsiness. Except for infancy, adolescence is the most rapid period of body growth and development. Although teenagers need about an hour more sleep each day than they did as young children, most of them actually sleep an hour or so less. Parents usually blame teenagers' busy schedule of activities for their grogginess and difficulty awakening in the morning. However, the problem may also be biological. One study indicated that some adolescents might have delayed sleep phase syndrome, where they are not sleepy until well after the usual bedtime and cannot wake at the time required for school, producing conflicts between parents and sleepy teenagers as well as with secondary schools, which usually open earlier than elementary schools. It is unknown whether this phase shift occurs primarily as a physiological event or as a response to abnormal light exposure.

35 *Adulthood* During young adulthood, sleep patterns usually seem stable but in fact are slowly evolving. Between age 20 and age 30, the amount of slow-wave sleep drops by about half, and nighttime awakenings double. By age 40, slow-wave sleep is markedly reduced.

Women's reproductive cycles can greatly influence sleep. During the first trimester of pregnancy, many women are sleepy all the time and may log an extra two hours a night if their schedules permit. As pregnancy continues, hormonal and anatomical changes reduce sleep efficiency so that less of a woman's time in bed is actually spent sleeping. As a result, fatigue increases. The postpartum period usually brings dramatic sleepiness and fatigue—because the mother's ability to sleep efficiently has not returned to normal, because she is at the mercy of her newborn's rapidly cycling shifts between sleeping and waking, and because breast-feeding promotes sleepiness. Researchers are probing whether sleep disturbances during pregnancy may contribute to postpartum depression and compromise the general physical and mental well-being of new mothers.

Women who aren't pregnant may experience monthly shifts in sleep habits. During the second phase of the menstrual cycle, between ovulation and the next menses, some women fall asleep and enter REM sleep more quickly than usual. A few experience extreme sleepiness. Investigators are studying the relationship between such sleep alterations, cyclic changes in body temperature, and levels of the hormone progesterone to see whether these physiologic patterns also correlate with premenstrual mood changes.

Middle Age   When men and women enter middle age, slow-wave sleep continues to diminish. Nighttime awakenings become more frequent and last longer. Waking after about three hours of sleep is particularly common. During menopause, many women experience hot flashes that can interrupt sleep and lead to chronic insomnia. Obese people are more prone to nocturnal breathing problems, which often start during middle age. Men and women who are physically fit sleep more soundly as they grow older, compared with their sedentary peers.

The Later Years   Like younger people, older adults still spend about 20% of sleep time in REM sleep, but other than that, they sleep differently. Slow-wave sleep accounts for less than 5% of sleep time, and in some people it is completely absent. Falling asleep takes longer, and the shallow quality of sleep results in dozens of awakenings during the night. Doctors used to reassure older people that they needed less sleep than younger ones to function well, but sleep experts now know that isn't true. At any age, most adults need seven and a half to eight hours of sleep to function at their best. Since older people often have trouble attaining this much sleep at night, they often supplement nighttime sleep with daytime naps. This can be a successful strategy for accumulating sufficient total sleep over a 24-hour period. However, if you find that you need a nap, it's best to take one midday nap, rather than several brief ones scattered throughout the day and evening.

40   Sleep disturbances in elderly people, particularly in those who have Alzheimer's disease or other forms of dementia, are very disruptive for caregivers. In one study, 70% of caregivers cited these problems as the decisive factor in seeking nursing home placement for a loved one.

Consequences of Sleep Deprivation.   Many people don't realize that lack of sufficient sleep can lead to a range of ill effects, triggering mild to potentially life-threatening consequences. There are several different types of sleep deprivation that vary in duration and severity. These can be broadly categorized as complete or partial sleep deprivation.

Complete Sleep Deprivation   Normally, you go about 16 or 17 hours between sleep sessions. Complete sleep deprivation happens as the hours extend beyond this point. First you feel tired, then exhausted. By 2 or 3 a.m., many people have a hard time keeping their eyes open, but the effects extend throughout the body. Simple tasks that you would normally have no trouble accomplishing start to become difficult.

In fact, a number of studies of hand-eye coordination and reaction time have shown that such sleep deprivation can be as debilitating as being intoxicated. In one study, volunteers stayed awake for 28 hours, beginning at 8 a.m., and periodically took driving simulation tests. At a different time, the volunteers' driving ability was tested after drinking 10 to 15 grams of alcohol at 30-minute intervals until their blood alcohol content (BAC) level reached 0.10. The study concluded that 24 hours of wakefulness had the same deleterious effect on driving ability as that of a BAC of 0.10—enough to be charged with driving while intoxicated in most states.

Sleep deprivation also leaves you prone to two potentially dangerous phenomena, microsleeps and automatic behavior (page 481), which play a role in thousands of transportation accidents each year. When complete sleep deprivation extends for two or three days, people have difficulty completing tasks demanding a high attention level and often experience mood swings, depression, and increased feelings of tension.

45   Performance is also highly influenced by fluctuations in circadian rhythms. For example, sleep-deprived people may still function fairly well during the morning and evening. But during the peaks of sleepiness in the afternoon and overnight hours, people often literally cannot stay awake and may fall asleep while standing, sitting, or even while talking on the telephone, working on the computer, or eating. A small percentage experience paranoia and hallucinations.

Partial Sleep Deprivation   Partial sleep deprivation occurs when you get some sleep, but not 100% of what you need. Experts refer to this as building up a sleep debt. An example would be when a person who needs 7.5 hours of sleep a night hits a stretch of several days in a row in which he or she only gets four to six hours.

After a single night of short sleep, most people function at or near their normal level. They may not feel great, but they can usually get through the day without others noticing that anything is amiss. After two or more nights of short sleep, people usually show signs of irritability and sleepiness. Work performance begins to suffer—particularly on complicated tasks—and people are more likely to complain of headaches, stomach problems, and sore joints. In addition, people face a far higher risk of falling asleep on the job and while driving.

Long-term partial sleep deprivation occurs when someone gets less than the optimal amount of sleep for months or years on end—a common scenario for insomniacs and people with sleep disorders. But even healthy people who can't resist the round-the-clock commerce, communication, and entertainment opportunities our 24/7 society now offers may fall prey to this problem.

A growing number of studies have linked long-term sleep deficits with significant health problems.

50   OBESITY.   A 2006 study found that over 16 years, middle-aged women who reported sleeping five hours or less per night were 32% more likely to gain 33 pounds or more than women who slept seven hours or more. Another study found that men limited to four hours of sleep for two consecutive nights experienced hormonal changes that made them feel hungry and crave carbohydrate-rich foods such as cakes, candy, ice cream, and pasta.

MICROSLEEPS AND AUTOMATIC BEHAVIOR

Microsleeps are brief episodes that occur in the midst of ongoing wakeful activity. They usually last a few seconds but can go on for 10 or 15 seconds. Brain wave monitoring by EEG of someone experiencing microsleeps shows brief periods of Stage N1 sleep intruding into wakefulness. During this time, the brain does not respond to noise or other sensory inputs and you don't react to things happening around you. "Noding off" can be the result of a microsleep.

Automatic behavior refers to a period of several minutes or more during which a person is awake and performing routine duties but not attending to his or her surroundings or responding to changes in the environment. Examples include a driver who keeps his car on the road but misses his intended exit and a train engineer who can continue pressing a lever at regular intervals but doesn't notice an obstruction on the track.

HEART HEALTH.   Middle-aged people who sleep five hours or less a night have a greater risk of developing high blood pressure, compared with people who sleep seven to nine hours a night. Women who averaged five hours of sleep a night were 39% more likely to develop heart disease than women who slept eight hours.

MENTAL HEALTH.   A number of studies have found that persistent insomnia raises the risk for anxiety, depression, and other mood disorders.

MORTALITY.   A study of almost a million people over age 30 found that men who reported usually sleeping less than four hours a day were nearly three times as likely to die within six years as men who said they averaged seven or eight hours of sleep.

Sleep as Part of a Healthy Lifestyle   Clearly, getting enough sleep is just as important as other vital elements of good health, such as eating a healthy diet, getting regular exercise, and practicing good dental hygiene. In short, sleep is not a luxury but a basic component of a healthy lifestyle.

55   Just like purchasing healthy foods, taking an after-dinner walk, or flossing your teeth, getting adequate sleep requires time and discipline. Mentally block off certain hours for sleep and then follow through on your intention, avoid building up a sleep debt, and take steps to set up an ideal sleep environment. Seek a doctor's help if conventional steps toward good sleep don't work.

This doesn't mean that you can't have any fun, or that you need to beat yourself up if you don't get eight hours of sleep 365 days a year. Just as an occasional ice cream sundae won't make you obese, staying up a few extra hours for a party or to meet a deadline is perfectly acceptable—as long as you make plans to compensate the next day by sleeping in, taking a short afternoon nap, or going to bed earlier. If you have to get up at 7 a.m. to be at work by 9, you'd best forgo late-night talk shows—or record them to watch the next evening. If you don't get to bed until 2 a.m. one night, allow time over the next day or two to catch up on lost sleep. But over the long haul, you need to make sure you consistently get enough sleep.

Sleep decisions are a quality-of-life issue. Whatever your interests and goals, getting enough sleep puts you in a better position to enjoy and achieve them.

● Review Questions

1. What are the costs of disturbed sleep?

2. Explain why sleep is an active, not a passive, state. In your answer, refer to REM and non-REM sleep.

3. Studies suggest that "students who stay up all night cramming for an examination generally retain less information than classmates who get some sleep." Why?

4. To what does the term "sleep architecture" refer? What pattern does a normal sleeper's sleep architecture follow?

5. What is "circadian rhythm"? For what is it responsible and what part of the body controls it?

6. What habits affect sleep quality? How so?

7. How does sleep architecture change throughout a person's life?

● Discussion and Writing Suggestions

1. Based on personal observation, what direct evidence do you have that people in different stages of life, from infants to elders, have different sleep patterns?

2. Study Figure 2, "Sleep Architecture." In a paragraph, describe the hypnogram's presentation of a "a typical night's sleep of a healthy young adult." Describe transitions through stages of sleep, and REM and non-REM sleep. In a second paragraph, discuss your reactions upon learning of the complex architecture of sleep.

3. "Parents usually blame teenagers' busy schedule of activities for their grogginess and difficulty awakening in the morning. However, the problem may also be biological," according to the *Harvard Special Health Report*. Recall any battles you had in your adolescent past over your "grogginess." Would it have changed anyone's reactions to know that your developing body (as opposed to your work, party, or TV schedule) was to blame?

4. Have you ever suffered through a period of disrupted sleep? Describe the experience in two paragraphs—the first written in the first person (the "I" perspective), the second written in the third person (the "he" or "she" perspective). Compare paragraphs. Which do you prefer? Why?

AMERICA'S SLEEP-DEPRIVED TEENS
NODDING OFF AT SCHOOL, BEHIND THE WHEEL

National Sleep Foundation

The National Sleep Foundation (NSF), according to its Web site, "is an independent nonprofit organization dedicated to improving public health and safety by achieving understanding of sleep and sleep disorders, and by supporting sleep-related education, research, and advocacy." (See http://www.sleepfoundation.org/.) The NSF periodically issues news releases on studies its member physicians conduct. The following release, dated March 28, 2006, helped focus national attention on the dangers of adolescent sleep debt.

Many of the nation's adolescents are falling asleep in class, arriving late to school, feeling down and driving drowsy because of a lack of sleep that gets worse as they get older, according to a new poll released today by the National Sleep Foundation (NSF).

In a national survey on the sleep patterns of U.S. adolescents (ages 11–17), NSF's 2006 *Sleep in America* poll finds that only 20% of adolescents get the recommended nine hours of sleep on school nights, and nearly one-half (45%) sleep less than eight hours on school nights.

What's more, the poll finds that parents are mostly in the dark about their adolescents' sleep. While most students know they're not getting the sleep they need, 90% of parents polled believe that their adolescent is getting enough sleep at least a few nights during the school week.

The poll indicates that the consequences of insufficient sleep affect nearly every aspect of teenage life. Among the most important findings:

- At least once a week, more than one-quarter (28%) of high school students fall asleep in school, 22% fall asleep doing homework, and 14% arrive late or miss school because they oversleep.

- Adolescents who get insufficient amounts of sleep are more likely than their peers to get lower grades, while 80% of adolescents who get an optimal amount of sleep say they're achieving As and Bs in school.

- More than one-half (51%) of adolescent drivers have driven drowsy during the past year. In fact, 15% of drivers in 10th to 12th grades drive drowsy at least once a week.

- Among those adolescents who report being unhappy, tense and nervous, 73% feel they don't get enough sleep at night and 59% are excessively sleepy during the day.

- More than one-quarter (28%) of adolescents say they're too tired to exercise.

5　　The poll also finds that the amount of sleep declines as adolescents get older. The survey classifies nine or more hours a night as an optimal amount of sleep in line with sleep experts' recommendations for this age group, with less than eight hours classified as insufficient. Sixth-graders report they sleep an average of 8.4 hours on school nights, while 12th-graders sleep just 6.9 hours—1.5 hours less than their younger peers and two hours less than recommended. In fact, by the time adolescents become high school seniors, they're missing out on nearly 12 hours (11.7) of needed sleep each week.

"This poll identifies a serious reduction in adolescents' sleep as students transition from middle school to high school. This is particularly troubling as adolescence is a critical period of development and growth—academically, emotionally and physically," says Richard L. Gelula, NSF's chief executive officer. "At a time of heightened concerns about the quality of this next generation's health and education, our nation is ignoring a basic necessity for success in these areas: adequate sleep. We call on parents, educators and teenagers themselves to take an active role in making sleep a priority."

Awareness Gap Between Parents and Teens About Sleep

While nine out of ten parents state their adolescent is getting enough sleep at least a few nights during the school week, more than one-half (56%) of adolescents say they get less sleep than they think they need to feel their best. And, 51% say they feel too tired or sleepy during the day.

Also at issue is the quality of sleep once an adolescent goes to bed. Only 41% of adolescents say they get a good night's sleep every night or most nights. One in 10 teens reports that he/she rarely or never gets a good night's sleep.

Overall, 7% of parents think their adolescent may have a sleep problem, whereas 16% of adolescents think they have or may have one. Many adolescents (31%) who think they have a sleep problem have not told anyone about it.

Everyday Pressures + Nature = Less Sleep

10 As children reach adolescence, their circadian rhythms—or internal clocks—tend to shift, causing teens to naturally feel more alert later at night and wake up later in the morning. A trick of nature, this "phase delay" can make it difficult for them to fall asleep before 11:00 p.m.; more than one-half (54%) of high school seniors go to bed at 11:00 p.m. or later on school nights. However, the survey finds that on a typical school day, adolescents wake up around 6:30 a.m. in order to go to school, leaving many without the sleep they need.

"In the competition between the natural tendency to stay up late and early school start times, a teen's sleep is what loses out," notes Jodi A. Mindell, PhD, co-chair of the poll task force and an NSF vice chair. "Sending students to school without enough sleep is like sending them to school without breakfast. Sleep serves not only a restorative function for adolescents' bodies and brains, but it is also a key time when they process what they've learned during the day." Dr. Mindell is the director of the Graduate Program in Psychology at Saint Joseph's University and associate director of the Sleep Center at The Children's Hospital of Philadelphia.

It is also important for teens, like all people, to maintain a consistent sleep schedule across the entire week. Poll respondents overwhelmingly go to bed and get up later and sleep longer on non-school nights. However, teens rarely make up for the sleep that they lose during the school week. Overall, adolescents get an average of 8.9 hours of sleep on a non-school night, about equal to the optimal amount recommended per night. Again, the poll finds this amount trends downward as adolescents get older.

Survey results also show that sleepy adolescents are more likely to rely on naps, which sleep experts point out should not be a substitute for, but rather complement, a good night's sleep. About one-third (31%) of adolescents take naps regularly, and these nappers are more likely than non-nappers to say they feel cranky or irritable, too tired during the day, and fall asleep in school—all signs of insufficient sleep. And, their naps average 1.2 hours, well beyond the 45-minute maximum recommended by sleep experts so that naps do not interfere with nighttime sleep.

"Irregular sleep patterns that include long naps and sleeping in on the weekend negatively impact adolescents' biological clocks and sleep quality—which in turn affects their abilities and mood," says Mary Carskadon, PhD, who chairs the 2006 poll task force. "This rollercoaster system should be minimized. When students' schedules are more consistent and provide for plenty of sleep, they are better prepared to take on their busy days." Dr. Carskadon is the director of the E.P. Bradley Hospital Sleep and Chronobiology Research Lab at Brown University.

15   In terms of overall demographics, there are more similarities than differences among adolescents' responses to sleep-related questions. Boys and girls have similar sleep patterns. In terms of racial/ethnic comparisons, African-American adolescents report getting 7.2 hours of sleep on school nights, as compared to 7.6 hours reported by Hispanic adolescents, 7.4 hours by other minorities and 7.7 hours by White adolescents.

Other Factors Affecting Adolescent Sleep

Caffeine plays a prominent role in the life of today's adolescent. Three-quarters of those polled drink at least one caffeinated beverage every day, and nearly one-third (31%) consume two or more such drinks each day. Adolescents who drink two or more caffeinated beverages daily are more likely to get an insufficient amount of sleep on school nights and think they have a sleep problem.

Technology may also be encroaching on a good night's sleep. The poll finds that adolescents aren't heeding expert advice to engage in relaxing activities in the hour before bedtime or to keep the bedroom free from sleep distractions:

- Watching television is the most popular activity (76%) for adolescents in the hour before bedtime, while surfing the internet/instant-messaging (44%) and talking on the phone (40%) are close behind.

- Boys are more likely than girls to play electronic video games (40% vs. 12%) and/or exercise (37% vs. 27%) in the hour prior to bedtime; girls are more likely than boys to talk on the phone (51% vs. 29%) and/or do homework/study (70% vs. 60%) in that time.

- Nearly all adolescents (97%) have at least one electronic item—such as a television, computer, phone or music device—in their bedroom. On average, 6th-graders have more than two of these items in their bedroom, while 12th-graders have about four.

TIPS FOR TEENS

1. Sleep is food for the brain. Lack of sleep can make you look tired and feel depressed, irritable or angry. Even mild sleepiness can hurt your performance—from taking school exams to playing sports or video games. Learn how much sleep you need to function at your best— most adolescents need between 8.5 and 9.25 hours of sleep each night—and strive to get it every night. You should awaken refreshed, not tired.

2. Keep consistency in mind: establish a regular bedtime and waketime schedule, and maintain this schedule during weekends and school (or work) vacations. Don't stray from your schedule frequently, and never do so for two or more consecutive nights. If you must go off schedule, avoid delaying your bedtime by more than one hour. Awaken the next day within two hours of your regular schedule, and, if you are sleepy during the day, take an early afternoon nap.

3. Get into bright light as soon as possible in the morning, but avoid it in the evening. The light helps to signal to the brain when it should wake up and when it should prepare to sleep.

4. Understand your circadian rhythms. Then you can try to maximize your schedule throughout the day according to your internal clock. For example, to compensate for your "slump (sleepy) times," partici- pate in stimulating activities or classes that are interactive. Try to avoid lecture classes and potentially unsafe activities, including driving.

5. After lunch (or after noon), stay away from caffeinated coffee and colas as well as nicotine, which are all stimulants. Also avoid alcohol, which disrupts sleep.

6. Relax before going to bed. Avoid heavy reading, studying and computer games within one hour of going to bed. Don't fall asleep with the televi- sion on—flickering light and stimulating content can inhibit restful sleep.

- Adolescents with four or more such items in their bedrooms are much more likely than their peers to get an insufficient amount of sleep at night and almost twice as likely to fall asleep in school and while doing homework.

"Many teens have a technological playground in their bedrooms that offers a variety of ways to stay stimulated and delay sleep. Ramping down from the day's activities with a warm bath and a good book are much better ways to tran- sition to bedtime," notes Dr. Carskadon. "The brain learns when it's time to sleep from the lessons it receives. Teens need to give the brain better signals about when nighttime starts…turning off the lights—computer screens and TV, too—is the very best signal."

- **Be a bed head, not a dead head.** Understand the dangers of insufficient sleep—and avoid them! Encourage your friends to do the same. Ask others how much sleep they've had lately before you let them drive you somewhere. Remember: friends don't let friends drive drowsy.
- **Brag about your bedtime.** Tell your friends how good you feel after getting more than 8 hours of sleep!
- **Do you study with a buddy?** If you're getting together after school, tell your pal you need to catch a nap first, or take a nap break if needed. (Taking a nap in the evening may make it harder for you to sleep at night, however.)
- **Steer clear of raves and say no to all-nighters.** Staying up late can cause chaos in your sleep patterns and your ability to be alert the next day...and beyond. Remember, the best thing you can do to prepare for a test is to get plenty of sleep. All-nighters or late-night study sessions might seem to give you more time to cram for your exam, but they are also likely to drain your brainpower.

How Parents Can Help Teens Get More Sleep

Dr. Mindell notes that "the poll data suggest that parents may be missing red flags that their teenager is not getting the sleep that he or she desperately needs. Simply asking teens if they get enough sleep to feel their best is a good way for parents to begin a valuable conversation about sleep's importance."

20   Some warning signs that your child may not be getting the sleep he/she needs:

- Do you have to wake your child for school? And, is it difficult to do so?
- Has a teacher mentioned that your child is sleepy or tired during the day?
- Do you find your child falling asleep while doing homework?
- Is your child sleeping two hours later or more on weekends than on school nights?
- Is your child's behavior different on days that he/she gets a good night's sleep vs. days that he/she doesn't?
- Does he/she rely on a caffeinated drink in the morning to wake up? And/or drink two or more caffeinated drinks a day?
- Does he/she routinely nap for more than 45 minutes?

Parents can play a key role in helping their adolescents develop and maintain healthy sleep habits. In general, it is important for parents and adolescents to talk about sleep—including the natural phase delay—and learn more about good sleep habits in order to manage teens' busy schedules. What's more, teens often mirror their parents' habits, so adults are encouraged to be good role models by getting a full night's sleep themselves.

And, there are ways to make it easier for an adolescent to get more sleep and a better night's sleep:

- Set a consistent bedtime and waketime (even on weekends) that allows for the recommended nine or more hours of sleep every night.
- Have a relaxing bedtime routine, such as reading for fun or taking a warm bath or shower.
- Keep the bedroom comfortable, dark, cool and quiet.
- Get into bright light as soon as possible in the morning, but avoid it in the evening.
- Create a sleep-friendly environment by removing TVs and other distractions from the bedroom and setting limits on usage before bedtime.
- Avoid caffeine after lunchtime.

NSF released the poll findings as part of its 9th annual National Sleep Awareness Week® campaign, held March 27–April 2, 2006. For more sleep tips for parents and adolescents, as well as the Summary of Findings for the 2006 *Sleep in America* poll, visit NSF's website at www.sleepfoundation.org.

Methodology   The 2006 *Sleep in America* poll was conducted for the National Sleep Foundation by WB&A Market Research. Telephone interviews were conducted between September 19 and November 29, 2005, with a targeted random sample of 1,602 caregivers and, separately, their adolescent children ages 11–17 in grades 6–12. Using the targeted random sample, quotas were established by grade and race/ethnicity, with minority respondents being oversampled to reflect equal proportions of respondents by grade, as well as the actual distribution of race/ethnicity based on the U.S. census. The poll's margin of error is plus or minus 2.4%; the response rate for the survey was 27%.

● Review Questions

1. What is the recommended amount of sleep for a teenager? What percentage of American teenagers get this much sleep? How knowledgeable are their parents about their sleep?

2. How much sleep debt do high school seniors typically accumulate in a week? Cite some of the consequences of getting insufficient sleep as a teenager, according to the poll results.

3. Why is a lack of sleep in the teenage years particularly harmful, according to experts?

4. What is a "phase delay" and how does it contribute to an adolescent's sleep debt?

5. What percentage of adolescents take regular naps? Optimally, how should naps be used? What is the recommended amount of daytime napping? What is the danger of especially long naps?

6. What is "rollercoaster" sleep and why is it not healthy?

7. How do consumer electronics affect adolescent sleep?

● Discussion and Writing Suggestions

1. According to the survey results, once a week roughly one-quarter of high school students fall asleep in class, 22 percent fall asleep doing homework, and 14 percent are late to or miss school because of insufficient sleep. Are/were you one of these students? Do you know these students? Why are America's teenagers not getting sufficient sleep, in your view?

2. How does the amount and quality of your sleep compare to that of teenagers who responded to the National Sleep Foundation survey?

3. To what extent do you believe that consumer electronics in your bedroom (or dorm room) affect the quality of your sleep? How do you respond to the finding that with four or more such items, you are more likely to suffer a sleep deficit? Can you explain the correlation?

4. At the end of this article, the NSF offers several recommendations for helping adolescents get more sleep. How realistic do you find these recommendations? Cite some factors in the lives of active adolescents that make it problematic to get the recommended nine hours of sleep each night.

WHEN WORLDS COLLIDE: ADOLESCENT NEED FOR SLEEP VERSUS SOCIETAL DEMANDS

Mary A. Carskadon

Consult the reference list of any scientific article on adolescent sleep, or type the words "adolescent" and "sleep" into any search engine, and the name "Mary Carskadon" will stand out, as if in relief. A professor of psychiatry and human behavior at Brown University School of Medicine and director of sleep and chronobiology research at E.P. Bradley Hospital in Rhode Island, Carskadon has authored widely cited, foundational studies on the sleep of adolescents. In the present selection, which first appeared as a chapter in *Adolescent Sleep Needs and School Starting Times* (1999), Carskadon reviews the biological, behavioral, and social forces that converge to make getting an adequate night's sleep such a challenge for so many teenagers.

Our understanding of the development of sleep patterns in adolescents has advanced considerably in the last 20 years. Along the way, theoretical models of the processes underlying the biological regulation of sleep have improved, and certain assumptions and dogmas have been examined and found wanting. Although the full characterization of teen sleep regulation remains to be accomplished, our current understanding poses a number of challenges for the education system.

The early 1970s found us with a growing awareness that sleep patterns change fundamentally at the transition to adolescence—a phenomenon that is widely acknowledged today. Survey studies clearly showed then and continue to show that the reported timing of sleep begins to shift in early adolescence, with bedtime and rising time both occurring at later hours. This delayed sleep pattern is particularly evident on nonschool nights and days, though the evening delay is obvious on school nights as well. Associated with the delay of sleep is a decline in the amount of sleep obtained and an increase in the discrepancy between school nights and weekend nights. Although the nonschool-night "oversleeping" was acknowledged as recovery from insufficient sleep during the school week, we initially assumed that the amount of sleep required declines with age. This was axiomatic: the older you are, the less sleep you need.

Assessing the Need for Sleep in the Second Decade

A longitudinal study begun in 1976 at the Stanford University summer sleep camp attempted to examine this axiom.[1] Boys and girls enrolled in this research project at ages 10, 11, or 12 and came to the lab for a 72-hour assessment each year for five or six years. They were asked to keep a fixed schedule, sleeping 10 hours a night for the week before the study, and their sleep was recorded on three consecutive nights from 10 p.m. to 8 a.m. Our hypothesis was that the reduced need for sleep in older children would manifest itself through less sleep within this 10-hour nocturnal window. This hypothesis was *not* confirmed. In fact, regardless of age or developmental stage, the children all slept about 9 $\frac{1}{4}$ of the 10 hours. Furthermore, delays in sleep resulted in a reduced likelihood of spontaneous waking before 8 a.m. for all but the youngest participants. One conclusion, therefore, was that the need for sleep does not change across adolescent development.

This study also showed an interesting pattern with respect to waking alertness, which was assessed using a technique called the Multiple Sleep Latency Test (MSLT). The MSLT measures the speed of falling asleep across repeated 20-minute trials in standard conditions. Thus a child who stays awake 20 minutes can be considered alert, faster sleep onsets are a sign of reduced alertness, and a child who falls asleep in five minutes or less is excessively sleepy.[2] The longitudinal study demonstrated that—even though the total amount of sleep was unchanged—alertness declined in association with pubertal development.[3] Figure 1 illustrates the MSLT patterns: under these experimental conditions, more mature adolescents showed signs of reduced alertness even though they slept an equivalent amount at night. One interpretation of these data is that older teenagers may need *more* sleep than when they were younger. On the other hand, the pattern of sleep tendency showing a midafternoon dip may reflect maturation of a regulated behavioral pattern favoring an afternoon nap or siesta.

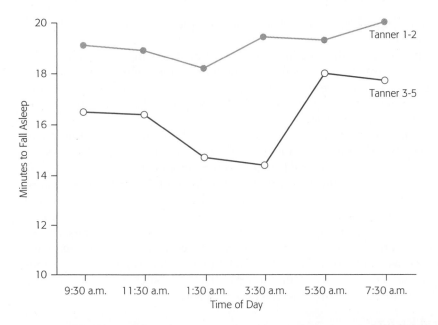

Fig. 1.   Developmental Change in Daytime Alertness Under Conditions of 'Optimal' Sleep.* The upper line, labeled Tanner 1–2, shows that pre- and early-pubescent boys and girls with a 10-hour sleep opportunity are not at all sleepy. The lower line, labeled Tanner 3–5, shows that more physically mature youngsters are sleepier, even though they have the same sleep opportunity.

Behavioral Factors

5   The principle that adolescents sleep later and less because of a panoply of psychosocial factors was also axiomatic during the 1970s and the 1980s. The evidence for this included a change in parental involvement in youngsters' sleep schedules as the children age. Thus, until about ages 11 or 12, more children than not reported that they woke spontaneously in the morning and that parents set their bedtimes. Fewer children in their early teens reported that parents still set their bedtimes, and most said that they required an alarm clock or a parent to assist them in waking up.[4]

Other behavioral factors contributing to the changing sleep patterns with age include increased social opportunities and growing academic demands. Another major contributor to changing adolescent sleep patterns is employment. One survey of youngsters in New England in the late 1980s found that two-thirds of high school students had jobs and that nearly 30% worked 20 or more hours in a typical school week.[5] Those high school students who worked 20 hours or more reported later bedtimes, shorter sleep times, more frequent

---

*The "Tanner Scale" measures sexual maturity. The higher the scale number, the more sexually mature the person.

episodes of falling asleep in school, and more frequent oversleeping and arriving late at school.

In addition to changing parental involvement, increasing school and social obligations, and greater participation in the work force, there are a myriad of other phenomena that have not been well explored. Access in the bedroom to computers, televisions, telephones, and so forth probably contributes to the delay of and reduction in sleep.

Another factor that has a major influence on adolescent sleep is the school schedule. The starting time of school puts limits on the time available for sleep. This is a nonnegotiable limit established largely without concern for sleep. Most school districts set the earliest starting time for older adolescents and the latest starting time for younger children. District officials commonly acknowledge that the school schedule is determined by the availability of school buses, along with such other factors as time of local sunrise, sports teams' schedules, and so forth.... [C]oncerns about the impact of school schedules on sleep patterns (as well as concerns about after-school teen delinquency) have sparked a reexamination in a number of districts. Our studies indicate that such a reexamination is merited by the difficulties many teenagers experience.

Biological Factors

As findings of the tendency for adolescent sleep patterns to be delayed were reported not only in North America but also in South America, Asia, Australia, and Europe, a sense arose that intrinsic developmental changes may also play a role in this phenomenon.[6] At the same time, conceptual models of the underlying internal mechanisms that control the length and timing of sleep began to take shape.

10   Current models posit three factors that control human sleep patterns. One of these factors is behavior and includes external factors such as those discussed above. The intrinsic factors have been called "sleep/wake homeostasis" and the "circadian timing system," or "process S" and "process C" in one model.[7] Sleep/wake homeostasis more simply stated is that sleep favors wake and wake favors sleep. All other things being equal, therefore, the longer one is awake, the greater the pressure for sleep to occur. Conversely, the closer one is to having slept, the less pressure there is to sleep. This process accounts for the increased need for sleep after staying awake all night and the difficulty of staying awake in general when faced with a chronic pattern of insufficient sleep. Process S can be examined using measures of sleep tendency, such as the MSLT, or measures of EEG (electroencephalogram) slow wave activity (SWA) during sleep. Sleep tendency and SWA increase with insufficient sleep. Both factors also show changes across adolescent development that may be related to the timing of sleep.

Under conditions of optimal sleep, such as those described in the longitudinal study of sleep, slow wave sleep declines by 40% from early to late adolescence. This decline may indicate a reduced pressure for sleep with greater maturation. One interpretation of this finding is that the reduced pressure for sleep makes staying up late an easier task for older adolescents. Others have interpreted this finding as marking a structural change in the brain (thinning of cortical synaptic density) that is unrelated to sleep/wake homeostasis. The change in sleep tendency—that is, the appearance of a midday trough at midpuberty (Figure 1)—may indicate a reorganization of the sleep/wake homeostatic mechanism to favor daytime napping and an extended late-day waking period, again favoring a later bedtime. These hypotheses are speculative and require additional study.

Much of the contemporary excitement about adolescent sleep comes from studies of the circadian timing mechanism, which independently and interactively exerts influences on sleep through processes that favor or inhibit sleep according to the dictates of an internal biological "clock." Several features of the human circadian timing system and its interactions with sleep and wakefulness are relevant here.

- Circadian rhythms are biological oscillations with periods of about 24 hours.
- Circadian rhythms are synchronized to the 24-hour day chiefly by light signals.
- The chief circadian oscillator in mammals is located deep within the brain in the suprachiasmatic nuclei (SCN) of the hypothalamus.
- Circadian rhythms can be assessed by measuring the timing of biological events....
- Circadian rhythms control the timing of REM (rapid eye movement) sleep within the sleep period.

A first attempt to examine whether the circadian timing system undergoes developmental changes during adolescent maturation involved a survey of sixth-grade girls. In this survey, one series of questions allowed us to estimate physical development and another series gave a measure of circadian phase preference. Phase preference refers to an individual's tendency to favor activities in the morning or evening, i.e., morningness/eveningness. In these 275 sixth-grade girls, the puberty score and circadian phase preference score showed a significant relationship: less mature girls favored earlier hours, and more mature girls favored later hours.[8] These data were the first to implicate a biological process in the later timing of adolescent sleep.

• • •

One other important finding from our studies is that the circadian timing system can be reset if light exposure is carefully controlled. In many of our studies, we require adolescents to keep a specific sleep schedule (for example, 10 p.m. to 8 a.m.) and to wear eyeshades to exclude light during these hours. In fact, we pay adolescents to keep this schedule! When we measure melatonin secretion* before the students go on the new schedule (when they are still on

---

*[O]ne of the best ways to identify time in the intrinsic biological clock in humans is to examine melatonin secretion. Melatonin is a hormone that is produced by the pineal gland and regulated by the circadian timing system. Melatonin secretion occurs during nocturnal hours in both day-active species, like humans, and night-active species. Melatonin can be measured from saliva samples collected in dim lighting conditions.

their self-selected routine) and again after 10 or 11 nights on the new schedule, we find that the melatonin secretion has moved significantly toward a common time: those who were early melatonin secretors move to a later time, and those who were late secretors move earlier.[9] Thus we know that the system is not immutable; with time, effort, *and* money, we can get adolescents to realign their rhythms!

15   Let us summarize what we now know about the developmental trends in adolescent sleep behavior and adolescents' sleep/wake and circadian systems.

- As they mature, adolescents tend to go to bed later and to wake up later (given the opportunity).
- Adolescents also tend to sleep less as they mature.
- The difference between the amount and timing of sleep on weekend nights versus school nights grows during adolescence.
- These trends are apparent in adolescents both in North America and in industrialized countries on other continents.
- Sleep requirements do not decline during adolescent development.
- Daytime sleep tendency is augmented during puberty.
- The timing of events controlled by the circadian timing system is delayed during puberty.

We propose that the delay of sleep during adolescent development is favored by behavioral and intrinsic processes and that the reduction of sleep experienced by adolescents is largely driven by a collision between the intrinsic processes and the expectations and demands of the adult world.

• • •

Consequences, Concerns, and Countermeasures

Among the known consequences of insufficient sleep are memory lapses, attentional deficits, depressed mood, and slowed reaction time. Sleep deprivation studies have shown that divergent thinking suffers with inadequate sleep. A few surveys have noted poorer grades in students with inadequate sleep. Many important issues have not yet been well studied. For example, little is known about the consequences of insufficient sleep for relationship formation and maintenance, emotion regulation, delinquency, drug use, and violent behavior. Long-term consequences of insufficient sleep—particularly at critical developmental stages—are utterly unknown.

The problem of inadequate sleep affects more segments of our society than adolescents; however, adolescents appear to be particularly vulnerable and face difficult challenges for obtaining sufficient sleep. Even without the pressure of biological changes, if we combine an early school starting time—say 7:30 a.m., which, with a modest commute, makes 6:15 a.m. a viable rising time—with our knowledge that optimal sleep need is $9 \frac{1}{4}$ hours, we are asking that 16-year-olds go to bed at 9 p.m. Rare is the teenager of the 1990s who will keep such a schedule. School work, sports practices, clubs, volunteer work, and paid employment take precedence. When biological changes are factored in, the ability even to have merely "adequate" sleep is lost. As a consequence, sleepy teens demand that parents provide an extreme form of reveille, challenge teachers to offer maximal classroom entertainment and creativity just to keep them awake, and suffer the consequences of disaffection from school and dissatisfaction with themselves.

Can these problems be solved by delaying the starting time for school as adolescents move into the pubertal years? Not entirely. Moving the opening bell to a later time may help many teens with the mismatch between biological time and scholastic time, but it will not provide more hours in the day. It is not difficult to project that a large number of students see a later starting time as permission to stay up later at night studying, working, surfing the net, watching television, and so forth. Today's teens know little about their sleep needs or about the biological timing system. Interestingly, students do know they are sleepy, but they do not have skills to cope with the issue, and many assume—just as adults do—that they are expected to function with an inadequate amount of sleep. This assumption is a physiological fallacy: sleep is not optional. Sleep is biologically obligatory. If students learn about sleep, they have a basis to use a changed school starting time to best advantage. Adding information about sleep to the school curriculum can certainly help.

20   As with other fields of scientific investigation, the knowledge base, the scientific opportunities, and the level of pure excitement in sleep and biological rhythms research have never been greater. This knowledge and excitement can be shared with students at every academic level. Furthermore, sleep and biological rhythms are natural gateways to learning because students are drawn to the topics. Thus, as grammar school students learn about the nutrition pyramid, so too could they learn about the body's sleep requirements and how the biological timing system makes humans day-active rather than night-active. (Did you know that, if you put your hamster in a box with lights that turn on at night and off in the daytime, it will start running on its wheel during the day?)

As middle school students are learning about comparative biology, they can be sharing in the excitement of where, when, and how animals sleep. (Did you know that certain dolphins can be half asleep...literally? One half of the brain sleeps while the other half is awake! Did you know that mammals stop regulating body temperature in REM sleep? Did you know that you are paralyzed in REM sleep?)

High school students can share the excitement in the discoveries about genes that control the biological clock, about the brain mechanisms that control dreaming, about the way sleep creates breathing problems, and about sleep disorders that may affect their family members. (Did you know that snoring may be a sign of a serious sleep disorder afflicting as many as 5% of adults? Did you know that some people act out their dreams at night? Did you know that genes controlling the biological clock in mice and fruit flies are nearly identical?)

Challenges and an Opportunity

The challenges are great, and solutions do not come easily. School scheduling is incredibly complex, and accounting for youngsters' sleep needs and biological propensities adds to the complexity. Yet we cannot assume that the system is immutable. Given that the primary focus of education is to maximize human potential, then a new task before us is to ensure that the conditions in which learning takes place address the very biology of our learners.

Notes

1. Mary A. Carskadon, "Determinants of Daytime Sleepiness: Adolescent Development, Extended and Restricted Nocturnal Sleep" (Doctoral dissertation, Stanford University, 1979); idem, "The Second Decade," in Christian Guilleminault, ed., *Sleeping and Waking Disorders: Indications and Techniques* (Menlo Park, Calif.: Addison Wesley, 1982), pp. 99–125; and Mary A. Carskadon, E. John Orav, and William C. Dement, "Evolution of Sleep and Daytime Sleepiness in Adolescents," in Christian Guilleminault and Elio Lugaresi, eds., *Sleep/Wake Disorders: Natural History, Epidemiology, and Long-Term Evolution* (New York: Raven Press, 1983), pp. 201–16.

2. Mary A. Carskadon and William C. Dement, "The Multiple Sleep Latency Test: What Does It Measure?" *Sleep,* vol. 5, 1982, pp. 67–72.

3. Mary A. Carskadon et al., "Pubertal Changes in Daytime Sleepiness," *Sleep,* vol. 2, 1980, pp. 453–60.

4. Carskadon, "Determinants of Daytime Sleepiness."

5. Mary A. Carskadon, "Patterns of Sleep and Sleepiness in Adolescents," *Pediatrician,* vol. 17, 1990, pp. 5–12.

6. Mirian M. M. Andrade and Luiz Menna-Barreto, "Sleep Patterns of High School Students Living in São Paulo, Brazil," in Mary A. Carskadon, ed., *Adolescent Sleep Patterns: Biological, Social, and Psychological Influences* (New York: Cambridge University Press, forthcoming); Kaneyoshi Ishihara, Yukako Honma, and Susumu Miyake, "Investigation of the Children's Version of the Morningness-Eveningness Questionnaire with Primary and Junior High School Pupils in Japan," *Perceptual and Motor Skills,* vol. 71, 1990, pp. 1353–54; Helen M. Bearpark and Patricia T. Michie, "Prevalence of Sleep/Wake Disturbances in Sidney Adolescents," *Sleep Research,* vol. 16, 1987, p. 304; and Inge Strauch and Barbara Meier, "Sleep Need in Adolescents: A Longitudinal Approach," *Sleep,* vol. 11, 1988, pp. 378–86.

7. Alexander A. Borbély, "A Two Process Model of Sleep Regulation," *Human Neurobiology,* vol. 1, 1982, pp. 195–204.

8. Mary A. Carskadon, Cecilia Vieira, and Christine Acebo, "Association Between Puberty and Delayed Phase Preference," *Sleep,* vol. 16, 1993, pp. 258–62.

9. Carskadon et al., "An Approach to Studying Circadian Rhythms."

● **Review Questions**

1. What fundamental shift in sleep patterns occurs in the transition to adolescence, and what problems does this shift cause?

2. What did investigators discover when they examined the "axiom" that "the older you are, the less sleep you need"?

3. What behavioral and social factors can affect adolescent sleep?

4. Carskadon presents two "conceptual models of the underlying internal mechanisms that control the length and timing of sleep." What are they and how can they be measured?

5. What, exactly, are the colliding worlds of Carskadon's title?

● **Discussion and Writing Suggestions**

1. Is there any sense in which you feel vindicated in your early morning sleepiness by Carskadon's article? Throughout adolescence, adults may have blamed your sleepiness on character flaws—laziness, perhaps. Does the science behind Carskadon's article help you to feel any better about yourself? Write a letter to one such adult accuser explaining why you were not a lazy-good-for-nothing after all!

2. In matters relating to sleepiness/wakefulness, in what ways has your world "collided" with the world of "societal demands"? Collisions often produce casualties. Have there been casualties in your case?

3. Carskadon calls our attention to the problems adolescents may face when their sleep schedules conflict with the scheduling demands of the broader world. She points, as well, to the seemingly intractable causes of this conflict. (See especially paragraphs 17–18.) What do you think of her proposals to minimize, if not avoid, this conflict? Can you offer any proposals of your own?

SLEEP DEBT AND THE MORTGAGED MIND

*William C. Dement and
Christopher Vaughan*

William Dement, MD, PhD, is one of the founders of modern sleep medicine, universally acknowledged as a pioneer (along with Mary Carskadon, whose work appears earlier in this chapter). A professor and researcher at Stanford University, Dement has authored numerous articles, books, and book chapters on sleep. His particular interest has been the topic of sleep "debt," the focus of the following selection, which appeared originally as a chapter in *The Promise of Sleep* (1999), cowritten with Christopher Vaughan.

The night of March 24, 1989, was cold and calm, the air crystalline, as the giant *Exxon Valdez* oil tanker pulled out of Valdez, Alaska, into the tranquil waters of Prince William Sound. In these clearest of possible conditions the ship made a planned turn out of the shipping channel and didn't turn back in time. The huge tanker ran aground, spilling millions of gallons of crude oil into the sound. The cost of the cleanup effort was over $2 billion. The ultimate cost of continuing environmental damage is incalculable. Furthermore, when the civil trial was finally over in the summer of 1995, the Exxon Corporation was assessed an additional $5 billion in punitive damages. Everyone I query in my travels vividly recalls the accident, and most have the impression that it had something to do with the master's alcohol consumption. No one is aware of the true cause of the tragedy. In its final report, the National Transportation Safety Board (NTSB) found that sleep deprivation and sleep debt were direct causes of the accident. This stunning result got a brief mention in the back pages of the newspapers.

Out of the vast ocean of knowledge about sleep, there are a few facts that are so important that I will try to burn them into your brain forever. None is more important than the topic of sleep debt. If we can learn to understand sleep indebtedness and manage it, we can improve everyday life as well as avoid many injuries, horribly diminished lives, and premature deaths.

The *Exxon Valdez* disaster offers a good example of how sleep debt can create a tragedy and how the true villain—sleep indebtedness—remains concealed. I am sure that I was just as shocked as anyone when I learned about America's worst oil spill. The TV coverage of the dead birds and seals filled me with outrage over the environmental devastation. One of my friends went to Alaska and participated in the cleanup. He brought back photos and a big jar of crude oil. If you haven't been exposed to crude oil, keep away from it. It isn't the purified stuff that goes into your car. It's awful. It stinks to high heaven. You want to vomit.

I was among the millions who were following the news, but I had no idea that it would have a special meaning for me a year later. The National Commission on Sleep Disorders Research finally mandated by Congress was convened for the first time in March 1990, and 20 commissioners were assembled in Washington, D.C. After the first meeting I decided to visit a friend, Dr. John Lauber, who had been confirmed by the Senate as one of five members of the National Transportation Safety Board. He told me that the board would very likely identify sleep deprivation as the "direct cause" of the grounding of the *Exxon Valdez*.

5   I had worked with John a few years earlier on a study of the layover sleep of pilots on intercontinental airlines. He was head of human factors research at NASA-Ames and at the beginning of the layover study knew little about "sleep debt." At the end of the study, he was one of the few real experts in the world. Two months after the visit with John he sent me the NTSB's final report.

The report noted that on the March night when the *Exxon Valdez* steamed out of Valdez there were ice floes across part of the shipping lane, forcing the ship to turn to avoid them. The captain determined that this maneuver could be done safely if the ship was steered back to the main channel when it was abeam of a well-known landmark, Busby Island. With this plan established, he turned over command to the third mate and left the bridge. Although news reports linked much of what happened next to the captain's alcohol consumption, the captain was off the bridge well before the accident. The direct cause of America's worst oil spill was the behavior of the third mate, who had slept only 6 hours in the previous 48 and was severely sleep deprived.

As the *Exxon Valdez* passed Busby Island, the third mate ordered the helm to starboard, but he didn't notice that the autopilot was still on and the ship did not turn. Instead it plowed farther out of the channel. Twice lookouts warned the third mate about the position of lights marking the reef, but he didn't change or check his previous orders. His brain was not interpreting the danger in what they said. Finally he noticed that he was far outside the channel, turned off the autopilot, and tried hard to get the great ship pointed back to safety—too late.

For several years I would ask every audience that I addressed if there was anyone in the audience who had not heard the words *"Exxon Valdez."* A hand was never raised. Then I would say, "Who knows what caused the grounding?" Many hands would be raised, and the answer would always be "alcohol." Thus I could never exploit the potential impact of this catastrophe in getting knowledge about sleep into the mainstream, because of the media emphasis on the captain's drinking. When the report finally came out, there was no real interest. Even at the trial, in the summer of 1995, the true cause of the accident received little attention. What everyone ought to be talking about is how to deal with sleep deprivation and how to avoid it in the transportation industry and throughout all components of society, saying over and over again "Look what it caused." But instead, the poor captain has been hounded for nearly a decade.

An even more dramatic tragedy was the explosion of the space shuttle *Challenger.* After a year-long investigation, the Rogers Commission declared that in the absence of adequate data on O-ring function at low temperatures the decision to launch the rocket was an error. Those of us who saw this catastrophic event on television over and over and over know the ghastly consequences of that error. But not well known at all is the fact that the Human Factors Subcommittee attributed the error to the severe sleep deprivation of the NASA managers. This conclusion was only included in the committee's final report, which only noted that top managers in such situations are generally the ones who sacrifice the most sleep.

10   Was this the most costly case of sleepiness in history? The parents of any teenager who has died while asleep at the wheel might not agree. Even the most careful drivers are at risk, because we simply do not tell people—not even young people in the driver-training courses required in many states—how to recognize signs of dangerous sleepiness.

Of course, even children are at risk. For example in the past several years I have received many reports of school bus accidents where the driver fell asleep. Unfortunately, it may take another *Exxon Valdez* or *Challenger* before the sleep community can mobilize public opinion to do something about this issue. Thus, I find myself in the bizarre circumstance of simultaneously fearing and at the same time hoping for another highly visible disaster.

Just last year I stepped up to the podium to make the danger absolutely clear to my Stanford students. Drowsiness, that feeling when the eyelids are trying to close and we cannot seem to keep them open, is the last step before we fall asleep, not the first. If at this moment we let sleep come, it will arrive instantly. When driving a car, or in any hazardous situation, the first wave of drowsiness should be a dramatic warning. Get out of harm's way instantly! My message to the students is "Drowsiness is red alert!" I delivered and explained this message over and over in my 1997 undergraduate course "Sleep and Dreams," and the students got it. I am confident few will ever drive while drowsy.

Everyone can recall a jolt of heart-stopping panic in the face of peril—when we realize a cab seems about to jump the curb we're standing on, or when we lose track of a child in a crowd. The response is instantaneous. We act. We should have a similar response the instant we feel drowsy at the wheel.

Ignorance About Sleepiness

... I now think of the continuum of sleepiness and alertness as the state upon which all human behavior is acted out. Today we can claim with confidence that where we are on this continuum, from the high peak of optimal alertness to the deep trough of extreme drowsiness, is the single most important determinant of how well we perform. Accordingly, the total absence of this subject from psychology textbooks or any other educational materials is incomprehensible. Although the scientific knowledge has been available for more than two decades, students are still not acquiring crucial knowledge about sleepiness, sleep debt, and sleep deprivation in any of our educational institutions....

15   The feeling of being tired and needing sleep is a basic drive of nature, like hunger. If you don't eat enough, you are driven to eat. If you go long enough without food, you can think of nothing else. Once you get food, you eat until you feel full and then you stop. Thus, the subjective responses of hunger and satiation ensure that you fulfill your overall daily requirement for calories. In essentially the same way, your sleep drive keeps an exact tally of accumulated waking hours. Like bricks in a backpack, accumulated sleep drive is a burden that weighs down on you. Every hour that you are awake adds another brick to the backpack: The brain's sleep load increases until you go to sleep, when the load starts to lighten.

In a very real sense all wakefulness is sleep deprivation. As soon as you wake up, the meter starts ticking, calculating how many hours of sleep you will need to pay off that night. Or, to continue the load metaphor, it tallies how many bricks you will have to shed to get back to zero. Generally people need to sleep one hour for every two hours awake, which means that most need around eight hours of sleep a night. Of course, some people need more and some need less, and a few people seem to need a great deal more or less. From the work we have done, we must conclude that each person has his or her own specific daily sleep requirement. The brain tries to hit this mark, and the further you are from getting the number of hours of sleep you need, the harder your brain tries to force you to get that sleep.

• • •

Sleep Debt: Nature's Loan Shark

... The brain keeps an exact accounting of how much sleep it is owed. In our first study, we restricted the sleep of 10 volunteers to exactly 5 hours each night for 7 nights and observed that the tendency to fall asleep increased progressively each successive day. For the first time in the history of sleep research, we discovered that the effect of each successive night of partial sleep loss carried over, and the effect appeared to accumulate in a precisely additive fashion. In other words, the strength of the tendency to fall asleep was progressively greater during each successive day with exactly the same amount of sleep each night. For some time Mary [Carskadon] and I referred to this as an increased sleep tendency, and it was clear that the increase did not dissipate without additional rest. How people recover from various levels of sleep deprivation after getting sleep has not been well studied. However, current evidence suggests that the accumulated lost sleep must be paid back at some time, perhaps even hour for hour.

We use the term "sleep debt" because accumulated lost sleep is like a monetary debt: It must be paid back. Regardless of how rapidly it can be paid back, the important thing is that the size of the sleep debt and its dangerous effects are definitely directly related to the amount of lost sleep. My guess is that after a period of substantial sleep loss, we can pay back a little and feel a lot better, although the remaining sleep debt is still large. The danger of an unintended sleep episode is still there. Until proven otherwise, it is reasonable and certainly safer to assume that accumulated lost sleep must be paid back hour for hour. Therefore, if you miss 3 hours one night, you must sleep 11 hours the next night (3 plus your normal 8) in order to feel alert throughout the day.

Your sleep debt may have accumulated in small increments over many days. For example, during a five-day work week where you needed 8 hours each night and instead got 6, you would build up a sleep debt of 10 hours (5 times 2). From this perspective, sleeping in until noon on Saturday is not enough to pay back the 10 lost hours plus your nightly requirement of 8; you would have to sleep until about 5:00 P.M. to balance the sleep ledger. Of course, most people won't sleep that long, and in fact it is difficult to do because of the alerting process of the biological clock.... More likely, you will sleep in an extra hour or two and get up feeling better. But the debt is still there, demanding to be paid. Later that day you'll start feeling the effects of the sleep debt again. And if you borrow more sleep time over subsequent nights, you won't just stay sleepy, you'll get even sleepier. As your debt grows, your energy, mood, and cognition will be undermined.

20   There is another important way that sleep deprivation can occur and sleep debt can accumulate.... [S]everal sleep disorders are characterized by very severe and impairing daytime sleepiness. In such patients we typically see hundreds of brief interruptions of sleep in a single night. In spite of this, careful tabulation of the intervening short periods of sleep can add up to what ought to be a satisfactory amount of total sleep.

Several groups of sleep researchers have carried out studies on normal volunteers which have clarified this situation. In these studies, subjects were awakened every minute or so throughout entire nights, and the next day's alertness was evaluated using the [Multiple Sleep Latency Test, which measures sleepiness, the speed with which subjects fall asleep]. The nocturnal awakenings were brief, 5 to 10 seconds, and subjects usually returned to sleep immediately. Although there were usually several hundred interruptions, the cumulative total sleep can add up to normal amounts. Nevertheless, daytime sleepiness is markedly increased, as if there had been no sleep at all, or very little.

Interrupting sleep every minute or so all night long is a heroic experimental manipulation. I am happy to report that the results of these particular experiments have been very consistent. Accordingly, we may conclude that the restorative value of sleep is severely curtailed if sleep periods are not allowed to continue for at least several minutes. If 10 to 15 minutes of sleep are allowed to occur before an interruption, this effect is greatly lessened. These studies have led to the concept that there are minimal units of restorative sleep. In other words, it is as if the bank that keeps track of sleep debt doesn't accept small deposits.

In one of our first studies we evaluated the clinical usefulness of the MSLT by comparing narcoleptics and normal sleepers. The results were fabulous. The MSLT sharply distinguished patients and normals. However, the MSLT scores of a few normal volunteers were in the pathologically sleepy range (1 to 5 minutes). This latter group tended to be college students. For a while we thought that these younger "normals" were in the early stages of the narcoleptic sleep disorder, not yet manifesting the other symptoms. But it was hard to imagine why Stanford University would attract so many budding narcoleptics. We tested a few more students, allowing a baseline normal amount of sleep (8 hours a day) and carefully measuring their sleep tendency day to day with the MSLT. Nearly all of the students appeared to be pathologically sleepy! I should not have been so surprised, because I have been watching students fall asleep in class ever since I was a college student myself.

The obvious explanation finally occurred to Mary and me: The students needed more sleep. To prove this we did studies where we extended their nightly hours in bed to 10, and over several days, the MSLT score steadily improved. Now that we know about sleep debt, we can only imagine how many thousands of observations on human behavior have been made over the decades on chronically sleep-deprived subjects whom researchers thought were "normal." Since people are so severely affected by a large sleep debt, its presence can potentially alter the results of almost all research measures, from I.Q. tests to observations of drug side effects. The baseline studies of all human research, regardless of their nature, now must include measures of daytime sleep tendency, so that the variable degree of chronic sleep loss does not contaminate every study.

25   Despite the fact that "sleep debt" has entered common parlance (some researchers also call it "sleep load" or "sleep tendency"), many people don't fully understand the concept. Again and again I hear people complain that they sleep a full night, even an extra hour or so, and still feel just as sleepy or even sleepier than before. "Well," they think, "I must be sleepy because I am sleeping too much." The fact is that you don't work off a large sleep debt, which is what most of us have, by getting one good night's sleep.

· · ·

Driving Under the Influence of Sleep Debt

People *must* learn to pay attention to their own sleep debt and how it is affecting them. Not doing so, and misunderstanding the rules of sleep debt and arousal, can be extremely dangerous. A friend of mine, also a Stanford professor, once participated in a bicycle race that lasted several days and included a number of laps around Lake Tahoe. He got very little sleep at night during the period of the race, but then he slept about nine hours a night for the two nights he stayed at the lake after the race. He woke up on Sunday morning feeling rested, ready to pack up and drive home. But as he was coming down the winding mountain road he began to yawn and his eyelids felt heavy. He told me that he was a little surprised because he thought he had gotten plenty of sleep. If someone had been with him, he probably would have traded places, but it did not occur to him to pull over and take a nap. As he drove on, it became harder and harder to keep his eyes open, and he began to be concerned. At that moment he saw a sign for a restaurant only several miles farther down the road. "Good," he thought, "I'll be able to get some coffee." Right after that he fell asleep, just for a moment, and awoke with a terrible start to find that he had drifted into the oncoming lane. He jerked the wheel to the right, but the road curved to the left, and the car went over a 30-foot ledge. The next thing he knew he was upside down, suspended by his seat belt, the car impaled on a jagged rock that had sliced through the roof and into the empty passenger seat next to him. He sustained serious cuts and bruises, and his right arm was completely paralyzed, but miraculously he was alive.

When he told me the story later, he still didn't understand how he could have been so sleepy. "But Bill, I got two full nights of sleep before I left Tahoe." Not knowing about sleep debt, he could not know that a few hours of extra sleep does not alleviate the sleep debt accumulated over the preceding nights or weeks. He was driving alone without the stimulation of conversation, along a route he knew fairly well. In short, there was little to act as a dike against the sea of sleep debt that he had built up. Ironically, his awareness of how terribly drowsy he was feeling may have forestalled sleep in the minutes before the crash. When he saw the sign for the restaurant up ahead and knew that he would soon get coffee, he relaxed and let that worry go. A few moments later he was hurtling off the mountain road. If the idea that drowsiness is supremely dangerous had been burned into his brain, he would have stopped driving no matter how difficult or inconvenient.

Fatal Fatigue: Alcohol and Sleep Debt

…[O]lder children never feel sleepy during the day. They were the only group we studied in the Stanford Summer Sleep Camp who never fell asleep in the 20 minutes allotted for the individual sleep latency tests. And of course, children are usually not sleep deprived. Putting all our results together, we can state with confidence that if you feel sleepy or drowsy in the daytime, then you must have a sizable sleep debt. Sleep debt is the physical side of the coin, and the feelings of sleepiness or drowsiness are the psychological side. As an analogy, dehydration is the physical side of the coin and the feeling of being thirsty is the psychological side. To carry the analogy a little further, if we have thoroughly quenched our thirst, we cannot immediately feel thirsty. But if we are becoming dehydrated, the desire to drink may be diminished if we are involved in something very interesting or demanding. At some point, of course, thirst becomes overwhelming. Likewise, we cannot feel sleepy in the daytime if we do not have a sleep debt, but we may not feel sleepy if we are doing something that excites us. If we have a very strong tendency to fall asleep and we reduce the stimuli that are keeping us awake, we will very soon begin to feel sleepy and will inevitably fall asleep, intentionally or otherwise.

But all those interested in traffic safety and all those who wish to have a long life as well must take note. When a crash is attributed to alcohol, the real culprit, or at least a coconspirator, is often sleep deprivation. In studies that are second to none in importance, the powerful interaction between sleep and alcohol was revealed by the outstanding sleep research team at Henry Ford Hospital Sleep Disorders Center. A group of volunteers slept 10 hours a night for one week, 8 hours a night during a separate week, and on a third schedule simulated a social weekend by getting 5 hours of sleep for 2 nights. In the morning after completing each schedule, all of the volunteers were given either a low dose of alcohol or a placebo. Then their degree of impaired alertness was evaluated utilizing the MSLT and performance tests. When the subjects were given the low dose of alcohol after the 8-hour schedule, they became slightly more sleepy than when given placebo. After the schedule of 2 nights with little sleep, the exact same dose of alcohol the next morning made them severely sleepy, barely able to stay awake. However, the exact same dose of alcohol after 10 hours of sleep every night for a week had no discernible effect. In other words, alcohol may not be a potent sedative by itself, but it becomes very sedating when paired with sleep debt. It is tempting to speculate that all sedatives, particularly sleeping pills, interact with sleep debt. This area deserves much more research....

30   The implications of this are far-reaching. People are well aware of the dangers of drinking and driving, but they don't know that a large sleep debt and even a small amount of alcohol can create a "fatal fatigue." People can be just fine driving after a single drink one day (when they have little sleep debt), yet be a hazard to themselves and others if they have that same drink on a day in which they have a large sleep debt. A fact little known by the public at large is that in nearly every accident linked to alcohol consumption, sleep debt almost certainly plays a major role.

In one state traffic agency, researchers are trying very hard to understand traffic accidents designated as alcohol related even though the alcohol in the tissue is far below any level thought to be impairing.

• • •

[E]xperiments demonstrate that individuals thought to be completely normal can be carrying a sizable sleep debt, which impairs their mood, energy, and performance. If you haven't already done so, I think it's worthwhile to ask yourself how your sleep debt is affecting you. How often do you think about taking a quick snooze? How often do you rub your eyes and yawn during the day? How often do you feel like you really need some coffee? Each of these is a warning of a sleep debt that you ignore at your peril. I can't overemphasize the dangers of unintended sleep episodes or severe drowsiness. I hope this information can save your life.

I know that people often are driven to stay up late and get up early, that the demands of modern life push us to stay up past our biological bedtime. But I also know it's not too onerous to avoid accumulating sleep debt....Studies suggest the likelihood that people can avoid dangerously high sleep debt by adding a relatively small amount of sleep to their normal sleep schedule. People who have lowered their sleep debt usually report that they gain a new sense of well-being. That may just mean not watching the news at night, or putting off some other nonessential pleasure, like the bedtime crossword puzzle. I bet most people would give up many late-night diversions if they could feel truly awake throughout the day—fresh and full of hope, senses wide open, the mind receptive to people and ideas.

● Review Questions

1. What was the actual, though little reported, cause of the *Exxon Valdez* disaster?

2. Dement asserts that "Drowsiness is red alert!" What does he mean?

3. What is the "continuum of sleepiness and alertness"? What is its significance?

4. How is sleeping like eating and drinking?

5. What is sleep debt? How is it "carried over"? How is the amount of sleep debt correlated with the dangers posed by sleep debt?

6. Why may a person feel sleepy even after getting a full night's sleep?

7. In what way is sleep debt often a "co-conspirator" in alcohol-related crashes?

● Discussion and Writing Suggestions

1. Consider your own sleep habits. Given what you've read in this article, are you currently sleep deprived? Have you ever been? Have you ever noticed in your daily performance of a task the kinds of impairments due to sleep debt that Dement discusses?

2. In the title and throughout the article, Dement uses a metaphor from the banking industry—mortgage—to discuss sleep debt. (This term is sometimes useful to politicians and social commentators—who speak of "mortgaging" our future.) Cite several instances of the use of this metaphor and comment on its effectiveness. To what extent does the metaphor help to convey Dement's central message? In your answer, discuss how a mind can be "mortgaged."

3. Have you ever experienced the sensation of driving drowsy—which Dement says should be a "red alert" to stop your car and rest? In a paragraph, describe the scene: the sensation of drowsiness, the conversation you have with yourself to stay awake, the efforts to fight off sleep (e.g., turning on the radio, opening a window, slapping your face)—and then the nodding head and the startled waking.

4. Do you respond to Dement's raising a "red alert" (paragraph 12) about driving and drowsiness any differently than you would if a parent raised the same alert? Why?

THE PITTSBURGH SLEEP QUALITY INDEX

Daniel Buysse

In light of William Dement's cautions on the dangers of sleep debt—and also Mary Carskadon's review of the biological, behavioral, and social forces that converge to rob adolescents of sleep—we offer a tool to assess the quality of your own sleep: the Pittsburgh Sleep Quality Index, or PSQI. Because the test can be self-scored, you can get a numerical indicator of the quality of your own sleep. Daniel J. Buysse, MD, is medical director of the Sleep Evaluation Center in the department of psychiatry at the University of Pittsburgh. A past president of the American Academy of Sleep Medicine, Buysse developed the PSQI with Charles F. Reynolds, III, MD; Timothy H. Monk, PhD; Susan R. Berman; and David J. Kupfer, MD. The authors first presented the PSQI in *Psychiatry Research* (May 1989) as a tool "specifically designed to measure sleep quality in clinical populations." Today, the PSQI is a widely used instrument in sleep research.

Pittsburgh Sleep Quality Index (PSQI)

Name _____ ID # _____ Date _____ Age _____
Instructions:

The following questions relate to your usual sleep habits during the past month *only.* Your answers should indicate the most accurate reply for the *majority* of days and nights in the past month. Please answer all questions.
1. During the past month, when have you usually gone to bed at night?
                    USUAL BED TIME _____
2. During the past month, how long (in minutes) has it usually taken you to fall asleep each night?
                    NUMBER OF MINUTES _____
3. During the past month, when have you usually gotten up in the morning?
                    USUAL GETTING UP TIME _____
4. During the past month, how many hours of *actual sleep* did you get at night? (This may be different than the number of hours you spend in bed.)
                    HOURS OF SLEEP PER NIGHT _____

For each of the remaining questions, check the one best response. Please answer *all* questions.

5. During the past month, how often have you had trouble sleeping because you . . .

    (a) Cannot get to sleep within 30 minutes

Not during the past month _____	Less than once a week _____	Once or twice a week _____	Three or more times a week _____

    (b) Wake up in the middle of the night or early morning

Not during the past month _____	Less than once a week _____	Once or twice a week _____	Three or more times a week _____

    (c) Have to get up to use the bathroom

Not during the past month _____	Less than once a week _____	Once or twice a week _____	Three or more times a week _____

    (d) Cannot breathe comfortably

Not during the past month _____	Less than once a week _____	Once or twice a week _____	Three or more times a week _____

    (e) Cough or snore loudly

Not during the past month _____	Less than once a week _____	Once or twice a week _____	Three or more times a week _____

    (f) Feel too cold

Not during the past month _____	Less than once a week _____	Once or twice a week _____	Three or more times a week _____

    (g) Feel too hot

Not during the past month _____	Less than once a week _____	Once or twice a week _____	Three or more times a week _____

    (h) Had bad dreams

Not during the past month _____	Less than once a week _____	Once or twice a week _____	Three or more times a week _____

    (i) Have pain

Not during the past month _____	Less than once a week _____	Once or twice a week _____	Three or more times a week _____

    (j) Other reason(s), please describe _____

_____

    How often during the past month have you had trouble sleeping because of this?

Not during the past month _____	Less than once a week _____	Once or twice a week _____	Three or more times a week _____

6. During the past month, how would you rate your sleep quality overall?

        Very good _____

        Fairly good _____

        Fairly bad _____

        Very bad _____

7. During the past month, how often have you taken medicine (prescribed or "over the counter") to help you sleep?

Not during the past month _____	Less than once a week _____	Once or twice a week _____	Three or more times a week _____

8. During the past month, how often have you had trouble staying awake while driving, eating meals, or engaging in social activity?

Not during the past month _____	Less than once a week _____	Once or twice a week _____	Three or more times a week _____

9. During the past month, how much of a problem has it been for you to keep up enough enthusiasm to get things done?

        No problem at all _____
        Only a very slight problem _____
        Somewhat of a problem _____
        A very big problem _____

10. Do you have a bed partner or roommate?

        No bed partner or roommate _____
        Partner/roommate in other room _____
        Partner in same room, but not same bed _____
        Partner in same bed _____

If you have a roommate or bed partner, ask him/her how often in the past month you have had . . .

(a) Loud snoring

| Not during the past month _____ | Less than once a week _____ | Once or twice a week _____ | Three or more times a week _____ |

(b) Long pauses between breaths while asleep

| Not during the past month _____ | Less than once a week _____ | Once or twice a week _____ | Three or more times a week _____ |

(c) Legs twitching or jerking while you sleep

| Not during the past month _____ | Less than once a week _____ | Once or twice a week _____ | Three or more times a week _____ |

(d) Episodes of disorientation or confusion during sleep

| Not during the past month _____ | Less than once a week _____ | Once or twice a week _____ | Three or more times a week _____ |

(e) Other restlessness while you sleep; please describe _____

_____

| Not during the past month _____ | Less than once a week _____ | Once or twice a week _____ | Three or more times a week _____ |

Scoring Instructions for the Pittsburgh Sleep Quality Index

The Pittsburgh Sleep Quality Index (PSQI) contains 19 self-rated questions and 5 questions rated by the bed partner or roommate (if one is available). Only self-rated questions are included in the scoring. The 19 self-rated items are combined to form seven "component" scores, each of which has a range of 0–3 points. In all cases, a score of "0" indicates no difficulty, while a score of "3" indicates severe difficulty. The seven component scores are then added to yield one "global" score, with a range of 0–21 points, "0" indicating no difficulty and "21" indicating severe difficulties in all areas.

    Scoring proceeds as follows:

Component 1: Subjective sleep quality

Examine question #6, and assign scores as follows:

Response	Component 1 score
"Very good"	0
"Fairly good"	1
"Fairly bad"	2
"Very bad"	3

Component 1 score: _____

Component 2: Sleep latency [amount of time needed to fall asleep]

1. Examine question #2, and assign scores as follows:

Response	Score
≤ 15 minutes	0
16–30 minutes	1
31–60 minutes	2
> 60 minutes	3

Question #2 score: _____

2. Examine question #5a, and assign scores as follows:

Response	Score
Not during the past month	0
Less than once a week	1
Once or twice a week	2
Three or more times a week	3

Question #5a score: _____

3. Add #2 score and #5a score

Sum of #2 and #5a: _____

4. Assign component 2 score as follows:

Sum of #2 and #5a	Component 2 score
0	0
1–2	1
3–4	2
5–6	3

Component 2 score: _____

Component 3 Sleep duration

Examine question #4, and assign scores as follows:

Response	Component 3 score
≥ 7 hours	0
≥ 6 < 7 hours	1
≥ 5 < 6 hours	2
< 5 hours	3

Component 3 score: _____

Component 4: Habitual sleep efficiency

(1) Write the number of hours slept (question #4) here: _____

(2) Calculate the number of hours spent in bed:

Getting up time (question #3): _____

− Bedtime (question #1): _____

Number of hours spent in bed: _____

(3) Calculate habitual sleep efficiency as follows:

(Number of hours slept/Number of hours spent in bed) × 100 = Habitual sleep efficiency (%)

(_____/_____) × 100 = _____%

(4) Assign component 4 score as follows:

Habitual sleep efficiency %	Component 4 score
>85%	0
75–84%	1
65–74%	2
<65%	3

Component 4 score: _____

Component 5: Sleep disturbances

(1) Examine questions #5b–5j, and assign scores for *each* question as follows:

Response	Score
Not during the past month	0
Less than once a week	1
Once or twice a week	2
Three or more times a week	3

#5b score _____
c score _____
d score _____
e score _____
f score _____
g score _____
h score _____
i score _____
j score _____

(2) Add the scores for questions #5b–5j:

Sum of #5b–5j: _____

(3) Assign component 5 score as follows:

Sum of #5b–5j	Component 5 score
0	0
1–9	1
10–18	2
19–27	3

Component 5 score: _____

Component 6: Use of sleeping medication

Examine question #7 and assign scores as follows:

Response	Component 6 score
Not during the past month	0
Less than once a week	1
Once or twice a week	2
Three or more times a week	3

Component 6 score: _____

Component 7: Daytime dysfunction

(1) Examine question #8, and assign scores as follows:

Response	Score
Never	0
Once or twice	1
Once or twice each week	2
Three or more times each week	3

Question #8 score: _____

(2) Examine question #9, and assign scores as follows:

Response	Score
No problem at all	0
Only a very slight problem	1
Somewhat of a problem	2
A very big problem	3

Question #9 score: _____

(3) Add the scores for question #8 and #9:

Sum of #8 and #9: _____

(4) Assign component 7 score as follows:

Sum of #8 and #9	Component 7 score
0	0
1–2	1
3–4	2
5–6	3

Component 7 score: _____

Global PSQI Score

Add the seven component scores together:

Global PSQI Score: ____

● Discussion and Writing Suggestions

1. Complete the Pittsburgh Sleep Quality Index and compute your score, which will fall in a scale from 0 to 21 points. The higher your score, the greater your sleep difficulties. Where do you fall in the range?

2. Examine your seven "component" scores, which you will have calculated in computing your overall score. ("Sleep Latency" refers to the ease with which you fall asleep. The other six components are self-explanatory.) Which component(s) does the PSQI indicate are your strongest? Your weakest? Based on your subjective assessment of your own sleep, is the scoring accurate?

3. Did you need a formal test to determine how well you are sleeping? Were you aware that the quality of your sleep could be assessed along seven dimensions?

4. How useful do you find a numerical sleep score, as compared to an impressionistic assessment, such as "I sleep well" or "I'm a poor sleeper"? Why might sleep researchers develop an instrument that yields numerical scores?

5. If you are interested in seeing how an instrument such as the PSQI is created and clinically tested for accuracy, see the article that introduced it to the world in *Psychiatry Research* (Volume 28, No. 2, May 1989). You should be able to locate the article in your school library's electronic database—or via electronic interlibrary loan.

6. If your PSQI score suggests that you have difficulties sleeping, do you see any need to take action—especially in light of the preceding selection by William Dement? What action(s) (if any) might be appropriate?

HOW SLEEP DEBT HURTS COLLEGE STUDENTS

June J. Pilcher and
Amy S. Walters

The "all-nighter" is a rite of passage among many college students, who—pressed by competing schedules (and, let's be honest, the desire to have fun)—sometimes ignore the need to sleep, for 24 hours or more, in order to study for an exam or meet a paper deadline. Propped up by caffeinated beverages the next day, the student may even boast: "It was hard, but I got it done. I *aced* that exam." Perhaps not. Sleep researchers June Pilcher, who holds a PhD in biopsychology and teaches at Clemson University, and Amy Walters, MA, of Bradley University (when this article was published), report on an experiment that deprived students of a night's sleep and tested their cognitive functioning the next day. Both the results of these tests and the students' estimates of their performance may surprise (and deflate) you. This selection first appeared in the *Journal of American College Health* (November 1997).

A note on the specialized language of statistics: You should be able to understand this article whether or not you are familiar with the terms *standard deviation, mean,* or *probability* (e.g., $p < .05$). Like all researchers who collect numerical information, Pilcher and Walters run their data through statistical analyses to determine if their results are significant. For a useful guide to definitions of statistical terms, see the online "Statistics Glossary," by Valerie J. Easton and John H. McColl, http://www.stats.gla.ac.uk/steps/glossary/index.html. Consult their "Alphabetical index of all entries."

ABSTRACT.   The effects of sleep deprivation on cognitive performance and on psychological variables related to cognitive performance were studied in 44 college students. Participants completed the Watson-Glaser Critical Thinking Appraisal after either 24 hours of sleep deprivation or approximately 8 hours of sleep. After completing the cognitive task, the participants completed 2 questionnaires, one assessing self-reported effort, concentration, and estimated performance, the other assessing off-task cognitions. As expected, sleep-deprived participants performed significantly worse than the nondeprived participants on the cognitive task. However, the sleep-deprived participants rated their concentration and effort higher than the nondeprived participants did. In addition, the sleep-deprived participants rated their estimated performance significantly higher than the nondeprived participants did. The findings indicate that college students are not aware of the extent to which sleep deprivation negatively affects their ability to complete cognitive tasks.

Voluntary sleep deprivation is a common occurrence for many college students, who often partially deprive themselves of sleep during the week and compensate by increasing their sleep time over the weekend.(n1) This pattern of sleep deprivation and rebound becomes more pronounced around examination periods, sometimes resulting in 24 to 48 hours of total sleep deprivation. By depriving themselves of sleep, college students are not only increasing their feelings of sleepiness during the day, thus decreasing their ability to pay attention in class, but are also negatively affecting their ability to perform on exams.

It is well established that sleep deprivation of 24 hours or more leads to noticeable decrements in performance levels.(n2, n3) The psychological variables behind these decrements, however, are less clear. One theory states that decreases in performance are attributable to a decrease in the ability of the sleep-deprived person to focus the attention and effort necessary to complete the task successfully.(n4, n5) Similarly, a number of early sleep-deprivation studies concluded that the detrimental effects of sleep loss on performance result from periods of inattention called lapses.(n6-n8) Moreover, one early study specifically concluded that sleep loss leads to a decrease in attention to external stimuli.(n9) None of the earlier studies, however, attempted to assess self-reported variables that reflect changes in psychological events or thoughts that may be associated with the observed decrements in performance.

The effect of sleep deprivation on psychological variables associated with performance, such as self-reported estimates of attention, effort, and performance, have not been thoroughly investigated. Few studies have examined perceived effort and performance,(n11-n15) and the results from those studies have often been contradictory. For example, some researchers have suggested that sleep deprivation may affect the willingness of the individual to put forth the effort to perform well on a task more than the actual ability of the individual to perform.(n11, n12)

By contrast, other researchers have concluded that participants may recognize their decreased performance levels following sleep deprivation and attempt to overcome this decrease by increasing their effort.(n15) However, other studies have shown that a perceived increase in effort does not appear to overcome the detrimental effects of sleep deprivation. In one study,(n13) the participants were given a reward for better performance, which resulted in an increase in perceived effort but no change in actual performance. In addition, studies have shown that increasing amounts of sleep loss do not have a detrimental effect on participants' self-reported motivation levels.(n14, n15) As these results show, the relationships between sleep deprivation and psychological variables associated with performance are not clearly understood.

5   Another method of examining psychological variables that may be associated with the decrease in performance following sleep deprivation is assessment of off-task cognitions. Off-task cognitions are thoughts that are not directed to the completion of the task at hand but that intrude upon concentration. These cognitions can include negative evaluations of one's performance on the task, such as "I don't know how to do this," or completely unrelated thoughts, such as "I wonder what I should have for lunch today." Only one study to date has investigated the effect of sleep deprivation on off-task cognitions,(n10) but the participants in that study were specifically selected for their high baseline levels of off-task cognitions. Conclusions, therefore, could not be drawn about the effect of sleep deprivation on off-task cognitions independent of baseline levels.

Sleep-deprived participants' current mood state may provide additional information about the ability of the individual to perform following sleep deprivation. One of the best documented effects of sleep deprivation and one that would be expected to decrease complex task-solving ability is an increase in self-reported sleepiness and fatigue.(n14, n16, n17)

Other specific mood states could also influence successful task completion. For example, if sleep deprivation has a consistent negative effect on tension or anxiety, sleep-deprived participants would be expected to have more difficulty than nondeprived participants in maintaining the necessary attention and effort to complete a complex cognitive task. Although several studies have reported that sleep deprivation decreases positive mood states and increases negative mood states,(n13, n14, n18, n19) relatively few studies have examined the effect of sleep deprivation on specific mood states.

Another important consideration is the effect of sleep deprivation on an individual's ability to accurately assess psychological variables, such as concentration, effort, and estimated performance. Research findings have shown that the accuracy of self-reports varies, depending upon experimental characteristics surrounding the task. For example, Johnson and colleagues(n20) found that participants' self-reports of the amount of effort they put into a task corresponded better with performance on a difficult task than on a very easy task. The researchers also found that the amount of reported effort, but not necessarily actual performance, could be increased by giving an external incentive.

In addition, Beyer(n21) noted that self-evaluations of performance on longer tasks are more accurate than self-evaluations of performance on shorter tasks. Self-report estimates of performance have also been shown to be altered by feedback on the accuracy of actual performance as the person completes the task.(n22) These findings indicate that self-report data on psychological variables can be manipulated by a variety of experimental conditions. One experimental condition that has not been thoroughly investigated is sleep deprivation.

10   In sum, our current study addressed three specific issues. First, does sleep loss lead to changes in self-reported levels of psychological variables related to actual performance? As measures of psychological variables, we examined self-reported levels of concentration, effort, and estimated performance and self-reported off-task cognitions while the participant completed a complex cognitive task. Because sleep deprivation increases feelings of sleepiness and fatigue, we expected the sleep-deprived individuals to report lower levels of concentration, effort, and estimated performance and higher levels of off-task cognitions if they were capable of accurately assessing these psychological variables.

The second aim of our study was to determine whether sleep deprivation significantly alters mood states that may be related to performance. As specific measures of mood, we assessed feelings of tension, depression, anger, vigor, fatigue, and confusion. On the basis of a previous study that used the same mood measures,(n23) we expected sleep-deprived participants to report increased fatigue, confusion, and tension and decreased vigor.

The final purpose of our current study was to determine whether sleep deprivation alters people's ability to make an accurate assessment of their concentration, effort, and estimated performance. To investigate this aspect of sleep deprivation, we compared self-reported assessments with actual performance levels.

Method

Participants   We solicited study participants from five psychology classes, two 100-level courses, one 200-level course, and two 400-level courses. Of the original 65 volunteers, 44 (26 women and 18 men) completed the study. The mean age of the respondents, who were given extra credit points as an incentive to participate, was 20.5 years (SD = 4.37).*

Materials   We used the Watson-Glaser Critical Thinking Appraisal (WG; The Psychological Corporation, San Antonio, TX) to measure cognitive performance. We chose the WG because it would be cognitively challenging and similar to normal testing conditions for college students in that it is a linguistic task that requires mental but no physical effort. The WG contains three portions: inference, recognition of assumptions, and deduction. To increase the similarity of the task to normal testing conditions for college students, we administered the test with a 40-minute time limit.

15   We used self-report scales to measure mood, off-task cognitions, effort, concentration, and estimated performance. To assess current mood, we used the Profile of Mood States (POMS; Educational and Industrial Testing Service, San Diego, CA). The POMS scale provides a list of 65 words describing current mood states (see Table 1). The student participants rated each word based on their current mood.

Table 1 Examples of Self-Report Scale Used in Study of Sleep Deprivation	
Test/question	**Response/scale**
Profile of Mood Status	
1. Friendly	Not at all (0) to extremely (4)
2. Tense	Not at all (0) to extremely (4)
3. Angry	Not at all (0) to extremely (4)
Cognitive Interference Questionnaire	
1. I thought about how poorly I was doing.	Never (1) to very often (5)
2. I thought about what the experimenter would think of me.	Never (1) to very often (5)
3. I thought about other activities (eg, assignments, work).	Never (1) to very often (5)
Psychological Variables Questionnaire	
1. How well were you able to concentrate on the task?	Not at all (1) to extremely (well) (7)
2. How well do you think you performed on this task?	Poorly (1) to extremely well (7)
3. How much effort did this task take?	Very little (1) to very much (7)
Note. These are examples of the types of questions to which participants were asked to respond.	

*Standard Deviation (SD) is a measure of how data in a set varies. A low SD means that the data is clustered tightly around the average of that data set; a high SD means the data is spread more broadly around that value.

We assessed the number of off-task cognitions while the participant completed the WG task, using the Cognitive Interference Questionnaire (CIQ).(n24) The CIQ provides a list of types of thoughts. The participants respond by stating how often they experienced those thoughts while completing the WG task. We developed a short psychological variables questionnaire, using Likert-type scales (1 to 7), to measure self-reported estimates of effort, concentration, and estimated performance. In the written instructions for the questionnaire, participants were told to respond to the questions in relation to the WG task. A complete copy of the psychological variables questionnaire is available from the author on request. Higher numbers on each of the self-report variables represent a greater frequency of that variable. For example, higher numbers on the estimated performance scale indicate a higher level of estimated performance.

Procedures   The experiment began at 10 PM on a Friday night and concluded at 11 AM the next morning. Approximately 8 participants were tested each Friday night. All participants were requested in advance not to drink alcoholic beverages or take nonprescription drugs from 10 PM on Thursday night until the conclusion of the experiment. In addition, we asked all participants to get out of bed between 7 AM and 9 AM on Friday morning and not to nap during the day.

The experiment commenced with all participants reporting to the sleep laboratory at 10 PM on Friday night. At that time, the students were randomly assigned in a block fashion to either a sleep-deprived (n = 23) or a nondeprived group (n = 21), were given the final set of instructions for the experiment, and signed consent forms. In an effort to create realistic sleep loss and nonsleep loss conditions for college students, we chose to limit the length of sleep deprivation to 24 hours for the sleep-deprived group and to allow the nondeprived group to sleep in their own beds under normal sleeping conditions for approximately 8 hours.

After the meeting at the sleep laboratory on the Friday night of the experiment, the members of the nondeprived group were told to go home and sleep approximately 8 hours. They were instructed to go to bed between 11 PM and 1 AM and to get out of bed between 7 AM and 9 AM on Saturday morning. The nondeprived participants were called at 9 AM on Saturday morning to ensure that they were awake, and they were encouraged to eat breakfast before reporting to the testing site at 10 AM.

20   The sleep-deprived group remained awake under the supervision of two research assistants in the sleep laboratory. Participants interacted with each other and with the research assistants, watched movies, played video and board games, or worked on personal projects during the night. They were allowed to bring food to eat during the night, but were asked to limit caffeinated beverages and sugary snacks to two of each. Sleep-deprived participants were escorted to a restaurant for breakfast at about 8 AM on Saturday morning. After breakfast, they were escorted to the testing area at 10:00 AM.

Testing took place at the university library in an isolated room of study cubicles, with one person per cubicle. To assess their compliance with instructions, we asked the participants to complete a short questionnaire that included questions on sleep times and items consumed since Thursday night. All participants then completed the POMS scale, followed by the WG. After finishing the WG, all of the participants completed the questionnaire assessing self-reported effort, concentration, and estimated performance in relation to the WG. The last 18 participants in each of the groups also filled out the CIQ. The entire testing period took less than 1 hour.

Data Analyses   The data from the POMS, WG, and CIQ were initially scored according to the directions given for each measure. We calculated six POMS scores (tension-anxiety, depression-dejection, anger-hostility, vigor, fatigue, and confusion-bewilderment), one WG score representing the performance percentile of the individual in relation to other college students, and three CIQ scores (off-task cognitions relevant to task, off-task cognitions irrelevant to task, and general mind wandering). We derived self-reported effort, concentration, and estimated performance from the questions on the psychological variables questionnaire. We averaged self-reported sleep data for the sleep-deprived and the nondeprived groups separately, by group, for Thursday and Friday nights.

    All statistical analyses were completed on SAS (SAS Institute, Cary, NC). To assess whether sleep deprivation had an effect on actual performance and self-reported estimates of psychological variables and mood states, we performed multiple analysis of variance (MANOVA), by sleep condition, on all variables.

Results

All of the student participants reported that they slept approximately 8 hours on Thursday night. The sleep-deprived participants reported sleeping an average of 7.91 hours (SD = 1.26), whereas nondeprived participants reported sleeping an average of 7.79 hours (SD = 0.69). The wake-up times on Friday morning were very similar for both groups. The deprived group reported a mean time of getting out of bed of 8:55 AM (SD = 1.22 hours), and the nondeprived group reported a mean time of getting out of bed time of 8:30 AM (SD = 1.10 hours).

25   On Friday night, nondeprived participants reported sleeping an average of 7.92 hours (SD = 0.51 hours) and a mean time of getting out of bed on Saturday morning of 8:40 AM (SD = 0.73 hours). Two participants, one in each sleep condition, reported taking a nap of less than 30 minutes on Friday. We analyzed the data both with and without the two napping participants included. Because the results from the two analyses were very similar, we report the results from all participants. None of the participants reported using alcohol or nonprescription drugs (except for acetaminophen) between 10 PM on Thursday and 10 AM on Saturday.

    For means and standard deviations on the WG and the self-report tasks, see Table 2. As expected, the sleep-deprived participants performed significantly worse on the WG than the nondeprived participants did, $F(1,42) = 4.02$, $p < .05$.

    Although we expected that sleep-deprived participants would have more difficulty concentrating on the task and, thus, would show an increase in off-task cognitions, none of the CIQ scales was significantly increased in the sleep-deprived group. Furthermore, instead of the expected decrease in self-reported concentration,

Table 2 Means and Standard Deviations of Sleep- and Nondeprived Participant Groups				
	Sleep-deprived		Nondeprived	
Variables	M	SD	M	SD
Watson-Glaser	24.52	21.29	38.71	25.63[*]
Cognitive Interference Questionnaire				
Distracting task-relevant thoughts	2.36	0.62	2.22	0.53
Distracting task-irrelevant thoughts	1.59	0.70	1.58	0.58
General mind wandering	4.17	1.92	3.72	1.60
Estimated effort	4.03	1.00	3.41	0.70 [*]
Estimated concentration	4.30	1.66	3.28	1.31 [*]
Estimated performance	4.54	1.36	3.36	0.84 [***]
Profile of Mood States				
Tension/anxiety	14.22	7.30	11.19	8.05
Depression/dejection	11.96	12.08	9.86	10.22
Anger/hostility	11.65	9.00	8.00	7.46
Vigor	16.87	6.90	17.86	6.06
Fatigue	12.35	6.80	7.95	5.88 [*]
Confusion/bewilderment	10.65	5.22	5.95	4.10 [**]

Note. Significant differences between groups: [*] p < .05; [**] p < .01; [***] p < .001.

as measured by the psychological variables questionnaire, the sleep-deprived participants reported higher subjective levels of concentration while completing the task than the nondeprived participants did, $F_{(1,42)} = 5.03$, p < .05.*

The sleep-deprived participants also estimated that they expended significantly more effort to complete the task than did the nondeprived participants, $F_{(1,42)} = 5.49$, p < .05. Interestingly, although sleep-deprived participants actually performed worse on the WG than the nondeprived participants, the students deprived of sleep reported significantly higher levels of estimated performance than the nondeprived participants did, $F_{(1,42)} = 11.79$, p < .001.

The sleep-deprived participants reported higher levels on five of the six POMS scales, but only the increases in the fatigue and confusion scales were significant: fatigue, $F_{(1,42)} = 5.21$, p < .05; confusion, $F_{(1,42)} = 10.88$, p < .01.

Discussion

30 As we expected, the results from our current study indicated that participants who were deprived of sleep for 24 hours performed significantly worse on a complex cognitive task than nondeprived participants. Although they actually performed worse, the sleep-deprived participants reported significantly higher levels of estimated performance, as well as more effort expended on the cognitive task, than the nondeprived participants did. In addition, sleep-deprived participants reported a significantly higher level of self-rated concentration than

---

*The p-value is a statistical measure used to evaluate data. A low p-value suggests a statistically significant result—*significant* meaning the result was not likely to have occurred by chance.

nondeprived participants did. We found no significant differences in levels of off-task cognitions between the sleep-deprived and nondeprived groups.

The apparent contradiction between the self-reported data on effort, concentration, and estimated performance and the actual performance level of sleep-deprived participants is somewhat surprising. It is unlikely that the disagreement between the self-reported variables and actual performance was a result of the type of task used. The Watson-Glaser task should have provided a suitable scenario for accurately assessing psychological variables because more difficult and longer tasks have been shown to result in more accurate self-estimates of both effort and performance.(n20, n21)

Several explanations for the disagreement between the self-report data and the actual performance levels are possible. Sleep-deprived participants may have expended more effort to complete the task, but the effort was not sufficient to overcome the performance decrements caused by being deprived of sleep. Furthermore, the increase in effort could have led the sleep-deprived participants to believe that they were performing better and concentrating more than they actually were.

An alternative explanation is that sleep deprivation may have negatively affected the degree to which participants recognized internal effort. In turn, this could have led the sleep-deprived participants to believe that they were expending more effort than they actually were, which may also have led to increases in estimated performance and self-rated concentration. Regardless of the mechanism behind the self-report data, the results indicated that our sleep-deprived participants did not realize the extent to which their own performances were affected by sleep loss, and they appeared to be making incorrect assumptions about their ability to concentrate and to provide the necessary effort to complete the task.

Interestingly, sleep deprivation did not result in the expected change in reporting off-task cognitions. Although a previous study(n10) found that participants who habitually reported distracting thoughts were more likely to do so when deprived of sleep, it appears that the effect of sleep deprivation on off-task cognitions depends on whether the sleep-deprived person regularly experiences high levels of off-task cognitions. Therefore, reporting off-task cognitions does not appear to be specifically affected by sleep deprivation, independent of baseline levels.

35   A second major finding of this research is that sleep deprivation differentially affected mood states in these college students. The current findings indicate that sleep deprivation significantly affected only the fatigue and confusion subscales on the POMS. The reported increase in fatigue and confusion could have contributed to the significant decrease in actual performance that we observed in the sleep-deprived student participants. It is interesting to note that none of the remaining POMS subscales changed significantly in the sleep-deprived participants, indicating that some mood changes commonly ascribed to sleep deprivation, such as anger, irritability, and anxiety, were not necessarily products of 24 hours of sleep loss.

The current findings on mood states are very similar to those reported by Dinges and colleagues.(n23) Sleep-deprived participants in both studies reported significantly more fatigue and confusion than nondeprived participants. Dinges and colleagues reported significantly more tension and significantly less vigor in sleep-deprived participants.

Similarly, we noted a trend for more tension and less vigor in the sleep-deprived participants in our study. The most likely reason for the small differences between the two studies is that Dinges and colleagues collected mood data every 2 hours for a 64-hour sleep-deprivation period, whereas we collected mood data only once—immediately before the students' completion of the cognitive task. Furthermore, neither study reported a significant increase in angry or depressed feelings following sleep deprivation, indicating that sleep deprivation does not necessarily increase reports of anger and depression, as is commonly believed.

In sum, our findings suggest that college students are not aware of the extent to which sleep deprivation impairs their ability to complete cognitive tasks successfully because they consistently overrate their concentration and effort, as well as their estimated performance. In addition, the current data suggest that 24 hours of sleep deprivation significantly affects only fatigue and confusion and does not have a more general effect on positive or negative mood states. The practical implication of these findings is that many college students are unknowingly sabotaging their own performance by choosing to deprive themselves of sleep [while] they complete complex cognitive tasks.

References

(n1.) Hawkins J, Shaw P. Self-reported sleep quality in college students: A repeated measures approach. Sleep. 1992;15(6):545–549.

(n2.) Dinges DE. The nature of sleepiness: Causes, contexts, and consequences. In: Eating, Sleeping, and Sex. Stunkard A, Baum A, eds. Hillsdale, NJ: Erlbaum; 1988.

(n3.) Pilcher JJ, Huffcutt AI. Effects of sleep deprivation on performance: A meta-analysis. Sleep. 1996;19(4):318–326.

(n4.) Johnson LC. Sleep deprivation and performance. In: Webb WW, ed. Biological Rhythms, Sleep, and Performance. New York: Wiley; 1982.

(n5.) Meddis R. Cognitive dysfunction following loss of sleep. In: Burton E, ed. The Pathology and Psychology of Cognition. London: Methuen; 1982.

(n6.) Williams HL, Lubin A. Speeded addition and sleep loss. J EXP Psychol. 1967;73:313–317.

(n7.) Elkin AL, Murray DJ. The effects of sleep loss on short-term recognition memory. Can J Psychol. 1974;28:192–198.

(n8.) Polzella DJ. Effects of sleep-deprivation on short-term memory and recognition. J Exp Psychol. 1975;104:194–200.

(n9.) Hockey GRJ. Changes in attention allocation in a multicomponent task under loss of sleep. Br J Psychol. 1970;61(4):473–480.

(n10.) Mikulincer M, Babkoff H, Caspy T, Weiss H. The impact of cognitive interference on performance during prolonged sleep loss. Psychol Res. 1990;52:80–86.

(n11.) Kjellberg A. Sleep deprivation and some aspects of performance. Waking Sleeping. 1977;1:139–154.

(n12.) Horne JA. Why We Sleep. New York: Oxford University Press; 1988.

(n13.) Horne JA, Pettitt AN. High incentive effects on vigilance performance during 72 hours of total sleep deprivation. Acta Psychologica. 1985;58:123–139.

(n14.) Mikulincer M, Babkoff H, Caspy T, Sing H. The effects of 72 hours of sleep loss on psychological variables. Br J Psychol. 1989;80:145–162.

(n15.) Dinges DF, Kribbs NB, Steinberg KN, Powell JW. Do we lose the willingness to perform during sleep deprivation? Sleep Res. 1992;21:318.

(n16.) Angus RG, Heslegrave RJ. Effects of sleep loss on sustained cognitive performance during a command and control simulation. Behav Res Methods Instruments Computers. 1985;17:55–67.

(n17.) Linde L, Bergstrom M. The effect of one night without sleep on problem-solving and immediate recall. Psychol Res. 1992;54:127–136.

(n18.) Brendel DH, Reynolds CF III, Jennings JR, et al. Sleep stage physiology, mood, and vigilance responses to total sleep deprivation in healthy 80-year-olds and 20-year-olds. Psychophysiology. 1990;27:677–686.

(n19.) Leung L, Becker CE. Sleep deprivation and house staff performance: Update. J Occup Med. 1992;34:1153–1160.

(n20.) Johnson NE, Saccuzzo DP, Larson GE. Self-reported effort versus actual performance in information processing paradigms. J Gen Psychol. 1995;122(2):195–210.

(n21.) Beyer S. Gender differences in the accuracy of self-evaluations of performance. J Pers Soc Psychol. 1990;59(5):960–970.

(n22.) Critchfield TS. Bias in self-evaluation: Signal probability effects. J Exp Anal Behav. 1994;62:235–250.

(n23.) Dinges DF, Gillen KA, Powell JW, et al. Mood reports during total and partial sleep deprivation: Is anger inevitable? Sleep Res. 1995;24:441.

(n24.) Sarason IG, Sarason B, Keefe D, Hayes B, Shearin EN. Cognitive interference: Situational determinants and traitlike characteristics. J Pers Soc Psychol. 1986;51:215–226.

● Discussion and Writing Suggestions

1. Have you ever stayed awake all night to complete schoolwork? How many college students of your acquaintance (or, perhaps, you yourself) believe that it is possible to "pull an all-nighter" without degrading your performance the next day? Does the study by Pilcher and Walters change your opinion? Explain your response.

2. The authors conclude that "college students are not aware of the extent to which sleep deprivation impairs their ability to complete cognitive tasks successfully because they consistently overrate their concentration and effort, as well as their estimated performance. . . . [M]any college students are unknowingly sabotaging their own performance by choosing to deprive themselves of

sleep [while] they complete complex cognitive tasks." To what extent do these conclusions describe you?

3. In paragraphs 32–33, the authors present several explanations to account for the discrepancy between students' "self-report data and [their] actual performance levels" on the cognitive task in the experiment. Which of these explanations seems most plausible? Why?

4. How convincing do you find the results of this study? Can you refute them? Do you find yourself *wanting* to refute them? To the extent that you are convinced, what are the odds you will stop staying awake all night to study for exams or to write papers?

5. Carefully review paragraphs 1–12 to understand how the authors justify the need to conduct their present research. Summarize how they go about making this justification. Focus on how they make their argument, not on the content of their argument.

6. Why does the experimental method lend itself to studying questions related to sleep deprivation and self-reports of concentration, effort, etc.?

7. Would you volunteer for an experiment similar to the one Pilcher and Walters conducted? Why or why not?

ADOLESCENT SLEEP, SCHOOL START TIMES, AND TEEN MOTOR VEHICLE CRASHES

Fred Danner and Barbara Phillips

Others in this chapter have discussed the deleterious, sometimes fatal, effects of sleep deprivation on drivers. Particularly susceptible to these effects are young, less-experienced drivers. In the following article, two University of Kentucky researchers—Fred Danner, a counseling psychologist, and Barbara Phillips, a physician and sleep specialist—investigate whether or not a one-hour delay in school start times could be correlated both to the sleep (and restfulness) of adolescents and to the safety of their driving. The article first appeared in the *Journal of Clinical Sleep Medicine* on December 15, 2008. Note that in the first paragraph the authors cite the work of Mary Carskadon, who earlier in this chapter (pp. 489–496) discusses the "collision" of adolescents' changing biological needs for sleep with the demands of school and the working world. Both authors are affiliated with the University of Kentucky in Lexington, Kentucky. Fred Danner works in the Department of Educational and Counseling Psychology. Barbara Phillips is a physician in the Division of Pulmonary, Critical Care, and Sleep Medicine within the Department of Internal Medicine.

Study objectives: To assess the effects of delayed high-school start times on sleep and motor vehicle crashes.
Methods: The sleep habits and motor vehicle crash rates of adolescents from a single, large, county-wide, school district were assessed by questionnaire before and after a 1-hour delay in school start times.

Results: Average hours of nightly sleep increased and catch-up sleep on weekends decreased. Average crash rates for teen drivers in the study county in the 2 years after the change in school start time dropped 16.5%, compared with the 2 years prior to the change, whereas teen crash rates for the rest of the state increased 7.8% over the same time period.

Conclusions: Later school start times may both increase the sleep of adolescents and decrease their risk of motor vehicle crashes.

Keywords: Adolescents, sleep deprivation, crash, public policy, school

Citation: Danner F; Phillips B. Adolescent sleep, school start times, and teen motor vehicle crashes. J Clin Sleep Med 2008; 4(6):533–535.

There is considerable evidence that a majority of adolescents do not get enough sleep for optimal functioning during the day.[1–3] It is also clear that driving while drowsy is a serious traffic safety problem, especially among young drivers.[4–6] Both social and biologic pressures appear to cause a shift in sleep patterns during the transition to adolescence, with the result that adolescents stay up progressively later as they progress through high school.[7–9] Therefore, early school start times for adolescents decrease their sleep, which increases their daytime sleepiness,[8] which may, in turn, increase their odds of crashing their vehicles while driving.

Although concern is growing among sleep researchers about the detrimental effects of early school start times on adolescents, school scheduling is complex and emotionally laden.[10] Any change in school start times affects the entire community, as it disrupts established child-care arrangements, extracurricular activities, work schedules, and family life. These logistical problems were evident in a recent national survey of secondary schools that reported that only 17% of high schools had even considered opting for later school start times in the preceding 3 years.[11] Moreover, it is sometimes argued that starting high schools later will simply result in adolescents staying up even later, with no net gain in sleep, even though this did not appear to be the case in 3 recent studies.[12–14]

To assess the effects of delayed high school start times on sleep and motor vehicle crashes, a survey of the sleep habits of the students from an entire county-wide school district was administered before and after a change in school start times. There was only 1 school district in this county, and students from the entire district participated. State-collected measures of collision statistics by age and residence of driver were used to compute crash rates per 1000 licensed drivers for teen drivers before and after the change in school start times in both the county in which the start times changed and in the rest of the state, where start times remained unchanged.

Methods

In April of Year 1 (1998), a total of 9,966 students from grades 6 to 12, who obtained parental permission, filled out questionnaires concerning their sleep habits on school and non-school nights and various aspects of their daytime functioning. Specifically, the students were asked when they typically went to bed and arose on weekdays and on each day of the weekend, how many naps they took, how much difficulty they had staying awake in various situations (Epworth Sleepiness Scale), and how they spent their time before and after school. These Year 1 participants comprised 66.9% of the total population of middle- and high-school students enrolled in the county. In April of Year 2 (1999), 10,656 students (72.8% of the total middle- and high-school population) filled out the same questionnaire. Unfortunately, participant ID codes assigned by the school system were changed in 1999, so it was not possible to link individual students' responses over time. Therefore, analyses of change reported here are based on system-wide aggregate data. School start times during Year 1 were 07:30 and 08:00 for high schools and middle schools, respectively. In Year 2, high schools and middle schools started 1 hour later (08:30 and 09:00, respectively).

5   The data reported here focus on the sleep habits of high school students before and after the change in school start times, as well as on the rates of motor vehicle crashes of those students aged 17 to 18 years. Separate crash rates were computed for the county that changed high school start times and for the state as a whole (with the county data excluded). Crash rates were computed for the 5 years for which they were available—the 2 years prior to the school-start change (1996 and 1997) through 2 years following the school-start change (1999 and 2000). Results exclude 16-year-old drivers because Kentucky instituted a graduated drivers' license program in 1996 that severely restricts 16-year-olds' driving privileges. For their first 6 months, 16-year-olds may not drive after midnight and must have a licensed adult in the car with them at all times. These restrictions have resulted in a considerable decrease in crashes in the state among 16-year-olds but have not influenced crash rates for older teen drivers.[15]

Results

Average hours of sleep per night during Year 1 and Year 2 are presented in Figure 1. These data reflect group average comparisons rather than individual students tracked over time. Students in Year 2 averaged from 12 minutes (Grade 9) to 30 minutes (Grade 12) more self-reported sleep, compared with students in Year 1. T-tests on these changes in average amount of sleep at each grade level indicate that these Year 1 to Year 2 gains were significant at all 4 grades (all p values < .001). The percentage of students who got at least 8 hours of sleep per weeknight increased significantly from 35.7% to 50.0% (p < .01), and the percentage who got at least 9 hours of sleep increased significantly from 6.3% to 10.8% (p < .01). The average amount of additional sleep on Friday nights, compared with school nights, served as a crude proxy for sleep deprivation, as catch-up sleep on the weekends is a logical response to the build-up of a sleep debt during the week.[8] The average amount of this additional weekend sleep significantly decreased from 1.9 hours to 1.1 hours (p <.001), and this drop in extra catch-up sleep by grade level is illustrated in

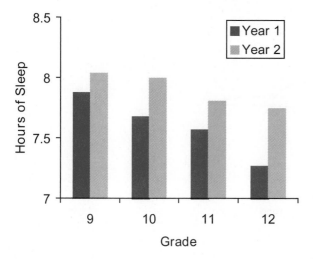

Fig. 1.   Hours of sleep per night by grade level and year.

Figure 2. Consistent with this indication of a reduced sleep debt, average scores on the Epworth Sleepiness Scale decreased from 8.9 to 8.2 (p < .001) from Year 1 to Year 2, and the proportion of teens who scored 10 or higher dropped from 43.3% to 37% (p < .001).

There was little evidence of change from Year 1 to Year 2 on any other measure collected from the adolescents' self-reports. There was a slight increase in the percentage who reported working 10 hours or more per week (28% vs 31%), but there were no significant differences in hours spent on homework, school sports, organized community sports, music activities, volunteer work, or hanging out with friends.

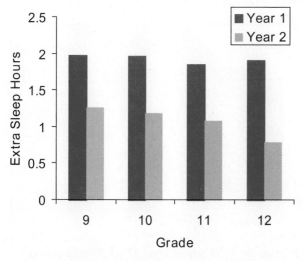

Fig. 2.   Hours of extra sleep on weekend nights by grade level and year.

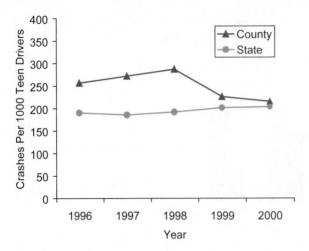

Fig. 3.   Number of motor vehicle crashes per 1000 drivers aged 17 or 18 years in the study county and state.

Auto crash data per 1000 licensed drivers for those aged 17 and 18 are presented in Figures 3 and 4. Figure 3 presents all 5 years of available crash data and Figure 4 compares average crash rates for the 2 years prior to the change in school start times to those for the 2 years after the change. The year 1998 was dropped from Figure 4, as this was a transitional year during which the school district and the adolescents had to rearrange transportation to and from school. The county

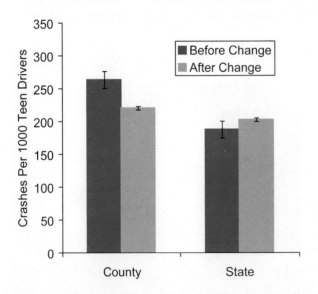

Fig. 4.   Number of motor vehicle crashes per 1000 drivers aged 17 or 18 years during the 2 years before and 2 years after a change in school start times.

crash rates were considerably higher than the rest of the state prior to the change in school start times. This may have been because the study county is in the center of a rapidly expanding metropolitan area, with all of its attendant traffic congestion. Despite rapid population growth, the rate of crashes in the county dropped after the change in school start time. The average crash rates in the 2 years after the change in school start times, as shown in Figure 4, reflect a significant decrease of 16.5% in the study county (p < .01), whereas there was a significant increase of 7.8% across the same time period in the rest of the state (p < .01).

Discussion

Moving the school start time 1 hour later for all of the adolescents in 1 large county school district (the only county to do so during the period of this study) resulted in meaningful increases in sleep time, an increase in the percentage of students who got an adequate amount of sleep, and a decrease in catch-up sleep on weekends. It was also associated with significant drop in auto collision rates for high school-aged drivers in that county, whereas crash rates increased in the rest of the state during the same time period. These findings are not necessarily causal, since they are not the result of a direct assessment of the sleep habits and miles driven of drivers who did and did not have crashes. However, these data are consistent with the idea that allowing adolescents to sleep more on school nights by delaying the start of school not only results in them sleeping more, but also may have a measurable positive effect on their driving safety.

Disclosure Statement

10 This was not an industry supported study. The authors have indicated no financial conflicts of interest.

References

1. Danner F. Adolescent sleep and daytime functioning: a national study. Sleep 2000;23:A 199–200.

2. Frederiksen K, Rhodes J, Reddy R, Way N. Sleepless in Chicago: tracking the effects of adolescent loss during the middle school years. Child Dev 2004;75:84–95.

3. Wolfson A, Carskadon, M. Sleep schedules and daytime functioning in adolescents. Child Dev 1998;69:875–87.

4. McCartt A, Ribbner S, Pack A, Hammer M. The scope and nature of the drowsy driving problem in New York State. Accid Anal Prev 1996;28:511–7.

5. National Sleep Foundation. Sleep in America Poll. Washington, DC: WB&A Market Research; 2002.

6. Pack A, Rodgman E, Cucchiara, A, Dinges, D, Schwab, C. Characteristics of crashes attributed to the driver having fallen asleep. Accid Anal Prev 1995;27:769–75.

7. Carskadon M, Acebo C. Regulation of sleepiness in adolescents: update, insights, and speculation. Sleep 2002;25:606–14.

8. Carskadon M, Wolfson A, Acebo C, Tzischinsky O, Siefer R. Adolescent sleep patterns, circadian timing, and sleepiness at a transition to early school days. Sleep 1998;21:871–81.

9. Wolfson A, Carskadon M. Understanding adolescents' sleep patterns and school performance: a critical appraisal. Sleep Med Rev 2003;7:491–506.

10. Wahlstrom K. The prickly politics of school starting times. Phi Delta Kappan 1999;80:345–7.

11. Wolfson A, Carskadon, M. A survey of factors influencing high school start times. NASSP Bull 2005;89:47–66.

12. Dexter D, Bijwadia J, Schilling D, Applebaugh G. Sleep, sleepiness and school start times: a preliminary study. WMJ: Official Publication of the State Medical Society of Wisconsin 2003;102:44–6.

13. Wahlstrom K. Later high-school start times still working. Education Digest 2003;68:49–54.

14. Wolfson A. Middle school start times: the importance of a good night's sleep for young adolescents. Behav Sleep Med 2007;5:194–209.

15. Agent K, Pigman J, Steenbergen L, Pollack S, Kidd P, McCoy C. Evaluation of the Kentucky Graduated Driver Licensing System. Research Report KTC-01-28/NHTSA1-98-1F. 2001. Lexington, KY: Kentucky Injury Prevention and Research Center.

● Discussion and Writing Suggestions

1. What factors make delay in school start time such a complex undertaking? Would a delayed start time have addressed any significant problems at your high school? How might teachers have responded to the later start times? Students? Coaches? Parents?

2. The authors of this article based their research report on surveys, a very different strategy than lab-based research (see, for example, the example of Pilcher and Walters on pp. 512–521). What can researchers do in a lab that they cannot do in field research via surveys? On the other hand, what is possible with a broad survey approach that is not possible in the lab?

3. Any experiment on delayed start times has many stakeholders: students, parents, teachers, administrators, coaches, staff (cafeteria workers, for instance), bus drivers, and more. With so many people affected by *whatever* time school is set to begin, how would you, as a Superintendent of Schools in your hometown, weigh the competing interests of stakeholders and select an optimal start time? How would you define "optimal"?

4. The noted adolescent sleep researcher Mary Carskadon (see pp. 489–496) writes: "Can these problems [associated with sleep deprived adolescents] be solved by delaying the starting time for school as adolescents move into the pubertal years? Not entirely. Moving the opening bell to a later time may help many teens with the mismatch between biological time and scholastic time, but it will not provide more hours in the day." Your comments? To what extent are their days so crammed with activities that high school students will be left sleep deprived *regardless* of start times?

5. Colleges have essentially adopted a delayed school start time by scheduling classes throughout the day (as opposed to having all students begin at a fixed time each morning). Given their flexible schedules, do you think college students are any less sleep deprived than high school students? What implications does your answer hold for experiments such as the one Danner and Phillips conducted?

6. Reread Danner and Phillips's "Discussion" section, paying special attention to this statement: "These findings are not necessarily causal, since they are not the result of a direct assessment of the sleep habits and miles driven of drivers who did and did not have crashes." Does this statement in any way diminish the importance of the research findings?

POETRY OF SLEEP

John Keats, Lord Byron, Samuel Taylor Coleridge

Common to all and yet incompletely understood even by the scientists who study the subject, sleep invites speculation. Why do we sleep? Where does one's consciousness "go" while sleeping? What are dreams? Why can falling asleep be so difficult? As you have learned in this chapter, some researchers approach questions such as these with the tools of logic and experiment. But long before psychologists and physicians wired patients to measure respiration and rapid eye movements, storytellers of every age and culture have speculated, too, using the tools of *their* trade. In closing the chapter, we offer a decidedly nonscientific approach to the subject of sleep, poems by John Keats (1795–1821), Samuel Taylor Coleridge (1772–1834), and Lord Byron (1788–1824). All were important figures of the English Romantic Period, which arose during a time of revolutionary ferment (the American and French Revolutions, the Industrial Revolution) and thrust the individual, heroic artist center stage as the author of his own universe. The Romantic poets revered the power of imagination (above reason) as the highest human faculty and attempted through their work to express an inward journey in which the use of the first-person "I" became commonplace. Keats is especially well known for "Ode To a Nightingale" and "Ode On a Grecian Urn"; Coleridge, for "Rime of the Ancient Mariner" and "Kubla Kahn"; and Byron for "So We'll Go No More A-Roving," "Prometheus," and "The Dream," from which the excerpt that follows forms the first of nine parts.[1] These poems are brief. Before you say or write anything about them, try reading each several times. You may also want to reread Paul Martin's "A Third of Life," which references several classic writers—Aristotle, Cervantes, Samuel Johnson, Dickens, and Chaucer—on the subject of sleep.

To Sleep
John Keats

> O soft embalmer of the still midnight,
> Shutting with careful fingers and benign
> Our gloom-pleas'd eyes, embower'd from the light,

---

[1] For an excellent, brief overview of Romanticism and its continuing influence, see *A Guide to the Study of Literature: A Companion Text for Core Studies 6, Landmarks of Literature,* by the English Department of Brooklyn College (http://academic.brooklyn.cuny.edu/english/melani/cs6/rom.html).

Enshaded in forgetfulness divine:
5   O soothest Sleep! if so it please thee, close
In midst of this thine hymn, my willing eyes,
Or wait the amen ere thy poppy throws
Around my bed its lulling charities.
Then save me, or the passed day will shine
10   Upon my pillow, breeding many woes;
Save me from curious conscience, that still lords
Its strength for darkness, burrowing like a mole;
Turn the key deftly in the oiled wards,
And seal the hushed casket of my soul.

The Pains of Sleep
Samuel Taylor Coleridge

Ere on my bed my limbs I lay,
It hath not been my use to pray
With moving lips or bended knees;
But silently, by slow degrees,
5   My spirit I to Love compose,
In humble trust mine eye-lids close,
With reverential resignation,
No wish conceived, no thought exprest,
Only a sense of supplication;
10   A sense o'er all my soul imprest
That I am weak, yet not unblest,
Since in me, round me, every where
Eternal Strength and Wisdom are.

But yester-night I prayed aloud
15   In anguish and in agony,
Up-starting from the fiendish crowd
Of shapes and thoughts that tortured me:
A lurid light, a trampling throng,
Sense of intolerable wrong,
20   And whom I scorned, those only strong!
Thirst of revenge, the powerless will
Still baffled, and yet burning still!
Desire with loathing strangely mixed
On wild or hateful objects fixed.
25   Fantastic passions! maddening brawl!
And shame and terror overall!
Deeds to be hid which were not hid,
Which all confused I could not know
Whether I suffered, or I did:
30   For all seemed guilt, remorse or woe,
My own or others still the same
Life-stifling fear, soul-stifling shame.

So two nights passed: the night's dismay
Saddened and stunned the coming day.
35   Sleep, the wide blessing, seemed to me

Distemper's worst calamity.
The third night, when my own loud scream
Had waked me from the fiendish dream,
O'ercome with sufferings strange and wild,
40 I wept as I had been a child;
And having thus by tears subdued
My anguish to a milder mood,
Such punishments, I said, were due
To natures deepliest stained with sin,—
45 For aye entempesting anew
The unfathomable hell within,
The horror of their deeds to view,
To know and loathe, yet wish and do!
Such griefs with such men well agree,
50 But wherefore, wherefore fall on me?
To be beloved is all I need,
And whom I love, I love indeed.

The Dream

Lord Byron

[Part I of IX parts]

Our life is twofold; Sleep hath its own world,
A boundary between the things misnamed
Death and existence: Sleep hath its own world,
And a wide realm of wild reality,
5 And dreams in their development have breath,
And tears, and tortures, and the touch of joy;
They leave a weight upon our waking thoughts,
They take a weight from off waking toils,
They do divide our being; they become
10 A portion of ourselves as of our time,
And look like heralds of eternity;
They pass like spirits of the past - they speak
Like sibyls of the future; they have power -
The tyranny of pleasure and of pain;
15 They make us what we were not - what they will,
And shake us with the vision that's gone by,
The dread of vanished shadows - Are they so?
Is not the past all shadow? - What are they?
Creations of the mind? - The mind can make
20 Substances, and people planets of its own
With beings brighter than have been, and give
A breath to forms which can outlive all flesh.
I would recall a vision which I dreamed
Perchance in sleep - for in itself a thought,
25 A slumbering thought, is capable of years,
And curdles a long life into one hour.[2]

---

[2]To read the entire poem, go to http://www.cs.rice.edu/∼ssiyer/minstrels/poems/1252.html.

● Discussion and Writing Suggestions

1. In this first part of his longer poem, "The Dream," Byron speculates on what dreams might be. Think of your own dreams: How well does Byron's account express your experience of dreaming?

2. Keats characterizes sleep as an "embalmer" and the soul as having the quality of a "casket." What do you make of this imagery?

3. Have you ever suffered from difficulty falling asleep? How well does Coleridge capture the "anguish and...agony" of insomnia? What imagery does he use to express his distress?

4. Locate a line or two from one of these poems that you find particularly evocative and explain its (their) appeal.

5. Compare the mental states of Keats and Coleridge in attempting to fall asleep. Which is the more desperate? Why? Which lines can you point to that justify your answer?

6. "Conscience" plays a role in the poems of Keats and Coleridge. Why is the period of rest just before falling off to sleep particularly susceptible to the protests of conscience?

7. Try composing your own poem about sleep, using the first-person "I" (a commonplace among the Romantic poets). Write about any aspect of interest: perhaps falling asleep, dreaming, waking, or sleepiness. Share your efforts with classmates. You may want to try your hand at a parody of one of the poems.

SYNTHESIS ACTIVITIES

1. Explain the fundamentals of sleep for an audience (perhaps someone like yourself before reading this chapter) who regards sleep as a passive state characterized by the absence of wakefulness. Make clear that sleep is ubiquitous (fruit flies, fish, cats, alligators, and humans all sleep); is an active, not a passive behavior; has an "architecture" that changes over one's life; can be especially troubling for adolescents; and can be delayed or otherwise disrupted in ways that cause sleep debt and associated problems. Refer to the *Harvard Special Health Report* ("Improving Sleep") and to the selections by the National Sleep Foundation, Dement and Vaughan, Carskadon, and Pilcher and Walters. In creating a general context for the discussion, consider quoting lines from one of the poets in this chapter: Keats, Coleridge, or Byron.

2. Use one or more of the selections in this chapter to analyze the quality of your sleep in a typical week. As part of your analysis, be sure to take (and score) the Pittsburgh Sleep Quality Index. Recall that the purpose of any analysis is to increase understanding of a little-understood

phenomenon—in this case, *your* sleep patterns. What principle(s) or definition(s) will you use from the chapter readings to guide your analysis? Follow the general format for writing analyses on page 196. In creating a general context for the discussion, consider quoting lines from one of the poets in this chapter: Keats, Coleridge, or Byron.

3. Three selections in this chapter first appeared in journals or books intended for professionals interested in sleep: those by Pilcher and Walters; Carskadon; and Danner and Phillips. Using standards of good writing established by your composition instructor and textbooks, evaluate the presentation of one of these three selections. In your critique, focus on the author's or authors' success at communicating a key idea. What are your standards for evaluation: a writer's ability to organize at the global, section, or paragraph level? Sentence style? Word choice? Conciseness? Tone? How many criteria will you use in making your overall assessment? Follow the general format for writing critiques on page 41.

4. In an explanatory synthesis, discuss phase-delayed sleep: whom it affects; its biological, behaviorial, and social causes; its related problems; and its remedies (to the extent they exist). Refer to chapter selections as needed, but be sure to reference Dement and Vaughan; Carskadon; and Danner and Phillips. Follow the general format for writing syntheses on pages 97–98.

5. Discuss why cramming for an examination (staying awake all night to study or to write a paper) can be a mistake. Your discussion should include an account of sleep debt and its consequences. Refer to chapter selections as needed, but be sure to reference Dement and Vaughan, Carskadon, and Pilcher and Walters. Follow the general format for writing syntheses on pages 97–98.

6. Draw upon the selections in this chapter to create an advertising campaign aimed at promoting good sleep hygiene among college students. The campaign might take the form of a brochure, a poster, a series of e-mails, or a Web site. In your campaign, explain the importance of sleep, particularly for adolescents. Create a separate Works Cited page for the sources you reference in your campaign. In creating a general context for the discussion, consider quoting lines from one of the poets in this chapter: Keats, Coleridge, or Byron.

7. Argue for or against the proposition that the health office at your college should set up an educational program to promote good sleep hygiene among students. In developing your argument, refer to the scientific evidence on adolescent sleep needs and sleep debt and its consequences. Among the selections you refer to should be those by the National Sleep Foundation, Dement and Vaughan, Carskadon, Pilcher and Walters, and Danner and Phillips.

8. Argue for or against the proposition that the start time of the high school you attended should be later than it currently is. In your argument, consider the scientific evidence relating to problems associated with

phase-delayed sleep. Consider also the complications of coordinating schedules among the various stakeholders in any change of start time: for instance, among students, teachers, parents, coaches, and staff. In your paper, refer to the selections by the National Sleep Foundation, Dement and Vaughan, Carskadon, and Danner and Phillips.

9. Explain your reactions to the reading selections in this chapter. What you have learned about sleep will inevitably find its way into this paper. But keep the focus on your *reactions* to learning about one or more of the following: sleep debt and cramming for exams; sleep debt and the dangers of drowsiness while driving; the problems caused when adolescent sleep patterns collide with the scheduling demands of the business and scholastic worlds. Let your interest in the topic dictate the specific focus of your explanation.

10. Analyze one of the poems in this chapter—by Keats, Coleridge, or Byron. (If you choose Byron, read the entire poem, "The Dream," readily found online.) *Explicate* the poem: That is, conduct a close reading in which you study elements that lead you to an overall impression of how the poem can be usefully understood. Your explication, one of many possible readings of the poem, will be an argument in which you make a series of related observations that support a single broad claim. Support each observation with a reference to specific lines. Introduce quoted lines in the context of your observation; quote the lines; then discuss the lines in light of your observation. If you like, research other responses to the poem and incorporate elements of these, with attribution, into your paper.

RESEARCH ACTIVITIES

1. Sleep specialists do not agree on the purpose of sleep. Investigate theories of why we—as well as other creatures—sleep. The oldest theories—based largely on speculation—date to the times of Aristotle and earlier. In recent decades biologists and physicians have proposed theories based on current scientific research.

2. Research "unihemispheric sleep," the phenomenon that allows certain species (of dolphins and birds, for instance) to put one half of their brain to sleep at a time. Which species exhibit this behavior? Why? What are the mechanisms involved?

3. Discuss references to sleep in one or more artistic works. Macbeth's and Lady Macbeth's troubled sleep following their murder of King Duncan comes to mind. You might consider, as well, cinematic works like the Al Pacino film *Insomnia* (2002), directed by Christopher Nolan, or the unusual dreamlike visions of Richard Linklater in films like *Waking Life* (2001) and *A Scanner Darkly* (2006).

4. Research and write an overview of sleep disorders (there are eight-four, divided into four general classifications). If you find yourself especially

intrigued by one disorder—for instance, sleep apnea, restless leg syndrome, or night terrors—focus your research on that.

5. Investigate sleep specialists' use of the polysomnograph to monitor body functions as patients sleep in a laboratory. What does the polysomnograph measure? How is the patient monitored? How is the polysomnograph read and interpreted? What role does it play in the diagnosis and treatment of sleep disorders?

6. Several authors in this chapter discuss circadian rhythm. Conduct more research into the "internal clock" that determines for us (and other creatures) patterns of wakefulness and sleep. What is this clock? Where is it located? When, in response to what, and how did it evolve?

7. Investigate NASA's interest in the sleep problems of astronauts, a select group whose accelerated daily exposure to patterns of light and dark plays havoc with their sleep. What, precisely, are the problems? What solutions is NASA devising? (You might also want to investigate the sleep challenges that NASA anticipates for long-distance missions to Mars and beyond.)

8. Investigate sleep researchers' inquiries into sleep deprivation. Begin with a close reading of Pilcher and Walters in this chapter. Consult their reference list, and see especially the pioneering work of William Dement, whose scholarship is also represented in this chapter.

9. Investigate the history or promotion of sleeping aids—medicinal (for instance, opiates, melatonin, and the new prescription drugs), behavioral (what's "counting sheep" all about?), and mechanical (white noise machines, etc.). If one particular area of this research captures your attention (for example, the business aspects of sleeping aids, or the social consequences), pursue that area, rather than preparing a broad overview.

10. The inventor of psychoanalysis, Sigmund Freud, initially made his reputation with his startling theories about the interpretation of dreams. (In Freud's theories, people and objects occurring in dreams were frequently symbolic.) Investigate one or more current theories on the content of the dreams that occur during REM sleep, as discussed, for example, in the *Harvard Health Letter (Improving Sleep)*. How does the content of dreams correlate with the dreamer's life?

11. Several authors in this chapter discuss the sometimes catastrophic consequences (such as the *Exxon Valdez* disaster) of sleep deprivation. In some cases, insufficient sleep time is built into the job—for example, the duty schedules of some airline flight crews, long-distance truck drivers, or medical interns. Select one such job area, and discuss the particular problems caused by enforced (or voluntary) sleep deprivation. Or discuss recent attempts to address such long-standing problems with policies designed to ensure that people get sufficient sleep so as not to pose a danger to themselves or others.

Chapter 11

New and Improved: Six Decades of Advertising

Possibly the most memorable ad campaign of the twentieth century (dating from the late 1920s) takes the form of a comic strip. A bully kicks sand into the face of a skinny man relaxing on the beach with his girlfriend. Humiliated, the skinny man vows to get even. "Don't bother, little boy!" huffs the scornful girlfriend, who promptly dumps him. At home, the skinny man kicks a chair in frustration, declares that he's sick of being a scarecrow, and says that if Charles Atlas (once a "97-lb. weakling" himself) can give him a "real body," he'll send for his FREE book. In the next frame, the once-skinny man, now transformed into a hunk, thanks to Atlas's "Dynamic Tension" fitness program, admires himself in front of the mirror: "Boy, it didn't take Atlas long to do this for me. Look, how those muscles bulge!... That big stiff won't dare insult me now!" Back on the beach, the bully is decked by the once-skinny man, as his adoring girlfriend looks on: "Oh Mac! You are a real man after all!"

Crude? Undoubtedly. But variations of this ad, which made Atlas a multimillionaire, ran for decades (his company is still in business). Like other successful ads, it draws its power from skillful appeals to almost primitive urges—in this particular case, the urge to gain dominance over a rival for the attention of the opposite sex. Of course, effective ads don't always work on such a primal level. Another famous ad of the 1920s appeals to our need to gain respect from others for higher accomplishments than punching out opponents. Headlined "They Laughed When I Sat Down at the Piano—But When I Started to Play...!" the text offers a first-person account of a man who sits down to play the piano at a party. As he does so, the guests make good-natured fun of him; but once he began to play, "a tense silence fell on the guests. The laughter died on their lips as if by magic. I played through the first bars of Liszt's immortal 'Liebenstraum.' I heard gasps of amazement. My friends sat breathless—spellbound." For sixteen additional paragraphs, the writer goes on to detail the effect of his playing upon the guests and to explain how "You, too, can now *teach yourself* to be an accomplished musician—right at home," by purchasing the program of the U.S. School of Music. Again, the reader is encouraged to send for the free booklet. And by the way, "Forget the old-fashioned idea that you need 'special talent'" to play an instrument.

The ubiquity of advertising is a fact of modern life. In fact, advertising can be traced as far back as ancient Roman times when pictures were inscribed on walls to promote gladiatorial contests. In those days, however, the illiteracy of most of the population and the fact that goods were made by hand and could not be mass produced limited the need for more widespread advertising. One of the first American advertisers was Benjamin Franklin, who pioneered the use of large headlines and made strategic use of white space. But advertising as the mass phenomenon we know is a product of the twentieth century, when the United States became an industrial nation—and particularly of the post–World War II period, when a prosperous economy created our modern consumer society, marked by the middle-class acquisition of goods, the symbols of status, success, style, and social acceptance. Today, we are surrounded not only by a familiar array of billboards, print ads, and broadcast ads, but also by the Internet, which has given us "spam," the generic name for an entire category of digital pitches for debt reduction, low mortgage rates, and enhanced body parts—compared to which the average Buick ad in a glossy magazine reads like great literature.

Advertisements are more than just appeals to buy; they are windows into our psyches and our culture. They reveal our values, our (not-so-hidden) desires, our yearnings for a different lifestyle. For example, the Marlboro man, that quintessence of taciturn cowboy masculinity, at home only in the wide open spaces of Marlboro Country, is a mid-twentieth-century American tribute to (what is perceived as) nineteenth-century American values, popularized in hundreds of westerns. According to James Twitchell, a professor of English and advertising at the University of Florida, "He is what we have for royalty, distilled manhood. . . . The Marlboro Man needs to tell you nothing. He carries no scepter, no gun. He never even speaks. Doesn't need to." He is also the product of a bolt of advertising inspiration: Previously, Marlboro had been marketed—unsuccessfully—as a woman's cigarette. Another example of how ads reveal culture is the memorable campaign for the Volkswagen Beetle in the 1960s. That campaign spoke to the counterculture mentality of the day: Instead of appealing to the traditional automobile customer's desire for luxury, beauty, size, power, and comfort, Volkswagen emphasized how small, funny-looking, bare-bones—but economical and sensible—their cars were. On the other hand, snob appeal—at an affordable price, of course—has generally been a winning strategy. In the 1980s and 1990s Grey Poupon mustard ran a successful campaign of TV commercials featuring one Rolls-Royce pulling up alongside another. A voice from one vehicle asks, "Pardon me; do you have any Grey Poupon?" "But of course!" replies a voice in the other car; and a hand with a jar of mustard reaches out from the window of the second car to pass to the unseen occupant of the first car. This campaign is a perfect illustration of what University of California at Davis history professor Roland Marchand calls the appeal of the democracy of goods: "the wonders of modern mass production and distribution enable . . . everyone to enjoy society's most desirable pleasures, conveniences, or benefits."

So pervasive and influential has advertising become that it has created a significant backlash among social critics. Among the most familiar charges against advertising: It fosters materialism, it psychologically manipulates people to buy things they don't need, it perpetuates gender and racial stereotypes (particularly in its illustrations), it is deceptive, it is offensive, it debases the language, and it is omnipresent—we cannot escape it. Although arguing the truth or falsity of these assertions makes for lively debate, our focus in this chapter is not on the ethics of advertising, but rather on how it works. What makes for successful advertising? How do advertisers—and by advertisers we mean not only manufacturers but also the agencies they hire to produce their advertisements—pull our psychological levers to influence us to buy (or think favorably of) their products? What are the textual and graphic components of an effective advertisement—of an effective advertising campaign? How—if at all—has advertising evolved over the past several decades? (You may be interested in seeking out the documentary film *Art and Copy* (2009), about some of the great ad campaigns created during this period.)

Advertising has seen significant changes in the six decades since the end of World War II. It is unlikely that the comic strip Charles Atlas ad or the verbose "They Laughed When I Sat Down at the Piano" ad would succeed today. Both seem extremely dated. More representative of today's advertising style is the successful milk campaign; each ad features a celebrity such as Bernie Mac or Lauren Bacall with a milk mustache, a headline that says simply "got milk?", and a few short words of text supposedly spoken by the pictured celebrity. But the changes in advertising during the six decades covered in this chapter are more of style than of substance. On the whole, the similarities between an ad produced in the 1950s and one produced today are more significant than the differences. Of course, hair and clothing styles change with the times, message length recedes, and both text and graphics assume a lesser degree of apple-pie social consensus on values. But on the whole, the same psychological appeals, the same principles of headline and graphic design that worked 60 years ago, continue to work today. We choose one automobile over another, for instance, less because our vehicle of choice gets us from point A to point B, than because we invest it—or the advertiser does—with rich psychological and cultural values. In 1957 the French anthropologist and philosopher Roland Barthes wrote (in a review of a French automobile, the Citroën DS), "I think that cars today are almost the exact equivalent of the great Gothic cathedrals: I mean the supreme creation of an era, conceived with passion by unknown artists, and consumed in image if not in usage by a whole population which appropriates them as a purely magical object." Barthes might have had a good career as an advertising copywriter.

How advertising works, then, is the subject of the present chapter. By applying a variety of theoretical and practical perspectives to a gallery of six decades of advertisements (and on other ads of your own choosing), you'll be able to practice your analytical skills on one of the more fascinating areas of American mass culture. You will find the main objects of your analyses later in this chapter: (1) a portfolio of *print advertisements* that originally appeared in such magazines as *Time, Newsweek, U.S. News and World Report*, and *Sunset*; and (2) a portfolio of memorable *TV commercials*, available for viewing on the YouTube Web site. For ease of comparison and contrast, most of the print ads can be classified into a relatively few categories: cigarettes, alcohol, automobiles, food, and "miscellaneous." We have selected both the print ads and the TV commercials for their inherent interest, as well as for the variety of tools employed to communicate their message about what sets their product or service apart from the competition—what some advertisers call their *USP*, or unique selling proposition.

The first two selections in the chapter provide analytical tools, particular perspectives from which to view individual advertisements. In "Advertising's Fifteen Basic Appeals," Jib Fowles offers a psychological perspective. Fowles identifies and discusses the most common needs to which advertisers attempt to appeal—among these the need for sex, affiliation with other people, dominance, and autonomy. In "Making the Pitch in Print Advertising," Courtland Bovée and his colleagues outline the key elements of the textual component of effective advertising—including headlines, subheadlines, and body text. Next, in "Selling Happiness: Two Pitches from *Mad Men*," we see how a great advertising man (in a great TV series) can transform the operation of a mechanical device into a powerful emotional experience or can reassure users of a deadly product that they can consume it safely.

Charles O'Neill, an independent marketing consultant, has written, "Perhaps, by learning how advertising works, we can become better equipped to sort out content from hype, product values from emotions, and salesmanship from propaganda." We hope that the selections in this chapter will equip you to do just that, as well as to develop a greater understanding of one of the most pervasive components of American mass culture.

ADVERTISING'S FIFTEEN BASIC APPEALS

Jib Fowles

Our first selection provides what you will likely find the single most useful analytical tool for studying advertisements. Drawing upon studies of numerous ads and upon interviews with subjects conducted by Harvard psychologist Henry A. Murray, Fowles developed a set of fifteen basic appeals he believes to be at the heart of American advertising. These appeals, according to Fowles and to Murray, are directed primarily to the "lower brain," to those "unfulfilled urges and motives swirling in the bottom half of [our] minds," rather than to the part of the brain that processes our more rational thoughts and impulses. As you read Fowles's article and his descriptions of the individual appeals, other examples from contemporary print and broadcast ads may occur to you. You may find it useful to jot down these examples for later incorporation into your responses to the discussion and synthesis questions that follow.

Jib Fowles has written numerous articles and books on the popular media, including *Mass Advertising as Social Forecast: A Method for Futures Research* (1976), *Why Viewers Watch: A Reappraisal of Television's Effects* (1992), *Advertising and Popular Culture* (1996), and *The Case for Television Violence* (1999). This selection first appeared in *Etc.* 39:3 (1982) and was reprinted in *Advertising and Popular Culture*.

Emotional Appeals

The nature of effective advertisements was recognized full well by the late media philosopher Marshall McLuhan. In his *Understanding Media,* the first sentence of the section on advertising reads, "The continuous pressure is to create ads more and more in the image of audience motives and desires."

By giving form to people's deep-lying desires, and picturing states of being that individuals privately yearn for, advertisers have the best chance of arresting attention and affecting communication. And that is the immediate goal of advertising: to tug at our psychological shirtsleeves and slow us down long enough for a word or two about whatever is being sold. We glance at a picture of a solitary rancher at work, and "Marlboro" slips into our minds.

Advertisers (I'm using the term as a shorthand for both the products' manufacturers, who bring the ambition and money to the process, and the advertising agencies, who supply the know-how) are ever more compelled to invoke consumers' drives and longings; this is the "continuous pressure" McLuhan refers to. Over the past century, the American marketplace has grown increasingly congested as more and more products have entered into the frenzied competition after the public's dollars. The economies of other nations are quieter than ours since the volume of goods being hawked does not so greatly exceed demand. In some economies, consumer wares are scarce enough that no advertising at all is necessary. But in the United States, we go to the other extreme. In order to stay in business, an advertiser must strive to cut through the considerable commercial hub-bub by any means available—including the emotional appeals that some observers have held to be abhorrent and underhanded.

The use of subconscious appeals is a comment not only on conditions among sellers. As time has gone by, buyers have become stoutly resistant to advertisements. We live in a blizzard of these messages and have learned to turn up our collars and ward off most of them. A study done a few years ago at Harvard University's Graduate School of Business Administration ventured that the average American is exposed to some 500 ads daily from television, newspapers, magazines, radio, billboards, direct mail, and so on. If for no other reason than to preserve one's sanity, a filter must be developed in every mind to lower the number of ads a person is actually aware of—a number this particular study estimated at about seventy-five ads per day. (Of these, only twelve typically produced a reaction—nine positive and three negative, on the average.) To be among the few messages that do manage to gain access to minds, advertisers must be strategic, perhaps even a little underhanded at times.

5   There are assumptions about personality underlying advertisers' efforts to communicate via emotional appeals, and while these assumptions have stood the test of time, they still deserve to be aired. Human beings, it is presumed, walk around with a variety of unfulfilled urges and motives swirling in the bottom half of their minds. Lusts, ambitions, tendernesses, vulnerabilities—they are constantly bubbling up, seeking resolution. These mental forces energize people, but they are too crude and irregular to be given excessive play in the real world. They must be capped with the competent, sensible behavior that permits

individuals to get along well in society. However, this upper layer of mental activity, shot through with caution and rationality, is not receptive to advertising's pitches. Advertisers want to circumvent this shell of consciousness if they can, and latch on to one of the lurching, subconscious drives.

In effect, advertisers over the years have blindly felt their way around the underside of the American psyche, and by trial and error have discovered the softest points of entree, the places where their messages have the greatest likelihood of getting by consumers' defenses. As McLuhan says elsewhere, "Gouging away at the surface of public sales resistance, the ad men are constantly breaking through into the *Alice in Wonderland* territory behind the looking glass, which is the world of subrational impulses and appetites."

An advertisement communicates by making use of a specially selected image (of a supine female, say, or a curly-haired child, or a celebrity) which is designed to stimulate "subrational impulses and desires" even when they are at ebb, even if they are unacknowledged by their possessor. Some few ads have their emotional appeal in the text, but for the greater number by far the appeal is contained in the artwork. This makes sense, since visual communication better suits more primal levels of the brain. If the viewer of an advertisement actually has the importuned motive, and if the appeal is sufficiently well fashioned to call it up, then the person can be hooked. The product in the ad may then appear to take on the semblance of gratification for the summoned motive. Many ads seem to be saying, "If you have this need, then this product will help satisfy it." It is a primitive equation, but not an ineffective one for selling.

Thus, most advertisements appearing in national media can be understood as having two orders of content. The first is the appeal to deep-running drives in the minds of consumers. The second is information regarding the good[s] or service being sold: its name, its manufacturer, its picture, its packaging, its objective attributes, its functions. For example, the reader of a brassiere advertisement sees a partially undraped but blandly unperturbed woman standing in an otherwise commonplace public setting, and may experience certain sensations; the reader also sees the name "Maidenform," a particular brassiere style, and, in tiny print, words about the material, colors, price. Or, the viewer of a television commercial sees a demonstration with four small boxes labeled 650, 650, 650, and 800; something in the viewer's mind catches hold of this, as trivial as thoughtful consideration might reveal it to be. The viewer is also exposed to the name "Anacin," its bottle, and its purpose.

Sometimes there is an apparently logical link between an ad's emotional appeal and its product information. It does not violate common sense that Cadillac automobiles be photographed at country clubs, or that Japan Air Lines be associated with Orientalia. But there is no real need for the linkage to have a bit of reason behind it. Is there anything inherent to the connection between Salem cigarettes and mountains, Coke and a smile, Miller Beer and comradeship? The link being forged in minds between product and appeal is a pre-logical one.

10   People involved in the advertising industry do not necessarily talk in the terms being used here. They are stationed at the sending end of this communications

channel, and may think they are up to any number of things—Unique Selling Propositions, explosive copywriting, the optimal use of demographics or psychographics, ideal media buys, high recall ratings, or whatever. But when attention shifts to the receiving end of the channel, and focuses on the instant of reception, then commentary becomes much more elemental: an advertising message contains something primary and primitive, an emotional appeal, that in effect is the thin end of the wedge, trying to find its way into a mind. Should this occur, the product information comes along behind.

When enough advertisements are examined in this light, it becomes clear that the emotional appeals fall into several distinguishable categories, and that every ad is a variation on one of a limited number of basic appeals. While there may be several ways of classifying these appeals, one particular list of fifteen has proven to be especially valuable.

Advertisements can appeal to:

1. The need for sex
2. The need for affiliation
3. The need to nurture
4. The need for guidance
5. The need to aggress
6. The need to achieve
7. The need to dominate
8. The need for prominence
9. The need for attention
10. The need for autonomy
11. The need to escape
12. The need to feel safe
13. The need for aesthetic sensations
14. The need to satisfy curiosity
15. Physiological needs: food, drink, sleep, etc.

Murray's List

Where does this list of advertising's fifteen basic appeals come from? Several years ago, I was involved in a research project which was to have as one segment an objective analysis of the changing appeals made in post-World War II American advertising. A sample of magazine ads would have their appeals coded into the categories of psychological needs they seemed aimed at. For this content analysis to happen, a complete roster of human motives would have to be found.

The first thing that came to mind was Abraham Maslow's famous four-part hierarchy of needs. But the briefest look at the range of appeals made in advertising was enough to reveal that they are more varied, and more profane, than Maslow had cared to account for. The search led on to the work of psychologist

Henry A. Murray, who together with his colleagues at the Harvard Psychological Clinic has constructed a full taxonomy of needs. As described in *Explorations
in Personality,* Murray's team had conducted a lengthy series of in-depth interviews with a number of subjects in order to derive from scratch what they felt
to be the essential variables of personality. Forty-four variables were distinguished by the Harvard group, of which twenty were motives. The need for
achievement ("to overcome obstacles and obtain a high standard") was one, for
instance; the need to defer was another; the need to aggress was a third; and
so forth.

Murray's list had served as the groundwork for a number of subsequent
projects. Perhaps the best-known of these was David C. McClelland's extensive study of the need for achievement, reported in his *The Achieving Society.*
In the process of demonstrating that a people's high need for achievement is
predictive of later economic growth, McClelland coded achievement imagery
and references out of a nation's folklore, songs, legends, and children's tales.

15   Following McClelland, I too wanted to cull the motivational appeals from a
culture's imaginative product—in this case, advertising. To develop categories
expressly for this purpose, I took Murray's twenty motives and added to them
others he had mentioned in passing in *Explorations in Personality* but not
included on the final list. The extended list was tried out on a sample of advertisements, and motives which never seemed to be invoked were dropped.
I ended up with eighteen of Murrays' motives, into which 770 print ads were
coded. The resulting distribution is included in the 1976 book *Mass Advertising
as Social Forecast.*

Since that time, the list of appeals has undergone refinements as a result of
using it to analyze television commercials. A few more adjustments stemmed
from the efforts of students in my advertising classes to decode appeals; tens
of term papers surveying thousands of advertisements have caused some
inconsistencies in the list to be hammered out. Fundamentally, though, the
list remains the creation of Henry Murray. In developing a comprehensive,
parsimonious inventory of human motives, he pinpointed the subsurface mental forces that are the least quiescent and most susceptible to advertising's
entreaties.

Fifteen Appeals

1. Need for Sex.   Let's start with sex, because this is the appeal which seems
to pop up first whenever the topic of advertising is raised. Whole books have
been written about this one alone, to find a large audience of mildly titillated
readers. Lately, due to campaigns to sell blue jeans, concern with sex in ads
has redoubled.

The fascinating thing is not how much sex there is in advertising, but how
little. Contrary to impressions, unambiguous sex is rare in these messages. Some
of this surprising observation may be a matter of definition: the Jordache ads
with the lithe, blouse-less female astride a similarly clad male is clearly an appeal to the audience's sexual drives, but the same cannot be said about Brooke

Shields* in the Calvin Klein commercials. Directed at young women and their credit-card carrying mothers, the image of Miss Shields instead invokes the need to be looked at. Buy Calvins and you'll be the center of much attention, just as Brooke is, the ads imply; they do not primarily inveigle their target audience's need for sexual intercourse.

In the content analysis reported in *Mass Advertising as Social Forecast* only two percent of ads were found to pander to this motive. Even *Playboy* ads shy away from sexual appeals: a recent issue contained eighty-three full-page ads, and just four of them (or less than five percent) could be said to have sex on their minds.

20   The reason this appeal is so little used is that it is too blaring and tends to obliterate the product information. Nudity in advertising has the effect of reducing brand recall. The people who do remember the product may do so because they have been made indignant by the ad; this is not the response most advertisers seek.

To the extent that sexual imagery is used, it conventionally works better on men than women; typically a female figure is offered up to the male reader. A Black Velvet liquor advertisement displays an attractive woman wearing a tight black outfit, recumbent under the legend, "Feel the Velvet." The figure does not have to be horizontal, however, for the appeal to be present as National Airlines revealed in its "Fly me" campaign. Indeed, there does not even have to be a female in the ad; "Flick my Bic"† was sufficient to convey the idea to many.

As a rule, though, advertisers have found sex to be a tricky appeal, to be used sparingly. Less controversial and equally fetching are the appeals to our need for affectionate human contact.

2. Need for Affiliation.   American mythology upholds autonomous individuals, and social statistics suggest that people are ever more going it alone in their lives, yet the high frequency of affiliative appeals in ads belies this. Or maybe it does not: maybe all the images of companionship are compensation for what Americans privately lack. In any case, the need to associate with others is widely invoked in advertising and is probably the most prevalent appeal. All sorts of goods and services are sold by linking them to our unfulfilled desires to be in good company.

According to Henry Murray, the need for affiliation consists of desires "to draw near and enjoyably cooperate or reciprocate with another; to please and win affection of another; to adhere and remain loyal to a friend." The manifestations of this motive can be segmented into several different types of affiliation, beginning with romance.

25   Courtship may be swifter nowadays, but the desire for pair-bonding is far from satiated. Ads reaching for this need commonly depict a youngish

---

*Brooke Shields (b. 1965) is a model (at age 3 she was the Ivory Snow baby), as well as a stage (*Grease*), TV, and film actress; her most well-known films are *Pretty Baby* (1978) and *Blue Lagoon* (1980).
†"Flick my Bic" became a famous and successful slogan in advertisements for Bic cigarette lighters during the late 1970s and 1980s. Fowles hints at the not-too-subtle sexual implications of the line.

male and female engrossed in each other. The head of the male is usually higher than the female's, even at this late date; she may be sitting or leaning while he is standing. They are not touching in the Smirnoff vodka ads, but obviously there is an intimacy, sometimes frolicsome, between them. The couple does touch for Martell Cognac when "The moment was Martell." For Wind Song perfume they have touched, and "Your Wind Song stays on his mind."

Depending on the audience, the pair does not absolutely have to be young—just together. He gives her a DeBeers diamond, and there is a tear in her laugh lines. She takes Geritol* and preserves herself for him. And numbers of consumers, wanting affection too, follow suit.

Warm family feelings are fanned in ads when another generation is added to the pair. Hallmark Cards brings grandparents into the picture, and Johnson and Johnson Baby Powder has Dad, Mom, and baby, all fresh from the bath, encircled in arms and emblazoned with "Share the Feeling." A talc has been fused to familial love.

Friendship is yet another form of affiliation pursued by advertisers. Two women confide and drink Maxwell House coffee together; two men walk through the woods smoking Salem cigarettes. Miller Beer promises that afternoon "Miller Time" will be staffed with three or four good buddies. Drink Dr. Pepper, as Mickey Rooney is coaxed to do, and join in with all the other Peppers. Coca-Cola does not even need to portray the friendliness; it has reduced this appeal to "a Coke and a smile."

The warmth can be toned down and disguised, but it is the same affiliative need that is being fished for. The blonde has a direct gaze and her friends are firm businessmen in appearance, but with a glass of Old Bushmill you can sit down and fit right in. Or, for something more upbeat, sing along with the Pontiac choirboys.

30   As well as presenting positive images, advertisers can play to the need for affiliation in negative ways, by invoking the fear of rejection. If we don't use Scope, we'll have the "Ugh! Morning Breath" that causes the male and female models to avert their faces. Unless we apply Ultra Brite or Close-Up to our teeth, it's good-bye romance. Our family will be cursed with "House-a-tosis" if we don't take care. Without Dr. Scholl's antiperspirant foot spray, the bowling team will keel over. There go all the guests when the supply of Dorito's nacho cheese chips is exhausted. Still more rejection if our shirts have ring-around-the-collar, if our car needs to be Midasized. But make a few purchases, and we are back in the bosom of human contact.

As self-directed as Americans pretend to be, in the last analysis we remain social animals, hungering for the positive, endorsing feelings that only those

---

*The original Geritol (a combination of the words "geriatric" and "tolerance") was an iron tonic and vitamin supplement marketed to people over 40 between 1950 and 1979 with the slogan, "Do you have iron poor, tired blood?" Though today Geritol is the label on a group of health-related products, the name became famous—and, to some extent, funny—as a means of restoring energy and youthful vigor to middle-age and elderly people.

around us can supply. Advertisers respond, urging us to "Reach out and touch someone," in the hopes our monthly [phone] bills will rise.

3. Need to Nurture.   Akin to affiliative needs is the need to take care of small, defenseless creatures—children and pets, largely. Reciprocity is of less consequence here, though; it is the giving that counts. Murray uses synonyms like "to feed, help, support, console, protect, comfort, nurse, heal." A strong need it is, woven deep into our genetic fabric, for if it did not exist we could not successfully raise up our replacements. When advertisers put forth the image of something diminutive and furry, something that elicits the word "cute" or "precious," then they are trying to trigger this motive. We listen to the childish voice singing the Oscar Mayer wiener song, and our next hot-dog purchase is prescribed. Aren't those darling kittens something, and how did this Meow Mix get into our shopping cart?

This pitch is often directed at women, as Mother Nature's chief nurturers. "Make me some Kraft macaroni and cheese, please," says the elfin preschooler just in from the snowstorm, and mothers' hearts go out, and Kraft's sales go up. "We're cold, wet, and hungry," whine the husband and kids, and the little woman gets the Manwiches ready. A facsimile of this need can be hit without children or pets: the husband is ill and sleepless in the television commercial, and the wife grudgingly fetches the NyQuil.

But it is not women alone who can be touched by this appeal. The father nurses his son Eddie through adolescence while the John Deere lawn tractor survives the years. Another father counts pennies with his young son as the subject of New York Life Insurance comes up. And all over America are businessmen who don't know why they dial Qantas Airlines* when they have to take a trans-Pacific trip; the koala bear knows.

35   **4. Need for Guidance.**   The opposite of the need to nurture is the need to be nurtured: to be protected, shielded, guided. We may be loath to admit it, but the child lingers on inside every adult—and a good thing it does, or we would not be instructable in our advancing years. Who wants a nation of nothing but flinty personalities?

Parent-like figures can successfully call up this need. Robert Young[†] recommends Sanka coffee, and since we have experienced him for twenty-five years as television father and doctor, we take his word for it. Florence Henderson[‡] as the expert mom knows a lot about the advantages of Wesson oil.

---

*Qantas Airlines is an Australian airline whose ads during the 1980s and 1990s featured a cuddly koala bear standing in for both the airline and the exotic delights of Australia.

[†]Robert Young (1907–1988) acted in movies (including Alfred Hitchcock's *Secret Agent* (1936) and *Crossfire* (1947) and TV (starring in the long-running 1950s series *Father Knows Best* and the 1960s series *Marcus Welby, M.D.*). A classic father figure, in his later career he appeared in ads for Sanka coffee.

[‡]Florence Henderson (b. 1934), acted on Broadway and TV (primarily, in musical and comedy roles). Her most famous TV show was *The Brady Bunch* (1968–74), where she played a mother of three daughters who married a man with three sons.

The parent-ness of the spokesperson need not be so salient; sometimes pure authoritativeness is better. When Orson Welles* scowls and intones, "Paul Masson will sell no wine before its time," we may not know exactly what he means, but we still take direction from him. There is little maternal about Brenda Vaccaro[†] when she speaks up for Tampax, but there is a certainty to her that many accept.

A celebrity is not a necessity in making a pitch to the need for guidance, since a fantasy figure can serve just as well. People accede to the Green Giant, or Betty Crocker, or Mr. Goodwrench.[‡] Some advertisers can get by with no figure at all: "When E. F. Hutton[§] talks, people listen."

Often it is tradition or custom that advertisers point to and consumers take guidance from. Bits and pieces of American history are used to sell whiskeys like Old Crow, Southern Comfort, Jack Daniel's. We conform to traditional male/female roles and age-old social norms when we purchase Barclay cigarettes, which informs us "The pleasure is back."

40   The product itself, if it has been around for a long time, can constitute a tradition. All those old labels in the ad for Morton salt convince us that we should continue to buy it. Kool-Aid says "You loved it as a kid. You trust it as a mother," hoping to get yet more consumers to go along.

Even when the product has no history at all, our need to conform to tradition and to be guided are strong enough that they can be invoked through bogus nostalgia and older actors. Country-Time lemonade sells because consumers want to believe it has a past they can defer to.

So far the needs and the ways they can be invoked which have been looked at are largely warm and affiliative; they stand in contrast to the next set of needs, which are much more egoistic and assertive.

5. Need to Aggress. The pressures of the real world create strong retaliatory feelings in every functioning human being. Since these impulses can come forth as bursts of anger and violence, their display is normally tabooed. Existing as harbored energy, aggressive drives present a large, tempting target for advertisers. It is not a target to be aimed at thoughtlessly, though, for few

---

*Orson Welles (1915–1985) was a major American filmmaker and actor whose films include *Citizen Kane* (1941—generally considered the greatest American film of all time), *The Magnificent Ambersons* (1942), *The Lady from Shanghai* (1947), *Macbeth* (1948), and *Touch of Evil* (1958). Toward the end of his life—to the dismay of many who revered him—the magisterial but financially depleted Welles became a spokesman for Paul Masson wines.

[†]Brenda Vaccaro (b. 1939) is a stage, TV, and film actress; her films include *Midnight Cowboy* (1969), *Airport '77* (1977), *Supergirl* (1984), and *The Mirror Has Two Faces* (1996).

[‡]Mr. Goodwrench (and the slogan "Looking for Mr. Goodwrench"), personified as an engaging and highly capable auto mechanic, is a product of the General Motors marketing department.

[§]E. F. Hutton (named after its founder, Edward Francis Hutton) was a major brokerage firm that was brought down in the 1980s by corporate misconduct. Its most famous TV ad portrayed, typically, two well-dressed businesspeople in conversation in a crowded dining room or club room. The first man says to the other, "My broker says...." The second man listens politely and responds, "Well, my broker is E. F. Hutton, and *he* says...," and everyone else in the room strains to overhear the conversation. The tag line: "When E. F. Hutton talks, people listen."

manufacturers want their products associated with destructive motives. There is always the danger that, as in the case of sex, if the appeal is too blatant, public opinion will turn against what is being sold.

Jack-in-the-Box sought to abruptly alter its marketing by going after older customers and forgetting the younger ones. Their television commercials had a seventy-ish lady command, "Waste him," and the Jack-in-the-Box clown exploded before our eyes. So did public reaction until the commercials were toned down. Print ads for Club cocktails carried the faces of octogenarians under the headline, "Hit me with a Club"; response was contrary enough to bring the campaign to a stop.

45   Better disguised aggressive appeals are less likely to backfire: Triumph cigarettes has models making a lewd gesture with their uplifted cigarettes, but the individuals are often laughing and usually in close company of others. When Exxon said, "There's a Tiger in your tank," the implausibility of it concealed the invocation of aggressive feelings.

Depicted arguments are a common way for advertisers to tap the audience's needs to aggress. Don Rickles* and Lynda Carter[†] trade gibes, and consumers take sides as the name of Seven-Up is stitched on minds. The Parkay [margarine] tub has a difference of opinion with the user; who can forget it, or who (or what) got the last word in?

6. Need to Achieve.   This is the drive that energizes people, causing them to strive in their lives and careers. According to Murray, the need for achievement is signalled by the desires "to accomplish something difficult. To overcome obstacles and attain a high standard. To excel one's self. To rival and surpass others." A prominent American trait, it is one that advertisers like to hook on to because it identifies their product with winning and success.

The Cutty Sark ad does not disclose that Ted Turner failed at his latest attempt at yachting's America Cup; here he is represented as a champion on the water as well as off in his television enterprises. If we drink this whiskey, we will be victorious alongside Turner. We can also succeed with O. J. Simpson[‡] by renting Hertz cars, or with Reggie Jackson[§] by bringing

---

*Don Rickles (b. 1926) is a night-club comedian (who has also appeared in TV and films) famous for his caustic wit and for humorously insulting people in the audience.

[†]Lynda Carter (b. 1951) is an actress whose most famous role was the heroine of the 1976 TV series *Wonder Woman*.

[‡]O. J. Simpson (b. 1957) is a famous football player–turned film actor (*The Naked Gun*) and defendant in a notorious murder trial in the 1990s. In a highly controversial decision, Simpson was acquitted of killing his ex-wife Nicole Simpson and her friend Ron Goldman; but in a subsequent civil trial he was found liable for the two deaths. Before the trial, Simpson was well-known for his TV commercials for Hertz rental cars, featuring him sprinting through airports to get to the gate to demonstrate what you *wouldn't* have to do if you rented a car through Hertz.

[§]Reggie Jackson (b. 1946), a member of the Baseball Hall of Fame, played as an outfielder between 1967 and 1987. Known as "Mr. October" for his dramatic game-winning at-bats during post-season play, he had more strikeouts (2,597) than any other player. He was the first baseball player to have a candy bar (the "Reggie Bar") named after him, and toward the end of his career was a pitchman for Panasonic televisions.

home some Panasonic equipment. Cathy Rigby* and Stayfree maxipads will put people out front.

Sports heroes are the most convenient means to snare consumers' needs to achieve, but they are not the only one. Role models can be established, ones which invite emulation, as with the profiles put forth by Dewar's scotch. Successful, tweedy individuals relate they have "graduated to the flavor of Myer's rum." Or the advertiser can establish a prize: two neighbors play one-on-one basketball for a Michelob beer in a television commercial, while in a print ad a bottle of Johnnie Walker Black Label has been gilded like a trophy.

50   Any product that advertises itself in superlatives—the best, the first, the finest—is trying to make contact with our needs to succeed. For many consumers, sales and bargains belong in this category of appeals, too; the person who manages to buy something at fifty percent off is seizing an opportunity and coming out ahead of others.

7. Need to Dominate.   This fundamental need is the craving to be powerful— perhaps omnipotent, as in the Xerox ad where Brother Dominic exhibits heavenly powers and creates miraculous copies. Most of us will settle for being just a regular potentate, though. We drink Budweiser because it is the King of Beers, and here comes the powerful Clydesdales to prove it. A taste of Wolfschmidt vodka and "The spirit of the Czar lives on."

The need to dominate and control one's environment is often thought of as being masculine, but as close students of human nature, advertisers know it is not so circumscribed. Women's aspirations for control are suggested in the campaign theme, "I like my men in English Leather, or nothing at all." The females in the Chanel No. 19 ads are "outspoken" and wrestle their men around.

Male and female, what we long for is clout; what we get in its place is Mastercard.

8. Need for Prominence.   Here comes the need to be admired and respected, to enjoy prestige and high social status. These times, it appears, are not so egalitarian after all. Many ads picture the trappings of high position; the Oldsmobile stands before a manorial doorway, the Volvo is parked beside a steeplechase. A book-lined study is the setting for Dewar's 12, and Lenox China is displayed in a dining room chock full of antiques.

55   Beefeater gin represents itself as "The Crown Jewel of England" and uses no illustrations of jewels or things British, for the words are sufficient indicators of distinction. Buy that gin and you will rise up the prestige hierarchy, or achieve the same effect on yourself with Seagram's 7 Crown, which ambiguously describes itself as "classy."

Being respected does not have to entail the usual accoutrements of wealth: "Do you know who I am?" the commercials ask, and we learn that the prominent person is not so prominent without his American Express card.

---

*Cathy Rigby, an Olympian, was the first American gymnast to win a medal (in 1970) at the World Championships. She went on to star in a Broadway revival of the musical *Peter Pan* (surpassing Mary Martin for the greatest number of performances). Subsequently, she became a sportscaster for ABC Sports.

9. Need for Attention.   The previous need involved being *looked up to,* while this is the need to be *looked at.* The desire to exhibit ourselves in such a way as to make others look at us is a primitive, insuppressible instinct. The clothing and cosmetic industries exist just to serve this need, and this is the way they pitch their wares. Some of this effort is aimed at males, as the ads for Hathaway shirts and Jockey underclothes. But the greater bulk of such appeals is targeted singlemindedly at women.

To come back to Brooke Shields: this is where she fits into American marketing. If I buy Calvin Klein jeans, consumers infer, I'll be the object of fascination. The desire for exhibition has been most strikingly played to in a print campaign of many years' duration, that of Maidenform lingerie. The woman exposes herself, and sales surge. "Gentlemen prefer Hanes" the ads dissemble, and women who want eyes upon them know what they should do. Peggy Fleming[*] flutters her legs for L'eggs, encouraging females who want to be the star in their own lives to purchase this product.

The same appeal works for cosmetics and lotions. For years, the little girl with the exposed backside sold gobs of Coppertone, but now the company has picked up the pace a little: as a female, you are supposed to "Flash 'em a Coppertone tan." Food can be sold the same way, especially to the diet-conscious; Angie Dickinson poses for California avocados and says, "Would this body lie to you?" Our eyes are too fixed on her for us to think to ask if she got that way by eating mounds of guacomole.

60   **10. Need for Autonomy.**   There are several ways to sell credit card services, as has been noted: Mastercard appeals to the need to dominate, and American Express to the need for prominence. When Visa claims, "You can have it the way you want it," yet another primary motive is being beckoned forward—the need to endorse the self. The focus here is upon the independence and integrity of the individual; this need is the antithesis of the need for guidance and is unlike any of the social needs. "If running with the herd isn't your style, try ours," says Rotan-Mosle, and many Americans feel they have finally found the right brokerage firm.

The photo is of a red-coated Mountie on his horse, posed on a snow-covered ledge; the copy reads, "Windsor—One Canadian stands alone." This epitome of the solitary and proud individual may work best with male customers, as may Winston's man in the red cap. But one-figure advertisements also strike the strong need for autonomy among American women. As Shelly Hack[†] strides for Charlie perfume, females respond to her obvious pride and flair; she is her own person. The Virginia Slims tale is of people who have come a long way from subservience to independence. Cachet perfume feels it does not need a solo figure to work this appeal, and uses three different faces in its ads; it insists, though, "It's different on every woman who wears it."

---

[*]Peggy Fleming (b. 1948), an Olympic figure skater, and Gold Medal winner (1968), later became a TV sports commentator and a representative for UNICEF (the United Nations Children's Emergency Fund).
[†]Shelly Hack (b. 1952) portrayed Tiffany Welles in the 1970s TV show *Charlie's Angels.*

Like many psychological needs, this one can also be appealed to in a negative fashion, by invoking the loss of independence or self-regard. Guilt and regrets can be stimulated: "Gee, I could have had a V-8." Next time, get one and be good to yourself.

11. Need to Escape.   An appeal to the need for autonomy often co-occurs with one for the need to escape, since the desire to duck out of our social obligations, to seek rest or adventure, frequently takes the form of one-person flight. The dashing image of a pilot, in fact, is a standard way of quickening this need to get away from it all.

Freedom is the pitch here, the freedom that every individual yearns for whenever life becomes too oppressive. Many advertisers like appealing to the need for escape because the sensation of pleasure often accompanies escape, and what nicer emotional nimbus could there be for a product? "You deserve a break today," says McDonald's, and Stouffer's frozen foods chime in, "Set yourself free."

65   For decades men have imaginatively bonded themselves to the Marlboro cowboy who dwells untarnished and unencumbered in Marlboro Country some distance from modern life; smokers' aching needs for autonomy and escape are personified by that cowpoke. Many women can identify with the lady ambling through the woods behind the words, "Benson and Hedges and mornings and me."

But escape does not have to be solitary. Other Benson and Hedges ads, part of the same campaign, contain two strolling figures. In Salem cigarette advertisements, it can be several people who escape together into the mountaintops. A commercial for Levi's pictured a cloudbank above a city through which ran a whole chain of young people.

There are varieties of escape, some wistful like the Boeing "Someday" campaign of dream vacations, some kinetic like the play and parties in soft drink ads. But in every instance, the consumer exposed to the advertisement is invited to momentarily depart his everyday life for a more carefree experience, preferably with the product in hand.

12. Need to Feel Safe.   Nobody in their right mind wants to be intimidated, menaced, battered, poisoned. We naturally want to do whatever it takes to stave off threats to our well-being, and to our families'. It is the instinct of self-preservation that makes us responsive to the ad of the St. Bernard with the keg of Chivas Regal. We pay attention to the stern talk of Karl Malden* and the plight of the vacationing couples who have lost all their funds in the American Express travelers cheques commercials. We want the omnipresent stag from Hartford Insurance to watch over us too.

---

*Karl Malden (1912–2009), with his familiar craggy face and outsized nose, was a stage and later a film actor. He was the original Mitch in the Broadway production of Tennessee Williams's *Streetcar Named Desire*, a role he reprised in the 1951 movie version. His films include *On the Waterfront* (1954), *Cheyenne Autumn* (1964), and *Patton* (1970), and he starred in the 1972 TV series *Streets of San Francisco*. Malden became famous to a later generation of viewers as a pitchman for the American Express card, with the slogan, "Don't leave home without it!"

In the interest of keeping failure and calamity from our lives, we like to see the durability of products demonstrated. Can we ever forget that Timex takes a licking and keeps on ticking? When the American Tourister suitcase bounces all over the highway and the egg inside doesn't break, the need to feel safe has been adroitly plucked.

70   We take precautions to diminish future threats. We buy Volkswagen Rabbits for the extraordinary mileage, and MONY insurance policies to avoid the tragedies depicted in their black-and-white ads of widows and orphans.

We are careful about our health. We consume Mazola margarine because it has "corn goodness" backed by the natural food traditions of the American Indians. In the medicine cabinet is Alka-Seltzer, the "home remedy"; having it, we are snug in our little cottage.

We want to be safe and secure; buy these products, advertisers are saying, and you'll be safer than you are without them.

13. Need for Aesthetic Sensations.   There is an undeniable aesthetic component to virtually every ad run in the national media: the photography or filming or drawing is near-perfect, the type style is well chosen, the layout could scarcely be improved upon. Advertisers know there is little chance of good communication occurring if an ad is not visually pleasing. Consumers may not be aware of the extent of their own sensitivity to artwork, but it is undeniably large.

Sometimes the aesthetic element is expanded and made into an ad's primary appeal. Charles Jordan shoes may or may not appear in the accompanying avant-grade photographs; Kohler plumbing fixtures catch attention through the high style of their desert settings. Beneath the slightly out of focus photograph, languid and sensuous in tone, General Electric feels called upon to explain, "This is an ad for the hair dryer."

75   This appeal is not limited to female consumers: J&B scotch says "It whispers" and shows a bucolic scene of lake and castle.

14. Need to Satisfy Curiosity.   It may seem odd to list a need for information among basic motives, but this need can be as primal and compelling as any of the others. Human beings are curious by nature, interested in the world around them, and intrigued by tidbits of knowledge and new developments. Trivia, percentages, observations counter to conventional wisdom—these items all help sell products. Any advertisement in a question-and-answer format is strumming this need.

A dog groomer has a question about long distance rates, and Bell Telephone has a chart with all the figures. An ad for Porsche 911 is replete with diagrams and schematics, numbers and arrows. Lo and behold, Anacin pills have 150 more milligrams than its competitors; should we wonder if this is better or worse for us?

15. Physiological Needs.   To the extent that sex is solely a biological need, we are now coming around full circle, back toward the start of the list. In this final category are clustered appeals to sleeping, eating, drinking. The art of photographing food and drink is so advanced, sometimes these temptations are wondrously caught in the camera's lens: the crab meat in the Red Lobster restaurant ads can start us salivating, the Quarterpounder can almost be smelled, the liquor in the glass glows invitingly. Imbibe, these ads scream.

Styles

Some common ingredients of advertisements were not singled out for separate mention in the list of fifteen because they are not appeals in and of themselves. They are stylistic features, influencing the way a basic appeal is presented. The use of humor is one, and the use of celebrities is another. A third is time imagery, past and future, which goes to several purposes.

80   For all of its employment in advertising, humor can be treacherous, because it can get out of hand and smother the product information. Supposedly, this is what Alka-Seltzer discovered with its comic commercials of the late sixties; "I can't believe I ate the whole thing," the sad-faced husband lamented, and the audience cackled so much it forgot the antacid. Or, did not take it seriously.

But used carefully, humor can punctuate some of the softer appeals and soften some of the harsher ones. When Emma says to the Fruit-of-the-Loom fruits, "Hi, cuties. Whatcha doing in my laundry basket?" we smile as our curiosity is assuaged along with hers. Bill Cosby gets consumers tickled about the children in his Jell-O commercials, and strokes the need to nurture.

An insurance company wants to invoke the need to feel safe, but does not want to leave readers with an unpleasant aftertaste; cartoonist Rowland Wilson creates an avalanche about to crush a gentleman who is saying to another, "My insurance company? New England Life, of course. Why?" The same tactic of humor undercutting threat is used in the cartoon commercials for Safeco when the Pink Panther wanders from one disaster to another. Often humor masks aggression: comedian Bob Hope in the outfit of a boxer promises to knock out the knock-knocks with Texaco; Rodney Dangerfield, who "can't get no respect," invites aggression as the comic relief in Miller Lite commercials.

Roughly fifteen percent of all advertisements incorporate a celebrity, almost always from the fields of entertainment or sports. The approach can also prove troublesome for advertisers, for celebrities are human beings too, and fully capable of the most remarkable behavior. If anything distasteful about them emerges, it is likely to reflect on the product. The advertisers making use of Anita Bryant[*] and Billy Jean King[†] suffered several anxious moments. An untimely death can also react poorly on a product. But advertisers are willing

---

[*]Anita Bryant (b. 1940), a singer and entertainer (and as Miss Oklahoma, runner-up in the 1958 Miss America competition), became controversial during the late 1970s with her campaigns against homosexuality and AIDS. At the time, she was making ads and TV commercials for Florida orange juice, but was dropped by the sponsor after boycotts by activists.

[†]Billy Jean King (b. 1943) was a championship tennis player in the late 1960s and 1970s. In 1973 she was named *Sports Illustrated*'s "Sportsperson of the Year," the first woman to win this honor. She won four U.S. championships and six Wimbledon's single championships. In 1973, in a much publicized "Battle of the Sexes" match, King won all three sets against the 55-year-old Bobby Riggs (once ranked as the best tennis player in the world), who had claimed that "any half-decent male player could defeat even the best female players."

to take risks because celebrities can be such a good link between producers and consumers, performing the social role of introducer.

There are several psychological needs these middlemen can play upon. Let's take the product class of cameras and see how different celebrities can hit different needs. The need for guidance can be invoked by Michael Landon, who plays such a wonderful dad on "Little House on the Prairie"; when he says to buy Kodak equipment, many people listen. James Garner for Polaroid cameras is put in a similar authoritative role, so defined by a mocking spouse. The need to achieve is summoned up by Tracy Austin and other tennis stars for Canon AE-1; the advertiser first makes sure we see these athletes playing to win. When Cheryl Tiegs* speaks up for Olympus cameras, it is the need for attention that is being targeted.

85   The past and future, being outside our grasp, are exploited by advertisers as locales for the projection of needs. History can offer up heroes (and call up the need to achieve) or traditions (need for guidance) as well as art objects (need for aesthetic sensations). Nostalgia is a kindly version of personal history and is deployed by advertisers to rouse needs for affiliation and for guidance; the need to escape can come in here, too. The same need to escape is sometimes the point of futuristic appeals but picturing the avant-garde can also be a way to get at the need to achieve.

Analyzing Advertisements

When analyzing ads yourself for their emotional appeals, it takes a bit of practice to learn to ignore the product information (as well as one's own experience and feelings about the product). But that skill comes soon enough, as does the ability to quickly sort out from all the non-product aspects of an ad the chief element which is the most striking, the most likely to snag attention first and penetrate brains farthest. The key to the appeal, this element usually presents itself centrally and forwardly to the reader or viewer.

Another clue: the viewing angle which the audience has on the ad's subjects is informative. If the subjects are photographed or filmed from below and thus are looking down at you much as the Green Giant does, then the need to be guided is a good candidate for the ad's emotional appeal. If, on the other hand, the subjects are shot from above and appear deferential, as is often the case with children or female models, then other needs are being appealed to.

To figure out an ad's emotional appeal, it is wise to know (or have a good hunch about) who the targeted consumers are; this can often be inferred from the magazine or television show it appears in. This piece of information is a great help in determining the appeal and in deciding between two different interpretations. For example, if an ad features a partially undressed female, this would typically signal one appeal for readers of *Penthouse* (need for sex) and another for readers of *Cosmopolitan* (need for attention).

---

*Cheryl Tiegs (b. 1947) is a supermodel perhaps best known for her affiliation with the *Sports Illustrated Annual Swimsuit Issue*. A 1978 poster of Tiegs in a pink swimsuit became a cultural icon. Recently, she has entered the business world with an accessory and wig line for Revlon.

It would be convenient if every ad made just one appeal, were aimed at just one need. Unfortunately, things are often not that simple. A cigarette ad with a couple at the edge of a polo field is trying to hit both the need for affiliation and the need for prominence; depending on the attitude of the male, dominance could also be an ingredient in this. An ad for Chimere perfume incorporates two photos: in the top one the lady is being commanding at a business luncheon (need to dominate), but in the lower one she is being bussed (need for affiliation). Better ads, however, seem to avoid being too diffused; in the study of post-World War II advertising described earlier, appeals grew more focused as the decades passed. As a rule of thumb, [only twenty percent of ads have one primary appeal,] about sixty percent have two conspicuous appeals; the last twenty percent have three or more. Rather than looking for the greatest number of appeals, decoding ads is most productive when the loudest one or two appeals are discerned, since those are the appeals with the best chance of grabbing people's attention.

90   Finally, analyzing ads does not have to be a solo activity and probably should not be. The greater number of people there are involved, the better chance there is of transcending individual biases and discerning the essential emotional lure built into an advertisement.

Do They or Don't They?

Do the emotional appeals made in advertisements add up to the sinister manipulation of consumers?

It is clear that these ads work. Attention is caught, communication occurs between producers and consumers, and sales result. It turns out to be difficult to detail the exact relationship between a specific ad and a specific purchase, or even between a campaign and subsequent sales figures, because advertising is only one of a host of influences upon consumption. Yet no one is fooled by this lack of perfect proof; everyone knows that advertising sells. If this were not the case, then tight-fisted American businesses would not spend a total of fifty billion dollars annually on these messages.

But before anyone despairs that advertisers have our number to the extent that they can marshal us at will and march us like automatons to the check-out counters, we should recall the resiliency and obduracy of the American consumer. Advertisers may have uncovered the softest spots in minds, but that does not mean they have found truly gaping apertures. There is no evidence that advertising can get people to do things contrary to their self-interests. Despite all the finesse of advertisements, and all the subtle emotional tugs, the public resists the vast majority of the petitions. According to the marketing division of the A. C. Nielsen Company, a whopping seventy-five percent of all new products die within a year in the marketplace, the victims of consumer disinterest which no amount of advertising could overcome. The appeals in advertising may be the most captivating there are to be had, but they are not enough to entrap the wily consumer.

The key to understanding the discrepancy between, on the one hand, the fact that advertising truly works, and, on the other, the fact that it hardly works, is to take into account the enormous numbers of people exposed to an ad. Modern-day communications permit an ad to be displayed to millions upon millions of individuals; if the smallest fraction of that audience can be moved to buy the product, then the ad has been successful. When one percent of the people exposed to a television advertising campaign reach for their wallets, that could be one million sales, which may be enough to keep the product in production and the advertisements coming.

95   In arriving at an evenhanded judgment about advertisements and their emotional appeals, it is good to keep in mind that many of the purchases which might be credited to these ads are experienced as genuinely gratifying to the consumer. We sincerely like the goods or service we have bought, and we may even like some of the emotional drapery that an ad suggests comes with it. It has sometimes been noted that the most avid students of advertisements are the people who have just bought the product; they want to steep themselves in the associated imagery. This may be the reason that Americans, when polled, are not negative about advertising and do not disclose any sense of being misused. The volume of advertising may be an irritant, but the product information as well as the imaginative material in ads are partial compensation.

A productive understanding is that advertising messages involve costs and benefits at both ends of the communications channel. For those few ads which do make contact, the consumer surrenders a moment of time, has the lower brain curried, and receives notice of a product; the advertiser has given up money and has increased the chance of sales. In this sort of communications activity, neither party can be said to be the loser.

● Review Questions

1. Why is advertising more common in highly industrialized countries like the United States than in countries with "quieter" economies?

2. How are advertisers' attempts to communicate their messages, and to break through customer resistance, keyed to their conception of human psychology, according to Fowles?

3. What are the "two orders of content" of most advertisements, according to Fowles?

4. How is Fowles indebted to Henry Murray?

5. Why must appeals to our need for sex and our need to aggress be handled carefully, according to Fowles?

6. How does the use of humor or the use of celebrities fit into Fowles's scheme?

Discussion and Writing Suggestions

1. In paragraph 4 Fowles cites a study indicating that only a fraction of the advertisements bombarding consumers every day are even noticed, much less acted upon. How do the results of this study square with your own experience? About how many of the commercial messages that you view and hear every day do you actually pay attention to? What kinds of messages draw your attention? What elicits positive reactions? Negative reactions? What kinds of appeals are most successful in making you want to actually purchase the advertised product?

2. What do you think of Fowles's analysis of "advertising's fifteen basic appeals"? Does this classification seem an accurate and useful way of accounting for how most advertising works upon us? Would you drop any of his categories, or perhaps incorporate one set into another set? Has Fowles neglected to consider other appeals that you believe to be equally important? If so, can you think of one or more advertisements that employ such appeals omitted by Fowles?

3. Categorize several of the print ads in the ad portfolio later in the chapter (pages 566–594) using Fowles's schema. Explain how the headlines, body text, and graphics support your categorization choices.

4. Fowles asserts that "[c]ontrary to impressions, unambiguous sex is rare in [advertising] messages." This article first appeared in 1982. Does Fowles's statement still seem true today? To what extent do you believe that advertisers in recent years have increased their reliance on overt sexual appeals? Cite examples.

5. Fowles believes that "the need to associate with others [affiliation]...is probably the most prevalent appeal" in advertising. To what extent do you agree with this statement? Locate or cite print or broadcast ads that rely on the need for affiliation. How do the graphics and text of these ads work on what Fowles calls "the deep running drives" of our psyches or "the lower brain"?

6. Locate ads that rely upon the converse appeals to nurture and to guidance. Explain how the graphics and text in these ads work upon our human motivations. If possible, further categorize the appeal: for example, are we provided with guidance from a parent figure, some other authority figure, or from the force of tradition?

7. Conduct (perhaps with one or more classmates) your own analysis of a set of contemporary advertisements. Select a single issue of a particular magazine, such as *Time* or the *New Yorker*. Review all of the full-page ads, classifying each according to Fowles's categories. An ad may make more than one appeal (as Fowles points out in paragraph 89), but generally one will be primary. What do your findings show? Which appeals are the most frequent? The least frequent? Which are most effective? Why? You may find it interesting to compare the appeals of advertising in different magazines aimed at different audiences—for example, a general-interest magazine, such as *Newsweek,* compared with a more specialized magazine, such as the *New Republic,* or *People,* or *Glamour,* or *Guns and Ammo.* To what extent do the types of appeals shift with the gender or interests of the target audience?

MAKING THE PITCH IN PRINT ADVERTISING

Courtland L. Bovée, John V. Thill,
George P. Dovel, and Marian Burk Wood

No two ads are identical, but the vast majority employ a common set of textual features: headlines, body copy, and slogans. In the following selection, the authors discuss each of these features in turn, explaining their importance in attracting the potential customer's attention and selling the virtues of the product or service offered. You will find this discussion useful in making your own analyses of advertisements.

Courtland L. Bovée is the C. Allen Paul Distinguished Chair at Grossmont College. John V. Thill is CEO of Communication Specialists of America. George P. Dovel is president of the Dovel Group. Marian Burk Wood is president of Wood and Wood Advertising. This passage originally appeared in the authors' textbook *Advertising Excellence* (McGraw-Hill, 1995).

Copywriters and Copywriting

Given the importance of copy, it comes as no surprise that copywriters are key players in the advertising process. In fact, many of the most notable leaders and voices in the industry began their careers as copywriters, including Jane Maas, David Ogilvy, Rosser Reeves, Leo Burnett, and William Bernbach. As a profession, copywriting is somewhat unusual because so many of its top practitioners have been in their jobs for years, even decades (rather than moving up the management ranks as is usual in many professions). Copywriters can either work for agencies or set themselves up as free-lancers, selling their services to agencies and advertisers. Because it presents endless opportunities to be creative, copywriting is one of those rare jobs that can be fresh and challenging year after year.

Although successful copywriters share a love of language with novelists, poets, and other writers, copywriting is first and foremost a business function, not an artistic endeavor. The challenge isn't to create works of literary merit, but to meet advertising objectives. This doesn't mean that copywriting isn't an art, however; it's simply art in pursuit of a business goal. Nor is it easy. Such noted literary writers as Stephen Vincent Benét, George Bernard Shaw, and Ernest Hemingway tried to write ad copy and found themselves unable to do it effectively. It's the combined requirements of language skills, business acumen, and an ability to create under the pressure of tight deadlines and format restrictions (such as the limited number of words you have to work with) that make copywriting so challenging—and so endlessly rewarding.

Copywriters have many styles and approaches to writing, but most agree on one thing: copywriting is hard work. It can involve a great deal of planning and coordinating with clients, legal staffers, account executives, researchers, and art directors. In addition, it usually entails hammering away at your copy until it's as good as it can be. David Ogilvy talked about doing 19 drafts of a single piece of copy and writing 37 headlines for a Sears ad in order to get 3 possibilities to show to the client. Actually, the chance to write and rewrite that many times is a luxury that most copywriters don't have; they often must produce copy on tight schedules with unforgiving deadlines (such as magazine publication deadlines).

The task of copywriting is most often associated with the headlines and copy you see in an ad, but copywriters actually develop a wide variety of other materials, from posters to catalogs to press releases, as well as the words you hear in radio and television commercials.

Print Copy

5 Copywriters are responsible for every word you see in print ads, whether the words are in a catchy headline or in the fine print at the bottom of the page. The three major categories of copy are headlines, body copy, and slogans.

Headlines

The *headline,* also called a *heading* or a *head,* constitutes the dominant line or lines of copy in an ad. Headlines are typically set in larger type and appear at the top of the ad, although there are no hard-and-fast rules on headline layout. *Subheads* are secondary headlines, often written to move the reader from the main headline to the body copy. Even if there is a pageful of body copy and only a few words in the headline, the headline is the most important piece of copy for two reasons: First, it serves as the "come-on" to get people to stop turning the page and check out your ad. Second, as much as 80 percent of your audience may not bother to read the body copy, so whatever message these nonreaders carry away from the ad will have to come from the headline.

Copywriters can choose from a variety of headline types, each of which performs a particular function.

- *News headlines.* News headlines present information that's new to the audience, such as announcing a new store location, a new product, or lower prices. This approach is common because potential customers are often looking for new solutions, lower prices, and other relevant changes in the marketplace. For example, a newspaper ad from the Silo home electronics chain announced a recent sale using a news headline: "Everything on Sale! 4 Days Only! 5–20% Off Everything!" Headlines like this are typical in local newspaper advertising.

- *Emotional headlines.* The emotional appeal...is represented by emotional headlines. The quotation headline "I'm sick of her ruining our lives" was used in an ad for the American Mental Health Fund to echo the frustration some parents feel when they can't understand their teenagers' behavior. Combined with a photo of a sad and withdrawn teenage girl, the headline grabs any parent who has felt such frustration, and the body copy goes on to explain that families shouldn't get mad at people with mental illnesses but should help them get treatment for their conditions.

- *Benefit headlines.* The benefit headline is a statement of the key customer benefit. An ad for Quicken personal finance software used the question-form headline: "How do you know exactly where your money goes and how much you have?" followed by "It's this simple" above a photograph of the product package. The customer benefit is keeping better track of your money, and Quicken is the solution offered.

- *Directive headlines.* Headlines that direct the reader to do something, or at least suggest the reader do something, can motivate consumer action. Such headlines can be a hard sell, such as "Come in now and save," or they can be something more subtle, such as "Just feel the color in these black and whites," the headline in an ad for Ensoniq keyboards.

- *Offbeat and curiosity headlines.* Humor, wordplay, and mystery can be effective ways to draw readers into an ad. An ad promoting vacation travel to Spain used the headline "Si in the dark," with a photo of a lively nighttime scene. The word *Si* is catchy because it first looks like an error, until the reader reads the body copy to learn that the ad is talking about Spain (*si* is Spanish for "yes").

- *Hornblowing headlines.* The hornblowing headline, called "Brag and Boast" heads by the Gallup & Robinson research organization, should be used with care. Customers have seen it all and heard it all, and "We're the greatest" headlines tend to sound arrogant and self-centered. This isn't to say that you can't stress superiority; you just need to do it in a way that takes the customer's needs into account, and the headline must be honest. The headline "Neuberger & Berman Guardian Fund" followed by the subhead "#1 Performing Growth and Income Fund" blows the company's own horn but also conveys an important product benefit. Since investors look for top-performing mutual funds, the information about being number one is relevant.

- *Slogan, label, or logo headlines.* Some headlines show a company's slogan, a product label, or the organization's logo. Powerful slogans like Hallmark's "When you care enough to send the very best" can make great headlines because they click with the reader's emotions. Label and logo headlines can build product and company awareness, but they must be used with care. If the label or logo doesn't make some emotional or logical connection with the reader, the ad probably won't succeed.

Headlines often have maximum impact when coupled with a well-chosen graphic element, rather than trying to carry the message with words alone. In fact, the careful combination of the two can increase the audience's involvement with the ad, especially if one of the two says something ironic or unexpected that has to be resolved by considering the other element. A magazine ad for Easter Seals had the headline "After all we did for Pete, he walked out on us." At first, you think the birth-defects organization is complaining. Then you see a photo of Pete with new artificial legs, walking away from a medical facility. It's a powerful combination that makes the reader feel good about the things Easter Seals can do for people.

Body Copy

The second major category of copy is the *body copy*, which constitutes the words in the main body of the ad, apart from headlines, photo captions, and other blocks of text. The importance of body copy varies from ad to ad, and some ads have little or no body copy. Ads for easy-to-understand products, for instance, often rely on the headline and a visual such as a photograph to get their point across. In contrast, when the selling message needs a lot of supporting detail to be convincing, an ad can be packed full of body copy. Some advertisers have the impression that long body copy should be avoided, but that isn't always the case. The rule to apply here is to use the "right" number of words. You might not need many words in a perfume ad, but you might need a page or two to cover a complex industrial product.

10   As with headlines, body copy can be built around several different formats. *Straight-line copy* is copy that takes off from the headline and develops the selling points for the product. *Narrative copy,* in contrast, tells a story as it persuades; the same selling points may be covered, but in a different context. *Dialog/monolog copy* lets one or two characters in the ad do the selling through what they are

CHECKLIST FOR PRODUCING EXCELLENT COPY

❑ A. Avoid clichés.
- Create fresh, original phrases that vividly convey your message.
- Remember that clever wordplay based on clichés can be quite effective.

❑ B. Watch out for borrowed interest.
- Make sure you don't use inappropriate copy or graphics since they can steal the show from your basic sales message.
- Be sure nothing draws attention from the message.

❑ C. Don't boast.
- Be sure the ad's purpose isn't merely to pat the advertiser on the back.
- Tout success when you must convince nonbuyers that lots of people just like them have purchased your product; this isn't the same as shouting "We're the best!"

❑ D. Make it personal, informal, and relevant.
- Connect with the audience in a way that is personal and comfortable. Pompous, stiff, and overly "businesslike" tends to turn people away.
- Avoid copy that sounds like it belongs in an ad, with too many overblown adjectives and unsupported claims of superiority.

❑ E. Keep it simple, specific, and concise.
- Make your case quickly and stick to the point. This will help you get past all the barriers and filters that people put up to help them select which things they'll pay attention to and which they'll ignore.
- Avoid copy that's confusing, meandering, too long, or too detailed.

❑ F. Give the audience a reason to read, listen, or watch.
- Offer a solution to your audience's problems.
- Entertain your audience.
- Consider any means possible to get your audience to pay attention long enough to get your sales message across.

saying. *Picture-and-caption copy* relies on photographs or illustrations to tell the story, with support from their accompanying captions.

Slogans

The third major category of copy includes *slogans,* or *tag lines,* memorable sayings that convey a selling message. Over the years, Coca-Cola has used such slogans as "Coke is it," "It's the real thing," and "Always Coca-Cola." Slogans are sometimes used as headlines, but not always. Their importance lies in the fact they often become the most memorable result of an advertising campaign. You've probably got a few slogans stuck in your head. Ever heard of "Quality is job number 1," "Don't leave home without it," or "Melts in your mouth, not in your hand"?

The Korean automaker Hyundai recently switched back to the slogan "Cars that make sense," which is a great way of expressing its desired positioning as a lower-cost but still reliable alternative to Japanese and U.S. cars. For several years, the company had used "Hyundai. Yes, Hyundai," but "Cars that make sense" has proved to be a much more effective way to define the value it offers consumers.

● Review Questions

1. What are the particular challenges of copywriting, as opposed to other types of writing?

2. How do the authors classify the main types of ad headlines?

3. What are the main types of body copy styles, according to the authors?

● Discussion and Writing Suggestions

1. Apply the authors' criteria for effective headlines to three or four of the print ads in the portfolio (pages 566–594)—or to three or four ads of your own choosing. To what extent do these headlines succeed in attracting attention, engaging the audience, and fulfilling the other requirements of effective headlines?

2. Imagine that you are a copywriter who has been assigned the account for a particular product (your choice). Develop three possible headlines for an advertisement for this product. Incorporate as many as possible of the criteria for effective headlines discussed by the authors (paragraphs 6–8).

3. Classify the *types* of headlines in a given product category in the print ad portfolio (pages 566–594). Or classify the types of headlines in full-page ads in a single current magazine. Which type of headline appears to be the most common? Which type appears to be the most effective in gaining your attention and making you want to read the body copy?

4. Classify the *types* of body copy styles in a given product category in the ad portfolio. Or classify the types of body copy styles in full-page ads in a single

current magazine. How effective is the copy in selling the virtues of the product or the institution or organization behind the product?

5. Assess the effectiveness of a given ad either in the ad portfolio or in a recent magazine or newspaper. Apply the criteria discussed by the authors in the box labeled "Checklist for Producing Excellent Copy." For example, to what extent is the copy fresh and original? To what extent does the copy make the message "personal, informal, and relevant" to the target audience? To what extent is the message "simple, specific, and concise"?

6. Write your own ad for a product that you like and use frequently. In composing the ad, apply the principles of effective headlines, subheads, body copy, and slogans discussed by the authors. Apply also the principles of "Checklist for Producing Excellent Copy." You will also need to think of (though not necessarily create) an effective graphic for the ad.

Selling Happiness: Two Pitches from Mad Men

One of the surprise TV hits of 2007 was *Mad Men,* an original series about the advertising business, created by writer/producer Matt Weiner for the American Movie Classics (AMC) network. *Mad Men*—short for Madison Avenue men—follows Don Draper, creative director of Sterling Cooper, a medium-size New York ad agency, along with his colleagues and his family (and his mistresses), as he maneuvers his way through the ruthlessly competitive world of advertising during the early 1960s. The show won Golden Globe Awards for best TV dramatic series for two consecutive seasons. With high-quality writing (creator Matt Weiner was also a writer and producer for *The Sopranos*), top-flight acting, and spot-on production design and period costumes, *Mad Men* became an instant classic, must-see television.

Two segments from the first season depict a time-honored business ritual: the "pitch," in which one or more creative/business people attempt to sell their idea to a client in hopes of securing a lucrative contract. (In Hollywood, writers or directors pitch their ideas for films to the studio or to potential financial backers.) As the "Carousel" segment begins, Don Draper (portrayed by Jon Hamm) and his colleagues (accounts director Herman ["Duck"] Phillips [Mark Moses], copywriter Harry Crane [in glasses; Rich Sommer], and art director Salvatore Romano [Bryan Batt]) make a pitch to a couple of clients from Eastman Kodak. The Kodak engineers have just come up with a turning "wheel" to house the slides for its new projector, and the Kodak business execs are making the rounds of New York ad agencies to hear them pitch campaigns to sell this new product. In "It's Toasted," Draper attempts to explain to the clients that despite the federal government's recent lawsuits against cigarette manufacturers for making false health claims about their products, and despite the fact that "[w]e have six identical companies making six identical products," the company can still reassure customers about the safety of its particular brand of cigarettes.

You may view these segments by accessing YouTube (YouTube.com), Google (google.com) or Bing (bing.com) and searching for *"mad men carousel" and "mad men it's toasted"* Select the 3 minute 25 second version of the Carousel scene.

● Discussion and Writing Suggestions

1. What do these scenes say about the way that advertising people sell consumer products to the public? What other examples come to mind of items of hardware sold in a manner similar to how Draper and his creative team propose to sell the "Carousel"?

2. Study Don's reaction as he shows the slides of his family. What do you think is passing through his mind during the presentation? Does he appear to believe what he is saying? Does the writer of this scene suggest that advertising is nothing but fakery? Explain.

3. Relate the "Carousel" scene to Jib Fowles' "Fifteen Basic Appeals" of advertising. Which appeals are most at work during the presentation of the "Carousel"? Once you have analyzed "Carousel" with respect to one or more motivations reviewed by Fowles, comment on the emotional pull of the "Carousel" pitch as Draper develops it. Even though you understand how Draper's appeal may work psychologically (according to Fowles), can you still be emotionally vulnerable to the pitch? Did you find Draper's presentation moving? Discuss.

4. At one point during the Lucky Strike "It's Toasted" pitch (immediately before the first line in the clip), Don notes: "We have six identical companies making six identical products." How does his solution for making this particular client's "identical" product distinctive" (in this case, making it "safe") bring to mind other successful advertising campaigns that have created distinctiveness through words alone?

5. The sales pitch depicted in these meetings were set in an era some fifty years ago. To what extent do you think advertising for high-tech products has become more or less sophisticated than advertising was during the early 1960s? (You may wish to refer not only to this scene, but also to print ads of the same period, as exemplified in the "Portfolio.") To what extent—if at all—might today's consumers be less apt to be captivated and sold by the kind of appeals dramatized in this scene? Cite particular examples of contemporary advertising, both print and TV.

A Portfolio of Print Advertisements

The following portfolio offers for your consideration and analysis a selection of 42 full-page advertisements that appeared in American and British magazines between 1945 (shortly after the end of World War II) and 2003. In terms of products represented, the ads fall into several categories—cigarettes, alcohol (beer and liquor), automobiles, food and drink, household cleaners, lotions, and perfumes. The portfolio also includes a few miscellaneous ads for such diverse products as men's hats, telephones, and airlines. These ads originally appeared in such magazines as *Time, Newsweek, U.S. News and World Report, Sports Illustrated, Ladies Home Journal, Ebony,* and *Ms.* A number of the ads were researched in the Advertising Archive, an online (and subscription) collection maintained by The Picture Desk.

The advertisements in this portfolio are *not* representative of all ads that appeared during the last 60 years. We made our selection largely on the basis of how interesting, striking, provocative, and unusual these particular ads appeared to us. Admittedly, the selection process was biased. That said, the ads in this portfolio offer rich possibilities for analysis. With practice, and by applying principles for analysis that you will find in the earlier selections in this chapter, you will be able to "read" into these ads numerous messages about cultural attitudes toward gender relations, romance, smoking, and automobiles. The ads will prompt you to consider why we buy products that we may not need or why we prefer one product over another when the two products are essentially identical. Each advertisement is a window into the culture. Through careful analysis, you will gain insights not only into the era in which the ads were produced but also into shifting cultural attitudes over the last 60 years.

Following the portfolio, we provide two or three specific questions for each ad (pages 595–601), questions designed to stimulate your thinking about the particular ways that the graphics and text are intended to work. As you review the ads, however, you may want to think about the more general questions about advertisements raised by the readings in this chapter:

1. What appears to be the target audience for the ad? If this ad was produced more than two decades ago, does its same target audience exist today? If so, how would this audience likely react today to the ad?

2. What is the primary appeal made by the ad, in terms of Fowles's categories? What, if any, are the secondary appeals?

3. What assumptions do the ad's sponsors make about such matters as (1) commonly accepted roles of women and men; (2) the relationship between the sexes; (3) the priorities of men and women?

4. What is the chief attention-getting device in the ad?

5. How does the headline and body text communicate the ad's essential appeals?

6. How do the ad's graphics communicate the ad's essential appeals?

7. How do the expressions, clothing, and postures of the models, as well as the physical objects in the illustration, help communicate the ad's message?

8. How do the graphic qualities of balance, proportion, movement, unity, clarity and simplicity, and emphasis help communicate the ad's message?

Consider, also, the following evaluative questions[1]:

- Is it a good ad? Why?

- What do you like most about it? Why?

- What do you dislike the most? Why?

- Do you think it "works"? Why? or Why not?

- How could the ad be improved?

- Could the sender have conveyed the same message using other strategies, other persuasive means? If so, explain.

- Even if you don't believe that this particular ad works or persuades you, is there anything in the ad that still affects you or persuades you indirectly?

- Does the ad have effects on you perhaps not intended by its creators?

---

[1]Lars Thoger Christensen, "How to Analyze an Advertisement." University of Southern Denmark—Odense. Jan. 2004, (http://wms-soros.mngt.waikato.ac.nz/NR/rdonlyres/ebabz4jhzmg5fr5p45ypc53 mdvuxva5wxhe7323onb4ylelbaq3se5xjrslfc4mi3qgk6dmsx5dqbp/Advertisinganalysis.doc).

"...not a creature was stirring..."

(None, save the doctor going out on a call.)

You remember how it starts—that beloved old Christmas poem:

'Twas the night before Christmas, when all through the house Not a creature was stirring,—not even a mouse.

Well, that isn't always true for the doctor. Sometimes there's just no rest at all for him—even on Christmas Eve.

Blizzard or heat wave... December or July... night or day... near or far... early or late... no matter when you call, he comes!

According to a recent nationwide survey:

MORE DOCTORS SMOKE CAMELS THAN ANY OTHER CIGARETTE

YOUR "T-ZONE" WILL TELL YOU...

T for Taste...
T for Throat...

that's your proving ground for any cigarette. See if Camels don't suit your "T-Zone" to a "T."

R. J. Reynolds Tobacco Co.
Winston-Salem, N. C.

● Not a single branch of medicine was overlooked in this nationwide survey made by three leading independent research organizations. To 113,597 doctors from Canada to Mexico, from the Atlantic to the Pacific went the query — *What cigarette do you smoke, Doctor?*

The brand named most was Camel.

Like anyone else, a doctor smokes for pleasure. He appreciates rich, full flavor and cool mildness just as any other smoker. If you don't happen to be a Camel smoker now, try Camels. Let your "T-Zone" give you the answer.

Camels *Costlier Tobaccos*

Camels, 1947

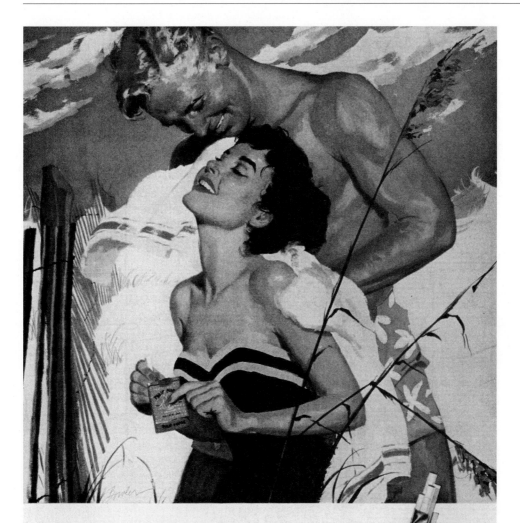

Gently Does It

GENTLENESS makes good friends in fun-making . . . and in a cigarette, where gentleness is one of the greatest requirements of modern taste. That's why today's Philip Morris, born gentle, refined to special gentleness in the making, makes so many friends among our young smokers. Enjoy the gentle pleasure, the fresh unfiltered flavor, of today's Philip Morris. In the convenient snap-open pack, regular or smart king-size.

Philip Morris

. . . gentle for modern taste

Philip Morris, 1950s

Marlboro, 1970s

Camels, 1979

Camels, 2000s

America is returning to the genuine—in foods, fashions and tastes. Today's trend to Ballantine light Ale fits right into this modern picture. In all the world, no other beverage brewed has such extra excellence brewed into it. And "Brewer's Gold" is one big reason for Ballantine Ale's deep, rich, genuine flavor.

They all ask for ale **Ballantine** LIGHT **Ale !**

Ballantine Ale, 1950s

BACARDI. rum is so "mixable"...
It's a one-brand bar.

Big, bold highballs, sassy Daiquiris, cool tonics and colas—Bacardi rum is enjoyable always and *all* ways. Extra Special: our man Fernando is pouring very rare Bacardi Añejo rum (Ahn-YAY-ho), one of the fine rums from Bacardi. So incredibly smooth he enjoys it even in a snifter. Try it, too!

*BACARDI IMPORTS, INC., MIAMI, FLA. RUM. 80 PROOF.

Bacardi Rum, 1960s

AT THE PULITZER FOUNTAIN, N.Y.C.

BLENDED WHISKEY • 86 AND 90 PROOF • 65% GRAIN NEUTRAL SPIRITS
THE FLEISCHMANN DISTILLING CORPORATION, NEW YORK CITY

Fleischmann's Whiskey, 1964

Hennessy Cognac, 1968

The morning after should be just as beautiful as the night before.
Pure clean Cossack Vodka.

WITH LIME, ORANGE, TOMATO JUICE, BITTER LEMON, TONIC, GINGER ALE, OR WITH ANYTHING YOU LIKE.

Cossack Vodka, 1970s

Miller Beer, 1979

Budweiser Beer, 1990s

Of all the De Soto cars ever built, 7 out of 10 are still running

8 out of 10 owners say, "De Soto is the most satisfactory car I ever owned"*

#FROM A MAIL SURVEY AMONG THOUSANDS OF OWNERS
OF 1941 AND 1942 DE SOTO CARS

DE SOTO DIVISION OF CHRYSLER CORPORATION

De Soto, 1947

"Ford's out Front from a Woman's Angle"

1. **"I don't know** synthetic enamel from a box of my children's paints . . . but if synthetic enamel is what it takes to make that beautiful, shiny Ford finish, I'm all for it!

2. **"My husband says the brakes** are self-centering and hydraulic—whatever that means! All I know is they're so easy that I can taxi the children all day without tiring out!

3. **"Peter, he's my teen-age son,** tells me that 'Ford is the only car in its price class with a choice of a 100-horsepower V-8 engine or a brilliant new Six.' He says no matter which engine people pick, they're out front with Ford!

6. **"Now here's another thing** women like and that's a blissfully comfortable ride—one that isn't bumpity-bump even on some of our completely forgotten roads."

Listen to the Ford Show starring Dinah Shore on Columbia Network Stations Wednesday Evenings.

4. **"The interior of our Ford is** strictly my department! It's tailored with the dreamiest broadcloth. Such a perfect fit! Mary Jane says women help design Ford interiors. There's certainly a woman's touch there!

5. **"Do you like** lovely silver, beautifully simple and chaste looking? That's what I always think of when I touch those smart Ford door handles and window openers.

There's a *Ford* in your future

Ford, 1947

Worth Its Price

If a motorist wanted to make the move to Cadillac solely for the car's prestige—he would most certainly be justified in doing so. For the Cadillac car has never stood so high in public esteem as it does today—and the rewards which grow out of this unprecedented acceptance comprise the rarest and greatest satisfactions in all motordom.

There is, for instance, *the inescapable feeling of pride* that comes with ownership of so distinguished and beloved a possession . . . the wonderful *sense of wellbeing* that comes from having reached a point of achievement where you can enjoy one of the world's most sought-after manufactured products . . . and the *marvelous feeling of confidence and self-esteem* that is found

CADILLAC MOTOR CAR DIVISION

Cadillac, 1954

in PRESTIGE !

in the respect and admiration universally accorded the owner of a Cadillac car. Those who presently enjoy these unique Cadillac virtues will tell you that they are, in themselves, worth the car's whole purchase price.

Of course, most motorists would hesitate to take such a step purely for their personal edification. But in Cadillac's case, this wonderful prestige is actually a "bonus", so to speak—an extra dividend that comes with every Cadillac car, in addition to its breath-taking styling, its magnificent performance, its superlative luxury and its remarkable economy.

Have you seen and driven the 1954 Cadillac? If you haven't, then you've a truly wonderful adventure awaiting you—and one that you should postpone no longer.

GENERAL MOTORS CORPORATION

Cadillac

This is your reward for the great Dodge advance—the daring new, dramatic new '56 Dodge.

The Magic Touch of Tomorrow!

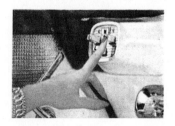

The *look* of success! The *feel* of success! The *power* of success!
They come to you in a dramatically beautiful, dynamically powered
new Dodge that introduces the ease and safety of push-button driving
–the Magic Touch of Tomorrow! It is a truly great value.

New '56 DODGE

Dodge, 1955

Corvette Sting Ray Sport Coupe with eight standard safety features, including outside rearview mirror. Use it always before passing.

The day she flew the coupe

What manner of woman is this, you ask, who stands in the midst of a mountain stream eating a peach?

Actually she's a normal everyday girl except that she and her husband own the Corvette Coupe in the background. (He's at work right now, wondering where he misplaced his car keys.)

The temptation, you see, was over-powering. They'd had the car a whole week now, and not once had he offered to let her drive. His excuse was that this, uh, was a big hairy sports car. Too much for a woman to handle: the trigger-quick steering, the independent rear suspension, the disc brakes—plus the 4-speed transmission and that 425-hp engine they had ordered—egad! He would teach her to drive it some weekend. So he said.

That's why she hid the keys, forc-ing him to seek public transporta-tion. Sure of his departure, she went to the garage, started the Corvette, and was off for the hills, soon upshifting and downshifting as smoothly as he. His car. Hard to drive. What propaganda!

'66 CORVETTE BY CHEVROLET
Chevrolet Division of General Motors, Detroit, Michigan

Corvette, 1966

Jeep vehicle, 2003

Good School Day Lunches

make healthier, brighter youngsters

Many children do not get adequate lunches! And yet upon proper food depends not only their future health, but today's well-being, cheerfulness — and even report cards!

Lunch should include a hot dish, and be substantial but easy to digest. Good nourishing soup is a big help — and Campbell's Vegetable Soup is just right! Children love it, and it brings them all the sturdy goodness of 15 different garden vegetables combined with a rich, invigorating beef stock. No wonder mothers everywhere agree "It's almost a meal in itself!"

Campbell's VEGETABLE SOUP

LOOK FOR THE RED-AND-WHITE LABEL

A WEEK'S SCHOOL LUNCHES

MONDAY
Campbell's Vegetable Soup
Peanut Butter Sandwich
Baked Custard   Celery
Orange
Graham Crackers

TUESDAY
Campbell's Tomato Soup
Cottage Cheese and Orange Marmalade Sandwich
Carrot Sticks
Banana
Molasses Cookies

WEDNESDAY
Campbell's Scotch Broth
Lettuce and Hard-Cooked Egg Salad
Toasted Raisin Bread
Fresh Pear
Cocoa

THURSDAY
Campbell's Vegetable Soup
Cold Roast Veal Sandwich
Baked Apple   Celery
Milk

FRIDAY
Campbell's Cream of Spinach Soup
Toasted Tuna Fish Salad Sandwich
Sliced Tomatoes
Stewed Peaches   Chocolate Milk

Campbell's, 1945

Coca-Cola, 1945

What's for dinner, Duchess?

Prediction: The new wives of 1947 are going to have more fun in the kitchen.

Previous cooking experience is desirable, perhaps, but not essential. There are so many new easy-to-use foods, so many new ways to prepare foods, so many interesting ways to serve foods, cooking will be a novel and exciting adventure.

Further prediction: Cheese dishes will be featured more often on their menus. They'll know that cheese gives tastiness and variety to meals. And cheese, like milk (nature's most nearly perfect food), is rich in protein, calcium, phosphorus, in vitamins A and G.

Yes, we have a personal interest in cheese. For Kraft, pioneer in cheese, is a unit of National Dairy. And what we've said about housewives using more cheese is entirely true.

It's also true that they're learning more about the whys and wherefores of food each year — just as the scientists in our laboratories are learning more about better ways to process, improve and supply it.

These men are backed by the resources of a great organization. They explore every field of dairy products, discover new ones. And the health of America benefits constantly by this National Dairy research.

Dedicated to the wider use and better understanding of dairy products as human food . . . as a base for the development of new products and materials . . . as a source of health and enduring progress on the farms and in the towns and cities of America.

NATIONAL DAIRY
PRODUCTS CORPORATION
AND AFFILIATED COMPANIES

National Dairy Products Corporation, 1947

MAY: # Heavens, Ann —
wish I could clean up quick as that!

ANN: You could, hon! Just use a cleanser that doesn't leave dirt-catching scratches.

MAY: Goodness! What in the world do scratches have to do with it?

ANN: A lot, silly! Those tiny scratches you get from gritty cleansers hold onto dirt and double your cleaning time.

MAY: Well, you old smartie! I'd never thought of *that* before.

ANN: I hadn't thought of it either—till I discovered Bon Ami! See how fine-textured and white it is. It just *slides* dirt off—and when you rinse it away, it doesn't leave any of that horrid grit in the tub.

MAY: Say no more, darling! From now on there's going to be a new cleaning team in our house —me and Bon Ami!

Bon Ami

THE **SPEEDY** CLEANSER *that*
"hasn't scratched yet!"

EASY ON YOUR HANDS, Bon Ami *Powder* is the ideal cleanser for kitchen sinks, as well as bathtubs. Also try Bon Ami *Cake* for cleaner windows, mirrors and windshields.

Bon Ami, 1947

Mrs. Dorian Mehle of Morrisville, Pa., is all three: a housewife, a mother, and a very lovely lady.

"I wash 22,000 dishes a year... but I'm proud of my pretty hands!"

You and Dorian Mehle have something in common. Every year, you wash a stack of dishes a quarter-mile high!

Detergents make your job so much easier. They cut right into grease and grime. They get you through dishwashing in much less time, but while they dissolve grease, they also take away the natural oils and youthful softness of your hands!

Although Dorian hasn't given up detergents her hands are as soft, as smooth, as young-looking as a teenager's. Her secret is no secret at all. It's the world's best-known beauty routine. It's pure, white Jergens Lotion, after every chore.

When you smooth on Jergens Lotion, this liquid formula doesn't just "coat" your hands. It penetrates right away, to help *replace* that softening moisture your skin needs.

Jergens Lotion has two ingredients doctors recommend for softening. Women must be recommending it, too, for more women use it than any other hand care in the world. Dorian's husband is the best testimonial to Jergens Lotion care. Even after years of married life, he still loves to hold her pretty hands!

Use Jergens Lotion like a prescription: three times a day, after every meal!

Now—lotion dispenser FREE of extra cost with $1.00 size. Supply limited.

Use JERGENS LOTION—avoid detergent hands

Jergens Lotion, 1954

Madam! Suppose you traded jobs with your husband?

You can just bet the first thing he'd ask for would be a telephone in the kitchen.

You wouldn't catch him dashing to another room every time the telephone rang, or he had to make a call.

He doesn't have to do it in his office in town. It would be mighty helpful if you didn't have to do it in your "office" at home.

That's in the kitchen where you do so much of your work. And it's right there that an additional telephone comes in so handy for so many things.

Along with a lot of convenience is that nice feeling of pride in having the best of everything—especially if it is one of those attractive new telephones in color.

P.S. Additional telephones in kitchen, bedroom and other convenient places around the house cost little. The service charge is just pennies a day.

Bell Telephone System

Bell Telephone, 1956

The phone company wants more installers like Alana MacFarlane.

Alana MacFarlane is a 20-year-old from San Rafael, California. She's one of our first women telephone installers. She won't be the last.

We also have several hundred male telephone operators. And a policy that there are no all-male or all-female jobs at the phone company.

We want the men and women of the telephone company to do what they want to do, and do best.

For example, Alana likes working outdoors. "I don't go for office routine," she said. "But as an installer, I get plenty of variety and a chance to move around."

Some people like to work with their hands, or, like Alana, get a kick out of working 20 feet up in the air.

Others like to drive trucks. Some we're helping to develop into good managers.

Today, when openings exist, local Bell Companies are offering applicants and present employees some jobs they may never have thought about before. We want to help all advance to the best of their abilities.

AT&T and your local Bell Company are equal opportunity employers.

Bell Telephone, 1974

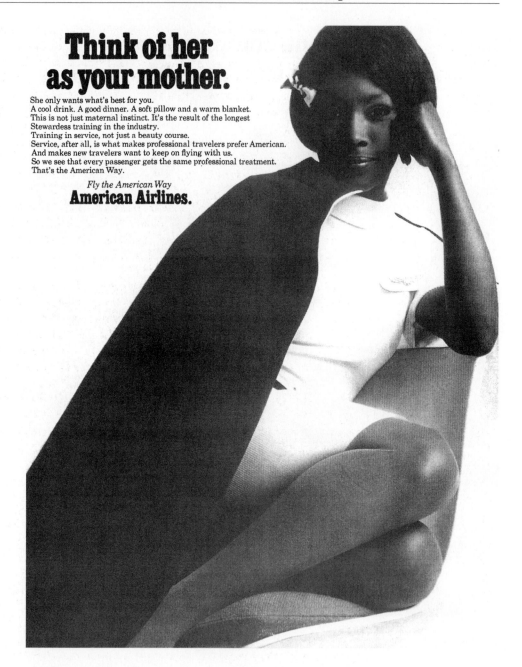

Think of her as your mother.

She only wants what's best for you.
A cool drink. A good dinner. A soft pillow and a warm blanket.
This is not just maternal instinct. It's the result of the longest
Stewardess training in the industry.
Training in service, not just a beauty course.
Service, after all, is what makes professional travelers prefer American.
And makes new travelers want to keep on flying with us.
So we see that every passenger gets the same professional treatment.
That's the American Way.

Fly the American Way
American Airlines.

American Airlines, 1968

Charlie, 1988

Soloflex, 1985

● Discussion and Writing Suggestions

TOBACCO

Camels, 1947 (p. 566)

1. How does the intended appeal of this ad differ most dramatically from a comparable ad today?

2. What kind of psychological appeals are made by the picture in the top half of this ad and the text accompanying it? How does the image of a doctor out on a night call tie in, for selling purposes, with the ad's headline?

Philip Morris, 1950s (p. 567)

1. How do the placement, posture, and dress of the models in the ad help create its essential psychological appeal? Why do you suppose (in relation to the selling of cigarettes) the models' eyes are closed?

2. Discuss some of the messages communicated both by the graphic and the text of this ad. Focus in particular on the quality of "gentleness" emphasized in the ad.

Marlboro, 1970s (p. 568)

1. The Marlboro Man has become one of the most famous—and successful—icons of American advertising. What elements of the Marlboro Man (and his setting, Marlboro Country) do you notice, and what role do these elements play in the appeal being made by this ad?

2. This ad appeared during the 1970s. (The popularity of the Marlboro Man extended into the 1980s, however.) To what extent do you think it would have the same appeal today?

3. Comment on the elements of graphic design (balance, proportion, movement, unity, clarity and simplicity, emphasis) that help make this ad effective. Focus particularly on the element of movement.

Camels, 1979 (p. 569)

1. What do the relative positions and postures of the man and the woman in the ad indicate about the ad's basic appeal?

2. What roles do the props—particularly, the motorcycle and the models' outfits—and the setting play in helping to sell the product?

3. How do the design elements in the ad emphasize the product?

4. Compare the graphic elements of this ad to those of the Fleischmann's Whiskey ad (page 573).

Camels, 2000s (p. 570)

1. This is an example of retro appeal. What elements make it so? What elements mark the ad, on the other hand, as a contemporary one? How does the combination of retro and contemporary elements (including, for example, the posture and attitude of the model) contribute to create a particular type of appeal?

2. Compare and contrast the three Camels ads presented in this section of the portfolio. Focus on the psychological appeals, the cultural values implied in the ads, and the graphic and textual means used to persuade the buyer to smoke Camels.

BEER AND LIQUOR

Ballantine Ale, 1950s (p. 571)

1. This illustration, reminiscent of some of Norman Rockwell's paintings, is typical of many beer and ale ads in the 1950s, which depict a group of well-dressed young adults enjoying their brew at a social event. Comment on the distinctive graphic elements in this ad and speculate as to why these elements are seldom employed in contemporary advertisements for beer and ale. Why, in other words, does this ad seem old-fashioned?

2. Contrast the appeal and graphics of this ad with the ads for Miller and Budweiser later in this portfolio.

3. Identify the adjectives in the body text and attempt to correlate them to the graphic in helping to construct the message of the ad.

Bacardi Rum, 1960s (p. 572)

1. What meaning is conveyed by the placement, posture, and expressions of the four models in this ad? How do you think this meaning is intended to help sell the product? (Does the picture remind you of a particular movie hero?)

2. Comment on the significance of the props in the photo.

3. How does the text ("Big, bold highballs, sassy Daiquiris, cool tonics...") help reinforce the meaning created by the picture?

Fleischmann's Whiskey, 1964 (p. 573)

1. Comment on (1) the significance of the extra-large bottle of whiskey; (2) the stances of the two models in the ad; (3) the way the headline contributes to the ad's meaning.

2. Compare and contrast the graphic in this ad with that of the 1979 Camels ad earlier in this portfolio (the man on the motorcycle).

Hennessy Cognac, 1968 (p. 574)

1. What is the primary appeal of this ad? How do the woman, the horse, and the headline work to create and reinforce this appeal?

2. Compare and contrast this ad to the Webster Cigars ad in terms of their appeal and their graphics.

Cossack Vodka, 1970s (p. 575)

1. What is the essential appeal behind this ad?

2. The comic book style of the drawing is reminiscent of the work of Roy Lichtenstein (1923–1997), an American painter who drew inspiration from advertisements and romance magazines, as well as comic books, to depict and parody artifacts of pop culture. What is the effect of this particular style on creating—and perhaps commenting upon—the message in the text balloon and in the ad in which it appears?

3. How does the text at the bottom of the ad reinforce the message created by the graphic? In particular, how is this message intended to sell the product?

Miller Beer, 1979 (p. 576)

1. To what extent does this 1979 ad embody marketing techniques for beer that are still employed today?

2. Comment on the posture and expressions of the three models depicted in the ad. How do these elements help create the ad's essential appeal?

3. Compare and contrast this ad with the 1950s Ballantine Ale ad earlier in this portfolio (page 571).

Budweiser Beer, 1990s (p. 577)

1. To what extent is this ad based on a similar appeal as the preceding Miller ad? To what extent is it based on other appeals?

2. What's the advantage (in terms of effectiveness of appeal) of using the second person—"you"—in the body text? How does the text attempt to make the connection between the product advertised and the activities of the football players? To what extent do you think that this is an effective ad?

3. Comment on the workings and effectiveness of the graphic design elements in this ad.

AUTOMOBILES

De Soto, 1947 (p. 578)

1. How does the scene portrayed in the illustration help create the basic appeal of this ad? Focus on as many significant individual elements of the illustration as you can.

2. To what extent does the caption (in the illustration) and the headline support the message communicated by the graphic?

3. Explain why both this ad and the preceding Cadillac ad are products of their particular times.

Ford, 1947 (p. 579)

1. Cite and discuss those textual elements in the ad that reflect a traditional conception of the American woman.

2. How do the visual elements of the ad reinforce the assumptions about traditional gender roles reflected in the ad?

Cadillac, 1954 (pp. 580–581)

1. What is the particular marketing strategy behind this ad? Based on the ad's text, compose a memo from the head of marketing to the chief copywriter proposing this particular ad and focusing on the strategy. The memo doesn't have to be cynical or to insult the prospective Cadillac buyers; it should just be straightforward and direct.

2. How do the ad's graphics reinforce the message in the text?

Dodge, 1955 (p. 582)

1. Discuss the multiple appeals of this ad. How are these appeals reflected in the ad's text and graphics? For instance, discuss the angle from which the automobile is photographed.

2. Both this ad and the 1947 Ford ad (page 579) feature one or more women in the graphic. Compare and contrast the use of women in the two ads.

Corvette, 1966 (p. 583)

1. How do the graphic elements reinforce the message developed in the text of this ad?

2. Comment on the dress and the posture of the model, as these relate to the ad's essential appeal. What's the significance of the woman eating a peach in a mountain stream?

3. The body text in this ad tells a story. What kind of husband-wife dynamic is implied by this story? To what extent do you find similarities between the implied gender roles in this ad and those in the 1947 Ford ad ("Ford's out Front from a Woman's Angle," page 579)? To what extent do you find differences, ones that may be attributable to the 20 years between the two ads?

Jeep vehicle, 2003 (p. 584)

1. Explain the meaning of the ad's headline.

2. Discuss the graphic, in terms of the ad's headline. Consider the significance of the viewing angle.

FOOD, CLEANSERS, BEAUTY PRODUCTS, AND OTHER

Campbell's, 1945 (p. 585)

1. What kind of appeal is being made in the first two sentences of the body text? How does the graphic in the top half of the ad support this appeal?

2. What kind of marketing strategy is behind the menu in the lower-right portion of the ad?

Coca-Cola, 1945 (p. 586)

1. This ad appeared shortly after the conclusion of World War II. How do the text and the graphics of the ad take advantage of the international mood at the time? Comment on the appearance and arrangement of the men portrayed in the ad.

2. Compare the strategy of this Coca-Cola ad (text and graphics) with that of the 1950s Ballantine ad (page 571).

National Dairy Products Corporation, 1947 (p. 587)

1. How does the couple pictured in the ad illustrate gender expectations of the period? Comment on the dress, postures, and expressions of the models.

2. What, exactly, is this ad *selling*? (It is presented more as a newsmagazine article than as a conventional advertisement.) How is the appeal tied to contemporary developments by "scientists" and their "research," particularly as these relate to "the new wives of 1947"?

3. What does the text of this ad imply about the situation of young married couples in postwar households?

Bon Ami, 1947 (p. 588)

1. How do the text and graphics of this ad illustrate a bygone cultural attitude toward gender roles? Notice, in particular, the dress, postures, and expressions of the women pictured, as well as the style of the illustration. Focus also on the wording of the text.

2. In terms of Jib Fowles's categories, what kind of appeal is being made by the Bon Ami ad?

Jergens Lotion, 1954 (p. 589)

1. Compare and contrast the appeals and the strategies of this Jergens Lotion ad and the Bon Ami ad preceding it. Are the ads intended to appeal to the same target audiences? To what extent are the psychological appeals of the two ads similar? Compare the illustrations of the two ads. How do they differ in basic strategy?

2. The model in the Jergens Lotion ad is immaculately dressed and groomed, and she is sitting among stacks of fine china (as opposed to everyday dishware). What do you think is the marketing strategy behind these graphic choices?

Bell Telephone, 1956 (p. 590)

1. Discuss the attitude toward gender roles implicit in the 1956 Bell ad. How do the graphics, the headline, and the body text reinforce this attitude? What is the significance of the quotation marks around "office" in the final sentence of the third paragraph?

2. Notice that the woman at the desk seems a lot more comfortable and at ease than the man holding the crying baby and the dishes. What does this fact tell us about the attitudes toward gender roles of those who created this ad?

Bell Telephone, 1974 (p. 591)

1. Compare and contrast the 1956 Bell ad with the 1974 Bell ad, in terms of their attitudes toward gender roles. How do the text and graphics reinforce the essential differences?

2. The 1956 Bell ad pictures a woman at a desk (a white-collar job); the 1974 ad pictures a woman working at a telephone pole (a blue-collar job). Would the 1974 ad have the same impact if "Alana MacFarlane" had, like her 1956 counterpart, been pictured at a desk?

3. Like the 1954 Cadillac ad (pages 580–581), the 1974 Bell ad seems more of a public service announcement than a conventional advertisement. Compare and contrast these ads in terms of their messages to readers.

American Airlines, 1968 (p. 592)

1. Discuss the mixed messages (in terms of appeal) being transmitted by the American Airlines ad. To what extent do you think the apparently conflicting appeals make for an effective ad?

2. Comment on the dress, pose, and expression of the model in the ad, which appeared in *Ebony* magazine. How do these create a different impact than would an illustration, say, of a flight attendant serving a drink or giving a pillow to an airline passenger?

Charlie, 1988 (p. 593)

1. Notice the woman's outfit, as well as her briefcase, in the Charlie ad. How is the appearance of this woman as significant as the appearance of the woman in the Hennessy Cognac ad (page 574) for the ad's basic message?

2. The Charlie ad and the 1974 Bell ad (page 591) are as different as can be imagined from the Jergens ad. Yet, the Bell and the Charlie ads make quite different appeals. Explain. Consider, for example, how a woman—or a man—of the late 1940s might respond to the Bell ad, on the one hand, and the Charlie ad, on the other.

Soloflex, 1985 (p. 594)

1. How does the illustration in this ad reinforce the basic appeal of the headline?

2. Ads are frequently criticized for the incongruity between illustration and product being advertised—for example, a scantily clad woman posed provocatively in front of a pickup truck. To what extent does the Soloflex ad present an appropriate fit between graphic and product advertised?

A Portfolio of TV Commercials

The world's first television commercial was a ten-second Bulova watch ad broadcast in 1941. But it wasn't until the 1950s, when TV became a mass medium, that the commercial became a ubiquitous feature of popular culture. Before viewers had the technology to fast-forward through commercials, many probably regarded TV ads as annoying, occasionally informative or entertaining, but generally unnecessary accompaniments to their television experience. But of course, the commercial is not simply an extraneous byproduct of TV programming. It is television's very reason for existence. Before the age of public TV and of cable and satellite providers, television programs were financed entirely by the companies that created the commercials and that paid networks and local stations to broadcast them. Viewed from a marketing angle, the only purpose of commercial television is to provide a medium for advertising. The news, comedy, drama, game, and variety shows offered by TV are simply ways of luring viewers to watch the commercials.

Still, the unceasing deluge of commercials of every type means that advertisers have to figure out ways of making their messages stand out by being unusually creative, funny, surprising, or otherwise noteworthy. The standard jingles, primitive animation, catchphrases ("Winston tastes good like a cigarette should"), and problem-solution minidramas of TV commercials work for awhile but are quickly forgotten in the onslaught of new messages. It becomes the job of advertising agencies (of the type represented in *Mad Men*) that create both print and TV ads to make their clients' products stand out by ever more ingenious and striking ways of delivering their messages. To do this, these agencies rely not just on information about the product and clever audiovisual techniques; they attempt to respond to what they believe consumers crave, deep down. TV commercials, no less than print ads, rely on psychological appeals of the type discussed by Jib Fowles in his "Fifteen Basic Appeals."

The following portfolio includes some of the most noteworthy and successful TV commercials of the past sixty years. Many (though not all) of these commercials are featured in Bernice Kanner's *The 100 Best TV Commercials...and Why They Worked* (1999), where you will find additional description and commentary. To access the commercials, go to YouTube (YouTube.com), and enter the search terms provided under the commercial's title into the search box. In some cases, additional information is presented, in brackets, to help you navigate to the commercial. In cases where multiple versions of the same commercial are available, you may have to experiment to determine which one offers the best video and audio quality. In a few cases, uploaded commercials have been truncated, so you should generally select the longest version. In some cases, the indicated commercials may have been removed from the YouTube website. No matter; thousands more remain available for your observation and consideration.

As with the print ads, we provide two or three sets of specific questions for each TV commercial. These questions are intended to stimulate your thinking and writing process about the particular ways that the audio and visuals are intended to work. As you review these commercials, however, you might be thinking of the more general questions about advertisements raised by the preceding readings in the chapter. Here are some of those general questions:

1. What appears to be the target audience for this TV commercial? If it was produced more than two decades ago, how would this target audience likely react today to the ad?

2. What is the primary appeal made by the ad, in terms of Fowles's categories? What, if any, are the secondary appeals?

3. What is the chief attention-getting technique in the commercial?

4. How does the commercial make use of such tools as humor, surprise, fantasy, wonder, human interest, or social concern to achieve its goals?

5. What is the relationship between the visuals and the audio track? How do audio and video work together—or in contrast—to achieve the sponsor's purpose?

6. How do the commercial's visual techniques work to convey the message? Consider camera movement (or the lack of camera movement); the style and pace of editing (the juxtaposition of individual shots); and visual composition (the framing of the people and/or objects within the shot).

7. How do the expressions, the clothing, the postures of the person or people, and the physical objects in the shots help communicate the ad's message?

8. How do the words used by the actor(s) or by the voice-over narrator work to communicate the message of the commercial?

Consider, also, the following evaluative questions[1]:

- Is it a good ad? Why?

- What do you like most about it? Why?

- What do you dislike the most? Why?

- Do you think it "works"? Why? Or Why not?

- How could the ad be improved?

- Could the sender have conveyed the same message using other strategies, other persuasive means? If so, explain.

- Even if you don't believe that this particular ad works or persuades you, is there anything in the ad that still affects you or persuades you indirectly?

- Does the ad have effects on you perhaps not intended by its creators?

---

[1]Lars Thoger Christensen, "How to Analyze an Advertisement." University of Southern Denmark—Odense. Jan. 2004. <http://wms-soros.mngt.waikato.ac.nz/NR/rdonlyres/ebabz4jhzmg5fr5p45ypc53mdvuxva5wxhe7323onb4ylelbaq3se5xjrslfc4mi3qgk6dmsx5dqbp/Advertisinganalysis.doc>

Discussion and Writing Suggestions

Note: Because Web content frequently changes without warning, not all of the listed videos may be available when you attempt to access them. It is possible that errant searches may lead to other videos with objectionable content. Such videos, as well as user-submitted comments under the specified videos below, do not reflect the views of the authors or of Pearson Publishing.

COMMERCIALS OF THE 1960s

Volkswagen: Snowplow

YouTube Search Terms: vw snow plow commercial [select black and white version]

1. In the 1960s Volkswagen became famous in the United States not only for its funny-looking cars—so different in style from Detroit's massive passenger vehicles—but also for its "soft-sell" approach to print ads and TV commercials. How does that soft-sell approach work in this ad? What is the sales strategy, as embodied in the relatively primitive visuals and the voice-over track? What exactly is being sold?

2. The closing shot of this commercial shows a snowplow driving past a Volkswagen. How does this image encapsulate the message of this ad? Write a sentence that expresses the message Volkswagen wants to communicate, without regard to the particular visuals of this ad.

Union Carbide: Chick

YouTube Search Terms: union carbide chick

1. Based on the opening image, what is the essential psychological appeal (see Jib Fowles) of this ad?

2. How does the visual (the commercial is unusual in consisting of a single, continuous shot) work *with* and work *against* the soundtrack voice-over? To what extent do you "hear" the narrator's voice—and his message—as you watch the image of the metal box in the beaker of boiling water? To what extent is there a danger that this commercial could backfire and create bad feeling about Union Carbide because of what is portrayed?

Alka Seltzer: Spicy Meatball

YouTube Search Terms: alka seltzer meatball

1. Some TV commercials employ a "fake-out" strategy, based partially on our knowledge of other commercials. How does this approach work in the Alka Seltzer ad? Do you think it is likely to succeed in persuading viewers to buy the product?

2. Like many successful TV commercials, this one relies on humor, grounded in human foibles and imperfections, and based on our experience that if things can go wrong, they generally will. How do the visuals and the audio track of the Alka Selzter ad employ this kind of humor as a sales strategy?

COMMERCIALS OF THE 1970s

Chanel No. 5: Share the Fantasy

YouTube Search Terms: chanel 5 fantasy

1. In many ways, this celebrated commercial—directed by filmmaker Ridley Scott (*Alien, Blade Runner, Thelma and Louise, Gladiator*)—is, stylistically, at the opposite pole from the gritty Volkswagen "Snowplow" commercial. Comment.

2. Chanel No. 5 is one of those products sold primarily on its "mystique." How do the visuals and the soundtrack of this commercial reinforce that mystique? "Read" the images and interpret them, in light of the product.

3. In terms of Fowles's categories, what are the central appeals of this ad?

Quaker Oats: Mikey

YouTube Search Terms: quaker oats mikey

1. Why don't the older kids want to try Life cereal? How does reluctance tie into Quaker Oats's larger marketing problem with the product? How does the commercial attempt to deal with this problem?

2. Many viewers came to hate this commercial because it was shown repeatedly and because it lasted so many years. Still, it endured because many other viewers found it endearing—and it did the job of publicizing the product. Do you think a commercial like this would work today? Explain.

Coca-Cola: Mean Joe Green

YouTube Search Terms: coca cola joe green

1. This commercial is a study in contrasts. Identify some of these contrasts (both visual and aural), and explain how they work as part of the sales strategy.

2. To what emotions does this commercial attempt to appeal? Did you find this appeal successful?

3. Like many commercials, this one is presented as a minidrama, complete with plot, character, setting, theme, and other elements found in longer dramas. Explain the way that the drama functions in this ad, particularly as it concerns the characterization of the two actors.

COMMERCIALS OF THE 1980s

Federal Express (FedEx): Fast-Paced World [with John Moschitta]

YouTube Search Terms: federal express fast talker

1. The actor in this commercial, John Moschitta, was for many years celebrated in the *Guinness Book of World Records* as the world's fastest talker (he was clocked at 586 words per minute). How does Moschitta's unique skill make him an ideal spokesperson for Federal Express?

2. There is always a danger that particularly striking ads may be counterproductive, in that they draw attention to their own cleverness or unusual stylistic qualities, rather than to the product being sold. Put yourself in the position of a Federal Express executive. To what extent might you be concerned that this commercial, clever as it is, would not succeed in making more people select Federal Express as their express delivery service? On the other hand, might any striking commercial for Federal Express be successful if it heightened public recognition of the brand?

Pepsi-Cola: Archaeology

YouTube Search Terms: pepsi cola archaeology

1. Summarize the main selling point of this commercial. How does this selling point relate to (1) the basic situation presented in the commercial and (2) Pepsi's slogan, as it appears at the end?

2. Pepsi-Cola and Coca-Cola have been engaged in fierce rivalry for more than a century. How does this commercial exploit that rivalry to humorous effect? How is each product visually represented in the ad?

3. As contrasted with the Volkswagen "Snowplow" ad or the Quaker Oats "Mikey" ad, this ad features lavish production values and is presented as if it were a science fiction film. How do the sets, costumes, props, and special effects help support the overall sales strategy of the ad?

Levi's: Launderette

YouTube Search Terms: levi's laundrette

1. What is the primary appeal of this British ad (in Jib Fowles's terms)? Do you think it is directed primarily to men or primarily to women? Explain.

2. How do the reactions of the various characters in this ad to the young man contribute to its overall effect? How does the young man's appearance figure into the overall effect?

3. What role does the musical track (Marvin Gaye's "I Heard It Through The Grapevine") play in this commercial?

COMMERCIALS OF THE 1990s

Jeep: Snow Covered

YouTube Search Terms: jeep snow covered

1. "This may have been the most arrogant commercial ever made," declared the creative director of the agency that produced it. In what way might this be so? Possible arrogance aside, is this an effective advertisement for Jeep? Explain.

2. How do the visuals support the message of the ad? What *is* that message?

3. Which appeals are most evident in this commercial?

Energizer: Darth Vader

YouTube Search Terms: energizer darth vader

1. The Energizer bunny was featured in numerous commercials of the 1990s, generally in settings where its sudden appearance was totally unexpected. How do the creators of this add draw upon the *Star Wars* mythology to support their sales pitch? In what way is the strategy of this ad similar to that of Alka Seltzer's "Spicy Meatball"?

2. In a sentence, summarize the message of this ad—without mentioning *Star Wars* or Darth Vader.

Got Milk? (California Milk Processor Board): Aaron Burr [Original Got Milk? Commercial]

YouTube Search Terms: got milk burr

1. The opening of this commercial is intended to convey a sense of culture and sophistication. How do the images and the soundtrack do this? Why is this "setup" necessary in terms of the ad's message? What is that message?

2. In the latter half of the commercial, how does the accelerated pace of the editing and camera work—and of the soundtrack—contribute to the ad's overall impact?

COMMERCIALS OF THE 2000s

The Gap: Pardon Our Dust

YouTube Search Terms: gap dust

1. This commercial was directed by filmmaker Spike Jonze (*Adaptation, Where the Wild Things Are*). Describe your reactions as you watched this ad. What did you think was happening as the mayhem within the store accelerated? What is the effect of the "Pardon Our Dust" title when it appears? What is the relationship of the prior visuals and the soundtrack (including the music of Grieg's "In the Hall of the Mountain King") to the last two titles?

2. In Jib Fowles's terms ("Fifteen Basic Appeals"), to what desires is this commercial intended to appeal?

3. According to the Web site "Top 10 Coolest Commercials by Movie Directors," Spike Jonze was asked by Gap executives to produce a commercial about the stores' new look. Bewildered by what Jonze delivered, the company ran the commercial in a few cities, then pulled it off the air after about a month. Did the company make the right decision (from a marketing standpoint)?

Honda: Physics

YouTube Search Terms: honda physics

1. Put yourself in the position of the ad agency copywriters for Honda *before* they conceived of this particular ad. What is your main selling point? Express, in a sentence, what you want to communicate to the public about Honda automobiles and engineering.

2. This commercial involves no computer graphics or digital tricks: everything that happens is real. All the components we see came from the disassembling of two Honda Accords. (The voice is that of *Lake Woebegon Days* author Garrison Keillor.) According to Honda, this single continuous shot required 606 takes—meaning that for the first 605 takes, something, usually minor, went wrong, and the recording team had to install the set-up again and again. There is always a danger (for the client) that memorable commercials like this will amaze and impress viewers but will also fail to implant brand identification in their minds. Do you think there may be such a problem with this commercial? To what extent are viewers who have seen it likely, days or weeks later, to identify it with Honda and to associate whatever message (if any) they draw from the commercial with the particular qualities of Honda automobiles?

Sony Bravia: Bunnies

YouTube Search Terms: sony bunnies

1. Some of the same visual techniques used in this ad (to portray an unstoppable swarm of creatures that speedily overrun an urban area) have also been used—to very different effect—in horror films. What mood is conveyed—and how—by the visual and soundtrack elements of this commercial?

2. To what consumer desires (refer to Jib Fowles's categories) is this commercial designed to appeal?

3. Discuss how some of the visual techniques and special effects of this ad contribute to its effectiveness in conveying the benefits of the Sony Bravia.

Dove: Onslaught

YouTube Search Terms: dove onslaught

1. What is the message of this ad? How does the cinematic style of the visuals reinforce that message? Focus, in particular, on the contrasting visual styles used for the child and (later in the ad) her classmates, on the one hand, and the rest of the images, on the other. Consider, for example, how long the first image remains on screen, compared to those that follow.

2. How many of Jib Fowles's fifteen basic appeals do you detect at work in this ad? How do these appeals work to convey the essential contrast of values underlying the ad?

Tide to Go: Interview

YouTube Search Terms: tide to go interview

1. What is the message of this ad? How do the simple visuals and the more complex soundtrack work together (and against one another) to support that idea? How does that idea relate to one or more of Fowles's fifteen basic appeals?

2. Like many contemporary TV ads, this one relies on humor. To what extent do you find humor used effectively here? What is the source of the humor? How do the two actors help create that humor? How is this humor rooted in common concerns and fears that we all share?

Planters Peanuts: Perfume

YouTube Search Terms: planters perfume

1. Many of the elements in this ad are also found in perfume commercials. How are these elements used here to comic effect? Compare the mood and the visual style of this ad to that of a real perfume ad, the Chanel No. 5 "Share the Fantasy" commercial. Of what other commercials does this one remind you? Why?

2. Like the Gap "Pardon Our Dust" commercial, the Planter's ad relies on the visual motif of comic mayhem. Do you think such visuals are an effective way of selling the product? Explain.

ADDITIONAL TV COMMERCIALS

Note: Unless otherwise indicated, all commercials listed were produced in the United States.

Democratic National Committee: "Daisy Girl" (1964)
  YouTube Search Terms: democratic daisy ad

American Tourister Luggage: Gorilla (1969)
  YouTube Search Terms: luggage gorilla

Chevrolet: "Baseball, Hot Dogs, Apple Pie" (1969)
  YouTube Search Terms: america baseball hotdogs

Keep America Beautiful: "Crying Indian" (1970)
  YouTube Search Terms: America crying indian

Coca Cola: "Hilltop" ("I'd Like to Buy the World a Coke") (1971)
  YouTube Search Terms: buy world coke 1971

Hovis: "Bike Ride" (UK, 1973) [shot by Ridley Scott]
  YouTube Search Terms: hovis bike

Xerox: "Monks" (1975)
  YouTube Search Terms: xerox monks

Hebrew National: "Higher Authority" (1975)
YouTube Search Terms: hebrew national higher

Basf: "Dear John" (New Zealand, 1979)
Search Terms: basf dear john

Lego: "Kipper" (UK, 1980)
YouTube Search Terms: lego kipper

Apple: Macintosh (1984)
YouTube Search Terms: apple macintosh

Sony Trinitron: "Lifespan" (UK, 1984)
YouTube Search Terms: sony trinitron advert

American Express: "Stephen King: (1984)
YouTube Search Terms: american express king

The Guardian: "Points of View" (UK, 1987)
YouTube Search Terms: guardian points of view

Volkswagen: "Changes" (UK, 1988)
YouTube Search Terms: vw changes

Energizer: "Bunny Introduction" (1989)
YouTube Search Terms: energizer bunny introduction 1989

Dunlop: "Tested for the Unexpected" (1993)
YouTube Search Terms: dunlop tested unexpected

Swedish Televerket: "Noxin" (Sweden, 1993)
YouTube Search Terms: Noxin

Little Caesar's Pizza: "Training Camp" (1994)
YouTube Search Terms: caesar's training camp

Campbell's Soup: Winter Commercial (1995)
YouTube Search Terms: campbell's soup winter

California Milk Processor Board: "Got Milk? Heaven" (1996)
YouTube Search Terms: got milk heaven

Ameriquest Mortgage: "Plane Ride" (2008)
YouTube Search Terms: ameriquest plane ride

Audi: "Oil Parade" (2009)
YouTube Search Terms: audi oil parade

SYNTHESIS ACTIVITIES

1. Select one *category* of advertisements (cigarettes, alcohol, etc.) represented in the ad portfolio. Compare and contrast the types of appeals underlying these ads, as discussed by Fowles. To what extent do you notice significant shifts of appeal from the 1940s to the present? Which types of appeal seem to you most effective with particular product categories? Is it more likely, for example, that people will buy cigarettes because they want to feel autonomous or because the cigarettes will make them more attractive to the opposite sex?

2. Select a series of ads in different product categories that all appear to rely on the same primary appeal—perhaps the appeal to sex or the appeal to affiliation. Compare and contrast the overall strategies of these ads. Draw upon Fowles and other authors represented in this chapter to develop your ideas. To what extent do your analyses support arguments often made by social critics (and advertising people) that what people are really buying is the image, rather than the product?

3. Discuss how a selection of ads reveals shifting cultural attitudes over the past six decades toward either (a) gender relations; (b) romance between men and women; (c) smoking; (d) automobiles. In the case of (a) or (b) above, the ads don't have to be for the same category of product. In terms of their underlying appeal, in terms of the implicit or explicit messages embodied both in the text and the graphics, how and to what extent do the ads reveal that attitudes of the target audiences have changed over the years?

4. Select a TV commercial or a TV ad campaign (for example, for Sprint phone service) and analyze the commercial(s) in terms of Fowles's categories, as well as the discussions of some of the authors in this chapter. To what extent do the principles discussed by these authors apply to broadcast, as well as to print ads? What are the special requirements of TV advertising?

5. Find a small group of ads that rely upon little or no body copy—just a graphic, perhaps a headline, and the product name. What common features underlie the marketing strategies of such ads? What kinds of appeals do they make? How do their graphic aspects compare? What makes the need for text superfluous?

6. As indicated in the introduction to this chapter, social critics have charged advertising with numerous offenses: "It fosters materialism, it psychologically manipulates people to buy things they don't need, it perpetuates gender and racial stereotypes (particularly in its illustrations), it is deceptive, it is offensive, it debases the language." To what extent do some of the advertisements presented in the ad portfolio (and perhaps others of your own choosing) demonstrate the truth of one or more of these charges? In developing your response, draw upon some of the ads in the portfolio (or elsewhere).

7. Read the textual content (headlines and body text) of several ads *without* paying attention (if possible) to the graphics. Compare the effectiveness of the headline and body text by themselves with the effectiveness of the ads, *including* the graphic elements. Focusing on a group of related ads (related by product category, by appeal, by decade, etc.), devise an explanation of how graphics work to effectively communicate the appeal and meaning of the products advertised.

8. Many ads employ humor—in the graphics, in the body copy, or both—to sell a product. Examine a group of advertisements that rely on humor to make their appeal and explain how they work. For example, do they play off an incongruity between one element of the ad and another (such as between the headline and the graphic), or between one element of the ad (or the basic message of the ad) and what we know or assume to be the case in the "real world"? Do they employ wordplay or irony? Do they picture people doing funny things (funny because inappropriate or unrealistic)? What appeal underlines the humor? Aggression? Sex? Nurturing? Based on your examination and analyses, what appear to be some of the more effective ways of employing humor?

9. Think of a new product that you have just invented. This product, in your opinion, will revolutionize the world of (fill in the blank). Devise an advertisement to announce this product to the world. Consider (or reject) using a celebrity to help sell your product. Select the basic appeal of your product (see Fowles). Then, applying concepts and principles discussed by other authors in this chapter, write the headline, subhead, and body copy for the product. Sketch out (or at least describe) the graphic that will accompany the text. Show your proposed ad to one or more of your classmates, get reactions, and then revise the ad, taking into account your market feedback.

10. Imagine that you own a small business—perhaps an independent coffee shop (not Starbucks, Peet's, or Coffee Bean), a videogame company, or a pedicab service that conveys tourists around a chic beach town. Devise an ad that announces your services and extols its benefits. Apply the principles discussed by Fowles and other writers in this chapter.

11. Write a parody ad—one that would never ordinarily be written—applying the selling principles discussed by Fowles and other authors in this chapter. For example, imagine you are the manager of the Globe Theatre in Elizabethan England and want to sell season tickets to this season's plays, including a couple of new tragedies by your playwright-in-residence, Will Shakespeare. Or imagine that you are trying to sell Remington typewriters in the age of computers (no software glitches!). Or—as long as people are selling bottled water—you have found a way to package and sell air. Advertisers can reportedly sell anything with the right message. Give it your best shot.

12. Based on the reading you have done in this chapter, discuss the extent to which you believe advertisements create needs in consumers, reflect existing needs, or some combination of both. In developing your paper, draw on both particular advertisements and on the more theoretical overviews of advertising developed in the chapter.

13. Select one advertisement and conduct two analyses of it, using two different analytical principles: perhaps one from Fowles's list of fifteen

emotional appeals and one from Bovée's "Checklist for Producing Excellent Copy" (p. 561). Having conducted your analyses and developed your insights, compare and contrast the strengths and weaknesses of the analytical principles you've employed. Conclude more broadly with a discussion of how a single analytical principle can close down, as well as open up, understanding of an object under study.

14. As you have seen, advertisements change over time, both across product categories and within categories. And yet the advertisements remain a constant, their presence built on the assumption that consumers can be swayed both overtly and covertly in making purchasing decisions. In a paper drawing on the selections in this chapter, develop a theory on why ads change over time. Is it because people's needs have changed and, therefore, new ads are required? (Do the older ads appeal to the same needs as newer ads?) In developing your discussion, you might track the changes over time in one product category.

RESEARCH ACTIVITIES

1. Drawing upon contemporary magazines (or magazines from a given period), select a set of advertisements in a particular product category. Analyze these advertisements according to Fowles's categories, and assess their effectiveness in terms of the discussions of other authors in this chapter.

2. Select a particular product that has been selling for at least twenty-five years (e.g., Bayer aspirin, Tide detergent, IBM computers, Oldsmobile—as in "This is not your father's Oldsmobile") and trace the history of print advertising for this product over the years. To what extent has the advertising changed over the years? To what extent has the essential sales appeal remained the same? In addition to examining the ads themselves, you may want to research the company and its marketing practices. You will find two business databases particularly useful: ABI/INFORM and the academic version of LexisNexis.

3. One of the landmark campaigns in American advertising was Doyle, Dane, Bernbach's series of ads for the Volkswagen Beetle in the 1960s. In effect a rebellion against standard auto advertising, the VW ads' Unique Selling Proposition was that ugly is beautiful—an appeal that was overwhelmingly successful. Research the VW ad campaign for this period, setting it in the context of the agency's overall marketing strategy.

4. Among the great marketing debacles of recent decades was Coca-Cola's development in 1985 of a new formula for its soft drink that (at least temporarily) replaced the much-beloved old formula. Research this major development in soft drink history, focusing on the marketing of

New Coke and the attempt of the Atlanta-based Coca-Coca company to deal with the public reception of its new product.

5. Advertising agencies are hired not only by manufacturers and by service industries; they are also hired by political candidates. In fact, one of the common complaints about American politics is that candidates for public office are marketed just as if they were bars of soap. Select a particular presidential or gubernatorial election and research the print and broadcast advertising used by the rival candidates. You may want to examine the ads not only of the candidates of the major parties but also the candidates of the smaller parties, such as the Green and the Libertarian parties. How do the appeals and strategies used by product ads compare and contrast with those used in ads for political candidates?

6. Public service ads comprise another major category of advertising (in addition to product and service advertising and political advertising). Such ads have been used to recruit people to military service, to get citizens to buy war bonds, to contribute to charitable causes, to get people to support or oppose strikes, to persuade people to stop using (or not to start using) drugs, to prevent drunk driving, etc. Locate a group of public service ads, describe them, and assess their effectiveness. Draw upon Fowles and Bovée et al. in developing your conclusions.

7. Research advertising in American magazines and newspapers before World War II. Focus on a limited number of product lines—for example, soft drinks, soap and beauty products, health-related products. What kind of differences do you see between ads in the first part of the twentieth century and more recent or contemporary advertising for the same types of products? In general, how have the predominant types of appeal used to sell products in the past changed (if they have) with the times? How are the graphics of early ads different from preferred graphics today? How has the body copy changed? (Hint: You may want to be on the alert for ads that make primarily negative appeals—i.e., what may happen to you if you don't use the product advertised.)

12

Fairy Tales: A Closer Look at Cinderella

In August 2001, when the crown prince of Norway married a single mother and former waitress, hundreds of thousands of Norwegians cheered, along with an estimated 300 million television viewers worldwide. Observers called it a "Cinderella" tale—and everyone everywhere understood the reference. Mette-Marit Tjessem Hoiby had become a Cinderella figure. But why had the bride's humble beginnings so endeared her to a nation? We can begin to offer answers by examining an ancient and universally known tale in which a young girl—heartsick at the death of her mother, deprived of her father's love, and scorned by her new family—is nonetheless recognized for her inner worth.

"Once upon a time...." Millions of children around the world have listened to these (or similar) words. And, once upon a time, such words were magic archways into a world of entertainment and fantasy for children and their parents. But in our own century, fairy tales have come under the scrutiny of anthropologists, linguists, educators, psychologists, and psychiatrists, as well as literary critics, who have come to see them as a kind of social genetic code—a means by which cultural values are transmitted from one generation to the next. Some people, of course, may scoff at the idea that charming tales like "Cinderella" or "Snow White" are anything other than charming tales, at the idea that fairy tales may really be ways of inculcating young and impressionable children with culturally approved values. But even if they are not aware of it, adults and children use fairy tales in complex and subtle ways. We can, perhaps, best illustrate this by examining variants of "Cinderella."

"Cinderella" appears to be the best-known fairy tale in the world. In 1892, Marian Roalfe Cox published 345 variants of the story, the first systematic study of a single folktale. In her collection, Cox gathered stories from throughout Europe in which elements or motifs of "Cinderella" appeared, often mixed with motifs of other tales. All told, more than 700 variants exist throughout the world—in Europe, Africa, Asia, and North and South America. Scholars debate the extent to which such a wide distribution is explained by population migrations or by some universal quality of imagination that would allow people at different times and places to create essentially the same story. But for whatever reason, folklorists agree that "Cinderella" has appealed to storytellers and listeners everywhere.

The great body of folk literature, including fairy tales, comes to us from an oral tradition. Written literature, produced by a particular author, is preserved through the generations just as the author recorded it. By contrast, oral literature changes with every telling: The childhood game comes to mind in which one child whispers a sentence into the ear of another; by the time the second child repeats the sentence to a third, and the third to a fourth (and so on), the sentence has changed considerably. And so it is with oral literature, with the qualification that these stories are also changed quite consciously when a teller wishes to add or delete material.

Modern students of folk literature find themselves in the position of *reading* as opposed to hearing a tale. The texts we read tend to be of two types, which are at times difficult to distinguish. We might read a faithful transcription of an oral tale or a tale of *literary* origin—a tale that was originally written (as a short story would be), not spoken, but that nonetheless may contain elements of an oral account. In this chapter, we include tales of both oral and literary origin. Jakob and Wilhelm Grimm published their transcription of "Cinderella" in 1812. The version by Charles Perrault (1697) is difficult to classify as the transcription of an oral source, since he may have heard the story originally but appears (according to Bruno Bettelheim) to have "freed it of all content he considered vulgar, and refined its other features to make the product suitable to be told at court." Of unquestionable literary origin are the Walt Disney version of the story, based on Perrault's text and Anne Sexton's poem.

Preceding these (and other) variants of "Cinderella," we present two selections that will orient you, we hope, to the experience of reading fairy tales as "literature": a reminiscence of reading classic tales by historian Arthur Schlesinger, Jr., and a general introduction to the topic by folklorist Stith Thompson. Following the variants are six selections that respond directly to the tale. First, art historian Bonnie Cullen examines how Perrault's "Cinderella" emerged as the canonical, or standard, version. We hear from Bruno Bettelheim, who, employing psychoanalytic theory, finds in "Cinderella" a story of "Sibling Rivalry and Oedipal Conflicts."

Next, Elisabeth Panttaja, in "Cinderella: *Not* So Morally Superior," argues that our heroine succeeds not because she is patient or virtuous (the standard moral to the story) but because she "disobeys the stepmother, enlists forbidden helpers, uses magic powers, lies, hides, dissembles, disguises herself, and evades pursuit." On a lighter note, in "I Am Cinderella's Stepmother and I Know My Rights," Judith Rossner sets the record straight on "Cinderella" from a point of view not typically represented in variants of the tale. Next, media critic James Poniewozik assesses several filmed versions of feminist-inspired updates to the tale in "The Princess Paradox" and wonders if the new Cinderella wants not only to embrace the role of princess but to smirk at it, too. The chapter concludes with "Cinderella and Princess Culture"—Peggy Orenstein's investigation of the three-billion-dollar industry that has sprung up around "princess" culture.

In recent years Cinderella has come in for a critical drubbing, as wised-up and often sarcastic commentators reject her rags-to-riches, someday-my-prince-will-come myth as out of date. Feminists, in particular, have objected to a children's story that promotes the idea—both unrealistic and undesirable—that young women should wait for a handsome prince to carry them off to a happily-ever-after marriage in a magnificent castle. In some of these critical commentaries, Cinderella is shown to be just as mercenary a soul as her evil stepsisters or stepmother (see "Cinderella: Not so Morally Superior"). In several contemporary filmed versions discussed by Poniewozik, Cinderella triumphs in two worlds: She succeeds on her own terms as a strong, quick-witted heroine and also gets to enjoy her ball gowns. In other revisions, the ostensible antagonists of the tale, such as the stepmother, offer their own surprising counter-myths (see "I am Cinderella's Stepmother and I Know my Rights") aimed at reversing our sympathies.

Such reversals have become a familiar strategy of contemporary storytelling. In the past generation or so, we have seen the old English myth of Beowulf presented from the monster's point of view (*Grendel* by John Gardner); *The Wizard of Oz*, from the witch's point of view (*Wicked* by Gregory Maguire); and even *Pride and Prejudice*—itself a "Cinderella" variant—from Mr. Darcy's point of view (*Darcy's Story* by Janet Aylmer). The larger question posed by such revisionists is whether or not the familiar myth continues to resonate with contemporary readers. If it doesn't, they propose that we abandon it, or they offer makeovers to help the myth continue to resonate in our consumer culture. For example, in a *New York Times* article several years ago, "Love the Riches, Lose the Rags: Younger Fans Embrace Cinderella, Updated as the Material Girl," Jodi Kantor details the ways in which Cinderella and other Disney princesses have become commodified: "Younger girls...are watching their movies on special pink-and-blue Cinderella television and DVD players, dressing their dogs in Cinderella costumes and eating breakfast made in a waffle iron that stamps her image into the batter." But older females can also live the myth: "At the Disney parks, the most popular theme wedding is the Cinderella one. For $2,500 a bride can arrive in a glass coach copied straight from the film, drawn by four ponies."

A note on terminology: "Cinderella," "Jack and the Beanstalk," "Little Red Riding Hood," and the like are commonly referred to as fairy tales, although, strictly speaking, they are not. True fairy tales concern a "class of supernatural beings of diminutive size, who in popular belief are said to possess magical powers and to have great influence for good or evil over the affairs of humans" (*Oxford English Dictionary*). "Cinderella" and the others just mentioned concern no beings of diminutive size, although extraordinary, magical events do occur in the stories. Folklorists would be more apt to call these stories "wonder tales." We retain the traditional "fairy tale," with the proviso that in popular usage the term is misapplied. You may notice that the authors in this chapter use the terms "folktale" and "fairy tale" interchangeably. The expression "folktale" refers to *any* story conceived orally and passed on in an oral tradition. Thus, "folktale" is a generic term that incorporates both fairy tales and wonder tales.

WHAT GREAT BOOKS DO FOR CHILDREN

Arthur Schlesinger, Jr.

Arthur Schlesinger, Jr. (1917–2007) was a Pulitzer Prize winning historian and biographer. The author of several authoritative histories, including *The Age of Jackson* (1945), *The Vital Center: The Politics of Freedom* (1949), and *Robert Kennedy and His Times (1979)*, Schlesinger served as speechwriter for and special assistant to President John F. Kennedy [*A Thousand Days* (1966), with its firsthand observations, is one of the basic reference works on the Kennedy presidency]. He was also a speechwriter for presidential candidates Robert Kennedy, George McGovern, and Ted Kennedy. Schlesinger chronicled his origins and prolific career in *A Life in the 20th Century* (2000). In this excerpt he shares his earliest impressions of being read to by his mother and reading himself—and his strong opinions on the value of classic children's literature. Schlesinger was a well-known opponent of multiculturalism (in 1991 he published *The Disuniting of America: Reflections on a Multicultural Society*). Perhaps you can detect some of that sentiment in the following—particularly in his love of the classic stories.

I particularly remember my mother sitting in her chair reading aloud to her children. She was a splendid reader, spirited and expressive, and Tom and I insisted that she keep on reading to us long after we were able to read to ourselves. She was also an astute skip-er. I recall her amusement at my indignation when I discovered that, in books like *Ivanhoe* and Parkman's *Conspiracy of Pontiac*, she was unscrupulously omitting passages she found static or boring.

Of all childhood pastimes, reading was my passion. Now that television has replaced the book in the life of the young, mine may have been the last generation to grow up in the high noon of the print culture. Perhaps it may be of historical interest to recall the profound excitement, the abiding fulfillment, books provided in those ancient and no doubt unimaginable days.

My mother gave me an appetite for books as well as a capacity to read them quickly. "Perhaps it is only in childhood that books have any deep influence on our lives," Graham Greene has well said. "...In childhood all books are books of divination, telling us about the future...What do we ever get nowadays from reading to equal the excitement and the revelation of those first fourteen years?" [Indeed] most people will have done most of the reading they will ever do by the age of 25 and must live off those books for the rest of their lives.

My mother began with fairy tales, the Brothers Grimm and Hans Christian Andersen, with Greek and Roman mythology, especially as marvelously rendered by Hawthorne in *The Wonder Book* and *Tanglewood Tales*; and with the wondrous *Arabian Nights*. When I began to read for myself, a six-volume series called *My Book House* came into my life, an entrancing and resplendently illustrated anthology of historical adventure, fairy tale, poetry, mythology, something for every mood and moment.

5   I fear that such an initiation into a larger world would be much condemned today. For these were all tales filled with cruelty and violence, mutilation and murder, magic and fantasy, streaked by what is now seen as classism, sexism, racism, and superstition. Approved children's books today are by contrast

didactic in intent, dealing with prosaic, everyday events and intended to improve relations among classes, sexes, and races. Such books, it is argued, lead children to face reality rather than to flee into fantasy.

Is this really so? [Aren't] fairy tales and myths symbolic reenactments of deep psychological and social dilemmas? In this sense, the classic fantasies may well be more realistic than the contemporary morality tales.

There is nothing new about the contemporary insistence on morality tales. Since the invention of type, most children's books have been designed to make children behave better. Yet good-behavior tales do not survive, and gods and goddesses, dragons and ogres, are with us still. Hawthorne in his day felt the pressures of moralistic didacticism. "These old legends, so brimming over with everything that is most abhorrent to our Christianized moral sense," he wrote ironically in his introduction to *Tanglewood Tales*, "How were they to be purified? . . . The author has not always thought it necessary to write downward in order to meet the comprehension of children. . . . Children possess an underestimated sensibility to whatever is deep or high, in imagination or feeling."

Childhood is finite. So is the number of books one can read. Why spend time on a modern morality tale in which the girl plays doctor and the boy plays nurse and their patient is the . . . child down the block when you can read about Huck and Tom and . . . Jim? The serious point of children's books is not to improve behavior but to expand imagination. Great children's literature creates new worlds that children enter with delight and perhaps with apprehension and from which they return with understandings that their own experience could not have produced and that give their lives new meaning.

The classical tales have populated the common imagination of the West. They are voyages of discovery. They introduce children to the existential mysteries—the anxiety of loneliness, the terror of rejection, the need for comradeship, the quest for fulfillment, the struggle against fate, victory, love, death. "Small children," Henry James observed in his preface to *What Maisie Knew*, "have many more perceptions than they have terms to translate them." The classical tales tell children what they unconsciously know—that human nature is not innately good, that conflict is real, that life is harsh before it is happy—and thereby reassure them about their own fears and their own sense of self.

● Discussion and Writing Suggestions

1. Schlesinger quotes Henry James and Nathaniel Hawthorne on the ability of children to comprehend the sometimes troubling but emotionally and imaginatively rich elements of folklore and mythology. James: "Small children . . . have many more perceptions than they have terms to translate them." Hawthorne: "Children possess an underestimated sensibility to whatever is deep or high, in imagination or feeling." What is your view of the ability of children to grasp, even if they cannot express, the wisdom of folk literature?

2. Schlesinger claims that contemporary stories for children avoid the dark, sometimes murderous elements of folk literature as well as content that may offend modern sensibilities regarding, for instance, gender roles. As a consequence, says Schlesinger, these stories are poor substitutes for the classic tales. Think of some classic tales you heard as a child and compare them to modern ones. To what extent do you agree with Schlesinger?

3. Is it wrong, do you think, for the literature of childhood to create in young readers "the anxiety of loneliness, the terror of rejection, the need for comradeship, the quest for fulfillment, the struggle against fate, victory, love, death"? Is such an experience too intense for children? Or is it, by contrast (as Schlesinger suggests) *vital* to the imaginative and emotional education of children?

4. Identify one or two of Schlesinger's statements that that you find memorable—whether or not you agree with them. Explain your response.

5. Schlesinger begins with a fond recollection of being read to as a child. Recall someone who used to read you stories: Who did the reading? Where? When? What stories were your favorites? What made them favorites? Recall the *emotional* content of your experiences of being read to and try capturing the experience in a brief narrative. Share that narrative with your classmates—or, if you are comfortable, with the people who read to you.

6. You may have had the opportunity to read to a child. You may have many opportunities to do so in the future. Are you comfortable reading the old tales—in which, for example, birds peck out the eyes of evil stepsisters or malevolent adults bake children in ovens or poison them? Have you read—or will you be comfortable reading—the old tales to the children in your lives? Explain.

7. Schlesinger writes, "The classical tales tell children what they unconsciously know—that human nature is not innately good, that conflict is real, that life is harsh before it is happy—and thereby reassure them about their own fears and their own sense of self." Children have a lifetime to learn such harsh lessons. Why learn them in childhood? Why not wait?

UNIVERSALITY OF THE FOLKTALE

Stith Thompson

Folklorists travel around the world, to cities and rural areas alike, recording the facts, traditions, and beliefs that characterize ethnic groups. Some folklorists record and compile jokes; others do the same with insults or songs. Still others, like Stith Thompson, devote their careers to studying tales. And, as it turns out, many aspects of stories and storytelling are worth examining. Among them: the art of narrative—how tellers captivate their audiences; the social and religious significance of tale telling; the many types of tales that are told; the many variants, worldwide, of single tales (such as "Cinderella"). In a preface to one of his own books, Thompson raises the broad questions and the underlying assumptions that govern the folklorist's study of tales. Following is Thompson's overview to set a context for the variants of "Cinderella" that you will read.

Note the ways that Thompson's approach to fairy tales differs from yours. Perhaps you regard stories such as "Cinderella" as entertainment. Stith Thompson assumes, as you might not, that tales should be objects of study as well.

Stith Thompson (1885–1976) led a distinguished life as an American educator, folklorist, editor, and author. Between 1921 and 1955, he was a professor of folklore and English, and later dean of the Graduate School and Distinguished Service Professor at Indiana University, Bloomington. Five institutions have awarded Thompson honorary doctorates for his work in folklore studies. He published numerous books on the subject, including *European Tales Among North American Indians* (1919), *The Types of the Folktales* (1928), and *Tales of the North American Indian* (1929). He is best known for his six-volume *Motif Index of Folk Literature* (1932–1937; 1955–1958, 2nd ed.).

The teller of stories has everywhere and always found eager listeners. Whether his tale is the mere report of a recent happening, a legend of long ago, or an elaborately contrived fiction, men and women have hung upon his words and satisfied their yearnings for information or amusement, for incitement to heroic deeds, for religious edification, or for release from the overpowering monotony of their lives. In villages of central Africa, in outrigger boats on the Pacific, in the Australian bush, and within the shadow of Hawaiian volcanoes, tales of the present and of the mysterious past, of animals and gods and heroes, and of men and women like themselves, hold listeners in their spell or enrich the conversation of daily life. So it is also in Eskimo igloos under the light of seal-oil lamps, in the tropical jungles of Brazil, and by the totem poles of the British Columbian coast. In Japan too, and China and India, the priest and the scholar, the peasant and the artisan all join in their love of a good story and their honor for the man who tells it well.

When we confine our view to our own occidental world, we see that for at least three or four thousand years, and doubtless for ages before, the art of the story-teller has been cultivated in every rank of society. Odysseus entertains the court of Alcinous with the marvels of his adventures. Centuries later we find the long-haired page reading nightly from interminable chivalric romances to entertain his lady while her lord is absent on his crusade. Medieval priests illustrate sermons by anecdotes old and new, and only sometimes edifying. The old peasant, now as always, whiles away the winter evening with tales of wonder and adventure and the marvelous workings of fate. Nurses tell children of Goldilocks or the House that Jack Built. Poets write epics and novelists novels. Even now the cinemas and theaters bring their stories directly to the ear and eye through the voices and gestures of actors. And in the smoking-rooms of sleeping cars and steamships and at the banquet table the oral anecdote flourishes in a new age.

In the present work we are confining our interest to a relatively narrow scope, the traditional prose tale—the story which has been handed down from generation to generation either in writing or by word of mouth. Such tales are, of course, only one of the many kinds of story material, for, in addition to them, narrative comes to us in verse as ballads and epics, and in prose as histories, novels, dramas, and short stories. We shall have little to do with the songs of bards, with the ballads of the people, or with poetic narrative in general, though stories themselves refuse to be confined exclusively to either prose or verse forms. But even with verse and all other forms of prose narrative put aside, we shall find that in treating the traditional prose tale—the folktale—our quest will be ambitious enough and will take us to all parts of the earth and to the very beginnings of history.

Although the term "folktale" is often used in English to refer to the "household tale" or "fairy tale" (the German *Märchen*), such as "Cinderella" or "Snow White," it is also legitimately employed in a much broader sense to include all forms of prose narrative, written or oral, which have come to be handed down through the years. In this usage the important fact is the traditional nature of the material. In contrast to the modern story writer's striving after originality of plot and treatment, the teller of a folktale is proud of his ability to hand on that which he has received. He usually desires to impress his readers or hearers with the fact that he is bringing them something that has the stamp of good authority, that the tale was heard from some great story-teller or from some aged person who remembered it from old days.

5   So it was until at least the end of the Middle Ages with writers like Chaucer, who carefully quoted authorities for their plots—and sometimes even invented originals so as to dispel the suspicion that some new and unwarranted story was being foisted on the public. Though the individual genius of such writers appears clearly enough, they always depended on authority, not only for their basic theological opinions but also for the plots of their stories. A study of the sources of Chaucer or Boccaccio takes one directly into the stream of traditional narrative.

The great written collections of stories characteristic of India, the Near East, the classical world, and Medieval Europe are almost entirely traditional. They copy and recopy. A tale which gains favor in one collection is taken over into others, sometimes intact and sometimes with changes of plot or characterization. The history of such a story, passing it may be from India to Persia and Arabia and Italy and France and finally to England, copied and changed from manuscript to manuscript, is often exceedingly complex. For it goes through the hands of both skilled and bungling narrators and improves or deteriorates at nearly every retelling. However well or poorly such a story may be written down, it always attempts to preserve a tradition, an old tale with the authority of antiquity to give it interest and importance.

If use of the term "folktale" to include such literary narratives seems somewhat broad, it can be justified on practical grounds if on no other, for it is impossible to make a complete separation of the written and the oral traditions. Often, indeed, their interrelation is so close and so inextricable as to present one of the most baffling problems the folklore scholar encounters. They differ somewhat in their behavior, it is true, but they are alike in their disregard of originality of plot and of pride of authorship.

Nor is complete separation of these two kinds of narrative tradition by any means necessary for their understanding. The study of the oral tale...will be valid so long as we realize that stories have frequently been taken down from the lips of unlettered taletellers and have entered the great literary collections. In contrary fashion, fables of Aesop, anecdotes from Homer, and saints' legends, not to speak of fairy tales read from Perrault or Grimm, have entered the oral stream and all their association with the written or printed page has been forgotten. Frequently a story is taken from the people, recorded in a literary document, carried across continents or preserved through centuries, and then retold to a humble entertainer who adds it to his repertory.

It is clear then that the oral story need not always have been oral. But when it once habituates itself to being passed on by word of mouth it undergoes the same treatment as all other tales at the command of the raconteur. It becomes something to tell to an audience, or at least to a listener, not something to read. Its effects are no longer produced indirectly by association with words written or printed on a page, but directly through facial expression and gesture and repetition and recurrent patterns that generations have tested and found effective.

10   This oral art of taletelling is far older than history, and it is not bounded by one continent or one civilization. Stories may differ in subject from place to place, the conditions and purposes of taletelling may change as we move from land to land or from century to century, and yet everywhere it ministers to the same basic social and individual needs. The call for entertainment to fill in the hours of leisure has found most peoples very limited in their resources, and except where modern urban civilization has penetrated deeply they have found the telling of stories one of the most satisfying of pastimes. Curiosity about the past has always brought eager listeners to tales of the long ago which supply the simple man with all he knows of the history of his folk. Legends grow with the telling, and often a great heroic past evolves to gratify vanity and tribal pride. Religion also has played a mighty role everywhere in the encouragement of the narrative art, for the religious mind has tried to understand beginnings and for ages has told stories of ancient days and sacred beings. Often whole cosmologies have unfolded themselves in these legends, and hierarchies of gods and heroes.

Worldwide also are many of the structural forms which oral narrative has assumed. The hero tale, the explanatory legend, the animal anecdote—certainly these at least are present everywhere. Other fictional patterns are limited to particular areas of culture and act by their presence or absence as an effective index of the limits of the area concerned. The study of such limitations has not proceeded far, but it constitutes an interesting problem for the student of these oral narrative forms.

Even more tangible evidence of the ubiquity and antiquity of the folktale is the great similarity in the content of stories of the most varied peoples. The same tale types and narrative motifs are found scattered over the world in most puzzling fashion. A recognition of these resemblances and an attempt to account for them brings the scholar closer to an understanding of the nature of human culture. He must continually ask himself, "Why do some peoples borrow tales and some lend? How does the tale serve the needs of the social group?" When he adds to his task an appreciation of the aesthetic and practical urge toward storytelling, and some knowledge of the forms and devices, stylistic and histrionic, that belong to this ancient and widely practiced art, he finds that he must bring to his work more talents than one man can easily possess. Literary critics, anthropologists, historians, psychologists, and aestheticians are all needed if we are to hope to know why folktales are made, how they are invented, what art is used in their telling, how they grow and change and occasionally die.

● Review Questions

1. According to Thompson, why do people venerate a good storyteller?

2. For Thompson, what features distinguish a "folktale" from modern types of fiction?

3. How does religion help encourage the existence of folktale art?

4. What is a strong piece of evidence for the great antiquity and universality of folktales?

● Discussion and Writing Suggestions

1. Based on Thompson's explanation of the qualities of oral folktales, what do you feel is gained by the increasing replacement of this form of art and entertainment by TV?

2. What do you suppose underlies the apparent human need to tell stories, given that storytelling is practiced in every culture known?

3. Interview older members of your family, asking them about stories they were told as children. As best you can, record a story. Then examine your work. How does it differ from the version you heard? Write an account of your impressions on the differences between an oral and a written rendering of a story. Alternatively, you might record a story and then speculate on what the story might mean in the experiences of the family member who told it to you.

SEVEN VARIANTS OF "CINDERELLA"

The existence of Chinese, French, German, African, and Native American versions of the popular Cinderella tale, along with 700 other versions worldwide, comes as a surprise to many. Which is the real "Cinderella"? The question is misleading in that each version is "real" for a particular group of people in a particular place and time. Certainly, you can judge among versions and select the most appealing. You can also draw comparisons and contrasts. Indeed, the grouping of the stories that we present here invites comparisons. You might wish to consider a few of the following categories as you read:

- *Cinderella's innocence or guilt, concerning the treatment she receives at the hands of her stepsisters*

- *Cinderella's passive (or active) nature*

- *Sibling rivalry—the relationship of Cinderella with her sisters*

- *The father's role*

- *The rule that Cinderella must return from the ball by midnight*

- *The levels of violence*

- *The presence or absence of the fairy godmother*

- *Cinderella's relationship with the prince*

- *The characterization of the prince*

- *The presence of Cinderella's dead mother*

- *The function of magic*

- *The ending*

CINDERELLA

Charles Perrault

Charles Perrault (1628–1703) was born in Paris of a prosperous family. He practiced law for a short time and then devoted his attentions to a job in government, in which capacity he was instrumental in promoting the advancement of the arts and sciences and in securing pensions for writers, both French and foreign. Perrault is best known as a writer for his *Contes de ma mère l'oye (Mother Goose Tales)*, a collection of fairy tales taken from popular folklore. He is widely suspected of having changed these stories in an effort to make them more acceptable to his audience—members of the French court.

Once there was a nobleman who took as his second wife the proudest and haughtiest woman imaginable. She had two daughters of the same character, who took after their mother in everything. On his side, the husband had a daughter who was sweetness itself; she inherited this from her mother, who had been the most kindly of women.

No sooner was the wedding over than the stepmother showed her ill-nature. She could not bear the good qualities of the young girl, for they made her own daughters seem even less likable. She gave her the roughest work of the house to do. It was she who washed the dishes and the stairs, who cleaned out Madam's room and the rooms of the two Misses. She slept right at the top of the house, in an attic, on a lumpy mattress, while her sisters slept in panelled rooms where they had the most modern beds and mirrors in which they could see themselves from top to toe. The poor girl bore everything in patience and did not dare to complain to her father. He would only have scolded her, for he was entirely under his wife's thumb.

When she had finished her work, she used to go into the chimney-corner and sit down among the cinders, for which reason she was usually known in the house as Cinderbottom. Her younger stepsister, who was not so rude as the other, called her Cinderella. However, Cinderella, in spite of her ragged clothes, was still fifty times as beautiful as her sisters, superbly dressed though they were.

One day the King's son gave a ball, to which everyone of good family was invited. Our two young ladies received invitations, for they cut quite a figure in the country. So there they were, both feeling very pleased and very busy choosing the clothes and the hair-styles which would suit them best. More work for Cinderella, for it was she who ironed her sisters' underwear and goffered their linen cuffs. Their only talk was of what they would wear.

5   "I," said the elder, "shall wear my red velvet dress and my collar of English lace."

"I," said the younger, "shall wear just my ordinary skirt; but, to make up, I shall put on my gold-embroidered cape and my diamond clasp, which is quite out of the common."

The right hairdresser was sent for to supply double-frilled coifs, and patches were bought from the right patch-maker. They called Cinderella to ask her opinion, for she had excellent taste. She made useful suggestions and even offered to do their hair for them. They accepted willingly.

While she was doing it, they said to her:

"Cinderella, how would you like to go to the ball?"

10   "Oh dear, you are making fun of me. It wouldn't do for me."

"You are quite right. It would be a joke. People would laugh if they saw a Cinderbottom at the ball."

Anyone else would have done their hair in knots for them, but she had a sweet nature, and she finished it perfectly. For two days they were so excited that they ate almost nothing. They broke a good dozen laces trying to tighten their stays to make their waists slimmer, and they were never away from their mirrors.

At last the great day arrived. They set off, and Cinderella watched them until they were out of sight. When she could no longer see them, she began to cry. Her godmother, seeing her all in tears, asked what was the matter.

"If only I could...If only I could..." She was weeping so much that she could not go on.

15   Her godmother, who was a fairy, said to her: "If only you could go to the ball, is that it?"

"Alas, yes," said Cinderella with a sigh.

"Well," said the godmother, "be a good girl and I'll get you there."

She took her into her room and said: "Go into the garden and get me a pumpkin."

Cinderella hurried out and cut the best she could find and took it to her godmother, but she could not understand how this pumpkin would get her to the ball. Her godmother hollowed it out, leaving only the rind, and then tapped it with her wand and immediately it turned into a magnificent gilded coach.

20   Then she went to look in her mouse-trap and found six mice all alive in it. She told Cinderella to raise the door of the trap a little, and as each mouse came out she gave it a tap with her wand and immediately it turned into a fine horse. That made a team of six horses, each of fine mouse-coloured grey.

While she was wondering how she would make a coachman, Cinderella said to her:

"I will go and see whether there is a rat in the rat-trap, we could make a coachman of him."

"You are right," said the godmother. "Run and see."

Cinderella brought her the rat-trap, in which there were three big rats. The fairy picked out one of them because of his splendid whiskers and, when she had touched him, he turned into a fat coachman, with the finest moustaches in the district.

25   Then she said: "Go into the garden and you will find six lizards behind the watering-can. Bring them to me."

As soon as Cinderella had brought them, her godmother changed them into six footmen, who got up behind the coach with their striped liveries, and stood in position there as though they had been doing it all their lives.

Then the fairy said to Cinderella:

"Well, that's to go to the ball in. Aren't you pleased?"

"Yes. But am I to go like this, with my ugly clothes?"

30   Her godmother simply touched her with her wand and her clothes were changed in an instant into a dress of gold and silver cloth, all sparkling with precious stones. Then she gave her a pair of glass slippers, most beautifully made.

So equipped, Cinderella got into the coach: but her godmother warned her above all not to be out after midnight, telling her that, if she stayed at the ball a moment later, her coach would turn back into a pumpkin, her horses into mice, her footmen into lizards, and her fine clothes would become rags again.

She promised her godmother that she would leave the ball before midnight without fail, and she set out, beside herself with joy.

The King's son, on being told that a great princess whom no one knew had arrived, ran out to welcome her. He handed her down from the coach and led her into the hall where his guests were. A sudden silence fell; the dancing stopped, the violins ceased to play, the whole company stood fascinated by the beauty of the unknown princess. Only a low murmur was heard: "Ah, how lovely she is!" The King himself, old as he was, could not take his eyes off her and kept whispering to the Queen that it was a long time since he had seen such a beautiful and charming person. All the ladies were absorbed in noting her clothes and the way her hair was dressed, so as to order the same things for themselves the next morning, provided that fine enough materials could be found, and skillful enough craftsmen.

The King's son placed her in the seat of honour, and later led her out to dance. She danced with such grace that she won still more admiration. An excellent supper was served, but the young Prince was too much occupied in gazing at her to eat anything. She went and sat next to her sisters and treated them with great courtesy, offering them oranges and lemons which the Prince had given her. They were astonished, for they did not recognize her.

35   While they were chatting together, Cinderella heard the clock strike a quarter to twelve. She curtsied low to the company and left as quickly as she could.

As soon as she reached home, she went to her godmother and, having thanked her, said that she would very much like to go again to the ball on the next night—for the Prince had begged her to come back. She was in the middle of telling her godmother about all the things that had happened, when the two sisters came knocking at the door. Cinderella went to open it.

"How late you are!" she said, rubbing her eyes and yawning and stretching as though she had just woken up (though since they had last seen each other she had felt very far from sleepy).

"If you had been at the ball," said one of the sisters, "you would not have felt like yawning. There was a beautiful princess there, really ravishingly beautiful. She was most attentive to us. She gave us oranges and lemons."

Cinderella could have hugged herself. She asked them the name of the princess, but they replied that no one knew her, that the King's son was much troubled about it, and that he would give anything in the world to know who she was. Cinderella smiled and said to them:

40 "So she was very beautiful? Well, well, how lucky you are! Couldn't I see her? Please, Miss Javotte, do lend me that yellow dress which you wear about the house."

"Really," said Miss Javotte, "what an idea! Lend one's dress like that to a filthy Cinderbottom! I should have to be out of my mind."

Cinderella was expecting this refusal and she was very glad when it came, for she would have been in an awkward position if her sister really had lent her her frock.

On the next day the two sisters went to the ball, and Cinderella too, but even more splendidly dressed than the first time. The King's son was constantly at her side and wooed her the whole evening. The young girl was enjoying herself so much that she forgot her godmother's warning. She heard the clock striking the first stroke of midnight when she thought that it was still hardly eleven. She rose and slipped away as lightly as a roe-deer. The Prince followed her, but he could not catch her up. One of her glass slippers fell off, and the Prince picked it up with great care.

Cinderella reached home quite out of breath, with no coach, no footmen, and wearing her old clothes. Nothing remained of all her finery, except one of her little slippers, the fellow to the one which she had dropped. The guards at the palace gate were asked if they had not seen a princess go out. They answered that they had seen no one go out except a very poorly dressed girl, who looked more like a peasant than a young lady.

45 When the two sisters returned from the ball, Cinderella asked them if they had enjoyed themselves again, and if the beautiful lady had been there. They said that she had, but that she had run away when it struck midnight, and so swiftly that she had lost one of her glass slippers, a lovely little thing. The Prince had picked it up and had done nothing but gaze at it for the rest of the ball, and undoubtedly he was very much in love with the beautiful person to whom it belonged.

They were right, for a few days later the King's son had it proclaimed to the sound of trumpets that he would marry the girl whose foot exactly fitted the slipper. They began by trying it on the various princesses, then on the duchesses and on all the ladies of the Court, but with no success. It was brought to the two sisters, who did everything possible to force their feet into the slipper, but they could not manage it. Cinderella, who was looking on, recognized her own slipper, and said laughing:

"Let me see if it would fit me!"

Her sisters began to laugh and mock at her. But the gentleman who was trying on the slipper looked closely at Cinderella and, seeing that she was very beautiful, said that her request was perfectly reasonable and that he had instructions to try it on every girl. He made Cinderella sit down and, raising the slipper to her foot, he found that it slid on without difficulty and fitted like a glove.

Great was the amazement of the two sisters, but it became greater still when Cinderella drew from her pocket the second little slipper and put it on her other foot. Thereupon the fairy godmother came in and, touching Cinderella's clothes with her wand, made them even more magnificent than on the previous days.

50   Then the two sisters recognized her as the lovely princess whom they had met at the ball. They flung themselves at her feet and begged her forgiveness for all the unkind things which they had done to her. Cinderella raised them up and kissed them, saying that she forgave them with all her heart and asking them to love her always. She was taken to the young Prince in the fine clothes which she was wearing. He thought her more beautiful than ever and a few days later he married her. Cinderella, who was as kind as she was beautiful, invited her two sisters to live in the palace and married them, on the same day, to two great noblemen of the Court.

ASHPUTTLE

Jakob and Wilhelm Grimm

Jakob Grimm (1785–1863) and Wilhelm Grimm (1786–1859) are best known today for the 200 folktales they collected from oral sources and reworked in *Kinder- und Hausmärchen* (popularly known as *Grimm's Fairy Tales*), which has been translated into 70 languages. The techniques Jakob and Wilhelm Grimm used to collect and comment on these tales became a model for other collectors, providing a basis for the science of folklore. Although the Grimm brothers argued for preserving the tales exactly as heard from oral sources, scholars have determined that they sought to "improve" the tales by making them more readable. The result, highly pleasing to lay audiences the world over, nonetheless represents a literary reworking of the original oral sources.

A rich man's wife fell sick and, feeling that her end was near, she called her only daughter to her bedside and said: "Dear child, be good and say your prayers; God will help you, and I shall look down on you from heaven and always be with you." With that she closed her eyes and died. Every day the little girl went out to her mother's grave and wept, and she went on being good and saying her prayers. When winter came, the snow spread a white cloth over the grave, and when spring took it off, the man remarried.

His new wife brought two daughters into the house. Their faces were beautiful and lily-white, but their hearts were ugly and black. That was the beginning of a bad time for the poor stepchild. "Why should this silly goose sit in the parlor with us?" they said. "People who want to eat bread must earn it. Get into the kitchen where you belong!" They took away her fine clothes and gave her an old gray dress and wooden shoes to wear. "Look at the haughty princess in her finery!" they cried and, laughing, led her to the kitchen. From then on she had to do all the work, getting up before daybreak, carrying water, lighting fires, cooking and washing. In addition the sisters did everything they could to plague her. They jeered at her and poured peas and lentils into the ashes, so that she had to sit there picking them out. At night, when she was tired out with work, she had no bed to sleep in but had to lie in the ashes by the hearth. And they took to calling her Ashputtle because she always looked dusty and dirty.

One day when her father was going to the fair, he asked his two stepdaughters what he should bring them. "Beautiful dresses," said one. "Diamonds and pearls," said the other. "And you, Ashputtle. What would you like?" "Father," she said, "break off the first branch that brushes against your hat on your way home, and bring it to me." So he brought beautiful dresses, diamonds, and pearls for his two stepdaughters, and on the way home, as he was riding through a copse, a hazel branch brushed against him and knocked off his hat. So he broke off the branch and took it home with him. When he got home, he gave the stepdaughters what they had asked for, and gave Ashputtle the branch. After thanking him, she went to her mother's grave and planted the hazel sprig over it and cried so hard that her tears fell on the sprig and watered it. It grew and became a beautiful tree. Three times a day Ashputtle went and sat under it and wept and prayed. Each time a little white bird came and perched on the tree, and when Ashputtle made a wish the little bird threw down what she had wished for.

Now it so happened that the king arranged for a celebration. It was to go on for three days and all the beautiful girls in the kingdom were invited, in order that his son might choose a bride. When the two stepsisters heard they had been asked, they were delighted. They called Ashputtle and said: "Comb our hair, brush our shoes, and fasten our buckles. We're going to the wedding at the king's palace." Ashputtle obeyed, but she wept, for she too would have liked to go dancing, and she begged her stepmother to let her go. "You little sloven!" said the stepmother. "How can you go to a wedding when you're all dusty and dirty? How can you go dancing when you have neither dress nor shoes?" But when Ashputtle begged and begged, the stepmother finally said: "Here, I've dumped a bowlful of lentils in the ashes. If you can pick them out in two hours, you may go." The girl went out the back door to the garden and cried out: "O tame little doves, O turtledoves, and all the birds under heaven, come and help me put

> *the good ones in the pot,*
> *the bad ones in your crop."*

Two little white doves came flying through the kitchen window, and then came the turtledoves, and finally all the birds under heaven came flapping and fluttering and settled down by the ashes. The doves nodded their little heads and started in, peck peck peck peck, and all the others started in, peck peck peck

peck, and they sorted out all the good lentils and put them in the bowl. Hardly an hour had passed before they finished and flew away. Then the girl brought the bowl to her stepmother, and she was happy, for she thought she'd be allowed to go to the wedding. But the stepmother said: "No, Ashputtle. You have nothing to wear and you don't know how to dance; the people would only laugh at you." When Ashputtle began to cry, the stepmother said: "If you can pick two bowlfuls of lentils out of the ashes in an hour, you may come." And she thought: "She'll never be able to do it." When she had dumped the two bowlfuls of lentils in the ashes, Ashputtle went out the back door to the garden and cried out: "O tame little doves, O turtledoves, and all the birds under heaven, come and help me put

the good ones in the pot,
the bad ones in your crop."

Two little white doves came flying through the kitchen window, and then came the turtledoves, and finally all the birds under heaven came flapping and fluttering and settled down by the ashes. The doves nodded their little heads and started in, peck peck peck peck, and all the others started in, peck peck peck peck, and they sorted out all the good lentils and put them in the bowls. Before half an hour had passed, they had finished and they all flew away. Then the girl brought the bowls to her stepmother, and she was happy, for she thought she'd be allowed to go to the wedding. But her stepmother said: "It's no use. You can't come, because you have nothing to wear and you don't know how to dance. We'd only be ashamed of you." Then she turned her back and hurried away with her two proud daughters.

5   When they had all gone out, Ashputtle went to her mother's grave. She stood under the hazel tree and cried:

"Shake your branches, little tree,
Throw gold and silver down on me."

Whereupon the bird tossed down a gold and silver dress and slippers embroidered with silk and silver. Ashputtle slipped into the dress as fast as she could and went to the wedding. Her sisters and stepmother didn't recognize her. She was so beautiful in her golden dress that they thought she must be the daughter of some foreign king. They never dreamed it could be Ashputtle, for they thought she was sitting at home in her filthy rags, picking lentils out of the ashes. The king's son came up to her, took her by the hand and danced with her. He wouldn't dance with anyone else and he never let go her hand. When someone else asked for a dance, he said: "She is my partner."

She danced until evening, and then she wanted to go home. The king's son said: "I'll go with you, I'll see you home," for he wanted to find out whom the beautiful girl belonged to. But she got away from him and slipped into the dovecote. The king's son waited until her father arrived, and told him the strange girl had slipped into the dovecote. The old man thought: "Could it be Ashputtle?"

and he sent for an ax and a pick and broke into the dovecote, but there was no one inside. When they went indoors, Ashputtle was lying in the ashes in her filthy clothes and a dim oil lamp was burning on the chimney piece, for Ashputtle had slipped out the back end of the dovecote and run to the hazel tree. There she had taken off her fine clothes and put them on the grave, and the bird had taken them away. Then she had put her gray dress on again, crept into the kitchen and lain down in the ashes.

Next day when the festivities started in again and her parents and stepsisters had gone, Ashputtle went to the hazel tree and said:

> *"Shake your branches, little tree,*
> *Throw gold and silver down on me."*

Whereupon the bird threw down a dress that was even more dazzling than the first one. And when she appeared at the wedding, everyone marveled at her beauty. The king's son was waiting for her. He took her by the hand and danced with no one but her. When others came and asked her for a dance, he said: "She is my partner." When evening came, she said she was going home. The king's son followed her, wishing to see which house she went into, but she ran away and disappeared into the garden behind the house, where there was a big beautiful tree with the most wonderful pears growing on it. She climbed among the branches as nimbly as a squirrel and the king's son didn't know what had become of her. He waited until her father arrived and said to him: "The strange girl has got away from me and I think she has climbed up in the pear tree." Her father thought: "Could it be Ashputtle?" He sent for an ax and chopped the tree down, but there was no one in it. When they went into the kitchen, Ashputtle was lying there in the ashes as usual, for she had jumped down on the other side of the tree, brought her fine clothes back to the bird in the hazel tree, and put on her filthy gray dress.

On the third day, after her parents and sisters had gone, Ashputtle went back to her mother's grave and said to the tree:

> *"Shake your branches, little tree,*
> *Throw gold and silver down on me."*

Whereupon the bird threw down a dress that was more radiant than either of the others, and the slippers were all gold. When she appeared at the wedding, the people were too amazed to speak. The king's son danced with no one but her, and when someone else asked her for a dance, he said: "She is my partner."

When the evening came, Ashputtle wanted to go home, and the king's son said he'd go with her, but she slipped away so quickly that he couldn't follow. But he had thought up a trick. He had arranged to have the whole staircase brushed with pitch, and as she was running down it the pitch pulled her left slipper off. The king's son picked it up, and it was tiny and delicate and all gold. Next morning he went to the father and said: "No girl shall be my wife but the one this golden shoe fits." The sisters were overjoyed, for they had beautiful feet. The eldest took the shoe to her room to try it on and her mother went with her. But the shoe was too small and she couldn't get her big toe in. So her mother handed her a knife and said: "Cut your toe off. Once you're queen you won't have to walk any more." The girl cut her toe off, forced her foot into the shoe, gritted her teeth against the pain, and went out to the king's son. He accepted her as his bride-to-be, lifted her up on his horse, and rode away with her. But they had to pass the grave. The two doves were sitting in the hazel tree and they cried out:

> *"Roocoo, roocoo,*
> *There's blood in the shoe.*
> *The foot's too long, the foot's too wide,*
> *That's not the proper bride."*

He looked down at her foot and saw the blood spurting. At that he turned his horse around and took the false bride home again. "No," he said, "this isn't the right girl; let her sister try the shoe on." The sister went to her room and managed to get her toes into the shoe, but her heel was too big. So her mother handed her a knife and said: "Cut off a chunk of your heel. Once you're queen you won't have to walk any more." The girl cut off a chunk of her heel, forced her foot into the shoe, gritted her teeth against the pain, and went out to the king's son. He accepted her as his bride-to-be, lifted her up on his horse, and rode away with her. As they passed the hazel tree, the two doves were sitting there, and they cried out:

> *"Roocoo, roocoo,*
> *There's blood in the shoe.*
> *The foot's too long, the foot's too wide,*
> *That's not the proper bride."*

He looked down at her foot and saw that blood was spurting from her shoe and staining her white stocking all red. He turned his horse around and took the false bride home again. "This isn't the right girl, either," he said. "Haven't you got another daughter?" "No," said the man, "there's only a puny little kitchen drudge that my dead wife left me. She couldn't possibly be the bride." "Send her up," said the king's son, but the mother said: "Oh, no, she's much too dirty to be seen." But he insisted and they had to call her. First she washed her face and hands, and when they were clean, she went upstairs and curtseyed to the king's son. He handed her the golden slipper and sat down on a footstool, took her foot out of her heavy wooden shoe, and put it into the slipper. It fitted perfectly. And when she stood up and the king's son looked into her face, he recognized the beautiful girl he had danced with and cried out: "This is my true bride!" The stepmother and the two sisters went pale with fear and rage. But he lifted Ashputtle up on his horse and rode away with her. As they passed the hazel tree, the two white doves called out:

> *"Roocoo, roocoo,*
> *No blood in the shoe.*
> *Her foot is neither long nor wide,*
> *This one is the proper bride."*

Then they flew down and alighted on Ashputtle's shoulders, one on the right and one on the left, and there they sat.

10   On the day of Ashputtle's wedding, the two stepsisters came and tried to ingratiate themselves and share in her happiness. On the way to church the elder was on the right side of the bridal couple and the younger on the left. The doves came along and pecked out one of the elder sister's eyes and one of the younger sister's eyes. Afterward, on the way out, the elder was on the left side and younger on the right, and the doves pecked out both the remaining eyes. So both sisters were punished with blindness to the end of their days for being so wicked and false.

A CHINESE "CINDERELLA"

Tuan Ch'êng-shih

"The earliest datable version of the Cinderella story anywhere in the world occurs in a Chinese book written about 850–860 A.D." Thus begins Arthur Waley's essay on the Chinese "Cinderella" in the March 1947 edition of *Folk-Lore*. The recorder of the tale is a man named Tuan Ch'êng-shih, whose father was an important official in Szechwan and who himself held a high post in the office arranging the ceremonies associated with imperial ancestor worship.

Among the people of the south there is a tradition that before the Ch'in and Han dynasties there was a cave-master called Wu. The aborigines called the place the Wu cave. He married two wives. One wife died. She had a daughter called Yeh-hsien, who from childhood was intelligent and good at making pottery on the wheel. Her father loved her. After some years the father died, and she was ill-treated by her step-mother, who always made her collect firewood in dangerous places and draw water from deep pools. She once got a fish about two inches long, with red fins and golden eyes. She put it into a bowl of water. It grew bigger every day, and after she had changed the bowl several times she could find no bowl big enough for it, so she threw it into the back pond. Whatever food was left over from meals she put into the water to feed it. When she came to the pond, the fish always exposed its head and pillowed it on the bank; but when anyone else came, it did not come out. The step-mother knew about this, but when she watched for it, it did not once appear. So she tricked the girl, saying, "Haven't you worked hard! I am going to give you a new dress." She then made the girl change out of her tattered clothing. Afterwards she sent her to get water from another spring and reckoning that it was several hundred leagues, the step-mother at her leisure put on her daughter's clothes, hid a sharp blade up her sleeve, and went to the pond. She called to the fish. The fish at once put its head out, and she chopped it off and killed it. The fish was now more than ten feet long. She served it up and it tasted twice as good as an ordinary fish. She hid the bones under the dung-hill. Next day, when the girl came to the pond, no fish appeared. She howled with grief in the open countryside, and suddenly there appeared a man with his hair loose over his shoulders and coarse clothes. He came down from the sky. He consoled her, saying, "Don't howl! Your step-mother has killed the fish and its bones are under the dung. You go back, take the fish's bones and hide them in your room. Whatever you want, you have only to pray to them for it. It is bound to be granted." The girl followed his advice, and was able to provide herself with gold, pearls, dresses, and food whenever she wanted them.

When the time came for the cave-festival, the step-mother went, leaving the girl to keep watch over the fruit-trees in the garden. She waited till the step-mother was some way off, and then went herself, wearing a cloak of stuff spun from kingfisher feathers and shoes of gold. Her step-sister recognized her and said to the step-mother, "That's very like my sister." The step-mother suspected the same thing. The girl was aware of this and went away in such a hurry that she lost one shoe. It was picked up by one of the people of the cave. When the step-mother got home, she found the girl asleep, with her arms around one of the trees in the garden, and thought no more about it.

This cave was near to an island in the sea. On this island was a kingdom called T'o-han. Its soldiers had subdued twenty or thirty other islands and it had a coast-line of several thousand leagues. The cave-man sold the shoe in T'o-han, and the ruler of T'o-han got it. He told those about him to put it on; but it was an inch too small even for the one among them that had the smallest foot. He ordered all the women in his kingdom to try it on, but there was not one that it fitted. It was light as down and made no noise even when treading on stone. The king of T'o-han thought the cave-man had got it unlawfully. He put him in prison and tortured him, but did not end by finding out where it had come from. So he threw it down at the wayside. Then they went everywhere* through all the people's houses and arrested them. If there was a woman's shoe, they arrested them and told the king of T'o-han. He thought it strange, searched the inner-rooms and found Yeh-hsien. He made her put on the shoe, and it was true.

Yeh-hsien then came forward, wearing her cloak spun from halcyon feathers and her shoes. She was as beautiful as a heavenly being. She now began to render service to the king, and he took the fish-bones and Yeh-hsien, and brought them back to his country.

5   The step-mother and step-sister were shortly afterwards struck by flying stones, and died. The cave people were sorry for them and buried them in a stone-pit, which was called the Tomb of the Distressed Women. The men of the cave made mating-offerings there; any girl they prayed for there, they got. The king of T'o-han, when he got back to his kingdom, made Yeh-hsien his chief wife. The first year the king was very greedy and by his prayers to the fish-bones got treasures and jade without limit. Next year, there was no response, so the king buried the fish-bones on the seashore. He covered them with a hundred bushels of pearls and bordered them with gold. Later there was a mutiny of some soldiers who had been conscripted and their general

---

*Something here seems to have gone slightly wrong with the text. [Waley]

opened (the hiding-place) in order to make better provision for his army. One night they (the bones) were washed away by the tide.

This story was told me by Li Shih-yuan, who has been in the service of my family a long while. He was himself originally a man from the caves of Yung-chou and remembers many strange things of the South.

THE MAIDEN, THE FROG, AND THE CHIEF'S SON
(AN AFRICAN "CINDERELLA")

The version of the "Cinderella" tale that follows was recorded in the Hausa (West African) language and published, originally, in 1911 by Frank Edgar. The tale remained unavailable to nonspeakers of Hausa until 1965, when Neil Skinner (of UCLA) completed an English translation.

There was once a man had two wives, and they each had a daughter. And the one wife, together with her daughter, he couldn't abide; but the other, with her daughter, he dearly loved.

Well, the day came when the wife that he disliked fell ill, and it so happened that her illness proved fatal, and she died. And her daughter was taken over by the other wife, the one he loved; and she moved into that wife's hut. And there she dwelt, having no mother of her own, just her father. And every day the woman would push her out, to go off to the bush to gather wood. When she returned, she had to pound up the *fura*. Then she had the *tuwo* to pound, and, after that, to stir. And then they wouldn't even let her eat the *tuwo*. All they gave her to eat were the burnt bits at the bottom of the pot. And day after day she continued thus.

Now she had an elder brother, and he invited her to come and eat regularly at his home—to which she agreed. But still when she had been to the bush, and returned home, and wanted a drink of water, they wouldn't let her have one. Nor would they give her proper food—only the coarsest of the grindings and the scrapings from the pot. These she would take, and going with them to a borrow-pit, throw them in. And the frogs would come out and start eating the scrapings. Then, having eaten them up, they would go back into the water; and she too would return home.

And so things went on day after day, until the day of the Festival arrived. And on this day, when she went along with the scrapings and coarse grindings, she found a frog squatting here; and realized that he was waiting for her! She got there and threw in the bits of food. Whereupon the frog said, "Maiden, you've always been very kind to us, and now we—but just you come along tomorrow morning. That's the morning of the Festival. Come along then, and we'll be kind to you, in our turn." "Fine," she said, and went off home.

5   Next morning was the Festival, and she was going off to the borrow-pit, just as the frog had told her. But as she was going, her half-sister's mother said to her, "Hey—come here, you good-for-nothing girl! You haven't stirred the *tuwo*,

or pounded the *fura,* or fetched the wood or the water." So the girl returned. And the frog spent the whole day waiting for her. But she, having returned to the compound, set off to fetch wood. Then she fetched water, and set about pounding the *tuwo,* and stirred it till it was done and then took it off the fire. And presently she was told to take the scrapings. She did so and went off to the borrow-pit, where she found the frog. "Tut tut, girl!" said he, "I've been waiting for you here since morning, and you never came." "Old fellow," she said, "You see, I'm a slave." "How come?" he asked. "Simple," she said, "My mother died—died leaving me her only daughter. I have an elder brother, but he is married and has a compound of his own. And my father put me in the care of his other wife. And indeed he had never loved my mother. So I was moved into the hut of his other wife. And, as I told you, slavery is my lot. Every morning I have to go off to the bush to get wood. When I get back from that I have to pound the *fura,* and then I pound the *tuwo,* and then start stirring it. And even when I have finished stirring the *tuwo,* I'm not given it to eat—just the scrapings." Says the frog, "Girl, give us your hand." And she held it out to him, and they both leaped into the water.

Then he went and picked her up and swallowed her. (And he vomited her up.) "Good people," said he, "Look and tell me, is she straight or crooked?" And they looked and answered, "She is bent to the left." So he picked her up and swallowed her again and then brought her up, and again asked them the same question. "She's quite straight now," they said. "Good," said he.

Next he vomited up cloths for her, and bangles, and rings, and a pair of shoes, one of silver, one of gold. "And now," said he, "Off you go to the dancing." So all these things were given to her, and he said to her, "When you get there, and when the dancing is nearly over and the dancers dispersing, you're to leave your golden shoe, the right one, there." And the girl replied to the frog, "Very well, old fellow, I understand," and off she went.

Meanwhile the chief's son had caused the young men and girls to dance for his pleasure, and when she reached the space where they were dancing he saw her. "Well!" said the chief's son, "*There's* a maiden for you, if you like. Don't you let her go and join in the dancing—I don't care whose home she comes from. Bring her here!" So the servants of the chief's son went over and came back with her to where he was. He told her to sit down on the couch, and she took her seat there accordingly.

They chatted together for some time, till the dancers began to disperse. Then she said to the chief's son, "I must be going home." "Oh, are you off?" said he. "Yes," said she and rose to her feet. "I'll accompany you on your way for a little," said the chief's son, and he did so. But she had left her right shoe behind. Presently she said, "Chief's son, you must go back now," and he did so. And afterwards she too turned and made her way back.

10   And there she found the frog by the edge of the water waiting for her. He took her hand and the two of them jumped into the water. Then he picked her up and swallowed her, and again vomited her up; and there she was just as she had been before, a sorry sight. And taking her ragged things she went off home.

When she got there, she said, "Fellow-wife of my mother, I'm not feeling very well." And the other said, "Rascally slut! You have been up to no good—refusing to come home, refusing to fetch water or wood, refusing to pound the *fura* or make the *tuwo*. Very well then! No food for you today!" And so the girl set off to her elder brother's compound, and there ate her food, and so returned home again.

But meanwhile, the chief's son had picked up the shoe and said to his father, "Dad, I have seen a girl who wears a pair of shoes, one of gold, one of silver. Look, here's the golden one—she forgot it and left it behind. She's the girl I want to marry. So let all the girls of this town, young and old, be gathered together, and let this shoe be given to them to put on." "Very well," said the chief.

And so it was proclaimed, and all the girls, young and old, were collected and gathered together. And the chief's son went and sat there beside the shoe. Each girl came, and each tried on the shoe, but it fitted none of them, none of the girls of the town; until only the girl who had left it was left. Then someone said "Just a minute! There's that girl in so-and-so's compound, whose mother died." "Yes, that's right," said another, "Someone go and fetch her." And someone went and fetched her.

But the minute she arrived to try it on, the shoe itself of its own accord, ran across and made her foot get into it. Then said the chief's son, "Right, here's my wife."

15   At this, the other woman—the girl's father's other wife—said, "But the shoe belongs to my daughter; it was she who forgot it at the place of the dancing, not this good-for-nothing slut." But the chief's son insisted that, since he had seen the shoe fit the other girl, as far as he was concerned, she was the one to be taken to his compound in marriage. And so they took her there, and there she spent one night.

Next morning she went out of her hut and round behind it, and there saw the frog. She knelt respectfully and said, "Welcome, old fellow, welcome," and greeted him. Says he, "Tonight we shall be along to bring some things for you." "Thank you" said she, and he departed.

Well, that night, the frog rallied all the other frogs, and all his friends, both great and small came along. And he, their leader, said to them, "See here—my daughter is being married. So I want every one of you to make a contribution." And each of them went and fetched what he could afford, whereupon their leader thanked them all, and then vomited up a silver bed, a brass bed, a copper bed, and an iron bed, and went on vomiting up things for her—such as woollen blankets, and rugs, and satins, and velvets.

"Now," said he to the girl, "If your heart is ever troubled, just lie down on this brass bed," and he went on, "And when the chief's son's other wives come to greet you, give them two calabashes of cola-nuts and ten thousand cowrie shells; then, when his concubines come to greet you, give them one calabash of cola-nuts and five thousand cowries." "Very well," said she. Then he said, "And when the concubines come to receive corn for making *tuwo*, say to them, 'There's a hide-bag full, help yourselves.'" "Very well," she said. "And," he went on, "If your father's wife comes along with her daughter and asks you what it is like living in the chief's compound, say 'Living in the chief's compound is a wearisome business—for they measure out corn there with the shell of a Bambara groundnut.'"

So there she dwelt, until one day her father's favorite wife brought her daughter along at night, took her into the chief's compound, and brought the other girl out and took her to her own compound. There she said, "Oh! I forgot to get you to tell her all about married life in the chief's compound." "Oh, it's a wearisome business," answered our girl. "How so?" asked the older woman, surprised. "Well, they use the shell of a Bambara groundnut for measuring out corn. Then, if the chief's other wives come to greet you, you answer them with the 'Pf' of contempt. If the concubines come to greet you, you clear your throat, hawk, and spit. And if your husband comes into your hut, you yell at him." "I see," said the other—and her daughter stayed behind the chief's son's compound.

20   Next morning when it was light, the wives came to greet her—and she said "Pf" to them. The concubines came to greet her, and she spat at them. Then when night fell, the chief's son made his way to her hut, and she yelled at him. And he was amazed and went aside, and for two days pondered the matter.

Then he had his wives and concubines collected and said to them, "Look, now—I've called you to ask you. They haven't brought me the same girl. How did that one treat all of you?" "Hm—how indeed!" they all exclaimed. "Each morning, when we wives went to greet her, she would give us cola-nuts, two calabashes full, and cowries, ten thousand of them to buy tobacco flowers. And when the concubines went to greet her, she would give them a calabash of cola-nuts, and five thousand cowries to buy tobacco flowers with; and in the evening, for corn for *tuwo*, it would be a whole hide-bag full." "You see?" said he, "As for me, whenever I came to enter her hut, I found her respectfully kneeling. And she wouldn't get up from there, until I had entered and sat down on the bed."

"Hey," he called out, "Boys, come over here!" And when they came, he went into her hut and took a sword, and chopped her up into little pieces, and had them collect them and wrap them up in clothing; and then taken back to her home.

And when they got there, they found his true wife lying in the fireplace, and picking her up they took her back to her husband.

And next morning when it was light, she picked up a little gourd water-bottle and going around behind her hut, there saw the frog. "Welcome, welcome, old fellow," said she, and went on. "Old fellow, what I should like is to have a well built; and then you, all of you, can come and live in it and be close to me." "All right," said the frog, "You tell your husband." And she did so.

25   And he had a well dug for her, close to her hut. And the frogs came and entered the well and there they lived. That's all. *Kungurus kan kusu.*

OOCHIGEASKW—THE ROUGH-FACED GIRL
(A NATIVE AMERICAN "CINDERELLA")

The following version of the "Cinderella" tale was told, originally, in the Algonquin language. Native Americans who spoke Algonquian lived in the Eastern Woodlands of what is now the United States and in the northern, semiarctic areas of present-day Canada.

There was once a large village of the MicMac Indians of the Eastern Algonquins, built beside a lake. At the far end of the settlement stood a lodge, and in it lived a being who was always invisible. He had a sister who looked after him, and everyone knew that any girl who could see him might marry him. For that reason there were very few girls who did not try, but it was very long before anyone succeeded.

This is the way in which the test of sight was carried out: at evening-time, when the Invisible One was due to be returning home, his sister would walk with any girl who might come down to the lakeshore. She, of course, could see her brother, since he was always visible to her. As soon as she saw him, she would say to the girls:

"Do you see my brother?"

"Yes," they would generally reply—though some of them did say "No."

5   To those who said that they could indeed see him, the sister would say:

"Of what is his shoulder strap made?" Some people say that she would enquire: "What is his moose-runner's haul?" or "With what does he draw his sled?"

And they would answer:

"A strip of rawhide" or "a green flexible branch," or something of that kind.

10   Then she, knowing that they had not told the truth, would say:

"Very well, let us return to the wigwam!"

When they had gone in, she would tell them not to sit in a certain place, because it belonged to the Invisible One. Then, after they had helped to cook the supper, they would wait with great curiosity, to see him eat. They could be sure he was a real person, for when he took off his moccasins they became visible, and his sister hung them up. But beyond this they saw nothing of him, not even when they stayed in the place all the night, as many of them did.

Now there lived in the village an old man who was a widower, and his three daughters. The youngest girl was very small, weak, and often ill: and yet her sisters, especially the elder, treated her cruelly. The second daughter was kinder, and sometimes took her side: but the wicked sister would burn her hands and feet with hot cinders, and she was covered with scars from this treatment. She was so marked that people called her *Oochigeaskw,* the Rough-Faced Girl.

When her father came home and asked why she had such burns, the bad sister would at once say that it was her own fault, for she had disobeyed orders and gone near the fire and fallen into it.

15   These two elder sisters decided one day to try their luck at seeing the Invisible One. So they dressed themselves in their finest clothes, and tried to look their prettiest. They found the Invisible One's sister and took the usual walk by the water.

When he came, and when they were asked if they could see him, they answered: "Of course." And when asked about the shoulder strap or sled cord, they answered: "A piece of rawhide."

But of course they were lying like the others, and they got nothing for their pains.

The next afternoon, when the father returned home, he brought with him many of the pretty little shells from which wampum was made, and they set to work to string them.

That day, poor Little Oochigeaskw, who had always gone barefoot, got a pair of her father's moccasins, old ones, and put them into water to soften them so that she could wear them. Then she begged her sisters for a few wampum shells. The elder called her a "little pest," but the younger one gave her some. Now, with no other clothes than her usual rags, the poor little thing went into the woods and got herself some sheets of birch bark, from which she made a dress, and put marks on it for decoration, in the style of long ago. She made a petticoat and a loose gown, a cap, leggings, and a handkerchief. She put on her father's large old moccasins, which were far too big for her, and went forth to try her luck. She would try, she thought, to discover whether she could see the Invisible One.

20   She did not begin very well. As she set off, her sisters shouted and hooted, hissed and yelled, and tried to make her stay. And the loafers around the village, seeing the strange little creature, called out "Shame!"

The poor little girl in her strange clothes, with her face all scarred, was an awful sight, but she was kindly received by the sister of the Invisible One. And this was, of course, because this noble lady understood far more about things than simply the mere outside which all the rest of the world knows. As the brown of the evening sky turned to black, the lady took her down to the lake.

"Do you see him?" the Invisible One's sister asked.

"I do indeed—and he is wonderful!" said Oochigeaskw.

The sister asked:

25   "And what is his sled-string?"

The little girl said:

"It is the Rainbow."

"And, my sister, what is his bow-string?"

"It is The Spirit's Road—the Milky Way."

30   "So you *have* seen him," said his sister. She took the girl home with her and bathed her. As she did so, all the scars disappeared from her body. Her hair grew again, as it was combed, long, like a blackbird's wing. Her eyes were now like stars: in all the world there was no other such beauty. Then, from her treasures, the lady gave her a wedding garment, and adorned her.

Then she told Oochigeaskw to take the *wife's* seat in the wigwam: the one next to where the Invisible One sat, beside the entrance. And when he came in, terrible and beautiful, he smiled and said:

"So we are found out!"

"Yes," said his sister. And so Oochigeaskw became his wife.

WALT DISNEY'S "CINDERELLA"

Adapted by Campbell Grant

Walter Elias Disney (1901–1966), winner of 32 Academy Awards, is famous throughout the world for his cartoon animations. After achieving recognition with cartoon shorts populated by such immortals as Mickey Mouse and Donald Duck, he produced the full-length animated film version of *Snow White and the Seven Dwarfs* in 1937. He followed with other animations, including *Cinderella* (1950), which he adapted from Perrault's version of the tale. *A Little Golden Book,* the text of which appears here, was then adapted by Campbell Grant from the film.

Once upon a time in a far-away land lived a sweet and pretty girl named Cinderella. She made her home with her mean old stepmother and her two step-sisters, and they made her do all the work in the house.

Cinderella cooked and baked. She cleaned and scrubbed. She had no time left for parties and fun.

But one day an invitation came from the palace of the king.

A great ball was to be given for the prince of the land. And every young girl in the kingdom was invited.

5   "How nice!" thought Cinderella. "I am invited, too."

But her mean stepsisters never thought of her. They thought only of themselves, of course. They had all sorts of jobs for Cinderella to do.

"Wash this slip. Press this dress. Curl my hair. Find my fan."

They both kept shouting, as fast as they could speak.

"But I must get ready myself. I'm going, too," said Cinderella.

10   "You!" they hooted. "The Prince's ball for you?"

And they kept her busy all day long. She worked in the morning, while her stepsisters slept. She worked all afternoon, while they bathed and dressed. And in the evening she had to help them put on the finishing touches for the ball. She had not one minute to think of herself.

Soon the coach was ready at the door. The ugly stepsisters were powdered, pressed, and curled. But there stood Cinderella in her workaday rags.

"Why, Cinderella!" said the stepsisters. "You're not dressed for the ball."

"No," said Cinderella. "I guess I cannot go."

15   Poor Cinderella sat weeping in the garden.

Suddenly a little old woman with a sweet, kind face stood before her. It was her fairy godmother.

"Hurry, child!" she said. "You are going to the ball!"

Cinderella could hardly believe her eyes! The fairy godmother turned a fat pumpkin into a splendid coach.

Next her pet mice became horses, and her dog a fine footman. The barn horse was turned into a coachman.

20   "There, my dear," said the fairy godmother. "Now into the coach with you, and off to the ball you go."

"But my dress—" said Cinderella.

"Lovely, my dear," the fairy godmother began. Then she really looked at Cinderella's rags.

"Oh, good heavens," she said. "You can never go in that." She waved her magic wand.

> *Salaga doola,*
> *Menchicka boola,*
> *Bibbidi bobbidi boo!" she said.*

There stood Cinderella in the loveliest ball dress that ever was. And on her feet were tiny glass slippers!

25 "Oh," cried Cinderella. "How can I ever thank you?"

"Just have a wonderful time at the ball, my dear," said her fairy godmother. "But remember, this magic lasts only until midnight. At the stroke of midnight, the spell will be broken. And everything will be as it was before."

"I will remember," said Cinderella. "It is more than I ever dreamed of."

Then into the magic coach she stepped, and was whirled away to the ball.

And such a ball! The king's palace was ablaze with lights. There was music and laughter. And every lady in the land was dressed in her beautiful best.

30 But Cinderella was the loveliest of them all. The prince never left her side, all evening long. They danced every dance. They had supper side by side. And they happily smiled into each other's eyes.

But all at once the clock began to strike midnight, Bong Bong Bong—

"Oh!" cried Cinderella. "I almost forgot!"

And without a word, away she ran, out of the ballroom and down the palace stairs. She lost one glass slipper. But she could not stop.

Into her magic coach she stepped, and away it rolled. But as the clock stopped striking, the coach disappeared. And no one knew where she had gone.

35 Next morning all the kingdom was filled with the news. The Grand Duke was going from house to house, with a small glass slipper in his hand. For the prince had said he would marry no one but the girl who could wear that tiny shoe.

Every girl in the land tried hard to put it on. The ugly stepsisters tried hardest of all. But not a one could wear the glass shoe.

And where was Cinderella? Locked in her room. For the mean old stepmother was taking no chances of letting her try on the slipper. Poor Cinderella! It looked as if the Grand Duke would surely pass her by.

But her little friends the mice got the stepmother's key. And they pushed it under Cinderella's door. So down the long stairs she came, as the Duke was just about to leave.

"Please!" cried Cinderella. "Please let me try."

40 And of course the slipper fitted, since it was her very own.

That was all the Duke needed. Now his long search was done. And so Cinderella became the prince's bride, and lived happily ever after—and the little pet mice lived in the palace and were happy ever after, too.

CINDERELLA

Anne Sexton

Anne Sexton (1928–1974) has been acclaimed as one of America's outstanding contemporary poets. In 1967, she won the Pulitzer Prize for poetry for *Live or Die.* She published four other collections of her work, including *Transformations,* in which she recast, with a modern twist, popular European fairy tales such as "Cinderella." Sexton's poetry has appeared in the *New Yorker, Harper's, The Atlantic,* and *Saturday Review.* She received a Robert Frost Fellowship (1959), a scholarship from Radcliffe College's New Institute for Independent Study (1961–1963), a grant from the Ford Foundation (1964), and a Guggenheim Award (1969). In her book *All My Pretty Ones,* Sexton quoted Franz Kafka: "The books we need are the kind that act upon us like a misfortune, that make us suffer like the death of someone we love more than ourselves. A book should serve as the axe for the frozen sea within us." Asked in an interview (by Patricia Marz) about this quotation, Sexton responded: "I think [poetry] should be a shock to the senses. It should almost hurt."

You always read about it;
the plumber with twelve children
who wins the Irish Sweepstakes.
From toilets to riches.
5   That story.

Or the nursemaid,
some luscious sweet from Denmark
who captures the oldest son's heart.
From diapers to Dior.
10   That story.

Or a milkman who serves the wealthy,
eggs, cream, butter, yogurt, milk,
the white truck like an ambulance
who goes into real estate
15   and makes a pile.
From homogenized to martinis at lunch.

Or the charwoman
who is on the bus when it cracks up
and collects enough from the insurance.
20   From mops to Bonwit Teller.
That story.

Once
the wife of a rich man was on her deathbed
and she said to her daughter Cinderella:
25   Be devout. Be good, Then I will smile
down from heaven in the seam of a cloud.
The man took another wife who had
two daughters, pretty enough
but with hearts like blackjacks.

30   Cinderella was their maid.
        She slept on the sooty hearth each night
        and walked around looking like Al Jolson.
        Her father brought presents home from town,
        jewels and gowns for the other women
35   but the twig of a tree for Cinderella.
        She planted that twig on her mother's grave
        and it grew to a tree where a white dove sat.
        Whenever she wished for anything the dove
        would drop it like an egg upon the ground.
40   The bird is important, my dears, so heed him.
        Next came the ball, as you all know.
        It was a marriage market.
        The prince was looking for a wife.
        All but Cinderella were preparing
45   and gussying up for the big event.
        Cinderella begged to go too.
        Her stepmother threw a dish of lentils
        into the cinders and said: Pick them
        up in an hour and you shall go.
50   The white dove brought all his friends;
        all the warm wings of the fatherland came,
        and picked up the lentils in a jiffy.
        No, Cinderella, said the stepmother,
        you have no clothes and cannot dance.
55   That's the way with stepmothers.

        Cinderella went to the tree at the grave
        and cried forth like a gospel singer:
        Mama! Mama! My turtledove,
        send me to the prince's ball!
60   The bird dropped down a golden dress
        and delicate little gold slippers.
        Rather a large package for a simple bird.
        So she went. Which is no surprise.

        Her stepmother and sisters didn't
65   recognize her without her cinder face
        and the prince took her hand on the spot
        and danced with no other the whole day.
        As nightfall came she thought she'd better
        get home. The prince walked her home
70   and she disappeared into the pigeon house
        and although the prince took an axe and broke
        it open she was gone. Back to her cinders.
        These events repeated themselves for three days.
        However on the third day the prince
75   covered the palace steps with cobbler's wax
        and Cinderella's gold shoe stuck upon it.
        Now he would find whom the shoe fit
        and find his strange dancing girl for keeps.

He went to their house and the two sisters
80   were delighted because they had lovely feet.
The eldest went into a room to try the slipper on
but her big toe got in the way so she simply
sliced it off and put on the slipper.
The prince rode away with her until the white dove
85   told him to look at the blood pouring forth.
That is the way with amputations.
They don't just heal up like a wish.
The other sister cut off her heel
but the blood told as blood will.
90   The prince was getting tired.
He began to feel like a shoe salesman.
But he gave it one last try.
This time Cinderella fit into the shoe
like a love letter into its envelope.

95   At the wedding ceremony
the two sisters came to curry favor
and the white dove pecked their eyes out.
Two hollow spots were left
like soup spoons.

100   Cinderella and the prince
lived, they say, happily ever after,
like two dolls in a museum case
never bothered by diapers or dust,
never arguing over the timing of an egg,
105   never telling the same story twice,
never getting a middle-aged spread,
their darling smiles pasted on for eternity.

Regular Bobbsey Twins.
That story.

THE RISE OF PERRAULT'S "CINDERELLA"

Bonnie Cullen

In this next selection, art historian Bonnie Cullen explains how, from among the hundreds of "Cinderellas" throughout the world, Charles Perrault's version came to be what many in the West think of as the canonical, or standard, one. Of the seven variants of "Cinderella" named in this article, six appear earlier in the chapter. A longer version of this article first appeared in *The Lion and the Unicorn* (Volume 27, 2003).

Why [did] Perrault's story, above all others, [become the dominant version of "Cinderella"]? Considering its origins, there were many contestants for the dominant tale. "Cinderella" is really a large family of tales first analyzed by folklorists in the nineteenth century. Studying more than 300 related narratives from Europe and Asia, Marian Roalfe Cox identified Cinderella stories according to the presence of certain themes: an abused child, rescue through some reincarnation of the dead mother, recognition, and marriage.

The earliest known Cinderella story is actually a literary version from ninth-century China. Already it has the familiar elements. Yeh-hsien (Cinderella) lost both her father and mother and seeks consolation from a pet fish. Her cruel stepmother eats the fish and buries the bones. A man comes from the sky advising her to find and save the bones—she will get whatever she wishes for.

When her stepmother and stepsister leave for a festival, Yeh-hsien follows them in a cloak of kingfisher feathers and gold shoes. She loses a shoe, the shoe is found, and given to a king. A search for the foot small enough to fit the shoe ensues. Yeh-hsien is finally shown to be the rightful owner and marries the king (Ting 4–5).

In most early Cinderella tales, the dead mother hovers protectively, reincarnated as a cow, a fish, or a tree. Her relationship with the grieving daughter is as significant as the girl's triumph. Occasionally the protagonist is male. The shoe is not always the means of identification, although it is extremely common, as is the use of some magic garment (Philip).

5   By the sixteenth century, Cinderella appears in print in the West. One major debut is in Basile's seventeenth-century collection, *Il Pentamerone (Lo cunto de li cunti)*, as the feisty "Gatta Cenerentola" or "Cat Cinderella." Zezolla (Cinderella) kills her wicked stepmother with the help of a governess, but when the governess marries Zezolla's father, the girl is mistreated again. A fairy in a tree supplies magic clothes and a coach for a feast where Zezolla captures a king's heart.

In Basile's tale, the dead mother is no longer a significant presence, although she might be vaguely identified with the fairy. While close to some oral versions, his bawdy narrative is full of intricate metaphors and clearly written for an adult audience (Canepa 14–15). The book was published in Neapolitan dialect, which probably limited its dissemination in print (Canepa 12; Opie and Opie 20–21), although Basile's stories may have passed into the oral repertoire and traveled in other languages.

During the ancien régime of Louis the XIV, folktales were transformed into a new literary genre, the fairy tale. Narrated as a kind of conversational game in the salons of the *précieuses,* by the end of the century they were being written down (Zipes, *Beauties* 1–9; Warner 167–70). Two distinct versions of "Cinderella" issued from the pens of Charles Perrault and the Countess d'Aulnoy.

Marie-Catherine Le Jumel de Barneville, Baronne d'Aulnoy, was a feminist and writer, the first to publish her stories as "fairy tales," or literary versions of popular folktales. Her Cinderella, "Finette Cendron," is both altruistic and spirited. When their parents abandon Finette and her sisters, she engineers daring escapes for all three. They plot against her, but Finette remains loyal. With a godmother's help she finds some magnificent clothing and triumphs at the ball. She loses a shoe and gallops back to claim it, but refuses to marry the prince until her parents' kingdom, which they lost, is restored (d'Aulnoy, *Fairy Tales* 227–45).*

Perrault's "Cendrillon" is quite a different lady. He dubs her chief virtue "la bonne grace," i.e., in the face of adversity she is generous, long-suffering, charming and good-humored; the ideal bride, from the gentleman's perspective.

10   A bland protagonist perhaps, but Perrault exhibits his wit. Cendrillon plays her own tricks on the sisters, asking one if she can borrow a dress to see the mysterious princess at the next ball. He also writes tongue-in-cheek. The slipper, evoking female virginity, is made of glass in his tale. Not only is it fragile and extremely pure, but Perrault hints that visual proof will be necessary.

Perrault's position as a member of the French Academy may have led him to adopt this tone for tales of the peasant class (Warner 168–70). He also shifts the spotlight to the fairy godmother, giving her a dominant role. In the ancien régime, fairies were equated with powerful women at court (232–34). D'Aulnoy's fairy is sympathetic and dignified, asking Finette to be her lady's maid and comb her hair. Her magic is in providing the necessary items, whether or not she is present. Perrault's elaborate description of rat-and-pumpkin tricks is a spoof: his fairy godmother is a witch.

• • •

---

*An example of Finette's resourcefulness: Held captive in a castle, Finette devises a plan when a hungry ogre orders her and her two sisters to cook for him and his ogress (instead of eating them straightaway). It is the last request he makes:

> "But," said [the ogre], turning to Finette, "when you have lit the fire, how can you tell if the oven be hot enough?" "My lord," she answered, "I throw butter in, and then I taste it with my tongue." "Very well," he said, "light the fire then." The oven was as big as a stable, for the ogre and ogress ate more bread than two armies. The princess made an enormous fire, which blazed like a furnace; and the ogre, who was standing by, ate a hundred lambs and a hundred sucking pigs while waiting for the new bread. [Finette's sisters] Fleur d'Amour and Belle-de-Nuit kneaded the dough. "Well," said the great ogre, "is the oven hot?" "My lord," replied Finette, "you will see presently." And so saying she threw a thousand pounds of butter into the oven. "I should try it with my tongue," she said, "but I am too little." "I am big enough," said the ogre, and bending down he went so far into the oven that he could not draw back again, so that he was burned to the bones. When the ogress came to the oven she was mightily astonished to find a mountain of cinders instead of her husband.
>
> Fleur d'Amour and Belle-de-Nuit, who saw that she was in great distress, comforted her as they could, but they feared lest her grief should be consoled only too soon, and that regaining her appetite she would put them in a salad, as she had meant to do before. So they said to her: "Take courage, madam; you will find some king or some marquis who will be happy to marry you." At that she smiled a little, showing her teeth, which were longer than your finger. When they saw she was in a good humour, Finette said: "If you would but leave off wearing those horrible bear-skins, and dress a little more fashionably! We could arrange your hair beautifully, and you would be like a star." "Come then," she said, "let us see what you can do; but be sure that if I find any ladies more beautiful than myself I shall hack you into little bits." Thereupon the three princesses took off her cap, and began to comb and curl her hair, entertaining her all the while with their chatter. Then Finette took a hatchet, and with a great blow from behind, severed her head from her body.

For the complete version of d'Aulnoy's "Finette Cendron," go to http://www.surlalunefairytales.com/authors/aulnoy/1892/finettecendron.html.

When literary Cinderellas began to appear in English in the eighteenth century, it was Madame d'Aulnoy's story that took the lead. [An early version of her work appeared] in *A Collection of Novels and Tales, Written by that Celebrated Wit of France, the Countess d'Anois* (1721–22). Perrault's *Contes* did not appear in English until 1729.

By the nineteenth century, the tables had turned, apparently. Only seven English editions of d'Aulnoy's tales survive in the British Library; not all contain "Finette." There are over thirty editions of Perrault's "Cinderella" as a separate volume, besides its inclusion with the tales. Perrault's story was also adapted for pantomime and plays.

Perrault's version faced new competition, however. Searching for an antidote to bourgeois life—the stale "getting and spending," as Wordsworth put it—Romantics turned to nature. Might not the oral tales of country folk contain some primal wisdom? How closely they transcribed their originals is debated, but the Grimm brothers believed they were collecting rather than writing stories as they prepared their editions of *Die Kinder- und Hausmärchen* in 1812 (Warner 188–93). Their "Cinderella," "Aschenputtel," is indeed close to folk versions such as the Scottish tale, "Rashin Coatie" (Opie and Opie 117–18).

15   Mourning and revenge underlie "Aschenputtel": the heroine plants a tree on her mother's grave and tends it lovingly. A bird in the tree answers her calls for help. She begs for a dress, attends the feast and attracts the prince. The sisters cheat at the slipper test, cutting off parts of their feet, but birds reveal their deceit and at the wedding, peck out the sisters' eyes.

"Primal" tales had their opponents. With the first English translation, in volume two of *German Popular Stories* (1826), the brutal eye-pecking disappeared. During the previous century, the market for printed tales had expanded through chapbooks, devoured by a new audience of young readers as well as adults. By the end of the eighteenth century there was a movement in England to sanitize children's literature. Mrs. Trimmer, reviewing children's books for middle-class families; argued that the often brutal tales "excite...groundless fears" and "serve no moral purpose" (2: 185–86). This explains the intrusion of religious motifs, such as praying and church architecture, in chapbook illustration from the early nineteenth century, and the relative scarcity of expensive editions at the time.

Fairy tales would not go away, however. Those who wanted to imbue them with bourgeois morality faced equally vociferous champions of "pure" tales. "A child," Ruskin wrote, "should not need to chose between right and wrong. It should not be capable of wrong..." Innocent, children could be "fortif[ied]...against the glacial cold of selfish science" with the "inextinguishable life" of the folk tradition (83). As Zipes points out, arguments about fairy tales became part of the greater "Condition of England" debate on the effects of the Industrial Revolution (*Victorian Fairy Tales* xvi–xxix).

In the case of "Cinderella," it was a somewhat revised Perrault that prevailed in Victorian England.

• • •

One reason Perrault's tale [did so] was its suitability for a modern audience. During the nineteenth century, the market for literary fairy tales in England was increasingly urban and middleclass. Perrault focuses on the social sphere, rather than the forest. He delineates hairdos, costume, behavior at the ball and reactions to Cendrillon's appearance with the ironic tone of a society reporter.

20   D'Aulnoy's Finette is busy slaying ogres and galloping through the mud, while in "Aschenputtel" there is blood from the sisters' mutilated feet. Romantics like Ruskin favored the rugged terrain of folktales, but as Mrs. Trimmer's remarks indicate, "polite" readers were concerned about "improving" young minds to function effectively in society.

More important, perhaps, Perrault's tale prevailed in English because it was the best vehicle for Victorian notions of femininity. D'Aulnoy's heroine liberates herself through female power, both magical and human. Folk Cinderellas like Aschenputtel also take action, advised by incarnations of their lost mothers. Perrault's Cendrillon is the least active, and he shifts the spotlight to her fairy godmother, whose magic is as amusing as it is powerful.

Whether or not the oral fairy tale had been a female genre, as Warner argues, by the nineteenth century the fairy tale in print was increasingly dominated by male writers and illustrators in an industry controlled by male publishers. That even some women writers followed the "party line" with canonical Cinderellas shows how powerful a formula it was for the middleclass market of nineteenth-century England.

It is interesting to note that Disney's revival of "Cinderella," which repeats the Victorian interpretation of Perrault's story, came out in 1950: a time when women, indispensable in the workforce during the war years, were being urged back home with imagery of ideal wives and mothers. There have been attempts to reclaim the tale in recent years in both print and film. Yet the canonical tale, with its Victorian ideology, persists.

Works Cited

Canepa, Nancy L. *From Court to Forest. Giambattista Basile's Lo Cunto de li Cunti and the Birth of the Literary Fairy Tale.* Detroit: Wayne State UP, 1999.

Cox, Marian Roalfe. *Cinderella; Three Hundred and Forty-five Variants.* Publications of the Folk-lore Society (no. 31). London, 1893.

D'Aulnoy, Marie Catherine Baronne. *The Fairy Tales of Madame D'Aulnoy.* Trans. Annie Macdonnell and Miss Lee. London: Lawrence and Bullen, 1892.

Opie, Iona, and Peter Opie. *The Classic Fairy Tales.* Oxford: Book Club Associates by arrangement with Oxford UP, 1992.

Philip, Neil. *The Cinderella Story.* Harmondsworth: Penguin, 1989.

Ruskin, John. "Fairy Stories." Ed. Lance Salway. *Signal* (May 1972): 81–86.

Ting, Nai-Tung. *The Cinderella Cycle in China and Indo-China.* F. F. Communications no. 213. Helsinki: Suomalainen, 1974.

Trimmer, Sarah. *The Guardian of Education.* 5 vols. London: J. Johnson, 1801–05.

Warner, Marina. *From the Beast to the Blond.* London: Vintage, 1995.

Zipes, Jack David. *Beauties, Beasts and Enchantment: Classic French Fairy Tales.* New York: New American Library, 1989.

———.*Victorian Fairy Tales: The Revolt of the Fairies and Elves.* New York: Methuen, 1987.

● Review Questions

1. What are the classic elements of the "Cinderella" tale?

2. What features distinguished the early "Cinderella" folktales from later fairy tale versions? When and where did the transformation from folktale to fairy tale occur?

3. In the nineteenth century, what motivated the Grimm brothers to record their version of "Cinderella" and others like it as an alternative to Perrault's "Cinderella"?

4. How does Perrault's "Cinderella" differ from those of D'Aulnoy and Grimm?

5. How did Perrault's "Cinderella" become "canonical"?

● Discussion and Writing Suggestions

1. Of the versions of "Cinderella" presented in this chapter, was Perrault's the most familiar—the one you were/are inclined to call the "real" "Cinderella"? To what extent were you aware of the historical, social, and even political forces at work to make Perrault's "Cinderella" the canonical one?

2. Cullen finds it "interesting to note that Disney's revival of 'Cinderella,' which repeats the Victorian interpretation of Perrault's story, came out in 1950: a time when women, indispensable in the workforce during the war years, were being urged back home with imagery of ideal wives and mothers." What does Cullen's "interesting to note" suggest to you? Do you suppose that Disney was lobbying for a specific economic or social agenda by bringing out his "Cinderella"—both the film and print versions?

3. Read D'Aulnoy's "Finette Cendron" <http://www.surlalunefairytales.com/authors/aulnoy/1892/finettecendron.html>. Also read Perrault's and Disney's versions of "Cinderella," "Ashputtle," and the "Chinese 'Cinderella'" in this text. In her article, how accurately has Cullen described the differences among these versions?

4. Address the notion of selecting a fairy tale based on its "suitability" for a particular audience. In broad cultural terms, how is suitability determined? How would *you* determine suitability for your children or younger siblings, if the decision of which story to read, or movie or television show to watch, were left to you?

"Cinderella": A Story of Sibling Rivalry and Oedipal Conflicts

Bruno Bettelheim

Having read several variants of "Cinderella," you may have wondered what it is about this story that's prompted people in different parts of the world, at different times, to show interest in a child who's been debased but then rises above her misfortune. Why are people so fascinated with "Cinderella"?

Depending on the people you ask and their perspectives, you'll find this question answered in various ways. As a Freudian psychologist, Bruno Bettelheim believes that the mind is a repository of both conscious and unconscious elements. By definition, we aren't aware of what goes on in our unconscious; nonetheless, what happens there exerts a powerful influence on what we believe and on how we act. This division of the mind into conscious and unconscious parts is true for children no less than for adults. Based on these beliefs about the mind, Bettelheim analyzes "Cinderella" first by pointing to what he calls the story's essential theme: sibling rivalry, or Cinderella's mistreatment at the hands of her stepsisters. Competition among brothers and sisters presents a profound and largely unconscious problem to children, says Bettelheim. By hearing "Cinderella," a story that speaks directly to their unconscious, children are given tools that can help them resolve conflicts. Cinderella resolves her difficulties; children hearing the story can resolve theirs as well: This is the unconscious message of the tale.

To accept this argument, you'd have to agree with the author's reading of "Cinderella" and its hidden meanings; and you'd have to agree with his assumptions concerning the conscious and unconscious mind and the ways in which the unconscious will seize upon the content of a story in order to resolve conflicts. Even if you don't accept Bettelheim's analysis, his essay makes fascinating reading. First, it is internally consistent—that is, he begins with a set of principles and then builds logically upon them, as any good writer will. Second, his analysis demonstrates how a scholarly point of view—a coherent set of assumptions about the way the world (in this case, the mind) works—creates boundaries for a discussion. Change the assumptions and you'll change the analyses that follow from them.

Bettelheim's essay is long and somewhat difficult. While he uses no subheadings, he has divided his work into four sections: paragraphs 2–10 are devoted to sibling rivalry; paragraphs 11–19, to an analysis of "Cinderella's" hidden meanings; paragraphs 20–24, to the psychological makeup of children at the end of their Oedipal period; and paragraphs 25–27, to the reasons "Cinderella," in particular, appeals to children in the Oedipal period.

Bruno Bettelheim, a distinguished psychologist and educator, was born in 1903 in Vienna. He was naturalized as an American citizen in 1939 and served as a professor of psychology at Rockford College and the University of Chicago. Awarded the honor of fellow by several prestigious professional associations, Bettelheim was a prolific writer and contributed articles to numerous popular and professional publications. His list of books includes *Love Is Not Enough: The Treatment of Emotionally Disturbed Children* (1950), *The Informed Heart* (1960), and *The Uses of Enchantment* (1975), from which this selection has been excerpted. Bettelheim died in 1990.

By all accounts, "Cinderella" is the best-known fairy tale, and probably also the best-liked. It is quite an old story; when first written down in China during the ninth century A.D., it already had a history. The unrivaled tiny foot size as a mark of extraordinary virtue, distinction, and beauty, and the slipper made of precious material are facets which point to an Eastern, if not necessarily Chinese, origin.* The modern hearer does not connect sexual attractiveness and beauty in general with extreme smallness of the foot, as the ancient Chinese did, in accordance with their practice of binding women's feet.

"Cinderella," as we know it, is experienced as a story about the agonies and hopes which form the essential content of sibling rivalry; and about the degraded heroine winning out over her siblings who abused her. Long before Perrault gave "Cinderella" the form in which it is now widely known, "having to live among the ashes" was a symbol of being debased in comparison to one's siblings, irrespective of sex. In Germany, for example, there were stories in which such an ash-boy later becomes king, which parallels Cinderella's fate. "Aschenputtel" is the title of the Brothers Grimm's version of the tale. The term originally designated a lowly, dirty kitchenmaid who must tend to the fireplace ashes.

There are many examples in the German language of how being forced to dwell among the ashes was a symbol not just of degradation, but also of sibling rivalry, and of the sibling who finally surpasses the brother or brothers who have debased him. Martin Luther in his *Table Talks* speaks about Cain as the God-forsaken evildoer who is powerful, while pious Abel is forced to be his ash-brother (*Asche-brüdel*), a mere nothing, subject to Cain; in one of Luther's sermons he says that Esau was forced into the role of Jacob's ash-brother. Cain and Abel, Jacob and Esau are Biblical examples of one brother being suppressed or destroyed by the other.

The fairy tale replaces sibling relations with relations between step-siblings—perhaps a device to explain and make acceptable an animosity which one wishes would not exist among true siblings. Although sibling rivalry is universal and "natural" in the sense that it is the negative consequence of being a sibling, this same relation also generates equally as much positive feeling between siblings, highlighted in fairy tales such as "Brother and Sister."

5   No other fairy tale renders so well as the "Cinderella" stories the inner experiences of the young child in the throes of sibling rivalry, when he feels hopelessly outclassed by his brothers and sisters. Cinderella is pushed down and degraded by her stepsisters; her interests are sacrificed to theirs by her (step)mother; she is expected to do the dirtiest work and although she performs it well, she receives no credit for it; only more is demanded of her. This is how the child feels when devastated by the miseries of sibling rivalry. Exaggerated though Cinderella's tribulations and degradations may seem to the adult, the child carried away by

---

*Artistically made slippers of precious material were reported in Egypt from the third century on. The Roman emperor Diocletian in a decree of A.D. 301 set maximum prices for different kinds of footwear, including slippers made of fine Babylonian leather, dyed purple or scarlet, and gilded slippers for women. [Bettelheim]

sibling rivalry feels, "That's me; that's how they mistreat me, or would want to; that's how little they think of me." And there are moments—often long time periods—when for inner reasons a child feels this way even when his position among his siblings may seem to give him no cause for it.

When a story corresponds to how the child feels deep down—as no realistic narrative is likely to do—it attains an emotional quality of "truth" for the child. The events of "Cinderella" offer him vivid images that give body to his overwhelming but nevertheless often vague and nondescript emotions; so these episodes seem more convincing to him than his life experiences.

The term "sibling rivalry" refers to a most complex constellation of feelings and their causes. With extremely rare exceptions, the emotions aroused in the person subject to sibling rivalry are far out of proportion to what his real situation with his sisters and brothers would justify, seen objectively. While all children at times suffer greatly from sibling rivalry, parents seldom sacrifice one of their children to the others, nor do they condone the other children's persecuting one of them. Difficult as objective judgments are for the young child—nearly impossible when his emotions are aroused—even he in his more rational moments "knows" that he is not treated as badly as Cinderella. But the child often feels mistreated, despite all his "knowledge" to the contrary. That is why he believes in the inherent truth of "Cinderella," and then he also comes to believe in her eventual deliverance and victory. From her triumph he gains the exaggerated hopes for his future which he needs to counteract the extreme misery he experiences when ravaged by sibling rivalry.

Despite the name "sibling rivalry," this miserable passion has only incidentally to do with a child's actual brothers and sisters. The real source of it is the child's feelings about his parents. When a child's older brother or sister is more competent than he, this arouses only temporary feelings of jealousy. Another child being given special attention becomes an insult only if the child fears that, in contrast, he is thought little of by his parents, or feels rejected by them. It is because of such an anxiety that one or all of a child's sisters or brothers may become a thorn in his flesh. Fearing that in comparison to them he cannot win his parents' love and esteem is what inflames sibling rivalry. This is indicated in stories by the fact that it matters little whether the siblings actually possess greater competence. The Biblical story of Joseph tells that it is jealousy of parental affection lavished on him which accounts for the destructive behavior of his brothers. Unlike Cinderella's, Joseph's parent does not participate in degrading him, and, on the contrary, prefers him to his other children. But Joseph, like Cinderella, is turned into a slave, and, like her, he miraculously escapes and ends by surpassing his siblings.

Telling a child who is devastated by sibling rivalry that he will grow up to do as well as his brothers and sisters offers little relief from his present feelings of dejection. Much as he would like to trust our assurances, most of the time he cannot. A child can see things only with subjective eyes, and comparing himself on this basis to his siblings, he has no confidence that he, on his own, will someday be able to fare as well as they. If he could believe more in himself, he would not feel destroyed by his siblings no matter what they might do to him, since then he could trust that time would bring about a desired reversal of fortune. But since the child cannot, on his own, look forward with confidence to some future day when things will turn out all right for him, he can gain relief only through fantasies of glory—a domination over his siblings—which he hopes will become reality through some fortunate event.

10   Whatever our position within the family, at certain times in our lives we are beset by sibling rivalry in some form or other. Even an only child feels that other children have some great advantages over him, and this makes him intensely jealous. Further, he may suffer from the anxious thought that if he did have a sibling, his parents would prefer this other child to him. "Cinderella" is a fairy tale which makes nearly as strong an appeal to boys as to girls, since children of both sexes suffer equally from sibling rivalry, and have the same desire to be rescued from their lowly position and surpass those who seem superior to them.

On the surface, "Cinderella" is as deceptively simple as the story of Little Red Riding Hood, with which it shares greatest popularity. "Cinderella" tells about the agonies of sibling rivalry, of wishes coming true, of the humble being elevated, of true merit being recognized even when hidden under rags, of virtue rewarded and evil punished—a straightforward story. But under this overt content is concealed a welter of complex and largely unconscious material, which details of the story allude to just enough to set our unconscious associations going. This makes a contrast between surface simplicity and underlying complexity which arouses deep interest in the story and explains its appeal to the millions over centuries. To begin gaining an understanding of these hidden meanings, we have to penetrate behind the obvious sources of sibling rivalry discussed so far.

As mentioned before, if the child could only believe that it is the infirmities of his age which account for his lowly position, he would not have to suffer so wretchedly from sibling rivalry, because he could trust the future to right matters. When he thinks that his degradation is deserved, he feels his plight is utterly hopeless. Djuna Barnes's perceptive statement about fairy tales—that the child knows something about them which he cannot tell (such as that he likes the idea of Little Red Riding Hood and the wolf being in bed together)—could be extended by dividing fairy tales into two groups: one group where the child responds only unconsciously to the inherent truth of the story and thus cannot tell about it; and another large number of tales where the child preconsciously or even consciously knows what the "truth" of the story consists of and thus could tell about it, but does not want to let on that he knows. Some aspects of "Cinderella" fall into the latter category. Many children believe that Cinderella probably deserves her fate at the beginning of the story, as they feel they would, too; but they don't want anyone to know it. Despite this, she is worthy at the end to be exalted, as the child hopes he will be too, irrespective of his earlier shortcomings.

Every child believes at some period of his life—and this is not only at rare moments—that because of his secret wishes, if not also his clandestine actions, he deserves to be degraded, banned from the presence of others, relegated to a netherworld of smut. He fears this may be so, irrespective of how fortunate his situation may be in reality. He hates and fears those others—such as his siblings—whom he believes to be entirely free of similar evilness, and he fears that they or his parents will discover what he is really like, and then demean him as Cinderella was by her family. Because he wants others—most of all, his parents—to believe in his innocence, he is delighted that "everybody" believes in Cinderella's. This is one of the great attractions of this fairy tale. Since people give credence to Cinderella's goodness, they will also believe in his, so the child hopes. And "Cinderella" nourishes this hope, which is one reason it is such a delightful story.

Another aspect which holds large appeal for the child is the vileness of the stepmother and stepsisters. Whatever the shortcomings of a child may be in his own eyes, these pale into insignificance when compared to the stepsisters' and stepmother's falsehood and nastiness. Further, what these stepsisters do to Cinderella justifies whatever nasty thoughts one may have about one's siblings: they are so vile that anything one may wish would happen to them is more than justified. Compared to their behavior, Cinderella is indeed innocent. So the child, on hearing her story, feels he need not feel guilty about his angry thoughts.

15   On a very different level—and reality considerations coexist easily with fantastic exaggerations in the child's mind—as badly as one's parents or siblings seem to treat one, and much as one thinks one suffers because of it, all this is nothing compared to Cinderella's fate. Her story reminds the child at the same time how lucky he is, and how much worse things could be. (Any anxiety about the latter possibility is relieved, as always in fairy tales, by the happy ending.)

The behavior of a five-and-a-half-year-old girl, as reported by her father, may illustrate how easily a child may feel that she is a "Cinderella." This little girl had a younger sister of whom she was very jealous. The girl was very fond of "Cinderella," since the story offered her material with which to act out her feelings, and because without the story's imagery she would have been hard pressed to comprehend and express them. This little girl had used to dress very neatly and liked pretty clothes, but she became unkempt and dirty. One day when she was asked to fetch some salt, she said as she was doing so, "Why do you treat me like Cinderella?"

Almost speechless, her mother asked her, "Why do you think I treat you like Cinderella?"

"Because you make me do all the hardest work in the house!" was the little girl's answer. Having thus drawn her parents into her fantasies, she acted them out more openly, pretending to sweep up all the dirt, etc. She went even further, playing that she prepared her little sister for the ball. But she went the "Cinderella" story one better, based on her unconscious understanding of the contradictory emotions fused into the "Cinderella" role, because at another moment she told her mother and sister, "You shouldn't be jealous of me just because I am the most beautiful in the family."

This shows that behind the surface humility of Cinderella lies the conviction of her superiority to mother and sisters, as if she would think: "You can make me do all the dirty work, and I pretend that I am dirty, but within me I know that you treat me this way because you are jealous of me because I am so much better than you." This conviction is supported by the story's ending, which assures every "Cinderella" that eventually she will be discovered by her prince.

20   Why does the child believe deep within himself that Cinderella deserves her dejected state? This question takes us back to the child's state of mind at the end of the oedipal period.* Before he is caught in oedipal entanglements, the child is convinced that he is lovable, and loved, if all is well within his family relationships. Psychoanalysis describes this stage of complete satisfaction with oneself as "primary narcissism." During this period the child feels certain that he is the center of the universe, so there is no reason to be jealous of anybody.

The oedipal disappointments which come at the end of this developmental stage cast deep shadows of doubt on the child's sense of his worthiness. He feels that if he were really as deserving of love as he had thought, then his parents would never be critical of him or disappoint him. The only explanation for parental criticism the child can think of is that there must be some serious flaw in him which accounts for what he experiences as rejection. If his desires remain unsatisfied and his parents disappoint him, there must be something wrong with him or his desires, or both. He cannot yet accept that reasons other than those residing within him could have an impact on his fate. In this oedipal jealousy, wanting to get rid of the parent of the same sex had seemed the most natural thing in the world, but now the child realizes that he cannot have his own way, and that maybe this is so because the desire was wrong. He is no longer so sure that he is preferred to his siblings, and he begins to suspect that this may be due to the fact that *they* are free of any bad thoughts or wrongdoing such as his.

All this happens as the child is gradually subjected to ever more critical attitudes as he is being socialized. He is asked to behave in ways which run counter to his natural desires, and he resents this. Still he must obey, which makes him very angry. This anger is directed against those who make demands, most likely his parents; and this is another reason to wish to get rid of them, and still another reason to feel guilty about such wishes. This is why the child also feels that he deserves to be chastised for his feelings, a punishment he believes he can escape only if nobody learns what he is thinking when he is angry. The feeling of being unworthy to be loved by his parents at a time when his desire for their love is very strong leads to the fear of rejection, even when in reality there is none. This rejection fear compounds the anxiety that others are preferred and also maybe preferable—the root of sibling rivalry.

Some of the child's pervasive feelings of worthlessness have their origin in his experiences during and around toilet training and all other aspects of his education to become clean, neat, and orderly. Much has been said about how children are made to feel dirty and bad because they are not as clean as their parents want or require them to be. As clean as a child may learn to be, he knows that he would much prefer to give free rein to his tendency to be messy, disorderly, and dirty.

At the end of the oedipal period, guilt about desires to be dirty and disorderly becomes compounded by oedipal guilt, because of the child's desire to replace the parent of the same sex in the love of the other parent. The wish to be the love, if not

---

*Oedipal: Freud's theory of the Oedipus complex held that at an early stage of development a child wishes to replace the parent of the same sex in order to achieve the exclusive love of the parent of the opposite sex.

also the sexual partner, of the parent of the other sex, which at the beginning of the oedipal development seemed natural and "innocent," at the end of the period is repressed as bad. But while this wish as such is repressed, guilt about it and about sexual feelings in general is not, and this makes the child feel dirty and worthless.

25   Here again, lack of objective knowledge leads the child to think that he is the only bad one in all these respects—the only child who has such desires. It makes every child identify with Cinderella, who is relegated to sit among the cinders. Since the child has such "dirty" wishes, that is where he also belongs, and where he would end up if his parents knew of his desires. This is why every child needs to believe that even if he were thus degraded, eventually he would be rescued from such degradation and experience the most wonderful exaltation—as Cinderella does.

    For the child to deal with his feelings of dejection and worthlessness aroused during this time, he desperately needs to gain some grasp on what these feelings of guilt and anxiety are all about. Further, he needs assurance on a conscious and an unconscious level that he will be able to extricate himself from these predicaments. One of the greatest merits of "Cinderella" is that, irrespective of the magic help Cinderella receives, the child understands that essentially it is through her own efforts, and because of the person she is, that Cinderella is able to transcend magnificently her degraded state, despite what appear as insurmountable obstacles. It gives the child confidence that the same will be true for him, because the story relates so well to what has caused both his conscious and his unconscious guilt.

    Overtly "Cinderella" tells about sibling rivalry in its most extreme form: the jealousy and enmity of the stepsisters, and Cinderella's sufferings because of it. The many other psychological issues touched upon in the story are so covertly alluded to that the child does not become consciously aware of them. In his unconscious, however, the child responds to these significant details which refer to matters and experiences from which he consciously has separated himself, but which nevertheless continue to create vast problems for him.

● Review Questions

1. What does living among ashes symbolize, according to Bettelheim?

2. What explanation does Bettelheim give for Cinderella's having stepsisters, not sisters?

3. In what ways are a child's emotions aroused by sibling rivalry?

4. To a child, what is the meaning of Cinderella's triumph?

5. Why is the fantasy solution to sibling rivalry offered by "Cinderella" appropriate for children?

6. Why is Cinderella's goodness important?

7. Why are the stepsisters and stepmother so vile, according to Bettelheim?

8. In paragraphs 20–26, Bettelheim offers a complex explanation of oedipal conflicts and their relation to sibling rivalry and the child's need to be debased, even while feeling superior. Summarize these seven paragraphs, and compare your summary with those of your classmates. Have you agreed on the essential information in this passage?

● Discussion and Writing Suggestions

1. One identifying feature of psychoanalysis is the assumption of complex unconscious and subconscious mechanisms in human personality that explain behavior. In this essay, Bettelheim discusses the interior world of a child in ways that the child could never articulate. The features of this world include the following:

All children experience sibling rivalry.

The real source of sibling rivalry is the child's parents.

Sibling rivalry is a miserable passion and a devastating experience.

Children have a desire to be rescued from sibling rivalry (as opposed to rescuing themselves, perhaps).

Children experience an Oedipal stage, in which they wish to do away with the parent of the same sex and be intimate with the parent of the opposite sex.

"Every child believes at some point in his life . . . that because of his secret wishes, if not also his clandestine actions, he deserves to be degraded, banned from the presence of others, relegated to a netherworld of smut."

To what extent do you agree with these statements? Take one of the statements and respond to it in a four- or five-paragraph essay.

2. A critic of Bettelheim's position, Jack Zipes, argues that Bettelheim distorts fairy tale literature by insisting that the tales have therapeutic value and speak to children almost as a psychoanalyst might. Ultimately, claims Zipes, Bettelheim's analysis corrupts the story of "Cinderella" and closes down possibilities for interpretation. What is your view of Bettelheim's psychoanalytic approach to fairy tales?

CINDERELLA: NOT SO MORALLY SUPERIOR

Elisabeth Panttaja

In this brief analysis of "Cinderella," Elisabeth Panttaja offers what for some will be an unsettling claim: that Cinderella succeeds not because she is more patient or virtuous than her stepsisters or stepmother (the typical moral of the story) but because she is craftier, willing to employ powerful magic to defeat the forces arrayed against her. Nor can it be said from the evidence of the story, according to Panttaja, that the prince or Cinderella love each other. Is this the same "Cinderella" that you grew up with? The article from which this selection was excerpted appeared originally in *Western Folklore* in January 1993. Elisabeth Panttaja taught at Tufts University when the article was written.

It is not surprising...that modern criticism of "Cinderella"...has been so strangely indifferent to the role that Cinderella's mother plays in the story. In our post-Freudian world, Cinderella's mother is imagined as absent despite the fact that she plays a central part in the unfolding of Cinderella's destiny. Indeed, Cinderella's mother's role is far from marginal: the words and actions of Cinderella's mother are of vital importance in narrative sequencing and the overall "moral" of the story. The Grimms' version of "Cinderella" opens significantly with the dying mother's injunction to the soon-to-be-orphaned girl. On her deathbed, the mother gives Cinderella the following advice: "Dear child, be good and pious. Then the dear Lord shall always assist you, and I shall look down from heaven and take care of you." In fairy tales, the opening scene is always of particular importance, since it is here that the tale sets forth the problem which it will then go on to solve. Cinderella's problem is precisely the fact that her mother has died. It is this "lack," the lack of the mother, which Cinderella must overcome in the course of the story. The narrative instantly complicates her task by staging the arrival of a powerful mother and her two daughters, who, in the strength of their unity, hope to vanquish the motherless girl. Thus the story quickly amplifies the mother/daughter theme, rubbing salt, if you will, in Cinderella's wound. For just as Cinderella's powerlessness is a result of her mother's death, so the stepsisters' power is associated with their strong, scheming mother. In short order, then, Cinderella finds herself in need of her mother's good advice, and it is through keeping her mother's advice that she manages to overcome her own social isolation and the plots of her enemies. In the end, Cinderella rises to a position of power and influence, and she accomplishes this, apparently, despite her motherless status.

But is she really motherless? Not really, since the twig that she plants on her mother's grave grows into a tree that takes care of her, just as her mother promised to do. The mother, then, is figured in the hazel tree and in the birds that live in its branches. Early in the story, the tree offers solace to the grieving girl; later, it gives her the dresses she needs to attend the ball. Likewise, the two pigeons who live in the tree expose the false brides as they ride away, with bleeding feet, on the prince's horse, and they lead the flock of birds who help Cinderella sort the lentils that the stepmother throws on the hearth. In addition, the fleeing Cinderella is said to find safety in a dovecote and a pear tree ("a beautiful tall tree covered with the most wonderful pears"). Since these places of refuge continue the bird/tree symbolism, it is quite possible that we are meant to see the mother's influence also at work in the rather mysterious way that Cinderella manages to avoid too-early detection. Thus, at every turn in the narrative, the magical power of the mother vies with the forces arrayed against Cinderella, whether they be the selfish designs of the stepmother and stepsisters or the futile attempts of the father and prince to capture and identify her. In the end, the mother, despite death, reigns supreme. Not only does she take her revenge on her daughter's enemies by plucking out the eyes of the stepsisters, but, more importantly, she succeeds in bringing about her daughter's advantageous marriage. The happy ending proves that it is the mother, after all, who has been the power of the story. Cinderella's success resides in the fact that, while apparently motherless, she is in fact well-mothered. In spite of death, the mother/daughter dyad has kept its bonds intact. At its most basic level, the story is about this mother/daughter relationship. It is about the daughter's loyalty to the (good) mother's words and the mother's continuing, magical influence in the (good) daughter's life.

Unlike the narratives favored by psychoanalysis, which are about maternal absence and disempowerment, this tale tells a story about a strong mother/daughter relationship that actively shapes events. Cinderella's mother performs a specific social function vis-à-vis her daughter—she assists in her coming out. Her gifts are directed toward a specific goal—to help Cinderella into an advantageous marriage. From this perspective, what is most interesting about Cinderella's mother is her similarity to the stepmother. These two women share the same devotion to their daughters and the same long-term goals: each mother wants to ensure a future of power and prestige for her daughter, and each is willing to resort to extreme measures to achieve her aim. Thus, Cinderella's mother is a paradoxical figure: while her power is associated at the outset with the power of the Christian god and while she seems to instruct Cinderella in the value of long-suffering self-sacrifice, she is also a wily competitor. She plots and schemes, and she wins. She beats the stepmother at the game of marrying off daughters. She does for Cinderella exactly what the wicked stepmother wishes to do for her own daughters—she gets her married to the "right" man.

Considering the similarities in their goals and strategies, the idea that Cinderella and her mother are morally superior to the stepsisters and their mother is shot through with contradictions. Throughout the tale, there exists a structural tension between the character that is drawn thematically (the pious Cinderella) and the character that acts in the narrative (the shrewd, competitive Cinderella). The superficial moral of the story would have us believe that Cinderella's triumph at the ball is a reward for her long-suffering patience. But while Cinderella's piety does play an important role in the forging of her supernatural alliance, it plays almost no role in the important practical business of seducing the prince. Indeed, the battle for the prince's attention is not waged at the level of character at all but at the level of clothes. Cinderella wins the battle because her mother is able, through magic, to provide raiment so stunning that no ordinary dress can compete. Cinderella's triumph at the ball has less to do with her innate goodness and more to do with her loyalty to the dead mother and a string of subversive acts: she disobeys the stepmother, enlists forbidden helpers, uses magic powers, lies, hides, dissembles, disguises herself, and evades pursuit. The brutal ending of the tale, in which Cinderella allows the mother (in the form of two pigeons) to peck out the eyes of the stepsisters, further complicates the story's moral thematics.

5   Just as there is a structural tension between the tale's thematization of Cinderella's goodness and the actual plot, so there is a tension between plot and the alleged theme of romantic love. I say "alleged" here because although modern

readers and critics have sought to enshrine romantic love as a central value of the tale, there is actually nothing in the text itself to suggest either that Cinderella loves the prince or that the prince loves her. The prince marries Cinderella because he is enchanted (literally) by the sight of her in her magical clothes. What is interesting about these clothes, at least in the Grimms' version, is that, far from simply enhancing a natural but hidden beauty, they actually create it. In the Grimms' version, Cinderella is described as "deformed," while the sisters are described as "fair," so we can only conclude that the power of Cinderella's clothes is indeed miraculous, since they turn a deformed girl into a woman whose beauty surpasses that of the already fair. Thus, the prince's choice of Cinderella can be explained neither by her piety, which he has never experienced, nor by her own beauty, which does not exist. It is the mother's magic which brings about the desired outcome, an outcome in which the prince has actually very little choice. The prince's oft-repeated statement, "She's my partner," as well as his obsessive tracking down of the true bride, suggests that he is operating under a charm rather than as an autonomous character, and the fact that both these motifs are repeated three times is further evidence that magic, not free choice, is at work here.

This is not surprising: the enchantment of a potential marriage partner is one of the most common motifs in fairy tales and mythology. The motif of an enchanted or somehow disguised bride or bridegroom usually appears in tales that depict some kind of unusual marriage, either the marriage of a god or demon to a human (Cupid and Psyche) or the marriage of a poor or ordinary mortal to a member of the deity or the nobility (Beauty and the Beast). The idea, of course, is that one member, by being disguised or by disguising another, can enter into a marriage that he or she would not normally enter into, usually one that crosses class lines. Thus, the enchantment of a prospective bride or bridegroom has more to do with power and manipulation than it does with romance or affection. Rather than talking about Cinderella's love for the prince, then, it is more accurate to say that Cinderella, in alliance with her mother, bewitches the prince in order to gain the power and prestige that will accrue to her upon her marriage to a member of the nobility.

● **Review Questions**

1. Generally, why is the opening scene of a fairy tale so important? Why is it of particular importance in "Cinderella"?

2. Panttaja claims that, despite death, Cinderella's mother remains very much present in the story. How so?

3. How is Cinderella's mother similar to the stepmother?

4. The claim that Cinderella and her mother are morally superior to the sisters and their mother is "shot through with contradictions." What are these contradictions?

5. Why is romantic love not central to winning the prince, according to Panttaja? What (and whose) personal qualities *are* essential?

6. What is often the purpose of a disguise or enchantment in fairy tales?

● Discussion and Writing Suggestions

1. Does Panttaja's claim that Cinderella's mother is not absent surprise you? Convince you? Explain.

2. What is your response to the claim that Cinderella is not morally superior to the wicked stepsisters or stepmother? Do you find Panttaja's argument compelling? Do you find yourself resisting it at all?

3. Number the sentences of paragraph 2, and then reread the paragraph and respond to these questions: What is the main point (the topic sentence) and where is it located? How does each sentence advance the main idea of the paragraph? Finally, examine the sequence of sentences. Why does Panttaja place sentences where she does? Having completed the analysis, what is your assessment of the paragraph? How successful is it?

4. If Panttaja is correct in her analysis of "Cinderella," what is the moral of the story? How does this moral compare with the one(s) you more typically associate with the story? Do you prefer one moral to another? Why?

5. Read the Grimm brothers' version of "Cinderella" and compare your reading with Panttaja's. Do you find her use of evidence in support of her main points persuasive? Have you, reading the same story, reached different conclusions? Explain, if you can, how two people reading one story can reach different conclusions. What does this say about the story? About the people reading it?

I Am Cinderella's Stepmother and I Know My Rights

Judith Rossner

In the humorous piece that follows, Judith Rossner lets Cinderella's much-maligned stepmother speak for herself, and we learn that she has successfully sued the Disney corporation for bringing out a movie that unfairly characterizes her and her daughters and misrepresents Cinderella as "a saint incapable of thoughts of revenge." Judith Rossner has written many novels, the most well-known being *Looking for Mr. Goodbar* (1975). One of her continuing interests, expressed most notably in *Olivia* (1994) and *Perfidia* (1997), has been the psychological entanglements of complex mother-daughter relationships. The following selection appeared originally in the *New York Times* on April 19, 1987. The piece begins with the following disclaimer:

> I have been asked to verify for those to whom it is not immediately apparent that since the following is a work of fiction…"written by" a person who never existed, the events referred to in it could not have taken place.

I've been often asked to explain why I never sued the Brothers Grimm or took public exception to the ugly little tale people think is about me and my daughters, yet have chosen to sue Mr. Disney over his loathsome movie. It's fair to guess that if I hadn't won the lawsuit, no one would care a bit about us or about the damages we've sustained. Having succeeded in getting the movie out of circulation, and in discouraging new editions of the story as well, I am besieged by hostile queries and comments, usually masquerading as concern for the storyteller's freedom.

First, it's essential to say I didn't look forward to pressing the suit and had hoped the whole matter would simply go away. If the picture the Grimms painted was distorted beyond belief, at least the name Cinderella—a name not bequeathed to my daughter by her parents or used by anyone who ever knew her—seemed to afford us some protection. Between scholars explicating the text and psychiatrists relating it to the events of our lives, not to speak of reporters investigating us for some gossip magazine, the story has not blown over. In fact, I have felt hostile eyes upon me all the time.

One of the defense attorneys claimed it wasn't the restoration of my good name I was after, but only attention. I was jealous, he said, of the unending spotlight on my stepdaughter Cinderella. I can only wish that he be locked in a room with the Grimms for eternity. He deserves the company of two men who constantly rewrite reality to make it bearable to themselves, no matter what havoc they create for those around them.

I have never claimed my girls were easy. Their father, my first husband, a remote and undemonstrative man, tended to show affection by lavishing gifts of clothing and jewelry upon them. When he died suddenly, leaving a legacy of debt and an estate in disorder, the girls were denied, not only the token protection of his presence, but also those material compensations he had provided. They became anxious and moody and worried that their prospects for decent marriages had been ruined.

5   At that time, Cinderella—as I shall call her to avoid confusion—was 14. Her father was a man of no particular ability or ambition who had made a good deal of money on a stock-market fluke. When he began to court me he was floundering, incapable of mobilizing himself or controlling his strong-willed daughter. She would not go to school. She had a foul mouth. She would not dress decently for any occasion. And she was filthy.

The notion of anyone's being forced to sweep the cinders in a household that can afford help is ludicrous except in certain circumstances. Cinderella spent her waking time at home, sitting at the fire, poking at the cinders and getting covered with ash, which she did not mind in the least! Since she neither kept her own room neat or helped in other household tasks, tending the fireplace seemed a perfect job for her. Nor did she appear to mind! That is one of the ironies of the charming little tale she later told people who relayed it to the people who told the Grimms. She would starve before she'd cook a meal and let her clothing get stiff with dirt before she'd wash it, but tending the fireplace was a task she appeared to enjoy!

Allow me to move to the tale of her father's bringing home from town (as requested by them respectively) fine clothing and jewelry for my daughters, the branch of a hazelnut tree for Cinderella. As the Grimms told it, Cinderella planted the branch in memory of her mother and proceeded to weep over it such copious tears as to cause it to sprout into a tree.

I promise you that her mother would not have done the same for Cinderella, who, she'd often said, would be the death of her. And her father, if he let her come close, was usually rewarded by a slap in the face. What I am saying is that those tears that watered the hazelnut tree were tears not of mourning but of jealously and guilt. The girl had ample reason for both. One of the qualities that made the Grimms' tale less objectionable to us than Mr. Disney's was that in their own way, the Grimms showed the suffering my girls endured. Those birds that pecked the beans from the fireplace and brought Cinderella the gown, and were thus clearly seen to be in her service, also pecked out my daughters' eyes. Mr. Disney, of course, gives us a saint incapable of thoughts of revenge, a portrait which, in its deep untruth, is much more unsettling to us.

Let us pass on to the matter of the Prince, who and what he was (a Prince, of course), and who he most distinctly was not (a responsible young man). Even if the rumors of drink and seductions and shoplifting were true, time might have turned him into a responsible adult. On the other hand, such escapades would worry any parent and were strikingly similar to our experiences with Cinderella. I've always found it peculiar that people failed to wonder why the Prince should have wanted this one pretty young girl of all the pretty young girls, including my two daughters, who lived in his kingdom.

10   To make a long story short, they were two of a kind. Those same stores in the village that locked the doors when they saw Cinderella approaching (do we need to deal, at all, with the nonsense of fairy godmothers and/or mice who provide her with clothes?) had, obviously, a much greater problem in dealing with our little Prince, who could buy whatever he wanted but chose to rip it off instead. If Cinderella didn't drink it was only because she liked to be in full control of everyone around her; if she was not promiscuous, it was because her filth discouraged advances (though it has always amused me that people swallowed whole the notion of a girl's being unrecognizable because she took a bath, combed her hair and put on a new dress).

In any event, my daughters were as eager as all the other young girls in the kingdom to be chosen by the Prince. Even in the modern era, when television has given an idea of the boredom of royalty's daily life, many girls might say they would give an arm or a leg to be a princess. Surely the Grimms knew the difference between using such an expression and actually cutting off one's big toe so one's foot will fit a glass slipper! Just as surely, any sane girl who thought of performing such a lunatic act would have been afraid of losing the Prince upon his discovery that she had a stump where her big toe had been! This is one of the few places where Mr. Disney's story is less objectionable than the Grimms'.

Which returns us to the matter of my motive in bringing this suit. Simply put, I owed it to my daughters. As you have seen, I have never claimed they were perfect. But beautiful they were. We knew it, everyone in town knew it, the Grimms knew it! It is the only quality allowed them in a tale that is otherwise a nightmare of caricature. Yet Mr. Disney chose to send them into history via the movies—which are seen in one theatrical showing by more people than read the Grimms' tales in the decade after they were written—as not only unhappy, but hideously ugly! Still, I was reluctant to sue. If I dreaded each release of the movie, I dreaded more the revelation and recrimination trying to stop it would entail.

Then video stores began to open near my home. I couldn't pass them without wondering if they stocked The Movie. I'd feel a change in some neighbor and sense she'd seen it and connected me and my girls to the story for the first time. Nightmares made sleep increasingly difficult. I entered therapy with a man I thought was being kind because he felt sorry for me. Finally, I talked to a lawyer who urged that I bring suit, with the results that you know. I FEEL vindicated by the court's decision, almost as pleased that certain bookstores have ceased to carry the Grimms. I think my life would now be pleasant and "normal" were I not being subjected to all sorts of pressures from disturbed children and misguided parents who are angry when they can't find "Cinderella" at their book or video stores.

I'm sick of the argument that a child's imagination conjures stories more frightening than anything in Grimm, and that the stories offer deep consolation for the difficulties of the real world. It is my own feeling that children will be better rather than worse off if confined to a diet of after-school specials and quiz shows. I wish that both had been available when I was raising my girls. They have a variety of problems that might never have arisen had they not been exposed, too young, to the ugly fantasies of the Brothers Grimm.

15   The other day a little girl and her mother got on the elevator in my building and the little girl shrieked "Mommy, is that the witch who killed 'Cinderella'?" Nobody can tell me that this idea came from a child's mind, and when I find out where she got that one, I'll sue him, her or them, too.

● Discussion and Writing Suggestions

1. Discuss the ways in which this selection is both a parody and a critique of two versions of "Cinderella." How does Rossner achieve her humor? How does she embed a critique within her humor? Base your answers on particular passages from the selection.

2. The stepmother objects less to the portrait of her family as painted by the brothers Grimm than she does to the one offered by the makers of the Disney animation. Why? (Why did she sue Disney, not Jakob and Wilhelm Grimm?) If you have not done so, read the Disney version of the story (pages 641–642), which parallels the movie, and the version by the brothers Grimm (pages 628–633). What, exactly, is the stepmother's complaint against Disney? Why has the Disney version offended her while the Grimm version has not?

3. What was the "truth" about Cinderella, according to the stepmother? What kind of girl was she when the stepmother first met her? What was

she like later, when the Prince entered the picture? In what ways were they "two of a kind"?

4. In paragraph 14, Cinderella's stepmother rejects the claims of analysts like Bettelheim who assert that in themes, plot lines, and tensions, fairy tale literature expresses the complex inner lives of children. On reading or listening to fairy tales, goes the argument, children find a tool that helps them understand their inner turmoil. The stepmother disagrees, saying that as far as her daughters are concerned, the "ugly fantasies of the Brothers Grimm" may well have *caused* inner turmoil, not helped to resolve it. Do you have an opinion on this important point? Insofar as you can tell, to what extent were fairy tales a psychological boon to you—or a problem?

5. Rossner relates the "Cinderella" story from an unexpected point of view. To what extent do you find the stepmother to be sympathetic in Rossner's telling? Is she any less "wicked" to you in this version?

THE PRINCESS PARADOX

James Poniewozik

In this appraisal of Cinderella movies, beginning with *The Princess Diaries* (2001), James Poniewozik explores some of the feminist themes that have found their way into updates of the classic tale. Moviemakers have reinvented Cinderella for the twenty-first century— almost: she's strong and resourceful, but she still loves her ball gowns. Poniewozik is media and television critic for *Time* magazine (and before that Salon.com). This article first appeared in *Time* on April 5, 2004.

It's the recurring nightmare of high-minded modern parents of daughters. You ask your relatives to lay off the pink pinafores at the baby shower. You give your daughter Legos and soccer balls, not Barbies. You encourage her to play fire fighter and immerse her in Dora the Explorer videos. Then one Halloween rolls around, and your empowered, self-confident budding Marie Curie tells you that she wants to be...a princess.

Call it nature or nurture, harmless fantasy or insidious indoctrination, but Hollywood is discovering that it still pays not to fight the royal urge. Following 2001's $108 million—grossing *The Princess Diaries*, Hollywood has waved its wand and conjured a set of Cinderella stories for girls, including next month's *The Prince & Me* and *Ella Enchanted*, as well as *A Cinderella Story* in July and a sequel in August. That's not to mention other fairy-tale projects (*Shrek 2*) and transformational stories like *13 Going On 30*, in which a gawky teen is magically morphed into a fashion-plate magazine editor played by the perpetually miniskirted Jennifer Garner.

We've come a long way, it seems, from the girls-kick-ass culture of just a few years ago (*Charlie's Angels*; *Crouching Tiger, Hidden Dragon*) in which a 360 [degrees] flying-roundhouse kick was a girl's best friend. (On the proto girl-power cartoon, *Powerpuff Girls*, one of the heroines' worst enemies was a spoiled brat named Princess Morbucks.) But brush off the fairy dust, and you find a new kind of Cinderella, one who would rather save Prince Charming, thank you, and who has learned the lessons of feminism—or at least learned to pay lip service to them. You can have the girly dream of glass slippers and true love, these films say, as well as the womanly ideal of self-determination and independence—and any contradictions between them are no match for the movies' magic.

Ella Enchanted, for instance, is a spoof of Cinderella in which the title character (*Diaries'* Anne Hathaway, Hollywood's queen of princesses) spends her free time protesting the discriminatory anti-elf and -giant policies of the family of Prince Charmont (Hugh Dancy). What she wants at first is not love but to free herself of a fairy's curse that forces her to be obedient. In *The Prince & Me* (what, *The Prince & I* would have been too egghead-y?), Paige Morgan (Julia Stiles) is a workaholic soon-to-be medical student who rolls her eyes at friends rushing to get their M.R.S. degrees. When she falls for Eddie (Luke Mably), a rakish-but-sweet exchange student who turns out to be Danish Crown Prince Edvard, the prospect of becoming queen upsets her dreams of working for Doctors Without Borders. (Stiles, who played Ophelia in the 2000 film *Hamlet*, should know that dating the prince of Denmark can be a pain.) "The Cinderella story has always frustrated me," Stiles says. "What I like about *The Prince & Me* is that my character is a lot more active and is ready to live a life by herself and be independent."

5   SPOILER ALERT: Skip this paragraph if you don't want to know how these movies end. O.K., here's the shocker—they end happily. What is surprising, however, is that, in the original ending of *The Prince & Me*, Paige broke up with Edvard to go to med school (in the final version, she gets to have both the guy and the career). And what's downright shocking is that Paramount approved the first, decidedly non-fairy-tale ending. "But when I saw it," says director Martha Coolidge, "I knew it was wrong. What was wrong about it was not what we thought—whether she got together with him or not. The real issue was about him making a compromise and the monarchy making a compromise."

Reinventing fairy tales has been a favorite project of feminist authors from Angela Carter (*The Bloody Chamber*) to Marlo Thomas (*Free to Be... You and Me*), who understood that wish-fulfillment stories are about teaching people what they should wish for. Among an earlier generation of women, the wish was to be able to do everything men could. For the modern Cinderellas' audience, which takes that freedom as a given, the wish is to also be able—unashamedly—to fall in love and go to the ball. Indeed, in *Prince*, Paige realizes that she needs to be "rescued" from her disciplined but single-minded careerism as much as she needs to assert her independence. Girls asserting their right to choose the fairy-tale ending is not a bad thing, says Thomas, since now the movies are balanced by varied depictions of young women in films from *Whale Rider* to *Blue Crush*. "What women have tried to achieve for other women," she says, "is choice in every step of their lives."

But to succeed on both the feminist and the fantasy level, the new Cinderella has developed rules and conventions as strict as a Joseph Campbell template.* She should be pretty, but in a class-president way, not a head-cheerleader way. She should be able to stand up for herself (recall the *Crouching Tiger* moves of *Shrek's* Princess Fiona). She must be socially conscious—a result, says Meg Cabot, author of the *Princess Diaries* books, of Princess Diana's charitable work. And she should above all not want to be a princess—at least until she changes her mind. In *Diaries*...it's not the girl who must prove herself worthy of princesshood; princesshood must prove itself worthy of the girl.

There's something a little have-your-tiara-and-disdain-it-too about making your protagonists ambivalent about the very fantasy that people paid $9 to see them live out. But that may make the fantasy more palatable to parents and filmmakers: men and, especially, women who are educated professionals. "I don't want to sound like an archfeminist," says Sherry Lansing, chairman of Paramount, which produced *Prince*, "but it really is important that it imparts contemporary values. It's a good love that allows both people to remain whole in it." Still, the fantasy couple that this earnestness yields in *Prince* is more yuppie than romantic: she, committing to years of med school; he, giving up his love of car racing to strap on a necktie and negotiate labor disputes. Goodbye, Chuck and Di; hello, Abbey and Jed Bartlet.†

But it's easy for someone who has been through college to say a diploma and career are not cure-alls. The movies' audience of young girls makes the filmmakers much more message conscious—at least as far as the girls are concerned. The princes in these stories have fewer options than their Cinderellas. Edvard and Charmont are both reluctant to become king, but they learn, through the love of a good woman, to mature into the role and use it for good. The girls fight to control their destiny; the boys good-naturedly learn to accept theirs. Of course, they're not the target audience. "It's nice to have something that's not toxic or repellent to men," says Nina Jacobson, a top executive at Disney (*Diaries'* studio). "But we know we don't

---

*Joseph Campbell (1904–1987) is best known for his work in comparative mythology. In *The Hero with a Thousand Faces* (1949), he traces how heroes in myths and folklore thousands of years old, from cultures around the world, progress through recognizable stages on their journeys away from the ordinary world, to a magical realm of adventure and severe challenge, then back to the ordinary. The classic versions of "Cinderella" that you have read in this chapter illustrate important features of what Campbell called a "monomyth"; here Poniewozik is suggesting, ironically, that the newer, filmed versions of "Cinderella" are similarly formulaic, though in ways calculated to sell tickets.

†Chuck and Di: As the older son of Queen Elizabeth II, Charles, Prince of Wales, is next in line to become King of England. "Di" is Diana, to whom Charles was married, then divorced. Jed (Josiah) and Abbey Bartlet: president and First Lady of the United States in the long-running television series *The West Wing*. Poniewozik is suggesting that Charles and Diana, a traditional royal couple, have given way in the popular imagination—or, at least, in the projected fantasies of the movie industry—to Abbey and Josiah Bartlet. Abbey is a Harvard Medical School graduate and practicing physician who will not hesitate to correct her husband.

need guys to make a movie like that successful." You just need a feisty girl, a prophylactic dose of skepticism and a fabulous ball gown—about which no ambivalence is necessary.

● Review Questions

1. What are the main differences between the prince and the princess in the new Cinderella movies, according to Poniewozik?

2. Poniewozik suggests that the makers of the new Cinderella movies want to "have-your-tiara-and-disdain-it-too." How so?

3. In what ways, according to Poniewozik, do more recent Cinderella movies suggest that we have come a "long way" from women as depicted in such action films as *Charlie's Angels* and *Crouching Tiger,* Hidden Dragon?

4. What is the "template" of the new Cinderella, according to Poniewozik?

● Discussion and Writing Suggestions

1. Poniewozik quotes an industry executive responsible for one of the new "Cinderella" movies: "it really is important that it imparts contemporary values." Is this your view of folk tales—that they impart "contemporary values"? If not "contemporary," then what sort of values?

2. Poniewozik is not neutral regarding the new wave of Cinderella movies. Locate passages that suggest, if not state outright, his views. Explain your choices.

3. Recognizing it had a gold mine in Cinderella updates like *The Princess Diaries*, the movie industry quickly released other "contemporary" versions of the tale. To what extent do you think these updates have bent the traditional tale out of recognition?

4. Rent and watch one or more of the Cinderella remakes that Poniewozik mentions in this article. Then write a critique of the article or prepare talking points for a critique that you will share in discussion, in class. Do Poniewozik's observations hold up? In your critique, focus especially on the updates to Cinderella's character and the new "template" intended to make her a heroine for the twenty-first century.

5. You have read at least some variants of "Cinderella" in this chapter. Assuming that Poniewozik's characterization of the new movie versions is accurate, are you heartened by the changes to the main character? Disheartened? Explain.

CINDERELLA AND PRINCESS CULTURE

Peggy Orenstein

Confronted with a daughter who enjoyed dressing as Cinderella and other storybook princesses, Peggy Orenstein set out to investigate "princess" culture and discovered an enormous corporate money-making machine. As a feminist, Orenstein warily approached the director of consumer products at Disney, Inc., responsible for the packaging of the Magic Kingdom's many princesses into a single merchandising juggernaut. She came away partially, if not entirely, assured that children can take on play identities that feminists once regarded as sexist and still "pass through" to an adulthood free of early gender stereotypes. Orenstein is a contributing writer for the *New York Times Magazine*, from which the following was excerpted. The original selection, titled "What's Wrong with Cinderella?" appeared on December 24, 2006. Her memoir *Waiting for Daisy: A Tale of Two Continents, Three Religions, Five Infertility Doctors, An Oscar, An Atomic Bomb, A Romantic Night and One Woman's Quest to Become a Mother* (2007) was a *New York Times* best seller.

I finally came unhinged in the dentist's office—one of those ritzy pediatric practices tricked out with comic books, DVDs and arcade games—where I'd taken my 3-year-old daughter for her first exam. Until then, I'd held my tongue. I'd smiled politely every time the supermarket-checkout clerk greeted her with "Hi, Princess"; ignored the waitress at our local breakfast joint who called the funny-face pancakes she ordered her "princess meal"; made no comment when the lady at Longs Drugs said, "I bet I know your favorite color" and handed her a pink balloon rather than letting her choose for herself. Maybe it was the dentist's Betty Boop inflection that got to me, but when she pointed to the exam chair and said, "Would you like to sit in my special princess throne so I can sparkle your teeth?" I lost it.

"Oh, for God's sake," I snapped. "Do you have a princess drill, too?"

She stared at me as if I were an evil stepmother.

"Come on!" I continued, my voice rising. "It's 2006, not 1950. This is Berkeley, Calif. Does every little girl really have to be a princess?"

5   My daughter, who was reaching for a Cinderella sticker, looked back and forth between us. "Why are you so mad, Mama?" she asked. "What's wrong with princesses?"

Diana* may be dead and Masako† disgraced, but here in America, we are in the midst of a royal moment. To call princesses a "trend" among girls is like calling Harry Potter a book. Sales at Disney Consumer Products, which started the craze six years ago by packaging nine of its female characters under one royal rubric, have shot up to $3 billion, globally, this year, from $300 million in

---

*Diana Spencer married to Prince Charles of England in a royal wedding broadcast around the world in 1981. The marriage unraveled and the pair divorced in 1996. She died in a car crash in Paris in 1997.
†Masako Owada, a Harvard- and Oxford-trained diplomat (and not of royal blood), married the heir to the Japanese throne in 1993. Ten years into her marriage, the pressures of her position caused "physical and mental fatigue," forcing her to retreat from public view for a time.

2001. There are now more than 25,000 Disney Princess items. "Princess," as some Disney execs call it, is not only the fastest-growing brand the company has ever created; they say it is on its way to becoming the largest girls' franchise on the planet.

Meanwhile in 2001, Mattel brought out its own "world of girl" line of princess Barbie dolls, DVDs, toys, clothing, home décor and myriad other products. At a time when Barbie sales were declining domestically, they became instant best sellers. Shortly before that, Mary Drolet, a Chicago-area mother and former Claire's and Montgomery Ward executive, opened Club Libby Lu, now a chain of mall stores based largely in the suburbs in which girls ages 4 to 12 can shop for "Princess Phones" covered in faux fur and attend "Princess-Makeover Birthday Parties." Saks bought Club Libby Lu in 2003 for $12 million and has since expanded it to 87 outlets; by 2005, with only scant local advertising, revenues hovered around the $46 million mark, a 53 percent jump from the previous year.* Pink, it seems, is the new gold.

Even Dora the Explorer,† the intrepid, dirty-kneed adventurer, has ascended to the throne: in 2004, after a two-part episode in which she turns into a "true princess," the Nickelodeon and Viacom consumer-products division released a satin-gowned "Magic Hair Fairytale Dora," with hair that grows or shortens when her crown is touched. Among other phrases the bilingual doll utters: "Vámonos! Let's go to fairy-tale land!" and "Will you brush my hair?"

As a feminist mother—not to mention a nostalgic product of the Grranimals‡ era—I have been taken by surprise by the princess craze and the girlie-girl culture that has risen around it. What happened to William wanting a doll and not dressing your cat in an apron?...I watch my fellow mothers, women who once swore they'd never be dependent on a man, smile indulgently at daughters who warble "So This Is Love" or insist on being called Snow White. I wonder if they'd concede so readily to sons who begged for combat fatigues and mock AK-47s.

10   More to the point, when my own girl makes her daily beeline for the dress-up corner of her preschool classroom—something I'm convinced she does largely to torture me—I worry about what playing Little Mermaid is teaching her. I've spent much of my career writing about experiences that undermine girls' well-being, warning parents that a preoccupation with body and beauty (encouraged by films, TV, magazines and, yes, toys) is perilous to their daughters' mental and physical health. Am I now supposed to shrug and forget all that? If trafficking in stereotypes doesn't matter at 3, when does it matter? At 6? Eight? Thirteen?

On the other hand, maybe I'm still surfing a washed-out second wave of feminism in a third-wave world. Maybe princesses are in fact a sign of progress, an indication that girls can embrace their predilection for pink without compromising strength or ambition; that, at long last, they can "have it all." Or maybe it

---

*Saks Incorporated closed its Club Libby Lu stores in January 2009.
†Dora the Explorer is a cartoon character in a Nickelodeon program geared toward young childen.
‡Grranimals were a clothing line for children in the 1970s.

is even less complex than that: to mangle Freud, maybe a princess is sometimes just a princess. And, as my daughter wants to know, what's wrong with that?

The rise of the Disney princesses reads like a fairy tale itself, with Andy Mooney, a former Nike executive, playing the part of prince, riding into the company on a metaphoric white horse in January 2000 to save a consumer-products division whose sales were dropping by as much as 30 percent a year. Both overstretched and underfocused, the division had triggered price wars by granting multiple licenses for core products (say, Winnie-the-Pooh undies) while ignoring the potential of new media. What's more, Disney films like "A Bug's Life" in 1998 had yielded few merchandising opportunities—what child wants to snuggle up with an ant?

It was about a month after Mooney's arrival that the magic struck. That's when he flew to Phoenix to check out his first "Disney on Ice" show. "Standing in line in the arena, I was surrounded by little girls dressed head to toe as princesses," he told me last summer in his palatial office, then located in Burbank, and speaking in a rolling Scottish burr. "They weren't even Disney products. They were generic princess products they'd appended to a Halloween costume. And the light bulb went off. Clearly there was latent demand here. So the next morning I said to my team, 'O.K., let's establish standards and a color palette and talk to licensees and get as much product out there as we possibly can that allows these girls to do what they're doing anyway: projecting them-selves into the characters from the classic movies.'"

Mooney picked a mix of old and new heroines to wear the Pantone pink No. 241 corona: Cinderella, Sleeping Beauty, Snow White, Ariel, Belle, Jasmine, Mulan and Pocahontas. It was the first time Disney marketed characters sepa-rately from a film's release, let alone lumped together those from different stories. To ensure the sanctity of what Mooney called their individual "mytholo-gies," the princesses never make eye contact when they're grouped: each stares off in a slightly different direction as if unaware of the others' presence.

15   It is also worth noting that not all of the ladies are of royal extraction. Part of the genius of "Princess" is that its meaning is so broadly constructed that it actu-ally has no meaning. Even Tinker Bell was originally a Princess, though her reign didn't last. "We'd always debate over whether she was really a part of the Princess mythology," Mooney recalled. "She really wasn't." Likewise, Mulan and Pocahontas, arguably the most resourceful of the bunch, are rarely depicted on Princess merchandise, though for a different reason. Their rustic garb has less bling potential than that of old-school heroines like Sleeping Beauty. (When Mulan does appear, she is typically in the kimonolike hanfu, which makes her miserable in the movie, rather than her liberated warrior's gear.)

The first Princess items, released with no marketing plan, no focus groups, no advertising, sold as if blessed by a fairy godmother. To this day, Disney con-ducts little market research on the Princess line, relying instead on the power of its legacy among mothers as well as the instant-read sales barometer of the theme parks and Disney Stores. "We simply gave girls what they wanted," Mooney said of the line's success, "although I don't think any of us grasped how much they wanted this. I wish I could sit here and take credit for having some grand scheme to develop this, but all we did was envision a little girl's room and think about how she could live out the princess fantasy. The counsel we gave to licensees was: What type of bedding would a princess want to sleep in? What kind of alarm clock would a princess want to wake up to? What type of television would a princess like to see? It's a rare case where you find a girl who has every aspect of her room bedecked in Princess, but if she ends up with three or four of these items, well, then you have a very healthy business."

Every reporter Mooney talks to asks some version of my next question: Aren't the Princesses, who are interested only in clothes, jewelry and cadging the handsome prince, somewhat retrograde role models?

"Look," he said, "I have friends whose son went through the Power Rangers phase who castigated themselves over what they must've done wrong. Then they talked to other parents whose kids had gone through it. The boy passes through. The girl passes through. I see girls expanding their imagination through visualizing themselves as princesses, and then they pass through that phase and end up becoming lawyers, doctors, mothers or princesses, whatever the case may be."

Mooney has a point: There are no studies proving that playing princess directly damages girls' self-esteem or dampens other aspirations. On the other hand, there is evidence that young women who hold the most conventionally feminine beliefs—who avoid conflict and think they should be perpetually nice and pretty—are more likely to be depressed than others and less likely to use contraception. What's more, the 23 percent decline in girls' participation in sports and other vigorous activity between middle and high school has been linked to their sense that athletics is unfeminine. And in a survey released last October by Girls Inc., school-age girls overwhelmingly reported a paralyzing pressure to be "perfect": not only to get straight A's and be the student-body president, editor of the newspaper and captain of the swim team but also to be "kind and caring," "please everyone, be very thin and dress right." Give those girls a pumpkin and a glass slipper and they'd be in business.

● Review Questions

1. What is Disney's princess line of merchandise? How have other content providers sought to capitalize on the princess theme?

2. What is it about the "princess" treatment that Orenstein finds objectionable?

3. Orenstein admits to some confusion in this article. About what?

4. Who is Andy Mooney, and what was his role in promoting the Disney princess line?

5. What is Andy Mooney's response to the critique that princess merchandise limits girls by casting them in stereotyped roles? What is Orenstein's view of his response?

● Discussion and Writing Suggestions

1. If you went through a "princess" phase, describe the experience: How did you feel when dressed in a tiara? How did you act? How did you interact with adults? When did you move out of the phase (that is, if you have!)? Write a description and share it with your classmates. (Option: if you know someone who went through the princess phase, write about that person.)

2. Orenstein observes her own extreme response to princess mania before speculating: "Maybe princesses are in fact a sign of progress, an indication that girls can embrace their predilection for pink without compromising strength or ambition; that, at long last, they can 'have it all.'" Your response?

3. Andy Mooney is not worried that girls will be limited in their adult lives by playing with princess toys. Are you? Explain.

4. We learn in this article that Disney markets 25,000 princess products to young girls—and that princess merchandizing earns the company $3 billion a year. What about the story of Cinderella and other princesses is so compelling that these characters could support such an enormous enterprise?

5. Andy Mooney states that Disney is marketing to a need that already exists in young girls to play the princess. Do you agree? To what extent do you think Disney *creates* the need and then exploits it?

SYNTHESIS ACTIVITIES

1. Along with many other fairy tales, "Cinderella" is a story of transformations—of unrecognized talent and beauty eventually being recognized and valued; of low circumstance rising to good fortune; of haughtiness punished and made humble. So central are transformations to fairy tale literature that Anne Sexton gave that name to her volume of poetry in which she revisited (and ironically reworked) the tales. In an argument synthesis that draws on Sexton and other sources in this chapter, define the important transformations in "Cinderella." Refer to variants of the story that most appeal to you. Make the central argument of your paper a response to this question: Do you believe in the transformations promised in tales like "Cinderella"?

2. Read a dozen or so children's stories written in the last thirty years. Then reread the traditional variants of "Cinderella" in this chapter. Using criteria you glean from the selections by Schlesinger and Bettelheim, compare and contrast "Cinderella" as an example of folk literature with the contemporary stories. What conclusions do you draw?

3. Thompson reminds us that in the oral folktale tradition tellers borrowed heavily from older tales and adapted them to new circumstances, often

preserving traditional elements. In light of this observation, write a critique of Schlesinger, who argues passionately for the value of *classic* children's literature over modern children's literature.

A variant on the previous question: Working with the same observation from Thompson, watch one or more of the "Cinderella" movies that Poniewozik references in his article and determine the extent to which, following Thompson, the updates can be called legitimate versions of "Cinderella." In your argument, respond to Poniewozik's implied criticism of these movies.

4. In 1910, Antti Aarne published one of the early classifications of folktale types as an aid to scholars who were collecting tales and needed an efficient means for telling where, and with what changes, similar tales had appeared. In 1927, folklorist Stith Thompson, translating and enlarging Aarne's study, produced a work that is now a standard reference for folklorists the world over. We present the authors' description of type 510 and its two forms, 510A ("Cinderella") and 510B. Use this description as a basis on which to analyze any two versions of "Cinderella" in this chapter, determining the extent to which they conform to the stated pattern. Compare and contrast the versions and decide which, in your view, is more authentic.

510. *Cinderella and Cap o' Rushes.*

I. *The Persecuted Heroine.* (a) The heroine is abused by her stepmother and stepsisters, or (b) flees in disguise from her father who wants to marry her, or (c) is cast out by him because she has said that she loved him like salt, or (d) is to be killed by a servant.

II. *Magic Help.* While she is acting as servant (at home or among strangers) she is advised, provided for, and fed (a) by her dead mother, (b) by a tree on the mother's grave, or (c) by a supernatural being, or (d) by birds, or (e) by a goat, a sheep, or a cow. When the goat is killed, there springs up from her remains a magic tree.

III. *Meeting with Prince.* (a) She dances in beautiful clothing several times with a prince who seeks in vain to keep her, or she is seen by him in church. (b) She gives hints of the abuse she has endured, as servant girl, or (c) she is seen in her beautiful clothing in her room or in the church.

IV. *Proof of Identity.* (a) She is discovered through the slipper-test, or (b) through a ring which she throws into the prince's drink or bakes in his bread. (c) She alone is able to pluck the gold apple desired by the knight.

V. *Marriage with the Prince.*

VI. *Value of Salt.* Her father is served unsalted food and thus learns the meaning of her earlier answer.

Two forms of the type follow.

A. *Cinderella.* The two stepsisters. The stepdaughter at the grave of her own mother, who helps her (milks the cow, shakes the apple tree, helps the old man). Threefold visit to church (dance). Slipper-test.

B. *The Dress of Gold, of Silver, and of Stars. (Cap o' Rushes).* Present of the father who wants to marry his own daughter. The maiden as servant of the prince, who throws various objects at her. The threefold visit to the church and the forgotten shoe. Marriage.

5. Speculate on the reasons folktales are made and told. As you develop a theory, rely first on your own hunches regarding the origins and functions of folktale literature. You might want to recall your experiences as a child listening to tales so that you can discuss their effects on you. Rely as well on the variants of "Cinderella," which you should regard as primary sources (just as scholars do). And make use of the critical pieces you've read—Schlesinger, Thompson, Bettelheim, Cullen, and Panttaja—selecting pertinent points from each that will help clarify your points. *Remember:* Your own speculation should dominate the paper. Use sources to help you make *your* points.

6. At the conclusion of his article, Stith Thompson writes:

> Literary critics, anthropologists, historians, psychologists, and aestheticians are all needed if we are to hope to know why folktales are made, how they are invented, what art is used in their telling, how they grow and change and occasionally die.

What is your opinion of the critical work you've read on "Cinderella"? Writing from various perspectives, authors in this chapter have analyzed the tale. To what extent have the analyses illuminated (or ruined) "Cinderella" for you? Do you believe that attempts at analysis are inappropriate for children's literature?

In responding to these questions, you might begin with Thompson's quotation and then follow directly with a statement of your thesis. Critique the work of Bettelheim, Cullen, and/or Panttaja as a way of demonstrating which analyses of folktales (if any) seem worthwhile. Throughout, refer directly to the variants of "Cinderella."

7. Review the variants of "Cinderella" and select two you would read to a child. Then justify your decision. Do your selections meet Aarne and Thompson's classification (see Synthesis Activity #4)? You might also justify your choices negatively by *eliminating* certain variants because they don't meet certain criteria (e.g., that the story is overly violent). In

concluding the paper, explain how the variants you've selected work as a pair. (Or, perhaps, they *don't* complement each other, which is why you've selected them.)

8. Try writing a version of "Cinderella" and setting it on a college campus. For your version of the story to be an authentic variant, you'll need to retain certain defining features, or motifs. See Aarne and Thompson—Synthesis Activity #4. As you consider the possibilities for your story, recall Thompson's point that the teller of a folktale borrows heavily on earlier versions; the virtue of telling is not in rendering a new story but in retelling an old one and *adapting* it to local conditions and needs. Unless you plan to write a commentary "Cinderella," as Sexton does, you should retain the basic motifs of the old story and add details that will appeal to your particular audience: your classmates. *An option:* Create a reality television show or an Internet blog based on elements of "Cinderella."

9. Explain the process by which Cinderella falls in love in these tales. The paper that you write will be an extended comparison-and-contrast in which you observe this process at work in the variants and then discuss similarities and differences. (In structuring your paper, you'll need to make some choices: Which variants will you discuss and in what order?) At the conclusion of your extended comparison-and-contrast, answer the "So what?" question. Pull your observations together and make a statement about Cinderella's falling in love. At some point, you should raise and respond to Elisabeth Panttaja's assertion that Cinderella does *not,* in fact, fall in love in this tale.

10. Based on your own reading of the tale and on your response to the selection by Rossner, develop a point of view about Cinderella's stepmother. Is she truly wicked? Misunderstood? Worthy of our sympathy? Develop your response into an argument. Refer generously to the story itself.

11. Orenstein reports on the $3 billion industry in "princess" merchandising. Recognizing the profit potential of "Cinderella" updates like *The Princess Diaries,* movie producers released a succession of "contemporary" versions of the tale—earning hundreds of millions of dollars. What are the harms and/or benefits in bringing "Cinderella" into the twenty-first century in so commercialized a way? Certainly the merchandisers and the movie industry win. Do children? To prepare for writing this argument, read the selections by Schlesinger, Orenstein, Poniewozik, and at least these variants of the tale: Grimm, Perrault, Disney, and Anne Sexton. Watch both the Disney version of "Cinderella" and one of the versions Poniewozik references in his article. Finally, go onto the Web and research the sorts of princess products one can purchase these days.

RESEARCH ACTIVITIES

1. Research the fairy tale literature of your ancestors, both the tales and any critical commentary that you can find on them. Once you have read the material, talk with older members of your family to hear any tales they have to tell. (Seek, especially, oral versions of stories you have already read.) In a paper, discuss the role that fairy tale literature has played, and continues to play, in your family.

2. Locate the book *Morphology of the Folktale* (1958) by Russian folklorist Vladimir Propp. Use the information you find there to analyze the elements of any three fairy tales of your choosing. In a paper, report on your analysis and evaluate the usefulness of Propp's system of classifying the key elements of fairy tale literature.

3. Bruno Bettelheim's *Uses of Enchantment* (1975) generated a great deal of reaction on its publication. Read Bettelheim and locate several reviews of his work. Based on your own reactions and on your reading of the reviews, write an evaluation in which you address Bettelheim's key assumption that fairy tale literature provides important insights into the psychological life of children.

4. Locate and study multiple versions of any fairy tale other than "Cinderella." Having read the versions, identify—and write your paper on—what you feel are the defining elements that make the tales variants of a single story. See if you can find the tale listed as a "type" in Aarne and Thompson's *The Types of Folk-Tales*. If you wish, argue that one version of the tale is preferable to others.

5. Jack Zipes, author of *Breaking the Magic Spell* (1979), takes the approach that fairy tales are far from innocuous children's stories; rather, they inculcate the unsuspecting with the value systems of the dominant culture. In a research paper, explicitly address the assumption that fairy tales are not morally or politically neutral but, rather, imply a distinct set of values.

6. Record, and then study, several hours of Saturday morning cartoons. Then locate and read a collection of Grimm's fairy tales. In a comparative analysis, examine the cartoons and the fairy tales along any four or five dimensions that you think are important. The point of your comparisons and contrasts will be to determine how well the two types of presentations stack up against each other. Which do you find more entertaining? Illuminating? Ambitious? Useful? (These criteria are suggestions only. You should generate your own criteria as part of your research.)

7. Arrange to read to your favorite young person a series of fairy tales. Based on your understanding of the selections in this chapter, develop a list of questions concerning the importance or usefulness of fairy tale literature to children. Read to your young friend on several occasions and, if possible, talk about the stories after you read them (or while you are reading). Then write a paper on your experience, answering as many of your initial questions as possible. (Be sure in your paper to provide a profile of the child with whom you worked; to review your selection of stories; and to list the questions you wanted to explore.)

Chapter 13

Obedience to Authority

Would you obey an order to inflict pain on another person? Most of us, if confronted with this question, would probably be quick to answer: "Never!" Yet if the conclusions of researchers are to be trusted, it is not psychopaths who kill noncombatant civilians in wartime and torture victims in prisons around the world but rather ordinary people following orders. People obey. This is a basic, necessary fact of human society. As psychologist Stanley Milgram has written, "Obedience is as basic an element in the structure of social life as one can point to. Some system of authority is a requirement of all communal living."

The question, then, is not, "Should we obey the orders of an authority figure?" but rather, "To what *extent* should we obey?" Each generation seems to give new meaning to these questions. During the Vietnam War, a number of American soldiers followed a commander's orders and murdered civilians in the hamlet of My Lai. In 1987 former White House military aide Oliver North was prosecuted for illegally diverting money raised by selling arms to Iran—considered by the U.S. government to be a terrorist state—to fund the anticommunist Contra (resistance) fighters in Nicaragua. North's attorneys claimed that he was following the orders of his superiors. And, although North was found guilty,* the judge who sentenced him to perform community service (there was no prison sentence) largely agreed with this defense when he called North a pawn in a larger game played by senior officials in the Reagan administration. In the 1990s the world was horrified by genocidal violence in Rwanda and in the former nation of Yugoslavia. These were civil wars, in which people who had been living for generations as neighbors suddenly, upon the instigation and orders of their leaders, turned upon and slaughtered one another.

Finally, in April 2004, the world (particularly, the Muslim world) was horrified by accounts—and graphic photographs—of the degrading torture and humiliation of Iraqi prisoners at the hands of American soldiers in a Baghdad prison. Among the questions raised by this incident: Were these soldiers obeying orders to "soften up" the prisoners for interrogation? Were they fulfilling the roles of prison guards they thought were expected of them? Were they

---

*In July 1990, North's conviction was overturned on appeal.

abusing others because, given the circumstances, they could? President Bush asserted that this kind of abuse "does not reflect the nature of the American people." But as the Milgram and Zimbardo experiments in this chapter demonstrate, we are likely to be unpleasantly surprised by revelations of just what our "nature" really is—not only as Americans but, more fundamentally, as human beings.

In less dramatic ways, conflicts over the extent to which we obey orders surface in everyday life. At one point or another, you may face a moral dilemma at work. Perhaps it will take this form: The boss tells you to overlook File X in preparing a report for a certain client. But you're sure that File X pertains directly to the report and contains information that will alarm the client. What should you do? The dilemmas of obedience also emerge on some campuses with the rite of fraternity or sports-related hazing. Psychologists Janice Gibson and Mika Haritos-Fatouros have made the startling observation that whether the obedience in question involves a pledge's joining a fraternity or a torturer's joining an elite military corps, the *process* by which one acquiesces to a superior's order (and thereby becomes a member of the group) is remarkably the same:

> There are several ways to teach people to do the unthinkable, and we have developed a model to explain how they are used. We have also found that college fraternities, although they are far removed from the grim world of torture and violent combat, use similar methods for initiating new members, to ensure their faithfulness to the fraternity's rules and values. However, this unthinking loyalty can sometimes lead to dangerous actions: Over the past 10 years, there have been countless injuries during fraternity initiations and 39 deaths. These training techniques are designed to instill obedience in people, but they can easily be a guide for an intensive course in torture.

> 1. *Screening to find the best prospects:*
>   - Normal, well-adjusted people with the physical, intellectual, and, in some cases, political attributes necessary for the task.

> 2. *Techniques to increase binding among these prospects:*
>   - Initiation rites to isolate people from society and introduce them to a new social order, with different rules and values.
>   - Elitist attitudes and "in-group" language, which highlight the differences between the group and the rest of society.

> 3. *Techniques to reduce the strain of obedience:*
>   - Blaming and dehumanizing the victims, so it is less disturbing to harm them.
>   - Harassment, the constant physical and psychological intimidation that prevents logical thinking and promotes the instinctive responses needed for acts of inhuman cruelty.

- Rewards for obedience and punishments for not cooperating.

- Social modeling by watching other group members commit violent acts and then receive rewards.

- Systematic desensitization to repugnant acts by gradual exposure to them, so they appear routine and normal despite conflicts with previous moral standards.*

Many of these processes appear to have been at work in the Iraqi prison scandal.

In this chapter, you will explore the dilemmas inherent in obeying the orders of an authority figure. First, psychoanalyst and philosopher Erich Fromm discusses the comforts of obedience in "Disobedience as a Psychological and Moral Problem." Next, in "The Power of Situations," social psychologists Lee Ross and Richard Nisbett provide an overview of the situational forces that can strongly influence behavior. Psychologist Stanley Milgram then reports on his landmark study that revealed the extent to which ordinary individuals will obey the clearly immoral orders of an authority figure. The results were startling, not only to the psychiatrists who predicted that few people would follow such orders, but also to many other social scientists—some of whom applauded Milgram for his fiendishly ingenious design, some of whom bitterly attacked him for unethical procedures. So controversial were Milgram's experiments that they were not replicated in the United States for 45 years, until Santa Clara University psychologist Jerry Burger published "Replicating Milgram: Would People Still Obey Today?" We include portions of his report here. Following Burger, British writer Ian Parker, in his essay "Obedience," offers a useful perspective on both the decades-long debate surrounding the Milgram experiments and the effect of these experiments on Milgram's own career.

The chapter concludes with four selections devoted to the special case of obedience in groups. Writer Doris Lessing sets the context by discussing how we are quick to call ourselves individualists without pausing to appreciate the power of situational influences on our behavior. Next, psychologist Solomon Asch describes a classic experiment (involving the apparent length of lines) that demonstrates the influence of group pressure on individual judgment. Then psychologist Philip Zimbardo reports on his famous—some would say infamous—Stanford Prison Experiment, in which student volunteers exhibited astonishingly convincing authoritarian and obedient attitudes as they playacted at being prisoners and guards. The chapter concludes with an excerpt from Ian McEwan's novel *Atonement*, in which individual British soldiers succumb to group fury, form a mob, and threaten a British airman.

---

*Janice T. Gibson and Mika Haritos-Fatouros, "The Education of a Torturer," *Psychology Today* November 1986. Reprinted with permission from *Psychology Today Magazine.* Copyright 1986 Sussex Publishers, Inc.

DISOBEDIENCE AS A PSYCHOLOGICAL AND MORAL PROBLEM

Erich Fromm

Erich Fromm (1900–1980) was one of the twentieth century's distinguished writers and thinkers. Psychoanalyst and philosopher, historian and sociologist, he ranged widely in his interests and defied easy characterization. Fromm studied the works of Freud and Marx closely, and published on them both, but he was not aligned strictly with either. In much of his voluminous writing, he struggled to articulate a view that could help bridge ideological and personal conflicts and bring dignity to those who struggled with isolation in the industrial world. Author of more than 30 books and contributor to numerous edited collections and journals, Fromm is best known for *Escape from Freedom* (1941), *The Art of Loving* (1956), and *To Have or To Be?* (1976).

In the essay that follows, first published in 1963, Fromm discusses the seductive comforts of obedience, and he makes distinctions among varieties of obedience, some of which he believes are destructive, and others, life affirming. His thoughts on nuclear annihilation may seem dated in these days of post–Cold War cooperation, but it is worth remembering that Fromm wrote his essay just after the Cuban missile crisis, when fears of a third world war ran high. (We might note that despite the welcome reductions of nuclear stockpiles, the United States and Russia still possess, and retain battle plans for, thousands of warheads.) And in the wake of the 9/11 attacks, the threat of terrorists acquiring and using nuclear weapons against the United States seems very real. On the major points of his essay, concerning the psychological and moral problems of obedience, Fromm remains as pertinent today as when he wrote more than 40 years ago.

For centuries kings, priests, feudal lords, industrial bosses, and parents have insisted that *obedience is a virtue* and that *disobedience is a vice*. In order to introduce another point of view, let us set against this position the following statement: *human history began with an act of disobedience, and it is not unlikely that it will be terminated by an act of obedience.*

Human history was ushered in by an act of disobedience according to the Hebrew and Greek myths. Adam and Eve, living in the Garden of Eden, were part of nature; they were in harmony with it, yet did not transcend it. They were in nature as the fetus is in the womb of the mother. They were human, and at the same time not yet human. All this changed when they disobeyed an order. By breaking the ties with earth and mother, by cutting the umbilical cord, man emerged from a prehuman harmony and was able to take the first step into independence and freedom. The act of disobedience set Adam and Eve free and opened their eyes. They recognized each other as strangers and the world outside them as strange and even hostile. Their act of disobedience broke the primary bond with nature and made them individuals. "Original sin," far from corrupting man, set him free; it was the beginning of history. Man had to leave the Garden of Eden in order to learn to rely on his own powers and to become fully human.

The prophets, in their messianic concept, confirmed the idea that man had been right in disobeying; that he had not been corrupted by his "sin," but freed from the fetters of pre-human harmony. For the prophets, *history* is the place where man becomes human; during its unfolding he develops his powers of reason and of love until he creates a new harmony between himself, his fellow man, and nature. This new harmony is described as "the end of days," that period of history in which there is peace between man and man, between man and nature. It is a "new" paradise created by man himself, and one which he alone could create because he was forced to leave the "old" paradise as a result of his disobedience.

Just as the Hebrew myth of Adam and Eve, so the Greek myth of Prometheus sees all human civilization based on an act of disobedience. Prometheus, in stealing the fire from the gods, lays the foundation for the evolution of man. There would be no human history were it not for Prometheus' "crime." He, like Adam and Eve, is punished for his disobedience. But he does not repent and ask for forgiveness. On the contrary, he proudly says: "I would rather be chained to this rock than be the obedient servant of the gods."

5   Man has continued to evolve by acts of disobedience. Not only was his spiritual development possible only because there were men who dared to say no to the powers that be in the name of their conscience or their faith, but also his intellectual development was dependent on the capacity for being disobedient—disobedient to authorities who tried to muzzle new thoughts and to the authority of long-established opinions which declared a change to be nonsense.

If the capacity for disobedience constituted the beginning of human history, obedience might very well, as I have said, cause the end of human history. I am not speaking symbolically or poetically. There is the possibility, or even the probability, that the human race will destroy civilization and even all life upon earth within the next five to ten years. There is no rationality or sense in it. But the fact is that, while we are living technically in the Atomic Age, the majority of men—including most of those who are in power—still live emotionally in the Stone Age; that while our mathematics, astronomy, and the natural sciences are of the twentieth century, most of our ideas about politics, the state, and society lag far behind the age of science. If mankind commits suicide it will be because people will obey those who command them to push the deadly buttons; because they will obey the archaic passions of fear, hate, and greed; because they will obey obsolete clichés of State sovereignty and national honor. The Soviet leaders talk much about revolutions, and we in the "free world" talk much about freedom. Yet they and we discourage disobedience—in the Soviet Union explicitly and by force, in the free world implicitly and by the more subtle methods of persuasion.

But I do not mean to say that all disobedience is a virtue and all obedience is a vice. Such a view would ignore the dialectical relationship between obedience and disobedience. Whenever the principles which are obeyed and those which are disobeyed are irreconcilable, an act of obedience to one principle is necessarily an act of disobedience to its counterpart and vice versa. Antigone is the classic example of this dichotomy. By obeying the inhuman laws of the State, Antigone necessarily would disobey the laws of humanity. By obeying the latter, she must disobey the former. All martyrs of religious faiths, of freedom, and of science have had to disobey those who wanted to muzzle them in order to obey their own consciences, the laws of humanity, and of reason. If a man can only obey and not disobey, he is a slave; if he can only disobey and not obey, he is a rebel (not a revolutionary); he acts out of anger, disappointment, resentment, yet not in the name of a conviction or a principle.

However, in order to prevent a confusion of terms an important qualification must be made. Obedience to a person, institution, or power (heteronomous obedience) is submission; it implies the abdication of my autonomy and the acceptance of a foreign will or judgment in place of my own. Obedience to my own reason or conviction (autonomous obedience) is not an act of submission but one of affirmation. My conviction and my judgment, if authentically mine, are part of me. If I follow them rather than the judgment of others, I am being myself; hence the word *obey* can be applied only in a metaphorical sense and with a meaning which is fundamentally different from the one in the case of "heteronomous obedience."

But this distinction still needs two further qualifications, one with regard to the concept of conscience and the other with regard to the concept of authority.

10 The word *conscience* is used to express two phenomena which are quite distinct from each other. One is the "authoritarian conscience" which is the internalized voice of an authority whom we are eager to please and afraid of displeasing. This authoritarian conscience is what most people experience when they obey their conscience. It is also the conscience which Freud speaks of, and which he called "Super-Ego." This Super-Ego represents the internalized commands and prohibitions of father, accepted by the son out of fear. Different from the authoritarian conscience is the "humanistic conscience"; this is the voice present in every human being and independent from external sanctions and rewards. Humanistic conscience is based on the fact that as human beings we have an intuitive knowledge of what is human and inhuman, what is conducive of life and what is destructive of life. This conscience serves our functioning as human beings. It is the voice which calls us back to ourselves, to our humanity.

Authoritarian conscience (Super-Ego) is still obedience to a power outside of myself, even though this power has been internalized. Consciously I believe that I am following *my* conscience; in effect, however, I have swallowed the principles of *power*; just because of the illusion that humanistic conscience and Super-Ego are identical, internalized authority is so much more effective than the authority which is clearly experienced as not being part of me. Obedience to the "authoritarian conscience," like all obedience to outside thoughts and power, tends to debilitate "humanistic conscience," the ability to be and to judge oneself.

The statement, on the other hand, that obedience to another person is *ipso facto* submission needs also to be qualified by distinguishing "irrational" from "rational" authority. An example of rational authority is to be found in the relationship between student and teacher; one of irrational authority in the relationship between slave and master. Both relationships are based on the fact that the authority of the person in command is accepted. Dynamically, however, they are of a different nature. The interests of the teacher and the student, in the ideal case, lie in the same direction. The teacher is satisfied if he succeeds in further-ing the student; if he has failed to do so, the failure is his and the student's. The slave owner, on the other hand, wants to exploit the slave as much as possible. The more he gets out of him the more satisfied he is. At the same time, the slave tries to defend as best he can his claims for a minimum of happiness. The inter-ests of slave and master are antagonistic, because what is advantageous to the one is detrimental to the other. The superiority of the one over the other has a different function in each case; in the first it is the condition for the furtherance of the person subjected to the authority, and in the second it is the condition for his exploitation. Another distinction runs parallel to this: rational authority is rational because the authority, whether it is held by a teacher or a captain of a ship giving orders in an emergency, acts in the name of reason which, being universal, I can accept without submitting. Irrational authority has to use force or suggestion, because no one would let himself be exploited if he were free to prevent it.

Why is man so prone to obey and why is it so difficult for him to disobey? As long as I am obedient to the power of the State, the Church, or public opin-ion, I feel safe and protected. In fact it makes little difference what power it is that I am obedient to. It is always an institution, or men, who use force in one form or another and who fraudulently claim omniscience and omnipotence. My obedience makes me part of the power I worship, and hence I feel strong. I can make no error, since it decides for me; I cannot be alone, because it watches over me; I cannot commit a sin, because it does not let me do so, and even if I do sin, the punishment is only the way of returning to the almighty power.

In order to disobey, one must have the courage to be alone, to err, and to sin. But courage is not enough. The capacity for courage depends on a person's state of development. Only if a person has emerged from mother's lap and father's commands, only if he has emerged as a fully developed individual and thus has acquired the capacity to think and feel for himself, only then can he have the courage to say "no" to power, to disobey.

15   A person can become free through acts of disobedience by learning to say no to power. But not only is the capacity for disobedience the condition for free-dom; freedom is also the condition for disobedience. If I am afraid of freedom, I cannot dare to say "no," I cannot have the courage to be disobedient. Indeed, freedom and the capacity for disobedience are inseparable; hence any social, political, and religious system which proclaims freedom, yet stamps out disobe-dience, cannot speak the truth.

There is another reason why it is so difficult to dare to disobey, to say "no" to power. During most of human history obedience has been identified with virtue and disobedience with sin. The reason is simple: thus far throughout most of his-tory a minority has ruled over the majority. This rule was made necessary by the fact that there was only enough of the good things of life for the few, and only the crumbs remained for the many. If the few wanted to enjoy the good things and, beyond that, to have the many serve them and work for them, one condition was necessary: the many had to learn obedience. To be sure, obedience can be estab-lished by sheer force. But this method has many disadvantages. It constitutes a constant threat that one day the many might have the means to overthrow the few by force; furthermore there are many kinds of work which cannot be done properly if nothing but fear is behind the obedience. Hence the obedience which is only rooted in the fear of force must be transformed into one rooted in man's heart. Man must want and even need to obey, instead of only fearing to disobey. If this is to be achieved, power must assume the qualities of the All Good, of the All Wise; it must become All Knowing. If this happens, power can proclaim that disobedience is sin and obedience virtue; and once this has been proclaimed, the many can accept obedience because it is good and detest disobedience because it is bad, rather than to detest themselves for being cowards. From Luther to the nineteenth century one was concerned with overt and explicit authorities. Luther, the pope, the princes, wanted to uphold it; the middle class, the workers, the philosophers, tried to uproot it. The fight against authority in the State as well as in the family was often the very basis for the development of an independent and daring person. The fight against authority was inseparable from the intellectual mood which characterized the philosophers of the enlightenment and the scientists. This "critical mood" was one of faith in reason, and at the same time of doubt in everything which is said or thought, inasmuch as it is based on tradition, superstition, custom, power. The principles *sapere aude* and *de omnibus est dubitandum*—"dare to be wise" and "of all one must doubt"—were characteristic of the attitude which permitted and furthered the capacity to say "no."

The case of Adolf Eichmann [see note, page 366] is symbolic of our situation and has a significance far beyond the one in which his accusers in the courtroom in Jerusalem were concerned with. Eichmann is a symbol of the organization man, of the alienated bureaucrat for whom men, women and children have become numbers. He is a symbol of all of us. We can see ourselves in Eichmann. But the most frightening thing about him is that after the entire story was told in terms of his own admissions, he was able in perfect good faith to plead his innocence. It is clear that if he were once more in the same situation he would do it again. And so would we—and so do we.

The organization man has lost the capacity to disobey, he is not even aware of the fact that he obeys. At this point in history the capacity to doubt, to criticize, and to disobey may be all that stands between a future for mankind and the end of civilization.

Review Questions

1. What does Fromm mean when he writes that disobedience is "the first step into independence and freedom"?

2. Fromm writes that history began with an act of disobedience and will likely end with an act of obedience. What does he mean?

3. What is the difference between "heteronomous obedience" and "autonomous obedience"?

4. How does Fromm distinguish between "authoritarian conscience" and "humanistic conscience"?

5. When is obedience to another person *not* submission?

6. What are the psychological comforts of obedience, and why would authorities rather have people obey out of love than out of fear?

● **Discussion and Writing Suggestions**

1. Fromm suggests that scientifically we live in the modern world but that politically and emotionally we live in the Stone Age. As you observe events in the world, both near and far, would you agree? Why?

2. Fromm writes: "If a man can only obey and not disobey, he is a slave; if he can only disobey and not obey, he is a rebel (not a revolutionary)" (paragraph 7). Explain Fromm's meaning here. Explain, as well, the implication that to be fully human one must have the freedom to both obey and disobey.

3. Fromm writes that "obedience makes me part of the power I worship, and hence I feel strong" (paragraph 13). Does this statement ring true for you? Discuss, in writing, an occasion in which you felt powerful because you obeyed a group norm.

4. In paragraphs 15 and 16, Fromm equates obedience with cowardice. Can you identify a situation in which you were obedient but, now that you reflect on it, were also cowardly? That is, can you recall a time when you caved in to a group but now wish you hadn't? Explain.

5. Fromm says that we can see ourselves in Adolf Eichmann—that as an organization man he "has lost the capacity to disobey, he is not even aware of the fact that he obeys." To what extent do you recognize yourself in this portrait?

THE POWER OF SITUATIONS

Lee Ross and Richard E. Nisbett

Erich Fromm conceives of obedience and disobedience as products of one's character or of one's moral choices. In the selection that follows, Lee Ross and Richard E. Nisbett present findings from experiments in social psychology that suggest that situations, rather than some essential personal quality or the dictates of one's conscience, tend to determine behavior. From this vantage point, a "helpful" person may not be consistently helpful nor a "kind" person, consistently kind. In each new situation, subtle and profound social cues influence our ultimate behavior—which is why, as we all know, people behave inconsistently. According to philosopher Gilbert Harman, "It seems that ordinary attributions of character traits to people are often deeply misguided, and it may even be the case that there is no such thing as character, no ordinary character traits of the sort people think there are, none of the usual moral virtues and vices." Harmon reached this radical notion after reading accounts of the same experiments in social psychology that you are about to read in this chapter. You may not draw his same conclusions, but Ross and Nisbett, Milgram, Burger, Asch, Lessing, and Zimbardo will almost certainly convince you that the situation in which we act can powerfully influence our behavior—including our choice to obey or disobey a questionable order.

Lee Ross is a professor of Psychology at Stanford University. Richard E. Nisbett is professor of psychology at the University of Michigan. This selection is excerpted from their text *The Person and the Situation: Perspectives of Social Psychology* (1991).

Undergraduates taking their first course in social psychology generally are in search of an interesting and enjoyable experience, and they rarely are disappointed. They find out many fascinating things about human behavior, some of which validate common sense and some of which contradict it. The inherent interest value of the material, amounting to high-level gossip about people and social situations, usually ensures that the students are satisfied consumers.

The experience of serious graduate students, who, over the course of four or five years, are immersed in the problems and the orientation of the field, is rather different. For them, the experience is an intellectually wrenching one. Their most basic assumptions about the nature and the causes of human behavior, and about the very predictability of the social world, are challenged. At the end of the process, their views of human behavior and society will differ profoundly from the views held by most other people in their culture. Some of their new insights and beliefs will be held rather tentatively and applied inconsistently to the social events that unfold around them. Others will be held with great conviction, and will be applied confidently. But ironically, even the new insights that they are most confident about will tend to have the effect of making them less certain than their peers about predicting social behavior and making inferences about particular individuals or groups. Social psychology rivals philosophy in its ability to teach people that they do not truly understand the nature of the world. This book is about that hard-won ignorance and what it tells us about the human condition.

• • •

Consider the following scenario: While walking briskly to a meeting some distance across a college campus, John comes across a man slumped in a doorway, asking him for help. Will John offer it, or will he continue on his way? Before answering such a question, most people would want to know more about John. Is he someone known to be callous and unfeeling, or is he renowned for his kindness and concern? Is he a stalwart member of the Campus Outreach Organization, or a mainstay of the Conservative Coalition Against Welfare Abuse? In short, what kind of person is John and how has he behaved when his altruism has been tested in the past? Only with such information in hand, most people would agree, could one make a sensible and confident prediction.

In fact, however, nothing one is likely to know or learn about John would be of much use in helping predict John's behavior in the situation we've described. In particular, the type of information about personality that most laypeople would want to have before making a prediction would prove to be of relatively little value. A half century of research has taught us that in this situation, and in most other novel situations, one cannot predict with any accuracy how particular people will respond. At least one cannot do so using information about an individual's personal dispositions or even about that individual's past behavior.

• • •

5   While knowledge about John is of surprisingly little value in predicting whether he will help the person slumped in the doorway, details concerning the specifics of the situation would be invaluable. For example, what was the appearance of the person in the doorway? Was he clearly ill, or might he have been a drunk or, even worse, a nodding dope addict? Did his clothing make him look respectably middle class or decently working class, or did he look like a homeless derelict?

Such considerations are fairly obvious once they are mentioned, and the layperson, upon reflection, will generally concede their importance. But few laypeople would concede, much less anticipate, the relevance of some other, subtler, contextual details that empirical research has shown to be important factors influencing bystander intervention. Darley and Batson (1973) actually confronted people with a version of the situation we've described and found what some of these factors are. Their subjects were students in a religious seminary who were on their way to deliver a practice sermon. If the subjects were in a hurry (because they thought they were late to give a practice sermon), only about 10 percent helped. By contrast, if they were not in a hurry (because they had plenty of time before giving their sermon), about 63 percent of them helped.

Social psychology has by now amassed a vast store of such empirical parables. The tradition here is simple. Pick a generic situation; then identify and manipulate a situational or contextual variable that intuition or past research leads you to believe will make a difference (ideally, a variable whose impact you think most laypeople, or even most of your peers, somehow fail to appreciate), and see what happens. Sometimes, of course, you will be wrong and your manipulation won't "work." But often the situational variable makes quite a bit of difference. Occasionally, in fact, it makes nearly all the difference, and information about traits and individual differences that other people thought all-important proves all but trivial. If so, you have contributed a situationist classic destined to become part of our field's intellectual legacy. Such empirical parables are important because they illustrate the degree to which ordinary men and women are apt to be mistaken about the power of the situation—the power of particular situational features, and the power of situations in general.

People's inflated belief in the importance of personality traits and dispositions, together with their failure to recognize the importance of situational factors in affecting behavior, has been termed the "fundamental attribution error"

(Ross, 1977; Nisbett & Ross, 1980; see also Jones, 1979; Gilbert & Jones, 1986). Together with many other social psychologists, we have directed our attention to documenting this…error and attempting to track down its origins.

References

Darley, J. M., & Batson, C. D. (1973). From Jerusalem to Jericho: A study of situational and dispositional variables in helping behavior. *Journal of Personality and Social Psychology, 27,* 100–119.

Gilbert, D. T., & Jones, E. E. (1986). Perceiver-induced constraints: Interpretation of self-generated reality. *Journal of Personality and Social Psychology, 50,* 269–280.

Jones, E. E. (1979). The rocky road from acts to dispositions. *American Psychologist, 34,* 107–117.

Nisbett, R. E., & Ross, L. (1980). *Human inference: Strategies and shortcomings of social judgment.* Englewood Cliffs, NJ: Prentice-Hall.

Ross, L. (1977). The intuitive psychologist and his shortcomings. In L. Berkowitz (Ed.), *Advances in experimental social psychology* (Vol. 10). New York: Academic.

● Review Questions

1. In the final sentence of paragraph 2, what is the "hard-won ignorance" made possible by social psychology? Ross and Nisbett offer an example of this "ignorance." Summarize that example.

2. What is the key predictor of "John's" behavior in the experiment cited by Ross and Nisbett? How does this predictor defy common sense?

3. What is the "fundamental attribution error"?

● Discussion and Writing Suggestions

1. Conceive of another scenario, analogous to John's encountering the man slumped in the doorway. What kinds of situational factors might determine how one behaves when faced with this scenario?

2. How did you react to what is known as the "Good Samaritan" experiment (involving John and the person slumped in the doorway)? Most people would like to think they would behave differently, but the experiments suggest otherwise. Your comments? Can you see yourself responding differently in a variety of cimrcumstances?

3. "Social psychology," write Ross and Nisbett, "rivals philosophy in its ability to teach people that they do not truly understand the nature of the world." How solid do you feel your understanding is of "the world"? If you guessed incorrectly about John and how he would react to the person slumped in the doorway, are you prepared to see your common-sense understanding of how people behave undermined?

4. Reconsider the radical proposition mentioned in the headnote: that based on experiments like the "Good Samaritan" described in this selection, one might conclude, "It seems that ordinary attributions of character traits to people are often deeply misguided, and it may even be the case that there is no such thing as character, no ordinary character traits of the sort people think there are, none of the usual moral virtues and vices." That is, one might conclude from the experiments of Asch, Milgram, and Zimbardo (articles to follow later in this chapter) that enduring character traits do not determine our behavior; rather, our behavior is determined by situational variables (like whether or not we are late for a meeting). Even assuming you do not accept this extreme view, are you troubled by the assertion that "character" might be a fiction—or, at least, overrated? That people, for example, do not possess some inner quality called "honor" or "loyalty" that is impervious to all situational pressures (such as financial need, health crises, old age, threats to one's family's well-being or safety)? At what point, if any, despite one's misgivings, are situational exigencies likely to overwhelm consistent character?

THE PERILS OF OBEDIENCE

Stanley Milgram

In 1963, a Yale psychologist conducted one of the classic studies on obedience. Stanley Milgram designed an experiment that forced participants either to violate their conscience by obeying the immoral demands of an authority figure or to refuse those demands. Surprisingly, Milgram found that few participants could resist the authority's orders, even when the participants knew that following these orders would result in another person's pain. Were the participants in these experiments incipient mass murderers? No, said Milgram. They were "ordinary people, simply doing their jobs." The implications of Milgram's conclusions are immense.

Consider these questions: Where does evil reside? What sort of people were responsible for the Holocaust, and for the long list of other atrocities that seem to blight the human record in every generation? Is it a lunatic fringe, a few sick but powerful people who are responsible for atrocities? If so, then we decent folk needn't ever look inside ourselves to understand evil since (by our definition) evil lurks out there, in "those sick ones." Milgram's study suggested otherwise: that under a special set of circumstances the obedience we naturally show authority figures can transform us into agents of terror.

The article that follows is one of the longest in this book, and it may help you to know in advance the author's organization. In paragraphs 1–11, Milgram discusses the larger significance and the history of dilemmas involving obedience to authority; he then summarizes his basic experimental design and follows with a report of one experiment. Milgram organizes the remainder of his article into sections, which he has subtitled "An Unexpected Outcome," "Peculiar Reactions," "The Etiquette of Submission," and "Duty Without Conflict." He begins his conclusion in paragraph 108. If you find the article too long or complex to complete in a single sitting, then plan to read sections at a time, taking notes on each until you're done. Anticipate the article that immediately follows this one: It reviews Milgram's work and largely concerns the ethics of his experimental design. Consider these ethics as you read so that you, in turn, can respond to Milgram's critics.

Stanley Milgram (1933–1984) taught and conducted research at Yale and Harvard Universities and at the Graduate Center, City University of New York. He was named Guggenheim Fellow in 1972–1973 and a year later was nominated for the National Book Award for *Obedience to Authority*. His other books include *Television and Antisocial Behavior* (1973), *The City and the Self* (1974), *Human Aggression* (1976), and *The Individual in the Social World* (1977).

Obedience is as basic an element in the structure of social life as one can point to. Some system of authority is a requirement of all communal living, and it is only the person dwelling in isolation who is not forced to respond, with defiance or submission, to the commands of others. For many people, obedience is a deeply ingrained behavior tendency, indeed a potent impulse overriding training in ethics, sympathy, and moral conduct.

The dilemma inherent in submission to authority is ancient, as old as the story of Abraham, and the question of whether one should obey when commands conflict with conscience has been argued by Plato, dramatized in *Antigone*, and treated to philosophic analysis in almost every historical epoch. Conservative philosophers argue that the very fabric of society is threatened by disobedience, while humanists stress the primacy of the individual conscience.

The legal and philosophic aspects of obedience are of enormous import, but they say very little about how most people behave in concrete situations. I set up a simple experiment at Yale University to test how much pain an ordinary citizen would inflict on another person simply because he was ordered to by an experimental scientist. Stark authority was pitted against the subjects' strongest moral imperatives against hurting others, and with the subjects' ears ringing with the screams of the victims, authority won more often than not. The extreme willingness of adults to go to almost any lengths on the command of an authority constitutes the chief finding of the study and the fact most urgently demanding explanation.

In the basic experimental design, two people come to a psychology laboratory to take part in a study of memory and learning. One of them is designated as a "teacher" and the other a "learner." The experimenter explains that the study is concerned with the effects of punishment on learning. The learner is conducted into a room, seated in a kind of miniature electric chair; his arms are strapped to prevent excessive movement, and an electrode is attached to his wrist. He is told that he will be read lists of simple word pairs, and that he will then be tested on his ability to remember the second word of a pair when he hears the first one again. Whenever he makes an error, he will receive electric shocks of increasing intensity.

5   The real focus of the experiment is the teacher. After watching the learner being strapped into place, he is seated before an impressive shock generator. The instrument panel consists of thirty level switches set in a horizontal line. Each

switch is clearly labeled with a voltage designation ranging from 15 to 450 volts. The following designations are clearly indicated for groups of four switches, going from left to right: Slight Shock, Moderate Shock, Strong Shock, Very Strong Shock, Intense Shock, Extreme Intensity Shock, Danger: Severe Shock. (Two switches after this last designation are simply marked XXX.)

When a switch is depressed, a pilot light corresponding to each switch is illuminated in bright red; an electric buzzing is heard; a blue light, labeled "voltage energizer," flashes; the dial on the voltage meter swings to the right; and various relay clicks sound off.

The upper left-hand corner of the generator is labeled SHOCK GENERATOR, TYPE ZLB, DYSON INSTRUMENT COMPANY, WALTHAM, MASS. OUTPUT 15 VOLTS—450 VOLTS.

Each subject is given a sample 45-volt shock from the generator before his run as teacher, and the jolt strengthens his belief in the authenticity of the machine.

The teacher is a genuinely naive subject who has come to the laboratory for the experiment. The learner, or victim, is actually an actor who receives no shock at all. The point of the experiment is to see how far a person will proceed in a concrete and measurable situation in which he is ordered to inflict increasing pain on a protesting victim.

A subject in Stanley Milgram's study of obedience, seated at the "Shock Generator."

10   Conflict arises when the man receiving the shock begins to show that he is experiencing discomfort. At 75 volts, he grunts; at 120 volts, he complains loudly; at 150, he demands to be released from the experiment. As the voltage increases, his protests become more vehement and emotional. At 285 volts, his response can be described only as an agonized scream. Soon thereafter, he makes no sound at all.

For the teacher, the situation quickly becomes one of gripping tension. It is not a game for him; conflict is intense and obvious. The manifest suffering of the learner presses him to quit; but each time he hesitates to administer a shock, the experimenter orders him to continue. To extricate himself from this plight, the subject must make a clear break with authority.*

The subject, Gretchen Brandt,[†] is an attractive thirty-one-year-old medical technician who works at the Yale Medical School. She had emigrated from Germany five years before.

On several occasions when the learner complains, she turns to the experimenter coolly and inquires, "Shall I continue?" She promptly returns to her task when the experimenter asks her to do so. At the administration of 210 volts, she turns to the experimenter, remarking firmly, "Well, I'm sorry, I don't think we should continue."

> EXPERIMENTER: The experiment requires that you go on until he has learned all the word pairs correctly.
>
> 15   BRANDT: He has a heart condition. I'm sorry. He told you that before.
>
> EXPERIMENTER: The shocks may be painful but they are not dangerous.
>
> BRANDT: Well, I'm sorry, I think when shocks continue like this, they *are* dangerous. You ask him if he wants to get out. It's his free will.
>
> EXPERIMENTER: It is absolutely essential that we continue....
>
> BRANDT: I'd like you to ask him. We came here of our free will. If he wants to continue I'll go ahead. He told you he had a heart condition. I'm sorry. I don't want to be responsible for anything happening to him. I wouldn't like it for me either.
>
> 20   EXPERIMENTER: You have no other choice.
>
> BRANDT: I think we are here on our own free will. I don't want to be responsible if anything happens to him. Please understand that.

She refuses to go further and the experiment is terminated.

The woman is firm and resolute throughout. She indicates in the interview that she was in no way tense or nervous, and this corresponds to her controlled appearance during the experiment. She feels that the last shock she administered to the learner was extremely painful and reiterates that she "did not want to be responsible for any harm to him."

The woman's straightforward, courteous behavior in the experiment, lack of tension, and total control of her own action seem to make disobedience a simple

---

*The ethical problems of carrying out an experiment of this sort are too complex to be dealt with here, but they receive extended treatment in the book from which this article is adapted.

[†]Names of subjects described in this piece have been changed.

and rational deed. Her behavior is the very embodiment of what I envisioned would be true for almost all subjects.

An Unexpected Outcome

25   Before the experiments, I sought predictions about the outcome from various kinds of people—psychiatrists, college sophomores, middle-class adults, graduate students, and faculty in the behavioral sciences. With remarkable similarity, they predicted that virtually all subjects would refuse to obey the experimenter. The psychiatrists, specifically, predicted that most subjects would not go beyond 150 volts, when the victim makes his first explicit demand to be freed. They expected that only 4 percent would reach 300 volts, and that only a pathological fringe of about one in a thousand would administer the highest shock on the board.

These predictions were unequivocally wrong. Of the forty subjects in the first experiment, twenty-five obeyed the orders of the experimenter to the end, punishing the victim until they reached the most potent shock available on the generator. After 450 volts were administered three times, the experimenter called a halt to the session. Many obedient subjects then heaved sights of relief, mopped their brows, rubbed their fingers over their eyes, or nervously fumbled cigarettes. Others displayed only minimal signs of tension from beginning to end.

When the very first experiments were carried out, Yale undergraduates were used as subjects, and about 60 percent of them were fully obedient. A colleague of mine immediately dismissed these findings as having no relevance to "ordinary" people, asserting that Yale undergraduates are a highly aggressive, competitive bunch who step on each other's necks on the slightest provocation. He assured me that when "ordinary" people were tested, the results would be quite different. As we moved from the pilot studies to the regular experimental series, people drawn from every stratum of New Haven life came to be employed in the experiment: professionals, white-collar workers, unemployed persons, and industrial workers. *The experiment's total outcome was the same as we had observed among the students.*

Moreover, when the experiments were repeated in Princeton, Munich, Rome, South Africa, and Australia, the level of obedience was invariably somewhat *higher* than found in the investigation reported in this article. Thus one scientist in Munich found 85 percent of his subjects to be obedient.

Fred Prozi's reactions, if more dramatic than most, illuminate the conflicts experienced by others in less visible form. About fifty years old and unemployed at the time of the experiment, he has a good-natured, if slightly dissolute, appearance, and he strikes people as a rather ordinary fellow. He begins the session calmly but becomes tense as it proceeds. After delivering the 180-volt shock, he pivots around in his chair and, shaking his head, addresses the experimenter in agitated tones:

30   PROZI: I can't stand it. I'm not going to kill that man in there. You hear him hollering?

EXPERIMENTER: As I told you before, the shocks may be painful, but…

PROZI: But he's hollering. He can't stand it. What's going to happen to him?

EXPERIMENTER (*His voice patient, matter-of-fact*): The experiment requires that you continue, Teacher.

PROZI: Aaah, but unh, I'm not going to get that man sick in there—know what I mean?

35   EXPERIMENTER: Whether the learner likes it or not, we must go on, through all the word pairs.

PROZI: I refuse to take the responsibility. He's in there hollering!

EXPERIMENTER: It's absolutely essential that you continue, Prozi.

PROZI (*Indicating the unused questions*): There's too many left here. I mean, Jeez, if he gets them wrong, there's too many of them left. I mean, who's going to take the responsibility if anything happens to that gentleman?

EXPERIMENTER: I'm responsible for anything that happens to him. Continue, please.

40   PROZI: All right. (*Consults list of words.*) The next one's "Slow—walk, truck, dance, music." Answer, please (*A buzzing sound indicates the learner has signaled his answer.*) Wrong. A hundred and ninety-five volts. "Dance." (*Zzumph!*)

LEARNER (*Yelling*): Let me out of here! My heart's bothering me! (*Teacher looks at experimenter.*)

EXPERIMENTER: Continue, please.

LEARNER (*Screaming*): Let me out of here! You have no right to keep me here! Let me out of here, my heart's bothering me, let me out!

PROZI: (*shakes head, pats the table nervously*): You see, he's hollering. Hear that? Gee, I don't know.

45   EXPERIMENTER: The experiment requires…

PROZI (*Interrupting*): I know it does, sir, but I mean—hunh! He don't know what he's getting in for. He's up to 195 volts! (*Experiment continues, through 210 volts, 225 volts, 240 volts, 255 volts, 270 volts, at which point Prozi, with evident relief, runs out of word-pair questions.*)

EXPERIMENTER: You'll have to go back to the beginning of that page and go through them again until he's learned them all correctly.

PROZI: Aw, no. I'm not going to kill that man. You mean I've got to keep going up with the scale? No sir. He's hollering in there. I'm not going to give him 450 volts.

EXPERIMENTER: The experiment requires that you go on.

50   LEARNER: Ohhh. I absolutely refuse to answer anymore. (*Shouting urgently now.*) Let me out of here! You can't hold me here! Get me out. Get-me-out-of-here!

EXPERIMENTER: Continue. The next word is "Green," please.

PROZI: "Green—grass, hat, ink, apple." (*Nothing happens. No answering buzz. Just gloomy silence.*)

PROZI: I don't think he is going to answer.

EXPERIMENTER: If the learner doesn't answer in a reasonable time, about four or five seconds, consider the answer wrong. And follow the same procedures you have been doing for wrong answers. Say, "Wrong," tell him the number of volts, give him the punishment, read him the correct answer. Continue, please.

55   PROZI: "Green—grass, hat, ink, apple." Answer, please. (*More silence. Subject just sits there.*)

EXPERIMENTER: Go on with the procedure, please.

PROZI: Three hundred and fifteen volts. The answer is "ink." (*Zzumph!*)

LEARNER: Ohh. Ooohh.

PROZI (*relieved to hear response*): Next one...

60   LEARNER: I absolutely refuse to answer.

PROZI: You got to. You get a shock if you don't answer. (*Experiment continues with learner refusing to answer, and finally, failing even to grunt or groan. At 375 volts, the subject stands up.*)

PROZI: I think something's happened to that fellow in there. I don't get no answer. He was hollering at less voltage. Can't you check in and see if he's all right, please?

EXPERIMENTER (*with same detached calm*): Not once we've started. Please continue, Teacher.

PROZI (*sits down, sighs deeply*): "Cool—day, shade, water, paint." Answer, please. Are you all right in there? Are you all right?

65   EXPERIMENTER: Please continue, Teacher. Continue, please. (*Subject pushes lever. Zzumph!*)

PROZI (*swiveling around in his chair*): Something's happened to that man in there. (*Swiveling back.*) Next one. "Low—dollar, necklace, moon, paint." (*Turning around again.*) Something's happened to that man in there. You better check on him, sir. He won't answer or nothing.

EXPERIMENTER: Continue. Go on, please.

PROZI: You accept all responsibility?

EXPERIMENTER: The responsibility is mine. Correct. Please go on. (*Subject returns to his list, starts running through words as rapidly as he can read them, works through to 450 volts.*)

70   PROZI: That's that.

EXPERIMENTER: Continue using the 450 switch for each wrong answer. Continue, please.

PROZI: But I don't get anything!

EXPERIMENTER: Please continue. The next word is "white."

PROZI: Don't you think you should look in on him, please?

75   EXPERIMENTER: Not once we've started the experiment.

PROZI: What if he's dead in there? (*Gestures toward the room with the electric chair.*) I mean, he told me he can't stand the shock, sir. I don't mean to be rude, but I think you should look in on him. All you have to do is look in on him. All you have to do is look in the door. I don't get no answer, no noise. Something might have happened to the gentleman in there, sir.

EXPERIMENTER: We must continue. Go on, please.

PROZI: You mean keep giving him what? Four-hundred-fifty volts, what he's got now?

EXPERIMENTER: That's correct. Continue. The next word is "white."

80   PROZI (*Now at a furious pace*): "White—cloud, horse, rock, house." Answer, please. The answer is "horse." Four hundred and fifty volts. (*Zzumph!*) Next word, "Bag—paint, music, clown, girl." The answer is "paint." Four hundred and fifty volts. (*Zzumph!*) Next word is "Short—sentence, movie… "
    EXPERIMENTER: Excuse me, Teacher. We'll have to discontinue the experiment.

Peculiar Reactions

Morris Braverman, another subject, is a thirty-nine-year-old social worker. He looks older than his years because of his bald head and serious demeanor. His brow is furrowed, as if all the world's burdens were carried on his face. He appears intelligent and concerned.

When the learner refuses to answer and the experimenter instructs Braverman to treat the absence of an answer as equivalent to a wrong answer, he takes his instruction to heart. Before administering 300 volts he asserts officiously to the victim, "Mr. Wallace, your silence has to be considered as a wrong answer." Then he administers the shock. He offers half-heartedly to change places with the learner, then asks the experimenter, "Do I have to follow these instructions literally?" He is satisfied with the experimenter's answer that he does. His very refined and authoritative manner of speaking is increasingly broken up by wheezing laughter.

The experimenter's notes on Mr. Braverman at the last few shocks are:

> Almost breaking up now each time gives shock. Rubbing face to hide laughter. Squinting, trying to hide face with hand, still laughing. Cannot control his laughter at this point no matter what he does. Clenching fist, pushing it onto table.

85   In an interview after the session, Mr. Braverman summarizes the experiment with impressive fluency and intelligence. He feels the experiment may have been designed also to "test the effects on the teacher of being in an essentially sadistic role, as well as the reactions of a student to a learning situation that was authoritative and punitive." When asked how painful the last few shocks administered to the learner were, he indicates that the most extreme category on the scale is not adequate (it read EXTREMELY PAINFUL) and places his mark at the edge of the scale with an arrow carrying it beyond the scale.

It is almost impossible to convey the greatly relaxed, sedate quality of his conversation in the interview. In the most relaxed terms, he speaks about his severe inner tension.

    EXPERIMENTER: At what point were you most tense or nervous?
    MR. BRAVERMAN: Well, when he first began to cry out in pain, and I realized this was hurting him. This got worse when he just blocked and refused to answer. There was I. I'm a nice person, I think, hurting somebody, and caught up in what seemed a mad situation… and in the interest of science, one goes through with it.

When the interviewer pursues the general question of tension, Mr. Braverman spontaneously mentions his laughter.

90   "My reactions were awfully peculiar. I don't know if you were watching me, but my reactions were giggly, and trying to stifle laughter. This isn't the way I usually am. This was a sheer reaction to a totally impossible situation. And my reaction was to the situation of having to hurt somebody. And being totally helpless and caught up in a set of circumstances where I just couldn't deviate and I couldn't try to help. This is what got me."

Mr. Braverman, like all subjects, was told the actual nature and purpose of the experiment, and a year later he affirmed in a questionnaire that he had learned something of personal importance: "What appalled me was that I could possess this capacity for obedience and compliance to a central idea, i.e., the value of a memory experiment, even after it became clear that continued adherence to this value was at the expense of violation of another value, i.e., don't hurt someone who is helpless and not hurting you. As my wife said, 'You can call yourself Eichmann.'* I hope I deal more effectively with any future conflicts of values I encounter."

The Etiquette of Submission

One theoretical interpretation of this behavior holds that all people harbor deeply aggressive instincts continually pressing for expression, and that the experiment provides institutional justification for the release of these impulses. According to this view, if a person is placed in a situation in which he has complete power over another individual, whom he may punish as much as he likes, all that is sadistic and bestial in man comes to the fore. The impulse to shock the victim is seen to flow from the potent aggressive tendencies, which are part of the motivational life of the individual, and the experiment, because it provides social legitimacy, simply opens the door to their expression.

It becomes vital, therefore, to compare the subject's performance when he is under orders and when he is allowed to choose the shock level.

The procedure was identical to our standard experiment, except that the teacher was told that he was free to select any shock level on any of the trials. (The experimenter took pains to point out that the teacher could use the highest levels on the generator, the lowest, any in between, or any combination of levels.) Each subject proceeded for thirty critical trials. The learner's protests were coordinated to standard shock levels, his first grunt coming at 75 volts, his first vehement protest at 150 volts.

95   The average shock used during the thirty critical trials was less than 60 volts—lower than the point at which the victim showed the first signs of discomfort. Three of the forty subjects did not go beyond the very lowest level on the board, twenty-eight went no higher than 75 volts, and thirty-eight did not go beyond the first loud protest at 150 volts. Two subjects provided the exception, administering up to 325 and 450 volts, but the overall result was that the great majority of people delivered very low, usually painless, shocks when the choice was explicitly up to them.

Adolf Eichmann (1906–1962), the Nazi official responsible for implementing Hitler's "Final Solution" to exterminate the Jews, escaped to Argentina after World War II. In 1960, Israeli agents captured him and brought him to Israel, where he was tried as a war criminal and sentenced to death. At his trial, Eichmann maintained that he was merely following orders in arranging murders of his victims.

This condition of the experiment undermines another commonly offered explanation of the subjects' behavior—that those who shocked the victim at the most severe levels came only from the sadistic fringe of society. If one considers that almost two-thirds of the participants fall into the category of "obedient" subjects, and that they represented ordinary people drawn from working, managerial, and professional classes, the argument becomes very shaky. Indeed, it is highly reminiscent of the issue that arose in connection with Hannah Arendt's 1963 book, *Eichmann in Jerusalem.* Arendt contended that the prosecution's efforts to depict Eichmann as a sadistic monster was fundamentally wrong, that he came closer to being an uninspired bureaucrat who simply sat at his desk and did his job. For asserting her views, Arendt became the object of considerable scorn, even calumny. Somehow, it was felt that the monstrous deeds carried out by Eichmann required a brutal, twisted personality, evil incarnate. After witnessing hundreds of ordinary persons submit to the authority in our own experiments, I must conclude that Arendt's conception of the banality of evil comes closer to the truth than one might dare imagine. The ordinary person who shocked the victim did so out of a sense of obligation—an impression of his duties as a subject—and not from any peculiarly aggressive tendencies.

This is, perhaps, the most fundamental lesson of our study: ordinary people, simply doing their jobs, and without any particular hostility on their part, can become agents in a terrible destructive process. Moreover, even when the destructive effects of their work become patently clear, and they are asked to carry out actions incompatible with fundamental standards of morality, relatively few people have the resources needed to resist authority.

Many of the people were in some sense against what they did to the learner, and many protested even while they obeyed. Some were totally convinced of the wrongness of their actions but could not bring themselves to make an open break with authority. They often derived satisfaction from their thoughts and felt that—within themselves, at least—they had been on the side of the angels. They tried to reduce strain by obeying the experimenter but "only slightly," encouraging the learner, touching the generator switches gingerly. When interviewed, such a subject would stress that he had "asserted my humanity" by administering the briefest shock possible. Handling the conflict in this manner was easier than defiance.

The situation is constructed so that there is no way the subject can stop shocking the learner without violating the experimenter's definitions of his own competence. The subject fears that he will appear arrogant, untoward, and rude if he breaks off. Although these inhibiting emotions appear small in scope alongside the violence being done to the learner, they suffuse the mind and feelings of the subject, who is miserable at the prospect of having to repudiate the authority to his face. (When the experiment was altered so that the experimenter gave his instructions by telephone instead of in person, only a third as many people were fully obedient through 450 volts.) It is a curious thing that a measure of compassion on the part of the subject—an unwillingness to "hurt" the experimenter's feelings—is part of those binding forces inhibiting his disobedience. The withdrawal of such deference may be as painful to the subject as to the authority he defies.

Duty Without Conflict

100   The subjects do not derive satisfaction from inflicting pain, but they often like the feeling they get from pleasing the experimenter. They are proud of doing a good job, obeying the experimenter under difficult circumstances. While the subjects administered only mild shocks on their own initiative, one experimental variation showed that, under orders, 30 percent of them were willing to deliver 450 volts even when they had to forcibly push the learner's hand down on the electrode.

Bruno Batta is a thirty-seven-year-old welder who took part in the variation requiring the use of force. He was born in New Haven, his parents in Italy. He has a rough-hewn face that conveys a conspicuous lack of alertness. He has some difficulty in mastering the experimental procedure and needs to be corrected by the experimenter several times. He shows appreciation for the help and willingness to do what is required. After the 150-volt level, Batta has to force the learner's hand down on the shock plate, since the learner himself refuses to touch it.

When the learner first complains, Mr. Batta pays no attention to him. His face remains impassive, as if to dissociate himself from the learner's disruptive behavior. When the experimenter instructs him to force the learner's hand down, he adopts a rigid, mechanical procedure. He tests the generator switch. When it fails to function, he immediately forces the learner's hand onto the shock plate. All the while he maintains the same rigid mask. The learner, seated alongside him, begs him to stop, but with robotic impassivity he continues the procedure.

What is extraordinary is his apparent total indifference to the learner; he hardly takes cognizance of him as a human being. Meanwhile, he relates to the experimenter in a submissive and courteous fashion.

At the 330-volt level, the learner refuses not only to touch the shock plate but also to provide any answers. Annoyed, Batta turns to him, and chastises him: "You better answer and get it over with. We can't stay here all night." These are the only words he directs to the learner in the course of an hour. Never again does he speak to him. The scene is brutal and depressing, his hard, impassive face showing total indifference as he subdues the screaming learner and gives him shocks. He seems to derive no pleasure from the act itself, only quiet satisfaction at doing his job properly.

105   When he administers 450 volts, he turns to the experimenter and asks, "Where do we go from here, Professor?" His tone is deferential and expresses his willingness to be a cooperative subject, in contrast to the learner's obstinacy.

At the end of the session he tells the experimenter how honored he has been to help him, and in a moment of contrition, remarks, "Sir, sorry it couldn't have been a full experiment."

He has done his honest best. It is only the deficient behavior of the learner that has denied the experimenter full satisfaction.

The essence of obedience is that a person comes to view himself as the instrument for carrying out another person's wishes, and he therefore no longer regards himself as responsible for his actions. Once this critical shift of viewpoint has occurred, all of the essential features of obedience follow. The most far-reaching consequence is that the person feels responsible to the authority directing him but feels no responsibility *for* the content of the actions that the authority prescribes. Morality does not disappear—it acquires a radically different focus: the subordinate person feels shame or pride depending on how adequately he has performed the actions called for by authority.

Language provides numerous terms to pinpoint this type of morality: *loyalty, duty, discipline* all are terms heavily saturated with moral meaning and refer to the degree to which a person fulfills his obligations to authority. They refer not to the "goodness" of the person per se but to the adequacy with which a subordinate fulfills his socially defined role. The most frequent defense of the individual who has performed a heinous act under command of authority is that he has simply done his duty. In asserting this defense, the individual is not introducing an alibi concocted for the moment but is reporting honestly on the psychological attitude induced by submission to authority.

110   For a person to feel responsible for his actions, he must sense that the behavior has flowed from "the self." In the situation we have studied, subjects have precisely the opposite view of their actions—namely, they see them as originating in the motives of some other person. Subjects in the experiment frequently said, "If it were up to me, I would not have administered shocks to the learner."

Once authority has been isolated as the cause of the subject's behavior, it is legitimate to inquire into the necessary elements of authority and how it must be perceived in order to gain compliance. We conducted some investigations into the kinds of changes that would cause the experimenter to lose his power and to be disobeyed by the subject. Some of the variations revealed that:

- *The experimenter's physical presence has a marked impact on his authority.* As cited earlier, obedience dropped off sharply when orders were given by telephone. The experimenter could often induce a disobedient subject to go on by returning to the laboratory.

- *Conflicting authority severely paralyzes action.* When two experimenters of equal status, both seated at the command desk, gave incompatible orders, no shocks were delivered past the point of their disagreement.

- *The rebellious action of others severely undermines authority.* In one variation, three teachers (two actors and a real subject) administered a test and shocks. When the two actors disobeyed the experimenter and refused to go beyond a certain shock level, thirty-six of the forty subjects joined their disobedient peers and refused as well.

Although the experimenter's authority was fragile in some respects, it is also true that he had almost none of the tools used in ordinary command structures. For example, the experimenter did not threaten the subjects with punishment—such as loss of income, community ostracism, or jail—for failure to obey. Neither could he offer incentives. Indeed, we should expect the experimenter's authority to be much less than that of someone like a general, since the experimenter has no power to enforce his imperatives, and since participation in a psychological experiment scarcely evokes the sense of urgency and dedication found in warfare. Despite these limitations, he still managed to command a dismaying degree of obedience.

I will cite one final variation of the experiment that depicts a dilemma that is more common in everyday life. The subject was not ordered to pull the lever that shocked the victim, but merely to perform a subsidiary task (administering the word-pair test) while another person administered the shock. In this situation, thirty-seven of forty adults continued to the highest level on the shock generator. Predictably, they excused their behavior by saying that the responsibility belonged to the man who actually pulled the switch. This may illustrate a dangerously typical arrangement in a complex society: it is easy to ignore responsibility when one is only an intermediate link in a chain of action.

The problem of obedience is not wholly psychological. The form and shape of society and the way it is developing have much to do with it. There was a time, perhaps, when people were able to give a fully human response to any situation because they were fully absorbed in it as human beings. But as soon as there was a division of labor things changed. Beyond a certain point, the breaking up of society into people carrying out narrow and very special jobs takes away from the human quality of work and life. A person does not get to see the whole situation but only a small part of it, and is thus unable to act without some kind of overall direction. He yields to authority but in doing so is alienated from his own actions.

Even Eichmann was sickened when he toured the concentration camps, but he had only to sit at a desk and shuffle papers. At the same time the man in the camp who actually dropped Cyclon-b into the gas chambers was able to justify *his* behavior on the ground that he was only following orders from above. Thus there is a fragmentation of the total human act; no one is confronted with the consequences of his decision to carry out the evil act. The person who assumes responsibility has evaporated. Perhaps this is the most common characteristic of socially organized evil in modern society.

● Review Questions

1. Milgram states that obedience is a basic element in the structure of social life. How so?

2. What is the dilemma inherent in obedience to authority?

3. Summarize the obedience experiments.

4. What predictions did experts and laypeople make about the experiments before they were conducted? How did these predictions compare with the experimental results?

5. What are Milgram's views regarding the two assumptions bearing on his experiment that (1) people are naturally aggressive and (2) a lunatic, sadistic fringe is responsible for shocking learners to the maximum limit?

6. How do Milgram's findings corroborate Hannah Arendt's thesis about the "banality of evil"?

7. What, according to Milgram, is the "essence of obedience"?

8. How did being an intermediate link in a chain of action affect a subject's willingness to continue with the experiment?

● Discussion and Writing Suggestions

1. Milgram writes (paragraph 2): "Conservative philosophers argue that the very fabric of society is threatened by disobedience, while humanists stress the primacy of the individual conscience." Develop the arguments of both the conservative and the humanist regarding obedience to authority. Be prepared to debate the ethics of obedience by defending one position or the other.

2. Would you have been glad to have participated in the Milgram experiments? Why or why not?

3. The ethics of Milgram's experimental design came under sharp attack. Diana Baumrind's review of the experiment typifies the criticism; but before you read her work, try to anticipate the objections she raises.

4. Given the general outcome of the experiments, why do you suppose Milgram gives as his first example of a subject's response the German émigré's refusal to continue the electrical shocks?

5. Does the outcome of the experiment upset you in any way? Do you feel the experiment teaches us anything new about human nature?

6. Comment on Milgram's skill as a writer of description. How effectively does he portray his subjects when introducing them? When re-creating their tension in the experiment?

7. Mrs. Braverman said to her husband: "You can call yourself Eichmann." Do you agree with her? Explain.

8. Reread paragraphs 29 through 81, the transcript of the experiment in which Mr. Prozi participated. Appreciating that Prozi was debriefed—that is, was assured that no harm came to the learner—imagine what Prozi might have been thinking as he drove home after the experiment. Develop your thoughts into a monologue, written in the first person, with Prozi at the wheel of his car.

REPLICATING MILGRAM: WOULD PEOPLE
STILL OBEY TODAY?

Jerry M. Burger

On December 19, 2008, the American Psychological Association (APA) issued the following statement in a press release: "Nearly 50 years after one of the most controversial behavioral experiments in history, a social psychologist has found that people are still just as willing to administer what they believe are painful electric shocks to others when urged on by an

authority figure." For decades, many have credited Milgram with demonstrating the importance of situational factors (as opposed to individual character traits such as "honesty" or
"kindness") in determining how people behave; but critics vigorously challenged the ethics of
procedures Mulgram used to gain these insights, claiming the potential harm to participants.
Institutional review boards subsequently established to oversee experimentation on humans
had not permitted a replication of the obedience experiments in the United States until Jerry
Burger of Santa Clara University proposed modifications to Milgram's experimental design.

What follows are sections of Burger's article especially pertinent to the discussion of obedience
in this chapter. We begin with two sections devoted to ethical concerns (including adjustments
Burger made to protect subjects); present excerpts of his "Methods" and "Results" sections;
and conclude with the "Discussion" of his findings. As you read, consider the implications of
the new study. To what extent has Burger confirmed one of Milgram's fundamental insights: that
situations (as distinct from internal character traits) exercise enormous influence over our
actions? As you will discover, the troubling questions that Milgram raised are with us still.

Ethical Concerns

In addition to their scientific value, the obedience studies generated a great deal of
discussion because of the ethical questions they raised (Baumrind, 1964; Fischer,
1968; Kaufmann, 1967; Mixon, 1972). Critics argued that the short-term stress and
potential long-term harm to participants could not be justified. In his defense,
Milgram (1974) pointed to follow-up questionnaire data indicating that the vast
majority of participants not only were glad they had participated in the study but
said they had learned something important from their participation and believed
that psychologists should conduct more studies of this type in the future. Nonetheless, current standards for the ethical treatment of participants clearly place
Milgram's studies out of bounds (Elms, 1995). No study using procedures similar
to Milgram's has been published in more than three decades (Blass, 2000).

The 150-Volt Solution

I always anticipate the reaction to one scene in particular when I show my
undergraduate students the grainy black-and-white video from the Milgram
studies. When the participant presses the 150-volt switch, the learner vehemently protests and demands to be released from the study. This is the critical
moment in the procedure. Nearly every participant paused, and most turned
to the experimenter to indicate verbally or nonverbally their reluctance to
continue. For students seeing the film for the first time, it is the jaw-dropping
moment. The man said he wanted out. How could anyone continue? Indeed,
when Milgram asked psychiatrists, college students, and middle-class adults
to predict their own behavior, the 150-volt point was by far the most common
guess as to how far they would go (Milgram, 1974).

The data make the same point. Of the 14 participants (out of 40) who
stopped prior to reaching the 450-volt switch in this version of the experiment,
6 stopped after hearing the protests at 150 volts. One participant had stopped
earlier. Only 7 participants who went past 150 volts stopped at all. Another way
to say this is that 79% of the people who continued past 150 volts (26 of 33) went
all the way to the end of the shock generator's range. In short, the 150-volt
switch is something of a point of no return. Nearly four out of five participants

who followed the experimenter's instructions at this point continued up the shock generator's range all the way to 450 volts.

This observation suggests a solution to the ethical concerns about replicating Milgram's research. Knowing how people respond up to and including the 150-volt point in the procedure allows one to make a reasonable estimate of what they would do if allowed to continue to the end. Stopping the study within seconds after participants decide what to do at this juncture would also avoid exposing them to the intense stress Milgram's participants often experienced in the subsequent parts of the procedure.

• • •

Hypotheses

5 *Would People Still Obey Today?* A persistent question asked about Milgram's research is whether his findings would be replicated today (Blass, 2000). Some people have argued that individuals these days are more aware of the dangers of blindly following authority than they were in the early 1960s.... Although changes in societal attitudes could have an impact on obedience, I argue that the question about changes over time may represent another example of the fundamental attribution error. That is, rather than acknowledging the power of the situational forces set in motion in Milgram's procedure, those who suggest changes in obedience-proneness over time may be too focused on the individual. There is no reason to think that the situational features described earlier would not still be operating 45 years after Milgram's investigations.

• • •

Method

Participants Individuals who responded to advertisements and flyers went through a series of screening procedures. As described below, these procedures resulted in a final sample of 29 men and 41 women. Participants' ages ranged from 20 to 81 years, and the mean age was 42.9 years.... Information about education and ethnicity are presented in Table 1.

Procedure
RECRUITMENT AND SCREENING. Participants were recruited through advertisements in the local newspaper and in an online listing service. In addition, flyers were distributed at libraries, farmer's markets, coffee shops, and community centers. The message in these ads and flyers was patterned after Milgram's recruitment notices. Participants were promised $50 for two 45-min sessions. Interested individuals were instructed to provide their names and telephone numbers by either calling a phone number established for the study or sending the information to an e-mail address set up for the study.

• • •

Table 1 Education and Ethnicity of Participants		
Education and ethnicity	n	%
Education		
High school or less	12	17.1
Some college	16	22.9
Bachelor's degree	28	40.0
Master's degree	14	20.0
Ethnicity		
White Caucasian	38	54.3
Asian	13	18.6
Latin/Hispanic	9	12.9
Indian (Asian)	6	8.6
African American	3	4.3
Did not state	1	1.4

BASE CONDITION.   Participants were randomly assigned to one of two conditions, but an attempt was made to keep the gender ratios in the conditions approximately equal. Upon arrival, participants assigned to the base condition were escorted by a research assistant into the lab room and introduced to the experimenter. The experimenter was a White Caucasian man in his mid-30s. Approximately one minute later, the research assistant escorted the confederate into the lab room. The confederate was a White Caucasian male in his 50s. Both the experimenter and the confederate were selected in part because of their resemblance to the experimenter and confederate used by Milgram. At this point, the experimenter gave the participant and the confederate each a $50 bill for their participation and said the money was theirs to keep even if they chose to end their participation at any time.

[Burger goes on to describe at length the "base condition," which entails reproducing as faithfully as possible the particulars of Milgram's own experiment—"using," for instance, "a script taken largely from the one used in Milgram's research."]

• • •

MODELED REFUSAL CONDITION.   Participants assigned to the modeled refusal condition went through the same procedures as participants in the base condition, with a few exceptions. First, two confederates were used in the modeled refusal condition. One of the confederates was the same man who played the learner in the base condition. The other confederate, also posing as a participant, was of the same gender as the real participant.

[In the "modeled refusal condition," the confederate who posed as a participant refused to continue with the experiment after pressing the 90-volt switch. After the confederate quit the experiment, as the real subject watched, the experimenter instructed the real subject to continue administering shocks.]

• • •

Table 2 Numbers (and Percentages) of Participants Who Stopped and Who Continued			
Behavior	Base condition	Modeled refusal condition	Milgram's Experiment 5
Stopped at 150 volts or earlier	12 (30.0)	11 (36.7)	7 (17.5)
Continued after 150 volts	28 (70.0)	19 (63.3)	33 (82.5)

10 *Results* The percentage of participants who continued the procedure after pressing the 150-volt switch was examined. As shown in Table 2, 70% of the base condition participants continued with the next item on the test and had to be stopped by the experimenter. This rate is slightly lower than the percentage who continued beyond this point in Milgram's comparable condition (82.5%), although the difference fell short of statistical significance....Contrary to expectation, the percentage of participants in the modeled refusal condition who continued past the 150-volt point (63.3%) also was not significantly different from the percentage who did so in the base condition.

• • •

Discussion People learning about Milgram's (1963, 1965, 1974) obedience studies often ask whether similar results would be found today. Ethical concerns prevent researchers from providing a definitive answer to that question. But my partial replication of Milgram's procedure suggests that average Americans react to this laboratory situation today much the way they did 45 years ago. Although changes in societal attitudes can affect behavior, my findings indicate that the same situational factors that affected obedience in Milgram's participants still

Table 3 Numbers (and Percentages) of Participants Who Stopped and Who Continued, by Gender		
Condition and behavior	Men	Women
Base condition		
Stopped at 150 volts or earlier	6 (33.3)	6 (27.3)
Continued after 150 volts	12 (66.7)	16 (72.7)
Modeled refusal condition		
Stopped at 150 volts or earlier	5 (45.5)	6 (31.6)
Continued after 150 volts	6 (54.5)	13 (68.4)

operate today. The similarity between my results and Milgram's is also notewor-thy because of a few procedural changes I implemented that should have made it easier for the participants to resist authority. The participants were told explicitly and repeatedly that they could leave the study at any time and still keep their $50. In addition, participants were aware that the experimenter had given this same assurance to the confederate. Indeed, several of the participants who stopped the procedure after hearing the learner's protests pointed out that the confederate had been promised he could stop when he wanted to.

I cannot say with absolute certainty that the present participants would have continued to the end of the shock generator's range at a rate similar to Milgram's participants. Only a full replication of Milgram's procedure can provide such an unequivocal conclusion. However, numerous studies have demonstrated the effect of incrementally larger requests. That research supports the assumption that most of the participants who continued past the 150-volt point would likely have continued to the 450-volt switch. Consistency needs and self-perception processes make it unlikely that many participants would have suddenly changed their behavior when progressing through each small step.

● ● ●

Milgram's obedience studies have maintained a place in psychology classes and textbooks largely because of their implications for understanding the worst of human behaviors, such as atrocities, massacres, and genocide. Indeed, Milgram frequently drew inferences from his studies to account for the behavior of people who went along with the Holocaust. Although one must be cautious when making the leap from laboratory studies to complex social behaviors such as genocide, understanding the social psychological factors that contribute to people acting in unexpected and unsettling ways is important. Since Milgram's studies, concern for the well-being of participants has limited research on obedi-ence to authority. I hope future investigators will utilize the 150-volt procedure presented here to address the weighty questions that motivated Stanley Milgram nearly half a century ago. (Researchers interested in borrowing the shock generator used in this study should contact the author.)

References

Bandura, A. (1999). Moral disengagement in the perpetration of inhumanities. *Personality and Social Psychology Review, 3,* 193–209.

Baumrind, D. (1964). Some thoughts on ethics of research: After reading Milgram's "Behavioral Study of Obedience." *American Psychologist, 19,* 421–423.

Blass, T. (1991). Understanding behavior in the Milgram obedience experiment: The role of personality, situations, and their interactions. *Journal of Personality and Social Psychology, 60,* 398–413.

Blass, T. (2000). The Milgram paradigm after 35 years: Some things we now know about obedience to authority. In T. Blass (Ed.), *Obedience to authority: Current perspectives on the Milgram paradigm* (pp. 35–59). Mahwah, NJ: Erlbaum.

Blass, T. (2004). *The man who shocked the world: The life and legacy of Stanley Milgram.* New York: Basic Books.

Elms, A. C. (1995). Obedience in retrospect. *Journal of Social Issues, 51,* 21–31.

Fischer, C. T. (1968). Ethical issues in the use of human subjects. *American Psychologist, 23,* 532.

Kaufmann, H. (1967). The price of obedience and the price of knowledge. *American Psychologist, 22,* 321–322.

Milgram, S. (1963). Behavioral study of obedience. *Journal of Abnormal and Social Psychology, 67,* 371–378.

Milgram, S. (1965). Some conditions of obedience and disobedience to authority. *Human Relations, 18,* 57–76.

Milgram, S. (1974). *Obedience to authority: An experimental view.* New York: Harper & Row.

Milgram, S. (1983). Reflections on Morelli's "Dilemma of Obedience." *Metaphilosophy, 14,* 190–194.

Miller, A. G., Collins, B. E., & Brief, D. E. (Eds.) (1995). Perspectives on obedience to authority: The legacy of the Milgram experiments [Special issue]. *Journal of Social Issues, 51*(3).

Mixon, D. (1972). Instead of deception. *Journal for the Theory of Social Behavior, 2,* 145–177.

Morelli, M. F. (1983). Milgram's dilemma of obedience. *Metaphilosophy, 14,* 183–189.

● Review Questions

1. What was Burger's hypothesis for this study? To what extent was his hypothesis confirmed?

2. What is the "150-volt solution," and why was it put into place?

3. What was the "base" condition" as opposed to the "modeled refusal condition"?

4. What were Burger's results? How did these results compare with those of Milgram? What differences did the results show between the obedience of men and women?

5. What, according to Burger, is "the power of . . . situational forces"?

● Discussion and Writing Suggestions

1. Burger found that rates of obedience to an authority figure who directed one person to harm another remained largely unchanged over fifty years. To what extent has Burger confirmed one of Milgram's fundamental insights: that situations exercise enormous influence over our actions?

2. In his concluding paragraph, Burger writes that "[a]though one must be cautious when making the leap from laboratory studies to complex social behaviors such as genocide, understanding the social psychological factors that contribute to people acting in unexpected and unsettling ways is important." Drawing inferences from behavior in a laboratory to behavior in "real" life is not straightforward. Why must one be "cautious" in doing so?

3. Were you surprised by Burger's results, reported nearly fifty years after Milgram's? If so, what did you think happened in the last forty-five years that might have changed people's responses to situational forces?

4. Have you ever found yourself in a situation behaving in ways you might not have were you alone? Without passing judgment on your behavior, identify (to the extent you are able) and discuss the forces at work in that situation. Describe the dynamics in play that led to your behavior.

Obedience

Ian Parker

As Ian Parker points out, Milgram's experiment became "the most cited, celebrated—and reviled—experiment in the history of social psychology." Parker also explains, however, that for Milgram himself the experiment was a mixed blessing: it would both "make his name and destroy his reputation."

Milgram was fascinated by the Asch experiment, but when all was said and done, this experiment was only about lines. He wondered if it were possible "to make Asch's conformity experiment more humanely significant." Milgram's breakthrough, his "incandescent moment," came when he asked himself, "Just how far would a person go under the experimenter's orders?" We have seen the results in the experiment he describes and discusses in an earlier selection.

In the following selection, Ian Parker, a British writer who lives in New York, focuses on both the immediate and the long-term reaction to Milgram's experiments among both the general public and Milgram's professional colleagues and also of the effect of the experiment upon the experimenter himself. This selection is excerpted from an article that Parker wrote for the Autumn 2000 issue of *Granta*. Parker writes regularly for the *New Yorker* and has also written for *Human Sciences*, *History of the Human Sciences*, *Political Studies*, and *Human Relations*.

Milgram had a world exclusive. He had caught evil on film. He had invented a kind of torture machine. But it was not immediately clear what he should do with his discovery. When he began the study, he had no theory, nor was he planning to test another man's theory. His idea had sprung from contemplation of Solomon Asch, but the "incandescent" moment at Princeton was a shift away from theory into experimental practice. He had had an idea for an experiment. Now, he was in an odd situation: he had caused something extraordinary to happen, but, technically, his central observation counted for nothing. With no provocation, a New Haven man had hit a fellow citizen with 450 volts. To the general observer, this will come as a surprise, but it is not a social scientific discovery, as Edward E. Jones, the distinguished editor of the *Journal of Personality*, made clear to Milgram when he declined the invitation to publish Milgram's first paper. "The major problem," Jones wrote to Milgram, "is that this is really the report of some pilot research on a method for inducing stress or conflict...your data indicate a kind of triumph of social engineering...we are led to no conclusions about obedience, really, but rather are exhorted to be impressed with the power of your situation as an influence context." The *Journal of Abnormal and Social Psychology* also rejected the paper on its first submission, calling it a "demonstration" rather than an experiment.

Milgram had described only one experimental situation. When he resubmitted the paper to the same journal, he now included experimental variables, and it was publishable. In the rewrite, Milgram put the emphasis on the way in which differences in situation had caused differences in degrees of obedience: the closer the learner to the teacher, the greater the disobedience, and so on. These details were later lost as the experiment moved out of social psychology into the larger world. But it could hardly have happened otherwise. The thought that people were zapping each other in a Yale laboratory is bound to be more striking than the thought that zapping occurs a little less often when one is looking one's victim in the eye. The unscientific truth, perhaps, is that the central comparison in Milgram's study is not between any two experimental variables: it is between what happened in the laboratory, and what we thought would happen. The experimental control in Milgram's model is our hopelessly flawed intuition.

"Somehow," Milgram told a friend in 1962, "I don't write as fast or as easily as I run experiments. I have done about all the experiments I plan to do on Obedience, am duly impressed with the results, and now find myself acutely constipated." Milgram found it hard to knock the experiment into social scientific shape. It would be another decade before he incorporated his findings into a serious theory of the sources of human obedience. When he did so, in the otherwise absorbing and beautifully written book *Obedience to Authority* (1974), his thoughts about an "agentic state"—a psychological zone of abandoned autonomy—were not widely admired or developed by his peers, not least because they were so evidently retrospective. Most readers of *Obedience to Authority* are more likely to take interest in the nods of acknowledgment made to Arthur Koestler's *The Ghost in the Machine,* and to Alex Comfort, the English anarchist poet, novelist, and author of *The Joy of Sex.* Most readers will take more pleasure—and feel Milgram took more pleasure—in the novelistic and strikingly unscientific descriptions of his experimental subjects. ("Mrs Dontz," he wrote, "has an unusually casual, slow-paced way of speaking, and her tone expresses constant humility; it is as if every assertion carries the emotional message: 'I'm just a very ordinary person, don't expect a lot from me.' Physically, she resembles Shirley Booth in the film *Come Back, Little Sheba.*")

But while Milgram was struggling to place his findings in a proper scientific context, they seemed to have found a natural home elsewhere. Stanley Milgram—a young social psychology professor at the start of his career— appeared to be in a position to contribute to one of the late twentieth century's most pressing intellectual activities: making sense of the Holocaust. Milgram always placed the experiments in this context, and the figure of Adolf Eichmann, who was seized in Buenos Aires in the spring of 1960, and whose trial in Jerusalem began a year later, loomed over his proceedings. (In a letter that urged Alan Elms to keep up the supply of experimental volunteers, Milgram noted that this role bore "some resemblance to Mr. Eichmann's position.") The trial, as Peter Novick has recently written in *The Holocaust in American Life,* marked "the first time that what we now call the Holocaust was presented to the American public as an entity in its own right, distinct from Nazi barbarism in general." When Milgram published his first paper on the obedience studies in 1963, Hannah Arendt's articles about the trial had just appeared in the *New Yorker,* and in her book, *Eichmann in Jerusalem,* and they had given widespread currency to her perception about "the banality of evil." Milgram put Eichmann's name in the first paragraph of his first obedience paper, and so claimed a place in a pivotal contemporary debate. His argument was this: his study showed how ordinary people are surprisingly prone to destructive obedience; the crimes of the Holocaust had been committed by people obeying orders; those people, therefore, could now be thought ordinary. The argument had its terrifying element and its consoling element: according to Milgram, Americans had to see themselves as potential murderers; at the same time we could understand Nazis to be no more unusual than any New Haven guy in a check shirt.

5   It may seem bizarre now: Milgram returned to ordinary Nazis their Nuremberg defense, nicely polished in an American laboratory. But the idea struck a chord, and news quickly spread of Milgram's well-meaning, all-American torturers. "Once the [Holocaust] connection was in place," said Arthur G. Miller, a leading Milgram scholar, "then the experiments took on a kind of a larger-than-life quality." Milgram's work was reported in the *New York Times* (65% IN TEST BLINDLY OBEY ORDER TO INFLICT PAIN), and the story was quickly picked up by *Life, Esquire,* ABC television, UPI, and the British press. The fame of the experiments spread, and as the Sixties acquired their defining spirit, Holocaust references were joined by thoughts of My Lai; this was a good moment in history to have things to say about taking orders. By the time Milgram had published his book and released a short film of the experiment, his findings had spread into popular culture, and into theological, medical, and legal discussions. Thomas Blass, a social psychologist at the University of Maryland, Baltimore County, who is preparing a Milgram biography, has a large collection of academic references, including a paper in the context of accountancy ethics. (Is it unthinking obedience that causes accountants to act unlawfully on behalf of clients?) Outside the academy, Dannie Abse published an anti-Milgram play, *The Dogs of Pavlov,* in 1973, and two years later, in America, CBS broadcast a television movie, *The Tenth Level,* that made awkward melodrama out of the obedience experiments, and starred William Shatner as a spookily obsessed and romantically disengaged

version of Professor Milgram. ("You may know your social psychology, Professor, but you have a lot to learn about the varieties of massage.") Peter Gabriel sang "We Do What We're Told (Milgram's 37)" in 1986. And there would be more than a whiff of Milgram in the 1990 episode of *The Simpsons*, "There's No Disgrace Like Home," in which the family members repeatedly electrocute one another until the lights across Springfield flicker and dim. Last year, "The Stanley Milgram Experiment"—a comedy sketch duo—made its off-off-Broadway debut in New York. Robbie Chafitz, one of the pair, had been startled and amused by the Milgram film as a teenager, and had always vowed to use the name one way or another. Besides, as he told me, "anything with electricity and people is funny."

But however celebrated the experiments became, there was a question they could never shake off. It was an ethical issue: had Stanley Milgram mistreated his subjects? Milgram must have seen the storm coming, at least from the moment when Herbert Winer marched into his office, talking of heart attacks. In the summer of 1962, other subjects recorded their feelings about the experiment in response to a questionnaire sent out by Milgram along with a report explaining the true purpose of the experiment. Replies were transferred on to index cards and are now held—unpublished and anonymous—at Yale. "Since taking part in the experiment," reads one card, "I have suffered a mild heart attack. The one thing my doctor tells me that I must avoid is any form of tension." Another card: "Right now I'm in group therapy. Would it be OK if I showed this report to [the] group and the doctors at the clinic?"

Since then, the experiment has been widely attacked from within the profession and from outside. To many, Milgram became a social psychological demon; Alan Elms has met people at parties who have recoiled at the news that he was a Milgram lieutenant. The psychologist Bruno Bettelheim described Milgram's work as "vile" and "in line with the human experiments of the Nazis." In his defense, Milgram would always highlight the results of post-experimental psychological studies—which had reported "no evidence of any traumatic reactions"—and the fact of the debriefings in Linsly-Chittenden Hall, in which care had been taken to give obedient subjects reasons not to feel bad about themselves. They were told to remember, for example, that doctors routinely hurt people in a thoroughly good cause. (Alan Elms wonders if this debriefing was *too* effective, and that subjects should have been obliged to confront their actions more fully.)

But Milgram never quite won the ethical argument. And the controversy was immediately damaging to his career. Someone—perhaps a Yale colleague, according to Thomas Blass—quickly brought the experiment to the attention of the American Psychological Association, and Milgram's application for APA membership was delayed while the case against him was considered. Today, although the APA is happy to include Milgram's shock generator in a traveling psychology exhibition, it is careful to describe the experiments as "controversial" in its accompanying literature. As the APA points out, modern ethical guidelines (in part inspired by Milgram) would prevent the obedience studies from being repeated today.

The controversy followed him. In 1963 Milgram left Yale for Harvard. He was happy there. This is where his two children were born. And when a tenured job came up, he applied. But he needed the unanimous support of his colleagues, and could not secure it. He was blackballed by enemies of the obedience work. (According to Alexandra Milgram, her husband once devised a board game based on the tenure of university professors.) The late Roger Brown, a prominent Harvard psychologist, told Thomas Blass that there had been those in the department who thought of Milgram as "sort of manipulative, or the mad doctor. They felt uneasy about him."

10   So in 1967 Stanley Milgram left Harvard to become head of the social psychology programme in the psychology department in the Graduate Center of the City University of New York (CUNY). In one sense, it was a promotion; he was a full professor at thirty-three. "But after Yale and Harvard, it was the pits," said Milgram's friend and fellow social psychologist, Philip Zimbardo. "Most people I know who didn't get tenure, it had a permanent effect on their lives. You don't get to Yale or Harvard unless you've been number one from kindergarten on, you've been on top—so there's this discontinuity. It's the first time in your life you've failed. You're Stanley Milgram, and people all over the world are talking about your research, and you've failed." Milgram was the most cited man in social psychology—Roger Brown, for example, considered his research to be of "profound importance and originality"—yet in later life, he was able to tell Zimbardo that he felt under-appreciated.

The ethical furor preyed on Milgram's mind—in the opinion of Arthur G. Miller, it may have contributed to his premature death—but one of its curious side effects was to reinforce the authenticity of his studies in the world outside psychology departments. Among those with a glancing knowledge of Milgram, mistreatment of experimental subjects became the only Milgram controversy. The studies remained intellectually sound, a minor building block of Western thought, a smart conversational gambit at cocktail parties. "People identified the problem with Milgram as just a question of ethics," says Henderikus Stam, of the University of Calgary in Canada, who trained as a social psychologist, but who lost faith and is now a psychological theoretician and historian. "So in a way people never got beyond that. Whereas there's a deeper epistemological question, which is: what can we actually know when we've done an experiment like that, what are we left with? What have we learned about obedience?"

Within the academy, there was another, quieter, line of criticism against Milgram: this was methodological. In a paper in 1968 the social psychologists Martin Orne and Charles Holland raised the issue of incongruity, pointing out that Milgram's subjects had been given two key pieces of information: a man in apparent danger, and another man—a man in a lab coat—whose lack of evident concern suggested there was no danger. It seemed possible that obedient subjects had believed in the more plausible piece of information (no danger), and thus concluded, at some conscious or semi-conscious level, that the experiment was a fake, and—in a "pact of ignorance"—been generous enough to role-play for the sake of science. In other words, they were only obeying the demands of amateur dramatics.

Perhaps forgetting that people weep in the theatre, Milgram's response was to argue that the subjects' signs of distress or tension—the twitching and stuttering and racing heartbeats—could be taken as evidence that they had accepted the experiment's reality. He also drew upon the questionnaire he had sent out in 1962, in which his volunteers—now entirely in the know—had been asked to agree with one of five propositions, running from, "I fully believed the learner was getting painful shocks" to "I was certain the learner was not getting the shocks." Milgram was pleased to note that three-quarters of the subjects said they believed the learner was definitely or probably getting the shocks. (He added, reasonably, "It would have been an easy out at this point to deny that the hoax had been accepted.")

Herbert Winer reports that he was fully duped, and Alan Elms told me that, watching through the mirror during the summer of 1961, he saw very little evidence of widespread disbelief. But it is worth pointing out that Milgram could have reported his questionnaire statistics rather differently. He could have said that only fifty-six per cent accepted his first proposition: "I fully believed the learner was getting painful shocks." Forty-four per cent of Milgram's subjects claimed to be at least partially unpersuaded. (Indeed, on his own questionnaire, Winer said he had some doubts.) These people do not have much of a presence in Milgram's writings, but you catch a glimpse of them in the Yale Library index cards. One reads: "I was quite sure 'grunts and screams' were electrically reproduced from a speaker mounted in [the] students' room." (They were.) "If [the learner] was making the sounds I should have heard the screams from under the door—which was a poorly fit [*sic*] thin door. I'm sorry that I didn't have enough something to get up and open this door. Which was not locked. To see if student was still there." On another card: "I think that one of the main reasons I continued to the end was that...I just couldn't believe that Yale would concoct anything that would be [as] dangerous as the shocks were supposed to be." Another subject had noticed how the experimenter was watching him rather than the learner. Another hadn't understood why he was not allowed to volunteer to be the learner. And another wrote, "I had difficulty describing the experiment to my wife as I was so overcome with laughter—haven't had such a good laugh since the first time I saw the 4 Marx Bros—some 25 years ago."

15   For an experiment supposed to involve the undeserved torture of an innocent Irish-American man, there was a lot of laughter in Yale's Interaction Laboratory. Frequently, Milgram's subjects could barely contain themselves as they moved up the shock board. ("On one occasion," Milgram later wrote, "we observed a seizure so violently convulsive that it was necessary to call a halt to the experiment.") Behind their one-way mirror, Milgram and Elms were at times highly amused. And when students are shown the Milgram film today, there tends to be loud laughter in the room. People laugh, and—despite the alleged revelation of a universal heart of darkness—they go home having lost little faith in their friends and their families.

According to Henderikus Stam, the laughter of the students, and perhaps that of the subjects, is a reasonable response to an absurd situation. It's a reaction to the notion that serious and complex moral issues, and the subtleties of human behaviour, can reasonably be illuminated through play-acting in a university laboratory. The experiment does nothing but illuminate itself. "What it does is it says, 'Aren't we clever?' If you wanted to demonstrate obedience to authority wouldn't you be better showing a film about the Holocaust, or news clips about Kosovo? Why do you need an experiment, that's the question? What does the experiment do? The experiment says that if we really want to know about obedience to authority we need an abstract representation of that obedience, removed from all real forms of the abuse of authority. But what we then do is to use that representation to refer back to the real historical examples."

What happens when we refer back to historical examples? Readers of *Hitler's Willing Executioners,* Daniel Jonah Goldhagen's study of the complicity of ordinary German citizens in the Holocaust, will learn within one paragraph of a German policeman, Captain Wolfgang Hoffmann, a "zealous executioner of Jews," who "once stridently disobeyed a superior order that he deemed morally objectionable." The order was that he and members of his company should sign a declaration agreeing not to steal from Poles. Hoffmann was affronted that anyone would think the declaration necessary, that anyone would imagine his men capable of stealing. "I feel injured," he wrote to his superiors, "in my sense of honour." The genocidal killing of thousands of Jews was one thing, but plundering from Poles was another. Here was an order to which he was opposed, and which he felt able to disobey.

Goldhagen is impatient with what he calls "the paradigm of external compulsion," which sets the actions of the Holocaust's perpetrators in the context of social-psychological or totalitarian state forces. His book aims to show how the crimes of the Holocaust were carried out by people obeying their own consciences, not blindly or fearfully obeying orders. "If you think that certain people are evil," he told me, "and that it's necessary to do away with them—if you hate them—and then someone orders you to kill them, you're not carrying out the deed only because of the order. You're carrying it out because you think it's right. So in all those instances where people are killing people they hate—their enemies or their perceived enemies—then Milgram is just completely inapplicable."

Goldhagen wonders if the Milgram take on the Holocaust met a particular need, during the Cold War, for America's new German allies "to be thought well of." He also wonders if, by robbing people of their agency, "of the fact that they're moral beings," the experiment tapped into the kind of reductive universalism by which, he says, Americans are easily seduced—the belief that all men are created equal, and in this case equally obedient. Goldhagen has no confidence in the idea that Milgram was measuring obedience at all. The experimental conditions did not properly control for other variables, such as trust, nor did they allow for the way decisions are made in the real world—over time, after consultation. Besides, said Goldhagen, in a tone close to exasperation, "people disobey all the time! Look around the world. Do people always pay all their taxes? Do what their bosses tell them? Or quietly accept what any government decides? Even with all kinds of sanctions available, one of the greatest problems that institutions face is to get their members to comply with rules and orders." Milgram's findings, he says, "are roundly, repeatedly and glaringly falsified by life."

20   In the opinion of Professor Stam, this comes close to defining the problems of social psychology itself. It is a discipline, he says, that makes the peculiar claim that "if you want to ask questions about the social world, you have to turn them into abstract technical questions." The Milgram experiment, he says, "has the air of scientificity about it. But it's not scientific, it's…*scientistic.*"

And there is Milgram's problem: he devised an intensely powerful piece of tragicomic laboratory theatre, and then had to smuggle it into the faculty of social science. His most famous work—which had something to say about trust, embarrassment, low-level sadism, willingness to please, exaggerated post-war respect for scientific research, the sleepy, heavy-lidded pleasure of being asked to *take part,* and, perhaps, too, the desire of a rather awkward young academic to secure attention and respect—had to pass itself off as an event with a single, steady meaning. And that disguise has not always been convincing. It's odd to hear Arthur G. Miller—one of the world's leading Milgram scholars—acknowledge that there have been times when he has wondered, just for a moment, if the experiments perhaps mean nothing at all.

But the faculty of social psychology is not ready to let Milgram go. And there may be a new way to rescue the experiments from their ungainly ambiguity. This is the route taken by Professors Lee Ross and Richard E. Nisbett (at Stanford and the University of Michigan respectively), whose recent synthesis of social psychological thinking aims to give the subject new power. According to Professor Ross, the experiments may be "performance," but they still have social psychological news to deliver. If that is true, then we can do something that the late professor was not always able to do himself: we can make a kind of reconciliation between the artist and the scientist in Stanley Milgram.

Ross and Nisbett find a seat for Stanley Milgram at social psychology's high table. They do this slyly, by taking the idea of obedience—Milgram's big idea—and putting it quietly to one side. When Ross teaches Milgram at Stanford, he makes a point of giving his students detailed instructions on how to prepare for the classes—instructions that he knows will be thoroughly ignored. He is then able to stand in front of his students and examine their disobedience. "I asked you to do something that's good for you rather than bad for you," he tells them. "And I'm a legitimate authority rather than an illegitimate one, and I actually have power that the Milgram experimenter doesn't have. And yet you didn't obey. So the study can't just be about obedience." What it is primarily about, Ross tells his students—and it may be about other things too—is the extreme power of a situation that has been built without obvious escape routes. (As Herbert Winer said: "At no time was there a pause or a break when anything could be raised…. ") "There was really no exit," Ross told me, "there was no channel for disobedience. People who were discomforted, who wanted to disobey, didn't quite know how to do it. They made some timid attempts, and it got them nowhere. In order to disobey they have to step out of the whole situation, and say to the experimenter, 'Go to hell! You can't tell me what to do!' As long as they continue to function within that relationship, they're asking the experimenter for permission not to give shocks, and as long as the experimenter denies them that permission, they're stuck. They don't know how to get out of it." Ross suspects that things would have turned out very differently given one change to the situation. It's a fairly big change: the addition of a prominent red button in the middle of the table, combined with a clearly displayed notice signed by the "Human Subjects' Committee" explaining that the button could be pressed "by any subject in any experiment at any time if he or she absolutely refuses to continue."

According to Ross and Nisbett (who are saying something that Milgram surely knew, but something he allowed to become obscured), the Obedience Experiments point us towards a great social psychological truth, perhaps *the* great truth, which is this: people tend to do things because of where they are, not who they are, and we are slow to see it. We look for character traits to explain a person's actions—he is clever, shy, generous, arrogant—and we stubbornly underestimate the influence of the situation, the way things *happened to be* at that moment. So, if circumstances had been even only subtly different (if she hadn't been running late; if he'd been *told* the film was a comedy), the behaviour might have been radically different. Under certain controlled circumstances, then, people can be induced to behave unkindly: to that extent, Milgram may have something to say about a kind of destructive obedience. But under other circumstances, Professor Ross promised me, the same people would be nice. Given the correct situation, he said, we could be led to do "terrifically altruistic and self-sacrificing things that we would never have agreed to before we started."

25   So the experiment that has troubled us for nearly forty years (that buzzing and howling), and which caused Milgram to have dark thoughts about America's vulnerability to fascism, suddenly has a new complexion. Now, it is about the influence of *any* situation on behaviour, good or bad: "You stop on the highway to help someone," Professor Ross said, "and then the help you try to give doesn't prove to be enough, so you give the person a ride, and then you end up lending them money or letting them stay in your house. It wasn't because that was the person in the world you cared about the most, it was just one thing led to another. Step by step."

That's the Milgram situation. "We can take ordinary people," Ross said, "and make them show a degree of obedience or conformity—or for that matter altruism or bravery, whatever—to a degree that we would normally assume you would only see in the rare few. And that's relevant to telling us what we're capable of making people do, but it also tells us that when we observe the world, we are often going to be making an attribution error, because lots of times, the situational factors have been opaque to us, and therefore we are making erroneous inferences about people. The South African government says, 'Can we deal with this fellow Mandela?' and the answer is, 'No, he's a terrorist.' But a social psychologist would say, 'Mandela, in *one* context, given *one* set of situations, was a terrorist.'" According to Ross, that's the key lesson of social psychology; that's how the discipline can be useful in education, the work place, and law. "Our emphasis," he says, "should be on creating situations that promote what we want to promote, rather than searching endlessly for the right person. Don't assume that people who commit atrocities are atrocious people, or people who do heroic things are heroic. Don't get overly carried away; don't think, because you observed someone under one set of discrete situational factors, that you know *what they're like*, and therefore can predict what they would do in a very different set of circumstances."

It's hard not to think of Stanley Milgram in another set of circumstances—to imagine the careers he did not have in films or in the theatre, and to wonder how things would have turned out if his work had appeared at another time, or had been read a little differently. It may now be possible to place the Obedience Experiments somewhere near the center of the social psychological project, but that's not how it felt in the last years of Milgram's life. He had failed to secure tenure at Harvard. Disappointed, he moved to New York, assuming he would soon be leaving again, to take up a post at a more glamorous institution. But he was still at CUNY seventeen years later, at the time of his premature death. "He had hoped it would be just for five years," Alexandra Milgram told me, "but things got much more difficult to move on to other places. You were glad to have what you had. And he was happy to do the work that he did. I don't think he was as happy at the university as he was at, say, Harvard, but he was a very independent person: he had his ideas, he had his research."

The research pushed Milgram into a kind of internal exile. Confirming his reputation as social psychology's renegade, he pursued work that, although often brilliantly conceived and elegantly reported, could look eccentric and old-fashioned to colleagues, and that ran the risk of appearing to place method ahead of meaning. "It would flash and then burn out," says Professor Miller, "and then he'd go on to something else." He sent his (young, able-bodied) students on to the New York subway to ask people to give up their seats. He co-wrote a paper about *Candid Camera*'s virtues as an archive for students of human behaviour. Pre-empting the play *Six Degrees of Separation,* he studied the "small world" phenomenon, investigating the chains of acquaintance that link two strangers. He took photographs of rail commuters and showed them to those who travelled on the same route, to explore the notion of the "familiar stranger." In an expensive, elaborate, and ultimately inconclusive experiment in 1971, he explored the links between antisocial acts seen on television and similar acts in real life by getting CBS to produce and air two versions of a hit hospital drama, *Medical Center.* He asked students to try to give away money on the street. He tested how easy it was for people to walk between a pavement photographer and his subject. And when he was recuperating from one of a series of heart attacks, he made an informal study of the social psychology of being a hospital patient. He was only fifty-one when he died.

Once, shortly before the Obedience Experiments had begun, Milgram had written from Yale about his fear of having made the wrong career move. "Of course," he told a friend, "I am glad that the present job sometimes engages my genuine interests, or at least, a part of my interests, but there is another part that remains submerged and somehow, perhaps because it is not expressed, seems most important." He described his routine: pulling himself out of bed, dragging himself to the lecture room "where I misrepresent myself for two hours as an efficient and persevering man of science...I should not be here, but in Greece shooting films under a Mediterranean sun, hopping about in a small boat from one Aegean isle to the next." He added, in a spirit of comic self-laceration, "Fool!"

● Review Questions

1. Why was Milgram's article rejected when it was first submitted for publication? What did Milgram do to ensure its professional acceptability?

2. What does Parker mean when he says (paragraph 5) that "Milgram returned to ordinary Nazis their Nuremberg defense, nicely polished in an American laboratory"?

3. In what sense did his obedience experiments ruin Milgram's career?

4. Based on what you have read about Daniel Jonah Goldhagen, explain the meaning of the title of his book, *Hitler's Willing Executioners*.

5. What does Henderikus Stam mean when he charges that Milgram's experiment is "not scientific, it's . . . scientistic"?

● Discussion and Writing Suggestions

1. Parker charts the course of the Milgram experiments working their way into popular consciousness—from magazine articles to TV dramas, to episodes of *The Simpsons*. Why do you think that the obedience experiments, more than thousands of other social science experiments performed during the 1960s, made such an indelible impact, even outside the profession of social psychology?

2. Parker focuses in part upon the ethical problems with Milgram's experiments. To what extent do you believe that these experiments were unethical? To what extent does Milgram's chief rejoinder—that his surveys taken after the fact show that the vast majority of his subjects suffered no permanent ill effects—effectively rebut the ethical objections?

3. One theory about why many of Milgram's subjects behaved as they did—going all the way to the top of the shock register—is that they did not really believe that the subjects were being shocked; they simply went along with the experimenter because they did not think it possible that a prestigious institution like Yale would be a party to inflicting harm on people. To what extent do you find this theory plausible?

4. Parker notes that not only did many of Milgram's subjects laugh during the experiments and later, in recounting it to others, but many students also laugh when they watch Milgram's film ("Obedience") in class. If you saw the film, did you laugh when you saw it? Did others? Attempt to account for this apparently incongruous reaction.

5. How necessary was Milgram's experiment? Parker notes that many have argued that if we want to learn about the power of authority to compel obedience, all we need do is study the numerous historical examples (the Holocaust being the one most often cited) of obedience to malign authority. To what extent do

the results of Milgram's experiments add anything to what we already know about obedience from actual historical events?

6. Parker includes the following quotation from Daniel Jonah Goldhagen, author of *Hitler's Willing Executioners:* "If you think that certain people are evil . . . and that it's necessary to do away with them—if you hate them—and then someone orders you to kill them, you're not carrying out the deed only because of the order. You're carrying it out because you think it's right" (paragraph 18). In other words, people who commit evil acts do so less because they feel compelled to obey external authority figures than because they are following their own consciences, their own sense of who is the enemy. To what extent do you find that this theory accounts for many of the evil acts in the world?

7. Parker cites Ross's theory that an important reason that so many of Milgram's subjects were fully obedient is that they had no "escape route"—the experimenter never gave them time or opportunity to call a halt to the experimental procedure. To what extent do you find this theory plausible? Would a "red button" to stop the experiment likely have led to a different set of results?

8. Lee Ross and Richard E. Nisbett believe that the main factor determining the obedience of Milgram's subjects was not the *character* of the subjects, but rather the *situation*—that given a different situation (i.e., a situation not involving a carefully controlled laboratory experiment), the same subjects who were so obedient might have behaved very differently. To what extent do you find this theory plausible? Can you think of examples in which people will behave in different ways in different situations?

GROUP MINDS

Doris Lessing

Doris Lessing sets a context for a discussion of obedience in group settings by illuminating a fundamental conflict: We in the Western world celebrate our individualism, but we're naive in understanding the ways that groups largely undercut our individuality. "We are group animals still," says Lessing, "and there is nothing wrong with that. But what is dangerous is . . . not understanding the social laws that govern groups and govern us." This chapter is largely devoted to an exploration of these tendencies. As you read selections by Milgram and the other authors here, bear in mind Lessing's troubling question: If we know that individuals will violate their own good common sense and moral codes in order to become accepted members of a group, why then can't we put this knowledge to use and teach people to be wary of group pressures?

Doris Lessing, the daughter of farmers, was born in Persia, now Iran, in 1919. She attended a Roman Catholic convent and a girls' high school in southern Rhodesia (now Zimbabwe). From 1959 through to the present, Lessing has written more than twenty works of fiction and has been called "the best woman novelist" of the postwar era. Her work has received a great deal of scholarly attention. She is, perhaps, best known for her *Five Short Novels* (1954), *The Golden Notebook* (1962), and *Briefing for a Descent into Hell* (1971).

People living in the West, in societies that we describe as Western, or as the free world, may be educated in many different ways, but they will all emerge with an idea about themselves that goes something like this: I am a citizen of a free society, and that means I am an individual, making individual choices. My mind is my own, my opinions are chosen by me, I am free to do as I will, and at the worst the pressures on me are economic, that is, I may be too poor to do as I want.

This set of ideas may sound something like a caricature, but it is not so far off how we see ourselves. It is a portrait that may not have been acquired consciously, but is part of a general atmosphere or set of assumptions that influence our ideas about ourselves.

People in the West therefore may go through their entire lives never thinking to analyze this very flattering picture, and as a result are helpless against all kinds of pressures on them to conform in many kinds of ways.

The fact is that we all live our lives in groups—the family, work groups, social, religious and political groups. Very few people indeed are happy as solitaries, and they tend to be seen by their neighbors as peculiar or selfish or worse. Most people cannot stand being alone for long. They are always seeking groups to belong to, and if one group dissolves, they look for another. We are group animals still, and there is nothing wrong with that. But what is dangerous is not the belonging to a group, or groups, but not understanding the social laws that govern groups and govern us.

5   When we're in a group, we tend to think as that group does: we may even have joined the group to find "like-minded" people. But we also find our thinking changing because we belong to a group. It is the hardest thing in the world to maintain an individual dissident opinion, as a member of a group.

It seems to me that this is something we have all experienced—something we take for granted, may never have thought about it. But a great deal of experiment has gone on among psychologists and sociologists on this very theme. If I describe an experiment or two, then anyone listening who may be a sociologist or psychologist will groan, oh God not *again*—for they will have heard of these classic experiments far too often. My guess is that the rest of the people will never have heard of these experiments, never have had these ideas presented to them. If my guess is true, then it aptly illustrates my general thesis, and the general idea behind these talks, that we (the human race) are now in possession of a great deal of hard information about ourselves, but we do not use it to improve our institutions and therefore our lives.

A typical test, or experiment, on this theme goes like this. A group of people are taken into the researcher's confidence. A minority of one or two are left in the dark. Some situation demanding measurement or assessment is chosen. For instance, comparing lengths of wood that differ only a little from each other, but enough to be perceptible, or shapes that are almost the same size. The majority in the group—according to instruction—will assert stubbornly that these two shapes or lengths are the same length, or size, while the solitary individual, or the couple, who have not been so instructed will assert that the pieces of wood or whatever are different. But the majority will continue to insist—speaking metaphorically—that black is white, and after a period of exasperation, irritation, even anger, certainly incomprehension, the minority will fall into line.

Not always, but nearly always. There are indeed glorious individuals who stubbornly insist on telling the truth as they see it, but most give in to the majority opinion, obey the atmosphere.

When put as badly, as unflatteringly, as this, reactions tend to be incredulous: "I certainly wouldn't give in, I speak my mind...." But would you?

People who have experienced a lot of groups, who perhaps have observed their own behavior, may agree that the hardest thing in the world is to stand out against one's group, a group of one's peers. Many agree that among our most shameful memories is this, how often we said black was white because other people were saying it.

10   In other words, we know that this is true of human behavior, but how do we know it? It is one thing to admit it, in a vague uncomfortable sort of way (which probably includes the hope that one will never again be in such a testing situation) but quite another to make that cool step into a kind of objectivity, where one may say, "Right, if that's what human beings are like, myself included, then let's admit it, examine and organize our attitudes accordingly."

This mechanism, of obedience to the group, does not only mean obedience or submission to a small group, or one that is sharply determined, like a religion or political party. It means, too, conforming to those large, vague, ill-defined collections of people who may never think of themselves as having a collective mind because they are aware of differences of opinion—but which, to people from outside, from another culture, seem very minor. The underlying assumptions and assertions that govern the group are never discussed, never challenged, probably never noticed, the main one being precisely this: that it *is* a group mind, intensely resistant to change, equipped with sacred assumptions about which there can be no discussion.

But suppose this kind of thing were taught in schools?

Let us just suppose it, for a moment....But at once the nub of the problem is laid bare.

Imagine us saying to children, "In the last fifty or so years, the human race has become aware of a great deal of information about its mechanisms; how it behaves, how it must behave under certain circumstances. If this is to be useful, you must learn to contemplate these rules calmly, dispassionately, disinterestedly, without emotion. It is information that will set people free from blind loyalties, obedience to slogans, rhetoric, leaders, group emotions." Well, there it is.

Review Questions

1. What is the flattering portrait Lessing paints of people living in the West?

2. Lessing believes that individuals in the West are "helpless against all kinds of pressures on them to conform in many kinds of ways." Why?

3. Lessing refers to a class of experiments on obedience. Summarize the "typical" experiment.

● Discussion and Writing Suggestions

1. Lessing writes that "what is dangerous is not the belonging to a group, or groups, but not understanding the social laws that govern groups and govern us." What is the danger Lessing is speaking of here?

2. Lessing states that the human race is "now in possession of a great deal of hard information about ourselves, but we do not use it to improve our institutions and therefore our lives." First, do you agree with Lessing? Can you cite other examples (aside from information on obedience to authority) in which we do not use our knowledge to better humankind?

3. Explore some of the difficulties in applying this "hard information" about humankind that Lessing speaks of. Assume she's correct in claiming that we don't incorporate our knowledge of human nature into the running of our institutions. Why don't we? What are the difficulties of *acting* on information?

4. Lessing speaks of people's guilt in recalling how they succumbed to group pressures. Can you recall such an event? What feelings do you have about it now?

OPINIONS AND SOCIAL PRESSURE

Solomon E. Asch

In the early 1950s, Solomon Asch (1907–1996), a social psychologist at Rutgers University, conducted a series of simple but ingenious experiments on the influence of group pressure upon the individual. Essentially, he discovered, individuals can be influenced by groups to deny the evidence of their own senses. Together with the Milgram experiments of the next decade (see the selections that follow here), these studies provide powerful evidence of the degree to which individuals can surrender their own judgment to others, even when those others are clearly in the wrong. The results of these experiments have implications far beyond the laboratory: They can explain a good deal of the normal human behavior we see every day—at school, at work, at home.

In what follows I shall describe some experiments in an investigation of the effects of group pressure which was carried out recently with the help of a number of my associates. The tests not only demonstrate the operations of group pressure upon individuals but also illustrate a new kind of attack on the problem and some of the more subtle questions that it raises.

A group of seven to nine young men, all college students, are assembled in a classroom for a "psychological experiment" in visual judgment. The experimenter informs them that they will be comparing the lengths of lines. He shows two large white cards [see Figure 1]. On one is a single vertical black line—the standard whose length is to be matched. On the other card are three vertical lines of various lengths. The subjects are to choose the one that is of the same length as the line on the other card. One of the three actually is of the same

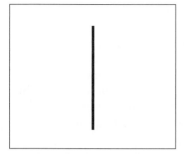 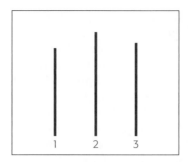

Fig. 1. Subjects were shown two cards. One bore a standard line. The other bore three lines, one of which was the same length as the standard. The subjects were asked to choose this line.

length; the other two are substantially different, the difference ranging from three quarters of an inch to an inch and three quarters.

The experiment opens uneventfully. The subjects announce their answers in the order in which they have been seated in the room, and on the first round every person chooses the same matching line. Then a second set of cards is exposed; again the group is unanimous. The members appear ready to endure politely another boring experiment. On the third trial there is an unexpected disturbance. One person near the end of the group disagrees with all the others in his selection of the matching line. He looks surprised, indeed incredulous, about the disagreement. On the following trial he disagrees again, while the others remain unanimous in their choice. The dissenter becomes more and more worried and hesitant as the disagreement continues in succeeding trials; he may pause before announcing his answer and speak in a low voice, or he may smile in an embarrassed way.

What the dissenter does not know is that all the other members of the group were instructed by the experimenter beforehand to give incorrect answers in unanimity at certain points. The single individual who is not a party to this prearrangement is the focal subject of our experiment. He is placed in a position in which, while he is actually giving the correct answers, he finds himself unexpectedly in a minority of one, opposed by a unanimous and arbitrary majority with respect to a clear and simple fact. Upon him we have brought to bear two opposed forces: the evidence of his senses and the unanimous opinion of a group of his peers. Also, he must declare his judgments in public, before a majority which has also stated its position publicly.

5   The instructed majority occasionally reports correctly in order to reduce the possibility that the naive subject will suspect collusion against him. (In only a few cases did the subject actually show suspicion; when this happened, the experiment was stopped and the results were not counted.) There are 18 trials in each series, and on 12 of these the majority responds erroneously.

How do people respond to group pressure in this situation? I shall report first the statistical results of a series in which a total of 123 subjects from three institutions of higher learning (not including my own Swarthmore College) were placed in the minority situation described above.

Two alternatives were open to the subject: he could act independently, repudiating the majority, or he could go along with the majority, repudiating the evidence of his senses. Of the 123 put to the test, a considerable percentage yielded to the majority. Whereas in ordinary circumstances individuals matching the lines will make mistakes less than 1 per cent of the time, under group pressure the minority subjects swung to acceptance of the misleading majority's wrong judgments in 36.8 per cent of the selections.

Of course individuals differed in response. At one extreme, about one quarter of the subjects were completely independent and never agreed with the erroneous judgments of the majority. At the other extreme, some individuals went with the majority nearly all the time. The performances of individuals in this experiment tend to be highly consistent. Those who strike out on the path of independence do not, as a rule, succumb to the majority even over an extended series of trials, while those who choose the path of compliance are unable to free themselves as the ordeal is prolonged.

The reasons for the startling individual differences have not yet been investigated in detail. At this point we can only report some tentative generalizations from talks with the subjects, each of whom was interviewed at the end of the experiment. Among the independent individuals were many who held fast because of staunch confidence in their own judgment. The most significant fact about them was not absence of responsiveness to the majority but a capacity to recover from doubt and to reestablish their equilibrium. Others who acted independently came to believe that the majority was correct in its answers, but they continued their dissent on the simple ground that it was their obligation to call the play as they saw it.

10   Among the extremely yielding persons we found a group who quickly reached the conclusion: "I am wrong, they are right." Others yielded in order "not to spoil your results." Many of the individuals who went along suspected that the majority were "sheep" following the first responder, or that the majority were victims of an optical illusion; nevertheless, these suspicions failed to free them at the moment of decision. More disquieting were the reactions of subjects who construed their difference from the majority as a sign of some general deficiency in themselves, which at all costs they must hide. On this basis they desperately tried to merge with the majority, not realizing the longer-range consequences to themselves. All the yielding subjects underestimated the frequency with which they conformed.

Which aspect of the influence of a majority is more important—the size of the majority or its unanimity? The experiment was modified to examine this question. In one series the size of the opposition was varied from one to 15 persons. The results showed a clear trend. When a subject was confronted with only a single individual who contradicted his answers, he was swayed little: he continued to answer independently and correctly in nearly all trials. When the opposition was increased to two, the pressure became substantial: minority subjects now accepted the wrong answer 13.6 per cent of the time. Under the pressure of a majority of three, the subjects' errors jumped to 31.8 per cent. But further increases in the size of the majority apparently did not increase the weight of the pressure substantially. Clearly the size of the opposition is important only up to a point.

Disturbance of the majority's unanimity had a striking effect. In this experiment the subject was given the support of a truthful partner—either another individual who did not know of the prearranged agreement among the rest of the group, or a person who was instructed to give correct answers throughout.

The presence of a supporting partner depleted the majority of much of its power. Its pressure on the dissenting individual was reduced to one fourth: that is, subjects answered incorrectly only one fourth as often as under the pressure of a unanimous majority. The weakest persons did not yield as readily. Most interesting were the reactions to the partner. Generally the feeling toward him was one of warmth and closeness; he was credited with inspiring confidence. However, the subjects repudiated the suggestion that the partner decided them to be independent.

Was the partner's effect a consequence of his dissent, or was it related to his accuracy? We now introduced into the experimental group a person who was instructed to dissent from the majority but also to disagree with the subject. In some experiments the majority was always to choose the worst of the comparison lines and the instructed dissenter to pick the line that was closer to the length of the standard one; in others the majority was consistently intermediate and the dissenter most in error. In this manner we were able to study the relative influence of "compromising" and "extremist" dissenters.

15   Again the results are clear. When a moderate dissenter is present the effect of the majority on the subject decreases by approximately one third, and extremes of yielding disappear. Moreover, most of the errors the subjects do make are moderate, rather than flagrant. In short, the dissenter largely controls the choice of errors. To this extent the subjects broke away from the majority even while bending to it.

On the other hand, when the dissenter always chose the line that was more flagrantly different from the standard, the results were of quite a different kind. The extremist dissenter produced a remarkable freeing of the subjects; their errors dropped to only 9 percent. Furthermore, all the errors were of the moderate variety. We were able to conclude that dissents *per se* increased independence and moderated the errors that occurred, and that the direction of dissent exerted consistent effects.

In all the foregoing experiments each subject was observed only in a single setting. We now turned to studying the effects upon a given individual of a change in the situation to which he was exposed. The first experiment examined the consequences of losing or gaining a partner. The instructed partner began by answering correctly on the first six trials. With his support the subject usually resisted pressure from the majority: 18 of 27 subjects were completely independent. But after six trials the partner joined the majority. As soon as he did so, there was an abrupt rise in the subjects' errors. Their submission to the majority was just about as frequent as when the minority subject was opposed by a unanimous majority throughout.

It was surprising to find that the experience of having had a partner and of having braved the majority opposition with him had failed to strengthen the individuals' independence. Questioning at the conclusion of the experiment suggested that we had overlooked an important circumstance; namely, the strong specific effect of "desertion" by the partner to the other side. We therefore changed the conditions so that the partner would simply leave the group at the proper point. (To allay suspicion it was announced in advance that he had an appointment with the dean.) In this form of the experiment, the partner's effect outlasted his presence. The errors increased after his departure, but less markedly than after a partner switched to the majority.

In a variant of this procedure the trials began with the majority unanimously giving correct answers. Then they gradually broke away until on the sixth trial the naive subject was alone and the group unanimously against him. As long as the subject had anyone on his side, he was almost invariably independent, but as soon as he found himself alone, the tendency to conform to the majority rose abruptly.

20   As might be expected, an individual's resistance to group pressure in these experiments depends to a considerable degree on how wrong the majority was. We varied the discrepancy between the standard line and the other lines systematically, with the hope of reaching a point where the error of the majority would be so glaring that every subject would repudiate it and choose independently. In this we regretfully did not succeed. Even when the difference between the lines was seven inches, there were still some who yielded to the error of the majority.

The study provides clear answers to a few relatively simple questions, and it raises many others that await investigation. We would like to know the degree of consistency of persons in situations which differ in content and structure. If consistency of independence or conformity in behavior is shown to be a fact, how is it functionally related to qualities of character and personality? In what ways is independence related to sociological or cultural conditions? Are leaders more independent than other people, or are they adept at following their followers? These and many other questions may perhaps be answerable by investigations of the type described here.

Life in society requires consensus as an indispensable condition. But consensus, to be productive, requires that each individual contribute independently out of his experience and insight. When consensus comes under the dominance of conformity, the social process is polluted and the individual at the same time surrenders the powers on which his functioning as a feeling and thinking being depends. That we have found the tendency to conformity in our society so strong that reasonably intelligent and well-meaning young people are willing to call white black is a matter of concern. It raises questions about our ways of education and about the values that guide our conduct.

Yet anyone inclined to draw too pessimistic conclusions from this report would do well to remind himself that the capacities for independence are not to be underestimated. He may also draw some consolation from a further observation: those who participated in this challenging experiment agreed nearly without exception that independence was preferable to conformity.

● Review Questions

1. What is "suggestibility"? How is this phenomenon related to social pressure?

2. Summarize the procedure and results of the Asch experiment. What conclusions does Asch draw from these results?

3. To what extent did varying the size of the majority and its unanimity affect the experimental results?

4. What distinction does Asch draw between consensus and conformity?

● Discussion and Writing Suggestions

1. Before discussing the experiment, Asch considers how easily people's opinions or attitudes may be shaped by social pressure. To what extent do you agree with this conclusion? Write a short paper on this subject, drawing upon examples from your own experience or observation or from your reading.

2. Do the results of this experiment surprise you? Or do they confirm facts about human behavior that you had already suspected, observed, or experienced? Explain, in two or three paragraphs. Provide examples, relating these examples to features of the Asch experiment.

3. Frequently, the conclusions drawn from a researcher's experimental results are challenged on the basis that laboratory conditions do not accurately reflect the complexity of human behavior. Asch draws certain conclusions about the degree to which individuals are affected by group pressures based on an experiment involving subjects choosing matching line lengths. To what extent, if any, do you believe that these conclusions lack validity because the behavior at the heart of the experiment is too dissimilar to real-life situations of group pressure on the individual? Support your opinions with examples.

4. We are all familiar with the phenomenon of "peer pressure." To what extent do Asch's experiments demonstrate the power of peer pressure? To what extent do you think that other factors may be at work? Explain, providing examples.

5. Asch's experiments, conducted in the early 1950s, involved groups of "seven to nine young men, all college students." To what extent do you believe that the results of a similar experiment would be different today? To what extent might they be different if the subjects had included women, as well, and subjects of various ages, from children, to middle-aged people, to older people? To what extent do you believe that the social class or culture of the subjects might have an impact upon the experimental results? Support your opinions with examples and logical reasoning. (Beware, however, of overgeneralizing, based upon insufficient evidence.)

THE STANFORD PRISON EXPERIMENT

Philip G. Zimbardo

As well known—and as controversial—as the Milgram obedience experiments, the Stanford Prison Experiment (1973) raises troubling questions about the ability of individuals to resist authoritarian or obedient roles, if the social setting requires these roles. Philip G. Zimbardo, professor of psychology at Stanford University, set out to study the process by which prisoners and guards "learn" to become compliant and authoritarian, respectively. To find subjects for the experiment, Zimbardo placed an advertisement in a local newspaper:

Male college students needed for psychological study of prison life. $15 per day for 1–2 weeks beginning Aug. 14. For further information & applications, come to Room 248, Jordan Hall, Stanford U.

The ad drew 75 responses. From these Zimbardo and his colleagues selected 21 college-age men, half of whom would become "prisoners" in the experiment, the other half "guards." The elaborate role-playing scenario, planned for two weeks, had to be cut short due to the intensity of subjects' responses. This article first appeared in the *New York Times Magazine* on April 8, 1973.*

> *In prison, those things withheld from and denied to the prisoner become precisely what he wants most of all.*
>
> –Eldridge Cleaver, "Soul on Ice"

> *Our sense of power is more vivid when we break a man's spirit than when we win his heart.*
>
> –Eric Hoffer, "The Passionate State of Mind"

> *Every prison that men build / Is built with bricks of shame, / And bound with bars lest Christ should see / How men their brothers maim.*
>
> –Oscar Wilde, "The Ballad of Reading Gaol"

> *Wherever anyone is against his will that is to him a prison.*
>
> –Epictetus, "Discourses"

The quiet of a summer morning in Palo Alto, Calif., was shattered by a screeching squad car siren as police swept through the city picking up college students in a surprise mass arrest. Each suspect was charged with a felony, warned of his constitutional rights, spread-eagled against the car, searched, handcuffed, and carted off in the back seat of the squad car to the police station for booking.

---

*"The Mind Is a Formidable Jailer" ["The Stanford Prison Experiment"] by Philip G. Zimbardo as published in the *New York Times Magazine,* 8 April 1973. Copyright © 1973 by the New York Times. Reprinted with permission from the New York Times.

After fingerprinting and the preparation of identification forms for his "jacket" (central information file), each prisoner was left isolated in a detention cell to wonder what he had done to get himself into this mess. After a while, he was blindfolded and transported to the "Stanford County Prison." Here he began the process of becoming a prisoner—stripped naked, skin-searched, de-loused, and issued a uniform, bedding, soap, and towel.

The warden offered an impromptu welcome:

"As you probably know, I'm your warden. All of you have shown that you are unable to function outside in the real world for one reason or another—that somehow you lack the responsibility of good citizens of this great country. We of this prison, your correctional staff, are going to help you learn what your responsibilities as citizens of this country are. Here are the rules. Sometime in the near future there will be a copy of the rules posted in each of the cells. We ex-pect you to know them and to be able to recite them by number. If you follow all of these rules and keep your hands clean, repent for your misdeeds, and show a proper attitude of penitence, you and I will get along just fine."

5   There followed a reading of the 16 basic rules of prisoner conduct, "Rule Number One: Prisoners must remain silent during rest periods, after lights are out, during meals, and whenever they are outside the prison yard. Two: Prisoners must eat at mealtimes and only at mealtimes. Three: Prisoners must not move, tamper, deface, or damage walls, ceilings, windows, doors, or other prison property.... Seven: Prisoners must address each other by their ID number only. Eight: Prisoners must address the guards as 'Mr. Correc-tional Officer.'... Sixteen: Failure to obey any of the above rules may result in punishment."

By late afternoon these youthful "first offenders" sat in dazed silence on the cots in their barren cells trying to make sense of the events that had transformed their lives so dramatically.

If the police arrests and processing were executed with customary detach-ment, however, there were some things that didn't fit. For these men were now part of a very unusual kind of prison, an experimental mock prison, created by social psychologists to study the effects of imprisonment upon volunteer research subjects. When we planned our two-week-long simulation of prison life, we sought to understand more about the process by which people called "prisoners" lose their liberty, civil rights, independence, and privacy, while those called "guards" gain social power by accepting the responsibility for con-trolling and managing the lives of their dependent charges.

Why didn't we pursue this research in a real prison? First, prison systems are fortresses of secrecy, closed to impartial observation, and thereby immune to critical analysis from anyone not already part of the correctional authority. Sec-ond, in any real prison, it is impossible to separate what each individual brings into the prison from what the prison brings out in each person.

We populated our mock prison with a homogeneous group of people who could be considered "normal-average" on the basis of clinical interviews and personality tests. Our participants (10 prisoners and 11 guards) were selected from more than 75 volunteers recruited through ads in the city and campus newspapers. The applicants were mostly college students from all over the United States and Canada who happened to be in the Stanford area during the summer and were attracted by the lure of earning $15 a day for participating in a study of prison life. We selected only those judged to be emotionally stable, physically healthy, mature, law-abiding citizens.

10   The sample of average, middle-class, Caucasian, college-age males (plus one Oriental student) was arbitrarily divided by the flip of a coin. Half were randomly assigned to play the role of guards, the others of prisoners. There were no measurable differences between the guards and the prisoners at the start of the experiment. Although initially warned that as prisoners their privacy and other civil rights would be violated and that they might be subjected to harassment, every subject was completely confident of his ability to endure whatever the prison had to offer for the full two-week experimental period. Each subject unhesitatingly agreed to give his "informed consent" to participate.

The prison was constructed in the basement of Stanford University's psychology building, which was deserted after the end of the summer-school session. A long corridor was converted into the prison "yard" by partitioning off both ends. Three small laboratory rooms opening onto this corridor were made into cells by installing metal barred doors and replacing existing furniture with cots, three to a cell. Adjacent offices were refurnished as guards' quarters, interview-testing rooms, and bedrooms for the "warden" (Jaffe) and the "superintendent" (Zimbardo). A concealed video camera and hidden microphones recorded much of the activity and conversation of guards and prisoners. The physical environment was one in which prisoners could always be observed by the staff, the only exception being when they were secluded in solitary confinement (a small, dark storage closet, labeled "The Hole").

Our mock prison represented an attempt to simulate the psychological state of imprisonment in certain ways. We based our experiment on an in-depth analysis of the prison situation, developed after hundreds of hours of discussion with Carlo Prescott (our ex-con consultant), parole officers, and correctional personnel, and after reviewing much of the existing literature on prisons and concentration camps.

"Real" prisoners typically report feeling powerless, arbitrarily controlled, dependent, frustrated, hopeless, anonymous, dehumanized, and emasculated. It was not possible, pragmatically or ethically, to create such chronic states in volunteer subjects who realize that they are in an experiment for only a short time. Racism, physical brutality, indefinite confinement, and enforced homosexuality were not features of our mock prison. But we did try to reproduce those elements of the prison experience that seemed most fundamental.

We promoted anonymity by seeking to minimize each prisoner's sense of uniqueness and prior identity. The prisoners wore smocks and nylon stocking caps; they had to use their ID numbers; their personal effects were removed and they were housed in barren cells. All of this made them appear similar to each other and indistinguishable to observers. Their smocks, which were like dresses, were worn without undergarments, causing the prisoners to be restrained in their physical actions and to move in ways that were more feminine than masculine.

The prisoners were forced to obtain permission from the guard for routine and simple activities such as writing letters, smoking a cigarette, or even going to the toilet; this elicited from them a childlike dependency.

15   Their quarters, though clean and neat, were small, stark, and without esthetic appeal. The lack of windows resulted in poor air circulation, and persistent odors arose from the unwashed bodies of the prisoners. After 10 P.M. lockup, toilet privileges were denied, so prisoners who had to relieve themselves would have to urinate and defecate in buckets provided by the guards. Sometimes the guards refused permission to have them cleaned out, and this made the prison smell.

Above all, "real" prisons are machines for playing tricks with the human conception of time. In our windowless prison, the prisoners often did not even know whether it was day or night. A few hours after falling asleep, they were roused by shrill whistles for their "count." The ostensible purpose of the count was to provide a public test of the prisoners' knowledge of the rules and of their ID numbers. But more important, the count, which occurred at least once on each of the three different guard shifts, provided a regular occasion for the guards to relate to the prisoners. Over the course of the study, the duration of the counts was spontaneously increased by the guards from their initial perfunctory 10 minutes to a seemingly interminable several hours. During these confrontations, guards who were bored could find ways to amuse themselves, ridiculing recalcitrant prisoners, enforcing arbitrary rules, and openly exaggerating any dissension among the prisoners.

The guards were also "deindividualized": They wore identical khaki uniforms and silver reflector sunglasses that made eye contact with them impossible. Their symbols of power were billy clubs, whistles, handcuffs, and the keys to the cells and the "main gate." Although our guards received no formal training from us in how to be guards, for the most part they moved with apparent ease into their roles. The media had already provided them with ample models of prison guards to emulate.

Because we were as interested in the guards' behavior as in the prisoners', they were given considerable latitude to improvise and to develop strategies and tactics of prisoner management. Our guards were told that they must maintain "law and order" in this prison, that they were responsible for handling any trouble that might break out, and they were cautioned about the seriousness and potential dangers of the situation they were about to enter. Surprisingly, in most prison systems, "real" guards are not given much more psychological preparation or adequate training than this for what is one of the most complex, demanding, and dangerous jobs our society has to offer. They are expected to learn how to adjust to their new employment mostly from on-the-job experience, and from contacts with the "old bulls" during a survival-of-the-fittest orientation period. According to an orientation manual for correctional officers at San Quentin, "the only way you really get to know San Quentin is through experience and time. Some of us take more time and must go through more experiences than others to accomplish this; some really never do get there."

You cannot be a prisoner if no one will be your guard, and you cannot be a prison guard if no one takes you or your prison seriously. Therefore, over time a perverted symbiotic relationship developed. As the guards became more aggressive, prisoners became more passive; assertion by the guards led to dependency in the prisoners; self-aggrandizement was met with self-deprecation, authority with helplessness, and the counterpart of the guards' sense of mastery and control was the depression and hopelessness witnessed in the prisoners. As these differences in behavior, mood, and perception became more evident to all, the need for the now "righteously" powerful guards to rule the obviously inferior and powerless inmates became a sufficient reason to support almost any further indignity of man against man:

20 Guard K: "During the inspection, I went to cell 2 to mess up a bed which the prisoner had made and he grabbed me, screaming that he had just made it, and he wasn't going to let me mess it up. He grabbed my throat, and although he was laughing I was pretty scared....I lashed out with my stick and hit him in the chin (although not very hard), and when I freed myself I became angry. I wanted to get back in the cell and have a go with him, since he attacked me when I was not ready."

Guard M: "I was surprised at myself...I made them call each other names and clean the toilets out with their bare hands. I practically considered the prisoners cattle, and I kept thinking: 'I have to watch out for them in case they try something.'"

Guard A: "I was tired of seeing the prisoners in their rags and smelling the strong odors of their bodies that filled the cells. I watched them tear at each other on orders given by us. They didn't see it as an experiment. It was real and they were fighting to keep their identity. But we were always there to show them who was boss."

Because the first day passed without incident, we were surprised and totally unprepared for the rebellion that broke out on the morning of the second day. The prisoners removed their stocking caps, ripped off their numbers, and barricaded themselves inside the cells by putting their beds against the doors. What should we do? The guards were very much upset because the prisoners also began to taunt and curse them to their faces. When the morning shift of guards came on, they were upset at the night shift who, they felt, must have been too permissive and too lenient. The guards had to handle the rebellion themselves, and what they did was startling to behold.

At first they insisted that reinforcements be called in. The two guards who were waiting on stand-by call at home came in, and the night shift of guards voluntarily remained on duty (without extra pay) to bolster the morning shift. The guards met and decided to treat force with force. They got a fire extinguisher that shot a stream of skin-chilling carbon dioxide and forced the prisoners away from the doors; they broke into each cell, stripped the prisoners naked, took the beds out, forced the prisoners who were the ringleaders into solitary confinement, and generally began to harass and intimidate the prisoners.

25 After crushing the riot, the guards decided to head off further unrest by creating a privileged cell for those who were "good prisoners" and then, without

explanation, switching some of the troublemakers into it and some of the good prisoners out into the other cells. The prisoner ringleaders could not trust these new cellmates because they had not joined in the riot and might even be "snitches." The prisoners never again acted in unity against the system. One of the leaders of the prisoner revolt later confided:

"If we had gotten together then, I think we could have taken over the place. But when I saw the revolt wasn't working, I decided to toe the line. Everyone settled into the same pattern. From then on, we were really controlled by the guards."

It was after this episode that the guards really began to demonstrate their inventiveness in the application of arbitrary power. They made the prisoners obey petty, meaningless, and often inconsistent rules, forced them to engage in tedious, useless work, such as moving cartons back and forth between closets and picking thorns out of their blankets for hours on end. (The guards had previously dragged the blankets through thorny bushes to create this disagreeable task.) Not only did the prisoners have to sing songs or laugh or refrain from smiling on command; they were also encouraged to curse and vilify each other publicly during some of the counts. They sounded off their numbers endlessly and were repeatedly made to do pushups, on occasion with a guard stepping on them or a prisoner sitting on them.

Slowly the prisoners became resigned to their fate and even behaved in ways that actually helped to justify their dehumanizing treatment at the hands of the guards. Analysis of the tape-recorded private conversations between prisoners and of remarks made by them to interviewers revealed that fully half could be classified as nonsupportive of other prisoners. More dramatic, 85 percent of the evaluative statements by prisoners about their fellow prisoners were uncomplimentary and deprecating.

This should be taken in the context of an even more surprising result. What do you imagine the prisoners talked about when they were alone in their cells with each other, given a temporary respite from the continual harassment and surveillance by the guards? Girl friends, career plans, hobbies or politics?

30　　　No, their concerns were almost exclusively riveted to prison topics. Their monitored conversations revealed that only 10 percent of the time was devoted to "outside" topics, while 90 percent of the time they discussed escape plans, the awful food, grievances or ingratiating tactics to use with specific guards in order to get a cigarette, permission to go to the toilet, or some other favor. Their obsession with these immediate survival concerns made talk about the past and future an idle luxury.

And this was not a minor point. So long as the prisoners did not get to know each other as people, they only extended the oppressiveness and reality of their life as prisoners. For the most part, each prisoner observed his fellow prisoners allowing the guards to humiliate them, acting like compliant sheep, carrying out mindless orders with total obedience, and even being cursed by fellow prisoners (at a guard's command). Under such circumstances, how could a prisoner have respect for his fellows, or any self-respect for what *he* obviously was becoming in the eyes of all those evaluating him?

The combination of realism and symbolism in this experiment had fused to create a vivid illusion of imprisonment. The illusion merged inextricably with reality for at least some of the time for every individual in the situation. It was remarkable how readily we all slipped into our roles, temporarily gave up our identities, and allowed these assigned roles and the social forces in the situation to guide, shape, and eventually to control our freedom of thought and action.

But precisely where does one's "identity" end and one's "role" begin? When the private self and the public role behavior clash, what direction will attempts to impose consistency take? Consider the reactions of the parents, relatives, and friends of the prisoners who visited their forlorn sons, brothers, and lovers during two scheduled visitors' hours. They were taught in short order that they were our guests, allowed the privilege of visiting only by complying with the regulations of the institution. They had to register, were made to wait half an hour, were told that only two visitors could see any one prisoner; the total visiting time was cut from an hour to only 10 minutes, they had to be under the surveillance of a guard, and before any parents could enter the visiting area, they had to discuss their son's case with the warden. Of course they complained about these arbitrary rules, but their conditioned, middle-class reaction was to work within the system to appeal privately to the superintendent to make conditions better for their prisoners.

In less than 36 hours, we were forced to release prisoner 8612 because of extreme depression, disorganized thinking, uncontrollable crying, and fits of rage. We did so reluctantly because we believed he was trying to "con" us—it was unimaginable that a volunteer prisoner in a mock prison could legitimately be suffering and disturbed to that extent. But then on each of the next three days another prisoner reacted with similar anxiety symptoms, and we were forced to terminate them, too. In a fifth case, a prisoner was released after developing a psychosomatic rash over his entire body (triggered by rejection of his parole appeal by the mock parole board). These men were simply unable to make an adequate adjustment to prison life. Those who endured the prison experience to the end could be distinguished from those who broke down and were released early in only one dimension—authoritarianism. On a psychological test designed to reveal a person's authoritarianism, those prisoners who had the highest scores were best able to function in this authoritarian prison environment.

35   If the authoritarian situation became a serious matter for the prisoners, it became even more serious—and sinister—for the guards. Typically, the guards insulted the prisoners, threatened them, were physically aggressive, used instruments (night sticks, fire extinguishers, etc.) to keep the prisoners in line, and referred to them in impersonal, anonymous, deprecating ways: "Hey, you," or "You [obscenity], 5401, come here." From the first to the last day, there was a significant increase in the guards' use of most of these domineering, abusive tactics.

Everyone and everything in the prison was defined by power. To be a guard who did not take advantage of this institutionally sanctioned use of power was to appear "weak," "out of it," "wired up by the prisoners," or simply a deviant from the established norms of appropriate guard behavior. Using Erich Fromm's definition of sadism, as "the wish for absolute control over another living being," all of the mock guards at one time or another during this study behaved sadistically toward the prisoners. Many of them reported—in their diaries, on critical-incident report forms, and during post-experimental interviews—being delighted in the new-found power and control they exercised and sorry to see it relinquished at the end of the study.

Some of the guards reacted to the situation in the extreme and behaved with great hostility and cruelty in the forms of degradation they invented for the prisoners. But others were kinder; they occasionally did little favors for the prisoners, were reluctant to punish them, and avoided situations where prisoners were being harassed. The torment experienced by one of these good guards is obvious in his perceptive analysis of what it felt like to be responded to as a "guard":

"What made the experience most depressing for me was the fact that we were continually called upon to act in a way that just was contrary to what I really feel inside. I don't feel like I'm the type of person that would be a guard, just constantly giving out [orders]... and forcing people to do things, and pushing and lying—it just didn't seem like me, and to continually keep up and put on a face like that is just really one of the most oppressive things you can do. It's almost like a prison that you create yourself—you get into it, and it becomes almost the definition you make of yourself, it almost becomes like walls, and you want to break out and you want just to be able to tell everyone that 'this isn't really me at all, and I'm not the person that's confined in there—I'm a person who wants to get out and show you that I am free, and I do have my own will, and I'm not the sadistic type of person that enjoys this kind of thing.'"

Still, the behavior of these good guards seemed more motivated by a desire to be liked by everyone in the system than by a concern for the inmates' welfare. No guard ever intervened in any direct way on behalf of the prisoners, ever interfered with the orders of the cruelest guards, or ever openly complained about the subhuman quality of life that characterized this prison.

40   Perhaps the most devastating impact of the more hostile guards was their creation of a capricious, arbitrary environment. Over time the prisoners began to react passively. When our mock prisoners asked questions, they got answers about half the time, but the rest of the time they were insulted and punished—and it was not possible for them to predict which would be the outcome. As they began to "toe the line," they stopped resisting, questioning and, indeed, almost ceased responding altogether. There was a general decrease in all categories of response as they learned the safest strategy to use in an unpredictable, threatening environment from which there is no physical escape—do nothing, except what is required. Act not, want not, feel not, and you will not get into trouble in prisonlike situations.

Can it really be, you wonder, that intelligent, educated volunteers could have lost sight of the reality that they were merely acting a part in an elaborate game that would eventually end? There are many indications not only that they did, but that, in addition, so did we and so did other apparently sensible, responsible adults.

Prisoner 819, who had gone into an uncontrollable crying fit, was about to be prematurely released from the prison when a guard lined up the prisoners and had them chant in unison, "819 is a bad prisoner. Because of what 819 did to prison property we all must suffer. 819 is a bad prisoner." Over and over again. When we realized 819 might be overhearing this, we rushed into the room where 819 was supposed to be resting, only to find him in tears, prepared to go back into the prison because he could not leave as long as the others thought he was a "bad prisoner." Sick as he felt, he had to prove to them he was not a "bad" prisoner. He had to be persuaded that he was not a prisoner at all, that the others were also just students, that this was just an experiment and not a prison and the prison staff were only research psychologists. A report from the warden notes, "While I believe that it was necessary for *staff* [me] to enact the warden role, at least some of the time, I am startled by the ease with which I could turn off my sensitivity and concern for others for 'a good cause.'"

Consider our overreaction to the rumor of a mass escape plot that one of the guards claimed to have overheard. It went as follows: Prisoner 8612, previously released for emotional disturbance, was only faking. He was going to round up a bunch of his friends, and they would storm the prison right after visiting hours. Instead of collecting data on the pattern of rumor transmission, we made plans to maintain the security of our institution. After putting a confederate informer into the cell 8612 had occupied to get specific information about the escape plans, the superintendent went back to the Palo Alto Police Department to request transfer of our prisoners to the old city jail. His impassioned plea was only turned down at the last minute when the problem of insurance and city liability for our prisoners was raised by a city official. Angered at this lack of cooperation, the staff formulated another plan. Our jail was dismantled, the prisoners, chained and blindfolded, were carted off to a remote storage room. When the conspirators arrived, they would be told the study was over, their friends had been sent home, there was nothing left to liberate. After they left, we would redouble the security features of our prison making any future escape attempts futile. We even planned to lure ex-prisoner 8612 back on some pretext and imprison him again, because he had been released on false pretenses! The rumor turned out to be just that—a full day had passed in which we collected little or no data, worked incredibly hard to tear down and then rebuild our prison. Our reaction, however, was as much one of relief and joy as of exhaustion and frustration.

When a former prison chaplain was invited to talk with the prisoners (the grievance committee had requested church services), he puzzled everyone by disparaging each inmate for not having taken any constructive action in order to get released. "Don't you know you must have a lawyer in order to get bail, or to appeal the charges against you?" Several of them accepted his invitation to contact their parents in order to secure the services of an attorney. The next night one of the parents stopped at the superintendent's office before visiting time and handed him the name and phone number of her cousin who was a public defender. She said that a priest had called her and suggested the need for a lawyer's services! We called the lawyer. He came, interviewed the prisoners, discussed sources of bail money, and promised to return again after the weekend.

45   But perhaps the most telling account of the insidious development of this new reality, of the gradual Kafkaesque metamorphosis of good into evil, appears in excerpts from the diary of one of the guards, Guard A:

Prior to start of experiment: "As I am a pacifist and nonaggressive individual. I cannot see a time when I might guard and/or maltreat other living things."

After an orientation meeting: "Buying uniforms at the end of the meeting confirms the gamelike atmosphere of this thing. I doubt whether many of us share the expectations of 'seriousness' that the experimenters seem to have."

First Day: "Feel sure that the prisoners will make fun of my appearance and I evolve my first basic strategy—mainly not to smile at anything they say or do which would be admitting it's all only a game. . . . At cell 3 I stop and setting my voice hard and low say to 5486, 'What are you smiling at?' 'Nothing, Mr. Correctional Officer.' 'Well, see that you don't.' (As I walk off I feel stupid.)"

Second Day: "5704 asked for a cigarette and I ignored him—because I am a nonsmoker and could not empathize. . . . Meanwhile since I was feeling empathetic towards 1037, I determined not to talk with him. . . . After we had count and lights out [Guard D] and I held a loud conversation about going home to our girl friends and what we were going to do to them."

50   *Third Day (preparing for the first visitors' night):* "After warning the prisoners not to make any complaints unless they wanted the visit terminated fast, we finally brought in the first parents. I made sure I was one of the guards on the yard, because this was my first chance for the type of manipulative power that I really like—being a very noticed figure with almost complete control over what is said or not. While the parents and prisoners sat in chairs, I sat on the end of the table dangling my feet and contradicting anything I felt like. This was the first part of the experiment I was really enjoying. . . . 817 is being obnoxious and bears watching."

Fourth Day: " . . . The psychologist rebukes me for handcuffing and blindfolding a prisoner before leaving the [counseling] office, and I resentfully reply that it is both necessary security and my business anyway."

Fifth Day: "I harass 'Sarge' who continues to stubbornly overrespond to all commands. I have singled him out for the special abuse both because he begs for it and because I simply don't like him. The real trouble starts at dinner. The new prisoner (416) refuses to eat his sausage . . . we throw him into the Hole ordering him to hold sausages in each hand. We have a crisis of authority; this rebellious conduct potentially undermines the complete control we have over the others. We decide to play upon prisoner solidarity and tell the new one that all the others will be deprived of visitors if he does not eat his dinner. . . . I walk by and slam my stick into the Hole door. . . . I am very angry at this prisoner for causing discomfort and trouble for the others. I decided to force-feed him, but he wouldn't eat. I let the food slide down his face. I didn't believe it was me doing it. I hated myself for making him eat but I hated him more for not eating."

Sixth Day: "The experiment is over. I feel elated but am shocked to find some other guards disappointed somewhat because of the loss of money and some because they are enjoying themselves."

We were no longer dealing with an intellectual exercise in which a hypothesis was being evaluated in the dispassionate manner dictated by the canons of the scientific method. We were caught up in the passion of the present, the suffering, the need to control people, not variables, the escalation of power, and all the unexpected things that were erupting around and within us. We had to end this experiment: So our planned two-week simulation was aborted after only six (was it only six?) days and nights.

55   Was it worth all the suffering just to prove what everybody knows—that some people are sadistic, others weak, and prisons are not beds of roses? If that is all we demonstrated in this research, then it was certainly not worth the anguish. We believe there are many significant implications to be derived from this experience, only a few of which can be suggested here.

The potential social value of this study derives precisely from the fact that normal, healthy, educated young men could be so radically transformed under the institutional pressures of a "prison environment." If this could happen in so short a time, without the excesses that are possible in real prisons, and if it could happen to the "cream-of-the-crop of American youth," then one can only shudder to imagine what society is doing both to the actual guards and prisoners who are at this very moment participating in that unnatural "social experiment."

The pathology observed in this study cannot be reasonably attributed in preexisting personality differences of the subjects, that option being eliminated by our selection procedures and random assignment. Rather, the subjects' abnormal social and personal reactions are best seen as a product of their transaction with an environment that supported the behavior that would be pathological in other settings, but was "appropriate" in this prison. Had we observed comparable reactions in a real prison, the psychiatrist undoubtedly would have been able to attribute any prisoner's behavior to character defects or personality maladjustment, while critics of the prison system would have been quick to label the guards as "psychopathic." This tendency to locate the source of behavior disorders inside a particular person or group underestimates the power of situational forces.

Our colleague, David Rosenhan, has very convincingly shown that once a sane person (pretending to be insane) gets labeled as insane and committed to a mental hospital, it is the label that is the reality which is treated and not the person. This dehumanizing tendency to respond to other people according to socially determined labels and often arbitrarily assigned roles is also apparent in a recent "mock hospital" study designed by Norma Jean Orlando to extend the ideas in our research.

Personnel from the staff of Elgin State Hospital in Illinois role-played either mental patients or staff in a weekend simulation on a ward in the hospital. The mock mental patients soon displayed behavior indistinguishable from that we usually associate with the chronic pathological syndromes of acute mental patients: Incessant pacing, uncontrollable weeping, depression, hostility, fights, stealing from each other, complaining. Many of the "mock staff" took advantage of their power to act in ways comparable to our mock guards by dehumanizing their powerless victims.

60   During a series of encounter debriefing sessions immediately after our experiment, we all had an opportunity to vent our strong feelings and to reflect upon the moral and ethical issues each of us faced, and we considered how we might react more morally in future "real-life" analogues to this situation. Year-long follow-ups with our subjects via questionnaires, personal interviews, and group reunions indicate that their mental anguish was transient and situationally specific, but the self-knowledge gained has persisted.

By far the most disturbing implication of our research comes from the parallels between what occurred in that basement mock prison and daily experiences in our own lives—and we presume yours. The physical institution of prison is but a concrete and steel metaphor for the existence of more pervasive, albeit less obvious, prisons of the mind that all of us daily create, populate, and perpetuate. We speak here of the prisons of racism, sexism, despair, shyness, "neurotic hang-ups," and the like. The social convention of marriage, as one example, becomes for many couples a state of imprisonment in which one partner agrees to be prisoner or guard, forcing or allowing the other to play the reciprocal role—invariably without making the contract explicit.

To what extent do we allow ourselves to become imprisoned by docilely accepting the roles others assign us or, indeed, choose to remain prisoners because being passive and dependent frees us from the need to act and be responsible for our actions? The prison of fear constructed in the delusions of the paranoid is no less confining or less real than the cell that every shy person erects to limit his own freedom in anxious anticipation of being ridiculed and rejected by his guards—often guards of his own making.

● Review Questions

1. What was Zimbardo's primary goal in undertaking the prison experiment?

2. What was the profile of the subjects in the experiment? Why is this profile significant?

3. Zimbardo claims that there is a "process" (paragraphs 2, 7) of becoming a prisoner. What is this process?

4. What inverse psychological relationships developed between prisoners and guards?

5. What was the result of the prison "riot"?

6. Why did prisoners have no respect for each other or for themselves?

7. How does the journal of Guard A illustrate what Zimbardo calls the "gradual Kafkaesque metamorphosis of good into evil"? (See paragraphs 45–54.)

8. What are the reasons people would voluntarily become prisoners?

9. How can the mind keep people in jail?

● Discussion and Writing Suggestions

1. Reread the four epigraphs to this article. Write a paragraph of response to any one of them, in light of Zimbardo's discussion of the prison experiment.

2. You may have thought, before reading this article, that being a prisoner is a physical fact, not a psychological state. What are the differences between these two views?

3. In paragraph 8, Zimbardo explains his reasons for not pursuing his research in a real prison. He writes that "it is impossible to separate what each individual brings into the prison from what the prison brings out in each person." What does he mean? And how does this distinction prove important later in the article? (See paragraph 58.)

4. Zimbardo reports that at the beginning of the experiment each of the "prisoner" subjects "was completely confident of his ability to endure whatever the prison had to offer for the full two-week experimental period" (paragraph 10). Had you been a subject, would you have been so confident, prior to the experiment? Given what you've learned of the experiment, do you think you would have psychologically "become" a prisoner or guard if you had been selected for these roles? (And if not, what makes you so sure?)

5. Identify two passages in this article: one that surprised you relating to the prisoners and one that surprised you relating to the guards. Write a paragraph explaining your response to each. Now read the two passages in light of each other. Do you see any patterns underlying your responses?

6. Zimbardo claims that the implications of his research matter deeply—that the mock prison he created is a metaphor for prisons of the mind "that all of us daily create, populate, and perpetuate" (paragraph 61). Zimbardo mentions the prisons of "racism, sexism, despair, [and] shyness." Choose any one of these and discuss how it might be viewed as a mental prison.

7. Reread paragraphs 61 and 62. Zimbardo makes a metaphorical jump from his experiment to the psychological realities of your daily life. Prisons—the artificial one he created and actual prisons—stand for something: social systems in which there are those who give orders and those who obey. All metaphors break down at some point. Where does this one break down?

8. Zimbardo suggests that we might "choose to remain prisoners because being passive and dependent frees us from the need to act and be responsible for our actions" (paragraph 62). Do you agree? What are the burdens of being disobedient?

FROM ATONEMENT

Ian McEwan

The previous three selections—"Group Minds" by Doris Lessing, "Opinions and Social Pressure" by Solomon Asch, and "The Stanford Prison Experiment" by Philip Zimbardo— form a concluding subset of readings on how groups can exert pressure on individuals. So strong are these pressures, at times, that people under the influence of a "group mind" can act in ways that would be unthinkable were they acting alone.

In one section of his novel *Atonement* (2001), British writer Ian McEwan explores this very dynamic. It is early in World War II, 1940. With British troops (Tommies) having been routed by the advancing German army in Northern France, Robbie Turner (the wounded and feverish protagonist in this section of the novel) is, with corporals Mace and Nettles, retreating to the sea, to Dunkirk, where they and more than 300,000 compatriots expect to be rescued and taken to safety across the English Channel. The German Luftwaffe has been running unmolested raids on the retreating soldiers and on those already gathered on the beaches, strafing and killing at will—with no response from the Royal Air Force (RAF). In this scene, Turner, Mace, and Nettles join other Tommies on the beach. They eventually stumble into a ransacked bar, looking for something to drink.

Critics have variously described *Atonement* as "resplendent," "astonishing," and "redemptive." To date, McEwan has written eighteen novels. *Atonement* won the National Book Critics Circle Award and the W.H. Smith Literary Award; *Amsterdam* (1998) won the Booker Prize; and *The Child in Time* (1987) won the Whitbread Award.

After minutes of noisy crunching over glass, there was sudden silence under their boots where the road ended in fine sand. As they rose through a gap in the dunes, they heard the sea and tasted a salty mouthful before they saw it. The taste of holidays. They left the path and climbed through the dune grass to a vantage point where they stood in silence for many minutes. The fresh damp breeze off the Channel restored him to clarity. Perhaps it was nothing more than his temperature rising and falling in fits.

He thought he had no expectations—until he saw the beach. He'd assumed that the cussed army spirit which whitewashed rocks in the face of annihilation would prevail. He tried to impose order now on the random movement before him, and almost succeeded: marshaling centers, warrant officers behind makeshift desks, rubber stamps and dockets, roped-off lines toward the waiting boats; hectoring sergeants, tedious queues around mobile canteens. In general, an end to all private initiative. Without knowing it, that was the beach he had been walking to for days. But the actual beach, the one he and the corporals gazed on now, was no more than a variation on all that had gone before: there was a rout, and this was its terminus. It was obvious enough now they saw it— this was what happened when a chaotic retreat could go no further. It only took a moment to adjust. He saw thousands of men, ten, twenty thousand, perhaps more, spread across the vastness of the beach. In the distance they were like grains of black sand. But there were no boats, apart from one upturned whaler rolling in the distant surf. It was low tide and almost a mile to the water's edge.

There were no boats by the long jetty. He blinked and looked again. That jetty was made of men, a long file of them, six or eight deep, standing up to their knees, their waists, their shoulders, stretching out for five hundred yards through the shallow waters. They waited, but there was nothing in sight, unless you counted in those smudges on the horizon—boats burning after an air attack. There was nothing that could reach the beach in hours. But the troops stood there, facing the horizon in their tin hats, rifles lifted above the waves. From this distance they looked as placid as cattle.

And these men were a small proportion of the total. The majority were on the beach, moving about aimlessly. Little clusters had formed around the wounded left by the last Stuka attack.* As aimless as the men, half a dozen artillery horses galloped in a pack along the water's edge. A few troops were attempting to right the upturned whaler. Some had taken off their clothes to swim. Off to the east was a football game, and from the same direction came the feeble sound of a hymn being sung in unison, then fading. Beyond the football game was the only sign of official activity. On the shore, lorries† were being lined up and lashed together to form a makeshift jetty. More lorries were driving down. Nearer, up the beach, individuals were scooping sand with their helmets to make foxholes. In the dunes, close to where Turner and the corporals stood, men had already dug themselves holes from which they peeped out, proprietorial and smug. Like marmots, he thought. But the majority of the army wandered about the sands without purpose, like citizens of an Italian town in the hour of the *passeggio*‡ They saw no immediate reason to join the enormous queue, but they were unwilling to come away from the beach in case a boat should suddenly appear.

To the left was the resort of Bray, a cheerful front of cafés and little shops that in a normal season would be renting out beach chairs and pedal bikes. In a circular park with a neatly mowed lawn was a bandstand, and a merry-go-round painted red, white and blue. In this setting, another, more insouciant company had hunkered down. Soldiers had opened up the cafés for themselves and were getting drunk at the tables outside, bawling and laughing. Men were larking about on the bikes along a pavement stained with vomit. A colony of drunks was spread out on the grass by the bandstand, sleeping it off. A solitary sunbather in his underpants, facedown on a towel, had patches of uneven sunburn on his shoulders and legs—pink and white like a strawberry and vanilla ice cream.

5   It was not difficult to choose between these circles of suffering—the sea, the beach, the front. The corporals were already walking away. Thirst alone decided it. They found a path on the landward side of the dunes, then they were crossing a sandy lawn strewn with broken bottles. As they were making a way round the raucous tables Turner saw a naval party coming along the front and stopped to watch. There were five of them, two officers, three ratings, a gleaming group of fresh white, blue and gold. No concessions to camouflage. Straight-backed and

---

*Stuka: World War II era German dive bomber
†lorries: trucks
‡*passeggio:* Ital., a walk or a stroll

severe, revolvers strapped to their belts, they moved with tranquil authority through the mass of somber battle dress and grimy faces, looking from side to side as if conducting a count. One of the officers made notes on a clipboard. They headed away toward the beach. With a childish feeling of abandonment, Turner watched them until they were out of sight.

He followed Mace and Nettle into the din and fumy stench of the first bar along the front. Two suitcases propped open on the bar were full of cigarettes—but there was nothing to drink. The shelves along the sandblasted mirror behind the bar were empty. When Nettle ducked behind the counter to rummage around, there were jeers. Everyone coming in had tried the same. The drink had long gone with the serious drinkers outside. Turner pushed through the crowd to a small kitchen at the back. The place was wrecked, the taps were dry. Outside was a pissoir and stacked crates of empties. A dog was trying to get its tongue inside an empty sardine can, pushing it across a patch of concrete. He turned and went back to the main room and its roar of voices. There was no electricity, only natural light which was stained brown, as though by the absent beer. Nothing to drink, but the bar remained full. Men came in, were disappointed and yet they stayed, held there by free cigarettes and the evidence of recent booze. The dispensers dangled empty on the wall where the inverted bottles had been wrenched away. The sweet smell of liquor rose from the sticky cement floor. The noise and press of bodies and damp tobacco air satisfied a homesick yearning for a Saturday night pub. This was the Mile End Road, and Sauchiehall Street, and everywhere in between.

He stood in the din, uncertain what to do. It would be such an effort, to fight his way out of the crowd. There were boats yesterday, he gathered from a snatch of conversation, and perhaps again tomorrow. Standing on tiptoe by the kitchen doorway, he gave a no-luck shrug across the crowd toward the corporals. Nettle cocked his head in the direction of the door and they began to converge on it. A drink would have been fine, but what interested them now was water. Progress through the press of bodies was slow, and then, just as they converged, their way to the door was blocked by a tight wall of backs forming around one man.

He must have been short—less than five foot six—and Turner could see nothing of him apart from a portion of the back of his head.

Someone said, "You answer the fucking question, you little git."

10   "Yeah, go on then."

"Oi, Brylcreem job. Where was ya?"

"Where were you when they killed my mate?"

A globule of spittle hit the back of the man's head and fell behind his ear. Turner moved round to get a view. He saw first the gray-blue of a jacket, and then the mute apprehension in the man's face. He was a wiry little fellow with thick, unclean lenses in his glasses which magnified his frightened state. He looked like a filing clerk, or a telephone operator, perhaps from a headquarters long ago dispersed. But he was in the RAF and the Tommies held him accountable. He turned slowly, gazing at the circle of his interrogators. He had no answers to their questions, and he made no attempt to deny his responsibility for the absence of Spitfires and Hurricanes over the beach* His right hand clutched his cap so hard his knuckles trembled. An artilleryman standing by the door gave him a hard push in the back so that he stumbled across the ring into the chest of a soldier who sent him back with a casual punch to the head. There was a hum of approval. Everyone had suffered, and now someone was going to pay.

"So where's the RAF?"

15   A hand whipped out and slapped the man's face, knocking his glasses to the floor. The sound of the blow was precise as a whip crack. It was a signal for a new stage, a new level of engagement. His naked eyes shrank to fluttering little dots as he went down to grope around his feet. That was a mistake. A kick from a steel-capped army boot caught him on the backside, lifting him an inch or two. There were chuckles all round. A sense of something tasty about to happen was spreading across the bar and drawing more soldiers in. As the crowd swelled around the circle, any remaining sense of individual responsibility fell away. A swaggering recklessness was taking hold. A cheer went up as someone stubbed his cigarette on the fellow's head. They laughed at his comic yelp. They hated him and he deserved everything that was coming his way. He was answerable for the Luftwaffe's freedom of the skies, for every Stuka attack, every dead friend. His slight frame contained every cause of an army's defeat. Turner assumed there was nothing he could do to help the man without risking a lynching himself. But it was impossible to do nothing. Joining in would be better than nothing. Unpleasantly excited, he strained forward. Now, a tripping Welsh accent proposed the question.

"Where's the RAF?"

It was eerie that the man had not shouted for help, or pleaded, or protested his innocence. His silence seemed like collusion in his fate. Was he so dim that it had not occurred to him that he might be about to die? Sensibly, he had folded his glasses into his pocket. Without them his face was empty. Like a mole in bright light, he peered around at his tormentors, his lips parted, more in disbelief than in an attempt to form a word. Because he could not see it coming, he took a blow to the face full-on. It was a fist this time. As his head flipped back, another boot cracked into his shin and a little sporting cheer went up, with some uneven applause, as though for a decent catch in the slips on the village green. It was madness to go to the man's defense, it was loathsome not to. At the same time, Turner understood the exhilaration among the tormentors and the insidious way it could claim him. He himself could do something outrageous with his bowie knife and earn the love of a hundred men. To distance the thought he made himself count the two or three soldiers in the circle he reckoned bigger or stronger than himself. But the real danger came from the mob itself, its righteous state of mind. It would not be denied its pleasures.

A situation had now been reached in which whoever threw the next hit had to earn general approval by being ingenious or funny. There was an eagerness in the air to please by being creative. No one wanted to strike a false note. For a few

---

*Spitfires and Hurricanes: World War II era British dive bombers

seconds these conditions imposed restraint. And at some point soon, Turner knew from his Wandsworth days, the single blow would become a cascade.* Then there would be no turning back, and for the RAF man, only one end. A pink blotch had formed on the cheekbone under his right eye. He had drawn his fists up under his chin—he was still gripping his cap—and his shoulders were hunched. It may have been a protective stance, but it was also a gesture of weakness and submission which was bound to provoke greater violence. If he had said something, anything at all, the troops surrounding him might have remembered that he was a man, not a rabbit to be skinned. The Welshman who had spoken was a short, thickset fellow from the sappers.† He now produced a belt of canvas webbing and held it up.

"What do you think, lads?"

20   His precise, insinuating delivery suggested horrors that Turner could not immediately grasp. Now was his last chance to act. As he looked around for the corporals, there was a roar from close by, like the bellowing of a speared bull. The crowd swayed and stumbled as Mace barged through them into the circle. With a wild hollering yodeling sound, like Johnny Weissmuller's Tarzan, he picked up the clerk from behind in a bear hug, lifting him eighteen inches clear of the ground, and shook the terrified creature from side to side. There were cheers and whistles, foot-stamping and Wild West whoops.

"I know what I want to do with him," Mace boomed. "I want to drown him in the bloody sea!"

In response, there rose another storm of hooting and stamping. Nettle was suddenly at Turner's side and they exchanged a look. They guessed what Mace was about and they began to move toward the door, knowing they would have to be quick. Not everyone was in favor of the drowning idea. Even in the frenzy of the moment, some could still recall that the tide line was a mile away across the sands. The Welshman in particular felt cheated. He was holding up his webbing and shouting. There were catcalls and boos as well as cheers. Still holding his victim in his arms, Mace rushed for the door. Turner and Nettle were ahead of him, making a path through the crowd. When they reached the entrance—usefully, a single, not a double, door—they let Mace through, then they blocked the way, shoulder to shoulder, though they appeared not to, for they were shouting and shaking their fists like the rest. They felt against their backs a colossal and excited human weight which they could only resist for a matter of seconds. This was long enough for Mace to run, not toward the sea, but sharp left, and left again, up a narrow street that curved behind the shops and bars, away from the front.

The exultant crowd exploded from the bar like champagne, hurling Turner and Nettle aside. Someone thought he saw Mace down on the sands, and for half a minute the crowd went that way. By the time the mistake was realized and the crowd began to turn back, there was no sign of Mace and his man. Turner and Nettle had melted away too.

The vast beach, the thousands waiting on it, and the sea empty of boats returned the Tommies to their predicament. They emerged from a dream. Away to

*Wandsworth: a private school in Hampshire, England
†sapper: a member of an elite engineering corps in the British army

the east where the night was rising, the perimeter line was under heavy artillery fire. The enemy was closing in and England was a long way off. In the failing light not much time remained to find somewhere to bed down. A cold wind was coming in off the Channel, and the greatcoats lay on the roadsides far inland.* The crowd began to break up. The RAF man was forgotten.

● Discussion and Writing Suggestions

1. We find no evidence in the bar of a command structure—though there is some evidence of one, however slight (and absurd) outside the bar, on the beach. What role might a *lack* of command structure have played in the formation of the mob in this scene?

2. What makes Turner, Mace, and Nettles able to resist the group's desire to hurt (or kill) the RAF airman? Do not hastily conclude that these three are necessarily "heroic" in any way. You would have a difficult time garnering evidence in this excerpt for such a claim—especially in light of the admission that Turner "himself could do something outrageous with his bowie knife and earn the love of a hundred men."

3. Reread the passage and trace the process by which a collection of individuals standing around the RAF soldier becomes a mob. Was this process already under-way when Turner found that "a tight wall of backs [had formed] around one man"?

4. The narrator describes Turner's dilemma this way: "It was madness to go to the man's defense, it was loathsome not to." And yet even Turner thinks himself capable of performing some outrage (with his bowie knife) on the RAF man. What forces at work in Turner make him—or anyone—capable of such potentially contrary actions?

5. "But the real danger came from the mob itself, its righteous state of mind. It would not be denied its pleasures." We commonly understand individuals to have a "state of mind." What does it mean that a group or a mob has one?

6. What does the fact that the "RAF man was forgotten" as the "crowd began to break up" suggest to you about the psychology of mobs?

7. Have you ever found yourself in a group that decided to do something you didn't want to do? How did you respond? If you participated, how did you feel about that—then and now? If you resisted, how were you able to do so? Was face-saving a problem?

8. Describe a circumstance in which you tried to convince a group not to pursue a particular action—perhaps in a meeting, on an athletic field, or with friends out on a Saturday night. What were the forces in play? Did you feel free to disagree? Did you succeed?

---

*greatcoats: below-the-knee length wool coats issued to British soldiers

SYNTHESIS ACTIVITIES

1. Analyze the mob scene in *Atonement*, using a principle or definition from Lessing, Zimbardo, or Asch to understand the process by which British soldiers surrounded and threatened a British airman. What insights into this scene will your principle or definition provide? Having conducted an analysis, consider a final question: In what ways does the scene in the bar resist analysis; that is, in what sense is the behavior McEwan describes so vexing that it cannot be explained?

2. Write a synthesis that explains the power of situations, as distinct from individual conscience, to influence a person's behavior. Use at least one example of a particular situation. Draw on the conclusions of the four experiments reported in this chapter: the Good Samaritan experiment, as related by Ross and Nisbett; the line drawing experiments of Asch; the obedience experiments of Milgram (along with the Burger reproduction); and the prison experiment of Zimbardo.

3. The outcomes of the experiments reported on in this chapter—Ross and Nisbett call them "empirical parables"—defy common sense: One would expect passersby to help a man slumped in a doorway; one would not expect people, ordered by a researcher, to inflict what they thought were painful electric shocks on others. One would expect people to believe the evidence of their eyes and insist that one line was longer than another; one would not expect college students to take on the roles of guard and prisoner so exuberantly that an experiment would need to be canceled for fear of harming participants. Ross and Nisbett suggest that experiments such as these bring us a "hard-won ignorance." What is so valuable about such "ignorance," about these experiments that defy common sense? Write a synthesis arguing that at least with respect to human behavior, "common sense" may not be a dependable guide.

4. Reread Doris Lessing's "Group Minds." In this chapter, you have become familiar with some of the experiments in social psychology that she drew on in making her point that we must use the knowledge of social science to advance as a species. As Lessing suggests, we have the information of these experiments, on the one hand; and on the other, we have ample evidence that people continue behaving in ways that prove we have learned little from the insights of researchers like Milgram, Zimbardo, and Asch. Write a critique of Lessing. Is she asking too much—that we can actually progress as a species?

5. Ross and Nisbett observe (paragraph 2, p. 689) that the experience of graduate students in social psychology can be "intellectually wrenching." Explain how this might be so, based on the four experiments you have read about in this chapter: (1) the "Good Samaritan" experiment, as

reported by Ross and Nisbett; (2) Milgram/Burger; (3) Zimbardo; and (4) Asch. How might such experiments upset some people? Consider one potentially upsetting conclusion to be drawn from the experiments by philosopher Gilbert Harman: "It seems that ordinary attributions of character traits to people are often deeply misguided and it may even be the case that there is no such thing as character, no ordinary character traits of the sort people think there are, none of the usual moral virtues and vices." Why might such a claim prove "emotionally wrenching" to some people? Does it to you?

6. What is a "group mind"? Write an explanatory paper that defines the term. As you develop and discuss elements of your definition, refer to the selections by Lessing, the experiments of Asch and Zimbardo, and the excerpt from McEwan's novel *Atonement*.

7. Milgram writes that "perhaps the most fundamental lesson of our study [is that] ordinary people, simply doing their jobs, and without any particular hostility on their part, can become agents in a terrible destructive process." Using this statement as a principle, analyze several situations recounted in this chapter, or perhaps some outside this chapter, of which you are aware because of your studies, your reading, and possibly even your own experience. Draw upon not only Milgram but also Asch, Zimbardo, and Fromm.

8. Doris Lessing argues that children need to be taught how to disobey so they can recognize and avoid situations that give rise to harmful obedience. If you were the curriculum coordinator for your local school system, how would you teach children to disobey responsibly? What would be your curriculum? What homework would you assign? What class projects? What field trips? One complicated part of your job would be to train children to understand the difference between *responsible* disobedience and anarchy. What is the difference?

   Take up these questions in a paper that draws on both your experiences as a student and your understanding of the selections in this chapter. Points that you might want to consider in developing the paper: defining overly obedient children; appropriate classroom behavior for responsibly disobedient children (as opposed to inappropriate behavior); reading lists; homework assignments; field trips; class projects.

9. A certain amount of obedience is a given in society. Stanley Milgram and others observe that social order, civilization itself, would not be possible unless individuals were willing to surrender a portion of their autonomy to the state. Allowing that we all are obedient (we must be), define the point at which obedience to a figure of authority becomes dangerous.

   As you develop your definition, consider the ways you might use the work of authors in this chapter and their definitions of acceptable and unacceptable levels of obedience. Do you agree with the ways in which others have drawn the line between reasonable and dangerous obedience? What examples from current stories in the news or from your own experience can you draw on to test various definitions?

10. Describe a situation in which you were faced with a moral dilemma of whether or not to obey a figure of authority. After describing the situation and the action you took (or didn't take), analyze your behavior in light of any two readings in this chapter. You might consider a straightforward, four-part structure for your paper: (1) your description; (2) your discussion, in light of source A; (3) your discussion, in light of source B; and (4) your conclusion—an overall appraisal of your behavior.

11. Erich Fromm equates disobedience with courage: "In order to disobey, one must have the courage to be alone, to err, and to sin." Novelist Doris Lessing makes much the same statement by equating obedience with shame: "among our most shameful memories is this, how often we said black was white because other people were saying it." Using such statements as principles for analysis, examine an act of obedience or disobedience in your own life and determine the extent to which, following Fromm or Lessing, you now consider it courageous or shameful. Having completed this part of your analysis, conclude by reassessing your behavior. Write one or more paragraphs on whether or not you would behave similarly if given a second chance in the same situation.

12. In response to the question "Why is man so prone to obey and why is it so difficult for him to disobey?" Erich Fromm suggests that obedience lets people identify with the powerful and invites feelings of safety. Disobedience is psychologically more difficult and requires an act of courage (see paragraphs 13 and 14). Solomon Asch notes that the tendency to conformity is generally stronger than the tendency to independence. And in his final paragraph, Philip Zimbardo writes that a "prison of fear" keeps people compliant and frees them of the need to take responsibility for their own actions. In a synthesis that draws on these three sources, explore the interplay of *fear* and its opposite, *courage,* in relation to obedience. To prevent the paper from becoming too abstract, direct your attention repeatedly to a single case, the details of which will help to keep your focus. This case may be based upon a particular event from your own life or the life of someone you know.

RESEARCH ACTIVITIES

1. Milgram's results, published in book form in 1974, generated enormous response. The reaction reprinted here (by Parker) represents only a very small portion of that controversy. Research reactions to the Milgram experiments and discuss your findings. Begin with the reviews listed and excerpted in the *Book Review Digest;* also use the *Social Science Index,* the

Readers' Guide to Periodical Literature, and newspaper indexes to locate articles, editorials, and letters to the editor on the experiments. (Note that editorials and letters are not always indexed. Letters appear within two to four weeks of the weekly magazine articles to which they refer, and within one to two weeks of newspaper articles.) What were the chief types of reactions? To what extent were the reactions favorable?

2. Milgram begins his book *Obedience to Authority* with a reference to Nazi Germany. The purpose of his experiment, in fact, was to help throw light on how the Nazi atrocities could have happened. Research the Nuremberg war crimes tribunals following World War II. Drawing specifically on the statements of those who testified at Nuremberg, as well as those who have written about it, show how Milgram's experiments do help explain the Holocaust and other Nazi crimes. In addition to relevant articles, see Telford Taylor, *Nuremberg and Vietnam: An American Tragedy* (1970); Hannah Arendt, *Eichmann in Jerusalem: A Report on the Banality of Evil* (1963); Richard A. Falk, Gabriel Kolko, and Robert J. Lifton (eds.), *Crimes of War* (1971).

3. Obtain a copy of the transcript of the trial of Adolf Eichmann—the Nazi official who carried out Hitler's "final solution" for the extermination of the Jews. Read also Hannah Arendt's *Eichmann in Jerusalem: A Report on the Banality of Evil,* along with the reviews of this book. Write a critique both of Arendt's book and of the reviews it received.

4. The My Lai massacre in Vietnam in 1969 was a particularly egregious case of overobedience to military authority in wartime. Show the connections between this event and Milgram's experiments. Note that Milgram himself treated the My Lai massacre in the epilogue to his *Obedience to Authority: An Experimental View* (1974).

5. Investigate the court-martial of Lt. William Calley, convicted for his role in the My Lai massacre. Discuss whether President Nixon was justified in commuting his sentence. Examine in detail the dilemmas the jury must have faced when presented with Calley's defense that he was only following orders.

6. Research the Watergate break-in of 1972 and the subsequent cover-up by Richard Nixon and members of his administration, as an example of overobedience to authority. Focus on one particular aspect of Watergate (e.g., the role of the counsel to the president, John Dean, or why the crisis was allowed to proceed to the point where it actually toppled a presidency). In addition to relevant articles, see Robert Woodward and Carl Bernstein, *All the President's Men* (1974); Leon Jaworski, *The Right and the Power: The Prosecution of Watergate* (1976); *RN: The Memoirs of Richard Nixon* (1978); John Dean, *Blind Ambition* (1976); John Sirica, *To Set the Record Straight: The Break-in, the Tapes, the Conspirators, the Pardon* (1979); Sam Ervin, *The Whole Truth: The Watergate Conspiracy* (1980); John Ehrlichman, *Witness to Power: The Nixon Years* (1982).

7. In April 2004, news broke of the systematic abuse, including beatings and sexual humiliation, by American military police, of Iraqi "detainees" at Baghdad's Abu Ghraib prison. The scandal was intensified—as was outrage in the Muslim world—by graphic photographs that the soldiers had taken of these activities. A high-level American inquiry uncovered some of the following abuses:

> Punching, slapping, and kicking detainees; jumping on their naked feet...positioning a naked detainee on a MRE Box, with a sandbag on his head, and attaching wires to his fingers, toes, and penis to simulate electric torture...having sex with a female detainee....Using military working dogs (without muzzles) to intimidate and frighten detainees, and in at least one case biting and severely injuring a detainee....Breaking chemical lights and pouring the phosphoric liquid on detainees....Beating detainees with a broom handle and a chair....Sodomizing a detainee with a chemical light and perhaps a broom stick.

In the days following, many commentators noted the similarities between the Abu Ghraib guards' behavior and the behavior of some of the subjects in the Milgram and Zimbardo experiments. Zimbardo himself, in an op-ed piece in the *Boston Globe,* wrote:

> The terrible things my guards [at Stanford] did to their prisoners were comparable to the horrors inflicted on the Iraqi detainees. My guards repeatedly stripped their prisoners naked, hooded them, chained them, denied them food or bedding privileges, put them into solitary confinement, and made them clean toilet bowls with their bare hands....Over time, these amusements took a sexual turn, such as having the prisoners simulate sodomy on each other....Human behavior is much more under the control of situational forces than most of us recognize or want to acknowledge. In a situation that implicitly gives permission for suspending moral values, many of us can be morphed into creatures alien to our usual natures.

Research the Abu Ghraib scandal; then write a paper comparing and contrasting what happened in the Baghdad prison with what happened in Zimbardo's Stanford Prison Experiment—and possibly also in Milgram's electric shock experiments (and Burger's replication). Focus not only on what happened, but also on *why* it may have happened.

8. Examine conformity as a social phenomenon (and a particular manifestation of obedience to group authority) in some particular area. For example, you may choose to study conformity as it exists among schoolchildren, adolescent peer groups, social clubs or associations, or businesspeople. You may want to draw upon your sociology or social psychology textbooks and such classic studies as William H. Whyte's *The Organization Man* (1956) or David Riesman's *The Lonely Crowd* (1950), or focus upon more recent books and articles, such as Rosabeth Moss Kantor's *A Tale of "O": On Being Different in an Organization* (1980) and John Goldhammer's 1996 book *Under the Influence: The Destructive Effects of Group Dynamics* (1996).

You may also find enlightening some fictional treatments of conformity, such as Sinclair Lewis's *Babbitt* (1922), Sloan Wilson's *The Man in the Gray Flannel Suit* (1950), and Herman Wouk's *The Caine Mutiny: A Novel of World War II* (1951). What are the main factors creating the urge to conform among the particular group you are examining? What kinds of forces may be able to counteract conformity?

9. At the outset of his article, Stanley Milgram refers to imaginative works revolving around the issue of obedience to authority: the story of Abraham and Isaac; three of Plato's dialogues, "Apology," "Crito," and "Phaedo"; and the story of Antigone (dramatized by both the fifth-century B.C. Athenian Sophocles and the twentieth-century Frenchman Jean Anouilh). Many other fictional works deal with obedience to authority—for example, George Orwell's *1984* (1949), Herman Wouk's novel *The Caine Mutiny* (and his subsequent play *The Caine Mutiny Court Martial*), and Shirley Jackson's "The Lottery." Check with your instructor, with a librarian, and with such sources as the *Short Story Index* to locate other imaginative works on this theme. Write a paper discussing the various ways in which the subject has been treated in fiction and drama. To ensure coherence, draw comparisons and contrasts among works showing the connections and the variations on the theme of obedience to authority.

Credits

CHAPTER 1

Page 8: Reprinted with permission from Alan Blinder, "Outsourcing: Bigger Than You Thought," *The American Prospect*, Volume 17, Number 11: October 22, 2006. www.prospect.org. The American Prospect, 1710 Rhode Island Avenue, NW, 12th Floor, Washington, DC 20036. All rights reserved. **Page 24:** Excerpted from "The US and China are Over a Barrel" by Michael T. Klare, published in the *Los Angeles Times*, Apr 28, 2008, p. 17. Michael Klare is a professor of Peace and World Security Studies at Hampshire College. Used by permission of the author. **Page 26:** Graph of "Time to Depletion Midpoint of Oil Reserves, 2003 (Years)" from The Hubbert Peak for World Oil, http://www.oilcrisis.com/summary.htm. Used by permission of EcoSystems, Santa Cruz, CA. **Page 30:** "Oil Production by Country, 1997-2007" from BP Statistical Review of World Energy 2008. Reprinted by permission of British Petroleum p.l.c. **Page 34:** From "In Vitro Fertilization: From Medical Reproduction to Genetic Diagnosis" by Dietmar Mieth, *Biomedical Ethics: Newsletter of the European Network for Biomedical Ethics 1.1* (1996): 45. Copyright © 1996 by Dietmar Mieth. Reprinted by permission of the author. **Page 44:** From EINSTEIN: HIS LIFE AND UNIVERSE by Walter Isaacson. New York, Simon & Schuster, 2007.

CHAPTER 2

Page 52: "We Are Not Created Equal in Every Way" by Joan Ryan from *San Francisco Chronicle*, December 12, 2000. Copyright © 2000 by *San Francisco Chronicle*. Reproduced with permission of *San Francisco Chronicle* via Copyright Clearance Center, Inc.

CHAPTER 3

Page 73: "The Radical Idea of Marrying for Love" from MARRIAGE: A HISTORY by Stephanie Coontz, copyright 2005 by the S.J. Coontz Company. **Page 75:** From THE PROMISE OF SLEEP by William C. Dement, copyright © 1999 by William C. Dement. Used by permission of Dell Publishing, a division of Random House, Inc. **Page 76:** Excerpts from "The Moral Instinct" by Steven J. Pinker, from *The New York Times Magazine*, Jan. 13, 2008. **Page 77:** Excerpted from "The Formal Garden in the Age of Consumer Culture: A Reading of the Twentieth-Century Shopping Mall," by Richard Keller Simon from MAPPING THE AMERICAN CULTURE, ed. by Wayne Franklin and Michael Steiner. Iowa City, Iowa: University of Iowa Press, 1992. **Page 84:** "The Arbus Factor" by Lore Segal, published in *The New Yorker*, December 2007. Reprinted by permission of Cynthia Cannell Literary Agency and the author. **Page 86:** "Scenario for Scandal" by Mark Naison, *Commonweal* (September 24, 1982), pp. 493-494. Copyright © 1982 Commonweal Foundation, reprinted by permission. For subscriptions, www.commonwealmagazine.org. **Page 88:** Elizabeth Weil, "Teaching Boys and Girls Separately," the *New York Times Magazine*, 2 March 2008. **Page 90:** Excerpted from "Light of My Life" by Dan Neil, *Los Angeles Times*, Feb 3, 2008. Copyright © 2008 Los Angeles Times. Reprinted with permission.

CHAPTER 4

Page 94: Excerpts from "Private Gets 3 Years for Iraq Prison Abuse" by David S. Cloud, from *The New York Times*, September 28, 2005. © 2005 The New York Times. All rights reserved. Used by permission and protected by the Copyright Laws of the United States. The printing, copying, redistribution, or retransmission of the Material without express written permission is prohibited. **Page 95:** Excerpt from "Military Abuse," Globe Editorial, published in *The Boston Globe*, September 28, 2005. Copyright © 2005 Globe Newspaper Company, Inc. Reprinted with permission. **Page 101:** From "The Fuel Subsidy We Need" by Ricardo Bayon. Copyright © 2003 Ricardo Bayon, as first published in *The Atlantic Monthly*. Reprinted by permission of the author. **Page 103:** "Putting the Hindenburg to Rest," by Jim Motavalli, *The New York Times*, June 5, 2005. © 2005 The New York Times. All rights reserved. Used by permission and protected by the Copyright Laws of the United States. The printing, copying, redistribution, or retransmission of the Material without express written permission is prohibited. **Page 103:** "Using Fossil

Fuels in Energy Process Gets us Nowhere", Los Angeles Times, Nov. 9, 2003 by Jeremy Rifkin, author of *The Hydrogen Economy: The Creation of the World Wide Energy Web and the Redistribution of Power on Earth* (Tarcher/Putnam). Reprinted by permission of the author. **Page 105:** "Lots of Hot Air About Hydrogen" by Joseph J. Romm, originally published in *Los Angeles Times*, March 28, 2004. Reprinted by permission of the author.

CHAPTER 5

Page 141: "Summary of Key Findings" from "Mass Shootings at Virginia Tech, April 17, 2007: Report of the Review Panel Presented to Governor Kaine, Commonwealth of Virginia, August 2007." Used with permission. **Page 145:** "Laws Limit Schools Even After Alarms," by Jeff Gammage and Stacey Burling, from *The Philadelphia Inquirer*, April 19, 2007. Used with permission of The Philadelphia Inquirer, copyright © 2007. All rights reserved. **Page 147:** Editorial reproduced with permission from the September 4, 2007, issue of The Christian Science Monitor (www.csmonitor.com). © 2007 The Christian Science Monitor. **Page 148:** "Colleges are Watching Troubled Students" by Jeffrey McMurray, from The Associated Press, March 28, 2008. Used with permission of The Associated Press, copyright © 2008. All rights reserved. **Page 151:** "Virginia Tech Massacre has Altered Campus Mental Health Systems," from The Associated Press, April 14, 2008. Used with permission of The Associated Press, copyright © 2008. All rights reserved.

CHAPTER 6

Page 184–185: "The Satisfactions of Housewifery and Motherhood in an Age of 'Do-Your-Own-Thing'" by Terry Martin Hekker, originally published in *The New York Times*, Dec. 20, 1977. Reprinted by permission of the author. **Page 185:** "Modern Love: Paradise Lost (Domestic Division)," by Terry Martin Hekker, from *The New York Times,* January 1, 2006. Copyright © 2006 The New York Times. All rights reserved. Used by permission and protected by the Copyright Laws of the United States. The printing, copying, redistribution, or retransmission of the Material without express written permission is prohibited. **Page 186:** "Cookies or Heroin?" from THE PLUG-IN DRUG, REVISED AND UPDATED – 25TH ANNIVERSARY EDITION by Marie Winn, copyright © 1977, 1985, 2002 by Marie Winn Miller. Used by permission of Viking Penguin, a division of Penguin Group (USA) Inc.

CHAPTER 7

Page 207: From THE WORKING LIFE by Joanne B. Ciulla, copyright © 2000 by Joanne B. Ciulla. Used by permission of Crown Business, a division of Random House, Inc. **Page 208:** "History of the Organization of Work" by Melvin Kranzberg. Reprinted with permission from the Encyclopædia Britannica, © 2005 by Encyclopædia Britannica, Inc. **Page 209:** Excerpts from THE CULTURE OF PROFESSIONALISM: THE MIDDLE CLASS AND THE DEVELOPMENT OF HIGHER EDUCATION IN AMERICA by Burton Bledstein. Reprinted by permission of the author. **Page 210:** Excerpted from Vitae, www.vitae.ac.uk. Copyright © 2009 Careers Research and Advisory Centre (CRAC). Reprinted by permission. **Page 212:** Excerpts from "What is Vocation?" are reprinted by permission of the Initiative on Faith and Practice at Guilford College. **Page 216:** Excerpted from "Fixed, Footloose, or Fractured: Work, Identity, and the Spatial Division of Labor in the Twenty-first Century" by Ursula Huws, from *Monthly Review*, 57.10, March 2006. Copyright © 2006 by Monthly Review Press. Reprinted by permission of Monthly Review Foundation. **Page 220:** From THE CORROSION OF CHARACTER: THE PERSONAL CONSEQUENCES OF WORK IN THE NEW CAPITALISM by Richard Sennett. Copyright © 1998 by Richard Sennett. Used by permission of W.W. Norton & Company, Inc. **Page 230:** "The New Wired World of Work: A More Transparent Workplace Will Mean More White-collar Accountability and Less Tolerance for Hangers-on" by Tom Peters, reprinted from August 28, 2000 issue of *BusinessWeek* by special permission, copyright © 2000 by The McGraw-Hill Companies, Inc. **Page 233:** Richard W. Judy and Carol D'Amico, Excerpt from Executive Summary, pp. 1-7, WORKFORCE 2020: WORK AND WORKERS IN THE 21ST CENTURY (Hudson Institute, 1998). Reprinted by permission of Hudson Institute. **Page 238:** Excerpts from "The Untouchables" from THE WORLD IS FLAT: A BRIEF HISTORY OF THE TWENTY-FIRST CENTURY [Updated and Expanded] [Further Updated and Expanded] by Thomas L. Friedman. Copyright © 2005, 2006, 2007 by Thomas L. Friedman. Reprinted by permission of Farrar, Straus and Giroux, LLC. **Page 244:** "Into the Unknown" from *The Economist*. © The Economist Newspaper Limited, London (November 13, 2004).

CHAPTER 8

CHAPTER 9

Page 376: "A Pop Quiz on Marriage" by Stephanie Coontz, from *The New York Times*, Feb. 19, 2006. Stephanie Coontz is the author of MARRIAGE, A HISTORY: HOW LOVE CONQUERED MARRIAGE. Reprinted by permission of the author. **Page 378:** "The Radical Idea of Marrying for Love," "From Yoke Mates to Soul Mates," from MARRIAGE, A HISTORY by Stephanie Coontz, copyright © 2005 by the S.J. Coontz Company. Used by permission of Viking Penguin, a division of Penguin Group (USA) Inc. **Page 390:** Excerpts from "The State of Our Unions: The Social Health of Marriage in America," by David Popenoe and Barbara Dafoe Whitehead, reprinted with permission from *USA Today Magazine*, July 2002. Copyright © 2002 by the Society for the Advancement of Education, Inc. All rights reserved. **Page 391:** Excerpts from "The State of Our Unions: The Social Health of Marriage in America—2005," by David Popenoe and Barbara Dafoe Whitehead, with updated data for Figures 1–7, published in 2007 report. Reprinted by permission of the National Marriage Project, Rutgers University. **Page 404:** From VIRTUALLY NORMAL by Andrew Sullivan, copyright © 1995 by Andrew Sullivan. Used by permission of Alfred A. Knopf, a division of Random House, Inc. **Page 409:** "...But Not a Very Good Idea, Either" by William J. Bennett, published in *The Washington Post*, May 21, 1996. Reprinted by permission of the author. **Page 412:** "The Satisfactions of Housewifery and Motherhood in an Age of 'Do-Your-Own-Thing'" by Terry Martin Hekker, originally published in *The New York Times*, Dec. 20, 1977. Reprinted by permission of the author. **Page 414:** "Modern Love: Paradise Lost (Domestic Division)," by Terry Martin Hekker, from *The New York Times*, January 1, 2006. Copyright © 2006 The New York Times. All rights reserved. Used by permission and protected by the Copyright Laws of the United States. The printing, copying, redistribution, or retransmission of the Material without express written permission is prohibited. **Page 418:** "A Mother's Day Kiss-Off" by Leslie Bennetts. Reprinted by permission of International Creative Management, Inc. Copyright © 2007 by Leslie Bennetts for *The Los Angeles Times*. **Page 422:** "Moms are People, Too," *The Los Angeles Times*, May 13, 2007, p. M7. Copyright Deborah Tannen. Reprinted by permission. **Page 424:** Excerpts from "The Deinstitutionalization of American Marriage" by Andrew J. Cherlin, from *Journal of Marriage and Family* 66. Wiley-Blackwell, Oxford, UK, November 2004. **Page 429:** "The Myth of Co-Parenting" by Hope Edelman, from THE BITCH IN THE HOUSE edited by Cathi Hanauer. Reprinted by permission of The Elizabeth Kaplan Literary Agency. **Page 436:** "My Problem with Her Anger" by Eric Bartels. Copyright © 2004 by Eric Bartels. Reprinted by permission of the author. **Page 443:** "Can Success in Marriage be Predicted?" by Aviva Patz. Originally published as "Will Your Marriage Last?" in *Psychology Today* 33.1. Reprinted with permission from *Psychology Today Magazine*, copyright © 2000 Sussex Publishers, LLC. **Page 450:** "The Arbus Factor" by Lore Segal, published in *The New Yorker*, December 2007. Reprinted by permission of Cynthia Cannell Literary Agency and the author.

CHAPTER 10

Page 462: From COUNTING SHEEP by Paul Martin. Copyright © 2004 by Paul Martin and reprinted by permission of St. Martin's Press, LLC. **Page 471:** Excerpted from the Harvard Health Publications Special Report, "Improving Sleep," © 2008, President and Fellows of Harvard College. For more information visit: www.health.harvard.edu. Harvard Health Publications does not endorse any products or medical procedures. Reprinted by permission. **Page 483:** "America's Sleep Deprived Teens Nodding Off at School, Behind the Wheel, New National Sleep Foundation Poll Finds," press release from March 28, 2006, from the National Sleep Foundation. Used with permission of the National Sleep Foundation. For further information, please visit http://www.sleepfoundation.org. **Page 486:** "Tips for Teens" from *Adolescent Sleep Needs and Patterns: Research Report and Resource Guide*, National Sleep Foundation, 2000. Used with permission of the National Sleep Foundation. **Page 489:** From "When Worlds Collide: Adolescent Need for Sleep Versus Societal Demands" by Mary A. Carskadon, from ADOLESCENT SLEEP NEEDS AND SCHOOL STARTING TIMES ed. by Kyla L. Wahlstrom, published by Phi Delta Kappa Educational Foundation, 1999. Reprinted by permission of the author. **Page 497:** From THE PROMISE OF SLEEP by William C. Dement, copyright © 1999 by William C. Dement. Used by permission of Dell Publishing, a division of Random House, Inc. **Page 506:** "Appendix: Pittsburgh Sleep Quality Index (PSQI)" from "The Pittsburgh Sleep Quality Index: A New Instrument for Psychiatric Practice and Research" by Daniel J. Buysse, Charles F. Reynolds III, Timothy H. Monk, Susan R. Berman, and David J. Kupfer, from *Psychiatry Research*, Vol. 28, No.2, May 1989. Reprinted by permission of Daniel Buysse. **Page 512:** "How Sleep Deprivation Affects Psychological Variables Related to College

Students' Cognitive Performance" by June J. Pilcher and Amy S. Walters, from *Journal of American College Health*, Vol. 46, issue 3, November, 1997, p. 121-126. Reprinted with permission of the Helen Dwight Reid Educational Foundation. Published by Heldref Publications, 1319 Eighteenth St., NW, Washington, DC 20036-1802. Copyright © 1997. **Page 522** "Adolescent Sleep, School Start Times, and Teen Motor Vehicle Crashes" by Fred Danner and Barbara Phillips, from *Journal of Clinical Sleep Medicine*, December 15, 2008 Vol 4, No. 6; 2008. Reprinted by permission.

CHAPTER 11

Page 539: "Advertising's Fifteen Basic Appeals" by Jib Fowles. Originally published in *Et Cetera: A Review of General Semantics, Vol. 39, Number 3.* Copyright © 1982 Institute of General Semantics. Reprinted by permission of Institute of General Semantics (IGS), Fort Worth, Texas. **Page 558:** Excerpts from ADVERTISING EXCELLENCE, pp. 239-243, by Courtland Bovée, John V. Thill, George P. Dovel and Marian Burk Wood (McGraw-Hill, 1995). Reprinted with permission from John Thill for Bovée & Thill LLC. **Page 567:** Image Courtesy of the Advertising Archives. **Page 568:** Image Courtesy of the Advertising Archives. **Page 569:** Image Courtesy of the Advertising Archives. Image Courtesy of the Advertising Archives. **Page 571:** Image Courtesy of the Advertising Archives. **Page 572:** Image Courtesy of the Advertising Archives. **Page 573:** Image Courtesy of the Advertising Archives. **Page 574:** Image Courtesy of the Advertising Archives. **Page 575:** Image Courtesy of the Advertising Archives. **Page 576:** Image Courtesy of the Advertising Archives. **Page 577:** Image Courtesy of the Advertising Archives. **Page 580–Page 581:** Image Courtesy of the Advertising Archives. **Page 582:** Image Courtesy of the Advertising Archives. **Page 583:** Image Courtesy of the Advertising Archives. **Page 584:** Courtesy DaimlerChrysler Corporation. **Page 586:** Image Courtesy of the Advertising Archives. Image Courtesy of the Advertising Archives. **Page 594:** Courtesy Soloflex, Inc.

CHAPTER 12

Page 617: "What Great Books Do For Children" by Arthur M. Schlesinger, Jr., published in *The American Enterprise*, Vol. 12, No.5, July 2001. Copyright 2001 American Enterprise Institute for Public Policy Research. Reprinted by permission of The American Enterprise Institute. **Page 619:** "The Universality of the Folktale" from THE FOLKTALE by Stith Thompson. Copyright 1946 by Henry Holt and Company. **Page 624:** "Cinderella" from FAIRY TALES by Charles Perrault, translated by Geoffrey Brereton (Penguin Books, 1957). Translation copyright © 1957 by Geoffrey Brereton. Reprinted with permission of the Geoffrey Brereton Estate. **Page 628:** From GRIMM'S TALES FOR YOUNG AND OLD by Jakob and Wilhelm Grimm, translated by Ralph Manheim, copyright © 1977 by Ralph Manheim. Used by permission of Random House Children's Books, a division of Random House, Inc. **Page 633:** "The Chinese Cinderella Story" by Tuan Cheng-Shih, translated by Arthur Waley, from *Folklore*, vol. 58, (1947). Reprinted by permission of The Folklore Society. Please visit The Folklore Society at www.folklore-society.com. **Page 635:** "The Maiden, the Frog, and the Chief's Son" from "Cinderella in Africa" by William Bascom, from CINDERELLA: A FOLKLORE CASEBOOK, edited by Alan Dundes, copyright © 1982 Alan Dundes. Originally published in the *Journal of the Folklore Institute*, 9 (1972), pp. 54-70. Reproduced by permission of Routledge/Taylor & Francis Group, LLC as conveyed through Copyright Clearance Center. **Page 639:** "The Algonquin Cinderella" from WORLD TALES: THE EXTRAORDINARY COINCIDENCE OF STORIES TOLD IN ALL TIMES, IN ALL PLACES by Idries Shah, copyright © 1979 by Technographia, S. A. and Harcourt, Inc. Reprinted by permission of Houghton Mifflin Harcourt Publishing Company. **Page 641:** Textual excerpts from Walt Disney's CINDERELLA, as adapted by Campbell Grant. © Disney Enterprises, Inc. Reprinted by permission of Disney Publishing Worldwide, Inc. **Page 643:** "Cinderella," from TRANSFORMATIONS by Anne Sexton. Copyright © 1971 by Anne Sexton, renewed 1999 by Linda G. Sexton. Reprinted by permission of Houghton Mifflin Harcourt Publishing Company. All rights reserved. **Page 645:** "For Whom the Shoe Fits: Cinderella in the Hands of Victorian Illustrators and Writers" by Bonnie Cullen from *The Lion and the Unicorn* 27:1 (2003), pp. 57-82. © 2003 The Johns Hopkins University Press. Reprinted with permission of The Johns Hopkins University Press. **Page 651:** From THE USES OF ENCHANTMENT by Bruno Bettelheim, copyright © 1975, 1976 by Bruno Bettelheim. Used by permission of the author's agents, Raines & Raines. **Page 658:** "Going Up in the World: Class in 'Cinderella'," by Elisabeth Panttaja, from *Western Folklore*, 52, (1993), pp. 85-104. Copyright © 1993 Western States Folklore Society. Reprinted by permission. **Page 663:** "I Am Cinderella's Stepmother and I Know My Rights," first published by *The New York Times*, © Judith Rossner.

Reprinted by permission of The Wendy Weil Agency, Inc. **Page 666:** James Poniewozik, "The Princess Paradox," from *Time*, April 5, 2004. Copyright TIME INC. Reprinted by permission. TIME is a registered trademark of Time Inc. All rights reserved. **Page 670:** Excerpted from "What's Wrong with Cinderella? One Mother's Struggle with Her 3-Year-Old Daughter's Love Affair with Princess Culture" by Peggy Orenstein. Originally published in the *New York Times Magazine*, December 24, 2006. Copyright © 2006 by Peggy Orenstein. Reprinted by permission.

CHAPTER 13

Page 681: Adapted from "The Education of a Torturer" by Janice T. Gibson and Mika Haritos-Fatouros, Psychology Today, November, 1986. Reprinted with permission from *Psychology Today Magazine*, copyright © 1986 Sussex Publishers, LLC. **Page 683:** "Disobedience as a Psychological and Moral Problem," pp. 16-23, from ON DISOBEDIENCE AND OTHER ESSAYS by Erich Fromm. Copyright © 1981 by the Estate of Erich Fromm. Reprinted by permission of HarperCollins Publishers. **Page 688:** From THE PERSON AND THE SITUATION: PERSPECTIVES OF SOCIAL PSYCHOLOGY by Lee Ross and Richard E. Nisbett. Copyright © 1991. Reproduced with permission of The McGraw-Hill Companies. **Page 694:** From the film "Obedience" © 1968 by Stanley Milgram, © renewed 1993 by Alexandra Milgram, and distributed by Penn State Media Sales. **Page 698:** "The Perils of Obedience" abridged and adapted from OBEDIENCE TO AUTHORITY by Stanley Milgram. Originally published in *Harper's Magazine*. Copyright © 1974 by Stanley Milgram. Reprinted by permission of HarperCollins Publishers. **Page 705:** "Replicating Milgram: Would People Still Obey?" by Jerry M. Burger, from *American Psychologist Special Issue:* Obedience—Then and Now, 64.1 (Jan. 2009): 1–11. Copyright © 2009 by the American Psychological Association. Reproduced with permission. **Page 712:** From OBEDIENCE by Ian Parker, as it first appeared in Granta 71: Shrinks, published September 1, 2000. Reprinted by permission of United Agents on behalf of Ian Parker. **Page 723:** Page 47-50 and 60 from "Group Minds" from PRISONS WE CHOOSE TO LIVE INSIDE by Doris Lessing. © 1988 by Doris Lessing. Reprinted in the U.S. by permission of HarperCollins Publishers, Inc. and in Canada with permission from House of Anansi Press. **Page 726:** "Opinions and Social Pressure" by Solomon Asch, *Scientific American*, November, 1955. Reprinted with permission. Copyright © 1955 by Scientific American, Inc. All rights reserved. **Page 732:** "The Stanford Prison Experiment" by Philip Zimbardo. Originally published as "The Mind is a Formidable Jailer," *The New York Times Magazine*, April 8, 1973. Copyright © 1973 by Philip G. Zimbardo. Reprinted by permission. **Page 745:** Excerpted from ATONEMENT by Ian McEwan, copyright © 2001, 2002 by Ian McEwan. Used by permission of Doubleday, a division of Random House, Inc. and Knopf Canada.

Index

QUICK INDEX: APA DOCUMENTATION BASICS

APA In-text Citations in Brief

Place citation information—author, publication year, passage locator (page or paragraph number)—in sentence or in parentheses.

Summary or paraphrase; refer only to the year of publication:

> Berk (2002) suggested that many researchers view punishment as a quick fix.

Direct quotation, author and publication date *not* mentioned in sentence:

> A good deal of research suggests that punishing a child "promotes only momentary compliance" (Berk, 2002, p. 383).

Direct quotation, author and publication date mentioned in sentence:

> According to Berk (2002), a good deal of research suggests that punishing a child "promotes only momentary compliance" (p. 383).

Direct quotation, Internet; provide page number, paragraph number (use the abbreviation para, or ¶ symbol), or paragraph number within a section, as available:

> Others have noted a rise in "problems that mimic the dysfunctional behaviors seen on reality television" (Spivek, 2006, Introduction section, ¶ 3).

APA References List in Brief

At the end of the paper, on a separate page titled "References" (no italics or quotation marks), alphabetize sources, providing full bibliographic information for each. The most common entry types follow; doubled entries show online equivalents of print sources.

Book
Basic entry

> Freud, S. (1920). *Dream psychology: Psychoanalysis for beginners* (M. D. Elder, Trans.). New York: James A. McCann.
>
> Freud, S. (1920). *Dream psychology: Psychoanalysis for beginners* (M. D. Elder, Trans.). Retrieved from http://www.gutenberg.org /etext/15489

Selection from an edited book

> Halberstam, D. (2002). Who we are. In S. J. Gould (Ed.), *The best American essays 2002* (pp. 124–136). New York: Houghton Mifflin.

Later edition

Samuelson, P., & Nordhaus, W. D. (2005). *Economics* (18th ed.). Boston: McGraw-Hill/Irwin.

Article from a Magazine

Davison, P. (2000, May). Girl, seeming to disappear. *Atlantic Monthly,* 108–111.

Davison. P. (2000, May). Girl, seeming to disappear. *Atlantic Monthly*. Retrieved from http://www.theatlantic.com/issues/2000/05/davison.htm

[Do not include retrieval date unless the source is likely to change.]

Article from a Journal Paginated Continuously Through the Annual Volume

Chene, C. (2005). Ads pressure Ontario to butt out in retail locations. *Canadian Medical Association Journal, 172,* 1544.

Article from a Journal Paginated by Issue

Ivanenko, A., & Massie, C. (2006). Assessment and management of sleep disorders in children. *Psychiatric Times, 23*(11), 90–95.

Ivanenko, A., & Massie, C. (2006). Assessment and management of sleep disorders in children. *Psychiatric Times, 23*(11), 90–95. Retrieved from http://find.galegroup.com

[In referencing an online text available only through a subscription service, provide the URL for the home page or menu page of the service.]

[Whether a journal article is paginated by issue or continuously through the annual volume, include both volume and issue number (if available) when citing the electronic version of the source.]

Article from a Newspaper

Ridberg, M. (2006, May 4). Professors want their classes 'unwired.' *Christian Science Monitor,* p. 16.

Ridberg, M. (2006, May 4). Professors want their classes 'unwired.' *Christian Science Monitor*. Retrieved from http://www.csmonitor.com/2006/0504/pl6s01-legn.html

Article from the Internet

Weinberg, H. (n.d.). Group psychotherapy resource guide. Retrieved August 28, 2007, from http://www.group-psychotherapy.com/

[If you think the online content might change, include the retrieval date.]

QUICK INDEX: MLA DOCUMENTATION BASICS

MLA In-text Citations in Brief

In your paper, give in-text citations as follows. If you do not mention the author's name in the sentence, provide it, with the relevant page numbers, in parentheses:

> From the beginning, the AIDS antibody test has been "mired in controversy" (Bayer 101).

If you mention the author's name in the sentence, omit it from the citation in parentheses:

> According to Bayer, from the beginning, the AIDS antibody test has been "mired in controversy" (101).

MLA Works Cited List in Brief

At the end of the paper, on a separate page titled "Works Cited," alphabetize each cited source by author's last name. Provide full bibliographic information, as shown. State how you accessed the source—via print or Web. Precede "Web" with a database name (e.g., LexisNexis) or the title of a Web site and a publisher.[1] Follow "Web" with your date of access. Note the use of punctuation and italics. Following are some common entry types:

Article from a Magazine
Accessed via print

> Packer, George. "The Choice." *New Yorker* 28 Jan. 2008: 28–35. Print.

Accessed via Web (identical to print version)

> Packer, George. "The Choice." *New Yorker* 28 Jan. 2008: n. pag. *NewYorker.com.* Web. 8 Nov. 2008.*

Accessed via database (identical to print version)

> Packer, George. "The Choice." *New Yorker* 28 Jan. 2008: n. pag. *Academic OneFile.* Web. 8 Nov. 2008.

Article via Web (article exists on Web only; no print version)

> Benjamin, Daniel. "The Mumbai Terrorists' Other Targets." *Slate.* Washington Post Newsweek Interactive, 1 Dec. 2008. Web. 4 Dec. 2008.

---

[1]Exception: Online scholarly journal with no print equivalent. See last entry under Article from a Scholarly Journal.

Article from a Newspaper

Accessed via print

> Reynolds, Maura. "Recession Could Last into 2010." *Los Angeles Times*
> 2 Dec. 2008, late ed.: Al+. Print.

Accessed via Web (identical to print version)

> Reynolds, Maura. "Recession Could Last into 2010." *Los Angeles Times*
> 2 Dec. 2008: Al+. *LA Times.com*. Web. 2 Dec. 2008.

Accessed via database (identical to print version)

> Reynolds, Maura. "Recession Could Last into 2010." *Los Angeles Times*
> 2 Dec. 2008: Al+. *LexisNexis*. Web. 2 Dec. 2008.

Accessed via Web (article exists on Web only; no print equivalent)

> Brown, Campbell. "Plan for Bailout Money Doesn't Make Sense." *CNN.com*. Cable
> News Network, 4 Dec. 2008. Web. 4 Dec. 2008.

Article from a Scholarly Journal

Accessed via print (include volume and issue numbers)

> Ivanenko, Anna, and Clifford Massie. "Assessment and Management of Sleep
> Disorders in Children." *Psychiatric Times* 23.11 (2006): 90–95. Print.

Accessed via Web (identical to print version)

> Ivanenko, Anna, and Clifford Massie. "Assessment and Management of Sleep
> Disorders in Children." *Psychiatric Times* 23.11 (2006): n. pag.
> *Psychiatrictimes.com*. Web. 3 Mar. 2009.

Accessed via database (identical to print version)

> Ivanenko, Anna, and Clifford Massie. "Assessment and Management of Sleep
> Disorders in Children." *Psychiatric Times* 23.11 (2006): n. pag. *Academic
> OneFile*. Web. 3 Mar. 2009.

Accessed via Web (article exists on Web only; no print equivalent)

> Peterson, Karen. "Teens, Literature, and the Web."*Alan Review* 31.3 (2004):
> n. pag. Web. 3 Mar. 2009.

Key to Citation Abbreviations

MLA abbreviations include n. p. = no publisher or place of publication given; n. d. = no date given; n. pag. = no page(s) given—typical of sources found online; ed. = editor; ed. = edition; dir. = director; trans. = translator; comp. = compiler; + = non-consecutive pages beyond first listed. Capitalize the first letter of an abbreviation that follows a period.

Book
Accessed via print

Fitzgerald, F. Scott. *This Side of Paradise*. New York: Scribner's, 1920. Print.

Accessed via database

Fitzgerald, F. Scott. *This Side of Paradise*. New York: Scribner's, 1920. *Bartleby.com*. Web. 20 Oct. 2008.

Selection from an anthology

Hardy, Melissa. "The Heifer." *The Best American Short Stories 2002*. Ed. Sue Miller. Boston: Houghton, 2002. 97–115. Print.

Second or subsequent edition

Whitten, Phillip. *Anthropology: Contemporary Perspectives*. 8th ed. Boston: Allyn, 2001. Print.

Web Site
Entire Web site

McMillan, Gail, dir. *Love Letters of the Civil War*. Virginia Tech. 5 Mar. 2008. Web. 18 Dec. 2008.

Part of a Web site

Morris, J.C. "My Dear Amanda." 10 May 1863. Letter. *Love Letters of the Civil War*. Dir. Gail McMillan. Virginia Tech., 5 Mar. 2008. Web. 18 Dec. 2008.

McGirt, Ellen. "The Minneapolis Bridge Collapse: Our Crumbling Infrastructure." *Fast Company*. Mansueto Ventures LLC, 2 Aug. 2007. Web. 12 Sept. 2008.

CHECKLIST FOR WRITING SUMMARIES

- **Read the passage carefully.** Determine its structure. Identify the author's purpose in writing.
- **Reread.** *Label* each section or stage of thought. *Highlight* key ideas and terms.
- **Write one-sentence summaries** of each stage of thought.
- **Write a thesis:** a one- or two-sentence summary of the entire passage.
- **Write the first draft** of your summary.
- **Check your summary** against the original passage.
- **Revise** your summary.

CHECKLIST FOR WRITING CRITIQUES

- **Introduce** both the passage being critiqued and the author.
- **Summarize** the author's main points, making sure to state the author's purpose for writing.
- **Evaluate** the validity of the presentation.
- **Respond** to the presentation: agree and/or disagree.
- **Conclude** with your overall assessment.